World of Chemistry

FLORIDA TEACHER'S EDITION

World of Chemistry

FLORIDA TEACHER'S EDITION

Steven S. Zumdahl
University of Illinois

Susan L. Zumdahl
University of Illinois

Donald J. DeCoste
University of Illinois

McDougal Littell
A Houghton Mifflin Company
Evanston, Illinois • Boston • Dallas

Library of Congress Catalog Card Number: 2004118263

ISBN: 0-618-57064-0

1 2 3 4 5 6 7 8 9-DOW-09 08 07 06 05

Teacher Panel

Robert Blaus
York High School
Elmhurst, Illinois

Bernadette Gruca-Peal
Archdiocese of Chicago Schools
Queen of Peace High School
Chicago, Illinois

Janet Jones
Chicago Public Schools
Sullivan High School
Chicago, Illinois

Ray Lesniewski
Jones Academic Magnet High School
Chicago, Illinois

Ann Levinson
Niles Township Community High School
Skokie, Illinois

Lee Slick
Morgan Park High School
Chicago, Illinois

Carl Wasik
Chicago Public Schools
Curie High School
Chicago, Illinois

Teacher Reviewers

Donna Bettinelli
Bay Shore High School
Bay Shore, New York

Charles Busenhart
St. Louis University High School
St. Louis, Missouri

Ray Lesniewski
Jones Academic Magnet High School
Chicago, Illinois

Lee Slick
Morgan Park High School
Chicago, Illinois

Greg Thompson, Ph.D.
Lewiston High School
Lewiston, Idaho

About the Authors

Steven S. Zumdahl earned a B.S. in Chemistry from Wheaton College (IL) and a Ph.D from the University of Illinois, Urbana-Champaign. He has been a faculty member at the University of Colorado-Boulder, Parkland College (IL) and the University of Illinois at Urbana-Champaign (UIUC) where he is currently Professor of Chemistry, Associate Head of Chemistry and Director of the General Chemistry Program. He has received numerous awards including the National Catalyst Award for excellence in chemical education, the University of Illinois Teaching Award, the UIUC Liberal Arts and Sciences Award for Excellence in Teaching, the UIUC Liberal Arts and Sciences Advising Award and the School of Chemical Sciences Teaching Award (five times). He is author of several chemistry textbooks. In his leisure time he enjoys traveling and collecting and restoring classic cars.

Susan Zumdahl is Director of the Merit Program for Emerging Scholars in Chemistry at University of Illinois, Urbana-Champaign. In this program, which covers the first two years of college chemistry, she uses active learning techniques to teach students and she also trains teachers in these methods. In addition, she is involved in the development of a sophisticated web-based electronic homework system for teaching chemistry. She has taught chemistry at the middle school, high school, community college and university levels for 30 years. She earned her Bachelors and Masters degrees in chemistry at California State University at Fullerton and she has coordinated and led workshops and programs for science teachers from elementary through college levels that encourage and support active learning and creative science teaching techniques. For several years she was Director of an Institute for Chemical Education Field Center in Southern California and has authored several chemistry textbooks. Susan enjoys traveling, classic automobiles, and gardening in her spare time.

Don DeCoste is a chemistry instructor at the University of Illinois at Urbana-Champaign. He has been teaching at the high school and college levels for 14 years. He earned his B.S. in Chemistry and PhD. in Science Education from the University of Illinois. He has led workshops for secondary teachers and graduate student teaching assistants, discussing the methods and benefits of getting the students more actively involved in class. He has developed a data base of class discussion questions to encourage students to use active learning in their study of chemistry. Don enjoys spending time with his family and has had an on-off relationship with an acoustic guitar for the past ten years.

A Word From the Authors

Because our experience tells us that learning chemistry is not a spectator sport, this curriculum is designed to put the student in the center of the learning process. To learn in a meaningful way, the student must be a participant in the process. A knowledge of chemistry is not something a teacher gives to a student—it is something the student must construct for herself or himself with the help of the teacher, the textbook, laboratory exploration and the other materials provided.

Also, our experience tells us that there is no better way to learn than to teach someone else. When we try to teach a concept to someone, it soon becomes obvious whether we truly understand the concept or not. Teaching someone exposes our own misconceptions and motivates us to "fix" them. However, successful peer teaching activities require much more than simply assigning the students to work in groups. The quality of the problems they work on in groups is critical. Based on our extensive experience with active learning in Introductory Chemistry at the University of Illinois, we have designed **Team Learning Worksheets,** which contain the type of conceptual questions that produce discussion and meaningful learning in a group setting.

One of the great advantages of effective active learning is that it directs the students to the textbook. When students confront a concept in group work that they do not understand, they learn much more effectively if they struggle with it rather that having the teacher simply supply the answer. One of the major adjustments that students have to make in going from high school to college is the need to be much more independent learners, especially by using textbooks. Students who never learned to use textbooks effectively in high school have a much more difficult time adjusting to college. Students who are not college bound also need to know how to learn from books since changing job markets necessitate retraining.

Therefore, one of our main goals in constructing this learning package was to make the textbook readable and useful to students and to provide learning materials that direct the students to the textbook. We feel that it's very important that the textbook is a central learning resource for the students. To that end the text has **Focus Questions** to help the students read the book in a meaningful way. These questions, which occur after two or three sections that form a natural segment, are meant to be completed by the students before they come to class to discuss the topic. These questions will help the student focus on the main ideas in the segment. The text also contains many features to help the students connect the chemistry they are learning to their daily lives. **Chemical Impacts** feature interesting and timely applications of chemistry, **Celebrity Chemicals** emphasize especially important chemicals and the **Top Ten** and **What If** features highlight interesting connections between classroom studies and "real life".

The text contains hundreds of worked out **examples** that show the systematic thinking needed to solve chemical problems. These examples always emphasize understanding concepts rather than rote memorization. The **end-of-chapter problems** were carefully designed to help the students assess their understanding of the concepts covered in the chapter. The problems vary in level from simple drill and practice exercises to those that combine several ideas to develop the students' critical thinking skills.

To encourage in-class exploration, we have included several **Chemistry in Action** activities for each chapter. These activities can be used to introduce students to the concepts in a hands-on format. The **laboratory program** for *World of Chemistry* provides experiments that include in-text, traditional, microscale and CBL formats. All of these labs have been class tested and were constructed to provide an effective balance between structure and exploration. In addition, we have provided **leveled chapter review worksheets** that are designed for students at various stages in their learning of chemistry. There are basic worksheets for students who need extra help, standard worksheets for students at the average level and challenge worksheets for students with higher than average understanding. We also have designed a **Chapter Test** for each chapter and have included a computerized **Test Item File** for designing your own tests and quizzes.

Our goals are to interest and motivate the students, making them active participants in the process of truly understanding this fascinating and important subject.

Acknowledgments

This was a massive project and we are indebted to many people for their help. We are especially grateful to Richard Stratton, Senior Sponsoring Editor at Houghton Mifflin, who has championed this project from the beginning and supported us cheerfully and enthusiastically in every possible way. We very much appreciate the professional and efficient work of Tamela Ambush, Senior Production Editor, who managed the production of this very complex project in a smooth way. We are also indebted to Marisa Papile, Editorial Assistant, who coordinated the production of all the ancillaries and to Karen O'Connor, Editorial Associate, who handled many of the editorial questions that arose during the project. We appreciate the efforts of Chere Bemelmans, Software Producer, who worked so hard to put together the technology for the package, including the Web site, video and animations, and CD. We also very much appreciate the support we have received from the people at McDougal Littell. Dan Rogers, Vice President and Editorial Director for Science, read the manuscript and offered very helpful comments. Jan Powers, Product Manager for Science, and Chris Tabbert, Director of Special Markets, were always supportive and offered valuable advice about marketing issues.

We are especially grateful to John Little, St. Mary's High School, Stockton, California, and Connie Grosse, El Dorado High School, Placentia, California, who supplied creative and innovative laboratory experiments and who gave us much valuable advice along the way. We also greatly appreciate the efforts of Steve Nelson, Addison Trail High School, Addison, Illinois, who wrote the excellent chapter assessment materials. We are indebted to Cathie Keenan, Chaffey College, California, who did a very thorough job checking the material for the Teacher's Edition. Special thanks to Tim Loftus, who checked many of the experiments.

Finally we are grateful to all our friends who teach high school who have done so much to encourage and enlighten us over the years. You are a very dedicated, highly professional group of people whom we admire greatly.

Brief Contents

Contents

Radioactivity and Nuclear Energy 606

Chapter **20**

Organic Chemistry 632

Chapter 21

Biochemistry 682

Appendices A1

Answers to End-to-Chapter Problems A13

Glossary A15

Photo/Illustration Credits A23

Index A27

CELEBRITY CHEMICAL

TOP TEN LISTS

CHEMICAL IMPACT
Science, Technology, and Society

Connection to Biology

Consumer Connections

Connection to History

Connection to Astronomy

Connection to Archeology

CHEMISTRY in ACTION

CHEMISTRY in the LABORATORY

Program Overview

THE VISION FOR HIGH SCHOOL CHEMISTRY

The Balanced Equation

Our high school chemistry program presents the right balance of concepts and applications, emphasizing active learning and encouraging students to solve problems creatively.

Teacher's Edition Content Overview

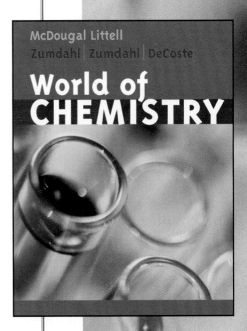

McDougal Littell
Zumdahl | Zumdahl | DeCoste
World of CHEMISTRY

Student Edition

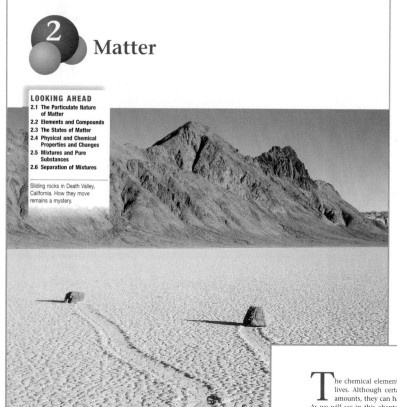

2   Matter

LOOKING AHEAD
2.1 The Particulate Nature of Matter
2.2 Elements and Compounds
2.3 The States of Matter
2.4 Physical and Chemical Properties and Changes
2.5 Mixtures and Pure Substances
2.6 Separation of Mixtures

Sliding rocks in Death Valley, California. How they move remains a mystery.

20

◀ Each **Chapter Opener** provides an engaging full-page photograph tied to the chapter content, plus **Looking Ahead**, a chapter outline that gives students a preview of the topics to be explored.

The chapter begins with a general introduction that connects the chapter content to students' prior knowledge and everyday experiences. This reinforces the text's emphasis on conceptual understanding and helps draw students comfortably into the material. ▶

A straightforward **Objective** or two lead off each section, giving students a context for their reading. ▶

The chemical elements are very important to each of us in our daily lives. Although certain elements are present in our bodies in tiny amounts, they can have profound effects on our health and behavior. As we will see in this chapter, lithium can be a miracle treatment for someone with manic-depressive disease and our cobalt levels can have a remarkable impact on whether we behave violently.

Since ancient times, humans have used chemical changes to their advantage. The processing of ores to produce metals for ornaments and tools and the use of embalming fluids are two applications of chemistry that were used before 1000 B.C.

The Greeks were the first to try to explain why chemical changes occur. By about 400 B.C. they had proposed that all matter was composed of four fundamental substances: fire, earth, water, and air.

The next 2000 years of chemical history were dominated by alchemy. Some alchemists were mystics and fakes who were obsessed with the idea of turning cheap metals into gold. However, many alchemists were sincere scientists and this period saw important events: the elements mercury, sulfur, and antimony were discovered, and alchemists learned how to prepare acids.

The first scientist to recognize the importance of careful measurements was the Irishman Robert Boyle (1627–1691). Boyle is best known for his pioneering work on the properties of gases, but his most important contribution to science was probably his insistence that science should be firmly grounded in experiments. For example, Boyle held no preconceived notions about how many elements there might be. His definition of the term *element* was based on experiments: a substance was an element unless it could be broken down into two or more simpler substances. For example, air could not be an element as the Greeks believed, because it could be broken down into many pure substances.

As Boyle's experimental definition of an element became generally accepted, the list of known elements grew, and the Greek system of four elements died. But although Boyle was an excellent scientist, he was not always right. For some reason he ignored his own definition of an element and clung to the alchemists' views that metals were not true elements and that a way would be found eventually to change one metal into another.

Robert Boyle at 62 years of age.

3.1   The Elements

Objectives: *To learn about the relative abundances of the elements.*
To learn the names of some elements.

As we saw in Chapter 2, all of the materials of the earth (and other parts of the universe) can be broken down chemically into about 100 different elements. At first it might seem amazing that the millions of known substances are composed of so few fundamental elements. Fortunately for those trying to understand and systematize it, nature often uses a relatively small number of fundamental units to assemble even extremely complex materials. For example, proteins, a group of substances that serve the human

3.1 The Elements   **47**

Margin Notes appear throughout the text to clarify concepts and terms. ▶

Important Rules and Steps are set off from the text in colored boxes and are clearly enumerated for easy reference. ▶

Oxidation: Loss of electrons

Reduction: Gain of electrons

Oxidizing Agent:
Accepts electrons
Contains element reduced

Reducing Agent:
Furnishes electrons
Contains element oxidized

In a redox reaction, an oxidizing agent is reduced (gains electrons) and a reducing agent is oxidized (loses electrons).

With this background, we can now define *oxidation* and *reduction* in terms of oxidation states. **Oxidation** is an *increase* in oxidation state (a loss of electrons). **Reduction** is a *decrease* in oxidation state (a gain of electrons). Thus in the reaction

$$2Na(s) + Cl_2(g) \rightarrow 2NaCl(s)$$

sodium is oxidized and chlorine is reduced. Cl_2 is called the **oxidizing agent (electron acceptor)** and Na is called the **reducing agent (electron donor)**. We can also define the *oxidizing agent* as the reactant containing the element that is reduced (gains electrons). The *reducing agent* can be defined similarly as the reactant containing the element that is oxidized (loses electrons).

Concerning the reaction

$$CH_4(g) + 2O_2(g) \rightarrow CO_2(g) + 2H_2O(g)$$

we can say the following:

1. Carbon is oxidized because there is an increase in its oxidation state (carbon has apparently lost electrons).

2. The reactant CH_4 contains the carbon that is oxidized, so CH_4 is the reducing agent. It is the reactant that furnishes the electrons (those lost by carbon).

3. Oxygen is reduced because there has been a decrease in its oxidation state (oxygen has apparently gained electrons).

4. The reactant that contains the oxygen atoms is O_2, so O_2 is the oxidizing agent. That is, O_2 accepts the electrons.

Note that when the oxidizing or reducing agent is named, the *whole compound* is specified, not just the element that undergoes the change in oxidation state.

Rules for Assigning Oxidation States

1. The oxidation state of an atom in an uncombined element is 0.
2. The oxidation state of a monatomic ion is the same as its charge.
3. Oxygen is assigned an oxidation state of -2 in most of its covalent compounds. Important exception: peroxides (compounds containing the O_2^{2-} group), in which each oxygen is assigned an oxidation state of -1.
4. In its covalent compounds with nonmetals, hydrogen is assigned an oxidation state of $+1$.
5. In binary compounds, the element with the greater electronegativity is assigned a negative oxidation state equal to its charge as an anion in its ionic compounds.
6. For an electrically neutral compound, the sum of the oxidation states must be zero.
7. For an ionic species, the sum of the oxidation states must equal the overall charge.

eduction Reactions and Electrochemistry

3.11 Compounds That Contain Ions

Objective: *To describe how ions combine to form neutral compounds.*

Chemists have good reasons to believe that many chemical compounds contain ions. For instance, consider some of the properties of common table salt, sodium chloride (NaCl). It must be heated to about 800 °C to melt and to almost 1500 °C to boil (compare to water, which boils at 100 °C). As a solid, salt will not conduct an electric current, but when melted it is a very good conductor. Pure water will not conduct electricity (will not allow an electric current to flow), but when salt is dissolved in water, the resulting solution readily conducts electricity (see **Figure 3.20**).

Figure 3.20
(a) Pure water does not conduct a current, so the circuit is not complete and the bulb does not light. (b) Water containing a dissolved salt conducts electricity and the bulb lights.

(a)

(b)

🧪 **CHEMISTRY**
Melting means that the solid, where the ions are locked into place, is changed to a liquid, where the ions can move.

Chemists have come to realize that we can best explain these properties of sodium chloride (NaCl) by picturing it as containing Na^+ ions and Cl^- ions packed together as shown in **Figure 3.21**. Because the positive and negative charges attract each other very strongly, salt must be heated to a very high temperature (800 °C) before it melts.

Figure 3.21
(a) The arrangement of sodium ions (Na^+) and chloride ions (Cl^-) in the ionic compound sodium chloride. (b) Solid sodium chloride highly magnified.

(a)

(b)

🧪 **CHEMISTRY**
A substance containing ions that can move can conduct an electric current.

To explore further the significance of the electrical conductivity results, we need to discuss briefly the nature of electric currents. An electric current can travel along a metal wire because *electrons are free to move* through the wire; the moving electrons carry the current. In ionic substances the ions carry the current. Thus substances that contain ions can conduct an electric current *only if the ions can move*—the current travels by the movement of the

3.11 Compounds That Contain Ions **75**

◀ A comprehensive **Art Program** provides hundreds of photographs and illustrations that clearly represent chemical reactions, phenomena and processes, both to reinforce the text's explanations and to make the material more engaging for students.

Physical and Chemical Changes

1. A *physical change* involves a change in one or more physical properties, but no change in the fundamental components that make up the substance. The most common physical changes are changes of state: solid ⇔ liquid ⇔ gas.
2. A *chemical change* involves a change in the fundamental components of the substance; a given substance changes into a different substance or substances. Chemical changes are called **reactions**: silver tarnishes by reacting with substances in the air; a plant forms a leaf by combining various substances from the air and soil; and so on.

◀ **Key terms and concepts*** are highlighted and clearly defined to focus students' attention on them.

*See SE in Planning Guide.

Example 2.2

Identifying Physical and Chemical Changes

Classify each of the following as a physical or a chemical change.

a. Iron metal is melted.
b. Iron combines with oxygen to form rust.
c. Wood burns in air.
d. A rock is broken into small pieces.

Solution

a. Melted iron is just liquid iron and could cool again to the solid state. This is a physical change.
b. When iron combines with oxygen, it forms a different substance (rust) that contains iron and oxygen. This is a chemical change because a different substance forms.
c. Wood burns to form different substances (as we will see later, they include carbon dioxide and water). After the fire, the wood is no longer in its original form. This is a chemical change.
d. When the rock is broken up, all the [ ] composition as the whole rock. Each r[ ] inal only in size and shape. This is a [ ]

Oxygen combines with the chemicals in wood to produce flames. Is a physical or chemical change taking place?

 Self-Check Exercise 2.2

Classify each of the following as a chemical [ ] a combination of the two.

a. Milk turns sour.
b. Wax is melted over a flame and then [ ]

2.4 Physical and Chemic[ ]

The **Periodic Table** is emphasized throughout. When various elements are introduced in the text, their locations in the periodic table are highlighted visually.

For example, copper is a typical metal. It is lustrous (although it tarnishes readily); it is an excellent conductor of electricity (it is widely used in electrical wires); and it is readily formed into various shapes, such as pipes for water systems. Copper is one of the transition metals—the metals shown in the center of the periodic table. Iron, aluminum, and gold are other familiar elements that have metallic properties. All of the elements shown to the left and below of the heavy "stair-step" black line in Figure 3.11 are classified as metals, except for hydrogen (**Figure 3.12**).

A copper kettle and burner from the Bethnal Green Museum in London.

The relatively small number of elements that appear in the upper righthand corner of the periodic table (to the right of the heavy line in Figures 3.11 and 3.12) are called **nonmetals.** Nonmetals generally lack those properties that characterize metals and show much more variation in their properties than metals do. Whereas almost all metals are solids at normal temperatures, many nonmetals (such as nitrogen, oxygen, chlorine, and neon) are gaseous and one (bromine) is a liquid. Several nonmetals (such as carbon, phosphorus, and sulfur) are also solids.

The elements that lie close to the "stair-step" line in Figure 3.11 often show a mixture of metallic and nonmetallic properties. These elements, which are called **metalloids** or **semimetals,** include silicon, germanium, arsenic, antimony, and tellurium.

As we continue our study of chemistry, we will see that the periodic table is a valuable tool for organizing accumulated knowledge and that it helps us predict the properties we expect a given element to exhibit. We will also develop a model for atomic structure that will explain why there are groups of elements with similar chemical properties.

Figure 3.12
The elements classified as metals and as nonmetals.

Nonmetals

Metals

CHEMISTRY
Nonmetals sometimes have one or more metallic properties. For example, solid iodine is lustrous, and graphite (a form of pure carbon) conducts electricity.

Indonesian men carrying chunks of elemental sulfur in baskets.

66 Chapter 3 Chemical Foundations: Elements, Atoms, and Ions

Example 3.5

Interpreting the Periodic Table

For each of the following elements, use the periodic table in the back of the book to give the symbol and atomic number and to specify whether the element is a metal or a nonmetal. Also give the named family to which the element belongs (if any).

   a. iodine

   b. magnesium

   c. gold

   d. lithium

Solution

   a. Iodine (symbol I) is element 53 (its atomic number is 53). Iodine lies to the right of the stair-step line in Figure 3.12 and thus is a nonmetal. Iodine is a member of Group 7, the family of halogens.

   b. Magnesium (symbol Mg) is element 12 (atomic number 12). Magnesium is a metal and is a member of the alkaline earth metal family (Group 2).

   c. Gold (symbol Au) is element 79 (atomic number 79). Gold is a metal and is not a member of a named vertical family. It is classed as a transition metal.

   d. Lithium (symbol Li) is element 3 (atomic number 3). Lithium is a metal in the alkali metal family (Group 1).

 Self-Check Exercise 3.5

Give the symbol and atomic number for each of the following elements. Also indicate whether each element is a metal or a nonmetal and whether it is a member of a named family.

   a. argon

   b. chlorine

   c. barium

   d. cesium

3.9 Natural States of the Elements

Objective: *To learn the natures of the common e*

A gold nugget weighing 13 lb, 7 oz, which came to be called Tom's Baby, was found by Tom Grove near Breckenridge, Colorado, on July 23, 1887.

As we have noted, the matter around Most often these mixtures contain co different elements are bound together. M their atoms tend to combine with those o pounds quite readily. Thus we do not of pure form—uncombined with other eleme exceptions. The gold nuggets found at

3.9   Nat

Examples, titled for easy reference, model a thoughtful, step-by-step approach to problem solving.

Most examples are followed by **Self-Check Exercises**, which provide students with opportunities to practice the skills they have just learned. The solutions to these exercises are found at the back of the book.

We can summarize the description of matter given in this chapter with the diagram shown in **Figure 2.18**. Note that a given sample of matter can be a pure substance (either an element or a compound) or, more commonly, a mixture (homogeneous or heterogeneous). We have seen that all matter exists as elements or can be broken down into elements, the most fundamental substances we have encountered up to this point. We will have more to say about the nature of elements in the next chapter.

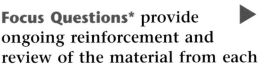

Figure 2.18
The organization of matter.

Focus Questions **Sections 2.4–2.6**

  1. Classify the following as *physical* or *chemical* changes.
    a. Mothballs gradually vaporize in a closet.
    b. Hydrofluoric acid attacks glass and is used to etch calibration marks on glass laboratory utensils.
    c. Calcium chloride lowers the temperature at which water freezes and can be used to melt ice on city sidewalks and roadways.
    d. An antacid tablet fizzes and releases carbon dioxide gas when it comes in contact with hydrochloric acid in the stomach.
    e. A flashlight battery corrodes and leaks on prolonged storage.
    f. Chemistry majors usually get holes in the cotton jeans they wear to lab because of the acids used in many experiments.
    g. Whole milk curdles if you add vinegar to it.
    h. A piece of rubber stretches when you pull it.
    i. Rubbing alcohol evaporates quickly from the skin.
    j. Acetone is used to dissolve and remove nail polish.
  2. Identify the following as *mixtures* or *pure substances*.
    a. milk
    b. the paper on which this book is printed
    c. a teaspoon of sugar
    d. a teaspoon of sugar dissolved in a glass of water
    e. steel
  3. Classify the following mixtures as *homogeneous* or *heterogeneous*.
    a. vanilla ice cream
    b. "rocky road" ice cream
    c. Italian salad dressing
    d. kitty litter
  4. Are all physical changes accompanied by chemical changes? Are all chemical changes accompanied by physical changes? Explain.

Focus Questions* provide ongoing reinforcement and review of the material from each learning segment of the text. Each learning segment consists of two or more closely related sections. (These divisions are clearly identified on the chapter planning pages.)

*See **SE** in Planning Guide.

Student Edition

Celebrity Chemical* introduces ▶ students to the properties and uses of various key elements and compounds.

◀ **Chemical Impact* boxes** discuss the latest real-world applications of chemistry to a variety of fields, including science and technology, consumer issues, and history.

*See **SE** in Planning Guide.

Help Notes appear in the margin throughout the text, providing tips that assist students in solving problems, doing calculations, and understanding concepts.

PROBLEM SOLVING
To convert pressure to the units needed, remember

1.000 atm

760.0 mm Hg
760.0 torr
14.69 psi
101,325 Pa

The SI unit for pressure is the **pascal** (abbreviated Pa).

1 standard atmosphere = 101,325 Pa

Thus 1 atmosphere is about 100,000 or 10^5 pascals. Because the pascal is so small we will use it sparingly in this book. A unit of pressure that is employed in the engineering sciences and that we use for measuring tire pressure is pounds per square inch, abbreviated psi.

1.000 atm = 14.69 psi

Sometimes we need to convert from one unit of pressure to another. We do this by using conversion factors. The process is illustrated in Example 13.1.

Example 13.1

Checking the air pressure in a tire.

Pressure Unit Conversions

The pressure of the air in a tire is measured to be 28 psi. Represent this pressure in atmospheres, torr, and pascals.

Solution

To convert from pounds per square inch to atmospheres, we need the equivalence statement

1.000 atm = 14.69 psi

which leads to the conversion factor

$$\frac{1.000 \text{ atm}}{14.69 \text{ psi}}$$

$$28 \text{ psi} \times \frac{1.000 \text{ atm}}{14.69 \text{ psi}} = 1.9 \text{ atm}$$

To convert from atmospheres to torr, we use the equivalence statement

1.000 atm = 760.0 torr

which leads to the conversion factor

$$\frac{760.0 \text{ torr}}{1.000 \text{ atm}}$$

$$1.9 \text{ atm} \times \frac{760.0 \text{ torr}}{1.000 \text{ atm}} = 1.4 \times 10^3 \text{ torr}$$

change from torr to pascals, we need the equivalence statement

1.000 atm = 101,325 Pa

hich leads to the conversion factor

$$\frac{101,325 \text{ Pa}}{1.000 \text{ atm}}$$

$$1.9 \text{ atm} \times \frac{101,325 \text{ Pa}}{1.000 \text{ atm}} = 1.9 \times 10^5 \text{ Pa}$$

TABLE 3.1
Distribution (Mass Percent) of the 18 Most Abundant Elements in the Earth's Crust, Oceans, and Atmosphere

Element	Mass Percent	Element	Mass Percent
oxygen	49.2	titanium	0.58
silicon	25.7	chlorine	0.19
aluminum	7.50	phosphorus	0.11
iron	4.71	manganese	0.09
calcium	3.39	carbon	0.08
sodium	2.63	sulfur	0.06
potassium	2.40	barium	0.04
magnesium	1.93	nitrogen	0.03
hydrogen	0.87	fluorine	0.03
		all others	0.49

The sand in these dunes at Death Valley National Monument is composed of silicon and oxygen atoms.

The number of elements changes regularly as new elements are made in particle accelerators.

TOP TEN
Elements in the Human Body

Element	Mass Percent
1. Oxygen	65.0
2. Carbon	18.0
3. Hydrogen	10.0
4. Nitrogen	3.0
5. Calcium	1.4
6. Phosphorus	1.0
7. Magnesium	0.50
8. Potassium	0.34
9. Sulfur	0.26
10. Sodium	0.14

body in almost uncountable ways, are all made by linking together a few fundamental units to form huge molecules. A nonchemical example is the English language, where hundreds of thousands of words are constructed from only 26 letters. Compounds are made by combining atoms of the various elements, just as words are constructed from the 26 letters of the alphabet. And just as you had to learn the letters of the alphabet before you could learn to read and write, you need to learn the names and symbols of the chemical elements before you can read and write chemistry.

Presently about 115 different elements are known, 88 of which occur naturally. (The rest have been made in laboratories.) The elements vary tremendously in abundance. In fact, only 9 elements account for most of the compounds found in the earth's crust. In **Table 3.1**, the elements are listed in order of abundance (mass percent) in the earth's crust, oceans, and atmosphere. Note that nearly half of the mass is accounted for by oxygen alone. Also note that the 9 most abundant elements account for over 98% of the total mass.

Oxygen, in addition to accounting for about 20% of the earth's atmosphere (where it occurs as O_2 molecules), is also found in virtually all the rocks, sand, and soil on the earth's crust. In these latter materials, oxygen is not present as O_2 molecules but exists in compounds that usually contain silicon and aluminum atoms. The familiar substances of the geological world, such as rocks and sand, contain large groups of silicon and oxygen atoms bound together to form huge clusters.

The list of elements found in living matter is very different from that for the earth's crust. The Top Ten list shows the distribution of the most abundant elements in the human body. Oxygen, carbon, hydrogen, and nitrogen form the basis for all biologically important molecules. Some elements found in the body (called trace elements) are crucial for life, even though they are present in relatively small amounts. For example, chromium helps the body use sugars to provide energy.

One more general comment is important at this point. As we have seen, elements are fundamental to understanding chemistry. However, students are oftentimes confused by the many different ways that chemists use the term *element*. Sometimes when we say *element*, we mean a single atom of that element. We might call this the microscopic form of an element. Other times

Top Ten Lists* offer interesting applications and connections to chemical concepts.

*See 🔵 in Planning Guide.

What If?* boxes feature open-ended, critical-thinking questions for students to consider. These are particularly useful for generating class discussion. ▶

*See <img SE> in Planning Guide.

8.2 Reactions in Which a Solid Forms

Objective: To learn to identify the solid that forms in a

One driving force for a chemical reaction is the process called **precipitation**. The solid that [forms is called a precipi-]**tate**, and the reaction is known as a **precipitatio**[n reaction. For example,] when an aqueous (water) solution of potassium chr[omate, $K_2CrO_4(aq)$, which] is yellow, is added to a colorless aqueous solution of [barium nitrate,] $Ba(NO_3)_2(aq)$, a yellow solid forms (see **Figure 8.1**). [This yellow solid] tells us that a reaction—a chemical change—has o[ccurred. We have] a situation where

Reactants → Products

What is the equation that describes this chemical c[hange? To write the equa-]tion, we must decipher the identities of the reacta[nts and products. The re-]actants have already been described: $K_2CrO_4(aq)$ and $Ba(NO_3)_2(aq)$. Is there some way in which we can predict the identities of the products? What is the yellow solid? The best way to predict the identity of this solid is to first *consider what products are possible.* To do this we need to know what chemical species are present in the solution that results when the reactant solutions are mixed. First, let's think about the nature of each reactant in an aqueous solution.

What Happens When an Ionic Compound Dissolves in Water?

The designation $Ba(NO_3)_2(aq)$ means that barium nitrate (a white solid) has been dissolved in water. Note from its formula that barium nitrate contains the Ba^{2+} and NO_3^- ions. *In virtually every case when a solid containing ions*

Figure 8.1
The precipitation reaction that occurs when yellow potassium chromate, $K_2CrO_4(aq)$, is mixed with a colorless barium nitrate solution, $Ba(NO_3)_2(aq)$.

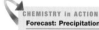

CHEMISTRY in ACTION
Forecast: Precipitation

1. Make two sets of flashcards with names of ions on one side and symbol and charge on the other (use the cards from the Chapter 4 activities if you have them).
   Set 1: all of the alkali and alkaline earth metals, and iron(II), iron(III), lead(II), and silver.
   Set 2: all of the nonmetals from Groups 5, 6, and 7, and the polyatomic ions listed in Table 4.4.
2. Randomly pick one card from set 1 and one card from set 2. Write the formula for the ionic compound that would form and name the compound.
3. Repeat step 2. Are both ionic compounds soluble? If so, go to step 4; if not, go back to step 2.
4. Use the two soluble ionic compounds as reactants. Write the names and formulas for the possible products of the reaction, the molecular equation, and the complete ionic equation. Is at least one of the products insoluble? If so, go to step 5; if not, go back to step 2.
5. Write the net ionic equation for the reaction. Go back to step 2 and continue this process until you have five net ionic equations.

Energy is the essence of our very existence as individuals and as a society. The food that we eat furnishes the energy to live, work, and play, just as the coal and oil consumed by manufacturing and transportation systems power our modern industrialized civilization.

Huge quantities of carbon-based fossil fuels have been available for the taking. This abundance of fuels has led to a world society with a voracious appetite for energy, consuming millions of barrels of petroleum every day. We are now dangerously dependent on the dwindling supplies of oil, and this dependence is an important source of tension among nations in today's world. In an incredibly short time we have moved from a period of ample and cheap supplies of petroleum to one of high prices and uncertain supplies. If our present standard of living is to be maintained, we must find alternatives to petroleum. To do this, we need to know the relationship between chemistry and energy, which we explore in this chapter.

10.1 The Nature of Energy

Objective: To understand the general properties of energy.

Although energy is a familiar concept, it is difficult to define precisely. For our purposes we will define **energy** as *the ability to do work or produce heat.* We will define these terms below.

Energy can be classified as either potential or kinetic energy. **Potential energy** is energy due to position or composition. For example, water behind a dam has potential energy that can be converted to work when the water flows down through turbines, thereby creating electricity. Attractive and repulsive forces also lead to potential energy. The energy released when gasoline is burned results from differences in attractive forces between the nuclei and electrons in the reactants and products. The **kinetic energy** of an object is energy due to the motion of the object and depends on the mass of the object m and its velocity v: $KE = \frac{1}{2}mv^2$.

One of the most important characteristics of energy is that it is conserved. The **law of conservation of energy** states *that energy can be converted from one form to another but can be neither created nor destroyed.* That is, the energy of the universe is constant.

Although the energy of the universe is constant, it can be converted from one form to another. Consider the two balls in **Figure 10.1a**. Ball A, because of its initially higher position, has more potential energy than ball B.

When ball A is released, it moves down the hill and strikes ball B. Eventually, the arrangement shown in **Figure 10.1b** is achieved. What has happened in going from the initial to the final arrangement? The potential energy of A has decreased because its position was lowered. However, this energy cannot disappear. Where is the energy lost by A?

WHAT IF?
What if energy were not conserved? How would it affect our lives?

—Held in place

(a) Initial

(b) Final

Figure 10.1
(a) In the initial positions, ball A has a higher potential energy than ball B. (b) After A has rolled down the hill, the potential energy lost by A has been converted to random motions of the components of the hill (frictional heating) and to an increase in the potential energy of B.

10.1 The Nature of Energy **289**

◀ **Chemistry in Action†** provides hands-on activities that can be performed quickly and easily with readily available materials.

†See in Planning Guide.

CHEMISTRY in the LABORATORY
Physical and Chemical Changes

Problem
How do physical changes differ from chemical changes?

Introduction
Matter can undergo both physical and chemical changes. Physical changes involve changes in one or more physical properties. Chemical changes involve changes in the composition of the substance.

The following are clues that indicate that a chemical change may have occurred: a color change, the evolution of bubbles, the formation of a solid, and heat absorbed or produced.

In this lab you will carry out four procedures (Parts I–IV) and make observations. Then you will decide how well the clues enable you to determine whether a chemical reaction occurred. In addition, you will develop molecular definitions of physical and chemical changes.

Prelab Assignment
Read the entire laboratory experiment before you begin.

Materials

Goggles	Spatula
Apron	Sponge
250-mL beakers (2)	Well plate
100-mL beakers (3)	Tongs
Graduated cylinder	Barium nitrate
Bunsen burner	Potassium sulfate
Matches	HCl (3.0 M)
Ring stand	Magnesium ribbon
Ring	Food coloring
Wire gauze	Water

Safety
1. The 3.0 M HCl is corrosive. Handle it with extreme care.
2. If you come in contact with any solution, wash the contacted area thoroughly.
3. You are working with a flame in this lab. Tie back hair and loose clothing.
4. Do not drop matches into the sink. Dispose of burned matches in the trashcan after they are cool.

Procedure
Part I
1. Add about 100 mL of water to a 250-mL beaker.
2. Add a few drops of food coloring to a beaker of water.
3. Make observations for several minutes.

42

Part II
1. Dissolve a spatula-tip amount of barium nitrate in a small amount of water (about 10 mL) in a 100-mL beaker.
2. Dissolve a spatula-tip amount of potassium sulfate in a small amount of water (about 10 mL) in a 100-mL beaker.
3. Pour the solutions from steps 1 and 2 together into an empty 100-mL beaker. Make careful observations.

Ring stand
Beaker
Wire gauze
Ring
Bunsen burner
Setup to boil water.

Part III
1. Add about 100 mL of water to a 250-mL beaker.
2. Arrange the beaker and ring stand as shown in the figure.
3. Light the Bunsen burner and place it under the beaker. Adjust the burner so that the hottest part of the flame touches the bottom of the beaker.
4. Bring the water to a boil. Make careful observations.
5. Use the tongs to hold the sponge over the beaker for a couple of minutes as the water boils.
6. Place the sponge on the lab bench and let it cool.
7. Squeeze the sponge. Record your observations.

Part IV
1. Place a few drops of 3.0 M HCl in one of the wells.
2. Add a small piece of magnesium ribbon to the acid. Make careful observations.

...rash your hands thoroughly.

...or each of the four parts of

...one provided here. Discuss ...hysical or chemical with your ...onclusions in the table. Jus- ...e table.

	That a ...cal Change ...d	Chemical or Physical Change?
...o water		
Mixing two solutions		
Boiling water		
Adding Mg to HCl		

2. Sometimes a physical change produces the same clues as those normally associated with chemical changes. Did this happen in any of your procedures? Which ones?
3. What was the purpose of the sponge in Part III? How did it help you decide whether the procedure involved a physical or chemical change?
4. Make microscopic drawings of each of the four procedures. Discuss how these explain your observations.
5. Develop definitions of chemical change and physical change using atoms and molecules in your definitions.

Something Extra
Chemists have learned that a chemical change always includes a rearrangement of the ways in which atoms are grouped. Explain what this statement means and discuss whether your observations support this statement.

◀ **Chemistry in the Laboratory*** concludes each chapter. These laboratory activities, which are also found in the Laboratory Manual, are exploratory and introductory.

Key Terms* are boldfaced and defined within the text when they first appear. They are also listed by section in the **Chapter Review*** and in the glossary at the back of the textbook.

Each chapter has a **Summary** section to reinforce key concepts and applications.

*See in Planning Guide.

 Chapter Review

Key Terms

matter (2.1)	chemical properties (2.4)
atom (2.2)	physical change (2.4)
compound (2.2)	chemical change (2.4)
molecule (2.2)	reaction (2.4)
element (2.2)	mixture (2.5)
graphite (2.2)	alloy (2.5)
diamond (2.2)	pure substance (2.5)
buckminsterfullerene (2.2)	homogeneous mixture (2.5)
solid (2.3)	solution (2.5)
liquid (2.3)	heterogeneous mixture (2.5)
gas (2.3)	distillation (2.6)
physical properties (2.4)	filtration (2.6)

Summary

1. Matter can exist in three states—solid, liquid, and gas—and can be described in terms of its physical and chemical properties. Chemical properties describe a substance's ability to undergo a change to a different substance. Physical properties are the characteristics a substance exhibits as long as no chemical change occurs.

2. A physical change involves a change in one or more physical properties, but no change in composition. A chemical change transforms a substance into a new substance or substances.

3. A mixture has variable composition. A homogeneous mixture has the same properties throughout; a heterogeneous mixture does not. A pure substance always has the same composition. We can physically separate mixtures of pure substances by distillation and filtration.

4. Pure substances are of two types: elements, which cannot be broken down chemically into simpler substances, and compounds, which can be broken down chemically into elements.

5. Elements are composed of tiny particles called atoms. Each element has a characteristic type of atom.

6. Compounds are composed of different types of atoms. Many compounds contain molecules—particles that are composed of atoms bonded to one another.

Chapter Review **43**

Student Edition

Questions and Problems

All exercises with blue numbers have answers in the back of this book.

2.1 The Particulate Nature of Matter

Questions

1. How do we "know" that matter is composed of atoms?

2. Why can't we see atoms with the naked eye?

2.2 Elements and Compounds

Questions

3. What does it mean to say that a given compound always has the same composition?

4. How do the properties of a compound, in general, compare to the properties of the elements of which it is composed? Give an example of a common compound and the elements of which it is composed to illustrate your answer.

2.3 The States of Matter

Questions

5. Consider three 10-g samples of water: one as ice, one as a liquid, and one as vapor. How do the volumes of these three samples compare with one another? How is this difference in volume related to the physical state involved?

6. In a sample of a gaseous substance, more than 99% of the overall volume of the sample is empty space. How is this fact reflected in the properties of a gaseous substance, compared with the properties of a liquid or solid substance?

2.4 Physical and Chemical Properties and Changes

Questions

7. Copper is a reddish-brown metal that is easily stretched to make wires. These characteristics are examples of (physical/chemical) properties of copper.

8. When copper metal is heated in concentrated nitric acid, the copper dissolves to form a deep blue solution, and a brown gas is evolved from the acid. These characteristics are examples of (physical/chemical) changes.

(For Exercises 9 and 10) Solutions of the substance potassium dichromate are bright orange in color. If a potassium dichromate solution is added to an acidic solution of iron(II) sulfate, the orange color of the potassium dichromate disappears, and the mixture takes on a bright green color as chromium(III) ion forms.

9. From the information above, indicate one *physical* property of potassium dichromate in solution.

10. From the information above, indicate one *chemical* property of potassium dichromate in solution.

11. What is meant by *electrolysis?* Are the changes produced by electrolysis chemical or physical in nature? Give an example to show your reasoning.

12. Classify the following as *physical* or *chemical* changes/properties.
    a. A shirt scorches when you leave the iron on one spot too long.
    b. The tires on your car seem to be getting flat in very cold weather.
    c. Your grandmother's silver tea set gets black with tarnish over time.
    d. Spray-on oven cleaner converts grease in the oven into a soapy material.
    e. An ordinary flashlight battery begins to leak with age and can't be recharged.
    f. Acids produced by bacteria in plaque cause teeth to decay.
    g. Sugar will char if overheated while making homemade candy.
    h. Hydrogen peroxide fizzes when applied to a wound.
    i. Dry ice "evaporates" without melting as time passes.
    j. Chlorine laundry bleaches will sometimes change the color of brightly colored clothing.

2.5 Mixtures and Pure Substances

Questions

13. Give three examples of heterogeneous *mixtures* and three examples of *solutions* that you might use in everyday life.

14. Classify the following as *mixtures* or as *pure substances*.
    a. a multivitamin tablet
    b. the blue liquid in your car's windshield washer
    c. a Spanish omelet
    d. a diamond

15. Classify the following mi[...] erogeneous.
    a. gasoline
    b. a jar of jelly beans
    c. chunky peanut butt[...]
    d. margarine
    e. the paper on which[...]

2.6 Separation of Mi[...]

Questions

16. Describe how the proces[...] to separate a solution int[...] Give an example.

17. Describe how the process of *filtration* could be used to separate a mixture into its components. Give an example.

18. In a common laboratory experiment in general chemistry, students are asked to determine the relative amounts of benzoic acid and charcoal in a solid mixture. Benzoic acid is relatively soluble in hot water, but charcoal is not. Devise a method for separating the two components of this mixture.

19. Describe the process of distillation depicted in Figure 2.14. Does the separation of the components of a mixture by distillation represent a chemical or a physical change?

Critical Thinking

20. Pure substance X is melted, and the liquid is placed in an electrolysis apparatus like that shown in Figure 2.8. When an electric current is passed through the liquid, a brown solid forms in one chamber and a white solid forms in the other chamber. Is substance X a compound or an element?

21. If a piece of hard white blackboard chalk is heated strongly in a flame, the mass of the piece of chalk will decrease, and eventually the chalk will crumble into a fine white dust. Does this change suggest that the chalk is composed of an element or a compound?

22. During a very cold winter, the temperature may remain below the freezing point for extended periods. However, fallen snow can still disappear, even though it cannot melt. This is possible because a solid can vaporize directly, without passing through the liquid state. Is this process (sublimation) a physical or a chemical change?

23. Discuss the similarities and differences between a liquid and a gas.

24. In gaseous substances, the individual molecules are relatively (close/far apart) and are moving freely, rapidly, and randomly.

25. The fact that the substance copper(II) sulfate pentahydrate is bright blue is an example of a _____ property.

26. The fact that the substance copper(II) sulfate pentahydrate combines with ammonia in solution to form a new compound is an example of a _____ property.

◀ **Questions and Problems** are keyed to chapter sections. Answers to blue highlighted exercises appear at the back of the book. Answers to all questions and problems are found at point-of-use in the Teacher's Edition. Complete solutions to all questions and problems are found in the Solutions Guide.

See **SE** in Planning Guide.

Critical Thinking Questions ▶ enrich and extend the text's exercise sets, encouraging a deeper conceptual understanding. Answers are found in the Teacher's Edition; complete solutions are provided in the Solutions Guide.

Reading Chemistry

Chemistry textbooks are written differently from non–technical textbooks. With this in mind, be aware that reading five pages in a chemistry textbook will probably take much more time than reading five pages in an English or a history textbook.

If you want to understand this chemistry text, prepare to spend a great deal of time reading each section within a chapter. If you flip through this book, you will notice many examples, explanations, diagrams, charts, symbols, and photos to read, analyze, and interpret. You should read the text in each section and incorporate these visuals in your reading. You will quickly find that these visuals are very useful in helping you understand the subject matter.

Use these suggestions to become an efficient and effective reader of chemistry.

1. **Preview your textbook.**

   To become familiar with the design and structure of your textbook, take a look at these key features:

   - Information about the authors, page vi
   - Tables of Contents and List of Features, pages vii–xxi
   - Appendices, pages A1–A11
   - Glossary, pages A47–A54
   - Index, pages A59–A76
   - Periodic Table, inside back cover

2. **Plan when and where you read.**

   Although you might find that relaxing on the couch at night is a comfortable and convenient place to do some of your homework, it will not be a good place to read about a chemistry concept.

   - Try to read your chemistry section during daylight hours, or in a well-lit area.
   - Sit in a straight-backed chair, such as th[...] a kitchen chair, or a desk chair.
   - Read in a quiet atmosphere; turn off th[...]
   - Remember that reading chemistry requ[...] Make sure that you have a pencil, notel[...] necessary items to help you study.
   - Allow plenty of time to read through ea[...] section is short, it still requires deep co[...]

xxii

◀ **Reading Chemistry** provides support to help students become active readers and to promote reading comprehension. Tips are provided and can be implemented at the onset of the course, as well as before, during, and after each chapter.

Writing Chemistry introduces ▶ students to technical writing by comparing and contrasting creative and technical styles of writing. Expectations for the style of writing required in this course are explained, and students are given a list of hints to strengthen their technical writing skills.

Writing Chemistry

Up to this point in your studies, you have learned and practiced many different types and styles of writing. In this class, you will be expected to use technical writing. Technical writing differs from essay, report, letter, and creative writing in many ways. Technical writing is factual, precise, clear, and free of bias and personal opinion. Sentences should be specific and to the point.

For instance, if you were asked to write about the current weather conditions in your area for a technical course, your description should use the technical writing style shown in Example 1, rather than the creative style shown in Example 2.

Example 1 • Technical Writing Sample

 The temperature is 75°F. It is sunny with minimal cloud coverage. The wind is blowing north to northwest at 15 miles per hour.

Note that the writer in Example 1 states factual information regarding the temperature and wind speed, includes units of measure, and writes without bias and personal opinion.

Example 2 • Creative Writing Sample

 It is a beautiful spring day! The sun is shining without a cloud in the sky, the air is light and breezy, and the temperature is simply perfect for a picnic in the park.

Although the writer in Example 2 paints a visual picture of the weather conditions, it would not be an appropriate description in a technical course. There are too many adjectives, there are not enough detailed facts, and the writing contains personal opinion about the weather.

When writing a response to a laboratory question, get right to the point. There is no need for extra words. For instance, you may be asked: "What evidence did you observe that indicates a reaction occurred?"

A good technical response would be:

 A yellow precipitate formed in the container.

The wordy response below would be inappropriate:

 After we observed the reaction for a few minutes, we saw something yellow starting to form at the bottom of the glass. We think that is how we know that a reaction occurred.

xxiv

Student Edition

Testing in Chemistry

The key to earning a successful grade on a chemistry test is to be actively involved in learning the content and to be well-prepared for every class. Chemistry is a cumulative subject, meaning that each section builds on the one before it. Preparation cannot begin the night before the test, but must be ongoing from the first day of class to the last day of class.

Designate a notebook for your chemistry notes and homework. Review your class notes with the corresponding section in the textbook, every day. If you are having trouble remembering new vocabulary words, chemical structures, or formulas, create a set of flashcards. Study your flashcards as often as possible.

Keep in mind that if you find yourself "cramming" for a chemistry test, it is likely that your test grade will reflect a lack of effort. Many of the concepts that you will be learning in this chemistry course will be unfamiliar and challenging. Embrace this challenge by organizing your approach to studying for this course.

Follow these test preparation tips to help you achieve a successful test score.

Before a Chemistry Test

- Read the course outline to know when your tests are scheduled.
- Review your class notes daily, and review the entire section after you have completed it in class. Do not put off reviewing material until right before test time; review needs to be ongoing.
- As you review, ask yourself questions about the material that is difficult for you.
- Create and answer your own test questions about what the teacher emphasized in class.
- Create and study your flashcards.
- Rework any homework problems that you solved incorrectly.
- Find out from your teacher what topics will be covered on the test, the style of the test, and whether a formula ref
- Get a good night's sleep before the test. Eat the test so that you can think, process, and
- Remember to take pencils, erasers, a calcula

During a Chemistry Test

- Relax!
- Read the test directions before you start ans
- Look through the test so that you know ho are, the style of the test items, and what ref This will help determine how much time y question.

xxvi

Testing in Chemistry provides test-preparation tips for testing in the chemistry content area. Students can refer to this material throughout the course, before chapter assessments, and before taking a standardized test.

Specific strategies targeted to achieving success in test-taking are explained in detail for each phase of testing: *Before* a test, *During* a test, and *After* a test.

Gridded Response

When a test item requires you to place your answer in a grid, you must answer the test item correctly *and* fill out accurately the grid on your answer sheet, or the item will be marked as incorrect. The answer to a gridded response test item can be only a positive numerical value, such as a positive integer, a fraction, an improper fraction, or a decimal.

After you work the test item and determine the answer, you must write your answer in the answer boxes at the top of the grid. You must then fill in the corresponding bubble under each box.

- Write your answer with the first digit in the far left answer box, or with the last digit in the far right answer box.
- Write only one digit or symbol in each answer box.
- Do not leave a blank in the middle of an answer.
- Include the decimal point or the fraction bar if it is part of the answer.
- Fill in only one bubble for each answer box that has a number or symbol. Bubbles should be filled in by making a solid black mark.
- Do not grid a mixed number. You must first convert the mixed number to an improper fraction.

Examples

xxviii

The Gridded Response includes section detailed information about the most common types of standardized test items students may encounter on a state or national chemistry test. Test-taking strategies and detailed examples are provided to help students respond to these types of test items.

*A resourceful Teacher's Edition, that is straightforward
and uncomplicated, provides helpful tools
and ideas for effective classroom integration.*

Teacher's Edition Features

- Entire content of the Student Edition

- Complete section-by-section Chapter Planning Guide

- *Integrating Reading Strategies and Chemistry Concepts* feature is presented at the beginning of each chapter

- Wraparound margin notes, including:

  - Chapter Overview

  - Teaching Tips

  - Additional Examples for each worked text example

  - Background material

  - Suggestions for setting up and performing in-class demonstrations and activities

  - References to print and technology resources at point-of-use

  - Answers to all questions and problems within text

  - Suggestions for integrating text features

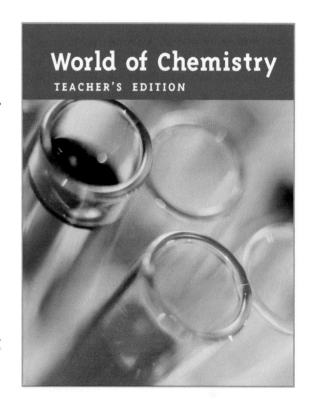

World of Chemistry
TEACHER'S EDITION

Teacher's Edition

◀ Each **Chapter Planning Guide** provides a section-by-section detailed guide to help with classroom planning and time-management. Placements of labs, activities, features, assessments, technology sources, and strategies for all learners are clearly indicated for quick reference.

An **Overview** is provided on each chapter opener page. This feature clearly defines the goals for the chapter, allowing for a quick determination of the objectives accomplished within the chapter. ▶

◀ At the beginning of each section is an outline listing the implied **Themes** of the section, the necessary **Skills**, tips for **Student Preparation, Active Learning** suggestions and activities, and applicable **Laboratory** experiments.

In-depth **Teaching Tips** provide information and strategies to help present concepts to students who have various learning styles, skill levels, and interests. These ideas can also help trigger prior knowledge, reinforce concepts, and extend the material.

Group Activities and other inclusion strategies appear in appropriate locations throughout the text, providing valuable suggestions to reach all learners.

Misconceptions are highlighted throughout the text, and tips are given to clarify misinterpretations, caution students against common mistakes, and to clear up confusion about terms and symbols.

Teacher's Edition

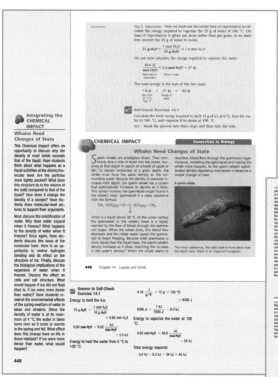

▶ Wraparound notes, such as **Integrating the Chemical Impact**, provide additional discussion topics and questions, activity ideas, and topics for further research.

▲ **Teaching Support** boxes are featured at the bottom of the page, highlighting **Demonstrations**, **Background Information**, and **Historical Information**. These are particularly useful for enhancing class discussion.

◀ Additional information about the materials and purpose of each **Chemistry in Action** feature helps implement these hands-on activities quickly and efficiently. Class discussion ideas are presented and questions posed in the activity are answered in detail.

▲ **Additional Examples** corresponding to a specific in-text example problem can be used to reinforcement new concepts. These examples are similar in style and in substance to the examples in the student text, and all answers are provided.

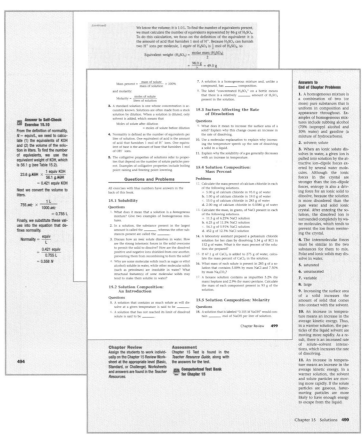

Answers to the Focus Questions, Self-Check Exercises, Questions and Problems, and Critical Thinking Questions are found at point-of-use. ▶

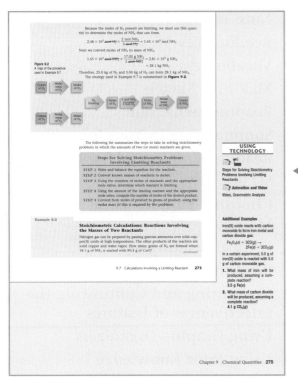

▲ Point-of-use transparencies and videotapes are called out in the **Using Technology** feature. The title of each item is clearly labeled for easy reference.

Focus On Reading

◀ **Integrating Reading Strategies and Chemistry Concepts** provides strategies and suggestions at the beginning of each chapter for teachers to implement throughout the course. Twenty-one specific reading strategies are explained in detail to help you meet the individual needs of your students.

Each chapter is associated with one type of reading strategy. Any of these strategies, however, can be implemented for any chapter. It is recommended that you preview the list of reading strategies and introduce strategies in an order that is best suited for your class.

Chp	Integrating Reading Strategies and Chemistry Concepts Features
1	Previewing the Textbook
2	Reading Laboratory Experiments
3	Creating and Using Flashcards
4	Reading Symbols
5	Reading Math
6	Reading Example Problems
7	Reading Chemical Equations
8	Note Taking
9	Reading Key Words
10	Vocabulary
11	Making a Sketch
12	Reading a Diagram
13	Summarizing in Your Journal
14	Reading Graphs and Tables
15	SQ3R
16	Choosing Supplemental Reading Materials
17	Critical Reading Skills
18	Reading Rules
19	Comparing and Contrasting the Effectiveness of Features
20	Using Graphic Organizers
21	Using Prior Knowledge

All of the Elements for Success

The *World of Chemistry* program includes all of the elements for a successful learning experience. In addition to the Student Edition and the Teacher's Edition, the curriculum includes the tools listed to the right.

Laboratory Experiment Program

This program is designed to help students learn chemistry by exploring the chemical nature of matter. In addition to the labs and demonstrations explained in the text, the program includes the following items.

Accessible Content
Creative Problem Solving
Active Learning
Real-World Connections

Laboratory Experiment Program
Assessment Program
Teacher Resource Program
Technology Program
All Learners Program
Student Resource Program

LABORATORY EXPERIMENTS *for* World of CHEMISTRY
McDougal Littell
Zumdahl Zumdahl DeCoste

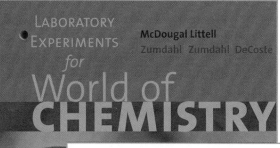

◄ **Laboratory Experiments for World of Chemistry***
This Laboratory Manual provides 91 engaging experiments, which are organized to match the topics in the text. The manual includes the 21 in-text labs found in the text, plus 30 additional experiments of a traditional nature, 27 microscale labs, and 13 computer-based labs. All experiments have been class-tested and have undergone a safety review to ensure their appropriateness for high school chemistry students. Complete lab safety guidelines are provided throughout the manual.

*See **LM** in Planning Guide.

Experiment 39

Synthesis of Manganese(II) Chloride

Problem
What special techniques are needed to synthesize a pure sample of a metal halide?

Introduction
In this experiment you will synthesize manganese(II) chloride by allowing a known mass of manganese metal to react with an excess of hydrochloric acid. From the theoretical yield (calculated from the mass of metal used) and the actual mass of product recovered, you will calculate the percentage yield. The balanced equation for the reaction is:

$$Mn(s) + 2 HCl(aq) \rightarrow MnCl_2(aq) + H_2(g)$$

According to the equation, one mole (54.94 grams) of manganese will generate precisely one mole (125.84 grams) of manganese(II) chloride. Regardless of the actual mass of manganese used, the mass of reactant and product must be in this same ratio. Once the synthesis is complete and you have isolated your product, you will determine your actual yield by weighing the flask and product. You will then compare it with the expected yield (called the *theoretical yield*), by applying the ratio of the molar masses of the product and metal. From these two, you will calculate your percentage yield. As part of your error analysis, you will try to account for any deviation between the actual and theoretical yields.

Evaporation of the solution remaining in the flask after reaction will yield solid manganese(II) chloride. The product is very hygroscopic (water absorbing), so it will be necessary for it to cool in a location that will not allow absorption of atmospheric moisture. Such dry-atmosphere cooling chambers are called *desiccators*.

Prelaboratory Assignment
✓ Read the **Introduction** and **Procedure** before you begin.
✓ Answer the Prelaboratory Questions.
  1. Explain the difference between *theoretical yield* and *actual yield*.
  2. Why is it important for the manganese to react entirely before proceeding at step 5?
  3. What is a desiccator, and why is it needed in this experiment?
  4. a. If 10 M HCl(aq) accidentally spills or splashes on your skin or clothing, describe in detail what you should do.
     b. What, if anything, would you do differently if the acid spilled on the surface of the lab bench or hood?
  5. When you are done with the manganese(II) chloride, how should you dispose of the product?

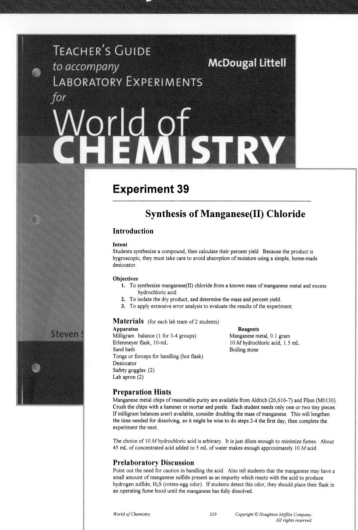

TEACHER'S GUIDE
to accompany
LABORATORY EXPERIMENTS
for
McDougal Littell
World of
CHEMISTRY

Steven

◄ Teacher's Guide to Accompany Laboratory Experiments* This helpful guide includes general notes about each experiment, detailed hints for teacher laboratory preparation and cleanup, hints for pre- and post-laboratory discussions, lists of materials required, and a key for the student report sheet that contains sample data as well as detailed answers for the questions and calculations.

Experiment 39

Synthesis of Manganese(II) Chloride

Introduction

Intent
Students synthesize a compound, then calculate their percent yield. Because the product is hygroscopic, they must take care to avoid absorption of moisture using a simple, home-made desiccator.

Objectives
1. To synthesize manganese(II) chloride from a known mass of manganese metal and excess hydrochloric acid.
2. To isolate the dry product, and determine the mass and percent yield.
3. To apply extensive error analysis to evaluate the results of the experiment.

Materials (for each lab team of 2 students)

Apparatus	Reagents
Milligram balance (1 for 3-4 groups)	Manganese metal, 0.1 gram
Erlenmeyer flask, 10-mL	10 M hydrochloric acid, 1.5 mL
Sand bath	Boiling stone
Tongs or forceps for handling (hot flask)	
Desiccator	
Safety goggles (2)	
Lab apron (2)	

Preparation Hints
Manganese metal chips of reasonable purity are available from Aldrich (26,616-7) and Flinn (M0130). Crush the chips with a hammer or mortar and pestle. Each student needs only one or two tiny pieces. If milligram balances aren't available, consider doubling the mass of manganese. This will lengthen the time needed for dissolving, so it might be wise to do steps 2-4 the first day, then complete the experiment the next.

The choice of 10 M hydrochloric acid is arbitrary. It is just dilute enough to minimize fumes. About 45 mL of concentrated acid added to 5 mL of water makes enough approximately 10 M acid.

Prelaboratory Discussion
Point out the need for caution in handling the acid. Also tell students that the manganese may have a small amount of manganese sulfide present as an impurity which reacts with the acid to produce hydrogen sulfide, H_2S (rotten-egg odor). If students detect this odor, they should place their flask in an operating fume hood until the manganese has fully dissolved.

World of Chemistry   219   *Copyright © Houghton Mifflin Company.*

REPORT SHEETS
to accompany
LABORATORY EXPERIMENTS
for
McDougal Littell
World of
CHEMISTRY

Report Sheets to Accompany Laboratory Experiments* Student report sheets are provided for all of the experiments in Laboratory Experiments for World of Chemistry. The report sheet is an organized form for students to use for answering Prelaboratory Questions, recording their data/observations, and completing their analysis and conclusions. ▶

For teachers who prefer that their students write their own lab reports, the experiments are written to include prelaboratory questions, information on preparing data tables and tables for results, and analysis questions.

*See Ⓛ in Planning Guide.

Name_____

Section_____Date_____

Report for Experiment 36

The Calcium Content of Milk

Prelaboratory Questions
1. Why would you expect the calcium in milk to be present as calcium ions, rather than as elemental calcium?

2. According to one source, one cup (~240 mL) of whole milk contains 291 mg of calcium. Use this to calculate the mass percent of calcium in whole milk. Assume the density of milk is 1.0 g/mL.

3. Would you expect the density of milk to be affected by its fat content? Explain. Would increased fat content raise or lower the density? Explain.

J. DeCoste

Data/Observations

Data Table

Titration 1:

Initial mass of milk pipet	g	Initial mass of EDTA pipet	g
Final mass of milk pipet	g	Final mass of EDTA pipet	g
Mass of milk used	g	Mass of EDTA used	g

Titration 2:

Initial mass of milk pipet	g	Initial mass of EDTA pipet	g
Final mass of milk pipet	g	Final mass of EDTA pipet	g
Mass of milk used	g	Mass of EDTA used	g

World of Chemistry   123   *Copyright © Houghton Mifflin Company.*

Assessment Program

This program includes multiple ways to assess student comprehension. Included within the Student Edition are Self-Check Exercises, Focus Questions, end-of-chapter problems, and critical thinking exercises. In addition, the assessment program includes the following items.

This **Chapter Test*** resource booklet contains chapter tests for each chapter of *World of Chemistry.*

Included in each chapter test are various styles of test items to allow for a complete, comprehensive assessment of students' understanding of the chapter material:
- Matching
- Multiple choice
- Fill-in-the-blank
- Free response

Answers are provided at the end of the booklet.

*See **RP** in Planning Guide.

TEACHER RESOURCES
CHAPTER TESTS
to accompany
McDougal Littell

World of
CHEMISTRY

Name_____ Section_____ Date_____

_____ 16. For a constant number of moles of a gas, volume varies:

a) directly with the absolute temperature and inversely with pressure
b) inversely with the absolute temperature and directly with pressure
c) directly with the absolute temperature and directly with pressure
d) inversely with the absolute temperature and inversely with pressure

_____ 17. Consider the following: You have 2 liters of neon gas at a pressure of 2 atmospheres, 2 liters of carbon dioxide gas at a pressure of 3 atmospheres, and 2 liters of nitrogen gas at a pressure of 4 atmospheres. All three samples are at room temperature. If you transfer all 3 gases to the same rigid 2 liter container, what is the pressure exerted by the nitrogen in the final mixture?

a) 2 atm   c) 4 atm
b) 3 atm   d) 9 atm

Name_____ Section_____ Date_____

II. Multiple Choice

Choose the one best answer and write its letter in the blank.

_____ 9. If the temperature is held constant, what will happen to the pressure exerted by a gas if the volume of the container is decreased?

a) increase   c) remain the same
b) decrease   d) increase, or decrease (it depends)

_____ 10. Which of the following is NOT true about pressure?

Name_____ Section_____ Date_____

Chapter 13
Gases

I.   Matching

Match the description in Column B with the correct term in Column A. Write the letter in the blank provided. Each term matches with only one description, so be sure to choose the best description for each term.

Column A

_____ 1. absolute zero

_____ 2. universal gas constant

_____ 3. Boyle's law

_____ 4. Charles's law

_____ 5. Avogadro's law

_____ 6. combined gas law

_____ 7. Dalton's law of partial pressures

_____ 8. molar volume of ideal gas at STP

Column B

A. at constant temperature, the volume of a given amount of gas is inversely proportional to its pressure.

B. the total pressure of a mixture of gases is the sum of the pressures that each gas would exert if alone in the container.

C. temperature at which a gas theoretically occupies zero volume.

D. $\dfrac{P_1V_1}{T_1} = \dfrac{P_2V_2}{T_2}$

E. at constant temperature and pressure, the volume of a gas is directly proportional to the number of moles of gas.

F. 22.4 liters

G. at constant pressure, the volume of a given amount of gas is directly proportional to its kelvin temperature.

H. 0.08206 $\dfrac{L \cdot atm}{mol \cdot K}$

Assessment

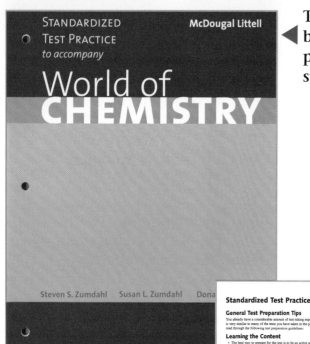

STANDARDIZED
TEST PRACTICE
to accompany

McDougal Littell

World of CHEMISTRY

Steven S. Zumdahl   Susan L. Zumdahl   Dona...

The **Standardized Test Practice*** booklet is a tool to help students prepare for national and state-specific standardized testing.

▼ This resource provides general test preparation tips and test-taking strategies for different types of test items that students may see on a standardized chemistry test.

The booklet contains 21 multiple-choice chapter tests that correspond to the chapters within the text. It includes a wide variety of problems, ranging from basic to challenging, typical of what the students will experience on a standardized test. Answers to each test are provided at the end of the booklet.

A student scantron sheet is provided and can be copied and distributed for each test.

*See **AR** in Planning Guide.

Standardized Test Practice

General Test Preparation Tips

You already have a considerable amount of test-taking experience. For the most part, a standardized test in chemistry is very similar to many of the tests you have taken in the past. However, in order to make sure that you do your best, read through the following test preparation guidelines:

Learning the Content

- The best way to prepare for the test is to be an active and involved learner throughout the school year. Keep up with your class work, take good notes, and ask questions when you do not understand something.
- Before taking the test, thoroughly review your class notes. If there are topics you do not understand, ask your friends and your teacher for help. You may also want to reread the chapter from your textbook that covers the material.
- If possible, take several practice standardized tests.
- You may want to create a special test preparation notebook. In it, list important terms and their definitions, illustrate concepts and processes, and summarize key equations and relationships that you will need to know.
- Study with your friends or join a test-prep study group. Having someone new explain a concept may make a confusing concept clear; different people's understandings of a concept can be very helpful. If possible, take practice tests together and compare answers.
- Make sure you know what topics will and will not be covered on the test. Although all of the topics covered in your class are important to your overall understanding of chemistry, it is also important to realize that studying topics that are not covered on the test is unlikely to improve your test score.

The Night Before the Test

- Try to avoid last minute cramming.
- Organize the things you will need for the test, such as pencils, an eraser, a calculator, and your glasses.
- Get a good night's sleep.

Test Day—Taking the Test

- Eat a good breakfast. Your thinking will be sharper and more focused if you are not hungry and have gotten a good night's sleep.
- Arrive on time and prepared to take the test.
- Read the directions carefully and pace yourself. It is important that you give yourself enough time to answer all of the questions on the test. Be careful, however, not to rush through the test. It is a good strategy to answer the questions you know first, while allowing yourself enough time to return to and think about the questions you are unsure of.

Strategies for Answering Test Questions

You will encounter several types of questions on the test, from typical multiple choice questions, to questions requiring the review and interpretation of diagrams, charts, tables, and graphs, to short answer (constructed-response) questions, ... chemistry-related reading. The strategies below may be helpful in answering these ... given question type, not all of the strategies will need to be applied.

...ring Multiple Choice Questions
...tion before considering the answers.
...note key words and phrases in the questions that indicate what you should
...es. This strategy works best for questions with long introductions.
...es reading the answer choices.

- Read all of the answer choices before making a decision. Eliminate choices that you know are incorrect. Pay special attention to answer choices such as "all of the above" or "none of the above." It is possible to eliminate these choices as soon as an answer that does not fit is found.
- If you are confused about the possible answer after reading the answer choices, move on to the next question. Sometimes other questions on the test will give you additional information and insight needed to answer the question. Remember to leave yourself enough time to return to the question later. If you are still unsure after returning to the question, go with your best guess.

Strategies for Answering Diagram-based Questions

Some of the questions on the test will be related to informational diagrams. The diagrams may look realistic or they may represent a process in schematic form. Schematic drawings show relationships among parts and/or the sequence of a process.

- Study the diagram before reading the question and/or the related passage.
- Analyze the information the diagram provides. Be sure to note the information given in the title and labels.
- Read the question and then follow the strategies given for answering multiple choice or reading-based questions.

Strategies for Answering Data Table-based Questions

Some of the questions on the test will be related to data tables. Data tables generally contain information summarizing a topic or the results of an experiment. The information in the table is organized into horizontal rows and vertical columns. Column headings name the type of information contained in the table.

- Note the title of the data table. The title should be located across the top of the table.
- Analyze the rows and columns in the table and determine their purpose. Generally, you should read across the rows and down the columns to determine the relationships in the data.
- Read the question and then follow the strategies given for answering multiple choice or reading-based questions.

Strategies for Answering Graph-based Questions

Some of the questions on the test will be related to graphs. A graph is a visual representation of data that should make the relationships in data easier to see. Typical types of graphs include line graphs, circle graphs, and bar graphs. Line graphs typically show the relationship between two quantities, or variables; one quantity is changed in a controlled manner (the independent variable, plotted on the x-axis), while the second quantity varies in response to this change (the dependent variable, plotted on the y-axis). Circle graphs usually depict relationships between components of a whole and are often expressed in percentages. Bar graphs are usually used to compare how several quantities vary as another quantity is changed.

- Study the graph before reading the question and/or the related passage.
- Analyze the information given in the graph. Note the information given in the title of the graph and identify the dependent and independent variables.
- What happens to the dependent variable as the independent variable is changed? Try to determine the relationship between the variables.
- Read the question and then follow the strategies given for answering multiple choice or reading-based questions.

Name _____   Section _____   Date _____

Chapter 16   Standardized Test Practice

1. The pH of a substance is defined as:
   A. log[H^+].   **B.** −log[H^+].   **C.** −log[H^+].   **D.** −log[OH^-].

2. Which of the following relationships is correct?
   F. pH + pOH = K_w **H.** [H^+][OH^-] = 1.0×10^{-14}
   G. K_w = −log[H^+]   **J.** none of the above

3. If the pOH of a solution is 5.25, what is [H^+]?
   A. 8.75 M **B.** 5.25 M **C.** 5.6×10^{-6} M **D.** 1.8×10^{-9} M

4. Which of the following pairings is incorrect?
   F. neutral : pH = 7   **H.** basic : [H^+] < [OH^-]
   G. acidic : [H^+] > [OH^-]   **J.** none of the above

Passage I

Use the following passage and graph to answer questions 5–8.

A student conducted a titration experiment by gradually adding 0.10 M NaOH to a flask containing an unknown solution. She used a pH meter during the procedure to measure the pH of the solution. Her experimental results are shown in the graph below.

(graph: pH vs 0.10 M NaOH added (mL), showing a titration curve with "Equivalence point" labeled)

5. Based on the graph, which of the following statements is true?
   A. At the equivalence point, [H^+] > [OH^-].
   B. The titration curve indicates that the unknown liquid is a weak base.
   C. The titration curve indicates that the unknown liquid is a weak acid.
   D. At the equivalence point, −log[H^+] = 7.

McDougal Littell Test Generator* Available on CD-ROM for Macintosh or Windows, the computerized test bank augments the printed Chapter Tests resource by providing a wealth of questions from which teachers can select questions to create quizzes and tests. This powerful, easy-to-use program can produce multiple-choice, true/false, short-answer, matching, fill-in-the-blank, and essay questions. Teachers can select questions according to chapter, question format, type, and/or topic.

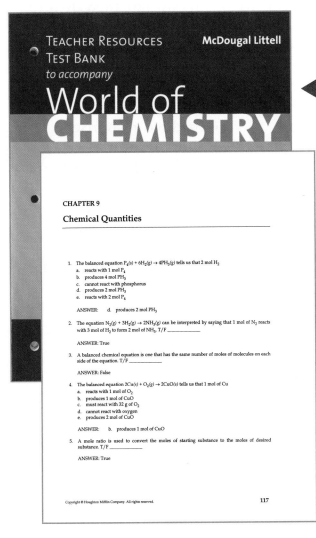

◀ **Test Bank*** This teacher resource contains printed versions of approximately 1600 items from the computerized test bank. The questions for each chapter are arranged by section. The test items consist of multiple-choice, true-false, short-answer, matching, fill-in-the-blank and essay questions. The questions do not repeat any items from the Chapter Test resource booklet.

*See 🅡🅟 in Planning Guide.

Assessment

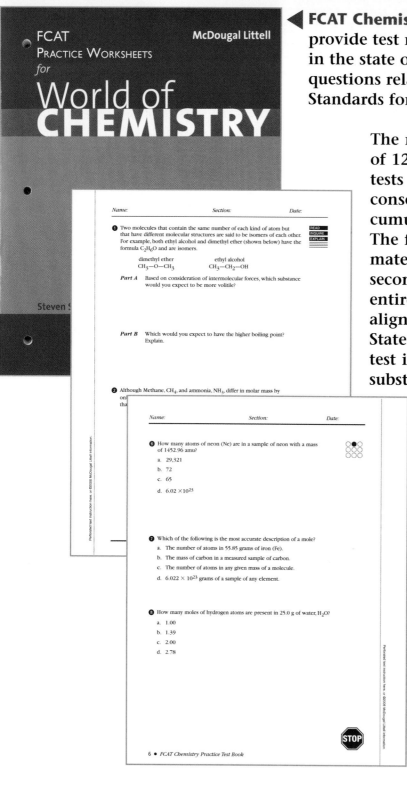

◀ FCAT Chemistry Practice Worksheets* provide test materials to help students in the state of Florida prepare for FCAT questions related to the Sunshine State Standards for high school chemistry.

The resource book includes a total of 12 tests. Each of ten chapter tests covers materials from two consecutive chapters. Two cumulative tests are also provided. The first cumulative test covers material from Chapters 1–10; the second covers material from the entire text. Each test question aligns with the Florida Sunshine State Standards. Test format and test items are similar in style and substance to the actual FCAT exam.

Each test includes these types of test items:
- Multiple choice
- Gridded response
- Short response
- Extended response

An answer key is provided at the end of the book.

*See 🌑 in Planning Guide.

Teacher Resource Program

This program provides teachers with the additional resources needed for classroom assistance and management.

Lesson Plans to accompany *World of Chemistry** These lesson plans are provided to map out the information and resources available for presenting a particular section of the textbook. Each lesson plan provides the following information.

- Section and corresponding textbook page numbers

- Section objectives

- Time schedule for periods and block

- National Science Content Standards

- *Focus:* Includes suggested classroom demonstrations

- *Teach:* Includes teaching tips, all learner strategies, examples, and other in-text features

- *Laboratory Activity:* Corresponding lab resources needed

- *Assess:* Suggests assessment resources

- *Close:* Suggests worksheets for discussion

- *Homework:* Suggested assignments

- *Resources:* Includes technology resources

- *Notes:* An area for teacher comments

*See 🅛🅟 in Planning Guide.

Teacher Resources

Transparencies* This package features 86 full-color overhead transparency acetates of key illustrations from the text. Each transparency is clearly labeled with the table number or figure number from the text. Point-of-use for each transparency is provided in the Teacher's Edition.

These visual aids help reinforce important concepts and are particularly helpful to the visual learner.

***See** in Planning Guide.

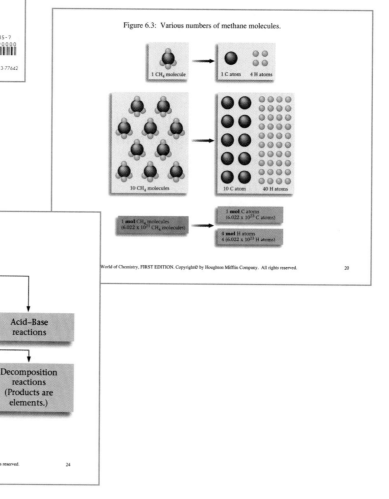

Figure 6.3: Various numbers of methane molecules.

1 CH₄ molecule → 1 C atom   4 H atoms

10 CH₄ molecules → 10 C atom   40 H atoms

1 **mol** CH₄ molecules
(6.022 x 10²³ CH₄ molecules)

1 **mol** C atoms
(6.022 x 10²³ C atoms)

4 **mol** H atoms
4 (6.022 x 10²³ H atoms)

World of Chemistry, FIRST EDITION. Copyright© by Houghton Mifflin Company. All rights reserved.   20

Figure 8.12: Summary of classes of reactions.

```
                    Chemical
                    reactions
        ┌──────────────┼──────────────┐
        ↓              ↓              ↓
   Precipitation  Oxidation–Reduction   Acid–Base
    reactions        reactions          reactions
        ┌──────────────┼──────────────┐
        ↓              ↓              ↓
   Combustion      Synthesis      Decomposition
    reactions      reactions        reactions
                 (Reactants are   (Products are
                   elements.)       elements.)
```

Zumdahl / World of Chemistry, FIRST EDITION. Copyright© by Houghton Mifflin Company. All rights reserved.   24

Classroom Activities and Projects* This teacher resource contains templates, guidelines, teaching notes, and suggested activities designed to supplement discussions and explanations in the text. Most of the activities and projects are cross-referenced with the appropriate chapters in the text. This resource also includes a special Spring Project designed for independent student work.

This **Solutions Guide*** contains completely worked-out solutions to all of the questions, problems, and critical thinking questions contained in the text at the end of each chapter. Solutions are written in a manner that complements the explanations in the textbook.

*See ⓡⓟ in Planning Guide.

Technology

Technology Program

This program provides a comprehensive collection of technology resources to help make your classroom presentations exciting, engaging, and interesting. Resources include CD-ROMs, videotapes, and Web site links.

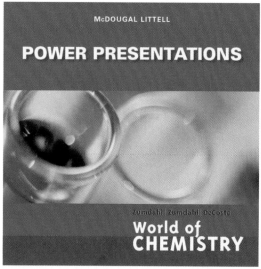

◀ **Video and Animations CD-Rom***
Chemistry Videos and Animations are available on both DVD and CD-ROM. The disks feature video clips of chemical phenomena and dozens of animations of molecular-level processes and key chemical concepts. The Teacher's Edition offers point-of-use suggestions for integrating these visuals in classroom presentations.

- The video: **video** clips of chemical phenomena and dozens of **animations** of molecular level processes and key chemical concepts, which are intended for use in classroom presentations. Point of use is indicated in the Teacher's Edition.

*See ▣ in Planning Guide.

◀ **PowerPresentations CD** The PowerPresentations CD-ROM contains PowerPoint slides of key figures from the text for use in classroom presentations.

Chemistry in Motion Videotape* ▶
This item contains 34 videos of popular classroom chemical demonstrations. The Teacher's Edition offers point-of-use suggestions for integrating these videos in classroom presentations.

*See ▣ in Planning Guide.

easyPlanner CD-ROM, Florida Edition

The Florida Edition of the easyPlanner CD contains:
- Florida Teacher's Edition
- Teaching Resources
- The FCAT Practice Worksheets
- State and national standards
- Customizeable lesson plans

This CD-ROM can be used to view, edit, and customize pre-made lesson plans.

Access to all printed teaching resources is available by skill level and by topic.

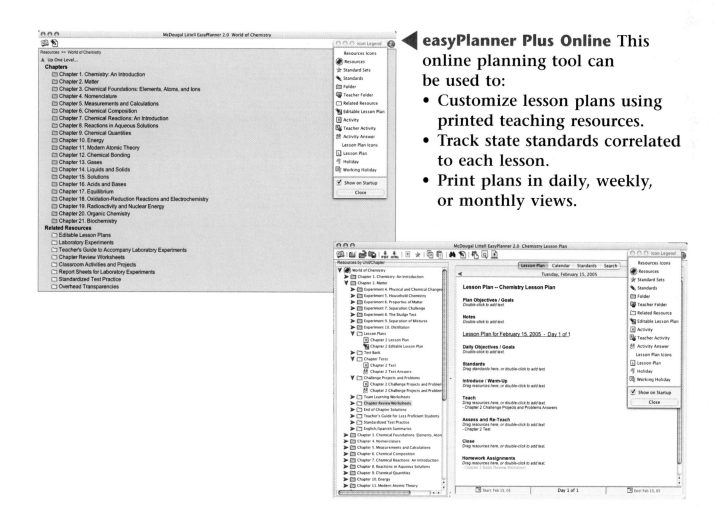

easyPlanner Plus Online This online planning tool can be used to:
- Customize lesson plans using printed teaching resources.
- Track state standards correlated to each lesson.
- Print plans in daily, weekly, or monthly views.

All Learners Program

World of Chemistry helps all learners learn chemistry by providing universal access. The program includes resources designed to meet the individual needs of all students. Chapter features and critical thinking problems are provided in the textbook. Teaching tip activities and reading strategies are found in the Teacher's Edition. Technology aids and other teacher resources make up the All Learners program.

Challenge Projects and Problems*
Challenge projects and problems give the students the opportunity to apply their chemistry knowledge to real-world situations. Each project can be assigned as a group activity or as an individual activity for students who will benefit from extra challenging material.

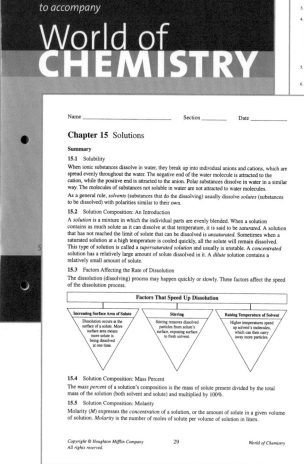

Teacher's Guide for Less Proficient Students* This tool includes easy-to-read chapter summaries and additional basic-level focus questions designed to help students who are having difficulty comprehending a section.

*See **AB** in Planning Guide.

Team Learning Worksheets* These worksheets provide questions to engage students in small-group discussions to encourage active learning. These worksheets can be used in the classroom as an integral part of the learning process and for presentation of new concepts.

*See 🅡🅟 in Planning Guide.

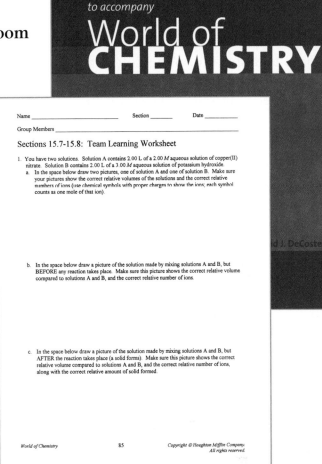

TEACHER RESOURCES
TEAM LEARNING WORKSHEETS
to accompany

McDougal Littell

World of CHEMISTRY

d J. DeCoste

Name _____ Section _____ Date _____

Group Members _____

Sections 15.7-15.8: Team Learning Worksheet

1. You have two solutions. Solution A contains 2.00 L of a 2.00 M aqueous solution of copper(II) nitrate. Solution B contains 2.00 L of a 3.00 M aqueous solution of potassium hydroxide.
   a. In the space below draw two pictures, one of solution A and one of solution B. Make sure your pictures show the correct relative volumes of the solutions and the correct relative numbers of ions (use chemical symbols with proper charges to show the ions; each symbol counts as one mole of that ion).

   b. In the space below draw a picture of the solution made by mixing solutions A and B, but BEFORE any reaction takes place. Make sure this picture shows the correct relative volume compared to solutions A and B, and the correct relative number of ions.

   c. In the space below draw a picture of the solution made by mixing solutions A and B, but AFTER the reaction takes place (a solid forms). Make sure this picture shows the correct relative volume compared to solutions A and B, and the correct relative number of ions, along with the correct relative amount of solid formed.

World of Chemistry   85

ENGLISH/ SPANISH SUMMARIES *to accompany*   McDougal Littell

World of CHEMISTRY

Ste

15 Chapter Review

Key Terms

solution (p. 467)
solvent (p. 467)
solute (p. 467)
aqueous solutions (p. 467)
saturated (15.2)
unsaturated (15.2)
supersaturated (15.2)
concentrated (15.2)
dilute (15.2)
mass percent (15.4)

molarity (M) (15.5)
standard solution (15.5)
dilution (15.6)
neutralization reaction(15.8)
equivalent of an acid (15.9)
equivalent of a base (15.9)
equivalent weight (15.9)
normality (N) (15.9)
colligative property (15.10)

Summary

1. A solution is a homogeneous mixture. The solubility of a solute in a given solvent depends on the interactions between the solvent and solute particles. Water dissolves many ionic compounds and compounds with polar molecules, because strong forces occur between the solute and the polar water molecules. Nonpolar solvents tend to dissolve nonpolar solutes. "Like dissolves like."

2. Solution composition can be described in many ways. Two of the most important are in terms of mass percent of solute.

   $$\text{Mass percent} = \frac{\text{mass of solute}}{\text{mass of solution}} \times 100\%$$

   and molarity:

   $$\text{Molarity} = \frac{\text{moles of solute}}{\text{liters of solution}}$$

3. A standard solution is one whose concentration is accurately known. Solutions are often made from a stock solution by dilution. When a solution diluted, only solvent is added, which means that

   Moles of solute after dilution
     = moles of solute before dilution

4. Normality is defined as the number of equivalents per liter of solution. One equivalent of acid is the amount of acid that furnishes 1 mol of H⁺ ions. One equivalent of base is the amount of base that furnishes 1 mol of OH⁻ ions.

5. The colligative properties of solutions refer to properties that depend on the number of solute particles present. Examples of colligative properties include boiling point raising and freezing point lowering.

15 Repaso del capítulo

Vocabulario

solución (pág. 467)
disolvente (pág. 467)
soluto (pág. 467)
solución acuosa (pág. 467)
solución saturada (15.2)
solución insaturada (15.2)
solución supersaturada (15.2)
solución concentrada (15.2)
solución diluida (15.2)
porcentaje de masa (15.4)
molaridad (M) (15.5)

solución estándar (15.5)
dilución (15.6)
reacción
  de neutralización (15.8)
equivalente
  de un ácido (15.9)
equivalente de una
  base (15.9)
equivalente por peso (15.9)
normalidad (N) (15.9)
propiedad coligativa (15.10)

Resumen

1. Las soluciones son mezclas homogéneas. La solubilidad de un soluto en un disolvente dado depende de la interacción entre las partículas que los forman. El agua es capaz de disolver muchos compuestos iónicos y compuestos de moléculas polarizadas debido a las fuerzas de gran magnitud que se crean entre el soluto y las moléculas polarizadas del agua. Los disolventes no polarizados tienden a disolver los solutos no polarizados. En otras palabras, disolventes semejantes disuelven solutos semejantes.

2. La composición de las soluciones se describe de diversas maneras. A continuación se resumen dos de las principales:

   $$\text{Porcentaje de} \atop \text{masa del soluto} = \frac{\text{masa del soluto}}{\text{masa de la solución}} \times 100\%$$

   $$\text{Molaridad:} = \frac{\text{moles de soluto}}{\text{litros de la solución}}$$

3. Las soluciones estándar son las que tienen una concentración conocida. Muchas veces, las soluciones se hacen por dilución a partir de soluciones previamente mezcladas. En este caso, las diluciones se preparan agregando disolvente exclusivamente, por lo que el número de moles del soluto es igual antes y después de la dilución.

4. El término *normalidad* se define como el número de equivalentes por litro de solución. Un equivalente de ácido es la cantidad de ácido necesaria para producir 1 mol de iones H⁺. Un equivalente de base es la cantidad de base necesaria para producir 1 mol de iones OH⁻.

5. Las propiedades coligativas de las soluciones son las que dependen del número de partículas de soluto presentes. Entre los ejemplos de propiedades coligativas se encuentran la elevación del punto de ebullición y la depresión del punto de congelación.

◀ **English/Spanish Summaries*** These copymasters contain translations of chapter summaries and key terms to help Spanish-speaking students and English learners understand key concepts.

*See 🅐🅡 in Planning Guide.

Student Resources

Student Resource Program

To encourage students to be active participants in the learning process, a Web site supporting the *World of Chemistry* program is available for student use any time.

Student Web Site* classzone.com

This text-specific Web site contains a variety of useful materials that supplement classroom learning. It features

- ACE quizzes, a self-testing program: containing two or three multiple-choice quizzes per chapter. Students can quiz themselves on chapter content and receive an immediate score and feedback on their answers.

- A flashcard study tool, offering key terms and definitions.

- PowerPoint slides of art from each chapter for use as a study and review aide.

Also available for student learning:

eEdition CD-ROM*

This learning tool contains PDF files of the student textbook. Students can access prereading, postreading, and homework assignments, as well as review for quizzes or tests. The eEdition CD features a classzone.com toolbar button for quick access to the program's Web site.

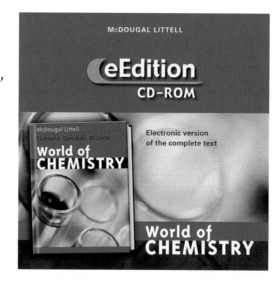

*See ⬛ in Planning Guide.

National Science Education Standards (NSES) Correlation to *World of Chemistry*

The table shows the *World of Chemistry* segment correlation to the National Science Education Standards. For additional information, see each chapter planner in the Teacher's Edition interleaf pages.

Code	STANDARD	TEACHING SEGMENT
UNIFYING CONCEPTS AND PROCESSES		
UCP1	Systems, order, and organization	1A (pp. 3–11), 1B (pp. 11–16), 2A (pp. 21–29), 2B (pp. 29–41), 3A (pp. 47–53), 3B (pp. 54–63), 3C (pp. 63–78), 4A (pp. 85–100), 4B (pp. 100–106), 5A (pp. 113–121), 5B (pp. 122–129), 5C (pp. 130–146), 6A (pp. 153–164), 6B (pp. 165–170), 6C (pp. 171–185), 7A (pp. 193–207) (pp. 193–207), 11A (pp. 323–327), 11C (pp. 333–339), 11D (pp. 339–352), 12B (pp. 365–371), 13A (pp. 398–415), 13B (pp. 415–425), 14A (pp. 442–449), 15A (pp. 467–473), 15B (pp. 474–485), 15D (pp. 491–496), 16A (pp. 503–513), 16B (pp. 513–524), 17A (pp. 537–547), 17B (pp. 548–554), 17C (pp. 554–567), 18A (pp. 575–584), 18B (pp. 585–594), 19A (pp. 608–618), 19B (pp. 618–627), 20A (pp. 634–648), 20B (pp. 648–653), 20C (pp. 654–659), 20E (pp. 664–668), 20F (pp. 669–674), 21A (pp. 684–690), 21B (pp. 690–697), 21C (pp. 697–707)
UCP2	Evidence, models, and explanation	1A (pp. 3–11), 1B (pp. 11–16), 2A (pp. 21–29), 2B (pp. 29–41), 3A (pp. 47–53), 3B (pp. 54–63), 6A (pp. 153–164), 11B (pp. 328–332), 11C (pp. 333–339), 12A (pp. 359–365), 12B (pp. 365–371), 12C (pp. 371–381), 12D (pp. 381–392), 13C (pp. 425–433), 14C (pp. 454–461), 16A (pp. 503–513), 16B (pp. 513–524), 16C (pp. 524–529), 17A (pp. 537–547), 17B (pp. 548–554), 20A (pp. 634–648), 20B (pp. 648–653), 20D (pp. 660–664)
UCP3	Change, consistency, and measurements	2B (pp. 29–41), 3B (pp. 54–63), 3C (pp. 63–78), 4A (pp. 85–100), 4B (pp. 100–106), 5B (pp. 122–129), 5C (pp. 130–146), 6A (pp. 153–164), 6B (pp. 165–170), 6C (pp. 171–185), 7A (pp. 193–207) (pp. 193–207), 8A (pp. 213–223), 8B (pp. 223–230), 8C (pp. 231–243), 9A (pp. 251–258), 9B (pp. 258–268), 9C (pp. 268–279), 11D (pp. 339–352), 12B (pp. 365–371), 13A (pp. 398–415), 13B (pp. 415–425), 13C (pp. 425–433), 14A (pp. 442–449), 14B (pp. 449–453), 15B (pp. 474–485), 15C (pp. 485–491), 15D (pp. 491–496), 16B (pp. 513–524), 16C (pp. 524–529), 17A (pp. 537–547), 17B (pp. 548–554), 17C (pp. 554–567), 18B (pp. 585–594), 18C (pp. 595–600), 19A (pp. 608–618), 19B (pp. 618–627), 20D (pp. 660–664), 20E (pp. 664–668), 20F (pp. 669–674), 21A (pp. 684–690)
UCP4	Evolution and equilibrium	14B (pp. 449–453), 17A (pp. 537–547), 17B (pp. 548–554), 17C (pp. 554–567)
UCP5	Form and function	2A (pp. 21–29), 3A (pp. 47–53), 3B (pp. 54–63), 3C (pp. 63–78), 6C (pp. 171–185), 8B (pp. 223–230), 8C (pp. 231–243), 12A (pp. 359–365), 12B (pp. 365–371), 12C (pp. 371–381), 12D (pp. 381–392), 14A (pp. 442–449), 14B (pp. 449–453), 14C (pp. 454–461), 16A (pp. 503–513), 16C (pp. 524–529), 18B (pp. 585–594), 18C (pp. 595–600), 19B (pp. 618–627), 20A (pp. 634–648), 20B (pp. 648–653), 20C (pp. 654–659), 20D (pp. 660–664), 20E (pp. 664–668), 20F (pp. 669–674), 21A (pp. 684–690), 21B (pp. 690–697), 21C (pp. 697–707)
SCIENCE AS INQUIRY		
A1	Abilities necessary to do scientific inquiry	1A (pp. 3–11), 1B (pp. 11–16), 2A (pp. 21–29), 2B (pp. 29–41), 3A (pp. 47–53), 3B (pp. 54–63), 3C (pp. 63–78), 4A (pp. 85–100), 4B (pp. 100–106), 5A (pp. 113–121), 5B (pp. 122–129), 5C (pp. 130–146), 6A (pp. 153–164), 6B (pp. 165–170), 6C (pp. 171–185), 7A (pp. 193–207) (pp. 193–207), 8A (pp. 213–223), 8B (pp. 223–230), 8C (pp. 231–243), 9A (pp. 251–258), 9B (pp. 258–268), 9C (pp. 268–279), 10A (pp. 289–293), 10B (pp. 293–301), 10C (pp. 301–305), 10D (pp. 306–315), 11A (pp. 323–327), 11B (pp. 328–332), 11C (pp. 333–339), 11D (pp. 339–352), 12A (pp. 359–365), 12B (pp. 365–371), 12C (pp. 371–381), 12D (pp. 381–392), 13A (pp. 398–415), 13B (pp. 415–425), 13C (pp. 425–433), 14A (pp. 442–449), 14B (pp. 449–453), 14C15A, 15B (pp. 474–485), 15C (pp. 485–491), 15D (pp. 491–496),16A (pp. 503–513), 16B (pp. 513–524), 16C (pp. 524–529), 17A (pp. 537–547), 17B (pp. 548–554), 17C (pp. 554–567), 18A (pp. 575–584), 18B (pp. 585–594), 18C (pp. 595–600),19A (pp. 608–618), 19B (pp. 618–627), 20A (pp. 634–648), 20B (pp. 648–653), 20C (pp. 654–659), 20D (pp. 660–664), 20E (pp. 664–668), 20F (pp. 669–674), 21A (pp. 684–690), 21B (pp. 690–697)

Standards: NSES

Code	STANDARD	TEACHING SEGMENT
A2	Understanding about scientific inquiry	1A (pp. 3–11), 1B (pp. 11–16), 2A (pp. 21–29), 2B (pp. 29–41), 3A (pp. 47–53), 3B (pp. 54–63), 3C (pp. 63–78), 4A (pp. 85–100), 4B (pp. 100–106), 5A (pp. 113–121), 5B (pp. 122–129), 5C (pp. 130–146), 6A (pp. 153–164), 6B (pp. 165–170), 6C (pp. 171–185), 7A (pp. 193–207) (pp. 193–207), 8A (pp. 213–223), 8B (pp. 223–230), 8C (pp. 231–243), 9A (pp. 251–258), 9B (pp. 258–268), 9C (pp. 268–279), 10A (pp. 289–293), 10B (pp. 293–301), 10C (pp. 301–305), 10D (pp. 306–315), 11A (pp. 323–327), 11B (pp. 328–332), 11C (pp. 333–339), 11D (pp. 339–352), 12A (pp. 359–365), 12B (pp. 365–371), 12C (pp. 371–381), 12D (pp. 381–392), 13A (pp. 398–415), 13B (pp. 415–425), 13C (pp. 425–433), 14A (pp. 442–449), 14B (pp. 449–453), 14C, 15A, 15B (pp. 474–485), 15C (pp. 485–491), 15D (pp. 491–496),16A (pp. 503–513), 16B (pp. 513–524), 16C (pp. 524–529), 17A (pp. 537–547), 17B (pp. 548–554), 17C (pp. 554–567), 18A (pp. 575–584), 18B (pp. 585–594), 18C (pp. 595–600),19A (pp. 608–618), 19B (pp. 618–627)

PHYSICAL SCIENCE

Code	STANDARD	TEACHING SEGMENT
B1	Structure of atoms	2A (pp. 21–29), 3B (pp. 54–63), 6A (pp. 153–164), 6B (pp. 165–170), 6C (pp. 171–185), 11A (pp. 323–327), 12A (pp. 359–365), 12B (pp. 365–371), 12C (pp. 371–381), 12D (pp. 381–392), 19A (pp. 608–618), 19B (pp. 618–627), 20A (pp. 634–648)
B2	Structure and properties of matter	2A (pp. 21–29), 2B (pp. 29–41), 3A (pp. 47–53), 3B (pp. 54–63), 3C (pp. 63–78), 4A (pp. 85–100), 6A (pp. 153–164), 6B (pp. 165–170), 6C (pp. 171–185), 9A (pp. 251–258), 9B (pp. 258–268), 9C (pp. 268–279), 11A (pp. 323–327), 11D (pp. 339–352), 12A (pp. 359–365), 12B (pp. 365–371), 12C (pp. 371–381), 12D (pp. 381–392), 13A, 13B, 13C (pp. 425–433), 14A (pp. 442–449), 14B (pp. 449–453), 14C (pp. 454–461), 15A (pp. 467–473), 15B (pp. 474–485), 15C (pp. 485–491), 15D (pp. 491–496), 16A (pp. 503–513), 16B (pp. 513–524), 16C (pp. 524–529), 18A (pp. 575–584), 18B (pp. 585–594), 18C (pp. 595–600), 19A (pp. 608–618), 19B (pp. 618–627), 20A (pp. 634–648), 20B (pp. 648–653), 20C (pp. 654–659), 20D (pp. 660–664), 20E (pp. 664–668), 20F (pp. 669–674), 21A (pp. 684–690), 21B (pp. 690–697), 21C (pp. 697–707)
B3	Chemical reactions	1A (pp. 3–11), 2B (pp. 29–41), 3A (pp. 47–53), 3C (pp. 63–78), 4A (pp. 85–100), 4B (pp. 100–106), 6A (pp. 153–164), 6B (pp. 165–170), 6C (pp. 171–185), 7A (pp. 193–207) (pp. 193–207), 8A (pp. 213–223), 8B (pp. 223–230), 8C (pp. 231–243), 9A (pp. 251–258), 9B (pp. 258–268), 9C (pp. 268–279), 15C (pp. 485–491), 16A (pp. 503–513), 16C (pp. 524–529), 17A (pp. 537–547), 17B (pp. 548–554), 17C (pp. 554–567), 18A (pp. 575–584), 18B (pp. 585–594), 18C (pp. 595–600), 20A (pp. 634–648), 20B (pp. 648–653), 20C (pp. 654–659), 20D (pp. 660–664), 20E (pp. 664–668), 20F (pp. 669–674), 21B (pp. 690–697)
B4	Motions and forces	13A (pp. 398–415), 13B (pp. 415–425), 13C (pp. 425–433), 14A (pp. 442–449), 14B (pp. 449–453)
B5	Conservation of energy and increase in disorder	10A (pp. 289–293), 10B (pp. 293–301), 10C (pp. 301–305), 10D (pp. 306–315), 14A (pp. 442–449), 14B (pp. 449–453), 14C (pp. 454–461)
B6	Interactions of energy and matter	10A (pp. 289–293), 10B (pp. 293–301), 10C (pp. 301–305), 10D (pp. 306–315), 11A (pp. 323–327), 11B (pp. 328–332), 11C (pp. 333–339), 11D (pp. 339–352), 17A (pp. 537–547)

LIFE SCIENCE

Code	STANDARD	TEACHING SEGMENT
C2	Molecular basis of heredity	21C (pp. 697–707)
C4	Interdependence of organisms	16A (pp. 503–513), 17C (pp. 554–567)
C5	Matter, energy, and organization in living systems	8C (pp. 231–243), 9B (pp. 258–268), 10A (pp. 289–293), 10B (pp. 293–301), 14A (pp. 442–449), 17C (pp. 554–567), 20A (pp. 634–648)
C6	Behavior of organisms	3A (pp. 47–53), 4B (pp. 100–106), 7A (pp. 193–207) (pp. 193–207), 9B (pp. 258–268), 10C (pp. 301–305), 14A (pp. 442–449), 16A (pp. 503–513), 20C (pp. 654–659), 21A (pp. 684–690), 21B (pp. 690–697)

EARTH AND SPACE SCIENCE

Code	STANDARD	TEACHING SEGMENT
D2	Geochemical cycles	8B (pp. 223–230), 10C (pp. 301–305)
D3	Origin and evolution of the earth system	6C (pp. 171–185), 19A (pp. 608–618), 19B (pp. 618–627)
D4	Origin and evolution of the universe	19B (pp. 618–627)

Code	STANDARD	TEACHING SEGMENT
SCIENCE AND TECHNOLOGY		
E1	Abilities of technological design	3A (pp. 47–53), 3B (pp. 54–63), 3C (pp. 63–78), 5B (pp. 122–129), 5C (pp. 130–146), 6A (pp. 153–164), 7A (pp. 193–207) (pp. 193–207), 8C (pp. 231–243), 9B (pp. 258–268), 10D (pp. 306–315), 11A (pp. 323–327), 11C (pp. 333–339), 11D (pp. 339–352), 12B (pp. 365–371), 12C (pp. 371–381), 12D (pp. 381–392), 13C (pp. 425–433), 14C (pp. 454–461), 16A (pp. 503–513), 16B (pp. 513–524), 17A (pp. 537–547), 17C (pp. 554–567), 18A (pp. 575–584), 18B (pp. 585–594), 18C (pp. 595–600), 19A (pp. 608–618), 19B (pp. 618–627), 20A (pp. 634–648), 20B (pp. 648–653), 20E (pp. 664–668), 20F (pp. 669–674), 21B (pp. 690–697), 21C (pp. 697–707)
E2	Understanding about science and technology	1A (pp. 3–11), 3A (pp. 47–53), 3B (pp. 54–63), 3C (pp. 63–78), 5A (pp. 113–121), 5B (pp. 122–129), 5C (pp. 130–146), 6A (pp. 153–164), 7A (pp. 193–207) (pp. 193–207), 8C (pp. 231–243), 9B (pp. 258–268), 10D (pp. 306–315), 11A (pp. 323–327), 11C (pp. 333–339), 11D (pp. 339–352), 12B (pp. 365–371), 12C (pp. 371–381), 12D (pp. 381–392), 13C (pp. 425–433), 14C (pp. 454–461), 16B (pp. 513–524), 17A (pp. 537–547), 17C (pp. 554–567), 18A (pp. 575–584), 18C (pp. 595–600), 19A (pp. 608–618), 19B (pp. 618–627), 20B (pp. 648–653), 20E (pp. 664–668), 20F (pp. 669–674), 21B (pp. 690–697), 21C (pp. 697–707)
SCIENCE IN PERSONAL AND SOCIAL PERSPECTIVES		
F1	Personal and community health	4A (pp. 85–100), 6C (pp. 171–185), 7A (pp. 193–207) (pp. 193–207), 8C (pp. 231–243), 9B (pp. 258–268), 13C (pp. 425–433), 14C (pp. 454–461), 15A (pp. 467–473), 16C (pp. 524–529), 17C (pp. 554–567), 19A (pp. 608–618), 20A (pp. 634–648)
F2	Population growth	21B (pp. 691–697), 21C (pp. 697–707)
F3	Natural resources	3A (pp. 47–53), 9B (pp. 258–268), 10C (pp. 301–305), 10D (pp. 306–315), 11C (pp. 333–339), 15A (pp. 467–473), 18B (pp. 585–594), 18C (pp. 595–600), 19B (pp. 618–627), 20B (pp. 648–653)
F4	Environmental quality	5B (pp. 122–129), 10C (pp. 301–305), 10D (pp. 306–315), 11C (pp. 333–339), 13C (pp. 425–433), 15A (pp. 467–473), 16C (pp. 524–529), 17A (pp. 537–547), 17C (pp. 554–567), 18C (pp. 595–600), 19B (pp. 618–627), 20B (pp. 648–653)
F5	Natural and human-induced hazards	7A (pp. 193–207) (pp. 193–207), 9B (pp. 258–268), 13C (pp. 425–433), 15A (pp. 467–473), 15C (pp. 485–491), 16C (pp. 524–529), 17C (pp. 554–567), 20B (pp. 648–653)
F6	Science and technology in local, national, and global challenges	5B (pp. 122–129), 8C (pp. 231–243), 9B (pp. 258–268), 9C (pp. 268–279), 10C (pp. 301–305), 10D (pp. 306–315), 11A (pp. 323–327), 11C (pp. 333–339), 12B (pp. 365–371) 12C (pp. 371–381), 12D (pp. 381–392), 13C (pp. 425–433), 14C (pp. 454–461), 15A (pp. 467–473), 16B (pp. 513–524), 16C (pp. 524–529), 17A (pp. 537–547), 18C (pp. 595–600), 19A (pp. 608–618), 19B (pp. 618–627), 20A (pp. 634–648), 20B (pp. 648–653), 20E (pp. 664–668), 20F (pp. 669–674), 21C (pp. 697–707)
SCIENCE AS INQUIRY		
G1	Science as a human endeavor	1A (pp. 3–11), 1B (pp. 11–16), 2B (pp. 29–41), 3A (pp. 47–53), 3B (pp. 54–63), 6A (pp. 153–164), 6C (pp. 171–185), 8B (pp. 223–230), 11B (pp. 328–332), 11D (pp. 339–352), 12C (pp. 371–381), 13A (pp. 398–415), 16B (pp. 513–524), 18A (pp. 575–584), 18B (pp. 585–594), 18C (pp. 595–600), 19A (pp. 608–618), 19B (pp. 618–627), 20A (pp. 634–648), 20F (pp. 669–674)
G2	Nature of scientific knowledge	1A (pp. 3–11), 1B (pp. 11–16), 2B (pp. 29–41), 3A (pp. 47–53), 3B (pp. 54–63), 6A (pp. 153–164), 6C (pp. 171–185), 8B (pp. 223–230), 11A (pp. 323–327), 11B (pp. 328–332), 11D (pp. 339–352), 12C (pp. 371–381), 13A (pp. 398–415), 14C (pp. 454–461), 16B (pp. 513–524), 18A (pp. 575–584), 18B (pp. 585–594), 18C (pp. 595–600), 19A (pp. 608–618), 19B (pp. 618–627), 20A (pp. 634–648), 20F (pp. 669–674)
G3	Historical perspectives	1B (pp. 11–16), 2B (pp. 29–41), 3A (pp. 47–53), 3B (pp. 54–63), 5B (pp. 122–129), 6A (pp. 153–164), 6C (pp. 171–185), 7A (pp. 193–207) (pp. 193–207), 8B (pp. 223–230), 9B (pp. 258–268), 11A (pp. 323–327), 11B (pp. 328–332), 11D (pp. 339–352), 12C (pp. 371–381), 13A (pp. 398–415), 13C (pp. 425–433), 15C (pp. 485–491), 16B (pp. 513–524), 17A (pp. 537–547), 18A (pp. 575–584), 18B (pp. 585–594), 18C (pp. 595–600), 19A (pp. 608–618), 19B (pp. 618–627), 20A (pp. 634–648), 20F (pp. 669–674)

Florida Sunshine State Standards (SSS)

Florida	CHEMISTRY I 2003340	PAGE REFERENCES
Apply knowledge of the nature of science and scientific habits of mind to solve problems, and employ sage and effective use of laboratory technologies		
SC.H.1.4.1	knows that investigations are conducted to explore new phenomena, to check on previous results, to test how well a theory predicts, and to compare different theories.	5–6, 8–11, 11–13, 49, 55–57, 79, 103, 198, 237, 265, 267, 308–310, 330–331, 327, 337, 368, 377, 383, 403–406, 407–413, 420–422, 434, 458, 460, 497–498, 503–505, 510, 516, 523, 529–531, 539–541, 555, 597, 598–600, 600, 623–624, 625–627, 612–613, 618–619, 620–621, 621–623, 633, 646, 659, 668, 673, 683, 692, 705–708
SC.H.1.4.2	knows that from time to time, major shifts occur in the scientific view of how the world works, but that more often the changes that take place in the body of scientific knowledge are small modifications of prior knowledge.	12–14, 36, 55–57, 59, 60–63, 85, 226–227, 237, 265, 267, 307–309, 311, 323–324, 330–331, 331–332, 337–339, 368, 458, 503–504, 595–597, 600, 612–614, 624, 626, 633, 648–649
SC.H.1.4.3	understands that no matter how well one theory fits observations, a new theory might fit them as well or better, or might fit a wider range of observations, because in science, the testing, revising, and occasional discarding of theories, new and old, never ends and leads to an increasingly better understanding of how things work in the world, but not to absolute truth.	9–11, 12–13, 14, 17–18, 19, 36, 52–53, 55–57, 58, 323–324, 327, 330–331, 331–332, 380–381, 458, 503–504, 555, 597, 600, 613, 621–623, 624, 648–649, 692
SC.H.1.4.4	knows that scientists in any one research group tend to see things alike and that therefore scientific teams are expected to seek out the possible sources of bias in the design of their investigations and in their data analysis.	14, 19, 26, 58, 160, 265, 330–331, 331–332, 541, 597, 600, 613, 624, 692, 696
SC.H.1.4.5	understands that new ideas in science are limited by the context in which they are conceived, are often rejected by the scientific establishment, sometimes spring from unexpected findings, and usually grow slowly from many contributors.	13–14, 19, 47, 52–53, 121, 330–331, 510, 575, 597, 600, 613, 621–623, 624, 626, 668
SC.H.1.4.6	understands that, in the short run, new ideas that do not mesh well with mainstream ideas in science often encounter vigorous criticism and that, in the long run, theories are judged by how they fit with other theories, the range of observations they explain, how well they explain observations, and how effective they are in predicting new findings.	12–14, 52–53, 55–57, 330–331, 331–332, 458, 503–504, 600, 622–623, 633
SC.H.1.4.7	understands the importance of a sense of responsibility, a commitment to peer review, truthful reporting of the methods and outcomes of investigations, and making the public aware of the findings.	4–6, 14, 19, 160, 198, 368, 380–381, 471, 525, 597, 622–623, 624, 625–627, 648–649, 692, 704
SC.H.2.4.1	knows that scientists assume that the universe is a vast system in which basic rules exist that may range from very simple to extremely complex, but that scientists operate on the belief that the rules can be discovered by careful, systemic study.	11–14, 14–16, 91, 366, 613, 622–623
SC.H.2.4.2	knows that scientists control conditions in order to obtain evidence, but when that is not possible for practical or ethical reasons, they try to observe a wide range of natural occurrences to discern patterns.	613, 621–623, 623–624, 626

Florida	CHEMISTRY I 2003340	PAGE REFERENCES
Demonstrate understanding of matter, its classifications, structure, and changes.		
SC.A.1.4.1	knows that the electron configuration in atoms determines how a substance reacts and how much energy is involved in its reactions.	59, 339–342, 343–347, 365–367, 504
SC.A.1.4.3	knows that a change from one phase of matter to another involves a gain or loss of energy.	28–29, 30–31, 197–199, 241–242, 292–293, 304–306, 312–315, 441, 444–445, 446–449, 449–451, 452–453, 462, 558–561
Demonstrate understanding of atomic theory.		
SC.A.2.4.1	knows that the number and configuration of electrons will equal the number of protons in an electrically neutral atom and when an atom gains or loses electrons, the charge is unbalanced.	56–57, 59, 60–63, 71–74, 75–78, 89–94, 100–101, 231–234, 236–237, 239, 343–347, 365–368, 371–375, 375–381
SC.A.2.4.3	knows that a number of elements have heavier, unstable nuclei that decay, spontaneously giving off smaller particles and waves that result in a small loss of mass and release a large amount of energy.	608–612, 612–614, 614–615, 616–618
SC.A.2.4.4	knows that nuclear energy is released when small, light atoms are fused into heavier ones.	619, 620–621, 621–623, 623–624
SC.A.2.4.6	understands that matter may act as a wave, a particle, or something else entirely different with its own characteristic behavior.	324–325, 326–327, 328–329, 331–332, 337–339, 346–347
SC.C.2.4.4	knows that the forces that hold the nucleus of an atom together are much stronger than electromagnetic force and that this is the reason for the great amount of energy released from the nuclear reactions in the sun and other stars.	607, 619, 620–621, 623–624
Demonstrate understanding of the application of the periodic table.		
SC.A.2.4.5	knows that elements are arranged into groups and families based on similarities in electron structure and that their physical and chemical properties can be predicted.	42–43, 63–67, 67–70, 74, 75–77, 323, 339–343, 343–347, 348–352, 355–357, 456
Demonstrate understanding of covalent and ionic bonding.		
SC.A.1.4.2	knows that the vast diversity of the properties of materials is primarily due to variations in the forces that hold molecules together.	68–70, 359–361, 361–363, 364–365, 369–371, 383–386, 390–391, 441, 442–444, 454–455, 456–461, 663–664, 664–665, 693–695, 701–704
SC.A.1.4.5	knows that connections (bonds) form between substances when outer-shell electrons are either transferred or shared between their atoms, changing the properties of substances.	359–361, 371–375, 375–381, 383–389, 390–392, 509, 575–576, 577, 634, 635–637, 638–640, 651–653, 654, 664–665, 671–674, 685–687
SC.C.2.4.2	knows that electrical forces exist between any two charged objects.	56–57, 75–78, 214–217, 364–365, 506–509, 542, 575–576, 577–579, 591–594, 595–597
SC.C.2.4.5	knows that most observable forces can be traced to electric forces acting between atoms or molecules.	56–57, 79, 226–230, 231–235, 359–361, 506–509, 575–576, 577–579, 591–594, 595–597
Use chemical formulas to write balanced equations and predict reaction products.		
SC.A.2.4.2	knows the difference between an element, a molecule, and a compound.	24–27, 47–49, 50–51, 54–55, 67–70, 75–78
SC.B.1.4.2	understand that there is conservation of mass and energy when matter is transformed.	52, 196–200, 200–207, 252–264, 289, 290, 293–294, 486–490, 585–590, 608–612

Florida	CHEMISTRY I 2003340	PAGE REFERENCES
Explain the behavior of gases in terms of gas laws and kinetic molecular theory.		
SC.B.1.4.3	knows that temperature is a measure of the average translational kinetic energy of motion of the molecules in an object.	427–428, 437, 449–451, 452–453
Demonstrate understanding of reaction rates and equilibrium.		
SC.A.1.4.4	experiments and determines that the rates of reaction among atoms and molecules depend on the concentration, pressure, and temperature of the reactants and the presence or absence of catalysts.	473, 476, 477–485, 538–540, 541–543, 560–561, 691–693
SC.G.2.4.2	knows that changes in a component of an ecosystem will have unpredictable effects on the entire system but that the components of the system tend to react in a way that will restore the ecosystem to its original condition.	543–547, 548–551, 552–553, 562
Demonstrate understanding of the dynamics of energy.		
SC.B.1.4.1	understands how knowledge of energy is fundamental to all the scientific disciplines (e.g., the energy required for biological processes in living organisms and the energy required for the building, erosion, and rebuilding of the Earth).	289–290, 297, 307–312, 448, 648–649, 683–684, 690–691, 693
SC.B.1.4.6	knows that the first law of thermodynamics relates the transfer of energy to the work done and the heat transferred.	293–294, 306
SC.B.1.4.7	knows that the total amount of usable energy always decreases, even though the total amount of energy is conserved in any transfer.	289, 292–293, 293–294, 294–300, 303–305, 306
SC.G.2.4.1	knows that layers of energy-rich organic materials have been gradually turned into great coal beds and oil pools (fossil fuels) by the pressure of the overlying earth and that humans burn fossil fuels to release the stored energy as heat and carbon dioxide.	240, 288, 307, 309–310, 312, 427, 648–649
Demonstrate understanding of the interactions of chemistry with technology and society.		
SC.B.1.4.5	knows that each source of energy presents advantages and disadvantages to its use in society (e.g., political and economic implications may determine a society's selection of renewable or nonrenewable energy sources).	5–6, 288, 307–312, 368, 471, 541, 575, 597, 620–621, 621–623, 624–625, 626–627, 648–649
SC.H.3.4.1	knows that performance testing is often conducted using small-scale models, computer simulations, or analogous systems to reduce the chance of system failure.	265, 368, 523, 597, 620–621, 646, 692
SC.H.3.4.2	knows that technological problems often create a demand for new scientific knowledge and that new technologies make it possible for scientists to extend their research in a way that advances science.	9, 53, 58, 87, 123, 205, 368, 432, 460, 472, 516, 521–522, 523, 539–541, 575, 597, 618–619, 624, 648–649
SC.H.3.4.3	knows that scientists can bring information, insights, and analytical skills to matters of public concern and help people understand the possible causes and effects of events.	5–6, 53, 87, 265, 429, 460, 471, 525, 541, 555, 575, 597, 617
SC.H.3.4.4	knows that funds for science research come from federal government agencies, industry, and private foundations and that this funding often influences the areas of discovery.	53, 87, 117, 265, 277, 472, 523, 541, 597, 620–621, 646, 648–649, 668 673
SC.H.3.4.5	knows that the value of a technology may differ for different people and at different times.	5–6, 58, 155, 357–358, 460, 523, 525, 529, 575, 594–595, 597, 683–684
SC.H.3.4.6	knows that scientific knowledge is used by those who engage in design and technology to solve practical problems, taking human values and limitations into account.	89, 123, 198, 237, 311, 342, 432, 460, 523, 529, 541, 576, 597, 618–619, 625–627, 637, 646, 663–664, 668, 673, 683–684, 705

World of Chemistry

FLORIDA TEACHER'S EDITION

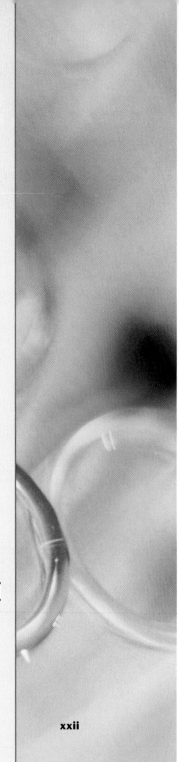

Overview

In this section our goals are for students to

- Understand the importance of reading a chemistry textbook.

- Become efficient and effective readers of chemistry.

- Develop technical writing skills.

- Learn and implement test preparation tips for before, during, and after a test.

- Become familiar with various styles of test items.

- Know how to answer or respond to standardized test items.

Skills

Prereading, making comparisons, evaluating

Student Preparation

Have the students read these reading support pages before coming to class.

Active Learning

After discussing the information in this feature, place the students in small groups and have them work together to preview the textbook.

TEACHING TIPS

- Use the strategies in Chapter 1's **Integrating Reading Strategies and Chemistry Concepts: Previewing the Textbook** to supplement this feature.

- Ask the students to write a reading agreement in their journals to show their commitment to the demands of the course. Have the students sign their agreements.

Reading Chemistry

Chemistry textbooks are written differently from non–technical textbooks. With this in mind, be aware that reading five pages in a chemistry textbook will probably take much more time than reading five pages in an English or a history textbook.

If you want to understand this chemistry text, prepare to spend a great deal of time reading each section within a chapter. If you flip through this book, you will notice many examples, explanations, diagrams, charts, symbols, and photos to read, analyze, and interpret. You should read the text in each section and incorporate these visuals in your reading. You will quickly find that these visuals are very useful in helping you understand the subject matter.

Use these suggestions to become an efficient and effective reader of chemistry.

1. **Preview your textbook.**

   To become familiar with the design and structure of your textbook, take a look at these key features:

   - Information about the authors, page vi
   - Tables of Contents and List of Features, pages vii–xxi
   - Appendices, pages A1–A11
   - Glossary, pages A47–A54
   - Index, pages A59–A76
   - Periodic Table, inside back cover

2. **Plan when and where you read.**

   Although you might find that relaxing on the couch at night is a comfortable and convenient place to do some of your homework, it will not be a good place to read about a chemistry concept.

   - Try to read your chemistry section during daylight hours, or in a well-lit area.
   - Sit in a straight-backed chair, such as the chairs in the classroom, a kitchen chair, or a desk chair.
   - Read in a quiet atmosphere; turn off the television or radio.
   - Remember that reading chemistry requires active participation. Make sure that you have a pencil, notebook, and any other necessary items to help you study.
   - Allow plenty of time to read through each section. Even if a section is short, it still requires deep concentration and focus.

3. Preview each chapter.

When you start a new chapter, be sure to preview it before you begin reading a section within the chapter. Taking time to get an overview of the concepts within the chapter will help you become a more efficient learner.

- Read the title of the chapter and the "Looking Ahead" box. Ask yourself what you have learned previously that may apply to these new concepts.
- Read the first paragraph of the chapter. This paragraph will give you a quick preview of what will be covered and why this chapter material is important.
- Read each section title and the corresponding objectives.
- Glance at the highlighted features, photos, graphs, charts, and symbols in the chapter, to get a sense of the content.
- Read the Chapter Review found at the end of each chapter. This indicates what is most important and what material you will most likely have to master.

4. Read each section prior to class.

Make sure that you read a section before it is presented in class. By previewing the section, you will be better prepared for class.

- Note the section title and objectives in your notebook.
- Make a list of questions you have about the section and of any concepts you need to clarify.
- Write down any vocabulary, symbols, or structures that you have difficulty interpreting.
- Try to work through the example problems, and note any steps that confuse you.
- Attempt to answer the Focus Questions if they appear at the end of a section.

5. Reread each section after class.

To reinforce the concepts explained during class, read the section again.

- Highlight in your notes the concepts your teacher emphasized during class.
- Make flashcards to help you memorize structures, symbols, and vocabulary. Review your flashcards daily.
- Work through each example problem, and complete the Self-Check Exercises at the end of each example.
- Write a summary of the section. Putting the material in your own words will help you to learn this new information.

Additional Activity

Use this feature to begin focusing on how chemistry and reading are integrated. Create a bulletin board highlighting a reading strategy of your choice for each chapter. Highlight its function and importance.

TEACHING TIPS

- Now is a good time to tell the students that they will need a notebook designated for this course.
- Use the strategies in Chapter 3's **Integrating Reading Strategies and Chemistry Concepts: Creating and Using Flashcards** to supplement this feature.
- Ask the students to write a paragraph in their journals about the similarities and differences between reading a textbook for a technical course versus reading a novel.
- Use the information and the questions that the students have from their previewing of a section to determine the technology aids to use.
- Review the strategies explained in the **Integrating Reading Strategies and Chemistry Concepts** feature before each chapter in the Teacher's Edition to determine the strategies best suited to your class.

Additional Activity

Distribute magazines and scientific journals. Have the students compare and contrast creative styles of writing with technical writing. Ask the students to rewrite one creatively written paragraph as a technical statement.

WHAT IF

Ask the students: What if scientists did not conform to a certain style of writing? How could this varying style affect the interpretation of a scientist's research?

Discuss how words can be used to persuade. Point out that research results explained in various styles of writing could lead to a range of interpretations.

Explain how the scientific community relies on clear, quantitative technical descriptions to record, analyze, and explain results.

Additional Examples

To practice technical writing, have the students rewrite these statements.

1. Every minute, the temperature got hotter and hotter by twelve K.

   [The temperature increased at a rate of 12 K per minute.]

2. People can use distillation or filtration to separate the things in a mixture. Either method will work just fine.

   [The substances that make up mixtures can be separated by two methods: distillation and filtration.]

Writing Chemistry

Up to this point in your studies, you have learned and practiced many different types and styles of writing. In this class, you will be expected to use technical writing. Technical writing differs from essay, report, letter, and creative writing in many ways. Technical writing is factual, precise, clear, and free of bias and personal opinion. Sentences should be specific and to the point.

For instance, if you were asked to write about the current weather conditions in your area for a technical course, your description should use the technical writing style shown in Example 1, rather than the creative style shown in Example 2.

Example 1 • Technical Writing Sample

 The temperature is 75°F. It is sunny with minimal cloud coverage. The wind is blowing north to northwest at 15 miles per hour.

Note that the writer in Example 1 states factual information regarding the temperature and wind speed, includes units of measure, and writes without bias and personal opinion.

Example 2 • Creative Writing Sample

 It is a beautiful spring day! The sun is shining without a cloud in the sky, the air is light and breezy, and the temperature is simply perfect for a picnic in the park.

Although the writer in Example 2 paints a visual picture of the weather conditions, it would not be an appropriate description in a technical course. There are too many adjectives, there are not enough detailed facts, and the writing contains personal opinion about the weather.

When writing a response to a laboratory question, get right to the point. There is no need for extra words. For instance, you may be asked: "What evidence did you observe that indicates a reaction occurred?"

A good technical response would be:

 A yellow precipitate formed in the container.

The wordy response below would be inappropriate:

 After we observed the reaction for a few minutes, we saw something yellow starting to form at the bottom of the glass. We think that is how we know that a reaction occurred.

To strengthen your skills in technical writing for this chemistry course, as well as for other technical courses, follow these helpful hints.

- Write in third person. Do not use *I, we, our, your, my,* or *us.*
- Be specific. Do not ramble to make a point.
- Use the correct verb tense. Use present tense when writing research papers and lab reports and when analyzing data. Use past tense to describe objectives and experimental results.
- Responses to questions should be organized, logical, and precise. A reader should be able to follow clearly your train of thought.
- Avoid stating your opinion. Most of your descriptions and observations should be based on things that can be measured. Keep in mind that your writing should be based on facts, not on the opinion of the observer.
- Write numbers as numerals when they are greater than 10 or when they are linked with a measurement. For example: 230, six, 6 cm.
- Avoid beginning sentences with a number, unless the number is part of a chemical name.
- Include units of measure as part of your data. For example: 50°F, not 50°; 0.025 M, not 0.025.
- Use scientific notation when appropriate.
- Use the correct number of significant figures when reporting your data.
- Use lowercase for chemical names, unless they are at the beginning of a sentence.
- Tables, graphs, and diagrams used to help explain a response should be completely and accurately labeled.
- Describe a laboratory procedure in enough detail that another person can repeat the experiment.
- Make sure that a summary of an experiment includes the meaning of your results and how they are the basis for your conclusions. Incorporate possible sources of error in your description.
- Cite all references.

xxv

Additional Activity

Have the students research a winner of the Nobel Prize in Chemistry and submit a short technical report.

TEACHING TIPS

- Assess students on their technical writing skills in their laboratory reports and in their responses to Critical Thinking Questions, Chemistry in Action features, and What If features.
- Tell the students to revisit these helpful hints before they turn in a written assignment.
- Review how to cite a reference properly.
- Review the strategies explained in Chapter 14's **Integrating Reading Strategies and Chemistry Concepts: Reading Graphs and Tables.**
- Demonstrate to the students how reading aloud what they write can help them identify problems with logic and organization.

Student Activity

For one of the features in the text, such as a **Chemistry in Action** feature or a **What If** feature, have the students exchange written responses with another student. Each student should then make suggestions for improving the technical style of the partner's response.

- Highlight testing dates in your course outline.

- Review the strategies explained in Chapter 3's **Integrating Reading Strategies and Chemistry Concepts: Creating and Using Flashcards.**

- Additional materials, such as the Teacher's Guide for Less Proficient Students and the English/Spanish Summaries, can be used as tools to help struggling students better comprehend the main points of a chapter.

- Encourage the students to write in their journals about fears or apprehension they experience before a test. Help students develop a plan to calm their fears.

- During the week of a test, tell the students the style of the test and the approximate number of questions. You may wish to distribute a sample test to give students a visual idea of what to expect.

- Distribute a reference sheet several days before the test so that the students will not spend time memorizing unnecessary information.

- Refer the students to pages iv–vi of the Standardized Test Practice booklet for additional test preparation tips.

xxvi

Testing in Chemistry

The key to earning a successful grade on a chemistry test is to be actively involved in learning the content and to be well-prepared for every class. Chemistry is a cumulative subject, meaning that each section builds on the one before it. Preparation cannot begin the night before the test, but must be ongoing from the first day of class to the last day of class.

Designate a notebook for your chemistry notes and homework. Review your class notes with the corresponding section in the textbook, every day. If you are having trouble remembering new vocabulary words, chemical structures, or formulas, create a set of flashcards. Study your flashcards as often as possible.

Keep in mind that if you find yourself "cramming" for a chemistry test, it is likely that your test grade will reflect a lack of effort. Many of the concepts that you will be learning in this chemistry course will be unfamiliar and challenging. Embrace this challenge by organizing your approach to studying for this course.

Follow these test preparation tips to help you achieve a successful test score.

Before a Chemistry Test

- Read the course outline to know when your tests are scheduled.
- Review your class notes daily, and review the entire section after you have completed it in class. Do not put off reviewing material until right before test time; review needs to be ongoing.
- As you review, ask yourself questions about the material that is difficult for you.
- Create and answer your own test questions about what the teacher emphasized in class.
- Create and study your flashcards.
- Rework any homework problems that you solved incorrectly.
- Find out from your teacher what topics will be covered on the test, the style of the test, and whether a formula reference sheet will be provided.
- Get a good night's sleep before the test. Eat a good breakfast the day of the test so that you can think, process, and recall quickly and accurately.
- Remember to take pencils, erasers, a calculator, and a watch.

During a Chemistry Test

- Relax!
- Read the test directions before you start answering the test questions.
- Look through the test so that you know how many test questions there are, the style of the test items, and what references you have available. This will help determine how much time you should spend on each question.

- If a test question is too hard or too time consuming, skip it and return to it later. Sometimes you may be reminded about a concept or have a thought triggered by another test item. Circle any test items that you skip so that when you go back over the test, you will quickly know which items are not completed.
- Try to save time at the end of the testing period to review and check your answers. Verify that you have completed all parts of each question and that your answers are written clearly.

After a Chemistry Test

- Correct any wrong or incomplete answers.
- If necessary, make changes to your study habits or to your organization to prepare better for the next test.
- Do not give up! Chemistry concepts and applications can be tough to grasp, but with steadfast effort, you will be successful.

Strategies for Various Styles of Test Items

When taking a standardized test, you may encounter various styles of test items, such as multiple choice, gridded response, short answer, and extended response. Each style of question assesses your knowledge and understanding of chemistry, but each is graded differently.

Multiple Choice

A multiple choice test item consists of a test question and four answer choices, such as the following:

> *A compound contains 16% carbon and 84% sulfur by mass.*
>
> *What is the empirical formula of this compound?*
>
> **A** CS_2 **B** C_2S_2 **C** CS **D** C_2S

To answer a multiple choice question:

- Read the entire question slowly before considering any of the answer choices. Take note of key words that indicate what you are being asked to do.
- Try to determine an answer to the question before looking at the answer choices. Be sure to read all of the answer choices before selecting an answer.
- If you are not sure of the answer, try methods such as eliminating answer choices or working backward from the answer choices provided to make an educated guess.
- Completely fill in the correct answer choice on the answer sheet. Verify that the test item number matches the item number on the answer sheet.

xxvii

Review these math skills to help the students grid their answer correctly:

- Converting a mixed number to an improper fraction.
- Writing a percentage as a decimal or as a fraction.
- Converting between a fraction and a decimal.

Additional Examples

Have the students grid each of the following.

1. 25%

2. 17.25%

3. $2\frac{3}{4}$

4. $\frac{1}{2}$%

5. 3×10^{-3}

Review the various correct ways to grid each number.

Gridded Response

When a test item requires you to place your answer in a grid, you must answer the test item correctly *and* fill out accurately the grid on your answer sheet, or the item will be marked as incorrect. The answer to a gridded response test item can be only a positive numerical value, such as a positive integer, a fraction, an improper fraction, or a decimal.

After you work the test item and determine the answer, you must write your answer in the answer boxes at the top of the grid. You must then fill in the corresponding bubble under each box.

- Write your answer with the first digit in the far left answer box, or with the last digit in the far right answer box.
- Write only one digit or symbol in each answer box.
- Do not leave a blank in the middle of an answer.
- Include the decimal point or the fraction bar if it is part of the answer.
- Fill in only one bubble for each answer box that has a number or symbol. Bubbles should be filled in by making a solid black mark.
- Do not grid a mixed number. You must first convert the mixed number to an improper fraction.

Response Grid

Answer boxes
Fraction bar bubbles
Decimal point bubbles
Number bubbles

Examples

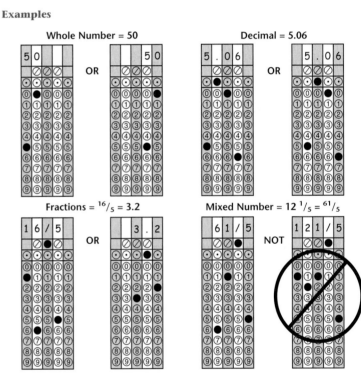

Whole Number = 50   Decimal = 5.06

Fractions = $^{16}/_5$ = 3.2   Mixed Number = 12 $^1/_5$ = $^{61}/_5$

2.

3.

4.

5.

Short Response

Short response test items are structured questions designed to test comprehension and understanding. In a multiple choice or gridded response test item, you simply solve a problem and select or write your answer. In a short response question, however, you must show your work and describe your reasoning process in order to receive full credit.

- Before responding to a short response test item, take time to thoroughly read the question. You may find it helpful to underline key words that signal what should be included in your answer.
- Use the margin of your test page to write a brief outline of your response.
- Use your technical writing skills to write an organized and logical description or explanation.
- Verify that any needed units of measure are included in your answer and that your response contains complete sentences that are free of spelling and grammatical errors.

Extended Response

Extended response test items are usually multi-part questions that require a high level of thinking. Because the extended response questions are longer and more involved, your answer may be scored using several points and may involve partial credit.

The following is a sample scoring rubric (method) used to score an answer to an extended response test item.

A Sample Scoring Rubric (Method)

4 points: Student shows a thorough understanding of the concept, correctly answers the question and provides a complete, detailed explanation.

3 points: Student shows most of the work and provides an explanation but has a minor error OR student shows all work and arrives at a correct response, but does not provide an explanation.

2 points: Student shows work but makes major errors resulting in an incorrect response or explanation. Explanation is missing, incorrect, or incomplete.

1 point: Student shows some work and has an incorrect response without an explanation OR student does not follow directions.

To answer this type of test item, follow the same suggestions given for short response test items. You must also pay attention to the number of parts in the question. Underline key words or phrases in the question, such as *List, Explain, Solve, Compare, Contrast, Design, Identify,* and so on to help you include all aspects of the question in your response.

xxix

World of Chemistry

1 Chemistry: An Introduction

	Section	Text Features & Components	Labs, Demonstrations & Activities
Teaching Segment 1A **1.5 blocks** pp. 3–11	1.1 The Importance of Learning Chemistry	**LP** Lesson Plans (Sec 1.1–1.4) **SE** Top Ten Reasons for Taking Chemistry *p. 4* **TE** Celebrity Chemical: Helium *p. 5*	**TE** Teaching Support: Demonstrations *p. 6*
	1.2 What is Chemistry?		**LM** Experiment 1: Experiment of Fire Lab Manual Report Sheets Teacher's Lab Guide
	1.3 Solving Problems Using a Scientific Approach	**SE** Chemical Impact: Land Mine Buzzers *p. 9*	**LM** Experiment 2: Scientific Observations Lab Manual Report Sheets Teacher's Lab Guide
	1.4 Using Scientific Thinking to Solve a Problem	**SE** Chemical Impact: Observations, Theories, and the Planets *p. 13*	**TE** Teaching Support: Additional Activity *pp. 10–11*
Teaching Segment 1B **1 block** pp. 11–16	1.5 The Scientific Method	**LP** Lesson Plans (Sec 1.5–1.6) **SE** Chemical Impact: Learn Chemistry—Prepare for Life *p. 15*	**SE** Chemistry in the Lab: Observations and Explanations *p. 17* **TE** Teaching Support: Additional Activity *p. 12* **LM** Experiment 3: Observations and Explanations Lab Manual Report Sheets Teacher's Lab Guide
	1.6 Learning Chemistry		**TE** Teaching Support: Additional Activity *pp. 14–15* **TE** Analogies for Teaching and Learning Demonstration *pp. 15–16*

Key

SE Student Edition
TE Teacher Edition
RP Teacher Resource Package
LM Lab Materials
LP Lesson Plans
AR Additional Resources
 Florida Specific

Technology and Media

 Transparencies
Figure 1.1, 1.2

PowerPoint Slides

 Chemistry in Motion
(10) Oxygen—Hydrogen Soap Bubbles and Balloons
(33) Sulfuric Acid and Sugar

eEdition CD-ROM
Easy Planner CD-ROM
English Summaries CD
Spanish Summaries CD

Web Site classzone.com
McDougal Littell Test Generator

Chapter Planning Guide

All Learners	Review & Assessment	Standards
CM Chemistry in Motion (33) **AR** Less Proficient Students *p. 1*	**SE** Questions and Problems *p. 18*	**TE** **NSES** UCP1, UCP2, A1, A2, B3, E2, G1, G2 **SSS** SC.H.1.4.1, SC.H.1.4.3, SC.H.1.4.7, SC.B.1.4.5, SC.H.3.4.2, SC.H.3.4.3, SC.H.3.4.5
TE Teaching Tips *p. 8* **AR** Less Proficient Students *p. 1*	**SE** Key Terms *p. 18* **SE** Questions and Problems *p. 18*	
TE Team Activity *p. 8* **AR** Less Proficient Students *p. 1*	**SE** Questions and Problems *p. 19*	
RP Team Learning Worksheets (Sec 1.1–1.4) *p. 1* **AR** Less Proficient Students *p. 1*	**SE** Focus Questions (Sec 1.1–1.4) *p. 11* **SE** Questions and Problems *p. 19*	
TE Active Learning *p. 11* **CM** Chemistry in Motion (10) **TR** Transparency: Figure 1.1 *p. 12* **TE** Correcting Misconceptions *p. 14* **AR** Less Proficient Students *pp. 1–2*	**SE** What if . . . *p. 14* **SE** Key Terms *p. 18* **SE** Questions and Problems *p. 19*	**TE** **NSES** UCP1, UCP2, A1, A2, B3, E2, G1, G2 **SSS** SC.H.1.4.1, SC.H.1.4.2, SC.H.1.4.3, SC.H.1.4.4, SC.H.1.4.5, SC.H.1.4.6, SC.H.1.4.7, SC.H.2.4.1
TR Transparency: Figure 1.2 *p. 16* **RP** Team Learning Worksheets (Sec 1.5–1.6) *p. 3* **AR** Less Proficient Students *p. 2*	**SE** Focus Questions (Sec 1.5–1.6) *p. 16* **SE** Questions and Problems *p. 19*	

Chapter Materials

TE Reading Strategy	**SE** Chapter Summary *p. 18*
AR English/Spanish Summaries *p. 2*	**RP** Solutions Guide
RP Classroom Activities and Projects: Element Mobile/Report *pp. 1–8*	**RP** Chapter Tests
AR Challenge Projects/Problems *p. 1*	**RP** Test Bank
English Summary Audio	McDougal Littell Test Generator
Spanish Summary Audio	**AR** Standardized Test Practice
RP Chapter Review Worksheets: (Basic, Review, Challenge)	**FCAT Test 1**

1 Integrating Reading Strategies and Chemistry Concepts

Chapter 1: Previewing the Textbook

Before Distributing Student Textbooks

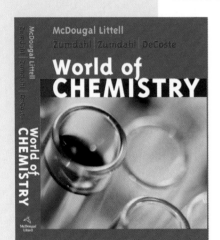

Before distributing the textbooks, hold up a copy in front of the class and start a discussion about the book's cover. Inform students that the cover shows top and side views of various test tubes.

Ask the students if they know any chemists and what that person does at his or her job. Tell the students that although laboratory research is one traditional career of a chemist, chemists contribute in many other industries such as education, medicine, law, sales, marketing, consulting, purchasing, biotechnology, health and safety, food, and environmental science.

Share with the students the information about the authors from pages vi–viii of the Teacher's Edition. Talk about the authors' backgrounds and emphasize their enthusiasm for writing the text in a way that will be readable and useful. Tell the students that the textbook has numerous resources within it to help explain, review, and clarify difficult material.

> ### A Word From the Authors
>
> Because our experience tells us that learning chemistry is not a spectator sport, this curriculum is designed to put the student in the center of the learning process. To learn in a meaningful way, the student must be a participant in the process. A knowledge of chemistry is not something a teacher gives to a student—it is something the student must construct for herself or himself with the help of the teacher, the textbook, laboratory exploration and the other materials provided.
>
> Also, our experience tells us that there is no better way to learn than to teach someone else. When we try to teach a concept to someone, it soon becomes obvious whether we truly understand the concept or not. Teaching someone exposes our own misconceptions and motivates us to "fix" them. However, successful peer teaching activities require much more than simply assigning the students to work in groups. The quality of the problems they work on in groups is critical. Based on our extensive experience with active learning in Introductory Chemistry at the University of Illinois, we have designed **Team Learning Worksheets,** which contain the type of conceptual questions that produce discussion and meaningful learning in a group setting.

In order to help the students become active participants in learning chemistry, consider guiding them in exploration of the textbook. Knowledge of how the chemistry text is organized is essential to the students' understanding of the course objectives.

While Distributing Student Textbooks

As you distribute books, allow the students time to look through the text. Note any initial reactions that could indicate student excitement or apprehensiveness regarding the subject matter.

Tips for Previewing the Textbook

• Direct the students to the **Table of Contents** on pages ix–xvi. Ask them to note the number of chapters and the chapter titles. Ask the students to describe which chapter title sounds most interesting and ask them to explain their choice.

• Point out that each chapter is divided into short sections. Each chapter is followed by a laboratory experiment that uses the ideas in the chapter to support what students will learn. Distribute your course outline, if applicable, and allow the students time to compare it to the table of contents.

- Discuss with the students the visual material used throughout the text: photos, graphs, tables, diagrams, sketches, and figures. Direct the students' attention to the various examples of visuals and explain that each type provides significant content information. Emphasize the importance of visual material in a chemistry text, and tell the students that you will help them develop the necessary skills for reading and interpreting visual material in chemistry.

- Note that Section 1.6 is provided specifically to help students develop successful strategies for learning chemistry.

- Have the students follow along as you guide them through the text. Point out and explain the importance of each chapter feature listed in the table on this page. Page numbers are given for quick reference.

- Ask the students to turn to the **Appendices** of the textbook, pages A1–A11. Point out that these references may be used for reviewing skills or as a resource for important rules, factors, and other significant data that they will use frequently.

- Text pages A13–A45 show solutions to the **Self-Check Exercises** and to some of the **End-of-Chapter Problems**. Encourage the students to use these pages to check their solutions or as a guide to obtain a solution as necessary.

Chapter Features

- Chapter Title and Chapter Title Page, p. 20
- Looking Ahead box that provides quick reference to section titles for the chapter, p. 20
- Numbered Section Titles and Objectives at beginning of each section, p. 21
- Box Features such as Celebrity Chemical, Chemical Impact, Top Ten, and Chemistry in Action, pp. 23, 26, 28
- Focus Questions, p. 29
- Example Problems and Self-Check Exercises, p. 30
- Chemistry in the Laboratory feature, pp. 42–43
- Chapter Review: Key Terms, Summary, Questions and Problems, and Critical Thinking Problems pp. 43–45

- Demonstrate use of the **Glossary**, found on pages A47–A54. Ask the students to define the words "buret" or "ketone". Emphasize that vocabulary will be introduced throughout the course and that the glossary is a quick source for definitions.

- Direct students to the **Index**, found on pages A59–A76, and have them practice using it to locate topics. Point out how this feature saves time when searching for a particular concept or topic.

- Point out that the inside back cover contains the **Periodic Table**. Explain that this table will soon become a valuable reference.

- Conclude the review of the text by directing the students to the feature found on pages xxii–xxix of the student book (pp. lxiv–lxxi in the Teacher's Edition): Reading Chemistry, Writing Chemistry, and Testing in Chemistry. Allow time for students to read this material. Encourage students to revisit these pages and Section 1.6 of the text periodically, as these pages contain helpful tips for successful completion of the chemistry course.

Chapter 1

Overview

In this Chapter our goals are for the students to:

- Understand the importance of learning chemistry

- Define chemistry

- Recognize the general steps scientists use in solving problems

- Illustrate the scientific method

- Develop successful strategies for learning chemistry

1 Chemistry: An Introduction

Chemistry deals with the natural world.

Did you ever see a fireworks display on the Fourth of July and wonder how it's possible to produce those beautiful, intricate designs in the air? Have you read about dinosaurs—how they ruled the earth for millions of years and then suddenly disappeared? Although the extinction happened 65 million years ago and may seem unimportant, could the same thing happen to us? Have you ever wondered why an ice cube (pure water) floats in a glass of water (also pure water)? Did you know that the "lead" in your pencil is made of the same substance (carbon) as the diamond in an engagement ring? Did you ever wonder how a corn plant or a palm tree grows seemingly by magic, or why leaves turn beautiful colors in autumn? Do you know how the battery works to start your car or run your calculator? Surely some of these things and many others in the world around you have intrigued you. The fact is that we can explain all of these things in convincing ways using the models of chemistry and the related physical and life sciences.

Fireworks are a beautiful illustration of chemistry in action.

1.1 The Importance of Learning Chemistry

Objective: *To understand the importance of learning chemistry.*

Although chemistry might seem to have little to do with dinosaurs, knowledge of chemistry was the tool that enabled paleontologists like Luis W. Alvarez and his coworkers from the University of California at Berkeley to "crack the case" of the disappearing dinosaurs. The key was the relatively high level of iridium found in the sediment that represents the boundary between the earth's Cretaceous (K) and Tertiary (T) periods—the time when the dinosaurs disappeared virtually overnight (on the geological scale). The Berkeley researchers knew that meteorites also have unusually high iridium content (relative to the earth's composition), which led them to suggest that a large meteorite hit the earth 65 million years ago, causing the climatic changes that wiped out the dinosaurs.

1.1　The Importance of Learning Chemistry　**3**

Section 1.1

Themes
Organization, Form and Function

Skills
Interpreting data, making comparisons, evaluating

Student Preparation
Assign the students to read Sections 1.1 to 1.4 and to answer the Focus Questions at the end of Section 1.4 before coming to class.

Active Learning
After introducing the material in Sections 1.1 to 1.4 in class, place the students in groups and have them work together on Sections 1.1–1.4: Team Learning Worksheet. Answers and/or discussion of these questions are located in the *Teacher Resources*.

Using the TOP TEN

Ask students to design their own Top Ten Reasons for Taking Chemistry. Place the list in their portfolios for later review and revision or in a file for review later in the year.

TOP TEN

Reasons for Taking Chemistry

1. Do experiments using fire and chemicals
2. Learn to answer chemistry questions on game shows
3. Learn to solve problems
4. See cool demonstrations in class
5. Learn to safely use and dispose of household chemicals
6. Wear fashionable lab aprons and goggles
7. Learn to think like a scientist
8. Impress your friends by using words like "molarity" and "stoichiometry"
9. Find a practical use for the math you've been learning
10. Meet the most interesting people—the people who teach it!

Why Study Chemistry?

A knowledge of chemistry is useful to almost everyone—chemistry occurs all around us all of the time, and an understanding of chemistry is useful to doctors, lawyers, mechanics, business people, firefighters, and poets among others. Chemistry is important—there is no doubt about that. It lies at the heart of our efforts to produce new materials that make our lives safer and easier, to produce new sources of energy that are abundant and non-polluting, and to understand and control the many diseases that threaten us and our food supplies. Even if your future career does not require the daily use of chemical principles, your life will be greatly influenced by chemistry.

Although a strong case can be made that the use of chemistry has greatly enriched all of our lives, there is also a dark side to the story. Our society has used its knowledge of chemistry to kill and destroy. It is important to understand that the principles of chemistry are inherently neither good nor bad—it's what we do with this knowledge that really matters. Although humans are clever, resourceful, and concerned about others, they also can be greedy, selfish, and ignorant. In addition, we tend to be shortsighted; we concentrate too much on the present and do not think enough about the long-range implications of our actions. This type of thinking has already caused us a great deal of trouble—severe environmental damage has occurred on many fronts. We cannot place all the responsibility on the chemical companies, because everyone has contributed to these problems. However, it is less important to lay blame than to figure out how to solve these problems. An important part of the answer must rely on chemistry.

A Real-World Chemist

One of the "hottest" fields in the chemical sciences is environmental chemistry—an area that involves studying our environmental ills and finding creative ways to address them. For example, meet Bart Eklund, who works in the atmospheric chemistry field for Radian Corporation in Austin, Texas. Bart's interest in a career in environmental science started with two environmental chemistry courses and two ecology courses he took as a college undergraduate. The multidisciplinary nature of environmental problems has since allowed Bart to pursue his interest in several fields at the same time. You might say that he specializes in being a generalist.

The environmental consulting field appeals to Bart for a number of reasons: the chance to define and solve a number of research problems; the simultaneous work on a number of diverse projects; the mix of desk, field, and laboratory work; the travel; and the opportunity to perform rewarding work that has a positive effect on people's lives.

Among Bart's career highlights are the following:

Bart Eklund checking air quality at a hazardous waste site.

- Spending a winter month doing air sampling in the Grand Tetons, where he also met his wife and learned to ski;

- Driving sampling pipes by hand into the rocky ground of Death Valley Monument in California;

- Working regularly with experts in their fields and with people who enjoy what they do;

- Doing vigorous work in 100 °F weather while wearing a rubberized suit, double gloves, and a respirator; and

- Getting to work in and see Alaska, Yosemite Park, Niagara Falls, Hong Kong, the People's Republic of China, Mesa Verde, New York City, and dozens of other interesting places.

Bart Eklund's career demonstrates how chemists are helping to solve our environmental problems. It is how we use our chemical knowledge that makes all the difference.

Real-World Chemistry

An example that shows how technical knowledge can be a "double-edged sword" is the case of chlorofluorocarbons (CFCs). When the compound called Freon-12 was first synthesized, it was hailed as a near-miracle substance. Because of its noncorrosive nature and its unusual ability to resist decomposition, Freon-12 seemed ideal for refrigeration and air-conditioning systems, cleaning applications, the blowing of foams used for insulation and packing materials, and many other applications. For years everything seemed fine—the CFCs actually replaced more dangerous materials, such as the ammonia

CELEBRITY CHEMICAL

Helium (He)

Have you ever heard recordings of deep-sea diver's voices? They sound a lot like Donald Duck. It's the helium gas mixed with the oxygen gas in the "air" that the divers are breathing that produces the effect. Normal air is about 8/10 nitrogen and 2/10 oxygen. This mixture doesn't work for diving, because too much nitrogen dissolves in the blood at the high pressures under the ocean. When the diver returns to the surface, this nitrogen can form bubbles leading to the "bends"— a terribly painful condition that can be fatal. Helium does not dissolve in the blood so easily and thus it does not lead to the bends so readily.

Helium is a very interesting substance. You are no doubt familiar with it, because you have had balloons filled with helium. If you let go of a helium-filled balloon, it floats up and away from you. That's because helium is lighter than air.

Helium is unique in another way—it was discovered on the sun before it was discovered on earth. In fact, the word "helium" comes from the Greek word for the sun. Although helium is the second most abundant substance in the universe, very little helium is found on earth. Helium is so light that the earth's gravitational field cannot hold it. The tiny amount of helium present in our atmosphere forms from natural radioactive processes and it is continuously lost to outer space.

The helium we use for deep-sea diving and filling balloons is separated from natural gas as it is brought to the surface. This helium was formed in the depths of the earth by radioactive decay and remains trapped with the natural gas deposits.

Helium has many uses. For example, it is used to fill blimps and weather balloons. In addition, because of its very low boiling point (-452 °F), it is used as an extreme coolant in scientific experiments.

For a "light-weight," helium is pretty important.

Spiderman-balloon filled with helium.

CELEBRITY CHEMICAL

Helium (He)

Encourage students to recognize that they are already familiar with uses of elements and compounds in their daily lives. These features highlight uses of chemicals.

Additional Activity: Use this feature to begin focusing on an Element of the Week. Feature a bulletin board with a celebrity element each week. Highlight its properties, uses, and characteristics.

Student Project: Assign an element to each student. Have the students create mobiles for their elements, including their names, symbols, properties, uses, and characteristics. Use the mobiles to decorate the classroom for parent night.

formerly used in refrigeration systems. The CFCs were definitely viewed as "good guys." But then a problem was discovered—the ozone in the upper atmosphere that protects us from the high-energy radiation of the sun began to decline. What was happening to cause the destruction of the vital ozone?

Much to everyone's amazement, the culprits turned out to be the seemingly beneficial CFCs. Inevitably, large quantities of CFCs had leaked into the atmosphere. No one was very worried about this development, however, because these compounds seemed totally benign. In fact, the great stability of the CFCs (a tremendous advantage for their various applications) was in the end a great disadvantage when they were released into the environment. Professor F. S. Rowland and his colleagues at the University of California at Irvine demonstrated that the CFCs eventually drifted to high altitudes in the atmosphere, where the energy of the sun stripped off chlorine atoms. These chlorine atoms, in turn, promoted the decomposition of the ozone in the upper atmosphere. Thus a substance that possessed many advantages in earthbound applications turned against us in the atmosphere. Who could have guessed it would end this way?

The good news is that the U.S. chemical industry is leading the way to find environmentally safe alternatives to CFCs, and the levels of CFCs in the atmosphere are already dropping.

The story of the CFCs shows that we can respond relatively quickly to a serious environmental problem if we decide to do so. Also, it is important to understand that chemical manufacturers have a new attitude about the environment—they are now among the leaders in finding ways to address our environmental problems. The industries that apply the chemical sciences are now determined as being part of the solution rather than being part of the problem.

A chemist in the laboratory.

Learning Chemistry

As you can see, learning chemistry is both interesting and important. A chemistry course can do more than simply help you learn the principles of chemistry, however. A major by-product of your study of chemistry is that you will become a better problem solver. One reason chemistry has the reputation of being "tough" is that it often deals with rather complicated systems that require some effort to figure out. Although this complexity might seem like a disadvantage at first, you can turn it to your advantage if you have the right attitude. Employers maintain that one of the first things they look for in a prospective employee is the ability to solve problems. We will spend a good deal of time solving various types of problems in this book by using a systematic, logical approach that will help you solve any kind of problem in any field. Keep this broader goal in mind as you learn to solve the specific problems connected with chemistry.

Although learning chemistry is often not easy, it's never impossible. In fact, anyone who is interested, patient, and willing to work can learn chemistry. In this book we will try very hard to help you understand what chemistry is and how it works and to point out how chemistry applies to the things going on in your life.

Our sincere hope is that this text will motivate you to learn chemistry, make its concepts understandable to you, and demonstrate how interesting and vital the study of chemistry is.

1.2 What Is Chemistry?

Objective: *To define chemistry.*

Section 1.2

Themes
Organization, Models, Form and Function

Skills
Classifying, making inferences

Laboratory
Experiment 1:
Chemistry of Fire, Traditional

Chemistry can be defined as *the science that deals with the materials of the universe and the changes that these materials undergo.* Chemists are involved in activities as diverse as examining the fundamental particles of matter, looking for molecules in space, synthesizing and formulating new materials of all types, using bacteria to produce such chemicals as insulin, and inventing new diagnostic methods for early detection of disease.

Chemistry is often called the central science—and with good reason. Most of the phenomena that occur in the world around us involve chemical changes, changes where one or more substances become different substances. Here are some examples of chemical changes:

Wood burns in air, forming water, carbon dioxide, and other substances.

A plant grows by assembling simple substances into more complex substances.

The steel in a car rusts.

Eggs, flour, sugar, and baking powder are mixed and baked to yield a cake.

The definition of the term *chemistry* is learned and stored in the brain.

Emissions from a power plant lead to the formation of acid rain.

As we proceed, you will see how the concepts of chemistry allow us to understand the nature of these and other changes and thus help us manipulate natural materials to our benefit.

To understand these processes and the many others that occur around us, chemists take a special view of things. Chemists "look inside" ordinary objects to see how the fundamental components are behaving.

To understand how this approach works, consider a tree. When we view a tree from a distance, we see the tree as a whole. The trunk, the branches, and the leaves all blend together to give the tree. We call this overall view of the tree the *macroscopic* picture.

As we get closer to the tree, we begin to see the detail— pieces of bark, individual leaves, large and tiny branches, and so on. Now imagine that we examine a single leaf. We see veins, variation in color, surface irregularities, and more. Our curiosity is whetted. What lies inside the leaf? What causes it to change from a bud in the spring to a green leaf in the summer and then to a red or golden color in the fall? To answer these questions, we need a microscope. As we examine the leaf under a microscope, we see cells and motion. Because we don't "live" in this *microscopic* world, the commonplace leaf becomes fascinating and mysterious.

The launch of the space shuttle gives clear indications that chemical reactions are occurring.

can be disposed of in a trashcan. The beaker can be cleaned with soap and water.

Alternative If you do not have a fume hood, this demonstration is found on the *Chemistry in Motion* videotape or videodisc (Demonstration 33).

- Connecting the real world to the atomic/molecular world is difficult for many students. Encourage students to visualize the atomic/molecular world by drawing pictures.

- Discuss students' ideas of what everyday objects look like on an atomic/molecular level. Include in your discussion examples such as air, water, salt, and sugar. Don't worry about the details here. The idea is to get students thinking and ready to continue with Chapter 2. Further detail will be developed there. The student responses will give you an idea of their entering perceptions.

1.3 Section 1.3

Themes
Organization

Skills
Developing hypotheses, evaluating, problem solving

Laboratory
Experiment 2:
Scientific Observations, Traditional

Team Activity
Group students in pairs or triples. Have each team discuss and present its solutions to the questions in the text.

When we speak of "motion" in the macroscopic world, we refer to the swaying of the tree and the rustling of the leaves. In the microscopic world, "motion" refers to the cells acting as tiny machines that absorb energy from the sun and nutrients from the air and the soil. We are now in the microscopic world, but as chemists, we want to go even further. What are the building blocks of the cells and what are the components of the water that contains the dissolved nutrients?

Think about water, a very familiar substance. In the macroscopic world, it flows and splashes over rocks in mountain streams and freezes on ponds in the winter. What is the microscopic nature of water? As you may know already, water is composed of tiny molecules that we can represent as

Here H represents a hydrogen atom and O represents an oxygen atom. We often write this molecule as H_2O because it contains two hydrogens (H) and one oxygen (O).

This is the microscopic world of the chemist—a world of molecules and atoms. This is the world we will explore in this book. One of our main goals is to connect the macroscopic world in which you live to the microscopic world that makes it all work. We think you will enjoy the trip!

The macroscopic view of water (the mountain stream) and the microscopic view (the individual water molecules).

1.3 Solving Problems Using a Scientific Approach

Objective: *To recognize the general steps scientists use in solving problems.*

One of the most important things we do in everyday life is solve problems. In fact, most of the decisions you make each day can be described as solving problems.

> It's 8:30 A.M. on Friday. Which is the best way to drive to school to avoid traffic congestion?
>
> You have two tests on Monday. Should you divide your study time equally or allot more time to one than to the other?
>
> Your car stalls at a busy intersection and your little brother is with you. What should you do next?

These are everyday problems of the type we all face. What process do we use to solve them? You may not have thought about it before, but there are several steps that almost everyone uses to solve problems:

1. Recognize the problem and state it clearly. Some information becomes known, or something happens that requires action. In science we call this step *making an observation*.

2. Propose *possible* solutions to the problem or *possible* explanations for the observation. In scientific language, suggesting such a possibility is called *formulating a hypothesis*.

8 Chapter 1 Chemistry: An Introduction

CHEMICAL IMPACT | Science, Technology, and Society

Land Mine Buzzers

An estimated 100 million plastic land mines are scattered throughout the earth on former battlefields. Every day, these hidden mines kill or maim 60 people. Finding these mines is very difficult—they were designed to resist detection. Scientists are now enthusiastic about a new way to identify the mines—with honeybees. Previous work has shown that bees foraging in chemically contaminated areas carry these substances back to their hives. The hope is that bees searching for food in mined areas will bring back traces of the explosives from "leaky"

mines, alerting people of nearby danger. Scientists also plan to train bees to seek out explosives by associating the scents of the explosive compounds with food. The researchers will keep track of the bees' movements by fitting electronic identification tags (about the size of a grain of rice) on the bees' backs.

If this idea works, it would be a cheap, safe method for characterizing a minefield. These "mine buzzers" would be much safer than the current practice of prodding the soil with pokers.

3. Decide which of the solutions is the best or decide whether the explanation proposed is reasonable. To do this we search our memory for any pertinent information or we seek new information. In science we call searching for new information *performing an experiment.*

As we will discover in the next section, citizens as well as scientists use these same procedures to study what happens in the world around us. The important point here is that scientific thinking can help you in all parts of your life. It's worthwhile to learn how to think scientifically—whether you want to be a scientist, an auto mechanic, a doctor, a politician, or a poet!

1.4 Using Scientific Thinking to Solve a Problem

Objective: *To illustrate the scientific method.*

To illustrate how science helps us solve problems, consider a true story about two people, David and Susan (not their real names). Several years ago David and Susan were healthy 40-year-olds living in California, where David was serving in the Air Force. Gradually Susan became quite ill, showing flulike symptoms including nausea and severe muscle pains. Even her personality changed: she became uncharacteristically grumpy. She seemed like a totally different person from the healthy, happy woman of a few months earlier. Following her doctor's orders, she rested and drank a lot of fluids, including large quantities of coffee and orange juice from her favorite mug, part of a 200-piece set of pottery dishes recently purchased in Italy. However, she just got sicker, developing extreme abdominal cramps and severe anemia.

During this time David also became ill and exhibited symptoms much like Susan's: weight loss, excruciating pain in his back and arms, and uncharacteristic fits of temper. The disease became so serious that he retired early from the Air Force and the couple moved to Seattle. For a short time their health improved, but after they unpacked all their belongings (including those pottery dishes), their health began to deteriorate again. Susan's body became so sensitive that she could not tolerate the weight of a blanket. She was near death. What was wrong? The doctors didn't know, but one of them suggested that she might have porphyria, a rare blood disease.

Italian pottery.

Desperate, David began to search the medical literature himself. One day while he was reading about porphyria, a phrase jumped off the page: "Lead poisoning can sometimes be confused with porphyria." Could the problem be lead poisoning?

We have described a very serious problem with life-or-death implications. What should David do next? Overlooking for a moment the obvious response of calling the couple's doctor immediately to discuss the possibility of lead poisoning, could David solve the problem by scientific thinking? Let's use the three steps described in Section 1.3 to attack the problem one part at a time. This is important: usually we solve complex problems by breaking them down into manageable parts. We can then assemble the solution to the overall problem from the answers we have found "piecemeal."

In this case there are many parts to the overall problem:

What is the disease?

Where is it coming from?

Can it be cured?

Let's attack "What is the disease?" first.

Observation: David and Susan are ill with the symptoms described. Is the disease lead poisoning?

Hypothesis: The disease is lead poisoning.

Experiment: If the disease is lead poisoning, the symptoms must match those known to characterize lead poisoning. Look up the symptoms of lead poisoning. David did this and found that they matched the couple's symptoms almost exactly.

This discovery points to lead poisoning as the source of their problem, but David needed more evidence.

Observation: Lead poisoning results from high levels of lead in the bloodstream.

Hypothesis: The couple have high levels of lead in their blood.

Experiment: Perform a blood analysis. Susan arranged for such an analysis, and the results showed high lead levels for both David and Susan.

This test confirms that lead poisoning is probably the cause of the trouble, but the overall problem is still not solved. David and Susan are likely to die unless they find out where the lead is coming from.

Observation: There is lead in the couple's blood.

Hypothesis: The lead is in their food or drink when they buy it.

Experiment: Find out whether anyone else who shopped at the same store was getting sick (no one was). Also note that moving to a new area did not solve the problem.

Observation: The food they buy is free of lead.

Hypothesis: The dishes they use are the source of the lead poisoning.

Experiment: Find out whether their dishes contain lead. David and Susan learned that lead compounds are often used to put a shiny finish on pottery objects. And laboratory analysis of their Italian pottery dishes showed that lead was present in the glaze.

10   Chapter 1   Chemistry: An Introduction

Observation: Lead is present in their dishes, so the dishes are a possible source of their lead poisoning.

Hypothesis: The lead is being leached into their food.

Experiment: Place a beverage, such as orange juice, in one of the cups and then analyze the beverage for lead. The results showed high levels of lead in drinks that had come in contact with the pottery cups.

After many applications of the scientific method, the problem is solved. We can summarize the answer to the problem (David and Susan's illness) as follows: the Italian pottery they used for everyday dishes contained a lead glaze that contaminated their food and drink with lead. This lead accumulated in their bodies to the point where it interfered seriously with normal functions and produced severe symptoms. This overall explanation, which summarizes the hypotheses that agree with the experimental results, is called a *theory* in science. This explanation accounts for the results of all the experiments performed.*

We could continue to use the scientific method to study other aspects of this problem, such as the following:

What types of food or drink leach the most lead from the dishes?

Do all pottery dishes with lead glazes produce lead poisoning?

As we answer questions using the scientific method, other questions naturally arise. By repeating the three steps over and over, we can come to understand a given phenomenon thoroughly.

Focus Questions Sections 1.1–1.4

Focus Questions are designed to help you concentrate on the most important ideas as you read the text and should be answered before class. See page 16 for more information.

1. How do CFCs illustrate that technical knowledge can be a "double-edged" sword?

2. Why is chemistry often called the central science?

3. Describe how you would set up an experiment to test the relationship between doing chemistry homework and the final grade received in the course. Apply a scientific approach to solving this problem. Label each of your steps appropriately.

 ## 1.5 The Scientific Method

Objective: *To describe the method scientists use to study nature.*

In the last two sections we began to see how the methods of science are used to solve problems. In this section we will further examine this approach.

Science is a framework for gaining and organizing knowledge. Science is not simply a set of facts but also a plan of action—a *procedure* for processing

---

*"David" and "Susan" recovered from their lead poisoning and are now publicizing the dangers of using lead-glazed pottery. This happy outcome is the answer to the third part of their overall problem, "Can the disease be cured?" They simply stopped eating from that pottery!

more confident as we make more observations that fit. After many different names have been presented, the "female five-letter name" category will become apparent. Discuss how this exercise relates to the scientific method (students made observations, looked for patterns, and developed a hypothesis; they then used new observations to refine the theory).

 ## Section 1.5

Themes
Organization

Skills
Developing hypotheses, evaluating, problem solving

Student Preparation
Assign the students to read Sections 1.5 and 1.6 and to answer the Focus Questions at the end of Section 1.6 before coming to class.

Active Learning
After introducing the material in Sections 1.5 and 1.6 in class, place the students in groups and have them work together on Sections 1.5–1.6: Team Learning Worksheet. Answers and/or discussion of these questions are located in the *Teacher Resources*.

 Laboratory
Experiment 3:
Observations and Explanations, In Text

and understanding certain types of information. Although scientific thinking is useful in all aspects of life, in this text we will use it to understand how the natural world operates. The process that lies at the center of scientific inquiry is called the **scientific method.** As we saw in Section 1.3, it consists of the following steps:

Quantitative observations involve a number. Qualitative ones do not.

Steps in the Scientific Method

1. *State the problem and collect data (make observations).* Observations may be *qualitative* (the sky is blue; water is a liquid) or *quantitative* (water boils at 100 °C; a certain chemistry book weighs 4.5 pounds). A qualitative observation does not involve a number. A quantitative observation is called a **measurement** and does involve a number (and a unit, such as pounds or inches). We will discuss measurements in detail in Chapter 5.
2. *Formulate hypotheses.* A hypothesis is a *possible* explanation for the observation.
3. *Perform experiments.* An experiment is something we do to test the hypothesis. We gather new information that allows us to decide whether the hypothesis is supported by the new information we have learned from the experiment. Experiments always produce new observations, and these observations bring us back to the beginning of the process.

To explain the behavior of a given part of nature, we repeat these steps many times. Gradually we gather the knowledge necessary to understand what is going on.

Once we have a set of hypotheses that agrees with our various observations, we assemble them into a theory that is often called a *model*. A **theory** (model) is a set of tested hypotheses that gives an overall explanation of some part of nature (see **Figure 1.1**).

It is important to distinguish between observations and theories. An observation is something that is witnessed and can be recorded. A theory is an *interpretation*—a possible explanation of *why* nature behaves in a particular way. Theories inevitably change as more information becomes available. For example, the motions of the sun and stars have remained virtually the same over the thousands of years during which humans have been observing them, but our explanations—our theories—have changed greatly since ancient times.

The point is that we don't stop asking questions just because we have devised a theory that seems to account satisfactorily for some aspect of natural behavior. We continue doing experiments to refine our theories. We do this by using the theory to make a prediction and then performing an experiment (making a new observation) to see whether the results match this prediction.

Always remember that theories (models) are human inventions. They represent our attempts to explain observed natural behavior in terms of our human experiences. We must continue to do experiments and refine our theories to be consistent with new knowledge if we hope to approach a more nearly complete understanding of nature.

As we observe nature, we often see that the same observation applies to many different systems. For example, studies of innumerable chemical changes

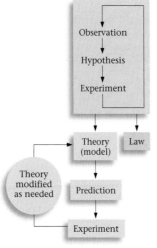

Figure 1.1
The various parts of the scientific method.

Connection to Astronomy

Observations, Theories, and the Planets

Humans have always been fascinated by the heavens—by the behavior of the sun by day and the stars by night. Although more accurately measured now thanks to precise instruments, our basic *observations* of their behavior have remained the same over the past 4000 years. However, our *interpretations* of these observations have changed dramatically. For example, around 2000 B.C. the Egyptians thought that the sun was a boat inhabited by the god Ra, who daily sailed across the sky.

Over the years, patterns in the changes in the heavens were recognized and, through marvelous devices such as Stonehenge in England, were connected to the seasons of the year. People also noticed that seven objects seemed to move against the background of "fixed stars." These objects (actually the sun, the moon, and the planets Mercury, Venus, Mars, Jupiter, and Saturn) were called the "wanderers." The planets generally seemed to move from west to east, but sometimes they seemed to slow down and even to move backward for a few weeks.

Eudoxus, born in 400 B.C., tried to explain these observations. He imagined the earth as fixed in space and the planets as attached to a set of transparent spheres, each slightly larger than the previous one, that moved at different rates around the earth. The stars were attached to a fixed outermost sphere. This model, although clever, still did not account for the "backward" movement of some of the planets. Five hundred years later Ptolemy, a Greek scholar, worked out a plan more complex than that of Eudoxus, in which the planets were attached to the edges of spheres that "rolled around" the spheres of Eudoxus. This model accounted for the observed behavior of all the planets, including the apparent reversals in their motions.

Because of a natural human prejudice that the earth should be the center of the universe, Ptolemy's model was assumed to be correct for more than a thousand years, and its wide acceptance actually in-

The Egyptian sun-god, Ra (drawn on papyrus).

TOP TEN

Most Massive Bodies in the Solar System

Body	Mass (kg)
1. Sun	2.4×10^{28}
2. Jupiter	2.3×10^{25}
3. Saturn	7.0×10^{24}
4. Neptune	1.2×10^{24}
5. Uranus	1.1×10^{24}
6. Earth	7.4×10^{22}
7. Venus	6.0×10^{22}
8. Mars	7.9×10^{21}
9. Mercury	4.1×10^{21}
10. Pluto	1.6×10^{20}

hibited the advancement of astronomy. Finally, in 1543, the Polish cleric Nicholas Copernicus postulated that the earth was only one of the planets, all of which revolved around the sun. This suggestion by Copernicus that the earth might not be at the center of the universe produced violent opposition to his model. In fact, Copernicus's writings were "corrected" by religious officials before scholars were allowed to use them.

However, the Copernican theory persisted and was finally given a solid mathematical base by Johannes Kepler. Kepler's hypotheses were in turn further refined 36 years after his death by Isaac Newton, who recognized that the concept of gravity could account for the positions and motions of the planets. However, even the brilliant models of Newton were discovered to be incomplete by Albert Einstein, who showed that Newton's ideas were just a part of a much more general model.

Thus the same basic observations were made for several thousand years, but the explanations—the models—changed remarkably from the Egyptians' boat of Ra to Einstein's relativity.

The lesson is that our models (theories) inevitably change and that we should expect them to do so. They can help us make scientific progress, or they can inhibit our progress if we become too attached to them. Although the observations of chemistry will remain the same, the models given in a chemistry text written in 2100 will certainly be quite different from the ones presented here.

1.5 The Scientific Method **13**

Law: A summary of observed behavior.

Theory: An explanation of behavior.

have shown that the total mass of the materials involved is the same before and after the change. We often summarize such generally observed behavior into a statement called a **natural law.** The observation that the total mass of materials is not affected by a chemical change in those materials is called the law of conservation of mass.

You must recognize the difference between a law and a theory. A law is a summary of observed (measurable) behavior, whereas a theory is an explanation of behavior. *A law tells what happens; a theory (model) is our attempt to explain why it happens.*

In this section, we have described the scientific method (which is summarized in Figure 1.1) as it might ideally be applied. However, it is important to remember that science does not always progress smoothly and efficiently. Scientists are human. They have prejudices; they misinterpret data; they can become emotionally attached to their theories and thus lose objectivity; and they play politics. Science is affected by profit motives, budgets, fads, wars, and religious beliefs. Galileo, for example, was forced to deny his astronomical observations in the face of strong religious resistance. Lavoisier, the father of modern chemistry, was beheaded because of his political affiliations. And great progress in the chemistry of nitrogen fertilizers resulted from the desire to produce explosives to fight wars. The progress of science is often slowed more by the frailties of humans and their institutions than by the limitations of scientific measuring devices. The scientific method is only as effective as the humans using it. It does not automatically lead to progress.

1.6 Learning Chemistry

Objective: *To develop successful strategies for learning chemistry.*

Chemistry courses have a universal reputation for being difficult. There are some good reasons for this. For example, as we have already discussed, we live in the macroscopic world but to understand this world we need to think in terms of the unfamiliar microscopic world. In addition, the language of chemistry is unfamiliar in the beginning; many terms and definitions need to be memorized. As with any language, *you must know the vocabulary* before you can communicate effectively. We will try to help you by pointing out those things that need to be memorized.

But memorization is only the beginning. Don't stop there or your experience with chemistry will be frustrating. Memorization is not the same as understanding. We can teach a parrot to say anything we can say, but the parrot does not understand the meaning of its words. You need to memorize facts, but you also need to strive to understand the fundamental ideas—the models of chemistry. Be willing to do some thinking, and learn to trust yourself to figure things out. To solve a typical chemistry problem, you must sort through the given information and decide what is really crucial.

It is important to realize that chemical systems tend to be complicated—there are typically many components—and we must make approximations in describing them. Therefore, trial and error play a major role in solving chemical problems. In tackling a complicated system, a practicing chemist really does not expect to be right the first time he or she analyzes the problem. The usual practice is to make several simplifying assumptions and then give it a try. If the answer obtained doesn't make sense, the chemist adjusts the assumptions, using feedback from the first attempt, and tries again. The point is this: in dealing with chemical systems, do not expect to understand immediately everything that is going on. In fact, it is typical (even for an experienced chemist) *not* to understand at first. Make an attempt to solve the problem and then analyze the feedback. *It is no disaster to make a mistake as long as you learn from it.*

The only way to develop your confidence as a problem solver is to practice solving problems. To help you, this book contains many examples worked out in detail. Follow these through carefully, making sure you understand each step. These examples are usually followed by a similar exercise (called a self-check exercise) that you should try on your own (detailed solutions of the self-check exercises are given at the end of each chapter). Use the self-check exercises to test whether you are understanding the material as you go along.

CHEMICAL IMPACT

Consumer Connection

Learn Chemistry—Prepare for Life

What is the purpose of education? Because you are spending considerable time and energy pursuing an education, this is an important question.

Some people seem to equate education with the storage of facts in the brain. These people apparently believe that education simply means memorizing the answers to all of life's present and future problems. Although this idea is clearly unreasonable, many students seem to behave as though it were their guiding principle. These students want to memorize lists of facts and to reproduce them on tests. They regard as unfair any exam questions that require some original thought or some processing of information. Indeed, it might be tempting to reduce education to a simple filling up with facts, because that approach can produce short-term satisfaction for both student and teacher. Of course, storing facts in the brain *is* important. You cannot function without knowing that red means stop, electricity is dangerous, ice is slippery, and so on.

However, mere recall of abstract information, without the ability to process it, makes you little better than a talking encyclopedia. Former students always seem to bring the same message when they return. The characteristics that are most important to their success are a knowledge of the fundamentals of their fields, the ability to recognize and solve problems, and the ability to communicate effectively. They also emphasize the importance of a high level of motivation.

How does studying chemistry help you achieve these characteristics? The fact that chemical systems are complicated is really a blessing, though one that is well disguised. Studying chemistry will

not by itself make you a good problem solver, but it can help you develop a positive, aggressive attitude toward problem solving and it can help boost your confidence. Learning to "think like a chemist" can be valuable to anyone in any field. People who were trained as chemists often excel not only in chemical research and production but also in personnel, marketing, sales, development, finance, and management. The point is that much of what you learn in this course can be applied to any career. So be careful not to take too narrow a view of this course. Try to look beyond short-term frustration to long-term benefits. It may not be easy to learn to be a good problem solver, but it's well worth the effort.

Learning chemistry is both fun and important.

their role is to simply remember what you say and what is in the text without assimilating it.

To complete the point, go to the students in a different order to show that the tape recorder is no longer correct. Ask a question such as "Why is the sky blue?" When the tape recorder answers "Bob," discuss the fact that the tape recorder does not even know what is being asked. Inform students that a major

goal this year is to learn to think scientifically, and that they cannot achieve this goal if they are merely tape recorders.

Many students have the wrong goals when learning chemistry. Most understand and accept that they will have to commit some material to memory (the language of chemistry). However, students generally do not really recognize what it means to "understand." For many stu-

dents, simply knowing (that is, memorizing) constitutes understanding.

Integrating the CHEMICAL IMPACT

Learn Chemistry— Prepare for Life

This feature helps students see that learning chemistry has value beyond the next test. Learning to be a creative problem solver is valuable in any career. Becoming adept at chemistry requires the kind of critical thinking that serves someone well in all walks of life.

ANALOGIES FOR TEACHING AND LEARNING

You will need:
Water	0.10 *M* HCl
0.10 *M* NaOH	Vegetable
Universal	oil
indicator	250-mL
1-L Erlenmeyer	Erlenmeyer
flask	flask (4)

Empty Pitcher: Show the students a large flask filled with water and an empty 250-mL flask. Explain that in this analogy the teacher is the large flask, the small flask is the student, and the water is knowledge. In this analogy, the student starts out empty (knowing nothing). The teacher pours knowledge into the student. Discuss the problems with this analogy. First, students do come into class with ideas about the subject material, even if some are mistaken. Second, the knowledge that students attain is not the same as the knowledge the teacher has; knowledge is not simply transferred. Finally, learning is not a passive activity.

Oil and Water: Once again, a flask of water represents the teacher. Another flask with some vegetable oil represents the student. This exercise shows that students come with knowledge and that this knowledge is different from the teacher's knowledge. The knowledge (water) flows from the teacher to the student, and it takes a lot of work to get it to mix with the student's initial knowledge. This analogy is demonstrated by capping the flask, which represents the student, and mixing it vigorously. Show the students the product of this work and let them watch as the water and oil slowly sepa-

(continued)

(continued)

rate. "This is a lot of work for nothing. If learning is truly like this—that is, 'cram as much as you can in your head for a test, and then let it out afterwards'—then we are all wasting our time." In this analogy the teacher is doing all of the work.

Active Learning: In this case, the teacher's knowledge is represented by an aqueous acidic solution. The student is represented by a basic solution containing several drops of universal indicator. When the acidic solution (knowledge) flows, the students' knowledge changes (shown by a change in color). As in the oil and water analogy, the student begins with some knowledge (different from the teacher). The students do not just take the knowledge, but the new knowledge interacts with what the students already know. The new knowledge changes their understanding, and they don't end up just like the teacher. The interaction is achieved by the students taking an active role in understanding the material.

USING TECHNOLOGY

Figure 1.2

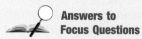

Answers to Focus Questions

1. An observation can be witnessed and recorded. A theory is an interpretation of why something occurred or why nature behaves in a particular way. Students will have various observations and theories. Try to have them explain their examples.

2. Text
   Experiments
   Activities
   Guided interactive learning
   Team worksheets
   Homework
   Quizzes/exams
   Teacher
   Classmates

3. Knowledge of fundamentals in the field
   Ability to recognize and solve problems
   Ability to communicate effectively
   High level of motivation

Learning Chemistry: It's Your Job

In the process of learning chemistry you are at the center. No one can learn it for you, but there are many ways we can help you.

To learn something new you first need to gather information. One way to do so is by making your own observations. The **Chemistry in Action** activities and **Chemistry in the Laboratory** experiments have exactly that goal. Another way to collect information is to read a book. Because textbooks contain lots of information, it is important, especially at first, to focus on the main ideas. We have designed questions, called **Focus Questions,** to help you concentrate on the most important ideas as you read the text. These Focus Questions should be answered *before* you go to class. Don't worry if you can't answer all of them completely—they are just meant to get you started thinking about the material.

Once you have done the initial reading and attempted to answer the Focus Questions, then you are ready for class. In class your teacher will help you to better understand these ideas. Then you will work with your classmates on the **Team Worksheets,** teaching and learning from each other. The Team Worksheets enable you to check your understanding with the help of other members of your class.

Next you can practice individually by doing homework problems that give you a chance to see how much you understand and which ideas you need to work on.

Once you have completed your homework, you are ready for a quiz, which gives you the chance to show what you know. Now you are ready to apply your knowledge to your further study of chemistry. This student-centered method for learning chemistry is summarized in **Figure 1.2.**

Figure 1.2
Student-centered learning.

Focus Questions Sections 1.5–1.6

1. What is the difference between an observation and a theory? Give an example of each (different from the ones in your book!).

2. What resources are available to help you learn chemistry?

3. What characteristics do former chemistry students find most important to their success? Which characteristics are the easiest for you to achieve? Which are the most difficult?

16 Chapter 1 Chemistry: An Introduction

Students' answers regarding their personal strengths and weaknesses will vary.

CHEMISTRY in the LABORATORY

Observations and Explanations

Objectives

1. To make observations

2. To differentiate between an observation and a theory

Lab Skills

Observing, classifying, interpreting data, making comparisons, designing experiments

Prelab Discussion

Students should tie back their hair and loose clothing whenever they work with a flame in the lab. Students will often deposit matches in the sink. Remind them to dispose of burned matches in the trashcan after they are cool.

Safety Tips

Students will often deposit matches in the sink. Remind them to dispose of burned matches in the trashcan after they are cool.

Procedure Hints

Have students work in pairs. For Part II one student is the observer and the other is the recorder. For Part III they switch roles.

Post-Lab Discussion

Many students are familiar with the

Problem

Why does a flame burn? How does an observation differ from a theory?

Introduction

Observation is an important part of science but it is often misunderstood by beginners. Many students believe that "observing" is the same as "seeing." In fact, observing involves much more than seeing. For example, at the scene of an accident different witnesses will often give different testimony as to what they saw. The witnesses all saw the same thing, but some are more observant than others.

This lab consists of a simple system—a burning candle. You have undoubtedly *seen* a burning candle many times. In this lab, you will *observe* the burning candle.

Prelab Assignment

Read the entire laboratory experiment before you begin.

Materials

Goggles
Apron
Candle
Matches
Drinking glass or beaker (taller than the candle)
3″ × 5″ index card
Watch or clock (with second hand)

Safety

1. You are working with a flame in this lab. Tie back hair and loose clothing.
2. Do not drop matches into the sink. Dispose of burned matches in the trashcan after they are cool.

Procedure

Part I

1. Light a candle.
2. Drip some wax onto a 3″ × 5″ card and stand the candle in the melted wax. Hold the candle upright until it can stand alone.
3. Observe the burning candle for a few minutes.

Part II

1. Place a drinking glass upside down over the candle.
2. Observe the candle for a few minutes. Record the time it takes for the flame to almost go out.
3. Lift the glass from the candle and place it on the table (mouth side down).
4. Replace the glass over the candle. Record the time it takes for the flame to go out.

Part III

1. Remove the glass and place it mouth side down on the table.
2. Light the candle again.
3. Lift the glass from the table and lower the mouth of the glass over the burning candle.
4. Observe what happens.

Cleaning Up

Clean up all materials.

Data/Observations

Part I

1. Make a list of your observations of the burning candle.

Part II

1. What happens to the flame when the candle is covered?
2. How long does it take for the flame to almost go out after the candle is covered?
3. What happens to the flame when you lift the glass?
4. How long does it take for the flame to go out after the candle is covered again?

Part III

1. Do you observe anything on the inside of the glass? Discuss.
2. What happens to the flame when you lower the glass over the candle?

Analysis and Conclusions

1. Compare your list of observations from Part I with those of another group of students. Which observations did you make that they did not? Which observations did they make that you did not?
2. Compare the times from Part II, questions 2 and 4, in the Data/Observations section.
3. Develop a theory that explains your observations when the candle is covered with the glass. Make sure to address the following:
   a. Support your theory with specific observations.
   b. How does your theory explain the differences in times when covering the candle (in Part II)?
   c. No theories answer all questions. What are two questions that your theory does not answer or address?

(continued) **17**

Part III

1. There should be drops of clear liquid on the inside of the glass. The glass should also be filled with smoke.
2. The flame eventually goes out.

Analysis and Conclusions

1. Answers will vary.
2. Answers will vary. The time in question 4 should be less than the time in question 2.
3. Answers could vary. The first choice given below is correct, but the second one explains the observations.

The flame goes out because oxygen in the air is used up in the reaction and fire requires oxygen.

   a. The flame gets dim when covered. When oxygen is reintroduced (by lifting the glass), the flame goes back to its original size and brightness.
   b. There is less oxygen in the glass after it has been over the candle. When it is replaced over the candle, little oxygen is left and it doesn't take as long to use up this smaller amount of oxygen.
   c. Must all of the oxygen be used up for the flame to go out? Does the smoke have anything to do with the flame going out? What happens to the oxygen? What is the identity of the clear liquid?

The smoke that is produced by the flame smothers it.

   a. Smoke is given off when the flame burns and the flame goes out as the glass fills with smoke.
   b. The glass is filled with smoke when it is placed back over the candle and the candle goes out more quickly.
   c. What is the identity of the smoke? Is anything used up? What is the identity of the clear liquid? Why is there a flame in the first place?
4. The flame is a result of a release of energy as the wick reacts with oxygen (burns).
   (continued)

idea that a flame requires oxygen and observe that "the oxygen is being used up." Tell students that they have really good eyes to be able to see this! Use this opportunity to discuss the differences between an observation (what we see) and a theory (an explanation of what we see).

This experiment can be used as an introduction to the idea of a chemical change—something new is formed during the burning process.

Sample Data/Answers

Part I

1. Heat, light, smoke, and flame appear to "tug" at the wick. Wax melts and drips down the side of the candle (solidifies as it runs down the candle).

Part II

1. The flame gets smaller and dimmer.

2. Answers will vary depending on the size of the glass and the flame.
3. The flame returns to the original size and brightness.
4. Answers will vary depending on the size of the glass and the flame. The time should be shorter than in question 2.

When the oxygen concentration around the wick is sufficiently low, the reaction will stop and the flame will go out. The less oxygen there is, the dimmer the flame will be.

5. An observation describes what happened. It is something we see; it is a fact. A theory is an attempt to explain why a phenomenon happened. "The flame went out" is an observation; "the oxygen was used up and caused the flame to go out" is a theory.

Chapter Review
Assign the students to work individually on the Chapter 1 Review Worksheet at the appropriate level (Basic, Standard, or Challenge). Answers are found in the *Teacher Resources.*

Assessment
Chapter 1 Test is found in the *Teacher Resources,* along with the answers for the test.

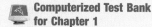 **Computerized Test Bank for Chapter 1**

---

4. Why does a flame burn? Explain how your observations support your answer.

5. What is the difference between a theory and an observation? Give an example of each from this experiment.

Something Extra

A few hundred years ago (before oxygen was discovered), scientists proposed a theory of burning that relied on a substance called phlogiston. In this theory, substances that burned were said to contain phlogiston. Burning resulted in the release of phlogiston, a substance that could not burn. Thus the flame of a burning candle placed under a glass will eventually go out because the glass will become filled with phlogiston. Design an experiment to disprove the theory of phlogiston.

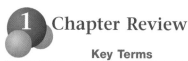 **Chapter Review**

Key Terms

chemistry (1.2)
scientific method (1.5)
measurement (1.5)
theory (1.5)
natural law (1.5)

Summary

1. Chemistry *should make sense* to you. As you learn chemistry, you should be able to understand, explain, and predict the phenomena of the macroscopic world using the models of the microscopic world. Remember that these models are consistent with one another. As you learn a new model, think about how it connects to what you already know.

2. *Understanding is different from memorizing.* Learning facts and understanding the models of chemistry should go hand in hand. You need both to be successful in chemistry.

3. *Models are not the same as reality.* Models represent our attempts to explain the phenomena in the world around us. In chemistry these models are always based on the properties of atoms and molecules. When a chemist is asked to explain a given phenomenon, you can bet that "movies" of atoms and molecules are playing in his or her brain. We hope to help you see these same "movies."

4. Learning chemistry takes time. Use all the resources available to you and study on a regular basis. Don't expect too much of yourself too soon. You may not understand everything at first, and you may not be able to do many of the problems the first time you try them. This is normal. It doesn't mean you can't learn chemistry. Just remember to keep working and to keep learning from your mistakes, and you will make steady progress.

Questions and Problems

All exercises with blue numbers have answers in the back of this book.

1.1 The Importance of Learning Chemistry

Questions

1. The first few paragraphs of this book asked you if you had ever wondered how and why various things in everyday life behave the way they do. Surely there are many other such phenomena that have intrigued you. Make a list of five such things and present them in class for discussion with your instructor and fellow students.

2. Chemistry is used in many professions, and a basic understanding of chemistry is of great importance. Suggest two ways persons practicing each of the following professions might make use of chemistry in their jobs.
   - **a.** physician
   - **b.** lawyer
   - **c.** pharmacist
   - **d.** artist
   - **e.** photographer
   - **f.** farmer
   - **g.** nurse

3. This section presents several ways our day-to-day lives have been enriched by chemistry. List three materials or processes involving chemistry that you feel have contributed to such an enrichment, and explain your choices.

4. The text admits that there has also been a "dark side" to our use of chemicals and chemical processes, and uses the example of chlorofluorocarbons (CFCs) to explain this. List three additional improper or unfortunate uses of chemicals or chemical processes, and explain your reasoning.

18   Chapter 1   Chemistry: An Introduction

Answers to End of Chapter Problems

1. Answers will vary.

2. (a) physician (cellular processes; drug mechanisms); (b) lawyer (understanding forensic reports; examination of the crime scene); (c) pharmacist (drug interactions; dosages); (d) artist (properties of paints and thinners; properties of sculpture media); (e) photographer (film-developing process; properties of papers and coatings); (f) farmer (fertilizers; plant hormones); (g) nurse (drug interactions; dosages)

3. Answers will vary. New drugs and treatments and new materials (such as special plastics and comfortable contact lenses) are probable answers.

4. Unfortunately, many examples exist. Chemical and biological weapons are produced in some countries. Although the development of plastics has been a boon in many endeavors, their use also depletes fossil fuel reserves and increases our solid waste problems. Although biotechnology has produced many exciting new drugs and treatments, the testing procedures that have been developed for determining whether a person has a genetic likelihood of developing a particular disease may also be used to make it difficult or impossible for that person to obtain health or life insurance.

1.2 What Is Chemistry?

Questions

5. This textbook provides a specific definition of chemistry: the study of the materials of which the universe is made and the transformations that these materials undergo. Obviously, such a general definition has to be very broad and nonspecific. From your point of view at this time, how would *you* define chemistry? In your mind, what are "chemicals"? What do "chemists" do?

6. We use chemical reactions in our everyday lives, not just in the science laboratory. Give at least five examples of chemical transformations that you make use of in your daily activities. Indicate what the "chemical" is in each of your examples, and how you recognize that a chemical change has taken place.

1.3 Solving Problems Using a Scientific Approach

Questions

7. Discuss several situations in which you have analyzed a problem such as those presented in this section. What hypotheses did you suggest? How did you test those hypotheses?

1.4 Using Scientific Thinking to Solve a Problem

Questions

8. For the lead poisoning case given in this section, discuss how David and Susan analyzed the situation, arriving at the theory that the lead glaze on the pottery was responsible for their symptoms.

1.5 The Scientific Method

Questions

9. What are the three operations involved in applying the scientific method? How does the scientific method help us to understand our observations of nature?

10. Which of the following are quantitative observations and which are qualitative observations?
   a. My waist size is 31 inches.
   b. My eyes are blue.
   c. My right index finger is 1/4 inch longer than my left.
   d. The leaves of most trees are green in summer.
   e. An apple consists of over 95% water.
   f. Chemistry is an easy subject.
   g. I got 90% on my last Chem exam.

11. What is the difference between a *hypothesis* and a *theory?* How are the two similar? How do they differ?

12. What is a *natural law?* Give examples of such laws. How does a law differ from a theory?

13. Discuss several political, social, or personal considerations that might affect a scientist's evaluation of a theory. Give examples of how such external forces have influenced scientists in the past. Discuss methods by which such bias might be excluded from future scientific investigations.

1.6 Learning Chemistry

Questions

14. In some academic subjects, it may be possible to receive a good grade primarily by memorizing facts. Why is chemistry not one of these subjects?

15. Why is the ability to solve problems important in the study of chemistry? Why is it that the *method* used to attack a problem is as important as the answer to the problem itself?

16. Students approaching the study of chemistry must learn certain basic facts (such as the names and symbols of the most common elements), but it is much more important that they learn to think critically and to go beyond the specific examples discussed in class or in the textbook. Explain how learning to do this might be helpful in any career, even one far removed from chemistry.

13. When a scientist formulates a hypothesis, he or she wants it to be proved correct. Financial success and prestige are dependent on publishing and producing such ideas.

14. Most applications of chemistry are oriented toward the interpretation of observations that solve problems. Although memorization of facts may *aid* in these endeavors, it is the ability to combine, relate, and synthesize information that is most important in the study of chemistry.

15. When we study chemistry, at least in the beginning, we try to be as general as possible. In this way the basic principles learned can be applied to many situations. By learning to interpret and solve less complex problems, students can extend this strategy to more complex real-life situations.

16. In real-life situations, the problems and applications likely to be encountered are not simple textbook examples. You must be able to observe an event, hypothesize a cause, and then test this hypothesis. You must be able to carry what has been learned in class forward to new, different situations.

5. Answers will vary.

6. Answers will depend on students' choices.

7. Answers will depend on students' experience.

8. David and Susan first recognized the problem (unexplained medical problems). A possible explanation was then proposed (the glaze on their china might be causing the lead poisoning). The explanation was tested by experiment (it was determined that the china did contain lead). A full scenario is given in the text.

9. Recognizing the problem and stating it clearly; proposing possible solutions to or explanations of the problem; performing experiments to test the solutions or explanations and then refining or changing the solution or explanation

10. (a) quantitative; (b) qualitative; (c) quantitative; (d) qualitative; (e) quantitative; (f) qualitative; (g) quantitative

11. A hypothesis is a possible explanation of a single observed phenomenon. A theory or model consists of a set of tested hypotheses that give an overall explanation of some part of nature.

12. A natural law is a summary of observed, measurable behavior that occurs repeatedly and consistently. A theory is an attempt to explain such behavior.

2 Matter

Section	Text Features & Components	Labs, Demonstrations & Activities
Teaching Segment 2A **0.5 block** **pp. 21–29** **2.1 The Particulate Nature of Matter**	🄛 Lesson Plans (Sec 2.1–2.3)	🆂🄴 Chemistry in Action: Full or Empty? *p. 23*
2.2 Elements and Compounds	🆂🄴 Celebrity Chemical: Hydrogen Peroxide *p. 26* 🆂🄴 Top Ten Elements in the Universe *p. 26* 🆂🄴 Chemical Impact: Carbon—Element of Many Forms *p. 28*	🅃🄴 Teaching Support: Demonstration *p. 26* 🅃🄴 Mini Demo *pp. 26, 27*
2.3 The States of Matter		🅃🄴 Teaching Support: Demonstration *pp. 28–29* 🅃🄴 Mini Demo *p. 28*
Teaching Segment 2B **4 blocks** **pp. 29–41** **2.4 Physical and Chemical Properties and Changes**	🄛 Lesson Plans (Sec 2.4–2.6)	🆂🄴 Chemistry in the Lab: Physical and Chemical Changes *p. 42* 🄛🄼 Experiments 4–5 Lab Manual Report Sheets Teacher's Lab Guide
2.5 Mixtures and Pure Substances	🆂🄴 Chemical Impact: Alchemical Cymbals *p. 36* 🅃🄴 Teaching Support: Historical Notes *p. 36*	🆂🄴 Chemistry in Action: Mysterious Mixing *p. 34* 🆂🄴 Chemistry in the Lab: Physical and Chemical Changes *p. 42* 🅃🄴 Mini Demos *p. 37*
2.6 Separation of Mixtures		🅃🄴 Teaching Support: Demonstration *p. 40* 🄛🄼 Experiments 6–10 Lab Manual Report Sheets Teacher's Lab Guide

Technology and Media

 Transparencies
Top Ten Elements in the Universe
Figure 2.7, 2.18

PowerPoint Slides

 Animation States of Matter

 Video Paper Chromatography
Chemistry in Motion
(30) Electrolysis of Water

 eEdition CD-ROM
Easy Planner CD-ROM
English Summaries CD
Spanish Summaries CD

 Web Site classzone.com
McDougal Littell Test Generator

Chapter Planning Guide

All Learners	Review & Assessment	Standards
(TE) Active Learning *p. 21* (TE) Misconceptions *p. 22* (AR) Less Proficient Students *p. 3*	(SE) What if . . . *p. 21* (SE) Key Terms *p. 43* (SE) Questions and Problems *p. 44*	(TE) **NSES** UCP1, UCP2, UCP5, A1, A2, B1, B2 (●) **SSS** SC.A.1.4.3, SC.A.2.4.2
(▱) Transparency: Top Ten Elements in the Universe *p. 26* (AR) Less Proficient Students *p. 3*	(SE) Key Terms *p. 43* (SE) Questions and Problems *p. 44*	
(▱) Animation: States of Matter (RP) Team Learning Worksheets (Sec 2.1–2.3) *pp. 5–6* (AR) Less Proficient Students *p. 3*	(SE) What if . . . *p. 29* (SE) Focus Questions (Sec 2.1–2.3) *p. 29* (SE) Key Terms *p. 43* (SE) Questions and Problems *p. 44*	
(TE) Active Learners *p. 30* (▱) Transparency: Figure 2.7 *p. 31* (▱) Chemistry in Motion (30) (TE) Teaching Tips *p. 33* (AR) Less Proficient Students *p. 3*	(TE) Additional Examples *pp. 30, 33* (SE) Self Check *pp. 30, 33* (SE) Key Terms *p. 43* (SE) Questions and Problems *p. 44*	(TE) **NSES** UCP1, UCP2, UCP3, A1, A2, B2, B3, G1, G2, G3 (●) **SSS** SC.H.1.4.2, SC.A.1.4.3
(TE) Misconceptions *p. 35* (AR) Less Proficient Students *p. 4*	(TE) Additional Examples *p. 38* (SE) Self Check *p. 39* (SE) Key Terms *p. 43* (SE) Questions and Problems *p. 44*	
(▱) Video: Paper Chromatography (▱) Transparency: Figure 2.18 *p. 41* (RP) Team Learning Worksheets (Sec 2.4–2.6) *pp. 7–8* (AR) Less Proficient Students *p. 4*	(SE) Focus Questions (Sections 2.4–2.6) *p. 41* (SE) Key Terms *p. 43* (SE) Questions and Problems *pp. 43–44*	

Chapter Materials

(TE) Reading Strategy (AR) English/Spanish Summaries *p. 3* (RP) Classroom Activities and Projects: Element Report *pp. 3–8* (AR) Challenge Projects/Problems *pp. 2–3* (◉) English Summary Audio (◉) Spanish Summary Audio (RP) Chapter Review Worksheets (Basic, Review, Challenge)	(SE) Chapter Summary *p. 18* (SE) Critical Thinking *p. 45* (RP) Solutions Guide (RP) Chapter Tests (RP) Test Bank (▱) McDougal Littell Test Generator (AR) Standardized Test Practice (●) **FCAT Test 1**

2 Integrating Reading Strategies and Chemistry Concepts

Chapter 2: Reading Laboratory Experiments

 CHEMISTRY in the LABORATORY
Physical and Chemical Changes

Problem
How do physical changes differ from chemical changes?

Introduction
Matter can undergo both physical and chemical changes. Physical changes involve changes in one or more physical properties. Chemical changes involve changes in the composition of the substance.

The following are clues that indicate that a chemical change may have occurred: a color change, the evolution of bubbles, the formation of a solid, and heat absorbed or produced.

In this lab you will carry out four procedures (Parts I–IV) and make observations. Then you will decide how well the clues enable you to determine whether a chemical reaction occurred. In addition, you will develop molecular definitions of physical and chemical changes.

Prelab Assignment
Read the entire laboratory experiment before you begin.

Materials

Goggles	Spatula
Apron	Sponge
250-mL beakers (2)	Well plate
100-mL beakers (3)	Tongs
Graduated cylinder	Barium nitrate
Bunsen burner	Potassium sulfate
Matches	HCl (3.0 M)
Ring stand	Magnesium ribbon
Ring	Food coloring
Wire gauze	Water

Safety
1. The 3.0 M HCl is corrosive. Handle it with extreme care.
2. If you come in contact with any solution, wash the contacted area thoroughly.
3. You are working with a flame in this lab. Tie back hair and loose clothing.
4. Do not drop matches into the sink. Dispose of burned matches in the trashcan after they are cool.

Procedure
Part I
1. Add about 100 mL of water to a 250-mL beaker.
2. Add a few drops of food coloring to a beaker of water.
3. Make observations for several minutes.

42

Part II
1. Dissolve a spatula-tip amount of barium nitrate in a small amount of water (about 10 mL) in a 100-mL beaker.
2. Dissolve a spatula-tip amount of potassium sulfate in a small amount of water (about 10 mL) in a 100-mL beaker.
3. Pour the solutions from steps 1 and 2 together into an empty 100-mL beaker. Make careful observations.

Setup to boil water.

Part III
1. Add about 100 mL of water to a 250-mL beaker.
2. Arrange the beaker and ring stand as shown in the figure.
3. Light the Bunsen burner and place it under the beaker. Adjust the burner so that the hottest part of the flame touches the bottom of the beaker.
4. Bring the water to a boil. Make careful observations.
5. Use the tongs to hold the sponge over the beaker for a couple of minutes as the water boils.
6. Place the sponge on the lab bench and let it cool.
7. Squeeze the sponge. Record your observations.

Part IV
1. Place a few drops of 3.0 M HCl in one of the wells.
2. Add a small piece of magnesium ribbon to the acid. Make careful observations.

For a productive laboratory experience, assign students to read the laboratory experiment *before* coming to class. The lab will run more efficiently and the lab experience will be more satisfying if the students read the experiment ahead of time. Encourage the students to generate a list of any parts of the experiment that are not clear to them.

Each laboratory experiment in this course is organized according to the same format. This consistency aids in the readability of the experiments, allowing the students to become familiar with an organized plan for each lab. Use the following descriptions of the format to explain what each section of an experiment covers, and why it is important to pre-read each section before doing the lab. *If time is an issue, direct students to read page ix of the Laboratory Experiments workbook.*

Laboratory Experiment Format

Problem This section presents the question(s) to be answered in the experiment. The students should be aware that they will need to answer the question(s) in their laboratory report. If more than one question is posed, guide the students to create a table to keep information organized.

Introduction This section gives the information and background necessary to comprehend the experiment, such as definitions of terms, nomenclature, necessary formulas, diagrams, and so on. Encourage the students to read this section carefully and to refer to the textbook to clarify any questions they have.

Prelab Assignment The students should read and complete this assignment before conducting the experiment. Explain the importance of preparation.

Pre-reading Assessment Ideas

Before they begin an experiment, give the students a short quiz to verify that they have read the material and understand the theory and the goals of the experiment.

For the lab in Chapter 2, pose questions such as these:

What is a physical change?

What is a chemical change?

What type of change occurs if you see the formation of bubbles?

How should you dispose of a used match?

Materials Explain to the students that the materials list identifies the chemicals and materials needed for the experiment. Although you will be providing these items, it is important for the students to read the list before beginning the lab and to identify any unfamiliar items. For instance, in the lab for Chapter 2, if a student does not know what a Bunsen burner is or how it is used, you should review this piece of equipment with the class prior to beginning the lab.

Safety This section lists the potential safety hazards in the experiment. Prereading this section will create awareness of risks and allow for a safer laboratory experience. For a more general discussion of laboratory safety, encourage the students to read *Appendix A: Laboratory Safety Handbook* on pages A3–A4 of the student text. As needed, create an imaginary scenario of a lab accident and ask students to describe how the situation should be handled and what could have been done to prevent the accident.

Procedure Inform the students that they will be required to have a solid understanding of the procedure before they begin the experiment. Show the students that this section gives a detailed, organized plan for performing the experiment. The lab procedure is broken into parts to guide the students through the observation process. For some labs, you may find it beneficial to have the students read the first part of the procedure and then predict what they may observe. Then guide the students to read the next part of the procedure and make another prediction, and so on. This prediction technique helps the students understand that the experiment is performed in parts rather than as a whole. In addition to having the students preread the experiment, consider asking them to submit time estimates for each part of the Procedure section. You can use this information to assess whether each student comprehends the task.

Cleaning Up Reading this section before the laboratory will help the students understand what is expected of them in regard to clean-up so they can budget their time effectively.

Data/Observations This section teaches the students how to organize their data and observations. Ask the students to identify how data and observations for a specific lab should be recorded. [Answer: tables, diagrams, or charts.] Encourage the students to prepare blank tables, diagrams, or charts before they begin the experiment or before coming to class. Have students use a dictionary to explain the difference between quantitative and qualitative observations.

Analysis and Conclusions This section helps the students to interpret the results of the experiment and to form conclusions. By reading this section before conducting the experiment, the students will be able to identify key points in the lab procedure that will help them answer these questions and understand the concepts the lab is exploring.

Something Extra (when applicable) This section describes a way of extending the investigation.

Chapter 2

2 Matter

Sliding rocks in Death Valley, California. How they move remains a mystery.

20

As you look around you, you must wonder about the properties of matter. How do plants grow and why are they green? Why is the sun hot? Why does a hot dog get hot in a microwave oven? Why does wood burn whereas rocks do not? What is a flame? How does soap work? Why does soda fizz when you open the bottle? When iron rusts, what's happening? And why doesn't aluminum rust? How does a cold pack for an athletic injury, which is stored for weeks or months at room temperature, suddenly get cold when you need it? How does a hair permanent work?

The answers to these and endless other questions lie in the domain of chemistry. In this chapter we begin to explore the nature of matter: how it is organized and how and why it changes. We will also consider the energy that accompanies these changes.

Why does soda fizz when you open the bottle?

2.1 The Particulate Nature of Matter

Objective: *To learn about the composition of matter.*

Matter, the "stuff" of which the universe is composed, has two characteristics: it has mass and it occupies space. Matter comes in a great variety of forms: the stars, the air that you are breathing, the gasoline that you put in your car, the chair on which you are sitting, the turkey in the sandwich you may have eaten for lunch, the tissues in your brain that enable you to read and comprehend this sentence, and so on.

As we look around in the macroscopic world, we are impressed by the great diversity of matter. Given the many forms and types of matter, it seems difficult to believe that all matter is composed of a small number of fundamental particles. It is surprising that the fundamental building blocks in chocolate cake are very similar to the components of air.

The Atomic Nature of Matter

How do we know that matter is composed of the tiny particles we call atoms? After all, they are far too small to be seen with the naked eye. It turns out that after literally thousands of years of speculation, we can finally "see" the atoms that are present in matter. In recent years scientists have developed a device called a scanning tunneling microscope (STM) that, although it works quite differently from an optical microscope, can produce images of atoms.

2.1   The Particulate Nature of Matter   **21**

Themes
Organization, Form and Function

Skills
Making comparisons, classifying, evaluating

Student Preparation
Assign the students to read Sections 2.1 to 2.3 and to answer the Focus Questions at the end of Section 2.3 before coming to class.

Active Learning
After introducing the material in Sections 2.1 to 2.3 in class, place the students in groups and have them work together on Sections 2.1–2.3: Team Learning Worksheet. Answers and/or discussion of these questions are located in the *Teacher Resources*.

WHAT IF Comments

There are many ways to support a particulate theory of matter. For example, the fact that we smell food as it is cooking is evidence of the existence of particles (molecules) that are released into the air. In addition, students may discuss the significance of the activity in which they add food coloring to water. They may also discuss the law of definite proportions or the law of multiple proportions, both of which summarize the historical observations that lead us to believe in atoms.

Figure 2.1
The surface of the copper penny shown on the left, is made of copper atoms represented on the right, as through the lens of a very powerful electronic microscope.

Figure 2.2
A scanning tunneling microscope image of nickel metal. Each peak represents a nickel atom.

Sand on a beach looks uniform from a distance, but up-close the irregular sand grains are visible.

For example, look at the picture of a penny shown in **Figure 2.1.** The objects on the right in Figure 2.1 represent tiny copper atoms. When chemists look at other metals using powerful microscopes, they see atoms in these substances as well. You can see an example of another metal in **Figure 2.2.** *Notice that, with ultra-high magnification, objects appear more similar. That is, all objects appear to be made up of small particles.*

All matter consists of tiny particles called atoms. But when you look at objects such as nails or pennies, you don't see these particles. Why not? The atoms are very tiny and can be seen only with a powerful magnifying instrument. You may have encountered the same concept in your life when you looked at a beach from a distance. The sand looks uniform—you can't see the separate particles. As you get close, however, the individual grains of sand become apparent. Or observe the Impressionist painting by Seurat shown in the photo on the following page. From a distance the scene looks normal. Only when you stand very close to the painting do you see that it is composed from tiny dots of paint.

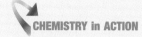

The painting 'Sunday Afternoon on the Island of La Grand Jatte' by Georges Seurat illustrates the Impressionist style.

So, the conclusion is that although objects in the macroscopic world typically look quite continuous and uniform, they are really particulate in nature—they are made of atoms. We can "see" them with powerful electronic microscopes.

CHEMISTRY in ACTION
Full or Empty?

Part I

1. Use clay to secure a funnel to an empty soft-drink bottle. Make sure that the mouth of the bottle is completely covered.
2. Pour water into the funnel.
3. Observe what happens to the water and list your observations.
4. Develop a method that allows the water to go smoothly into the bottle. Explain why it works.
5. Develop a method that allows the water to stay in the funnel. Explain why it works.
6. Develop a method that allows the water to periodically "squirt" into the bottle. Explain why it works.

Part II

1. Fill a plastic soft-drink bottle with water and replace the cap tightly.
2. Using a large safety pin, poke a hole in the side of the container. What happens? Why?
3. Hold the bottle over a sink and unscrew the cap. What happens? Why?
4. Relate your findings to those from Part I of this activity.

2.1   The Particulate Nature of Matter   **23**

CHEMISTRY in ACTION

Full or Empty?

Materials Each student/group will need a soft-drink bottle, a funnel, clay, and a long pin.

Purpose Students will understand that air is matter and therefore takes up space.

Discussion

Part I: Air is matter; it therefore has mass and takes up space. For water to enter the soft-drink bottle, air must leave. When students first pour the water into the funnel with clay completely covering the mouth of the bottle, water cannot easily enter the bottle.

Water does not enter the bottle: If the water is poured quickly such that no water initially enters, the water will stay in the funnel.

Water "squirts" into the bottle: If the water is added relatively slowly at first and some enters the bottle, it pushes air through the water that is being added to the funnel. A bubble of water goes through the water and starts a cycle of air leaving the bottle (bubbling through the water) and water entering the bottle. This cycle can be difficult to achieve.

Water flows smoothly into the bottle: Students should poke a hole through the clay next to the funnel. This hole allows air to continuously leave the bottle, and therefore the water will flow smoothly.

Part II: Water will not come out of the hole until the cap is loosened. For water to leave the bottle, air must enter.

Elements and Compounds

Objective: *To learn the difference between elements and compounds.*

In the last section we considered the most important idea in chemistry: matter is composed of tiny particles we call **atoms**. If all matter is made up of tiny particles called atoms, are all atoms alike? That is, is copper metal made of the same kind of atoms as gold? The answer is no. Copper atoms and gold atoms are different. Scientists have learned that all matter is composed from about 100 different types of atoms. For example, air is mostly gaseous oxygen and nitrogen. The nitrogen atoms are different from the oxygen atoms, which in turn are different from copper atoms, which themselves differ from gold atoms.

You can think of the matter in the universe like the words in a book. If you break all the words in this book apart into their component letters, you will end up with "large piles" of only 26 letters. The English alphabet allows you to construct thousands of words from just 26 letters. Similarly, all the matter in the universe is constructed by putting approximately 100 types of atoms together in various ways. The different types of matter are like the different words in a book. When we separate all of the universe into its atoms, we find approximately 100 different atoms. We call these 100 types of atoms the *elements* of the universe.

To illustrate this idea, consider the letters A, D, and M. Using these letters you can make many words, such as MAD, DAM, DAD, and MADAM (can you think of others?). Each word represents something very different. Thus, with only three letters, you can represent several unique things or ideas.

Compounds

In much the same way that we can use a few letters to make thousands of words, we can use a few types of atoms to construct all matter. For example, consider the atoms hydrogen, oxygen, and carbon:

Hydrogen   Oxygen   Carbon

Notice we represent atoms by circles. We get this idea from the highly magnified pictures of metals that show the atoms. Notice from Figure 2.1 that atoms look like spheres.

We can combine the hydrogen, oxygen, and carbon atoms in a variety of ways. Just as letters combine to form different words, atoms combine to form different compounds. **Compounds** are substances made by bonding atoms together in specific ways. These substances contain two or more different types of atoms bound together in a particular way. A specific compound consists of the same particles throughout.

Consider a glass of water. If you could magically travel inside the water and examine its individual parts, you would see particles consisting of two hydrogen atoms bonded to an oxygen atom:

Atom Combinations	Name	Characteristics
	carbon monoxide	Carbon monoxide is a poisonous gas.
	carbon dioxide	You breathe out carbon dioxide as a waste material and plants use carbon dioxide to make oxygen.
	water	Water is the most important liquid on Earth.
	hydrogen peroxide	Hydrogen peroxide is used to disinfect cuts and bleach hair.

We call this particle a molecule. A **molecule** is made up of atoms that are "stuck" together. A glass of water, for example, contains a huge number of molecules packed closely together (see **Figure 2.3**).

Carbon dioxide is another example of a compound. For example, "dry ice"—solid carbon dioxide—contains molecules of the type packed together as shown in **Figure 2.4.**

Figure 2.3
A glass of water contains millions of tiny water molecules packed closely together.

Figure 2.4
Dry ice contains ⬭ molecules packed closely together.

2.2   Elements and Compounds   **25**

Hydrogen Peroxide (H₂O₂)

A small change in the composition of a substance greatly changes its properties. For example, the properties of hydrogen peroxide (the celebrity chemical) and water are very different. Other examples are ethanol (CH_3CH_2OH) and methanol (CH_3OH), and carbon monoxide (CO) and carbon dioxide (CO_2).

CELEBRITY CHEMICAL

Hydrogen Peroxide (H₂O₂)

Hydrogen and oxygen atoms combine to form two different molecules: the very familiar water molecule (H_2O) and the hydrogen peroxide molecule (H_2O_2). Because these molecules have very similar compositions, you might think they should behave in very similar ways. In fact, the properties of water and hydrogen peroxide are very different.

You are already very familiar with water. We drink it, we swim in it, we cook vegetables in it, we wash with it, and so on. Water is essential for life. A few days without it and we die.

Hydrogen peroxide is very different from water. This corrosive liquid would poison us if we were foolish enough to drink it. It is most commonly used as a bleaching agent. For example, hydrogen peroxide bleaches hair by reacting with melanin, the substance responsible for the color of brown and black hair. Hydrogen peroxide changes the composition of melanin in a way that causes it to lose its color—it turns brown hair blonde. In addition, hydrogen peroxide is used to bleach fibers, such as silk, and to bleach flour, producing the ultra-white powder that consumers demand. Small amounts of hydrogen peroxide are also added to some toothpastes as whitening agents.

One of the most common uses of hydrogen peroxide is to prevent infections in cuts. Sometime in your life when you have cut or scraped yourself, a parent or a nurse probably has applied a liquid to the wound that foamed and burned. That substance was hydrogen peroxide—a powerful *antiseptic* (killer of microorganisms).

Surprisingly, hydrogen peroxide is also used by some plants for communication. For example, consider the shade-loving Arabidopsis plant. When this plant is exposed to excessive sunlight, its leaves defend themselves by producing chemicals that protect against sunlight damage. Even more interesting, the affected leaves make hydrogen peroxide, which travels through the air to leaves that are shaded from the sun and "tells" these leaves to prepare for possible sun damage. Thus the leaves directly affected by the light not only defend themselves, but also send a danger message to the rest of the plant via "cell phones" using H_2O_2 molecules traveling through the air.

Although it looks deceptively similar to water, hydrogen peroxide behaves very differently from water. A small change in the make-up of a molecule can produce big changes in behavior.

TOP TEN		
Elements in the Universe		
Element		Percent (by atoms)
1. Hydrogen		73.9
2. Helium		24.0
3. Oxygen		1.1
4. Carbon		0.46
5. Neon		0.13
6. Iron		0.11
7. Nitrogen		0.097
8. Silicon		0.065
9. Magnesium		0.058
10. Sulfur		0.044

Notice that the particles in water are all the same. Likewise, all the particles in dry ice are the same. However, the particles in water differ from the particles in dry ice. Water and carbon dioxide are different compounds.

Elements

Just as hydrogen, oxygen, and carbon can form the compounds carbon dioxide and water, atoms of the same type can also combine with one another to form molecules. For example, hydrogen atoms can pair up ⬤⬤ as can oxygen atoms ⬤⬤.

For reasons we will consider later, carbon atoms form much larger groups, leading to substances such as diamond, graphite, and buckminsterfullerene (see **Figure 2.5**).

Because each of these substances contains only one type of atom, the substances are called elemental substances or, more commonly, **elements.** Elements are substances that contain only one type of atom. For example, pure aluminum contains only aluminum atoms, elemental copper contains

26   Chapter 2   Matter

Diamond

Graphite

Carbon atoms

Buckminsterfullerene

Figure 2.5
The three forms of the element carbon: diamond, graphite, and buckminsterfullerene.

only copper atoms, and so on. Thus an element contains only one kind of atom; a sample of iron contains many atoms, but they are all iron atoms. Samples of certain pure elements do contain molecules; for example, hydrogen gas contains H—H (usually written H_2) molecules, and oxygen gas contains O—O (O_2) molecules. However, any pure sample of an element contains only atoms of that element, *never* any atoms of any other element.

A compound *always* contains atoms of *different* elements. For example, water contains hydrogen atoms and oxygen atoms, and there are always exactly twice as many hydrogen atoms as oxygen atoms because water consists of H—O—H molecules. A different compound, carbon dioxide, consists of CO_2 molecules and so contains carbon atoms and oxygen atoms (always in the ratio 1:2).

A compound, although it contains more than one type of atom, *always has the same composition*—that is, the same combination of atoms. The properties of a compound are typically very different from those of the elements it contains. For example, the properties of water are quite different from the properties of pure hydrogen and pure oxygen.

2.2   Elements and Compounds   **27**

Carbon—Element of Many Forms

Although the term is not used in this section, now might be a good time to introduce *allotrope*—used when an element exists in several forms. Carbon has three allotropes: diamond, graphite, and buckminsterfullerene. A piece of chicken wire serves as a useful model for graphite; a soccer ball makes a very nice model for buckminsterfullerene; and commercial models are available for diamond.

Other elements also exist as allotropes. Examples include:

Oxygen	oxygen and ozone
Phosphorus	white, red, and black phosphorus
Tin	white, gray, and brittle tin

Section 2.3

Themes
Organization, Models, Form and Function

Skills
Classifying, developing models, making comparisons

MINI-DEMO

Demonstrate the movement of the molecules in water by placing a drop of food coloring in a beaker of water and allowing it to mix without stirring.

MINI-DEMO

Use small (marble-size) Styrofoam balls to demonstrate the differences among solids, liquids, and gases at the atomic/molecular level. Glue a number of balls together in an orderly fashion to represent a solid. Place a handful of loose balls in a beaker to represent a liquid. The balls can be poured and flow over one another; the liquid will take the shape of its container. Place just a few balls in a quart jar with a lid and shake the jar to represent a gas. If you leave the top off the jar and shake it, the gas will escape from the container.

Carbon—Element of Many Forms

Did you know that the "lead" in your pencil and the diamond in an engagement ring are made of exactly the same thing—elemental carbon? It may come as a surprise to learn that the black, slippery material that makes up pencil "lead," which is called **graphite**, has the same composition as the brilliant, hard gemstone called **diamond**. Although both substances are made of carbon atoms, their properties vary dramatically because the carbon atoms are arranged differently in the two substances.

A third form of elemental carbon also exists—**buckminsterfullerene** (see Figure 2.5). This very strange name comes from a famous industrial designer, Buckminster Fuller, who popularized geodesic domes. The fundamental component of buckminsterfullerene is a C_{60} molecule that has framework like a geodesic dome. The C_{60} molecule also resembles a soccer ball with its interconnecting hexagons (six-sided polygons) and pentagons (five-sided polygons). Thus chemists have nicknamed this form of carbon "bucky balls." So there are three forms of elemental carbon: graphite, diamond, and buckminsterfullerene.

Because diamonds are so much more valuable than the other forms of carbon, it has long been the dream of entrepreneurs to make gem-quality diamonds from other carbon-based substances. In fact, we have been able to make artificial diamonds for about 50 years. One of the first crude diamonds was actually made by compressing peanut butter at high pressures and temperatures! General Electric now has the capacity to manufacture 150 million carats (30,000 kg) of diamonds per year, but most of these diamonds are diamond grit—industrial-grade diamonds used as coatings for cutting tools. The processes for making gem-quality diamonds are now being perfected to the point that artificial diamond gems will soon be cheaper than natural diamonds dug from the earth. This development has caused diamond merchants to scramble to find tests to distinguish natural diamonds from synthetic diamonds. The future of the diamond market should prove very interesting.

2.3 The States of Matter

Objective: *To define the three states of matter.*

The three states of water: solid (ice), liquid (water), and gas (water vapor in the air).

Water is one of the most familiar substances in our world. We recognize water in three different states: solid, liquid, and gas. If we lower the temperature of liquid water, it freezes—that is, it changes to ice (solid water). On the other hand, if we heat water to its boiling point, it "disappears" into the air as a gas.

The three states of water have distinctly different properties. If a pond freezes in the winter, you can walk across it. Solid water can support your weight. Conversely, you would never try to walk across the same pond in the summertime!

We can also highlight the differing properties of liquid and solid water with food coloring. A drop of food coloring placed on an ice cube just sits there on top of the ice. In contrast, a drop of food coloring placed in liquid water spreads throughout the liquid. The fact that the food

28   Chapter 2   Matter

TEACHING SUPPORT
Demonstration

States of Matter

Materials

Small wooden block	Several containers with interesting shapes
Colored water	
Balloon	

Procedure Show students the wooden block. Ask what state of matter it is. Discuss the fact that the block has a definite volume. Ask how its volume might be calculated. Then put the block in each of the different-shaped containers to illustrate that solids do not take the shape of their container.

Next, show students the colored water. Ask what state of matter it is. Pour the liquid from one container to another. Discuss the change in shape for a liquid. Ask if the volume is constant. How could it be measured?

Next, have a student blow up the balloon, but do not tie it closed. Ask what the state of matter is for the air in the balloon. Ask the student to pour the air into one of the containers. Continue pouring the air from container to container. Discuss the change in shape of the air. Discuss whether the volume of the air is constant.

Summarize the properties of the states of matter.

Figure 2.6
Liquid water takes the shape of its container.

USING TECHNOLOGY

 Animation and Video
Animation, States of Matter

WHAT IF?
Carnival balloons are filled with helium from a certain tank that can fill 200 balloons.

What if the person filling the balloons tells you that after filling 100 balloons the tank is only *half full* with helium? Does this statement make sense?

WHAT IF Comments

A specific tank has a maximum capacity due to the tank's limitations. Even if there is half as much gas as full capacity, the tank is still considered "full." This property is characteristic of gases. It may be a good idea to provide the students with a picture of a container with 20 particles of gas (randomly distributed) and ask them to draw what the container would look like with 10 particles of gas (they should still be randomly distributed, although some students may try to condense the sample). This activity will give you information about the students' understanding of gases.

coloring spreads in all directions in the liquid water indicates that the water molecules must be moving, bouncing the "food coloring molecules" around and keeping them suspended. This property is very different from that of ice, where the food coloring does not penetrate the surface. Also, we know that gaseous water is quite different from solid and liquid water because it is invisible to the naked eye unlike the other states of water.

Like water, all substances exist in the *three states of matter:* solid, liquid, and gas. A **solid** is rigid. It has a fixed shape and volume. A **liquid** has a definite volume but takes the shape of its container (see **Figure 2.6**). A **gas** has no fixed volume or shape. It uniformly fills any container.

Focus Questions

Sections 2.1–2.3

1. How do atoms, compounds, and elements differ?
2. Consider the letters in the word "chemistry." Use them to make as many word "compounds" as possible with nine elements. How does an element differ from a compound?
3. Draw an "atom" picture of a solid, a liquid, and a gas. Describe the essential differences between them.

Answers to Focus Questions

1. Atoms are the fundamental building blocks of matter. There are the same number of different types of atoms as there are elements. An atom is a single unit of an element. Atoms may be grouped together in elements as pairs or in larger groups. Compounds differ from both atoms and elements because they are composed of two or more different atoms bonded together. The properties of compounds are different from those of the atoms or elements from which they are composed. Millions of compounds exist, but only about 100 elements are known.

2.

mist	time	chit
hem	thyme	mister
cry	chest	sir
trim	shirt	sit
met	shim	miter
mite	stir	

3. See Figure 2.7 for molecular pictures of a solid, liquid, and gas. A solid has a fixed shape and volume. A liquid takes the shape of its container and has a fixed volume. A gas has neither a fixed shape nor a fixed volume.

2.4 Physical and Chemical Properties and Changes

Objectives: *To learn to distinguish between physical and chemical properties.*
To learn to distinguish between physical and chemical changes.

When you see a friend, you immediately respond and call him or her by name. We can recognize a friend because each person has unique characteristics or properties. The person may be thin and tall, may have brown hair and blue eyes, and so on. The characteristics just mentioned are examples of **physical properties.** Substances also have physical properties. The typical physical properties of a substance include odor, color, volume,

2.4 Physical and Chemical Properties and Changes   **29**

Extension Place several ice cubes in a beaker. Place the beaker on a hot plate, melt the ice, and bring the water to boiling to show students that one state can change into another. If you have access to dry ice, use a sample to illustrate that not all matter must be liquefied before turning to a gas. Dry ice sublimes directly from the solid state to the gaseous state.

Section 2.4

Themes
Organization, Patterns of Change

Skills
Developing hypotheses, evaluating, problem solving

Student Preparation
Assign the students to read Sections 2.4 to 2.6 and to answer the Focus Questions at the end of Section 2.6 before coming to class.

Active Learning
After introducing the material in Sections 2.4 to 2.6 in class, place the students in groups and have them work together on Sections 2.4–2.6: Team Learning Worksheet. Answers and/or discussion of these questions are located in the *Teacher Resources*.

Additional Examples

Classify each of the following as a physical or chemical property.

1. Ice melts at 0°C.
   Physical property

2. Propane burns in the air.
   Chemical property

3. Lead is a very dense metal.
   Physical property

4. Leaves turn colors in the Fall.
   Chemical property

Laboratory
Experiment 4:
Physical and Chemical Changes, In Text

Laboratory
Experiment 5:
Household Chemistry, Microscale

Answers to Self-Check Exercise 2.1

Items (a) and (c) are physical properties. When solid gallium melts, it forms liquid gallium. Items (b) and (d) reflect the ability to change composition and are chemical properties. Statement (b) means that platinum does not react with oxygen to form some new substance. Statement (d) means that copper reacts with air to form a new substance, which is green.

---

state (gas, liquid, or solid), density, melting point, and boiling point. We can also describe a pure substance in terms of its **chemical properties,** which refer to its ability to form new substances. An example of a chemical change is wood burning in a fireplace, giving off heat and gases and leaving a residue of ashes. In this process, the wood is changed to several new substances. Other examples of chemical changes include the rusting of the steel in our cars, the digestion of food in our stomachs, and the growth of grass in our yards. In a chemical change a given substance changes to a fundamentally different substance or substances.

Example 2.1

Identifying Physical and Chemical Properties

Classify each of the following as a physical or a chemical property.

  a. The boiling point of a certain alcohol is 78° C.
  b. Diamond is very hard.
  c. Sugar ferments to form alcohol.
  d. A metal wire conducts an electric current.

Solution

Items (a), (b), and (d) are physical properties; they describe inherent characteristics of each substance, and no change in composition occurs. A metal wire has the same composition before and after an electric current has passed through it. Item (c) is a chemical property of sugar. Fermentation of sugars involves the formation of a new substance (alcohol).

Self-Check Exercise 2.1

Which of the following are physical properties and which are chemical properties?

  a. Gallium metal melts in your hand.
  b. Platinum does not react with oxygen at room temperature.
  c. This page is white.
  d. The copper sheets that form the "skin" of the Statue of Liberty have acquired a greenish coating over the years.

Gallium metal has such a low melting point (30 °C) that it melts from the heat of a hand.

Matter can undergo changes in both its physical and its chemical properties. To illustrate the fundamental differences between physical and chemical changes, we will consider water. As we have seen, a sample of water contains a very large number of individual units (called molecules), each made

30   Chapter 2   Matter

up of two atoms of hydrogen and one atom of oxygen—the familiar H_2O, which can be represented as

or

Here the letters stand for atoms and the lines show attachments (called bonds) between atoms, and the molecular model (on the right) represents water in a more three-dimensional fashion.

What is really occurring when water undergoes the following changes?

When ice melts, the rigid solid becomes a mobile liquid that takes the shape of its container. Continued heating brings the liquid to a boil, and the water becomes a gas or vapor that seems to disappear into "thin air." The changes that occur as the substance goes from solid to liquid to gas are represented in **Figure 2.7.** In ice the water molecules are locked into fixed positions. In the liquid the molecules are still very close together, but some motion is occurring; the positions of the molecules are no longer fixed as they are in ice. In the gaseous state the molecules are much farther apart and move randomly, hitting each other and the walls of the container.

We will describe these changes of state precisely in Chapter 14, but you already know something about these processes because you have observed them many times.

USING TECHNOLOGY

Figure 2.7

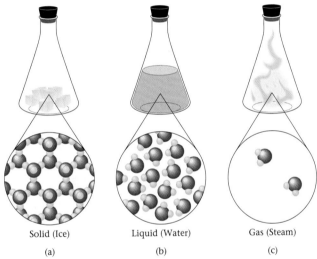

Solid (Ice)
(a)

Liquid (Water)
(b)

Gas (Steam)
(c)

Figure 2.7
The three states of water (where red spheres represent oxygen atoms and blue spheres represent hydrogen atoms). (a) Solid: the water molecules are locked into rigid positions and are close together. (b) Liquid: the water molecules are still close together but can move around to some extent. (c) Gas: the water molecules are far apart and move randomly.

2.4 Physical and Chemical Properties and Changes **31**

Water

Oxygen
gas forms

Hydrogen
gas forms

Electrode

Source of
direct current

Figure 2.8
Electrolysis, the decomposition of water by an electric current, is a chemical process.

The most important thing about all these changes is that the water molecules are still intact. The motions of individual molecules and the distances between them change, but *H$_2$O molecules are still present*. These changes of state are **physical changes** because they do not affect the composition of the substance. In each state we still have water (H$_2$O), not some other substance.

Now suppose we run an electric current through water as illustrated in **Figure 2.8.** Something very different happens. The water disappears and is replaced by two new gaseous substances, hydrogen and oxygen. An electric current actually causes the water molecules to come apart—the water *decomposes* to hydrogen and oxygen. We can represent this process as follows:

Electric
current

This is a **chemical change** because water (consisting of H$_2$O molecules) has changed into different substances: hydrogen (containing H$_2$ molecules) and oxygen (containing O$_2$ molecules). In this process, the H$_2$O molecules have been replaced by O$_2$ and H$_2$ molecules. Let us summarize as follows.

32   Chapter 2   Matter

> **Physical and Chemical Changes**
>
> 1. A *physical change* involves a change in one or more physical properties, but no change in the fundamental components that make up the substance. The most common physical changes are changes of state: solid ⇔ liquid ⇔ gas.
>
> 2. A *chemical change* involves a change in the fundamental components of the substance; a given substance changes into a different substance or substances. Chemical changes are called **reactions:** silver tarnishes by reacting with substances in the air; a plant forms a leaf by combining various substances from the air and soil; and so on.

Example 2.2

Identifying Physical and Chemical Changes

Classify each of the following as a physical or a chemical change.

 a. Iron metal is melted.
 b. Iron combines with oxygen to form rust.
 c. Wood burns in air.
 d. A rock is broken into small pieces.

Solution

 a. Melted iron is just liquid iron and could cool again to the solid state. This is a physical change.
 b. When iron combines with oxygen, it forms a different substance (rust) that contains iron and oxygen. This is a chemical change because a different substance forms.
 c. Wood burns to form different substances (as we will see later, they include carbon dioxide and water). After the fire, the wood is no longer in its original form. This is a chemical change.
 d. When the rock is broken up, all the smaller pieces have the same composition as the whole rock. Each new piece differs from the original only in size and shape. This is a physical change.

Oxygen combines with the chemicals in wood to produce flames. Is a physical or chemical change taking place?

 Self-Check Exercise 2.2

Classify each of the following as a chemical change, a physical change, or a combination of the two.

 a. Milk turns sour.
 b. Wax is melted over a flame and then catches fire and burns.

TEACHING TIP

To illustrate the difference between a physical and a chemical change, compare representations (b) and (c) from Figure 2.7 (a physical change from liquid water to gaseous water) to the chemical change that occurs when liquid water is electrolyzed to produce the gases H_2 and O_2. Use the equation in the text to represent the electrolysis of water as a chemical change.

Additional Examples

Classify each of the following as a chemical or physical change.

1. You make scrambled eggs. **Chemical change**

2. You step on a piece of chalk and it becomes powdered. **Physical change**

3. You light a candle when the electricity goes out. **Chemical change**

4. Steam from your hot shower condenses on a cold mirror. **Physical change**

Answers to Self-Check Exercise 2.2

a. Milk turns sour because new substances are formed. This is a chemical change.

b. Melting wax is a physical change (a change of state). When wax burns, new substances are formed. This is a chemical change.

Section 2.5

Themes
Organization, Form and
Function, Models

Skills
Classifying, making comparisons, developing models,
evaluating

CHEMISTRY in ACTION

Mysterious Mixing

Materials Each student group
will need a clear cup, water, and
food coloring.

Purpose Students will understand that water is made of constantly moving particles.

Discussion Liquid water is
macroscopically static but microscopically dynamic. This idea
surfaces frequently in chemistry
(for example, with gases, equilibrium, and kinetics). It will take
a few minutes for the food coloring to become homogeneously
mixed throughout the water, but
observations should begin immediately. The students should
study the directions that the food
coloring takes in mixing. While
gravity dictates that the drop
falls in the water, the food coloring also moves laterally, and will
sometimes even rise in the water. This movement indicates that
the water molecules are "pushing" the "food coloring molecules" around. By stirring the
water, the mixing occurs more
quickly, a result that molecular
theory is able to predict and explain (you could show the students
what happens when food coloring
is added to warm water—an introduction to the idea that temperature is a measure of kinetic
energy, which affects the velocity
of the molecules).

Have students draw molecular-
level pictures to give you some
insight into their ideas. For example, some students may draw
"clear" water molecules before
the food coloring is added, and
"colored" molecules after the
mixing has taken place. A correct
drawing would show water molecules and "food coloring molecules" mixed uniformly in solution. This exercise should lead to
a good discussion of physical
versus chemical changes.

34

2.5 Mixtures and Pure Substances

Objective: *To learn to distinguish between mixtures and pure substances.*

Virtually all of the matter around us consists of mixtures of substances. For example, if you closely observe a sample of soil, you will see that it has many types of components, including tiny grains of sand and rem-nants of plants. The air we breathe is a mixture, too. Even the water from a drinking fountain contains many substances besides water.

Mixtures

A **mixture** can be defined as something that has variable composition. For example, wood is a mixture (its composition varies greatly depending on the tree from which it originates); soda is a mixture (it contains many dissolved substances, including carbon dioxide gas); coffee is a mixture (it can be strong, weak, or bitter); and, although it looks very pure, water pumped from deep in the earth is a mixture (it contains dissolved minerals and gases). The most common example of a mixture is the air that surrounds us. If we collect a sample of air from a mountaintop where there is no pollution, we find a mix-ture containing the substances shown in **Figure 2.9.**

Figure 2.9
Air is composed of a variety of substances.

CHEMISTRY in ACTION
Mysterious Mixing

1. Half-fill a clear plastic cup with water.
2. Carefully place a drop of food coloring on top of the water.
3. Without disturbing the water, observe the food coloring for a few min-utes and make a list of your observations.
4. The water does not appear to be moving. What do your observations tell you about the water molecules? Explain your answer.
5. Draw molecular-level pictures that explain your observations.
6. Could you make the food coloring mix more quickly with the water? Design an experiment and discuss it with your teacher.
7. Perform your experiment and explain the results.

34   Chapter 2   Matter

When we examine each of the substances in air, we find the following:

Nitrogen contains molecules consisting of two atoms of nitrogen:

Oxygen contains molecules consisting of two atoms of oxygen:

Water contains molecules consisting of two hydrogen atoms and one oxygen atom:

Argon contains individual argon atoms:

Carbon dioxide contains molecules consisting of two oxygen atoms and one carbon atom:

Neon contains individual neon atoms:

Helium contains individual helium atoms:

As you can see from the figure, air is a mixture of elements and compounds. Although air has a similar composition everywhere on earth, differences arise depending on where the air is collected. For example, the amount of water vapor changes greatly. Air collected over a desert would include very little water vapor. In contrast, on a humid day in Florida, air holds a relatively large amount of water. Also, the carbon dioxide content of air would be higher in industrial areas due to the burning of fuels. Likewise, other substances (pollutants) would be present due to human activities such as driving cars. Thus air is not exactly the same everywhere. It has a somewhat different composition depending on where you get it. This variation is a characteristic of mixtures. *The composition of mixtures varies, but the composition of compounds is always the same.*

Air is only one of the many mixtures we encounter in our daily lives. For example, if you wear a gold ring, you are wearing a mixture. Pure gold, like that found in the bullion stored in Fort Knox, Kentucky, is really quite soft. Because it bends easily, the pure form is not useful for jewelry. Only when we mix gold with other metals such as silver and copper does it become sturdy enough to make rings and chains.

Your ring might be 14-karat gold—that is, it contains 36 atoms of gold for every 25 atoms of silver for every 39 atoms of copper. Or your ring might be 18-karat gold—that is, it contains 56 atoms of gold for every 20 atoms of silver for every 24 atoms of copper.

Mixtures of metals are called **alloys.** Many gold alloys exist, containing varying amounts of gold, silver, and copper atoms. Alloys are mixtures—their composition varies. They are not compounds like water. Compounds always

2.5   Mixtures and Pure Substances   **35**

Figure 2.10
Twenty-four-karat gold is an element. It contains only gold atoms. Fourteen- and 18-karat gold are alloys. They contain a mixture of different atoms.

24 karat gold   18 karat gold   14 karat gold

○ gold
● copper
◐ silver

Figure 2.11
Water is a compound. All the components are the same — H_2O molecules.

have the same atomic composition. These ideas are illustrated in **Figures 2.10** and **2.11**.

It is important to understand the difference between a compound and a mixture. A compound contains only particles of identical atomic composition. Therefore it always has the same composition. In contrast, a mixture is a collection of compounds and/or elements that are present in varying amounts. Thus the composition of a mixture depends on how much of each component is used when the mixture is formed.

Integrating the CHEMICAL IMPACT

Alchemical Cymbals

This feature presents an excellent opportunity to talk about alchemy. Alchemy, the pseudoscience that preceded chemistry, was founded on the premise that "base metals" could be transmuted into gold. This futile dream motivated alchemists and their financial supporters for 17 centuries. The power and influence of the alchemists was very great. In nearly every court in Europe, men were appointed to the task of discovering how to change lead and iron into gold. Many alchemists were so revered that they were almost raised to the level of nobility, working shoulder to shoulder with their sovereigns. Although many of the alchemists were simply "confidence men," some were genuine seekers of the truth—men like Bernard Trevisan and Philippus Aurelius Theophrastus Bombast von Hohenheim, better known as Paracelsus. More information on both alchemists is given below in the Historical Notes.

CHEMICAL IMPACT

Connection to History

Alchemical Cymbals

Chemistry is an ancient science dating back to at least 1000 B.C., when early "chemists" discovered how to isolate metals from ores and how to preserve bodies by using embalming fluids. The Greeks were the first to try to figure out why chemical changes occur. By 400 B.C., they had proposed a system of four elements: fire, earth, water, and air. The next 2000 years of chemical history was dominated by a pseudoscience called *alchemy*. Although many alchemists were fakes and mystics, some were serious scientists who made important discoveries.

In fact, did you know that the cymbals used by more than 60% of the rock bands in the world were invented by an alchemist? The story begins 377 years ago in Constantinople, when an alchemist named Avedis discovered an alloy that gave better-sounding cymbals. This development was important, because at that time cymbals were mainly used by armies to frighten their enemies. To honor his achievement, Avedis was given the name Zildjian, which meant "cymbal maker."

The descendants of that alchemist now run the Avedis Zildjian Company in Norwell, Massachusetts, which manufactures 2000 of the world's best cymbals every day. Although the alloy used in the cymbals (80% copper and 20% tin) is the standard recipe for making bells, the company maintains strict

secrecy about just how the metals are combined—the process discovered by Avedis Zildjian. Modern technology also contributes to the cymbals' special sound. In the last 20 years, the company has developed a special computer-controlled hammering process that brings out the specific sounds favored by drummers everywhere. The musical world—from classical to rock—truly loves alchemical cymbals.

Worker at Avedis Zildjian Company making cymbals.

TEACHING SUPPORT
Historical Notes

Bernard Trevisan Trevisan spent 70 years of his life and an immense fortune looking for the so-called philosopher's stone. Born into wealth in northern Italy in 1406, he spent his life following various teachers and performing labor-intensive experiments in his lab. In one case he spent eight years trying to

extract the magical potion for transmutation of base metal to gold from 2000 hen's eggs.

Paracelsus Paracelsus, who was born in 1493 as the son of a physician and teacher of alchemy, traveled the known world as a youth studying to become a physician. In his travels he became convinced of the folly of medicine as it was being practiced in his day. The shams perpetrated by the

pseudo-scientist physicians of the time convinced Paracelsus to become a rabid reformer. Not surprisingly, he met with bitter opposition and was forced to live underground, healing the sick and proclaiming through his writings the need for experimentation. Although Paracelsus appeared to be a failure when he died at age 48, his work pioneered the application of chemistry to medicine. On

The earth's atmosphere is a mixture containing many gases and water that condenses to form clouds.

Pure Substances

Whereas a mixture has variable composition, a **pure substance** always has the same composition. Pure substances are either elements or compounds. For example, pure water is a compound containing individual H_2O molecules. However, as we find it in nature, liquid water always contains other substances in addition to pure water—it is a mixture. This is obvious from the different tastes, smells, and colors of water samples obtained from various locations. However, if we take great pains to purify samples of water from various sources (such as oceans, lakes, rivers, and the earth's interior), we always end up with the same pure substance—water, which is made up of only H_2O molecules. Pure water always has the same physical and chemical properties and always consists of molecules containing hydrogen and oxygen in exactly the same proportions, regardless of the original source of the water. The properties of a pure substance make it possible to identify that substance conclusively.

Mixtures can be separated into pure substances: elements and/or compounds.

For example, we have seen that air can be separated into oxygen (element), nitrogen (element), water (compound), carbon dioxide (compound), argon (element), and other pure substances.

Figure 2.12
When table salt is stirred into water (left), a homogeneous mixture called a solution is formed (right).

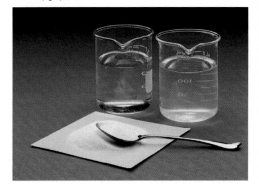

Homogeneous and Heterogeneous Mixtures

Mixtures can be classified as either homogeneous or heterogeneous. A **homogeneous mixture** is *the same throughout.* For example, when we dissolve some salt in water and stir well, all regions of the resulting mixture have the same properties. A homogeneous mixture is also called a **solution.** Of course, different amounts of salt and water can be mixed to form various solutions, but a homogeneous mixture (a solution) does not vary in composition from one region of the solution to another (see **Figure 2.12**).

The air around you is a solution—it is a homogeneous mixture of gases. Solid solutions also exist. Brass is a homogeneous mixture of the metals copper and zinc.

2.5 Mixtures and Pure Substances **37**

MINI-DEMO

Before class, prepare a mixture of iron filings and sulfur. Show students that a mixture can be separated by physical means—in this case, by using a magnet to separate the iron filings from the sulfur. Place a small amount of the mixture in a test tube. Heat the tube in the flame of a Bunsen burner until it changes to a reddish-brown color. Now show students that the compound, iron sulfide, cannot be separated into iron filings and sulfur by using a magnet.

TEACHING TIP

Although we say we can separate mixtures into pure substances, it is virtually impossible to separate mixtures into totally pure substances. No matter how hard we try, some impurities remain in each of the "pure substances."

his grave in Salzburg, Austria, are inscribed the following words: "Here is buried Philippus Theophrastus, distinguished Doctor of Medicine, who with wonderful art cured dire wounds, leprosy, gout, dropsy and other contagious diseases of the body."

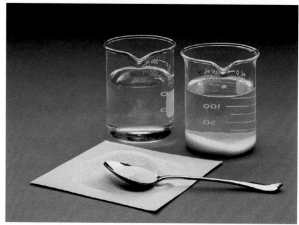

Figure 2.13
Sand and water do not mix to form a uniform mixture. After the mixture is stirred, the sand settles back to the bottom.

A **heterogeneous mixture** contains regions that have different properties from those of other regions. For example, when we pour sand into water, the resulting mixture has one region containing water and another, very different region containing mostly sand (see **Figure 2.13**).

Example 2.3

Distinguishing Between Mixtures and Pure Substances

Identify each of the following as a pure substance, a homogeneous mixture, or a heterogeneous mixture.

    a. gasoline
    b. a stream with gravel at the bottom
    c. air
    d. brass
    e. copper metal

Solution

    a. Gasoline is a homogeneous mixture containing many compounds.
    b. A stream with gravel on the bottom is a heterogeneous mixture.
    c. Air is a homogeneous mixture of elements and compounds.
    d. Brass is a homogeneous mixture containing the elements copper and zinc. Brass is not a pure substance because the relative amounts of copper and zinc are different in different brass samples.
    e. Copper metal is a pure substance (an element).

Self-Check Exercise 2.3

Classify each of the following as a pure substance, a homogeneous mixture, or a heterogeneous mixture.

a. maple syrup

b. the oxygen and helium in a scuba tank

c. oil and vinegar salad dressing

d. common salt (sodium chloride)

 ## 2.6 Separation of Mixtures

Objective: *To learn two methods of separating mixtures.*

We have seen that the matter found in nature is typically a mixture of pure substances. For example, seawater is water containing dissolved minerals. We can separate the water from the minerals by boiling, which changes the water to steam (gaseous water) and leaves the minerals behind as solids. If we collect and cool the steam, it condenses to pure water. This separation process, called **distillation**, is shown in **Figure 2.14**.

When we carry out the distillation of saltwater, water is changed from the liquid state to the gaseous state and then back to the liquid state. These changes of state are examples of physical changes. We are separating a mixture of

Figure 2.14
Distillation of a solution consisting of salt dissolved in water. (a) When the solution is boiled, steam (gaseous water) is driven off. If this steam is collected and cooled, it condenses to form pure water, which drips into the collection flask as shown. (b) After all of the water has been boiled off, the salt remains in the original flask and the water is in the collection flask.

Steam

Steam is condensed in a tube cooled by water.

Cooling water out

Saltwater

Cooling water in

Burner

Pure water

(a)

Salt

Pure water

(b)

2.6 Separation of Mixtures **39**

a. Maple syrup is a homogeneous mixture of sugar and other substances dispersed uniformly in water.

b. Helium and oxygen form a homogeneous mixture.

c. Oil and vinegar salad dressing is a heterogeneous mixture.

d. Common salt (sodium chloride) is a pure substance, so it always has the same composition. (Commercial iodized salt has iodine added to it and so would be a homogeneous mixture.)

 Section 2.6

Themes
Patterns of Change

Skills
Applying concepts, interpreting diagrams, designing experiments

Laboratory
Experiment 6:
Properties of Matter, Microscale

Laboratory
Experiment 7:
Separation Challenge, Microscale

Laboratory
Experiment 8:
Sludge Text, Traditional

Laboratory
Experiment 9:
Separation of Mixtures, Microscale

Laboratory
Experiment 10:
Distillation, Microscale

USING TECHNOLOGY

Animation and Video
Video, Paper Chromatography

Figure 2.15
No chemical change occurs when salt water is distilled.

Distillation
(physical method)

Saltwater solution
(homogeneous mixture)

Salt   +

Pure water

Mixture of
solid and
liquid

Stirring
rod

Funnel

Filter paper
traps solid

Filtrate (liquid
component
of the mixture)

Figure 2.16
Filtration separates a liquid from a solid. The liquid passes through the filter paper, but the solid particles are trapped.

Natural deposits of salt at Devil's Golf Course in Death Valley National Park, California, formed when the water evaporated from a saltwater sea.

substances, but we are not changing the composition of the individual substances. We can represent this as shown in **Figure 2.15.**

Suppose we scooped up some sand with our sample of seawater. This sample is a heterogeneous mixture, because it contains an undissolved solid as well as the saltwater solution. We can separate out the sand by simple **filtration.** We pour the mixture onto a mesh, such as a filter paper, which allows the liquid to pass through and leaves the solid behind (see **Figure 2.16**). The salt can then be separated from the water by distillation. The total separation process is represented in **Figure 2.17.** All the changes involved are physical changes.

Sand

Filtration
(physical
method)

+

Distillation
(physical
method)

Salt

+

Sand–saltwater
mixture

Saltwater
solution

Pure water

Figure 2.17
Separation of a sand–saltwater mixture.

40   Chapter 2   Matter

TEACHING SUPPORT
Demonstration

Simple Distillation

Materials

Distillation setup   50 mL 0.1 *M*
(Figure 2.14)   CuSO₄
                       solution

Procedure Place the copper sulfate solution in the flask over the burner. Begin heating the system. Be sure the condenser

has water running through it. After some time elapses and the copper sulfate solution is boiling gently, point out that the liquid collecting in the receiver flask is colorless. The blue color remains in the original flask. The water in the solution is turning to steam and then condensing and collecting in the receiving flask. If all of the water is boiled off (do not do this — it takes too long and you

may crack the flask), only crystals of copper sulfate will remain.

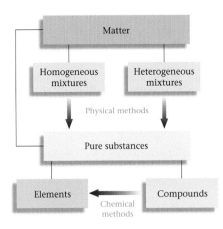

Figure 2.18
The organization of matter.

We can summarize the description of matter given in this chapter with the diagram shown in **Figure 2.18.** Note that a given sample of matter can be a pure substance (either an element or a compound) or, more commonly, a mixture (homogeneous or heterogeneous). We have seen that all matter exists as elements or can be broken down into elements, the most fundamental substances we have encountered up to this point. We will have more to say about the nature of elements in the next chapter.

Focus Questions

Sections 2.4–2.6

1. Classify the following as *physical* or *chemical* changes.
   a. Mothballs gradually vaporize in a closet.
   b. Hydrofluoric acid attacks glass and is used to etch calibration marks on glass laboratory utensils.
   c. Calcium chloride lowers the temperature at which water freezes and can be used to melt ice on city sidewalks and roadways.
   d. An antacid tablet fizzes and releases carbon dioxide gas when it comes in contact with hydrochloric acid in the stomach.
   e. A flashlight battery corrodes and leaks on prolonged storage.
   f. Chemistry students usually get holes in the cotton jeans they wear to lab because of the acids used in many experiments.
   g. Whole milk curdles if you add vinegar to it.
   h. A piece of rubber stretches when you pull it.
   i. Rubbing alcohol evaporates quickly from the skin.
   j. Acetone is used to dissolve and remove nail polish.

2. Identify the following as *mixtures* or *pure substances*.
   a. milk
   b. the paper on which this book is printed
   c. a teaspoon of sugar
   d. a teaspoon of sugar dissolved in a glass of water
   e. steel

3. Classify the following mixtures as *homogeneous* or *heterogeneous*.
   a. vanilla ice cream
   b. "rocky road" ice cream
   c. Italian salad dressing
   d. kitty litter

4. Are all physical changes accompanied by chemical changes? Are all chemical changes accompanied by physical changes? Explain.

 Answers to Focus Questions

1. **a.** physical   **f.** chemical
   b. chemical   **g.** chemical
   c. physical   **h.** physical
   d. chemical   **i.** physical
   e. chemical   **j.** physical

2. **a.** mixture   **d.** mixture
   b. mixture   **e.** mixture
   c. pure substance

3. **a.** homogeneous
   b. heterogeneous
   c. heterogeneous
   d. heterogeneous

4. Physical changes are not accompanied by chemical changes. In fact, the very nature of a physical change implies no change in the composition of the substance. Chemical changes, on the other hand, are accompanied by physical changes, because the composition of the substance is changed and thus will have new physical properties.

Focus Questions   **41**

Physical and Chemical Changes

Objectives

1. To observe physical and chemical changes

2. To classify each process as chemical or physical by analyzing observations

Lab Skills

Making observations, applying concepts, interpreting data, classifying, drawing conclusions

Preparation Hints

Place several small containers of each of the solids and solutions around the lab. This setup will make it easier and less time-consuming for the students.

Prelab Discussion

Tell students that 3.0 *M* HCl is corrosive. They should handle it with extreme care. If they come in contact with any solution, they need to wash the contacted area thoroughly. Make sure they know the locations of eyewashes.

Students should tie back their hair and loose clothing whenever they work with a flame in the lab. Students often deposit matches in the sink. Tell them to dispose of burned matches in the trashcan after they are cool.

Safety Tips

When working with chemicals, wear safety goggles and lab aprons. Collect all solutions and chemicals from the students and dispose of them properly.

Procedure Hints

The steam coming off of the water in Part III is very hot. Students should be careful when they are holding the sponge over the boiling water.

Post-Lab Discussion

Use a whole-class discussion to review the results. Students are still new at making observations and there will undoubtedly be differences among groups' results.

Sample Observations

Student observations will vary.

Part I: Eventually mixing, drops mix in all directions; water appears stationary.

Part II: Both salts dissolve and solutions are clear; a white solid forms in a clear liquid.

Part III: Bubbles form from bot-

Problem

How do physical changes differ from chemical changes?

Introduction

Matter can undergo both physical and chemical changes. Physical changes involve changes in one or more physical properties. Chemical changes involve changes in the composition of the substance.

The following are clues that indicate that a chemical change may have occurred: a color change, the evolution of bubbles, the formation of a solid, and heat absorbed or produced.

In this lab you will carry out four procedures (Parts I–IV) and make observations. Then you will decide how well the clues enable you to determine whether a chemical reaction occurred. In addition, you will develop molecular definitions of physical and chemical changes.

Prelab Assignment

Read the entire laboratory experiment before you begin.

Materials

Goggles	Spatula
Apron	Sponge
250-mL beakers (2)	Well plate
100-mL beakers (3)	Tongs
Graduated cylinder	Barium nitrate
Bunsen burner	Potassium sulfate
Matches	HCl (3.0 *M*)
Ring stand	Magnesium ribbon
Ring	Food coloring
Wire gauze	Water

Safety

1. The 3.0 *M* HCl is corrosive. Handle it with extreme care.

2. If you come in contact with any solution, wash the contacted area thoroughly.

3. You are working with a flame in this lab. Tie back hair and loose clothing.

4. Do not drop matches into the sink. Dispose of burned matches in the trashcan after they are cool.

Procedure

Part I

1. Add about 100 mL of water to a 250-mL beaker.

2. Add a few drops of food coloring to a beaker of water.

3. Make observations for several minutes.

Part II

1. Dissolve a spatula-tip amount of barium nitrate in a small amount of water (about 10 mL) in a 100-mL beaker.

2. Dissolve a spatula-tip amount of potassium sulfate in a small amount of water (about 10 mL) in a 100-mL beaker.

3. Pour the solutions from steps 1 and 2 together into an empty 100-mL beaker. Make careful observations.

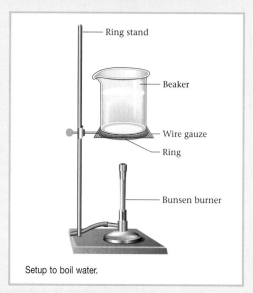

Setup to boil water.

Part III

1. Add about 100 mL of water to a 250-mL beaker.

2. Arrange the beaker and ring stand as shown in the figure.

3. Light the Bunsen burner and place it under the beaker. Adjust the burner so that the hottest part of the flame touches the bottom of the beaker.

4. Bring the water to a boil. Make careful observations.

5. Use the tongs to hold the sponge over the beaker for a couple of minutes as the water boils.

6. Place the sponge on the lab bench and let it cool.

7. Squeeze the sponge. Record your observations.

Part IV

1. Place a few drops of 3.0 *M* HCl in one of the wells.

2. Add a small piece of magnesium ribbon to the acid. Make careful observations.

---

tom to top, then burst at top; vapor disappears (steam), and sponge gets wet.

Part IV: Bubbles form; Mg disappears; a clear solution appears at the end; heat is generated.

Analysis and Conclusions

1. Fill in a table similar to the one provided at the right. Discuss whether each change is physical or chemical with your lab partner. Record your conclusions in the table. Justify each choice below the table.

2. Yes. Parts I and III are physical changes.

	Clues That a Chemical Change Occurred	Chemical or Physical Change?
Food coloring to water	Color change	Physical
Mixing two solutions	Formation of a solid	Chemical
Boiling water	1. Heat 2. Formation of a gas	Physical
Adding Mg to HCl	1. Heat 2. Formation of a gas	Chemical

3. The sponge collected the water. It showed that water was a product of boiling the water. Therefore boiling water is a physical process.

4. Answers will vary.

5. Answers will vary.

Something Extra

Answers will vary. In a chemical change the products are chemically different from the reactants. This fact was not directly observable in this lab.

Cleaning Up

Clean up all materials and wash your hands thoroughly.

Data/Observations

Make a list of observations for each of the four parts of the procedure.

Analysis and Conclusions

1. Fill in a table similar to the one provided here. Discuss whether each change is physical or chemical with your lab partner. Record your conclusions in the table. Justify each choice below the table.

	Clues That a Chemical Change Occurred	Chemical or Physical Change?
Food coloring to water		
Mixing two solutions		
Boiling water		
Adding Mg to HCl		

2. Sometimes a physical change produces the same clues as those normally associated with chemical changes. Did this happen in any of your procedures? Which ones?

3. What was the purpose of the sponge in Part III? How did it help you decide whether the procedure involved a physical or chemical change?

4. Make microscopic drawings of each of the four procedures. Discuss how these explain your observations.

5. Develop definitions of chemical change and physical change using atoms and molecules in your definitions.

Something Extra

Chemists have learned that a chemical change always includes a rearrangement of the ways in which atoms are grouped. Explain what this statement means and discuss whether your observations support this statement.

Chapter Review

Key Terms

matter (2.1)
atom (2.2)
compound (2.2)
molecule (2.2)
element (2.2)
graphite (2.2)
diamond (2.2)
buckminsterfullerene (2.2)
solid (2.3)
liquid (2.3)
gas (2.3)
physical properties (2.4)

chemical properties (2.4)
physical change (2.4)
chemical change (2.4)
reaction (2.4)
mixture (2.5)
alloy (2.5)
pure substance (2.5)
homogeneous mixture (2.5)
solution (2.5)
heterogeneous mixture (2.5)
distillation (2.6)
filtration (2.6)

Summary

1. Matter can exist in three states—solid, liquid, and gas—and can be described in terms of its physical and chemical properties. Chemical properties describe a substance's ability to undergo a change to a different substance. Physical properties are the characteristics a substance exhibits as long as no chemical change occurs.

2. A physical change involves a change in one or more physical properties, but no change in composition. A chemical change transforms a substance into a new substance or substances.

3. A mixture has variable composition. A homogeneous mixture has the same properties throughout; a heterogeneous mixture does not. A pure substance always has the same composition. We can physically separate mixtures of pure substances by distillation and filtration.

4. Pure substances are of two types: elements, which cannot be broken down chemically into simpler substances, and compounds, which can be broken down chemically into elements.

5. Elements are composed of tiny particles called atoms. Each element has a characteristic type of atom.

6. Compounds are composed of different types of atoms. Many compounds contain molecules—particles that are composed of atoms bonded to one another.

Chapter Review   **43**

1. We can "see" atoms with a scanning tunneling microscope.

2. Atoms are very tiny.

3. The molecules of that compound always contain the same type and number of atoms of its constituent elements.

4. In general, the properties of a compound are very different from the properties of its constituent elements. For example, the properties of water are very different from the properties of the elements (hydrogen gas and oxygen gas) that form it.

5. Gaseous water has a much larger volume than either the solid or the liquid form. There is a great deal of empty space in the gaseous sample.

6. Because gases are mostly open space, they can be compressed easily to smaller volumes. In solids and liquids, most of the sample's bulk volume is filled with the molecules, leaving little empty space.

7. physical

8. chemical

9. the orange color

10. The substance reacts with iron(II) sulfate.

11. Electrolysis is the passage of an electrical current through a substance or solution to force a chemical reaction to occur. For example, when an electrical current is passed through water, the water molecules undergo a chemical change to form hydrogen gas and oxygen gas.

12. (a) chemical; (b) physical; (c) chemical; (d) chemical; (e) chemical; (f) chemical; (g) chemical; (h) chemical; (i) physical; (j) chemical

13. Answers will vary. Possibilities for heterogeneous mixtures include salad dressing, candy, and pencils; possibilities for solutions include soft drinks, window cleaner, and shampoo.

14. (a) mixture; (b) mixture; (c) mixture; (d) pure substance

15. (a) homogeneous; (b) heterogeneous; (c) heterogeneous; (d) homogeneous; (e) homogeneous (basically)

Questions and Problems

All exercises with blue numbers have answers in the back of this book.

2.1 The Particulate Nature of Matter

Questions

1. How do we "know" that matter is composed of atoms?
2. Why can't we see atoms with the naked eye?

2.2 Elements and Compounds

Questions

3. What does it mean to say that a given compound always has the same composition?
4. How do the properties of a compound, in general, compare to the properties of the elements of which it is composed? Give an example of a common compound and the elements of which it is composed to illustrate your answer.

2.3 The States of Matter

Questions

5. Consider three 10-g samples of water: one as ice, one as a liquid, and one as vapor. How do the volumes of these three samples compare with one another? How is this difference in volume related to the physical state involved?
6. In a sample of a gaseous substance, more than 99% of the overall volume of the sample is empty space. How is this fact reflected in the properties of a gaseous substance, compared with the properties of a liquid or solid substance?

2.4 Physical and Chemical Properties and Changes

Questions

7. Copper is a reddish-brown metal that is easily stretched to make wires. These characteristics are examples of (physical/chemical) properties of copper.
8. When copper metal is heated in concentrated nitric acid, the copper dissolves to form a deep blue solution, and a brown gas is evolved from the acid. These characteristics are examples of (physical/chemical) changes.

(For Exercises 9 and 10) Solutions of the substance potassium dichromate are bright orange in color. If a potassium dichromate solution is added to an acidic solution of iron(II) sulfate, the orange color of the potassium dichromate disappears, and the mixture takes on a bright green color as chromium(III) ion forms.

9. From the information above, indicate one *physical* property of potassium dichromate in solution.
10. From the information above, indicate one *chemical* property of potassium dichromate in solution.
11. What is meant by *electrolysis*? Are the changes produced by electrolysis chemical or physical in nature? Give an example to show your reasoning.
12. Classify the following as *physical* or *chemical* changes/properties.
    a. A shirt scorches when you leave the iron on one spot too long.
    b. The tires on your car seem to be getting flat in very cold weather.
    c. Your grandmother's silver tea set gets black with tarnish over time.
    d. Spray-on oven cleaner converts grease in the oven into a soapy material.
    e. An ordinary flashlight battery begins to leak with age and can't be recharged.
    f. Acids produced by bacteria in plaque cause teeth to decay.
    g. Sugar will char if overheated while making homemade candy.
    h. Hydrogen peroxide fizzes when applied to a wound.
    i. Dry ice "evaporates" without melting as time passes.
    j. Chlorine laundry bleaches will sometimes change the color of brightly colored clothing.

2.5 Mixtures and Pure Substances

Questions

13. Give three examples of heterogeneous *mixtures* and three examples of *solutions* that you might use in everyday life.
14. Classify the following as *mixtures* or as *pure substances*.
    a. a multivitamin tablet
    b. the blue liquid in your car's windshield washer
    c. a Spanish omelet
    d. a diamond
15. Classify the following mixtures as *homogeneous* or *heterogeneous*.
    a. gasoline
    b. a jar of jelly beans
    c. chunky peanut butter
    d. margarine
    e. the paper on which this question is printed

2.6 Separation of Mixtures

Questions

16. Describe how the process of *distillation* could be used to separate a solution into its component substances. Give an example.

16. Consider a table salt solution (sodium chloride in water). Because water boils at a much lower temperature than sodium chloride does, the water can be boiled off from the solution, collected, and condensed back into the liquid state.

17. Consider a mixture of table salt (sodium chloride) and sand. Salt is soluble in water, but sand is not. The mixture is added to water, stirred to dissolve the salt, and then filtered. The salt solution passes through the filter, while the sand remains on the filter. The water can then be evaporated from the salt.

18. Add water to the sample and then heat the sample to boiling. This should dissolve the benzoic acid but not the charcoal. The hot sample can be filtered, which will remove the charcoal. As the filtered solution cools some of the benzoic acid will crystallize. The solution could also be heated carefully to boil off the water, leaving benzoic acid.

19. The solution is heated to vaporize (boil) the water. The water vapor is then cooled so that it condenses back to the liquid state, and the liquid is collected. After all the water is vaporized from the original sample, pure sodium chloride remains. The process consists of physical changes.

20. compound (two different solids form from a pure substance)

21. compound (loses mass when heated)

17. Describe how the process of *filtration* could be used to separate a mixture into its components. Give an example.

18. In a common laboratory experiment in general chemistry, students are asked to determine the relative amounts of benzoic acid and charcoal in a solid mixture. Benzoic acid is relatively soluble in hot water, but charcoal is not. Devise a method for separating the two components of this mixture.

19. Describe the process of distillation depicted in Figure 2.14. Does the separation of the components of a mixture by distillation represent a chemical or a physical change?

Critical Thinking

20. Pure substance X is melted, and the liquid is placed in an electrolysis apparatus like that shown in Figure 2.8. When an electric current is passed through the liquid, a brown solid forms in one chamber and a white solid forms in the other chamber. Is substance X a compound or an element?

21. If a piece of hard white blackboard chalk is heated strongly in a flame, the mass of the piece of chalk will decrease, and eventually the chalk will crumble into a fine white dust. Does this change suggest that the chalk is composed of an element or a compound?

22. During a very cold winter, the temperature may remain below the freezing point for extended periods. However, fallen snow can still disappear, even though it cannot melt. This is possible because a solid can vaporize directly, without passing through the liquid state. Is this process (sublimation) a physical or a chemical change?

23. Discuss the similarities and differences between a liquid and a gas.

24. In gaseous substances, the individual molecules are relatively (close/far apart) and are moving freely, rapidly, and randomly.

25. The fact that the substance copper(II) sulfate pentahydrate is bright blue is an example of a _____ property.

26. The fact that the substance copper(II) sulfate pentahydrate combines with ammonia in solution to form a new compound is an example of a _____ property.

22. physical

23. Liquids and gases flow freely and take the shape of their containers. The molecules in liquids are relatively close together and interact with each other. The molecules in a gas are far apart and do not interact with each other.

24. far apart

25. physical

26. chemical

3 Chemical Foundations: Elements, Atoms, and Ions

	Section	Text Features & Components	Labs, Demonstrations & Activities
Teaching Segment 3A 1.5 blocks pp. 47–53	3.1 The Elements	**LP** Lesson Plans (Sec 3.1–3.3) **SE** Top Ten Elements in the Human Body p. 48 **SE** Chemical Impact: Trace Elements—Small But Crucial p. 49	**TE** Mini Demo p. 49
	3.2 Symbols for the Elements	**SE** Celebrity Chemical: Iron p. 50	**TE** Teaching Support: Demonstration p. 50
	3.3 Dalton's Atomic Theory	**TE** Teaching Support: Historical Note p. 52 **SE** Chemical Impact: No Laughing Matter p. 53	**LM** Experiment 11: Aluminum Atoms Lab Manual Report Sheets Teacher's Lab Guide
Teaching Segment 3B 1 block pp. 54–63	3.4 Formulas of Compounds	**LP** Lesson Plans (Sec 3.4–3.7)	**LM** Experiment 12: Electrolysis Lab Manual Report Sheets Teacher's Lab Guide
	3.5 The Structure of the Atom	**TE** Teaching Support: Historical Notes p. 56 **SE** Chemical Impact: Glowing Tubes for Signs, Television Sets, and Computers p. 58	
	3.6 Introduction to the Modern Concept of Atomic Structure	**TE** Teaching Support: Background Information p. 58	**SE** Chemistry in Action: How Big Is An Atom? p. 59
	3.7 Isotopes		
	continued on next page		

Key **SE** Student Edition **TE** Teacher Edition **RP** Teacher Resource Package **LM** Lab Materials **LP** Lesson Plans **AR** Additional Resources ● Florida Specific

46a

Chapter Planning Guide

All Learners	Review & Assessment	Standards
(TE) Active Learning *p. 47* (⚑) Transparency: Elements in the Human Body *p. 48* (⚑) Transparency: Table 3.1 *p. 48* (TE) Teaching Tips *p. 48* (TE) Misconceptions *p. 49* (AR) Less Proficient Students *p. 5*	(SE) Questions and Problems *pp. 80–81*	(TE) **NSES** UCP1, UCP2, UCP5, A1, A2, B2, B3, C6, E1, E2, F3, G1, G2, G3 (◐) **SSS** SC.H.1.4.1, SC.H.1.4.3, SC.H.1.4.5, SC.H.1.4.6, SC.A.2.4.2, SC.B.1.4.2, SC.H.3.4.2, SC.H.3.4.4
(TE) Teaching Tips *p. 51* (⚑) Transparency: Table 3.3 *p. 51* (AR) Less Proficient Students *p. 5*	(SE) Key Terms *p. 80* (SE) Questions and Problems *p. 81*	
(AR) Less Proficient Students *p. 5*	(SE) Focus Questions (Sec 3.1–3.3) *p. 53* (SE) Key Terms *p. 80* (SE) Questions and Problems *p. 81*	
(TE) Teaching Tip *p. 54* (AR) Less Proficient Students *p. 5*	(TE) Additional Examples *p. 54* (SE) Self Check *p. 55* (SE) Key Terms *p. 80* (SE) Questions and Problems *p. 81*	(TE) **NSES** UCP1, UCP2, UCP3, UCP5, A1, A2, B1, B2, E1, E2, G1, G2, G3 (◐) **SSS** SC.H.1.4.1, SC.H.1.4.2, SC.H.1.4.3, SC.H.1.4.4, SC.H.1.4.6, SC.A.2.4.1, SC.C.2.4.2, SC.C.2.4.5, SC.A.2.4.2, SC.H.3.4.2, SC.H.3.4.5
(▢) Chemistry in Motion (1) (TE) Misconceptions *p. 56* (TE) Teaching Tips *p. 57* (▸) Animation: Scattering of Alpha Particles by Gold Foil (⚑) Transparency: Figure 3.5 *p. 56* (AR) Less Proficient Students *p. 5*	(SE) What if . . . *p. 57* (SE) Key Terms *p. 80* (SE) Questions and Problems *p. 81*	
(AR) Less Proficient Students *p. 5*	(SE) What if . . . *p. 59* (SE) Questions and Problems *p. 82*	
(RP) Team Learning Worksheets (Sec 3.1–3.7) *pp. 9–10* (AR) Less Proficient Students *p. 5*	(TE) Additional Examples *pp. 61–63* (SE) Self Check *pp. 62–63* (SE) Focus Questions (Sec 3.4–3.7) (SE) Key Terms *p. 80* (SE) Questions and Problems *p. 82*	

3 Chemical Foundations: Elements, Atoms, and Ions

Teaching Segment 3C
1.5 blocks
pp. 63–78

Section	Text Features & Components	Labs, Demonstrations & Activities
3.8 Introduction to the Periodic Table	Lesson Plans (Sec 3.8–3.12)	Experiment 13: Classifying Elements Lab Manual Report Sheets Teacher's Lab Guide Mini Demo *p. 65*
3.9 Natural States of the Elements	Chemical Impact: Miracle Coatings *p. 74*	Mini Demo *p. 70*
3.10 Ions		Teaching Support: Demonstration *pp. 74–75* Chemistry in the Laboratory Electric Solutions *p. 79* Experiment 14: Electric Solutions Lab Manual Report Sheets Teacher's Lab Guide
3.11 Compounds That Contain Ions		

Key

 Student Edition
 Teacher Edition
RP Teacher Resource Package
 Lab Materials
 Lesson Plans
AR Additional Resources
🔲 Florida Specific

Technology and Media

Transparencies
Table 3.1, 3.3, 3.5
Figure 3.5, 3.11, 3.12, 3.19
Elements in the Human Body

PowerPoint Slides

Animation Scattering of Alpha Particles by Gold Foil

Video Conductivity Parts 1, 2, 3
Chemistry in Motion (1) Cathode Ray Tube • (2) Conductivity of Aqueous Solutions

eEdition CD-ROM
Easy Planner CD-ROM
English Summaries CD
Spanish Summaries CD

Web Site classzone.com
McDougal Littell Test Generator

Chapter Planning Guide

All Learners

- **TE** Active Learning *p. 63*
- Transparency: Figure 3.11, 3.12
- **TE** Teaching Tips *p. 64*
- **AR** Less Proficient Students *p. 6*

- Transparency: Table 3.5 *p. 69*
- **AR** Less Proficient Students *p. 6*

- **TE** Teaching Tips *pp. 71, 74*
- Transparency: Figure 3.19 *p. 74*
- **AR** Less Proficient Students *p. 6*

- Video: Conductivity Parts 1, 2, 3
- Chemistry in Motion (2)
- **TE** Teaching Tips *p. 76*
- **RP** Team Learning Worksheets (Sec 3.8–3.11) *pp. 11–12*
- **AR** Less Proficient Students *p. 6*

Review & Assessment

- **TE** Additional Examples *p. 67*
- **SE** Self Check *p. 67*
- **SE** Key Terms *p. 80*
- **SE** Questions and Problems *p. 82*

- **SE** Key Terms *p. 80*
- **SE** Questions and Problems *p. 83*

- **SE** What if . . . *p. 76*
- **SE** Key Terms *p. 80*
- **SE** Questions and Problems *p. 83*

- **SE** What if . . . *p. 76*
- **TE** Additional Examples *p. 77*
- **SE** Self Check *p. 78*
- **SE** Focus Questions (Sec 3.8–3.11) *p. 78*
- **SE** Key Terms *p. 80*
- **SE** Questions and Problems *p. 83*

Standards

- **TE** **NSES** UCP1, UCP3, UCP5, A1, A2, B2, B3, E1, E2
- **SSS** SC.A.2.4.1, SC.A.2.4.5, SC.A.1.4.2, SC.C.2.4.2, SC.A.2.4.2

Chapter Materials

- **TE** Reading Strategy
- **AR** English/Spanish Summaries *pp. 4–5*
- **RP** Classroom Activities and Projects: Element Report/LED Tester *pp. 3–9*
- **AR** Challenge Projects/Problems *pp. 4–5*
- **AR** Less Proficient Students *p. 6*
- English Summary Audio
- Spanish Summary Audio
- **RP** Chapter Review Worksheets: (Basic, Review, Challenge)

- **SE** Chapter Summary *p. 80*
- **SE** Critical Thinking *p. 83*
- **RP** Solutions Guide
- **RP** Chapter Tests
- **RP** Test Bank
- McDougal Littell Test Generator
- **AR** Standardized Test Practice
- **FCAT Test 2**

3 Integrating Reading Strategies and Chemistry Concepts

Chapter 3: Creating and Using Flashcards

Your students are probably starting to comprehend that chemistry is a *cumulative* subject. Emphasize that because each new chapter will draw on knowledge from the previous chapters, chemistry students need ways to learn and recall information throughout the course.

Students may fear moving on to a new concept before they have mastered the concept that preceded it. Introduce the strategy of creating and using flashcards to help alleviate this fear. While students may not be receptive to the extra work of creating flashcards, the strategies below may help persuade them that creating flashcards will be worth their effort. There are also Chemistry in Action boxes in Chapters 3 and 4 that encourage students to make decks of flashcards for specific purposes. (See page 71, page 94).

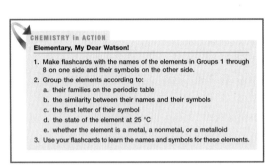

CHEMISTRY in ACTION
Elementary, My Dear Watson!
1. Make flashcards with the names of the elements in Groups 1 through 8 on one side and their symbols on the other side.
2. Group the elements according to:
   a. their families on the periodic table
   b. the similarity between their names and their symbols
   c. the first letter of their symbol
   d. the state of the element at 25 °C
   e. whether the element is a metal, a nonmetal, or a metalloid
3. Use your flashcards to learn the names and symbols for these elements.

CHEMISTRY in ACTION
Name Game I: Ionic Compounds
1. Make two sets of flashcards with names of ions on one side and symbol and charge on the other:
   Set 1: all of the alkali and alkaline earth metals, plus iron(II) and iron(III)
   Set 2: all of the nonmetals from Groups 5, 6, and 7
2. Randomly pick one card from set 1, and one card from set 2. Write the proper formula for the ionic compound made from these two ions, and name the compound.
3. Repeat the previous step until you correctly name ten compounds in a row. Make sure you can write formulas and names starting with either the names or the symbols and charges of the ions.

Creating Flashcards

Have the students reread Chapters 1 and 2 and their notes for those chapters. Challenge each of them to create a total of at least ten flashcards. Encourage the students to use index cards or some other heavy and durable paper. As you progress through Chapter 3, allow time for the students to add to their flashcards.

Reasons to Create and Use Flashcards

1. To understand and comprehend vocabulary, chemical names, elements, symbols, and structures.
2. To aid recall of commonly used formulas, chemical names, elements, and symbols.
3. To actively participate in the learning process by writing new material in your own words; which should make complex topics easier to interpret.
4. To involve senses other than vision in the learning process. For example, writing a flashcard and then reading the information on the card aloud can enhance your recall capability for the information.
5. To generate a convenient and comprehensive study tool that can be used anywhere and at any time.
6. To be better prepared for quizzes, tests, and exams, and to avoid the need to cram the night before.
7. To identify strong points and weak points in your knowledge. You can then spend your study time on those cards covering areas where you have the most difficulty.

Using Flashcards

If the students have completed flashcards for Chapters 1 through 3, each student should have a sizeable stack of cards. Consider having each student submit a written plan for using his or her flashcards as a study tool. Suggest the following ideas:

- Review cards at least three times each day, perhaps when riding the bus, waiting for class to begin, just before bedtime, and so on.
- Find a partner to quiz you using your cards. Have the partner separate the cards into two stacks: the cards you have mastered and the cards that require more studying.
- Read all the cards aloud at least three times each week.
- Trade flashcards with a classmate and study those cards. Encourage the students to discuss with the classmate the differences in the way they made their cards.

All Learners

If the students are having trouble creating or using the flashcards effectively, point out different styles of cards that can be created, and various ways of studying the cards that can be used, depending on a student's learning style.

Auditory Learners

Auditory Learners may benefit creating and reading aloud memory devices for important material. Have these students create flashcards by writing the vocabulary word on one side and the definition on the other side, or, the element on one side, and the symbol on the other side. Explain to the students that they can also create flashcards using a mnemonic, a song, or a rhyme to help them to learn.

Encourage the auditory learners to study the cards in a quiet place, read both sides of the flashcards aloud, close their eyes and then recite both sides of the card aloud. Tell the students to then repeat this process.

Visual Learners

Visual Learners are likely to benefit from flashcards if they are created using visual cues. Encourage these students to use pictures, diagrams, sketches, graphs, various colors, borders, symbols, and so on that will trigger a picture in their minds of the material they are trying to master. Tell these students to limit the information they write on a flashcard, so that when they study, they can more easily create a visual image of the material.

Kinesthetic/Tactile Learners

Encourage kinesthetic/tactile learners to make their own flashcards. These students will benefit as much from the act of making the card as they will from studying the material on the card. Encourage these students to limit the amount of information on each card, and to order their cards in a sequence that makes sense to them. For instance, if trying to learn a list of rules, the students should write one rule per card and then always study the cards in the same order. These students may also gain a better comprehension of the material if they use the flashcards in an interactive memory game.

Overview

In this Chapter our goals are for the students to:

- Learn the names and symbols for some elements

- Learn about the relative abundance for some elements

- Learn about Dalton's theory of atoms

- Understand the law of constant composition

- Learn about how a formula describes a compound's composition

- Understand Rutherford's experiment and its impact on atomic structure

- Describe important features of subatomic particles

- Learn about isotope, atomic number and mass number

- Understand the use of the symbol X

- Learn the various features of the periodic table

- Learn the properties of metals, nonmetals, and metalloids

- Describe the formation of ions from their parent atoms

- Predict which ion a given element forms by using the periodic table

- Describe how ions combine to form neutral compounds

3 Chemical Foundations: Elements, Atoms, and Ions

The new Guggenheim Museum in Bilbao, Spain. The museum's signature feature is a roof clad in titanium that forms a "metallic flower."

46

The chemical elements are very important to each of us in our daily lives. Although certain elements are present in our bodies in tiny amounts, they can have profound effects on our health and behavior. As we will see in this chapter, lithium can be a miracle treatment for someone with manic-depressive disease and our cobalt levels can have a remarkable impact on whether we behave violently.

Since ancient times, humans have used chemical changes to their advantage. The processing of ores to produce metals for ornaments and tools and the use of embalming fluids are two applications of chemistry that were used before 1000 B.C.

The Greeks were the first to try to explain why chemical changes occur. By about 400 B.C. they had proposed that all matter was composed of four fundamental substances: fire, earth, water, and air.

The next 2000 years of chemical history were dominated by alchemy. Some alchemists were mystics and fakes who were obsessed with the idea of turning cheap metals into gold. However, many alchemists were sincere scientists and this period saw important events: the elements mercury, sulfur, and antimony were discovered, and alchemists learned how to prepare acids.

The first scientist to recognize the importance of careful measurements was the Irishman Robert Boyle (1627–1691). Boyle is best known for his pioneering work on the properties of gases, but his most important contribution to science was probably his insistence that science should be firmly grounded in experiments. For example, Boyle held no preconceived notions about how many elements there might be. His definition of the term *element* was based on experiments: a substance was an element unless it could be broken down into two or more simpler substances. For example, air could not be an element as the Greeks believed, because it could be broken down into many pure substances.

Robert Boyle at 62 years of age.

As Boyle's experimental definition of an element became generally accepted, the list of known elements grew, and the Greek system of four elements died. But although Boyle was an excellent scientist, he was not always right. For some reason he ignored his own definition of an element and clung to the alchemists' views that metals were not true elements and that a way would be found eventually to change one metal into another.

3.1   The Elements

Objectives: *To learn about the relative abundances of the elements. To learn the names of some elements.*

As we saw in Chapter 2, all of the materials of the earth (and other parts of the universe) can be broken down chemically into about 100 different elements. At first it might seem amazing that the millions of known substances are composed of so few fundamental elements. Fortunately for those trying to understand and systematize it, nature often uses a relatively small number of fundamental units to assemble even extremely complex materials. For example, proteins, a group of substances that serve the human

3.1   The Elements   **47**

Section 3.1

Themes
Organization, Form and Function

Skills
Making comparisons, classifying, evaluating

Student Preparation
Assign the students to read Sections 3.1 to 3.7 and to answer the Focus Questions at the end of Section 3.7 before coming to class.

Active Learning
After introducing the material in Sections 3.1 to 3.7 in class, place the students in groups and have them work together on Sections 3.1–3.7: Team Learning Worksheet. Answers and/or discussion of these questions are located in the *Teacher Resources.*

The sand in these dunes at Death Valley National Monument is composed of silicon and oxygen atoms.

The number of elements changes regularly as new elements are made in particle accelerators.

TABLE 3.1

Distribution (Mass Percent) of the 18 Most Abundant Elements in the Earth's Crust, Oceans, and Atmosphere

Element	Mass Percent	Element	Mass Percent
oxygen	49.2	titanium	0.58
silicon	25.7	chlorine	0.19
aluminum	7.50	phosphorus	0.11
iron	4.71	manganese	0.09
calcium	3.39	carbon	0.08
sodium	2.63	sulfur	0.06
potassium	2.40	barium	0.04
magnesium	1.93	nitrogen	0.03
hydrogen	0.87	fluorine	0.03
		all others	0.49

body in almost uncountable ways, are all made by linking together a few fundamental units to form huge molecules. A nonchemical example is the English language, where hundreds of thousands of words are constructed from only 26 letters. Compounds are made by combining atoms of the various elements, just as words are constructed from the 26 letters of the alphabet. And just as you had to learn the letters of the alphabet before you could learn to read and write, you need to learn the names and symbols of the chemical elements before you can read and write chemistry.

Presently about 115 different elements are known, 88 of which occur naturally. (The rest have been made in laboratories.) The elements vary tremendously in abundance. In fact, only 9 elements account for most of the compounds found in the earth's crust. In **Table 3.1**, the elements are listed in order of abundance (mass percent) in the earth's crust, oceans, and atmosphere. Note that nearly half of the mass is accounted for by oxygen alone. Also note that the 9 most abundant elements account for over 98% of the total mass.

Oxygen, in addition to accounting for about 20% of the earth's atmosphere (where it occurs as O_2 molecules), is also found in virtually all the rocks, sand, and soil on the earth's crust. In these latter materials, oxygen is not present as O_2 molecules but exists in compounds that usually contain silicon and aluminum atoms. The familiar substances of the geological world, such as rocks and sand, contain large groups of silicon and oxygen atoms bound together to form huge clusters.

The list of elements found in living matter is very different from that for the earth's crust. The Top Ten list shows the distribution of the most abundant elements in the human body. Oxygen, carbon, hydrogen, and nitrogen form the basis for all biologically important molecules. Some elements found in the body (called trace elements) are crucial for life, even though they are present in relatively small amounts. For example, chromium helps the body use sugars to provide energy.

One more general comment is important at this point. As we have seen, elements are fundamental to understanding chemistry. However, students are oftentimes confused by the many different ways that chemists use the term *element*. Sometimes when we say *element*, we mean a single atom of that element. We might call this the microscopic form of an element. Other times

TOP TEN
Elements in the Human Body

Element	Mass Percent
1. Oxygen	65.0
2. Carbon	18.0
3. Hydrogen	10.0
4. Nitrogen	3.0
5. Calcium	1.4
6. Phosphorus	1.0
7. Magnesium	0.50
8. Potassium	0.34
9. Sulfur	0.26
10. Sodium	0.14

48 Chapter 3 Chemical Foundations: Elements, Atoms, and Ions

Trace Elements: Small but Crucial

We all know that certain chemical elements, such as calcium, carbon, nitrogen, phosphorus, and iron, are essential for humans to live. However, many other elements that are present in tiny amounts in the human body are also essential to life (see **Table 3.2**). Examples are chromium, cobalt, iodine, manganese, and copper. Chromium assists in the metabolism of sugars, cobalt is present in vitamin B_{12}, iodine is necessary for the proper functioning of the thyroid gland, manganese appears to play a role in maintaining the proper calcium levels in bones, and copper is involved in the production of red blood cells.

It is becoming clear that certain of the trace elements are very important in determining human behavior. For example, lithium (administered as lithium carbonate) has been a miracle drug for some people afflicted with manic-depressive syndrome, a disease in which a person's behavior varies between inappropriate "highs" and the blackest of depressions. Although its exact function remains unknown, lithium seems to balance out the levels of neurotransmitters (compounds that are essential to nerve function), relieving some of the extreme emotions in sufferers of manic-depressive disease.

In addition, a chemist named William Walsh has done some very interesting studies on the inmates of Stateville Prison in Illinois. By analyzing the trace elements in the hair of prisoners, he has found intriguing relationships between the behavior of the inmates and their trace element profile. For example, Walsh found an inverse relationship between the level of cobalt in the prisoner's body and the degree of violence in his behavior.

Besides the levels of trace elements in our bodies, our exposure to various substances in our water, our food, and the air we breathe also has great importance for our health. For example, many scientists are concerned about our exposure to aluminum, through aluminum compounds used in water purification, baked goods, and cheese (so that it melts easily when cooked), and the aluminum that dissolves from our cookware and utensils. The effects of exposure to low levels of aluminum on humans are not presently clear, but there are some indications that we should limit our intake of this element.

Another example of low-level exposure to an element is the fluoride placed in many water supplies and toothpastes to control tooth decay by making tooth enamel more resistant to dissolving. However, the exposure of large numbers of people to fluoride is quite controversial—some people think it is harmful.

The chemistry of trace elements is fascinating and important. Keep your eye on the news for further developments.

TABLE 3.2

Trace Elements in the Human Body

Trace Elements (in alphabetical order)

arsenic
chromium
cobalt
copper
fluorine
iodine
manganese
molybdenum
nickel
selenium
silicon
vanadium

---

when we use the term *element,* we mean a sample of the element large enough to weigh on a balance. Such a sample contains many, many atoms of the element, and we might call this the macroscopic form of the element. There is yet a further complication. As we will see in more detail in Section 3.9 the macroscopic forms of several elements contain molecules rather than individual atoms as the fundamental components. For example, chemists know that oxygen gas consists of molecules with two oxygen atoms connected together (represented as O—O or more commonly as O_2). Thus when we refer to the element oxygen we might mean a single atom of oxygen, a single O_2 molecule, or a macroscopic sample containing many O_2 molecules. Finally, we often use the term *element* in a generic fashion. When we say the human body contains the element sodium or lithium, we do not mean that free elemental sodium or lithium is present. Rather, we mean that atoms of these elements are present in some form. In this text we will try to make clear what we mean when we use the term *element* in a particular case.

3.1 The Elements **49**

Integrating the CHEMICAL IMPACT

Trace Elements: Small but Crucial

The "Trace Elements: Small but Crucial" feature points out that human behavior has an important chemical component. Elements that are present even in tiny amounts can have a crucial impact on the ways that a body functions. You can use this feature to integrate the study of chemistry with medicine, health, and biology.

MISCONCEPTIONS

Students often have difficulty understanding what is meant by chemical terms such as *element*. It is important to emphasize the various ways we use the term *element* in chemistry. When we say "element," we might mean a single atom, a molecule such as N_2 or O_2, or a large sample such as a bar of aluminum or the graphite ("lead") in a pencil. Be sure to help students realize that chemists use terms in many ways and that they need to look at the context of the word to make sure that they understand what is intended. Chemists are accustomed to thinking about things at the macroscopic and microscopic levels simultaneously. Encourage students to think about what they read and to consider how the terms are being used.

Themes
Systems, Organization

Skills
Classifying, interpreting data

3.2 Symbols for the Elements

Objective: *To learn the symbols of some elements.*

Gold nuggets and gold bars.

The names of the chemical elements have come from many sources. Often an element's name is derived from a Greek, Latin, or German word that describes some property of the element. For example, gold was originally called *aurum,* a Latin word meaning "shining dawn," and lead was known as *plumbum,* which means "heavy." The names for chlorine and iodine come from Greek words describing their colors, and the name for bromine comes from a Greek word meaning "stench." In addition, it is very common for an element to be named for the place where it was discovered. You can guess where the elements francium, germanium, californium*, and americium* were first found. Some of the heaviest elements are named after famous scientists—for example, einsteinium* and nobelium.*

We often use abbreviations to simplify the written word. For example, it is much easier to put MA on an envelope than to write out Massachusetts, and we often write USA instead of United States of America. Likewise, chemists have invented a set of abbreviations or **element symbols** for the chemical elements. These symbols usually consist of the first letter or the first two letters of the element names. The first letter is always capitalized, and the second is not.

CELEBRITY CHEMICAL

Iron (Fe)

Iron is an essential element in the body. Every molecule of hemoglobin contains four ions of iron. Hemoglobin is the component of blood that carries oxygen from the lungs to the tissues of the body. Iron deficiency in the diet causes a person to be fatigued, have a lower resistance to disease, and experience increased heart rate and respiration. Healthy adults need about 18 mg of iron daily. Iron is found in greatest concentrations in foods such as liver and kidneys. As most students are not fans of these items, they may relate better to high-iron foods such as egg yolks, some vegetables, and shellfish. Humans cannot absorb metallic iron directly. However, metallic iron does react with the hydrochloric acid in the stomach to produce Fe^{2+} and Fe^{3+}, which can be absorbed by the small intestine and used by the body.

Cereals sometimes have iron added as a food supplement. The demonstration at the right graphically shows the iron in cereal, which students find amazing. This iron is metallic iron. In the past, iron deficiency in children was often treated by cooking their meals in an iron skillet. Enough iron reacts with the food being prepared to increase the child's supply of usable iron.

CELEBRITY CHEMICAL

Iron (Fe)

Iron is a very important element that lies at the very heart of the earth. In fact, molten iron is thought to be the main component of the earth's core. Iron is also the fourth most abundant element in the earth's crust, found mainly in compounds with oxygen.

The earliest evidence of human use of iron dates back to about 4000 B.C. and takes the form of iron beads that are thought to have come from meteors striking the earth. The first humans to obtain iron from the ores found in the earth's crust were the Hittite peoples of Asia Minor in the third millennium B.C. The way in which the Hittites made iron weapons was one of the great military secrets of the ancient world. The process became widely known only after the fall of the Hittites around 1200 B.C., leading to the "Iron Age."

Two iron age axes found in Spain.

Of course, the major importance of iron in the modern world relates to its presence in steel. Steel is an alloy composed mainly of iron mixed with carbon and other metals. The principal structural material of our civilization, its annual production amounts to nearly a billion tons.

Although iron is extremely important as a construction material, it is even more important to human chemistry. Without the iron compounds in our systems we would die immediately. Iron compounds in the blood absorb oxygen from the air and transport it to the tissues, where it is stored by other iron compounds. Still more iron compounds assist oxygen in reacting with the fuel from our food to provide us with the energy to live, work, and play. Iron is truly essential to our lives.

*These elements are made artificially. They do not occur naturally.

50   Chapter 3   Chemical Foundations: Elements, Atoms, and Ions

TEACHING SUPPORT
Demonstration

Check Out This Cereal!

Materials
Box of cereal (use one with 100% iron or "reduced iron" on the label) (Total or Special K works well)
Bar magnet or magnetic stirrer magnet
Large zip-lock bag
Large beaker

Magnetic stir plate (optional)

Procedure Place about a cup of the cereal in the zip-lock bag. Have a student crush the cereal into small pieces. Pour the crushed cereal into the beaker and cover it with water. Stir until the cereal becomes soggy. Place the magnetic stirrer into the beaker and place the setup on the stir plate. Start stirring and continue for 15 to 20 minutes. If not using a stir plate, at-

tach the stirrer to a pencil or paint stick and stir the mixture for about 10 minutes. Remove the magnet from the mixture and show the students the dark-colored iron filings on the magnet. You can then remove the filings to a piece of white paper and show the students that the filings are attracted to a magnet held under the paper.

For example,

fluorine	F	neon	Ne
oxygen	O	silicon	Si
carbon	C		

Sometimes, however, the two letters used are not the first two letters in the name. For example,

zinc	Zn	cadmium	Cd
chlorine	Cl	platinum	Pt

The symbols for some other elements are based on the original Latin or Greek name.

Current Name	Original Name	Symbol
gold	aurum	Au
lead	plumbum	Pb
sodium	natrium	Na
iron	ferrum	Fe

A list of the most common elements and their symbols is given in **Table 3.3.** You can also see the elements represented on a table in the inside back cover of this text. We will explain the form of this table (which is called the periodic table) in later chapters.

TABLE 3.3

The Names and Symbols of the Most Common Elements

Element	Symbol	Element	Symbol
aluminum	Al	lithium	Li
antimony (stibium)*	Sb	magnesium	Mg
argon	Ar	manganese	Mn
arsenic	As	mercury (hydrargyrum)	Hg
barium	Ba	neon	Ne
bismuth	Bi	nickel	Ni
boron	B	nitrogen	N
bromine	Br	oxygen	O
cadmium	Cd	phosphorus	P
calcium	Ca	platinum	Pt
carbon	C	potassium (kalium)	K
chlorine	Cl	radium	Ra
chromium	Cr	silicon	Si
cobalt	Co	silver (argentium)	Ag
copper (cuprum)	Cu	sodium (natrium)	Na
fluorine	F	strontium	Sr
gold (aurum)	Au	sulfur	S
helium	He	tin (stannum)	Sn
hydrogen	H	titanium	Ti
iodine	I	tungsten (wolfram)	W
iron (ferrum)	Fe	uranium	U
lead (plumbum)	Pb	zinc	Zn

*Where appropriate, the original name is shown in parentheses so that you can see the sources of some of the symbols.

CHEMISTRY

In the symbol for an element, only the first letter is capitalized.

TEACHING TIPS

- Water pipes were once made of lead. This is the origin of the word "plumber."

- The only way to learn the symbols for the elements is to memorize them. Some symbol pairs, such as Au/Ag, Na/S, K/P, and Mg/Mn, are easily confused. Have students make flash cards with the element name on one side and the symbol on the other.

- In class, make several groupings of the symbols for the elements, such as the following:

  Symbols unrelated to the name
  Elements beginning with *C*
  Elements with single-letter symbols
  Elements named after a place
  Elements named after a planet

  Such a system breaks the large group of elements into smaller groups that are easier to learn.

USING TECHNOLOGY

 Table 3.3

Section 3.3

Themes
Organization, Models, Patterns of Change

Skills
Applying concepts, developing models

Laboratory
Experiment 11:
Aluminum Atoms, Traditional

3.3 Dalton's Atomic Theory

Objectives: *To learn about Dalton's theory of atoms.*
To understand and illustrate the law of constant composition.

As scientists of the eighteenth century studied the nature of materials, several things became clear:

1. Most natural materials are mixtures of pure substances.

2. Pure substances are either elements or combinations of elements called compounds.

3. A given compound always contains the same proportions (by mass) of the elements. For example, water *always* contains 8 g of oxygen for every 1 g of hydrogen, and carbon dioxide *always* contains 2.7 g of oxygen for every 1 g of carbon. This principle became known as the **law of constant composition.** It means that a given compound always has the same composition, regardless of where it comes from.

John Dalton (**Figure 3.1**), an English scientist and teacher, was aware of these observations. In about 1808 he offered an explanation for them that became known as **Dalton's atomic theory.** The main ideas of this theory (model) can be stated as follow

Figure 3.1
John Dalton (1766–1844) was an English scientist who made his living as a teacher in Manchester. Although Dalton is best known for his atomic theory, he made contributions in many other areas, including meteorology (he recorded daily weather conditions for 46 years, producing a total of 200,000 data entries). A rather shy man, Dalton was colorblind to red (a special handicap for a chemist) and suffered from lead poisoning contracted from drinking stout (strong beer or ale) that had been drawn through lead pipes.

Dalton's Atomic Theory

1. Elements are made of tiny particles called **atoms.**

2. All atoms of a given element are identical.

3. The atoms of a given element are different from those of any other element.

4. Atoms of one element can combine with atoms of other elements to form compounds. A given compound always has the same relative numbers and types of atoms.

5. Atoms are indivisible in chemical processes. That is, atoms are not created or destroyed in chemical reactions. A chemical reaction simply changes the way the atoms are grouped together.

Dalton's model successfully explained important observations such as the law of constant composition. This law makes sense because if a compound always contains the same relative numbers of atoms, it will always contain the same proportions by mass of the various elements.

Like most new ideas, Dalton's model was not accepted immediately. However, Dalton was convinced he was right and *used his model to predict* how a given pair of elements might combine to form more than one compound. For example, nitrogen and oxygen might form a compound containing one atom of nitrogen and one atom of oxygen (written NO), a compound containing two atoms of nitrogen and one atom of oxygen (written N_2O), a compound containing one atom of nitrogen and two atoms of oxygen

52   Chapter 3   Chemical Foundations: Elements, Atoms, and Ions

---

No Laughing Matter

Sometimes solving one problem leads to another. One such example involves the catalytic converters now required on all automobiles sold in much of the world. The purpose of these converters is to remove harmful pollutants such as CO and NO_2 from automobile exhausts. The good news is that these devices are quite effective and have led to much cleaner air in congested areas. The bad news is that these devices produce significant amounts of nitrous oxide, N_2O, commonly known as laughing gas because when inhaled it produces relaxation and mild inebriation. It was long used by dentists to make their patients more tolerant of some painful dental procedures.

The problem with N_2O is not that it is an air pollutant but that it is a "greenhouse gas." Certain molecules, such as CO_2, CH_4, N_2O, and others, strongly absorb infrared light ("heat radiation"), which causes the earth's atmosphere to retain more of its heat energy. Human activities have significantly increased the concentrations of these gases in the atmosphere. Mounting evidence suggests that the earth is warming as a result, leading to possible dramatic changes in climate.

A recent study by the Environmental Protection Agency (EPA) indicates that N_2O now accounts for over 7% of the greenhouse gases in the atmosphere and that automobiles equipped with catalytic converters produce nearly half of this N_2O. Ironically, N_2O is not regulated, because the Clean Air Act of 1970 was written to control smog—not greenhouse gases. The United States and other industrialized nations are now negotiating to find ways to control global warming but no agreement is now in place.

The N_2O situation illustrates just how complex environmental issues are. Clean may not necessarily be "green."

Figure 3.2
Dalton pictured compounds as collections of atoms. Here NO, NO_2, and N_2O are represented. Note that the number of atoms of each type in a molecule is given by a subscript, except that the number 1 is always assumed and never written.

(written NO_2), and so on **(Figure 3.2)**. When the existence of these substances was verified, it was a triumph for Dalton's model. Because Dalton was able to predict correctly the formation of multiple compounds between two elements, his atomic theory became widely accepted.

Focus Questions

Sections 3.1–3.3

1. Give four different chemical meanings for the word *element* and an example of each.
2. How many of the Top Ten elements in the human body are also Top Ten elements in Earth's crust, ocean, and atmosphere? What are these elements?
3. List the elements that you think were named after a place.
4. What observations led Dalton to propose his model for the atom?
5. Did Dalton's model of the atom include protons, neutrons, and electrons inside the atoms? Why or why not?

3.3 Dalton's Atomic Theory   **53**

No Laughing Matter

"No Laughing Matter" brings up the problem of greenhouse gases. The topic is very much in the news and would make a good project for which the students go onto the Internet to search for information. A powerful new greenhouse gas (SF_5CF_3, trifluoromethyl sulfur pentafluoride) has recently been identified that absorbs 18,000 times as much infrared radiation as carbon dioxide does. The SF_5CF_3 is present in only tiny amounts (0.1 part per trillion) now, but its concentration seems to be increasing slowly due to leakage from high-voltage equipment, where it is formed from the reaction of the SF_6 gas and fluorinated hydrocarbons.

Answers to Focus Questions

1. 1. a single atom; an atom of aluminum
   2. a sample of measurable size; 5.0 g of potassium
   3. a molecule of an element; a molecule of oxygen
   4. one of the building blocks of the universe; helium

2. Six: oxygen, hydrogen, calcium, magnesium, potassium, sodium

3. The list could include berkelium, californium, dubnium, europium, francium, germanium, americium, neptunium, plutonium, polonium, and uranium.

4. The observations that led Dalton to propose his atomic theory are:
   1. Most natural materials are mixtures of pure substances.
   2. Pure compounds are either elements or compounds.
   3. A given compound always contains the same proportions (by mass) of the elements.

5. Dalton's model of the atom did not include protons, neutrons, or electrons, because they were not known at the time he developed his theory.

Themes
Organization, Patterns of Change

Skills
Using the writing process, applying concepts, making comparisons

Laboratory
Experiment 12:
Electrolysis, Traditional

TEACHING TIP

Relate the formulas of simple compounds to drawings of the molecules. Place a formula on the board and have the students draw a representation of it. Focus on the number and kind of atoms in the molecule; don't worry about shape at this time. Ideas for some interactive examples are H_2O, NH_3, CO_2, and CH_4.

Additional Examples

Write the formula for each of the following compounds, listing the elements in the order given:

1. A molecule containing six carbon atoms and six hydrogen atoms.
   C_6H_6

2. A compounud containing half as many calcium atoms as chlorine atoms.
   $CaCl_2$

3. A compound containing equal numbers of sodium and nitrogen atoms, but three times as many oxygen atoms as there are sodium atoms.
   $NaNO_3$

3.4 Formulas of Compounds

Objective: *To learn how a formula describes a compound's composition.*

Here, *relative* refers to ratios.

A compound is a distinct substance that is composed of the atoms of two or more elements and always contains exactly the same relative masses of those elements. In light of Dalton's atomic theory, this simply means that a compound always contains the same relative *numbers* of atoms of each element. For example, water always contains two hydrogen atoms for each oxygen atom.

The types of atoms and the number of each type in each unit (molecule) of a given compound are conveniently expressed by a **chemical formula**. In a chemical formula the atoms are indicated by the element symbols, and the number of each type of atom is indicated by a subscript, a number that appears to the right of and below the symbol for the element. The formula for water is written H_2O, indicating that each molecule of water contains two atoms of hydrogen and one atom of oxygen (the subscript 1 is always understood and not written). Following are some general rules for writing formulas:

Rules for Writing Formulas

1. Each atom present is represented by its element symbol.
2. The number of each type of atom is indicated by a subscript written to the right of the element symbol.
3. When only one atom of a given type is present, the subscript 1 is not written.

Example 3.1

Writing Formulas of Compounds

Write the formula for each of the following compounds, listing the elements in the order given.

a. Each molecule of a compound that has been implicated in the formation of acid rain contains one atom of sulfur and three atoms of oxygen.

b. Each molecule of a certain compound contains two atoms of nitrogen and five atoms of oxygen.

c. Each molecule of glucose, a type of sugar, contains six atoms of carbon, twelve atoms of hydrogen, and six atoms of oxygen.

Solution

c.

Symbol for carbon ⟶ ⟶ Symbol for hydrogen ⟶ ⟵ Symbol for oxygen

$$C_6H_{12}O_6$$

Six atoms of carbon — Twelve atoms of hydrogen — Six atoms of oxygen

 Self-Check Exercise 3.1

Write the formula for each of the following compounds, listing the elements in the order given.

a. A molecule contains four phosphorus atoms and ten oxygen atoms.

b. A molecule contains one uranium atom and six fluorine atoms.

c. A molecule contains one aluminum atom and three chlorine atoms.

3.5 The Structure of the Atom

Objectives: *To learn about the internal parts of an atom.*
To understand Rutherford's experiment to characterize the atom's structure.

Dalton's atomic theory, proposed in about 1808, provided such a convincing explanation for the composition of compounds that it became generally accepted. Scientists came to believe that *elements consist of atoms* and that *compounds are a specific collection of atoms* bound together in some way. As does any new theory, Dalton's model of the atom spawned many new questions, including: What causes atoms to "stick together" to form compounds? and What is an atom like? It might be a tiny ball of matter that is the same throughout with no internal structure—like a ball bearing. Or the atom might be composed of parts—it might be made up of a number of subatomic particles. But if the atom contains parts, there should be some way to break up the atom into its components.

Many scientists pondered the nature of the atom during the 1800s, but it was not until almost 1900 that convincing evidence became available to show that the atom has a number of different parts.

Thomson's Experiment

A physicist in England named J. J. Thomson showed in the late 1890s that the atoms of any element can be made to emit tiny negative particles. (He knew they had a negative charge because he could show that they were repelled by the negative part of an electric field.) Thus he concluded that all types of atoms must contain these negative particles, which are now called **electrons.**

On the basis of his results, Thomson wondered what an atom must be like. Although atoms contain these tiny negative particles, he also knew that whole atoms are not negatively *or* positively charged. Thus he concluded that the atom must also contain positive particles that balance exactly the negative charge carried by the electrons, giving the atom a zero overall charge.

3.5 The Structure of the Atom **55**

 Answers to Self-Check Exercise 3.1

a. P_4O_{10}

b. UF_6

c. $AlCl_3$

 Section 3.5

Themes
Organization, Form and Function, Models

Skills
Classifying, making comparisons, developing models, evaluating

USING TECHNOLOGY

Animation and Video

***Chemistry in Motion* Demonstration 1, Cathode Ray Tube**
The cathode ray tube can be used to show how the beam of particles (electrons) can be deflected by a magnet.

Figure 3.4
Ernest Rutherford (1871–1937) was born on a farm in New Zealand. In 1895 he placed second in a scholarship competition to attend Cambridge University but was awarded the scholarship when the winner decided to stay home and get married. Rutherford was an intense, hard-driving person who became a master at designing just the right experiment to test a given idea. He was awarded the Nobel Prize in chemistry in 1908.

The Plum Pudding Model

Another scientist pondering the structure of the atom was William Thomson (better known as Lord Kelvin and no relation to J. J. Thomson). Lord Kelvin got the idea (which might have occurred to him during dinner) that the atom might be something like plum pudding (a pudding with raisins randomly distributed throughout). Kelvin reasoned that the atom might be thought of as a uniform "pudding" of positive charge with enough negative electrons scattered within to counterbalance that positive charge (see **Figure 3.3**). Thus the plum pudding model of the atom came into being.

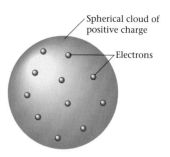

Figure 3.3
One of the early models of the atom was the plum pudding model, in which the electrons were pictured as embedded in a positively charged spherical cloud, much as raisins are distributed in an old-fashioned plum pudding.

Rutherford's Experiment

If you had taken this course in 1910, the plum pudding model would have been the only picture of the atom described. However, our ideas about the atom were changed dramatically in 1911 by a physicist named Ernest Rutherford **(Figure 3.4),** who learned physics in J. J. Thomson's laboratory in the late 1890s. By 1911 Rutherford had become a distinguished scientist with many important discoveries to his credit. One of his main areas of interest involved alpha particles (α particles), positively charged particles with a mass approximately 7500 times that of an electron. In studying the flight of these particles through air, Rutherford found that some of the α particles were deflected by something in the air. Puzzled by this, he designed an experiment that involved directing α particles toward a thin metal foil. Surrounding the foil was a detector coated with a substance that produced tiny flashes wherever it was hit by an α particle **(Figure 3.5).** The results of the experiment were very different from those Rutherford anticipated. Although most of the

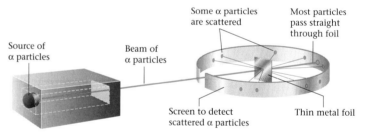

Figure 3.5
Rutherford's experiment on α-particle bombardment of metal foil.

α particles passed straight through the foil, some of the particles were
deflected at large angles, as shown in Figure 3.5, and some were reflected
backward.

This outcome was a great surprise to Rutherford. (He described this result
as comparable to shooting a gun at a piece of paper and having the bullet
bounce back.) Rutherford knew that if the plum pudding model of the atom
was correct, the massive α particles would crash through the thin foil like
cannonballs through paper (as shown in **Figure 3.6a**). So he expected the
α particles to travel through the foil experiencing, at most, very minor deflections of their paths.

Figure 3.6
(a) The results that the metal
foil experiment would have
yielded if the plum pudding
model had been correct.
(b) Actual results.

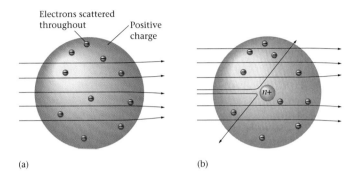

Electrons scattered throughout — Positive charge

(a)   (b)

CHEMISTRY
If the atom were expanded to
the size of a huge stadium like
the Astrodome, the nucleus
would be only about as big as
a fly at the center.

Rutherford concluded from these results that the plum pudding model
for the atom could not be correct. The large deflections of the α particles
could be caused only by a center of concentrated positive charge that would
repel the positively charged α particles, as illustrated in **Figure 3.6b.** Most
of the α particles passed directly through the foil because the atom is mostly
open space. The deflected α particles were those that had a "close encounter"
with the positive center of the atom, and the few reflected α particles were
those that scored a "direct hit" on the positive center. In Rutherford's mind
these results could be explained only in terms of a **nuclear atom**—an atom
with a dense center of positive charge (the **nucleus**) around which tiny electrons moved in a space that was otherwise empty.

He concluded that the nucleus must have a positive charge to balance
the negative charge of the electrons and that it must be small and dense.
What was it made of? By 1919 Rutherford concluded that the nucleus of an
atom contained what he called protons. A **proton** has the same magnitude
(size) of charge as the electron, but its charge is *positive*. We say that the
proton has a charge of 1+ and the electron a charge of 1−.

Rutherford reasoned that the hydrogen atom has a single proton at its
center and one electron moving through space at a relatively large distance
from the proton (the hydrogen nucleus). He also reasoned that other atoms
must have nuclei (the plural of *nucleus*) composed of many protons bound
together somehow. In addition, Rutherford and a coworker, James Chadwick,
were able to show in 1932 that most nuclei also contain a neutral particle
that they named the **neutron.** A neutron is slightly more massive than a proton but has no charge.

acknowledged the growing
women's rights movement by
allowing women to enter the
laboratory). Despite the prominence of Thomson and his laboratory, the suggestion that
these negative particles came
from inside atoms (that is, were
subatomic particles) was not
received with enthusiasm by
the scientific community. In
fact, in the 1890s many physicists did not even believe in the

existence of atoms.

TEACHING TIPS

- Emphasize the tiny size of the nucleus compared to the atom. One example is given in the text: If the nucleus were the size of a grape, the radius of the atom would be about one mile.

- Also emphasize that questioning theories is what science is all about. Theories are always questioned to refine and improve them or to cause them to be refuted.

CHEMICAL IMPACT

Glowing Tubes for Signs, Television Sets, and Computers

J. J. Thomson discovered that atoms contain electrons by using a device called a cathode ray tube (often abbreviated CRT today). When he did these experiments, he could not have imagined that he was making television sets and computer monitors possible. A cathode ray tube is a sealed glass tube that contains a gas and has separated metal plates connected to external wires **(Figure 3.7)**. When a source of electrical energy is applied to the metal plates, a glowing beam is produced **(Figure 3.8)**. Thomson became convinced that the glowing gas was caused by a stream of negatively charged particles coming from the metal plate. In addition, because Thomson always got the same kind of negative particles no matter what metal he used, he concluded that all types of atoms must contain these same negative particles (we now call them electrons).

Thomson's cathode ray tube has many modern applications. For example, "neon" signs consist of small-diameter cathode ray tubes containing different kinds of gases to produce various colors. For example, if the gas in the tube is neon, the tube glows with a red–orange color; if argon is present, a blue glow appears. The presence of krypton gives an intense white light.

A television picture tube or computer monitor is also fundamentally a cathode ray tube. In this case the electrons are directed onto a screen containing chemical compounds that glow when struck by fast-moving electrons. The use of various compounds that emit different colors when they are struck by the electrons makes color pictures possible on the screens of these CRTs.

Figure 3.7
Schematic of a cathode ray tube. A stream of electrons passes between the electrodes. The fast-moving particles excite the gas in the tube, causing a glow between the plates.

Figure 3.8
A CRT being used to display computer graphics.

TEACHING SUPPORT
Background Information

Radioactivity was discovered accidently by Antoine Henri Becquerel in 1896, when he stored a piece of potassium uranyl sulfate in a drawer with some photographic plates and found that the rock emitted radiation that exposed the plates. Although Becquerel was awarded a Nobel Prize for his discovery (in 1903), he didn't understand the composition of the radiation in 1896. The first clue to the nature of radioactivity came in 1897, when J. J. Thomson discovered the corpuscles of electricity now called electrons. The first person to study radioactivity in a systematic way, however, was Ernest Rutherford. In his studies at the Cavendish Laboratory, Rutherford learned that radioactive materials spewed out huge numbers of particles that traveled at thousands of miles per second. Rutherford found two distinct types of particles, which he named alpha and beta rays (now called particles). He found that while alpha particles were stopped by a sheet of paper, beta particles were highly penetrating. (In 1900, Becquerel showed that beta particles were

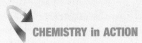
3.6 Introduction to the Modern Concept of Atomic Structure

Objective: *To describe some important features of subatomic particles.*

Nucleus

~10⁻¹³cm

~10⁻⁸cm

Figure 3.9
A nuclear atom viewed in cross section. (The symbol ~ means approximately.) This drawing does not show the actual scale. The nucleus is actually much smaller compared with the size of an atom.

CHEMISTRY

In this model the atom is called a nuclear atom because the positive charge is localized in a small, compact structure (the nucleus) and not spread out uniformly, as in the plum pudding view.

CHEMISTRY

The *chemistry* of an atom arises from its electrons.

WHAT IF?

The average diameter of an atom is 1.3×10^{-10} m.

What if the average diameter of an atom were 1 cm? How tall would you be?

In the years since Thomson and Rutherford, a great deal has been learned about atomic structure. The simplest view of the atom is that it consists of a tiny nucleus (about 10^{-13} cm in diameter) and electrons that move about the nucleus at an average distance of about 10^{-8} cm from it (**Figure 3.9**). To visualize how small the nucleus is compared with the size of the atom, consider that if the nucleus were the size of a grape, the electrons would be about one *mile* away on average. The nucleus contains protons, which have a positive charge equal in magnitude to the electrons' negative charge, and neutrons, which have almost the same mass as protons but no charge. The neutrons' function in the nucleus is not obvious. They may help hold the protons (which repel each other) together to form the nucleus, but we will not be concerned with that here. The relative masses and charges of the electron, proton, and neutron are shown in **Table 3.4**.

TABLE 3.4
The Mass and Charge of the Electron, Proton, and Neutron

Particle	Relative Mass*	Relative Charge
electron	1	1−
proton	1836	1+
neutron	1839	none

*The electron is arbitrarily assigned a mass of 1 for comparison.

An important question arises at this point: *If all atoms are composed of these same components, why do different atoms have different chemical properties?* The answer lies in the number and arrangement of the electrons. The space in which the electrons move accounts for most of the atomic volume. The electrons are the parts of atoms that "intermingle" when atoms combine to form molecules. Therefore, the number of electrons a given atom possesses greatly affects the way it can interact with other atoms. As a result, atoms of different elements, which have different numbers of electrons, show different chemical behavior. Although the atoms of different elements also differ in their numbers of protons, it is the number of electrons that really determines chemical behavior. We will discuss how this happens in later chapters.

CHEMISTRY in ACTION

How Big Is an Atom?

1. Get a strip of paper 11″ by 1″.
2. Cut the paper in half. Discard one piece.
3. Repeat step 2 until you can no longer cut the paper. How many times could you cut it?
4. How many times would you need to cut the paper to have a piece of paper remaining that is the same width as an atom? (Average atom diameter = 1.3×10^{-10} m.)

actually high-speed electrons.) In 1898, Rutherford moved to McGill University in Canada where he continued his life's work—the study of alpha particles. After four years of work Rutherford concluded that alpha particles are helium nuclei. One curious thing that Rutherford learned about alpha particles is that they don't travel in a straight line through air, because they are deflected by the oxygen and ni-

trogen molecules. After moving to the University of Manchester in 1907 and winning the Nobel Prize in 1908, Rutherford was determined to find out how alpha particles were deflected by matter. With the help of his assistant, Hans Geiger, and an undergraduate, Ernest Marsden, he set up an experiment in which alpha particles were directed at a thin metal foil, backed by a metal screen that gave flashes of light

when struck by an alpha particle. To see the tiny flashes the scientists had to sit in the absolute dark for more than an hour before the experiment. In 1909, Marsden was able to demonstrate that one in 8000 alpha particles rebounded from the foil—and the age of the nuclear atom was born.

CHEMISTRY in ACTION

How Big Is an Atom?

Materials Each student/group will need an 11″ by 1″ piece of paper, a pair of scissors, and a calculator.

Purpose Students will better appreciate the small size of an atom. In addition, they will get practice at problem solving.

Discussion A strip of paper 11″ long is 27.94 cm or 0.2794 m. If this number is divided in half 31 times, you get 1.3×10^{-10}.

A more systematic solution is (disregarding significant figures)

$0.2974 \text{ m}/2^x = 1.3 \times 10^{-10}$ m (x = the number of times the paper needs to be cut in half)

$0.2794 \text{ m}/1.3 \times 10^{-10}$ m = 2^x

$2.149 \times 10^9 = 2^x$

$\log(2.149 \times 10^9) = x\log 2$

$x = \log(2.149 \times 10^9)/\log 2$

= 31

Instead of measuring the paper, students can fold the paper in half to see where to cut it. After cutting the paper about six times it is hard to fold in half. After seven times it is hard to cut. Most students will find that eight or nine is the maximum number of cuts they can make. While 31 may seem like a small number of cuts to reach atomic size, this means that the students would have to cut that paper more than 20 more times to reach the size of an average atom.

WHAT IF Comments

Assume you are 6 feet tall (1.83 m). If atoms are simply stacked on top of each other, there would be approximately 1.4×10^{10} atoms [$1.83/(1.3 \times 10^{-10})$] from your head to your toes. If each atom were 1 cm, you would be 1.4×10^{10} cm tall, which is approximately 460 million feet tall.

Themes
Organization, Patterns of
Change, Form and Function

Skills
Applying concepts, interpreting
diagrams, making comparisons,
making predictions

TEACHING TIPS

- Students learned in Section 3.5 that the overall charge on an atom is zero. At this point you need to emphasize that the charge is zero because the number of negatively charged electrons equals the number of positively charged protons.

- The discussion of protons leads to an excellent example of how and why models change. Dalton's model of the atom did not account for isotopes, because he assumed that all atoms of an element are exactly alike. As knowledge expands, models change to accommodate the new information.

- The mass number represents the sum of the *numbers* of protons and neutrons. Students often believe that the mass number should be the sum of the masses of the protons and neutrons. Make sure they are clear on this point.

3.7 Isotopes

Objectives: *To learn about the terms* **isotope, atomic number,** *and* **mass number.**
To understand the use of the symbol ${}^{A}_{Z}X$ to describe a given atom.

CHEMISTRY

All atoms of same element have the same number of protons (the element's atomic number) and the same number of electrons.

In a free atom, the positive and negative charges always balance to yield a net zero charge.

Atomic number: the number of protons.

Mass number: the sum of protons and neutrons.

We have seen that an atom has a nucleus with a positive charge due to its protons and has electrons in the space surrounding the nucleus at relatively large distances from it.

As an example, consider a sodium atom, which has 11 protons in its nucleus. Because an atom has no overall charge, the number of electrons must equal the number of protons. Therefore, a sodium atom has 11 electrons in the space around its nucleus. It is *always* true that a sodium atom has 11 protons and 11 electrons. However, each sodium atom also has neutrons in its nucleus, and different types of sodium atoms exist that have different numbers of neutrons.

When Dalton stated his atomic theory in the early 1800s, he assumed all of the atoms of a given element were identical. This idea persisted for over 100 years, until James Chadwick discovered that the nuclei of most atoms contain neutrons as well as protons. (This is a good example of how a theory changes as new observations are made.) After the discovery of the neutron, Dalton's statement that all atoms of a given element are identical had to be changed to "All atoms of the same element contain the same number of protons and electrons, but atoms of a given element may have different numbers of neutrons."

To illustrate this idea, consider the sodium atoms depicted in **Figure 3.10.** These atoms are **isotopes,** or *atoms with the same number of protons but different numbers of neutrons.* The number of protons in a nucleus is called the atom's **atomic number.** The *sum* of the number of neutrons and the number of protons in a given nucleus is called the atom's **mass number.** To specify which of the isotopes of an element we are talking

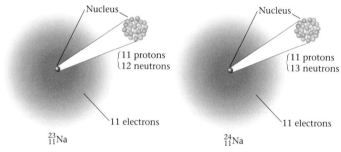

Figure 3.10
Two isotopes of sodium. Both have 11 protons and 11 electrons, but they differ in the number of neutrons in their nuclei.

60   Chapter 3   Chemical Foundations: Elements, Atoms, and Ions

about, we use the symbol

$$^A_Z X$$

where

> X = the symbol of the element

> A = the mass number (sum of protons and neutrons)

> Z = the atomic number (number of protons)

For example, the symbol for one particular type of sodium atom is written

Mass number
(sum of protons and neutrons)

$$^{23}_{11}\text{Na} \longleftarrow \text{Element symbol}$$

Atomic number
(number of protons)

The particular atom represented here is called sodium-23, because it has a mass number of 23. Let's specify the number of each type of subatomic particle. From the atomic number 11 we know that the nucleus contains 11 protons. And because the number of electrons is equal to the number of protons, we know that this atom contains 11 electrons. How many neutrons are present? We can calculate the number of neutrons from the definition of the mass number

> Mass number = number of protons + number of neutrons

or, in symbols,

> $A = Z +$ number of neutrons

We can isolate (solve for) the number of neutrons by subtracting Z from both sides of the equation

> $A - Z = Z - Z +$ number of neutrons

> $A - Z =$ number of neutrons

This is a general result. You can always determine the number of neutrons present in a given atom by subtracting the atomic number from the mass number. In this case ($^{23}_{11}\text{Na}$), we know that $A = 23$ and $Z = 11$. Thus

> $A - Z = 23 - 11 = 12 =$ number of neutrons

In summary, sodium-23 has 11 electrons, 11 protons, and 12 neutrons.

Example 3.2

Interpreting Symbols for Isotopes

In nature, elements are usually found as a mixture of isotopes. The three isotopes of elemental carbon are $^{12}_6C$ (carbon-12), $^{13}_6C$ (carbon-13), and $^{14}_6C$ (carbon-14). Determine the number of each of the three types of subatomic particles in each of these carbon atoms.

(continued)

Additional Examples

Determine the number of each of the three types of subatomic particles for each of the following:

1. $^{60}_{27}\text{Co}$

2. $^{37}_{17}\text{Cl}$

3. $^{238}_{92}\text{U}$

Answers (assumes each of the above are uncharged):

1. #protons = #electrons = 27, #neutrons = 33 (60 − 27)

2. #protons = #electrons = 2 = 17, #neutrons = 20 (37 = 17)

3. #protons = #electrons = 92, #neutrons = 146 (238 − 92)

(continued)

Solution

The number of protons and electrons is the same in each of the isotopes and is given by the atomic number of carbon, 6. The number of neutrons can be determined by subtracting the atomic number (Z) from the mass number:

$$A - Z = \text{number of neutrons}$$

The numbers of neutrons in the three isotopes of carbon are

$^{12}_{6}C$: number of neutrons = $A - Z = 12 - 6 = 6$

$^{13}_{6}C$: number of neutrons = $13 - 6 = 7$

$^{14}_{6}C$: number of neutrons = $14 - 6 = 8$

In summary,

Symbol	Number of Protons	Number of Electrons	Number of Neutrons
$^{12}_{6}C$	6	6	6
$^{13}_{6}C$	6	6	7
$^{14}_{6}C$	6	6	8

 Self-Check Exercise 3.2

Give the number of protons, neutrons, and electrons in the atom symbolized by $^{90}_{38}Sr$. Strontium-90 occurs in fallout from nuclear testing. It can accumulate in bone marrow and may cause leukemia and bone cancer.

 Self-Check Exercise 3.3

Give the number of protons, neutrons, and electrons in the atom symbolized by $^{201}_{80}Hg$.

Example 3.3

Magnesium burns in air to give a bright white flame.

Writing Symbols for Isotopes

Write the symbol for the magnesium atom (atomic number 12) with a mass number of 24. How many electrons and how many neutrons does this atom have?

Solution

The atomic number 12 means the atom has 12 protons. The element magnesium is symbolized by Mg. The atom is represented as

$^{24}_{12}Mg$

and is called magnesium-24. Because the atom has 12 protons, it must also have 12 electrons. The mass number gives the total number of protons and neutrons, which means that this atom has 12 neutrons ($24 - 12 = 12$).

62 Chapter 3 Chemical Foundations: Elements, Atoms, and Ions

 Answer to Self-Check Exercise 3.2

In the symbol $^{90}_{38}Sr$, the number 38 is the atomic number, which represents the number of protons in the nucleus of a strontium atom. Because the atom is neutral overall, it must also have 38 electrons. The number 90 (the mass number) represents the number of protons plus the number of neutrons. Thus the number of neutrons is $A - Z = 90 - 38 = 52$.

 Answer to Self-Check Exercise 3.3

The atom $^{201}_{80}Hg$ has 80 protons, 80 electrons, and $201 - 80 = 121$ neutrons.

Additional Examples

Write the symbol for each of the following atoms, and list the number of protons, neutrons, and electrons for each.

1. The cesium atom with a mass number of 132.

2. The iron atom with a mass number of 56.

Answers (assumes each are uncharged):

1. $^{132}_{55}Cs$,
   #protons = #electrons = 55,
   #neutrons = 77 (132 − 55)

2. $^{56}_{26}Fe$,
   #protons = #electrons = 26,
   #neutrons = 30 (56 − 26)

Example 3.4

Calculating Mass Number

Write the symbol for the silver atom ($Z = 47$) that has 61 neutrons.

Solution

The element symbol is $_{Z}^{A}Ag$, where we know that $Z = 47$. We can find A from its definition, $A = Z +$ number of neutrons. In this case,

$$A = 47 + 61 = 108$$

The complete symbol for this atom is $_{47}^{108}Ag$.

 Self-Check Exercise 3.4

Give the symbol for the phosphorus atom ($Z = 15$) that contains 17 neutrons.

 Focus Questions ⌕ **Sections 3.4–3.7**

1. How is Thomson's model of the atom different from Dalton's model of the atom? Draw a picture of each.
2. What caused Rutherford to propose a revised model of the atom? How is the Rutherford model different from the previous models?
3. What are the names, charges, and locations of the major subatomic particles in our modern model of the atom?
4. If all atoms contain the same types of subatomic particles, why do different atoms have different chemical properties?
5. In two isotopes of the same element, which of the following would be the same and which would be different?

    atomic number
    number of protons
    number of neutrons
    number of electrons
    element symbol

3.8   Introduction to the Periodic Table

Objectives: *To learn about various features of the periodic table.*
To learn some of the properties of metals, nonmetals, and metalloids.

In any room where chemistry is taught or practiced, you are almost certain to find a chart called the **periodic table** hanging on the wall. This chart shows all of the known elements and gives a good deal of information about each. As our study of chemistry progresses, the usefulness of the periodic table will become more obvious. This section will simply introduce it.

3.8   Introduction to the Periodic Table   **63**

Additional Examples

Write the symbol for each of the following:

1. The krypton atom that has 48 neutrons.
$_{36}^{84}Kr$

2. The nitrogen atom that has 6 neutrons.
$_{7}^{13}N$

 Answer to Self-Check Exercise 3.4

The atomic number for phosphorus is 15 and the mass number is $15 + 17 = 32$. Thus the symbol for the atom is $_{15}^{32}P$.

 Answers to Focus Questions

1. Thomson's model of the atom shows positive charges and negative charges uniformly distributed throughout the atoms. Neutral atoms have equal amounts of positive and negative charges. In Dalton's model atoms are not charged and are indivisible, containing no positive or negative areas within them.

2. Rutherford proposed a revised model of the atom when he could not explain how an alpha particle could be deflected when passing through a sheet of gold foil. In Rutherford's model of the atom, the mass of the atom is concentrated in a very small area in the center of the atom known as the nucleus. The remainder of the

---

atom is mostly empty space. In the previous models of the atom, the atom was believed to be of approximately uniform density.

3. A proton has a 1+ charge and is located in the nucleus. A neutron has no charge and is located in the nucleus. An electron has a 1− charge and is located in the space outside the nucleus.

4. The differences in chemical properties relate to the ways in which electrons interact with other atoms. The number of protons determines the type of atom and the number and arrangement of the electrons determine the type of chemical interaction that the atoms will undergo.

5. Things that are the same in two isotopes are atomic number, number of protons, number of electrons, and element symbol. Things that are different in two isotopes are number of neutrons and mass.

3.8 Section 3.8

Themes
Organization, Patterns of Change, Form and Function

Skills
Applying concepts, interpreting diagrams, making comparisons, making predictions

Student Preparation
Assign the students to read Sections 3.8 to 3.11 and to answer the Focus Questions at the end of Section 3.11 before coming to class.

Active Learning
After introducing the material in Sections 3.8 to 3.11 in class, place the students in groups and have them work together on Sections 3.8–3.11: Team Learning Worksheet. Answers and/or discussion of these questions are located in the *Teacher Resources*.

Laboratory
Experiment 13:
Classifying Elements, Microscale

TEACHING TIPS

- Use the transparency of Figure 3.11 to illustrate the important features of the periodic table. Be sure to include the groups and their names, the metals, nonmetals, and metalloids. Show students how many more metals there are than nonmetals. List the metalloids, as students may not know that aluminum is a metal and boron is a nonmetal. The other elements along both sides of the heavy stair-like line are metalloids. Discuss the location of hydrogen and the size of the table if the actinides and lanthanides were included in their proper places. Talk about the newly discovered elements from 110 to 112, and explain the three-letter symbols. These three-letter symbols are simply the number of the element written using Latin. For example, element 110 is called ununnillium, element 111 is unununnium, and so forth. Once the Union of Pure and Applied Chemists has agreed on a name for these elements, the number name will be changed. Students might be interested to know that these elements do not have official names yet because they are so new.

- Ask students to think of common metal items that illustrate the properties of metals. Examples include copper wire, aluminum foil, silver spoons, and hammered copper utensils.

- The reasons underlying the structure of the periodic table and the trends it shows are not introduced until Chapter 11. Focus students' attention on the location of groups of elements and the separation between metals and nonmetals.

- Students should learn the names of the common groups of the periodic table. This will simplify your discussion later in the course.

Noble gases

Alkaline earth metals

Halogens

1 1A																	18 8A
1 H	2 2A											13 3A	14 4A	15 5A	16 6A	17 7A	2 He
3 Li	4 Be											5 B	6 C	7 N	8 O	9 F	10 Ne
11 Na	12 Mg	3	4	5	6	7	8	9	10	11	12	13 Al	14 Si	15 P	16 S	17 Cl	18 Ar
19 K	20 Ca	21 Sc	22 Ti	23 V	24 Cr	25 Mn	26 Fe	27 Co	28 Ni	29 Cu	30 Zn	31 Ga	32 Ge	33 As	34 Se	35 Br	36 Kr
37 Rb	38 Sr	39 Y	40 Zr	41 Nb	42 Mo	43 Tc	44 Ru	45 Rh	46 Pd	47 Ag	48 Cd	49 In	50 Sn	51 Sb	52 Te	53 I	54 Xe
55 Cs	56 Ba	57 La*	72 Hf	73 Ta	74 W	75 Re	76 Os	77 Ir	78 Pt	79 Au	80 Hg	81 Tl	82 Pb	83 Bi	84 Po	85 At	86 Rn
87 Fr	88 Ra	89 Ac†	104 Rf	105 Db	106 Sg	107 Bh	108 Hs	109 Mt	110 Ds	111 Rg	112 Uub	113 Uut	114 Uuq	115 Uup			

Transition metals

Alkali metals

*Lanthanides	58 Ce	59 Pr	60 Nd	61 Pm	62 Sm	63 Eu	64 Gd	65 Tb	66 Dy	67 Ho	68 Er	69 Tm	70 Yb	71 Lu
†Actinides	90 Th	91 Pa	92 U	93 Np	94 Pu	95 Am	96 Cm	97 Bk	98 Cf	99 Es	100 Fm	101 Md	102 No	103 Lr

Figure 3.11
The periodic table.

A simple version of the periodic table is shown in **Figure 3.11.** Note that each box of this table contains a number written over one or two letters. The letters are the symbols for the elements. The number shown above each symbol is the atomic number (the number of protons and also the number of electrons) for that element. For example, carbon (C) has atomic number 6,

6
C

and lead (Pb) has atomic number 82,

82
Pb

Notice that elements 112 through 115 have unusual three-letter designations beginning with U. These are abbreviations for the systematic names of the atomic numbers of these elements. "Regular" names for these elements will be chosen eventually by the scientific community.

Note that the elements are listed on the periodic table in order of increasing atomic number. They are also arranged in specific horizontal rows and vertical columns. The elements were first arranged in this way in 1869 by Dmitri Mendeleev, a Russian scientist. Mendeleev arranged the elements in this way because of similarities in the chemical properties of various "families" of elements. For example, fluorine and chlorine are reactive gases that form similar compounds. It was also known that sodium and potassium behave very similarly. Thus the name *periodic table* refers to the fact that as we increase the atomic numbers, every so often an element occurs with properties similar to those of an earlier (lower-atomic-number) element. For example, the elements

9 F
17 Cl
35 Br
53 I
85 At

all show similar chemical behavior and so are listed vertically, as a "family" of elements.

These families of elements with similar chemical properties that lie in the same vertical column on the periodic table are called **groups.** Groups are often referred to by the number over the column (see Figure 3.11). Note that the group numbers are accompanied by the letter A on the periodic table in Figure 3.11 and the one inside the back cover of the text. For simplicity we will delete the As when we refer to groups in the text. Many of the groups have special names. For example, the first column of elements (Group 1) has the name **alkali metals.** The Group 2 elements are called the **alkaline earth metals,** the Group 7 elements are the **halogens,** and the elements in Group 8 are called the **noble gases.** A large collection of elements that spans many vertical columns consists of the **transition metals.**

Most of the elements are **metals.** Metals have the following characteristic physical properties:

Physical Properties of Metals

1. Efficient conduction of heat and electricity
2. Malleability (they can be hammered into thin sheets)
3. Ductility (they can be pulled into wires)
4. A lustrous (shiny) appearance

3.8 Introduction to the Periodic Table **65**

For example, copper is a typical metal. It is lustrous (although it tarnishes readily); it is an excellent conductor of electricity (it is widely used in electrical wires); and it is readily formed into various shapes, such as pipes for water systems. Copper is one of the transition metals—the metals shown in the center of the periodic table. Iron, aluminum, and gold are other familiar elements that have metallic properties. All of the elements shown to the left and below of the heavy "stair-step" black line in Figure 3.11 are classified as metals, except for hydrogen (**Figure 3.12**).

A copper kettle and burner from the Bethnal Green Museum in London.

USING TECHNOLOGY

 Figure 3.12

Figure 3.12
The elements classified as metals and as nonmetals.

Nonmetals

Metals

The relatively small number of elements that appear in the upper righthand corner of the periodic table (to the right of the heavy line in Figures 3.11 and 3.12) are called **nonmetals.** Nonmetals generally lack those properties that characterize metals and show much more variation in their properties than metals do. Whereas almost all metals are solids at normal temperatures, many nonmetals (such as nitrogen, oxygen, chlorine, and neon) are gaseous and one (bromine) is a liquid. Several nonmetals (such as carbon, phosphorus, and sulfur) are also solids.

The elements that lie close to the "stair-step" line in Figure 3.11 often show a mixture of metallic and nonmetallic properties. These elements, which are called **metalloids** or **semimetals,** include silicon, germanium, arsenic, antimony, and tellurium.

As we continue our study of chemistry, we will see that the periodic table is a valuable tool for organizing accumulated knowledge and that it helps us predict the properties we expect a given element to exhibit. We will also develop a model for atomic structure that will explain why there are groups of elements with similar chemical properties.

CHEMISTRY

Nonmetals sometimes have one or more metallic properties. For example, solid iodine is lustrous, and graphite (a form of pure carbon) conducts electricity.

Indonesian men carrying chunks of elemental sulfur in baskets.

Example 3.5

Interpreting the Periodic Table

For each of the following elements, use the periodic table in the back of the book to give the symbol and atomic number and to specify whether the element is a metal or a nonmetal. Also give the named family to which the element belongs (if any).

    a. iodine

    b. magnesium

    c. gold

    d. lithium

Solution

    a. Iodine (symbol I) is element 53 (its atomic number is 53). Iodine lies to the right of the stair-step line in Figure 3.12 and thus is a nonmetal. Iodine is a member of Group 7, the family of halogens.

    b. Magnesium (symbol Mg) is element 12 (atomic number 12). Magnesium is a metal and is a member of the alkaline earth metal family (Group 2).

    c. Gold (symbol Au) is element 79 (atomic number 79). Gold is a metal and is not a member of a named vertical family. It is classed as a transition metal.

    d. Lithium (symbol Li) is element 3 (atomic number 3). Lithium is a metal in the alkali metal family (Group 1).

 Self-Check Exercise 3.5

Give the symbol and atomic number for each of the following elements. Also indicate whether each element is a metal or a nonmetal and whether it is a member of a named family.

    a. argon

    b. chlorine

    c. barium

    d. cesium

3.9   Natural States of the Elements

Objective: *To learn the natures of the common elements.*

As we have noted, the matter around us consists mainly of mixtures. Most often these mixtures contain compounds, in which atoms from different elements are bound together. Most elements are quite reactive: their atoms tend to combine with those of other elements to form compounds quite readily. Thus we do not often find elements in nature in pure form—uncombined with other elements. However, there are notable exceptions. The gold nuggets found at Sutter's Mill in California that

A gold nugget weighing 13 lb, 7 oz, which came to be called Tom's Baby, was found by Tom Grove near Breckenridge, Colorado, on July 23, 1887.

For each of the following elements, use the periodic table to give the symbol and atomic number and to specify whether the element is a metal or nonmetal. Also give the named family to which the element belongs (if any).

1. strontium

2. silicon

3. xenon

Answers:

1. Sr, atomic number = 38. Strontium is a metal, and a member of the alkaline earth metal family (Group 2).

2. Si, atomic number = 14. Silicon is a metalloid and a member of Group 4.

3. Xe, atomic number = 54. Xenon is a nonmetal and a member of the noble gas family (Group 8).

 Answers to Self-Check Exercise 3.5

Element	Symbol	Atomic Number	Metal or Nonmetal	Family
Argon	Ar	18	Nonmetal	Noble gases
Chlorine	Cl	17	Nonmetal	Halogen
Barium	Ba	56	Metal	Alkaline earth metals
Cesium	Cs	55	Metal	Alkali metals

 Section 3.9

Themes
Organization, Patterns of Change, Form and Function

Skills
Applying concepts, interpreting diagrams, making comparisons

Platinum is a noble metal used in jewelry and in many industrial processes.

launched the Gold Rush in 1849 are virtually pure elemental gold. And platinum and silver are often found in nearly pure form.

Gold, silver, and platinum are members of a class of metals called *noble metals* because they are relatively unreactive. (The term *noble* implies a class set apart.)

Other elements that appear in nature in the uncombined state are the elements in Group 8: helium, neon, argon, krypton, xenon, and radon. Because the atoms of these elements do not combine readily with those of other elements, we call them the *noble gases*. For example, helium gas is found in uncombined form in underground deposits with natural gas.

When we take a sample of air (the mixture of gases that constitute the earth's atmosphere) and separate it into its components, we find several pure elements present. One of these is argon. Argon gas consists of a collection of separate argon atoms, as shown in **Figure 3.13.**

Air also contains nitrogen gas and oxygen gas. When we examine these two gases, however, we find that they do not contain single atoms, as argon does, but instead contain **diatomic molecules:** molecules made up of *two atoms*, as represented in **Figure 3.14.** In fact, any sample of elemental oxygen gas at normal temperatures contains O_2 molecules. Likewise, nitrogen gas contains N_2 molecules.

Hydrogen is another element that forms diatomic molecules. Although virtually all of the hydrogen found on earth is present in compounds with other elements (such as with oxygen in water), when hydrogen is prepared as a free element it contains diatomic H_2 molecules. For example, an electric

Figure 3.13
Argon gas consists of a collection of separate argon atoms.

The only elemental hydrogen found naturally on earth occurs in the exhaust gases of volcanoes.

CHEMISTRY
A molecule is a collection of atoms that behaves as a unit. Molecules are always electrically neutral (zero charge).

Figure 3.14
Gaseous nitrogen and oxygen contain diatomic (two-atom) molecules.

(a) Nitrogen gas contains N—N (N_2) molecules.

(b) Oxygen gas contains O—O (O_2) molecules.

Figure 3.15

The decomposition of two water molecules (H_2O) to form two hydrogen molecules (H_2) and an oxygen molecule (O_2). Note that only the grouping of the atoms changes in this process; no atoms are created or destroyed. There must be the same number of H atoms and O atoms before and after the process. Thus the decomposition of two H_2O molecules (containing four H atoms and two O atoms) yields one O_2 molecule (containing two O atoms) and two H_2 molecules (containing a total of four H atoms).

Water molecules → Electric current → Diatomic oxygen molecule + Diatomic hydrogen molecules

(a)

(b)

Figure 3.16

(a) Sodium chloride (common table salt) can be decomposed to the elements sodium metal and chlorine gas, shown in (b).

CHEMISTRY

~ means "approximately."

current can be used to decompose water (see **Figure 3.15**) into elemental hydrogen and oxygen containing H_2 and O_2 molecules, respectively.

Several other elements, in addition to hydrogen, nitrogen, and oxygen, exist as diatomic molecules. For example, when sodium chloride is melted and subjected to an electric current, chlorine gas is produced (along with sodium metal). This chemical change is represented in **Figure 3.16.** Chlorine gas is a pale green gas that contains Cl_2 molecules.

Chlorine is a member of Group 7, the halogen family. All the elemental forms of the Group 7 elements contain diatomic molecules. Fluorine is a pale yellow gas containing F_2 molecules. Bromine is a brown liquid made up of Br_2 molecules. Iodine is a lustrous, purple solid that contains I_2 molecules.

Table 3.5 lists the elements that contain diatomic molecules in their pure, elemental forms.

So far we have seen that several elements are gaseous in their elemental forms at normal temperatures (~25 °C). The noble gases (the Group 8 elements) contain individual atoms, whereas several other gaseous elements contain diatomic molecules (H_2, N_2, O_2, F_2, and Cl_2).

Group 7

| F |
| Cl |
| Br |
| I |

TABLE 3.5

Elements That Exist as Diatomic Molecules in Their Elemental Forms

Element Present	Elemental State at 25 °C	Molecule
hydrogen	colorless gas	H_2
nitrogen	colorless gas	N_2
oxygen	pale blue gas	O_2
fluorine	pale yellow gas	F_2
chlorine	pale green gas	Cl_2
bromine	reddish-brown liquid	Br_2
iodine	lustrous, dark purple solid	I_2

USING TECHNOLOGY

 Table 3.5

3.9 Natural States of the Elements **69**

Only two elements are liquids in their elemental forms at 25 °C: the nonmetal bromine (containing Br_2 molecules) and the metal mercury. The metals gallium and cesium almost qualify in this category; they are solids at 25 °C, but both melt at ~30 °C.

The other elements are solids in their elemental forms at 25 °C. For metals these solids contain large numbers of atoms packed together much like marbles in a jar (see **Figure 3.17**).

Figure 3.17
In solid metals, the spherical atoms are packed closely together.

The structures of solid nonmetallic elements are more varied than those of metals. In fact, different forms of the same element often occur. For example, solid carbon occurs in three forms. Different forms of a given element are called *allotropes*. The three allotropes of carbon are the familiar diamond and graphite forms plus a form that has only recently been discovered called buckminsterfullerene. These elemental forms have very different properties because of their different structures (see **Figure 3.18**). Diamond is the hardest natural substance known and is often used for industrial cutting tools. Diamonds are also valued as gemstones. Graphite, on the other hand, is a rather soft material useful for writing (pencil "lead" is really graphite) and (in the form of a powder) for lubricating locks. The rather odd name given to buckminsterfullerene comes from the structure of the C_{60} molecules of which it is composed. The soccer-ball-like structure contains five- and six-member rings reminiscent of the structure of geodesic domes suggested by the late industrial designer Buckminster Fuller. Other "fullerenes" containing molecules with more than 60 carbon atoms have also recently been discovered, leading to a new area of chemistry.

Liquid bromine in a flask with bromine vapor.

Graphite and diamond, two forms of carbon.

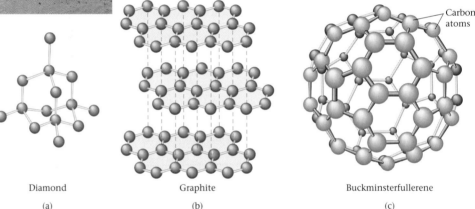

Diamond
(a)

Graphite
(b)

Buckminsterfullerene
(c)

Carbon atoms

Figure 3.18
The three solid elemental (allotropes) forms of carbon: (a) diamond, (b) graphite, and (c) buckminsterfullerene. The representations of diamond and graphite are just fragments of much larger structures that extend in all directions from the parts shown here. Buckminsterfullerene contains C_{60} molecules, one of which is shown.

MINI-DEMO

The allotropes of carbon can be illustrated using simple models. Diamond can be represented by a toothpick and gumdrop (or clay) model. Graphite can be shown by using pieces of chicken wire. Buckminsterfullerene can be illustrated by a soccer ball.

3.10 Ions

Objectives: *To describe the formation of ions from their parent atoms, and learn to name them.*
To predict which ion a given element forms by using the periodic table.

W e have seen that an atom has a certain number of protons in its nucleus and an equal number of electrons in the space around the nucleus. This results in an exact balance of positive and negative charges. We say that an atom is a neutral entity—it has *zero net charge.*

We can produce a charged entity, called an **ion,** by taking a neutral atom and adding or removing one or more electrons. For example, a sodium atom ($Z = 11$) has eleven protons in its nucleus and eleven electrons outside its nucleus.

If one of the electrons is lost, there will be eleven positive charges but only ten negative charges. This gives an ion with a net positive one (1+) charge: $(11+) + (10-) = 1+$. We can represent this process as follows: In shorthand form,

$$Na \rightarrow Na^+ + e^-$$

where Na represents the neutral sodium atom, Na^+ represents the 1+ ion formed, and e^- represents an electron.

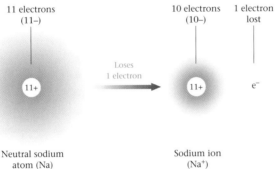

11 electrons
(11–)

10 electrons
(10–)

1 electron
lost

Loses
1 electron

11+

11+

e^-

Neutral sodium
atom (Na)

Sodium ion
(Na^+)

CHEMISTRY in ACTION
Elementary, My Dear Watson!

1. Make flashcards with the names of the elements in Groups 1 through 8 on one side and their symbols on the other side.
2. Group the elements according to:
   a. their families on the periodic table
   b. the similarity between their names and their symbols
   c. the first letter of their symbol
   d. the state of the element at 25 °C
   e. whether the element is a metal, a nonmetal, or a metalloid
3. Use your flashcards to learn the names and symbols for these elements.

Themes
Models, Patterns of Change, Form and Function

Skills
Applying concepts, interpreting diagrams, making comparisons, making predictions

 Laboratory
Experiment 14:
Electric Solutions, In Text

TEACHING TIPS

- Make sure that students realize the atoms of an element are neutral. Charge is shown only for ions.

- Emphasize that ions are formed by the gain and loss of electrons. This concept is difficult for students, because they tend to think about gain and loss using positive numbers. It is very important that they understand from the beginning that a positive ion is formed by *losing* electrons and a negative ion is formed by *gaining* electrons. In chemistry the positive number (protons) remains the same.

- Now is an excellent time to teach the notation for writing basic equations. $Na \rightarrow Na^+ + e^-$ shows how a neutral atom can lose an electron to have a positive charge. Students often have difficulty putting the electrons on the correct side when writing these equations.

- When naming ions, emphasize the difference in the suffix of the name. Students tend to slide over the ending and miss the *-ide,* which distinguishes the ion from an atom.

CHEMISTRY in ACTION

Elementary, My Dear Watson!

Materials Each student/group will need 44 (or more) index cards.

Purpose Students will become more familiar with the periodic table and will learn the names and symbols of some of the elements.

Discussion Although students will generally have access to a periodic table during most exams and quizzes, it is a good idea that they become familiar with the location of elements on the periodic table, some physical properties, and the names and symbols of at least the common elements. You may wish to include some of the more common transition metals in this activity (such as copper, zinc, and silver).

Cations and Anions

A positive ion, called a **cation** (pronounced *cat' eye on*), is produced when one or more electrons are *lost* from a neutral atom. We have seen that sodium loses one electron to become a 1+ cation. Some atoms lose more than one electron. For example, a magnesium atom typically loses two electrons to form a 2+ cation:

We usually represent this process as follows:

$$Mg \rightarrow Mg^{2+} + 2e^-$$

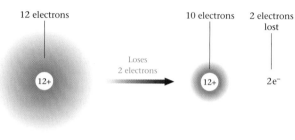

12 electrons   10 electrons   2 electrons lost

Loses 2 electrons

Neutral magnesium atom (Mg)
Magnesium ion (Mg²⁺)

Aluminum forms a 3+ cation by losing three electrons: That is,

$$Al \rightarrow Al^{3+} + 3e^-$$

13 electrons   10 electrons   3 electrons lost

Loses 3 electrons

Neutral aluminum atom (Al)
Aluminum ion (Al³⁺)

A cation is named using the name of the parent atom. Thus Na^+ is called the sodium ion (or sodium cation), Mg^{2+} is called the magnesium ion (or magnesium cation), and Al^{3+} is called the aluminum ion (or aluminum cation).

When electrons are *gained* by a neutral atom, an ion with a negative charge is formed. A negatively charged ion is called an **anion** (pronounced *an' ion*). An atom that gains one extra electron forms an anion with a 1− charge. An example of an atom that forms a 1− anion is the chlorine atom, which has seventeen protons and seventeen electrons.

CHEMISTRY

An ion has a net positive or negative charge.

That is,

$$Cl + e^- \rightarrow Cl^-$$

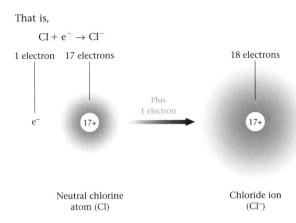

Neutral chlorine
atom (Cl)

Chloride ion
(Cl^-)

Note that the anion formed by chlorine has eighteen electrons but only seventeen protons, so the net charge is $(18-) + (17+) = 1-$. Unlike a cation, which is named for the parent atom, an anion is named by taking the root name of the atom and changing the ending. For example, the Cl^- anion produced from the Cl (chlorine) atom is called the *chlor*ide ion (or chloride anion). Notice that the word *chloride* is obtained from the root of the atom name (*chlor-*) plus the suffix *-ide*. Other atoms that add one electron to form 1− ions include the following:

fluorine $F + e^- \rightarrow F^-$ (*fluor*ide ion)

bromine $Br + e^- \rightarrow Br^-$ (*brom*ide ion)

iodine $I + e^- \rightarrow I^-$ (*iod*ide ion)

Note that the name of each of these anions is obtained by adding *-ide* to the root of the atom name.

Some atoms can add two electrons to form 2− anions. Examples include oxygen and sulfur:

oxygen $O + 2e^- \rightarrow O^{2-}$ (*ox*ide ion)

sulfur $S + 2e^- \rightarrow S^{2-}$ (*sulf*ide ion)

Note that the names for these anions are derived in the same way as those for the 1− anions.

It is important to recognize that ions are always formed by removing electrons from an atom (to form cations) or adding electrons to an atom (to form anions). *Ions are never formed by changing the number of protons in an atom's nucleus.*

It is essential to understand that isolated atoms do not form ions on their own. Most commonly, ions are formed when metallic elements combine with nonmetallic elements. As we will discuss in detail in Chapter 8, when metals and nonmetals react, the metal atoms tend to lose one or more electrons, which are in turn gained by the atoms of the nonmetal. Thus reactions between metals and nonmetals tend to form compounds that contain metal cations and nonmetal anions. We will have more to say about these compounds in Section 3.11.

Ion Charges and the Periodic Table

We find the periodic table very useful when we want to know what type of ion is formed by a given atom. **Figure 3.19** shows the types of ions formed by atoms in several of the groups on the periodic table. Note that the Group 1 metals all form 1+ ions (M^+), the Group 2 metals all form 2^+ ions (M^{2+}), and the Group 3 metals form 3^+ ions (M^{3+}). Thus for Groups 1 through 3 the charges of the cations formed are identical to the group numbers.

In contrast to the Group 1, 2, and 3 metals, most of the *transition metals* form cations with various positive charges. For these elements there is no easy way to predict the charge of the cation that will be formed.

Figure 3.19
The ions formed by selected members of Groups 1, 2, 3, 6, and 7.

CHEMISTRY
For Groups 1, 2, and 3, the charges of the cations equal the group numbers.

Note that metals always form positive ions. This tendency to lose electrons is a fundamental characteristic of metals. Nonmetals, on the other hand, form negative ions by gaining electrons. Note that the Group 7 atoms all gain one electron to form 1− ions and that all the nonmetals in Group 6 gain two electrons to form 2− ions.

At this point you should memorize the relationships between the group number and the type of ion formed, as shown in Figure 3.19. You will understand why these relationships exist after we further discuss the theory of the atom in Chapter 11.

CHEMICAL IMPACT

Consumer Connection

Miracle Coatings

Imagine a pair of plastic-lens sunglasses that are unscratchable, even if you drop them on concrete or rub them with sandpaper. Research may make such glasses possible, along with cutting tools that never need sharpening, special glass for windshields and buildings that cannot be scratched by wind-blown sand, and speakers that reproduce sound with a crispness unimagined until now. The secret of all these marvels is a thin diamond coating. Diamond is so hard that virtually nothing can scratch it. A thin diamond coating on a speaker cone limits resonance and gives a remarkably pure tone.

But how do you coat something with a diamond? It is nearly impossible to melt diamond (melting point, 3500 °C). And even if diamond were melted, the object being coated would itself melt immediately at this temperature. Surprisingly, a diamond coating can be applied quite easily to something even as fragile as plastic. First, the surface is bathed with a mixture of gaseous methane (CH_4) and hydrogen (H_2). Next, the methane is broken apart into its component elements by an energy source similar to that used in microwave ovens. The carbon atoms freed from the methane then form a thin diamond coating on the surface being treated.

The coating of soft, scratchable materials with a super-tough diamond layer should improve many types of consumer products in the near future.

74 Chapter 3 Chemical Foundations: Elements, Atoms, and Ions

3.11 Compounds That Contain Ions

Objective: *To describe how ions combine to form neutral compounds.*

Chemists have good reasons to believe that many chemical compounds contain ions. For instance, consider some of the properties of common table salt, sodium chloride (NaCl). It must be heated to about 800 °C to melt and to almost 1500 °C to boil (compare to water, which boils at 100 °C). As a solid, salt will not conduct an electric current, but when melted it is a very good conductor. Pure water will not conduct electricity (will not allow an electric current to flow), but when salt is dissolved in water, the resulting solution readily conducts electricity (see **Figure 3.20**).

Figure 3.20
(a) Pure water does not conduct a current, so the circuit is not complete and the bulb does not light. (b) Water containing a dissolved salt conducts electricity and the bulb lights.

(a)   (b)

Chemists have come to realize that we can best explain these properties of sodium chloride (NaCl) by picturing it as containing Na^+ ions and Cl^- ions packed together as shown in **Figure 3.21.** Because the positive and negative charges attract each other very strongly, salt must be heated to a very high temperature (800 °C) before it melts.

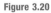

CHEMISTRY

Melting means that the solid, where the ions are locked into place, is changed to a liquid, where the ions can move.

Figure 3.21
(a) The arrangement of sodium ions (Na^+) and chloride ions (Cl^-) in the ionic compound sodium chloride. (b) Solid sodium chloride highly magnified.

(a)   (b)

CHEMISTRY

A substance containing ions that can move can conduct an electric current.

To explore further the significance of the electrical conductivity results, we need to discuss briefly the nature of electric currents. An electric current can travel along a metal wire because *electrons are free to move* through the wire; the moving electrons carry the current. In ionic substances the ions carry the current. Thus substances that contain ions can conduct an electric current *only if the ions can move*—the current travels by the movement of the

3.11   Compounds That Contain Ions   **75**

Themes
Patterns of Change, Form and Function

Skills
Applying concepts, interpreting diagrams, making predictions, evaluating

USING TECHNOLOGY

Animation and Video
Video, Conductivity Parts 1, 2, 3

Animation and Video
Chemistry in Motion
Demonstration 2, Conductivities of Aqueous Solutions

and sodium chloride solutions. Based on these results, have them predict what the HCl solution might look like at the molecular level. Finally, ask students to propose a hypothesis for how the acetic acid solution might differ from the HCl solution.

• Students need to think about ionic compounds on the molecular (ionic) level. Be sure to have them draw pictures when they begin writing formulas for these compounds. Emphasizing the idea that the compound is composed of both cations and anions lays a strong foundation for understanding the more advanced concepts later in the course. Once students can see the ions in a compound, making the total charge be a net of zero is more understandable. Students can then see how many of each ion are needed to attain a zero charge.

• Point out to students that atoms do not spontaneously gain or lose electrons. The gain and loss of electrons are always paired. One atom loses electrons simultaneously with another atom gaining electrons.

WHAT IF Comments

Metals and nonmetals form compounds (called ionic compounds) due to the transfer of one or more electrons (from the metal to the nonmetal). The ions formed in this way have a strong attraction for one another. Also, we can predict the formulas of ionic compounds because these compounds are electrically neutral. If subatomic particles had no charge, no ions would form and no ionic attraction would occur. Ionic compounds would be impossible. In fact, even perfectly covalent compounds are held together by the charged subatomic particles in their formation.

CHEMISTRY

Dissolving NaCl causes the ions to be randomly dispersed in the water, allowing them to move freely. Dissolving is not the same as melting, but both processes free the ions to move.

CHEMISTRY

An ionic compound cannot contain only anions or only cations, because the net charge of a compound must be zero.

CHEMISTRY

The net charge of a compound (zero) is the sum of the positive and negative charges.

CHEMISTRY

The subscript 1 in a formula is not written.

WHAT IF?

Thomson and Rutherford helped to show that atoms consist of subatomic particles, two of which are charged.

What if subatomic particles had no charge? How would it affect compounds formed between metals and nonmetals?

charged ions. In solid NaCl the ions are tightly held and cannot move. When the solid is melted and changed to a liquid, however, the structure is disrupted and the ions can move. As a result, an electric current can travel through the melted salt.

The same reasoning applies to NaCl dissolved in water. When the solid dissolves, the ions are dispersed throughout the water and can move around in the water, allowing it to conduct a current.

Thus we recognize substances that contain ions by their characteristic properties. They often have very high melting points, and they conduct an electric current when melted or when dissolved in water.

Many substances contain ions. In fact, whenever a compound forms between a metal and a nonmetal, it can be expected to contain ions. We call these substances **ionic compounds.**

One fact very important to remember is that *a chemical compound must have a net charge of zero.* This means that if a compound contains ions, then

1. There must be both positive ions (cations) and negative ions (anions) present.

2. The numbers of cations and anions must be such that the net charge is zero.

For example, note that the formula for sodium chloride is written NaCl, indicating one of each type of these elements. This makes sense because sodium chloride contains Na^+ ions and Cl^- ions. Each sodium ion has a 1+ charge and each chloride ion has a 1− charge, so they must occur in equal numbers to give a net charge of zero.

$$\text{Na}^+ \quad \text{Cl}^- \quad \rightarrow \quad \text{NaCl}$$

Charge: 1+   Charge: 1−   Net charge: 0

And for *any* ionic compound,

Total charge of cations + Total charge of anions = Zero net charge

Consider an ionic compound that contains the ions Mg^{2+} and Cl^-. What combination of these ions will give a net charge of zero? To balance the 2+ charge on Mg^{2+}, we will need two Cl^- ions to give a net charge of zero.

$$\text{Mg}^{2+} \quad \text{Cl}^- \quad \text{Cl}^- \quad \rightarrow \quad \text{MgCl}_2$$

Cation charge: 2+   +   Anion charge: 2 × (1−)   =   Compound net charge: 0

This means that the formula of the compound must be $MgCl_2$. Remember that subscripts are used to give the relative numbers of atoms (or ions).

Now consider an ionic compound that contains the ions Ba^{2+} and O^{2-}. What is the correct formula? These ions have charges of the same size (but opposite sign), so they must occur in equal numbers to give a net charge of zero. The formula of the compound is BaO, because $(2+) + (2-) = 0$.

Similarly, the formula of a compound that contains the ions Li^+ and N^{3-} is Li_3N, because three Li^+ cations are needed to balance the charge of the N^{3-} anion.

Positive charge:
$3 \times (1+)$ +   Negative charge: $(3-)$ =   Net charge: 0

Example 3.6

Writing Formulas for Ionic Compounds

The pairs of ions contained in several ionic compounds are listed below. Give the formula for each compound.

    a. Ca^{2+} and Cl^-

    b. Na^+ and S^{2-}

    c. Ca^{2+} and P^{3-}

Solution

    a. Ca^{2+} has a 2+ charge, so two Cl^- ions (each with the charge 1−) will be needed.

where   2+   +   2(1−)   = 0

The formula is $CaCl_2$.

    b. In this case S^{2-}, with its 2− charge, requires two Na^+ ions to produce a zero net charge.

where   2(1+)   +   2−   = 0

The formula is Na_2S.

    c. We have the ions Ca^{2+} (charge 2+) and P^{3-} (charge 3−). We must figure out how many of each is needed to balance exactly the positive and negative charges. Let's try two Ca^{2+} and one P^{3-}.

The resulting net charge is $2(2+) + (3-) = (4+) + (3-) = 1-$.

(continued)

Additional Examples

Use the pairs of ions below to give the formula for the compound containing these ions.

1. Ba^{2+} and O^{2-}
    BaO

2. Al^{3+} and S^{2+}
    Al_2S_3

3. K^+ and P^{3-}
    K_3P

3.11 Compounds That Contain Ions   **77**

**Answers to Self-Check
Exercise 3.6**

a. KI

$(1+) = (1-) = 0$

b. Al_2O_3

$2(3+) = 3(2-) = 0$

c. Mg_3N_2

$3(2+) = 2(3-) = 0$

 **Answers to
Focus Questions**

1. The properties of elements in vertical groups on the periodic table are similar, just like the characteristics of a particular human family are often similar.

2. The stair-step line on the periodic table marks the division between metals and nonmetals. Elements to the left of the line are metals, and those to the right are nonmetals. Directly adjacent, on either side of the line, are the metalloids.

3. Elements that form diatomic molecules are hydrogen, H_2; oxygen, O_2; nitrogen, N_2; fluorine, F_2; bromine, Br_2; chlorine, Cl_2; and iodine, I_2.

4. The gaseous elements are hydrogen, H_2; oxygen, O_2; nitrogen, N_2; fluorine, F_2; chlorine, Cl_2; helium, He; neon, Ne; argon, Ar; krypton, Kr; xenon, Xe; and radon, Rn.

5. $F + e^- \rightarrow F^-$

$Li \rightarrow Li^+ + e^-$

(continued) This doesn't work because the net charge is not zero. We can obtain the same total positive and total negative charges by having three Ca^{2+} ions and two P^{3-} ions.

where $3(2+)$ $+$ $2(3-)$ $= 0$

Thus the formula must be Ca_3P_2.

 Self-Check Exercise 3.6

Give the formulas for the compounds that contain the following pairs of ions.

   a. K^+ and I^- **b.** Mg^{2+} and N^{3-} **c.** Al^{3+} and O^{2-}

Focus Questions

Sections 3.8–3.11

1. Why are the elements in vertical groups on the periodic table called "families"?
2. What does the "stair-step" line on the periodic table tell you?
3. Which elements contain diatomic molecules? Write their formulas.
4. Which elements are gases at 25 °C? Write their formulas.
5. How is an ion formed?

       Show how F forms an anion.

       Show how Li forms a cation.

 **CHEMISTRY in the
LABORATORY**

Electric Solutions

Objectives

1. To test solutions to determine whether they conduct electricity
2. To classify substances as electrolytes or nonelectrolytes
3. To make a model for the composition of solutions

Lab Skills

Observing, applying concepts, classifying, developing models

Preparation Hints

You will need to make the paint-stick conductivity testers before this experiment. Directions for construction of the conductivity testers are found in the *Teacher Resources.*

Prelab Discussion

Tell students that if they come in contact with any solution, they need to

wash the contacted area thoroughly. Make sure they know the locations of eyewashes.

Safety Tips

When working with chemicals, wear safety goggles and lab aprons. Collect all solutions from the students and dispose of them properly.

Post-Lab Discussion

Students should realize that when sodium chloride is dissolved in water, the sodium ions and chloride ions dissociate from each other and

Electric Solutions

Problem

Which compounds contain ions?

Introduction

Some compounds contain ions. We can test for this condition by dissolving a compound in water. If the compound contains ions, the ions will be dispersed throughout the water and free to move. The movement of the ions in a solution enables them to conduct a current.

In this lab you will use a conductivity tester to determine which compounds contain ions.

Prelab Assignment

Read the entire laboratory experiment before you begin. Answer the following questions.

1. Why does the bulb light? What does it mean if the bulb doesn't light?

2. Why did we add nothing to a beaker of water and test it?

Materials

Goggles	HCl (0.10 M)
Apron	Potassium nitrate
Conductivity tester	Sodium chloride
Beakers (250 mL) or cups (11)	Vinegar
Plastic spoon	Sugar
Water	

Safety

If you come in contact with any solution, wash the contacted area thoroughly.

Procedure

1. Half-fill fix beakers or cups with water.

2. Add the following to each cup:

   Cup 1:   nothing
   Cup 2:   spoonful of sugar
   Cup 3:   spoonful of sodium chloride
   Cup 4:   spoonful of potassium nitrate
   Cup 5:   10 mL of 0.10 M HCl
   Cup 6:   10 mL vinegar

3. Use the conductivity testers provided by your teacher to test each cup. Carefully place the tips of the tester into the solution. Record your observations.

4. For the solutions that caused the bulb to light, pour a small amount (1 or 2 mL) of each solution into separate cups. Add water to each cup until it is almost filled.

5. Use the conductivity testers to test each solution. Record your observations.

Cleaning Up

Clean up all materials and wash your hands thoroughly. Dispose of all chemicals as instructed by your teacher.

Data/Observations

1. Record your observations in a table similar to the one below.

Substance	Did the Bulb Light?
water	
table sugar	
sodium chloride	
potassium nitrate	
HCl	
vinegar	

2. What happens when water is added to the solutions that originally caused the bulb to light?

Analysis and Conclusions

1. How are the compounds that caused the bulb to light similar to one another?

2. True or false: The reason a compound did not cause the bulb to light is because the substance did not dissolve in water. Explain your answer.

3. What do your observations tell you about the contents of each cup? Draw molecular-level pictures for each cup to explain your results.

4. Explain what happened when you added water to the solutions that originally caused the bulb to light by using molecular-level pictures.

5. How could we tell if a compound consisted of ions if it does not dissolve in water?

Something Extra

Test several household products to see if they contain ions. Get permission from your teacher first.

Data/Observations

1. Record your observations in a table similar to the one below.

Name	Did the Bulb Light?
Water	No
Table sugar	No
Sodium chloride	Yes
Potassium nitrate	Yes
HCl	Yes
Vinegar	Yes (but dim)

2. The bulb becomes more dim.

Analysis and Conclusions

1. All contained ions.

2. False. Sugar dissolves but does not cause the bulb to light. "Soluble" does not mean that a substance breaks up into ions.

3. The water contains only a tiny number of H^+ and OH^- ions, and table sugar solutions do not contain ions except for the small number from water. The other solutions do contain ions (although the concentration of ions is low in vinegar). The drawings will vary.

4. Answers will vary. They should show a lower concentration of ions when water is added.

5. One way is to melt the substance. Molten NaCl, for example, will conduct a current. In addition, ionic compounds have very high melting points.

Something Extra

Have the students pool their results and present them to the class.

become dispersed uniformly in the water. Their molecular-level pictures should show that the sodium chloride solution consists of dispersed ions and the sugar solution consists of dispersed molecules. When students are later confronted with stoichiometry problems involving solutions, they will need to understand what the reactants and products "look like" to be able to think about how to solve these problems.

Sample Data

The sodium chloride solution conducts a current, whereas the sugar solution and water do not. For a solution to conduct a current, free-flowing ions must be present. Thus sodium chloride dissociates into ions in solution, while the sugar does not.

Prelab Assignment

1. The bulb lights if a solution contains a relatively high concentration of ions. If the bulb does not light, either the substance does not consist of ions or the ions are at a very low concentration.

2. All of the solutions tested in the lab contain water. We test water to make sure that it does not cause the bulb to light. This step is called a control.

Assign the students to work individually on the Chapter 3 Review Worksheet at the appropriate level (Basic, Standard, or Challenge). Answers are found in the *Teacher Resources*.

Assessment

Chapter 3 Test is found in the *Teacher Resources* along with the answers for the test.

 Computerized Test Bank for Chapter 3

Answers to End of Chapter Problems

1. We still believe that matter is composed of a few simple substances and that the simple substances combine with each other in regular fixed manners. However, our notion of "element" is much different.

2. Alchemists discovered several previously unknown elements (mercury, sulfur, antimony) and were the first to prepare several common acids.

3. Boyle insisted that science be firmly grounded in experiment. His definition of the term *element* was based on observations and experimentation.

4. Approximately 115 elements are known (the number changes frequently); 88 occur naturally; the rest are man-made. Table 3.1 lists the most common elements on earth.

---

3 Chapter Review

Key Terms

element symbols (3.2)
law of constant
  composition (3.3)
Dalton's atomic
  theory (3.3)
atom (3.3)
compound (3.4)
chemical formula (3.4)
electron (3.5)
nuclear atom (3.5)
nucleus (3.5)
proton (3.5)
neutron (3.5)
isotopes (3.7)
atomic number, Z (3.7)
mass number, A (3.7)

periodic table (3.8)
groups (3.8)
alkali metals (3.8)
alkaline earth metals (3.8)
halogens (3.8)
noble gases (3.8)
transition metals (3.8)
metals (3.8)
nonmetals (3.8)
metalloids (semimetals) (3.8)
diatomic molecule (3.9)
ion (3.10)
cation (3.10)
anion (3.10)
ionic compound (3.11)

Summary

1. Of the approximately 115 different elements now known, only 9 account for about 98% of the total mass of the earth's crust, oceans, and atmosphere. In the human body, oxygen, carbon, hydrogen, and nitrogen are the most abundant elements.

2. Elements are represented by symbols that usually consist of the first one or two letters of the element's name. Sometimes, however, the symbol is taken from the element's original Latin or Greek name.

3. The law of constant composition states that a given compound always contains the same proportions by mass of the elements of which it is composed.

4. Dalton accounted for this law with his atomic theory. He postulated that all elements are composed of atoms; that all atoms of a given element are identical, but that atoms of different elements are different; that chemical compounds are formed when atoms combine; and that atoms are not created or destroyed in chemical reactions.

5. A compound can be represented by a chemical formula that uses the symbol for each type of atom and gives the number of each type of atom that appears in a molecule of the compound.

6. Atoms consist of a nucleus containing protons and neutrons, surrounded by electrons that occupy a large volume relative to the size of the nucleus. Electrons have a relatively small mass (1/1836 of the proton mass) and a negative charge. Protons have a positive charge equal in magnitude (but opposite in sign) to that of the electron. A neutron has a slightly greater mass than the proton but no charge.

7. Isotopes are atoms with the same number of protons but different numbers of neutrons.

8. The periodic table displays the elements in rows and columns in order of increasing atomic number. Elements that have similar chemical properties fall into vertical columns called groups. Most of the elements are metals. These occur on the left-hand side of the periodic table; the nonmetals appear on the right-hand side.

9. Each chemical element is composed of a given type of atom. These elements may exist as individual atoms or as groups of like atoms. For example, the noble gases contain single, separated atoms. However, elements such as oxygen, nitrogen, and chlorine exist as diatomic (two-atom) molecules.

10. When an atom loses one or more electrons, it forms a positive ion called a cation. This behavior is characteristic of metals. When an atom gains one or more electrons, it becomes a negatively charged ion called an anion. This behavior is characteristic of nonmetals. Oppositely charged ions form ionic compounds. A compound is always neutral overall—it has zero net charge.

11. The elements in Groups 1 and 2 on the periodic table form 1+ and 2+ cations, respectively. Group 7 atoms can gain one electron to form 1− ions. Group 6 atoms form 2− ions.

Questions and Problems

All exercises with blue numbers have answers in the back of this book.

3.1 The Elements

Questions

1. The ancient Greeks believed that all matter was composed of four fundamental substances: earth, air, fire, and water. How does this early conception of matter compare with our modern theories about matter?

2. Although they were not able to transform base metals into gold, what contributions did the alchemists make to the development of chemistry?

3. In addition to his important work on the properties of gases, what other valuable contributions did Robert Boyle make to the development of the study of chemistry?

4. In 2004, 115 elements were known. How many of these elements occur naturally, and how many are synthesized artificially? What are the most common elements present on the earth?

5. Oxygen, the most abundant element on the earth by mass, makes up a large percentage of the atmosphere. Where else is oxygen found? Is oxygen found more commonly as an element or in compounds?

---

5. Oxygen is found in the rivers, lakes, and oceans (combined with hydrogen in water molecules) and in the earth (most rocks and minerals are oxygen compounds). Oxygen is found most commonly in compounds.

6. The four most abundant elements in living creatures are oxygen, carbon, hydrogen, and nitrogen. In the nonliving world, the most abundant elements are oxygen, silicon, aluminum, and iron.

7. B (boron); C (carbon); F (fluo-

rine); H (hydrogen); I (iodine); K (potassium); N (nitrogen); O (oxygen); P (phosphorus); S (sulfur); U (uranium); V (vanadium); W (tungsten); Y (yttrium)

8. Sb (antimony); Cu (copper); Au (gold); Pb (lead); Hg (mercury); K (potassium); Ag (silver); Na (sodium); Sn (tin); W (tungsten); Fe (iron)

9. (a) Ne; (b) Ni; (c) K; (d) Si; (e) Ba; (f) Ag

10. iron; Cl; sulfur; U; neon; potassium

11. (a) copper; (b) cobalt; (c) calcium; (d) carbon; (e) chromium; (f) cesium; (g) chlorine; (h) cadmium

12. (a) False; most materials occur as mixtures of compounds. (b) False; a compound always contains the same relative number of atoms of its various elements. (c) False; molecules are made up of tiny "particles" called atoms.

13. According to Dalton, a given compound always consists of the same number and type of atoms;

6. What are the most abundant elements found in living creatures? Are these elements also the most abundant elements found in the nonliving world?

3.2 Symbols for the Elements

Note: Refer to the tables on the inside back cover when appropriate.

Questions

7. Give the symbols and names for the elements whose chemical symbols consist of only one letter.

8. In some cases, the symbol of an element does not seem to bear any relationship to the name we use for the element. Generally, the symbol for such an element is based on its name in another language. Give the symbols and names for five examples of such elements.

9. Give the chemical symbol for each of the following elements.
   a. neon   d. silicon
   b. nickel   e. barium
   c. potassium   f. silver

10. Give the name or symbol, as appropriate, for each of the following elements.

Symbol	Name
Fe	_____
_____	chlorine
S	_____
_____	uranium
Ne	_____
K	_____

11. Several elements have chemical symbols beginning with the letter C. For each of the following chemical symbols, give the name of the corresponding element.
   a. Cu   e. Cr
   b. Co   f. Cs
   c. Ca   g. Cl
   d. C   h. Cd

3.3 Dalton's Atomic Theory

Questions

12. Indicate whether each of the following statements is true or false. If a statement is false, correct the statement so that it becomes true.
   a. Most materials occur in nature as pure substances.
   b. A given compound usually contains the same relative number of atoms of its various elements.
   c. Atoms are made up of tiny particles called molecules.

13. What does the law of constant composition tell us? How did Dalton's atomic theory help to explain this law? Give examples.

3.4 Formulas of Compounds

Questions

14. What is a compound?

15. A given compound always contains the same relative masses of its constituent elements. How is this idea related to the relative numbers of each kind of atom present?

16. Write the formula for each of the following substances, listing the elements in the order given.
   a. a molecule containing one phosphorus atom and three chlorine atoms
   b. a molecule containing two boron atoms and six hydrogen atoms
   c. a compound containing one calcium atom for every two chlorine atoms
   d. a molecule containing one carbon atom and four bromine atoms
   e. a compound containing two iron atoms for every three oxygen atoms
   f. a molecule containing three hydrogen atoms, one phosphorus atom, and four oxygen atoms

3.5 The Structure of the Atom

Questions

17. Indicate whether each of the following statements is true or false. If a statement is false, correct the statement so that it becomes true.
   a. In his cathode ray tube experiments, J. J. Thomson obtained beams of different types of particles whose nature depended on which gas was contained in the tube.
   b. Thomson assumed that there must be positively charged particles in the atom, since isolated atoms have no overall charge.
   c. In the plum pudding model of the atom, the atom was envisioned as a sphere of negative charge in which positively charged electrons were randomly distributed.

18. Indicate whether each of the following statements is true or false. If false, correct the statement so that it becomes true.
   a. Rutherford's bombardment experiments with metal foil suggested that alpha particles were being deflected by coming near a large, negatively charged atomic nucleus.
   b. The proton and the electron have similar masses but opposite electrical charges.
   c. Most atoms also contain neutrons, which are slightly heavier than protons but carry no charge.

20. protons

21. The proton and neutron have similar (but not identical) masses. Either of these particles has a mass approximately 2000 times greater than the mass of an electron. The combination of the protons and the neutrons makes up the bulk of the mass of the atom. The electrons make the greatest contribution to the chemical properties of the atom.

22. electrons

23. False; atoms that have the same number of protons but different numbers of neutrons are called isotopes.

24. False; the mass number represents the total number of protons and neutrons in the nucleus.

25. Dalton's original theory proposed that all atoms of a given element were identical. We now know that this is not true—isotopes are possible.

26. Atoms of the same element (atoms with the same number of protons in the nucleus) may have different numbers of neutrons, and so will have different masses.

27. (a) 32; (b) 30; (c) 24; (d) 74; (e) 38; (f) 27; (g) 4; (h) 3

28. (a) $^{17}_{8}O$; (b) $^{37}_{17}Cl$; (c) $^{60}_{27}Co$; (d) $^{57}_{26}Fe$; (e) $^{131}_{53}I$; (f) $^{7}_{3}Li$

29. (a) 94p, 150n, 94e; (b) 95p, 146n, 95e; (c) 89p, 138n, 89e; (d) 55p, 78n, 55e; (e) 77p, 116n, 77e; (f) 25p, 31n, 25e

30.

Name	Symbol	Atomic Number	Mass Number	Neutrons
sodium	$^{23}_{11}Na$	11	23	12
nitrogen	$^{15}_{7}N$	7	15	8
barium	$^{136}_{56}Ba$	56	136	80
lithium	$^{9}_{3}Li$	3	9	6
boron	$^{11}_{5}B$	5	11	6

31. The elements in the periodic table are listed in order of increasing atomic number (number of protons in the nucleus). The periodic table was previously arranged on the basis of mass.

32. vertical; groups

33. Metals are excellent conductors of heat and electricity. They are also malleable, ductile, and generally shiny (lustrous) when a fresh surface is exposed.

thus the composition of the compound on a mass percentage basis is always the same.

14. A compound is a distinct substance that is composed of two or more elements and always contains exactly the same relative masses of those elements.

15. According to Dalton, all atoms of the same element are identical; in particular, every atom of a given element has the same mass as every other atom of that element. If a given compound always contains the same relative numbers of atoms of each kind, and those atoms always have the same masses, then the compound made from those elements always contains the same relative masses of its elements.

16. (a) PCl_3; (b) B_2H_6; (c) $CaCl_2$; (d) CBr_4; (e) Fe_2O_3; (f) H_3PO_4

17. (a) False; Thomson obtained beams of identical particles whose nature did not depend on what metal was used to generate them. (b) True. (c) False; the atom was envisioned as a sphere of positive charge in which negatively charged electrons were randomly distributed.

18. (a) False; Rutherford's bombardment experiments suggested that alpha particles were being deflected by a dense, positively charged nucleus. (b) False; The proton and electron do have opposite electrical charges, but the mass of the electron is much smaller than the mass of the proton. (c) True.

19. neutrons

34. Metallic elements are found toward the left and bottom of the periodic table; there are far more metallic elements than nonmetals.

35. Mercury is a liquid under normal conditions.

36. hydrogen, nitrogen, oxygen, fluorine, chlorine, plus all the Group 8 elements (noble gases)

37. The only metal that ordinarily exists as a liquid is mercury. The only nonmetallic element that exists as a liquid under normal conditions is bromine (Br_2). Oxygen and nitrogen are obtainable as liquids but only by compressing the gases at very low temperatures.

38. A metalloid is an element that has some properties common to both metallic and nonmetallic elements. The metalloids are found in the "stair-step" region marked on most periodic tables.

39. (a) 7, halogens; (b) 2, alkaline earth metals; (c) 1, alkali metals; (d) 1, alkali metals; (e) 8, noble gases; (f) 1, alkali metals; (g) 8, noble gases

40. (a) rubidium, Rb, atomic number 37, group number 1, metal; (b) germanium, Ge, atomic number 32, group number 4, metalloid; (c) magnesium, Mg, atomic number 12, group number 2, metal; (d) titanium, Ti, atomic number 22, transition metal; (e) iodine, I, atomic number 53, group number 7, nonmetal

41. Most of the elements are too reactive to be found in uncombined form in nature and are found only in compounds.

42. These elements are found uncombined in nature and do not react readily with other elements. Although these elements were once thought to form no compounds, this now has been shown to be untrue.

43. Diatomic gases: H_2, N_2, O_2, Cl_2, F_2; monatomic gases: He, Ne, Kr, Xe, Rn, Ar

44. liquids: bromine, gallium, mercury, cesium; gases: hydrogen, nitrogen, oxygen, fluorine, chlorine, the noble gases (helium, neon, argon, krypton, xenon, radon)

45. [1] b; [2] d; [3] b; [4] h; [5] f; [6] e; [7] a; [8] c; [9] g; [10] i

3.6 Introduction to the Modern Concept of Atomic Structure

Questions

19. What uncharged particles are found in the nuclei of most atoms?

20. What are the positively charged particles found in the nuclei of atoms called?

21. Do the proton and the neutron have exactly the same mass? How do the masses of the proton and the neutron compare to the mass of the electron? Which particles make the greatest contribution to the mass of an atom? Which particles make the greatest contribution to the chemical properties of an atom?

22. Although the nucleus of an atom is very important, it is the _____ of the atom that determine its chemical properties.

3.7 Isotopes

Questions

23. True or false? Atoms that have the same number of neutrons but different numbers of protons are called isotopes.

24. True or false? The mass number of a nucleus represents the number of protons in the nucleus.

25. How did Dalton's atomic theory have to be modified after the discovery that several isotopes of an element may exist?

26. Are all atoms of the same element identical? If not, how can they differ?

27. For each of the following elements, use the periodic table on the inside back cover of this book to write the element's atomic number.
   a. Ge
   b. zinc
   c. Cr
   d. tungsten
   e. Sr
   f. cobalt
   g. Be
   h. lithium

28. Write the atomic symbol ($^A_Z X$) for each of the isotopes described below.
   a. $Z = 8$, number of neutrons $= 9$
   b. the isotope of chlorine in which $A = 37$
   c. $Z = 27$, $A = 60$
   d. number of protons $= 26$, number of neutrons $= 31$
   e. the isotope of I with a mass number of 131
   f. $Z = 3$, number of neutrons $= 4$

29. How many protons and neutrons are contained in the nucleus of each of the following atoms? Assuming each atom is uncharged, how many electrons are present?
   a. $^{244}_{94}Pu$
   b. $^{241}_{95}Am$
   c. $^{227}_{89}Ac$
   d. $^{133}_{55}Cs$
   e. $^{193}_{77}Ir$
   f. $^{56}_{25}Mn$

82   Chapter 3   Chemical Foundations: Elements, Atoms, and Ions

30. Complete the following table.

Name	Symbol	Atomic Number	Mass Number	Neutrons
sodium	_____	11	23	_____
nitrogen	$^{15}_{7}N$			
_____	$^{136}_{56}Ba$	_____	_____	_____
lithium			_____	6
boron	_____	5	11	_____

3.8 Introduction to the Periodic Table

Questions

31. What property of the elements is considered when arranging the elements in the periodic table? Has the periodic table always been arranged based on this property?

32. In which direction on the periodic table, horizontal or vertical, are elements with similar chemical properties aligned? What are families of elements with similar chemical properties called?

33. List the characteristic physical properties that distinguish the metallic elements from the nonmetallic elements.

34. Where are the metallic elements found on the periodic table? Are there more metallic elements or nonmetallic elements?

35. Most, but not all, metallic elements are solids under ordinary laboratory conditions. Which metallic elements are *not* solids?

36. Give several examples of nonmetallic elements that occur in the gaseous state under ordinary conditions.

37. Under ordinary conditions, only a few pure elements occur as liquids. Give an example of a metallic and a nonmetallic element that ordinarily occur as liquids.

38. What is a *metalloid*? Where are the metalloids found on the periodic table?

39. Write the number and name (if any) of the group (family) to which each of the following elements belongs.
   a. iodine
   b. Ca
   c. Na
   d. lithium
   e. Kr
   f. sodium
   g. Ne

40. For each of the following elements, use the tables on the inside back cover of the book to give the chemical symbol, atomic number, and group number of each element, and to specify whether each element is a metal, metalloid, or nonmetal.
   a. rubidium
   b. germanium
   c. magnesium
   d. titanium
   e. iodine

46. (a) 27 protons, 25 electrons, CoO; (b) 27 protons, 24 electrons, Co_2O_3; (c) 17 protons, 18 electrons, $CaCl_2$; (d) 19 protons, 18 electrons, K_2O; (e) 16 protons, 18 electrons, CaS; (f) 38 protons, 36 electrons, SrO; (g) 13 protons, 10 electrons, Al_2O_3; (h) 15 protons, 18 electrons, Ca_3P_2

47. (a) Ca: 20 protons, 20 electrons; Ca^{2+}: 20 protons, 18 electrons; (b) P: 15 protons, 15 electrons; P^{3-}: 15 protons, 18 electrons; (c) Br: 35 protons, 35 electrons; Br^-: 35 protons, 36 elec-trons; (d) Fe: 26 protons, 26 electrons; Fe^{3+}: 26 protons, 23 electrons; (e) Al: 13 protons, 13 electrons; Al^{3+}: 13 protons, 10 electrons; (f) N: 7 protons, 7 electrons; N^{3-}: 7 protons, 10 electrons

48. (a) I^-; (b) Sr^{2+}; (c) Cs^+; (d) Ra^{2+}; (e) F^-; (f) Al^{3+}

49. A compound that has a high melting point (hundreds of degrees) and that conducts an electrical current when melted or dissolved in water almost certainly consists of ions.

50. In a solid state the ions are rigidly held in fixed positions in the crystal of the substance. For ionic substances to pass an electrical current, the ions must be able to move. This is possible in the liquid state.

51. The total number of positive charges must equal the total number of negative charges so that the crystals of an ionic compound have no net charge. A macroscopic sample of a compound ordinarily has no charge.

52. (a) FeP; (b) Fe_2S_3; (c) $FeCl_3$; (d) $MgCl_2$;

3.9 Natural States of the Elements

Questions

41. Are most of the chemical elements found in nature in the elemental form or combined in compounds? Why?

42. Why are the elements of Group 8 referred to as the noble or inert gas elements?

43. Give three examples of gaseous elements that exist as diatomic molecules. Give three examples of gaseous elements that exist as monatomic species.

44. Most of the elements are solids at 30 °C. Give three examples of elements that are *liquids* and three examples of elements that are *gases* at 30 °C.

3.10 Ions

Questions

45. For each of the positive ions listed in column 1, use the periodic table to find in column 2 the total number of electrons that ion contains. The same answer may be used more than once.

Column 1	Column 2
[1] Al^{3+}	[a] 2
[2] Fe^{3+}	[b] 10
[3] Mg^{2+}	[c] 21
[4] Sn^{2+}	[d] 23
[5] Co^{2+}	[e] 24
[6] Co^{3+}	[f] 25
[7] Li^+	[g] 36
[8] Cr^{3+}	[h] 48
[9] Rb^+	[i] 76
[10] Pt^{2+}	[j] 81

46. For each of the following ions, indicate the total number of protons and electrons in the ion. For the positive ions in the list, predict the formula of the simplest compound formed between each positive ion and the oxide ion, O^{2-}. For the negative ions in the list, predict the formula of the simplest compound formed between each negative ion and the calcium ion, Ca^{2+}.

a. Co^{2+} e. S^{2-}
b. Co^{3+} f. Sr^{2+}
c. Cl^- g. Al^{3+}
d. K^+ h. P^{3-}

47. For the following processes that show the formation of ions, use the periodic table to indicate the number of electrons and protons present in both the *ion* and the *neutral atom* from which the ion is made.

a. $Ca \rightarrow Ca^{2+} + 2e^-$ d. $Fe \rightarrow Fe^{3+} + 3e^-$
b. $P + 3e^- \rightarrow P^{3-}$ e. $Al \rightarrow Al^{3+} + 3e^-$
c. $Br + e^- \rightarrow Br^-$ f. $N + 3e^- \rightarrow N^{3-}$

48. For each of the following atomic numbers, use the periodic table to write the formula (including the charge) for the simple *ion* that the element is most likely to form.

a. 53   d. 88
b. 38   e. 9
c. 55   f. 13

3.11 Compounds That Contain Ions

Questions

49. List some properties of a substance that would lead you to believe it consists of ions. How do these properties differ from those of nonionic compounds?

50. Why does an ionic compound conduct an electric current when the compound is melted but not when it is in the solid state?

51. Why must the total number of positive charges in an ionic compound equal the total number of negative charges?

52. For the following pairs of ions, use the concept that a chemical compound must have a net charge of zero to predict the formula of the simplest compound that the ions are most likely to form.

a. Fe^{3+} and P^{3-} e. Mg^{2+} and O^{2-}
b. Fe^{3+} and S^{2-} f. Mg^{2+} and N^{3-}
c. Fe^{3+} and Cl^- g. Na^+ and P^{3-}
d. Mg^{2+} and Cl^- h. Na^+ and S^{2-}

Critical Thinking

53. What is the difference between the atomic number and the mass number of an element? Can atoms of two different elements have the same atomic number? Could they have the same mass number? Why or why not?

54. Which subatomic particles contribute the most to the atom's mass? Which subatomic particles determine the atom's chemical properties?

55. Is it possible for the same two elements to form more than one compound? Is this consistent with Dalton's atomic theory? Give an example.

56. Write the simplest formula for each of the following substances, listing the elements in the order given.

a. a molecule containing one carbon atom and two oxygen atoms
b. a compound containing one aluminum atom for every three chlorine atoms
c. perchloric acid, which contains one hydrogen atom, one chlorine atom, and four oxygen atoms
d. a molecule containing one sulfur atom and six chlorine atoms

(e) MgO; (f) Mg_3N_2; (g) Na_3P; (h) Na_2S

53. The atomic number represents the number of protons in the nucleus of an atom. The mass number represents the total number of protons and neutrons. No two elements have the same atomic number. If the total number of protons and neutrons happens to be the same for two atoms, the atoms will have the same mass number.

54. Most of the atom's mass is concentrated in the nucleus; thus the protons and neutrons contribute most to the mass of the atom. The chemical properties of an atom depend on the number and location of the electrons.

55. Yes. For example, carbon and oxygen form carbon monoxide (CO) and carbon dioxide (CO_2). This does not contradict Dalton's theory.

56. (a) CO_2; (b) $AlCl_3$; (c) $HClO_4$; (d) SCl_6

4 Nomenclature

Section	Text Features & Components	Labs, Demonstrations & Activities
Teaching Segment 4A 1 block pp. 85–100	4.1 Naming Compounds That Contain a Metal and a Nonmetal	**LP** Lesson Plans (Sec 4.1–4.3) **SE** Chemical Impact: Sugar of Lead *p. 87* **SE** Chemical Impact: How Can Water Be Hard or Soft? *p. 89*	**TE** Mini Demo *p. 90* **SE** Chemistry in Action: Name Game I: Ionic Compounds *p. 94*
	4.2–4.3 Naming Compounds That Contain Only Nonmetals (Type III) Naming Binary Compounds: A Review	**SE** Celebrity Chemical: Nitric Oxide (NO) *p. 96*	**LM** Experiment 15: Forming and Naming Ionic Compounds Lab Manual Report Sheets Teacher's Lab Guide
Teaching Segment 4B 1 block pp. 100–106	4.4 Naming Compounds That Contain Polyatomic Ions	**LP** Lesson Plans (Sec 4.4–4.6) **SE** Chemical Impact: Talking Tadpoles *p. 103*	**SE** Chemistry in Action: Name Game II: Polyatomic Ions *p. 104* **SE** Chemistry in the Laboratory: Grocery Store Nomenclature *p. 107* **LM** Experiment 16: Grocery Store Nomenclature Lab Manual Report Sheets Teacher's Lab Guide
	4.5 Naming Acids		**LM** Experiment 17: Energy Changes in Physical and Chemical Systems Lab Manual Report Sheets Teacher's Lab Guide
	4.6 Writing Formulas from Names	**SE** Top Ten First Letters of Last Names in the United States *p. 105*	

Key	Technology and Media	
SE Student Edition **TE** Teacher Edition **RP** Teacher Resource Package **LM** Lab Materials **LP** Lesson Plans **AR** Additional Resources **Florida Specific**	**Transparencies** Table 4.1, 4.2, 4.4 Figure 4.1, 4.2, 4.3 **PowerPoint Slides 4**	**eEdition CD-ROM** **Easy Planner CD-ROM** **English Summaries CD** **Spanish Summaries CD** **Web Site** classzone.com **McDougal Littell Test Generator**

Chapter Planning Guide

All Learners	Review & Assessment	Standards
TE Active Learning *p. 85* **TE** Teaching Tips *pp. 89, 90* Transparency: Table 4.1, 4.2 **AR** Less Proficient Students *p. 7*	**TE** Additional Examples *pp. 87, 91* **SE** Self Check *pp. 88, 93* **SE** What if . . . *p. 91* **SE** Self Check *p. 93* **SE** Key Terms *p. 108* **SE** Questions and Problems *p. 108*	**TE** **NSES** UCP1, UCP3, A1, A2, B2, B3, F1 **SSS** SC.H.1.4.2, SC.H.2.4.1, SC.A.2.4.1, SC.H.3.4.2, SC.H.3.4.3, SC.H.3.4.4, SC.H.3.4.6
TE Teaching Tips *pp. 95, 97* **RP** Team Learning Worksheets (Sec 4.1–4.3) *pp. 13–14* Transparency: Figure 4.1 *p. 98* **AR** Less Proficient Students *p. 7*	**SE** What if . . . *p. 97* **TE** Additional Examples *pp. 95, 97, 98* **SE** Self Check *pp. 95, 97, 99* **SE** Focus Questions (Sec 4.1–4.3) *p. 100* **SE** Questions and Problems *p. 108*	
TE Misconceptions *p. 101* Transparency: Table 4.4 *p. 100* Transparency: Figure 4.2 *p. 102* **AR** Less Proficient Students *p. 8*	**TE** Additional Examples *pp. 101, 103* **SE** Self Check *pp. 102, 103* **SE** Key Terms *p. 108* **SE** Questions and Problems *pp. 108–109*	**TE** **NSES** UCP1, UCP3, A1, A2, B2, B3, C6 **SSS** SC.H.1.4.1, SC.A.2.4.1
Transparency: Figure 4.3 *p. 105* **AR** Less Proficient Students *p. 8*	**TE** Additional Examples *p. 105* **SE** Key Terms *p. 108* **SE** Questions and Problems *p. 109*	
TE Teaching Tips *p. 105* **RP** Team Learning Worksheets (Sec 4.4–4.6) *pp. 15–17* **AR** Less Proficient Students *p. 8*	**TE** Additional Examples *p. 106* **SE** Self Check *p. 106* **SE** Focus Questions (Sec 4.4–4.6) *p. 106* **SE** Questions and Problems *p. 109*	

Chapter Materials

TE Reading Strategy
AR English/Spanish Summaries *p. 6*
AR Challenge Projects/Problems *pp. 6–7*
AR Less Proficient Students *p. 8*
English Summary Audio
Spanish Summary Audio
RP Chapter Review Worksheets (Basic, Review, Challenge)

SE Chapter Summary *p. 108*
SE Critical Thinking *pp. 109–111*
RP Solutions Guide
RP Chapter Tests
RP Test Bank
McDougal Littell Test Generator
AR Standardized Test Practice
FCAT Test 2

Integrating Reading Strategies and Chemistry Concepts

Chapter 4: Reading Symbols

So far the students have been exposed to a few important symbols. In Chapter 4, the students may struggle with their reading assignments if they do not correctly interpret these symbols. Tell the students that when they read, the symbols should not interrupt the flow pattern of their reading. The students should read the symbol as just another word in the sentence.

Before beginning this chapter, review with the students how to read the symbols they have learned to date.

SYMBOLS LEARNED TO DATE		
Symbols	**Meaning**	**Read as:**
H_2O	Two atoms of hydrogen bonded to one atom of oxygen	Water, or H 2 O
O_2	Two atoms of oxygen	Oxygen, or O 2
NO	One atom of nitrogen bonded to one atom of oxygen	Nitric oxide, nitrogen monoxide, or N O
Na^+	Sodium ion	Sodium ion, or sodium with a positive one charge, or sodium with a plus one charge
$2e^-$	Two electrons lost	Two electrons lost
Mg^{2+}	Magnesium ion	Magnesium ion, or magnesium plus two charge, or magnesium positive two charge
$C - O$	One atom of carbon bonded to one atom of oxygen	An atom of carbon bonded to an atom of oxygen

Remind the students that symbols are simply a shorthand notation established by chemists and that mastering the symbols' meaning will aid in their reading comprehension. Explain to the students that as they progress through the course, they will see combinations of symbols that they will need to be able to interpret accurately.

MISCONCEPTION Some of the students may confuse these symbols with those learned in mathematics. Explain that in a chemical formula a superscript indicates charge, not a power, and a subscript indicates the number of atoms. Also, tell the students that in a superscript the + and − symbols show charges, not addition and subtraction.

Reading Paragraphs Containing Symbols

Direct the students' attention to the second paragraph of Section 4.1 on page 85.

> In this section we will consider binary ionic compounds of two types based on the cations they contain. Certain metal atoms form only one cation. For example, the Na atom always forms Na^+, *never* Na^{2+} or Na^{3+}. Likewise, Cs always forms Cs^+, Ca always forms Ca^{2+}, and Al always forms Al^{3+}. We will call compounds that contain this type of metal atom Type I binary compounds and the cations they contain Type I cations. Examples of Type I cations are Na^+, Ca^{2+}, Cs^+, and Al^{3+}.

This paragraph contains important information, but some of the students may skip over it because they are intimidated by the symbols. Read the paragraph aloud so that the students can hear how to read the ion symbols. Then ask the students to read the next paragraph quietly aloud to a partner to determine whether there is an interruption of flow. Because Roman numerals are introduced at this point, you may want to quickly review them as well.

Memorizing Symbols

When they can correctly interpret and read the chemical symbols introduced thus far, the students are ready to learn and memorize common compounds. Tell the students that they will need to create more flashcards. As you cover the following sections, point out the charts that contain the material that the students should memorize.

Section 4.1 page 86

Section 4.2 page 90

Section 4.4 page 100

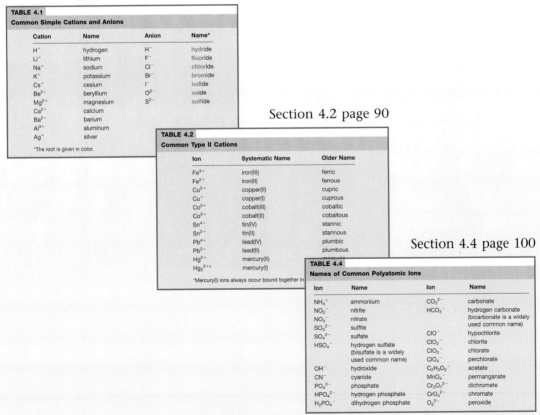

TABLE 4.1
Common Simple Cations and Anions

Cation	Name	Anion	Name*
H^+	hydrogen	H^-	hydride
Li^+	lithium	F^-	fluoride
Na^+	sodium	Cl^-	chloride
K^+	potassium	Br^-	bromide
Cs^+	cesium	I^-	iodide
Be^{2+}	beryllium	O^{2-}	oxide
Mg^{2+}	magnesium	S^{2-}	sulfide
Ca^{2+}	calcium		
Ba^{2+}	barium		
Al^{3+}	aluminum		
Ag^+	silver		

*The root is given in color.

TABLE 4.2
Common Type II Cations

Ion	Systematic Name	Older Name
Fe^{3+}	iron(III)	ferric
Fe^{2+}	iron(II)	ferrous
Cu^{2+}	copper(II)	cupric
Cu^+	copper(I)	cuprous
Co^{3+}	cobalt(III)	cobaltic
Co^{2+}	cobalt(II)	cobaltous
Sn^{4+}	tin(IV)	stannic
Sn^{2+}	tin(II)	stannous
Pb^{4+}	lead(IV)	plumbic
Pb^{2+}	lead(II)	plumbous
Hg^{2+}	mercury(II)	
Hg_2^{2+}	mercury(I)	

*Mercury(I) ions always occur bound together in

TABLE 4.4
Names of Common Polyatomic Ions

Ion	Name	Ion	Name
NH_4^+	ammonium	CO_3^{2-}	carbonate
NO_2^-	nitrite	HCO_3^-	hydrogen carbonate (bicarbonate is a widely used common name)
NO_3^-	nitrate		
SO_3^{2-}	sulfite		
SO_4^{2-}	sulfate	ClO^-	hypochlorite
HSO_4^-	hydrogen sulfate (bisulfate is a widely used common name)	ClO_2^-	chlorite
		ClO_3^-	chlorate
		ClO_4^-	perchlorate
OH^-	hydroxide	$C_2H_3O_2^-$	acetate
CN^-	cyanide	MnO_4^-	permanganate
PO_4^{3-}	phosphate	$Cr_2O_7^{2-}$	dichromate
HPO_4^{2-}	hydrogen phosphate	CrO_4^{2-}	chromate
$H_2PO_4^-$	dihydrogen phosphate	O_2^{2-}	peroxide

Chapter 4

In this Chapter our goals are for the students to:

- Learn to name binary compounds of a metal and a nonmetal

- Learn how to name binary compounds containing only nonmetals

- Learn the names of common polyatomic ions and how to use them in naming compounds

- Learn names for common acids and how the anion composition determines the acid's name

- Learn to write the formula of a compound, given its name

4 Nomenclature

Mineral towers in Mono Lake, California.

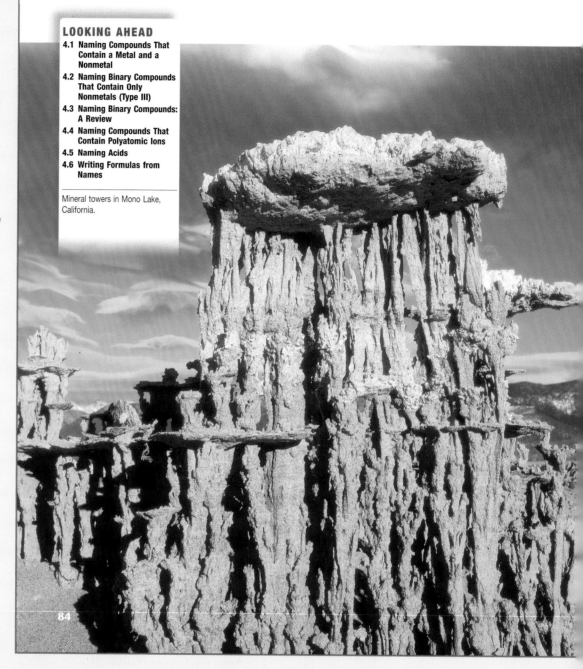

84

When chemistry was an infant science, there was no system for naming compounds. Names such as sugar of lead, blue vitriol, quicklime, Epsom salts, milk of magnesia, gypsum, and laughing gas were coined by early chemists. Such names are called *common names*. As our knowledge of chemistry grew, it became clear that using common names for compounds was not practical. More than four million chemical compounds are currently known. Memorizing common names for all these compounds would be impossible.

The solution, of course, is a *system* for naming compounds in which the name tells something about the composition of the compound. After learning the system, you should be able to name a compound when you are given its formula. Conversely, you should be able to construct a compound's formula, given its name. In the next few sections we will specify the most important rules for naming compounds other than organic compounds (those based on chains of carbon atoms).

We will begin by discussing the system for naming **binary compounds**—compounds composed of two elements. We can divide binary compounds into two broad classes:

1. Compounds that contain a metal and a nonmetal

2. Compounds that contain two nonmetals

Then we will describe the systems used for naming more complex compounds.

An artist using plaster of Paris, a gypsum plaster.

4.1 Naming Compounds That Contain a Metal and a Nonmetal

Objective: *To learn to name binary compounds of a metal and a nonmetal.*

As we saw in Section 3.11, when a metal such as sodium combines with a nonmetal such as chlorine, the resulting compound contains ions. The metal loses one or more electrons to become a cation, and the nonmetal gains one or more electrons to form an anion. The resulting substance is called a **binary ionic compound.** Binary ionic compounds contain a positive ion (cation), which is always written first in the formula, and a negative ion (anion). *To name these compounds we simply name the ions.*

In this section we will consider binary ionic compounds of two types based on the cations they contain. Certain metal atoms form only one cation. For example, the Na atom always forms Na^+, *never* Na^{2+} or Na^{3+}. Likewise, Cs always forms Cs^+, Ca always forms Ca^{2+}, and Al always forms Al^{3+}. We will call compounds that contain this type of metal atom Type I binary compounds and the cations they contain Type I cations. Examples of Type I cations are Na^+, Ca^{2+}, Cs^+, and Al^{3+}.

Other metal atoms can form two or more cations. For example, Cr can form Cr^{2+} and Cr^{3+} and Cu can form Cu^+ and Cu^{2+}. We will call such ions Type II cations and their compounds Type II binary compounds.

Themes
Organization, Systems

Skills
Classifying, evaluating

TEACHING TIP

Stress that learning the language of chemistry by naming compounds and writing their formulas is fundamental to being successful in chemistry. Tell students that they will use this skill for the remainder of the course in everything they do.

 Section 4.1

Themes
Systems, Organization

Skills
Classifying, interpreting data

Student Preparation
Assign the students to read Sections 4.1 to 4.3 and to answer the Focus Questions at the end of Section 4.3 before coming to class.

Active Learning
After introducing the material in Sections 4.1 to 4.3 in class, place the students in groups and have them work together on Sections 4.1–4.3: Team Learning Worksheet. Answers and/or discussion of these questions are located in the *Teacher Resources*.

CHEMISTRY

A simple cation has the same name as its parent element.

TABLE 4.1

Common Simple Cations and Anions

Cation	Name	Anion	Name*
H^+	hydrogen	H^-	hydride
Li^+	lithium	F^-	fluoride
Na^+	sodium	Cl^-	chloride
K^+	potassium	Br^-	bromide
Cs^+	cesium	I^-	iodide
Be^{2+}	beryllium	O^{2-}	oxide
Mg^{2+}	magnesium	S^{2-}	sulfide
Ca^{2+}	calcium		
Ba^{2+}	barium		
Al^{3+}	aluminum		
Ag^+	silver		

*The root is given in color.

In summary:

Type I compounds: The metal present forms only one type of cation.

Type II compounds: The metal present can form two (or more) cations that have different charges.

Some common cations and anions and their names are listed in **Table 4.1.** You should memorize these. They are an essential part of your chemical vocabulary.

Type I Binary Ionic Compounds

The following rules apply for Type I ionic compounds:

> **Rules for Naming Type I Ionic Compounds**
>
> 1. The cation is always named first and the anion second.
> 2. A simple cation (obtained from a single atom) takes its name from the name of the element. For example, Na^+ is called sodium in the names of compounds containing this ion.
> 3. A simple anion (obtained from a single atom) is named by taking the first part of the element name (the root) and adding *-ide*. Thus the Cl^- ion is called chloride.

We will illustrate these rules by naming a few compounds. For example, the compound NaI is called sodium iodide. It contains Na^+ (the sodium cation, named for the parent metal) and I^- (iodide: the root of iodine plus *-ide*). Similarly, the compound CaO is called calcium oxide because it contains Ca^{2+} (the calcium cation) and O^{2-} (the oxide anion).

The rules for naming binary compounds are also illustrated by the following examples.

86   Chapter 4   Nomenclature

CHEMICAL IMPACT

Sugar of Lead

In ancient Roman society it was common to boil fermented grape juice in a lead-lined vessel, driving off much of the water to produce a very sweet, viscous syrup called *sapa*. This syrup was often used as a sweetener for many types of food and drink.

We now realize that a major component of this syrup was lead acetate, $Pb(C_2H_3O_2)_2$. This compound has a very sweet taste—hence its original name, sugar of lead.

Many historians believe that the fall of the Roman Empire was due at least in part to lead poisoning, which causes lethargy and mental malfunctions. One major source of this lead was the sapa syrup. In addition, the Romans' highly advanced plumbing system employed lead water pipes, which allowed lead to be leached into their drinking water.

Sadly, this story is more relevant to today's society than you might think. Lead-based solder was widely used for many years to connect the copper pipes in water systems in homes and commercial buildings. There is evidence that dangerous amounts of lead can be leached from these soldered joints into drinking water. In fact, large quantities

A carving showing how lead-lined vessels were used.

of lead have been found in the water that some drinking fountains and water coolers dispense. In response to these problems, the U.S. Congress has passed a law banning lead from the solder used in plumbing systems for drinking water.

Compound	Ions Present	Name
NaCl	Na^+, Cl^-	sodium chloride
KI	K^+, I^-	potassium iodide
CaS	Ca^{2+}, S^{2-}	calcium sulfide
CsBr	Cs^+, Br^-	cesium bromide
MgO	Mg^{2+}, O^{2-}	magnesium oxide

It is important to note that in the *formulas* of ionic compounds, simple ions are represented by the element symbol: Cl means Cl^-, Na means Na^+, and so on. However, when *individual ions* are shown, the charge is always included. Thus the formula of potassium bromide is written KBr, but when the potassium and bromide ions are shown individually, they are written K^+ and Br^-.

Example 4.1

Naming Type I Binary Compounds

Name each binary compound.

    a. CsF   **b.** $AlCl_3$ **c.** MgI_2

(continued)

4.1 Naming Compounds That Contain a Metal and a Nonmetal **87**

Integrating the CHEMICAL IMPACT

Sugar of Lead

"Sugar of Lead" provides an interesting way to connect history to the chemistry classroom. Many reputable scholars believe that lead poisoning of the ruling classes of Rome was a contributing factor to the fall of the Roman Empire. The syrup called *sapa* was, in effect, the first artificial sweetener—and a very dangerous one at that.

Now might be a good time to discuss other incidences of heavy metal poisoning, such as the "Mad Hatters"—people working in the hat-making industry in England in the eighteenth century who suffered personality changes from being exposed to the mercury compounds then being used to change wool into felt. It has also been rumored that Charles II of England, an amateur chemist who had a lab in his castle, may have died from mercury poisoning. Some evidence indicates that Isaac Newton, who dabbled in chemistry as well as physics (and had the bad habit of tasting the new compounds he made in the lab), may have suffered mercury poisoning severe enough to cause him to interrupt his studies and go to the country for several months to recover.

Additional Examples

Name each binary compound.

1. KCl
   potassium chloride

2. ZnS
   zinc sulfide

3. $CaBr_2$
   calcium bromide

4. BaH_2
   barium hydride

5. Al_2S_3
   aluminum sulfide

(continued)

Solution

We will name these compounds by systematically following the rules given above.

a. CsF

Step 1   Identify the cation and anion. Cs is in Group 1, so we know it will form the 1+ ion Cs^+. Because F is in Group 7, it forms the 1− ion F^-.

Step 2   Name the cation. Cs^+ is simply called cesium, the same as the element name.

Step 3   Name the anion. F^- is called fluoride: we use the root name of the element plus -ide.

Step 4   Name the compound by combining the names of the individual ions. The name for CsF is cesium fluoride. (Remember that the name of the cation is always given first.)

b.

Compound	Ions Present	Ion Names	Comments
$AlCl_3$ — Cation	Al^{3+}	aluminum	Al (Group 3) always forms Al^{3+}.
— Anion	Cl^-	chloride	Cl (Group 7) always forms Cl^-.

The name of $AlCl_3$ is aluminum chloride.

c.

Compound	Ions Present	Ion Names	Comments
MgI_2 — Cation	Mg^{2+}	magnesium	Mg (Group 2) always forms Mg^{2+}.
— Anion	I^-	iodide	I (Group 7) gains one electron to form I^-.

The name of MgI_2 is magnesium iodide.

Self-Check Exercise 4.1

Name the following compounds.

a. Rb_2O **b.** SrI_2 **c.** K_2S

Example 4.1 reminds us of three things:

1. Compounds formed from metals and nonmetals are ionic.

2. In an ionic compound the cation is always named first.

3. The *net* charge on an ionic compound is always zero. Thus, in CsF, one of each type of ion (Cs^+ and F^-) is required: $(1+) + (1-) = 0$ charge. In $AlCl_3$, however, three Cl^- ions are needed to balance the charge of Al^{3+}: $(3+) + 3(1-) = 0$ charge. In MgI_2, two I^- ions are needed for each Mg^{2+} ion: $(2+) + 2(1-) = 0$ charge.

Answers to Self-Check Exercise 4.1

a. rubidium oxide
b. strontium iodide
c. potassium sulfide

CHEMICAL IMPACT

How Can Water Be Hard or Soft?

Water, like most liquids we use every day, is not 100% pure. Floating about in our tap water are all kinds of ions and molecules collected from the places where our water has been. Are these ions and molecules harmful to us? It depends on what they are. The most common impurities in tap water are calcium and magnesium ions. They dissolve into the water as it passes through soil rich in limestone. Calcium and magnesium ions are important in our diets, but when dissolved in water they can have some irritating properties as well. It is "hard" to get soaps to lather—and so we call water with lots of these ions "hard water."

The calcium and magnesium compounds in hard water also leave a white scale or residue inside tea kettles, coffee pots, irons, and other appliances that use water. This scale can build up and keep the appliance from working properly. When soap is used with hard water, a new compound is formed—calcium or magnesium stearate—that makes a ring in the bath or clouds clothes and keeps them from being bright.

How can we make water soft? Some homeowners install a water softener, which is really an ion exchanger. It is filled with sodium chloride (salt), which exchanges sodium ions for the calcium and magnesium ions in the hard water, making the water soft. How does this exchange alter the behavior of the water? The sodium ions do not react with carbonates to form the white scaly deposits or react with soaps to form soap scum. They produce no negative effects in drinking water, except in people who must limit their sodium intake because of high blood pressure or heart disease. A bonus—your shampoo and soap give much more lather, so less is needed to do the job!

Integrating the CHEMICAL IMPACT

How Can Water Be Hard or Soft?

"How Can Water Be Hard or Soft?" emphasizes again that the concept of a pure substance is really hypothetical—all substances are contaminated to some extent. This might be a good time to introduce the idea that ions in solution can react to form solids—in this case, soap scum. (The topic of precipitation reactions will be covered in detail in Chapter 8.) Water softening involves exchanging the ions, such as Ca^{2+} and Mg^{2+}, that form precipitates with soap for ions, such as Na^+, that do not form solids with the soap anions.

TEACHING TIPS

- We use Roman numerals only when they are required for clarity. It is not necessary, for example, to name NaCl "sodium(I) chloride," because the sodium ion always has a charge of 1+.

- Students often make the mistake of assuming that the Roman numeral tells us the number of ions present in the compound. In many cases, the Roman numeral is the same as one of the subscripts. Use an example such as iron(II) oxide with the formula FeO to show that the Roman numeral relates only to the charge.

Type II Binary Ionic Compounds

So far we have considered binary ionic compounds (Type I) containing metals that always give the same cation. For example, sodium always forms the Na^+ ion, calcium always forms the Ca^{2+} ion, and aluminum always forms the Al^{3+} ion. As we said in the previous section, we can predict with certainty that each Group 1 metal will give a 1+ cation and each Group 2 metal will give a 2+ cation. And aluminum always forms Al^{3+}.

However, many metals can form more than one type of cation. For example, lead (Pb) can form Pb^{2+} or Pb^{4+} in ionic compounds. Also, iron (Fe) can produce Fe^{2+} or Fe^{3+}, chromium (Cr) can produce Cr^{2+} or Cr^{3+}, gold (Au) can produce Au^+ or Au^{3+}, and so on. This means that if we saw the name gold chloride, we wouldn't know whether it referred to the compound AuCl (containing Au^+ and Cl^-) or the compound $AuCl_3$ (containing Au^{3+} and three Cl^- ions). Therefore, we need a way of specifying which cation is present in compounds containing metals that can form more than one type of cation.

Chemists have decided to deal with this situation by using a Roman numeral to specify the charge on the cation. To see how this works, consider the compound $FeCl_2$. Iron can form Fe^{2+} or Fe^{3+}, so we must first decide which of these cations is present. We can determine the charge on the iron cation, because we know it must balance the charge on the two 1− anions (the chloride ions). Thus if we represent the charges as

CHEMISTRY

Type II binary ionic compounds contain a metal that can form more than one type of cation.

we know that ? must represent 2 because $(2+) + 2(1-) = 0$

4.1 Naming Compounds That Contain a Metal and a Nonmetal **89**

CHEMISTRY

$FeCl_3$ must contain Fe^{3+} to balance the charge of three Cl^- ions.

Copper(II) sulfate crystals.

The compound $FeCl_2$, then, contains one Fe^{2+} ion and two Cl^- ions. We call this compound iron(II) chloride, where the II tells the charge of the iron cation. That is, Fe^{2+} is called iron(II). Likewise, Fe^{3+} is called iron(III). And $FeCl_3$, which contains one Fe^{3+} ion and three Cl^- ions, is called iron(III) chloride. Remember that the Roman numeral tells the *charge* on the ion, not the number of ions present in the compound.

Note that in the above examples the Roman numeral for the cation turned out to be the same as the subscript needed for the anion (to balance the charge). This is often not the case. For example, consider the compound PbO_2. Since the oxide ion is O^{2-}, for PbO_2 we have:

$$\underset{\substack{\text{Charge on} \\ \text{lead ion}}}{\boxed{?+}} \quad + \quad 2\underset{\substack{(4-) \\ \text{Charge on} \\ \text{two } O^{2-} \text{ ions}}}{\boxed{2-}} \quad = \quad \underset{\substack{\text{Net} \\ \text{charge}}}{0}$$

Thus the charge on the lead ion must be 4+ to balance the 4− charge of the two oxide ions. The name of PbO_2 is therefore lead(IV) oxide, where the IV indicates the presence of the Pb^{4+} cation.

There is another system for naming ionic compounds containing metals that form two cations. *The ion with the higher charge has a name ending in -ic, and the one with the lower charge has a name ending in -ous.* In this system, for example, Fe^{3+} is called the ferric ion, and Fe^{2+} is called the ferrous ion. The names for $FeCl_3$ and $FeCl_2$, in this system, are ferric chloride and ferrous chloride, respectively. **Table 4.2** gives both names for many Type II cations. We will use the system of Roman numerals exclusively in this text; the other system is falling into disuse.

To help distinguish between Type I and Type II cations, remember that Group 1 and 2 metals are always Type I. On the other hand, transition metals are almost always Type II.

TABLE 4.2

Common Type II Cations

Ion	Systematic Name	Older Name
Fe^{3+}	iron(III)	ferric
Fe^{2+}	iron(II)	ferrous
Cu^{2+}	copper(II)	cupric
Cu^+	copper(I)	cuprous
Co^{3+}	cobalt(III)	cobaltic
Co^{2+}	cobalt(II)	cobaltous
Sn^{4+}	tin(IV)	stannic
Sn^{2+}	tin(II)	stannous
Pb^{4+}	lead(IV)	plumbic
Pb^{2+}	lead(II)	plumbous
Hg^{2+}	mercury(II)	mercuric
Hg_2^{2+}*	mercury(I)	mercurous

*Mercury(I) ions always occur bound together in pairs to form Hg_2^{2+}.

90 Chapter 4 Nomenclature

Example 4.2

Naming Type II Binary Compounds

Give the systematic name of each of the following compounds.

    a. CuCl   **c.** Fe_2O_3 **e.** $PbCl_4$

    b. HgO   **d.** MnO_2

Solution

All these compounds include a metal that can form more than one type of cation; thus we must first determine the charge on each cation. We do this by recognizing that a compound must be electrically neutral; that is, the positive and negative charges must balance exactly. We will use the known charge on the anion to determine the charge of the cation.

    a. In CuCl we recognize the anion as Cl^-. To determine the charge on the copper cation, we invoke the principle of charge balance.

In this case, ?+ must be 1+ because $(1+) + (1-) = 0$. Thus the copper cation must be Cu^+. Now we can name the compound by using the regular steps.

WHAT IF?

We can use the periodic table to predict the stable ions formed by many atoms. For example, the atoms in column 1 always form 1+ ions. The transition metals, however, can form more than one type of stable ion.

What if each transition metal ion had only one possible charge? How would the naming of compounds be different?

Compound	Ions Present	Ion Names	Comments
CuCl — Cation →	Cu^+	copper(I)	Copper forms other cations (it is a transition metal), so we must include the I to specify its charge.
— Anion →	Cl^-	chloride	

The name of CuCl is copper(I) chloride.

    b. In HgO we recognize the O^{2-} anion. To yield zero net charge, the cation must be Hg^{2+}.

Compound	Ions Present	Ion Names	Comments
HgO — Cation →	Hg^{2+}	mercury(II)	The II is necessary to specify the charge.
— Anion →	O^{2-}	oxide	

The name of HgO is mercury(II) oxide.

    c. Because Fe_2O_3 contains three O^{2-} anions, the charge on the iron cation must be 3+.

$$2(3+) + 3(2-) = 0$$

Fe^{3+} O^{2-} Net charge

(continued)

4.1 Naming Compounds That Contain a Metal and a Nonmetal   **91**

Additional Examples

Name each binary compound.

1. $CoCl_3$
cobalt(III) chloride

2. CuI
copper(I) iodide

3. $SnBr_4$
tin(IV) bromide

4. $HgCl_2$
mercury(II) chloride

5. PbS
lead(II) sulfide

WHAT IF Comments

We modify the system for naming ionic compounds when a transition metal is present because most transition metals can have multiple charges. If transition metals had only one possible charge, a name such as iron oxide would be acceptable (just as potassium oxide is acceptable). We would not need to use the Roman numerals. It is important for students to realize that our rules are always as simple as possible. That is, we never use Roman numerals (or prefixes or suffixes) unless it is necessary to make the name clear. The idea that science keeps rules and models as simple as possible is an important one for students to understand.

Compound	Ions Present	Ion Names	Comments
Fe_2O_3 Cation	Fe^{3+}	iron(III)	Iron is a transition metal and requires a III to specify the charge on the cation.
Anion	O^{2-}	oxide	

The name of Fe_2O_3 is iron(III) oxide.

d. MnO_2 contains two O^{2-} anions, so the charge on the manganese cation is 4+.

$$(4+) + 2(2-) = 0$$
$$\underset{Mn^{4+}}{\uparrow} \qquad \underset{O^{2-}}{\uparrow} \quad \underset{Net\ charge}{\uparrow}$$

Compound	Ions Present	Ion Names	Comments
MnO_2 Cation	Mn^{4+}	manganese(IV)	Manganese is a transition metal and requires a IV to specify the charge on the cation.
Anion	O^{2-}	oxide	

The name of MnO_2 is manganese(IV) oxide.

e. Because $PbCl_4$ contains four Cl^- anions, the charge on the lead cation is 4+.

$$(4+) + 4(1-) = 0$$
$$\underset{Pb^{4+}}{\uparrow} \qquad \underset{Cl^-}{\uparrow} \quad \underset{Net\ charge}{\uparrow}$$

Compound	Ion Present	Ions Names	Comments
$PbCl_4$ Cation	Pb^{4+}	lead(IV)	Lead forms both Pb^{2+} and Pb^{4+}, so a Roman numeral is required.
Anion	Cl^-	chloride	

The name for $PbCl_4$ is lead(IV) chloride.

CHEMISTRY

Sometimes transition metals form only one ion, such as silver, which forms Ag^+; zinc, which forms Zn^{2+}; and cadmium, which forms Cd^{2+}. In these cases, chemists do not use a Roman numeral, although it is not "wrong" to do so.

The use of a Roman numeral in a systematic name for a compound is required only in cases where more than one ionic compound forms between a given pair of elements. This occurs most often for compounds that contain transition metals, which frequently form more than one cation. *Metals that form only one cation do not need to be identified by a Roman numeral.* Common metals that do not require Roman numerals are the Group 1 elements, which form only 1+ ions; the Group 2 elements, which form only 2+ ions; and such Group 3 metals as aluminum and gallium, which form only 3+ ions.

As shown in Example 4.2, when a metal ion that forms more than one type of cation is present, the charge on the metal ion must be determined by balancing the positive and negative charges of the compound. To do this, you must be able to recognize the common anions and you must know their charges (see Table 4.1).

Example 4.3

Naming Binary Ionic Compounds: Summary

Give the systematic name of each of the following compounds.

a. $CoBr_2$ **c.** Al_2O_3

b. $CaCl_2$ **d.** $CrCl_3$

Solution

Compound	Ions and Names	Compound Name	Comments
a. $CoBr_2$ → Co^{2+} cobalt(II) → Br^- bromide	cobalt(II) bromide	cobalt(II) bromide	Cobalt is a transition metal; the name of the compound must have a Roman numeral. The two Br^- ions must be balanced by a Co^{2+} cation.
b. $CaCl_2$ → Ca^{2+} calcium → Cl^- chloride	calcium chloride	calcium chloride	Calcium, an alkaline earth metal, forms only the Ca^{2+} ion. A Roman numeral is not necessary.
c. Al_2O_3 → Al^{3+} aluminum → O^{2-} oxide	aluminum oxide	aluminum oxide	Aluminum forms only Al^{3+}. A Roman numeral is not necessary.
d. $CrCl_3$ → Cr^{3+} chromium(III) → Cl^- chloride	chromium(III) chloride	chromium(III) chloride	Chromium is a transition metal. The name of the compound must have a Roman numeral. $CrCl_3$ contains Cr^{3+}.

✓ Self-Check Exercise 4.2

Give the names of the following compounds.

a. $PbBr_2$ and $PbBr_4$ **d.** Na_2S

b. FeS and Fe_2S_3 **e.** $CoCl_3$

c. $AlBr_3$

e. The compound $CoCl_3$ contains three Cl^- ions. Thus the cobalt cation must be Co^{3+}, which is named cobalt(III) because cobalt is a transition metal and can form more than one type of cation. Thus the name of $CoCl_3$ is cobalt(III) chloride.

Additional Examples

Name each binary compound.

1. SnI_4
   tin(IV) iodide

2. K_3N
   potassium nitride

3. HgO
   mercury(II) oxide

4. RbF
   rubidium fluoride

5. NaH
   sodium hydride

6. CrF_2
   chromium(II) fluoride

7. $MgBr_2$
   magnesium bromide

8. MnI_2
   manganese(II) iodide

9. Li_2O
   lithium oxide

4.1 Naming Compounds That Contain a Metal and a Nonmetal **93**

✓ Answers to Self-Check Exercise 4.2

a. The compound $PbBr_2$ must contain Pb^{2+}—named lead(II)—to balance the charges of the two Br^- ions. Thus the name is lead(II) bromide. The compound $PbBr_4$ must contain Pb^{4+}—named lead(IV)—to balance the charges of the four Br^- ions. The name is therefore lead(IV) bromide.

b. The compound FeS contains the S^{2-} ion (sulfide) and thus the iron cation present must be Fe^{2+}, iron(II). The name is iron(II) sulfide. The compound Fe_2S_3 contains three S^{2-} ions and two iron cations of unknown charge. We can determine the iron charge from the following:

$$2(?+) + 3(2-) = 0$$

$$\underset{\text{Iron charge}}{\uparrow} \qquad \underset{S^{2-} \text{ charge}}{\uparrow}$$

In this case, ? must be 3 because $2(3+) + 3(2-) = 0$. Thus Fe_2S_3

contains Fe^{3+} and S^{2-}, and its name is iron (III) sulfide.

c. The compound $AlBr_3$ contains Al^{3+} and Br^-. Because aluminum forms only one ion (Al^{3+}), no Roman numeral is required. The name is aluminum bromide.

d. The compound Na_2S contains Na^+ and S^{2-} ions. The name is sodium sulfide. Because sodium forms only Na^+, no Roman numeral is needed.

Chapter 4   Nomenclature   **93**

Section 4.2

Themes
Systems, Organization, Patterns of Change

Skills
Applying concepts, using the writing process, classifying

Laboratory
Experiment 15:
Forming and Naming Ionic Compounds, Microscale

The following flow chart is useful when you are naming binary ionic compounds:

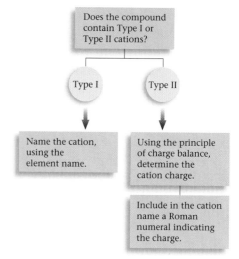

CHEMISTRY in ACTION

Name Game I: Ionic Compounds

1. Make two sets of flashcards with names of ions on one side and symbol and charge on the other:

   Set 1: all of the alkali and alkaline earth metals, plus iron(II) and iron(III)

   Set 2: all of the nonmetals from Groups 5, 6, and 7

2. Randomly pick one card from set 1, and one card from set 2. Write the proper formula for the ionic compound made from these two ions, and name the compound.

3. Repeat the previous step until you correctly name ten compounds in a row. Make sure you can write formulas and names starting with either the names or the symbols and charges of the ions.

4.2 Naming Binary Compounds That Contain Only Nonmetals (Type III)

Objective: *To learn how to name binary compounds containing only nonmetals.*

Binary compounds that contain only nonmetals are named in accordance with a system similar in some ways to the rules for naming binary ionic compounds, but there are important differences. *Type III binary compounds contain only nonmetals.* The following rules cover the naming of these compounds.

94 Chapter 4 Nomenclature

TABLE 4.3

Prefixes Used to
Indicate Numbers in
Chemical Names

Prefix	Number Indicated
mono-	1
di-	2
tri-	3
tetra-	4
penta-	5
hexa-	6
hepta-	7
octa-	8

Rules for Naming Type III Binary Compounds

1. The first element in the formula is named first, and the full element name is used.

2. The second element is named as though it were an anion.

3. Prefixes are used to denote the numbers of atoms present. These prefixes are given in **Table 4.3.**

4. The prefix *mono-* is never used for naming the first element. For example, CO is called carbon monoxide, *not* monocarbon monoxide.

We will illustrate the application of these rules in Example 4.4.

Example 4.4

Naming Type III Binary Compounds

Name the following binary compounds, which contain two nonmetals (Type III).

    a. BF_3 **b.** NO   **c.** N_2O_5

Solution

    a. BF_3

       Rule 1 Name the first element, using the full element name: boron.

       Rule 2 Name the second element as though it were an anion: fluoride.

       Rules 3 and 4 Use prefixes to denote numbers of atoms. One boron atom: do not use *mono-* in first position. Three fluorine atoms: use the prefix *tri-*.

       The name of BF_3 is boron trifluoride.

    b.

Compound	Individual Names	Prefixes	Comments
NO	nitrogen	none	*Mono-* is not used
	oxide	*mono-*	for the first element.

       The name for NO is nitrogen monoxide. Note that the second *o* in *mono-* has been dropped for easier pronunciation. The *common* name for NO, which is often used by chemists, is nitric oxide.

    c.

Compound	Individual Names	Prefixes	Comments
N_2O_5	nitrogen	*di-*	two N atoms
	oxide	*penta-*	five O atoms

       The name for N_2O_5 is dinitrogen pentoxide. The *a* in *penta-* has been dropped for easier pronunciation.

 Self-Check Exercise 4.3

Name the following compounds.

    a. CCl_4 **b.** NO_2 **c.** IF_5

4.2 Naming Binary Compounds That Contain Only Nonmetals (Type III)   **95**

TEACHING TIPS

- Students need to learn the prefixes given in Table 4.3. This effort will make naming compounds and writing formulas much easier.

- Like Roman numerals, prefixes are used only for clarity. For example, two "carbon oxides" are possible, and we must use prefixes to differentiate between them (carbon monoxide and carbon dioxide). We make the rules more complicated only when it is required.

- At times when naming Type III compounds, two vowels appear together (one from the prefix and one from the root name). We eliminate the vowel on the end of the prefix to make the pronunciation of the name easier. For example, tetraoxide becomes tetroxide and monooxide becomes monoxide.

Additional Examples

Name the following Type III compounds.

1. I_2O_7
   diiodine heptoxide

2. CO_2
   carbon dioxide

3. CF_4
   carbon tetrafluoride

4. NH_3
   ammonia

5. PCl_3
   phosphorus trichloride

 Answers to Self-Check Exercise 4.3

Compound	Individual Names	Prefixes	Name
a. CCl_4	carbon chloride	none tetra-	carbon tetrachloride
b. NO_2	nitrogen oxide	none di-	nitrogen dioxide
c. IF_5	iodine fluoride	none penta-	iodine pentafluoride

A piece of copper metal about to be placed in nitric acid (left). Copper reacts with nitric acid to produce colorless NO, which immediately reacts with the oxygen in the air to form reddish-brown NO_2 gas (right).

CHEMISTRY

Water and ammonia are always referred to by their common names.

The previous examples illustrate that, to avoid awkward pronunciation, we often drop the final *o* or *a* of the prefix when the second element is oxygen. For example, N_2O_4 is called dinitrogen tetroxide, *not* dinitrogen tetr*a*oxide, and CO is called carbon monoxide, *not* carbon mon*o*oxide.

Some compounds are always referred to by their common names. The two best examples are water and ammonia. The systematic names for H_2O and NH_3 are never used.

CELEBRITY CHEMICAL

Nitric Oxide (NO)

Until recently nitric oxide (NO, more correctly called nitrogen monoxide) was primarily viewed as an air pollutant. In the last few years, however, NO has been found to be a potent biological regulator. It turns out that this compound is produced in the body and regulates blood pressure by dilating blood vessels. Studies in the 1990s indicated that NO administered to patients with sickle-cell anemia may relieve serious symptoms of that disease. For example, it seems to benefit patients with acute chest syndrome—characterized by chest pain, fever, and high blood pressure in the lungs due to clogged blood vessels—which is the most life-threatening complication of sickle-cell disease, especially for children.

Sickle-cell anemia is a genetic disease that most often strikes people of West African descent. It causes the red blood cells to be misshapen ("sickle

shaped"), which in turn causes them to stick together and block blood flow. NO is thought to bind to a special site on the hemoglobin molecule (the molecule that carries O_2 from the lungs to the tissues). It is released when blood flow is impaired, causing dilation (expansion) of the blood vessels, thus helping to improve blood flow.

Further tests are now under way to try to discover exactly how NO works to relieve sickle-cell symptoms.

A mixture of normal and sickle-shaped red blood cells.

CELEBRITY CHEMICAL

Nitric Oxide (NO)

In the last few years NO has been found to be an important regulator molecule in the human body. Recently, it has been discovered that the "kissing bug," which is found in the tropics and sucks blood from humans much like a mosquito, actually releases NO with its bite. The NO delivered in the bug's saliva expands the victim's blood vessels and prevents clotting to ensure adequate blood flow. The same molecule in the bug's saliva that transports the NO also prevents the release of histamines, itch-inducing compounds produced by the body's immune system. If the histamines were released, victims would be made aware of the bite and the bug's meal would be interrupted—perhaps fatally.

To make sure you understand the procedures for naming binary non-metallic compounds (Type III), study Example 4.5 and then do Self-Check Exercise 4.4.

Example 4.5

Naming Type III Binary Compounds: Summary

Name each of the following compounds.

    a. PCl_5 **c.** SF_6 **e.** SO_2
    b. P_4O_6 **d.** SO_3 **f.** N_2O_3

Solution

Compound	Name
a. PCl_5	phosphorus pentachloride
b. P_4O_6	tetraphosphorus hexoxide
c. SF_6	sulfur hexafluoride
d. SO_3	sulfur trioxide
e. SO_2	sulfur dioxide
f. N_2O_3	dinitrogen trioxide

 Self-Check Exercise 4.4

Name the following compounds.

    a. SiO_2
    b. O_2F_2
    c. XeF_6

 4.3   Naming Binary Compounds: A Review

Objective: *To review the naming of Type I, Type II, and Type III binary compounds.*

Because different rules apply for naming various types of binary compounds, we will now consider an overall strategy to use for these compounds. We have considered three types of binary compounds, and naming each type requires a different procedure.

WHAT IF?

In this chapter, you have been learning a systematic way to name chemical compounds.

What if all compounds had only common names? What problems might arise?

Type I: Ionic compounds with metals that always form a cation with the same charge

Type II: Ionic compounds with metals (usually transition metals) that form cations with various charges

Type III: Compounds that contain only nonmetals

In trying to determine which type of compound you are naming, use the periodic table to help you identify metals and nonmetals and to determine which elements are transition metals.

WHAT IF Comments

Naming compounds requires certain rules. While some students think this chapter includes many rules, there really are only a few relative to the number of compounds that can be named. At least two major problems arise with common names. First, common names would require a great deal of memorization (the name of each compound would have to be memorized). With a systematic approach only the

rules must be learned. Second, common names are not really so "common." For example, asking people in different areas if they use a grocery "bag" or "sack," or if they drink "pop" or "soda," shows that "common names" differ from one place to another.

Name the following Type III compounds.

1. CO
    carbon monoxide

2. NO_2
    nitrogen dioxide

3. SeF_6
    selenium hexafluoride

4. SiO_2
    silicon dioxide

5. H_2O
    water

 Answers to Self-Check Exercise 4.4

a. silicon dioxide

b. dioxygen difluoride

c. xenon hexafluoride

 Section 4.3

Themes
Systems, Organization, Patterns of Change

Skills
Using the writing process, classifying

TEACHING TIPS

• Most students can name compounds if they are identified by type. This section provides an opportunity to review the types and have students practice on a variety of compounds rather than just those of a particular type.

• Figure 4.1 is a convenient flowchart to help students systematically name compounds. Students need to be encouraged to use this type of device to help them think through a difficult problem. The chart is also found in the transparency package.

Additional Examples

Name each of the following compounds:

1. AsF_3
   arsenic trifluoride

2. Al_2S_3
   aluminum sulfide

3. $SnBr_4$
   tin(IV) bromide

4. CS_2
   carbon disulfide

5. CdS
   cadmium sulfide

6. AgCl
   silver chloride

7. KI
   potassium iodide

8. NO
   nitrogen monoxide

9. P_2O_5
   diphosphorus pentoxide

10. $FeCl_3$
    iron(III) chloride

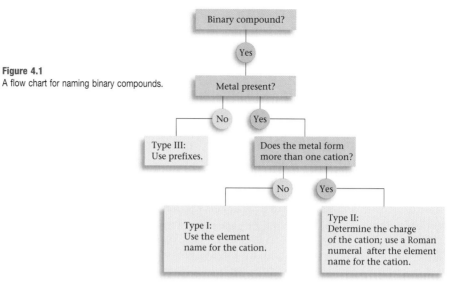

Figure 4.1
A flow chart for naming binary compounds.

The flow chart given in **Figure 4.1** should help you as you name binary compounds of the various types.

Example 4.6

Naming Binary Compounds: Summary

Name the following binary compounds.

a. CuO   c. B_2O_3 e. K_2S g. NH_3

b. SrO   d. $TiCl_4$ f. OF_2

Solution

a.

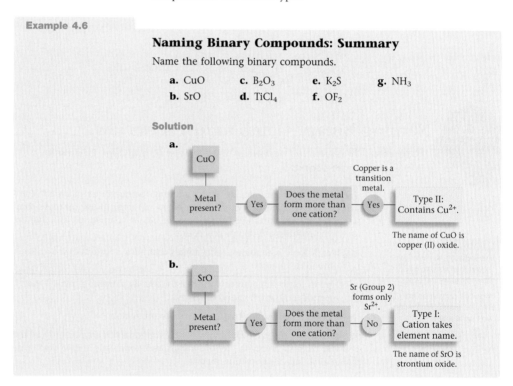

The name of CuO is copper (II) oxide.

b.

The name of SrO is strontium oxide.

c.

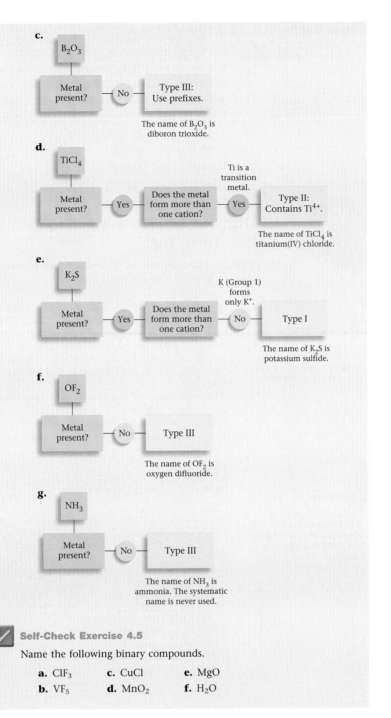

B_2O_3

Metal present? — No — Type III: Use prefixes.

The name of B_2O_3 is diboron trioxide.

d.

$TiCl_4$

Metal present? — Yes — Does the metal form more than one cation? — Yes — Ti is a transition metal. — Type II: Contains Ti^{4+}.

The name of $TiCl_4$ is titanium(IV) chloride.

e.

K_2S

Metal present? — Yes — Does the metal form more than one cation? — No — K (Group 1) forms only K^+. — Type I

The name of K_2S is potassium sulfide.

f.

OF_2

Metal present? — No — Type III

The name of OF_2 is oxygen difluoride.

g.

NH_3

Metal present? — No — Type III

The name of NH_3 is ammonia. The systematic name is never used.

✔ **Self-Check Exercise 4.5**

Name the following binary compounds.

a. ClF_3 c. CuCl e. MgO
b. VF_5 d. MnO_2 f. H_2O

4.3 Naming Binary Compounds: A Review **99**

✔ **Answers to Self-Check Exercise 4.5**

a. chlorine trifluoride
b. vanadium(V) fluoride
c. copper(I) chloride
d. manganese(IV) oxide
e. magnesium oxide
f. water

Answers to Focus Questions

1. A system for naming compounds is necessary because there are so many different compounds that it would be impossible to memorize all their names. A system makes it possible for each compound to have a unique name that can indicate its chemical composition.

2. A substance is a binary compound if it contains only two different elements.

3. The anions in all types of binary compounds have the ending *-ide*.

4. The cations in Type I compounds are named for the parent atom. In Type II compounds the cation has the parent atom name followed by a Roman numeral indicating its charge. In Type III compounds the first element is named as if it were a cation (the name of the parent atom) but it may have a prefix (indicating the number of atoms) if the formula contains more than one atom.

5. a. potassium bromide

b. tin(II) fluoride

c. carbon monoxide

d. copper(I) bromide

e. magnesium iodide

f. phosphorus trichloride

Section 4.4

Themes
Systems, Organization, Patterns of Change

Skills
Classifying, making comparisons, using the writing process

Student Preparation
Assign the students to read Sections 4.4 to 4.6 and to answer the Focus Questions at the end of Section 4.6 before coming to class.

Active Learning
After introducing the material in Sections 4.4 to 4.6 in class, place the students in groups and have them work together on Sections 4.4–4.6: Team Learning Worksheet. Answers and/or dis-

100

Focus Questions **Sections 4.1–4.3**

1. Why is a system for naming compounds necessary?
2. How can you tell if a substance is a binary compound?
3. How are the anions in all types of binary compounds similar?
4. How are the cations different in each type of binary compound?
5. Use Figure 4.1 to name the following compounds:

    a. KBr   **d.** CuBr
    b. SnF_2 **e.** MgI_2
    c. CO   **f.** PCl_3

4.4 Naming Compounds That Contain Polyatomic Ions

Objective: *To learn the names of common polyatomic ions and how to use them in naming compounds.*

CHEMISTRY
Ionic compounds containing polyatomic ions are not binary compounds, because they contain more than two elements.

A type of ionic compound that we have not yet considered is exemplified by ammonium nitrate, NH_4NO_3, which contains the **polyatomic ions** NH_4^+ and NO_3^-. As their name suggests, polyatomic ions are charged entities composed of several atoms bound together. Polyatomic ions are assigned special names that you *must memorize* to name the compounds containing them. The most important polyatomic ions and their names are listed in **Table 4.4.**

Note in Table 4.4 that several series of polyatomic anions exist that contain an atom of a given element and different numbers of oxygen atoms. These anions are called **oxyanions.** When there are two members in such a series, the name of the one with the smaller number of oxygen atoms ends

CHEMISTRY
The names and charges of polyatomic ions must be memorized. They are an important part of the vocabulary of chemistry.

TABLE 4.4
Names of Common Polyatomic Ions

Ion	Name	Ion	Name
NH_4^+	ammonium	CO_3^{2-}	carbonate
NO_2^-	nitrite	HCO_3^-	hydrogen carbonate (bicarbonate is a widely used common name)
NO_3^-	nitrate		
SO_3^{2-}	sulfite		
SO_4^{2-}	sulfate	ClO^-	hypochlorite
HSO_4^-	hydrogen sulfate (bisulfate is a widely used common name)	ClO_2^-	chlorite
		ClO_3^-	chlorate
		ClO_4^-	perchlorate
OH^-	hydroxide	$C_2H_3O_2^-$	acetate
CN^-	cyanide	MnO_4^-	permanganate
PO_4^{3-}	phosphate	$Cr_2O_7^{2-}$	dichromate
HPO_4^{2-}	hydrogen phosphate	CrO_4^{2-}	chromate
$H_2PO_4^-$	dihydrogen phosphate	O_2^{2-}	peroxide

100   Chapter 4   Nomenclature

---

cussion of these questions are also located in the *Teacher Resources.*

 Laboratory
Experiment 16:
Grocery Store Nomenclature, In Text

USING TECHNOLOGY

 Table 4.4

TEACHING TIPS
• Use Table 4.4 to help in learning the names of the polyatomic ions. Some groups of ions are related as part of a series, which makes remembering the names and charges easier. For example, nitrate and nitrite differ by only one oxygen atom, as do sulfate and sulfite. Show students that the charge is the same but the number of oxygen atoms changes. Also, point out that when hydro-

gen is added to a polyatomic ion (as in hydrogen sulfate or hydrogen carbonate), the charge on the polyatomic ion changes by 1.

• Chlorine is used to illustrate the series of ions formed between the halogens and oxygen. You can also show how other halogens (bromine, for example) form a series of anions with oxygen.

• If students learn the names and formulas for the *-ate* polyatomic ions and understand the concepts

CHEMISTRY

Note that the SO_3^{2-} anion has very different properties from SO_3 (sulfur trioxide), a pungent, toxic gas.

CHEMISTRY

Except for hydroxide, peroxide, and cyanide, the names of poly-atomic ions do not have an *-ide* ending.

CHEMISTRY

Certain transition metals form only one ion. Common examples are zinc (forms only Zn^{2+}) and silver (forms only Ag^+). For these cases the Roman numeral is omitted from the name.

in *-ite*, and the name of the one with the larger number ends in *-ate*. For example, SO_3^{2-} is sulfite and SO_4^{2-} is sulfate. When more than two oxyanions make up a series, *hypo-* (less than) and *per-* (more than) are used as prefixes to name the members of the series with the fewest and the most oxygen atoms, respectively. The best example involves the oxyanions containing chlorine:

ClO^-	*hypo*chlorite
ClO_2^-	chlorite
ClO_3^-	chlorate
ClO_4^-	*per*chlorate

Naming ionic compounds that contain polyatomic ions is very similar to naming binary ionic compounds. For example, the compound NaOH is called sodium hydroxide, because it contains the Na^+ (sodium) cation and the OH^- (hydroxide) anion. To name these compounds, *you must learn to recognize the common polyatomic ions.* That is, you must learn the *composition* and *charge* of each of the ions in Table 4.4. Then when you see the formula $NH_4C_2H_3O_2$, you should immediately recognize its two "parts":

The correct name is ammonium acetate.

When a metal is present that forms more than one cation, a Roman numeral is required to specify the cation charge, just as in naming Type II binary ionic compounds. For example, the compound $FeSO_4$ is called iron(II) sulfate, because it contains Fe^{2+} (to balance the 2^- charge on SO_4^{2-}). Note that to determine the charge on the iron cation, you must know that sulfate has a 2^- charge.

Example 4.7

Naming Compounds That Contain Polyatomic Ions

Give the systematic name of each of the following compounds.

a. Na_2SO_4 **c.** $Fe(NO_3)_3$ **e.** Na_2SO_3
b. KH_2PO_4 **d.** $Mn(OH)_2$

Solution

Compound	Ions Present	Ion Names	Compound Name
a. Na_2SO_4	two Na^+ SO_4^{2-}	sodium sulfate	sodium sulfate
b. KH_2PO_4	K^+ $H_2PO_4^-$	potassium dihydrogen phosphate	potassium dihydrogen phosphate
c. $Fe(NO_3)_3$	Fe^{3+} three NO_3^-	iron(III) nitrate	iron(III) nitrate

(continued)

Students should think of poly-atomic ions as a "unit." Many know that if NaCl is dissolved in water, Na^+ ions and Cl^- ions are present. However, students are often confused about the ions present when $NaNO_3$ is dissolved. Instead of the NO_3^- ion, students may think individual nitrogen and oxygen ions are present.

Additional Examples

Name each of these compounds.

1. $Cu(NO_3)_2$
   copper(II) nitrate

2. $PbCO_3$
   lead(II) carbonate

3. $KHSO_4$
   potassium hydrogen sulfate

4. NH_4I
   ammonium iodide

5. NaCN
   sodium cyanide

underlying the oxygen and hydro-gen anion series, they will be able to write formulas for almost all of the common polyatomic ions.

(continued)

d. $Mn(OH)_2$ Mn^{2+} manganese(II)   manganese(II)
              two OH^- hydroxide   hydroxide

e. Na_2SO_3 two Na^+ sodium   sodium sulfite
              $SO_3{}^{2-}$ sulfite

Answers to Self-Check Exercise 4.6

a. calcium hydroxide

b. sodium phosphate

c. potassium permanganate

d. ammonium dichromate

e. cobalt(II) perchlorate (Perchlorate has a 1− charge, so the cation must be Co^{2+} to balance the two $ClO_4{}^-$ ions.)

f. potassium chlorate

g. copper(II) nitrite (This compound contains two $NO_2{}^-$ (nitrite) ions and thus must contain a Cu^{2+} cation.)

Self-Check Exercise 4.6

Name each of the following compounds.

   a. $Ca(OH)_2$

   b. Na_3PO_4

   c. $KMnO_4$

   d. $(NH_4)_2Cr_2O_7$

   e. $Co(ClO_4)_2$

   f. $KClO_3$

   g. $Cu(NO_2)_2$

Example 4.7 illustrates that when more than one polyatomic ion appears in a chemical formula, parentheses are used to enclose the ion and a subscript is written after the closing parenthesis. Other examples are $(NH_4)_2SO_4$ and $Fe_3(PO_4)_2$.

In naming chemical compounds, use the strategy summarized in **Figure 4.2.** If the compound being considered is binary, use the procedure summarized in Figure 4.1. If the compound has more than two elements, ask yourself whether it has any polyatomic ions. Use Table 4.4 to help you recognize these ions until you have committed them to memory. If a polyatomic ion is present, name the compound using procedures very similar to those for naming binary ionic compounds.

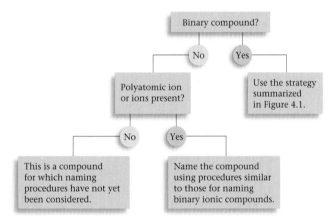

Figure 4.2
Overall strategy for naming chemical compounds.

Example 4.8

Summary of Naming Binary Compounds and Compounds That Contain Polyatomic Ions

Name the following compounds.

a. Na_2CO_3 d. PCl_3 e. $CuSO_4$

b. $FeBr_3$ c. $CsClO_4$

Solution

Compound	Name	Comments
a. Na_2CO_3	sodium carbonate	Contains $2Na^+$ and CO_3^{2-}.
b. $FeBr_3$	iron(III) bromide	Contains Fe^{3+} and $3Br^-$.
c. $CsClO_4$	cesium perchlorate	Contains Cs^+ and ClO_4^-.
d. PCl_3	phosphorus trichloride	Type III binary compound (both P and Cl are non-metals).
e. $CuSO_4$	copper(II) sulfate	Contains Cu^{2+} and SO_4^{2-}.

 Self-Check Exercise 4.7

Name the following compounds.

a. $NaHCO_3$ c. $CsClO_4$ e. $NaBr$ g. $Zn_3(PO_4)_2$

b. $BaSO_4$ d. BrF_5 f. $KOCl$

CHEMICAL IMPACT

Connection to Biology

Talking Tadpoles

It is well known that animals communicate by releasing chemicals that others of the same species receive and "understand." For example, ants use chemicals to signal news about food supplies and danger from predators, and honeybees "recognize" other bees from the same hive by their chemical signals. Now scientists at Yale University have shown that tadpoles send chemical signals to one another.

The experiment involved two groups of tadpoles of red-legged frogs. They were placed in an aquarium partitioned by a screen that allowed water to flow but blocked communications by sight and sound. When a wooden heron (a bird that preys on tadpoles) threatened the tadpoles in the one compartment, those on the other side moved away from the partition and ducked under a shelter. The researchers concluded that the frightened tadpoles signaled their fear to the tadpoles in other compartment by releasing a chemical signal that flowed to the other side in the water.

Other water-dwelling animals such as crayfish, hermit crabs, and a fish called the Iowa darter also have been observed to send chemical danger signals when they are threatened. Scientists think that the chemical used to send the signal is the ammonium ion, NH_4^+. Researchers are now trying to find out whether all aquatic species have a common chemical "language" to signal one another, just as ants and bees do.

A California red-legged frog tadpole.

Integrating the CHEMICAL IMPACT

Talking Tadpoles

Pheromones—the chemicals that a member of a particular species releases to communicate with other members of the species—are fascinating. It is interesting to speculate whether humans emit pheromones.

Plants use chemical signals as well. For example, when attacked by aphids the wild potato plant manufactures and emits the aphid alarm pheromone to scare off the invading aphids. Another interesting example is the *Orchidantha* plant in Borneo, which sports a purple flower that emits a foul odor attractive to dung beetles. The plant emits this special fragrance from 7:30 A.M. until midnight, attracting dung beetles to assist in the pollination process.

Name the following compounds.

1. $Ca(HCO_3)_2$
   calcium hydrogen carbonate

2. MgI_2
   magnesium iodide

3. $KMnO_4$
   potassium permanganate

4. Sb_2O_3
   antimony(III) oxide

5. $Fe(OH)_2$
   iron(II) hydroxide

Answers to Self-Check Exercise 4.7

Compound	Name
a. $NaHCO_3$ Contains Na^+ and HCO_3^-	Sodium hydrogen carbonate, often called sodium bicarbonate (common name)
b. $BaSO_4$ Contains Ba^{2+} and SO_4^{2-}	Barium sulfate
c. $CsClO_4$ Contains Cs^+ and ClO_4^-	Cesium perchlorate
d. BrF_5 Both nonmetals (Type III binary)	Bromine pentafluoride
e. $NaBr$ Contains Na^+ and Br^- (Type I binary)	Sodium bromide
f. $KOCl$ Contains K^+ and OCl^-	Potassium hypochlorite
g. $Zn_3(PO_4)_2$ Contains Zn^{2+} and PO_4^{3-}. Zn is a transition metal and officially requires a Roman numeral. However, because Zn forms only the Zn^{2+} cation, the II is usually omitted. Thus the name of the compound is usually given as zinc phosphate.	Zinc(II) phosphate

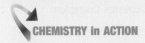

Name Game II: Polyatomic Ions

Materials Each student/group will need 22 index cards.

Purpose Students will learn the names, formulas, and charges of common polyatomic ions.

Discussion Understanding chemistry requires that students both understand fundamental principles and know the language of chemistry. They should be familiar with the periodic table, know names and symbols of some elements, and know how to name compounds. You can vary this activity to accommodate any time limit.

 Section 4.5

Themes
Systems, Organization, Patterns of Change

Skills
Classifying, making comparisons, using the writing process

 Laboratory
Experiment 17:
Energy Changes in Physical and Chemical Systems, Traditional

TEACHING TIPS

- Students are briefly introduced to acids in this chapter. Acids are reactants in many reactions in upcoming chapters and are used in early experiments, so this brief introduction is important.

- Students should be asked to name the oxyacids containing bromine as well as those containing chlorine. This activity provides an opportunity to review the naming system for the polyatomic ions and extend it to acids.

---

1. Make flashcards for the common polyatomic ions listed in Table 4.4. Write the name on one side and the formula (with charge) on the other.
2. Group all of the oxyanions together, and arrange them according to suffix (*-ate* or *-ite*). Notice the patterns.
3. Learn the names, formulas, and charges for all of the polyatomic ions listed in Table 4.4.

 ### 4.5 Naming Acids

Objectives: *To learn how the anion composition determines the acid's name. To learn names for common acids.*

When dissolved in water, certain molecules produce H^+ ions (protons). These substances, which are called **acids**, were first recognized by the sour taste of their solutions. For example, citric acid is responsible for the tartness of lemons and limes. Acids will be discussed in detail later. Here we simply present the rules for naming acids.

An acid can be viewed as a molecule with one or more H^+ ions attached to an anion. The rules for naming acids depend on whether the anion contains oxygen.

Rules for Naming Acids

1. If the *anion does not contain oxygen,* the acid is named with the prefix *hydro-* and the suffix *-ic* attached to the root name for the element. For example, when gaseous HCl (hydrogen chloride) is dissolved in water, it forms hydrochloric acid. Similarly, hydrogen cyanide (HCN) and dihydrogen sulfide (H_2S) dissolved in water are called hydrocyanic acid and hydrosulfuric acid, respectively.

2. When the *anion contains oxygen,* the acid name is formed from the root name of the central element of the anion or the anion name, with a suffix of *-ic* or *-ous.* When the anion name ends in *-ate,* the suffix *-ic* is used. For example,

Acid	Anion	Name
H_2SO_4	SO_4^{2-} (sulfate)	sulfuric acid
H_3PO_4	PO_4^{3-} (phosphate)	phosphoric acid
$HC_2H_3O_2$	$C_2H_3O_2^-$ (acetate)	acetic acid

When the anion name ends in *-ite,* the suffix *-ous* is used in the acid name. For example,

Acid	Anion	Name
H_2SO_3	SO_3^{2-} (sulfite)	sulfurous acid
HNO_2	NO_2^- (nitrite)	nitrous acid

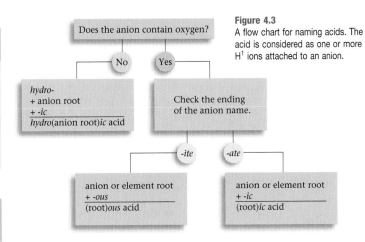

Figure 4.3
A flow chart for naming acids. The acid is considered as one or more H^1 ions attached to an anion.

The application of rule 2 can be seen in the names of the acids of the oxyanions of chlorine, as shown below. The rules for naming acids are given in schematic form in **Figure 4.3.** The names of the most important acids are given in **Table 4.5** and **Table 4.6.** These should be memorized.

Acid	Anion	Name
$HClO_4$	perchlor*ate*	perchlor*ic* acid
$HClO_3$	chlor*ate*	chlor*ic* acid
$HClO_2$	chlor*ite*	chlor*ous* acid
HClO	hypochlor*ite*	hypochlor*ous* acid

4.6 Writing Formulas from Names

Objective: *To learn to write the formula of a compound, given its name.*

So far we have started with the chemical formula of a compound and decided on its systematic name. Being able to reverse the process is also important. Often a laboratory procedure describes a compound by name, but the label on the bottle in the lab shows only the formula of the chemical it contains. It is essential that you are able to get the formula of a compound from its name. In fact, you already know enough about compounds to do this. For example, given the name calcium hydroxide, you can write the formula as $Ca(OH)_2$ because you know that calcium forms only Ca^{2+} ions and that, since hydroxide is OH^-, two of these anions are required to give a neutral compound. Similarly, the name iron(II) oxide implies the formula FeO, because the Roman numeral II indicates the presence of the cation Fe^{2+} and the oxide ion is O^{2-}.

We emphasize at this point that it is essential to learn the name, composition, and charge of each of the common polyatomic anions (and the NH_4^+ cation). If you do not recognize these ions by formula and by name, you will not be able to write the compound's name given its formula or the compound's formula given its name. You must also learn the names of the common acids.

4.6 Writing Formulas from Names   **105**

Write the correct formula for each compound.

1. sodium nitrate
   $NaNO_3$

2. ammonium dichromate
   $NH_4Cr_2O_7$

3. mercury(II) iodide
   HgI_2

4. barium carbonate
   $BaCO_3$

5. magnesium bromide:
   $MgBr_2$

6. hydrochloric acid
   $HCl(aq)$

7. carbon disulfide
   CS_2

8. nickel(II) perchlorate
   $Ni(ClO_4)_2$

9. cesium fluoride
   CsF

10. hypobromous acid
   $HBrO$

 Answers to Self-Check Exercise 4.8

Name	Chemical Formula
a. ammonium sulfate	$(NH_4)_2SO_4$

Two ammonium ions (NH_4^+) are required for each sulfate ion (SO_4^{2-}) to achieve charge balance.

b. vanadium(V) fluoride VF_5

The compound contains V^{5+} ions and requires five F^- ions for charge balance.

c. disulfur dichloride S_2Cl_2

The prefix *di-* indicates two of each atom.

d. rubidium peroxide Rb_2O_2

Because rubidium is in Group 1, it forms only 1^+ ions. Thus two Rb^+ ions are needed to balance the 2^- charge on the peroxide ion (O_2^{2-}).

e. aluminum oxide Al_2O_3

Aluminum forms only 3^+ ions. Two Al^{3+} ions are required to balance the charge on the three O^{2-} ions.

Example 4.9

Writing Formulas from Names

Give the formula for each of the following compounds.

    a. potassium hydroxide   **e.** calcium chloride
    b. sodium carbonate   **f.** lead(IV) oxide
    c. nitric acid   **g.** dinitrogen pentoxide
    d. cobalt(III) nitrate   **h.** ammonium perchlorate

Solution

Name	Formula	Comments
a. potassium hydroxide	KOH	Contains K^+ and OH^-.
b. sodium carbonate	Na_2CO_3	We need two Na^+ to balance CO_3^{2-}.
c. nitric acid	HNO_3	Common strong acid; memorize.
d. cobalt(III) nitrate	$Co(NO_3)_3$	Cobalt(III) means Co^{3+}; we need three NO_3^- to balance Co^{3+}.
e. calcium chloride	$CaCl_2$	We need two Cl^- to balance Ca^{2+}; Ca (Group 2) always forms Ca^{2+}.
f. lead(IV) oxide	PbO_2	Lead(IV) means Pb^{4+}; we need two O^{2-} to balance Pb^{4+}.
g. dinitrogen pentoxide	N_2O_5	*di-* means two; *pent(a)-* means five.
h. ammonium perchlorate	NH_4ClO_4	Contains NH_4^+ and ClO_4^-.

 Self-Check Exercise 4.8

Write the formula for each of the following compounds.

    a. ammonium sulfate   **d.** rubidium peroxide
    b. vanadium(V) fluoride   **e.** aluminum oxide
    c. disulfur dichloride

Focus Questions

Sections 4.4–4.6

1. What patterns can you see in Table 4.4 that reduce the number of polyatomic ions you need to memorize? (*Hint:* Try grouping the ions by common elements or suffixes.)

2. Once you have identified that a compound contains a polyatomic ion, how is naming it different from naming a binary compound?

3. How can you tell if a compound should be named an acid?

4. Use the flow chart in Figure 4.3 to name the following:

    a. $HClO_4$ **b.** HNO_2 **c.** HBr **d.** H_2SO_4

5. When writing a formula from a chemical name, how can you tell how many of each element or polyatomic ion to put in the formula?

Answers to Focus Questions

1. Ions can be grouped by the first element in the anion (such as sulfur, phosphorus, or nitrogen). The number of oxygen atoms varies, and the presence of hydrogen can also be incorporated into the series.

2. The compound containing a polyatomic ion is named by giving the name for the cation followed by the name for the polyatomic ion (except in the case of the ammonium ion, which is given first because it is a cation). The number of polyatomic ions present is not given in the name.

3. The formulas of compounds named as acids begin with H.

4. a. perchloric acid
    b. nitrous acid
    c. hydrobromic acid
    d. sulfuric acid

5. The number of each kind of element or polyatomic ion in a formula is determined by how many are needed to produce a compound that is neutral in charge.

Grocery Store Nomenclature (FIELD)

Problem

Can you determine which compounds are in your consumer products?

Introduction

Chemicals are not just used in chemistry class. We use chemicals every day and in everything we buy. In this activity you will determine the identity of a chemical based on clues given by your teacher. You will then find out which products contain these chemicals.

Prelab Assignment

Read the entire laboratory experiment before you begin.

Materials

List of clues   References

Procedure

1. Obtain a list of clues to the identities of five chemical compounds.
2. Use references (including your text, other books, and the Internet) to help you determine the identity of each chemical.
3. Find products in which each of the chemicals is present. You may find these items at home or you may need to go to a grocery store or drugstore.

Summary Table

Fill in a table similar to the one given below.

	Chemical Name	Chemical Formula	Justification	Products That Contain the Chemical
1				
2				
3				
4				
5				

Something Extra

Contact a company that manufactures a product that contains one of the chemicals on your list and find out the purpose of the chemical in the product.

107

CHEMISTRY in the LABORATORY

Grocery Store Nomenclature

Objectives

1. To name compounds
2. To find the purpose for compounds
3. To relate chemistry to real life

Skills

Classifying, applying concepts

Materials

List of clues   References

Preparation Hints

Give each student an individual list of five clues. Clues are printed in table form in the *Teacher's Guide for the Laboratory*.

Prelab Discussion

Tell students that all of the chemicals are compounds that they can name after studying Chapter 4.

Procedure Hints

Allow students time to visit a grocery store. Consider distributing the clues on Thursday or Friday and setting the due date for Monday.

Post-Lab Discussion

Once all of the students have turned in their reports, assemble a class set of data. Show students that many products contain compounds that they can name and identify by the formula.

Sample Data/Answers

Sample data are provided in the *Teacher's Guide for the Laboratory*.

Something Extra

Contact a company that makes a product containing one of the chemicals on your list and find out the purpose of the chemical in the product.

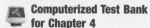

Chapter Review
Assign the students to work individually on the Chapter 4 Review Worksheet at the appropriate level (Basic, Standard, or Challenge). Answers are found in the *Teacher Resources*.

Assessment
Chapter 4 Test is found in the *Teacher Resources*, along with the answers for the test.

Computerized Test Bank for Chapter 4

Answers to End of Chapter Problems

1. A binary compound contains only two elements. Examples are sodium chloride, water, and carbon dioxide.

2. compounds containing a metal and a nonmetal; compounds containing two nonmetals

3. cation, anion

4. cation (positive ion)

5. Sodium chloride consists of Na^+ ions and Cl^- ions in an extended crystal lattice array. No discrete NaCl pairs are present.

6. (a) sodium iodide; (b) calcium fluoride; (c) aluminum sulfide; (d) calcium bromide; (e) strontium oxide; (f) silver(I) chloride (silver chloride); (g) cesium iodide; (h) lithium oxide

7. (a) incorrect; BaH_2 is barium hydride; (b) incorrect; Na_2O is sodium oxide; (c) correct; (d) incorrect; SiO_2 is silicon dioxide; (e) correct

8. (a) iron(III) iodide; (b) manganese(II) chloride; (c) mercury(II) oxide; (d) copper(I) oxide; (e) copper(II) oxide; (f) tin(IV) bromide

9. (a) cobaltous chloride; (b) chromic bromide; (c) plumbous oxide; (d) stannic oxide; (e) ferric oxide; (f) ferric chloride

10. (a) iodine pentafluoride; (b) arsenic trichloride; (c) selenium monoxide; (d) xenon tetrafluoride; (e) nitrogen triiodide; (f) diboron trioxide

11. (a) germanium tetrahydride; (b) dinitrogen tetrabromide; (c) diphosphorus pentasulfide; (d) selenium dioxide; (e) ammonia; (f) silicon dioxide

12. (a) diboron hexahydride, nonionic; (b) calcium nitride, ionic; (c) carbon tetrabromide, nonionic; (d) silver sulfide, ionic; (e) copper(II) chloride, ionic; (f) chlorine monofluoride, nonionic

13. (a) radium chloride, ionic; (b) selenium dichloride, nonionic; (c) phosphorus trichloride, nonionic; (d) sodium phosphide, ionic; (e) manganese(II) fluoride, ionic; (f) zinc oxide, ionic

14. An oxyanion contains a particular element plus oxygen. If there are two oxyanions of that element, the higher oxidation state is given the *-ate* ending and the lower oxidation state is given the *-ite* ending. If there are four

15. Which oxyanion of chlorine contains the most oxygen atoms: hypochlorite, chlorite, or perchlorate?

16. Complete the following list by filling in the missing names or formulas of the indicated oxyanions.

BrO^- _____
_____ iodate
IO_4^- _____
_____ hypoiodite

17. Write the formula for each of the following nitrogen-containing polyatomic ions, including the overall charge of the ion.
   a. nitrate
   b. nitrite
   c. ammonium
   d. cyanide

18. Write the formula for each of the following chlorine-containing ions, including the overall charge of the ion.
   a. chloride
   b. hypochlorite
   c. chlorate
   d. perchlorate

19. Write the formulas of the compounds below (see your answers to problem 18).
   a. magnesium chloride
   b. calcium hypochlorite
   c. potassium chlorate
   d. barium perchlorate

20. Give the name of each of the following polyatomic anions.
   a. MnO_4^-
   b. O_2^{2-}
   c. CrO_4^{2-}
   d. $Cr_2O_7^{2-}$
   e. NO_3^-
   f. SO_3^{2-}

21. Name each of the following compounds, which contain polyatomic ions.
   a. $Fe(NO_3)_3$
   b. $Co_3(PO_4)_2$
   c. $Cr(CN)_3$
   d. $Al_2(SO_4)_3$
   e. $Cr(C_2H_3O_2)_2$
   f. $(NH_4)_2SO_3$

4.5 Naming Acids

Questions

22. Give a simple definition of an *acid*.

23. Many acids contain the element _____ in addition to hydrogen.

24. Name each of the following acids.
   a. HCl
   b. H_2SO_4
   c. HNO_3
   d. HI
   e. HNO_2
   f. $HClO_3$
   g. HBr
   h. HF
   i. $HC_2H_3O_2$

4.6 Writing Formulas from Names

Problems

25. Write formulas for each of the following simple binary ionic compounds.
   a. lithium oxide
   b. aluminum iodide
   c. silver oxide
   d. potassium nitride
   e. calcium phosphide

f. magnesium fluoride
g. sodium sulfide
h. barium hydride

26. Write the formula for each of the following binary compounds of nonmetallic elements.
   a. carbon dioxide
   b. sulfur dioxide
   c. dinitrogen tetrachloride
   d. carbon tetraiodide
   e. phosphorus pentafluoride
   f. diphosphorus pentoxide

27. Write the formula for each of the following compounds that contain polyatomic ions. Be sure to enclose the polyatomic ion in parentheses if more than one such ion is needed.
   a. calcium phosphate
   b. ammonium nitrate
   c. aluminum hydrogen sulfate
   d. barium sulfate
   e. ferric nitrate
   f. copper(I) hydroxide

28. Write the formula for each of the following acids.
   a. hydrocyanic acid
   b. nitric acid
   c. sulfuric acid
   d. phosphoric acid
   e. hypochlorous acid
   f. hydrobromic acid
   g. bromous acid
   h. hydrofluoric acid

29. Write the formula for each of the following substances.
   a. lithium chloride
   b. cuprous carbonate
   c. hydrobromic acid
   d. calcium nitrate
   e. sodium perchlorate
   f. aluminum hydroxide
   g. barium hydrogen carbonate
   h. iron(II) sulfate
   i. diboron hexachloride
   j. phosphorus pentabromide
   k. potassium sulfite
   l. barium acetate

Critical Thinking

30. Before an electrocardiogram (ECG) is recorded for a cardiac patient, the ECG leads are usually coated with a moist paste containing sodium chloride. What property of an ionic substance such as NaCl is being made use of here?

31. What is a *binary* compound? What is a *polyatomic* anion? What is an *oxyanion*?

32. Name the following compounds.
   a. $AuBr_3$
   b. $Co(CN)_3$
   c. $MgHPO_4$
   d. B_2H_6
   e. NH_3
   f. Ag_2SO_4
   g. $Be(OH)_2$

(e) $NaClO_4$; (f) $Al(OH)_3$;
(g) $Ba(HCO_3)_2$; (h) $FeSO_4$;
(i) B_2Cl_6; (j) PBr_5; (k) K_2SO_3;
(l) $Ba(C_2H_3O_2)_2$

30. A moist paste of NaCl would contain Na^+ and Cl^- ions in solution and would serve as a conductor of electrical impulses.

31. A binary compound is a compound containing two—and only two—elements. A polyatomic anion is several atoms bonded together that, as a whole, carries a negative electrical charge. An oxyanion is a negative ion containing a particular element and one or more oxygen atoms.

32. (a) gold(III) bromide; (b) cobalt(III) cyanide; (c) magnesium hydrogen phosphate; (d) diboron hexahydride (diborane is the common name); (e) ammonia; (f) silver(I) sulfate (silver sulfate); (g) beryllium hydroxide

33. (a) ammonium carbonate; (b) ammonium hydrogen carbonate, ammonium bicarbonate; (c) calcium phosphate; (d) sulfurous acid; (e) manganese(IV) oxide; (f) iodic acid; (g) potassium hydride

34. (a) K_2O; (b) MgO; (c) FeO; (d) Fe_2O_3; (e) ZnO; (f) PbO; (g) Al_2O_3

35. M^+ compounds: MD, M_2E, M_3F; M^{2+} compounds: MD_2, ME, M_3F_2; M^{3+} compounds: MD_3, M_2E_3, MF

36. See Table 4.A in the *Solutions Guide*.

37. See Table 4.B in the *Solutions Guide*.

38. [1] e; [2] a; [3] a; [4] g; [5] g; [6] f; [7] g; [8] a; [9] e; [10] j

39. (a) Al (13e) → Al^{3+} (10e) + $3e^-$; (b) S(16e) + $2e^-$ → S^{2-} (18e); (c) Cu (29e) → Cu^+(28e) + $1e^-$; (d) F(9e) + e^- → F^-(10e); (e) Zn(30e) → Zn^{2+}(28e) + $2e^-$; (f) P(15e) + $3e^-$ → P^{3-} (18e)

40. (a) none likely; (b) Ga^{3+}; (c) Te^{2-}; (d) Tl^{3+}; (e) Br^-; (f) Fr^+

41. (a) Na_2S; (b) KCl; (c) BaO; (d) MgSe; (e) $CuBr_2$; (f) AlI_3; (g) Al_2O_3; (h) Ca_3N_2

42. (a) beryllium oxide; (b) magnesium iodide;

18. (a) Cl^-; (b) ClO^-; (c) ClO_3^-; (d) ClO_4^-

19. (a) $MgCl_2$; (b) $Ca(ClO)_2$; (c) $KClO_3$; (d) $Ba(ClO_4)_2$

20. (a) permanganate; (b) peroxide; (c) chromate; (d) dichromate; (e) nitrate; (f) sulfite

21. (a) iron(III) nitrate, ferric nitrate; (b) cobalt(II) phosphate, cobaltous phosphate; (c) chromium(III) cyanide, chromic phosphate; (d) aluminum sulfate; (e) chromium(II) acetate, chromous acetate; (f) ammonium sulfite

22. An acid is a substance that produces hydrogen ions, H^+, when dissolved in water.

23. oxygen

24. (a) hydrochloric acid; (b) sulfuric acid; (c) nitric acid; (d) hydroiodic acid; (e) nitrous acid; (f) chloric acid; (g) hydrobromic acid; (h) hydrofluoric acid; (i) acetic acid

25. (a) Li_2O; (b) AlI_3; (c) Ag_2O; (d) K_3N; (e) Ca_3P_2; (f) MgF_2; (g)Na_2S; (h) BaH_2

26. (a) CO_2; (b) SO_2; (c) N_2Cl_4; (d) CI_4; (e) PF_5; (f) P_2O_5

27. (a) $Ca_3(PO_4)_2$; (b) NH_4NO_3; (c) $Al(HSO_4)_3$; (d) $BaSO_4$; (e) $Fe(NO_3)_2$; (f) CuOH

28. (a) HCN; (b) HNO_3; (c) H_2SO_4; (d) H_3PO_4; (e) HClO or HOCl; (f) HBr; (g) $HBrO_2$; (h) HF

29. (a) LiCl; (b) Cu_2CO_3; (c) HBr; (d) $Ca(NO_3)_2$;

(c) sodium sulfide;
(d) aluminum iodide;
(e) hydrogen chloride
(gaseous), hydrochloric acid
(aqueous); (f) lithium
fluoride; (g) silver(I) sulfide,
usually called silver sulfide;
(h) calcium hydride

43. (a) incorrect (Si is
silicon); (b) incorrect (Co is
cobalt); (c) incorrect (calcium
hydride); (d) correct;
(e) incorrect (phosphorus
trihydride)

44. (a) iron(II) bromide;
(b) cobalt(II) sulfide;
(c) cobalt(III) sulfide;
(d) tin(IV) oxide;
(e) mercury(I) chloride;
(f) mercury(II) chloride

45. (a) xenon hexafluoride;
(b) oxygen difluoride;
(c) arsenic triiodide;
(d) dinitrogen tetraoxide
(tetroxide); (e) dichlorine
monoxide; (f) sulfur
hexafluoride

46. (a) iron(III) acetate;
(b) bromine monofluoride;
(c) potassium peroxide;
(d) silicon tetrabromide;
(e) copper(II) permanganate;
(f) calcium chromate

47. (a) lithium dihydrogen
phosphate; (b) copper(II)
cyanide; (c) lead(II) nitrate;
(d) sodium hydrogen
phosphate; (e) sodium
chlorite; (f) cobalt(III) sulfate

48. (a) $CaCl_2$; (b) Ag_2O;
(c) Al_2S_3; (d) $BeBr_2$; (e) H_2S;
(f) KH; (g) MgI_2; (h) CsF

49. (a) SO_2; (b) N_2O;
(c) XeF_4; (d) P_4O_{10}; (e) PCl_5;
(f) SF_6; (g) NO_2

50. (a) NaH_2PO_4; (b) $LiClO_4$;
(c) $Cu(HCO_3)_2$; (d) $KC_2H_3O_2$;
(e) BaO_2; (f) Cs_2SO_3

51. (a) $AgClO_4$; (b) $Co(OH)_3$;
(c) NaClO or NaOCl;
(d) $K_2Cr_2O_7$; (e) NH_4NO_2;
(f) $Fe(OH)_3$; (g) NH_4HCO_3;
(h) $KBrO_4$

33. Name the following compounds.
  a. $(NH_4)_2CO_3$ e. MnO_2
  b. NH_4HCO_3 **f.** HIO_3
  c. $Ca_3(PO_4)_2$ g. KH
  d. H_2SO_3

34. Most metallic elements form *oxides*, and often the oxide is the most common compound of the element that is found in the earth's crust. Write the formulas for the oxides of the following metallic elements.
  c. potassium   e. zinc
  b. magnesium   **f.** lead(II)
  c. iron(II)   g. aluminum
  d. iron(III)

35. Consider the hypothetical metallic element M, which is capable of forming stable simple cations that have charges of 1+, 2+, and 3+, respectively. Consider also the nonmetallic elements D, E, and F, which form anions that have charges of 1−, 2−, and 3−, respectively. Write the formulas of all possible compounds between metal M and nonmetals D, E, and F.

36. Complete Table 4.A (below) by writing the names and formulas for the ionic compounds formed when the cations listed across the top combine with the anions shown in the left-hand column.

37. Complete Table 4.B (below) by writing the formulas for the ionic compounds formed when the anions listed across the top combine with the cations shown in the left-hand column.

38. For each of the negative ions listed in column 1, use the periodic table to find in column 2 the total num-

TABLE 4.A

Ions	Fe^{2+}	Al^{3+}	Na^+	Ca^{2+}	NH_4^+	Fe^{3+}	Ni^{2+}	Hg_2^{2+}	Hg^{2+}
CO_3^{2-}	——	——	——	——	——	——	——	——	——
BrO_3^-	——	——	——	——	——	——	——	——	——
$C_2H_3O_2^-$	——	——	——	——	——	——	——	——	——
OH^-	——	——	——	——	——	——	——	——	——
HCO_3^-	——	——	——	——	——	——	——	——	——
PO_4^{3-}	——	——	——	——	——	——	——	——	——
SO_3^{2-}	——	——	——	——	——	——	——	——	——
ClO_4^-	——	——	——	——	——	——	——	——	——
SO_4^{2-}	——	——	——	——	——	——	——	——	——
O^{2-}	——	——	——	——	——	——	——	——	——
Cl^-	——	——	——	——	——	——	——	——	——

TABLE 4.B

Ions	nitrate	sulfate	hydrogen sulfate	dihydrogen phosphate	oxide	chloride
calcium	——	——	——	——	——	——
strontium	——	——	——	——	——	——
ammonium	——	——	——	——	——	——
aluminum	——	——	——	——	——	——
iron(III)	——	——	——	——	——	——
nickel(II)	——	——	——	——	——	——
silver(I)	——	——	——	——	——	——
gold(III)	——	——	——	——	——	——
potassium	——	——	——	——	——	——
mercury(II)	——	——	——	——	——	——
barium	——	——	——	——	——	——

ber of electrons the ion contains. A given answer may be used more than once.

Column 1	Column 2
[1] Se^{2-}	[a] 18
[2] S^{2-}	[b] 35
[3] P^{3-}	[c] 52
[4] O^{2-}	[d] 34
[5] N^{3-}	[e] 36
[6] I^-	[f] 54
[7] F^-	[g] 10
[8] Cl^-	[h] 9
[9] Br^-	[i] 53
[10] At^-	[j] 86

39. For each of the following processes that show the formation of ions, complete the process by indicating the number of electrons that must be gained or lost to form the ion. Indicate the total number of electrons in the ion, and in the atom from which it was made.
    a. $Al \rightarrow Al^{3+}$
    b. $S \rightarrow S^{2-}$
    c. $Cu \rightarrow Cu^+$
    d. $F \rightarrow F^-$
    e. $Zn \rightarrow Zn^{2+}$
    f. $P \rightarrow P^{3-}$

40. For each of the following atomic numbers, use the periodic table to write the formula (including the charge) for the simple *ion* that the element is most likely to form.
    a. 36
    b. 31
    c. 52
    d. 81
    e. 35
    f. 87

41. For the following pairs of ions, use the principle of electrical neutrality to predict the formula of the binary compound that the ions are most likely to form.
    a. Na^+ and S^{2-}
    b. K^+ and Cl^-
    c. Ba^{2+} and O^{2-}
    d. Mg^{2+} and Se^{2-}
    e. Cu^{2+} and Br^-
    f. Al^{3+} and I^-
    g. Al^{3+} and O^{2-}
    h. Ca^{2+} and N^{3-}

42. Give the name of each of the following simple binary ionic compounds.
    a. BeO
    b. MgI_2
    c. Na_2S
    d. Al_2O_3
    e. HCl
    f. LiF
    g. Ag_2S
    h. CaH_2

43. In which of the following pairs is the name incorrect?
    a. SiI_4, silver iodide
    b. $CoCl_2$, copper(II) chloride
    c. CaH_2, hydrocalcinic acid
    d. $Zn(C_2H_3O_2)_2$, zinc acetate
    e. PH_3, phosphoric trihydride

44. Write the name of each of the following ionic substances, using the system that includes a Roman numeral to specify the charge of the cation.
    a. $FeBr_2$
    b. CoS
    c. Co_2S_3
    d. SnO_2
    e. Hg_2Cl_2
    f. $HgCl_2$

45. Name each of the following binary compounds.
    a. XeF_6
    b. OF_2
    c. AsI_3
    d. N_2O_4
    e. Cl_2O
    f. SF_6

46. Name each of the following compounds.
    a. $Fe(C_2H_3O_2)_3$
    b. BrF
    c. K_2O_2
    d. $SiBr_4$
    e. $Cu(MnO_4)_2$
    f. $CaCrO_4$

47. Name each of the following compounds, which contain polyatomic ions.
    a. LiH_2PO_4
    b. $Cu(CN)_2$
    c. $Pb(NO_3)_2$
    d. Na_2HPO_4
    e. $NaClO_2$
    f. $Co_2(SO_4)_3$

48. Write the formula for each of the following simple binary ionic compounds.
    a. calcium chloride
    b. silver(I) oxide (usually called silver oxide)
    c. aluminum sulfide
    d. beryllium bromide
    e. hydrosulfuric acid
    f. potassium hydride
    g. magnesium iodide
    h. cesium fluoride

49. Write the formula for each of the following binary compounds of nonmetallic elements.
    a. sulfur dioxide
    b. dinitrogen monoxide
    c. xenon tetrafluoride
    d. tetraphosphorus decoxide
    e. phosphorus pentachloride
    f. sulfur hexafluoride
    g. nitrogen dioxide

50. Write the formula of each of the following ionic substances.
    a. sodium dihydrogen phosphate
    b. lithium perchlorate
    c. copper(II) hydrogen carbonate
    d. potassium acetate
    e. barium peroxide
    f. cesium sulfite

51. Write the formula for each of the following compounds, which contain polyatomic ions. Be sure to enclose the polyatomic ion in parentheses if more than one such ion is needed to balance the oppositely charged ion(s).
    a. silver(I) perchlorate (usually called silver perchlorate)
    b. cobalt(III) hydroxide
    c. sodium hypochlorite
    d. potassium dichromate
    e. ammonium nitrite
    f. ferric hydroxide
    g. ammonium hydrogen carbonate
    h. potassium perbromate

5 Measurements and Calculations

	Section	Text Features & Components	Labs, Demonstrations & Activities
Teaching Segment 5A 0.5 block pp. 113–121	5.1 Scientific Notation	**LP** Lesson Plans (Sec 5.1–5.3) **SE** Celebrity Chemical: Carvone *p. 114*	
	5.2 Units	**SE** Chemical Impact: Critical Units! *p. 117*	
	5.3 Measurements of Length, Volume, and Mass	**SE** Chemical Impact: What is a Meter, Anyway? *p. 121*	**TE** Mini Demo *p. 119*
Teaching Segment 5B 1.5 blocks pp. 122–129	5.4 Uncertainty in Measurement	**LP** Lesson Plans (Sec 5.4–5.5) **SE** Chemical Impact: Measuring Changes *p. 123*	**LM** Experiment 18: Measurement and the SI System Lab Manual Report Sheets Teacher's Lab Guide
	5.5 Significant Figures	**TE** Teaching Support: Background Information *p. 126*	**SE** Chemistry in the Laboratory: Measuring a Book? Precisely! **LM** Experiment 19: Measuring a Book? Precisely! Lab Manual Report Sheets Teacher's Lab Guide **RP** Classroom Activities and Projects *pp. 11–12*
	continued on next page		

continued on next page

Chapter Planning Guide

All Learners	Review & Assessment	Standards
(TE) Active Learning *p. 113* (TE) Teaching Tips *p. 113* (AR) Less Proficient Students *p. 9*	(TE) Additional Examples *pp. 115–116* (SE) Self Check *p. 116* (SE) Key Terms *p. 148* (SE) Questions and Problems *pp. 148–149*	(TE) **NSES** UCP1, A1, A2, E2 (⬤) **SSS** SC.H.1.4.5
(TE) Teaching Tips *p. 117* (�C) Transparency: Table 5.2 *p. 118* (AR) Less Proficient Students *p. 9*	(SE) What if . . . *p. 116* (SE) Key Terms *p. 148* (SE) Questions and Problems *p. 149*	
(�C) Transparency: Table 5.3 *p. 118* (�C) Transparency: Figure 5.1 *p. 119* (TE) Teaching Tips *p. 120* (RP) Team Learning Worksheets (Sec 5.1–5.3) *pp. 19–20* (AR) Less Proficient Students *p. 9*	(SE) Focus Questions (Sec 5.1–5.3) *p. 120* (SE) Key Terms *p. 148* (SE) Questions and Problems *p. 149*	
(TE) Active Learning *p. 122* (AR) Less Proficient Students *p. 9* (TE) Teaching Tips *p. 122*	(SE) Key Terms *p. 148* (SE) Questions and Problems *p. 149*	(TE) **NSES** UCP1, UCP3, A1, A2, E1, E2, F4, F6, G3 (⬤) **SSS** SC.H.3.4.2, SC.H.3.4.6
(TE) Teaching Tips *p. 124* (RP) Team Learning Worksheets (Sec 5.4–5.5) *pp. 21–22* (AR) Less Proficient Students *p. 9*	(TE) Additional Examples *pp. 125, 128* (SE) Self Check *pp. 126, 129* (SE) Focus Questions (Sec 5.4–5.5) *p. 129* (SE) Key Terms *p. 148* (SE) Questions and Problems *pp. 149–150*	

5 Measurements and Calculations

Section	Text Features & Components	Labs, Demonstrations & Activities
Teaching Segment 5C **1.5 blocks** **pp. 130–146** **5.6 Problem Solving and Dimensional Analysis**	**LP** Lesson Plans (Sec 5.6–5.8)	**SE** Chemistry in Action: Cooking in a Metric World *p. 135* **LM** Experiment 20: Conversion Factors Lab Manual Report Sheets Teacher's Lab Guide
5.7 Temperature Conversions: An Approach to Problem Solving	**SE** Chemical Impact: Ersatz Fog *p. 138*	**TE** Teaching Support: Graphing Temperature Scales *pp. 136–137*
5.8 Density	**SE** Top Ten Elements with Highest Densities *p. 144* **TE** Teaching Tips *p. 146*	**TE** Group Activity *p. 142* **TE** Mini Demo *p. 142* **TE** Teaching Support: Demonstration *pp. 142–143* **SE** Chemistry in Action: The Density of Clay *p. 143* **LM** Experiment 21: Measurement and Density Lab Manual Report Sheets Teacher's Lab Guide

Key

SE Student Edition

TE Teacher Edition

RP Teacher Resource Package

LM Lab Materials

LP Lesson Plans

AR Additional Resources

🔲 Florida Specific

Technology and Media

 Transparencies
Table 5.2, 5.3
Figure 5.1, 5.6

PowerPoint Slides 5

 Video Relative Densities of Pepsi and Diet Pepsi *p. 142*

 eEdition CD-ROM
Easy Planner CD-ROM
English Summaries CD
Spanish Summaries CD

 Web Site classzone.com
McDougal Littell Test Generator

Chapter Planning Guide

All Learners

- (TE) Active Learning *p. 130*
- (TE) Misconceptions *p. 131*
- (TE) Teaching Tips *pp. 130–131*
- (AR) Less Proficient Students *p. 10*

- (TE) Teaching Tip *p. 135*
- Transparency: Figure 5.6 *p. 136*
- (AR) Less Proficient Students *p. 10*

- (TE) Challenge Your Students *p. 146*
- Video: Relative Densities of Pepsi and Diet Pepsi *p. 142*
- (RP) Team Learning Worksheets (Sec 5.6–5.8) *pp. 23–24*
- (AR) Less Proficient Students *p. 10*

Review & Assessment

- (TE) Additional Examples *pp. 132–133*
- (SE) Self Check *pp. 133–134*
- (SE) Key Terms *p. 148*
- (SE) Questions and Problems *p. 150*

- (TE) Additional Examples *pp. 136–137, 140–141*
- (SE) Self Check *pp. 138, 140–14*
- (SE) Key Terms *p. 148*
- (SE) Questions and Problems *p. 150*

- (TE) Additional Examples *pp. 142, 144–145*
- (SE) Self Check *p. 144*
- (SE) Focus Questions (Sec 5.6–5.8) *p. 146*
- (SE) Key Terms *p. 148*
- (SE) Questions and Problems *p. 151*

Standards

- (TE) **NSES** UCP1, UCP3, A1, A2, E1, E2

Chapter Materials

- (TE) Reading Strategy
- (AR) English/Spanish Summaries *p. 7*
- (AR) Challenge Projects/Problems *pp. 8–9*
- (AR) Less Proficient Students *p. 10*
- English Summary Audio
- Spanish Summary Audio
- (RP) Chapter Review Worksheets (Basic, Review, Challenge)

- (SE) Chapter Summary *p. 148*
- (SE) Critical Thinking *p. 151*
- (RP) Solutions Guide
- (RP) Chapter Tests
- (RP) Test Bank
- McDougal Littell Test Generator
- (AR) Standardized Test Practice
- **FCAT Test 3**

5 Integrating Reading Strategies and Chemistry Concepts

Chapter 5: Reading Math

The material presented in Chapter 5 is an introduction to the math skills needed for success in problem solving and in recording quantitative observations in the laboratory. Point out to the students that math and chemistry are integrated and that previous skills learned in mathematics will help them in this course. Make sure that the students are aware of the Math Review section in Appendices B–E, pages A5–A8, and encourage them to use this reference.

Translating Math Symbols

The table shows some math symbols used in this course and their translations. Before beginning this chapter, quiz the students on what each symbol represents. Advise the students to create flashcards of any quiz item that they missed.

Encourage the students to translate and apply the symbols while they read. As you teach Section 5.1 on scientific notation, read aloud the numbers so that the students can hear how the notation is translated. For example, help the students translate between a numerical value, 1.7×10^3, and its spoken form, "one point seven times ten to the third (or ten cubed)." Be sure to include an example of a value with a power of 10 with a negative exponent: $8.9 \times 10^{-2} \rightarrow$ eight point nine times ten to the negative two.

MATH SYMBOLS	
Symbols	**Translates to**
=	equals, equivalent, is
°	degree
%	percent
≈	approximately
±	plus or minus
×	times, multiplied by, the product of
÷, /, —	divided by, per, ratio
Δ	delta, change in

Interpreting Units of Measure

When the students have a thorough understanding of Sections 5.2 and 5.3, explain the importance of reading and interpreting the unit of measure of a given quantity. Point out that a unit of measure indicates the type of measurement, and that when the students master this information, they will be better equipped to use dimensional analysis (Section 5.6) to solve problems. Encourage the students to generate a table similar to the one shown, summarizing typical units of various types of measures. After completing the chapter, tell the students to add to their tables the units of measure for temperature, density, and specific gravity.

UNITS OF MEASURE	
Measure	**Units**
length/width	mm, cm, m, km, in., ft, yd, mi
area	mm^2, cm^2, m^2, km^2, $in.^2$, ft^2, yd^2, mi^2
mass	mg, g, kg, lb
volume	mL, L, cm^3, m^3, $in.^3$, ft^3
temperature	°C, °F, K
density	$\dfrac{g}{mL}$, $\dfrac{g}{cm^3}$, $\dfrac{lb}{in.^3}$, $\dfrac{lb}{ft^3}$
specific gravity	No units

Misconceptions

To avoid possible confusion with symbol interpretation, point out that:

• there is a difference between the negative sign used for integers and for subtraction and the sign used to represent a negative charge on an ion.

• parentheses are used to represent multiplication, but not when used in a chemical equation to represent an element as a solid (*s*), liquid (*l*), gas (*g*), or aqueous solution (*aq*).

• there is a difference between the symbol used to indicate subtraction and that used to indicate a single bond between elements.

• subscripts on an element indicate number of atoms.

• a superscript on a number indicates a power. A superscript on an ion indicates a charge.

Interpreting Math in Questions and Problems

Explain that some of the questions and problems found at the end of each chapter will require the students to translate words or phrases into math problems in order to obtain an answer. Review these common key words and translations.

• *Is, equals, equivalent* all correspond to the equal sign.

• *Per* means "divided by."

• *Percent* means "amount per 100."

Direct the students' attention to Critical Thinking Problem #73, page 151. Have the students read the problem, and then ask the following questions:

> **73.** An organic solvent has density 1.31 g/mL. What volume is occupied by 50.0 g of the liquid?

• What measurements are given? [density = 1.31 g/mL; mass = 50.0 g]

• What is the unknown? [volume]

• What word indicates the equal sign? [is]

• What units of measure should the unknown measure have? [mL]

• How many digits are significant? [3]

Show the students how to use the answers to these questions to set up and solve the problem. $V = 50. \text{ g} \times \frac{\text{mL}}{1.31 \text{ g}} = 38.2 \text{ mL}$

Tell the students that it is also important to be able to distinguish significant information given in a question from extraneous information.

Direct the students' attention to Critical Thinking Problem #66, page 151.

> **66.** For a pharmacist dispensing pills or capsules, it is often easier to weigh the medication to be dispensed rather than to count the individual pills. If a single antibiotic capsule weighs 0.65 g, and a pharmacist weights out 15.6 g of capsules, how many capsules have been dispensed?

Ask the students to rewrite the problem with only the necessary information. [highlighted sentence above] Explain that reading a question and deciphering the key information is a skill that they must master for taking standardized tests.

Overview

In this Chapter our goals are for the students to:

- Show how numbers can be expressed in scientific notation

- Learn the English, metric, and SI systems of measurement

- Use the metric system to measure length, volume and mass

- Learn how uncertainty in a measurement arises and express uncertainty using significant figures

- Learn to determine the number of significant figures in a calculated result

- Learn how dimensional analysis can be used to solve various types of problems

- Learn the three temperature scales and how to convert from one to another

- Define density and its units

5 Measurements and Calculations

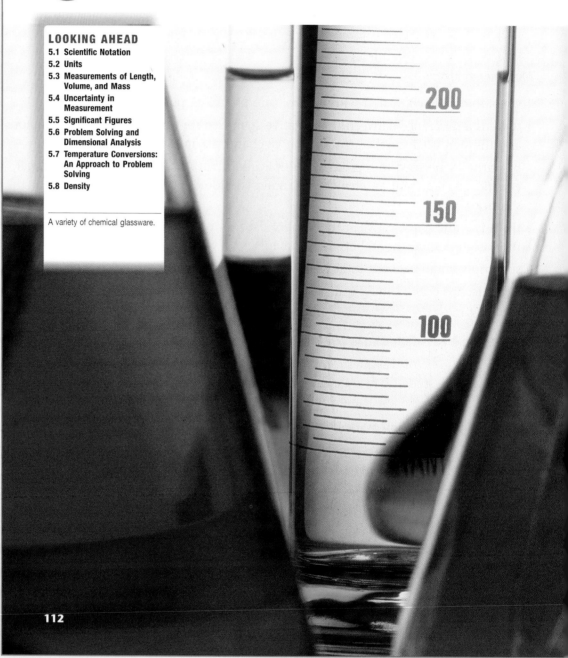

A variety of chemical glassware.

As we pointed out in Chapter 1, making observations is a key part of the scientific process. Sometimes observations are *qualitative* ("the substance is a yellow solid") and sometimes they are *quantitative* ("the substance weighs 4.3 grams"). A quantitative observation is called a **measurement.** Measurements are very important in our daily lives. For example, we pay for gasoline by the gallon so the gas pump must accurately measure the gas delivered to our fuel tank. The efficiency of the modern automobile engine depends on various measurements, including the amount of oxygen in the exhaust gases, the temperature of the coolant, and the pressure of the lubricating oil. In addition, cars with traction control systems have devices to measure and compare the rates of rotation of all four wheels. As we will see in the "Chemical Impact" discussion in this chapter, measuring devices have become very sophisticated in dealing with our fast-moving and complicated society.

As we will discuss in this chapter, a measurement always consists of two parts: a number and a unit. Both parts are necessary to make the measurement meaningful. For example, suppose a friend tells you that she saw a bug 5 long. This statement is meaningless as it stands. Five what? If it's 5 millimeters, the bug is quite small. If it's 5 centimeters, the bug is quite large. If it's 5 meters, run for cover!

The point is that for a measurement to be meaningful, it must consist of both a number and a unit that tells us the scale being used.

In this chapter we will consider the characteristics of measurements and the calculations that involve measurements.

A gas pump measures the amount of gasoline delivered.

5.1 Scientific Notation

Objective: *To show how very large or very small numbers can be expressed as the product of a number between 1 and 10 and a power of 10.*

A measurement must always consist of a number and a unit.

The numbers associated with scientific measurements are often very large or very small. For example, the distance from the earth to the sun is approximately 93,000,000 (93 million) miles. Written out, this number is rather bulky. Scientific notation is a method for making very large or very small numbers more compact and easier to write.

To see how this is done, consider the number 125, which can be written as the product

$$125 = 1.25 \times 100$$

Because $100 = 10 \times 10 = 10^2$, we can write

$$125 = 1.25 \times 100 = 1.25 \times 10^2$$

Similarly, the number 1700 can be written

$$1700 = 1.7 \times 1000$$

and because $1000 = 10 \times 10 \times 10 = 10^3$, we can write

$$1700 = 1.7 \times 1000 = 1.7 \times 10^3$$

5.1 Scientific Notation **113**

Section 5.1

Themes
Organization, Systems

Skills
Making comparisons, converting, evaluating

Student Preparation
Assign the students to read Sections 5.1 to 5.3 and to answer the Focus Questions at the end of Section 5.3 before coming to class.

Active Learning
After introducing the material in Sections 5.1 to 5.3 in class, place the students in groups and have them work together on Sections 5.1–5.3: Team Learning Worksheet. Answers and/or discussion of these questions are located in the *Teacher Resources*.

TEACHING TIPS

• You will find that the students have used scientific notation to some extent in their math classes. Point out that numbers in science are often very large or very small, so using scientific notation is very helpful. It makes an excellent shorthand way of writing numbers.

• Work out plenty of examples in class for each type of situation. This reinforcement will give students more confidence in doing problems on their own.

Scientific notation simply expresses a number as *a product of a number between 1 and 10 and the appropriate power of 10*. For example, the number 93,000,000 can be expressed as

$$93{,}000{,}000 = 9.3 \times 10{,}000{,}000 = 9.3 \times 10^7$$

Number between 1 and 10

Appropriate power of 10 ($10{,}000{,}000 = 10^7$)

The easiest way to determine the appropriate power of 10 for scientific notation is to start with the number being represented and count the number of places the decimal point must be moved to obtain a number between 1 and 10. For example, for the number

9 3 0 0 0 0 0 0
7 6 5 4 3 2 1

we must move the decimal point seven places to the left to get 9.3 (a number between 1 and 10). To compensate for every move of the decimal point to the left, we must multiply by 10. That is, each time we move the decimal point to the left, we make the number smaller by one power of 10. So for each move of the decimal point to the left, we must multiply by 10 to restore the number to its original magnitude. Thus moving the decimal point seven places to the left means we must multiply 9.3 by 10 seven times, which equals 10^7:

$$93{,}000{,}000 = 9.3 \times 10^7$$

We moved the decimal point seven places to the left, so we need 10^7 to compensate.

Remember: whenever the decimal point is moved to the *left*, the exponent of 10 is *positive*.

When describing very small distances, such as the diameter of a swine flu virus (shown here magnified 16,537 times), it is convenient to use scientific notation.

MATH

Keep one digit to the left of the decimal point.

MATH

Moving the decimal point to the left requires a positive exponent.

CELEBRITY CHEMICAL

Carvone (C₁₀H₁₄O)

Carvone is the main component of spearmint oil. It occurs naturally in caraway seeds, dill seeds, gingergrass, and spearmint. A pleasant-smelling liquid at room temperature, this chemical is often used as a flavoring agent in liqueurs and chewing gum and is added to soaps and perfumes to improve their aromas. Carvone is one of the "essential oils" that have been used in spices, perfumes, and medicines for thousands of years.

Carvone is a member of a class of compounds called *terpenes* that are produced by plants, often to attract beneficial insects. For example, certain plants give off these compounds when they are attacked by caterpillars. The released terpenes attract the attention of parasitic wasps that kill the caterpillars and inject their eggs. The caterpillar bodies then serve as food for the developing wasp larvae.

We can represent numbers smaller than 1 by using the same convention, but in this case the power of 10 is negative. For example, for the number 0.010 we must move the decimal point two places to the right to obtain a number between 1 and 10:

$$0.\underset{1\ 2}{\underbrace{0\ 1\ 0}}$$

This requires an exponent of -2, so $0.010 = 1.0 \times 10^{-2}$. Remember: whenever the decimal point is moved to the *right*, the exponent of 10 is *negative*.

Next consider the number 0.000167. In this case we must move the decimal point four places to the right to obtain 1.67 (a number between 1 and 10):

$$0.\underset{1\ 2\ 3\ 4}{\underbrace{0\ 0\ 0\ 1}}\ 6\ 7$$

Moving the decimal point four places to the right requires an exponent of -4. Therefore,

$$0.000167 \quad = \quad \underset{\substack{\text{We moved the decimal} \\ \text{point four places to the right.}}}{1.67 \times 10^{-4}}$$

We summarize these procedures below.

Using Scientific Notation

- Any number can be represented as the product of a number between 1 and 10 and a power of 10 (either positive or negative).

- The power of 10 depends on the number of places the decimal point is moved and in which direction. The *number of places* the decimal point is moved determines the *power of 10*. The *direction* of the move determines whether the power of 10 is *positive* or *negative*. If the decimal point is moved to the left, the power of 10 is positive; if the decimal point is moved to the right, the power of 10 is negative.

Example 5.1

Scientific Notation: Powers of 10 (Positive)

Represent the following numbers in scientific notation.

    a. 238,000

    b. 1,500,000

Solution

    a. First we move the decimal point until we have a number between 1 and 10—in this case 2.38.

$$\underset{5\ 4\ 3\ 2\ 1}{\underbrace{2\ 3\ 8\ 0\ 0\ 0}}\qquad\text{The decimal point was moved five places to the left.}$$

    Because we moved the decimal point five places to the left, the power of 10 is positive 5. Thus $238{,}000 = 2.38 \times 10^5$.

(continued)

Additional Examples

Express each number in scientific notation.

a. 12,500 1.25×10^4

b. 247 2.47×10^2

c. 10 1×10^1

d. 3,500,000 3.5×10^6

e. 1430 1.43×10^3

b. 1 5 0 0 0 0 0
  6 5 4 3 2 1   The decimal point was moved
               six places to the left, so
               the power of 10 is 6.

Thus $1,500,000 = 1.5 \times 10^6$.

Example 5.2

Scientific Notation: Powers of 10 (Negative)

Represent the following numbers in scientific notation.

   a. 0.00043

   b. 0.089

Solution

   a. First we move the decimal point until we have a number between 1 and 10—in this case 4.3.

     0 . 0 0 0 4 3
         1 2 3 4   The decimal point was moved four places to the right.

   Because we moved the decimal point four places to the right, the power of 10 is negative 4. Thus $0.00043 = 4.3 \times 10^{-4}$.

   b. 0 . 0 8 9
         1 2   The power of 10 is negative 2 because the decimal point was moved two places to the right.

   Thus $0.089 = 8.9 \times 10^{-2}$.

 Self-Check Exercise 5.1

Write the numbers 357 and 0.0055 in scientific notation. If you are having difficulty with scientific notation at this point, reread the Appendix.

5.2   Units

Objective: *To learn the English, metric, and SI systems of measurement.*

The **units** part of a measurement tells us what *scale* or *standard* is being used to represent the results of the measurement. From the earliest days of civilization, trade has required common units. For example, if a farmer from one region wanted to trade some of his grain for the gold of a miner who lived in another region, the two people had to have common standards (units) for measuring the amount of the grain and the weight of the gold.

The need for common units also applies to scientists, who measure quantities such as mass, length, time, and temperature. If every scientist had her

Critical Units!

How important are conversions from one unit to another? If you ask the National Aeronautic and Space Administration (NASA), very important! In 1999 NASA lost a $125 million Mars Climate Orbiter because of a failure to convert from English to metric units.

The problem arose because two teams working on the Mars mission were using different sets of units. NASA's scientists at the Jet Propulsion Laboratory in Pasadena, California, assumed that the thrust data for the rockets on the Orbiter they received from Lockheed Martin Astronautics in Denver, which built the spacecraft, were in metric units. In reality, the units were English. As a result the Orbiter dipped 100 kilometers lower into the Mars atmosphere than planned and the friction from the atmosphere caused the craft to burn up.

NASA's mistake refueled the controversy over whether Congress should require the United States to switch to the metric system. About 95% of the world now uses the metric system, and the United States is slowly switching from English to metric. For example, the automobile industry has adopted metric fasteners and we buy our soda in two-liter bottles.

Units can be very important. In fact, they can mean the difference between life and death on some occasions. In 1983, for example, a Canadian jetliner almost ran out of fuel when someone pumped 22,300 pounds of fuel into the aircraft instead of 22,300 kilograms. Remember to watch your units!

Artist's conception of the lost Mars Climate Orbiter.

or his own personal set of units, complete chaos would result. Unfortunately, although standard systems of units did arise, different systems were adopted in different parts of the world. The two most widely used systems are the **English system** used in the United States and the **metric system** used in most of the rest of the industrialized world.

The metric system has long been preferred for most scientific work. In 1960 an international agreement set up a comprehensive system of units called the **International System** (*le Système Internationale* in French), or **SI**. The SI units are based on the metric system and units derived from the metric system. The most important fundamental SI units are listed in **Table 5.1**. Later in this chapter we will discuss how to manipulate some of these units.

TABLE 5.1

Some Fundamental SI Units

Physical Quantity	Name of Unit	Abbreviation
mass	kilogram	kg
length	meter	m
time	second	s
temperature	kelvin	K

5.2　Units　**117**

TABLE 5.2

The Commonly Used Prefixes in the Metric System

Prefix	Symbol	Meaning	Power of 10 for Scientific Notation
mega	M	1,000,000	10^6
kilo	k	1000	10^3
deci	d	0.1	10^{-1}
centi	c	0.01	10^{-2}
milli	m	0.001	10^{-3}
micro	μ	0.000001	10^{-6}
nano	n	0.000000001	10^{-9}

Because the fundamental units are not always a convenient size, the SI system uses prefixes to change the size of the unit. The most commonly used prefixes are listed in **Table 5.2.** Although the fundamental unit for length is the meter (m), we can also use the decimeter (dm), which represents one-tenth (0.1) of a meter; the centimeter (cm), which represents one one-hundredth (0.01) of a meter; the millimeter (mm), which represents one one-thousandth (0.001) of a meter; and so on. For example, it's much more convenient to specify the diameter of a certain contact lens as 1.0 cm than as 1.0×10^{-2} m.

5.3 Measurements of Length, Volume, and Mass

Objective: *To use the metric system to measure length, volume, and mass.*

The fundamental SI unit of length is the meter, which is a little longer than a yard (1 meter = 39.37 inches). In the metric system fractions of a meter or multiples of a meter can be expressed by powers of 10, as summarized in **Table 5.3.**

The English and metric systems are compared on the ruler shown in **Figure 5.1.** Note that

1 inch = 2.54 centimeters

Other English–metric equivalences are given in Section 5.6.

TABLE 5.3

The Metric System for Measuring Length

Unit	Symbol	Meter Equivalent
kilometer	km	1000 m or 10^3 m
meter	m	1 m or 1 m
decimeter	dm	0.1 m or 10^{-1} m
centimeter	cm	0.01 m or 10^{-2} m
millimeter	mm	0.001 m or 10^{-3} m
micrometer	μm	0.000001 m or 10^{-6} m
nanometer	nm	0.000000001 m or 10^{-9} m

Figure 5.1
Comparison of English and metric units for length on a ruler.

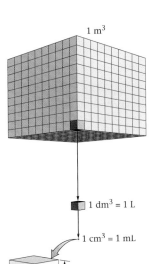

Figure 5.2
The largest drawing represents a cube that has sides 1 m in length and a volume of 1 m³. The middle-size cube has sides 1 dm in length and a volume of 1 dm³, or 1 L. The smallest cube has sides 1 cm in length and a volume of 1 cm³, or 1 mL.

Volume is the amount of three-dimensional space occupied by a substance. The fundamental unit of volume in the SI system is based on the volume of a cube that measures 1 meter in each of the three directions. That is, each edge of the cube is 1 meter in length. The volume of this cube is

$$1 \text{ m} \times 1 \text{ m} \times 1 \text{ m} = (1 \text{ m})^3 = 1 \text{ m}^3$$

or, in words, one cubic meter.

In **Figure 5.2** this cube is divided into 1000 smaller cubes. Each of these small cubes represents a volume of 1 dm³, which is commonly called the **liter** (rhymes with "meter" and is slightly larger than a quart) and abbreviated L.

The cube with a volume of 1 dm³ (1 liter) can in turn be broken into 1000 smaller cubes each representing a volume of 1 cm³. Thus each liter contains 1000 cm³. One cubic centimeter is called a **milliliter** (abbreviated mL), a unit of volume used very commonly in chemistry. This relationship is summarized in **Table 5.4.**

The *graduated cylinder* (see **Figure 5.3**), which is commonly used in chemical laboratories for measuring the volumes of liquids, is marked off in convenient units of volume (usually milliliters). The graduated cylinder is filled to the desired volume with the liquid, which then can be poured out.

Figure 5.3
A 100-mL graduated cylinder.

TABLE 5.4

The Relationship Between the Liter and Milliliter

Unit	Symbol	Equivalence
liter	L	1 L = 1000 mL
milliliter	mL	$\frac{1}{1000}$ L = 10^{-3} L = 1 mL

5.3   Measurements of Length, Volume, and Mass   **119**

- Now is an excellent time to discuss the difference between mass and weight. In daily life we often use these terms interchangeably. They have very different meanings to a chemist, however. Since our language does not have a verb for mass, we use the term "weigh" in chemistry to mean "finding the mass of the substance on a balance."

- Ask students to compare the relationship between a liter and a quart, a gram and a pound, and a kilometer and a mile. Try to get them to relate these ideas to the familiar objects in everyday life without actually converting the units.

TABLE 5.5

The Most Commonly Used Metric Units for Mass

Unit	Symbol	Gram Equivalent
kilogram	kg	$1000 \text{ g} = 10^3 \text{g} = 1 \text{ kg}$
gram	g	1 g
milligram	mg	$0.001 \text{ g} = 10^{-3} \text{g} = 1 \text{ mg}$

Figure 5.4
An electronic analytical balance used in chemistry labs.

Another important measurable quantity is **mass,** which can be defined as the quantity of matter present in an object. The fundamental SI unit of mass is the **kilogram.** Because the metric system, which existed before the SI system, used the gram as the fundamental unit, the prefixes for the various mass units are based on the **gram**, as shown in **Table 5.5.**

In the laboratory we determine the mass of an object by using a balance. A balance compares the mass of the object to a set of standard masses ("weights"). For example, the mass of an object can be determined by using a single-pan balance **(Figure 5.4).**

To help you get a feeling for the common units of length, volume, and mass, some familiar objects are described in **Table 5.6.**

TABLE 5.6

Some Examples of Commonly Used Units

length	A dime is 1 mm thick.
	A quarter is 2.5 cm in diameter.
	The average height of an adult man is 1.8 m.
mass	A nickel has a mass of about 5 g.
	A 120-lb woman has a mass of about 55 kg.
volume	A 12-oz can of soda has a volume of about 360 mL.
	A half gallon of milk is equal to about 2 L of milk.

Answers to Focus Questions

1. Qualitative observations are descriptive but do not usually contain numbers. Quantitative observations include both numbers and units.

2. positive, negative

3. **a.** 8.475×10^6

   b. 7.54×10^{-5}

   c. 1×10^3

   d. 3.5724×10^{-1}

4. Without a unit a number has no scale or standard to explain what is being measured.

5.

	English	Metric
Length	yard	meter
Volume	quart	liter
Mass	pound	kilogram

Focus Questions

Sections 5.1–5.3

1. What is the difference between a qualitative observation and a quantitative observation?

2. When you are writing numbers using scientific notation, very large numbers have _____ exponents and very small numbers have _____ exponents.

3. Change the following to scientific notation:

   a. 8,475,000   **c.** 1000
   b. 0.0000754   **d.** 0.35724

Connection to History

What Is a Meter, Anyway?

It is very important that everyone in the world have the same standards for measuring things. For example, if a company in the United States orders a part for a machine that must be exactly 0.1765 meter in length from a manufacturer in Germany, it is critical that the same definition of the meter is used in the United States and in Germany.

Although the world community now has universal standards of measurement, it has not always been this way. For example, in France in the 1780s, the units for measuring mass and length were a total mess—literally hundreds of local standards existed. To solve this problem a commission of prominent scientists recommended that the meter be defined as one ten-millionth of the distance (at sea level) from the North Pole to the equator. This suggestion made little sense because the errors in making this measurement would be much greater than the size of the meter (and besides, no one had ever been to the North Pole at this point!). Nevertheless this definition appealed to the prevailing notion that units should be "natural."

A huge project, comparable to NASA's program to reach the moon in our time, was set up to measure the meridian (the line on the earth's surface) from the North Pole to the equator. The idea was to measure a portion of the meridian and then use calculations to determine the entire length.

It took the surveyors about five years to measure this distance. In addition to the normal difficulties of such a job, the surveyors faced great personal risk because of the wars that were raging in that area. The effort was successful, however.

On November 28, 1798, an international meeting was held, at which the distance from the North Pole to the equator was agreed upon and the meter was defined as one ten-millionth of this distance. (The amazing thing about this 1798 measurement

is that it agrees within about 0.020% to modern measurements using satellites!) A platinum bar of this length was deposited in the French National Archives and became the standard meter in 1799. Because measuring this bar produced wear on the ends, in 1899 it was agreed that the meter should be defined in terms of a harder bar made of a platinum/iridium alloy, called the International Prototype. This bar was copied and the copies sent around the world to define the meter.

This definition of the meter persisted until 1969, when the world community agreed that the meter should be redefined in terms of the wavelength of light emitted by an isotope of krypton (^{86}Kr). In 1983, the meter was redefined once again as the distance light travels in a vacuum in exactly 1/299,792,458th of a second. That is, the speed of light is defined as exactly 299,792,458 meters per second. Thus the definition of the meter now depends on the definition of a second and hence on the accurate measurement of time.

This definition leads to another question: How do we measure time? Of course, the human concept of time is based on the periodic behavior of the sun. By the Middle Ages days had been divided into 24 hours, hours into 60 minutes, and minutes into 60 seconds. Because the earth's orbit is not circular and the axis of the earth is tilted, the sun appears to move more quickly during some parts of the year than others. Also the earth's rotational speed is not constant. These complications have led scientists to define time in terms of an "atomic clock" in which the second is defined in terms of the light absorbed by cesium-133. This atomic clock is kept at the National Institute of Standards and Technology (NIST) in Boulder, Colorado. It is accurate to one second in 20 million years!

What Is a Meter, Anyway?

"What Is a Meter, Anyway?" illustrates how our definition and the precision of the standard meter have changed as technology has changed. It is also interesting that the project to measure the distance from the North Pole to the equator was comparable in prominence in France in the 1780s to the U.S. effort in the 1960s to land a person on the moon. The portion of the meridian that the French chose to measure had to be selected carefully. The two ends of the segment to be measured had to be at sea level and the midpoint had to be near the middle of the North Pole-to-equator meridian. Only one segment satisfied these requirements—the one from Dunkirk, France, to Barcelona, Spain.

4. Why is a unit a necessary part of a measurement?

5. Complete the table below:

	English Unit	Metric Unit
Length		meter
Volume	quart	
Mass	pound	

Focus Questions **121**

Themes
Organization, Patterns of Change

Skills
Applying concepts, making comparisons

Student Preparation
Assign the students to read Sections 5.4 and 5.5 and to answer the Focus Questions at the end of Section 5.5 before coming to class.

Active Learning
After introducing the material in Sections 5.4 and 5.5 in class, place the students in groups and have them work together on Sections 5.4–5.5: Team Learning Worksheet. Answers and/or discussion of these questions are located in the *Teacher Resources*.

Laboratory
Experiment 18:
Measurement and the SI System, Traditional

TEACHING TIP

To illustrate uncertainty in measurements, bring to class several pieces of glassware used to measure volume. Show students the glassware. Draw the shape of a representative piece of the glassware on the board, marking the drawing to show the meniscus of a liquid between two of the lines. Because the volume falls between the lines, there is uncertainty involved in the reading. Have students write down the result of the measurement, then compare results. The number recorded for this measurement will vary from student to student only in the last digit. Thus there is only one uncertain digit.

5.4 Uncertainty in Measurement

Objectives: *To learn how uncertainty in a measurement arises.*
To learn to indicate a measurement's uncertainty by using significant figures.

Whenever a measurement is made with a device such as a ruler or a graduated cylinder, an estimate is required. We can illustrate this by measuring the pin shown in **Figure 5.5a.** We can see from the ruler that the pin is a little longer than 2.8 cm and a little shorter than 2.9 cm. Because there are no graduations on the ruler between 2.8 and 2.9, we must estimate the pin's length between 2.8 and 2.9 cm. We do this by *imagining* that the distance between 2.8 and 2.9 is broken into 10 equal divisions **(Figure 5.5b)** and estimating to which division the end of the pin reaches. The end of the pin appears to come about halfway between 2.8 and 2.9, which corresponds to 5 of our 10 imaginary divisions. So we estimate the pin's length as 2.85 cm. The result of our measurement is that the pin is approximately 2.85 cm in length, but we had to rely on a visual estimate, so it might actually be 2.84 or 2.86 cm.

Because the last number is based on a visual estimate, it may be different when another person makes the same measurement. For example, if five different people measured the pin, the results might be

Person	Result of Measurement
1	2.85 cm
2	2.84 cm
3	2.86 cm
4	2.85 cm
5	2.86 cm

Note that the first two digits in each measurement are the same regardless of who made the measurement; these are called the *certain* numbers of

Figure 5.5
Measuring a pin. (a) The length is between 2.8 cm and 2.9 cm. (b) Imagine that the distance between 2.8 and 2.9 is divided into 10 equal parts. The end of the pin occurs after about 5 of these divisions.

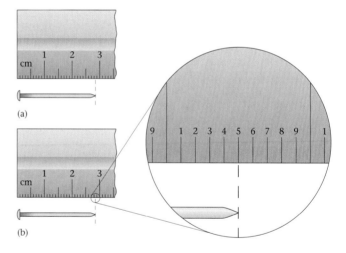

(a)

(b)

the measurement. However, the third digit is estimated and can vary; it is called an *uncertain* number. When one is making a measurement, the custom is to record all of the certain numbers plus the *first* uncertain number. It would not make any sense to try to measure the pin to the third decimal place (thousandths of a centimeter), because this ruler requires an estimate of even the second decimal place (hundredths of a centimeter).

CHEMISTRY

Every measurement has some degree of uncertainty.

It is very important to realize that *a measurement always has some degree of uncertainty*. The uncertainty of a measurement depends on the measuring device. For example, if the ruler in Figure 5.5 had marks indicating hundredths of a centimeter, the uncertainty in the measurement of the pin would occur in the thousandths place rather than the hundredths place—but some uncertainty would still exist.

CHEMICAL IMPACT

Consumer Connection

Measuring Changes

Measurement lies at the heart of doing science. We obtain the data for formulating laws and testing theories by doing measurements. Measurements also have very practical importance; they tell us if our drinking water is safe, whether we are anemic, and the exact amount of gasoline we put in our cars at the filling station.

Although the measuring devices we describe in this chapter are still widely used, new measuring techniques are being developed every day to meet the challenges of our increasingly sophisticated world. For example, engines in modern automobiles have oxygen sensors that analyze the oxygen content in the exhaust gases. This information is sent to the computer that controls the engine functions so that instantaneous adjustments can be made in spark timing and air–fuel mixtures to provide efficient power with minimum air pollution.

As another example, consider airline safety: How do we rapidly, conveniently, and accurately determine whether a given piece of baggage contains an explosive device? A thorough hand-search of each piece of luggage is out of the question. Scientists are now developing a screening procedure that bombards the luggage with high-energy particles that cause any substance present to emit radiation

A pollution control officer measuring the oxygen content of river water.

characteristic of that substance. This radiation is monitored to identify luggage with unusually large quantities of nitrogen, because most chemical explosives are based on compounds containing nitrogen.

Scientists are also examining the natural world to find supersensitive detectors because many organisms are sensitive to tiny amounts of chemicals in their environments—for example, the sensitive noses of bloodhounds. One of these natural measuring devices uses the sensory hairs from Hawaiian red swimming crabs, which are connected to electrical analyzers and used to detect hormones at levels as low as 10^{-8} g/L. Likewise, tissues from pineapple cores can be used to detect tiny amounts of hydrogen peroxide.

These types of advances in measuring devices have led to an unexpected problem: detecting all kinds of substances in our food and drinking water scares us. Although these substances were always there, we didn't worry so much when we couldn't detect them. Now that we know they are present, what should we do about them? How can we assess whether these trace substances are harmful or benign? Risk assessment has become much more complicated as our sophistication in taking measurements has increased.

5.4 Uncertainty in Measurement **123**

Integrating the CHEMICAL IMPACT

Measuring Changes

"Measuring Changes" provides the background for students to discuss the implications of measuring things ever more precisely. The discussion could include the benefits and hazards of measuring such small amounts. We have been able to create ever faster and more accurate computers by reducing the sizes of chips. We are able to detect minute amounts of chemicals in our food supply. Does the fact that we can now measure these contaminants mean that our food is less safe than it was 10 years ago, when we couldn't detect them? What effect does this knowledge have on our society? Should we be worried about these tiny amounts of chemicals in our daily lives? This discussion could be used in conjunction with a writing class or with a social science class.

Students working on a lab project.

The numbers recorded in a measurement (all the certain numbers plus the first uncertain number) are called **significant figures.** The number of significant figures for a given measurement is determined by the inherent uncertainty of the measuring device. For example, the ruler used to measure the pin can give results only to hundredths of a centimeter. Thus, when we record the significant figures for a measurement, we automatically give information about the uncertainty in a measurement. The uncertainty in the last number (the estimated number) is usually assumed to be ± 1 unless otherwise indicated. For example, the measurement 1.86 kilograms can be interpreted as 1.86 ± 0.01 kilograms, where the symbol ± means plus or minus. That is, it could be 1.86 kg − 0.01 kg = 1.85 kg or 1.86 kg + 0.01 kg = 1.87 kg.

Themes
Organization, Stability

Skills
Making comparisons, evaluating

Laboratory
Experiment 19:
Measuring a Book? Precisely!,
In Text

TEACHING TIPS

- Students have the most trouble determining whether zeros are significant. Be sure to do examples with zeros in various locations within the number.

- Students often have trouble determining which numbers qualify as "exact numbers." Discuss numbers that are exact as you encounter them in examples. Help students recognize numbers from definitions and from counting objects as exact.

- The easiest way to determine the number of significant figures in a number is to write the number in scientific notation. In this notation there are no leading zeros, all zeros in the middle of the number are significant, and trailing zeros are recorded only if they are significant.

5.5 Significant Figures

Objective: *To learn to determine the number of significant figures in a calculated result.*

We have seen that any measurement involves an estimate and thus is uncertain to some extent. We signify the degree of certainty for a particular measurement by the number of significant figures we record.

Because doing chemistry requires many types of calculations, we must consider what happens when we do arithmetic with numbers that contain uncertainties. It is important that we know the degree of uncertainty in the final result. Although we will not discuss the process here, mathematicians have studied how uncertainty accumulates and have designed a set of rules to determine how many significant figures the result of a calculation should have. You should follow these rules whenever you carry out a calculation. The first thing we need to do is learn how to count the significant figures in a given number. To do this we use the following rules:

MATH
Leading zeros are never significant figures.

Rules for Counting Significant Figures

1. *Nonzero integers.* Nonzero integers *always* count as significant figures. For example, the number 1457 has four nonzero integers, all of which count as significant figures.

2. *Zeros.* There are three classes of zeros:
   a. *Leading zeros* are zeros that *precede* all of the nonzero digits. They *never* count as significant figures. For example, in the number 0.0025, the three zeros simply indicate the position of the decimal point. The number has only two significant figures, the 2 and the 5.

124 Chapter 5 Measurements and Calculations

MATH

Captive zeros are always significant figures.

MATH

Trailing zeros are sometimes significant figures.

MATH

Exact numbers never limit the number of significant figures in a calculation.

b. *Captive zeros* are zeros that fall *between* nonzero digits. They *always* count as significant figures. For example, the number 1.008 has four significant figures.

c. *Trailing zeros* are zeros at the *right end* of the number. They are significant only if the number is written with a decimal point. The number one hundred written as 100 has only one significant figure, but written as 100., it has three significant figures.

3. *Exact numbers.* Often calculations involve numbers that were not obtained using measuring devices but were determined by counting: 10 experiments, 3 apples, 8 molecules. Such numbers are called *exact numbers*. They can be assumed to have an unlimited number of significant figures. Exact numbers can also arise from definitions. For example, 1 inch is defined as *exactly* 2.54 centimeters. Thus, in the statement 1 in. = 2.54 cm, neither 2.54 nor 1 limits the number of significant figures when it is used in a calculation.

Rules for counting significant figures also apply to numbers written in scientific notation. For example, the number 100. can be written as 1.00×10^2, and both versions have three significant figures. Scientific notation offers two major advantages: the number of significant figures can be indicated easily, and fewer zeros are needed to write a very large or a very small number. For example, the number 0.000060 is much more conveniently represented as 6.0×10^{-5}, and the number has two significant figures, written in either form.

Example 5.3

Counting Significant Figures

Give the number of significant figures for each of the following measurements.

  a. A sample of orange juice contains 0.0108 g of vitamin C.

  b. A forensic chemist in a crime lab weighs a single hair and records its mass as 0.0050060 g.

  c. The distance between two points was found to be 5.030×10^3 ft.

  d. In yesterday's bicycle race, 110 riders started but only 60 finished.

Solution

  a. The number contains three significant figures. The zeros to the left of the 1 are leading zeros and are not significant, but the remaining zero (a captive zero) is significant.

  b. The number contains five significant figures. The leading zeros (to the left of the 5) are not significant. The captive zeros between the 5 and the 6 are significant, and the trailing zero to the right of the 6 is significant because the number contains a decimal point.

  c. This number has four significant figures. Both zeros in 5.030 are significant.

(continued)

Additional Examples

Give the number of significant figures for each measurement.

1. The mass of a single eyelash is 0.000304 g. **(3)**

2. The length of a skidmark is 1.270×10^2 m. **(4)**

3. A 125-g sample of chocolate chip cookies contains 10 g of chocolate. **(3, 1)**

4. The volume of soda remaining in a can after a spill is 0.09020 L. **(4)**

5. A dose of antibiotic is 4.0×10^{-1} cm^3. **(2)**

5.5 Significant Figures   **125**

These rules reflect the way calculators round off.

MATH

Do not round off sequentially. The number 6.8347 rounded to three significant figures is 6.83, not 6.84.

(continued)

d. Both numbers are exact (they were obtained by counting the riders). Thus these numbers have an unlimited number of significant figures.

Self-Check Exercise 5.2

Give the number of significant figures for each of the following measurements.

    a. 0.00100 m
    b. 2.0800×10^2 L
    c. 480 cars

Rounding Off Numbers

When you perform a calculation on your calculator, the number of digits displayed is usually greater than the number of significant figures that the result should possess. So you must "round off" the number (reduce it to fewer digits). The rules for **rounding off** follow.

Rules for Rounding Off

1. If the digit to be removed
   a. is less than 5, the preceding digit stays the same. For example, 1.33 rounds to 1.3.
   b. is equal to or greater than 5, the preceding digit is increased by 1. For example, 1.36 rounds to 1.4, and 3.15 rounds to 3.2.
2. In a series of calculations, carry the extra digits through to the final result and *then* round off.* This means that you should carry all of the digits that show on your calculator until you arrive at the final number (the answer) and then round off, using the procedures in rule 1.

We need to make one more point about rounding off to the correct number of significant figures. Suppose the number 4.348 needs to be rounded to two significant figures. In doing this, we look at *only* the *first number* to the right of the 3:

4.348
    ↑
   Look at this
   number to round off
   to two significant figures.

The number is rounded to 4.3 because 4 is less than 5. It is incorrect to round sequentially. For example, do *not* round the 4 to 5 to give 4.35 and then round the 3 to 4 to give 4.4.

When rounding off, *use only the first number to the right of the last significant figure.*

---

*This practice will not be followed in the worked-out examples in this text, because we want to show the correct number of significant figures in each step of the example.

126   Chapter 5 Measurements and Calculations

Determining Significant Figures in Calculations

Next we will learn how to determine the correct number of significant figures in the result of a calculation. To do this we will use the following rules.

Rules for Using Significant Figures in Calculations

1. For *multiplication* or *division,* the number of significant figures in the result is the same as that in the measurement with the *smallest number* of significant figures. We say this measurement is *limiting,* because it limits the number of significant figures in the result. For example, consider this calculation:

$$4.56 \times 1.4 = 6.384 \quad \boxed{\text{Round off}} \Rightarrow \quad 6.4$$

Three significant figures   Limiting (two significant figures)   Two significant figures

Because 1.4 has only two significant figures, it limits the result to two significant figures. Thus the product is correctly written as 6.4, which has two significant figures. Consider another example. In the division $\frac{8.315}{298}$, how many significant figures should appear in the answer? Because 8.315 has four significant figures, the number 298 (with three significant figures) limits the result. The calculation is correctly represented as

Four significant figures

$$\frac{8.315}{298} = 0.0279027 \quad \boxed{\text{Round off}} \Rightarrow \quad 2.79 \times 10^{-2}$$

Limiting (three significant figures)   Result shown on calculator   Three significant figures

2. For *addition* or *subtraction,* the limiting term is the one with the smallest number of decimal places. For example, consider the following sum:

$$
\begin{array}{r}
12.11 \\
18.0 \quad \text{Limiting term (has one decimal place)}\\
1.013 \\
\hline
31.123
\end{array}
\quad \boxed{\text{Round off}} \Rightarrow \quad 31.1
$$

One decimal place

The correct result is 31.1 (it is limited to one decimal place because 18.0 has only one decimal place). Consider another example:

$$
\begin{array}{r}
0.6875 \\
-0.1 \quad \text{Limiting term (one decimal place)}\\
\hline
0.5875
\end{array}
\quad \boxed{\text{Round off}} \Rightarrow \quad 0.6
$$

Note that *for multiplication and division, significant figures are counted. For addition and subtraction, the decimal places are counted.*

Now we will put together the things you have learned about significant figures by considering some mathematical operations in the following examples.

Example 5.4

Counting Significant Figures in Calculations

Without performing the calculations, tell how many significant figures each answer should contain.

a. 5.19
1.9
0.842

b. $1081 - 7.25$

c. 2.3×3.14

d. the total cost of 3 boxes of candy at $2.50 per box

Solution

a. The answer will have one digit after the decimal place. The limiting number is 1.9, which has one decimal place, so the answer has two significant figures.

b. The answer will have no digits after the decimal point. The number 1081 has no digits to the right of the decimal point and limits the result, so the answer has four significant figures.

c. The answer will have two significant figures because the number 2.3 has only two significant figures (3.14 has three).

d. The answer will have three significant figures. The limiting factor is 2.50 because 3 (boxes of candy) is an exact number.

Example 5.5

Calculations Using Significant Figures

Carry out the following mathematical operations and give each result to the correct number of significant figures.

a. 5.18×0.0208

b. $(3.60 \times 10^{-3}) \times (8.123) \div 4.3$

c. $21 + 13.8 + 130.3$

d. $116.8 - 0.33$

e. $(1.33 \times 2.8) + 8.41$

Solution

Limiting terms   Round to this digit.

a. $5.18 \times 0.0208 = 0.107744 \Rightarrow 0.108$

The answer should contain three significant figures because each number being multiplied has three significant figures (rules 1). The 7 is rounded to 8 because the following digit is greater than 5.

Round to this digit.

b. $\dfrac{(3.60 \times 10^{-3})(8.123)}{4.3} = 6.8006 \times 10^{-3} \Rightarrow 6.8 \times 10^{-3}$

Limiting term

Additional Examples

Without performing the calculations, determine the correct number of significant figures in each answer.

1. $17.1 + 0.77 + 241$ (3)

2. $47.2 - 9 =$ (2)

3. $1.27 \times 3.1416 =$ (3)

4. $\dfrac{0.072}{4.36}$ (2)

5. cost of 2 tickets to a concert at $27.50 per ticket   (4)

Additional Examples

Give the correct power of 10 for each answer.

1. $(1.71 \times 10^3)(2.0 \times 10^2) =$
3.4 $\times$ _____
10^5

2. $\dfrac{1.64 \times 10^{-2}}{1.2 \times 10^{-2}} =$
1.4 $\times$ _____
10^0

3. Solve the following, giving the answer in scientific notation with the correct number of significant figures.

1. $(1.83 \times 10^{-4})(7.55 \times 10^7) =$ 1.38×10^4

2. $3.3 \times 5280 =$ 1.7×10^4

3. $\dfrac{(5.0 \times 10^{-4})(8.51 \times 10^{-2})}{2.92 \times 10^4} =$ 1.5×10^{-9}

4. $1.842 + 45.2 + 87.55 =$ 1.346×10^2

5. $714.3 - 18.56 =$ 6.957×10^2

Because 4.3 has the least number of significant figures (two), the result should have two significant figures (rule 1).

c.
```
   21
   13.8
  130.36
 ─────────
  165.16  ⇨ 165
```
In this case 21 is limiting (there are no digits after the decimal point). Thus the answer must have no digits after the decimal point, in accordance with the rule for addition (rule 2).

d.
```
  116.8
 − 0.33
 ─────────
  116.47 ⇨ 116.5
```
Because 116.8 has only one decimal place, the answer must have only one decimal place (rule 2). The 4 is rounded up to 5 because the digit to the right (7) is greater than 5.

e. $1.33 \times 2.8 = 3.724 \ ⇨ \ 3.7$
```
      3.7  ← Limiting term
    + 8.41
    ────────
     12.11 ⇨ 12.1
```

Note that in this case we multiplied and then rounded the result to the correct number of significant figures before we performed the addition so that we would know the correct number of decimal places.

 Self-Check Exercise 5.3

Give the answer for each calculation to the correct number of significant figures.

    a. 12.6×0.53

    b. $(12.6 \times 0.53) - 4.59$

    c. $(25.36 - 4.15) \div 2.317$

 Focus Questions   **Sections 5.4–5.5**

1. How has improving our ability to measure tiny amounts very accurately added stress to our lives?

2. Why are all measurements uncertain to some extent?

3. Mark the zeros that are significant figures in the following numbers.
   - **a.** 0.003042
   - **b.** 1.4030
   - **c.** 1000
   - **d.** 0.060
   - **e.** 50.0
   - **f.** 10.47020
   - **g.** 250.

4. How many significant figures are in each number in question 3?

5. Without doing the calculation, how many significant figures should be in each of the following results?
   - **a.** $3.2 + 4.17 + 1.243$
   - **b.** $1.3478 - 0.02$
   - **c.** 4.6×3.435
   - **d.** $(4.2 \times 10^{-5}) \times 3.74 \div 6.783$
   - **e.** $50 - 0.00473$

Focus Questions   **129**

 Answers to Self-Check Exercise 5.3

a. $12.6 \times 0.53 = 6.678 = 6.7$
Limiting

b. $12.6 \times 0.53 = 6.7$;   6.7   Limiting
Limiting
```
   −4.59
  ───────
    2.11 = 2.11
```

c.
```
   25.36
   −4.15
  ───────  = 9.154.8 = 9.154
   21.21
```

Answers to Focus Questions

1. We now worry about tiny amounts of chemicals that were not detectable years ago. We also worry about minute fluctuations in nutrients, weight, grades, and so forth.

2. All measurements are limited by the measuring device. Since these devices are not fully certain, neither are measurements made using them. Also, measurements are limited by our ability to accurately estimate the last digit.

3. Significant zeros are
   - **a.** between the 3 and 4
   - **b.** between the 4 and 3 and the last digit on the right
   - **c.** none
   - **d.** the last digit on the right
   - **e.** both are significant figures
   - **f.** all are significant
   - **g.** zero is significant

4. The number of significant figures in each case is
   - **a.** 4   **e.** 3
   - **b.** 5   **f.** 7
   - **c.** 1   **g.** 3
   - **d.** 2

5. The number of significant figures in each case is
   - **a.** 2   **d.** 2
   - **b.** 3   **e.** 1
   - **c.** 2

Example 5.8

5.6 Problem Solving and Dimensional Analysis

Objective: *To learn how dimensional analysis can be used to solve various types of problems.*

Suppose that the boss at the store where you work on weekends asks you to pick up 2 dozen doughnuts on the way to work. However, you find that the doughnut shop sells by the doughnut. How many doughnuts do you need?

This "problem" is an example of something you encounter all the time: converting from one unit of measurement to another. Examples of this occur in cooking (The recipe calls for 3 cups of cream, which is sold in pints. How many pints do I buy?); traveling (The purse costs 250 pesos. How much is that in dollars?); sports (A recent Tour de France bicycle race was 3215 kilometers long. How many miles is that?); and many other areas.

How do we convert from one unit of measurement to another? Let's explore this process by using the doughnut problem.

$$2 \text{ dozen doughnuts} = ? \text{ individual doughnuts}$$

where ? represents a number you don't know yet. The essential information you must have is the definition of a dozen:

$$1 \text{ dozen} = 12$$

You can use this information to make the needed conversion as follows:

$$2 \text{ dozen doughnuts} \times \frac{12}{1 \text{ dozen}} = 24 \text{ doughnuts}$$

You need to buy 24 doughnuts.

Note two important things about this process.

1. The factor $\frac{12}{1 \text{ dozen}}$ is a conversion factor based on the definition of the term *dozen*. This conversion factor is a ratio of the two parts of the definition of a dozen given above.

2. The unit dozen itself cancels.

Now let's generalize a bit. To change from one unit to another we will use a conversion factor.

$$\text{Unit}_1 \times \text{conversion factor} = \text{Unit}_2$$

The **conversion factor** is a ratio of the two parts of the statement that relates the two units. We will see this in more detail on the following pages.

Earlier in this chapter we considered a pin that measured 2.85 cm in length. What is the length of the pin in inches? We can represent this problem as

$$2.85 \text{ cm} \rightarrow ? \text{ in.}$$

The question mark stands for the number we want to find. To solve this problem, we must know the relationship between inches and centimeters. In **Table 5.7**, which gives several equivalents between the English and metric systems, we find the relationship

$$2.54 \text{ cm} = 1 \text{ in.}$$

TABLE 5.7

English-Metric and English-English Equivalents

Length	1 m = 1.094 yd
	2.54 cm = 1 in.
	1 mi = 5280. ft
	1 mi = 1760. yd
Mass	1 kg = 2.205 lb
	453.6 g = 1 lb
Volume	1 L = 1.06 qt
	1 ft³ = 28.32 L

This is called an **equivalence statement.** In other words, 2.54 cm and 1 in. stand for *exactly the same distance* (see Figure 5.1 on page 119). The respective numbers are different because they refer to different *scales (units)* of distance.

The equivalence statement 2.54 cm = 1 in. can lead to either of two conversion factors:

$$\frac{2.54 \text{ cm}}{1 \text{ in.}} \quad \text{or} \quad \frac{1 \text{ in.}}{2.54 \text{ cm}}$$

Note that these *conversion factors* are *ratios of the two parts of the equivalence statement* that relates the two units. Which of the two possible conversion factors do we need? Recall our problem:

$$2.85 \text{ cm} = ? \text{ in.}$$

That is, we want to convert from units of centimeters to inches:

$$2.85 \text{ cm} \times \text{conversion factor} = ? \text{ in.}$$

MATH

Units cancel just as numbers do.

We choose a conversion factor that cancels the units we want to discard and leaves the units we want in the result. Thus we do the conversion as follows:

$$2.85 \text{ cm} \times \frac{1 \text{ in.}}{2.54 \text{ cm}} = \frac{2.85 \text{ in.}}{2.54} = 1.12 \text{ in.}$$

Note two important facts about this conversion.

1. The centimeter units cancel to give inches for the result. This is exactly what we had wanted to accomplish. Using the other conversion factor $\left(2.85 \text{ cm} \times \dfrac{2.54 \text{ cm}}{1 \text{ in.}} \right)$ would not work because the units would not cancel to give inches in the result.

PROBLEM SOLVING

When you finish a calculation, always check to make sure that the answer makes sense.

2. As the units changed from centimeters to inches, the number changed from 2.85 to 1.12. Thus 2.85 cm has exactly the same value (is the same length) as 1.12 in. Notice that in this conversion, the number decreased from 2.85 to 1.12. This makes sense because the inch is a larger unit of length than the centimeter is. That is, it takes fewer inches to make the same length in centimeters.

The result in the previous conversion has three significant figures as required. Caution: Noting that the term 1 appears in the conversion, you might think that because this number appears to have only one significant figure, the result should have only one significant figure. That is, the answer should be given as 1 in. rather than 1.12 in. However, in the equivalence statement 1 in. = 2.54 cm, the 1 is an exact number (by definition). In other words, exactly 1 in. equals 2.54 cm. Therefore, the 1 does not limit the number of significant digits in the result.

PROBLEM SOLVING

When exact numbers are used in a calculation, they never limit the number of significant digits.

We have seen how to convert from centimeters to inches. What about the reverse conversion? For example, if a pencil is 7.00 in. long, what is its length in centimeters? In this case, the conversion we want to make is

$$7.00 \text{ in.} \rightarrow ? \text{ cm}$$

What conversion factor do we need to make this conversion?

Remember that two conversion factors can be derived from each equivalence statement. In this case, the equivalence statement 2.54 cm = 1 in. gives

$$\frac{2.54 \text{ cm}}{1 \text{ in.}} \quad \text{or} \quad \frac{1 \text{ in.}}{2.54 \text{ cm}}$$

5.6 Problem Solving and Dimensional Analysis **131**

TEACHING TIP

Asking students to consider whether their answer makes sense is good way to check on the magnitude and sign of the answer. Students are often reluctant to do so, which leads to many careless mistakes in calculations.

MISCONCEPTIONS

- Dimensional analysis is a double-edged sword: It is both extremely useful and quite dangerous. It is useful because it allows students to solve problems by considering only the units. It is dangerous for the same reason; that is, it can allow students to solve problems they do not understand.

- It is important to differentiate between achieving the correct answer and understanding the concepts underlying the problem. As an example, you may wish to give the students this problem:

  There are 2 igals in 1 odonku, and 6 odonkus in 4 falgers. If you have 3 igals, how many falgers is this?

Most students eventually get the answer "1 falger." Once they have solved the problem, ask them questions such as "What is an igal? An odonku? A falger?" While we expect students to be able to do the mathematical mechanics illustrated by this problem, they should also strive to understand the problems they are solving.

PROBLEM SOLVING

Consider the direction of the required change to select the correct conversion factor.

Again, we choose which to use by looking at the *direction* of the required change. For us to change from inches to centimeters, the inches must cancel. Thus the factor

$$\frac{2.54 \text{ cm}}{1 \text{ in.}}$$

is used, and the conversion is done as follows:

$$7.00 \text{ in.} \times \frac{2.54 \text{ cm}}{1 \text{ in.}} = (7.00)(2.54) \text{ cm} = 17.8 \text{ cm}$$

Here the inch units cancel, leaving centimeters as required.

Note that in this conversion, the number increased (from 7.00 to 17.8). This increase makes sense because the centimeter is a smaller unit of length than the inch. That is, it takes more centimeters to make the same length in inches. *Always take a moment to think about whether your answer makes sense.* It will help you avoid errors.

Changing from one unit to another via conversion factors (based on the equivalence statements between the units) is often called **dimensional analysis.** We will use this method throughout our study of chemistry.

We can now state some general steps for doing conversions by dimensional analysis.

Converting from One Unit to Another

STEP 1 To convert from one unit to another, use the equivalence statement that relates the two units. The conversion factor needed is a ratio of the two parts of the equivalence statement.

STEP 2 Choose the appropriate conversion factor by looking at the direction of the required change (make sure the unwanted units cancel).

STEP 3 Multiply the quantity to be converted by the conversion factor to give the quantity with the desired units.

STEP 4 Check that you have the correct number of significant figures.

STEP 5 Ask whether your answer makes sense.

We will now illustrate this procedure in Example 5.6.

Example 5.6

Conversion Factors: One-Step Problems

An Italian bicycle has its frame size given as 62 cm. What is the frame size in inches?

Solution

We can represent the problem as

$$62 \text{ cm} = ? \text{ in.}$$

Additional Examples

1. A new baby weighs 7.8 lb. What is its mass in kilograms?
3.5 kg

2. A piece of lumber is 88.4 cm long. What is its length in millimeters? In inches?
884 mm; 34.8 in.

3. A bottle of soda contains 2.0 L. What is the volume in quarts?
2.12 qt

In this problem we want to convert from centimeters to inches.

$$62 \text{ cm} \times \text{conversion factor} = ? \text{ in.}$$

Step 1 To convert from centimeters to inches, we need the equivalence statement 1 in. = 2.54 cm. This leads to two conversion factors:

$$\frac{1 \text{ in.}}{2.54 \text{ cm}} \quad \text{and} \quad \frac{2.54 \text{ cm}}{1 \text{ in.}}$$

Step 2 In this case, the direction we want is

Centimeters → inches

so we need the conversion factor $\frac{1 \text{ in.}}{2.54 \text{ cm}}$. We know this is the one we want because using it will make the units of centimeters cancel, leaving units of inches.

Step 3 The conversion is carried out as follows:

$$62 \text{ cm} \times \frac{1 \text{ in.}}{2.54 \text{ cm}} = 24 \text{ in.}$$

Step 4 The result is limited to two significant figures by the number 62. The centimeters cancel, leaving inches as required.

Step 5 Note that the number decreased in this conversion. This makes sense; the inch is a larger unit of length than the centimeter.

 Self-Check Exercise 5.4

Water is often bottled in 0.750-L containers. Using the appropriate equivalence statement from Table 5.7, calculate the volume of such a water bottle in quarts.

Next we will consider a conversion that requires several steps.

 Answer to Self-Check Exercise 5.4

$$0.750 \text{ L} \times \frac{1.06 \text{ qt}}{1 \text{ L}} = 0.795 \text{ qt}$$

Additional Examples

1. In the Olympics, one swimming event has a distance of 100 meters. How long is the race in feet?
   328 ft

2. How many seconds are in one day?
   86,400 s

3. Your car has a 5.00-L engine. What is the size of this engine in cubic inches?
   305 in^3

Example 5.7

Conversion Factors: Multiple-Step Problems

The length of the marathon race is approximately 26.2 mi. What is this distance in kilometers?

Solution

The problem before us can be represented as follows:

26.2 mi = ? km

We could accomplish this conversion in several different ways, but because Table 5.7 gives the equivalence statements 1 mi = 1760 yd and 1 m = 1.094 yd, we will proceed as follows:

Miles → yards → meters → kilometers

This process will be carried out one conversion at a time to make sure everything is clear.

(continued)

(continued)

Miles → Yards: We convert from miles to yards using the conversion factor $\dfrac{1760\ \text{yd}}{1\ \text{mi}}$.

$$26.2\ \cancel{\text{mi}} \times \frac{1760\ \text{yd}}{1\ \cancel{\text{mi}}} = 46{,}112\ \text{yd}$$

Result shown on calculator

$$46{,}112\ \text{yd}\ \boxed{\text{Round off}} \Rightarrow 46{,}100\ \text{yd} = 4.61 \times 10^4\ \text{yd}$$

Yards → Meters: The conversion factor used to convert yards to meters is $\dfrac{1\ \text{m}}{1.094\ \text{yd}}$.

$$4.61 \times 10^4\ \cancel{\text{yd}} \times \frac{1\ \text{m}}{1.094\ \cancel{\text{yd}}} = 4.213894 \times 10^4\ \text{m}$$

Result shown on calculator

$$4.213894 \times 10^4\ \text{m}\ \boxed{\text{Round off}} \Rightarrow 4.21 \times 10^4\ \text{m}$$

Meters → Kilometers: Because $1000\ \text{m} = 1\ \text{km}$, or $10^3\ \text{m} = 1\ \text{km}$, we convert from meters to kilometers as follows:

$$4.21 \times 10^4\ \cancel{\text{m}} \times \frac{1\ \text{km}}{10^3\ \cancel{\text{m}}} = 4.21 \times 10^1\ \text{km}$$

$$= 42.1\ \text{km}$$

Thus the marathon (26.2 mi) is 42.1 km.

Once you feel comfortable with the conversion process, you can combine the steps. For the above conversion, the combined expression is

$$\text{miles} \rightarrow \text{yards} \rightarrow \text{meters} \rightarrow \text{kilometers}$$

$$26.2\ \cancel{\text{mi}} \times \frac{1760\ \cancel{\text{yd}}}{1\ \cancel{\text{mi}}} \times \frac{1\ \cancel{\text{m}}}{1.094\ \cancel{\text{yd}}} \times \frac{1\ \text{km}}{10^3\ \cancel{\text{m}}} = 42.1\ \text{km}$$

Note that the units cancel to give the required kilometers and that the result has three significant figures.

PROBLEM SOLVING

Remember that we are rounding off at the end of each step to show the correct number of significant figures. However, in doing a multistep calculation, *you* should retain the extra numbers that show on your calculator and round off only at the end of the calculation.

Self-Check Exercise 5.5

Racing cars at the Indianapolis Motor Speedway now routinely travel around the track at an average speed of 225 mi/h. What is this speed in kilometers per hour?

Recap: Whenever you work problems, remember the following points:

1. Always include the units (a measurement always has two parts: a number *and* a unit).

2. Cancel units as you carry out the calculations.

3. Check that your final answer has the correct units. If it doesn't, you have done something wrong.

4. Check that your final answer has the correct number of significant figures.

5. Think about whether your answer makes sense.

PROBLEM SOLVING

Units provide a very valuable check on the validity of your solution. Always use them.

Answer to Self-Check Exercise 5.5

$$225\ \frac{\text{mi}}{\text{h}} \times \frac{1760\ \text{yd}}{1\ \text{mi}} \times \frac{1\ \text{m}}{1.094\ \text{yd}}$$

$$\times \frac{1\ \text{km}}{1000\ \text{m}} = 362\ \frac{\text{km}}{\text{h}}$$

1. Obtain a recipe card from your teacher.
2. Convert all of the measurements to metric units. Be careful in determining the number of significant figures in your answers.

5.7 Temperature Conversions: An Approach to Problem Solving

Objectives: *To learn the three temperature scales.*
To learn to convert from one scale to another.
To continue to develop problem-solving skills.

CHEMISTRY
Although 373 K is often stated
as 373 degrees Kelvin, it is
more correct to say 373 kelvins.

When the doctor tells you your temperature is 102 degrees and the
weather-person on TV says it will be 75 degrees tomorrow, they are
using the **Fahrenheit scale.** Water boils at 212 °F and freezes at 32 °F, and
normal body temperature is 98.6 °F (where °F signifies "Fahrenheit degrees").
This temperature scale is widely used in the United States and Great Britain,
and it is the scale employed in most of the engineering sciences. Another
temperature scale, used in Canada and Europe and in the physical and life
sciences in most countries, is the **Celsius scale.** In keeping with the metric
system, which is based on powers of 10, the freezing and boiling points of
water on the Celsius scale are assigned as 0 °C and 100 °C, respectively. On
both the Fahrenheit and the Celsius scales, the unit of temperature is called
a degree, and the symbol for it is followed by the capital letter representing
the scale on which the units are measured: °C or °F.

Still another temperature scale used in the sciences is the **absolute** or
Kelvin scale. On this scale water freezes at 273 K and boils at 373 K. On the
Kelvin scale, the unit of temperature is called a kelvin and is symbolized by
K. Thus, on the three scales, the boiling point of water is stated as 212 Fahren-
heit degrees (212 °F), 100 Celsius degrees (100 °C), and 373 kelvins (373 K).

The three temperature scales are compared in **Figure 5.6** on page 136.
There are several important facts you should note.

1. The size of each temperature unit (each degree) is the same for the
   Celsius and Kelvin scales. This follows from the fact that the *difference*
   between the boiling and freezing points of water is 100 units on both of
   these scales.

2. The Fahrenheit degree is smaller than the Celsius and Kelvin unit. Note
   that on the Fahrenheit scale there are 180 Fahrenheit degrees between
   the boiling and freezing points of water, as compared with 100 units on
   the other two scales.

3. The zero points are different on all three scales.

In your study of chemistry, you will sometimes need to convert from one
temperature scale to another. We will consider in some detail how this conversion is done. In addition to learning how to change temperature scales,
you should also use this section as an opportunity to further develop your
skills in problem solving.

5.7 Temperature Conversions: An Approach to Problem Solving **135**

Cooking in a Metric World

Materials Each student/group
needs one (or more) recipe
card(s) and a calculator. Save
recipe cards from magazines or
have the students bring them to
class. If you choose to have students bring them, announce this
fact early and set the due date
for a few days before you plan
to do this activity.

Purpose Students practice unit
conversions. In addition, they review rules for significant figures.

Discussion This activity can be
adapted to fit any time limit.

Section 5.7

Themes
Organization, Patterns of Change

Skills
Applying concepts, interpreting
diagrams, making comparisons,
solving problems

TEACHING TIP

This section provides an excellent opportunity to begin to emphasize relationships instead of
simply memorizing formulas.
The relationships among the
temperature scales can be related to graphing a straight line.
See Teaching Support on page
136. This idea relates to the student's math background. It is a
good opportunity for cross-curricular teaching with the math
department.

Figure 5.6
The three major temperature scales.

Converting Between the Kelvin and Celsius Scales

It is relatively simple to convert between the Celsius and Kelvin scales because the temperature unit is the same size; only the zero points are different. Look at Figure 5.6. To go from each Celsius temperature marked on the middle thermometer to the Kelvin temperature on the right thermometer, what do we need to do?

$$100\ °C + 273 = 373\ K$$
$$0\ °C + 273 = 273\ K$$
$$-18\ °C + 273 = 255\ K$$
$$-273\ °C + 273 = 0\ K$$

In each case we need to add 273 to the Celsius temperature. As 0 °C corresponds to 273 K, this addition of 273 corrects for the difference in zero points.

$$T_{°C} + 273 = T_K$$

We will illustrate this procedure in Example 5.8.

Example 5.8

MATH
The decimal point after the temperature reading indicates that the trailing zero is significant.

Temperature Conversion: Celsius to Kelvin

The boiling point of water at the top of Mt. Everest is 70. °C. Convert this temperature to the Kelvin scale.

Solution

Celsius-to-Kelvin conversions require us to adjust for different zero points using the formula

$$T_{°C} + 273 = T_K$$

136   Chapter 5   Measurements and Calculations

Using this formula to solve this problem gives

$$70. + 273 = 343$$

343 K is the correct answer. This conversion is summarized in **Figure 5.7**.

Figure 5.7
Converting 70. °C to units measured on the Kelvin scale.

We can summarize what we learned in Example 5.8 as follows: to convert from the Celsius to the Kelvin scale, we use the formula

$$T_{°C} + 273 = T_K$$

Temperature in Celsius degrees   Temperature in kelvins

Example 5.9

Temperature Conversion: Kelvin to Celsius

Liquid nitrogen boils at 77 K. What is the boiling point of nitrogen on the Celsius scale?

Solution

We solve this problem by using the formula

$$T_{°C} + 273 = T_K$$

However, in this case we want to solve for the Celsius temperature $T_{°C}$. That is, we want to isolate $T_{°C}$ on one side of the equals sign. To do this we use an important mathematical principle: doing *the same thing on both sides of the equals sign* preserves the equality. In other words, it's always okay to perform the same operation on both sides of the equals sign.

To isolate $T_{°C}$ we need to subtract 273 from both sides

$$T_{°C} + 273 - 273 = T_K - 273$$

↑　↑
Sum is zero

(continued)

points on the scales differ by 32. The equation for converting between Celsius and Fahrenheit is shown from the graph.

Now invent a temperature scale and ask the students to write an equation for converting from Celsius to your imaginary scale. The number of degrees between the boiling and freezing points of water should be different from the number of degrees for any of the common scales. The difference in the zero points should also be different from 273 and 32. If students understand the relationship between the imaginary scale and the Celsius scale, they should be able to write an equation for converting between the two.

(continued)

to give

$$T_{°C} = T_K - 273$$

Using this equation to solve the problem, we have

$$T_{°C} = T_K - 273 = 77 - 273 = -196$$

So we have shown that

$$77\ K = -196\ °C$$

Self-Check Exercise 5.6

Which temperature is colder, 172 K or −75 °C?

**Answer to Self-Check
Exercise 5.6**

The best way to solve this problem is to convert 172 K to Celsius degrees. To do so, we will use the formula $T_{°C} = T_K - 273 = 172 - 273 = -101$.

So 172 K = −101 °C, which is a lower temperature than −75 °C. Thus 172 K is colder than −75 °C.

In summary, because the Kelvin and Celsius scales have the same size unit, to switch from one scale to the other we must simply account for the different zero points. We must add 273 to the Celsius temperature to obtain the temperature on the Kelvin scale:

$$T_K = T_{°C} + 273$$

To convert from the Kelvin scale to the Celsius scale, we must subtract 273 from the Kelvin temperature:

$$T_{°C} = T_K - 273$$

CHEMICAL IMPACT

Science, Technology, and Society

Ersatz Fog

Did you know that a knowledge of chemistry might win you an Academy Award? In fact, James F. Foley, Charles E. Converse, and F. Edward Gardner of Praxair Corporation were given Technical Achievement Awards by the Academy of Motion Picture Arts and Sciences for their fake fog concoction used in the movie "Batman and Robin." The Praxair employees created a special low-lying fog for scenes involving the villain Mr. Freeze, played by Arnold Schwarzenegger. The fog resulted from a special mixture of steam, liquid nitrogen, and liquid oxygen. About 27.5 million cubic feet of the mixture was used in making the film. The liquid oxygen and nitrogen were hauled to the studio daily from a nearby Praxair air liquefaction plant using a cryogenic tank truck. A patent is now pending for the fog recipe, which looks like it has a "bright" future in Hollywood.

Note the ersatz fog behind Mr. Freeze.

Figure 5.8
Comparison of the Celsius and Fahrenheit scales.

Converting Between the Fahrenheit and Celsius Scales

The conversion between the Fahrenheit and Celsius temperature scales requires two adjustments:

1. For the different size units

2. For the different zero points

To see how to adjust for the different unit sizes, consider the diagram in **Figure 5.8.** Note that because 212 °F = 100 °C and 32 °F = 0 °C,

$$212 - 32 = 180 \text{ Fahrenheit degrees} = 100 - 0 = 100 \text{ Celsius degrees}$$

Thus

$$180. \text{ Fahrenheit degrees} = 100. \text{ Celsius degrees}$$

Dividing both sides of this equation by 100. gives

$$\frac{180.}{100.} \text{ Fahrenheit degrees} = \frac{100.}{100.} \text{ Celsius degrees}$$

or

$$1.80 \text{ Fahrenheit degrees} = 1.00 \text{ Celsius degree}$$

MATH
Remember, it's okay to do the same thing to both sides of the equation.

MATH
Note that because 180 and 100 here are both exact numbers obtained by counting the number of degrees, the ratio 180/100 has an unlimited number of significant digits. This ratio is typically shown as 1.80.

The factor 1.80 is used to convert from one degree size to the other.

Next we have to account for the fact that 0 °C is *not* the same as 0 °F. In fact, 32 °F = 0 °C. Although we will not show how to derive it, the equation to convert a temperature in Celsius degrees to the Fahrenheit scale is

$$\underset{\substack{\text{Temperature} \\ \text{in °F}}}{T_{°F}} = 1.80(\underset{\substack{\uparrow \\ \text{Temperature} \\ \text{in °C}}}{T_{°C}}) + 32$$

In this equation the term $1.80(T_{°C})$ adjusts for the difference in degree size between the two scales. The 32 in the equation accounts for the different zero points. We will now show how to use this equation.

5.7   Temperature Conversions: An Approach to Problem Solving   **139**

1. You're traveling in a metric country and get sick. Your temperature is 41 °C. What is it on the Fahrenheit scale?
   106 °F

2. Convert 32 °C to Fahrenheit degrees.
   89.6 °F

3. The boiling point of nitrogen is −196 °C. What is this temperature on the Fahrenheit scale?
   −321 °F

Example 5.10

Temperature Conversion: Celsius to Fahrenheit

On a summer day the temperature in the laboratory, as measured on a lab thermometer, is 28 °C. Express this temperature on the Fahrenheit scale.

Solution

This problem can be represented as 28 °C = ? °F. We will solve it using the formula

$$T_{°F} = 1.80(T_{°C}) + 32$$

In this case,

$$T_{°F} = ? °F = 1.80(\overset{T_{°C}}{\underset{\downarrow}{28}}) + 32 = 50.4 + 32$$

Rounds off to 50

$$= 50 + 32 = 82$$

Note that 28 °C is approximately equal to 82 °F. Because the numbers are just reversed, this is an easy reference point to remember for the two scales.

Thus 28 °C = 82 °F.

Example 5.11

Temperature Conversion: Celsius to Fahrenheit

Express the temperature −40. °C on the Fahrenheit scale.

Solution

We can express this problem as −40. °C = ? °F. To solve it we will use the formula

$$T_{°F} = 1.80(T_{°C}) + 32$$

In this case,

$$T_{°F} = ? °F = 1.80(\overset{T_{°C}}{\underset{\downarrow}{-40.}}) + 32$$
$$= -72 + 32 = -40$$

So −40 °C = −40 °F. This is a very interesting result and is another useful reference point.

 Self-Check Exercise 5.7

Hot tubs are often maintained at 41 °C. What is this temperature in Fahrenheit degrees?

Answer to Self-Check Exercise 5.7

The problem is 41 °C = ? °F.

Using the formula

$$T_{°F} = 1.80(T_{°C}) + 32$$

we have

$$T_{°F} = ? °F = 1.80(41) + 32$$
$$= 74 + 32 = 106$$

That is, 41 °C = 106 °F.

To convert from Celsius to Fahrenheit, we have used the equation

$$T_{°F} = 1.80(T_{°C}) + 32$$

To convert a Fahrenheit temperature to Celsius, we need to rearrange this equation to isolate Celsius degrees ($T_{°C}$). Remember we can always do the same operation to both sides of the equation. First subtract 32 from each side:

$$T_{°F} - 32 = 1.80(T_{°C}) + 32 - 32$$

Sum is zero

to give

$$T_{°F} - 32 = 1.80(T_{°C})$$

Next divide both sides by 1.80

$$\frac{T_{°F} - 32}{1.80} = \frac{1.80\,(T_{°C})}{1.80}$$

to give

$$\frac{T_{°F} - 32}{1.80} = T_{°C}$$

or

$$T_{°C} = \frac{\overset{\text{Temperature in °F}}{T_{°F}} - 32}{180}$$

$$\underset{\text{Temperature in °C}}{T_{°C}} = \frac{T_{°F} - 32}{180}$$

Example 5.12

Temperature Conversion: Fahrenheit to Celsius

One of the body's responses to an infection or injury is to elevate its temperature. A certain flu victim has a body temperature of 101 °F. What is this temperature on the Celsius scale?

Solution

The problem is 101 °F = ? °C. Using the formula

$$T_{°C} = \frac{T_{°F} - 32}{1.80}$$

yields

$$T_{°C} = ?\ °C = \frac{\overset{T_{°F}}{101} - 32}{1.80} = \frac{69}{1.80} = 38$$

That is, 101 °F = 38 °C.

 Self-Check Exercise 5.8

An antifreeze solution in a car's radiator boils at 239 °F. What is this temperature on the Celsius scale?

Additional Examples

1. Ray Bradbury wrote a book titled *Fahrenheit 451*. What is this temperature on the Celsius scale?
   233 °C

2. Pork is considered to be well cooked when its internal temperature reaches 160 °F. What is this temperature on the Celsius scale?
   71 °C

 Answer to Self-Check Exercise 5.8

This problem can be stated as 239 °F = ? °C.

Using the formula

$$T_{°C} = \frac{T_{°F} - 32}{1.80}$$

we have in this case

$$T_{°C} = ?\ °C = \frac{239 - 32}{1.80}$$

$$= \frac{207}{1.80} = 115$$

That is, 239 °F = 115 °C.

Themes
Organization, Stability

Skills
Applying concepts, solving problems, calculating

 Laboratory
Experiment 21:
Measurement and Density,
Traditional

USING TECHNOLOGY

 Animation and Video

Video, Relative Densities of Pepsi and Diet Pepsi

Additional Examples

A block has a volume of 25.3 cm³. Its mass is 21.7 g. Calculate the density of the block.
0.858 g/cm³

GROUP ACTIVITY

Have each team predict what would happen if they dropped a few raisins or small pieces of spaghetti into a container of carbonated liquid. Would the items sink or float? What if they waited for 30 seconds? Have students justify their predictions. Now have them test their predictions. Once the testing is complete, ask the teams if they want to change their thinking.

MINI-DEMO

Use a 1-L soda bottle to prepare a demonstration of density. Add 500 mL of vegetable oil and 500 mL of water (colored with food coloring) to the bottle. Tighten the top and shake. Allow the liquids to settle. Ask the students which liquid is more dense. You can extend your discussion to include an introduction to the immiscibility of oil and water. You can then ask students whether a density column could be made from different concentrations of the same substance. See Teaching Support for the construction of such a column.

142

In doing temperature conversions, you will need the following formulas.

Temperature Conversion Formulas	
Celsius to Kelvin	$T_K = T_{°C} + 273$
Kelvin to Celsius	$T_{°C} = T_K - 273$
Celsius to Fahrenheit	$T_{°F} = 1.80(T_{°C}) + 32$
Fahrenheit to Celsius	$T_{°C} = \dfrac{T_{°F} - 32}{1.80}$

5.8 Density

Objective: *To define density and its units.*

Lead has a greater density than feathers.

When you were in elementary school, you may have been embarrassed by your answer to the question, "Which is heavier, a pound of lead or a pound of feathers?" If you said lead, you were undoubtedly thinking about density, not mass. **Density** can be defined as the amount of matter present *in a given volume* of substance. That is, density is mass per unit volume, or the ratio of the mass of an object to its volume:

$$\text{Density} = \frac{\text{mass}}{\text{volume}}$$

It takes a much bigger volume to make a pound of feathers than to make a pound of lead. This is because lead has a much greater mass per unit volume—a greater density.

The density of a liquid can be determined easily by weighing a known volume of the substance as illustrated in Example 5.13.

Example 5.13

Calculating Density

Suppose a student finds that 23.50 mL of a certain liquid weighs 35.062 g. What is the density of this liquid?

Solution

We can calculate the density of this liquid simply by applying the definition

$$\text{Density} = \frac{\text{mass}}{\text{volume}} = \frac{35.062 \text{ g}}{23.50 \text{ mL}} = 1.492 \text{ g/mL}$$

This result could also be expressed as 1.492 g/cm³ because 1 mL = 1 cm³.

The volume of a solid object is often determined indirectly by submerging it in water and measuring the volume of water displaced. In fact, this is the most accurate method for measuring a person's percent body fat. The person is submerged momentarily in a tank of water, and the increase in volume is measured (see **Figure 5.9**). It is possible to calculate the body density by using the person's weight (mass) and the volume of the person's body determined by submersion. Fat, muscle, and bone have different densities (fat

142 Chapter 5 Measurements and Calculations

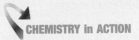

Figure 5.9
(a) Tank of water. (b) Person submerged in the tank, raising the level of the water.

(a)   (b)

is less dense than muscle tissue, for example), so the fraction of the person's body that is fat can be calculated. The more muscle and the less fat a person has, the higher his or her body density. For example, a muscular person weighing 150 lb has a smaller body volume (and thus a higher density) than a fat person weighing 150 lb.

The densities of various common substances are given in **Table 5.8.**

CHEMISTRY in ACTION

The Density of Clay

1. Obtain a piece of clay from your teacher.
2. Develop a method to determine the density of the clay and discuss it with your teacher. Also refer to Example 5.14 on page 144.
3. Determine the density of your clay.
4. Does the amount of clay you use in your determination affect the density you calculate? Why or why not?
5. Does the shape of the clay affect the density you calculate? Why or why not?
6. If you make a hollow ball out of clay, will it have the same density as you calculated previously? Explain.

TABLE 5.8

Densities of Various Common Substances at 20 °C

Substance	Physical State	Density (g/cm³)	Substance	Physical State	Density (g/cm³)
oxygen	gas	0.00133*	aluminum	solid	2.70
hydrogen	gas	0.000084*	iron	solid	7.87
ethanol	liquid	0.785	copper	solid	8.96
benzene	liquid	0.880	silver	solid	10.5
water	liquid	1.000	lead	solid	11.34
magnesium	solid	1.74	mercury	liquid	13.6
salt (sodium chloride)	solid	2.16	gold	solid	19.32

*At 1 atmosphere pressure

5.8 Density   **143**

CHEMISTRY in ACTION

The Density of Clay

Materials Each student/group will need a piece of clay. Have water, balances, graduated cylinders, and rulers available for students to use.

Purpose The purpose is for students to better understand the concept of density.

Discussion There are two common ways for students to determine the density of the clay. In both cases they need to determine the mass of the clay by using a balance. To determine the volume, a student may use water displacement, which means that he or she must understand that the clay will displace its volume of water. In this method, place some water in a graduated cylinder and note the volume reading. Then put the piece of clay into the cylinder, and determine the volume of water displaced. This volume is the volume of the clay. Another method would be to mold the clay into an easily measured geometric shape, such as a cube. Then the student can use a ruler, make the proper measurements, and calculate the volume. The density of the clay is the ratio of the mass to the volume.

Use modeling clay that does not readily absorb water for this activity. Clay is a useful material for such an activity because it allows for experimentation with density. For example, students should see that neither the shape of the object nor its size affects the density of the clay, as long as their object is not hollow. Many students confuse density with mass, and it is good for them to see that a large sample of clay has the same density as a small piece. When a piece of clay is formed with a cavity in its center, it has a much greater volume and essentially the same mass (although the mass of air adds a little to the total) and thus is less dense than a solid sample of clay.

bottom of the separatory funnel. Suspend the separatory funnel in an iron ring above the tall cylinder so that the hose reaches very near to the bottom of the cylinder. Fill the separatory funnel with red solution (the stopcock should be closed). Add the red solution to the cylinder, being careful to fill the tube completely with the solution. Close the stopcock just before all of the red solution drains out. Take the orange solution and slowly open the stopcock to add it to the column. Again, close the stopcock before all of the solution is drained out of the separatory funnel. Add the remaining solutions in the same manner in order of increasing concentration. You should end up with a rainbow column. The layers will remain visible for at least 24 hours if the column remains undisturbed. You can also stir the column at the end of the demonstration, which mixes the colors and shows students that the density was based on concentration, not miscibility.

Variation Students can construct their own columns by using 10-mL graduated cylinders and Beral pipets for the addition of the colors. They must add the solutions from most dense to least dense.

Example 5.14

CHEMISTRY

The most common units for density are g/mL = g/cm³.

TOP TEN

Elements with Highest Densities

Element	Year Discovered	Density (g/cm³)
1. Osmium	1804	22.59
2. Iridium	1804	22.56
3. Platinum	1748	21.45
4. Rhenium	1925	21.01
5. Neptunium	1940	20.47
6. Plutonium	1940	20.26
7. Gold	prehistoric	19.32
8. Tungsten	1783	19.26
9. Uranium	1789	19.05
10. Tantalum	1802	16.67

Determining Density

At a local pawn shop a student finds a medallion that the shop owner insists is pure platinum. However, the student suspects that the medallion may actually be silver and thus much less valuable. The student buys the medallion only after the shop owner agrees to refund the price if the medallion is returned within two days. The student, a chemistry student, then takes the medallion to her lab and measures its density as follows. She first weighs the medallion and finds its mass to be 55.64 g. She then places some water in a graduated cylinder and reads the volume as 75.2 mL. Next she drops the medallion into the cylinder and reads the new volume as 77.8 mL. Is the medallion platinum (density = 21.4 g/cm³) or silver (density = 10.5 g/cm³)?

Solution

The densities of platinum and silver differ so much that the measured density of the medallion will show which metal is present. Because by definition

$$\text{Density} = \frac{\text{mass}}{\text{volume}}$$

to calculate the density of the medallion, we need its mass and its volume. The mass of the medallion is 55.64 g. The volume of the medallion can be obtained by taking the difference between the volume readings of the water in the graduated cylinder before and after the medallion was added.

Volume of medallion = 77.8 mL − 75.2 mL = 2.6 mL

The volume appeared to increase by 2.6 mL when the medallion was added, so 2.6 mL represents the volume of the medallion. Now we can use the measured mass and volume of the medallion to determine its density:

$$\text{Density of medallion} = \frac{\text{mass}}{\text{volume}} = \frac{55.64 \text{ g}}{2.6 \text{ mL}} = 21 \text{ g/mL}$$

or

$$= 21 \text{ g/cm}^3$$

The medallion is really platinum.

 Self-Check Exercise 5.9

A student wants to identify the main component in a commercial liquid cleaner. He finds that 35.8 mL of the cleaner weighs 28.1 g. Of the following possibilities, which is the main component of the cleaner?

Substance	Density, g/cm³
chloroform	1.483
diethyl ether	0.714
isopropyl alcohol	0.785
toluene	0.867

Example 5.15

Using Density in Calculations

Mercury has a density of 13.6 g/mL. What volume of mercury must be taken to obtain 225 g of the metal?

Spherical droplets of mercury, a very dense liquid.

Solution

To solve this problem, start with the definition of density:

$$\text{Density} = \frac{\text{mass}}{\text{volume}}$$

Then rearrange this equation to isolate the required quantity. In this case we want to find the volume. Remember that we maintain an equality when we do the same thing to both sides. For example, if we multiply *both sides* of the density definition by volume,

$$\text{Volume} \times \text{density} = \frac{\text{mass}}{\text{volume}} \times \text{volume}$$

volume cancels on the right, leaving

$$\text{Volume} \times \text{density} = \text{mass}$$

We want the volume, so we now divide both sides by density:

$$\frac{\text{Volume} \times \text{density}}{\text{density}} = \frac{\text{mass}}{\text{density}}$$

to give

$$\text{Volume} = \frac{\text{mass}}{\text{density}}$$

Now we can solve the problem by substituting the given numbers:

$$\text{Volume} = \frac{225 \text{ g}}{13.6 \text{ g/mL}} = 16.5 \text{ mL}$$

We must take 16.5 mL of mercury to obtain an amount that has a mass of 225 g.

5.8   Density   **145**

Chapter 5   Measurements and Calculations   **145**

Besides being a tool for the identification of substances, density has many other uses. For example, the liquid in your car's lead storage battery (a solution of sulfuric acid) changes density because the sulfuric acid is consumed as the battery discharges. In a fully charged battery, the density of the solution is about 1.30 g/cm³. When the density falls below 1.20 g/cm³, the battery has to be recharged. Density measurement is also used to determine the amount of antifreeze, and thus the level of protection against freezing, in the cooling system of a car. Water and antifreeze have different densities, so the measured density of the mixture tells us how much of each is present. The device used to test the density of the solution—a hydrometer—is shown in **Figure 5.10.**

In certain situations, the term *specific gravity* is used to describe the density of a liquid. **Specific gravity** is defined as the ratio of the density of a given liquid to the density of water at 4 °C. Because it is a ratio of densities, specific gravity has no units.

Figure 5.10
A hydrometer being used to determine the density of the antifreeze solution in a car's radiator.

Focus Questions

Sections 5.6–5.8

1. What is an equivalence statement? How many conversion factors can be created from one equivalence statement? Choose an equivalence statement from Table 5.7 on page 130 and write all the conversion factors that can possibly be made from it.

2. How can you decide which conversion factor to choose in a problem?

3. Write a conversion factor or factors for these problems. Do not do the calculation.
  a. 37 cm × _____ = ? in.
  b. 4.2 qt × _____ = ? L
  c. 2.2 kg × _____ = ? pounds
  d. 3.5 mi × _____ = ? m

4. Consider the temperature conversion formulas shown below. Box the part of the formula that accounts for different zero points. Circle the part of the formula that accounts for different-size degrees.
  a. $T_K = T_{°C} + 273$
  b. $T_{°C} = T_K - 273$
  c. $T_{°F} = 1.80(T_{°C}) + 32$
  d. $T_{°C} = \frac{T_{°F} - 32}{1.80}$

5. When you make a temperature conversion, how many significant figures should be in the converted temperature?

Problem
How does the precision of an instrument affect measurements and calculations?

Introduction
Measurement is an important part of science, and an understanding of uncertainty is an important part of measurement.

In this activity you will compare measurements of your textbook with four different rulers, each with a different precision.

Prelab Assignment
Read the entire laboratory experiment before you begin.

Materials
4 special rulers   Chemistry textbook

Procedure
1. Measure the length and width of your chemistry textbook with each of the four special rulers.
2. Convert all measurements to centimeters (if necessary).
3. Using your measurements, calculate the perimeter (in cm) and area (in cm²) of the cover of your chemistry textbook.

Ruler Number	Length	Width	Length	Width	Perimeter	Area
1	ft	ft	cm	cm	cm	cm²
2	in	in	cm	cm	cm	cm²
3	cm	cm	cm	cm	cm	cm²
4	cm	cm	cm	cm	cm	cm²

Cleaning Up
Leave the rulers on the lab bench.

Analysis and Conclusions
1. Which ruler gives you the most precise measure of the perimeter and area of the cover of your chemistry textbook? Why?
2. Which ruler gives you the least precise measure of the perimeter and area of the cover of your chemistry textbook? Why?
3. Justify the number of significant figures in each of your measurements.
4. Justify the number of significant figures in each of your calculations.
5. Compare your measurements with other groups. For which ruler was there the most difference among groups? The least difference? Explain.
6. Compare your calculations with other groups. For which ruler was there the most difference among groups? The least difference? Explain.

Summary Table
Record your measurements and calculations in a table similar to the one shown below.

Something Extra
For each ruler, what is the largest length that you can measure that you would report as a measurement of zero? Explain.

147

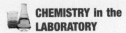
Measuring a Book? Precisely!

Objectives
1. To practice calculations and determine the correct number of significant figures
2. To understand uncertainty in measurement

Skills
Measuring, applying concepts (significant figures), making judgments, calculating, making comparisons, interpreting data

Materials
Four special rulers Textbook

Preparation Hints
Templates for the rulers are provided in the *Teacher Resources*. Make enough copies for each group of students to have one set.

Prelab Discussion
Make sure that students understand that there is only one uncertain digit in each measurement.

Procedure Hints
Have the students assemble class data once all measurements are converted to centimeters. If these results are incorrect, the calculations will be incorrect.

Post-Lab Discussion
Use a whole-class discussion to review the results. Students will still be relatively unfamiliar with uncertainty and there will undoubtedly be differences among the groups.

Analysis and Conclusions
1. Ruler 4 is the most precise. There is the greatest number of significant figures, and the precision is to the hundredths place.
2. Ruler 1 is the least precise. There is only one significant figure to the tenths place.
3. Answers will vary. There is always only one uncertain number in a measurement.
4. Answers will vary. Students should explain the rules for determining significant figures when adding numbers and multiplying numbers.

Summary Table
Actual numbers will depend on the size of the book used.

Ruler #	Length	Width	Length	Width	Perimeter	Area
1	0.8 ft	0.7 ft	20 cm	20 cm	80 cm	400 cm²
2	10.2 in	8.1 in	25.9 cm	21 cm	94 cm	540 cm²
3	26.1 cm	20.5 cm	26.1 cm	20.5 cm	93.2 cm	535 cm²
4	26.15 cm	20.59 cm	26.15 cm	20.59 cm	93.48 cm	538.4 cm²

Something Extra
For ruler 1, the measurement for any object that is shorter than 0.1 ft would be rounded to zero. For ruler 2, any measurement less than 0.1 in. is rounded to zero. For ruler 3, the measurement rounded to zero would be anything less than 0.1 cm. For ruler 4, anything less than 0.01 cm would be rounded to zero.

5. Answers will vary. There is a greater chance of differences with rulers 1 and 2 because of the smaller number of significant figures. Measurements for rulers 3 and 4 are probably closer among groups.

6. Answers will vary. See the explanation in question 5.

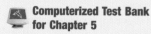
Chapter Review
Assign the students to work individually on the Chapter 5 Review Worksheet at the appropriate level (Basic, Standard, or
Challenge). Answers are found in
the *Teacher Resources*.

Assessment
Chapter 5 Test is found in the
Teacher Resources, along with
the answers for the test.

Computerized Test Bank
for Chapter 5

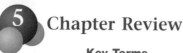

5 Chapter Review

Key Terms

measurement (p. 113)
scientific notation (5.1)
units (5.2)
English system (5.2)
metric system (5.2)
SI units (5.2)
volume (5.3)
liter (5.3)
milliliter (5.3)
kilogram (5.3)
gram (5.3)
mass (5.3)
significant figures (5.4)
rounding off (5.5)
conversion factor (5.6)
equivalence statement (5.6)
dimensional analysis (5.6)
Fahrenheit scale (5.7)
Celsius scale (5.7)
Kelvin (absolute) scale (5.7)
density (5.8)
specific gravity (5.8)

Summary

1. A quantitative observation is called a measurement and always consists of a number and a unit.

2. We can conveniently express very large or very small numbers using scientific notation, which represents the number as a number between 1 and 10 multiplied by 10 raised to a power.

3. Units give a scale on which to represent the results of a measurement. The three systems discussed are the English, metric, and SI systems. The metric and SI systems use prefixes (Table 5.2) to change the size of the units.

4. The mass of an object represents the quantity of matter in that object.

5. All measurements have a degree of uncertainty, which is reflected in the number of significant figures used to express them. Various rules are used to round off to the correct number of significant figures in a calculated result.

6. We can convert from one system of units to another by a method called dimensional analysis, in which conversion factors are used.

7. Temperature can be measured on three different scales: Fahrenheit, Celsius, and Kelvin. We can readily convert among these scales.

8. Density is the amount of matter present in a given volume (mass per unit volume). That is,

$$\text{Density} = \frac{\text{mass}}{\text{volume}}$$

Questions and Problems

All exercises with blue numbers have answers in the back of this book.

5.1 Scientific Notation

Questions

1. When the number 98,145 is written in standard scientific notation, the exponent indicating the power of 10 will be _____.

2. When the number 4.512×10^3 is written in ordinary decimal notation, it is expressed as _____.

Problems

3. Write each of the following as an "ordinary" decimal number.
   a. 6.235×10^{-2} c. 5.001×10^{-6}
   b. 7.229×10^3 d. 8.621×10^4

4. For each of the following numbers, if the number is rewritten in standard scientific notation, what will be the value of the exponent (for the power of 10)?
   a. 0.000067   c. 1/10,000
   b. 9,331,442   d. 163.1×10^2

5. Express each of the following numbers in *standard* scientific notation.
   a. 9,367,421   e. 6.24×10^2
   b. 7241   f. 6319×10^{-2}
   c. 0.0005519   g. 0.000000007215
   d. 5.408   h. 0.721

6. Express each of the following as an "ordinary" decimal number.
   a. 4.83×10^2 g. 9.999×10^3
   b. 7.221×10^{-4} h. 1.016×10^{-5}
   c. 6.1×10^0 i. 1.016×10^5
   d. 9.11×10^{-8} j. 4.11×10^{-1}
   e. 4.221×10^6 k. 9.71×10^4
   f. 1.22×10^{-3} l. 9.71×10^{-4}

7. Write each of the following numbers in *standard* scientific notation.
   a. 142.3×10^3 e. 0.0251×10^4
   b. 0.0007741×10^{-9} f. $97,522 \times 10^{-3}$
   c. 22.7×10^3 g. 0.0000097752×10^6
   d. 6.272×10^{-5} h. $44,252 \times 10^4$

8. Write each of the following numbers in *standard* scientific notation.

a. 1/0.00032
b. $10^3/10^{-3}$
c. $10^3/10^3$
d. 1/55,000
e. $(10^5)(10^4)(10^{-4})/(10^{-2})$
f. $43.2/(4.32 \times 10^{-5})$
g. $(4.32 \times 10^{-5})/432$
h. $1/(10^5)(10^{-6})$

5.2 Units

Questions

9. Indicate the meaning (as a power of 10) for each of the following metric prefixes.
   a. kilo
   b. centi
   c. milli
   d. deci
   e. nano
   f. micro

10. Give the metric prefix that corresponds to each of the following:
    a. 1,000,000
    b. 10^{-3}
    c. 10^{-9}
    d. 10^6
    e. 10^{-2}
    f. 0.000001

5.3 Measurements of Length, Volume, and Mass

Questions

11. Which distance is farther, 100 mi or 100 km?

12. One liter of volume in the metric system is approximately equivalent to one _____ in the English system.

13. The length 52.2 mm can also be expressed as _____ cm.

14. Who is taller, a man who is 1.62 m tall or a woman who is 5 ft 6 in. tall?

15. A 1-kg package of hamburger has a mass closest to which of the following?
    a. 8 oz
    b. 1 lb
    c. 2 lb
    d. 10 lb

16. A 2-L bottle of soda contains a volume closest to which of the following?
    a. 5 gal
    b. 1 qt
    c. 2 pt
    d. 2 qt

17. A recipe written in metric units calls for 250 mL of milk. Which of the following best approximates this amount?
    a. 1 qt
    b. 1 gal
    c. 1 cup
    d. 1 pt

18. Which metric system unit is most appropriate for measuring the distance between two cities?
    a. meters
    b. millimeters
    c. centimeters
    d. kilometers

For exercises 19 and 20 some examples of simple approximate metric–English equivalents are given in Table 5.6.

19. What is the value in dollars of a stack of dimes that is 10 cm high?

20. How many quarters would have to be lined up in a row to reach a length of 1 meter?

5.4 Uncertainty in Measurement

Questions

21. When a measuring scale is used properly to the limit of precision, the last significant digit recorded for the measurement is said to be *uncertain*. Explain.

22. For the pin shown in Figure 5.5, why is the third figure determined for the length of the pin uncertain? Considering that the third figure is uncertain, explain why the length of the pin is indicated as 2.85 cm rather than, for example, 2.83 or 2.87 cm.

23. Why can the length of the pin shown in Figure 5.5 not be recorded as 2.850 cm?

5.5 Significant Figures

Questions

24. Indicate the number of significant figures in each of the following:
    a. 1422
    b. 65,321
    c. 1.004×10^5
    d. 200
    e. 200.
    f. 2.00×10^2
    g. 435.662
    h. 56.341

25. Indicate the number of significant figures implied in each of the following statements:
    a. The population of the United States is 250 million.
    b. One hour is equivalent to 60 minutes.
    c. There are 5280 feet in 1 mile.
    d. Jet airliners fly at 500 mi/h.
    e. The "Daytona 500" is a 500-mile race.

Rounding Off Numbers

Questions

26. Round off each of the following numbers to three significant digits.
    a. 1,566,311
    b. 2.7651×10^{-3}
    c. 84,592
    d. 0.0011672
    e. 0.07759

27. Round off each of the following numbers to the indicated number of significant digits and write the answer in standard scientific notation.
    a. 0.00034159 to three digits
    b. 103.351×10^2 to four digits
    c. 17.9915 to five digits
    d. 3.365×10^5 to three digits

Determining Significant Figures in Calculations

Questions

28. When the calculation (0.0043)(0.0821)(298) is performed, the answer should be reported to _____ significant figures.

1. 4

2. 4512

3. (a) 0.06235; (b) 7229; (c) 0.000005001; (d) 86,210

4. (a) −5; (b) 6; (c) −4; (d) 4

5. (a) 9.367421×10^6; (b) 7.241×10^3; (c) 5.519×10^{-4}; (d) 5.408×10^0; (e) already in scientific notation; (f) 6.319×10^{-1}; (g) 7.215×10^{-9}; (h) 7.21×10^{-1}

6. (a) 483; (b) 0.0007221; (c) 6.1; (d) 0.0000000911; (e) 4,221,000; (f) 0.00122; (g) 9999; (h) 0.00001016; (i) 101,600; (j) 0.411; (k) 97,100; (l) 0.000971

7. (a) 1.423×10^5; (b) 7.741×10^{-13}; (c) 2.27×10^4; (d) already in scientific notation; (e) 2.51×10^2; (f) 9.7522×10^1; (g) 9.7752 (9.7752×10^0); (h) 4.4252×10^8

8. (a) 3.1×10^3; (b) 1×10^6; (c) 1 or 1×10^0; (d) 1.8×10^{-5}; (e) 1×10^7; (f) 1.00×10^6; (g) 1.00×10^{-7}; (h) 1×10^1

9. (a) 10^3; (b) 10^{-2}; (c) 10^{-3}; (d) 10^{-1}; (e) 10^{-9}; (f) 10^{-6}

10. (a) mega; (b) milli; (c) nano; (d) mega; (e) centi; (f) micro

11. 100 miles

12. quart

13. 5.22 cm

14. the woman

15. c

16. d

17. c

18. d

19. $10

20. 40 quarters

21. We estimate measurements between the smallest divisions on the scale; since this is our best estimate, the last significant digit recorded is uncertain.

22. It is given as 2.85 cm (rather than any other number) to indicate that the point of the pin appears to the observer to be halfway

between the smallest marked scale divisions.

23. The scale of the ruler is marked to the nearest tenth of a centimeter. Writing 2.850 would imply that the scale was marked to the nearest hundredth of a centimeter (and that the zero in the thousandths place had been estimated).

24. (a) four; (b) five; (c) four; (d) one; (e) three; (f) three; (g) six; (h) five

25. (a) probably only two; (b) infinite (definition); (c) infinite (definition); (d) probably only one; (e) three (the race is defined to be 500. miles)

26. (a) 1,570,000 or 1.57×10^6; (b) 2.77×10^{-3}; (c) 84,600 or 8.46×10^4; (d) 0.00117 or 1.17×10^{-3}; (e) 0.0776 or 7.76×10^{-2}

27. (a) 3.42×10^{-4}; (b) 1.034×10^4; (c) 1.7992×10^1; (d) 3.37×10^5

28. 2

29. 3

30. 1

31. none

32. (a) 641.0; (b) 1.327; (c) 77.34; (d) 3215

33. (a) 124; (b) 1.995×10^{-23}; (c) 1.14×10^{-2}; (d) 5.3×10^{-4}

34. (a) 2.045; (b) 3.8×10^3; (c) 5.19×10^{-5}; (d) 3.8418×10^{-7}

35. infinite (definition)

36. 1 mi/1760 yd; 1760 yd/1 mi

37. $0.79/1 lb

38. 1 lb/$0.79

39. (a) 2.44 yd; (b) 42.2 m; (c) 115 in; (d) 2238 cm; (e) 648.1 mi; (f) 716.9 km; (g) 0.0362 km; (h) 5.01×10^4 cm

40. (a) 0.2543 kg; (b) 2.75×10^3 g; (c) 6.06 lb; (d) 97.0 oz; (e) 1.177 lb; (f) 794 g; (g) 2.5×10^2 g; (h) 1.62 oz

41. DM 34.80; $57.47

42. 3.1×10^2 km; 3.1×10^5 m; 1.0×10^6 ft

43. The Boston–New York trains will be faster (the U.K. trains travel at a speed of 140. mi/h).

150

---

29. The quotient $(2.3733 \times 10^2)/(343)$ should be written with _____ significant figures.

30. How many digits after the decimal point should be reported when the calculation $(199.0354 + 43.09 + 121.2)$ is performed?

31. How many digits after the decimal point should be reported when the calculation $(10{,}434 - 9.3344)$ is performed?

Problems

Note: See the Appendix for help in doing mathematical operations with numbers that contain exponents.

32. Evaluate each of the following and write the answer to the appropriate number of significant figures.
 a. $212.2 + 26.7 + 402.09$
 b. $1.0028 + 0.221 + 0.10337$
 c. $52.331 + 26.01 - 0.9981$
 d. $2.01 \times 10^2 + 3.014 \times 10^3$

33. Evaluate each of the following and write the answer to the appropriate number of significant figures.
 a. $(4.031)(0.08206)(373.1)/(0.995)$
 b. $(12.011)/(6.022 \times 10^{23})$
 c. $(0.500)/(44.02)$
 d. $(0.15)/(280.62)$

34. Evaluate each of the following and write the answer to the appropriate number of significant figures.
 a. $(2.0944 + 0.0003233 + 12.22)/(7.001)$
 b. $(1.42 \times 10^2 + 1.021 \times 10^3)/(3.1 \times 10^{-1})$
 c. $(9.762 \times 10^{-3})/(1.43 \times 10^2 + 4.51 \times 10^1)$
 d. $(6.1982 \times 10^{-4})^2$

5.6 Problem Solving and Dimensional Analysis

Questions

35. How many significant figures are understood for the numbers in the following definition: 1 mi = 5280 ft?

36. Given that 1 mi = 1760 yd, determine what conversion factor is appropriate to convert 1849 yd to miles; to convert 2.781 mi to yards.

For exercises 37 and 38, apples cost $0.79 per pound.

37. What conversion factor is appropriate to express the cost of 5.3 lb of apples?

38. What conversion factor could be used to determine how many pounds of apples could be bought for $2.00?

Problems

39. Perform each of the following conversions, being sure to set up clearly the appropriate conversion factor in each case.
 a. 2.23 m to yards
 b. 46.2 yd to meters
 c. 292 cm to inches
 d. 881.2 in. to centimeters
 e. 1043 km to miles

---

 f. 445.5 mi to kilometers
 g. 36.2 m to kilometers
 h. 0.501 km to centimeters

40. Perform each of the following conversions, being sure to set up clearly the appropriate conversion factor in each case.
 a. 254.3 g to kilograms
 b. 2.75 kg to grams
 c. 2.75 kg to pounds
 d. 2.75 kg to ounces
 e. 534.1 g to pounds
 f. 1.75 lb to grams
 g. 8.7 oz to grams
 h. 45.9 g to ounces

41. If $1.00 is equivalent to 1.74 German marks, what is $20.00 worth in marks? What is the value in dollars of a 100-mark bill?

42. Boston and New York City are 190 miles apart. What is this distance in kilometers? in meters? in feet?

43. The United States will soon have high-speed trains running between Boston and New York capable of speeds up to 160 mi/h. Will these trains be faster or slower than the fastest trains in the United Kingdom, which reach speeds of 225 km/h?

5.7 Temperature Conversions

Questions

44. The normal boiling point of water is _____ °F, or _____ °C.

45. On both the Celsius and Kelvin temperature scales, there are _____ degrees between the normal freezing and boiling points of water.

46. On which temperature scale (°F, °C, or K) does 1 degree represent the smallest change in temperature?

Problems

47. Convert the following temperatures to kelvins.
 a. −155 °C   d. 101 °F
 b. 200 °C   e. −52 °F
 c. −52 °C   f. −196 °F

48. Convert the following Kelvin temperatures to Celsius degrees.
 a. 275 K   d. 77 K
 b. 445 K   e. 10,000. K
 c. 0 K   f. 2 K

49. Carry out the indicated temperature conversions.
 a. −40 °C to Fahrenheit degrees
 b. −40 °F to Celsius degrees
 c. 232 K to Celsius degrees
 d. 232 K to Fahrenheit degrees

50. Carry out the indicated temperature conversions.
 a. −201 °F to kelvins
 b. −201 °C to kelvins
 c. 351 °C to Fahrenheit degrees
 d. −150 °F to Celsius degrees

---

44. 212 °F; 100 °C

45. 100

46. Fahrenheit (F)

47. (a) 118 K; (b) 473 K; (c) 221 K; (d) 311 K; (e) 226 K; (f) 77 K

48. (a) 2 °C; (b) 172 °C; (c) −273 °C; (d) −196 °C; (e) 9727 °C; (f) −271 °C

49. (a) −40 °F ; (b) −40 °C; (c) −41 °C; (d) −42 °F

50. (a) 144 K; (b) 72 K;

(c) 664 °F; (d) −101 °C

51. volume

52. lead

53. low

54. Density is a characteristic property of a pure substance.

55. aluminum

56. (a) 20.1 g/cm³; (b) 1.05 g/cm³; (c) 0.907 g/cm³; (d) 1.30 g/cm³

57. 0.843 g/mL

58. 2.68 g/mL

59. float

60. 11.7 mL

61. (a) 23.1 cm³; (b) 3.68 cm³; (c) 56.8 cm³; (d) 4.76 cm³

62. (a) 966 g; (b) 394 g; (c) 567 g; (d) 135 g

63. (a) cm; (b) m; (c) km; (d) cm; (e) mm

64. highway: 19 km/L; city: 16 km/L

65. $1

66. 24 capsules

5.8 Density

Questions

51. The ratio of an object's mass to its _____ is called the *density* of the object.

52. A kilogram of lead occupies a much smaller volume than a kilogram of water, because _____ has a much higher density.

53. Typically, gases have very (high/low) densities compared to those of solids and liquids (see Table 5.8).

54. What property of density makes it useful as an aid in identifying substances?

55. Referring to Table 5.8, determine whether air, water, ethanol, or aluminum is the most dense.

Problems

56. For the masses and volumes indicated, calculate the density in grams per cubic centimeter.
    a. mass = 4.53 kg; volume = 225 cm³
    b. mass = 26.3 g; volume = 25.0 mL
    c. mass = 1.00 lb; volume = 500. cm³
    d. mass = 352 mg; volume = 0.271 cm³

57. If 89.2 mL of a liquid has a mass of 75.2 g, calculate the liquid's density.

58. A cube of metal weighs 1.45 kg and displaces 542 mL of water when immersed. Calculate the density of the metal.

59. A material will float on the surface of a liquid if the material has a density less than that of the liquid. Given that the density of water is approximately 1.0 g/mL, will a block of material having a volume of 1.2×10^4 in.³ and weighing 3.5 lb float or sink when placed in a reservoir of water?

60. The density of pure silver is 10.5 g/cm³ at 20 °C. If 5.25 g of pure silver pellets is added to a graduated cylinder containing 11.2 mL of water, to what volume level will the water in the cylinder rise?

61. Use the information in Table 5.8 to calculate the volume of 50.0 g of each of the following substances.
    a. sodium chloride
    b. mercury
    c. benzene
    d. silver

62. Use the information in Table 5.8 to calculate the mass of 50.0 cm³ of each of the following substances.
    a. gold
    b. iron
    c. lead
    d. aluminum

Critical Thinking

63. Which unit of length in the metric system would be most appropriate in size for measuring each of the following items?
    a. the dimensions of this page
    b. the size of the room in which you are sitting
    c. the distance from New York to London
    d. the diameter of a baseball
    e. the diameter of a common pin

64. Suppose your car is rated at 45 mi/gal for highway use and 38 mi/gal for city driving. If you wanted to write your friend in Spain about your car's mileage, what ratings in kilometers per liter would you report?

65. You are in Paris, and you want to buy some peaches for lunch. The sign in the fruit stand indicates that peaches are 11.5 francs per kilogram. Given that there are approximately 5 francs to the dollar, calculate what a pound of peaches will cost in dollars.

66. For a pharmacist dispensing pills or capsules, it is often easier to weigh the medication to be dispensed rather than to count the individual pills. If a single antibiotic capsule weighs 0.65 g, and a pharmacist weighs out 15.6 g of capsules, how many capsules have been dispensed?

67. For a material to float on the surface of water, the material must have a density less than that of water (1.0 g/mL) and must not react with the water or dissolve in it. A spherical ball has a radius of 0.50 cm and weighs 2.0 g. Will this ball float or sink when placed in water? (Note: Volume of a sphere = $\frac{4}{3}\pi r^3$.)

68. Ethanol and benzene dissolve in each other. When 100. mL of ethanol is dissolved in 1.00 L of benzene, what is the mass of the mixture? (See Table 5.8.)

69. For each of the following numbers, by how many places must the decimal point be moved to express the number in standard scientific notation? In each case, will the exponent be positive, negative, or zero?
    a. 55,651   d. 883,541
    b. 0.000008991   e. 0.09814
    c. 2.04

70. Which weighs more, 4.25 grams of gold or 425 milligrams of gold?

71. In the measurement of the length of the pin indicated in Figure 5.5, what are the *certain* numbers in the measurement shown?

72. Indicate the number of significant figures in each of the following:
    a. This book contains over 500 pages.
    b. A mile is just over 5000 ft.
    c. A liter is equivalent to 1.059 qt.
    d. The population of the United States is approaching 250 million.
    e. A kilogram is 1000 g.
    f. The Boeing 747 cruises at around 600 mi/h.

73. An organic solvent has density 1.31 g/mL. What volume is occupied by 50.0 g of the liquid?

74. A sample containing 33.42 g of metal pellets is poured into a graduated cylinder initially containing 12.7 mL of water, causing the water level in the cylinder to rise to 21.6 mL. Calculate the density of the metal.

67. The ball will sink ($d = 3.8$ g/cm³).

68. 959 g

69. (a) 4, positive; (b) 6, negative; (c) 0, zero; (d) 5, positive; (e) 2, negative

70. 4.25 grams

71. 2.8 (the hundredths place is estimated)

72. (a) one; (b) one; (c) four; (d) two; (e) infinite (definition); (f) one

73. 38.2 mL

74. 3.8 g/mL

6 Chemical Composition

Section	Text Features & Components	Labs, Demonstrations & Activities
Teaching Segment 6A **1 block** **pp. 153–164**	**6.1–6.2** ◓ Counting by Weighing Atomic Masses: Counting Atoms by Weighing	**LP** Lesson Plans (Sec 6.1–6.3) **TE** Teaching Support: Background Information *pp. 154–155* **SE** Chemical Impact: Plastic That Talks and Listens *p. 155*	**TE** Group Activity *p. 154* **SE** Chemistry in Action: Counting Pennies Without Counting *p. 158* **TE** Teaching Support: Demonstration *pp. 158–159*
	6.3 The Mole ◔	**TE** Teaching Support: Historical Note *p. 160*	**LM** Experiment 22: Bean Lab Lab Manual Report Sheets Teacher's Lab Guide **TE** Mini Demo *p. 160* **TE** Additional Activity *p. 161*
Teaching Segment 6B **0.5 block** **pp. 165–170**	**6.4 Molar Mass** ◔	**LP** Lesson Plans (Sec 6.4)	**SE** Chemistry in Action: Relative Masses *p. 170*
Teaching Segment 6C **1.5 blocks** **pp. 171–185**	**6.5–6.6** ◕ Percent Composition of Compounds Formulas of Compounds	**LP** Lesson Plans (Sec 6.5–6.8) **SE** Chemical Impact: Nutrition Facts *p. 171* • "Mauvelous" Chemistry *p. 174* **SE** Top Ten Elements in the Moon *p. 173* **TE** Teaching Support: Connection to Astronomy *p. 173*	**SE** Chemistry in Action: And the Winner Is . . . *p. 173* **TE** Mini Demo *p. 176*
	6.7–6.8 ◔ Calculation of Empirical Formulas Calculation of Molecular Formulas	**SE** Celebrity Chemical: Ammonia *p. 179* **SE** Chemical Impact: Using Chemistry to Understand Lost Worlds *p. 183*	**TE** Teaching Support: Demonstration *pp. 178–179* **SE** Chemistry in the Laboratory: Decomposing Copper Oxide *pp. 186–187* **LM** Experiment 23–24 Lab Manual Report Sheets Teacher's Lab Guide

Key

SE Student Edition
TE Teacher Edition
RP Teacher Resource Package
LM Lab Materials
LP Lesson Plans
AR Additional Resources
�', Florida Specific

Technology and Media

 Transparencies
Figure 6.3

PowerPoint Slides

 eEdition CD-ROM
Easy Planner CD-ROM
English Summaries CD
Spanish Summaries CD

 Web Site classzone.com
McDougal Littell Test Generator

Chapter Planning Guide

All Learners	Review & Assessment	Standards
TE Active Learning *p. 153* **TE** Teaching Tips *pp. 153–154, 156–157* **AR** Less Proficient Learners *p. 11*	**TE** Additional Examples *pp. 157–158* **SE** Self Check *pp. 157–158* **SE** Key Terms *p. 187* **SE** Questions and Problems *pp. 187–188*	**TE** **NSES** UCP1, UCP2, UCP3, A1, A2, B1, B2, B3, E1, E2, G1, G2, G3 **SSS** SC.H.3.4.5, SC.H.1.4.7
RP Team Learning Worksheets (Sec 6.1–6.3) *pp. 25–26* **AR** Less Proficient Learners *p. 11*	**SE** What if . . . *pp. 159, 163* **TE** Additional Examples *pp. 162–163* **SE** Self Check *p. 164* **SE** Focus Questions (Sec 6.1–6.3) *p. 164* **SE** Key Terms *p. 187* **SE** Questions and Problems *p. 188*	
TE Active Learning *p. 165* **⊏** Transparency: Figure 6.3 *p. 165* **TE** Misconceptions *p. 165* **TE** Using the Top Ten *p. 173* **RP** Team Learning Worksheets (Sec 6.4) *pp. 27–28* **AR** Less Proficient Learners *p. 11*	**TE** Additional Examples *pp. 166–169* **SE** Self Check *pp. 166, 168, 169* **SE** Focus Questions (Sec 6.4) *p. 170* **SE** Key Terms *p. 187* **SE** Questions and Problems *pp. 188–189*	**TE** **NSES** UCP1, UCP3, A1, A2, B1, B2, B3
TE Active Learning *p. 171* **TE** Teaching Tips *pp. 171–172* **TE** Using the Top Ten *p. 173* **AR** Less Proficient Learners *p. 11*	**TE** Additional Examples *pp. 172, 176* **SE** Self Check *p. 172* **SE** Key Terms *p. 187* **SE** Questions and Problems *p. 189*	**TE** **NSES** UCP1, UCP3, UCP5, A1, A2, B1, B2, B3, D3, F1, G1, G2, G3
TE Challenging Your Students *p. 185* **RP** Team Learning Worksheets *pp. 29–30* **AR** Less Proficient Learners *p. 12*	**TE** Additional Examples *pp. 178, 180–182, 184* **SE** Self Check *pp. 180–181, 183, 185* **SE** Focus Questions (Sec 6.5–6.8) *p. 185* **SE** Questions and Problems *p. 190*	

Chapter Materials

TE Reading Strategy
AR English/Spanish Summaries *p. 8*
RP Classroom Activities and Projects *pp. 13–16*
AR Challenge Projects/Problems *pp. 10–11*
AR Less Proficient Students *p. 12*
💿 English Summary Audio
💿 Spanish Summary Audio
RP Chapter Review Worksheets (Basic, Review, Challenge)

SE Chapter Summary *p. 187*
SE Critical Thinking *pp. 190–191*
RP Solutions Guide
RP Chapter Tests
RP Test Bank
▨ McDougal Littell Test Generator
AR Standardized Test Practice
● FCAT Test 3

Integrating Reading Strategies and Chemistry Concepts

Chapter 6: Reading Example Problems

Some students may avoid reading examples because they assume that the teacher will explain those problems during class. Make sure that the students recognize the value of example problems and the correlation of examples to problems that appear in homework or on tests and quizzes.

Before beginning this chapter, ask the students to look through the pages and briefly skim the example problems. Point out that the chapter contains several examples and that many of these require an entire page for the explanation and solution. Because the length of the solution may intimidate some students, emphasize that a significant portion of each example is devoted to explaining how to solve the problem.

Reasons to Read and Study Example Problems

1. Solving example problems clarifies concepts.

2. Complex information is more manageable when it is broken down into the step-by-step process shown in the examples.

3. Homework, quiz, and test problems are often similar to the example problems.

4. Detailed solutions to the example problems serve to fill in the gaps in note taking and class work.

5. Example problems provide great practice. When you study for a test, cover the solution and try to work each example problem. If your answer is incorrect, review the step-by-step process to determine where you made your mistake.

Remind the students that until now most of the examples have been based on key terms and general concepts or one- and two-step problems. Emphasize that as the material becomes more complex, the example problems will become even more important. These examples demonstrate how to work more complicated problems by using a systematic step-by-step process. Encourage the students to think about each step and understand it before continuing the process.

Encourage the students to reread the relevant sections of the text after working through each example. Point out that a careful reading of the text and a logical approach to problem solving will simplify their work and enhance their understanding of chemical properties and formulas.

How to Read the Example Problems

Direct the students' attention to Example 6.1 on page 157.

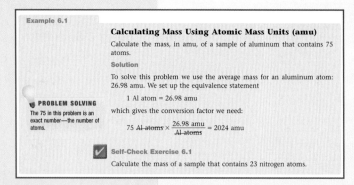

Example 6.1

Calculating Mass Using Atomic Mass Units (amu)

Calculate the mass, in amu, of a sample of aluminum that contains 75 atoms.

Solution

To solve this problem we use the average mass for an aluminum atom: 26.98 amu. We set up the equivalence statement

$$1 \text{ Al atom} = 26.98 \text{ amu}$$

PROBLEM SOLVING
The 75 in this problem is an exact number—the number of atoms.

which gives the conversion factor we need:

$$75 \text{ Al atoms} \times \frac{26.98 \text{ amu}}{\text{Al atoms}} = 2024 \text{ amu}$$

Self-Check Exercise 6.1

Calculate the mass of a sample that contains 23 nitrogen atoms.

Point out the boldface type at the top of the example, and ask students what this information tells them. [the type of problem the example demonstrates] Have the students skim the next several pages of the chapter to see whether this is always true. [yes]

Have the students read the first sentence in the example problem. Explain that in this textbook, the first sentence always states the goal of the problem.

Direct the students to read the first sentence in the **Solution** section of the example. Point out that the **Solution** section nearly always provides a strategy for solving the problem before beginning the actual solution.

Point out that each of the steps *and* the final solution include the appropriate units of measure. If the students write in the units only at the end of the problem, errors are more likely to occur. Encourage the students to carry units throughout their work, just as the example problem does.

Have the students read the **Self-Check Exercise**. Ask them how this problem relates to Example 6.1. [It is the same type of question and can be solved by the same method.] Inform the students that most of the examples in the text include a **Self-Check Exercise** and that solutions to these exercises are provided at the back of the text on pages A13–A31. These solutions are very similar to those provided in the example problems; they include a step-by-step process for each problem as well as the correct answer. Encourage the students to use these pages to check their solutions or as a guide to obtaining a solution.

Organizing Example Problems

To help the students create an effective study guide, encourage them to list the types of problems worked in each chapter. Tell the students to use abbreviations to keep the list short and to include the page number on which the example is worked. Doing so will help them locate specific types of questions quickly when they are doing homework or studying for a test. Consider having the students compile the list before you begin each chapter as a way of previewing the chapter material.

Type of Example Problem	Page
Calculating mass using AMU	157
Calculating # of atoms from mass	158
Calculating moles and # of atoms	162
Calculating # of atoms from mass	163
Calculating molar mass	166
Calculating mass from moles	167
Calculating moles from mass	168
Calculating # of molecules	169
Calculating mass percent	172
Writing empirical formulas	176
Calculating empirical formulas	178
Calculating empirical formulas for binary compounds	180
Calculating empirical formulas for compounds with 3 or more elements	181
Calculating empirical formulas from percent composition	182
Calculating molecular formulas	184

Chapter 6

Overview

In this Chapter our goals are for the students to:

- Understand the concept of average mass and explore how counting can be done by weighing

- Understand atomic mass and its experimental determination

- Understand the mole concept and Avogadro's number and convert among moles, mass and number of atoms in a sample

- Understand the definition of molar mass

- Learn to convert between moles and mass of a given sample of a chemical compound

- Learn to find the mass percent of an element in a compound

- Understand the meaning of empirical formulas

- Learn to calculate empirical formulas

- Learn to calculate the molecular formula of a compound, given its empirical formula and molar mass

6 Chemical Composition

Pearls are made of layers of calcium carbonate.

One very important chemical activity is the synthesis of new substances. Nylon, the artificial sweetener aspartame, Kevlar used in bulletproof vests and the body parts of exotic cars, polyvinyl chloride (PVC) for plastic water pipes, Teflon, Nitinol (the alloy that remembers its shape even after being severely distorted), and so many other materials that make our lives easier—all originated in some chemist's laboratory. Some of the new materials have truly amazing properties such as the plastic that listens and talks, described in the "Chemical Impact" on page 155. When a chemist makes a new substance, the first order of business is to identify it. What is its composition? What is its chemical formula?

In this chapter we will learn to determine a compound's formula. Before we can do that, however, we need to think about counting atoms. How do we determine the number of each type of atom in a substance so that we can write its formula? Of course, atoms are too small to count individually. As we will see in this chapter, we typically count atoms by weighing them. So let us first consider the general principle of counting by weighing.

This Italian car has composite body parts.

6.1 Counting by Weighing

Objective: *To understand the concept of average mass and explore how counting can be done by weighing.*

Suppose you work in a candy store that sells gourmet jelly beans by the bean. People come in and ask for 50 beans, 100 beans, 1000 beans, and so on, and you have to count them out—a tedious process at best. As a good problem solver, you try to come up with a better system. It occurs to you that it might be far more efficient to buy a scale and count the jelly beans by weighing them. How can you count jelly beans by weighing them? What information about the individual beans do you need to know?

Assume that all of the jelly beans are identical and that each has a mass of 5 g. If a customer asks for 1000 jelly beans, what mass of jelly beans would be required? Each bean has a mass of 5 g, so you would need 1000 beans × 5 g/bean, or 5000 g (5 kg). It takes just a few seconds to weigh out 5 kg of jelly beans. It would take much longer to count out 1000 of them.

In reality, jelly beans are not identical. For example, let's assume that you weigh 10 beans individually and get the following results:

Bean	Mass
1	5.1 g
2	5.2 g
3	5.0 g
4	4.8 g
5	4.9 g
6	5.0 g
7	5.0 g
8	5.1 g
9	4.9 g
10	5.0 g

Jellybeans can be counted by weighing.

153

6.1 **Section 6.1**

Themes
Models, Systems

Skills
Making comparisons, converting, evaluating

Student Preparation
Assign the students to read Sections 6.1 to 6.3 and to answer the Focus Questions at the end of Section 6.3 before coming to class.

Active Learning
After introducing the material in Sections 6.1 to 6.3 in class, place the students in groups and have them work together on Sections 6.1–6.3: Team Learning Worksheet. Answers and/or discussion of these questions are located in the *Teacher Resources*.

TEACHING TIPS

• Using analogies to cooking and daily life is helpful for beginning students.

• Students often spend so much time on the mechanics of solving these problems that they lose sight of the "big picture" of what they are trying to learn. Keep talking to them about the idea that we are determining chemical quantities to decide how much we will have or how much we may need of a particular substance.

MATH

To find an average, add up all the individual measurements and divide by the number of measurements.

Can we count these nonidentical beans by weighing? Yes. The key piece of information we need is the *average mass* of the jelly beans. Let's compute the average mass for our 10-bean sample.

$$\text{Average mass} = \frac{\text{total mass of beans}}{\text{number of beans}}$$

$$= \frac{5.1\text{ g} + 5.2\text{ g} + 5.0\text{ g} + 4.8\text{ g} + 4.9\text{ g} + 5.0\text{ g} + 5.0\text{ g} + 5.1\text{ g} + 4.9\text{ g} + 5.0\text{ g}}{10}$$

$$= \frac{50.0}{10} = 5.0\text{ g}$$

The average mass of a jelly bean is 5.0 g. Thus, to count out 1000 beans, we need to weigh out 5000 g of beans. This sample of beans, in which the beans have an average mass of 5.0 g, can be treated exactly like a sample where all of the beans are identical. Objects do not need to have identical masses to be counted by weighing. We simply need to know the average mass of the objects. For purposes of counting, the objects *behave as though they were all identical*, as though they each actually had the average mass.

Suppose a customer comes into the store and says, "I want to buy a bag of candy for each of my kids. One of them likes jelly beans and the other one likes mints. Please put a scoopful of jelly beans in a bag and a scoopful of mints in another bag." Then the customer recognizes a problem. "Wait! My kids will fight unless I bring home exactly the same number of candies for each one. Both bags must have the same number of pieces because they'll definitely count them and compare. But I'm really in a hurry, so we don't have time to count them here. Is there a simple way you can be sure the bags will contain the same number of candies?"

You need to solve this problem quickly. Suppose you know the average masses of the two kinds of candy:

Jelly beans: average mass = 5 g

Mints: average mass = 15 g

You fill the scoop with jelly beans and dump them onto the scale, which reads 500 g. Now the key question: What mass of mints do you need to give the same number of mints as there are jelly beans in 500 g of jelly beans? Comparing the average masses of the jelly beans (5 g) and mints (15 g), you realize that each mint has three times the mass of each jelly bean:

$$\frac{15\text{ g}}{5\text{ g}} = 3$$

This means that you must weigh out an amount of mints that is three times the mass of the jelly beans:

$$3 \times 500\text{ g} = 1500\text{ g}$$

You weigh out 1500 g of mints and put them in a bag. The customer leaves with your assurance that both the bag containing 500 g of jelly beans and the bag containing 1500 g of mints contain the same number of candies.

In solving this problem, you have discovered a principle that is very important in chemistry: two samples containing different types of components, A and B, both *contain the same number of components if the ratio of the sample masses is the same as the ratio of the masses of the individual components* of A and B.

154   Chapter 6   Chemical Composition

Let's illustrate this rather intimidating statement by using the example we just discussed. The individual components have the masses 5 g (jelly beans) and 15 g (mints). Consider several cases.

- Each sample contains 1 component:

    Mass of mint = 15 g
    Mass of jelly bean = 5 g

- Each sample contains 10 components:

$$10 \ \text{mints} \times \frac{15 \ \text{g}}{\text{mints}} = 150 \ \text{g of mints}$$

$$10 \ \text{jelly beans} \times \frac{5 \ \text{g}}{\text{jelly beans}} = 50 \ \text{g of jelly beans}$$

- Each sample contains 100 components:

$$100 \ \text{mints} \times \frac{15 \ \text{g}}{\text{mints}} = 1500 \ \text{g of mints}$$

$$100 \ \text{jelly beans} \times \frac{5 \ \text{g}}{\text{jelly beans}} = 500 \ \text{g of jelly beans}$$

CHEMICAL IMPACT

Science, Technology, and Society

Plastic That Talks and Listens

Imagine a plastic so "smart" that it can be used to sense a baby's breath, measure the force of a karate punch, sense the presence of a person 100 ft away, or make a balloon that sings. There is a plastic film capable of doing all these things. It's called *polyvinylidene difluoride (PVDF)*, which has the structure

When this polymer is processed in a particular way, it becomes piezoelectric and pyroelectric. A *piezoelectric* substance produces an electric current when it is physically deformed or, alternatively, undergoes a deformation when a current is applied. A *pyroelectric* material is one that develops an electrical potential in response to a change in its temperature.

Because PVDF is piezoelectric, it can be used to construct a paper-thin microphone; it responds to sound by producing a current proportional to the deformation caused by the sound waves. A ribbon of PVDF plastic one-quarter of an inch wide could be strung along a hallway and used to listen to all the conversations going on as people walk through. On the other hand, electric pulses can be applied to the PVDF film to produce a speaker. A strip of PVDF film glued to the inside of a balloon can play any song stored on a microchip attached to the film—hence a balloon that can sing "happy birthday" at a party. The PVDF film also can be used to construct a sleep apnea monitor, which, when placed beside the mouth of a sleeping infant, will set off an alarm if the breathing stops, thus helping to prevent sudden infant death syndrome (SIDS). The same type of film is used by the U.S. Olympic karate team to measure the force of kicks and punches as the team trains. Also, gluing two strips of film together gives a material that curls in response to a current, creating an artificial muscle. In addition, because the PVDF film is pyroelectric, it responds to the infrared (heat) radiation emitted by a human as far away as 100 ft, making it useful for burglar alarm systems. Making the PVDF polymer piezoelectric and pyroelectric requires some very special processing, which makes it costly ($10 per square foot), but this seems a small price to pay for its near-magical properties.

6.1 Counting by Weighing **155**

shell is drawn into the center. This change softens the center and hardens the shell. The driving force for this movement of water to the center is osmosis. The water flows toward the center, which is a more concentrated "solution" than the shell, trying to equalize the two concentrations. Osmosis also explains how pickles are made. When cucumbers are placed in a brine [NaCl(*aq*)] solution, water flows out of the cucumber into the brine, shrinking the cucumber into a pickle. Once again, water flows from the more dilute to the more concentrated solution.

Now that the curing process is understood, candymakers hope to find a way to speed up the jelly bean manufacturing process so that they do not have to store the jelly beans for several days, but can instead ship them quickly to market.

Note in each case that the ratio of the masses is always 3 to 1,

$$\frac{1500}{500} = \frac{150}{50} = \frac{15}{5} = \frac{3}{1}$$

which is the ratio of the masses of the individual components:

$$\frac{\text{Mass of mint}}{\text{Mass of jelly bean}} = \frac{15}{5} = \frac{3}{1}$$

Any two samples, one of mints and one of jelly beans, that have a *mass ratio* of $15/5 = 3/1$ will contain the same number of components. And these same ideas apply also to atoms, as we will see in the next section.

6.2 Atomic Masses: Counting Atoms by Weighing

Objective: *To understand atomic mass and its experimental determination.*

The balanced chemical equation for the reaction of solid carbon and gaseous oxygen to form gaseous carbon dioxide is as follows:

$$C(s) + O_2(g) \rightarrow CO_2(g)$$

Now suppose you have a small pile of solid carbon and want to know how many oxygen molecules are required to convert all of this carbon into carbon dioxide. The balanced equation tells us that one oxygen molecule is required for each carbon atom.

$$C(s) \qquad + \qquad O_2(g) \qquad \rightarrow \qquad CO_2(g)$$
1 atom reacts with 1 molecule   to yield   1 molecule

To determine the number of oxygen molecules required, we must know how many carbon atoms are present in the pile of carbon. But individual atoms are far too small to see. We must learn to count atoms by weighing samples containing large numbers of them.

In the last section we saw that we can easily count things like jelly beans and mints by weighing. Exactly the same principles can be applied to counting atoms.

Because atoms are so tiny, the normal units of mass—the gram and the kilogram—are much too large to be convenient. For example, the mass of a single carbon atom is 1.99×10^{-23} g. To avoid using terms like 10^{-23} when describing the mass of an atom, scientists have defined a much smaller unit of mass called the **atomic mass unit**, which is abbreviated **amu.** In terms of grams,

$$1 \text{ amu} = 1.66 \times 10^{-24} \text{ g}$$

Now let's return to our problem of counting carbon atoms. To count carbon atoms by weighing, we need to know the mass of individual atoms, just as we needed to know the mass of the individual jelly beans. Recall from Chapter 3 that the atoms of a given element exist as isotopes. The isotopes of carbon are $^{12}_{6}C$, $^{13}_{6}C$, and $^{14}_{6}C$. Any sample of carbon contains a mixture of these isotopes, always in the same proportions. Each of these isotopes has a slightly different mass. Therefore, just as with the nonidentical jelly beans,

Themes
Systems, Models

Skills
Making comparisons, evaluating, applying concepts, interpreting data

TEACHING TIPS

- Even though the students understand counting candy by weighing, it may be difficult for them to transfer the idea to counting atoms or molecules by mass. This concept seems much more abstract and confusing for them.

- We introduce counting atoms by weighing using atomic mass units. Students are not familiar with these units. It helps to reassure students that we will soon be working with more familiar units (grams).

- Refer back to the candy analogy or activity from Section 6.1. The average mass of a candy does not represent the mass of a particular candy. Similarly, the average mass of an atom does not represent the mass of an individual atom. This reasoning allows you to introduce the idea that atoms are slightly different in mass without developing the idea of isotopes at the same time.

- It is also helpful to point out to students that someone has already measured the masses of atoms and that we have a table for average atomic masses as a result of that work (the periodic table).

we need to use an average mass for the carbon atoms. The **average atomic mass** for carbon atoms is 12.01 amu. This means that any sample of carbon from nature *can be treated as though it were composed of identical carbon atoms*, each with a mass of 12.01 amu. Now that we know the average mass of the carbon atom, we can count carbon atoms by weighing samples of natural carbon. For example, what mass of natural carbon must we take to have 1000 carbon atoms present? Because 12.01 amu is the average mass,

PROBLEM SOLVING

Remember that 1000 is an exact number here.

$$\text{Mass of 1000 natural carbon atoms} = (1000 \; \cancel{\text{atoms}}) \left(\frac{12.01 \; \text{amu}}{\cancel{\text{atom}}} \right)$$

$$= 12{,}010 \; \text{amu} = 1.201 \times 10^4 \; \text{amu}$$

Now let's assume that when we weigh the pile of natural carbon mentioned earlier, the result is 3.00×10^{20} amu. How many carbon atoms are present in this sample? We know that an average carbon atom has the mass 12.01 amu, so we can compute the number of carbon atoms by using the equivalence statement

$$1 \; \text{carbon atom} = 12.01 \; \text{amu}$$

to construct the appropriate conversion factor,

$$\frac{1 \; \text{carbon atom}}{12.01 \; \text{amu}}$$

The calculation is carried out as follows:

$$3.00 \times 10^{20} \; \cancel{\text{amu}} \times \frac{1 \; \text{carbon atom}}{12.01 \; \cancel{\text{amu}}} = 2.50 \times 10^{19} \; \text{carbon atoms}$$

The principles we have just discussed for carbon apply to all the other elements as well. All the elements as found in nature typically consist of a mixture of various isotopes. So to count the atoms in a sample of a given element by weighing, we must know the mass of the sample and the average mass for that element. Some average masses for common elements are listed in **Table 6.1.**

TABLE 6.1

Average Atomic Mass Values for Some Common Elements

Element	Average Atomic Mass (amu)
Hydrogen	1.008
Carbon	12.01
Nitrogen	14.01
Oxygen	16.00
Sodium	22.99
Aluminum	26.98

Example 6.1

Calculating Mass Using Atomic Mass Units (amu)

Calculate the mass, in amu, of a sample of aluminum that contains 75 atoms.

Solution

To solve this problem we use the average mass for an aluminum atom: 26.98 amu. We set up the equivalence statement

$$1 \; \text{Al atom} = 26.98 \; \text{amu}$$

which gives the conversion factor we need:

$$75 \; \cancel{\text{Al atoms}} \times \frac{26.98 \; \text{amu}}{\cancel{\text{Al atoms}}} = 2024 \; \text{amu}$$

PROBLEM SOLVING

The 75 in this problem is an exact number—the number of atoms.

 Self-Check Exercise 6.1

Calculate the mass of a sample that contains 23 nitrogen atoms.

Additional Examples

1. Calculate the mass (in amu) of a sample of carbon that contains 62 atoms.
   744.6 amu

2. Calculate the mass (in amu) of a sample of iron that contains 15 atoms.
   837.8 amu

 Answer to Self-Check Exercise 6.1

The average mass of nitrogen is 14.01 amu. The appropriate equivalence statement is 1 N atom = 14.01 amu, which yields the conversion factor we need:

$$\underset{\text{(Exact)}}{23 \; \text{N atoms}} \times \frac{14.01 \; \text{amu}}{\text{N atom}}$$

$$= 322.2 \; \text{amu}$$

TEACHING TIPS

- You can use the Chemistry in Action activity, "Counting Pennies Without Counting" (Section 6.2), for a whole-class discussion. Show that if we weigh all of the pennies and divide the result by the mass of one penny, the calculation of the total number of pennies is close, but incorrect. We need to determine an average mass for the pennies. This leads to a good discussion of isotopes if you wish to introduce that concept at this time.

- The idea that different samples with identical mass ratios contain the same number of objects is a difficult one for the students. Consider using the following example.

- Suppose we have two blocks: a red block and a yellow block. The red block weighs 1.0 ounce, and the yellow block weighs 4.0 ounces. Now suppose we have 16 of each color block. What is the mass of each sample? The sample of red blocks weighs 16.0 ounces and the sample of yellow blocks weighs 64.0 ounces. Note, however, that 16.0 ounces is also 1.0 pound, so 64.0 ounces is 4.0 pounds. The relative masses of the blocks are

	One Block	Sixteen Blocks
Red	1.0 ounce	1.0 pound
Yellow	4.0 ounces	4.0 pounds

The relative masses stay the same (1:4) but the units are changed.

- You can draw an analogy between ounces and pounds in this case and atomic mass units and grams in the case of the periodic table. In the blocks example, the number 16 is analogous to Avogadro's number.

Chapter 6   Chemical Composition   **157**

158

Additional Examples

1. Calculate the number of copper atoms present in a sample that has a mass of 1779.4 amu.
   28.00 atoms

2. Calculate the number of argon atoms present in a sample that has a mass of 3755.3 amu.
   94.00 atoms

 Answer to Self-Check Exercise 6.2

The average mass of oxygen is 16.00 amu, which gives the equivalence statement 1 O atom = 16.00 amu. The number of oxygen atoms present is

$$288 \text{ amu} \times \frac{1 \text{ O atom}}{16.00 \text{ amu}}$$

$$= 18.0 \text{ O atom}$$

 CHEMISTRY in ACTION

Counting Pennies Without Counting

Materials Each student/group will need a sealed tub with a certain number of pennies (greater than 10), an empty tub similar to the sealed tub, 10 additional pennies, and a balance. Butter or margarine tubs work well for this activity.

Purpose Students will better understand the idea of counting by weighing, which is crucial in understanding the mole concept.

Discussion To determine the number of pennies, students must find the mass of just the pennies in the tub. They can do so by subtracting the mass of the empty tub from the mass of the sealed tub with pennies, assuming that the sealed tub and the empty tub are similar in mass. They also need to find the average mass of a penny (they should compare the mass of one penny and the average mass of a penny from the sample of 10). The students then divide the total mass of pennies in the sealed tub by the average mass of a penny to determine the number of pennies in the sealed tub.

Students should be able to determine the number of pennies in the tub quite accurately. They

(continued)

The opposite calculation can also be carried out. That is, if we know the mass of a sample, we can determine the number of atoms present. This procedure is illustrated in Example 6.2.

Calculating the Number of Atoms from the Mass

Calculate the number of sodium atoms present in a sample that has a mass of 1172.49 amu.

Solution

We can solve this problem by using the average atomic mass for sodium (see Table 6.1) of 22.99 amu. The appropriate equivalence statement is

1 Na atom = 22.99 amu

which gives the conversion factor we need:

$$1172.49 \text{ amu} \times \frac{1 \text{ Na atom}}{22.99 \text{ amu}} = 51.00 \text{ Na atoms}$$

 Self-Check Exercise 6.2

Calculate the number of oxygen atoms in a sample that has a mass of 288 amu.

To summarize, we have seen that we can count atoms by weighing if we know the average atomic mass for that type of atom. This is one of the fundamental operations in chemistry, as we will see in the next section.

The average atomic mass for each element is listed on the inside front cover of this book.

 CHEMISTRY in ACTION

Counting Pennies Without Counting

1. Obtain a sample of pennies in a sealed container. Do not count the pennies.
2. Obtain an empty container that is similar to the one containing the pennies and one additional penny. Devise a method using a balance to determine the number of pennies in the sealed container without opening it. Determine the number of pennies in the sealed container.
3. Repeat step 2 using ten additional pennies instead of one penny. Use your method to determine the number of pennies in the sealed container.
4. Open the sealed container and count the pennies.
5. Which method (using one penny or ten pennies) allowed you to more accurately determine the number of pennies in the sealed container? Why? How does this finding relate to counting atoms by weighing?

158 Chapter 6 Chemical Composition

TEACHING SUPPORT
Demonstration

Moles and Molecules

Materials
Four 500-mL beakers
Sugar
Sulfur
Water

Procedure Place the following in separate, labeled beakers:

   18 mL water (labeled 1 mol water)

342 g sugar (labeled 1 mol sugar)
256 g sulfur (labeled 1 mol sulfur)
342 mL water (labeled 342 g water)

Show students the beakers, each containing one mole. Note the differences in mass and volume. Note that the number of molecules (6.022×10^{23}) is the same in each case.

Now use the beaker containing sugar and the one containing 342 g water. Emphasize that they have the same mass. Ask students how the numbers of molecules in the beakers compare. The sugar contains 6.022×10^{23} molecules, and the water contains $19(6.022 \times 10^{23}) = 1.14 \times 10^{25}$ molecules of water.

Extending the Idea Ask students to determine the ratio of

6.3 The Mole

Objectives: *To understand the mole concept and Avogadro's number.*
To learn to convert among moles, mass, and number of atoms in a given sample.

In the previous section we used atomic mass units for mass, but these are extremely small units. In the laboratory a much larger unit, the gram, is the convenient unit for mass. In this section we will learn to count atoms in samples with masses given in grams.

Let's assume we have a sample of aluminum that has a mass of 26.98 g. What mass of copper contains exactly the same number of atoms as this sample of aluminum?

| 26.98 g aluminum | ←— Contains the same number of atoms —→ | ? grams copper |

To answer this question, we need to know the average atomic masses for aluminum (26.98 amu) and copper (63.55 amu). Which atom has the greater atomic mass, aluminum or copper? The answer is copper. If we have 26.98 g of aluminum, do we need more or less than 26.98 g of copper to have the same number of copper atoms as aluminum atoms? We need more than 26.98 g of copper because each copper atom has a greater mass than each aluminum atom. Therefore, a given number of copper atoms will weigh more than an equal number of aluminum atoms. How much copper do we need? Because the average masses of aluminum and copper atoms are 26.98 amu and 63.55 amu, respectively, 26.98 g of aluminum and 63.55 g of copper contain exactly the same number of atoms. So we need 63.55 g of copper. As we saw in Section 6.1 when we were discussing candy, *samples in which the ratio of the masses is the same as the ratio of the masses of the individual atoms always contain the same number of atoms.* In the case just considered, the ratios are

$$\underbrace{\frac{26.98\text{g}}{63.55\text{g}}}_{\substack{\text{Ratio of}\\\text{sample}\\\text{masses}}} = \underbrace{\frac{26.98\text{ amu}}{63.55\text{ amu}}}_{\substack{\text{Ratio of}\\\text{atomic}\\\text{masses}}}$$

Therefore, 26.98 g of aluminum contains the same number of aluminum atoms as 63.55 g of copper contains copper atoms.

Now compare carbon (average atomic mass, 12.01 amu) and helium (average atomic mass, 4.003 amu). A sample of 12.01 g of carbon contains the same number of atoms as 4.003 g of helium. In fact, if we weigh out samples of all the elements such that each sample has a mass equal to that element's average atomic mass in grams, these samples all contain the same number of atoms **(Figure 6.1).** This number (the number of atoms present

Figure 6.1
All these samples of pure elements contain the same number (a mole) of atoms: 6.022×10^{23} atoms.

WHAT IF?

What if you were offered $1 million to count from 1 to 6×10^{23} at a rate of one number each second?

Determine your hourly wage. Would you do it? Could you do it?

the number of molecules in the sugar beaker to the number of molecules in the water beaker. How does this ratio compare to the ratio of moles from sugar to water?

---

should notice that using the average mass of 10 pennies gives a more accurate number. It is a good idea to place more than 10 pennies in the tub because the masses of pennies vary. You can draw an analogy between the differences in the masses of pennies and isotopes (isotopes are why the atomic masses on the periodic table are averages).

 Section 6.3

Themes
Scale and Structure

Skills
Making comparisons, converting, evaluating, interpreting data

Laboratory
Experiment 22:
Bean Lab, Traditional

TEACHING TIPS

- This section provides a bridge between amu units and grams. The reasoning used to explain the relative atomic masses on the periodic table is the concept of mass ratios, which was introduced in Section 6.1. Students can memorize the definitions, but to ensure that they get a real understanding of the ideas presented here, you should proceed slowly using many examples.

- It is important for students to realize that a mole really describes the number of objects present, just as a dozen means 12. This connection between a mole as a number and the mass of a sample is essential, because we count atoms by weighing samples containing large numbers of them.

- The mole is a crucial concept in this chapter. An understanding of it is important for many later topics in the course.

WHAT IF Comments

6×10^{23} seconds is about 2×10^{20} hours (keeping track of significant figures) or about 2×10^{16} years. Thus the hourly wage is approximately 5×10^{-15} dollars/hour. Earning a penny would require on the order of hundreds

(continued)

of millions of years. In short, it would be impossible. Calculations such as these should help students appreciate the magnitude of the mole.

MINI-DEMO

Bring a dozen eggs, a gross of pencils, and a ream of paper to class. Show the students the eggs and ask them to determine how many eggs are in five dozen. Have a student explain how he or she got the answer. Do a similar thing with the pencils and the paper. Once students are familiar with calculating the number of objects of a given type, write the number of objects in a mole on the board. Ask the students to determine how many atoms of aluminum are in a mole of aluminum. Repeat this idea with several different elements and amounts. Make sure that students understand that the process used is the same regardless of the unit.

TEACHING TIPS

- We define the mole differently from the SI definition: "The mole is the amount of substance that contains as many entities as there are in exactly 0.012 kg of carbon 12." Our definition is "the mole is the number equal to the number of carbon atoms in 12.01 g of carbon." We believe that our definition is easier for students to understand at this point. It more strongly emphasizes both that the mole is fundamentally a number and that the periodic table contains average atomic masses.

- Make sure that students understand that *mol* means mole and not molecule.

- Students do not need to memorize the average atomic masses of elements. These masses are given in the periodic table.

CHEMISTRY
Avogadro's number (to four significant figures) is 6.022×10^{23}. One moles of *anything* is 6.022×10^{23} units of that substance.

CHEMISTRY
The mass of 1 mol of an element is equal to its average atomic mass in grams.

in all of these samples) assumes special importance in chemistry. It is called the mole, the unit all chemists use in describing numbers of atoms. The **mole** (abbreviated mol) can be defined as *the number equal to the number of carbon atoms in 12.01 grams of carbon.* Techniques for counting atoms very precisely have been used to determine this number to be 6.022×10^{23}. This number is called **Avogadro's number.** *One mole of something consists of 6.022×10^{23} units of that substance.*

Just as a dozen eggs is 12 eggs, a mole of eggs is 6.022×10^{23} eggs. And a mole of water contains 6.022×10^{23} H_2O molecules.

The magnitude of the number 6.022×10^{23} is very difficult to imagine. To give you some idea, 1 mol of seconds represents a span of time 4 million times as long as the earth has already existed! One mole of marbles is enough to cover the entire earth to a depth of 50 miles! However, because atoms are so tiny, a mole of atoms or molecules is a perfectly manageable quantity to use in a reaction **(Figure 6.2).**

Figure 6.2
One-mole samples of iron (nails), iodine crystals, liquid mercury, and powdered sulfur.

How do we use the mole in chemical calculations? Recall that Avogadro's number is defined such that a 12.01-g sample of carbon contains 6.022×10^{23} atoms. By the same token, because the average atomic mass of hydrogen is 1.008 amu (Table 6.1), 1.008 g of hydrogen contains 6.022×10^{23} hydrogen atoms. Similarly, 26.98 g of aluminum contains 6.022×10^{23} aluminum atoms. The point is that a sample of *any* element that weighs a number of grams equal to the average atomic mass of that element contains 6.022×10^{23} atoms (1 mol) of that element.

Table 6.2 shows the masses of several elements that contain 1 mol of atoms.

In summary, *a sample of an element with a mass equal to that element's average atomic mass expressed in grams contains 1 mol of atoms.*

To do chemical calculations, you *must* understand what the mole means and how to determine the number of moles in a given mass of a substance.

TABLE 6.2

Comparison of 1-Mol Samples of Various Elements

Element	Number of Atoms Present	Mass of Sample (g)
Aluminum	6.022×10^{23}	26.98
Gold	6.022×10^{23}	196.97
Iron	6.022×10^{23}	55.85
Sulfur	6.022×10^{23}	32.07
Boron	6.022×10^{23}	10.81
Xenon	6.022×10^{23}	131.3

160 Chapter 6 Chemical Composition

Naming the number 6.022×10^{23} as Avogadro's number honors Amadeo Avogadro (1776–1856), the Italian chemist who first realized that equal volumes of gases at the same pressure and temperature contain equal numbers of particles (atoms or molecules). This idea, known as Avogadro's hy-

pothesis, was advanced by Avogadro in 1811 but went unnoticed for about half a century. It was not until 1860, after Avogadro's death, that another Italian chemist, Stanislao Cannizzaro, used Avogadro's hypothesis to determine the molar masses of several compounds and in so doing proved the correctness of Avogadro's idea.

Have your students investigate the lives and careers of Avogadro and Cannizzaro to understand more fully their monumental contributions to chemistry.

However, before we do any calculations, let's be sure that the process of counting by weighing is clear. Consider the following "bag" of H atoms (symbolized by dots), which contains 1 mol (6.022×10^{23}) of H atoms and has a mass of 1.008 g. Assume the bag itself has no mass.

Contains 1 mol H atoms
(6.022×10^{23} atoms)

Sample A
Mass = 1.008 g

Now consider another "bag" of hydrogen atoms in which the number of hydrogen atoms is unknown.

Contains an unknown
number of H atoms

Sample B

A 1-mol sample of graphite (a form of carbon) weighs 12.01 g.

We want to find out how many H atoms are present in sample ("bag") B. How can we do that? We can do it by weighing the sample. We find the mass of sample B to be 0.500 g.

How does this measured mass help us determine the number of atoms in sample B? We know that 1 mol of H atoms has a mass of 1.008 g. Sample B has a mass of 0.500 g, which is approximately half the mass of a mole of H atoms.

| Sample A | Sample B |
| Mass = 1.008 g | Mass = 0.500 g |

Contains 1 mol
of H atoms
→
Because the mass of B is about half the mass of A

Must contain
about 1/2 mol
of H atoms

We carry out the actual calculation by using the equivalence statement

1 mol H atoms = 1.008 g H

to construct the conversion factor we need:

$$0.500 \text{ g H} \times \frac{1 \text{ mol H}}{1.008 \text{ g H}} = 0.496 \text{ mol H in sample B}$$

Let's summarize. We know the mass of 1 mol of H atoms, so we can determine the number of moles of H atoms in any other sample of pure hydrogen by weighing the sample and *comparing* its mass to 1.008 g (the mass of

6.3   The Mole   **161**

Additional Activity

Bring samples of several elements to class along with a balance. Weigh a sample of an element. Have students determine the number of moles and the number of atoms or molecules in the sample.

Remind students to express their answers in scientific notation with correct significant figures. This effort helps them remember that these considerations are important for every problem in chemistry.

1 mol of H atoms). We can follow this same process for any element, because we know the mass of 1 mol for each of the elements.

Also, because we know that 1 mol is 6.022×10^{23} units, once we know the *moles* of atoms present, we can easily determine the *number* of atoms present. In the case considered above, we have approximately 0.5 mol of H atoms in sample B. This means that about 1/2 of 6×10^{23}, or 3×10^{23}, H atoms are present. We carry out the actual calculation by using the equivalence statement

$$1 \text{ mol} = 6.022 \times 10^{23}$$

to determine the conversion factor we need:

$$0.496 \text{ mol H atoms} \times \frac{6.022 \times 10^{23} \text{ H atoms}}{1 \text{ mol H atoms}} =$$
$$2.99 \times 10^{23} \text{ H atoms in sample B}$$

These procedures are illustrated in Example 6.3.

Example 6.3

Calculating Moles and Number of Atoms

A bicycle with an aluminum frame.

Aluminum (Al), a metal with a high strength-to-weight ratio and a high resistance to corrosion, is often used for structures such as high-quality bicycle frames. Compute both the number of moles of atoms and the number of atoms in a 10.0-g sample of aluminum.

Solution

In this case we want to change from mass to moles of atoms:

$$\boxed{\begin{array}{c} 10.0 \text{ g} \\ \text{Al} \end{array}} \Rightarrow \boxed{\begin{array}{c} ? \text{ moles} \\ \text{of Al} \\ \text{atoms} \end{array}}$$

The mass of 1 mol (6.022×10^{23} atoms) of aluminum is 26.98 g. The sample we are considering has a mass of 10.0 g. Its mass is less than 26.98 g, so this sample contains less than 1 mol of aluminum atoms. We calculate the number of moles of aluminum atoms in 10.0 g by using the equivalence statement

$$1 \text{ mol Al} = 26.98 \text{ g Al}$$

to construct the appropriate conversion factor:

$$10.0 \text{ g Al} \times \frac{1 \text{ mol Al}}{26.98 \text{ g Al}} = 0.371 \text{ mol Al}$$

Next we convert from moles of atoms to the number of atoms, using the equivalence statement

$$6.022 \times 10^{23} \text{ Al atoms} = 1 \text{ mol Al atoms}$$

We have

$$0.371 \text{ mol Al} \times \frac{6.022 \times 10^{23} \text{ Al atoms}}{1 \text{ mol Al}} = 2.23 \times 10^{23} \text{ Al atoms}$$

Additional Examples

1. Calculate the number of moles of atoms and the number of atoms in a 25.0-g sample of calcium.
0.624 mol Ca;
3.76×10^{23} Ca atoms

2. Calculate the number of moles of atoms and the number of atoms in a 57.7-g sample of sulfur.
1.80 mol S;
1.08×10^{24} S atoms

TEACHING TIP

Either Avogadro's number or atomic masses can limit the number of significant figures in a result. Be sure that students recognize that these numbers are not exact.

We can summarize this calculation as follows:

$$\boxed{10.0 \text{ g Al}} \times \frac{1 \text{ mol}}{26.98 \text{ g}} \Rightarrow \boxed{0.371 \text{ mol Al}}$$

$$\boxed{0.371 \text{ mol Al atoms}} \times \frac{6.022 \times 10^{23} \text{ Al atoms}}{\text{mol}} \Rightarrow \boxed{2.23 \times 10^{23} \text{ Al atoms}}$$

Example 6.4

A silicon chip of the type used in electronic equipment.

Calculating the Number of Atoms

A silicon chip used in an integrated circuit of a microcomputer has a mass of 5.68 mg. How many silicon (Si) atoms are present in this chip? The average atomic mass for silicon is 28.09 amu.

Solution

Our strategy for doing this problem is to convert from milligrams of silicon to grams of silicon, then to moles of silicon, and finally to atoms of silicon:

Each arrow in the schematic represents a conversion factor. Because 1 g = 1000 mg, we have

$$5.68 \text{ mg Si} \times \frac{1 \text{ g Si}}{1000 \text{ mg Si}} = 5.68 \times 10^{-3} \text{ g Si}$$

Next, because the average mass of silicon is 28.09 amu, we know that 1 mol of Si atoms weighs 28.09 g. This leads to the equivalence statement

$$1 \text{ mol Si atoms} = 28.09 \text{ g Si}$$

Thus,

$$5.68 \times 10^{-3} \text{ g Si} \times \frac{1 \text{ mol Si}}{28.09 \text{ g Si}} = 2.02 \times 10^{-4} \text{ mol Si}$$

Using the definition of a mole (1 mol = 6.022×10^{23}), we have

$$2.02 \times 10^{-4} \text{ mol Si} \times \frac{6.022 \times 10^{23} \text{ atoms}}{1 \text{ mol Si}} = 1.22 \times 10^{20} \text{ Si atoms}$$

We can summarize this calculation as follows:

$$\boxed{5.68 \text{ mg Si}} \times \frac{1 \text{ g}}{1000 \text{ mg}} \Rightarrow \boxed{5.68 \times 10^{-3} \text{ g Si}}$$

$$\boxed{5.68 \times 10^{-3} \text{ g Si}} \times \frac{1 \text{ mol}}{28.09 \text{ g}} \Rightarrow \boxed{2.02 \times 10^{-4} \text{ mol Si}}$$

$$\boxed{2.02 \times 10^{-4} \text{ mol Si}} \times \frac{6.022 \times 10^{23} \text{ Si atoms}}{\text{mol}} \Rightarrow \boxed{1.22 \times 10^{20} \text{ Si atoms}}$$

(continued)

6.3   The Mole   **163**

WHAT IF?

What if you discovered Avogadro's number was not 6.02×10^{23} but 3.01×10^{23}?

Would your discovery affect the relative masses given on the periodic table? If so, how? If not, why not?

Additional Examples

1. Calculate the number of atoms in a 23.6-mg sample of zinc.
   2.17×10^{20} Zn atoms

2. Calculate the number of atoms in a 128.3-mg sample of silver.
   7.16×10^{20} Ag atoms

WHAT IF Comments

The value of Avogadro's number does not affect the relative masses of the atoms of the elements. Regardless of the value of Avogadro's number, the mass of an average carbon atom is always approximately 12 times as great as the mass of an average hydrogen atom.

✓ Answer to Self-Check Exercise 6.3

The sample of 5.00×10^{20} atoms of chromium contains less than 1 mol (6.022×10^{23} atoms) of chromium. What fraction of a mole it represents can be determined as follows:

$$5.00 \times 10^{20} \text{ atoms Cr}$$
$$\times \frac{1 \text{ mol Cr}}{6.022 \times 10^{23} \text{ atoms Cr}}$$
$$= 8.30 \times 10^{-4} \text{ mol Cr}$$

Because the mass of 1 mol of chromium atoms is 52.00 g, the mass of 5.00×10^{20} atoms can be determined as follows:

$$8.30 \times 10^{-4} \text{ mol Cr}$$
$$\times \frac{52.00 \text{ g Cr}}{1 \text{ mol Cr}}$$
$$= 4.32 \times 10^{-2} \text{ g Cr}$$

Answers to Focus Questions

1. Count out 10 nuts and 10 bolts. Weigh each sample and divide by 10 to find the average mass of a nut and the average mass of a bolt. Then multiply each average mass by 1200 to find the correct amount to be weighed out. Weigh out these amounts and deliver the nuts and bolts to your boss.

2. Not all atoms of a given element have identical masses. Therefore the average atomic mass of an element is not a whole number.

3. **a.** $1 \text{ mol} = 6.022 \times 10^{23}$ units

   b. The possible conversion factors are
   $$\frac{1 \text{ mol}}{6.022 \times 10^{23} \text{ units}} \text{ and}$$
   $$\frac{6.022 \times 10^{23} \text{ units}}{1 \text{ mol}}.$$

   c. The correct conversion factors are
   $$\frac{6.022 \times 10^{23} \text{ atoms Al}}{1 \text{ mol}}$$
   and
   $$\frac{1 \text{ mol}}{6.022 \times 10^{23} \text{ atoms Au}}.$$

4. **a.** 6.7 g Al

   b. 98.5 g Au

   c. 280 g Fe

   d. 8.0×10^2 g S

(continued)

 Self-Check Exercise 6.3

Chromium (Cr) is a metal that is added to steel to improve its resistance to corrosion (for example, to make stainless steel). Calculate both the number of moles in a sample of chromium containing 5.00×10^{20} atoms and the mass of the sample.

Problem Solving: Does the Answer Make Sense?

When you finish a problem, always think about the "reasonableness" of your answers. In Example 6.4, 5.68 mg of silicon is clearly much less than 1 mol of silicon (which has a mass of 28.09 g), so the final answer of 1.22×10^{20} atoms (compared to 6.022×10^{23} atoms in a mole) at least lies in the right direction. That is, 1.22×10^{20} atoms is a smaller number than 6.022×10^{23}. Also, always include the units as you perform calculations and make sure the correct units are obtained at the end. Paying careful attention to units and making this type of general check can help you detect errors such as an inverted conversion factor or a number that was incorrectly entered into your calculator.

CHEMISTRY

The values for the average masses of the atoms of the elements are listed inside the front cover of this book.

Focus Questions

Sections 6.1–6.3

1. Suppose you work in a hardware store. The manager asks you to get an order for a major customer who is waiting impatiently. You need 1200 matched sets of nuts and bolts. Unfortunately the nuts and bolts are not boxed—they are loose in big buckets. How can you earn a bonus from your boss and make the customer happy by giving him the nuts and bolts in less than 2 minutes?

2. Why isn't the average atomic mass of any element a whole number (for example, C, 12 amu; H, 1 amu; N, 14 amu)?

3. A mole of any substance contains Avogadro's number of units.
   a. Write an equivalence statement for this definition.
   b. Write the possible conversion factors from this relationship.
   c. To determine the following tell which conversion factor you would need to use:
      1. Moles Al from atoms Al
      2. Atoms Au from mol Au

4. Table 6.2 gives the mass (g) of a mole of some elements. Use this information and your conversion factors to find the mass of:
   a. 0.25 mol Al
   b. 0.500 mol Au
   c. 5.0 mol Fe
   d. 25 mol S

6.4 Molar Mass

Objectives: *To understand the definition of molar mass.*
To learn to convert between moles and mass of a given sample of a chemical compound.

CHEMISTRY

Note that when we say 1 mol of methane, we mean 1 mol of methane *molecules*.

MATH

Remember that the least number of decimal places limits the number of significant figures in addition.

A chemical compound is, fundamentally, a collection of atoms. For example, methane (the major component of natural gas) consists of molecules each containing one carbon atom and four hydrogen atoms (CH_4). How can we calculate the mass of 1 mol of methane? That is, what is the mass of 6.022×10^{23} CH_4 molecules? Because each CH_4 molecule contains one carbon atom and four hydrogen atoms, 1 mol of CH_4 molecules consists of 1 mol of carbon atoms and 4 mol of hydrogen atoms **(Figure 6.3)**. The mass of 1 mol of methane can be found by summing the masses of carbon and hydrogen present:

Mass of 1 mol of C = 1×12.01 g = 12.01 g
Mass of 4 mol of H = 4×1.008 g = <u>4.032 g</u>

Mass of 1 mol of CH_4 = 16.04 g

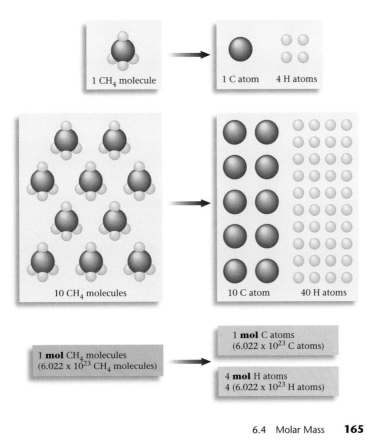

Figure 6.3
Various numbers of methane molecules showing their constituent atoms.

1 CH₄ molecule   1 C atom   4 H atoms

10 CH₄ molecules   10 C atom   40 H atoms

1 mol CH_4 molecules
(6.022×10^{23} CH_4 molecules)

1 mol C atoms
(6.022×10^{23} C atoms)

4 mol H atoms
$4 (6.022 \times 10^{23}$ H atoms)

6.4   Molar Mass   **165**

Themes
Organization, Scale and Structure

Skills
Applying concepts, making comparisons, interpreting data, calculating

Student Preparation
Assign the students to read Section 6.4 and to answer the Focus Questions at the end of Section 6.4 before coming to class.

Active Learning
After introducing the material in Section 6.4 in class, place the students in groups and have them work together on Section 6.4: Team Learning Worksheet. Answers and/or discussions of these questions are located in the *Teacher Resources*.

MISCONCEPTIONS

- The term *molar mass* has replaced "molecular weight" because molar mass more accurately describes the concept.

- Students are sometimes confused about which number from the periodic table to use to find molar mass. Remind them that atomic masses are used and not atomic numbers.

- Some students find it difficult to translate a formula into moles at this point. For example, 1 mol of methane molecules contains 4 mol of hydrogen atoms. Be sure to have students practice this translation and have them justify their answers.

- Emphasize that molar mass is the mass *per one mole* of substance. For example, one mole of diatomic oxygen gas has a mass of 32.00 g. A sample containing two moles of oxygen gas has a mass of 64.00 g.

USING TECHNOLOGY

  Figure 6.3

The quantity 16.04 g is called the molar mass for methane: the mass of 1 mol of CH_4 molecules. The **molar mass** of any substance is the *mass (in grams) of 1 mol of the substance*. The molar mass is obtained by summing the masses of the component atoms.

Example 6.5

Calculating Molar Mass

Calculate the molar mass of sulfur dioxide, a gas produced when sulfur-containing fuels are burned. Unless "scrubbed" from the exhaust, sulfur dioxide can react with moisture in the atmosphere to produce acid rain.

Solution

The formula for sulfur dioxide is SO_2. We need to compute the mass of 1 mol of SO_2 molecules—the molar mass for sulfur dioxide. We know that 1 mol of SO_2 molecules contains 1 mol of sulfur atoms and 2 mol of oxygen atoms:

Mass of 1 mol of S $= 1 \times 32.07 = 32.07$ g
Mass of 2 mol of O $= 2 \times 16.00 = \underline{32.00}$ g
Mass of 1 mol of SO_2 $= 64.07$ g = molar mass

The molar mass of SO_2 is 64.07 g. It represents the mass of 1 mol of SO_2 molecules.

 Self-Check Exercise 6.4

Polyvinyl chloride (called PVC), which is widely used for floor coverings ("vinyl") as well as for plastic pipes in plumbing systems, is made from a molecule with the formula C_2H_3Cl. Calculate the molar mass of this substance.

Some substances exist as a collection of ions rather than as separate molecules. For example, ordinary table salt, sodium chloride (NaCl), is composed of an array of Na^+ and Cl^- ions. There are no NaCl molecules present. In some books the term *formula weight* is used instead of molar mass for ionic compounds. However, in this book we will apply the term *molar mass* to both ionic and molecular substances.

To calculate the molar mass for sodium chloride, we must realize that 1 mol of NaCl contains 1 mol of Na^+ ions and 1 mol of Cl^- ions.

1 mol Na⁺
1 mol Cl⁻
1 mol NaCl

Na⁺
Cl⁻

CHEMISTRY

The mass of the electron is so small that Na⁺ and Na have the same mass for our purposes, even though Na⁺ has one electron less than Na. Also, the mass of Cl virtually equals the mass of Cl⁻ even though it has one more electron than Cl.

Therefore, the molar mass (in grams) for sodium chloride represents the sum of the mass of 1 mol of sodium ions and the mass of 1 mol of chloride ions.

$$\text{Mass of 1 mol of Na}^+ = 22.99 \text{ g}$$
$$\text{Mass of 1 mol of Cl}^- = \underline{35.45 \text{ g}}$$
$$\text{Mass of 1 mol of NaCl} = 58.44 \text{ g} = \text{molar mass}$$

The molar mass of NaCl is 58.44 g. It represents the mass of 1 mol of sodium chloride.

Example 6.6

Calculating Mass from Moles

Calcium carbonate, $CaCO_3$ (also called calcite), is the principal mineral found in limestone, marble, chalk, pearls, and the shells of marine animals such as clams.

  a. Calculate the molar mass of calcium carbonate.

  b. A certain sample of calcium carbonate contains 4.86 mol. What is the mass in grams of this sample?

Solution

  a. Calcium carbonate is an ionic compound composed of Ca^{2+} and CO_3^{2-} ions. One mole of calcium carbonate contains 1 mol of Ca^{2+} and 1 mol of CO_3^{2-} ions. We calculate the molar mass by summing the masses of the components.

$$\text{Mass of 1 mol of Ca}^{2+} = 1 \times 40.08 \text{ g} = 40.08 \text{ g}$$
Mass of 1 mol of CO_3^{2-} (contains 1 mol of C and 3 mol of O):
$$\text{1 mol of C} = 1 \times 12.01 \text{ g} = 12.01 \text{ g}$$
$$\text{3 mol of O} = 3 \times 16.00 \text{ g} = \underline{40.08 \text{ g}}$$
$$\text{Mass of 1 mol of CaCO}_3 = 100.09 \text{ g} = \text{molar mass}$$

  b. We determine the mass of 4.86 mol of $CaCO_3$ by using the molar mass,

$$4.86 \text{ mol CaCO}_3 \times \frac{100.09 \text{ g CaCO}_3}{1 \text{ mol CaCO}_3} = 486 \text{ g CaCO}_3$$

which can be diagrammed as follows:

$$\boxed{4.86 \text{ mol CaCO}_3} \times \frac{100.09 \text{ g}}{\text{mol}} \Rightarrow \boxed{486 \text{ g CaCO}_3}$$

Note that the sample under consideration contains nearly 5 mol and thus should have a mass of nearly 500 g, so our answer makes sense.

(continued)

6.4 Molar Mass **167**

TEACHING TIP

Students should not round off the atomic masses when calculating molar masses—for example, by using 1 for hydrogen and 12 for carbon. If the students develop this habit now, they will have trouble obtaining the correct answer to stoichiometry problems later in the course.

Additional Examples

1. Calculate the mass of 1.48 mol of potassium oxide. **139 g (K_2O)**

2. Calculate the mass of 4.85 mol of acetic acid, $HC_2H_3O_2$. Vinegar is a dilute solution of acetic acid. **291 g**

168

Answer to Self-Check Exercise 6.5

The formula for sodium sulfate is Na_2SO_4. One mole of Na_2SO_4 contains 2 mol of sodium ions and 1 mol of sulfate ions.

```
                          2 mol
1 mol of     ⎛ Na⁺  ⎞↗   Na⁺
Na₂SO₄ →     ⎝  SO₄²⁻ ⎠
1 mol of     ⎝ Na⁺  ⎠↘   1 mol
                          SO₄²⁻
```

Mass of 2 mol of Na^+
$= 2 \times 22.99$ $= 45.98$ g
Mass of 1 mol of SO_4^{2-}
$= 32.07 + 4(16.00)$ $= 96.07$ g
Mass of 1 mol of
Na_2SO_4 $= 142.05$ g

The molar mass for sodium sulfate is 142.05 g.

A sample of sodium sulfate with a mass of 300.0 g represents more than 1 mol. (Compare 300.0 g to the molar mass of Na_2SO_4.) We calculate the number of moles of Na_2SO_4 present in 300.0 g as follows:

$$300.0 \text{ g } \cancel{Na_2SO_4}$$
$$\times \frac{1 \text{ mol } Na_2SO_4}{142.05 \text{ g } \cancel{Na_2SO_4}}$$
$$= 2.112 \text{ mol } Na_2SO_4$$

Additional Examples

1. Formaldehyde, which in the past was used to preserve biological samples, has the formula H_2CO. How many moles of formaldehyde does a 7.55-g sample represent?
0.251 mol formaldehyde

2. How many moles of tetraphosphorus decoxide does a 250.0-g sample represent?
0.8805 mol

(continued)

✓ **Self-Check Exercise 6.5**

Calculate the molar mass for sodium sulfate, Na_2SO_4. A sample of sodium sulfate with a mass of 300.0 g represents what number of moles of sodium sulfate?

💡 **PROBLEM SOLVING**
For average atomic masses, look inside the front cover of this book.

In summary, the molar mass of a substance can be obtained by summing the masses of the component atoms. The molar mass (in grams) represents the mass of 1 mol of the substance. Once we know the molar mass of a compound, we can compute the number of moles present in a sample of known mass. The reverse, of course, is also true as illustrated in Example 6.7.

Example 6.7

Juglone, a natural herbicide, is produced from the husks of black walnuts.

Calculating Moles from Mass

Juglone, a dye known for centuries, is produced from the husks of black walnuts. It is also a natural herbicide (weed killer) that kills off competitive plants around the black walnut tree but does not affect grass and other noncompetitive plants. The formula for juglone is $C_{10}H_6O_3$.

a. Calculate the molar mass of juglone.

b. A sample of 1.56 g of pure juglone was extracted from black walnut husks. How many moles of juglone does this sample represent?

Solution

a. The molar mass is obtained by summing the masses of the component atoms. In 1 mol of juglone there are 10 mol of carbon atoms, 6 mol of hydrogen atoms, and 3 mol of oxygen atoms.

Mass of 10 mol of C $= 10 \times 12.01$ g $= 120.1$ g
Mass of 6 mol of H $= 6 \times 1.008$ g $= 6.048$ g
Mass of 3 mol of O $= 3 \times 16.00$ g $= \underline{48.00 \text{ g}}$

Mass of 1 mol of $C_{10}H_6O_3 = 174.1$ g $=$ molar mass

b. The mass of 1 mol of this compound is 174.1 g, so 1.56 g is much less than a mole. We can determine the exact fraction of a mole by using the equivalence statement

1 mol $= 174.1$ g juglone

to derive the appropriate conversion factor:

$$1.56 \text{ g } \cancel{juglone} \times \frac{1 \text{ mol juglone}}{174.1 \text{ g } \cancel{juglone}} = 0.00896 \text{ mol juglone}$$
$$= 8.96 \times 10^{-3} \text{ mol juglone}$$

$$\boxed{1.56 \text{ g juglone}} \times \frac{1 \text{ mol}}{174.1 \text{ g}} \Rightarrow \boxed{8.96 \times 10^{-3} \text{ mol juglone}}$$

Example 6.8

Calculating Number of Molecules

Isopentyl acetate, $C_7H_{14}O_2$, the compound responsible for the scent of bananas, can be produced commercially. Interestingly, bees release about 1 μg (1×10^{-6} g) of this compound when they sting. This attracts other bees, which then join the attack. How many moles and how many molecules of isopentyl acetate are released in a typical bee sting?

Solution

We are given a mass of isopentyl acetate and want the number of molecules, so we must first compute the molar mass.

$$7 \text{ mol C} \times 12.01 \frac{g}{mol} = 84.07 \text{ g C}$$

$$14 \text{ mol H} \times 1.008 \frac{g}{mol} = 14.11 \text{ g H}$$

$$2 \text{ mol O} \times 16.00 \frac{g}{mol} = \frac{32.00 \text{ g O}}{130.18 \text{ g}}$$

This means that 1 mol of isopentyl acetate (6.022×10^{23} molecules) has a mass of 130.18 g.

Next we determine the number of moles of isopentyl acetate in 1 μg, which is 1×10^{-6} g. To do this, we use the equivalence statement

1 mol isopentyl acetate = 130.18 g isopentyl acetate

which yields the conversion factor we need:

$$1 \times 10^{-6} \text{ g } C_7H_{14}O_2 \times \frac{1 \text{ mol } C_7H_{14}O_2}{130.18 \text{ g } C_7H_{14}O_2} = 8 \times 10^{-9} \text{mol } C_7H_{14}O_2$$

Using the equivalence statement 1 mol = 6.022×10^{23} units, we can determine the number of molecules:

$$8 \times 10^{-9} \text{ mol } C_7H_{14}O_2 \times \frac{6.022 \times 10^{23} \text{ molecules}}{1 \text{ mol } C_7H_{14}O_2} = 5 \times 10^{15} \text{ molecules}$$

This very large number of molecules is released in each bee sting.

 Self-Check Exercise 6.6

The substance Teflon, the slippery coating on many frying pans, is made from the C_2F_4 molecule. Calculate the number of C_2F_4 units present in 135 g of Teflon.

---

1. How many water molecules are in a 10.0-g sample of water?
   3.34×10^{23} water molecules

2. Sucrose, or table sugar, has the formula $C_{12}H_{22}O_{11}$. How many molecules of sugar are in a 5.00-lb bag of sugar?
   3.99×10^{24} sugar molecules

Answer to Self-Check Exercise 6.6

First we must compute the mass of 1 mol of C_2F_4 molecules (the molar mass). Because 1 mol of C_2F_4 contains 2 mol of C atoms and 4 mol of F atoms, we have

$$2 \text{ mol C} \times \frac{12.01 \text{ g}}{mol}$$
$$= 24.02 \text{ g C}$$

$$4 \text{ mol F} \times \frac{19.00 \text{ g}}{mol}$$
$$= 76.00 \text{ g F}$$

Mass of 1 mol of C_2F_4: 100.02 g = molar mass

Using the equivalence statement 100.02 g C_2F_4 = 1 mol C_2F_4, we calculate the moles of C_2F_4 units in 135 g of Teflon.

$$135 \text{ g } C_2F_4 \text{ units}$$
$$\times \frac{1 \text{ mol } C_2F_4}{100.02 \text{ g } C_2F_4}$$
$$= 1.35 \text{ mol } C_2F_4 \text{ units}$$

Next, using the equivalence statement 1 mol = 6.022×10^{23} units, we calculate the number of C_2F_4 units in 135 g of Teflon.

$$1.35 \text{ mol } C_2F_4$$
$$\times \frac{6.022 \times 10^{23} \text{ units}}{1 \text{ mol}}$$
$$= 8.13 \times 10^{23} C_2F_4 \text{ units}$$

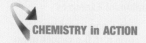

CHEMISTRY in ACTION

Relative Masses

Materials Each student/group will need some cotton balls (at least 20), some paper clips (at least 10), some rubber stoppers (all the same size, at least 5), a balance or scale, and a calculator.

Purpose Students will gain a better understanding of the concept of relative masses and the mole.

Discussion Students should notice that the numbers in the "Relative Mass of One Object" column and those in the "Mass of *n* Objects" column are the same (and in the same ratio as the numbers in the "Mass of One Object" column). This relationship shows that if we have equal numbers of different objects, the relative masses are the same as for single objects.

The relative mass of one object is analogous to relative atomic mass. The mass of *n* objects (in lb) is analogous to molar mass. This number tells us the mass of a certain number of objects (molar mass tells us the mass of one mole of atoms or molecules). The number *n* is analogous to Avogadro's number (the mole). It essentially converts a unitless number (like relative atomic mass) to a number with a mass (like molar mass). A sample table of answers is included below. In this case, $n = 1033$.

	Mass of One Object (g)	Relative Mass of One Object	Mass of *n* Objects (lb)
Cotton balls	0.44 g	$\frac{0.44}{0.44} = 1.0$	1.0 lb
Paper clips	1.42 g	$\frac{1.42}{0.44} = 3.2$	3.2 lb
Rubber stoppers	88 g	$\frac{88}{0.44} = 200$	200 lb

CHEMISTRY in ACTION

Relative Masses

1. Obtain cotton balls, paper clips, and rubber stoppers from your teacher.
2. Devise a method to find the average mass of each of these objects. Discuss this method with your teacher.
3. Copy the table below onto your paper.
4. Determine the average mass of each object and record it in your table.
5. Give your lightest object a relative mass of 1.0 in your table. Determine the relative masses of the remaining objects from your data.
6. How many of the lightest object would be needed to have 1 lb of that object? Call this number *n*.
7. If you had *n* of each of the other objects, how much would each sample weigh? Fill these numbers into your table.
8. Determine which columns correspond to the chemical terms "atomic mass" and "molar mass."
9. Which number represents "Avogadro's number?"

	Mass of One Object (g)	Relative Mass of One Object	Mass of *n* Objects
Cotton balls	g		lb
Paper clips	g		lb
Rubber stoppers	g		lb

Focus Questions

Section 6.4

1. How many moles of atoms of each element are present in the following amounts of each compound?
   a. 3 mol NH_3
   b. 0.25 mol H_2O
   c. 5.0 mol H_2SO_4
   d. 0.75 mol $Ca(NO_3)_2$

2. Determine the molar mass for each of the following:
   a. NH_3
   b. H_2O
   c. H_2SO_4
   d. $Ca(NO_3)_2$

3. Determine the mass of each sample in question 1.

4. Determine the number of molecules for the following:
   a. 3 mol NH_3
   b. 0.25 mol of H_2O

5. Determine the number of moles in the following:
   a. 100. g H_2SO_4
   b. 0.50 g $Ca(NO_3)_2$

170 Chapter 6 Chemical Composition

Answers to Focus Questions

1. a. 3 mol N, 9 mol H

   b. 0.50 mol H, 0.25 mol O

   c. 10.0 mol H, 5.0 mol S, 20.0 mol O

   d. 0.75 mol Ca, 1.50 mol N, 4.50 mol O

2. a. 17.03 g/mol

   b. 18.02 g/mol

   c. 98.09 g/mol

   d. 164.1 g/mol

3. a. 50 g

   b. 4.5 g

   c. 490 g

   d. 120 g

4. a. 1.807×10^{24} molecules

   b. 1.506×10^{23} molecules

5. a. 1.02 mol

   b. 3.0×10^{-3} mol

6.5 Percent Composition of Compounds

Objective: *To learn to find the mass percent of an element in a given compound.*

So far we have discussed the composition of compounds in terms of the numbers of constituent atoms. It is often useful to know a compound's composition in terms of the *masses* of its elements. We can obtain this information from the formula of the compound by comparing the mass of each element present in 1 mol of the compound to the total mass of 1 mol of the compound. The mass fraction for each element is calculated as follows:

MATH

$$\text{Percent} = \frac{\text{Part}}{\text{Whole}} \times 100\%$$

$$\text{Mass fraction for a given element} = \frac{\text{mass of the element present in 1 mol of compound}}{\text{mass of 1 mol of compound}}$$

The mass fraction is converted to *mass percent* by multiplying by 100%.

We will illustrate this concept using the compound ethanol, an alcohol obtained by fermenting the sugar in grapes, corn, and other fruits and grains. Ethanol is often added to gasoline as an octane enhancer to form a fuel called gasohol. The added ethanol has the effect of increasing the octane of the gasoline and also lowering the carbon monoxide in automobile exhaust.

Note from its formula that each molecule of ethanol contains two carbon atoms, six hydrogen atoms, and one oxygen atom. This means that each mole of ethanol contains 2 mol of carbon atoms, 6 mol of hydrogen atoms, and 1 mol of oxygen atoms. We calculate the mass of each element present and the molar mass for ethanol as follows:

CHEMISTRY

The formula for ethanol is written C_2H_5OH, although you might expect it to be written simply as C_2H_6O.

$$\text{Mass of C} = 2 \text{ mol} \times 12.01 \ \frac{g}{\text{mol}} = 24.02 \text{ g}$$

$$\text{Mass of H} = 6 \text{ mol} \times 1.008 \ \frac{g}{\text{mol}} = 6.048 \text{ g}$$

$$\text{Mass of O} = 1 \text{ mol} \times 16.00 \ \frac{g}{\text{mol}} = 16.00 \text{ g}$$

$$\text{Mass of 1 mol of } C_2H_5OH = 46.07 \text{ g} = \text{molar mass}$$

CHEMICAL IMPACT

Consumer Connection

Nutrition Facts

The food you eat contains all kinds of nutrients. But how much of what things? And is it healthful or "junk food"? To help you make informed decisions about the food you choose to eat, the U.S. Food and Drug Administration requires manufacturers to place nutrition facts on the packages for processed foods. Look at the label shown here (from a package of tortilla chips). Notice that the values of several substances are given as % RDA (recommended daily allowance). Because it is important to know the percent composition for food, the labels must describe the percentages of fats, proteins, carbohydrates, and other vital chemicals. You can use these guides to help you consume a healthy diet.

The law requires that the content of food (per serving) be printed on the label.

Section 6.5

Themes
Scale and Structure

Skills
Classifying, making comparisons, calculating, evaluating

Student Preparation
Assign the students to read Sections 6.5 to 6.8 and to answer the Focus Questions at the end of Section 6.8 before coming to class.

Active Learning
After introducing the material in Sections 6.5 to 6.8 in class, place the students in groups and have them work together on Sections 6.5–6.8: Team Learning Worksheet. Answers and/or discussion of these questions are located in the *Teacher Resources*.

TEACHING TIPS

• Bring a sample of a compound to class to use in discussing percent composition. Good examples include copper(II) nitrate, hydrogen peroxide, and potassium permanganate. Put the formula for the compound on the board and use it to illustrate the mass percent calculations.

• Remind students that a percentage is just a fraction multiplied by 100—it represents a part of the whole. You may need to spend some time in class working with students on the percent concept.

Integrating the CHEMICAL IMPACT

Nutrition Facts

Additional Activity The nutrition labels on snack foods list the mass of sodium per serving. Have students choose a snack food or drink and record the mass of sodium per serving and the number of servings in the container. In class have them determine the number of moles and atoms of sodium both per serving and for the whole container. Assemble the data for all of the snacks on the board. Which snacks contain the most sodium per serving? Which contain the least sodium?

The **mass percent** (sometimes called the weight percent) of carbon in ethanol can be computed by comparing the mass of carbon in 1 mol of ethanol with the total mass of 1 mol of ethanol and multiplying the result by 100%.

$$\text{Mass percent of C} = \frac{\text{mass of C in 1 mol } C_2H_5OH}{\text{mass of 1 mol } C_2H_5OH} \times 100\%$$

$$= \frac{24.02 \text{ g}}{46.07 \text{ g}} \times 100\% = 52.14\%$$

That is, ethanol contains 52.14% by mass of carbon. The mass percents of hydrogen and oxygen in ethanol are obtained in a similar manner.

$$\text{Mass percent of H} = \frac{\text{mass of H in 1 mol } C_2H_5OH}{\text{mass of 1 mol } C_2H_5OH} \times 100\%$$

$$= \frac{6.048 \text{ g}}{46.07 \text{ g}} \times 100\% = 13.13\%$$

$$\text{Mass percent of O} = \frac{\text{mass of O in 1 mol } C_2H_5OH}{\text{mass of 1 mol } C_2H_5OH} \times 100\%$$

$$= \frac{16.00 \text{ g}}{46.07 \text{ g}} \times 100\% = 34.73\%$$

PROBLEM SOLVING

Sometimes, because of rounding-off effects, the sum of the mass percents in a compound is not exactly 100%.

The mass percentages of all the elements in a compound add up to 100%, although rounding-off effects may produce a small deviation. Adding up the percentages is a good way to check the calculations. In this case, the sum of the mass percents is 52.14% + 13.13% + 34.73% = 100.00%.

Example 6.9

Calculating Mass Percent

Carvone is a substance that occurs in two forms, both of which have the same molecular formula ($C_{10}H_{14}O$) and molar mass. One type of carvone gives caraway seeds their characteristic smell; the other is responsible for the smell of spearmint oil. Compute the mass percent of each element in carvone.

Solution

MATH

The 120.1 limits the sum to one decimal place. Remember, in addition the number with the fewest decimal places determines the number of significant figures in the answer.

Because the formula for carvone is $C_{10}H_{14}O$, the masses of the various elements in 1 mol of carvone are

$$\text{Mass of C in 1 mol} = 10 \text{ mol} \times 12.01 \frac{g}{mol} = 120.1 \text{ g}$$

$$\text{Mass of H in 1 mol} = 14 \text{ mol} \times 1.008 \frac{g}{mol} = 14.11 \text{ g}$$

$$\text{Mass of O in 1 mol} = 1 \text{ mol} \times 16.00 \frac{g}{mol} = 16.00 \text{ g}$$

$$\text{Mass of 1 mol of } C_{10}H_{14}O = 150.21 \text{ g}$$
$$\text{Molar mass} = 150.2 \text{ g}$$

(rounding to the correct number of significant figures)

Next we find the fraction of the total mass contributed by each element and convert it to a percentage.

$$\text{Mass percent of C} = \frac{120.1 \text{ g C}}{150.2 \text{ g C}_{10}\text{H}_{14}\text{O}} \times 100\% = 79.96\%$$

$$\text{Mass percent of H} = \frac{14.11 \text{ g H}}{150.2 \text{ g C}_{10}\text{H}_{14}\text{O}} \times 100\% = 9.394\%$$

$$\text{Mass percent of O} = \frac{16.00 \text{ g O}}{150.2 \text{ g C}_{10}\text{H}_{14}\text{O}} \times 100\% = 10.65\%$$

Check: Add the individual mass percent values—they should total 100% within a small range due to rounding off. In this case, the percentages add up to 100.00%.

 Self-Check Exercise 6.7

Penicillin, an important antibiotic (antibacterial agent), was discovered accidentally by the Scottish bacteriologist Alexander Fleming in 1928, although he was never able to isolate it as a pure compound. This and similar antibiotics have saved millions of lives that would otherwise have been lost to infections. Penicillin, like many of the molecules produced by living systems, is a large molecule containing many atoms. One type of penicillin, penicillin F, has the formula $C_{14}H_{20}N_2SO_4$. Compute the mass percent of each element in this compound.

CHEMISTRY in ACTION
And the Winner Is . . .

1. Obtain three different types of sandwich cookies from your teacher.
2. Determine the percent composition of each cookie. Assume each cookie consists of two parts: the crunchy cookie and the cream filling. You will need a balance, foil, and a spoon. Do not place any part of the cookie or cream filling on the balance without the foil.
3. How do the percent compositions of the cookies compare?
4. Which would you say was the best cookie? Why?
5. Your teacher will tell you the price per cookie for each of the three types. Use this information to decide which cookie is the best buy. Defend your answer.

Photo of moon taken by Galileo space probe.

6.5 Percent Composition of Compounds **173**

Skills
Applying concepts, interpreting diagrams, making comparisons, calculating

TEACHING TIP

Students will have had no experience in determining the products of a chemical reaction. The approach in this section is to consider how a chemist determines the formula of a new compound. This topic leads to a discussion of getting chemical formulas from lab data.

Integrating the CHEMICAL IMPACT

"Mauvelous" Chemistry

"'Mauvelous' Chemistry" brings up the role of serendipity in chemical research. Many great discoveries were made by accident by an alert scientist. For example, indigo is a blue dye known and used by ancient civilizations. Prior to the 1890s, however, it had to be obtained from natural sources because no feasible synthesis was known. The commercially successful synthesis of indigo was discovered by accident when a mercury thermometer broke in a vat of naphthalene being heated with fuming sulfuric acid. The mercury reacted with the sulfuric acid to form mercury sulfate, a compound that catalyzes the transformation of naphthalene to phthalic anhydride, which can easily be converted (by a chemist) to indigo.

Examples of serendipity in science abound. The discovery of penicillin by Sir Alexander Fleming by accident is a well-known story. Another example is the discovery of Teflon in 1938, when a tank of tetrafluoroethylene accidently polymerized to form the white, waxy substance (Teflon) that has become so invaluable.

Another example of serendipity involves nylon. When nylon was first made, it seemed to possess

6.6 Formulas of Compounds

Objective: *To understand the meaning of the empirical formulas of compounds.*

Assume that you have mixed two solutions, and a solid product forms. How can you find out what the solid is? What is its formula? Although an experienced chemist can often predict the product expected in a chemical reaction, the only sure way to identify the product is to perform experiments. Usually we compare the physical properties of the product to the properties of known compounds.

Sometimes a chemical reaction gives a product that has never been obtained before. In such a case, a chemist determines what compound has been formed by determining which elements are present and how much of each is there. These data can be used to obtain the formula of the compound. In Section 6.5 we used the formula of the compound to determine the mass of

CHEMICAL IMPACT

Connection to History

"Mauvelous" Chemistry

Sometimes a little chemical knowledge can lead to a new and profitable career—as happened to a young chemistry student named William Perkin. In one of his chemistry lectures, Perkin's professor said it would be very desirable to make quinine artificially (in 1856, the only source for quinine—a drug effective against malaria—was the bark of the cinchona tree). Perkin, who was only 18 at the time, decided to make quinine artificially in his home laboratory as a project over Easter vacation.

To do so, he looked at the known formulas for quinine and toluidine (his starting reactant). Perkin recognized that he simply needed to add some carbon and hydrogen atoms and then several oxygens to get quinine. He had made some large oversimplifications and his reactions produced an ugly reddish-brown sludge. But Perkin didn't give up—he changed to a new starting material called aniline. This time he got an even worse-looking black solid. He was ready to throw the compound out when he noticed that it turned a beautiful purple color in water or alcohol.

Perkin liked the color so much that he became distracted from his original quest to make quinine. In testing the purple solutions, he found he could use them to dye cloth. He sent his synthetic dye to a dye works, which found that it worked well on silk and pretreated cotton.

Perkin decided to quit school (against the advice of his professors) and convinced his wealthy father to back his venture. He patented his dye and built a factory to produce it on a large scale. His dye eventually became known as mauve.

Until Perkin's discovery, all permanent purple or lavender dyes were outrageously expensive. The only source for the natural dye was a mollusk in the Mediterranean Sea. It took 9000 mollusks for 1g of dye—no wonder purple became the color associated with royalty. Perkin changed everything by producing a purple dye from coal tar that virtually everyone could afford and wear.

Perkin went on to develop another popular dye called alizarin in 1869. This red dye was being produced by the ton in his own factory by 1871.

Perkin sold his factory in 1874 and at age 36 had enough money to spend the rest of his life doing pure research. He bought a new house and continued working in his old laboratory. Eventually he made courmarin, the first perfume from coal tar and cinnamic acid. Perkin's work started an explosion in the manufacture of organic chemicals and research into their chemistry.

A portrait of Pliny wearing royal purple robes.

no useful properties. One day a scientist gathered a small part of a larger sample of nylon on a stirring rod and walked out the lab door and down the hall. He noticed that the resulting stretched material had a silky appearance and was thread-like. Eventually it was realized that stretching the nylon lined up the long polymer strands and turned it into the useful material used for so many purposes today.

For more information, see *Serendipity* by Royston M. Roberts (John Wiley and Sons, 1989).

each element present in a mole of the compound. To obtain the formula of an unknown compound, we do the opposite. That is, we use the measured masses of the elements present to determine the formula.

Recall that the formula of a compound represents the relative numbers of the various types of atoms present. For example, the molecular formula CO_2 tells us that for each carbon atom there are two oxygen atoms in each molecule of carbon dioxide. So to determine the formula of a substance we need to count the atoms. As we have seen in this chapter, we can do this by weighing. Suppose we know that a compound contains only the elements carbon, hydrogen, and oxygen, and we weigh out a 0.2015-g sample for analysis. Using methods we will not discuss here, we find that this 0.2015-g sample of compound contains 0.0806 g of carbon, 0.01353 g of hydrogen, and 0.1074 g of oxygen. We have just learned how to convert these masses to numbers of atoms by using the atomic mass of each element. We begin by converting to moles.

Carbon

$$(0.0806 \text{ g C}) \times \frac{1 \text{ mol C atoms}}{12.01 \text{ g C}} = 0.00671 \text{ mol C atoms}$$

Hydrogen

$$(0.01353 \text{ g H}) \times \frac{1 \text{ mol H atoms}}{1.008 \text{ g H}} = 0.01342 \text{ mol H atoms}$$

Oxygen

$$(0.1074 \text{ g O}) \times \frac{1 \text{ mol O atoms}}{16.00 \text{ g O}} = 0.006713 \text{ mol O atoms}$$

Let's review what we have established. We now know that 0.2015 g of the compound contains 0.00671 mol of C atoms, 0.01342 mol of H atoms, and 0.006713 mol of O atoms. Because 1 mol is 6.022×10^{23}, these quantities can be converted to actual numbers of atoms.

Carbon

$$(0.00671 \text{ mol C atoms}) \frac{(6.022 \times 10^{23} \text{ C atoms})}{1 \text{ mol C atom}} = 4.04 \times 10^{21} \text{ C atoms}$$

Hydrogen

$$(0.01342 \text{ mol H atoms}) \frac{(6.022 \times 10^{23} \text{ H atoms})}{1 \text{ mol H atom}} = 8.08 \times 10^{21} \text{ H atoms}$$

Oxygen

$$(0.006713 \text{ mol O atoms}) \frac{(6.022 \times 10^{23} \text{ O atoms})}{1 \text{ mol O atom}} = 4.043 \times 10^{21} \text{ O atoms}$$

These are the numbers of the various types of atoms *in 0.2015 g of compound*. What do these numbers tell us about the formula of the compound? Note the following:

1. The compound contains the same number of C and O atoms.

2. There are twice as many H atoms as C atoms or O atoms.

We can represent this information by the formula CH_2O, which expresses the *relative* numbers of C, H, and O atoms present. Is this the true formula for the compound? In other words, is the compound made up of CH_2O molecules? It may be. However, it might also be made up of $C_2H_4O_2$ molecules,

Additional Examples

Determine the empirical formula from each of the following molecular formulas.

1. H_2O_2, hydrogen peroxide, a substance commonly diluted with water and used as a disinfectant
HO

2. C_4H_{10}, butane, commonly used in lighters
C_2H_5

3. CCl_4, carbon tetrachloride, an organic solvent
CCl_4

TEACHING TIP

Remind students that subscripts outside the parentheses have an effect on the number of each atom inside the parentheses. You can relate this effect to the distributive property for multiplication over addition. This discussion will remind them to multiply the subscripts to obtain the number of atoms.

Figure 6.4
The glucose molecule. The molecular formula is $C_6H_{12}O_6$, as can be verified by counting the atoms. The empirical formula for glucose is CH_2O.

$C_3H_6O_3$ molecules, $C_4H_8O_4$ molecules, $C_5H_{10}O_5$ molecules, $C_6H_{12}O_6$ molecules, and so on. Note that each of these molecules has the required $1:2:1$ ratio of carbon to hydrogen to oxygen atoms (the ratio shown by experiment to be present in the compound).

When we break a compound down into its separate elements and "count" the atoms present, we learn only the ratio of atoms—we get only the *relative* numbers of atoms. The formula of a compound that expresses the smallest whole-number ratio of the atoms present is called the **empirical formula** or *simplest formula*. A compound that contains the molecules $C_4H_8O_4$ has the same empirical formula as a compound that contains $C_6H_{12}O_6$ molecules. The empirical formula for both is CH_2O. The actual formula of a compound—the one that gives the composition of the molecules that are present—is called the **molecular formula**. The sugar called glucose is made of molecules with the molecular formula $C_6H_{12}O_6$ **(Figure 6.4)**. Note from the molecular formula for glucose that the empirical formula is CH_2O. We can represent the molecular formula as a multiple (by 6) of the empirical formula:

$$C_6H_{12}O_6 = (CH_2O)_6$$

In the next section, we will explore in more detail how to calculate the empirical formula for a compound from the relative masses of the elements present. As we will see in Sections 6.7 and 6.8, we must know the molar mass of a compound to determine its molecular formula.

Example 6.10

Determining Empirical Formulas

In each case below, the molecular formula for a compound is given. Determine the empirical formula for each compound.

   a. C_6H_6. This is the molecular formula for benzene, a liquid commonly used in industry as a starting material for many important products.

   b. $C_{12}H_4Cl_4O_2$. This is the molecular formula for a substance commonly called dioxin, a powerful poison that sometimes occurs as a by-product in the production of other chemicals.

   c. $C_6H_{16}N_2$. This is the molecular formula for one of the reactants used to produce nylon.

PROBLEM SOLVING

When a subscript is outside of the parentheses, it applies to everything in the parentheses. Each subscript inside is multiplied by the subscript outside the parentheses.

Solution

   a. $C_6H_6 = (CH)_6$; CH is the empirical formula. Each subscript in the empirical formula is multiplied by 6 to obtain the molecular formula.

   b. $C_{12}H_4Cl_4O_2$; $C_{12}H_4Cl_4O_2 = (C_6H_2Cl_2O)_2$; $C_6H_2Cl_2O$ is the empirical formula. Each subscript in the empirical formula is multiplied by 2 to obtain the molecular formula.

   c. $C_6H_{16}N_2 = (C_3H_8N)_2$; C_3H_8N is the empirical formula. Each subscript in the empirical formula is multiplied by 2 to obtain the molecular formula.

176   Chapter 6   Chemical Composition

6.7 Calculation of Empirical Formulas

Objective: *To learn to calculate empirical formulas.*

As we said in the previous section, one of the most important things we can learn about a new compound is its chemical formula. To calculate the empirical formula of a compound, we first determine the relative masses of the various elements that are present.

One way to do this is to measure the masses of elements that react to form the compound. For example, suppose we weigh out 0.2636 g of pure nickel metal into a crucible and heat this metal in the air so that the nickel can react with oxygen to form a nickel oxide compound. After the sample has cooled, we weigh it again and find its mass to be 0.3354 g. The gain in mass is due to the oxygen that reacts with the nickel to form the oxide. Therefore, the mass of oxygen present in the compound is the total mass of the product minus the mass of the nickel:

| Total mass of nickel oxide | − | Mass of nickel originally present | = | Mass of oxygen that reacted with the nickel |

or

$$0.3354 \text{ g} \ - \ 0.2636 \text{ g} \ = \ 0.0718 \text{ g}$$

Note that the mass of nickel present in the compound is the nickel metal originally weighed out. So we know that the nickel oxide contains 0.2636 g of nickel and 0.0718 g of oxygen. What is the empirical formula of this compound?

To answer this question we must convert the masses to numbers of atoms, using atomic masses:

$$0.2636 \text{ g Ni} \times \frac{1 \text{ mol Ni atoms}}{58.69 \text{ g Ni}} = 0.004491 \text{ mol Ni atoms}$$

$$0.0718 \text{ g O} \times \frac{1 \text{ mol O atoms}}{16.00 \text{ g O}} = 0.00449 \text{ mol O atoms}$$

These mole quantities represent numbers of atoms (remember that a mole of atoms is 6.022×10^{23} atoms). It is clear from the moles of atoms that the compound contains an equal number of Ni and O atoms, so the formula is NiO. This is the *empirical formula;* it expresses the smallest whole-number (integer) ratio of atoms:

$$\frac{0.004491 \text{ mol Ni atoms}}{0.00449 \text{ mol O atoms}} = \frac{1 \text{ Ni}}{1 \text{ O}}$$

That is, this compound contains equal numbers of nickel atoms and oxygen atoms. We say the ratio of nickel atoms to oxygen atoms is 1:1 (1 to 1).

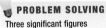

PROBLEM SOLVING
Four significant figures allowed.

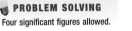

PROBLEM SOLVING
Three significant figures allowed.

Themes
Scale and Structure, Form and Function

Skills
Applying concepts, interpreting diagrams, calculating

Laboratory
Experiment 23:
Decomposing Copper Oxide, In Text

TEACHING TIP

The key concept in this section is that the mass of each element in a compound is an indicator of the number of atoms of that element in the compound, but only if the mass is converted to moles.

6.7 Calculation of Empirical Formulas **177**

1. A 1.500-g sample of a compound containing only carbon and hydrogen is found to contain 1.198 g of carbon. Determine the empirical formula for this compound. **CH₃**

2. A 3.450-g sample of nitrogen reacts with 1.970 g of oxygen. Determine the empirical formula for this compound. **N₂O**

TEACHING TIPS

- Students will often divide the mass of oxygen or mass percent of oxygen by 32.00 instead of 16.00. Let them know that we are determining the ratio of oxygen *atoms* in the compound.

- In these problems students worry when the ratio of moles of atoms is not an integer, thinking that the calculation may be incorrect. Warn them to be careful of calculation errors, but also to remember that a noninteger result is a fraction in decimal form. Some easily recognized fractions in decimal form are

$$\frac{1}{2} = 0.500$$

$$\frac{1}{3} = 0.333$$

$$\frac{1}{4} = 0.25$$

$$\frac{2}{3} = 0.667$$

$$\frac{3}{4} = 0.75$$

In cases in which a noninteger is obtained, students should look for one of these fractions and multiply each of the atom ratios by the denominator of the fraction to obtain a whole number.

Example 6.11

Calculating Empirical Formulas

An oxide of aluminum is formed by the reaction of 4.151 g of aluminum with 3.692 g of oxygen. Calculate the empirical formula for this compound.

Solution

We know that the compound contains 4.151 g of aluminum and 3.692 g of oxygen. But we need to know the relative numbers of each type of atom to write the formula, so we must convert these masses to moles of atoms to get the empirical formula. We carry out the conversion by using the atomic masses of the elements.

$$4.151 \text{ g Al} \times \frac{1 \text{ mol Al}}{26.98 \text{ g Al}} = 0.1539 \text{ mol Al atoms}$$

$$3.692 \text{ g O} \times \frac{1 \text{ mol O}}{16.00 \text{ g O}} = 0.2308 \text{ mol O atoms}$$

Because chemical formulas use only whole numbers, we next find the integer (whole-number) ratio of the atoms. To do this we start by dividing both numbers by the smallest of the two. This converts the smallest number to 1.

$$\frac{0.1539 \text{ mol Al}}{0.1539} = 1.000 \text{ mol Al atoms}$$

$$\frac{0.2308 \text{ mol O}}{0.1539} = 1.500 \text{ mol O atoms}$$

Note that dividing both numbers of moles of atoms by the *same* number does not change the *relative* numbers of oxygen and aluminum atoms. That is,

$$\frac{0.2308 \text{ mol O}}{0.1539 \text{ mol Al}} = \frac{1.500 \text{ mol O}}{1.000 \text{ mol Al}}$$

Thus we know that the compound contains 1.500 mol of O atoms for every 1.000 mol of Al atoms, or, in terms of individual atoms, we could say that the compound contains 1.500 O atoms for every 1.000 Al atom. However, because only *whole* atoms combine to form compounds, we must find a set of *whole numbers* to express the empirical formula. When we multiply both 1.000 and 1.500 by 2, we get the integers we need.

$$1.500 \text{ O} \times 2 = 3.000 = 3 \text{ O atoms}$$

$$1.000 \text{ Al} \times 2 = 2.000 = 2 \text{ Al atoms}$$

Therefore, this compound contains two Al atoms for every three O atoms, and the empirical formula is Al_2O_3. Note that the *ratio* of atoms in this compound is given by each of the following fractions:

$$\frac{0.2308 \text{ O}}{0.1539 \text{ Al}} = \frac{1.500 \text{ O}}{1.000 \text{ Al}} = \frac{\left(\frac{3}{2} \text{ O}\right)}{(1 \text{ Al})} \times \frac{2}{2} = \frac{3 \text{ O}}{2 \text{ Al}}$$

The smallest whole-number ratio corresponds to the subscripts of the empirical formula, Al_2O_3.

CHEMISTRY

We might express these data as:

$$Al_{1.000 \text{ mol}}O_{1.500 \text{ mol}}$$

or

$$Al_{2.000 \text{ mol}}O_{3.000 \text{ mol}}$$

or

$$Al_2O_3$$

MATH

Multiplying both the numerator and the denominator of a fraction (ratio) by the same number is just multiplying by 1

$$\frac{2}{2} = 1, \frac{3}{3} = 1, \text{ and so on}$$

It does not change the value of the fraction but it can help us get whole numbers in the ratio.

TEACHING SUPPORT
Demonstration

Properties of Ammonia

Materials
10 g ammonium chloride
10 g sodium hydroxide pellets
250-mL Erlenmeyer flask
One-holed rubber #5 stopper
glass tubing
Two 500-mL flasks and rubber stopper to fit

Red litmus paper
Hot plate or Bunsen burner
Shallow pan or baking dish

Preparation Before class insert the glass tubing through the #5 stopper. (Use glycerin for lubrication. Be sure to protect your hand during the process.) In the hood add the ammonium chloride and sodium hydroxide pellets to the 250-mL flask and stopper with your assembly. Heat the solids gently and in-

vert the 500-mL *dry* flask over the glass tube, filling the inverted flask with ammonia. (Test the mouth of the inverted flask with red litmus—when it turns blue the flask is full of ammonia.) Stopper the larger flask and remove the smaller flask from the heat.

Presentation Explain that you have brought a flask containing ammonia to class. Note the physical properties of the gas.

Ammonia (NH$_3$)

A mmonia is a colorless gas with a pungent odor that can be liquified at −34 °C. Ammonia (dissolved in water) is found in many household cleaning agents.

Ammonia is manufactured by combining the elements nitrogen and hydrogen:

$$3\ H_2(g) + N_2(g) \rightarrow 2\ NH_3(g)$$

The major use of ammonia is as a fertilizer to furnish nitrogen atoms to growing plants. Approximately 30 *billion* pounds of ammonia are produced every year for this purpose. For use as a fertilizer, the ammonia is liquified (at high pressures) and stored in mobile tanks that can be pulled through the fields by a tractor. It is then injected into the ground to serve as an additional source of nitrogen for the crop.

A cross section showing how ammonia is injected into the soil to act as a fertilizer.

Sometimes the relative numbers of moles you get when you calculate an empirical formula will turn out to be nonintegers, as was the case in Example 6.11. When this happens, you must convert to the appropriate whole numbers. This is done by multiplying all the numbers by the same small integer, which can be found by trial and error. The multiplier needed is almost always between 1 and 6. We will now summarize what we have learned about calculating empirical formulas.

Steps for Determining the Empirical Formula of a Compound

STEP 1 Obtain the mass of each element present (in grams).

STEP 2 Determine the number of moles of each type of atom present.

STEP 3 Divide the number of moles of each element by the smallest number of moles to convert the smallest number to 1. If all of the numbers so obtained are integers (whole numbers), they are the subscripts in the empirical formula. If one or more of these numbers are not integers, go on to step 4.

STEP 4 Multiply the numbers you derived in step 3 by the smallest integer that will convert all of them to whole numbers. This set of whole numbers represents the subscripts in the empirical formula.

6.7 Calculation of Empirical Formulas **179**

Unstopper the flask and place a piece of red litmus to the mouth of the flask. Restopper the flask and explain that moist red litmus turns blue when a base (in this case, ammonia) is present. Repeat this process with a flask containing air to show the difference.

Place the flask containing air in an inverted position in the shallow pan containing water. Observe that nothing happens.

This is just what the students would probably predict. Repeat this process with the flask containing the ammonia. The water should rush into the flask. Why? (Ammonia dissolves very easily in water thus lowering the pressure inside the flask.)

Relate these properties to the use of gaseous ammonia as a fertilizer in many parts of the country (see the photo in the Celebrity Chemical feature).

Why does the ammonia remain in the soil? It is dissolved in the water contained in the soil. What happens to the acidity of the soil? It is lowered by the dissolved ammonia.

Additional Examples

1. When a 2.000-g sample of iron metal is heated in air, it reacts with oxygen to achieve a final mass of 2.573 g. Determine the empirical formula for this iron oxide. **FeO [iron(II) oxide]**

2. A 4.550-g sample of cobalt reacts with 5.475 g chlorine to form a binary compound. Determine the empirical formula for this compound. **$CoCl_2$ [cobalt(II) chloride]**

Answer to Self-Check Exercise 6.8

Step 1 0.6884 g lead and 0.2356 g chlorine

Step 2 $0.6884 \text{ g Pb} \times \dfrac{1 \text{ mol Pb}}{207.2 \text{ g Pb}}$
$= 0.003322 \text{ mol Pb}$

$0.2356 \text{ g Cl} \times \dfrac{1 \text{ mol Cl}}{35.45 \text{ g Cl}}$
$= 0.006646 \text{ mol Cl}$

Step 3 $\dfrac{0.003322 \text{ mol Pb}}{0.003322}$
$= 1.000 \text{ mol Pb}$

$\dfrac{0.006646 \text{ mol Cl}}{0.003322}$
$= 2.001 \text{ mol Cl}$

These numbers are very close to integers, so step 4 is unnecessary. The empirical formula is $PbCl_2$.

Example 6.12

Calculating Empirical Formulas for Binary Compounds

When a 0.3546-g sample of vanadium metal is heated in air, it reacts with oxygen to achieve a final mass of 0.6330 g. Calculate the empirical formula of this vanadium oxide.

Solution

Step 1 All the vanadium that was originally present will be found in the final compound, so we can calculate the mass of oxygen that reacted by taking the following difference:

Total mass of compound	−	Mass of vanadium in compound	=	Mass of oxygen in compound
0.6330 g	−	0.3546 g	=	0.2784 g

Step 2 Using the atomic masses (50.94 for V and 16.00 for O), we obtain

$$0.3546 \text{ g V} \times \frac{1 \text{ mol V atoms}}{50.94 \text{ g V}} = 0.006961 \text{ mol V atoms}$$

$$0.2784 \text{ g O} \times \frac{1 \text{ mol O atoms}}{16.00 \text{ g O}} = 0.01740 \text{ mol O atoms}$$

Step 3 Then we divide both numbers of moles by the smaller, 0.006961.

$$\frac{0.006961 \text{ mol V atoms}}{0.006961} = 1.000 \text{ mol V atoms}$$

$$\frac{0.01740 \text{ mol O atoms}}{0.006961} = 2.500 \text{ mol O atoms}$$

Because one of these numbers (2.500) is not an integer, we go on to step 4.

Step 4 We note that $2 \times 2.500 = 5.000$ and $2 \times 1.000 = 2.000$, so we multiply both numbers by 2 to get integers.

$$2 \times 1.000 \text{ V} = 2.000 \text{ V} = 2 \text{ V}$$
$$2 \times 2.500 \text{ O} = 5.000 \text{ O} = 5 \text{ O}$$

This compound contains 2 V atoms for every 5 O atoms, and the empirical formula is V_2O_5.

MATH

$V_{1.000}O_{2.500}$ becomes V_2O_5 when we multiply both subscripts by 2.

Self-Check Exercise 6.8

In a lab experiment it was observed that 0.6884 g of lead combines with 0.2356 g of chlorine to form a binary compound. Calculate the empirical formula of this compound.

The same procedures we have used for binary compounds also apply to compounds containing three or more elements, as Example 6.13 illustrates.

180 Chapter 6 Chemical Composition

Example 6.13

Calculating Empirical Formulas for Compounds Containing Three or More Elements

A sample of lead arsenate, an insecticide used against the potato beetle, contains 1.3813 g of lead, 0.00672 g of hydrogen, 0.4995 g of arsenic, and 0.4267 g of oxygen. Calculate the empirical formula for lead arsenate.

Solution

Step 1 The compound contains 1.3813 g Pb, 0.00672 g H, 0.4995 g As, and 0.4267 g O.

Step 2 We use the atomic masses of the elements present to calculate the moles of each.

PROBLEM SOLVING
Only three significant figures are allowed because the mass of H has only three significant figures.

$$1.3813 \text{ g Pb} \times \frac{1 \text{ mol Pb}}{207.2 \text{ g Pb}} = 0.006667 \text{ mol Pb}$$

$$0.00672 \text{ g H} \times \frac{1 \text{ mol H}}{1.008 \text{ g H}} = 0.00667 \text{ mol H}$$

$$0.4995 \text{ g As} \times \frac{1 \text{ mol As}}{74.92 \text{ g As}} = 0.006667 \text{ mol As}$$

$$0.4267 \text{ g O} \times \frac{1 \text{ mol O}}{16.00 \text{ g O}} = 0.02667 \text{ mol O}$$

Step 3 Now we divide by the smallest number of moles.

$$\frac{0.006667 \text{ mol Pb}}{0.006667} = 1.000 \text{ mol Pb}$$

$$\frac{0.00667 \text{ mol H}}{0.006667} = 1.00 \text{ mol H}$$

$$\frac{0.006667 \text{ mol As}}{0.006667} = 1.000 \text{ mol As}$$

$$\frac{0.02667 \text{ mol O}}{0.006667} = 4.000 \text{ mol O}$$

The numbers of moles are all whole numbers, so the empirical formula is $PbHAsO_4$.

Self-Check Exercise 6.9

Sevin, the commercial name for an insecticide used to protect crops such as cotton, vegetables, and fruit, is made from carbamic acid. A chemist analyzing a sample of carbamic acid finds 0.8007 g of carbon, 0.9333 g of nitrogen, 0.2016 g of hydrogen, and 2.133 g of oxygen. Determine the empirical formula for carbamic acid.

When a compound is analyzed to determine the relative amounts of the elements present, the results are usually given in terms of percentages by masses of the various elements. In Section 6.5 we learned to calculate the percent composition of a compound from its formula. Now we will do the opposite. Given the percent composition, we will calculate the empirical formula.

Additional Examples

1. Phosphoric acid is found in some soft drinks. A sample of phosphoric acid contains 0.3086 g of hydrogen, 3.161 g of phosphorus, and 6.531 g of oxygen. Determine the empirical formula for phosphoric acid.
H_3PO_4

2. *Para*-dichlorobenzene is often used in chemistry labs when studying melting points. A sample of *para*-dichlorobenzene contains 5.657 g of carbon, 0.3165 g of hydrogen, and 5.566 g of chlorine. Determine the empirical formula for this compound.
C_3H_2Cl

Answer to Self-Check Exercise 6.9

Step 1 0.8007 g C, 0.9333 g N, 0.2016 g H, and 2.133 g O

Step 2 $0.8007 \text{ g C} \times$

$$\frac{1 \text{ mol C}}{12.01 \text{ g C}}$$

$$= 0.06667 \text{ mol C}$$

$$0.9333 \text{ g N} \times \frac{1 \text{ mol N}}{14.01 \text{ g N}}$$

$$= 0.06662 \text{ mol N}$$

$$0.2016 \text{ g H} \times \frac{1 \text{ mol H}}{1.008 \text{ g H}}$$

$$= 0.2000 \text{ mol H}$$

$$2.133 \text{ g O} \times \frac{1 \text{ mol O}}{16.00 \text{ g O}}$$

$$= 0.1333 \text{ mol O}$$

Step 3 $\dfrac{0.06667 \text{ mol C}}{0.06667}$

$$= 1.001 \text{ mol C}$$

$$\frac{0.06662 \text{ mol N}}{0.06667} = 1.000 \text{ mol N}$$

$$\frac{0.2000 \text{ mol H}}{0.06662} = 3.002 \text{ mol H}$$

$$\frac{0.1333 \text{ mol O}}{0.06662} = 2.001 \text{ mol O}$$

The empirical formula is CNH_3O_2.

CHEMISTRY

Percent by mass for a given element means the grams of that element in 100 g of the compound.

To understand this procedure, you must understand the meaning of *percent*. Remember that percent means parts of a given component per 100 parts of the total mixture. For example, if a given compound is 15% carbon (by mass), the compound contains 15 g of carbon per 100 g of compound.

Calculation of the empirical formula of a compound when one is given its percent composition is illustrated in Example 6.14.

Example 6.14

Calculating Empirical Formulas from Percent Composition

Cisplatin, the common name for a platinum compound that is used to treat cancerous tumors, has the composition (mass percent) 65.02% platinum, 9.34% nitrogen, 2.02% hydrogen, and 23.63% chlorine. Calculate the empirical formula for cisplatin.

Solution

Step 1 Determine how many grams of each element are present in 100 g of compound. Cisplatin is 65.02% platinum (by mass), which means there is 65.02 g of platinum (Pt) per 100.00 g of compound. Similarly, a 100.00-g sample of cisplatin contains 9.34 g of nitrogen (N), 2.02 g of hydrogen (H), and 26.63 g of chlorine (Cl).

If we have a 100.00-g sample of cisplatin, we have 65.02 g Pt, 9.34 g N, 2.02 g H, and 23.63 g Cl.

Step 2 Determine the number of moles of each type of atom. We use the atomic masses to calculate moles.

$$65.02 \text{ g Pt} \times \frac{1 \text{ mol Pt}}{195.1 \text{ g Pt}} = 0.3333 \text{ mol Pt}$$

$$9.34 \text{ g N} \times \frac{1 \text{ mol N}}{14.01 \text{ g N}} = 0.667 \text{ mol N}$$

$$2.02 \text{ g H} \times \frac{1 \text{ mol H}}{1.008 \text{ g H}} = 2.00 \text{ mol H}$$

$$23.63 \text{ g Cl} \times \frac{1 \text{ mol Cl}}{35.45 \text{ g Cl}} = 0.6666 \text{ mol Cl}$$

Step 3 Divide through by the smallest number of moles.

$$\frac{0.3333 \text{ mol Pt}}{0.3333} = 1.000 \text{ mol Pt}$$

$$\frac{0.667 \text{ mol N}}{0.3333} = 2.00 \text{ mol N}$$

$$\frac{2.00 \text{ mol H}}{0.3333} = 6.01 \text{ mol H}$$

$$\frac{0.6666 \text{ mol Cl}}{0.3333} = 2.000 \text{ mol Cl}$$

The empirical formula for cisplatin is $PtN_2H_6Cl_2$. Note that the number for hydrogen is slightly greater than 6 because of rounding-off effects.

Self-Check Exercise 6.10

The most common form of nylon (Nylon-6) is 63.68% carbon, 12.38% nitrogen, 9.80% hydrogen, and 14.14% oxygen. Calculate the empirical formula for Nylon-6.

Note from Example 6.14 that once the percentages are converted to masses, this example is the same as earlier examples in which the masses were given directly.

 ## 6.8 Calculation of Molecular Formulas

Objective: *To learn to calculate the molecular formula of a compound, given its empirical formula and molar mass.*

If we know the composition of a compound in terms of the masses (or mass percentages) of the elements present, we can calculate the empirical formula but not the molecular formula. For reasons that will become clear as we consider Example 6.15, to obtain the molecular formula we must know the molar mass. In this section we will consider compounds where both the percent composition and the molar mass are known.

CHEMICAL IMPACT

Connection to Archaeology

Using Chemistry to Understand Lost Worlds

Archaeology involves the study of past civilizations by examining the material remains of lost cultures. Usually it relies on digging. James E. Myster of Hamline University in Minnesota, however, does much of his archaeology through chemistry. Myster analyzes the soil to find out where buildings once stood and what the purposes of the structures were. This approach works because certain types of activities leave telltale elements in the soil. For example, a high phosphorus content in a given patch of soil indicates that animals may have been kept in that area—animal dung has a high phosphate content. When Myster finds an area characterized by high calcium and phosphorus content, he concludes that animals may have been butchered and processed there. Animal flesh contains large amounts of phosphorus, and bones and teeth contain a great deal of calcium. On the other hand, areas used for gardening typically show a depletion of calcium, magnesium, nitrogen, phosphorus, and sulfur.

Using soil analysis, Myster can even map where buildings once stood even though no trace of them remains. Soil inside the former structures contains elemental evidence of the activities that took place there. For instance, the former locations of privies show high phosphate content, whereas the soil under smokehouses has high sodium content from the salt used for the preservation of meat. The outlines of former buildings are also indicated by the way that pollutants, such as cadmium, chromium, lead, and nickel are distributed in the soil. The presence of a building would prevent these elements, which were scattered by the wind during the early Industrial Revolution, from being deposited in the soil.

One of the best things about chemical archaeology is that it is nondestructive. The soil analysis does not require digging up the site. Coupled with classical methods, chemical archaeology can be very revealing.

6.8 Calculation of Molecular Formulas **183**

 Answer to Self-Check Exercise 6.10

Step 1 In 100.00 g of Nylon-6 the masses of elements present are 63.68 g C, 12.38 g N, 9.80 g H, and 14.14 g O.

Step 2 $63.68 \text{ g C} \times \dfrac{1 \text{ mol C}}{12.01 \text{ g C}}$
$= 5.302 \text{ mol C}$

$12.38 \text{ g N} \times \dfrac{1 \text{ mol N}}{14.01 \text{ g N}}$
$= 0.8837 \text{ mol N}$

$9.80 \text{ g H} \times \dfrac{1 \text{ mol H}}{1.008 \text{ g H}}$
$= 9.72 \text{ mol H}$

$14.14 \text{ g O} \times \dfrac{1 \text{ mol O}}{16.00 \text{ g O}}$
$= 0.8838 \text{ mol O}$

Step 3 $\dfrac{5.302 \text{ mol C}}{0.8836} = 6.000 \text{ mol C}$

$\dfrac{0.8837 \text{ mol N}}{0.8837} = 1.000 \text{ mol N}$

$\dfrac{9.72 \text{ mol H}}{0.8837} = 11.0 \text{ mol H}$

$\dfrac{0.8838 \text{ mol O}}{0.8837} = 1.000 \text{ mol O}$

The empirical formula for Nylon-6 is $C_6NH_{11}O$.

 ## Section 6.8

Themes
Patterns of Change, Scale and Structure

Skills
Applying concepts, calculating, making predictions

Laboratory
Experiment 24: Formula of a Hydrate, Traditional

TEACHING TIPS

• Students should understand that unless they are given the molar mass for a compound they can calculate only the empirical formula for the compound.

• Tell them that they must first calculate the empirical formula before they can determine the molecular formula for a compound. This idea leads to a discussion of how the molar mass of an empirical formula can be used.

 Integrating the CHEMICAL IMPACT

Using Chemistry to Understand Lost Worlds

"Using Chemistry to Understand Lost Worlds" emphasizes the effects of human activity on the environment. Humans leave chemical signatures as they pursue their daily activities. Modern examples are landfill areas, the chemical fertilizers and pesticides used on farmlands, and residual petroleum contamination from leaky fuel tanks at gasoline stations. You might have your students list some examples they can think of from their own experiences. Also, have them suggest what these types of evidence might say about our culture if they were discovered far in the future by archaeologists.

1. A compound containing carbon, hydrogen, and oxygen is found to be 40.00% carbon and 6.700% hydrogen by mass. The molar mass of this compound is between 115 g/mol and 125 g/mol. Determine the molecular formula for this compound. $C_4H_8O_4$

2. Caffeine is a compound containing carbon, hydrogen, nitrogen, and oxygen. The mass percent composition of caffeine is 49.47% carbon, 5.191% hydrogen, 28.86% nitrogen, and 16.48% oxygen. The molar mass of caffeine is approximately 194 g/mol. Determine the molecular formula for caffeine. $C_8H_{10}N_4O_2$

Example 6.15

Calculating Molecular Formulas

A white powder is analyzed and found to have an empirical formula of P_2O_5. The compound has a molar mass of 283.88 g. What is the compound's molecular formula?

Solution

To obtain the molecular formula, we must compare the empirical formula mass to the molar mass. The empirical formula mass for P_2O_5 is the mass of 1 mol of P_2O_5 units.

$$
\begin{aligned}
&\overbrace{}^{\text{Atomic mass of P}}\\
&2 \text{ mol P: } 2 \times 30.97 \text{ g} = 61.94 \text{ g}\\
&5 \text{ mol O: } 5 \times 16.00 \text{ g} = \underline{80.00 \text{ g}}\\
&\underbrace{}_{\text{Atomic mass of O}} \qquad\qquad 141.94 \text{ g} \quad \text{Mass of 1 mol of } P_2O_5 \text{ units}
\end{aligned}
$$

Recall that the molecular formula contains a whole number of empirical formula units. That is,

$$\text{Molecular formula} = (\text{empirical formula})_n$$

where n is a small whole number. Now, because

$$\text{Molecular formula} = n \times \text{empirical formula}$$

then

$$\text{Molar mass} = n \times \text{empirical formula mass}$$

Solving for n gives

$$n = \frac{\text{molar mass}}{\text{empirical formula mass}}$$

Thus, to determine the molecular formula, we first divide the molar mass by the empirical formula mass. This tells us how many empirical formula masses are present in one molar mass.

$$\frac{\text{Molar mass}}{\text{Empirical formula mass}} = \frac{283.88 \text{ g}}{141.94 \text{ g}} = 2$$

This result means that $n = 2$ for this compound, so the molecular formula consists of two empirical formula units, and the molecular formula is $(P_2O_5)_2$, or P_4O_{10}. The structure of this interesting compound is shown in **Figure 6.5**.

Figure 6.5

The structure of P_4O_{10} as a "ball-and-stick" model. This compound has a great affinity for water and is often used as a desiccant, or drying agent.

Answer to Self-Check Exercise 6.11

Step 1 First we convert the mass percents to mass in grams. In 100.0 g of the compound, there are 71.65 g of chlorine, 24.27 g of carbon, and 4.07 g of hydrogen.

Step 2 We use these masses to compute the moles of atoms present.

$$71.65 \text{ g Cl} \times \frac{1 \text{ mol Cl}}{35.45 \text{ g Cl}}$$
$$= 2.021 \text{ mol Cl}$$

$$24.27 \text{ g C} \times \frac{1 \text{ mol C}}{12.01 \text{ g C}}$$
$$= 2.021 \text{ mol C}$$

$$4.07 \text{ g H} \times \frac{1 \text{ mol H}}{1.008 \text{ g H}}$$
$$= 4.04 \text{ mol H}$$

✓ **Self-Check Exercise 6.11**

A compound used as an additive for gasoline to help prevent engine knock shows the following percentage composition:

71.65% Cl   24.27% C   4.07% H

The molar mass is known to be 98.96 g. Determine the empirical formula and the molecular formula for this compound.

It is important to realize that the molecular formula is always an integer multiple of the empirical formula. For example, the sugar glucose (see Figure 6.4) has the empirical formula CH_2O and the molecular formula $C_6H_{12}O_6$. In this case there are six empirical formula units in each glucose molecule:

$$(CH_2O)_6 = C_6H_{12}O_6$$

In general, we can represent the molecular formula in terms of the empirical formula as follows:

$$(Empirical\ formula)_n = molecular\ formula$$

CHEMISTRY

Molecular formula = (empirical formula)$_n$, where n is an integer.

where n is an integer. If $n = 1$, the molecular formula is the same as the empirical formula. For example, for carbon dioxide the empirical formula (CO_2) and the molecular formula (CO_2) are the same, so $n = 1$. On the other hand, for tetraphosphorus decoxide the empirical formula is P_2O_5 and the molecular formula is $P_4O_{10} = (P_2O_5)_2$. In this case $n = 2$.

Focus Questions

Sections 6.5–6.8

1. Explain how you would find the mass percent of each element in water.
2. Is the empirical formula for a compound ever the same as its molecular formula? Explain.
3. Why are the subscripts in a chemical formula whole numbers—for example, N_2O_5 instead of $NO_{2.5}$?
4. What critical piece of information must be known (or given in the problem) to determine the molecular formula for a compound from its empirical formula?

Focus Questions   **185**

You might want to challenge your best students to determine the molecular formula for a compound when the molar mass for the compound is not given. Give them the mass of a sample of the compound and the number of moles of the compound contained in the sample. The students can then put together information on determining the molar mass of a compound with the information they have learned in this section to find the molecular formula for the compound.

Answers to Focus Questions

1. To find the mass percent of each element in water you would first need to determine the moles of each element in the formula. This means multiplying the atomic mass for hydrogen by 2, as there are two atoms of hydrogen in the formula. This mass of hydrogen in one mole of water should then be divided by the molar mass of water to determine the mass fraction of hydrogen in water. This value can then be converted to a percentage by multiplying by 100%. The process could be repeated for oxygen (omitting the step of multiplying by 2, as there is only one mole of oxygen per mole of water). Alternatively, the percentage of oxygen could be obtained by subtracting the percentage of hydrogen from 100%.

2. The empirical formula for a compound is the same as the molecular formula whenever the empirical molar mass is the same as the compound's molecular molar mass.

3. Because only whole numbers of atoms combine to form compounds, we use whole numbers to express the empirical formula.

4. To determine the molecular formula from the empirical formula, the molar mass of the compound must be known.

Step 3 Dividing each mole value by 2.021 (the smallest number of moles present), we obtain the empirical formula $ClCH_2$.

To determine the molecular formula, we must compare the empirical formula mass to the molar mass. The empirical formula mass is 49.48.

Cl:	35.45
C:	12.01
2 H:	2 × (1.008)
$ClCH_2$:	49.48 = empirical formula mass

The molar mass is known to be 98.96. We know that

Molar mass = n × (empirical formula mass)

So we can obtain the value of n as follows:

$$\frac{Molar\ mass}{Empirical\ formula\ mass}$$

$$= \frac{98.96}{49.48} = 2$$

Molecular formula = $(ClCH_2)_2$

$$= Cl_2C_2H_4$$

This substance is composed of molecules with the formula $Cl_2C_2H_4$.

Decomposing Copper Oxide

Objectives
To determine the formula for an oxide of copper by using percent composition data

Skills
Interpreting data, drawing conclusions, calculating, making comparisons

Materials
Goggles
Apron
Test tube
Bunsen burner
Matches
Balance
Two-holed rubber stopper
Glass tubing
Rubber tubing
Ringstand
Test tube clamp for ringstand
Copper oxide powder

Preparation Hints
The rubber stopper must fit snugly in the test tube, and the rubber tubing must fit snugly over the glass tubes in the rubber stopper. Otherwise, the Bunsen burners will not light and gas will escape into the room.

Prelab Discussion
Students should tie back their hair and loose clothing whenever they work with a flame in the lab. Students will often deposit matches in the sink. Tell them to dispose of burned matches in the trashcan after they are cool.

Hot glass and cold glass look the same. To avoid burns, students should allow plenty of time for the test tube to cool.

Tell students to avoid getting silver nitrate on their person since it produces brown stains.

Procedure Hints
Make sure that students do not heat the rubber stopper and melt it to the test tube.

Disposal
The copper can be scraped from the test tubes. In some cases it may melt onto the test tubes. Dispose of these test tubes.

Safety
When working with chemicals wear safety goggles and lab aprons. Collect all copper from the students. Either dispose of it properly or save it for future use.

Post-Lab Discussion
Make sure students understand how they can use their lab data

Problem
How is copper metal formed from a copper oxide? What is the formula of the copper oxide used in this experiment?

Introduction
Metals react with oxygen in the air to form metallic oxides. The process of rusting, for example, involves the reaction of iron and oxygen. As you learned in Chapter 4, many metals can form more than one type of cation. For example, copper (Cu) can form Cu^+ ions or Cu^{2+} ions in ionic compounds. You will be given a copper oxide and will determine whether it is copper(I) oxide or copper(II) oxide.

In this lab you will heat copper oxide powder in the absence of oxygen to form copper metal. From the masses of the original copper oxide and the copper metal you obtain, you can calculate the percent by mass of copper in the original compound. By comparing your result to the percent by mass of copper in copper(I) oxide and copper(II) oxide, you can decide which compound was the starting material.

Prelab Assignment
1. Read the entire lab experiment before you begin.
2. Calculate the percent copper by mass in copper(I) oxide.
3. Calculate the percent copper by mass in copper(II) oxide.

Materials
Goggles
Apron
Test tube
Bunsen burner
Matches
Balance
Two-holed rubber stopper fitted with glass tubing
Test tube clamp for ring stand
Rubber tubing
Ring stand
Copper oxide powder

Safety
1. You will work with a flame in this lab. Tie back hair and loose clothing.
2. Do not drop matches into the sink. Dispose of burned matches in the trashcan after they are cool.

Procedure
1. Accurately determine the mass of your test tube.
2. Measure between 3.00 and 4.00 g of copper oxide powder and place it in the test tube.
3. Clamp the test tube to the ring stand so that the tube is slightly angled. Make sure that a thin coating of copper oxide appears on the test tube and that the copper oxide is away from the mouth of the test tube.
4. Assemble the apparatus as shown in the figure below. The gas should flow through the test tube and into the Bunsen burner.
5. Light the Bunsen burner.

Setup to heat copper oxide in the absence of air.

6. Use the hottest part of the flame to heat the copper oxide in the test tube. Move the Bunsen burner back and forth over the length of the test tube containing the copper oxide. Keep the flame away from the rubber stopper.
7. Continue heating until all of the copper oxide has reacted.
8. Allow the test tube and its contents to cool in the absence of oxygen (move the Bunsen burner from underneath the test tube).
9. Accurately measure the mass of the test tube and copper. Determine the mass of copper formed.

Cleaning Up
Clean up all materials and wash your hands thoroughly.

---

to differentiate between copper(I) oxide and copper(II) oxide.

Sample Data/Answers
Prelab Assignment
2. Copper(I) oxide is 88.8% copper by mass.
3. Copper(II) oxide is 79.9% copper by mass.

Data/Observations
1. 3.50 g
2. 2.82 g

Analysis and Conclusions
1. The copper oxide powder is black. The copper is reddish brown. When all of the material in the test tube is reddish brown, the reaction is complete.
2. 80.6%
3. The difference between the lab result (from question 2) and the mass percent of copper(I) oxide is 8.2%.

4. The difference between the lab result (from question 2) and the mass percent of copper(II) oxide is 0.7%.
5. Copper(II) oxide, CuO, was formed as the lab result for percent copper was closest to that compound.
6. The iron bar has a greater mass after it rusts because it forms an oxide of iron. Because oxygen has mass, the oxide of iron has more mass than the iron alone.

Data/Observations

1. What is the mass of copper oxide that reacted?
2. What is the mass of copper produced?

Analysis and Conclusions

1. How could you tell when the reaction was completed?
2. Calculate the percent copper by mass in your original copper oxide.
3. Compare your result from question 2 to the mass percent of copper in copper(I) oxide by finding the difference between the two. *Note:* You calculated the mass percent of copper in copper(I) oxide in the prelab assignment.

4. Compare your result from question 2 to the mass percent of copper in copper(II) oxide by finding the difference between the two. *Note:* You calculated the mass percent of copper in copper(II) oxide in the prelab assignment.
5. What is the formula of the copper oxide you reacted? Justify your answer.
6. Which would have a larger mass, an iron bar before or after it rusts? Explain your answer.

Something Extra

Why was the gas sent through the test tube? Could this lab be performed with a test tube open to the air? Explain your answer.

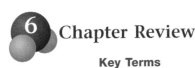

Chapter Review

Key Terms

atomic mass unit (6.2) molar mass (6.4)
average atomic mass (6.2) mass percent (6.5)
mole (6.3) empirical formula (6.6)
Avogadro's number (6.3) molecular formula (6.6)

Summary

1. We can count individual units by weighing if we know the average mass of the units. Thus, when we know the average mass of the atoms of an element as that element occurs in nature, we can calculate the number of atoms in any given sample of that element by weighing the sample.

2. A mole is a unit of measure equal to 6.022×10^{23}, which is called Avogadro's number. One mole of any substance contains 6.022×10^{23} units.

3. One mole of an element has a mass equal to the element's atomic mass expressed in grams. The molar mass of any compound is the mass (in grams) of 1 mol of the compound and is the sum of the masses of the component atoms.

4. Percent composition consists of the mass percent of each element in a compound:

Mass percent =
$$\frac{\text{mass of a given element in 1 mol of compound}}{\text{mass of 1 mol of compound}} \times 100\%$$

5. The empirical formula of a compound is the simplest whole-number ratio of the atoms present in the compound; it can be derived from the percent composition of the compound. The molecular formula is the exact formula of the molecules present; it is always an inte-

ger multiple of the empirical formula. The following diagram summarizes these different ways of expressing the same information.

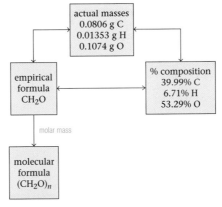

actual masses
0.0806 g C
0.01353 g H
0.1074 g O

empirical formula
CH_2O

% composition
39.99% C
6.71% H
53.29% O

molar mass

molecular formula
$(CH_2O)_n$

Questions and Problems*

All exercises with blue numbers have answers in the back of this book.

6.1 Counting by Weighing

Problems

1. Merchants usually sell small nuts, washers, and bolts by weight (like jelly beans!) rather than by individually counting the items. Suppose a particular type of washer weighs 0.110 g on the average. What would 100 such washers weigh? How many washers would there be in 100. g of washers?

---

*The element symbols and formulas are given in some problems but not in others to help you learn this necessary "vocabulary."

Chapter Review **187**

Chapter Review
Assign the students to work individually on the Chapter 6 Review Worksheet at the appropriate level (Basic, Standard, or Challenge). Answers are found in the *Teacher Resources*.

Assessment
Chapter 6 Test is found in the *Teacher Resources*, along with the answers for the test.

 Computerized Test Bank for Chapter 6

Answers to End of Chapter Problems

1. 11.0 g; 909 washers

2. 307 corks; 116 stoppers; 2640 g

3. The atomic mass unit (amu) is a unit of mass used to more simply describe relative masses on an atomic or molecular scale. One amu is equivalent to 1.66×10^{-24} g.

4. The average atomic mass is a weighted average including a contribution based on the mass of the individual isotopes of an element and their abundance in nature.

5. (a) 640. amu; (b) 2.319×10^6 amu; (c) 1642 amu; (d) 1.011×10^{25} amu; (e) 4.976×10^4 amu

6. (a) 1 B atom; (b) 10 S atoms; (c) 100 Au atoms; (d) 150 Xe atoms; (e) 133 Al atoms

7. 258 S atoms; 1.672×10^{26} amu

8. 1.205×10^{24}

9. Avogadro's number (6.022×10^{23})

10. 20.05 g Ca; 40.08 g

11. 177 g

12. 2.66×10^{-23} g

13. 0.50 mol O

14. (a) 0.133 mol Au; (b) 1.04 mol Ca; (c) 2.44×10^{-3} mol Ba; (d) 1.33×10^{-5} mol Pd; (e) 5.20×10^{-13} mol Ni; (f) 8.12 mol Fe; (g) 1.000 mol C

15. (a) 112 g Fe; (b) 30.6 g Ni; (c) 0.240 g Pt; (d) 1.50×10^4 g Pb; (e) 0.0248 g Mg; (f) 1.31×10^5 g Al; (g) 1468 g Li; (h) 3.95×10^{-5} g Na

16. (a) 1.05×10^{19} Co atoms; (b) 6.20×10^{20} Co atoms; (c) 0.0467 mol Co; (d) 0.00995 mol Co; (e) 249 g Co; (f) 2.55×10^{24} Co atoms; (g) 4.32×10^{22} Co atoms

17. molar mass

18. adding (summing)

19. (a) 82.98 g; (b) 76.15 g; (c) 97.94 g; (d) 46.07 g; (e) 82.09 g; (f) 98.09 g

20. (a) 336.2 g; (b) 120.38 g; (c) 278.1 g; (d) 187.57 g; (e) 260.5 g; (f) 94.11 g

21. (a) 6.14×10^{-4} mol SO_3; (b) 3.11×10^5 mol PbO_2; (c) 0.495 mol $CHCl_3$; (d) 2.45×10^{-8} mol $C_2H_3Cl_3$; (e) 0.167 mol LiOH

22. (a) 3.55×10^{-5} mol; (b) 5.26 mol; (c) 2700 mol; (d) 0.0697 mol; (e) 467 mol

23. (a) 612 g AlI_3; (b) 0.149 g C_6H_6; (c) 721 g $C_6H_{12}O_6$; (d) 2.10×10^7 g C_2H_5OH; (e) 373 g $Ca(NO_3)_2$

24. (a) 0.0559 g CO_2; (b) 4.96×10^5 g NCl_3; (c) 0.361 g NH_4NO_3; (d) 324 g H_2O; (e) 1.00×10^4 g $CuSO_4$

25. (a) 3.84×10^{24} molecules CO; (b) 1.37×10^{23} molecules CO; (c) 8.76×10^{16} molecules H_2O; (d) 1.58×10^{18} molecules H_2O; (e) 4.03×10^{22} molecules C_6H_6

26. (a) 0.0141 mol S; (b) 0.0159 mol S; (c) 0.0258 mol S; (d) 0.0254 mol S

2. A particular small laboratory cork weighs 1.63 g, whereas a rubber lab stopper of the same size weighs 4.31 g. How many corks would there be in 500. g of such corks? How many rubber stoppers would there be in 500. g of similar stoppers? How many grams of rubber stoppers would be needed to contain the same number of stoppers as there are corks in 1.00 kg of corks?

6.2 Atomic Masses: Counting Atoms by Weighing

Questions

3. Define the *amu*. What is one amu equivalent to in grams?

4. Why do we use the *average* atomic mass of the elements when performing calculations?

Problems

5. Using average atomic masses for each of the following elements (see the table inside the front cover of this book), calculate the mass, in amu, of each of the following samples.
   a. 635 atoms of hydrogen
   b. 1.261×10^4 atoms of tungsten
   c. 42 atoms of potassium
   d. 7.213×10^{23} atoms of nitrogen
   e. 891 atoms of iron

6. Using average atomic masses for each of the following elements (see the table inside the front cover of this book), calculate the number of atoms present in each of the following samples.
   a. 10.81 amu of boron
   b. 320.7 amu of sulfur
   c. 19,697 amu of gold
   d. 19,695 amu of xenon
   e. 3588.3 amu of aluminum

7. If an average atom of sulfur weighs 32.07 amu, how many sulfur atoms are contained in a sample with mass 8274 amu? What is the mass of 5.213×10^{24} sulfur atoms?

6.3 The Mole

Questions

8. In 24.02 g of carbon, there are _____ carbon atoms.

9. A sample equal to the atomic mass of an element in grams contains _____ atoms.

Problems

10. What mass of calcium metal contains the same number of atoms as 12.16 g of magnesium? What mass of calcium metal contains the same number of atoms as 24.31 g of magnesium?

11. What mass of cobalt contains the same number of atoms as 57.0 g of fluorine?

12. Calculate the average mass in grams of 1 atom of oxygen.

13. Which weighs more, 0.50 mol of oxygen atoms or 4 mol of hydrogen atoms?

14. Using the average atomic masses given inside the front cover of the text, calculate the number of *moles* of each element in samples with the following masses.
   a. 26.2 g of gold
   b. 41.5 g of calcium
   c. 335 mg of barium
   d. 1.42×10^{-3} g of palladium
   e. 3.05×10^{-5} μg of nickel
   f. 1.00 lb of iron
   g. 12.01 g of carbon

15. Using the average atomic masses given inside the front cover of the text, calculate the *mass in grams* of each of the following samples.
   a. 2.00 mol of iron
   b. 0.521 mol of nickel
   c. 1.23×10^{-3} mol of platinum
   d. 72.5 mol of lead
   e. 0.00102 mol of magnesium
   f. 4.87×10^3 mol of aluminum
   g. 211.5 mol of lithium
   h. 1.72×10^{-6} mol of sodium

16. Using the average atomic masses given inside the front cover of the text, calculate the indicated quantities.
   a. the number of cobalt atoms in 0.00103 g of cobalt
   b. the number of cobalt atoms in 0.00103 mol of cobalt
   c. the number of moles of cobalt in 2.75 g of cobalt
   d. the number of moles of cobalt represented by 5.99×10^{21} cobalt atoms
   e. the mass of 4.23 mol of cobalt
   f. the number of cobalt atoms in 4.23 mol of cobalt
   g. the number of cobalt atoms in 4.23 g of cobalt

6.4 Molar Mass

Questions

17. The _____ of a substance is the mass (in grams) of 1 mol of the substance.

18. The molar mass of a substance can be obtained by _____ the atomic weights of the component atoms.

Problems

19. Calculate the molar mass for each of the following substances.
   a. sodium nitride, Na_3N
   b. carbon disulfide, CS_2
   c. ammonium bromide, NH_4Br
   d. ethyl alcohol, C_2H_5OH
   e. sulfurous acid, H_2SO_3
   f. sulfuric acid, H_2SO_4

27. (a) 32.37% Na, 22.58% S, 45.05% O; (b) 36.48% Na, 25.44% S, 38.08% O; (c) 58.91% Na, 41.09% S; (d) 29.08% Na, 40.56% S, 30.36% O; (e) 55.26% K, 14.59% P, 30.15% O; (f) 44.90% K, 0.5787% H, 17.78% P, 36.74% O; (g) 28.73% K, 1.481% H, 22.76% P, 47.03% O; (h) 79.10% K, 20.88% P

28. (a) 28.45% Cu; (b) 44.29% Cu; (c) 44.06% Fe; (d) 34.43% Fe; (e) 18.84% Co; (f) 13.41% Co; (g) 88.12% Sn; (h) 78.77% Sn

29. (a) 49.32% C; (b) 35.00% N; (c) 49.47% C; (d) 52.56% Cl; (e) 71.92% C; (f) 39.99% C; (g) 85.03% C; (h) 52.14% C

30. (a) 33.73% NH_4^+; (b) 39.81% Cu^{2+}; (c) 64.94% Au^{3+}; (d) 63.51% Ag^+

31. The mass composition and the molar mass of a compound must be known.

32. The empirical formula represents the smallest whole-number ratio of the elements present in a compound. The molecular formula indicates the actual number of atoms of each element found in a molecule of the substance.

33. (a) NaO; (b) $C_4H_3O_2$; (c) $C_{12}H_{12}N_2O_3$; (d) C_2H_3Cl

20. Calculate the molar mass for each of the following substances.
  a. barium perchlorate
  b. magnesium sulfate
  c. lead(II) chloride
  d. copper(II) nitrate
  e. tin(IV) chloride
  f. phenol, C_6H_6O

21. Calculate the number of *moles* of the indicated substance in each of the following samples.
  a. 49.2 mg of sulfur trioxide
  b. 7.44×10^4 kg of lead(IV) oxide
  c. 59.1 g of chloroform, $CHCl_3$
  d. 3.27 μg of trichloroethane, $C_2H_3Cl_3$
  e. 4.01 g of lithium hydroxide

22. Calculate the number of *moles* of the indicated substance in each of the following samples.
  a. 4.26×10^{-3} g of sodium dihydrogen phosphate
  b. 521 g of copper(I) chloride
  c. 151 kg of iron
  d. 8.76 g of strontium fluoride
  e. 1.26×10^4 g of aluminum

23. Calculate the *mass in grams* of each of the following samples.
  a. 1.50 mol of aluminum iodide
  b. 1.91×10^{-3} mol of benzene, C_6H_6
  c. 4.00 mol of glucose, $C_6H_{12}O_6$
  d. 4.56×10^5 mol of ethanol, C_2H_5OH
  e. 2.27 mol of calcium nitrate

24. Calculate the *mass in grams* of each of the following samples.
  a. 1.27×10^{-3} mol of carbon dioxide
  b. 4.12×10^3 mol of nitrogen trichloride
  c. 0.00451 mol of ammonium nitrate
  d. 18.0 mol of water
  e. 62.7 mol of copper(II) sulfate

25. Calculate the number of *molecules* present in each of the following samples.
  a. 6.37 mol of carbon monoxide
  b. 6.37 g of carbon monoxide
  c. 2.62×10^{-6} g of water
  d. 2.62×10^{-6} mol of water
  e. 5.23 g of benzene, C_6H_6

26. Calculate the number of *moles* of sulfur atoms present in each of the following samples.
  a. 2.01 g of sodium sulfate
  b. 2.01 g of sodium sulfite
  c. 2.01 g of sodium sulfide
  d. 2.01 g of sodium thiosulfate, $Na_2S_2O_3$

6.5 Percent Composition of Compounds

Problems

27. Calculate the percent by mass of each element in the following compounds.
  a. sodium sulfate
  b. sodium sulfite
  c. sodium sulfide
  d. sodium thiosulfate, $Na_2S_2O_3$
  e. potassium phosphate
  f. potassium hydrogen phosphate
  g. potassium dihydrogen phosphate
  h. potassium phosphide

28. Calculate the percent by mass of the element listed *first* in the formulas for each of the following compounds.
  a. copper(II) bromide, $CuBr_2$
  b. copper(I) bromide, $CuBr$
  c. iron(II) chloride, $FeCl_2$
  d. iron(III) chloride, $FeCl_3$
  e. cobalt(II) iodide, CoI_2
  f. cobalt(III) iodide, CoI_3
  g. tin(II) oxide, SnO
  h. tin(IV) oxide, SnO_2

29. Calculate the percent by mass of the element listed *first* in the formulas for each of the following compounds.
  a. adipic acid, $C_6H_{10}O_4$
  b. ammonium nitrate, NH_4NO_3
  c. caffeine, $C_8H_{10}N_4O_2$
  d. chlorine dioxide, ClO_2
  e. cyclohexanol, $C_6H_{11}OH$
  f. dextrose, $C_6H_{12}O_6$
  g. eicosane, $C_{20}H_{42}$
  h. ethanol, C_2H_5OH

30. For each of the following ionic substances, calculate the *percentage* of the overall molar mass of the compound that is represented by the *positive ions* the compound contains.
  a. ammonium chloride
  b. copper(II) sulfate
  c. gold(III) chloride
  d. silver nitrate

6.6 Formulas of Compounds

Questions

31. What experimental evidence about a new compound must be known before its formula can be determined?

32. What does the *empirical* formula of a compound represent? How does the *molecular* formula differ from the empirical formula?

33. Give the empirical formula that corresponds to each of the following molecular formulas.
  a. sodium peroxide, Na_2O_2
  b. terephthalic acid, $C_8H_6O_4$
  c. phenobarbital, $C_{12}H_{12}N_2O_3$
  d. 1,4-dichloro-2-butene, $C_4H_6Cl_2$

34. Which of the following pairs of compounds have the same *empirical* formula?
  a. acetylene, C_2H_2, and benzene, C_6H_6
  b. ethane, C_2H_6, and butane, C_4H_{10}
  c. nitrogen dioxide, NO_2, and dinitrogen tetroxide, N_2O_4
  d. diphenyl ether, $C_{12}H_{10}O$, and phenol, C_6H_5OH

---

51. (1) c; (2) e; (3) j; (4) h; (5) b; (6) d; (7) a; (8) g; (9) i; (10) f

52. 5.00 g Al, 0.185 mol, 1.12×10^{23} atoms; 0.140 g Fe, 0.00250 mol, 1.51×10^{21} atoms; 270 g Cu, 4.3 mol, 2.6×10^{24} atoms; 0.00250 g Mg, 1.30×10^{-4} mol, 6.19×10^{19} atoms; 0.062 g Na, 2.7×10^{-3} mol, 1.6×10^{21} atoms; 3.95×10^{-18} g U, 1.66×10^{-20} mol, 1.00×10^4 atoms

53. 4.24 g C_6H_6, 0.0543 mol, 3.27×10^{22} molecules, 3.92×10^{23} atoms; 4.04 g H_2O, 0.224 mol, 1.35×10^{23} molecules, 4.05×10^{23} atoms; 1.98 g CO_2, 0.0450 mol, 2.71×10^{22} molecules, 8.13×10^{22} atoms; 45.9 g HCl, 1.26 mol, 7.59×10^{23} molecules, 1.52×10^{24} atoms; 126 g H_2O, 6.99 mol, 4.21×10^{24} molecules, 1.26×10^{25} atoms; 0.297 g CH_3OH, 0.00927 mol, 5.58×10^{21} molecules, 3.35×10^{22} atoms

54. Mg_3N_2; MgO

55. Cu_2O, CuO

56. (1) g; (2) c; (3) b; (4) a; (5) j; (6) i; (7) f; (8) h; (9) e; (10) d

57. 2.12 g Fe

58. 2.36 g Co

59. $CuSH_{10}O_9$ (usually written as $CuSO_4 \cdot 5H_2O$)

60. $C_3H_7N_2O$

61. HgO

62. $BaCl_2$

63. HNO_3

64. carbon (C)

65. empirical formula $C_4H_8O_4S$; molecular formula $C_4H_8O_4S$

---

34. (a) these have the same empirical formulas; (b) these do not have the same empirical formulas; (c) these have the same empirical formulas; (d) these do not have the same empirical formulas

35. C_3H_2OCl

36. CaO

37. $BaSO_4$

38. $AlCl_3$

39. Co_2S_3

40. $CaCl_2$

41. CuO

42. CuN_2O_6 [$Cu(NO_3)_2$]

43. Na_3N; NaN_3

44. The empirical formula represents the smallest whole-number relationship between the number and types of atoms in a compound. The molecular formula represents the actual number of atoms of each type in a true molecule of the substance. Water is an example of a compound that has the same empirical and molecular formulas.

45. molar mass

46. $C_3H_6O_3$

47. C_6H_{12}

48. $C_6H_{24}O_6$

49. empirical formula C_2H_2ON; molecular formula $C_6H_6O_3N_3$

50. empirical formula C_3H_3O; molecular formula $C_6H_6O_2$

6.7 Calculation of Empirical Formulas

Problems

35. A new compound has been prepared. A 0.4791-g sample was analyzed and was found to contain the following masses of elements: carbon, 0.1929 g; hydrogen, 0.01079 g; oxygen, 0.08566 g; chlorine, 0.1898 g. Determine the empirical formula of the new compound.

36. In an experiment, a 2.514-g sample of calcium was heated in a stream of pure oxygen, and was found to increase in mass by 1.004 g. Calculate the empirical formula of calcium oxide.

37. A compound has the following percentages by mass: barium, 58.84%; sulfur, 13.74%; oxygen, 27.43%. Determine the empirical formula of the compound.

38. If a 1.271-g sample of aluminum metal is heated in a chlorine gas atmosphere, the mass of aluminum chloride produced is 6.280 g. Calculate the empirical formula of aluminum chloride.

39. If cobalt metal is mixed with excess sulfur and heated strongly, a sulfide is produced that contains 55.06% cobalt by mass. Calculate the empirical formula of the sulfide.

40. If 2.461 g of metallic calcium is heated in a stream of chlorine gas, 4.353 g of Cl_2 is absorbed in forming the metal chloride. Calculate the empirical formula of calcium chloride.

41. If 10.00 g of copper metal is heated strongly in the air, the sample gains 2.52 g of oxygen in forming an oxide. Determine the empirical formula of this oxide.

42. A compound has the following percentage composition by mass: copper, 33.88%; nitrogen, 14.94%; oxygen, 51.18%. Determine the empirical formula of the compound.

43. Sodium and nitrogen form two binary compounds. The percentages of the elements in these compounds are:

  Compound 1:   83.12% Na; 16.88% N

  Compound 2:   35.36% Na; 64.64% N

Calculate the empirical formula of each of the compounds.

6.8 Calculation of Molecular Formulas

Questions

44. How does the molecular formula of a compound differ from the empirical formula? Can a compound's empirical and molecular formulas be the same? Explain.

45. What information do we need to determine the molecular formula of a compound if we know only the empirical formula?

Problems

46. A compound with the empirical formula CH_2O was found to have a molar mass between 89 and 91 g. What is the molecular formula of the compound?

47. A compound with the empirical formula CH_2 was found to have a molar mass of approximately 84 g. What is the molecular formula of the compound?

48. A compound with the empirical formula CH_4O was found in a subsequent experiment to have a molar mass of approximately 192 g. What is the molecular formula of the compound?

49. A compound having an approximate molar mass of 165–170 g has the following percentage composition by mass: carbon, 42.87%; hydrogen, 3.598%; oxygen, 28.55%; nitrogen, 25.00%. Determine the empirical and molecular formulas of the compound.

50. A compound consists of 65.45% C, 5.492% H, and 29.06% O on a mass basis and has a molar mass of approximately 110. Determine the molecular formula of the compound.

Critical Thinking

51. Use the periodic table inside the back cover of this text to determine the atomic mass (per mole) or molar mass of each of the substances in column 1, and find that mass in column 2.

Column 1	Column 2
(1) molybdenum	(a) 33.99 g
(2) lanthanum	(b) 79.9 g
(3) carbon tetrabromide	(c) 95.94 g
(4) mercury(II) oxide	(d) 125.84 g
(5) titanium(IV) oxide	(e) 138.9 g
(6) manganese(II) chloride	(f) 143.1 g
(7) phosphine, PH_3	(g) 156.7 g
(8) tin(II) fluoride	(h) 216.6 g
(9) lead(II) sulfide	(i) 239.3 g
(10) copper(I) oxide	(j) 331.6 g

52. Complete the following table.

Mass of Sample	Moles of Sample	Atoms in Sample
5.00 g Al	———	———
———	0.00250 mol Fe	———
———	———	2.6×10^{24} atoms Cu
0.00250 g Mg	———	———
———	2.7×10^{-3} mol Na	———
———	———	1.00×10^4 atoms U

53. Complete the following table.

Mass of Sample	Moles of Sample	Molecules in Sample	Atoms in Sample
4.24 g C_6H_6	———	———	———
———	0.224 mol H_2O	———	
———	———	2.71×10^{22} molecules CO_2	———
———	1.26 mol HCl	———	
———	———	4.21×10^{24} molecules H_2O	———
0.297 g CH_3OH	———	———	———

54. A binary compound of magnesium and nitrogen is analyzed, and 1.2791 g of the compound is found to contain 0.9240 g of magnesium. When a second sample of this compound is treated with water and heated, the nitrogen is driven off as ammonia, leaving a compound that contains 60.31% magnesium and 39.69% oxygen by mass. Calculate the empirical formulas of the two magnesium compounds.

55. When a 2.118-g sample of copper is heated in an atmosphere in which the amount of oxygen present is restricted, the sample gains 0.2666 g of oxygen in forming a reddish-brown oxide. However, when 2.118 g of copper is heated in a stream of pure oxygen, the sample gains 0.5332 g of oxygen. Calculate the empirical formulas of the two oxides of copper.

56. Find the item in column 2 that best explains or completes the statement or question in column 1.

Column 1

(1) 1 amu

(2) 1008 amu

(3) mass of the "average" atom of an element

(4) number of carbon atoms in 12.01 g of carbon

(5) 6.022×10^{23} molecules

(6) total mass of all atoms in 1 mol of a compound

(7) smallest whole-number ratio of atoms present in a molecule

(8) formula showing the actual number of atoms present in a molecule

(9) product formed when any carbon-containing compound is burned in O_2

(10) have the same empirical formulas, but different molecular formulas

Column 2

(a) 6.022×10^{23}

(b) atomic mass

(c) mass of 1000 hydrogen atoms

(d) benzene, C_6H_6, and acetylene, C_2H_2

(e) carbon dioxide

(f) empirical formula

(g) 1.66×10^{-24} g

(h) molecular formula

(i) molar mass

(j) 1 mol

57. Calculate the number of grams of iron that contain the same number of atoms as 2.24 g of cobalt.

58. Calculate the number of grams of cobalt that contain the same number of atoms as 2.24 g of iron.

59. A strikingly beautiful copper compound with the common name "blue vitriol" has the following elemental composition: 25.45% Cu, 12.84% S, 4.036% H, 57.67% O. Determine the empirical formula of the compound.

60. A 0.7221-g sample of a new compound has been analyzed and found to contain the following masses of elements: carbon, 0.2990 g; hydrogen, 0.05849 g; nitrogen, 0.2318 g; oxygen, 0.1328 g. Calculate the empirical formula of the compound.

61. When 4.01 g of mercury is strongly heated in air, the resulting oxide weighs 4.33 g. Calculate the empirical formula of the oxide.

62. When barium metal is heated in chlorine gas, a binary compound forms that consists of 65.95% Ba and 34.05% Cl by mass. Calculate the empirical formula of the compound.

63. A particular compound in the chemistry laboratory is found to contain 7.2×10^{24} atoms of oxygen, 56.0 g of nitrogen, and 4.0 mol of hydrogen. What is its empirical formula?

64. The compound A_2O is 63.7% A (a mystery element) and 36.3% oxygen. What is the identity of element A?

65. A molecule of an organic compound has twice as many hydrogen atoms as carbon atoms, the same number of oxygen atoms as carbon atoms, and one-eighth as many sulfur atoms as hydrogen atoms. The molar mass of the compound is 152 g/mol. What are the empirical and molecular formulas for this compound?

7 Chemical Reactions: An Introduction

	Section	Text Features & Components	Labs, Demonstrations & Activities
Teaching Segment 7A **3 blocks** **pp. 193–207**	7.1 Evidence for a ② Chemical Reaction	**LP** Lesson Plans (Sec 7.1–7.3) **SE** Chemical Impact: Unexpected Reactions! *p. 194*	**TE** Mini Demo *p. 194* **LM** Experiment 25–26 Lab Manual Report Sheets Teacher's Lab Guide
	7.2 Chemical Equations ●	**SE** Celebrity Chemical: Aspirin *p. 198*	**TE** Teaching Support: Demonstration *pp. 195–196*
	7.3 Balancing Chemical ● Equations ◑	**TE** Teaching Tips *p. 201* **SE** Chemical Impact: The Beetle That Shoots Straight *p. 202*	**TE** Teaching Support: Demonstration *p. 200* **SE** Chemistry in Action: Claymation Equations *p. 204* **LM** Experiment 27–28 Lab Manual Report Sheets Teacher's Lab Guide

Key

- **SE** Student Edition
- **TE** Teacher Edition
- **RP** Teacher Resource Package
- **LM** Lab Materials
- **LP** Lesson Plans
- **AR** Additional Resources
- 🔁 Florida Specific

Technology and Media

 Transparencies
Table 7.1
Figure 7.4

PowerPoint Slides

 Video Reaction of Copper with Nitric Acid
Chemistry in Motion
(3) Rxn of Metals with Acids • (4) Zinc and Iodine • (10) Hydrogen Soap Bubbles and Balloons • (11)Thermite Reaction • (22) Ammonium Dichromate Volcano • (28) Rxn of Nickel • (32) Barking Dogs

 eEdition CD-ROM
Easy Planner CD-ROM
English Summaries CD
Spanish Summaries CD

Web Site classzone.com
McDougal Littell Test Generator

Chapter Planning Guide

All Learners

- **TE** Active Learning *p. 193*
- **Video** Video: Reaction of Copper with Nitric Acid *p. 193*
- **Transparency** Transparency: Table 7.1 *p. 194*
- **Chemistry in Motion** Chemistry in Motion (3), (4), (10), (11), (22), (28), (32)
- **AR** Less Proficient Learners *p. 13*

- **TE** Teaching Tips *p. 195*
- **Chemistry in Motion** Chemistry in Motion, (10) *p. 196*
- **Transparency** Transparency: Figure 7.4 *p. 196*
- **AR** Less Proficient Learners *p. 13*

- **TE** Teaching Tips *p. 200*
- **Chemistry in Motion** Chemistry in Motion, (10) *p. 201*
- **RP** Team Learning Worksheets (Sec 7.1–7.3) *pp. 31–32*
- **AR** Less Proficient Learners *p. 13*

Review & Assessment

- **SE** What if . . . *p. 195*
- **SE** Questions and Problems *p. 209*

- **TE** Additional Examples *p. 198*
- **SE** Self Check *p. 199*
- **SE** Key Terms *p. 209*
- **SE** Questions and Problems *pp. 209–210*

- **SE** What if . . . *p. 201*
- **TE** Additional Examples *pp. 204–206*
- **SE** What if . . . *p. 205*
- **SE** Self Check *pp. 206–207*
- **SE** Focus Questions (Sec 7.1–7.3) *p. 207*
- **SE** Key Terms *p. 209*
- **SE** Questions and Problems *p. 210*

Standards

- **TE** **NSES** UCP1, UCP3, A1, A2, B3, C6, E1, E2, F1, F5, G3
- **SSS** SC.H.1.4.1, SC.H.1.4.7, SC.A.1.4.3, SC.B.1.4.2, SC.H.3.4.2, SC.H.3.4.6

Chapter Materials

- **TE** Reading Strategy
- **AR** English/Spanish Summaries *p. 10*
- **AR** Challenge Projects/Problems *pp. 12–13*
- **AR** Less Proficient Students *p. 13*
- **Audio** English Summary Audio
- **Audio** Spanish Summary Audio
- **RP** Chapter Review Worksheets (Basic, Review, Challenge)

- **SE** Chapter Summary *p. 209*
- **SE** Critical Thinking *p. 211*
- **RP** Solutions Guide
- **RP** Chapter Tests
- **RP** Test Bank
- McDougal Littell Test Generator
- **AR** Standardized Test Practice
- **FCAT Test 4**

7 Integrating Reading Strategies and Chemistry Concepts

Chapter 7: Reading Chemical Equations

Knowing how to read chemical equations may improve the students' understanding of previously learned concepts and aid in their comprehension of the material to come. Explain that the concepts involving elements, naming substances and ions, and writing chemical formulas will be expanded on in this chapter. Encourage the students to read the chapter summaries in Chapters 3 and 4 before they read Section 7.1.

Section 7.1 introduces the concept of chemical reactions, which students should relate to easily because of the real-world examples. Section 7.2, however, is the students' first exposure to how a chemical reaction is represented and they may initially be overwhelmed with the symbols and notation. Help the students understand that chemical equations are used to represent chemical reactions, just as symbols and formulas denote elements and compounds.

Learning the Key Terms

As you proceed through the chapter, encourage the students to write definitions of the vocabulary in their own words. Do not be concerned if the students' lists are not indicative of the definitions in the glossary. This strategy of writing their own definitions will help the students solidify the concepts. The key terms in this chapter are: reactant, product, coefficient, ratio, chemical reaction, chemical equation, unbalanced chemical equation, and balanced chemical equation.

Sample student definitions:

- products: the stuff to the right of the arrow, OR the things that are produced in the chemical reaction

- coefficient: the number in front of each component in the reaction

Misconception Alert: Differentiate the meaning of the words "product" and "coefficient" in this course versus their meanings in a mathematics course.

Interpreting Reaction Symbols and Notation

Guide the students to create a table in their notebooks titled "Reaction Symbols and Notation." Allow time for the students to fill in the table with the meanings for each symbol introduced in this chapter. Tell the students that they will be adding to this list as the course progresses. Check periodically—for instance, after Chapters 10, 17, and 20—to assess whether the students are keeping up with this strategy. By the end of the course, the students' tables should resemble the table shown here.

REACTION SYMBOLS AND NOTATION		
Symbol or Notation	**Represents**	**Chapter**
$\rightarrow$	yields, or produces	7
(s), (l), (g), (aq)	solid, liquid, gas, or aqueous solution	7
$+$	plus, added to, and	7
H_2O	dissolved in water	8
ΔH	enthalpy change	10
$\rightleftharpoons$	reversible reaction	16
catalyst	catalyst is present	17
hv	ultraviolet light is needed	20

Reading Unbalanced Equations

Direct the students to the unbalanced equation at the top of page 196. Read aloud various ways in which the equation can be read in word form.

Methane	Oxygen	Carbon dioxide	Water

$$CH_4 + O_2 \rightarrow CO_2 + H_2O$$

Reactants   Products

- Methane plus oxygen yields carbon dioxide plus water.
- Methane reacting with oxygen produces carbon dioxide and water.
- C H four plus O two yields C O two plus H two O.
- When you react methane and oxygen, the result is carbon dioxide and water.

Remind the students that the subscript written to the right of an element symbol in a formula represents the number of each type of atom. Point out that when only one atom is present, the subscript 1 is not written.

Pair students and give them the following equations to read. Have the students alternate between one partner reading the equation in word form and the other partner circling any part of the equation the reader does not interpret correctly.

- $NH_3(g) + HCl(g) \rightarrow NH_4Cl(s)$
- $HNO_3(l) \rightarrow NO_2(g) + H_2O(l) + O_2(g)$
- $Fe(s) + O_2(g) \rightarrow FeO(s)$

Reading Balanced Equations

$$CH_4 + 2O_2 \rightarrow CO_2 + 2H_2O$$

Direct the students to the balanced equation at the bottom of page 196. Point out the coefficients for each molecule. Explain that this value represents the number of molecules present in the reaction for atoms to be conserved. Tell the students that a coefficient of 1 is not written but is implied. Explain that when balancing an equation, the subscripts never change, only the coefficients change.

Read the equation aloud in word form, and compare and contrast the difference between reading an unbalanced equation and reading a balanced equation.

Translating Words to Equations

Direct the students to Example 7.1 on pages 198–199. Read aloud each reaction and then have the students create a list of key words and their meanings. Point out:

- "to form," "yields," "to produce," "makes," "generates," are represented by the arrow, $\rightarrow$
- "reacts with" is represented by the plus sign, +

Encourage the students to do the following for each reaction: write out each reaction as given, underline each key word in the sentence, and then correlate it to a symbol.

Solid mercury (II) oxide decomposes to produce liquid mercury metal and gaseous oxygen.

$$HgO(s) \qquad \rightarrow \qquad Hg(l) \qquad + \qquad O_2(g)$$

Assess the students' ability to translate words into symbols by assigning Focus Question #2 for Sections 7.1–7.3 on page 207.

Chapter 7

Overview

In this Chapter our goals are for the students to:

- Learn the signals that show a chemical reaction has occurred

- Learn to identify the characteristics of a chemical reaction and the information given by a chemical reaction

- Learn to write a balanced equation for a chemical reaction

7 Chemical Reactions: An Introduction

Aluminum reacting with bromine.

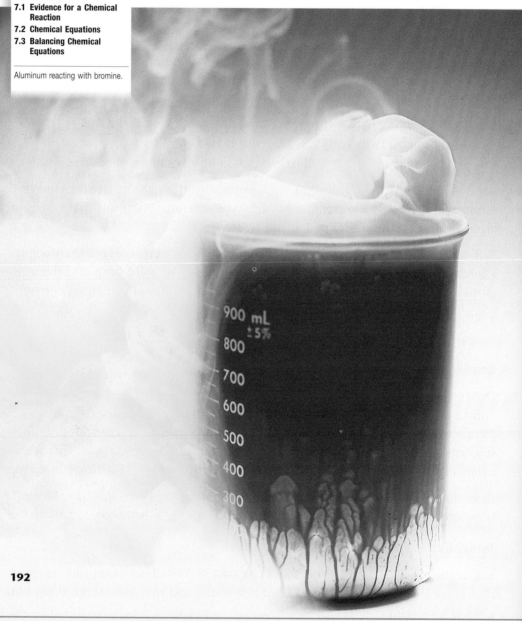

C hemistry is about change. Grass grows. Steel rusts. Hair is bleached, dyed, "permed," or straightened. Natural gas burns to heat houses. Nylon is produced for jackets, swimsuits, and pantyhose. Water is decomposed to hydrogen and oxygen gas by an electric current. The bombardier beetle concocts a toxic spray to shoot at its enemies (see "Chemical Impact" on page 202).

These are just a few examples of chemical changes that affect each of us. Chemical reactions are the heart and soul of chemistry, and in this chapter we will discuss the fundamental ideas about chemical reactions.

Nylon jackets are sturdy and dry quickly. These characteristics make them ideal for athletic wear.

Production of plastic film for use in containers such as soft drink bottles (left). Nylon being drawn from the boundary between two solutions containing different reactants (right).

7.1 Evidence for a Chemical Reaction

Objective: *To learn the signals that show a chemical reaction has occurred.*

H ow do we know when a chemical change (a reaction) has occurred? That is, what are the clues that a chemical change has taken place? A glance back at the processes in the introduction suggests that *chemical reactions often give a visual signal*. Steel changes from a smooth, shiny material to a reddish-brown, flaky substance when it rusts. Hair changes color when it

7.1   Evidence for a Chemical Reaction   **193**

Section 7.1

Themes
Organization, Patterns of Change

Skills
Observing, interpreting data

Student Preparation
Assign the students to read Sections 7.1 to 7.3 and to answer the Focus Questions at the end of Section 7.3 before coming to class.

Active Learning
After introducing the material in Sections 7.1 to 7.3 in class, place the students in groups and have them work together on Sections 7.1–7.3: Team Learning Worksheet. Answers and/or discussion of these questions are located in the *Teacher Resources*.

USING TECHNOLOGY

Animation and Video
Video, Reaction of Copper with Nitric Acid

Laboratory
 Experiment 25: Recognizing Chemical Reactions, Microscale

Laboratory
Experiment 26: Examples of Reactions, In Text

Figure 7.1
Bubbles of hydrogen and oxygen gas form when an electric current is used to decompose water.

is bleached. Solid nylon is formed when two particular liquid solutions are brought into contact. A blue flame appears when natural gas reacts with oxygen. Chemical reactions, then, often give *visual* clues: a color changes, a solid forms, bubbles are produced (see **Figure 7.1**), a flame occurs, and so on. However, reactions are not always visible. Sometimes the only signal that a reaction is occurring is a change in temperature as heat is produced or absorbed (see **Figure 7.2**).

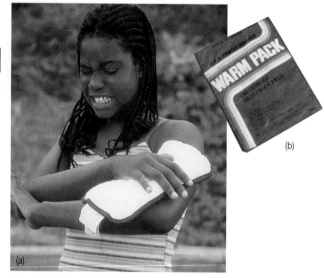

TABLE 7.1

Some Clues That a Chemical Reaction Has Occurred

1. The color changes.
2. A solid forms.
3. Bubbles form.
4. Heat and/or a flame is produced, or heat is absorbed.

Figure 7.2
(a) An injured girl using a cold pack to help prevent swelling. The pack is activated by breaking an ampule; this action initiates a chemical reaction that absorbs heat rapidly, lowering the temperature of the area to which the pack is applied. (b) A hot pack used to warm hands and feet in winter. When the package is opened, oxygen from the air penetrates a bag containing solid chemicals. The resulting reaction produces heat for several hours.

 CHEMICAL IMPACT　　　　　　　　　**Consumer Connection**

Unexpected Reactions!

Cleansers and cleaning products contain a wide variety of chemicals. When using them, it is important to be careful which cleansers you mix together. Mixing a strong oxidizer (such as bleach or products containing bleach) and a product containing ammonia can have dangerous results! They produce a toxic gas that can be very dangerous to

the person cleaning (especially in a tiny closed space like many bathrooms!). Other chemicals that are designed to remove iron or rust can also react with cleansers or cleaning solutions to produce gases that both smell bad and are toxic. Always read the warning labels on cleaning products before using them.

(a)

(b)

(c)

(d)

Figure 7.3
(a) When colorless hydrochloric acid is added to a red solution of cobalt(II) nitrate, the solution turns blue, a sign that a chemical reaction has taken place. (b) A solid forms when a solution of sodium dichromate is added to a solution of lead nitrate. (c) Bubbles of hydrogen gas form when calcium metal reacts with water. (d) Methane gas reacts with oxygen to produce a flame in a bunsen burner.

WHAT IF?

Table 7.1 gives clues that a chemical reaction has occurred.

What if someone uses this list as proof of a chemical reaction? What are some physical changes that such a person might mistakenly identify as chemical reactions?

Table 7.1 summarizes common clues to the occurrence of a chemical reaction, and **Figure 7.3** gives some examples of reactions that show these clues.

7.2 Chemical Equations

Objective: *To learn to identify the characteristics of a chemical reaction and the information given by a chemical equation.*

Chemists have learned that a chemical change always involves a rearrangement of the ways in which the atoms are grouped. For example, when the methane, CH_4, in natural gas combines with oxygen, O_2, in the air and burns, carbon dioxide, CO_2, and water, H_2O, are formed. Such a chemical change is called a **chemical reaction**. We represent a chemical reaction by writing a **chemical equation** in which the chemicals present before the reaction (the **reactants**) are shown to the left of an arrow and the chemicals formed by the reaction (the **products**) are shown to the right of an arrow. The arrow indicates the direction of the change and is read as "yields" or "produces":

Reactants → Products

7.2   Chemical Equations   **195**

WHAT IF Comments

Macroscopic clues are helpful but incomplete. We emphasize a microscopic perspective throughout the book because this model is a more powerful way to explain reactions. For example, if we rely on a color change as proof of a reaction, what about adding food coloring to water? Boiling water involves heat and results in the production of a gas, but it is not a chemical change. The production of a solid from the cooling of melted wax is also a physical change.

Section 7.2

Themes
Organization, Patterns of Change

Skills
Observing, interpreting data, interpreting diagrams, using the writing process

TEACHING TIP

In this section students learn that a chemical reaction involves rearrangement of the elements. It is very helpful to use simple models of the reactants that you can take apart and rearrange to show that atoms are conserved in a chemical reaction.

TEACHING SUPPORT
Demonstration

Elephant's Toothpaste

Materials
1-L cylinder
50 mL liquid detergent (Dawn works best)
50 mL 30% hydrogen peroxide
50 mL 6.0 *M* KI solution
Plastic dishwashing tub or tray

Preparation Make the KI solution by placing 8.3 g KI in 50 mL water. Premeasure all of the solutions for the demonstration.

Performance Place the cylinder in the plastic tub or tray (to catch the foam). Add the hydrogen peroxide to the cylinder. Add the liquid detergent to the cylinder and swirl to mix. Add the KI and step back. The reaction will occur and large amounts of foam will bubble out the top of the cylinder, forming the elephant's toothpaste.

Teaching Notes Discuss the evidence for a chemical reaction (the bubbles and the heat, seen as steam). There is also a color change to observe.

For the reaction of methane with oxygen, we have

Note from this equation that the products contain the same atoms as the reactants but that the atoms are associated in different ways. That is, a *chemical reaction involves changing the ways the atoms are grouped.*

It is important to recognize that **in a chemical reaction, atoms are neither created nor destroyed.** *All atoms present in the reactants must be accounted for among the products.* In other words, there must be the same number of each type of atom on the product side as on the reactant side of the arrow. Making sure that the equation for a reaction obeys this rule is called **balancing the chemical equation** for a reaction.

The equation that we have shown for the reaction between CH_4 and O_2 is not balanced. We can see that it is not balanced by taking the reactants and products apart.

The reaction cannot happen this way because, as it stands, this equation states that one oxygen atom is created and two hydrogen atoms are destroyed. A reaction is only a rearrangement of the way the atoms are grouped; atoms are not created or destroyed. The total number of each type of atom must be the same on both sides of the arrow. We can fix the imbalance in this equation by involving one more O_2 molecule on the left and by showing the production of one more H_2O molecule on the right.

This *balanced chemical equation* shows the actual numbers of molecules involved in this reaction (see **Figure 7.4**).

When we write the balanced equation for a reaction, we group like molecules together. Thus

$$CH_4 + O_2 + O_2 \rightarrow CO_2 + H_2O + H_2O$$

is written

$$CH_4 + 2O_2 \rightarrow CO_2 + 2H_2O$$

Figure 7.4
The reaction between methane and oxygen to give water and carbon dioxide. Note that there are four oxygen atoms in the products *and* in the reactants; none has been gained or lost in the reaction. Similarly, there are four hydrogen atoms and one carbon atom in the reactants *and* in the products. The reaction simply changes the way the atoms are grouped.

196   Chapter 7   Chemical Reactions: An Introduction

The chemical equation for a reaction provides us with two important types of information:

1. The identities of the reactants and products

2. The relative numbers of each

Physical States

Besides specifying the compounds involved in the reaction, we often indicate in the equation the *physical states* of the reactants and products by using the following symbols:

Symbol	*State*
(*s*)	solid
(*l*)	liquid
(*g*)	gas
(*aq*)	dissolved in water (in aqueous solution)

For example, when solid potassium reacts with liquid water, the products are hydrogen gas and potassium hydroxide; the latter remains dissolved in the water. From this information about the reactants and products, we can write the equation for the reaction. Solid potassium is represented by K(*s*); liquid water is written as $H_2O(l)$; hydrogen gas contains diatomic molecules and is represented as $H_2(g)$; potassium hydroxide dissolved in water is written as KOH(*aq*). So the *unbalanced* equation for the reaction is

Solid potassium		Water		Hydrogen gas		Potassium hydroxide dissolved in water
K(*s*)	+	$H_2O(l)$	$\rightarrow$	$H_2(g)$	+	KOH(*aq*)

This reaction is shown in **Figure 7.5.**

Figure 7.5
The reactants (a) potassium metal (stored in mineral oil to prevent oxidation) and (b) water. (c) The reaction of potassium with water. The flame occurs because the hydrogen gas, $H_2(g)$, produced by the reaction burns in air [reacts with $O_2(g)$] at the high temperatures caused by the reaction.

(a)

(b)

(c)

7.2   Chemical Equations   **197**

Aspirin ($C_9H_8O_4$)

It was about 2000 years before Hippocrates' advice to use willow bark as a painkiller was taken any further. In the 1820s an Italian chemist, Raffaele Piria, managed to isolate the compound salicin from willow bark and use it to make salicylic acid. It was later found that salicylic acid could also be obtained from the wildflower meadowsweet (*Spirea ulmaria*). Actually the name aspirin comes from this plant. The derivative acetylsalicylic acid—obtained from salicylic acid—was named a+ = spirea by the Bayer Corporation in Germany in the nineteenth century. Originally, acetylsalicylic acid, although known to be a potent painkiller, tasted unpleasant and caused burning in the mouth and stomach. These side effects were produced by contaminants that Bayer found a way to remove by 1893. At this point aspirin became a "wonder drug" and has been widely used ever since. People in the United States use 50 million aspirin per day—almost 2 billion aspirin per year. Many other painkillers are now available, but aspirin continues to be used by millions every day. It is more than a simple painkiller: It has the effect of "thinning" the blood (preventing clotting) and can protect people who have suffered heart attacks from recurrences.

Additional Examples

Write the *unbalanced* chemical equation for each of the following reactions.

1. Gaseous ammonia reacts with gaseous hydrogen chloride to form solid ammonium chloride.

   $NH_3(g) + HCl(g) \rightarrow NH_4Cl(s)$

2. Iron metal reacts with oxygen gas in the air to form solid iron(II) oxide.

   $Fe(s) + O_2(g) \rightarrow FeO(s)$

Aspirin ($C_9H_8O_4$)

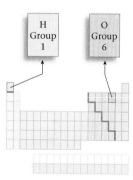

Pain is an unfortunate part of life, and humans have long searched for ways to suppress it. Originally plants were used as sources of painkillers. For example, Hippocrates, the ancient Greek medical pioneer, recommended the use of a substance derived from willow bark to ease the pain of childbirth. We now know that white willow bark contains salicin, which is converted in boiling water to salicylic acid—the active ingredient in aspirin, the most common modern painkiller. (Americans swallow about 2 billion aspirin tablets every year.)

Aspirin works by interfering with the production of prostaglandins, which are molecules that generate pain signals and cause inflammation. Besides masking pain and preventing inflammation, aspirin appears beneficial in preventing heart attacks and cataracts, the formation of certain proteins that cloud the lens of the eye.

Although aspirin is the most widely used painkiller in the United States, its use can prove dangerous in certain cases. In children and teenagers, use of aspirin can lead to Reye's syndrome, a rare but potentially fatal disease. Aspirin can also cause bleeding in the digestive tract.

The hydrogen gas produced in this reaction then reacts with the oxygen gas in the air, producing gaseous water and a flame. The *unbalanced* equation for this second reaction is

$$H_2(g) + O_2(g) \rightarrow H_2O(g)$$

Both of these reactions produce a great deal of heat. In Example 7.1 we will practice writing the unbalanced equations for reactions. Then, in the next section, we will discuss systematic procedures for balancing equations.

Example 7.1

CHEMISTRY

Because Zn forms only the Zn^{2+} ion, a Roman numeral is usually not used. Thus $ZnCl_2$ is commonly called zinc chloride.

Chemical Equations: Recognizing Reactants and Products

Write the *unbalanced* chemical equation for each of the following reactions.

a. Solid mercury(II) oxide decomposes to produce liquid mercury metal and gaseous oxygen.

b. Solid carbon reacts with gaseous oxygen to form gaseous carbon dioxide.

c. Solid zinc is added to an aqueous solution containing dissolved hydrogen chloride to produce gaseous hydrogen that bubbles out of the solution and zinc chloride that remains dissolved in the water.

Solution

a. In this case we have only one reactant, mercury(II) oxide. The name mercury(II) oxide means that the Hg^{2+} cation is present, so one O^{2-} ion is required for a zero net charge. Thus the formula is HgO, which is written $HgO(s)$ in this case because it is given as a solid. The products are liquid mercury, written $Hg(l)$, and gaseous oxygen, written $O_2(g)$. (Remember that oxygen exists as a diatomic molecule under normal conditions.) The unbalanced equation is

$$\underset{\text{Reactant}}{HgO(s)} \rightarrow \underset{\text{Products}}{Hg(l) \ + \ O_2(g)}$$

b. In this case, solid carbon, written $C(s)$, reacts with oxygen gas, $O_2(g)$, to form gaseous carbon dioxide, which is written $CO_2(g)$. The equation (which happens to be balanced) is

$$\underset{\text{Reactants}}{C(s) + O_2(g)} \rightarrow \underset{\text{Product}}{CO_2(g)}$$

c. In this reaction solid zinc, $Zn(s)$, is added to an aqueous solution of hydrogen chloride, which is written $HCl(aq)$ and called hydrochloric acid. These are the reactants. The products of the reaction are gaseous hydrogen, $H_2(g)$, and aqueous zinc chloride. The name zinc chloride means that the Zn^{2+} ion is present, so two Cl^- ions are needed to achieve a zero net charge. Thus zinc chloride dissolved in water is written $ZnCl_2(aq)$. The unbalanced equation for the reaction is

$$\underset{\text{Reactants}}{Zn(s) + HCl(aq)} \rightarrow \underset{\text{Products}}{H_2(g) + ZnCl_2(aq)}$$

Zinc metal reacts with hydrochloric acid to produce bubbles of hydrogen gas.

✓ **Self-Check Exercise 7.1**

Identify the reactants and products and write the *unbalanced* equation (including symbols for states) for each of the following chemical reactions.

a. Solid magnesium metal reacts with liquid water to form solid magnesium hydroxide and hydrogen gas.

b. Solid ammonium dichromate (review Table 4.4 if this compound is unfamiliar) decomposes to solid chromium(III) oxide, gaseous nitrogen, and gaseous water.

c. Gaseous ammonia reacts with gaseous oxygen to form gaseous nitrogen monoxide and gaseous water.

✓ **Answers to Self-Check Exercise 7.1**

a. $Mg(s) + H_2O(l) \rightarrow$ $Mg(OH)_2(s) + H_2(g)$
Note that magnesium (which is in Group 2) always forms the Mg^{2+} cation and thus requires two OH^- anions for a zero net charge.

b. Ammonium dichromate contains the polyatomic ions NH_4^+ and $Cr_2O_7^{2-}$ (students should memorize these ions). Because NH_4^+ has a $1+$ charge, two NH_4^+ cations are required for each $Cr_2O_7^{2-}$, with its $2-$ charge, to give the formula $(NH_4)_2Cr_2O_7$. Chromium(III) oxide contains Cr^{3+} ions—signified by chromium(III)—and O^{2-} ions (oxide ions). To achieve a net charge of zero, the solid must contain two Cr^{3+} ions for every three O^{2-} ions, so the formula is Cr_2O_3. Nitrogen gas contains diatomic molecules and is written $N_2(g)$, and gaseous water is written $H_2O(g)$. Thus the unbalanced equation for the decomposition of ammonium dichromate is

$(NH_4)_2Cr_2O_7(s) \rightarrow Cr_2O_3(s) +$ $N_2(g) + H_2O(g)$

c. Gaseous ammonia, $NH_3(g)$, and gaseous oxygen, $O_2(g)$, react to form nitrogen monoxide gas, $NO(g)$, plus gaseous water, $H_2O(g)$. The unbalanced equation is

$NH_3(g) + O_2(g) \rightarrow NO(g) +$ $H_2O(g)$

🧪 **Laboratory**
Experiment 27:
Interpreting Chemical Reactions, Microscale

🧪 **Laboratory**
Experiment 28:
Conservation of Mass, Traditional

TEACHING TIPS

- Remind students that they need to know the diatomic elements to write correct equations.

- Students often want to change the subscripts on the reactants or products to balance the equation. Remind them that this modification changes the substances in the reaction. Once they have decided on the reactants and products, they can change only the coefficients to balance the equation.

- Using recipes as analogies for chemical equations is a good idea. Recipes in which we are given only the ingredients (and product) involved are analogous to unbalanced equations. They are useful to a point, but we eventually need the amounts to do anything with the recipe (or the equation). Also, the amounts in a recipe can be changed, which requires all amounts to be changed by the same factor. Likewise, we can multiply all coefficients by 2, for example. (Of course, we can change a recipe by adding just a touch more salt, but this does not increase the amount of product.)

- Make it clear to students that the equation represents the *ratio* of the amounts of chemicals that react or are produced. An individual coefficient is as meaningless as a recipe that gives the required amount of only one ingredient.

7.3 Balancing Chemical Equations

Objective: *To learn how to write a balanced equation for a chemical reaction.*

As we saw in the previous section, an unbalanced chemical equation is not an accurate representation of the reaction that occurs. Whenever you see an equation for a reaction, you should ask yourself whether it is balanced. The principle that lies at the heart of the balancing process is that **atoms are conserved in a chemical reaction.** That is, atoms are neither created nor destroyed. They are just grouped differently. The same number of each type of atom is found among the reactants and among the products.

Chemists determine the identity of the reactants and products of a reaction by experimental observation. For example, when methane (natural gas) is burned in the presence of sufficient oxygen gas, the products are always carbon dioxide and water. **The identities (formulas) of the compounds must never be changed in balancing a chemical equation.** In other words, the subscripts in a formula cannot be changed, nor can atoms be added to or subtracted from a formula.

Most chemical equations can be balanced by trial and error—that is, by inspection. Keep trying until you find the numbers of reactants and products that give the same number of each type of atom on both sides of the arrow. For example, consider the reaction of hydrogen gas and oxygen gas to form liquid water. First, we write the unbalanced equation from the description of the reaction.

$$H_2(g) + O_2(g) \rightarrow H_2O(l)$$

We can see that this equation is unbalanced by counting the atoms on both sides of the arrow.

We have one more oxygen atom in the reactants than in the products. Because we cannot create or destroy atoms and because we *cannot change the formulas* of the reactants or products, we must balance the equation by adding more molecules of reactants and/or products. In this case we need one more oxygen atom on the right, so we add another water molecule (which contains one O atom). Then we count all of the atoms again.

💡 **PROBLEM SOLVING**
Trial and error is often useful for solving problems. It's okay to make a few wrong turns before you get to the right answer.

💡 **PROBLEM SOLVING**

Reactants	Products
2 H	2 H
2 O	1 O

💡 **PROBLEM SOLVING**

Reactants	Products
2 H	4 H
2 O	2 O

We have balanced the oxygen atoms, but now the hydrogen atoms have become unbalanced. There are more hydrogen atoms on the right than on the left. We can solve this problem by adding another hydrogen molecule (H_2) to the reactant side.

Animation and Video

Chemistry in Motion
**Demonstration 10,
Oxygen, Hydrogen, Soap
Bubbles and Balloons**

PROBLEM SOLVING

Reactants	Products
4 H	4 H
2 O	2 O

$$H_2(g) \quad + \quad H_2(g) \quad + \quad O_2(g) \quad \rightarrow \quad H_2O(l) \quad + \quad H_2O(l)$$

H H	H H	O O	H O H	H O H

Totals: 4 H   2 O | 4 H   2 O

The equation is now balanced. We have the same numbers of hydrogen and oxygen atoms represented on both sides of the arrow. Collecting like molecules, we write the balanced equation as

$$2H_2(g) + O_2(g) \rightarrow 2H_2O(l)$$

Consider next what happens if we multiply every part of this balanced equation by 2,

$$2 \times [2H_2(g) + O_2(g) \rightarrow 2H_2O(l)]$$

to give

$$4H_2(g) + 2O_2(g) \rightarrow 4H_2O(l)$$

WHAT IF?

What if mass was not conserved? How would it change how you balance equations?

This equation is balanced (count the atoms to verify this). In fact, we can multiply or divide *all parts* of the original balanced equation by any number to give a new balanced equation. Thus each chemical reaction has many possible balanced equations. Is one of the many possibilities preferred over the others? Yes.

The accepted convention is that the "best" balanced equation is the one with the *smallest integers (whole numbers)*. These integers are called the **coefficients** for the balanced equation. Therefore, for the reaction of hydrogen and oxygen to form water, the "correct" balanced equation is

$$2H_2(g) + O_2(g) \rightarrow 2H_2O(l)$$

The coefficients 2, 1 (never written), and 2, respectively, are the smallest *integers* that give a balanced equation for this reaction.

Next we will balance the equation for the reaction of liquid ethanol, C_2H_5OH, with oxygen gas to form gaseous carbon dioxide and water. This reaction, among many others, occurs in engines that burn a gasoline–ethanol mixture called gasohol.

PROBLEM SOLVING

In balancing equations, start by looking at the most complicated molecule.

The first step in obtaining the balanced equation for a reaction is always to identify the reactants and products from the description given for the reaction. In this case we are told that liquid ethanol, $C_2H_5OH(l)$, reacts with gaseous oxygen, $O_2(g)$, to produce gaseous carbon dioxide, $CO_2(g)$, and gaseous water, $H_2O(g)$. Therefore, the unbalanced equation is

$$C_2H_5OH(l) + O_2(g) \rightarrow CO_2(g) + H_2O(g)$$

Liquid   Gaseous   Gaseous   Gaseous
ethanol   oxygen   carbon dioxide   water

When one molecule in an equation is more complicated (contains more elements) than the others, it is best to start with that molecule. The most

WHAT IF Comments

We balance equations because atoms must be conserved. If atoms are conserved, mass is conserved.

TEACHING TIP

Students should indicate the states of the reactants and products in an equation so that this step becomes part of the process for writing and balancing the equation.

7.3 Balancing Chemical Equations **201**

PROBLEM SOLVING

C_2H_5OH

H
C H
H O H
C H
H

2 C, 6 H, 1 O

complicated molecule here is C_2H_5OH, so we begin by considering the products that contain the atoms in C_2H_5OH. We start with carbon. The only product that contains carbon is CO_2. Because C_2H_5OH contains two carbon atoms, we place a 2 before the CO_2 to balance the carbon atoms.

$$C_2H_5OH(l) + O_2(g) \rightarrow 2CO_2(g) + H_2O(g)$$

2 C atoms   2 C atoms

Remember, we cannot change the formula of any reactant or product when we balance an equation. We can only place coefficients in front of the formulas.

Next we consider hydrogen. The only product containing hydrogen is H_2O. C_2H_5OH contains six hydrogen atoms, so we need six hydrogen atoms on the right. Because each H_2O contains two hydrogen atoms, we need three H_2O molecules to yield six hydrogen atoms. So we place a 3 before the H_2O.

$$C_2H_5OH(l) + O_2(g) \rightarrow 2CO_2(g) + 3H_2O(g)$$

(5 + 1) H   (3 × 2) H
6 H   6 H

Finally, we count the oxygen atoms. On the left we have three oxygen atoms (one in C_2H_5OH and two in O_2), and on the right we have seven oxy-

---

CHEMICAL IMPACT

Connection to Biology

The Beetle That Shoots Straight

If someone said to you, "Name something that protects itself by spraying its enemies," your answer would almost certainly be "a skunk." Of course, you would be correct, but there is another correct answer—the bombardier beetle. When threatened, this beetle shoots a boiling stream of toxic chemicals at its enemy. How does this clever beetle accomplish this? Obviously, the boiling mixture cannot be stored inside the beetle's body all the time. Instead, when endangered, the beetle mixes chemicals that produce the hot spray. The chemicals involved are stored in two compartments. One compartment contains the chemicals hydrogen peroxide (H_2O_2) and methylhydroquinone ($C_7H_8O_2$). The key reaction is the decomposition of hydrogen peroxide to form oxygen gas and water:

$$2H_2O_2(aq) \rightarrow 2H_2O(l) + O_2(g)$$

Hydrogen peroxide also reacts with the hydroquinones to produce other compounds that become part of the toxic spray.

However, none of these reactions occurs very fast unless certain enzymes are present. (Enzymes are natural substances that speed up biological reactions by means we will not discuss here.) When the beetle mixes the hydrogen peroxide and hydroquinones with the enzyme, the decomposition of H_2O_2 occurs rapidly, producing a hot mixture pressurized by the formation of oxygen gas. When the gas pressure becomes high enough, the hot spray is ejected in one long stream or in short bursts. The beetle has a highly accurate aim and can shoot several attackers with one batch of spray.

A bombardier beetle defending itself.

202   Chapter 7   Chemical Reactions: An Introduction

TEACHING TIP

Encourage students to leave the elements and diatomic molecules until last when balancing equations. This choice simplifies the trial-and-error process.

gen atoms (four in $2CO_2$ and three in $3H_2O$). We can correct this imbalance if we have three O_2 molecules on the left. That is, we place a coefficient of 3 before the O_2 to produce the balanced equation.

$$C_2H_5OH(l) + 3O_2(g) \rightarrow 2CO_2(g) + 3H_2O(g)$$

$$1\,O \quad (3 \times 2)\,O \quad (2 \times 2)\,O \quad 3\,O$$

$$7\,O \qquad\qquad 7\,O$$

At this point you may have a question: why did we choose O_2 on the left when we balanced the oxygen atoms? Why not use C_2H_5OH, which has an oxygen atom? The answer is that if we had changed the coefficient in front of C_2H_5OH, we would have unbalanced the hydrogen and carbon atoms. Now we count all of the atoms as a check to make sure the equation is balanced.

$$C_2H_5OH(l) + 3O_2(g) \rightarrow 2CO_2(g) + 3H_2O(g)$$

Totals: 2 C   6 H   7 O   2 C   7 O   6 H

The equation is now balanced. We have the same numbers of all types of atoms on both sides of the arrow. Notice that these coefficients are the smallest integers that give a balanced equation.

The process of writing and balancing the equation for a chemical reaction consists of several steps:

How to Write and Balance Equations

STEP 1 Read the description of the chemical reaction. What are the reactants, the products, and their states? Write the appropriate formulas.

STEP 2 Write the *unbalanced* equation that summarizes the information from step 1.

STEP 3 Balance the equation by inspection, starting with the most complicated molecule. Proceed element by element to determine what coefficients are necessary so that the same number of each type of atom appears on both the reactant side and the product side. Do not change the identities (formulas) of any of the reactants or products.

STEP 4 Check to see that the coefficients used give the same number of each type of atom on both sides of the arrow. (Note that an "atom" may be present in an element, a compound, or an ion.) Also check to see that the coefficients used are the smallest integers that give the balanced equation. This can be done by determining whether all coefficients can be divided by the same integer to give a set of smaller *integer* coefficients.

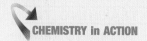

Claymation Equations

Materials Each student/group needs four different colors of modeling clay.

Purpose Students will better understand what the coefficients and subscripts represent in a balanced equation.

Discussion A subscript implies that atoms are bonded together in a molecule, and a coefficient tells us the relative number of molecules required or produced in the reaction. That is, the coefficients represent the ratio of reactants and products (generally the lowest whole-number ratio) in the reaction. Students should understand that changing a subscript changes the make-up of the molecule, and therefore we are balancing an entirely different equation from the original.

Additional Examples

Write the *balanced* chemical equation for each of the following reactions.

1. Nitrogen monoxide gas reacts with hydrogen gas to form nitrogen gas and water.
$$2NO(g) + 2H_2(g) \rightarrow N_2(g) + 2H_2O(l)$$

2. Lithium metal reacts with chlorine gas to form solid lithium chloride.
$$2Li(s) + Cl_2(g) \rightarrow 2LiCl(s)$$

1. Obtain four different colors of modeling clay.
2. Using the clay, make models of each of the reactants and products in the following reactions, and use these models to balance the equations.
   a. $N_2 + H_2 \rightarrow NH_3$
   b. $C_2H_6 + O_2 \rightarrow CO_2 + H_2O$
   c. $H_2 + O_2 \rightarrow H_2O$
   d. $O_2 \rightarrow O_3$
3. How do your models show the difference between a subscript and a coefficient?
4. How do your models show why we cannot change a subscript to balance an equation?

Example 7.2

Balancing Chemical Equations I

For the following reaction, write the unbalanced equation and then balance the equation: solid potassium reacts with liquid water to form gaseous hydrogen and potassium hydroxide that dissolves in the water.

Solution

Step 1　From the description given for the reaction, we know that the reactants are solid potassium, $K(s)$, and liquid water, $H_2O(l)$. The products are gaseous hydrogen, $H_2(g)$, and dissolved potassium hydroxide, $KOH(aq)$.

Step 2　The unbalanced equation for the reaction is

$$K(s) + H_2O(l) \rightarrow H_2(g) + KOH(aq)$$

Step 3　Although none of the reactants or products is very complicated, we will start with KOH because it contains the most elements (three). We will arbitrarily consider hydrogen first. Note that on the reactant side of the equation in step 2, there are two hydrogen atoms but on the product side there are three. If we place a coefficient of 2 in front of both H_2O and KOH, we now have four H atoms on each side.

$$K(s) + \underbrace{2H_2O(l)}_{\substack{4\,H \\ atoms}} \rightarrow \underbrace{H_2(g)}_{\substack{2\,H \\ atoms}} + \underbrace{2KOH(aq)}_{\substack{2\,H \\ atoms}}$$

Also note that the oxygen atoms balance.

$$K(s) + \underbrace{2H_2O(l)}_{\substack{2\,O \\ atom}} \rightarrow H_2(g) + \underbrace{2KOH(aq)}_{\substack{2\,O \\ atom}}$$

However, the K atoms do not balance; we have one on the left and two on the right. We can fix this easily by placing a coefficient of 2 in front of $K(s)$ to give the balanced equation:

$$2K(s) + 2H_2O(l) \rightarrow H_2(g) + 2KOH(aq)$$

Step 4

PROBLEM SOLVING

Reactants	Products
2 K	2 K
4 H	4 H
2 O	2 O

Check: There are 2 K, 4 H, and 2 O on both sides of the arrow, and the coefficients are the smallest integers that give a balanced equation. We know this because we cannot divide through by a given integer to give a set of smaller *integer* (whole-number) coefficients. For example, if we divide all of the coefficients by 2, we get

$$K(s) + H_2O(l) \rightarrow \tfrac{1}{2}H_2(g) + KOH(aq)$$

This is not acceptable because the coefficient for H_2 is not an integer.

Example 7.3

Balancing Chemical Equations II

Under appropriate conditions at 1000 °C, ammonia gas reacts with oxygen gas to produce gaseous nitrogen monoxide (common name, nitric oxide) and gaseous water. Write the unbalanced and balanced equations for this reaction.

Solution

PROBLEM SOLVING

Reactants	Products
1 N	1 N
3 H	2 H
2 O	1 O

Step 1   The reactants are gaseous ammonia, $NH_3(g)$, and gaseous oxygen, $O_2(g)$. The products are gaseous nitrogen monoxide, $NO(g)$, and gaseous water, $H_2O(g)$.

Step 2   The unbalanced equation for the reaction is

$$NH_3(g) + O_2(g) \rightarrow NO(g) + H_2O(g)$$

Step 3   In this equation there is no molecule that is obviously the most complicated. Three molecules contain two elements, so we arbitrarily start with NH_3. We arbitrarily begin by looking at hydrogen. A coefficient of 2 for NH_3 and a coefficient of 3 for H_2O give six atoms of hydrogen on both sides.

$$\underset{6\,H}{2NH_3(g)} + O_2(g) \rightarrow NO(g) + \underset{6\,H}{3H_2O(g)}$$

We can balance the nitrogen by giving NO a coefficient of 2.

$$\underset{2\,N}{2NH_3(g)} + O_2(g) \rightarrow \underset{2\,N}{2NO(g)} + 3H_2O(g)$$

PROBLEM SOLVING

$\frac{5}{2} = 2\frac{1}{2}$

O—O	$2\frac{1}{2}$ O_2
O—O	contains
O+O	5 O atoms

Finally, we note that there are two atoms of oxygen on the left and five on the right. The oxygen can be balanced with a coefficient of $\frac{5}{2}$ for O_2, because $\frac{5}{2} \times O_2$ gives five oxygen atoms.

$$2NH_3(g) + \underset{5\,O}{\tfrac{5}{2}O_2(g)} \rightarrow \underset{2\,O}{2NO(g)} + \underset{3\,O}{3H_2O(g)}$$

However, the convention is to have integer (whole-number) coefficients, so we multiply the entire equation by 2.

$$2 \times [2NH_3(g) + \tfrac{5}{2}O_2(g) \rightarrow 2NO(g) + 3H_2O(g)]$$

or

$$2 \times 2NH_3(g) + 2 \times \tfrac{5}{2}O_2(g) \rightarrow 2 \times 2NO(g) + 2 \times 3H_2O(g)$$

$$4NH_3(g) + 5O_2(g) \rightarrow 4NO(g) + 6H_2O(g)$$

(continued) **205**

WHAT IF?

What if a friend was balancing chemical equations by changing the values of the subscripts instead of using the coefficients? How would you explain to your friend that this tactic is the wrong approach to take?

Additional Examples

Write the *balanced* chemical equation for each of the following reactions.

1. Iron metal reacts with oxygen gas in the air to form iron(III) oxide.

   $$4Fe(s) + 3O_2(g) \rightarrow 2Fe_2O_3(s)$$

2. Diboron trioxide reacts with water to form boric acid, $B(OH)_3$.

   $$B_2O_3(s) + 3H_2O(l) \rightarrow 2B(OH)_3(aq)$$

WHAT IF Comments

Equations can be balanced mathematically by changing the subscripts (that is, the atoms will be conserved), but doing so changes the reaction. Coefficients tell us the ratio of the molecules involved in the reaction. Subscripts tell us the number of each type of atom in the molecules. A good example is water (H_2O) versus hydrogen peroxide (H_2O_2). Both consist solely of hydrogen and oxygen, but they have quite different properties. Chemical equations are often explained as recipes. In this analogy, changing the subscripts is like changing the ingredients.

Answer to Self-Check Exercise 7.2

Step 1 The reactants are propane, $C_3H_8(g)$, and oxygen, $O_2(g)$; the products are carbon dioxide, $CO_2(g)$, and water, $H_2O(g)$. All are in the gaseous state.

Step 2 The unbalanced equation for the reaction is

$$C_3H_8(g) + O_2(g) \rightarrow CO_2(g) + H_2O(g)$$

Step 3 We start with C_3H_8 because it is the most complicated molecule. C_3H_8 contains three carbon atoms per molecule, so a coefficient of 3 is needed for CO_2:

$$C_3H_8(g) + O_2(g) \rightarrow 3CO_2(g) + H_2O(g)$$

Also, each C_3H_8 molecule contains eight hydrogen atoms, so a coefficient of 4 is required for H_2O:

$$C_3H_8(g) + O_2(g) \rightarrow 3CO_2(g) + 4H_2O(g)$$

The final element to be balanced is oxygen. Note that the left side of the equation now has two oxygen atoms, and the right side has ten. We can balance the oxygen by using a coefficient of 5 for O_2:

$$C_3H_8(g) + 5O_2(g) \rightarrow 3CO_2(g) + 4H_2O(g)$$

Step 4 *Check:*

$$3\,C, 8\,H, 10\,O \rightarrow 3\,C, 8\,H, 10\,O$$
Reactant   Product
atoms   atoms

We cannot divide all coefficients by a given integer to give smaller integer coefficients.

Additional Examples

Write the *balanced* chemical equation for each of the following reactions.

1. Solid iron(III) oxide reacts with aqueous nitric acid to form aqueous iron(III) nitrate and water.
$$Fe_2O_3(s) + 6HNO_3(aq) \rightarrow 2Fe(NO_3)_3(aq) + 3H_2O(l)$$

2. Hydrogen sulfide gas reacts with aqueous lead(II) nitrate to form solid lead(II) sulfide and aqueous nitric acid.
$$H_2S(g) + Pb(NO_3)_2(aq) \rightarrow PbS(s) + 2HNO_3(aq)$$

PROBLEM SOLVING

Reactants	Products
4 N	4 N
12 H	12 H
10 O	10 O

Step 4

Check: There are 4 N, 12 H, and 10 O atoms on both sides, so the equation is balanced. These coefficients are the smallest integers that give a balanced equation. That is, we cannot divide all coefficients by the same integer and obtain a smaller set of *integers*.

Self-Check Exercise 7.2

Propane, C_3H_8, a liquid at 25 °C under high pressure, is often used for gas grills and as a fuel in rural areas where there is no natural gas pipeline. When liquid propane is released from its storage tank, it changes to propane gas that reacts with oxygen gas (it "burns") to give gaseous carbon dioxide and gaseous water. Write and balance the equation for this reaction.

Hint: This description of a chemical process contains many words, some of which are crucial to solving the problem and some of which are not. First sort out the important information and use symbols to represent it.

Example 7.4

Balancing Chemical Equations III

Decorations on glass are produced by etching with hydrofluoric acid.

Glass is sometimes decorated by etching patterns on its surface. Etching occurs when hydrofluoric acid (an aqueous solution of HF) reacts with the silicon dioxide in the glass to form gaseous silicon tetrafluoride and liquid water. Write and balance the equation for this reaction.

Solution

Step 1 From the description of the reaction we can identify the reactants:

hydrofluoric acid	HF(aq)
solid silicon dioxide	$SiO_2(s)$

and the products:

gaseous silicon tetrafluoride	$SiF_4(g)$
liquid water	$H_2O(l)$

Step 2 The unbalanced equation is

$$SiO_2(s) + HF(aq) \rightarrow SiF_4(g) + H_2O(l)$$

Step 3 There is no clear choice here for the most complicated molecule. We arbitrarily start with the elements in SiF_4. The silicon is balanced (one atom on each side), but the fluorine is not. To balance the fluorine, we need a coefficient of 4 before the HF.

$$SiO_2(s) + 4HF(aq) \rightarrow SiF_4(g) + H_2O(l)$$

Hydrogen and oxygen are not balanced. Because we have four hydrogen atoms on the left and two on the right, we place a 2 before the H_2O:

$$SiO_2(s) + 4HF(aq) \rightarrow SiF_4(g) + 2H_2O(l)$$

PROBLEM SOLVING

Reactants	Products
1 Si	1 Si
1 H	2 H
1 F	4 F
2 O	1 O

This balances the hydrogen *and* the oxygen (two atoms on each side).

Step 4

Check: $SiO_2(s) + 4HF(aq) \rightarrow SiF_4(g) + 2H_2O(l)$

Totals: 1 Si, 2 O, 4 H, 4 F → 1 Si, 4 F, 4 H, 2 O

All atoms check, so the equation is balanced.

Self-Check Exercise 7.3

Give the balanced equation for each of the following reactions.

a. When solid ammonium nitrite is heated, it produces nitrogen gas and water vapor.

b. Gaseous nitrogen monoxide (common name, nitric oxide) decomposes to produce dinitrogen monoxide gas (common name, nitrous oxide) and nitrogen dioxide gas.

c. Liquid nitric acid decomposes to reddish-brown nitrogen dioxide gas, liquid water, and oxygen gas. (This is why bottles of nitric acid become yellow upon standing.)

Focus Questions

Sections 7.1–7.3

1. What types of evidence indicate that a chemical reaction has taken place?

2. Write chemical equations for each of the following reactions:
   a. Gaseous chlorine reacts with an aqueous solution of potassium bromide to form liquid bromine and an aqueous solution of potassium chloride.
   b. Solid aluminum reacts with solid iodine to produce solid aluminum iodide.
   c. Solid magnesium reacts with an aqueous solution of hydrochloric acid to form an aqueous solution of magnesium chloride and bubbles of hydrogen gas.

3. Balance each of the chemical equations from question 2.

4. What is the difference between a coefficient and a subscript in a chemical equation? Which can be changed when balancing a chemical equation?

5. What is the difference between an aqueous solution and a liquid?

Focus Questions   **207**

Answers to Self-Check Exercise 7.3

a. $NH_4NO_2(s) \rightarrow N_2(g) + H_2O(g)$ (unbalanced)
   $NH_4NO_2(s) \rightarrow N_2(g) + 2H_2O(g)$ (balanced)

b. $NO(g) \rightarrow N_2O(g) + NO_2(g)$ (unbalanced)
   $3NO(g) \rightarrow N_2O(g) + NO_2(g)$ (balanced)

c. $HNO_3(l) \rightarrow NO_2(g) + H_2O(l) + O_2(g)$ (unbalanced)
   $4HNO_3(l) \rightarrow 4NO_2(g) + 2H_2O(l) + O_2(g)$ (balanced)

Answers to Focus Questions

1. The clues that indicate a reaction has occurred are a color change, formation of a solid, bubbles, production of heat or fire, or absorption of heat.

2. a. $Cl_2(aq) + KBr(aq) \rightarrow Br_2(l) + KCl(aq)$
   b. $Al(s) + I_2(s) \rightarrow AlI_3(s)$
   c. $Mg(s) + HCl(aq) \rightarrow MgCl_2(aq) + H_2(g)$

3. a. $Cl_2(aq) + 2KBr(aq) \rightarrow Br_2(l) + 2KCl(aq)$
   b. $2Al(s) + 3I_2(s) \rightarrow 2AlI_3(s)$
   c. $Mg(s) + 2HCl(aq) \rightarrow MgCl_2(aq) + H_2(g)$

4. A coefficient is placed in front of the formula for a reactant or product and indicates how many units of the substance are needed in the reaction. A subscript is found within a chemical formula and is written after an element and slightly below it. A subscript indicates how many atoms of that element are found in each unit of the reactant or product. Only coefficients can be changed when balancing a chemical equation.

5. An aqueous solution is a chemical that is dissolved in water. A liquid is a pure substance; it is not dissolved in water.

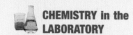
Examples of Reactions

Objectives

1. To carry out four chemical reactions and make observations

2. To decide which clues help to determine that a chemical reaction has taken place

Skills

Observing, applying concepts, interpreting data, drawing conclusions

Materials

Goggles	Hydrochloric
Apron	acid (3.0 *M*)
Bunsen burner	Iron(III) nitrate
Matches	(0.1 *M*)
Tongs	Potassium
Wooden splint	thiocyanate
Well plate	(0.1 *M*)
13 × 100 mm	Sodium
test tubes (2)	chloride
100-mL	Silver nitrate
beakers (2)	
Spatula	
Magnesium	
ribbon	

Preparation Hints

Place small amounts of each chemical in different places in the laboratory. In this way the students will not spend a lot of time waiting to gather materials.

Prelab Discussion

Students must wear safety goggles and lab aprons while in the lab. They should tie back their hair and loose clothing whenever they work with a flame in the lab. Students will often deposit matches in the sink. Tell them to dispose of burned matches in the trashcan after they are cool.

Remind students of the locations of eyewashes. If they come in contact with any solution, they should wash the contacted area thoroughly. The 3.0 *M* HCl is corrosive and should be handled with special care.

Tell students that hydrogen reacts readily with oxygen but only with a source of ignition. In Part I, students will produce hydrogen and should hear a "squeak" as it burns in air.

Disposal

Collect all solutions from the students and dispose of them properly.

Problem

What are some clues that accompany chemical changes?

Introduction

Chemical changes are accompanied by signals, many of which are visual. We can represent chemical reactions by writing chemical equations. Because atoms are neither created nor destroyed, we must balance these equations. In this lab you will carry out four chemical reactions and make careful observations to determine which clues accompany chemical changes.

Prelab Assignment

1. Read the entire lab experiment before you begin.

2. Write and balance chemical equations for the following reactions. Include the state for each substance in the equation.
   a. Solid magnesium reacts with aqueous hydrochloric acid to produce aqueous magnesium chloride and hydrogen gas.
   b. Aqueous sodium chloride reacts with aqueous silver nitrate to produce solid silver chloride and aqueous sodium nitrate.
   c. Solid magnesium burns in the air to form solid magnesium oxide.

Materials

Goggles	100-mL beakers (2)
Apron	Spatula
Bunsen burner	Magnesium ribbon
Matches	Hydrochloric acid (3.0 *M*)
Tongs	Iron(III) nitrate (0.1 *M*)
Wooden splint	Potassium thiocyanate
	(0.1 *M*)
Well plate	Sodium chloride
13 × 100 mm test tubes (2)	Silver nitrate

Safety

1. The 3.0 *M* HCl is corrosive. Handle it with extreme care.

2. If you come in contact with any solution, wash the contacted area thoroughly.

3. You will work with a flame in this lab. Tie back hair and loose clothing.

4. Do not drop matches into the sink. Dispose of burned matches in the trashcan after they are cool.

Procedure

Part I: Reacting Magnesium and Hydrochloric Acid

1. Place about 5 mL of 3.0 *M* aqueous hydrochloric acid in a test tube.

2. Add a 2- to 3-cm piece of magnesium ribbon to the acid. Make careful observations.

3. Place another test tube over the mouth of the test tube containing the acid and magnesium (the mouths should be the same size).

4. After the reaction is finished, light a wooden splint. Quickly turn over the top test tube (so that the mouth in pointing up) and place the burning wood splint near the mouth. Do not point the test tube toward anyone. Make careful observations.

Part II: Reacting Sodium Chloride and Silver Nitrate

1. Dissolve a spatula-tip amount of each of the solids in a small amount of water (about 10 mL) in separate 100-mL beakers.

2. Place a few drops of aqueous sodium chloride into one of the reaction wells.

3. Slowly add a few drops of aqueous silver nitrate to the aqueous sodium chloride. Make careful observations.

Part III: Reacting Magnesium and Oxygen

1. Light the Bunsen burner.

2. Use tongs to hold a 1- to 2-cm piece of magnesium ribbon in the flame. Do not look directly at the magnesium as it burns.

Part IV: $Fe^{3+} + SCN^- \rightarrow FeSCN^{2+}$

1. Place a few drops of aqueous iron(III) nitrate into a clean reaction well.

2. Slowly add a few drops of aqueous potassium thiocyanate to the aqueous iron(III) nitrate. Make careful observations.

Cleaning Up

Clean up all materials and wash your hands thoroughly.

Data/Observations

Include a list of observations for each of the four chemical reactions.

Analysis and Conclusions

1. For each of the reactions, which observations indicate that a chemical reaction was taking place?

2. What are some clues that accompany chemical changes?

Something Extra

List three chemical reactions from everyday life that demonstrate the clues that you observed in this lab.

Post-Lab Discussion

Gather a class list of observations from each part of the experiment. You may wish to use this lab to introduce different types of reactions (which will be studied in Chapter 8). The reaction in Part I is an oxidation–reduction reaction. In Part II, students carry out a precipitation reaction. The reaction in Part III is a combustion reaction (also an oxidation–reduction reaction).

Sample Data/Answers

Prelab Assignment

a. $Mg(s) + 2HCl(aq) \rightarrow MgCl_2(aq) + H_2(g)$

b. $NaCl(aq) + AgNO_3(aq) \rightarrow AgCl(s) + NaNO_3(aq)$

c. $2Mg(s) + O_2(g) \rightarrow 2MgO(s)$

Data/Observations

Answers will vary.

Analysis and Conclusions

1. Answers will vary. In Part I, students should have noticed bubbles, disappearance of magnesium (which does not dissolve in water), and possibly the production of heat. In Part II, a solid is formed. In Part III, light is given off and the product (MgO) is much different from the reactant (Mg). A color change accompanies Part IV.

2. Answers will vary. The formation of a gas, formation of a solid, gen-

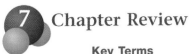

7 Chapter Review

Key Terms

chemical reaction (7.2)
chemical equation (7.2)
reactant (7.2)
product (7.2)

balancing a chemical
    equation (7.2)
coefficient (7.3)

Summary

1. Chemical reactions usually give some kind of visual signal—a color changes, a solid forms, bubbles form, heat and/or flame is produced.

2. A chemical equation represents a chemical reaction. Reactants are shown on the left side of an arrow and products on the right. In a chemical reaction, atoms are neither created nor destroyed; they are merely rearranged. A balanced chemical equation gives the relative numbers of reactant and product molecules.

3. A chemical equation for a reaction can be balanced by using a systematic approach. First identify the reactants and products and write the formulas. Next write the unbalanced equation. Then balance by trial and error, starting with the most complicated molecule(s). Finally, check to be sure the equation is balanced.

Questions and Problems

All exercises with blue numbers have answers in the back of this book.

7.1 Evidence for a Chemical Reaction

Questions

1. List some possible signals that a chemical reaction has occurred. Are these clues always visible? Can you think of any other indications that a chemical reaction has occurred?

2. If a piece of blackboard chalk is heated strongly, the mass of the chalk decreases substantially, and the chalk is converted into a fine powder. What evidence is there for a chemical reaction having taken place when the chalk is heated?

3. If you have had a clogged sink drain at your home, you might have tried using a commercial drain cleaner to dissolve the clog. What evidence is there that such drain cleaners work by chemical reaction?

4. If a bottle of aspirin is left open to air, eventually one of the products is acetic acid (vinegar is a mixture of acetic acid and water). Is there evidence that this change represents a chemical reaction?

7.2 Chemical Equations

Questions

5. The substances present before a chemical reaction takes place are called the _____, and the substances present after the reaction takes place are called the _____.

6. In an ordinary chemical reaction, _____ are neither created nor destroyed.

7. The notation "(g)" after a substance's formula indicates that the substance exists in the _____ state.

8. In a chemical equation for a reaction, the notation "(aq)" after a substance's formula means that the substance is dissolved in _____.

Problems

Note: In some of the following problems you will need to write a chemical formula from the name of the compound. Review Chapter 4 if you are having trouble.

9. If calcium carbonate is heated strongly, carbon dioxide gas is driven off, leaving a residue of calcium oxide. Write the unbalanced chemical equation for this process.

10. Liquefied propane gas is often used for cooking in suburban areas away from natural gas lines. Propane (C_3H_8) burns in oxygen gas, producing carbon dioxide gas, water vapor, and heat. Write the unbalanced chemical equation for this process.

11. If a sample of pure hydrogen gas is ignited very carefully, the hydrogen burns gently, combining with the oxygen gas of the air to form water vapor. Write the unbalanced chemical equation for this reaction.

12. Solid ammonium carbonate, $(NH_4)_2CO_3$, is used as the active ingredient in "smelling salts." When solid ammonium carbonate is heated, it decomposes into ammonia gas, carbon dioxide gas, and water vapor. Write the unbalanced chemical equation for this process.

13. Silver oxide may be decomposed by strong heating into silver metal and oxygen gas. Write the unbalanced chemical equation for this process.

14. Methanol (CH_3OH, wood alcohol) is an important industrial chemical. Methanol may be synthesized from carbon monoxide gas and hydrogen gas under certain conditions of temperature and pressure. Write the unbalanced chemical equation for this process.

15. Elemental boron is produced in one industrial process by heating diboron trioxide with magnesium metal, also producing magnesium oxide. Write the unbalanced chemical equation for this process.

16. Calcium metal is moderately reactive. If pieces of calcium are added to water, the metal begins to bubble as hydrogen gas is formed. The water begins to turn cloudy, as solid calcium hydroxide begins to form. Write the unbalanced chemical equation for the reaction of calcium metal with water.

Chapter Review   **209**

eration or absorption of heat, and a color change are some of the expected answers that are listed in the text. Others include the appearance of a new product or the disappearance of a reactant (that is not accounted for by dissolving).

Something Extra
Answers will vary. Possible answers include the cooking of food, the changing color of leaves in the fall, and the rusting of metal.

Chapter Review
Assign the students to work individually on the Chapter 7 Review Worksheet at the appropriate level (Basic, Standard, or Challenge). Answers are found in the *Teacher Resources.*

Assessment
Chapter 7 Test is found in the *Teacher Resources,* along with the answers for the test.

Computerized Test Bank for Chapter 7

Answers to End of Chapter Problems

1. Signals mentioned in the text include a change in color, formation of a solid, evolution of a gas, and absorption or evolution of heat. Other signals include a change in odor or separation of a reaction mixture into layers of visibly different composition.

2. decrease in mass; change in texture

3. The material in the drain does not dissolve in water until the drain cleaner is added. Heat may also be noticed.

4. change in odor as acetic acid is produced

5. reactants, products

6. atoms

7. gaseous

8. water

9. $CaCO_3(s) \rightarrow CaO(s) + CO_2(g)$

10. $C_3H_8(g) + O_2(g) \rightarrow CO_2(g) + H_2O(g)$

11. $H_2(g) + O_2(g) \rightarrow H_2O(g)$

12. $(NH_4)_2CO_3(s) \rightarrow NH_3(g) + CO_2(g) + H_2O(g)$

13. $Ag_2O(s) \rightarrow Ag(s) + O_2(g)$

14. $CO(g) + H_2(g) \rightarrow CH_3OH(l)$

15. $B_2O_3(s) + Mg(s) \rightarrow B(g) + MgO(s)$

16. $Ca(s) + H_2O(l) \rightarrow Ca(OH)_2(s) + H_2(g)$

17. $P_4(s) + Cl_2(g) \rightarrow PCl_3(g)$

18. $Mg(OH)_2(s) + HCl(aq) \rightarrow MgCl_2(aq) + H_2O(l)$

19. $NH_4NO_3(s) \rightarrow N_2O(g) + H_2O(g)$

20. $H_2S(g) + O_2(g) \rightarrow SO_2(g) + H_2O(g)$

21. $C_2H_2(g) + O_2(g) \rightarrow CO_2(g) + H_2O(g)$

Chapter 7   Chemical Reactions: An Introduction   **209**

22. $Fe_2O_3(s) + CO(g) \rightarrow Fe(l) + CO_2(g)$

23. $BaO(s) + Al(s) \rightarrow Ba(s) + Al_2O_3(s)$; $CaO(s) + Al(s) \rightarrow Ca(s) + Al_2O_3(s)$; $SrO(s) + Al(s) \rightarrow Sr(s) + Al_2O_3(s)$

24. $O_2(g) \rightarrow O_3(g)$

25. $CH_4(g) + Cl_2(g) \rightarrow CCl_4(l) + HCl(g)$

26. $NH_3(g) + HNO_3(g) \rightarrow NH_4NO_3(aq)$

27. $PbS(s) + O_2(g) \rightarrow PbO(s) + SO_2(g)$; $PbO(s) + C(s) \rightarrow Pb(l) + CO_2(g)$

28. $Xe(g) + F_2(g) \rightarrow XeF_4(g)$

29. $NH_4NO_3(s) \rightarrow N_2(g) + O_2(g) + H_2O(g)$

30. $Ag(s) + HNO_3(aq) \rightarrow AgNO_3(aq) + H_2(g)$

31. formula (subscripts)

32. whole numbers

33. (a) $2H_2O_2(aq) \rightarrow 2H_2O(l) + O_2(g)$; (b) $2Ag(s) + H_2S(g) \rightarrow Ag_2S(s) + H_2(g)$; (c) $2FeO(s) + C(s) \rightarrow 2Fe(l) + CO_2(g)$; (d) $Cl_2(g) + 2KI(aq) \rightarrow 2KCl(aq) + I_2(s)$; (e) $Na_2B_4O_7(s) + H_2SO_4(aq) + 5H_2O(l) \rightarrow 4H_3BO_3(s) + Na_2SO_4(aq)$; (f) $CaC_2(s) + 2H_2O(l) \rightarrow Ca(OH)_2(s) + C_2H_2(g)$; (g) $2NaCl(s) + H_2SO_4(l) \rightarrow 2HCl(aq) + Na_2SO_4(s)$; (h) $SiO_2(s) + 2C(s) \rightarrow Si(l) + 2CO(g)$

34. (a) $CaF_2(s) + H_2SO_4(l) \rightarrow CaSO_4(s) + 2HF(g)$; (b) $3KBr(s) + H_3PO_4(aq) \rightarrow K_3PO_4(aq) + 3HBr(g)$; (c) $TiCl_4(l) + 4Na(s) \rightarrow 4NaCl(s) + Ti(s)$; (d) $K_2CO_3(s) \rightarrow K_2O(s) + CO_2(g)$ (already balanced); (e) $4KO_2(s) + 2H_2O(l) \rightarrow 4KOH(aq) + 3O_2(g)$; (f) $2Na_2O_2(s) + H_2O(g) + 4CO_2(g) \rightarrow 4NaHCO_3(s) + O_2(g)$; (g) $2KNO_2(s) + 2C(s) \rightarrow 2K_2CO_3(s) + CO(g) + N_2(g)$; (h) $3BaO(s) + 2Al(s) \rightarrow 3Ba(s) + Al_2O_3(s)$

35. (a) $SiI_4(s) + 2Mg(s) \rightarrow Si(s) + 2MgI_2(s)$; (b) $MnO_2(s) + 2Mg(s) \rightarrow Mn(s) + 2MgO(s)$; (c) $8Ba(s) + S_8(s) \rightarrow 8BaS(s)$; (d) $4NH_3(g) + 3Cl_2(g) \rightarrow 3NH_4Cl(g) + NCl_3(g)$; (e) $8Cu_2S(s) + S_8(s) \rightarrow 16CuS(s)$; (f) $2Al(s) + 3H_2SO_4(g) \rightarrow Al_2(SO_4)_3(aq) + 3H_2(g)$; (g) $2NaCl(s) + 2H_2SO_4(l) \rightarrow 2HCl(g) + Na_2SO_4(s)$; (h) $2CO(g) + O_2(g) \rightarrow 2CO_2(g)$

17. Phosphorus trichloride is used in the manufacture of certain pesticides, and may be synthesized directly from its elements. Write the unbalanced chemical equation for this process.

18. Magnesium hydroxide has been used for many years as an antacid ("milk of magnesia") because it reacts with the hydrochloric acid in the stomach, producing magnesium chloride and water. Write the unbalanced chemical equation for this process.

19. Nitrous oxide gas (systematic name: dinitrogen monoxide) is used by some dentists as an anesthetic. Nitrous oxide (and water vapor) can be produced in small amounts in the laboratory by careful heating of ammonium nitrate. Write the unbalanced chemical equation for this reaction.

20. Hydrogen sulfide gas is responsible for the odor of rotten eggs. Hydrogen sulfide burns in air, producing sulfur dioxide gas and water vapor. Write the unbalanced chemical equation for this process.

21. Acetylene gas (C_2H_2) is often used by plumbers, welders, and glass blowers because it burns in oxygen with an intensely hot flame. The products of the combustion of acetylene are carbon dioxide and water vapor. Write the unbalanced chemical equation for this process.

22. If ferric oxide is heated strongly in a stream of carbon monoxide gas, it produces elemental iron and carbon dioxide gas. Write the unbalanced chemical equation for this process.

23. The Group 2 metals (Ba, Ca, Sr) can be produced in the elemental state by the reaction of their oxides with aluminum metal at high temperatures, also producing solid aluminum oxide. Write the unbalanced chemical equations for the reactions of barium oxide, calcium oxide, and strontium oxide with aluminum.

24. Ozone gas is a form of elemental oxygen containing molecules with *three* oxygen atoms, O_3. Ozone is produced from atmospheric oxygen gas, O_2, by the high-energy outbursts found in lightning storms. Write the unbalanced equation for the formation of ozone gas from oxygen gas.

25. Carbon tetrachloride was widely used for many years until its harmful properties became well established. Carbon tetrachloride may be prepared by the reaction of natural gas (methane, CH_4) and chlorine gas in the presence of ultraviolet light. Write the unbalanced chemical equation for this process.

26. Ammonium nitrate is used as a "high-nitrogen" fertilizer, despite the fact that it is quite explosive if not handled carefully. Ammonium nitrate can be synthesized by the reaction of ammonia gas and nitric acid. Write the unbalanced chemical equation for this process.

27. The principal natural ore of lead is galena, which is primarily lead(II) sulfide. Lead(II) sulfide can be converted to lead(II) oxide and sulfur dioxide gas by heat-

ing strongly in air. Lead(II) oxide can then be heated with elemental carbon (coke), producing pure lead metal and carbon dioxide gas. Write unbalanced chemical equations for the reaction of lead(II) sulfide with oxygen gas, and for the reaction of lead(II) oxide with carbon.

28. Although they were formerly called the inert gases, the heavier elements of Group 8 do form relatively stable compounds. For example, at high temperatures, xenon gas will combine directly with fluorine gas to produce solid xenon tetrafluoride. Write the unbalanced chemical equation for this process.

29. Ammonium nitrate is highly explosive if not handled carefully, breaking down into nitrogen gas, oxygen gas, and water vapor. The expansion of the three gases produced yields the explosive force in this case. Write the unbalanced chemical equation for this process.

30. Silver nitrate is used in "styptic pencils," which help to cauterize small nicks and cuts occurring during shaving. Silver nitrate can be prepared by dissolving metallic silver in concentrated nitric acid, with hydrogen gas being an additional product of the reaction. Write the unbalanced chemical equation for this process.

7.3 Balancing Chemical Equations

Questions

31. When balancing a chemical equation, one must never change the _____ of any reactant or product.

32. After balancing a chemical equation, we ordinarily make sure that the coefficients are the smallest _____ possible.

Problems

33. Balance each of the following chemical equations.
   a. $H_2O_2(aq) \rightarrow H_2O(l) + O_2(g)$
   b. $Ag(s) + H_2S(g) \rightarrow Ag_2S(s) + H_2(g)$
   c. $FeO(s) + C(s) \rightarrow Fe(l) + CO_2(g)$
   d. $Cl_2(g) + KI(aq) \rightarrow KCl(aq) + I_2(s)$

34. Balance each of the following chemical equations.
   a. $CaF_2(s) + H_2SO_4(l) \rightarrow CaSO_4(s) + HF(g)$
   b. $KBr(s) + H_3PO_4(aq) \rightarrow K_3PO_4(aq) + HBr(g)$
   c. $TiCl_4(l) + Na(s) \rightarrow NaCl(s) + Ti(s)$
   d. $K_2CO_3(s) \rightarrow K_2O(s) + CO_2(g)$

35. Balance each of the following chemical equations.
   a. $SiI_4(s) + Mg(s) \rightarrow Si(s) + MgI_2(s)$
   b. $MnO_2(s) + Mg(s) \rightarrow Mn(s) + MgO(s)$
   c. $Ba(s) + S_8(s) \rightarrow BaS(s)$
   d. $NH_3(g) + Cl_2(g) \rightarrow NH_4Cl(s) + NCl_3(g)$

36. Balance each of the following chemical equations.
   a. $Ba(NO_3)_2(aq) + Na_2CrO_4(aq) \rightarrow BaCrO_4(s) + NaNO_3(aq)$
   b. $PbCl_2(aq) + K_2SO_4(aq) \rightarrow PbSO_4(s) + KCl(aq)$
   c. $C_2H_5OH(l) + O_2(g) \rightarrow CO_2(g) + H_2O(l)$
   d. $CaC_2(s) + H_2O(l) \rightarrow Ca(OH)_2(s) + C_2H_2(g)$

36. (a) $Ba(NO_3)_2(aq) + Na_2CrO_4(aq) \rightarrow BaCrO_4(s) + 2NaNO_3(aq)$; (b) $PbCl_2(aq) + K_2SO_4(aq) \rightarrow PbSO_4(s) + 2KCl(aq)$; (c) $C_2H_5OH(l) + 3O_2(g) \rightarrow 2CO_2(g) + 3H_2O(l)$; (d) $CaC_2(s) + 2H_2O(l) \rightarrow Ca(OH)_2(s) + C_2H_2(g)$; (e) $Sr(s) + 2HNO_3(aq) \rightarrow Sr(NO_3)_2(aq) + H_2(g)$; (f) $BaO_2(s) + H_2SO_4(g) \rightarrow BaSO_4(s) + H_2O_2(aq)$; (g) $2AsI_3(s) \rightarrow 2As(s) + 3I_2(g)$; (h) $2CuSO_4(aq) + 4KI(s) \rightarrow 2CuI(s) + I_2(s) + K_2SO_4(aq)$

37. $Al(s) + O_2(g) \rightarrow Al_2O_3(s)$

38. $KNO_3(s) + C(s) \rightarrow K_2CO_3(s) + CO(g) + H_2(g)$

39. $C_{12}H_{22}O_{11}(aq) + H_2O(l) \rightarrow 4C_2H_5OH(l) + 4CO_2(g)$

40. $2H_2(g) + CO(g) \rightarrow CH_3OH(l)$

41. $2Al_2O_3(s) + 3C(s) \rightarrow 4Al(s) + 3CO_2(g)$

42. $Fe_3O_4(s) + 4H_2(g) \rightarrow 3Fe(s) + 4H_2O(g)$; $Fe_3O_4(s) + 4CO(g) \rightarrow 3Fe(s) + 4CO_2(g)$

43. $2Li(s) + S(s) \rightarrow Li_2S(s)$; $2Na(s) + S(s) \rightarrow Na_2S(s)$; $2K(s) + S(s) \rightarrow K_2S(s)$; $2Rb(s) + S(s) \rightarrow Rb_2S(s)$; $2Cs(s) + S(s) \rightarrow Cs_2S(s)$; $2Fr(s) + S(s) \rightarrow Fr_2S(s)$

44. $2KClO_3(s) \rightarrow 2KCl(s) + 3O_2(g)$

45. $2H_2O_2(aq) \rightarrow H_2O(g) + O_2(g)$

46. $CaSiO_3(s) + 6HF(g) \rightarrow CaF_2(aq) + SiF_4(g) + 3H_2O(l)$

47. Carbon dioxide gas is released.

Critical Thinking

37. Many ships are built with aluminum superstructures to save weight. Aluminum, however, burns in oxygen if there is a sufficiently hot ignition source, which has led to several tragedies at sea. Write the unbalanced chemical equation for the reaction of aluminum with oxygen, producing aluminum oxide as product.

38. Crude gunpowders often contain a mixture of potassium nitrate and charcoal (carbon). When such a mixture is heated until reaction occurs, a solid residue of potassium carbonate is produced. The explosive force of the gunpowder comes from the fact that two gases are also produced (carbon monoxide and nitrogen), which increase in volume with great force and speed. Write the unbalanced chemical equation for the process.

39. The sugar sucrose, which is present in many fruits and vegetables, reacts in the presence of certain yeast enzymes to produce ethyl alcohol (ethanol) and carbon dioxide gas. Balance the following equation for this reaction of sucrose.

$$C_{12}H_{22}O_{11}(aq) + H_2O(l) \rightarrow C_2H_5OH(aq) + CO_2(g)$$

40. Methanol (methyl alcohol), CH_3OH, is a very important industrial chemical. Today, methanol is synthesized from carbon monoxide and elemental hydrogen. Write the balanced chemical equation for this process.

41. The Hall process is an important method by which pure aluminum is prepared from its oxide (alumina, Al_2O_3) by indirect reaction with graphite (carbon). Balance the following equation, which is a simplified representation of this process.

$$Al_2O_3(s) + C(s) \rightarrow Al(s) + CO_2(g)$$

42. Iron oxide ores, commonly a mixture of FeO and Fe_2O_3, are given the general formula Fe_3O_4. They yield elemental iron when heated to a very high temperature with either carbon monoxide or elemental hydrogen. Balance the following equations for these processes.

$$Fe_3O_4(s) + H_2(g) \rightarrow Fe(s) + H_2O(g)$$
$$Fe_3O_4(s) + CO(g) \rightarrow Fe(s) + CO_2(g)$$

43. The elements of Group 1 all react with sulfur to form the metal sulfides. Write balanced chemical equations for the reactions of the Group 1 elements with sulfur.

44. A common experiment in chemistry classes involves heating a weighed mixture of potassium chlorate, $KClO_3$, and potassium chloride. Potassium chlorate decomposes when heated, producing potassium chloride and oxygen gas. By measuring the volume of oxygen gas produced in this experiment, students can calculate the relative percentage of $KClO_3$ and KCl in the original mixture. Write the balanced chemical equation for this process.

45. A common demonstration in chemistry classes involves adding a tiny speck of manganese(IV) oxide to a concentrated hydrogen peroxide, H_2O_2, solution. Hydrogen peroxide decomposes quite spectacularly under these conditions to produce oxygen gas and steam (water vapor). Manganese(IV) oxide speeds up the decomposition of hydrogen peroxide but is not consumed in the reaction. Write the balanced equation for the decomposition reaction of hydrogen peroxide.

46. Glass is a mixture of several compounds, but a major constituent of most glass is calcium silicate, $CaSiO_3$. Glass can be etched by treatment with hydrogen fluoride: HF attacks the calcium silicate of the glass, producing gaseous and water-soluble products (which can be removed by washing the glass). For example, the volumetric glassware in chemistry laboratories is often graduated by using this process. Balance the following equation for the reaction of hydrogen fluoride with calcium silicate.

$$CaSiO_3(s) + HF(g) \rightarrow CaF_2(aq) + SiF_4(g) + H_2O(l)$$

47. If you had a "sour stomach," you might try an over-the-counter antacid tablet to relieve the problem. Can you think of evidence that the action of such an antacid is a chemical reaction?

48. If solutions of potassium chromate and barium chloride are mixed, a bright yellow solid (barium chromate) forms and settles out of the mixture, leaving potassium chloride in solution. Write a balanced chemical equation for this process.

49. When a strip of magnesium metal is heated in oxygen, it bursts into an intensely white flame and produces a finely powdered dust of magnesium oxide. Write the unbalanced chemical equation for this process.

50. When copper(II) oxide is boiled in an aqueous solution of sulfuric acid, a strikingly blue solution of copper(II) sulfate forms along with additional water. Write the unbalanced chemical equation for this reaction.

51. When lead(II) sulfide is heated to high temperatures in a stream of pure oxygen gas, solid lead(II) oxide forms with the release of gaseous sulfur dioxide. Write the unbalanced chemical equation for this reaction.

52. Benzene, C_6H_6, is reacted with nitric acid. Two products are formed, one of which is water. The other product is an oily liquid with a molar mass of 213 g/mol. Analysis shows that the oily compound contains 33.8% C, 1.42% H, 19.7% N, and the remainder O. From this information, write a balanced equation for the reaction.

---

48. $K_2CrO_4(aq) + BaCl_2(aq) \rightarrow$ $BaCrO_4(s) + 2KCl(aq)$

49. $Mg(s) + O_2(g) \rightarrow MgO(s)$

50. $CuO(s) + H_2SO_4(aq) \rightarrow$ $CuSO_4(aq) + H_2O(l)$

51. $PbS(s) + O_2(g) \rightarrow PbO(s) +$ $SO_2(g)$

52. $C_6H_6(l) + 3HNO_3(aq) \rightarrow$ $C_6H_3N_3O_6(l) + 3H_2O(l)$

8 Reactions and Aqueous Solutions

Section	Text Features & Components	Labs, Demonstrations & Activities
Teaching Segment 8A **1 block** **pp. 213–223** 8.1–8.2 ◐ **Predicting Whether a Reaction Will Occur** **Reactions in Which a Solid Forms**	**LP** Lesson Plans (Sec 8.1–8.2) **TE** Teaching Support: Background Information *p. 212* **TE** Teaching Support: Background Information *pp. 214–215*	**SE** Chemistry in Action: Precipitation *p. 214* **TE** Mini Demo *p. 214* **TE** Teaching Support: Demonstration *pp. 216–217* **TE** Additional Activity *p. 218* **LM** Experiment 29: Precipitation Reaction Lab Manual Report Sheets Teacher's Lab Guide
Teaching Segment 8B **1 block** **pp. 223–230** 8.3 ◕ **Describing Reactions in Aqueous Solutions**	**LP** Lesson Plans (Sec 8.3–8.4) **SE** Chemical Impact: Instant Cooking-On Demand *p. 225*	**TE** Teaching Support: Demonstration *pp. 224–226*
	8.4 ◕ **Reactions That Form Water: Acids and Bases**	**TE** Teaching Support: Background Information: *pp. 226–227* **SE** Celebrity Chemical: Calcium Carbonate *p. 230*	**TE** Teaching Support: Demonstration *pp. 230–232* **TE** Mini Demo *p. 226*
Teaching Segment 8C **3 blocks** **pp. 231–243** 8.5 ◕ **Reactions of Metals with Nonmetals (Oxidation-Reduction)**	**LP** Lesson Plans (Sec 8.5–8.7) **TE** Teaching Tips *pp. 231–232*	**SE** Chemistry in Action: What's That in Your Water? *p. 234* **TE** Teaching Support *pp. 234–235*
	8.6 ◐ **Ways to Classify Reactions** ◑	**SE** Chemical Impact: Do We Age By Oxidation? *p. 237* **SE** Chemical Impact: Launching the Space Shuttle *p. 238*	**SE** Chemistry in the Laboratory *p. 244* **LM** Experiment 30–31 Lab Manual Report Sheets Teacher's Lab Guide
	8.7 ❷ **Other Ways to Classify Reactions**		**LM** Experiment 32–33 Lab Manual Report Sheets Teacher's Lab Guide

Key

SE Student Edition

TE Teacher Edition

RP Teacher Resource Package

LM Lab Materials

LP Lesson Plans

AR Additional Resources

 Florida Specific

Technology and Media

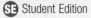 **Transparencies**
 Table 8.1   Figure 8.3, 8.12

PowerPoint Slides

 Animation
 Dissolution of a Solid in a Liquid
 Proton Transfer

 Video Potassium Metal Reaction with Water

Chemistry in Motion
 (4) Zinc and Iodine • (11) Thermite Reaction • (21) Sugar, Potassium Chlorate, and Sulfuric Acid • (22) Ammonium Dichromate Volcano

 eEdition CD-ROM
 Easy Planner CD-ROM
 English Summaries CD
 Spanish Summaries CD

 Web Site classzone.com
 McDougal Littell Test Generator

Chapter Planning Guide

All Learners	Review & Assessment	Standards
TE Active Learning *p. 213* **TE** Teaching Tips *p. 216* Animation: Dissolution of a Solid in a Liquid *p. 215* Transparency: Table 8. 1 *p. 218* Transparency: Figure 8.3 *p. 218* **RP** Team Learning Worksheets (Sec 8.1–8.2) *pp. 33–34* **AR** Less Proficient Students *p. 14*	**TE** Additional Examples *pp. 219, 221* **SE** Self Check *p. 223* **SE** Focus Questions (Sec 8.1–8.2) *p. 223* **SE** Key Terms *p. 245* **SE** Questions and Problems *p. 245*	**TE** NSES UCP3, A1, A2, B3 **SSS** SC.C.2.4.2
TE Active Learning *p. 223* **TE** Teaching Tips *p. 224* **AR** Less Proficient Students *p. 14*	**TE** Additional Examples *p. 225* **SE** Self Check *p. 226* **SE** Key Terms *p. 245* **SE** Questions and Problems *p. 246*	**TE** NSES UCP3, UCP5, A1, A2, B3, D2, G1, G2, G3 **SSS** SC.H.1.4.2, SC.C.2.4.5
Animation: Proton Transfer *p. 227* **RP** Team Learning Worksheets (Sec 8.3–8.4) *pp. 35–36* **AR** Less Proficient Students *p. 14*	**TE** Additional Examples *p. 228* **SE** Focus Questions (Sec 8.3–8.4) *p. 230* **SE** Key Terms *p. 245* **SE** Questions and Problems *pp. 246–247*	
TE Active Learning *p. 231* Chemistry in Motion (4), (11), (21), (22) Video: Potassium Metal Reaction with Water *p. 231* **AR** Less Proficient Students *p. 14*	**TE** Additional Examples *p. 233* **SE** Self Check *p. 234* **SE** Key Terms *p. 245* **SE** Questions and Problems *p. 247*	**TE** NSES UCP3, UCP5, A1, A2, B3, C5, E1, E2, F1, F6 **SSS** SC.H.1.4.1, SC.H.1.4.2, SC.A.1.4.3, SC.A.2.4.1, SC.C.2.4.5, SC.G.2.4.1, SC.H.3.4.6
TE Teaching Tips *pp. 236, 239* **AR** Less Proficient Students *p. 15*	**SE** Key Terms *p. 245* **SE** Questions and Problems *p. 247*	
Transparency: Figure 8.12 *p. 242* **RP** Team Learning Worksheets (Sec 8.5–8.7) *pp. 37–38* **AR** Less Proficient Students *p. 15*	**TE** Additional Examples *p. 242* **SE** Self Check *p. 243* **SE** What if . . . *p. 243* **SE** Focus Questions (Sec 8.5–8.7) *p. 243* **SE** Key Terms *p. 245* **SE** Questions and Problems *p. 248*	

Chapter Materials

TE Reading Strategy **AR** English/Spanish Summaries *pp. 11–12* **AR** Challenge Projects/Problems *pp. 14–15* **AR** Less Proficient Students *p. 13* English Summary Audio Spanish Summary Audio **RP** Chapter Review Worksheets (Basic, Review, Challenge)	**SE** Chapter Summary *p. 245* **SE** Critical Thinking *pp. 248–249* **RP** Solutions Guide **RP** Chapter Tests **RP** Test Bank McDougal Littell Test Generator **AR** Standardized Test Practice FCAT Test 4

8 Integrating Reading Strategies and Chemistry Concepts

Chapter 8: Note Taking

Your students probably know by now that understanding chemistry depends on being able to absorb a great deal of new and often complex information. Many students find the volume of information overwhelming and may feel anxious about taking and organizing their notes. Review various note-taking strategies to help the students become more confident and more efficient in organizing their thoughts.

Emphasize that different people take notes in different ways and that no one way is necessarily the best. Stress that it may take a while to discover which method works best for each individual but that the time spent taking and organizing notes will be worth their effort.

Note taking can be divided into two main categories: taking notes from written material, such as the textbook; and taking notes from verbal presentations, such as a class presentation. Point out that both types of note taking have advantages and that the students may want to try different methods before settling on one that works best.

Reasons to Take Notes from the Textbook

Notes ...

- prepare the students for the material that will be presented during class.

- help the students become familiar with basic concepts and vocabulary, making class presentations more understandable.

- enable the students to be better listeners because they recognize important points taken from the textbook.

- make reviewing for tests easier and more efficient.

Reasons to Take Notes During Class

Notes ...

- help the students concentrate throughout the class and avoid distractions.

- improve the students' listening skills.

- provide valuable hints as to what material the teacher considers important and therefore which items are likely to appear on a quiz or test.

- often contain information that is not provided in the textbook.

How to Organize Notes from Textbook Readings

Emphasize that notes need to be organized in a logical way. When taking notes from textbook readings, the students should first look through the chapter to see how it is organized and then decide on the best way to organize their own notes.

Tell the students to skim through Chapter 8. Then tell them to go back to the first page of the chapter and review the **Looking Ahead** box. Point out that every chapter contains a **Looking Ahead** box that can be a good starting point for organizing notes. Suggest that the students try to include at least one or two important points from each section of the chapter in their notes.

Have the students read the first section of the chapter, and ask them to summarize its key points. Provide hints as necessary. If time permits, repeat this exercise for the next few sections.

LOOKING AHEAD

8.1 Predicting Whether a Reaction Will Occur

8.2 Reactions in Which a Solid Forms

8.3 Describing Reactions in Aqueous Solutions

8.4 Reactions That Form Water: Acids and Bases

8.5 Reactions of Metals with Nonmetals (Oxidation–Reduction)

8.6 Ways to Classify Reactions

8.7 Other Ways to Classify Reactions

How to use the Cornell Note-Taking System during Class Presentations

The Cornell Note-Taking System is a method that is taught at a number of colleges and universities and is becoming more common in high schools. It involves the following steps: Record, Reduce, Recite, Reflect, and Review.

Have each student divide one notebook page into two columns by drawing a vertical line down the page. The left column, the "Recall Column," should be about 2.5 inches wide, and the right column, the "Recording Column," about 6 inches wide. Then have students draw a horizontal line across the bottom of the page, about 1 inch from the bottom. Explain to students the technique described in the diagram at right.

Recall Column | **Recording Column**

3. After reducing notes, cover the right-hand column. Look at the key terms in the left column and recite as much information as you can recall.

2. After class, reduce the notes you took in the Recording Column to key words and phrases.

1. During the presentation, record notes here. Write legibly and use abbreviations where possible. Don't try to write down everything; focus on key points. If the teacher writes notes on the board, be sure to include them.

4. After reciting the material, take a few minutes to reflect on your notes and make connections between them and previously learned concepts.

5. Review your notes by summarizing them in your own words in a couple of meaningful sentences. Doing so will help you retain the material.

Overview

In this Chapter our goals are for the students to:

- Learn about some of the factors that cause reactions to occur

- Learn to identify the solid that forms in a precipitation reaction

- Learn to describe reactions in solutions by writing molecular, complete ionic, and net ionic equations

- Learn the key characteristics of the reactions between strong acids and strong bases

- Learn the general characteristics of a reaction between a metal and a nonmetal

- Understand electron transfer as a driving force for a chemical reaction

- Learn various classification schemes for reactions

8 Reactions in Aqueous Solutions

LOOKING AHEAD

Potassium metal reacts vigorously with water.

212

TEACHING SUPPORT
Background Information

This chapter introduces the concept of a "driving force." Driving forces for natural processes are complex and we would not expect students to understand at this point the "why" of them. At this time students need to become aware that important driving forces exist and recognize what some of them are. The "why" of these forces usually is explained in terms of achieving the lowest possible randomness (entropy), but this idea would not make sense to students at this point in their study of chemistry.

The chemical reactions that are most important to us occur in water—in aqueous solutions. Virtually all of the chemical reactions that keep each of us alive and well take place in the aqueous medium present in our bodies. For example, the oxygen you breathe dissolves in your blood, where it associates with the hemoglobin in the red blood cells. While attached to the hemoglobin it is transported to your cells, where it reacts with fuel (from the food you eat) to provide energy for living. However, the reaction between oxygen and fuel is not direct—the cells are not tiny furnaces. Instead, electrons are transferred from the fuel to a series of molecules that pass them along (this is called the respiratory chain) until they eventually reach oxygen. Many other reactions are also crucial to our health and well-being. You will see numerous examples of these as you continue your study of chemistry.

In this chapter we will study some common types of reactions that take place in water, and we will become familiar with some of the driving forces that make these reactions occur. We will also learn how to predict the products for these reactions and how to write various equations to describe them.

Developing a photo involves several aqueous chemical reactions.

8.1 Predicting Whether a Reaction Will Occur

Objective: *To learn about some of the factors that cause reactions to occur.*

In this text we have already seen many chemical reactions. Now let's consider an important question: Why does a chemical reaction occur? What causes reactants to "want" to form products? As chemists have studied reactions, they have recognized several "tendencies" in reactants that drive them to form products. That is, there are several "driving forces" that pull reactants toward products—changes that tend to make reactions go in the direction of the arrow. The most common of these driving forces are

1. Formation of a solid

2. Formation of water

3. Transfer of electrons

4. Formation of a gas

When two or more chemicals are brought together, if any of these things can occur, a chemical change (a reaction) is likely to take place. Accordingly, when we are confronted with a set of reactants and want to predict whether a reaction will occur and what products might form, we will consider these driving forces. They will help us organize our thoughts as we encounter new reactions.

8.1 Predicting Whether a Reaction Will Occur **213**

Themes
Patterns of Change

Skills
Observing, applying concepts, making predictions

Student Preparation
Assign the students to read Sections 8.1 and 8.2 and to answer the Focus Questions at the end of Section 8.2 before coming to class.

Active Learning
After introducing the material in Sections 8.1 and 8.2 in class, place the students in groups and have them work together on Sections 8.1–8.2: Team Learning Worksheet. Answers and/or discussion of these questions are located in the *Teacher Resources.*

TEACHING TIPS

• Explain to students that chemists make predictions based on the driving forces in a reaction and their own databases (mostly in their memories) of chemical reactions. The more experience someone has, the easier it becomes to predict the correct products for a reaction.

• Now is an excellent time to review and reteach polyatomic ions. Students will need them to write the chemical equations in this chapter.

Themes
Patterns of Change

Skills
Observing, classifying, making predictions

Laboratory
Experiment 29:
Precipitation Reaction,
Microscale

TEACHING TIP

Many teachers identify precipitation reactions by the term "double-displacement reactions." Students are confused by this idea of double displacement, so we use only the term "precipitation" to emphasize the driving force in this type of reaction. The term "double displacement" is discussed as an alternative way to classify chemical reactions in Section 8.7.

MINI-DEMO

0.1 M K$_2$CrO$_4$ and 0.1 M Ba(NO$_3$)$_2$ can be used to illustrate the reaction shown in Figure 8.1. Place the yellow potassium chromate solution in a beaker and the barium nitrate solution in a graduated cylinder. Slowly pour the barium nitrate into the potassium chromate solution.

Note: You can also use many other combinations for this illustration. For example, another yellow precipitate is formed from KI and Pb(NO$_3$)$_2$.

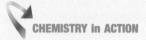

CHEMISTRY in ACTION

Forecast: Precipitation

Materials Each student/group will need the flashcards from the Chapter 4 activities and access to the solubility rules.

Purpose Students will practice interpreting the solubility rules and writing molecular, complete ionic, and net ionic equations. In addition, they will review writing formulas from ions.

Discussion This activity can be altered to fit any time limit. For example, you can have the students write a different number of net ionic equations.

8.2 Reactions in Which a Solid Forms

Objective: *To learn to identify the solid that forms in a precipitation reaction.*

One driving force for a chemical reaction is the formation of a solid, a process called **precipitation**. The solid that forms is called a **precipitate**, and the reaction is known as a **precipitation reaction**. For example, when an aqueous (water) solution of potassium chromate, K$_2$CrO$_4$(aq), which is yellow, is added to a colorless aqueous solution containing barium nitrate, Ba(NO$_3$)$_2$(aq), a yellow solid forms (see **Figure 8.1**). The fact that a solid forms tells us that a reaction—a chemical change—has occurred. That is, we have a situation where

Reactants → Products

What is the equation that describes this chemical change? To write the equation, we must decipher the identities of the reactants and products. The reactants have already been described: K$_2$CrO$_4$(aq) and Ba(NO$_3$)$_2$(aq). Is there some way in which we can predict the identities of the products? What is the yellow solid? The best way to predict the identity of this solid is to first *consider what products are possible*. To do this we need to know what chemical species are present in the solution that results when the reactant solutions are mixed. First, let's think about the nature of each reactant in an aqueous solution.

What Happens When an Ionic Compound Dissolves in Water?

The designation Ba(NO$_3$)$_2$(aq) means that barium nitrate (a white solid) has been dissolved in water. Note from its formula that barium nitrate contains the Ba^{2+} and NO$_3^-$ ions. *In virtually every case when a solid containing ions*

Figure 8.1
The precipitation reaction that occurs when yellow potassium chromate, K$_2$CrO$_4$(aq), is mixed with a colorless barium nitrate solution, Ba(NO$_3$)$_2$(aq).

CHEMISTRY in ACTION
Forecast: Precipitation

1. Make two sets of flashcards with names of ions on one side and symbol and charge on the other (use the cards from the Chapter 4 activities if you have them).

   Set 1: all of the alkali and alkaline earth metals, and iron(II), iron(III), lead(II), and silver.

   Set 2: all of the nonmetals from Groups 5, 6, and 7, and the polyatomic ions listed in Table 4.4.

2. Randomly pick one card from set 1 and one card from set 2. Write the formula for the ionic compound that would form and name the compound.

3. Repeat step 2. Are both ionic compounds soluble? If so, go to step 4; if not, go back to step 2.

4. Use the two soluble ionic compounds as reactants. Write the names and formulas for the possible products of the reaction, the molecular equation, and the complete ionic equation. Is at least one of the products insoluble? If so, go to step 5; if not, go back to step 2.

5. Write the net ionic equation for the reaction. Go back to step 2 and continue this process until you have five net ionic equations.

214   Chapter 8   Reactions in Aqueous Solutions

TEACHING SUPPORT
Background Information

One of the most valuable properties of water is its ability to dissolve many different substances. For example, salt "disappears" when you sprinkle it into the water used to cook vegetables, as does sugar when you add it to your iced tea. In each case the "disappearing"

substance is obviously still present—you can taste it. What happens when a solid dissolves? To understand this process, we need to consider the nature of water. Liquid water consists of a collection of H$_2$O molecules. An individual H$_2$O molecule is "bent" or V-shaped, with an H—O—H angle of approximately 105 degrees:

$$\overset{105°}{H\diagdown\underset{O}{\diagup}H}$$

The O—H bonds in the water molecule are covalent bonds formed by electron sharing between the oxygen and hydrogen atoms. However, the electrons of the bond are not shared equally between these atoms. For reasons we will discuss in later chapters, oxygen has a greater attraction for electrons than does hydrogen. If

Source of electric power

Pure water

(a) Pure water does not conduct an electric current. The lamp does not light.

Source of electric power

Free ions present in water

(b) When an ionic compound is dissolved in water, current flows and the lamp lights.

USING TECHNOLOGY

Animation and Video
The animation "Dissolution of a Solid in a Liquid" shows salt dissolving in water at the molecular level.

dissolves in water, the ions separate and move around independently. We say that the ions of the solid *dissociate* when the solid dissolves in water. That is, $Ba(NO_3)_2(aq)$ does not contain $Ba(NO_3)_2$ units. Rather, it contains separated Ba^{2+} and NO_3^- ions. In the solution there are two NO_3^- ions for every Ba^{2+} ion. Chemists know that separated ions are present in this solution because it is an excellent conductor of electricity (see **Figure 8.2**). Pure water does not conduct an electric current. Ions must be present in water for a current to flow.

When each unit of a substance that dissolves in water produces separated ions, the substance is called a **strong electrolyte.** Barium nitrate is a strong electrolyte in water, because each $Ba(NO_3)_2$ unit produces the separated ions $(Ba^{2+}, NO_3^-, NO_3^-)$.

Similarly, aqueous K_2CrO_4 also behaves as a strong electrolyte. Potassium chromate contains the K^+ and CrO_4^{2-} ions, so an aqueous solution of potassium chromate (which is prepared by dissolving solid K_2CrO_4 in water) contains these separated ions. That is, $K_2CrO_4(aq)$ does not contain K_2CrO_4 units but instead contains K^+ cations and CrO_4^{2-} anions, which move around independently. (There are two K^+ ions for each CrO_4^{2-} ion.)

The idea introduced here is very important: when ionic compounds dissolve, the *resulting solution contains the separated ions*. Therefore, we can represent the mixing of $K_2CrO_4(aq)$ and $Ba(NO_3)_2(aq)$ in two ways. We usually write these reactants as

$$K_2CrO_4(aq) + Ba(NO_3)_2(aq) \rightarrow \text{Products}$$

However, a more accurate representation of the situation is:

$K_2CrO_4(aq)$
Ions separate when the solid dissolves.

$Ba(NO_3)_2(aq)$
Ions separate when the solid dissolves.

Products

8.2   Reactions in Which a Solid Forms   **215**

the electrons were shared equally between the two atoms, both would be electrically neutral because, on average, the number of electrons around each would equal the number of protons in that nucleus. Because the oxygen atom has a greater attraction for electrons, the shared electrons tend to spend more time close to the oxygen than to either of the hydrogens. Thus the oxygen atom gains a slight excess of negative charge, and the hydrogen atoms become slightly positive. Because of this unequal charge distribution, water is said to be a **polar molecule.** This polarity gives water its great ability to dissolve compounds.

We can express this information in equation form as follows:

$$2K^+(aq) + CrO_4^{2-}(aq) + Ba^{2+}(aq) + 2NO_3^-(aq) \rightarrow \text{Products}$$

The ions in
$K_2CrO_4(aq)$

The ions in
$Ba(NO_3)_2(aq)$

Thus the *mixed solution* contains four types of ions: K^+, CrO_4^{2-}, Ba^{2+}, and NO_3^-. Now that we know what the reactants are, we can make some educated guesses about the possible products.

How to Decide What Products Form

Which of these ions combine to form the yellow solid observed when the original solutions are mixed? This is not an easy question to answer. Even an experienced chemist is not sure what will happen in a new reaction. The chemist tries to think of the various possibilities, considers the likelihood of each possibility, and then makes a prediction (an educated guess). Only after identifying each product experimentally can the chemist be sure what reaction actually has taken place. However, an educated guess is very useful because it indicates what kinds of products are most likely. It gives us a place to start. So the best way to proceed is first to think of the various possibilities and then to decide which of them is most likely.

What are the possible products of the reaction between $K_2CrO_4(aq)$ and $Ba(NO_3)_2(aq)$ or, more accurately, what reaction can occur among the ions K^+, CrO_4^{2-}, Ba^{2+}, and NO_3^-? We already know some things that will help us decide. We know that a *solid compound must have a zero net charge*. This means that the product of our reaction must contain *both anions and cations* (negative and positive ions). For example, K^+ and Ba^{2+} could not combine to form the solid because such a solid would have a positive charge. Similarly, CrO_4^{2-} and NO_3^- could not combine to form a solid because that solid would have a negative charge.

Something else that will help us is an observation that chemists have made by examining many compounds: *most ionic materials contain only two types of ions*—one type of cation and one type of anion. This idea is illustrated by the following compounds (among many others):

Compound	Cation	Anion
NaCl	Na^+	Cl^-
KOH	K^+	OH^-
Na_2SO_4	Na^+	SO_4^{2-}
NH_4Cl	NH_4^+	Cl^-
Na_2CO_3	Na^+	CO_3^{2-}

All the possible combinations of a cation and an anion to form uncharged compounds from among the ions K^+, CrO_4^{2-}, Ba^{2+}, and NO_3^- are shown below:

	NO_3^-	CrO_4^{2-}
K^+	KNO_3	K_2CrO_4
Ba^{2+}	$Ba(NO_3)_2$	$BaCrO_4$

So the following compounds *might* be the solid:

K_2CrO_4	$BaCrO_4$
KNO_3	$Ba(NO_3)_2$

TEACHING TIPS

- Review how ionic compounds are formed. Remind students that both positive and negative ions are needed to form a compound and that compounds must be electrically neutral.

- To help students decide which products can form, list all possible combinations and then eliminate the unlikely ones.

- Students sometimes have trouble remembering that they must eliminate the starting reactants as possible products. Use molecular-level drawings to show why these substances cannot be products in the reaction.

- Use the transparency for Figure 8.3 to help the students decide on the identity of the precipitate.

TEACHING SUPPORT
Demonstration

Lights Out!

Materials
Saturated $Ba(OH)_2$
3 *M* H_2SO_4
Beaker
Stirring plate and stir bar or student volunteer stirrer
Conductivity tester

Preparation Make saturated barium hydroxide by dissolving the maximum amount possible in distilled water. Decant the solution from the solid for use.

Presentation Place 25 mL distilled water and one drop of 3 *M* sulfuric acid in the beaker. Add the stirring bar and place the beaker on the stir plate. Place the conductivity tester in the beaker, out of the way of the spinning stir bar. Add the barium hydroxide solution dropwise, observing the light. Continue adding barium hydroxide until the light goes out. Stop and discuss this result with the students. End the demonstration by asking for a prediction of what will happen if more barium hydroxide is added to the solution. Add more barium hydroxide and discuss the results with the students.

Which of these possibilities is most likely to represent the yellow solid? We know it's not K_2CrO_4 or $Ba(NO_3)_2$; these are the reactants. They were present (dissolved) in the separate solutions that were mixed initially. The only real possibilities are KNO_3 and $BaCrO_4$. To decide which of these is more likely to represent the yellow solid, we need more facts. An experienced chemist, for example, knows that KNO_3 is a white solid. On the other hand, the CrO_4^{2-} ion is yellow. Therefore, the yellow solid must be $BaCrO_4$.

We have determined that one product of the reaction between $K_2CrO_4(aq)$ and $Ba(NO_3)_2(aq)$ is $BaCrO_4(s)$, but what happened to the K^+ and NO_3^- ions? The answer is that these ions are left dissolved in the solution. That is, KNO_3 does not form a solid when the K^+ and NO_3^- ions are present in water. In other words, if we took the white solid $KNO_3(s)$ and put it in water, it would totally dissolve (the white solid would "disappear," yielding a colorless solution). So when we mix $K_2CrO_4(aq)$ and $Ba(NO_3)_2(aq)$, $BaCrO_4(s)$ forms but KNO_3 is left behind in solution [we write it as $KNO_3(aq)$]. (If we poured the mixture through a filter to remove the solid $BaCrO_4$ and then evaporated all of the water, we would obtain the white solid KNO_3.)

After all this thinking, we can finally write the unbalanced equation for the precipitation reaction.

$$K_2CrO_4(aq) + Ba(NO_3)_2(aq) \rightarrow BaCrO_4(s) + KNO_3(aq)$$

We can represent this reaction in pictures as follows:

Solid $BaCrO_4$ forms.

Note that the K^+ and NO_3^- ions are not involved in the chemical change. They remain dispersed in the water before and after the reaction.

Using Solubility Rules

In the preceding example, we were finally able to identify the products of the reaction by using two types of chemical knowledge:

1. Knowledge of facts

2. Knowledge of concepts

For example, knowing the colors of the various compounds proved very helpful. This represents factual knowledge. Awareness of the concept that solids always have a net charge of zero was also essential. These two kinds of knowledge allowed us to make a good guess about the identity of the solid that formed. As you continue to study chemistry, you will see that a balance of factual and conceptual knowledge is always required. You must both *memorize* important facts and *understand* crucial concepts to succeed.

In the present case we are dealing with a reaction in which an ionic solid forms—that is, a process in which ions that are dissolved in water combine to give a solid. We know that for a solid to form, both positive and negative

Teaching Notes This demonstration provides a practical connection between the macroscopic and microscopic worlds. Draw the solutions before the reaction on a molecular level. Discuss how conductivity tells us that ions are present in the solution. Proceed with the demonstration until the light goes out. Now discuss on a molecular level what is present in the beaker (water and solid $BaSO_4$) and explain how this situation is different from that before the reaction. After the student predictions, explain that the light comes on again as a result of the addition of more barium and hydroxide ions, which do not form a precipitate because all of the sulfate has been consumed.

CHEMISTRY

Solids must contain both anions and cations in the relative numbers necessary to produce zero net charge.

ions must be present in relative numbers that give zero net charge. However, oppositely charged ions in water do not always react to form a solid, as we have seen for K$^+$ and NO$_3^-$. In addition, Na$^+$ and Cl$^-$ can coexist in water in very large numbers with no formation of solid NaCl. In other words, when solid NaCl (common salt) is placed in water, it dissolves—the white solid "disappears" as the Na$^+$ and Cl$^-$ ions are dispersed throughout the water. (You probably have observed this phenomenon in preparing salt water to cook food.) The following two statements, then, are really saying the same thing:

1. Solid NaCl is very soluble in water.

2. Solid NaCl does not form when one solution containing Na$^+$ is mixed with another solution containing Cl$^-$.

To predict whether a given pair of dissolved ions will form a solid when mixed, we must know some facts about the solubilities of various types of ionic compounds. In this text we will use the term **soluble solid** to mean a solid that readily dissolves in water; the solid "disappears" as the ions are dispersed in the water. The terms **insoluble solid** and **slightly soluble solid** are taken to mean the same thing: a solid where such a tiny amount dissolves in water that it is undetectable with the naked eye. The solubility information about common solids that is summarized in **Table 8.1** is based on observations of the behavior of many compounds. This is factual knowledge that you will need to predict what will happen in chemical reactions where a solid might form. This information is summarized in **Figure 8.3**.

TABLE 8.1

General Rules for Solubility of Ionic Compounds (Salts) in Water at 25 °C

1. Most nitrate (NO$_3^-$) salts are soluble.
2. Most salts of Na$^+$, K$^+$, and NH$_4^+$ are soluble.
3. Most chloride salts are soluble. Notable exceptions are AgCl, PbCl$_2$, and Hg$_2$Cl$_2$.
4. Most sulfate salts are soluble. Notable exceptions are BaSO$_4$, PbSO$_4$, and CaSO$_4$.
5. Most hydroxide compounds are only slightly soluble.* The important exceptions are NaOH and KOH. Ba(OH)$_2$ and Ca(OH)$_2$ are only moderately soluble.
6. Most sulfide (S^{2-}), carbonate (CO$_3^{2-}$), and phosphate (PO$_4^{3-}$) salts are only slightly soluble.*

*The terms *insoluble* and *slightly soluble* really mean the same thing: such a tiny amount dissolves that it is not possible to detect it with the naked eye.

Figure 8.3
Solubilities of common compounds.

(a) Soluble compounds

NO$_3^-$ salts		

Na$^+$, K$^+$, NH$_4^+$ salts		

Cl$^-$, Br$^-$, I$^-$ salts	Except for those containing	Ag$^+$, Hg$_2^{2+}$, Pb^{2+}

SO$_4^{2-}$ salts	Except for those containing	Ba^{2+}, Pb^{2+}, Ca^{2+}

(b) Insoluble compounds

S^{2-}, CO$_3^{2-}$, PO$_4^{3-}$ salts		

OH$^-$ salts	Except for those containing	Na$^+$, K$^+$, Ca^{2+}

Notice that in Table 8.1 and Figure 8.3 the term *salt* is used to mean *ionic compound*. Many chemists use the terms *salt* and *ionic compound* interchangeably. In Example 8.1, we will illustrate how to use the solubility rules to predict the products of reactions among ions.

Identifying Precipitates in Reactions Where a Solid Forms

When an aqueous solution of silver nitrate is added to an aqueous solution of potassium chloride, a white solid forms. Identify the white solid and write the balanced equation for the reaction that occurs.

Solution

First let's use the description of the reaction to represent what we know:

$$AgNO_3(aq) + KCl(aq) \rightarrow \text{White solid}$$

Remember, try to determine the essential facts from the words and represent these facts by symbols or diagrams. To answer the main question (What is the white solid?), we must establish what ions are present in the mixed solution. That is, we must know what the reactants are really like. Remember that *when ionic substances dissolve in water, the ions separate*. So we can write the equation

$$\underbrace{Ag^+(aq) + NO_3^-(aq)}_{\substack{\text{Ions in} \\ AgNO_3(aq)}} + \underbrace{K^+(aq) + Cl^-(aq)}_{\substack{\text{Ions in} \\ KCl(aq)}} \rightarrow \text{Products}$$

or use pictures

to represent the ions present in the mixed solution before any reaction occurs. In summary:

(continued)

(continued)

💡 **PROBLEM SOLVING**

Using a table like this one

	NO₃⁻	Cl⁻
Ag+	AgNO₃	AgCl
K⁺	KNO₃	KCl

helps to figure out the possible combinations.

Now we will consider what solid *might* form from this collection of ions. Because the solid must contain both positive and negative ions, the possible compounds that can be assembled from this collection of ions are

$$AgNO_3 \qquad AgCl$$
$$KNO_3 \qquad KCl$$

$AgNO_3$ and KCl are the substances already dissolved in the reactant solutions, so we know that they do not represent the white solid product. We are left with two possibilities:

$$AgCl \qquad KNO_3$$

Another way to obtain these two possibilities is by *ion interchange*. This means that in the reaction of $AgNO_3(aq)$ and $KCl(aq)$, we take the cation from one reactant and combine it with the anion of the other reactant.

$$Ag^+ + NO_3^- + K^+ + Cl^- \rightarrow Products$$

Possible solid products

Ion interchange leads to the following possible solids:

$$AgCl \text{ or } KNO_3$$

To decide whether $AgCl$ or KNO_3 is the white solid, we need the solubility rules (Table 8.1). Rule 2 states that most salts containing K^+ are soluble in water. Rule 1 says that most nitrate salts (those containing NO_3^-) are soluble. So the salt KNO_3 is water-soluble. That is, when K^+ and NO_3^- are mixed in water, a solid (KNO_3) does *not* form.

On the other hand, rule 3 states that although most chloride salts (salts that contain Cl^-) are soluble, $AgCl$ is an exception. That is, $AgCl(s)$ is insoluble in water. Thus the white solid must be $AgCl$. Now we can write

$$AgNO_3(aq) + KCl(aq) \rightarrow AgCl(s) + \text{?}$$

What is the other product?

To form $AgCl(s)$, we have used the Ag^+ and Cl^- ions:

$$Ag^+(aq) + NO_3^-(aq) + K^+(aq) + Cl^-(aq) \rightarrow AgCl(s)$$

This leaves the K^+ and NO_3^- ions. What do they do? Nothing. Because KNO_3 is very soluble in water (rules 1 and 2), the K^+ and NO_3^- ions remain separate in the water; the KNO_3 remains dissolved and we represent it as $KNO_3(aq)$. We can now write the full equation:

$$AgNO_3(aq) + KCl(aq) \rightarrow AgCl(s) + KNO_3(aq)$$

Figure 8.4 shows the precipitation of $AgCl(s)$ that occurs when this reaction takes place. In graphic form, the reaction is

Figure 8.4
Precipitation of silver chloride occurs when solutions of silver nitrate and potassium chloride are mixed. The K^+ and NO_3^- ions remain in solution.

The following strategy is useful for predicting what will occur when two solutions containing dissolved salts are mixed.

How to Predict Precipitates When Solutions of Two Ionic Compounds Are Mixed

STEP 1 Write the reactants as they actually exist before any reaction occurs. Remember that when a salt dissolves, its ions separate.

STEP 2 Consider the various solids that could form. To do this, simply *exchange the anions* of the added salts.

STEP 3 Use the solubility rules (Table 8.1) to decide whether a solid forms and, if so, to predict the identity of the solid.

Example 8.2

Using Solubility Rules to Predict the Products of Reactions

Using the solubility rules in Table 8.1, predict what will happen when the following solutions are mixed. Write the balanced equation for any reaction that occurs.

    a. $KNO_3(aq)$ and $BaCl_2(aq)$ **b.** $Na_2SO_4(aq)$ and $Pb(NO_3)_2(aq)$
    c. $KOH(aq)$ and $Fe(NO_3)_3(aq)$

Solution (a)

Step 1 $KNO_3(aq)$ represents an aqueous solution obtained by dissolving solid KNO_3 in water to give the ions $K^+(aq)$ and $NO_3^-(aq)$. Likewise, $BaCl_2(aq)$ is a solution formed by dissolving solid $BaCl_2$ in water to produce $Ba^{2+}(aq)$ and $Cl^-(aq)$. When these two solutions are mixed, the following ions will be present:

$$K^+, \quad NO_3^-, \qquad Ba^{2+}, \quad Cl^-$$

    From $KNO_3(aq)$ From $BaCl_2(aq)$

Step 2 To get the possible products, we exchange the anions.

$$K^+ \quad NO_3^- \quad Ba^{2+} \quad Cl^-$$

This yields the possibilities KCl and $Ba(NO_3)_2$. These are the solids that *might* form. Notice that two NO_3^- ions are needed to balance the 2+ charge on Ba^{2+}.

Step 3 The rules listed in Table 8.1 indicate that both KCl and $Ba(NO_3)_2$ are soluble in water. So no precipitate forms when $KNO_3(aq)$ and $BaCl_2(aq)$ are mixed. All of the ions remain dissolved in the solution. This means that no reaction takes place. That is, no chemical change occurs.

No solid forms.

(continued)

8.2 Reactions in Which a Solid Forms   **221**

(continued)

Solution (b)

Step 1   The following ions are present in the mixed solution before any reaction occurs:

$$Na^+, \quad SO_4^{2-}, \quad Pb^{2+}, \quad NO_3^-$$

From   From
$Na_2SO_4(aq)$ $Pb(NO_3)_2(aq)$

Step 2   Exchanging anions as follows:

$$Na^+ \quad SO_4^{2-} \quad Pb^{2+} \quad NO_3^-$$

yields the *possible* solid products $PbSO_4$ and $NaNO_3$.

Step 3   Using Table 8.1, we see that $NaNO_3$ is soluble in water (rules 1 and 2) but that $PbSO_4$ is only slightly soluble (rule 4). Thus, when these solutions are mixed, solid $PbSO_4$ forms. The balanced reaction is

$$Na_2SO_4(aq) + Pb(NO_3)_2(aq) \rightarrow PbSO_4(s) + 2NaNO_3(aq)$$

Remains dissolved

which can be represented as

Solution (c)

Step 1   The ions present in the mixed solution before any reaction occurs are

$$K^+, \quad OH^-, \quad Fe^{3+}, \quad NO_3^-$$

From KOH(aq)   From $Fe(NO_3)_3(aq)$

Step 2   Exchanging anions as follows:

$$K^+ \quad OH^- \quad Fe^{3+} \quad NO_3^-$$

yields the possible solid products KNO_3 and $Fe(OH)_3$.

Step 3   Rules 1 and 2 (Table 8.1) state that KNO_3 is soluble, whereas $Fe(OH)_3$ is only slightly soluble (rule 5). Thus, when these solutions are mixed, solid $Fe(OH)_3$ forms. The balanced equation for the reaction is

$$3KOH(aq) + Fe(NO_3)_3(aq) \rightarrow Fe(OH)_3(s) + 3KNO_3(aq)$$

222   Chapter 8   Reactions in Aqueous Solutions

Answers to Self-Check Exercise 8.1

a. The ions present are

$$Ba^{2+}(aq) + 2NO_3^-(aq) + Na^+(aq) + Cl^-(aq) \rightarrow$$

Ions in   Ions in
$Ba(NO_3)_2(aq)$ $NaCl(aq)$

Exchanging the anions gives the possible solid products $BaCl_2$ and $NaNO_3$. Using Table 8.1, we see that both substances are very

soluble (Rules 1, 2, and 3). Thus no solid forms.

b. The ions present in the mixed solution before any reaction occurs are

$$2Na^+(aq) + S^{2-}(aq) + Cu^{2+}(aq) + 2NO_3^-(aq) \rightarrow$$

Ions in   Ions in
$Na_2S(aq)$ $Cu(NO_3)_2(aq)$

Exchanging the anions gives the possible solid products CuS and $NaNO_3$ (soluble). By Rule 6, CuS is

insoluble, so it will precipitate. The balanced equation is

$$Na_2S(aq) + Cu(NO_3)_2(aq) \rightarrow$$
$$CuS(s) + 2NaNO_3(aq)$$

c. The ions present are

$$NH_4^+(aq) + Cl^-(aq) + Pb^{2+}(aq) + 2NO_3^-(aq) \rightarrow$$

Ions in   Ions in
$NH_4Cl(aq)$ $Pb(NO_3)_2(aq)$

Exchanging the anions gives the possible solid products NH_4NO_3 and $PbCl_2$. NH_4NO_3 is soluble

which can be represented as

Solid Fe(OH)₃
forms.

 Self-Check Exercise 8.1

Predict whether a solid will form when the following pairs of solutions are mixed. If so, identify the solid and write the balanced equation for the reaction.

    a. $Ba(NO_3)_2(aq)$ and $NaCl(aq)$

    b. $Na_2S(aq)$ and $Cu(NO_3)_2(aq)$

    c. $NH_4Cl(aq)$ and $Pb(NO_3)_2(aq)$

Focus Questions

Sections 8.1–8.2

1. What are the driving forces that indicate a chemical reaction is likely to occur?

2. Use the solubility rules in Table 8.1 or Figure 8.3 to predict which of the following will be soluble in water:
   a. potassium nitrate
   b. zinc hydroxide
   c. calcium carbonate
   d. ammonium chloride

3. Consider two separate beakers: one containing an aqueous solution of hydrochloric acid and one containing an aqueous solution of lead(II) nitrate.
   a. Draw a picture of each solution showing the ions present.
   b. Draw a picture after the solutions are mixed showing what is present.
   c. Predict the products for any reaction that occurs.
   d. Write an equation for the reaction.

8.3   Describing Reactions in Aqueous Solutions

Objective: *To learn to describe reactions in solutions by writing molecular, complete ionic, and net ionic equations.*

Much important chemistry, including virtually all of the reactions that make life possible, occurs in aqueous solutions. We will now consider the types of equations used to represent reactions that occur in water. For example, as we saw earlier, when we mix aqueous potassium chromate with aqueous barium nitrate, a reaction occurs to form solid barium chromate and

8.3   Describing Reactions in Aqueous Solutions   **223**

(Rules 1 and 2) and $PbCl_2$ is insoluble (Rule 3). Thus $PbCl_2$ will precipitate. The balanced equation is

$2NH_4Cl(aq) + Pb(NO_3)_2(aq) \rightarrow$
        $PbCl_2(s) + 2NH_4NO_3(aq)$

- Drawing molecular-level pictures when first discussing reactions in aqueous solutions is helpful for the students.

- Molecular equations can be considered to contain the complete formulas for all reactants and products. Complete ionic equations provide a window into the microscopic world. These equations show substances as they are in solution or at the molecular level.

- Remind students that a new product is often a solid and must not be written as ions if it is insoluble.

- Remind students that charges must be balanced in both ionic and net ionic equations.

dissolved potassium nitrate. One way to represent this reaction is by the equation

$$K_2CrO_4(aq) + Ba(NO_3)_2(aq) \rightarrow BaCrO_4(s) + 2KNO_3(aq)$$

This is called the **molecular equation** for the reaction; it shows the complete formulas of all reactants and products. However, although this equation shows the reactants and products of the reaction, it does not give a very clear picture of what actually occurs in solution. As we have seen, aqueous solutions of potassium chromate, barium nitrate, and potassium nitrate contain the individual ions, not molecules as is implied by the molecular equation. Thus the **complete ionic equation,**

$$2K^+(aq) + CrO_4{}^{2-}(aq) + Ba^{2+}(aq) + 2NO_3{}^-(aq) \rightarrow$$
$$BaCrO_4(s) + 2K^+(aq) + 2NO_3{}^-(aq)$$

better represents the actual forms of the reactants and products in solution. *In a complete ionic equation, all substances that are strong electrolytes are represented as ions.* Notice that $BaCrO_4$ is not written as the separate ions, because it is present as a solid; it is not dissolved.

The complete ionic equation reveals that only some of the ions participate in the reaction. Notice that the K^+ and $NO_3{}^-$ ions are present in solution both before and after the reaction. Ions such as these, which do not participate directly in a reaction in solution, are called **spectator ions.** The ions that participate in this reaction are the Ba^{2+} and $CrO_4{}^{2-}$ ions, which combine to form solid $BaCrO_4$:

$$Ba^{2+}(aq) + CrO_4{}^{2-}(aq) \rightarrow BaCrO_4(s)$$

This equation, called the **net ionic equation,** includes only those components that are directly involved in the reaction. Chemists usually write the net ionic equation for a reaction in solution, because it gives the actual forms of the reactants and products and includes only the species that undergo a change.

CHEMISTRY

A strong electrolyte is a substance that completely breaks apart into ions when dissolved in water. The resulting solution readily conducts an electric current.

CHEMISTRY

The net ionic equation includes only those components that undergo a change in the reaction.

Types of Equations for Reactions in Aqueous Solutions

Three types of equations are used to describe reactions in solutions.

1. The *molecular equation* shows the overall reaction but not necessarily the actual forms of the reactants and products in solution.

2. The *complete ionic equation* represents all reactants and products that are strong electrolytes as ions. All reactants and products are included.

3. The *net ionic equation* includes only those components that undergo a change. Spectator ions are not included.

To make sure these ideas are clear, we will do another example. In Example 8.2 we considered the reaction between aqueous solutions of lead nitrate and sodium sulfate. The molecular equation for this reaction is

$$Pb(NO_3)_2(aq) + Na_2SO_4(aq) \rightarrow PbSO_4(s) + 2NaNO_3(aq)$$

Integrating the CHEMICAL IMPACT

Instant Cooking— On Demand

Consumer Connection

Instant Cooking—On Demand

Can you think of foods you've recently prepared that were ready to go — except for adding water? From breakfast through dessert, chemists have found ways to prepare mixes that stay unreacted and ready to use on our shelves. All we need to do is place them in a bowl, add water, and cook! Why don't the ingredients react in the box?

Most of the ingredients used in mixes are solids. We've already seen that solids don't usually react until they are dissolved in water. So as long as moisture is kept out of the mix, it will remain unreacted. Sometimes manufacturers also dehydrate ingredients such as milk and eggs so they can be stored in unreactive form in the mix as well!

Angel food cake mix.

"Instant Cooking—On Demand" would be a good place to remind students about the importance of water as a reaction medium. Water dissolves all kinds of important chemicals, which allows reactions to occur that are essential to our everyday lives. You might have students make a list of some important reactions that occur in aqueous solutions.

Because any ionic compound that is dissolved in water is present as the separated ions, we can write the complete ionic equation as follows:

$$Pb^{2+}(aq) + 2NO_3^-(aq) + 2Na^+(aq) + SO_4^{2-}(aq) \rightarrow$$
$$PbSO_4(s) + 2Na^+(aq) + 2NO_3^-(aq)$$

The $PbSO_4$ is not written as separate ions because it is present as a solid. The ions that take part in the chemical change are the Pb^{2+} and the SO_4^{2-} ions, which combine to form solid $PbSO_4$. Thus the net ionic equation is

$$Pb^{2+}(aq) + SO_4^{2-}(aq) \rightarrow PbSO_4(s)$$

The Na^+ and NO_3^- ions do not undergo any chemical change; they are spectator ions.

Example 8.3

CHEMISTRY

Because silver is present as Ag^+ in all of its common ionic compounds, we usually delete the (I) when naming silver compounds.

Writing Equations for Reactions

For each of the following reactions, write the molecular equation, the complete ionic equation, and the net ionic equation.

a. Aqueous sodium chloride is added to aqueous silver nitrate to form solid silver chloride plus aqueous sodium nitrate.

b. Aqueous potassium hydroxide is mixed with aqueous iron(III) nitrate to form solid iron(III) hydroxide and aqueous potassium nitrate.

(continued)

Additional Examples

For each of the following reactions, write the balanced molecular equation, the balanced complete ionic equation, and the balanced net ionic equation.

1. Aqueous silver nitrate is added to aqueous sodium chromate to form solid silver chromate and aqueous sodium nitrate.

Molecular: $2AgNO_3(aq) + Na_2CrO_4(aq) \rightarrow Ag_2CrO_4(s) + 2NaNO_3(aq)$

Complete ionic:
$2Ag^+(aq) + 2NO_3^-(aq) + 2Na^+(aq) + CrO_4^{2-}(aq) \rightarrow Ag_2CrO_4(s) + 2Na^+(aq) + 2NO_3^-(aq)$

Net ionic: $2Ag^+(aq) + CrO_4^{2-}(aq) \rightarrow Ag_2CrO_4(s)$

2. Aqueous nickel(II) nitrate is added to aqueous potassium carbonate to form solid nickel(II) carbonate and aqueous potassium nitrate.

Molecular: $Ni(NO_3)_2(aq) + K_2CO_3(aq) \rightarrow NiCO_3(s) + 2KNO_3(aq)$

Complete ionic: $Ni^{2+}(aq) + 2NO_3^-(aq) + 2K^+(aq) + CO_3^{2-}(aq) \rightarrow NiCO_3(s) + 2K^+(aq) + 2NO_3^-(aq)$

Net ionic: $Ni^{2+}(aq) + CO_3^{2-}(aq) \rightarrow NiCO_3(s)$

8.3 Describing Reactions in Aqueous Solutions **225**

write an ionic equation for the reaction, and name the precipitate. Repeat for the remaining test tubes, pairing 3 and 4, 5 and 6, 7 and 8, 9 and 10, and 11 and 12.

Teaching Notes Students can write the molecular, complete ionic, and net ionic equations for each reaction as you perform the demonstration.

Silver nitrate and ammonium thiocyanate produce a brown precipitate, silver thiocyanate [all ions are (aq)]:

$Ag^+ + NO_3^- + NH_4^+ + SCN^- \rightarrow AgSCN(s) + NH_4^+ + NO_3^-$

(Ions such as K^+ and NO_3^-, which do not enter the reaction, are called spectator ions.)

Nickel(II) chloride and sodium carbonate produce a pale blue precipitate, nickel(II) carbonate.

$Ni^{2+} + 2Cl^- + 2Na^+ + CO_3^{2-} \rightarrow NiCO_3(s) + 2Cl^- + 2Na^+$

Lead(II) nitrate and potassium iodide produce a yellow precipitate, lead(II) iodide.

$Pb^{2+} + 2NO_3^- + 2K^+ + 2I^- \rightarrow PbI_2(s) + 2NO_3^- + 2K^+$

Sodium nitrate and potassium chloride produce no reaction.

$Na^+ + NO_3^- + K^+ + Cl^- \rightarrow N.R.$

(continued)

Answers to Self-Check Exercise 8.2

a. Molecular:

$Na_2S(aq) + Cu(NO_3)_2(aq) \rightarrow CuS(s) + 2NaNO_3(aq)$

Complete ionic:

$2Na^+(aq) + S^{2-}(aq) \rightarrow Cu^{2+}(aq) + 2NO_3^-(aq) \rightarrow CuS(s) + 2Na^+(aq) + 2NO_3^-(aq)$

Net ionic:

$S^{2-}(aq) + Cu^{2+}(aq) \rightarrow CuS(s)$

b. Molecular:

$2NH_4Cl(aq) + Pb(NO_3)_2(aq) \rightarrow PbCl_2(s) + 2NH_4NO_3(aq)$

Complete ionic:

$2NH_4^+(aq) + 2Cl^-(aq) + Pb^{2+}(aq) + 2NO_3^-(aq) \rightarrow PbCl_2(s) + 2NH_4^+(aq) + 2NO_3^-(aq)$

Net ionic:

$2Cl^-(aq) + Pb^{2+}(aq) \rightarrow PbCl_2(s)$

 Section 8.4

Themes
Patterns of Change, Form and Function

Skills
Observing, classifying, applying concepts, making predictions

---

MINI-DEMO

Use the conductivity apparatus to show that acids and bases in solution conduct electricity. You may also want to show students litmus paper and use it to test each solution. Be sure to test distilled water to show its lack of conductivity.

(continued)   **Solution**

a. *Molecular equation:*

$NaCl(aq) + AgNO_3(aq) \rightarrow AgCl(s) + NaNO_3(aq)$

Complete ionic equation:

$Na^+(aq) + Cl^-(aq) + Ag^+(aq) + NO_3^-(aq) \rightarrow AgCl(s) + Na^+(aq) + NO_3^-(aq)$

Net ionic equation:

$Cl^-(aq) + Ag^+(aq) \rightarrow AgCl(s)$

b. *Molecular equation:*

$3KOH(aq) + Fe(NO_3)_3(aq) \rightarrow Fe(OH)_3(s) + 3KNO_3(aq)$

Complete ionic equation:

$3K^+(aq) + 3OH^-(aq) + Fe^{3+}(aq) + 3NO_3^-(aq) \rightarrow Fe(OH)_3(s) + 3K^+(aq) + 3NO_3^-(aq)$

Net ionic equation:

$3OH^-(aq) + Fe^{3+}(aq) \rightarrow Fe(OH)_3(s)$

 Self-Check Exercise 8.2

For each of the following reactions, write the molecular equation, the complete ionic equation, and the net ionic equation.

a. Aqueous sodium sulfide is mixed with aqueous copper(II) nitrate to produce solid copper(II) sulfide and aqueous sodium nitrate.

b. Aqueous ammonium chloride and aqueous lead(II) nitrate react to form solid lead(II) chloride and aqueous ammonium nitrate.

8.4 Reactions That Form Water: Acids and Bases

Objective: *To learn the key characteristics of the reactions between strong acids and strong bases.*

CHEMISTRY
Don't taste chemicals!

In this section we encounter two very important classes of compounds: acids and bases. Acids were first associated with the sour taste of citrus fruits. In fact, the word *acid* comes from the Latin word *acidus,* which means "sour." Vinegar tastes sour because it is a dilute solution of acetic acid; citric acid is responsible for the sour taste of a lemon. Bases, sometimes called *alkalis,* are characterized by their bitter taste and slippery feel, like wet soap. Most commercial preparations for unclogging drains are highly basic.

Acids have been known for hundreds of years. For example, the *mineral acids* sulfuric acid, H_2SO_4, and nitric acid, HNO_3, so named because they were originally obtained by the treatment of minerals, were discovered around 1300. However, it was not until the late 1800s that the essential nature of

226 Chapter 8 Reactions in Aqueous Solutions

(continued)

Barium chloride and sodium sulfate produce a white precipitate, barium sulfate.

$Ba^{2+} + 2Cl^- + 2Na^+ + SO_4^{2-} \rightarrow BaSO_4(s) + 2Cl^- + 2Na^+$

Copper(II) chloride and sodium carbonate produce a pale blue precipitate, copper(II) carbonate.

$Cu^{2+} + 2Cl^- + 2Na^+ + CO_3^{2-} \rightarrow CuCO_3(s) + 2Cl^- + 2Na^+$

TEACHING SUPPORT
Background Information

Svante Arrhenius
The basis for the conductivity properties of solutions was first correctly identified by Svante Arrhenius (1859–1927), then a Swedish graduate student in physics, who carried out research on the nature of solutions at the University of Upp-

The marsh marigold is a beautiful but poisonous plant. Its toxicity results partly from the presence of erucic acid.

acids was discovered by Svante Arrhenius, then a Swedish graduate student in physics.

Arrhenius, who was trying to discover why only certain solutions could conduct an electric current, found that conductivity arose from the presence of ions. In his studies of solutions, Arrhenius observed that when the substances HCl, HNO_3, and H_2SO_4 were dissolved in water, they behaved as strong electrolytes. He suggested that this was the result of ionization reactions in water.

$$HCl \xrightarrow{H_2O} H^+(aq) + Cl^-(aq)$$

$$HNO_3 \xrightarrow{H_2O} H^+(aq) + NO_3^-(aq)$$

$$H_2SO_4 \xrightarrow{H_2O} H^+(aq) + HSO_4^-(aq)$$

Arrhenius proposed that an **acid** *is a substance that produces H^+ ions (protons) when it is dissolved in water.*

Studies show that when HCl, HNO_3, and H_2SO_4 are placed in water, *virtually every molecule* dissociates to give ions. This means that when 100 molecules of HCl are dissolved in water, 100 H^+ ions and 100 Cl^- ions are produced. Virtually no HCl molecules exist in aqueous solution (see **Figure 8.5**). Because these substances are strong electrolytes that produce H^+ ions, they are called **strong acids.**

Arrhenius also found that *aqueous solutions that exhibit basic behavior always contain hydroxide ions.* He defined a **base** as a *substance that produces hydroxide ions (OH^-) in water.* The base most commonly used in the chemical laboratory is sodium hydroxide, NaOH, which contains Na^+ and OH^- ions and is very soluble in water. Sodium hydroxide, like all ionic substances, produces separated cations and anions when it is dissolved in water.

$$NaOH(s) \xrightarrow{H_2O} Na^+(aq) + OH^-(aq)$$

Although dissolved sodium hydroxide is usually represented as NaOH(*aq*), you should remember that the solution really contains separated Na^+ and OH^- ions. In fact, for every 100 units of NaOH dissolved in water, 100 Na^+ ions and 100 OH^- ions are produced.

H Group 1   Cl Group 7

HCl

Water

Each HCl molecule dissociates when it dissolves in water.

Figure 8.5
When gaseous HCl is dissolved in water, each molecule dissociates to produce H^+ and Cl^- ions. That is, HCl behaves as a strong electrolyte.

8.4 Reactions That Form Water: Acids and Bases   **227**

sala in the early 1880s. Arrhenius came to believe that the conductivity of solutions arose from the presence of ions, an idea that was at first scorned by the majority of the scientific establishment. However, in the late 1890s when atoms were found to contain charged particles, the ionic theory suddenly made sense and became widely accepted.

As Arrhenius postulated, the extent to which a solution can conduct an electric current depends directly on the number of ions present. Some materials, such as sodium chloride, readily produce ions in aqueous solution and thus are strong electrolytes. Other substances, such as acetic acid, produce relatively few ions when dissolved in water and are weak electrolytes. A third class of materi-

als, such as sugar, form virtually no ions when dissolved in water and are nonelectrolytes.

Drain cleaners contain a strong base.

 CHEMISTRY

Hydrochloric acid is an aqueous solution that contains dissolved hydrogen chloride. It is a strong electrolyte.

Potassium hydroxide (KOH) has properties markedly similar to those of sodium hydroxide. It is very soluble in water and produces separated ions.

$$KOH(s) \xrightarrow{H_2O} K^+(aq) + OH^-(aq)$$

Because these hydroxide compounds are strong electrolytes that contain OH^- ions, they are called **strong bases.**

When strong acids and strong bases (hydroxides) are mixed, the fundamental chemical change that always occurs is that *H^+ ions react with OH^- ions to form water.*

$$H^+(aq) + OH^-(aq) \rightarrow H_2O(l)$$

Water is a very stable compound, as evidenced by the abundance of it on the earth's surface. Therefore, when substances that can form water are mixed, there is a strong tendency for the reaction to occur. In particular, the hydroxide ion OH^- has a high affinity for the H^+ ion to produce water.

The tendency to form water is the second of the driving forces for reactions that we mentioned in Section 8.1. Any compound that produces OH^- ions in water reacts vigorously to form H_2O with any compound that can furnish H^+ ions. For example, the reaction between hydrochloric acid and aqueous sodium hydroxide is represented by the following molecular equation:

$$HCl(aq) + NaOH(aq) \rightarrow H_2O(l) + NaCl(aq)$$

Because HCl, NaOH, and NaCl exist as completely separated ions in water, the complete ionic equation for this reaction is

$$H^+(aq) + Cl^-(aq) + Na^+(aq) + OH^-(aq) \rightarrow H_2O(l) + Na^+(aq) + Cl^-(aq)$$

Notice that the Cl^- and Na^+ are spectator ions (they undergo no changes), so the net ionic equation is

$$H^+(aq) + OH^-(aq) \rightarrow H_2O(l)$$

Thus the only chemical change that occurs when these solutions are mixed is that water is formed from H^+ and OH^- ions.

Example 8.4

Writing Equations for Acid–Base Reactions

Nitric acid is a strong acid. Write the molecular, complete ionic, and net ionic equations for the reaction of aqueous nitric acid and aqueous potassium hydroxide.

Solution

Molecular equation:

$$HNO_3(aq) + KOH(aq) \rightarrow H_2O(l) + KNO_3(aq)$$

Complete ionic equation:

$$H^+(aq) + NO_3^-(aq) + K^+(aq) + OH^-(aq) \rightarrow$$
$$H_2O(l) + K^+(aq) + NO_3^-(aq)$$

228 Chapter 8 Reactions in Aqueous Solutions

There are two important things to note as we examine the reaction of hydrochloric acid with aqueous sodium hydroxide and the reaction of nitric acid with aqueous potassium hydroxide:

1. The net ionic equation is the same in both cases; water is formed.

   $$H^+(aq) + OH^-(aq) \rightarrow H_2O(l)$$

2. Besides water, which is *always a product* of the reaction of an acid with OH^-, the second product is an ionic compound, which might precipitate or remain dissolved, depending on its solubility.

CHEMISTRY
Hydrochloric acid is an aqueous solution of HCl.

$$HCl(aq) + NaOH(aq) \rightarrow H_2O(l) + NaCl(aq)$$

Dissolved ionic compounds

$$HNO_3(aq) + KOH(aq) \rightarrow H_2O(l) + KNO_3(aq)$$

This ionic compound is called a **salt.** In the first case the salt is sodium chloride, and in the second case the salt is potassium nitrate. We can obtain these soluble salts in solid form (both are white solids) by evaporating the water.

CHEMISTRY
Both strong acids and strong bases are strong electrolytes.

Summary of Strong Acids and Strong Bases

The following points about strong acids and strong bases are particularly important.

1. The common strong acids are aqueous solutions of HCl, HNO_3, and H_2SO_4.

2. A strong acid is a substance that completely dissociates (ionizes) in water. (Each molecule breaks up into an H^+ ion plus an anion.)

3. A strong base is a metal hydroxide compound that is very soluble in water. The most common strong bases are NaOH and KOH, which completely break up into separated ions (Na^+ and OH^- or K^+ and OH^-) when they are dissolved in water.

4. The net ionic equation for the reaction of a strong acid and a strong base is always the same: it shows the production of water.

   $$H^+(aq) + OH^-(aq) \rightarrow H_2O(l)$$

5. In the reaction of a strong acid and a strong base, one product is always water and the other is always an ionic compound called a salt, which remains dissolved in the water. This salt can be obtained as a solid by evaporating the water.

6. The reaction of H^+ and OH^- is often called an acid–base reaction, where H^+ is the acidic ion and OH^- is the basic ion.

8.4   Reactions That Form Water: Acids and Bases   **229**

Calcium Carbonate (CaCO₃)

An easy way to remember which way stalactites and stalagmites point (for those of us who understand the rather archaic language) is as follows: As the "mites" go up, the "tights" come down.

Answers to Focus Questions

1. Molecular equations contain the complete formulas for all reactants and products. Complete ionic equations show substances as they are in solution.

2. A spectator ion is an ion that does not participate in the reaction in solution. Spectator ions are not shown in a net ionic equation.

3. **a.** $Na_2SO_4(aq) + BaBr_2(aq) \rightarrow BaSO_4(s) + 2NaBr(aq)$

   b. $2Na^+(aq) + SO_4^{2-}(aq) + Ba^{2+}(aq) + 2Br^-(aq) \rightarrow BaSO_4(s) + 2Na^+(aq) + 2Br^-(aq)$

   c. The spectator ions are sodium ions and bromide ions.

   d. $SO_4^{2-}(aq) + Ba^{2+}(aq) \rightarrow BaSO_4(s)$

4. The products are a salt and water. The evidence for a reaction is heat.

5. The acid drawing should contain H^+, NO_3^-, and water molecules. The base drawing should contain K^+, OH^-, and water molecules.

230

CELEBRITY CHEMICAL

Calcium Carbonate (CaCO₃)

Calcium carbonate, which contains the Ca^{2+} and CO_3^{2-} ions, is very common in nature, occurring in eggshells, limestone, marble, seashells, and coral. The spectacular formations seen in limestone caves are also composed of calcium carbonate.

Limestone caves form when underground limestone deposits come in contact with water made acidic by dissolved carbon dioxide. When rainwater absorbs CO_2 from the atmosphere, the following reaction occurs:

$$CO_2(g) + H_2O(l) \rightarrow H^+(aq) + HCO_3^-(aq)$$

This reaction leads to the presence of H^+ in the groundwater. The acidic groundwater then causes the limestone (which is made of $CaCO_3$) to dissolve:

$$CaCO_3(s) + H^+(aq) \rightarrow Ca^{2+}(aq) + HCO_3^-(aq)$$

Underground caverns then form. In the process of dissolving the limestone and creating the cave, the water containing the dissolved $CaCO_3$ drips from the ceiling of the cave. As the water forms drops, it tends to lose some of the dissolved CO_2, which lowers the amount of H^+ present (by the reversal of the first reaction), which in turn leads to the reversal of the second reaction, which then reforms the solid $CaCO_3$. This process causes stalactites to "grow" from the ceiling of the cave. Water that drips to the floor before losing its dissolved CO_2 forms stalagmites that build up from the floor of the cave.

Stalactites and stalagmites in Carlsbad Caverns, New Mexico.

Focus Questions

Sections 8.3–8.4

1. How does a molecular equation differ from a complete ionic equation?

2. What is a spectator ion and what happens to it in a net ionic equation?

3. Consider the following reaction: aqueous sodium sulfate is added to aqueous barium bromide to form solid barium sulfate and aqueous sodium bromide.
   a. Write the molecular equation.
   b. Write the complete ionic equation.
   c. List the spectator ions.
   d. Write the net ionic equation.

4. What are the products in a reaction between an acid and a base? How can you tell that a reaction has occurred?

5. Draw a microscopic picture of a strong acid solution of HNO_3 and a strong base solution of KOH in separate beakers.

230   Chapter 8   Reactions in Aqueous Solutions

TEACHING SUPPORT
Demonstration

Growing Crystals: A Magic Garden

Materials
Overhead projector
Large shallow dish for projector (large Petri dish or a beaker)
Sodium silicate solution
Universal indicator

Phenolphthalein
Thymolphthalein
$SrCl_2$ or $MnCl_2$
$CoCl_2$ or $Co(No_3)_2$
Droppers or Beral pipets (5)
Small plastic cups or beakers (5)

Preparation Sodium silicate can be prepared from a purchased sodium silicate solution or you can use the concentrated sodium silicate solution from a commercial kit such as Magic Rocks. If using a purchased so-

lution, dilute one part solution to two parts water and mix well. If using a kit, follow the directions on the kit. You will need enough to fill your container 1/4 inch deep.

Prepare the following solutions:
Solution A: 1 teaspoon of $SrCl_2$ or $MnCl_2$ in 50 mL water
Solution B: 1 teaspoon of $CoCl_2$ or $Co(NO_3)_2$ in 50 mL water

8.5 Reactions of Metals with Nonmetals (Oxidation–Reduction)

Objectives: *To learn the general characteristics of a reaction between a metal and a nonmetal.*
To understand electron transfer as a driving force for a chemical reaction.

In Chapter 3 we spent considerable time discussing ionic compounds—compounds formed in the reaction of a metal and a nonmetal. A typical example is sodium chloride, formed by the reaction of sodium metal and chlorine gas:

$$2Na(s) + Cl_2(g) \rightarrow 2NaCl(s)$$

Let's examine what happens in this reaction. Sodium metal is composed of sodium atoms, each of which has a net charge of zero. (The positive charges of the eleven protons in its nucleus are exactly balanced by the negative charges on the eleven electrons.) Similarly, the chlorine molecule consists of two uncharged chlorine atoms (each has seventeen protons and seventeen electrons). However, in the product (sodium chloride), the sodium is present as Na^+ and the chlorine as Cl^-. By what process do the neutral atoms become ions? The answer is that one electron is transferred from each sodium atom to each chlorine atom.

$$Na + Cl \rightarrow Na^+ + Cl^-$$

After the electron transfer, each sodium atom has ten electrons and eleven protons (a net charge of 1+), and each chlorine atom has eighteen electrons and seventeen protons (a net charge of 1−).

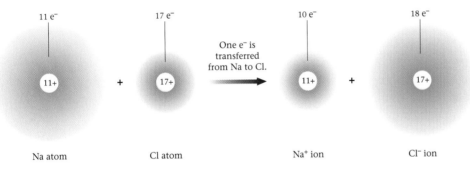

Na atom   Cl atom   Na⁺ ion   Cl⁻ ion

Thus the reaction of a metal with a nonmetal to form an ionic compound involves the transfer of one or more electrons from the metal (which forms a cation) to the nonmetal (which forms an anion). This tendency to transfer electrons from metals to nonmetals is the third driving force for reactions that we listed in Section 8.1. A reaction that *involves a transfer of electrons* is called an **oxidation–reduction reaction.**

8.5   Reactions of Metals with Nonmetals (Oxidation–Reduction)   **231**

8.5 **Section 8.5**

Themes
Patterns of Change, Form and Function

Skills
Classifying, making predictions, interpreting diagrams

Student Preparation
Assign the students to read Sections 8.5 to 8.7 and to answer the Focus Questions at the end of Section 8.7 before coming to class.

Active Learning
After introducing the material in Sections 8.5 to 8.7 in class, place the students in groups and have them work together on Sections 8.5–8.7: Team Learning Worksheet. Answers and/or discussion of these questions are located in the *Teacher Resources.*

USING TECHNOLOGY

 Animation and Video

Video, Potassium Metal Reaction with Water

TEACHING TIPS

- Discuss the importance of oxidation–reduction reactions in daily life. Batteries, corrosion, and combustion are all oxidation–reduction reactions.

- Point out that the loss or gain of electrons can take place only if another element is present to accept or donate electrons. If you do the demonstration "Making Salt," point out that chlorine gas doesn't react alone, nor does sodium metal. Yet if you ignite the sodium and place it in the chlorine gas, the two elements react to form ions.

- It is easier for students to begin with oxidation–reduction reactions between two elements. Once they understand this type of reaction, you can move on to more complicated reactions such as $2NaBr + Cl_2 \rightarrow 2NaCl + Br_2$. Reactions of this type are sometimes classified as single-displacement reactions. Students may be confused by this term, as they

(continued)

Solution C: 10 mL solution A and 3 drops universal indicator
Solution D: 10 mL solution A and 3 drops phenolphthalein
Solution E: 10 mL solution A and 3 drops thymolphthalein

Presentation Place the large shallow dish and the cups or beakers containing solutions A–E on the overhead projector.

Add sodium silicate to the large shallow dish to a depth of approximately ¼–½ inch. Point out solution A to students and identify its color. Using a dropper or Beral pipet, add several drops of solution A to the sodium silicate solution in the large dish. The students should see a white circular-shaped solid immediately. Repeat this process with each of the solutions B–E. Each time make sure

that students observe the color of the solution both before and after the addition.

Teaching Notes The crystals formed are a different color from the original solutions because the sodium silicate solution is basic and the original solutions were neutral. The color changes reflect the indicators used. The cobalt compound changes color because

(continued)

(continued)

do not understand how single displacement occurs when two elements are changing places. We choose to classify all oxidation–reduction reactions as reactions in which electrons are transferred between atoms. This terminology focuses students' attention on the driving force for the reaction. The term "single displacement" is discussed in Section 8.7 as an alternative way to classify reactions.

CHEMISTRY
This equation is read, "An aluminum atom yields an aluminum ion with a 3+ charge and three electrons."

There are many examples of oxidation-reduction reactions in which a metal reacts with a nonmetal to form an ionic compound. Consider the reaction of magnesium metal with oxygen,

$$2Mg(s) + O_2(g) \rightarrow 2MgO(s)$$

which produces a bright, white light useful in camera flash units. Note that the reactants contain uncharged atoms, but the product contains ions:

$$MgO$$
Contains Mg^{2+}, O^{2-}

Therefore, in this reaction, each magnesium atom loses two electrons ($Mg \rightarrow Mg^{2+} + 2e^-$) and each oxygen atom gains two electrons ($O + 2e^- \rightarrow O^{2-}$). We might represent this reaction as follows:

Another example is

$$2Al(s) + Fe_2O_3(s) \rightarrow 2Fe(s) + Al_2O_3(s)$$

which is a reaction (called the thermite reaction) that produces so much energy (heat) that the iron is initially formed as a liquid (see **Figure 8.6**). In this case the aluminum is originally present as the elemental metal (which contains uncharged Al atoms) and ends up in Al_2O_3, where it is present as Al^{3+} cations (the $2Al^{3+}$ ions just balance the charge of the $3O^{2-}$ ions). Therefore, in the reaction each aluminum atom loses three electrons.

$$Al \rightarrow Al^{3+} + 3e^-$$

The opposite process occurs with the iron, which is initially present as Fe^{3+} ions in Fe_2O_3 and ends up as uncharged atoms in the elemental iron. Thus each iron cation gains three electrons to form an uncharged atom:

$$Fe^{3+} + 3e^- \rightarrow Fe$$

Figure 8.6
The thermite reaction gives off so much heat that the iron formed is molten.

232   Chapter 8   Reactions in Aqueous Solutions

(continued)

the chloride and the silicates are different colors.

We can represent this reaction in schematic form as follows:

Example 8.5

Identifying Electron Transfer in Oxidation–Reduction Reactions

For each of the following reactions, show how electrons are gained and lost.

a. $2Al(s) + 3I_2(s) \rightarrow 2AlI_3(s)$ (This reaction is shown in **Figure 8.7**. Note the purple "smoke," which is excess I_2 being driven off by the heat.)

b. $2Cs(s) + F_2(g) \rightarrow 2CsF(s)$

Solution

a. In AlI_3 the ions are Al^{3+} and I^- (aluminum always forms Al^{3+}, and iodine always forms I^-). In $Al(s)$ the aluminum is present as uncharged atoms. Thus aluminum goes from Al to Al^{3+} by losing three electrons ($Al \rightarrow Al^{3+} + 3e^-$). In I_2 each iodine atom is uncharged. Thus each iodine atom goes from I to I^- by gaining one electron ($I + e^- \rightarrow I^-$). A schematic for this reaction is

Figure 8.7
When powdered aluminum and iodine (shown in the foreground) are mixed (and a little water added), they react vigorously.

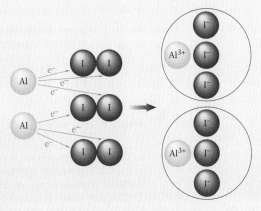

b. In CsF the ions present are Cs^+ and F^-. Cesium metal, $Cs(s)$, contains uncharged cesium atoms, and fluorine gas, $F_2(g)$, contains

(continued)

For each of the following reactions, show how electrons are gained and lost.

1. $4Al(s) + 3O_2(g) \rightarrow 2Al_2O_3(s)$
Each Al atom loses 3 electrons (for a total of 12 electrons). Each oxygen atom gains 2 electrons (for a total of 12 electrons).

2. $4Na(s) + O_2(g) \rightarrow 2Na_2O(s)$
Each Na atom loses 1 electron (for a total of 4 electrons). Each oxygen atom gains 2 electrons (for a total of 4 electrons).

Answers to Self-Check Exercise 8.3

a. The compound NaBr contains the ions Na^+ and Br^-. Each sodium atom loses one electron $(Na \rightarrow Na^+ + e^-)$, and each bromine atom gains one electron $(Br + e^- \rightarrow Br^-)$.

b. The compound CaO contains the Ca^{2+} and O^{2-} ions. Each calcium atom loses two electrons $(Ca \rightarrow Ca^{2+} + 2e^-)$, and each oxygen atom gains two electrons $(O + 2e^- \rightarrow O^{2-})$.

CHEMISTRY in ACTION

What's That in Your Water?

Materials Each student/group will need water samples and access to a solution of silver nitrate (~ 0.1 M). Empty film canisters work well for bringing in water samples (and drugstores will often give them to you in bulk).

Purpose Students will see that most water samples contain chloride ions. In addition, they will see an example of a precipitation reaction and write a net ionic equation.

Discussion Most likely, all of the water samples brought in by students will contain chloride ions to some extent (even bottled drinking water, which may surprise students). The distilled water from the school should be free of chloride ions. Before adding the silver nitrate, have students predict which samples will be high in chloride ions and which will be low. Then have them compare their predictions to the actual results.

The net ionic equation in all cases is

$Ag^+(aq) + Cl^-(aq) \rightarrow AgCl(s)$

(continued)

uncharged fluorine atoms. Thus in the reaction each cesium atom loses one electron $(Cs \rightarrow Cs^+ + e^-)$ and each fluorine atom gains one electron $(F + e^- \rightarrow F^-)$. The schematic for this reaction is

Self-Check Exercise 8.3

For each reaction, show how electrons are gained and lost.

a. $2Na(s) + Br_2(l) \rightarrow 2NaBr(s)$

b. $2Ca(s) + O_2(g) \rightarrow 2CaO(s)$

So far we have emphasized electron transfer (oxidation–reduction) reactions that involve a metal and a nonmetal. Electron transfer reactions can also take place between two nonmetals. We will not discuss these reactions in detail here. All we will say at this point is that one sure sign of an

CHEMISTRY in ACTION
What's That in Your Water?

1. Obtain samples of water from your home faucet, bottled water, distilled water from school, water from the school drinking fountain, and a swimming pool (if available).

2. Get a dropper bottle of silver nitrate solution from your teacher. (**Caution:** Silver nitrate solution will stain your skin!) Add a few drops of the silver nitrate solution to your samples of water.

3. What do you notice when you add the silver nitrate solution to your water samples? Compare your results with those of your classmates.

4. Write the net ionic equation for any reaction.

5. What does this test tell you about the water samples?

234 Chapter 8 Reactions in Aqueous Solutions

TEACHING SUPPORT
Demonstration

Making Salt

Materials
1-L cylinder filled one-third full with dry sand
Salt shaker filled with salt and with a wire attached long enough to reach out the top of the cylinder
Deflagrating spoon
Stopper to fit the cylinder

Na metal
Knife
Cl_2 gas (lecture bottle)
Tweezers
Wash bottle/water

Preparation Bury the salt shaker completely in the sand in the cylinder, with the wire extending up and out the top of the cylinder. In the hood, fill the cylinder with Cl_2 gas and stopper it firmly, catching the wire between the stopper and the glass.

Presentation Cut a small piece of sodium to fit in the deflagrating spoon. Use a paper towel to dry off the oil. Place the sodium in the deflagrating spoon. Squirt the sodium with a small amount of water to ignite it. Immediately remove the stopper from the cylinder and lower the deflagrating spoon into the cylinder. Once the sodium has gone out and white smoke is evident, remove the oxidation–reduction reaction between nonmetals is the presence of oxygen, $O_2(g)$, as a reactant or product. In fact, oxidation got its name from oxygen. Thus the reactions

$$CH_4(g) + 2O_2(g) \rightarrow CO_2(g) + 2H_2O(g)$$

and

$$2SO_2(g) + O_2(g) \rightarrow 2SO_3(g)$$

are electron transfer reactions, even though it is not obvious at this point.

We can summarize what we have learned about oxidation–reduction reactions as follows:

Characteristics of Oxidation–Reduction Reactions

1. When a metal reacts with a nonmetal, an ionic compound is formed. The ions are formed when the metal transfers one or more electrons to the nonmetal, the metal atom becoming a cation and the nonmetal atom becoming an anion. *Therefore, a metal–nonmetal reaction can always be assumed to be an oxidation–reduction reaction, which involves electron transfer.*

2. Two nonmetals can also undergo an oxidation–reduction reaction. At this point we can recognize these cases only by looking for O_2 as a reactant or product. When two nonmetals react, the compound formed is not ionic.

8.6   Ways to Classify Reactions

Objective: *To learn various classification schemes for reactions.*

So far in our study of chemistry we have seen many, many chemical reactions—and this is just Chapter 8. In the world around us and in our bodies, literally millions of chemical reactions are taking place. Obviously, we need a system for putting reactions into meaningful classes that will make them easier to remember and easier to understand.

In Chapter 8 we have so far considered the following "driving forces" for chemical reactions:

- Formation of a solid
- Formation of water
- Transfer of electrons

We will now discuss how to classify reactions involving these processes. For example, in the reaction

$$K_2CrO_4(aq) + Ba(NO_3)_2(aq) \rightarrow BaCrO_4(s) + 2KNO_3(aq)$$

Solution   Solution   Solid formed   Solution

solid $BaCrO_4$ (a precipitate) is formed. Because the *formation of a solid when two solutions are mixed* is called *precipitation*, we call this a *precipitation reaction.*

Section 8.6

Themes
Patterns of Change, Form and Function

Skills
Applying concepts, observing, classifying, making predictions

Laboratory
Experiment 30:
Activity Series for Metal, Microscale

Laboratory
Experiment 31:
Unknown Solutions, In Text

---

spoon. Ask the students what the product is. As they respond, pull the salt shaker out of the cylinder.

Teaching Notes Chlorine gas is toxic and choking. Be careful when removing the stopper. The reaction produces intense heat and light.

The reaction is:

$$2Na(s) + Cl_2(g) \rightarrow 2NaCl(s)$$

Notice in this reaction that two anions (NO_3^- and CrO_4^{2-}) are simply exchanged. Note that CrO_4^{2-} was originally associated with K^+ in K_2CrO_4 and that NO_3^- was associated with Ba^{2+} in $Ba(NO_3)_2$. In the products these associations are reversed. Because of this double exchange, we sometimes call this reaction a double-exchange reaction or **double-displacement reaction.** We might represent such a reaction as

$$AB + CD \rightarrow AD + CB$$

So we can classify a reaction such as this one as a precipitation reaction or as a double-displacement reaction. Either name is correct, but precipitation is commonly used by chemists.

In this chapter we have also considered reactions in which water is formed when a strong acid is mixed with a strong base. All of these reactions had the same net ionic equation:

$$H^+(aq) + OH^-(aq) \rightarrow H_2O(l)$$

The H^+ ion comes from a strong acid, such as $HCl(aq)$ or $HNO_3(aq)$, and the origin of the OH^- ion is a strong base, such as $NaOH(aq)$ or $KOH(aq)$. An ex-ample is

$$HCl(aq) + KOH(aq) \rightarrow H_2O(l) + KCl(aq)$$

We classify these reaction as **acid–base reactions.** You can recognize an acid–base reaction because it *involves an H^+ ion that ends up in the product water.*

The third driving force is electron transfer. We see evidence of this driv-ing force particularly in the "desire" of a metal to donate electrons to non-metals. An example is

$$2Li(s) + F_2(g) \rightarrow 2LiF(s)$$

where each lithium atom loses one electron to form Li^+, and each fluorine atom gains one electron to form the F^- ion. The process of electron transfer is also called oxidation–reduction. Thus we classify the above reaction as an *oxidation–reduction reaction.*

An additional driving force for chemical reactions that we have not yet discussed is *formation of a gas.* A reaction in aqueous solution that forms a gas (which escapes as bubbles) is pulled toward the products by this event. An example is the reaction

$$2HCl(aq) + Na_2CO_3(aq) \rightarrow CO_2(g) + H_2O(l) + 2NaCl(aq)$$

for which the net ionic equation is

$$2H^+(aq) + CO_3^{2-}(aq) \rightarrow CO_2(g) + H_2O(l)$$

Note that this reaction forms carbon dioxide gas as well as water, so it illus-trates two of the driving forces that we have considered. Because this reac-tion involves H^+ that ends up in the product water, we classify it as an acid–base reaction.

Consider another reaction that forms a gas:

$$Zn(s) + 2HCl(aq) \rightarrow H_2(g) + ZnCl_2(aq)$$

Do We Age by Oxidation?

People (especially those over age 30) seem obsessed about staying young, but the fountain of youth sought since the days of Ponce de Leon has proved elusive. The body inevitably seems to wear out after 70 or 80 years. Is this our destiny or can we find ways to combat aging?

Why do we age? No one knows for certain, but many scientists think that oxidation plays a major role. Although oxygen is essential for life, it can also have a detrimental effect. The oxygen molecule and other oxidizing substances in the body can extract single electrons from the large molecules that make up cell membranes (walls), thus causing them to become very reactive. In fact, these activated molecules can react with each other to change the properties of the cell membranes. If enough of these changes accumulate, the body's immune system comes to view the changed cell as "foreign" and destroys it. This action is particularly harmful to the organism if the cells involved are irreplaceable, such as nerve cells.

Because the human body is so complex, it is very difficult to pinpoint the cause or causes of aging. Scientists are therefore studying simpler life forms. For example, Rajundar Sohal and his coworkers at Southern Methodist University in Dallas are examining aging in common houseflies. Their

work indicates that the accumulated damage from oxidation is linked to both the fly's vitality and its life expectancy. One study showed that flies that were forced to be sedentary (couldn't fly around) showed much less damage from oxidation (because of their lower oxygen consumption) and lived twice as long as flies that had normal activities.

Accumulated knowledge from various studies indicates that oxidation is probably a major cause of aging. If this is true, how can we protect ourselves? The best way to approach the answer to this question is to study the body's natural defenses against oxidation. A recent study by Russel J. Reiter of the Texas Health Science Center at San Antonio has shown that melatonin—a chemical secreted by the pineal gland in the brain (but only at night)—protects against oxidation. In addition, it has long been known that vitamin E is an antioxidant. Studies have shown that red blood cells deficient in vitamin E age much faster than cells with normal vitamin E levels. On the basis of this type of evidence many people take daily doses of vitamin E to ward off the effects of aging.

Oxidation is only one possible cause of aging. Research continues on many fronts to find out why we get "older" as time passes.

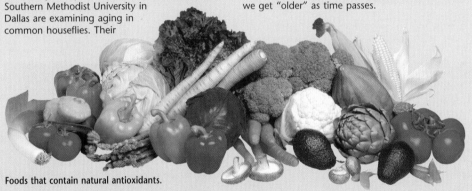

Foods that contain natural antioxidants.

Do We Age by Oxidation?

"Do We Age by Oxidation?" connects chemical reactions to the aging process. Accumulating evidence suggests that oxidation to form free radicals (a species with unpaired electrons) is the cause of some diseases (including cancer) and speeds up the aging of cells. Foods such as blueberries that contain natural reducing agents seem to protect us from disease and keep us healthier into old age.

The chemistry of nutrition is quite interesting. For example, although most students do not regard broccoli as a favorite food, good evidence indicates that it contains one or more chemicals that protect against cancer by blocking tumor formation. One such chemical from broccoli that has been identified is called sulforaphane and has the structure

$$CH_3 - \underset{\underset{O}{\overset{\|}{}}}{C} - (CH_2)_4 - NCS$$

Although this chemical doesn't look like something we should eat, in small amounts it seems quite beneficial.

How might we classify this reaction? A careful look at the reactants and products shows the following:

$$Zn(s) \ + \ 2HCl(aq) \ \rightarrow \ H_2(g) \ + \ ZnCl_2(aq)$$

Contains uncharged Zn atoms   Really $2H^+(aq) + 2Cl^-(aq)$ Contains uncharged H atoms   Really $Zn^{2+}(aq) + 2Cl^-(aq)$

8.6   Ways to Classify Reactions   **237**

Launching the Space Shuttle

"Launching the Space Shuttle" emphasizes the tremendous energy available from oxidation–reduction reactions. Virtually all of the reactions used in our society as energy sources are redox reactions. Examples include the reaction between the hydrocarbons in gasoline and the oxygen in the air used to power cars and trucks, the natural gas used to heat our homes (methane reacting with oxygen), and the decomposition of nitrogen-containing compounds such as TNT (trinitrotoluene) that act as explosives.

The solid-fuel rockets described in this Chemical Impact show that reactions can take place in the solid phase, although we almost always talk about reactions that occur in solutions.

CHEMICAL IMPACT

Launching the Space Shuttle

Launching into space a vehicle that weighs millions of pounds requires unimaginable quantities of energy—all furnished by oxidation–reduction reactions.

Notice from **Figure 8.8** that three cylindrical objects are attached to the shuttle orbiter. In the center is a tank about 28 feet in diameter and 154 feet long that contains liquid oxygen and liquid hydrogen (in separate compartments). These fuels are fed to the orbiter's rocket engines, where they react to form water and release a huge quantity of energy.

$$2H_2 + O_2 \rightarrow 2H_2O + \text{energy}$$

Note that we can recognize this reaction as an oxidation–reduction reaction because O_2 is a reactant.

Two solid-fuel rockets 12 feet in diameter and 150 feet long are also attached to the orbiter. Each rocket contains 1.1 million pounds of fuel: ammonium perchlorate (NH_4ClO_4) and powdered aluminum mixed with a binder ("glue"). Because the rockets are so large, they are built in segments and assembled at the launch site as shown in **Figure 8.9**. Each segment is filled with the syrupy propellant (**Figure 8.10**), which then solidifies to a consistency much like that of a hard rubber eraser.

The oxidation–reduction reaction between the ammonium perchlorate and the aluminum is represented as follows:

$$3NH_4ClO_4(s) + 3Al(s) \rightarrow$$
$$Al_2O_3(s) + AlCl_3(s) + 3NO(g)$$
$$+ 6H_2O(g) + \text{energy}$$

It produces temperatures of about 5700 °F (3150 °C) and 3.3 million pounds of thurst in each rocket.

Thus we can see that oxidation–reduction reactions furnish the energy to launch the space shuttle.

149.16 feet long,
12.17 feet in diameter

Figure 8.9
The solid-fuel rockets are assembled from segments to make loading the fuel more convenient.

Figure 8.10
A rocket segment being filled with the propellant mixture.

Figure 8.8
For launch, the space shuttle *Discovery* is attached to two solid-fuel rockets (left and right) and a fuel tank (center) that supplies hydrogen and oxygen to the orbiter's engines.

Note that in the reactant zinc metal, Zn exists as uncharged atoms, whereas in the product it exists as Zn^{2+}. Thus each Zn atom loses two electrons. Where have these electrons gone? They have been transferred to two H^+ ions to form H_2. The schematic for this reaction is

| Zn metal | Solution of HCl | H_2 molecule | Solution of $ZnCl_2$ |

This is an electron transfer process, so the reaction can be classified as an oxidation–reduction reaction.

Another way this reaction is sometimes classified is based on the fact that a *single* type of anion (Cl^-) has been exchanged between H^+ and Zn^{2+}. That is, Cl^- is originally associated with H^+ in HCl and ends up associated with Zn^{2+} in the product $ZnCl_2$. We can call this a **single-replacement reaction** in contrast to double-displacement reactions, in which two types of anions are exchanged. We can represent a single replacement as

$$A + BC \rightarrow B + AC$$

8.7 Other Ways to Classify Reactions

Objective: *To consider additional classes of chemical reactions.*

So far in this chapter we have classified chemical reactions is several ways. The most commonly used of these classifications are

- Precipitation reactions
- Acid–base reactions
- Oxidation–reduction reactions

However, there are still other ways to classify reactions that you may encounter in your future studies of chemistry. We will consider several of these in this section.

Combustion Reactions

Many chemical reactions that involve oxygen produce energy (heat) so rapidly that a flame results. Such reactions are called **combustion reactions.** We have considered some of these reactions previously. For example, the methane in natural gas reacts with oxygen according to the following balanced equation:

$$CH_4(g) + 2O_2(g) \rightarrow CO_2(g) + 2H_2O(g)$$

This reaction produces the flame of the common laboratory burner and is also used to heat most homes in the United States. Recall that we originally classified this reaction as an oxidation–reduction reaction in Section 8.5. Thus we can say that the reaction of methane with oxygen is both an

Figure 8.11
Classes of reactions. Combustion reactions are a special type of oxidation–reduction reaction.

oxidation–reduction reaction and a combustion reaction. Combustion reactions, in fact, are a special class of oxidation–reduction reactions (see **Figure 8.11**).

There are many combustion reactions, most of which are used to provide heat or electricity for homes or businesses or energy for transportation. Some examples are:

- Combustion of propane (used to heat some rural homes)

  $$C_3H_8(g) + 5O_2(g) \rightarrow 3CO_2(g) + 4H_2O(g)$$

- Combustion of gasoline* (used to power cars and trucks)

  $$2C_8H_{18}(l) + 25O_2(g) \rightarrow 16CO_2(g) + 18H_2O(g)$$

- Combustion of coal* (used to generate electricity)

  $$C(s) + O_2(g) \rightarrow CO_2(g)$$

Synthesis (Combination) Reactions

One of the most important activities in chemistry is the synthesis of new compounds. Each of our lives has been greatly affected by synthetic compounds such as plastic, polyester, and aspirin. When a given compound is formed from simpler materials, we call this a **synthesis** (or **combination**) **reaction.**

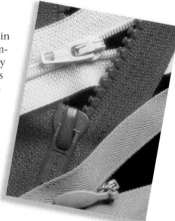

Formation of the colorful plastics used in these zippers is an example of a synthesis reaction.

---

*This substance is really a complex mixture of compounds, but the reaction shown is representative of what takes place.

In many cases synthesis reactions start with elements, as shown by the following examples:

- Synthesis of water $\quad\quad\quad\quad\quad\quad$ $2H_2(g) + O_2(g) \rightarrow 2H_2O(l)$
- Synthesis of carbon dioxide $\quad\quad$ $C(s) + O_2(g) \rightarrow CO_2(g)$
- Synthesis of nitrogen monoxide $\quad$ $N_2(g) + O_2(g) \rightarrow 2NO(g)$

Notice that each of these reactions involves oxygen, so each can be classified as an oxidation–reduction reaction. The first two reactions are also commonly called combustion reactions because they produce flames. The reaction of hydrogen with oxygen to produce water, then, can be classified three ways: as an oxidation–reduction reaction, as a combustion reaction, and as a synthesis reaction.

There are also many synthesis reactions that do not involve oxygen:

- Synthesis of sodium chloride $\quad\quad$ $2Na(s) + Cl_2(g) \rightarrow 2NaCl(s)$
- Synthesis of magnesium fluoride $\quad$ $Mg(s) + F_2(g) \rightarrow MgF_2(s)$

We have discussed the formation of sodium chloride before and have noted that it is an oxidation–reduction reaction; uncharged sodium atoms lose electrons to form Na^+ ions, and uncharged chlorine atoms gain electrons to form Cl^- ions. The synthesis of magnesium fluoride is also an oxidation–reduction reaction because Mg^{2+} and F^- ions are produced from the uncharged atoms.

We have seen that synthesis reactions in which the reactants are elements are oxidation–reduction reactions as well. In fact, we can think of these synthesis reactions as another subclass of the oxidation–reduction class of reactions.

Decomposition Reactions

In many cases a compound can be broken down into simpler compounds or all the way to the component elements. This is usually accomplished by heating or by the application of an electric current. Such reactions are called **decomposition reactions.** We have discussed decomposition reactions before, including

- Decomposition of water

$$2H_2O(l) \xrightarrow{\text{Electric current}} 2H_2(g) + O_2(g)$$

- Decomposition of mercury (II) oxide

$$2HgO(s) \xrightarrow{\text{Heat}} 2Hg(l) + O_2(g)$$

Because O_2 is involved in the first reaction, we recognize it as an oxidation–reduction reaction. In the second reaction, HgO, which contains Hg^{2+} and O^{2-} ions, is decomposed to the elements, which contain uncharged atoms. In this process each Hg^{2+} gains two electrons and each O^{2-} loses two electrons, so this is both a decomposition reaction and an oxidation–reduction reaction.

A decomposition reaction, in which a compound is broken down into its elements, is just the opposite of the synthesis (combination) reaction, in which elements combine to form the compound. For example, we have just

TEACHING TIP

Most students can write products for double-displacement and single-displacement reactions, but not for synthesis and decomposition reactions.

Figure 8.12
Summary of classes of reactions.

discussed the synthesis of sodium chloride from its elements. Sodium chloride can be decomposed into its elements by melting it and passing an electric current through it:

$$2NaCl(l) \xrightarrow[\text{current}]{\text{Electric}} 2Na(l) + Cl_2(g)$$

There are other schemes for classifying reactions that we have not considered. However, we have covered many of the classifications that are commonly used by chemists as they pursue their science in laboratories and industrial plants.

It should be apparent that many important reactions can be classified as oxidation–reduction reactions. As shown in **Figure 8.12,** various types of reactions can be viewed as subclasses of the overall oxidation–reduction category.

Example 8.6

Classifying Reactions

Classify each of the following reactions in as many ways as possible.

a. $2K(s) + Cl_2(g) \rightarrow 2KCl(s)$
b. $Fe_2O_3(s) + 2Al(s) \rightarrow Al_2O_3(s) + 2Fe(s)$
c. $2Mg(s) + O_2(g) \rightarrow 2MgO(s)$
d. $HNO_3(aq) + NaOH(aq) \rightarrow H_2O(l) + NaNO_3(aq)$
e. $KBr(aq) + AgNO_3(aq) \rightarrow AgBr(s) + KNO_3(aq)$
f. $PbO_2(s) \rightarrow Pb(s) + O_2(g)$

Solution

a. This is both a synthesis reaction (elements combine to form a compound) and an oxidation–reduction reaction (uncharged potassium and chlorine atoms are changed to K^+ and Cl^- ions in KCl).

Additional Examples

Classify each of the following reactions in as many ways as possible.

1. $2C_2H_2(s) + 5O_2(g) \rightarrow 4CO_2(g) + 2H_2O(g)$
Combustion, oxidation–reduction

2. $2Ni(s) + 4O_2(g) \rightarrow 2NiO(s)$
Synthesis, oxidation–reduction

b. This is an oxidation–reduction reaction. Iron is present in $Fe_2O_3(s)$ as Fe^{3+} ions and in elemental iron, $Fe(s)$, as uncharged atoms. So each Fe^{3+} must gain three electrons to form Fe. The reverse happens to aluminum, which is present initially as uncharged aluminum atoms, each of which loses three electrons to give Al^{3+} ions in Al_2O_3. Note that this reaction might also be called a single-replacement reaction because O is switched from Fe to Al.

c. This is both a synthesis reaction (elements combine to form a compound) and an oxidation–reduction reaction (each magnesium atom loses two electrons to give Mg^{2+} ions in MgO, and each oxygen atom gains two electrons to give O^{2-} in MgO).

d. This is an acid–base reaction. It might also be called a double-displacement reaction because NO_3^- and OH^- "switch partners."

e. This is a precipitation reaction that might also be called a double-displacement reaction in which the anions Br^- and NO_3^- are exchanged.

f. This is a decomposition reaction (a compound breaks down into elements). It also is an oxidation–reduction reaction, because the ions in PbO_2 (Pb^{4+} and O^{2-}) are changed to uncharged atoms in the elements $Pb(s)$ and $O_2(g)$. That is, electrons are transferred from O^{2-} to Pb^{4+} in the reaction.

 Self-Check Exercise 8.4

Classify each of the following reactions in as many ways as possible.

a. $4NH_3(g) + 5O_2(g) \rightarrow 4NO(g) + 6H_2O(g)$

b. $S_8(s) + 8O_2(g) \rightarrow 8SO_2(g)$

c. $2Al(s) + 3Cl_2(g) \rightarrow 2AlCl_3(s)$

d. $2AlN(s) \rightarrow 2Al(s) + N_2(g)$

e. $BaCl_2(aq) + Na_2SO_4(aq) \rightarrow BaSO_4(s) + 2NaCl(aq)$

f. $2Cs(s) + Br_2(l) \rightarrow 2CsBr(s)$

g. $KOH(aq) + HCl(aq) \rightarrow H_2O(l) + KCl(aq)$

h. $2C_2H_2(g) + 5O_2(g) \rightarrow 4CO_2(g) + 2H_2O(l)$

Focus Questions **Sections 8.5–8.7**

1. What is an oxidation–reduction reaction? How can you identify this type of reaction?

2. How do oxidation–reduction reactions lead to aging in humans?

3. What are the four driving forces for a chemical reaction?

4. What are four other ways to classify oxidation–reduction reactions?

5. Classify the following unbalanced reaction equations as precipitation, acid–base, or oxidation–reduction reactions.

a. $Fe(s) + H_2SO_4(aq) \rightarrow Fe_3(SO_4)_2(aq) + H_2(g)$
b. $HClO_4(aq) + RbOH(aq) \rightarrow RbClO_4(aq) + H_2O(l)$
c. $K_2SO_4(aq) + CaCl_2(aq) \rightarrow KCl(aq) + CaSO_4(s)$
d. $Ni(s) + Cl_2(g) \rightarrow NiCl_2(s)$

WHAT IF?

What if no ionic solids were soluble in water? Could reactions occur in aqueous solutions? Explain.

Focus Questions **243**

Answers to Self-Check Exercise 8.4

a. oxidation–reduction; combustion

b. synthesis; oxidation–reduction; combustion

c. synthesis; oxidation–reduction

d. decomposition; oxidation–reduction

e. precipitation (and double displacement)

f. synthesis; oxidation–reduction

g. acid–base (and double displacement)

h. combustion; oxidation–reduction

Answers to Focus Questions

1. An oxidation–reduction reaction involves the transfer of electrons. These reactions are typically reactions between metals and nonmetals or reactions between two nonmetals that have oxygen molecules as a reactant or a product.

2. Oxygen molecules can remove single electrons from the large molecules of the body, causing them to become very reactive. These reactions lead to changes in the cell membranes, which can lead to further deterioration of the cells.

3. The four driving forces for a chemical reaction are formation of a solid, formation of water, transfer of electrons, and formation of a gas.

4. Other ways to classify oxidation–reduction reactions include combustion, synthesis, decomposition, double displacement, and single displacement.

5. **a.** oxidation–reduction

b. acid–base

c. precipitation

d. oxidation–reduction

WHAT IF Comments

This feature specifically targets precipitation reactions. If no ionic solids were soluble, these reactions could not occur in solution. Precipitation reactions occur in solution because the ions separate when they dissolve in solution, which allows them to react. For example, potassium chloride solution is best thought of as separate potassium ions and chloride ions in solution. This case is another example illustrating the

importance of consistently emphasizing a microscopic perspective for chemical phenomena.

Unknown Solutions

Objective

To identify 10 unknown solutions using students' knowledge and understanding of chemistry

Skills

Observing, applying concepts, interpreting data, drawing conclusions, making inferences, designing experiments, analyzing clues

Materials

Goggles
Apron
Pipets
Phenolphthalein (an acid–base indicator)
Conductivity tester
10 unknown solutions:
   Table sugar
   Potassium nitrate
   Sulfuric acid
   Copper(II) nitrate
   Sodium chloride
   Silver nitrate
   Sodium hydroxide
   Barium nitrate
   Ammonium chloride
   Acetic acid

Preparation Hints

Distribute several sets of bottles with unknowns (labeled #1, #2, and so on) throughout the lab for easier access. Use 0.10 M solutions for all unknowns.

Prelab Discussion

Students must wear safety goggles and lab aprons while in the lab.

Remind the students of the locations of eyewashes. If students come in contact with any solution, they should wash the contacted area thoroughly.

Show students how phenolphthalein indicator acts in the presence of an acid and in the presence of a base.

Tell students that they will need to test only small amounts (drops) of each solution.

Procedure Hints

Tell students that some clues will be more helpful than others. For example, at this point students will not know that ammonium chloride is an acidic salt. They will find that there are three acidic solutions and should recognize sulfuric acid and acetic acid as being acidic. They will have to use other observations to narrow down the choices.

You may need to help students think about how to determine whether a solution is acidic, because the phenolphthalein will be colorless in both neutral and acidic solutions. One way is to find the basic solution, add phenolphthalein to a few drops of the base, and then add the same amount of another solution. If the pink solution turns colorless, the added solution is acidic.

Problem

How can you use chemical reactions and physical properties to identify unknown solutions?

Introduction

You have come a long way in your knowledge and understanding of chemistry. Now you are ready to use this knowledge and understanding to identify ten unknown solutions.

Prelab Assignment

1. Read the entire lab experiment before you begin. Review previous labs, class notes, and the text to find distinguishing characteristics for each of the solutions.
2. Write the formulas for all of the substances in the solutions (see the Materials section).
3. List methods to test the solutions. (*Hint:* Don't forget that you can react the solutions with each other.)

Materials

Goggles
Apron
Pipets
Phenolphthalein (an acid–base indicator)
Conductivity tester
Unknown solutions

Table sugar	Silver nitrate
Potassium nitrate	Sodium hydroxide
Sulfuric acid	Barium nitrate
Copper(II) nitrate	Ammonium chloride
Sodium chloride	Acetic acid

Safety

If you come in contact with any solution, wash the contacted area thoroughly.

Procedure

1. Discuss the procedures to test the solutions you have developed in the Prelab Assignment with your partner and your teacher.
2. Carry out the procedures.

Cleaning Up

Clean up all materials and wash your hands thoroughly.

Data/Observations

Record all procedures and results of your tests for each unknown solution in an orderly fashion.

Disposal

Collect all solutions from the students and dispose of them properly.

Post-Lab Discussion

Have students discuss their observations with each other to ensure that each student has a complete list of observations. Leave it to individual students or teams to decide how to use this information.

Analysis and Conclusions

List each observation and state the possibilities from each observation.

	Observations	Possibilities
Unknown #1		
Unknown #2		
. . .		
Unknown #10		

Summary Table

Fill in a table similar to the one provided here.

Unknown #	Name	Formula	Reason
1			
2			
. . .			
10			

Something Extra

Suppose you were given an unknown solution containing a mixture of two or more of the solutions used in this experiment. Describe what you could do to identify the components of this unknown solution.

Sample Data/Answers

Prelab Assignment

2. See the *Teacher's Guide* for the Laboratory.
3. Answers will vary. Look for tests that will limit the number of possibilities.

Analysis and Conclusions

Answers will vary; some possible answers are given in the *Teacher's Guide* for the Laboratory.

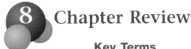

Chapter Review

Key Terms

precipitation (8.2)
precipitate (8.2)
precipitation reaction (8.2)
strong electrolyte (8.2)
soluble solid (8.2)
insoluble (slightly soluble)
  solid (8.2)
molecular equation (8.3)
complete ionic equation (8.3)
spectator ions (8.3)
net ionic equation (8.3)
acid (8.4)
strong acid (8.4)
base (8.4)

strong base (8.4)
salt (8.4)
oxidation-reduction
  reaction (8.5)
double–displacement
  reaction (8.6)
acid-base reaction (8.6)
single-replacement
  reaction (8.6)
combustion reaction (8.7)
synthesis (combination)
  reaction (8.7)
decomposition
  reaction (8.7)

Summary

1. Four driving forces that favor chemical change (chemical reaction) are formation of a solid, formation of water, transfer of electrons, and formation of a gas.

2. A reaction where a solid forms is called a precipitation reaction. General rules on solubility help predict whether a solid—and what solid—will form when two solutions are mixed.

3. Three types of equations are used to describe reactions in solution: (1) the molecular equation, which shows the complete formulas of all reactants and products; (2) the complete ionic equation, in which all reactants and products that are strong electrolytes are shown as ions; and (3) the net ionic equation, which includes only those components of the solution that undergo a change. Spectator ions (those ions that remain unchanged in a reaction) are not included in a net ionic equation.

4. A strong acid is a compound in which virtually every molecule dissociates in water to give an H^+ ion and an anion. Similarly, a strong base is a metal hydroxide compound that is soluble in water, giving OH^- ions and cations. The products of the reaction of a strong acid and a strong base are water and a salt.

5. Reactions of metals and nonmetals involve a transfer of electrons and are called oxidation–reduction reactions. A reaction between a nonmetal and oxygen is also an oxidation–reduction reaction. Combustion reactions involve oxygen and are a subgroup of oxidation–reduction reactions.

6. When a given compound is formed from simpler materials, such as elements, the reaction is called a synthesis or combination reaction. The reverse process,

which occurs when a compound is broken down into its component elements, is called a decomposition reaction. These reactions are also subgroups of oxidation–reduction reactions.

Questions and Problems

All exercises with blue numbers have answers in the back of this book.

8.1 Predicting Whether a Reaction Will Occur

Questions

1. Why is water an important solvent? Although you have not yet studied water in detail, can you think of some properties of water that make it so important?

2. What is a "driving force"? What are some of the driving forces discussed in this section that tend to make reactions likely to occur? Can you think of any other possible driving forces?

8.2 Reactions in Which a Solid Forms

Questions

3. When two solutions of ionic substances are mixed and a precipitate forms, what is the net charge of the precipitate? Why?

4. What does it mean to say that the ions of an electrolyte behave independently of one another when the electrolyte is dissolved in water?

5. What is meant by a *strong electrolyte?* Give two examples of substances that behave in solution as strong electrolytes.

6. When aqueous solutions of sodium chloride, NaCl, and silver nitrate, $AgNO_3$, are mixed, a precipitate forms, but this precipitate is *not* sodium nitrate. What does this reaction tell you about the solubility of $NaNO_3$ in water?

7. What do we mean when we say that a solid is "slightly" soluble in water? Is there a practical difference between *slightly* soluble and *in*soluble?

8. On the basis of the general solubility rules given in Table 8.1, predict which of the following substances are likely to be soluble in water.
   a. barium nitrate
   b. potassium carbonate
   c. sodium sulfate
   d. copper(II) hydroxide
   e. mercury(I) chloride
   f. ammonium phosphate
   g. chromium(III) sulfide
   h. lead(II) sulfate

Chapter Review **245**

uble); (h) insoluble (except for sulfate salts)

9. (a) rule 5: most hydroxide compounds are only slightly soluble; (b) rule 6: most carbonates are only slightly soluble; (c) rule 6: most phosphate salts are only slightly soluble; (d) rule 3: exception to the rule for chlorides

10. (a) calcium sulfate; (b) silver iodide; (c) lead(II) phosphate; (d) iron(III) hydroxide; (e) no precipitate: all potassium and sodium salts are soluble; (f) barium carbonate

11. (a) no precipitate;
(b) $(NH_4)_2S(aq) + CoCl_2(aq) \rightarrow$ $\underline{CoS(s)} + 2NH_4Cl(aq)$;
(c) $H_2SO_4(aq) + Pb(NO_3)_2(aq)$ $\rightarrow \underline{PbSO_4(s)} + 2HNO_3(aq)$;
(d) $CaCl_2(aq) + K_2CO_3(aq)$ $\rightarrow \underline{CaCO_3(s)} + 2KCl(aq)$;
(e) no precipitate;
(f) $Na_3PO_4(aq) + CrCl_3(aq)$ $\rightarrow \underline{CrPO_4(s)} + 3NaCl(aq)$

12.
(a) $2AgNO_3(aq) + H_2SO_4(aq) \rightarrow$ $Ag_2SO_4(s) + 2HNO_3(aq)$;
(b) $Ca(NO_3)_2(aq) + H_2SO_4(aq)$ $\rightarrow CaSO_4(s) + 2HNO_3(aq)$;
(c) $Pb(NO_3)_2(aq) + H_2SO_4(aq)$ $\rightarrow PbSO_4(s) + 2HNO_3(aq)$

13.
(a) $(NH_4)_2S(aq) + CoCl_2(aq) \rightarrow$ $CoS(s) + 2NH_4Cl(aq)$;
(b) $FeCl_3(aq) + NaOH(aq) \rightarrow$ $Fe(OH)_3(s) + 3NaCl(aq)$;
(c) $CuSO_4(aq) + Na_2CO_3(aq) \rightarrow$ $CuCO_3(s) + Na_2SO_4(aq)$

14. (a) $Ca^{2+}(aq) + SO_4^{2-}(aq)$ $\rightarrow CaSO_4(s)$; (b) $2Fe^{3+}(aq) +$ $3CO_3^{2-}(aq) \rightarrow Fe_2(CO_3)_3(s)$;
(c) $Ag^+(aq) + I^-(aq) \rightarrow AgI(s)$;
(d) $3Co^{2+}(aq) + 2PO_4^{3-}(aq)$ $\rightarrow Co_3(PO_4)_2(s)$;
(e) $Hg_2^{2+}(aq) + 2Cl^-(aq) \rightarrow$ $Hg_2Cl_2(s)$;
(f) $Pb^{2+}(aq) + 2Br^-(aq) \rightarrow$ $PbBr_2(s)$

15. $Ag^+(aq) + Cl^-(aq) \rightarrow$ $AgCl(s)$; $Pb^{2+}(aq) + 2Cl^-(aq)$ $\rightarrow PbCl_2(s)$; (e) $Hg_2^{2+}(aq) +$ $2Cl^-(aq) \rightarrow Hg_2Cl_2(s)$

16. $Ca^{2+}(aq) + C_2O_4^{2-}(aq) \rightarrow$ $CaC_2O_4(s)$

17. Strong acids are acids that completely ionize in water; thus strong acids are also strong electrolytes.

18. The strong bases are those hydroxide compounds that dissociate fully when dissolved in water. Strong bases that are highly soluble in water (NaOH, KOH) are also strong electrolytes.

246

9. On the basis of the general solubility rules given in Table 8.1, for each of the following compounds, indicate why the compound is *not* likely to be soluble in water. Indicate *which* of the solubility rules covers each substance's particular situation.
   a. iron(III) hydroxide
   b. calcium carbonate
   c. cobalt(III) phosphate
   d. silver chloride

10. On the basis of the general solubility rules given in Table 8.1, predict the identity of the precipitate that forms when aqueous solutions of the following substances are mixed. If no precipitate is likely, indicate which rules apply.
   a. sodium sulfate, Na_2SO_4, and calcium chloride, $CaCl_2$
   b. ammonium iodide, NH_4I, and silver nitrate, $AgNO_3$
   c. potassium phosphate, K_3PO_4, and lead(II) nitrate, $Pb(NO_3)_2$
   d. sodium hydroxide, NaOH, and iron(III) chloride, $FeCl_3$
   e. potassium sulfate, K_2SO_4, and sodium nitrate, $NaNO_3$
   f. sodium carbonate, Na_2CO_3, and barium nitrate, $Ba(NO_3)_2$

Problems

11. On the basis of the general solubility rules given in Table 8.1, write a balanced molecular equation for the precipitation reactions that take place when the following aqueous solutions are mixed. Underline the formula of the precipitate (solid) that forms. If no precipitation reaction is likely for the solutes given, so indicate.
   a. nitric acid, HNO_3, and barium chloride, $BaCl_2$
   b. ammonium sulfide, $(NH_4)_2S$, and cobalt(II) chloride, $CoCl_2$
   c. sulfuric acid, H_2SO_4, and lead(II) nitrate, $Pb(NO_3)_2$
   d. calcium chloride, $CaCl_2$, and potassium carbonate, K_2CO_3
   e. sodium acetate, $NaC_2H_3O_2$, and ammonium nitrate, NH_4NO_3
   f. sodium phosphate, Na_3PO_4, and chromium(III) chloride, $CrCl_3$

12. Balance each of the following equations that describe precipitation reactions.
   a. $AgNO_3(aq) + H_2SO_4(aq) \rightarrow Ag_2SO_4(s) + HNO_3(aq)$
   b. $Ca(NO_3)_2(aq) + H_2SO_4(aq) \rightarrow$ $CaSO_4(s) + HNO_3(aq)$
   c. $Pb(NO_3)_2(aq) + H_2SO_4(aq) \rightarrow$ $PbSO_4(s) + HNO_3(aq)$

13. For each of the following precipitation reactions, complete and balance the equation, indicating clearly which product is the precipitate.
   a. $(NH_4)_2S(aq) + CoCl_2(aq) \rightarrow$
   b. $FeCl_3(aq) + NaOH(aq) \rightarrow$
   c. $CuSO_4(aq) + Na_2CO_3(aq) \rightarrow$

8.3 Describing Reactions in Aqueous Solutions

Problems

14. Write balanced net ionic equations for the reactions that occur when the following aqueous solutions are mixed. If no reaction is likely to occur, so indicate.
   a. potassium sulfate and calcium nitrate
   b. iron(III) nitrate and sodium carbonate
   c. silver nitrate and calcium iodide
   d. ammonium phosphate and cobalt(II) sulfate
   e. strontium chloride and mercury(I) nitrate
   f. barium bromide and lead(II) nitrate

15. In the laboratory, students often learn to analyze mixtures of the common positive and negative ions, separating and confirming the presence of the particular ions in the mixture. One of the first steps in such an analysis is to treat the mixture with hydrochloric acid, which precipitates and removes silver ion, lead(II) ion, and mercury(I) ion from the aqueous mixture as the insoluble chloride salts. Write balanced net ionic equations for the precipitation reactions of these three cations with chloride ion.

16. Many plants are poisonous because their stems and leaves contain oxalic acid, $H_2C_2O_4$, or sodium oxalate, $Na_2C_2O_4$; when ingested, these substances cause swelling of the respiratory tract and suffocation. A standard analysis for determining the amount of oxalate ion, $C_2O_4^{2-}$, in a sample is to precipitate this species as calcium oxalate, which is insoluble in water. Write the net ionic equation for the reaction between sodium oxalate and calcium chloride, $CaCl_2$, in aqueous solution.

8.4 Reactions That Form Water: Acids and Bases

Questions

17. What is meant by a *strong acid?* Are the strong acids also *strong electrolytes?* Explain.

18. What is meant by a *strong base?* Are the strong bases also *strong electrolytes?* Explain.

19. If 1000 NaOH units were dissolved in a sample of water, the NaOH would produce _____ Na^+ ions and _____ OH^- ions.

19. 1000; 1000

20. $HBr(aq) \rightarrow H^+(aq) + Br^-(aq)$; $HClO_4(aq) \rightarrow H^+(aq) + ClO_4^-(aq)$

21. $RbOH(s) \rightarrow Rb^+(aq) +$ $OH^-(aq)$; $CsOH(s) \rightarrow Cs^+(aq) +$ $OH^-(aq)$

22. (a) $HCl(aq) + RbOH(aq) \rightarrow$ $H_2O(l) + \boxed{RbCl(aq)}$;
(b) $HClO_4(aq) + NaOH(aq) \rightarrow$ $H_2O(l) + \boxed{NaClO_4(aq)}$;
(c) $HBr(aq) + NaOH(aq) \rightarrow$ $H_2O(l) + \boxed{NaBr(aq)}$;
(d) $H_2SO_4(aq) + CsOH(aq) \rightarrow$

$2H_2O(l) + \boxed{Cs_2SO_4(aq)}$

23. (a) $H_2SO_4(aq) + 2NaOH(aq)$ $\rightarrow 2H_2O(l) + Na_2SO_4(aq)$; (b) $HNO_3(aq) + RbOH(aq) \rightarrow H_2O(l) +$ $RbNO_3(aq)$; (c) $HClO_4(aq) +$ $KOH(aq) \rightarrow 2H_2O(l) + KClO_4(aq)$; (d) $HCl(aq) + KOH(aq) \rightarrow H_2O(l) +$ $KCl(aq)$

24. A driving force tends to help convert reactants to products. A transfer of electrons from atoms of a metal (like sodium) to atoms of a nonmetal (like chlorine) is favored because metals tend to lose electrons and nonmetals tend to gain electrons.

25. the metal loses electrons, the nonmetal gains electrons

26. Each potassium atom would lose one electron to become a K^+ ion. Each sulfur atom would gain two electrons to become a S^{2-} ion. Two potassium ions would have to react for every one sulfur atom.

27. $AlBr_3$ is made up of Al^{3+} ions and Br^- ions. Aluminum atoms each lose three electrons and bromine atoms each gain one elec-

Problems

20. Along with the three strong acids emphasized in the chapter (HCl, HNO$_3$, and H$_2$SO$_4$), hydrobromic acid, HBr, and perchloric acid, HClO$_4$, are also strong acids. Write equations for the dissociation of each of these additional strong acids in water.

21. Along with the strong bases NaOH and KOH discussed in this chapter, the hydroxide compounds of other Group 1 elements also behave as strong bases when dissolved in water. Write equations for RbOH and CsOH that show which ions form when they dissolve in water.

22. Complete and balance each of the following molecular equations for strong acid/strong base reactions; circle the formula of the salt produced in each.
   a. HCl(aq) + RbOH(aq) →
   b. HClO$_4$(aq) + NaOH(aq) →
   c. HBr(aq) + NaOH(aq) →
   d. H$_2$SO$_4$(aq) + CsOH(aq) →

23. Below are indicated the formulas of some salts. Such salts could be formed by the reaction of the appropriate strong acid and strong base (with the other product of the reaction being, of course, water). For each salt, write an equation showing the formation of the salt from reaction of the appropriate strong acid and strong base.
   a. Na$_2$SO$_4$
   b. RbNO$_3$
   c. KClO$_4$
   d. KCl

8.5 Reactions of Metals with Nonmetals (Oxidation–Reduction)

Questions

24. What do we mean when we say that the transfer of electrons can be the "driving force" for a reaction? Give an example of a reaction where this happens.

25. If atoms of a metallic element (such as sodium) react with atoms of a nonmetallic element (such as sulfur), which element loses electrons and which element gains them?

26. If potassium atoms were to react with atoms of the nonmetal sulfur, how many electrons would each potassium atom lose? How many electrons would each sulfur atom gain? How many potassium atoms would have to react to provide enough electrons for one sulfur atom? What charges would the resulting potassium and sulfur ions have?

Problems

27. For the reaction 2Al(s) + 3Br$_2$(l) → 2AlBr$_3$(s), show how electrons are gained and lost by the atoms.

28. Balance each of the following oxidation–reduction chemical reactions.
   a. K(s) + F$_2$(g) → KF(s)
   b. K(s) + O$_2$(g) → K$_2$O(s)
   c. K(s) + N$_2$(g) → K$_3$N(s)
   d. K(s) + C(s) → K$_4$C(s)

29. Balance each of the following oxidation–reduction chemical reactions.
   a. Fe(s) + S(s) → Fe$_2$S$_3$(s)
   b. Zn(s) + HNO$_3$(aq) → Zn(NO$_3$)$_2$(aq) + H$_2$(g)
   c. Sn(s) + O$_2$(g) → SnO(s)
   d. K(s) + H$_2$(g) → KH(s)
   e. Cs(s) + H$_2$O(l) → CsOH(s) + H$_2$(g)

8.6 Ways to Classify Reactions

Questions

30. What is a *double*-displacement reaction? What is a *single*-displacement reaction? Write balanced chemical equations showing two examples of each type.

31. Two "driving forces" for reactions discussed in this section are the formation of water in an acid–base reaction and the formation of a gaseous product. Write balanced chemical equations showing two examples of each type.

32. Identify each of the following unbalanced reaction equations as belonging to one or more of the following categories: precipitation, acid–base, or oxidation–reduction.
   a. K$_2$SO$_4$(aq) + Ba(NO$_3$)$_2$(aq) → BaSO$_4$(s) + KNO$_3$(aq)
   b. HCl(aq) + Zn(s) → H$_2$(g) + ZnCl$_2$(aq)
   c. HCl(aq) + AgNO$_3$(aq) → HNO$_3$(aq) + AgCl(s)
   d. HCl(aq) + KOH(aq) → H$_2$O(l) + KCl(aq)
   e. Zn(s) + CuSO$_4$(aq) → ZnSO$_4$(aq) + Cu(s)
   f. NaH$_2$PO$_4$(aq) + NaOH(aq) → Na$_3$PO$_4$(aq) + H$_2$O(l)
   g. Ca(OH)$_2$(aq) + H$_2$SO$_4$(aq) → CaSO$_4$(s) + H$_2$O(l)
   h. ZnCl$_2$(aq) + Mg(s) → Zn(s) + MgCl$_2$(aq)
   i. BaCl$_2$(aq) + H$_2$SO$_4$(aq) → BaSO$_4$(s) + HCl(aq)

33. Identify each of the following unbalanced reaction equations as belonging to one or more of the following categories: precipitation, acid–base, or oxidation–reduction.
   a. H$_2$O$_2$(aq) → H$_2$O(l) + O$_2$(g)
   b. H$_2$SO$_4$(aq) + Cu(s) → CuSO$_4$(aq) + H$_2$(g)
   c. H$_2$SO$_4$(aq) + NaOH(aq) → Na$_2$SO$_4$(aq) + H$_2$O(l)
   d. H$_2$SO$_4$(aq) + Ba(OH)$_2$(aq) → BaSO$_4$(s) + H$_2$O(l)
   e. AgNO$_3$(aq) + CuCl$_2$(aq) → Cu(NO$_3$)$_2$(aq) + AgCl(s)
   f. KOH(aq) + CuSO$_4$(aq) → Cu(OH)$_2$(s) + K$_2$SO$_4$(aq)
   g. Cl$_2$(g) + F$_2$(g) → ClF(g)
   h. NO(g) + O$_2$(g) → NO$_2$(g)
   i. Ca(OH)$_2$(s) + HNO$_3$(aq) → Ca(NO$_3$)$_2$(aq) + H$_2$O(l)

---

tron (Br$_2$ gains two electrons).

28. (a) 2K(s) + F$_2$(g) → 2KF(s);
(b) 4K(s) + O$_2$(g) → K$_2$O(s);
(c) 6K(s) + N$_2$(g) → 2K$_3$N(s);
(d) 4K(s) + C(s) → K$_4$C(s)

29. (a) 2Fe(s) + 3S(s) → Fe$_2$S$_3$(s);
(b) Zn(s) + 2HNO$_3$(aq) →
Zn(NO$_3$)$_2$(aq) + H$_2$(g); (c) 2Sn(s) +
O$_2$(g) → 2SnO(s); (d) 2K(s) +
H$_2$(g) → 2KH(s); (e) 2Cs(s) +
2H$_2$O(l) → 2CsOH(s) + H$_2$(g)

30. In a double-displacement reaction, when two solutions of ionic solutes are mixed, the positive ions of the two solutes exchange anions. Two examples are

AgNO$_3$(aq) + HCl(aq) →
AgCl(s) + HNO$_3$(aq)

Pb(NO$_3$)$_2$(aq) + Li$_2$CO$_3$(aq) →
PbCO$_3$(aq) + 2LiNO$_3$(aq)

In a single-displacement reaction, a new element replaces a less active element in the compound. Examples are

Mg(s) + 2HCl(aq) → MgCl$_2$(aq) +
H$_2$(g)

Cu(s) + 2AgNO$_3$(aq) →
Cu(NO$_3$)$_2$(aq) + 2Ag(s)

31. Examples of the formation of water: H$_2$SO$_4$(aq) + 2NaOH(aq) →
2H$_2$O(l) + Na$_2$SO$_4$(aq); HClO$_4$(aq) +
KOH(aq) → 2H$_2$O(l) + KClO$_4$(aq)
Examples of formation of a gaseous product: Mg(s) + 2HCl(aq) →
MgCl$_2$(aq) + H$_2$(g); 2KClO$_3$(s) →
2KCl(s) + 3O$_2$(g)

32. (a) precipitation; (b) oxidation–reduction; (c) precipitation; (d) acid–base; (e) oxidation–reduction; (f) acid–base; (g) precipitation, acid–base; (h) oxidation–reduction; (i) precipitation

33. (a) oxidation–reduction; (b) oxidation–reduction; (c) acid–base; (d) acid–base, precipitation; (e) precipitation; (f) precipitation; (g) oxidation–reduction; (h) oxidation–reduction; (i) acid–base

34. A synthesis reaction represents the production of a given compound from simpler substances. An example is C(s) + O$_2$(g) → CO$_2$(g). This reaction can also be classified as an oxidation–reduction reaction and a combustion reaction. The reaction 2Fe(s) + 3Cl$_2$(g) → 2FeCl$_3$(s) is a synthesis reaction that can also be classified as an oxidation–reduction reaction but not a combustion reaction.

35. A decomposition reaction is one in which a given compound is broken down into simpler compounds or constituent elements. These reactions may be classified in other ways. For example, 2HgO(s) → 2Hg(l) + O$_2$(g) is both a decomposition reaction and an oxidation–reduction reaction.

36. (a) C$_2$H$_5$OH(l) + 3O$_2$(g) → 2CO$_2$(g) + 3H$_2$O(g);
(b) 2C$_6$H$_{14}$(l) + 19O$_2$(g) → 12CO$_2$(g) + 14H$_2$O(g);
(c) C$_6$H$_{12}$(l) + 9O$_2$(g) → 6CO$_2$(g) + 6H$_2$O(g)

37. (a) 2C$_2$H$_6$(g) + 7O$_2$(g) → 4CO$_2$(g) + 6H$_2$O(g);
(b) C$_2$H$_6$O(l) + 3O$_2$(g) → 2CO$_2$(g) + 3H$_2$O(g);
(c) 2C$_2$H$_6$O$_2$(l) + 5O$_2$(g) → 4CO$_2$(g) + 6H$_2$O(g)

38. (a) 2Co(s) + 3S(s) → Co$_2$S$_3$(s); (b) 2NO(g) + O$_2$(g) → 2NO$_2$(g);
(c) FeO(s) + CO$_2$(g) → FeCO$_3$(s); (d) 2Al(s) + 3F$_2$(g) → 2AlF$_3$(s);
(e) 2NH$_3$(g) + H$_2$CO$_3$(aq) → (NH$_4$)$_2$CO$_3$(s)

39. (a) 2NI$_3$(s) → N$_2$(g) + 3I$_2$(s); (b) BaCO$_3$(s) → BaO(s) + CO$_2$(g);
(c) C$_6$H$_{12}$O$_6$(s) → 6C(s) + 6H$_2$O(g); (d) Cu(NH$_3$)$_4$SO$_4$(s) → CuSO$_4$(s) + 4NH$_3$(g); (e) NaN$_3$(s) → Na$_3$N(s) + 4N$_2$(g)

40. A molecular equation uses the formulas for all reactants and products involved. The complete ionic equation shows the compounds broken into their respective ions (except for the product formed). The net ionic equation shows only those ions that form the product (an ionic solid, a gas, or water are the usual products). The net ionic equation most clearly shows the species that actually react with each other.

41. (a) silver ion: $Ag^+(aq) + Cl^-(aq) \rightarrow AgCl(s)$
lead(II) ion: $Pb^{2+}(aq) + 2Cl^-(aq) \rightarrow PbCl_2(s)$
mercury(I) ion: $Hg_2^{2+}(aq) + 2Cl^-(aq) \rightarrow Hg_2Cl_2(s)$
(b) sulfate ion: $Ca^{2+}(aq) + SO_4^{2-}(aq) \rightarrow CaSO_4(s)$
carbonate ion: $Ca^{2+}(aq) + CO_3^{2-}(aq) \rightarrow CaCO_3(s)$
phosphate ion: $3Ca^{2+}(aq) + 2PO_4^{3-}(aq) \rightarrow Ca_3(PO_4)_2(s)$
(c) hydroxide ion:
$Fe^{3+}(aq) + 3OH^-(aq) \rightarrow Fe(OH)_3(s)$
sulfide ion: $2Fe^{3+}(aq) + 3S^{2-}(aq) \rightarrow Fe_2S_3(s)$
phosphate ion: $Fe^{3+}(aq) + PO_4^{3-}(aq) \rightarrow FePO_4(s)$
(d) calcium ion: $Ca^{2+}(aq) + SO_4^{2-}(aq) \rightarrow CaSO_4(s)$
barium ion: $Ba^{2+}(aq) + SO_4^{2-}(aq) \rightarrow BaSO_4(s)$
lead(II) ion: $Pb^{2+}(aq) + SO_4^{2-}(aq) \rightarrow PbSO_4(s)$
(e) sulfide ion: $Hg_2^{2+}(aq) + S^{2-}(aq) \rightarrow Hg_2S(s)$
carbonate ion: $Hg_2^{2+}(aq) + 2CO_3^{2-}(aq) \rightarrow Hg_2CO_3(s)$
chloride ion: $Hg_2^{2+}(aq) + 2Cl^-(aq) \rightarrow Hg_2Cl_2(s)$
(f) chloride ion: $Ag^+(aq) + Cl^-(aq) \rightarrow AgCl(s)$
sulfide ion: $2Ag^+(aq) + S^{2-}(aq) \rightarrow Ag_2S(s)$ carbonate ion: $2Ag^+(aq) + 2CO_3^{2-}(aq) \rightarrow Ag_2CO_3(s)$

42. (a) $2Fe^{3+}(aq) + 3CO_3^{2-}(aq) \rightarrow Fe_2(CO_3)_3(s)$;
(b) $Hg_2^{2+}(aq) + 2Cl^-(aq) \rightarrow Hg_2Cl_2(s)$; (c) no precipitate;
(d) $Cu^{2+}(aq) + S^{2-}(aq) \rightarrow CuS(s)$; (e) $Pb^{2+}(aq) + 2Cl^-(aq) \rightarrow PbCl_2(s)$; (f) $Ca^{2+}(aq) + CO_3^{2-}(aq) \rightarrow CaCO_3(s)$; (g) $Au^{3+}(aq) + 3OH^-(aq) \rightarrow Au(OH)_3(s)$

43. (a) $HNO_3(aq) + KOH(aq) \rightarrow H_2O(l) + \underline{KNO_3}(aq)$;
(b) $H_2SO_4(aq) + Ba(OH)_2(aq) \rightarrow 2H_2O(l) + \underline{BaSO_4}(aq)$;
(c) $HClO_4(aq) + NaOH(aq) \rightarrow H_2O(l) + \underline{NaClO_4}(aq)$;
(d) $2HCl(aq) + Ca(OH)_2(aq) \rightarrow 2H_2O(l) + \underline{CaCl_2}(aq)$

44. Ag^+ ion: $AgCl$, Ag_2CO_3, $AgOH$, Ag_3PO_4, Ag_2S, Ag_2SO_4
Ba^{2+} ion: $BaCO_3$, $Ba(OH)_2$, $Ba_3(PO_4)_2$, BaS, $BaSO_4$
Ca^{2+} ion: $CaCO_3$, $Ca(OH)_2$, $Ca_3(PO_4)_2$, CaS, $CaSO_4$
Fe^{3+} ion: $Fe_2(CO_3)_3$, $Fe(OH)_3$, $FePO_4$, Fe_2S_3
Hg_2^{2+} ion: Hg_2Cl_2, Hg_2CO_3, $Hg_2(OH)_2$, $(Hg_2)_3(PO_4)_2$, Hg_2S
Na^+ ion: all common salts are soluble

248

8.7 Other Ways to Classify Reactions

Questions

34. What is a *synthesis* or *combination* reaction? Give an example. Can such reactions also be classified in other ways? Give an example of a synthesis reaction that is also a *combustion* reaction. Give an example of a synthesis reaction that is also an *oxidation–reduction* reaction, but which does not involve combustion.

35. What is a *decomposition* reaction? Give an example. Can such reactions also be classified in other ways?

Problems

36. Balance each of the following equations that describe combustion reactions.
a. $C_2H_5OH(l) + O_2(g) \rightarrow CO_2(g) + H_2O(g)$
b. $C_6H_{14}(l) + O_2(g) \rightarrow CO_2(g) + H_2O(g)$
c. $C_6H_{12}(l) + O_2(g) \rightarrow CO_2(g) + H_2O(g)$

37. Balance each of the following equations that describe combustion reactions.
a. $C_2H_6(g) + O_2(g) \rightarrow CO_2(g) + H_2O(g)$
b. $C_2H_6O(l) + O_2(g) \rightarrow CO_2(g) + H_2O(g)$
c. $C_2H_6O_2(l) + O_2(g) \rightarrow CO_2(g) + H_2O(g)$

38. Balance each of the following equations that describe synthesis reactions.
a. $Co(s) + S(s) \rightarrow Co_2S_3(s)$
b. $NO(g) + O_2(g) \rightarrow NO_2(g)$
c. $FeO(s) + CO_2(g) \rightarrow FeCO_3(s)$
d. $Al(s) + F_2(g) \rightarrow AlF_3(s)$
e. $NH_3(g) + H_2CO_3(aq) \rightarrow (NH_4)_2CO_3(s)$

39. Balance each of the following equations that describe decomposition reactions.
a. $NI_3(s) \rightarrow N_2(g) + I_2(s)$
b. $BaCO_3(s) \rightarrow BaO(s) + CO_2(g)$
c. $C_6H_{12}O_6(s) \rightarrow C(s) + H_2O(g)$
d. $Cu(NH_3)_4SO_4(s) \rightarrow CuSO_4(s) + NH_3(g)$
e. $NaN_3(s) \rightarrow Na_3N(s) + N_2(g)$

Critical Thinking

40. Distinguish between the *molecular* equation, the *complete ionic* equation, and the *net ionic* equation for a reaction in solution. Which type of equation most clearly shows the species that actually react with one another?

41. Using the general solubility rules given in Table 8.1, name three reactants that would form precipitates with each of the following ions in aqueous solution. Write the net ionic equation for each of your suggestions.
a. chloride ion
b. calcium ion
c. iron(III) ion
d. sulfate ion
e. mercury(I) ion, Hg_2^{2+}
f. silver ion

42. Without first writing a full molecular or ionic equation, write the net ionic equations for any precipitation reactions that occur when aqueous solutions of the following compounds are mixed. If no reaction occurs, so indicate.
a. iron(III) nitrate and sodium carbonate
b. mercurous nitrate and sodium chloride
c. sodium nitrate and ruthenium nitrate
d. copper(II) sulfate and sodium sulfide
e. lithium chloride and lead(II) nitrate
f. calcium nitrate and lithium carbonate
g. gold(III) chloride and sodium hydroxide

43. Complete and balance each of the following molecular equations for strong acid/strong base reactions. Underline the formula of the *salt* produced in each reaction.
a. $HNO_3(aq) + KOH(aq) \rightarrow$
b. $H_2SO_4(aq) + Ba(OH)_2(aq) \rightarrow$
c. $HClO_4(aq) + NaOH(aq) \rightarrow$
d. $HCl(aq) + Ca(OH)_2(aq) \rightarrow$

44. For the cations listed in the left-hand column, give the formulas of the precipitates that would form with each of the anions in the right-hand column. If no precipitate is expected for a particular combination, so indicate.

Cations	Anions
Ag^+	$C_2H_3O_2^-$
Ba^{2+}	Cl^-
Ca^{2+}	CO_3^{2-}
Fe^{3+}	NO_3^-
Hg_2^{2+}	OH^-
Na^+	PO_4^{3-}
Ni^{2+}	S^{2-}
Pb^{2+}	SO_4^{2-}

45. On the basis of the general solubility rules given in Table 8.1, write a balanced molecular equation for the precipitation reactions that take place when the following aqueous solutions are mixed. Underline the formula of the precipitate (solid) that forms. If no precipitation reaction is likely for the reactants given, so indicate.
a. silver nitrate and hydrochloric acid
b. copper(II) sulfate and ammonium carbonate
c. iron(II) sulfate and potassium carbonate
d. silver nitrate and potassium nitrate
e. lead(II) nitrate and lithium carbonate
f. tin(IV) chloride and sodium hydroxide

Ni^{2+} ion: $NiCO_3$, $Ni(OH)_2$, $Ni_3(PO_4)_2$, NiS
Pb^{2+} ion: $PbCl_2$, $PbCO_3$, $Pb(OH)_2$, $Pb_3(PO_4)_2$, PbS, $PbSO_4$

45. (a) $AgNO_3(aq) + HCl(aq) \rightarrow \underline{AgCl}(s) + HNO_3(aq)$; (b) $CuSO_4(aq) + (NH_4)_2CO_3(aq) \rightarrow \underline{CuCO_3}(s) + (NH_4)_2SO_4(aq)$; (c) $FeSO_4(aq) + K_2CO_3(aq) \rightarrow \underline{FeCO_3}(s) + K_2SO_4(aq)$; (d) no reaction; (e) $Pb(NO_3)_2(aq) + Li_2CO_3(aq) \rightarrow \underline{PbCO_3}(s) + 2LiNO_3(aq)$; (f) $SnCl_4(aq) + 4NaOH(aq) \rightarrow \underline{Sn(OH)_4}(s) +$

$4NaCl(aq)$

46. (a) $Ag^+(aq) + Cl^-(aq) \rightarrow AgCl(s)$; (b) $3Ca^{2+}(aq) + 2PO_4^{3-}(aq) \rightarrow Ca_3(PO_4)_2(s)$; (c) $Pb^{2+}(aq) + 2Cl^-(aq) \rightarrow PbCl_2(s)$; (d) $Fe^{3+}(aq) + 3OH^-(aq) \rightarrow Fe(OH)_3(s)$

47. See the *Teacher Resources*.

48. (a) one; (b) one; (c) two; (d) two; (e) three

49. (a) two; (b) one; (c) three; (d) one; (e) two

50. (a) $2C_3H_8OH(l) + 9O_2(g) \rightarrow 6CO_2(g) + 8H_2O(g)$; oxidation–reduction, combustion;
(b) $HCl(aq) + AgC_2H_3O_2(aq) \rightarrow AgCl(s) + HC_2H_3O_2(aq)$; precipitation, double-displacement;
(c) $3HCl(aq) + Al(OH)_3(s) \rightarrow AlCl_3(aq) + 3H_2O(l)$; acid–base, double-displacement;
(d) $N_2H_4(l) + O_2(g) \rightarrow N_2(g) + 2H_2O(g)$; oxidation–reduction, combustion

46. For each of the following *un*balanced molecular equations, write the corresponding *balanced net ionic equation* for the reaction.
    a. $HCl(aq) + AgNO_3(aq) \rightarrow AgCl(s) + HNO_3(aq)$
    b. $CaCl_2(aq) + Na_3PO_4(aq) \rightarrow$
       $Ca_3(PO_4)_2(s) + NaCl(aq)$
    c. $Pb(NO_3)_2(aq) + BaCl_2(aq) \rightarrow$
       $PbCl_2(s) + Ba(NO_3)_2(aq)$
    d. $FeCl_3(aq) + NaOH(aq) \rightarrow Fe(OH)_3(s) + NaCl(aq)$

47. Write a balanced oxidation–reduction equation for the reaction of each of the metals in the left-hand column with each of the nonmetals in the right-hand column.

Ba	O_2
K	S
Mg	Cl_2
Rb	N_2
Ca	Br_2
Li	

48. For each of the following metals, how many electrons will the metal atoms lose when the metal reacts with a nonmetal?
    a. sodium   d. barium
    b. potassium   e. aluminum
    c. magnesium

49. For each of the following nonmetals, how many electrons will each atom of the nonmetal gain in reacting with a metal?
    a. oxygen   d. chlorine
    b. fluorine   e. sulfur
    c. nitrogen

50. Classify the reactions represented by the following unbalanced equations by as many methods as possible. Balance the equations.
    a. $C_3H_8O(l) + O_2(g) \rightarrow CO_2(g) + H_2O(g)$
    b. $HCl(aq) + AgC_2H_3O_2(aq) \rightarrow$
       $AgCl(s) + HC_2H_3O_2(aq)$
    c. $HCl(aq) + Al(OH)_3(s) \rightarrow AlCl_3(aq) + H_2O(l)$
    d. $H_2O_2(aq) \rightarrow H_2O(l) + O_2(g)$
    e. $N_2H_4(l) + O_2(g) \rightarrow N_2(g) + H_2O(g)$

9 Chemical Quantities

	Section	Text Features & Components	Labs, Demonstrations & Activities
Teaching Segment 9A **0.5 block** pp. 251–258	**9.1–9.2** Information Given by Chemical Equations Mole–Mole Relationships	Lesson Plans (Sec 9.1–9.2)	**SE** Chemistry in Action: The Nuts and Bolts of Chemistry *p. 254*
Teaching Segment 9B **2 blocks** pp. 258–268	**9.3** Mass Calculations	**LP** Lesson Plans (Sec 9.3–9.5)	**LM** Experiment 34: Copper Wire in a Silver Nitrate Solution Lab Manual Report Sheets Teacher's Lab Guide
	9.4 Mass Calculations Using Scientific Notation	**SE** Top Ten Chemicals Used in the United States *p. 264* **SE** Chemical Impact: Methyl Alcohol: Fuel with a Future *p. 265*	**LM** Experiment 35: Mass Relationships in Chemical Compounds Lab Manual Report Sheets Teacher's Lab Guide
	9.5 Mass Calculations: Comparing Two Reactions	**SE** Celebrity Chemical: Lithium *p. 267*	**LM** Experiment 36: Calcium Content of Milk Lab Manual Report Sheets Teacher's Lab Guide
Teaching Segment 9C **2 blocks** pp. 268–279	**9.6–9.7** **2** The Concept of Limiting Reactants Calculations Involving a Limited Reactant	**LP** Lesson Plans (Sec 9.6–9.8)	**TE** Teaching Support: Demonstration *pp. 270–271* **SE** Chemistry in the Laboratory: Stoichiometry *pp. 280–281* **LM** Experiment 37–38 Lab Manual Report Sheets Teacher's Lab Guide
	9.8 Percent Yield	**SE** Chemical Impact: The "Golden" Dollar *p. 277*	**LM** Experiment 39: Synthesis of Manganese (II) Chloride Lab Manual Report Sheets Teacher's Lab Guide

Key

- **SE** Student Edition
- **TE** Teacher Edition
- **RP** Teacher Resource Package
- **LM** Lab Materials
- **LP** Lesson Plans
- **AR** Additional Resources
- Florida Specific

Technology and Media

Transparencies
Table 9.1
Steps for Solving Stoichiometry
Problems with Limiting Reactants

PowerPoint Slides

 Video Limiting Reagent
Gravimetric Analysis

 eEdition CD-ROM
Easy Planner CD-ROM
English Summaries CD
Spanish Summaries CD

Web Site classzone.com
McDougal Littell Test Generator

Chapter Planning Guide

All Learners

- **TE** Active Learning *p. 251*
- **TE** Teaching Tips *pp. 251, 255*
- **RP** Team Learning Worksheets (Sec 9.1–9.2) *pp. 39–40*
- **AR** Less Proficient Students *p. 16*

- **TE** Active Learning *p. 258*
- **TE** Teaching Tips *pp. 258–259*
- **AR** Less Proficient Students *p. 16*

- **TE** Using the Top Ten *p. 264*
- **AR** Less Proficient Students *p. 16*

- **RP** Team Learning Worksheets (Sec 9.3–9.5) *pp. 41–42*
- **AR** Less Proficient Students *p. 17*

- **TE** Active Learning *p. 268*
- **TE** Teaching Tips *p. 269*
- Video: Limiting Reagents *p. 270*
- Transparency: Figure 9.1 *p. 272*
- Transparency: Stoichiometry Problems *p. 275*
- Video: Gravimetric Analysis *p. 275*
- **AR** Less Proficient Students *p. 17*

- **TE** Teaching Tips *p. 277*
- **RP** Team Learning Worksheets (Sec 9.6–9.8) *pp. 43–44*
- **AR** Less Proficient Students *p. 17*

Review & Assessment

- **TE** Additional Examples *pp. 253, 255–257*
- **SE** Self Check *p. 257*
- **SE** Focus Questions (Sec 9.1–9.2) *p. 258*
- **SE** Key Terms *p. 281*
- **SE** Questions and Problems *pp. 281–282*

- **SE** What if . . . *p. 259*
- **TE** Additional Examples *p. 261*
- **SE** Self Check *pp. 260, 262*
- **SE** Questions and Problems *pp. 282– 283*

- **TE** Additional Examples *p. 263*
- **SE** Self Check *p. 264*
- **SE** Key Terms *p. 281*
- **SE** Questions and Problems *pp. 283–284*

- **SE** Self Check *p. 267*
- **SE** Focus Questions (Sec 9.3–9.5) *p. 268*
- **SE** Questions and Problems *p. 284*

- **SE** Key Terms *p. 281*
- **TE** Additional Examples *pp. 273, 275*
- **SE** Self Check *p. 276*
- **SE** Questions and Problems *pp. 284–285*

- **SE** What if . . . *p. 278*
- **TE** Additional Examples *p. 278*
- **SE** Self Check *p. 279*
- **SE** Focus Questions (Sec 9.6–9.8) *p. 279*
- **SE** Key Terms *p. 281*
- **SE** Questions and Problems *p. 285*

Standards

- **TE** NSES UCP3, A1, A2, B2, B3
- **SSS** SC.B.1.4.2

- **TE** NSES UCP3, A1, A2, B2, B3, C5, C6, E1, E2, F1, F3, F5, F6, G3
- **SSS** SC.H.1.4.1, SC.H.1.4.2, SC.H.1.4.4, SC.B.1.4.2, SC.H.3.4.1, SC.H.3.4.3

- **TE** NSES UCP3, A1, A2, B2, B3, F6

Chapter Materials

- **TE** Reading Strategy
- **AR** English/Spanish Summaries *p. 13*
- **AR** Challenge Projects/Problems *pp. 16–17*
- **AR** Less Proficient Students *p. 17*
- English Summary Audio
- Spanish Summary Audio
- **RP** Chapter Review Worksheets (Basic, Review, Challenge)

- **SE** Chapter Summary *p. 281*
- **SE** Critical Thinking *pp. 285–287*
- **RP** Solutions Guide
- **RP** Chapter Tests
- **RP** Test Bank
- McDougal Littell Test Generator
- **AR** Standardized Test Practice
- **FCAT Test 5**

9 Integrating Reading Strategies and Chemistry Concepts

Chapter 9: Reading Key Words

Recognizing key words is a reading strategy that may help the students read more efficiently and feel less overwhelmed. When the students use this strategy, expect to see an improvement in students' comprehension of the chapter objectives.

Explain that key words and phrases are those that are significant to the topic and that contribute to conveying the meaning of the material. Point out that these words or phrases are sometimes found in titles and subtitles, but are most often found in the text. Encourage the students to scan paragraphs to look for these items before they even begin reading a section. Show the students how identifying key words helps to define the focus of the section.

Advise students that key words are not limited to vocabulary words. Vocabulary words are usually presented in boldface or italic type or in a color different than the standard text.

Learning to Recognize Key Words and Other Important Material

Have the students turn to page 251 and skim the first few paragraphs at the top of the page.

Suppose you work for a consumer advocate organization and you want to test a company's advertising claims about the effectiveness of its antacid. The company claims that its product neutralizes ten times as much stomach acid per tablet as its nearest competitor. How would you test the validity of this claim?

Or suppose that some day you go to work for a chemical company that makes methanol (methyl alcohol), a substance used as a starting material for the manufacture of products such as antifreeze and aviation fuels and as a fuel in the cars that race in the Indianapolis 500 (see "Chemical Impact" on page 265). You are working with an experienced chemist who is trying to improve the company's process for making methanol from the reaction of gaseous hydrogen with carbon monoxide gas. The first day on the job, you are instructed to order enough hydrogen and carbon monoxide to produce 6.0 kg of methanol in a test run. How would you determine how much carbon monoxide and hydrogen you should order?

After you study this chapter, you will be able to answer these questions.

Methanol is a starting material for some jet fuels.

Ask these questions:

- What is the purpose of these paragraphs? [The material provides examples of how the information presented in this chapter might be used outside the classroom.]
- Is this material key to understanding the concepts presented in the rest of the chapter? [no]
- Do you need to spend time looking for key words in this section or taking notes? [no]
- Does each chapter in the text begin with a similar introduction? [yes]

Emphasize that the students should not skip the introductory material, but that they need not spend time looking for key words or taking notes on this type of material.

Next, have the students skim the first paragraph of Section 9.1 and write the key words and phrases in their notebooks. Remind the class that the goal is to capture the content of the paragraph in as few words as possible. Allow a few minutes for the students to complete the exercise, and then use this guide to review the paragraph.

As we saw in the last two chapters, chemistry is really about reactions. Chemical changes involve rearrangements of atom groupings as one or more substances change to new substances. Recall that reactions are described by equations that give the identities of the reactants and products and show how much of each reactant and product participates in the reaction. It is the numbers (coefficients) in the balanced chemical equation that enable us to determine just how much product we can get from a given quantity of reactants.

Have each student compare what they wrote with the material highlighted above. Point out that the students may have a few different words in their lists, but the general ideas should be the same as those shown above.

Tell the students to use only the key words and phrases highlighted above to rewrite the paragraph in list form.

- chemical changes involve rearrangements of atom groupings
- reactions are described by equations
- equations give reactants and products and show how much of each
- coefficients in balanced equation determine how much product from given reactants

Ask the students whether the list presents the same basic information as the paragraph. [yes] If the students disagree, have them explain what concepts they see in the paragraph that they do not see in the list.

If time permits, go through several more paragraphs, and guide the students to recognize appropriate key words and phrases.

If the students are have trouble grasping this strategy, read the material aloud and use your voice to emphasize the key points. Then have the students repeat this activity in pairs. Remind the students that identifying key words is an exercise in determining what is important in the text and can be a valuable tool when they are reading new and complex material.

Chemical Quantities

Overview

In this Chapter our goals are for the students to:

- Understand the molecular and mass information given in a balanced equation

- Learn to use a balanced equation to determine relationships between moles of reactants and moles of products

- Learn to relate masses of reactants and products in a chemical reaction

- Carry out mass calculations that involve scientific notation

- Understand the concept of limiting reactants

- Learn to recognize the limiting reactant in a reaction

- Learn to use the limiting reactant to do stoichiometric calculations

Herbicide chemicals must be mixed in exact quantities for treatment of plants such as sunflowers.

250

Suppose you work for a consumer advocate organization and you want to test a company's advertising claims about the effectiveness of its antacid. The company claims that its product neutralizes ten times as much stomach acid per tablet as its nearest competitor. How would you test the validity of this claim?

Or suppose that some day you go to work for a chemical company that makes methanol (methyl alcohol), a substance used as a starting material for the manufacture of products such as antifreeze and aviation fuels and as a fuel in the cars that race in the Indianapolis 500 (see "Chemical Impact" on page 265). You are working with an experienced chemist who is trying to improve the company's process for making methanol from the reaction of gaseous hydrogen with carbon monoxide gas. The first day on the job, you are instructed to order enough hydrogen and carbon monoxide to produce 6.0 kg of methanol in a test run. How would you determine how much carbon monoxide and hydrogen you should order?

After you study this chapter, you will be able to answer these questions.

Methanol is a starting material for some jet fuels.

9.1 Information Given by Chemical Equations

Objective: *To understand the molecular and mass information given in a balanced equation.*

As we saw in the last two chapters, chemistry is really about reactions. Chemical changes involve rearrangements of atom groupings as one or more substances change to new substances. Recall that reactions are described by equations that give the identities of the reactants and products and show how much of each reactant and product participates in the reaction. It is the numbers (coefficients) in the balanced chemical equation that enable us to determine just how much product we can get from a given quantity of reactants.

To explore this idea, consider a nonchemical analogy. Assume you are in charge of making deli sandwiches at a local fast-food restaurant. A particular type of sandwich requires 2 pieces of bread, 3 slices of meat, and 1 slice of cheese. You might represent making this sandwich by the following equation:

2 pieces bread + 3 slices meat + 1 slice cheese → 1 sandwich

Your boss sends you to the store to get enough ingredients to make 50 sandwiches. How do you figure out how much of each ingredient you need to buy? Because you need enough to make 50 sandwiches, you could multiply the preceding equation by 50.

50 (2 pieces bread) + 50 (3 slices meat) + 50 (1 slice cheese) →
50 sandwiches

That is,

100 pieces bread + 150 slices meat + 50 slices cheese → 50 sandwiches

9.1   Information Given by Chemical Equations   **251**

Section 9.1

Themes
Patterns of Change

Skills
Making comparisons, converting, evaluating

Student Preparation
Assign the students to read Sections 9.1 to 9.2 and to answer the Focus Questions at the end of Section 9.2 before coming to class.

Active Learning
After introducing the material in Sections 9.1 to 9.2 in class, place the students in groups and have them work together on Sections 9.1–9.2: Team Learning Worksheet. Answers and/or discussion of these questions are located in the *Teacher Resources.*

TEACHING TIPS

• Remind students that chemistry problems often require a balanced chemical equation. Remember to write the equation first, then to balance it before working the problem.

• Recipe analogies can help students relate to chemical equations and quantities. In a recipe (for chocolate chip cookies, for example) we need to know the ingredients, just as in a chemistry equation we need to know the reactants and products. An unbalanced chemical equation is like a recipe that lists the ingredients but not the amounts of each needed. Once a chemical equation is balanced, it is like a recipe that includes both the amounts and the identities of the ingredients. It can be increased or decreased by multiplying by the appropriate factor. For a cookie recipe you can double or halve the recipe, just as you can multiply a chemical equation by 2 or by $\frac{1}{2}$.

Notice that the numbers 100:150:50 correspond to the ratio 2:3:1, which represents the original numbers of bread, meat, and cheese ingredients in the equation for making a sandwich. If you needed the ingredients for 73 sandwiches, it would be easy to use the original sandwich equation to figure out what quantity of ingredients you need.

The equation for a chemical reaction gives you the same type of information. It indicates the relative numbers of reactant and product molecules required for the reaction to take place. Using the equation permits us to determine the amounts of reactants needed to give a certain amount of product or to predict how much product we can make from a given quantity of reactants.

To illustrate how this idea works, consider the reaction between gaseous carbon monoxide and hydrogen to produce liquid methanol, $CH_3OH(l)$. The reactants and products are

$$\text{Unbalanced: } \underset{\text{Reactants}}{CO(g) + H_2(g)} \rightarrow \underset{\text{Product}}{CH_3OH(l)}$$

Because atoms are just rearranged (not created or destroyed) in a chemical reaction, we must always balance a chemical equation. That is, we must choose coefficients that give the same number of each type of atom on both sides. Using the smallest set of integers that satisfies this condition gives the balanced equation

$$\text{Balanced: } CO(g) + 2H_2(g) \rightarrow CH_3OH(l)$$

Check: Reactants: 1 C, 1 O, 4 H; Products: 1 C, 1 O, 4 H

It is important to recognize that the coefficients in a balanced equation give the *relative* numbers of molecules. That is, we could multiply this balanced equation by any number and still have a balanced equation. For example, we could multiply by 12,

$$12[CO(g) + 2H_2(g) \rightarrow CH_3OH(l)]$$

to obtain

$$12CO(g) + 24H_2(g) \rightarrow 12CH_3OH(l)$$

This is still a balanced equation (check to be sure). Because 12 represents a dozen, we could even describe the reaction in terms of dozens:

$$1 \text{ dozen } CO(g) + 2 \text{ dozen } H_2(g) \rightarrow 1 \text{ dozen } CH_3OH(l)$$

We could also multiply the original equation by a very large number, such as 6.022×10^{23},

$$6.022 \times 10^{23}[CO(g) + 2H_2(g) \rightarrow CH_3OH(l)]$$

which leads to the equation

$$6.022 \times 10^{23} \, CO(g) + 2(6.022 \times 10^{23}) \, H_2(g) \rightarrow 6.022 \times 10^{23} \, CH_3OH(l)$$

CHEMISTRY

One mole is 6.022×10^{23} units. The mole was introduced in section 6.3.

Just as 12 is called a dozen, chemists call 6.022×10^{23} a *mole* (abbreviated mol). Our equation, then, can be written in terms of moles:

$$1 \text{ mol } CO(g) + 2 \text{ mol } H_2(g) \rightarrow 1 \text{ mol } CH_3OH(l)$$

Various ways of interpreting this balanced chemical equation are given in **Table 9.1.**

TABLE 9.1

Information Conveyed by the Balanced Equation for the Production of Methanol

$CO(g)$	+	$2H_2(g)$	$\rightarrow$	$CH_3OH(l)$
1 molecule CO	+	2 molecules H_2	$\rightarrow$	1 molecule CH_3OH
1 dozen CO molecules	+	2 dozen H_2 molecules	$\rightarrow$	1 dozen CH_3OH molecules
6.022×10^{23} CO molecules	+	$2(6.022 \times 10^{23})$ H_2 molecules	$\rightarrow$	6.022×10^{23} CH_3OH molecules
1 mol CO molecules	+	2 mol H_2 molecules	$\rightarrow$	1 mol CH_3OH molecules

Example 9.1

Relating Moles to Molecules in Chemical Equations

Propane is often
used as a fuel
for outdoor grills.

Propane, C_3H_8, is a fuel commonly used for cooking on gas grills and for heating in rural areas where natural gas is unavailable. Propane reacts with oxygen gas to produce heat and the products carbon dioxide and water. This combustion reaction is represented by the unbalanced equation

$$C_3H_8(g) + O_2(g) \rightarrow CO_2(g) + H_2O(g)$$

Give the balanced equation for this reaction, and state the meaning of the equation in terms of numbers of molecules and moles of molecules.

Solution

Using the techniques explained in Chapter 7, we can balance the equation.

$$C_3H_8(g) + 5O_2(g) \rightarrow 3CO_2(g) + 4H_2O(g)$$

Check: 3 C, 8 H, 10 O $\rightarrow$ 3 C, 8 H, 10 O

This equation can be interpreted in terms of molecules as follows:

1 molecule of C_3H_8 reacts with 5 molecules of O_2 to give 3 molecules of CO_2 plus 4 molecules of H_2O

Alternatively, it can be stated in terms of moles (of molecules):

1 mol C_3H_8 reacts with 5 mol O_2 to give 3 mol of CO_2 plus 4 mol H_2O

9.1   Information Given by Chemical Equations   **253**

TEACHING TIP

Emphasize that the coefficients in a balanced equation represent the mole *ratios*. An individual coefficient is meaningless (just as an amount of a single ingredient in a recipe is meaningless without the other amounts).

Additional Examples

Give the balanced equation for each of the following, and state the meaning of the equation in terms of numbers of molecules and moles of molecules.

1. $NO(g) + H_2(g) \rightarrow N_2(g) + H_2O(l)$
   $2NO(g) + 2H_2(g) \rightarrow N_2(g) + 2H_2O(l)$; 2 molecules (or 2 moles) of NO react with 2 molecules (or 2 moles) of hydrogen gas to give 1 molecule (or 1 mole) of nitrogen gas and 2 molecules (or 2 moles) of water.

2. $SiH_4(g) + NH_3(g) \rightarrow Si_3N_4(s) + H_2(g)$
   $3SiH_4(g) + 4NH_3(g) \rightarrow Si_3N_4(s) + 12H_2(g)$; 3 molecules (or 3 moles) of SiH_4 react with 4 molecules (or 4 moles) of ammonia to give 1 molecule (or 1 mole) of Si_3N_4 and 12 molecules (or 12 moles) of hydrogen gas.

CHEMISTRY in ACTION

CHEMISTRY in ACTION
The Nuts and Bolts of Chemistry

1. Obtain a cup of nuts and bolts from your teacher.
2. The nuts and bolts are the reactants. The product consists of two nuts on each bolt. Make as many products as possible.
3. Using N to symbolize a nut and B to symbolize a bolt, write an equation for the reaction. Pay attention to the difference between a subscript and a coefficient.
4. How many nuts did you have? How many bolts?
5. How many products could you make?
6. Which reactant (nut or bolt) was limiting? How did you make this determination?
7. The limiting reactant was the one that had (fewer/more) pieces. Explain.
8. An average mass of a bolt is 10.64 g and an average mass of a nut is 4.35 g. Suppose you are given "about 1500 g" of bolts and "about 1500 g" of nuts. Answer the following questions:
   a. How many bolts are in "about 1500 g"? How many nuts are in "about 1500 g"?
   b. Which reactant is limiting? Why is there a limiting reactant given that you have equal masses of each reactant?
   c. The limiting reactant was the one that had (fewer/more) pieces. Compare this answer to your answer in question 7. What does it tell you?
   d. What is the largest possible mass of product? How many products could you make?
   e. What is the mass of the leftover reactant?

9.2   Mole–Mole Relationships

Objective: *To learn to use a balanced equation to determine relationships between moles of reactants and moles of products.*

$2H_2O(l)$ $2H_2(g) + O_2(g)$

$4H_2O(l)$ $4H_2(g) + 2O_2(g)$

Now that we have discussed the meaning of a balanced chemical equation in terms of moles of reactants and products, we can use an equation to predict the moles of products that a given number of moles of reactants will yield. For example, consider the decomposition of water to give hydrogen and oxygen, which is represented by the following balanced equation:

$$2H_2O(l) \rightarrow 2H_2(g) + O_2(g)$$

This equation tells us that 2 mol of H_2O yields 2 mol of H_2 and 1 mol of O_2.

Now suppose that we have 4 mol of water. If we decompose 4 mol of water, how many moles of products do we get?

One way to answer this question is to multiply the entire equation by 2 (that will give us 4 mol of H_2O).

$$2[2H_2O(l) \rightarrow 2H_2(g) + O_2(g)]$$
$$4H_2O(l) \rightarrow 4H_2(g) + 2O_2(g)$$

Materials Each student/group will need a cup of nuts and bolts. The actual numbers do not matter, although it is a good idea to have more nuts than bolts, but fewer than twice as many. Thus there are more nuts, but they are still limiting (which is counter to a misconception that many students have).

Purpose Students will see a concrete example of the types of calculations involved in stoichiometry problems.

Discussion The equation for this "reaction" is $B + 2N \rightarrow BN_2$. Two nuts appear on each side, but the reactants are separate and the nuts are "bonded" together in the product. This activity should help the students better understand the difference between a subscript and a coefficient.

The answers to the first two questions (4 and 5) will vary depending on how many nuts and bolts you give to the students. Give the students quantities such that the answer to question 6 is the nut, and the answer to question 7 is "no." This choice forces students to confront the common misconception that the limiting reactant is always the lesser quantity.

For question 8, there are about 140 bolts (taking significant figures into account) and about 340 nuts. Using these numbers, the bolts are limiting. Having the same mass does not matter because the nuts and bolts "react" in terms of how many are present, not by mass (explicitly make the analogy to chemical reactions when discussing this point). In this case the limiting reactant is the lesser quantity. This fact, along with the activity, shows us that we always have to think about which reactant is limiting. Depending on the circumstances, it may be the larger quantity or the smaller quantity.

Important points to make:

- We must know the ratio of the parts needed. In this case, it was 1 bolt : 2 nuts. In chemistry we get this information from the balanced equation. For example, in the equation $2H_2 + O_2 \rightarrow 2H_2O$, we know that the ratio is 2:1:2.

- What we have is not the same as what we need. The ratio of bolts:nuts was 1:2. This is the ratio of what we need. It has **no** relation to what we are actually given.

- The calculations should make sense. For example, we did not calculate the number of products we could make from each component and then simply add those numbers together. Students should always think about what they are doing.

- It is not always true that the component present in the smallest numbers is used up first. It depends on how many of each component is needed. For example, with 7 bolts and 12 nuts we run out of nuts first, even though we have more nuts than bolts.

Section 9.2

Themes
Patterns of Change

Skills
Making comparisons, converting, evaluating

Now we can state that

4 mol of H_2O yields 4 mol of H_2 plus 2 mol of O_2

which answers the question of how many moles of products we get with 4 mol of H_2O.

Next, suppose we decompose 5.8 mol of water. What numbers of moles of products are formed in this process? We could answer this question by re-balancing the chemical equation as follows: First, we divide *all coefficients* of the balanced equation

$$2H_2O(l) \rightarrow 2H_2(g) + O_2(g)$$

by 2, to give

$$H_2O(l) \rightarrow H_2(g) + \tfrac{1}{2}O_2(g)$$

Now, because we have 5.8 mol of H_2O, we multiply this equation by 5.8.

$$5.8[H_2O(l) \rightarrow H_2(g) + \tfrac{1}{2}O_2(g)]$$

This gives

$$5.8H_2O(l) \rightarrow 5.8H_2(g) + 5.8(\tfrac{1}{2})O_2(g)$$

$$5.8H_2O(l) \rightarrow 5.8H_2(g) + 2.9O_2(g)$$

(Verify that this is a balanced equation.) Now we can state that

5.8 mol of H_2O yields 5.8 mol of H_2 plus 2.9 mol of O_2

This procedure of rebalancing the equation to obtain the number of moles involved in a particular situation always works, but it can be cumbersome. In Example 9.2 we will develop a more convenient procedure, which uses conversion factors, or **mole ratios**, based on the balanced chemical equation.

CHEMISTRY

This equation with noninteger coefficients makes sense only if the equation means moles (of molecules) of the various reactants and products.

Example 9.2

Determining Mole Ratios

What number of moles of O_2 will be produced by the decomposition of 5.8 mol of water?

Solution

Our problem can be diagrammed as follows:

| 5.8 mol H_2O | yields | ? mol of O_2 |

To answer this question, we need to know the relationship between moles of H_2O and moles of O_2 in the balanced equation (conventional form):

$$2H_2O(l) \rightarrow 2H_2(g) + O_2(g)$$

From this equation we can state that

| 2 mol H_2O | yields | 1 mol O_2 |

(continued)

Students sometimes have diffi-culty understanding what a mole ratio represents. Spend some time explaining that a mole ratio relates the moles of one sub-stance in the chemical equation to the moles of another sub-stance through an equivalence statement. The confusion arises when students assume that equivalence means equality. The moles on either side of an equiv-alence statement are not equal; they are equivalent amounts.

For example, in Example 9.2 the equivalence statement between H_2O and O_2 is

2 mol H_2O = 1 mol O_2

Thus, if you begin with 2 mol wa-ter, you will produce 1 mol oxy-gen. The moles are not equal to each other but they are equiva-lent for this equation.

Additional Examples

Methane burns in oxygen to form carbon dioxide and water ac-cording to the balanced equation

$$CH_4(g) + 2O_2(g) \rightarrow$$
$$CO_2(g) + 2H_2O(g)$$

1. What number of moles of oxygen gas is required to re-act with 7.4 mol of methane?
   14.8 mol $O_2(g)$

2. How many moles of carbon dioxide gas will be produced by reacting 2.6 mol of oxygen with excess methane?
   1.3 mol $CO_2(g)$

(continued)

CHEMISTRY

The statement 2 mol H_2O = 1 mol O_2 is obviously not true in a literal sense, but it correctly expresses the chemical equivalence between H_2O and O_2.

which can be represented by the following equivalence statement:

$$2 \text{ mol } H_2O = 1 \text{ mol } O_2$$

We now want to use this equivalence statement to obtain the conversion factor (mole ratio) that we need. Because we want to go from moles of H_2O to moles of O_2, we need the mole ratio

$$\frac{1 \text{ mol } O_2}{2 \text{ mol } H_2O}$$

so that mol H_2O will cancel in the conversion from moles of H_2O to moles of O_2.

$$5.8 \text{ mol } H_2O \times \frac{1 \text{ mol } O_2}{2 \text{ mol } H_2O} = 2.9 \text{ mol } O_2$$

So if we decompose 5.8 mol of H_2O, we will get 2.9 mol of O_2. Note that this is the same answer we obtained earlier when we rebalanced the equation to give

$$5.8H_2O(l) \rightarrow 5.8H_2(g) + 2.9O_2(g)$$

We saw in Example 9.2 that to determine the moles of a product that can be formed from a specified number of moles of a reactant, we can use the balanced equation to obtain the appropriate mole ratio. We will now extend these ideas in Example 9.3.

Example 9.3

Using Mole Ratios in Calculations

Calculate the number of moles of oxygen required to react exactly with 4.30 mol of propane, C_3H_8, in the reaction described by the following balanced equation:

$$C_3H_8(g) + 5O_2(g) \rightarrow 3CO_2(g) + 4H_2O(g)$$

Solution

In this case the problem can be stated as follows:

| 4.30 mol of C_3H_8 | requires | ? mol of O_2 |

To solve this problem, we need to consider the relationship between the reactants C_3H_8 and O_2. Using the balanced equation, we find that

$$1 \text{ mol of } C_3H_8 \text{ requires } 5 \text{ mol of } O_2$$

which can be represented by the equivalence statement

$$1 \text{ mol } C_3H_8 = 5 \text{ mol } O_2$$

Additional Examples

Hydrogen sulfide gas reacts with oxygen to produce sulfur dioxide gas and water according to the balanced equation

$$2H_2S(g) + 3O_2(g) \rightarrow$$
$$2SO_2(g) + 2H_2O(g)$$

1. How many moles of oxygen gas are required to react with 5.6 mol of hydrogen sulfide?
   8.4 mol $O_2(g)$

2. How many moles of sulfur dioxide gas will be produced by reacting 7.3 mol of hydrogen sulfide with excess oxygen?
   7.3 mol $SO_2(g)$

3. How many moles of sulfur dioxide gas will be produced by reacting 7.3 mol of oxygen with excess hydrogen sulfide?
   4.9 mol $SO_2(g)$

This leads to the required mole ratio

$$\frac{5 \text{ mol } O_2}{1 \text{ mol } C_3H_8}$$

for converting from moles of C_3H_8 to moles of O_2. We construct the conversion ratio this way so that mol C_3H_8 cancels:

$$4.30 \cancel{\text{ mol } C_3H_8} \times \frac{5 \text{ mol } O_2}{1 \cancel{\text{ mol } C_3H_8}} = 21.5 \text{ mol } O_2$$

We can now answer the original question:

4.30 mol of C_3H_8 requires 21.5 mol of O_2

 Self-Check Exercise 9.1

Calculate the moles of CO_2 formed when 4.30 mol of C_3H_8 reacts with the required 21.5 mol of O_2.

Hint: Use the moles of C_3H_8, and obtain the mole ratio between C_3H_8 and CO_2 from the balanced equation.

Example 9.4

Using Mole Ratios

Ammonia (NH_3) is used in huge quantities as a fertilizer. It is manufactured by combining nitrogen and hydrogen according to the following equation:

$$N_2(g) + 3H_2(g) \rightarrow 2NH_3(g)$$

Calculate the number of moles of NH_3 that can be made from 1.30 mol $H_2(g)$ reacting with excess $N_2(g)$.

Solution

We can represent this problem as follows:

| 1.30 mol H_2 | yields | ? mol NH_3 |

The problem states that we have excess $N_2(g)$, which means that we have more than is needed to react with all of the H_2 (1.30 mol).

From the balanced equation we see that

3 mol H_2 yields 2 mol NH_3

which can be represented by the equivalence statement

3 mol H_2 = 2 mol NH_3

This leads to the required mole ratio

$$\frac{2 \text{ mol } NH_3}{3 \text{ mol } H_2}$$

(continued)

The problem can be stated as follows:

4.30 mol $C_3H_8 \rightarrow$? mol CO_2
yields

From the balanced equation

$$C_3H_8(g) + 5O_2(g) \rightarrow 3CO_2(g) + 4H_2O(g)$$

we derive the equivalence statement

1 mol C_3H_8 = 3 mol CO_2

The appropriate conversion factor (moles of C_3H_8 must cancel) is 3 mol CO_2/1 mol C_3H_8, and the calculation is

$$4.30 \cancel{\text{ mol } C_3H_8} \times \frac{3 \text{ mol } CO_2}{1 \cancel{\text{ mol } C_3H_8}}$$
$$= 12.9 \text{ mol } CO_2$$

Thus we can say

4.30 mol C_3H_8 yields 12.9 mol CO_2

Additional Examples

Iron(II) oxide reacts with oxygen to form iron(III) oxide according to the balanced equation

$$4FeO(s) + O_2(g) \rightarrow 2Fe_2O_3(s)$$

1. What number of moles of oxygen gas is required to react with 2.4 mol of iron(II) oxide?
   0.60 mol $O_2(g)$

2. What number of moles of iron(III) oxide solid will be produced by reacting 9.2 mol of iron(II) oxide with excess oxygen?
   4.6 mol $Fe_2O_3(s)$

3. What number of moles of iron(III) oxide will be produced by reacting 9.2 mol of oxygen with excess iron(II) oxide?
   18.4 mol $Fe_2O_3(s)$

Answers to Focus Questions

1. The mole ratio is the key to determining the amount of product produced from a given amount of reactant.

2. Balancing a chemical equation is necessary so that the mole quantities for the various substances are known. This information allows the mole ratios for different relationships in the chemical equation to be determined.

3. The coefficient in a chemical equation can represent the number of molecules, moles or dozens of molecules, atoms, or ions.

4. The mole ratio gives the equivalence relationship between the reactant and the product. It essentially converts moles of reactant to moles of product.

5. 1.8 mol $O_2(g)$

Section 9.3

Themes
Patterns of Change, Stability

Skills
Applying concepts, interpreting data, converting, evaluating, calculating

Student Preparation
Assign the students to read Sections 9.3 to 9.5 and to answer the Focus Questions at the end of Section 9.5 before coming to class.

Active Learning
After introducing the material in Sections 9.3 to 9.5 in class, place the students in groups and have them work together on Sections 9.3–9.5: Team Learning Worksheet. Answers and/or discussion of these questions are located in the *Teacher Resources*.

Laboratory
Experiment 34:
Copper Wire in a Silver Nitrate Solution, Traditional

(continued)

for converting moles of H_2 to moles of NH_3:

$$1.30 \ \cancel{mol \ H_2} \times \frac{2 \ mol \ NH_3}{3 \ \cancel{mol \ H_2}} = 0.867 \ mol \ NH_3$$

Check: Notice that the number of moles of NH_3 that can be produced is less than 1.30. This answer makes sense because it takes 3 moles of H_2 to yield 2 moles of NH_3. Thus the number of moles of NH_3 produced (0.867) should be smaller than the number of moles of H_2 consumed (1.30).

Focus Questions   **Sections 9.1–9.2**

1. What part of a chemical equation allows us to determine how much product we can get from a known amount of reactants?

2. Why is it important to balance a chemical equation before answering any questions about it?

3. Give at least three different ways to interpret the coefficient in a chemical equation.

4. How does a mole ratio help to determine the amount of product produced from a known number of moles of reactant?

5. What number of moles of $O_2(g)$ is required to react with 3.6 mol $SO_2(g)$ in the following reaction?

$$2SO_2(g) + O_2(g) \rightarrow 2SO_3(g)$$

9.3 Mass Calculations

Objective: *To learn to relate masses of reactants and products in a chemical reaction.*

In the last section we saw how to use the balanced equation for a reaction to calculate the numbers of moles of reactants and products for a particular case. However, moles represent numbers of molecules, and we cannot count molecules directly. In chemistry we count by weighing. Therefore, in this section we will review the procedures for converting between moles and masses and will see how these procedures are applied to chemical calculations.

To develop these procedures we will consider the combustion of propane, C_3H_8. Propane, when used as a fuel, reacts with oxygen to produce carbon dioxide and water according to the following unbalanced equation:

$$C_3H_8(g) + O_2(g) \rightarrow CO_2(g) + H_2O(g)$$

What mass of oxygen will be required to react exactly with 44.1 g of propane?

PROBLEM SOLVING
Always balance the equation for the reaction first.

To deal with the amounts of reactants and products, we first need the balanced equation for this reaction:

$$C_3H_8(g) + 5O_2(g) \rightarrow 3CO_2(g) + 4H_2O(g)$$

258   Chapter 9   Chemical Quantities

TEACHING TIP

Now is an excellent time to ensure that students use units in solving problems. Without units, solving stoichiometry problems is very difficult. Many students are unaccustomed to using units in mathematics and so do not see any reason to use them in chemistry. This chapter illustrates the importance of using units in solving problems.

Your lab partner has made the observation that we always measure the mass of chemicals but then use mole ratios to balance equations.

What if your lab partner decided to balance equations by using masses as coefficients? Is this possible? Why or why not?

Next, let's summarize what we know and what we want to find.

What We Know:

- The balanced equation for the reaction
- The mass of propane available (44.1 g)

What We Want to Calculate:

- The mass of oxygen (O_2) required to react exactly with all the propane

Our problem, in schematic form, is

| 96.1 g propane | requires | ? grams of O_2 |

Our overall plan of attack is as follows:

1. We are given the number of grams of propane, so we must convert to moles of propane (C_3H_8), because the balanced equation deals in moles rather than grams.

2. Next, we can use the coefficients in the balanced equation to determine the moles of oxygen (O_2) required.

3. Finally, we will use the molar mass of O_2 to calculate grams of oxygen.

We can sketch this strategy as follows:

$$C_3H_8(g) \quad + \quad 5O_2(g) \quad \rightarrow \quad 3CO_2(g) \quad + \quad 4H_2O(g)$$

⇨ Thus the first question we must answer is, *How many moles of propane are present in 44.1 g of propane?* The molar mass of propane is 44.09 g ($3 \times 12.01 + 8 \times 1.008$). The moles of propane present can be calculated as follows:

$$44.1 \text{ g } C_3H_8 \times \frac{1 \text{ mol } C_3H_8}{44.09 \text{ g } C_3H_8} = 1.00 \text{ mol } C_3H_8$$

⇨ Next we recognize that each mole of propane reacts with 5 mol of oxygen. This gives us the equivalence statement

$$1 \text{ mol } C_3H_8 = 5 \text{ mol } O_2$$

from which we construct the mole ratio

$$\frac{5 \text{ mol } O_2}{1 \text{ mol } C_3H_8}$$

that we need to convert from moles of propane molecules to moles of oxygen molecules.

$$1.00 \text{ mol } C_3H_8 \times \frac{5 \text{ mol } O_2}{1 \text{ mol } C_3H_8} = 5.00 \text{ mol } O_2$$

9.3   Mass Calculations   **259**

WHAT IF Comments

Balancing in this way is not possible. Chemicals react by number. For example, each molecule of diatomic nitrogen requires three molecules of diatomic hydrogen to produce two molecules of ammonia. We do not use the masses as the coefficients (for example, in the ammonia case, we have about 28 amu of nitrogen and 6 amu of hydrogen as reactants and products). We can't balance equations by using masses because it does not conserve the atoms.

TEACHING TIPS

- Remind students that conversion factors such as 44.01 g C_3H_8 = 1 mol C_3H_8 and 32.00 g O_2 = 1 mol O_2 come from the circulation of molar masses. We use the coefficients in the balanced equation when relating two different substances.

- Use diagrams and flowcharts to help students think through these problems. Try to be consistent in your approach. Begin with the balanced equation each time and write down what is known and what is being sought.

260

Answer to Self-Check Exercise 9.2

The problem can be sketched as follows:

$$C_3H_8(g) \ + \ 5O_2(g) \ \rightarrow \ 3CO_2(g) + 4H_2O(g)$$

44.1g C_3H_8		Grams of CO_2

Use molar mass of C_3H_8 ↓ ↑ Use molar mass of CO_2

Moles of C_3H_8	→ Use mole ratio between CO_2 and C_3H_8 →	Moles of CO_2

We have already done the first step in Section 9.3:

44.1g C_3H_8	→	1 mol 44.09 g	→	1.00 mol C_3H_8

To find out how many moles of CO_2 can be produced from 1.00 mol of C_3H_8, we see from the balanced equation that 3 mol of CO_2 is produced for each mole of C_3H_8 reacted. The mole ratio we need is 3 mol CO_2/1 mol C_3H_8. The conversion is therefore

$$1.00 \ \text{mol } C_3H_8 \times \frac{3 \ \text{mol } CO_2}{1 \ \text{mol } C_3H_8}$$
$$= 3.00 \ \text{mol } CO_2$$

Next, using the molar mass of CO_2, which is 12.01 + 32.00 = 44.01 g, we calculate the mass of CO_2 produced.

$$3.00 \ \text{mol } CO_2 \times \frac{44.01 \ \text{g } CO_2}{1 \ \text{mol } CO_2}$$
$$= 132 \ \text{g } CO_2$$

The sequence of steps we took to find the mass of carbon dioxide produced from 44.1 g of propane is summarized in the following diagram.

44.1g C_3H_8	→	1 mol C_3H_8 44.09 g C_3H_8	→	1.00 mol C_3H_8

1.00 mol C_3H_8	→	3 mol CO_2 1 mol C_3H_8	→	3.00 mol CO_2

3.00 mol CO_2	→	44.01 g CO_2 1 mol CO_2	→	132 g CO_2

Mass   Moles

Notice that the mole ratio is set up so that the moles of C_3H_8 cancel and the resulting units are moles of O_2.

⇨ Because the original question asked for the *mass* of oxygen needed to react with 44.1 g of propane, we must convert the 5.00 mol of O_2 to grams, using the molar mass of O_2 (32.00 = 2 × 16.00).

$$5.00 \ \text{mol } O_2 \times \frac{32.0 \ \text{g } O_2}{1 \ \text{mol } O_2} = 160. \ \text{g } O_2$$

Therefore, 160 g of oxygen is required to burn 44.1 g of propane. We can summarize this problem by writing out a "conversion string" that shows how the problem was done.

$$44.1 \ \text{g } C_3H_8 \times \frac{1 \ \text{mol } C_3H_8}{44.09 \ \text{g } C_3H_8} \times \frac{5 \ \text{mol } O_2}{1 \ \text{mol } C_3H_8} \times \frac{32.0 \ \text{g } O_2}{1 \ \text{mol } O_2} = 160. \ \text{g } O_2$$

This is a convenient way to make sure the final units are correct. The procedure we have followed is summarized below.

This example illustrates in detail how to deal with masses of reactants in chemical equations. To see whether these ideas are clear to you, try the following Self-Check Exercises.

✓ PROBLEM SOLVING
Use units as a check to see that you have used the correct conversion factors (mole ratios).

✓ Self-Check Exercise 9.2

What mass of carbon dioxide is produced when 44.1 g of propane reacts with sufficient oxygen?

✓ Self-Check Exercise 9.3

Calculate the mass of water formed by the complete reaction of 44.1 g of propane with oxygen.

To illustrate how to deal with masses in a chemical equation, consider the following example.

260   Chapter 9   Chemical Quantities

✓ Answer to Self-Check Exercise 9.3

We sketch the problem as follows:

$$C_3H_8(g) + 5O_2(g) \rightarrow 3CO_2(g) + 4H_2O(g)$$

44.1g C_3H_8		Grams of H_2O

1 mole C_3H_8 44.09 g ↓ ↑ 18.02 g mol H_2O

Moles of C_3H_8	→	4 mol H_2O 1 mol C_3H_8	→	Moles of H_2O

Then we do the calculations.

44.1 g C_3H_8	→	1 mol C_3H_8 44.09 g	→	1.00 mol C_3H_8

1.00 mol C_3H_8	→	4 mol H_2O 1 mol C_3H_8	→	4.00 mol H_2O

4.00 mol H_2O	→	18.02 g mol H_2O	→	72.1 g H_2O

Therefore, 72.1 g of H_2O is produced from 96.1 g C_3H_8.

Example 9.5

Aluminum (*left*) and iodine (*right*) shown at the top, react vigorously to form aluminum iodide. The purple cloud results from excess iodine vaporized by the heat of the reaction.

Mass Relationships in Chemical Reactions

Consider the reaction of powdered aluminum metal and finely ground iodine to produce aluminum iodide. The balanced equation for this vigorous chemical reaction is

$$2Al(s) + 3I_2(s) \rightarrow 2AlI_3(s)$$

Calculate the mass of $I_2(s)$ needed to just react with 35.0 g Al(s).

Solution

Let's summarize what we know and what we need to calculate.

What We Know:

● The balanced equation for the reaction

● The mass of Al(s) available

What We Want to Calculate:

● The mass of iodine (I_2) required to react with all of the aluminum (35.0 g)

Let's summarize our plan:

1. We first need to convert from 35.0 g aluminum to moles of aluminum because the balanced equation deals in moles rather than grams.

2. We will use the balanced equation to find the moles of I_2 required to react with all of the aluminum.

3. Once we know the moles of $I_2(s)$ required, we will use the molar mass for iodine to calculate the mass of $I_2(s)$ required.

A schematic for this strategy is

$$2Al(s) \quad + \quad 3I_2(s) \quad \rightarrow \quad 2AlI_3(s)$$

35.0 g Al

⇩

? moles of Al

⇨

? grams I_2

⇧

? moles of I_2

Using the molar mass of aluminum (26.98 g), we will first calculate the moles of aluminum present in 35.0 g Al:

$$35.0 \ \text{g Al} \times \frac{1 \ \text{mol Al}}{26.98 \ \text{g Al}} = 1.30 \ \text{mol Al}$$

From the balanced equation for the reaction we see that

2 Al requires 3 I_2

(continued)

Solutions of sodium hydroxide absorb carbon dioxide from the air, forming sodium carbonate according to the balanced equation

$$2NaOH(aq) + CO_2(g) \rightarrow Na_2CO_3(g) + H_2O(l)$$

1. Calculate the mass of carbon dioxide gas that is required to react with a solution containing 10.0 g of sodium hydroxide.
5.50 g $CO_2(g)$

2. Calculate the mass of sodium carbonate that is produced when 10.0 g of sodium hydroxide reacts with an excess of carbon dioxide.
13.2 g $Na_2CO_3(g)$

(continued)

Thus the required conversion factor from Al to I_2 is

$$\frac{3 \text{ mol } I_2}{2 \text{ mol Al}}$$

Now we can determine the moles of I_2 required by 1.30 moles of Al:

$$1.30 \text{ mol Al} \times 3 \frac{\text{mol } I_2}{2 \text{ mol Al}} = 1.95 \text{ mol } I_2$$

We know the moles of I_2 required to react with the 1.30 mol of Al (35.0 g). The next step is to convert 1.95 mol of I_2 to grams so we will know how much to weigh out. We do so by using the molar mass of I_2. The atomic mass of iodine is 126.9 g (for 1 mol of I atoms), so the molar mass of I_2 is

$$2 \times 126.9 \text{ g/mol} = 253.8 \text{ g/mol} = \text{mass of 1 mol of } I_2$$

Now we convert the 1.95 mol of I_2 to grams of I_2.

$$1.95 \text{ mol } I_2 \times \frac{253.8 \text{ g } I_2}{\text{mol } I_2} = 495 \text{ g } I_2$$

We have solved the problem. We need to weigh out 495 g of iodine (contains I_2 molecules) to react exactly with the 35.0 g of aluminum.

This problem can be summarized as follows:

$$2Al(s) \quad + \quad 3I_2(s) \quad \rightarrow \quad 2AlI_3(s)$$

 Self-Check Exercise 9.4

Calculate the mass of $AlI_3(s)$ formed by the reaction of 35.0 g Al(s) with 495 g $I_2(s)$.

 Answer to Self-Check Exercise 9.4

1.30 mol Al → 1.30 mol AlI_3

$$1.30 \text{ mol } AlI_3 \times \frac{407.7 \text{ g } AlI_3}{\text{mol } AlI_3}$$

$$= 530. \text{ g } AlI_3$$

 Section 9.4

Themes
Patterns of Change

Skills
Applying concepts, interpreting data, converting, evaluating, calculating

Laboratory
Experiment 35:
Mass Relationships in Chemical Compounds, Traditional

9.4 Mass Calculations Using Scientific Notation

Objective: *To carry out mass calculations that involve scientific notation.*

So far in this chapter, we have spent considerable time "thinking through" the procedures for calculating the masses of reactants and products in chemical reactions. We can summarize these procedures in the following steps.

262   Chapter 9   Chemical Quantities

> ### Steps for Calculating the Masses of Reactants and Products in Chemical Reactions
>
> **STEP 1** Balance the equation for the reaction.
>
> **STEP 2** Convert the masses of reactants or products to moles.
>
> **STEP 3** Use the balanced equation to set up the appropriate mole ratio(s).
>
> **STEP 4** Use the mole ratio(s) to calculate the number of moles of the desired reactant or product.
>
> **STEP 5** Convert from moles back to mass.

The process of using a chemical equation to calculate the relative masses of reactants and products involved in a reaction is called **stoichiometry** (pronounced stoý·kē·om̓·ĕtry). Chemists say that the balanced equation for a chemical reaction describes the stoichiometry of the reaction.

We will now consider a few more examples that involve chemical stoichiometry. Because real-world examples often involve very large or very small masses of chemicals that are most conveniently expressed by using scientific notation, we will deal with such a case in Example 9.6.

Example 9.6

CHEMISTRY

For a review of writing formulas of ionic compounds, see Chapter 4.

Stoichiometric Calculations: Using Scientific Notation

Solid lithium hydroxide is used in space vehicles to remove exhaled carbon dioxide from the living environment. The products are solid lithium carbonate and liquid water. What mass of gaseous carbon dioxide can 1.00×10^3 g of lithium hydroxide absorb?

Solution

Step 1   Using the description of the reaction, we can write the unbalanced equation

$$LiOH(s) + CO_2(g) \rightarrow Li_2CO_3(s) + H_2O(l)$$

The balanced equation is

$$2LiOH(s) + CO_2(g) \rightarrow Li_2CO_3(s) + H_2O(l)$$

Check this for yourself.

Step 2   We convert the given mass of LiOH to moles, using the molar mass of LiOH, which is 6.941 g + 16.00 g + 1.008 g = 23.95 g.

$$1.00 \times 10^3 \ \cancel{\text{g LiOH}} \times \frac{1 \text{ mol LiOH}}{23.95 \ \cancel{\text{g LiOH}}} = 41.8 \text{ mol LiOH}$$

Step 3   The appropriate mole ratio is

$$\frac{1 \text{ mol CO}_2}{2 \text{ mol LiOH}}$$

(continued)

Additional Examples

Thionyl chloride, which is used as a drying agent in many synthetic chemistry experiments, reacts with water to form sulfur dioxide gas and hydrogen chloride gas:

$$SOCl_2(l) + H_2O(l) \rightarrow$$
$$SO_2(g) + 2HCl(g)$$

1. Calculate the mass of water consumed by the complete reaction of 3.50×10^2 g of thionyl chloride.
   53.0 g H$_2$O(l)

2. Calculate the mass of hydrogen chloride produced by the complete reaction of 3.50×10^2 g of thionyl chloride.
   2.14×10^2 g HCl(g)

(continued)

PROBLEM SOLVING

Carrying extra significant figures and rounding off only at the end gives an answer of 919 g CO_2.

Step 4 Using this mole ratio, we calculate the moles of CO_2 needed to react with the given mass of LiOH.

$$41.8 \text{ mol LiOH} \times \frac{1 \text{ mol } CO_2}{2 \text{ mol LiOH}} = 20.9 \text{ mol } CO_2$$

Step 5 We calculate the mass of CO_2 by using its molar mass (44.01 g).

$$20.9 \text{ mol } CO_2 \times \frac{44.01 \text{ g } CO_2}{1 \text{ mol } CO_2} = 920. \text{ g } CO_2 = 9.20 \times 10^2 \text{ g } CO_2$$

Thus 1.00×10^3 g of LiOH(s) can absorb 920. g of $CO_2(g)$.
We can summarize this problem as follows:

$$2LiOH(s) \quad + \quad CO_2(g) \rightarrow Li_2CO_3(s) + H_2O(l)$$

The conversion string is

$$1.00 \times 10^3 \text{ g LiOH} \times \frac{1 \text{ mol LiOH}}{23.95 \text{ g LiOH}} \times \frac{1 \text{ mol } CO_2}{2 \text{ mol LiOH}} \times \frac{44.01 \text{ g } CO_2}{1 \text{ mol } CO_2}$$

$$= 9.20 \times 10^2 \text{ g } CO_2$$

Astronaut Sidney M. Gutierrez changes the lithium hydroxide cannisters on space shuttle *Columbia*. The lithium hydroxide is used to purge carbon dioxide from the air in the shuttle's cabin.

 Self-Check Exercise 9.5

Hydrofluoric acid, an aqueous solution containing dissolved hydrogen fluoride, is used to etch glass by reacting with the silica, SiO_2, in the glass to produce gaseous silicon tetrafluoride and liquid water. The unbalanced equation is

$$HF(aq) + SiO_2(s) \rightarrow SiF_4(g) + H_2O(l)$$

a. Calculate the mass of hydrogen fluoride needed to react with 5.68 g of silica. *Hint:* Think carefully about this problem. What is the balanced equation for the reaction? What is given? What do you need to calculate? Sketch a map of the problem before you do the calculations.

b. Calculate the mass of water produced in the reaction described in part a.

TOP TEN

Chemicals Used in the United States (annually)

Chemical	Amount (kg)
1. Sulfur acid (H_2SO_4)	4.33×10^{10}
2. Nitrogen (N_2)	3.09×10^{10}
3. Oxygen (O_2)	2.43×10^{10}
4. Ethylene (C_2H_4)	2.13×10^{10}
5. Lime (CaO)	1.87×10^{10}
6. Ammonia (NH_3)	1.61×10^{10}
7. Phosphoric acid (H_3PO_4)	1.19×10^{10}
8. Sodium hydroxide (NaOH)	1.19×10^{10}
9. Propylene (C_3H_7)	1.17×10^{10}
10. Chlorine (Cl_2)	1.14×10^{10}

264 Chapter 9 Chemical Quantities

Using the TOP TEN

Divide students into teams. Give each team an equation using one of the Top Ten chemicals. Ask students to calculate the mass of another substance used or produced if all of the Top Ten chemical was used. You might even find some combinations of Top Ten chemicals that could be used later in the chapter as limiting reactant problems. Here are some possible unbalanced chemical equations for the Top Ten:

$$Ca_3(PO_4)_2 + H_2SO_4 \rightarrow H_3PO_4$$
$$C_2H_4 + O_2 \rightarrow CO_2 + H_2O$$
$$N_2 + H_2 \rightarrow NH_3$$
$$C_3H_7 + O_2 \rightarrow CO_2 + H_2O$$
$$Na + Cl_2 \rightarrow NaCl$$
$$CaCO_3 \rightarrow CaO + CO_2$$
$$NaOH + H_3PO_4 \rightarrow Na_3PO_4 + H_2O$$

Answers to Self-Check Exercise 9.5

a. We first write the balanced equation.

$$SiO_2(s) + 4HF(aq) \rightarrow SiF_4(g) + 2H_2O(l)$$

The map of the steps required is

We convert 5.68 g of SiO_2 to moles as follows:

$$5.68 \text{ g } SiO_2 \times \frac{1 \text{ mol } SiO_2}{60.09 \text{ g } SiO_2}$$
$$= 9.45 \times 10^{-2} \text{ mol } SiO_2$$

Using the balanced equation, we obtain the appropriate mole ratio and convert to moles of HF.

$$9.45 \times 10^{-2} \text{ mol } SiO_2$$
$$\times \frac{4 \text{ mol HF}}{1 \text{ mol } SiO_2}$$
$$= 3.78 \times 10^{-1} \text{ mol HF}$$

Finally, we calculate the mass of HF by using its molar mass.

$$3.78 \times 10^{-1} \text{ mol HF}$$
$$\times \frac{20.01 \text{ g HF}}{\text{mol HF}} = 7.56 \text{ g HF}$$

Science, Technology, and Society

Methyl Alcohol: Fuel with a Future?

Southern California is famous for many things, and among them, unfortunately, is smog. Smog is produced when pollutants in the air are trapped near the ground and are caused to react by sunlight. A step being considered by the state of California to help solve the smog problem is to replace gasoline with methyl alcohol (usually called methanol). One advantage of methanol is that it reacts more nearly completely than gasoline with oxygen in a car's engine, thus releasing lower amounts of unburned fuel into the atmosphere. Methanol also produces less carbon monoxide (CO) in the exhaust than does gasoline. Carbon monoxide not only is toxic itself but also encourages the formation of nitrogen dioxide by the reaction

$$CO(g) + O_2(g) + NO(g) \rightarrow CO_2(g) + NO_2(g)$$

Nitrogen dioxide is a reddish-brown gas that leads to ozone formation and acid rain.

Using methanol as a fuel is not a new idea. For example, it is the only fuel allowed in the open-wheeled race cars used in the Indianapolis 500 and in similar races. Methanol works very well in racing engines because it has outstanding antiknock characteristics, even at the tremendous speeds at which these engines operate.

The news about methanol is not all good, however. One problem is lower fuel mileage. Because it

A crewman adds methanol fuel to a race car in the Indianapolis 500 during a pit stop.

takes about twice as many gallons of methanol as gasoline to travel a given distance, a methanol-powered car's fuel tank must be twice the usual size. However, although costs vary greatly depending on market conditions, the cost of methanol averages about half that of gasoline, so the net cost is about the same for both fuels.

A second disadvantage of methanol is that its high affinity for water causes condensation from the air, which leads to increased corrosion of the fuel tank and fuel lines. This problem can be solved by using more expensive stainless steel for these parts.

The most serious problem with methanol may be its tendency to form formaldehyde, HCHO, when it is combusted. Formaldehyde has been implicated as a carcinogen (a substance that causes cancer). Formaldehyde can also lead to ozone formation in the air, which causes even more severe smog. Researchers are now working on catalytic converters for exhaust systems to help decompose the formaldehyde.

To test the feasibility of methanol as a motor fuel, California has operated several hundred vehicles on methanol since 1980. Because accessibility to methanol is limited, cars are now being prepared that can run on methanol or gasoline. These vehicles are being tested on a large scale in California. So if you live in southern California, in a few years your neighborhood "gas station" may actually be pumping methanol.

Integrating the CHEMICAL IMPACT

Methyl Alcohol: Fuel with a Future?

"Methyl Alcohol: Fuel with a Future?" can be used to foster a discussion about various alternative fuels for cars and trucks that are under consideration, such as ethanol, hydrogen, and vegetable oil (for trucks, buses, and farm tractors). You might discuss with students the advantages and disadvantages of each. For example, ethanol produces the greenhouse gas CO_2 and cannot be used as a pure liquid in cold climates because it becomes too nonvolatile. On the other hand, ethanol comes from a renewable source (corn). Hydrogen is very difficult to store but it produces only H_2O as a combustion product.

9.5 Section 9.5

Themes
Patterns of change

Skills
Making comparisons, evaluating

Laboratory
Experiment 36:
Calcium Content of Milk, Microscale

MINI-DEMO

The reaction between baking soda and an acid is a quick, fun demonstration to illustrate a neutralization reaction. Use a 2-L soda bottle with a stopper to fit. Wrap a teaspoon of baking soda in a tissue in a cigar shape with the ends twisted closed. Make the "cigar" thin enough to fit through the opening in the soda bottle. Place 100 mL of vinegar in the soda bottle before the demonstration. When you are ready to do the demonstration, stuff the "cigar" into the bottle and stopper it. Shake gently to mix and don't aim at any people. The stopper should shoot across the room. You might then discuss the reaction:

$$NaHCO_3(s) + HC_2H_3O_2(aq)$$
$$\rightarrow NaC_2H_3O_2(aq) + H_2O(l)$$
$$+ CO_2(g)$$

You can also discuss what might happen to the carbon dioxide gas if this reaction were to occur in the stomach.

9.5 Mass Calculations: Comparing Two Reactions

Objective: *To compare the stoichiometry of two reactions.*

In this section we will consider the relative effectiveness of two antacids to illustrate how chemical calculations can be important in daily life.

Baking soda, $NaHCO_3$, is often used as an antacid. It neutralizes excess hydrochloric acid secreted by the stomach. The balanced equation for the reaction is

$$NaHCO_3(s) + HCl(aq) \rightarrow NaCl(aq) + H_2O(l) + CO_2(g)$$

9.5 Mass Calculations: Comparing Two Reactions **265**

b. The map for this problem is

$$SiO_2(s) + 4HF(aq) \rightarrow SiF_4(g) + 2H_2O(l)$$

5.68 g SiO₂		Grams of H₂O
↓ Use molar mass of SiO₂		↑ Use molar mass of H₂O
Moles of SiO₂	→ Use mole ratio between H₂O and SiO₂ →	Moles of H₂O

We have already accomplished the first conversion in part a. Using the balanced equation, we obtain moles of H_2O as follows:

$$9.45 \times 10^{-2} \text{ mol } SiO_2$$
$$\times \frac{2 \text{ mol } H_2O}{1 \text{ mol } SiO_2}$$
$$= 1.89 \times 10^{-1} \text{ mol } H_2O$$

The mass of water formed is

$$1.89 \times 10^{-1} \text{ mol } H_2O$$
$$\times \frac{18.02 \text{ g } H_2O}{\text{mol } H_2O}$$
$$= 3.41 \text{ g } H_2O$$

Chapter 9 Chemical Quantities **265**

Two antacid tablets containing HCO_3^- dissolve to produce CO_2 gas.

Milk of magnesia, which is an aqueous suspension of magnesium hydroxide, $Mg(OH)_2$, is also used as an antacid. The balanced equation for its reaction is

$$Mg(OH)_2(s) + 2HCl(aq) \rightarrow 2H_2O(l) + MgCl_2(aq)$$

Which antacid can consume the most stomach acid, 1.00 g of $NaHCO_3$ or 1.00 g of $Mg(OH)_2$?

Before we begin, let's think about the problem to be solved. The question we must ask for each antacid is, *How many moles of HCl will react with 1.00 g of each antacid?* The antacid that reacts with the larger number of moles of HCl is more effective because it will neutralize more moles of acid. A schematic for this procedure is

Antacid   +   HCl   →   Products

1.00 g
antacid

⇩

Use molar mass
of antacid

⇩

Moles of antacid ⇨ Use mole ratio from balanced equation ⇨ Moles of HCl

Notice that in this case we do not need to calculate how many grams of HCl react; we can answer the question with moles of HCl. We will now solve this problem for each antacid. Both of the equations are balanced, so we can proceed with the calculations.

Using the molar mass of $NaHCO_3$, which is 22.99 g + 1.008 g + 12.01 g + 3(16.00 g) = 84.01 g, we determine the moles of $NaHCO_3$ in 1.00 g of $NaHCO_3$.

$$1.00 \text{ g NaHCO}_3 \times \frac{1 \text{ mol NaHCO}_3}{84.01 \text{ g NaHCO}_3} = 0.0119 \text{ mol NaHCO}_3$$
$$= 1.19 \times 10^{-2} \text{ mol NaHCO}_3$$

Next we determine the moles of HCl, using the mole ratio $\dfrac{1 \text{ mol HCl}}{1 \text{ mol NaHCO}_3}$.

$$1.19 \times 10^{-2} \text{ mol NaHCO}_3 \times \frac{1 \text{ mol HCl}}{1 \text{ mol NaHCO}_3} = 1.19 \times 10^{-2} \text{ mol HCl}$$

Thus 1.00 g of $NaHCO_3$ neutralizes 1.19×10^{-2} mol of HCl. We need to compare this to the number of moles of HCl that 1.00 g of $Mg(OH)_2$ neutralizes.

Answer to Self-Check Exercise 9.6

In this problem, we know the mass of the product to be formed by the reaction

$$CO(g) + 2H_2(g) \rightarrow CH_3OH(l)$$

and we want to find the masses of reactants needed. The procedure is the same one we have been following. We must first convert the mass of CH_3OH to moles, then use the balanced equation to obtain moles of H_2 and CO needed, and then convert these moles to masses. Using the molar mass of CH_3OH (32.04 g/mol), we convert to moles of CH_3OH.

First we convert kilograms to grams.

$$6.0 \text{ kg CH}_3\text{OH} \times \frac{1000 \text{ g}}{\text{kg}}$$
$$= 6.0 \times 10^3 \text{ g CH}_3\text{OH}$$

Next we convert 6.0×10^3 g CH_3OH to moles of CH_3OH, using the conversion factor 1 mol CH_3OH/32.04 g CH_3OH.

$$6.0 \times 10^3 \text{ g CH}_3\text{OH}$$
$$\times \frac{1 \text{ mol CH}_3\text{OH}}{32.04 \text{ g CH}_3\text{OH}}$$
$$= 1.9 \times 10^2 \text{ mol CH}_3\text{OH}$$

Then we have two questions to answer:

To answer these questions, we use the balanced equation

$$CO(g) + 2H_2(g) \rightarrow CH_3OH(l)$$

to obtain mole ratios between the reactants and the products. In the balanced equation the coefficients for

both CO and CH_3OH are 1, so we can write the equivalence statement

$$1 \text{ mol CO} = 1 \text{ mol CH}_3\text{OH}$$

Using the mole ratio 1 mol CO/1 mol CH_3OH, we can now convert from moles of CH_3OH to moles of CO.

$$1.9 \times 10^2 \text{ mol CH}_3\text{OH}$$
$$\times \frac{1 \text{ mol CO}}{1 \text{ mol CH}_3\text{OH}}$$
$$= 1.9 \times 10^2 \text{ mol CO}$$

To calculate the moles of H_2 required, we construct the equivalence statement between CH_3OH and H_2, using the coefficients in the balanced equation.

$$2 \text{ mol H}_2 = 1 \text{ mol CH}_3\text{OH}$$

Using the mole ratio 2 mol H_2/1 mol CH_3OH, we can convert moles of CH_3OH to moles of H_2.

$$1.9 \times 10^2 \text{ mol CH}_3\text{OH}$$
$$\times \frac{2 \text{ mol H}_2}{1 \text{ mol CH}_3\text{OH}}$$
$$= 3.8 \times 10^2 \text{ mol H}_2$$

Using the molar mass of $Mg(OH)_2$, which is 24.31 g + 2(16.00 g) + 2(1.008 g) = 58.33 g, we determine the moles of $Mg(OH)_2$ in 1.00 g of $Mg(OH)_2$.

$$1.00 \text{ g } Mg(OH)_2 \times \frac{1 \text{ mol } Mg(OH)_2}{58.33 \text{ g } Mg(OH)_2} = 0.0171 \text{ mol } Mg(OH)_2$$

$$= 1.71 \times 10^{-2} \text{ mol } Mg(OH)_2$$

To determine the moles of HCl that react with this amount of $Mg(OH)_2$, we use the mole ratio $\dfrac{2 \text{ mol HCl}}{1 \text{ mol } Mg(OH)_2}$.

$$1.71 \times 10^{-2} \text{ mol } Mg(OH)_2 \times \frac{2 \text{ mol HCl}}{1 \text{ mol } Mg(OH)_2} = 3.42 \times 10^{-2} \text{ mol HCl}$$

Therefore, 1.00 g of $Mg(OH)_2$ neutralizes 3.42×10^{-2} mol of HCl. We have already calculated that 1.00 g of $NaHCO_3$ neutralizes only 1.19×10^{-2} mol of HCl. Therefore, $Mg(OH)_2$ is a more effective antacid than $NaHCO_3$ on a mass basis.

 Self-Check Exercise 9.6

In this section we have answered one of the questions we posed in the introduction to this chapter. Now let's see if you can answer the other question posed there. Determine what mass of carbon monoxide and what mass of hydrogen are required to form 6.0 kg of methanol by the reaction

$$CO(g) + 2H_2(g) \rightarrow CH_3OH(l)$$

CELEBRITY CHEMICAL

Lithium (Li)

For the first 150 years after its discovery in 1817, lithium was a rather humble element. It seemed to have very few uses. In the last 30 years, however, lithium has been found to be a powerful psychoactive drug.

The psychological effects of lithium were discovered in the 1940s by accident by an Australian psychiatrist named John Cade. Cade was studying patients with manic-depressive syndrome, a disease that causes its victims to experience extreme feelings ranging from high mania to deep depression. Cade thought the disease might be due to problems in metabolizing uric acid. Consequently, he administered lithium salts of uric acid along with lithium carbonate to animals. The result was a dra-

matic calming effect. Cade noticed similar effects when he tried these treatments on himself and on a few patients with manic-depressive disease. It was not until a decade later that a Danish doctor, Mogens Schou, discovered that lithium—not the uric acid—caused the dramatic effects.

In the last 50 years, lithium has become the most popular drug for treating manic depression. Despite the fact that it has helped millions of people, we are still not sure how this element controls mania and relieves depression. Lithium appears to help regulate the levels of certain chemicals that transmit messages in the brain. Studies continue to explore how this once underrated element alters extreme moods so profoundly.

CELEBRITY CHEMICAL

Lithium (Li)

Lithium ion produces a beautiful red flame. To demonstrate its generation, place a lithium salt in a glass Petri dish or evaporating dish, and add a few milliliters of methanol. Stir the mixture, ignite it with a burner or a match, and turn the lights down. Your students will enjoy the intense red flame.

We now have the moles of reactants required to produce 6.0 kg of CH_3OH. Since we need the masses of reactants, we must use the molar masses to convert from moles to mass.

$$1.9 \times 10^2 \text{ mol CO}$$
$$\times \frac{28.01 \text{ g CO}}{1 \text{ mol CO}}$$
$$= 5.3 \times 10^3 \text{ g CO}$$
$$3.8 \times 10^2 \text{ mol } H_2$$
$$\times \frac{2.016 \text{ g } H_2}{1 \text{ mol } H_2}$$
$$= 7.7 \times 10^2 \text{ g } H_2$$

Therefore, we need 5.3×10^3 g CO to react with 7.7×10^2 g H_2 to form 6.0×10^3 g (6.0 kg) of CH_3OH. This whole process is depicted in the following diagram.

Answers to Focus Questions

1. A mole represents a huge number of molecules. Because we cannot count molecules directly, we count by weighing. The mass we determine must then be converted to moles so we can keep track of the number of molecules in the reaction.

2. 2.75 g CO_2 can be absorbed.

3. Methanol reacts more completely with oxygen than gasoline and it releases less unburned fuel into the atmosphere. Methanol also produces less CO in exhaust than gasoline does. It has good antiknock characteristics at high speeds.

4. In a stoichiometry problem the amount of a particular chemical needed to produce a certain amount of a second chemical is calculated by converting the mass of the first chemical to moles and using the mole ratio to find the moles of the second chemical and then its mass. In the supermarket you might determine the best buy by taking the mass of each product and using the cost per package to find the cost per gram of the product. This calculation could be done for both products and then used to determine which package provides the most product per gram.

Section 9.6

Themes
Patterns of Change

Skills
Applying concepts, making comparisons, making predictions, calculating

Student Preparation
Assign the students to read Sections 9.6 to 9.8 and to answer the Focus Questions at the end of Section 9.8 before coming to class.

Active Learning
After introducing the material in Sections 9.6 to 9.8 in class, place the students in groups and have them work together on Sections 9.6–9.8: Team Learning Worksheet. Answers and/or

discussion of these questions are located in the *Teacher Resources.*

1. Why do we need to convert mass to moles in stoichiometry problems?

2. Solutions of sodium hydroxide cannot be kept for very long because they absorb carbon dioxide from the air, forming sodium carbonate. The unbalanced equation is

$$NaOH(aq) + CO_2(g) \rightarrow Na_2CO_3(aq) + H_2O(l).$$

Calculate the number of grams of carbon dioxide that can be absorbed by complete reaction with a solution that contains 5.00 g of sodium hydroxide.

3. Why would methanol make a good alternative fuel? What are its limitations?

4. Show how the steps used in solving a stoichiometry problem are similar to a method that could be used to determine which of two products would be the best buy in a supermarket?

9.6 The Concept of Limiting Reactants

Objective: *To understand the concept of limiting reactants.*

Earlier in this chapter we discussed making sandwiches. Recall that the sandwich-making process could be described as follows:

2 pieces bread + 3 slices meat + 1 slice cheese → sandwich

In our earlier discussion, we always purchased the ingredients in the correct ratios so that we used up all of the components, with nothing left over.

Now assume you came to work one day and found the following quantities of ingredients:

20 slices of bread

24 slices of meat

12 slices of cheese

How many sandwiches can you make? What will be left over?

To solve this problem let's see how many sandwiches we can make with each component.

Bread:

$$20 \text{ slices bread} \times \frac{1 \text{ sandwich}}{2 \text{ slices bread}} = 10 \text{ sandwiches}$$

Meat:

$$24 \text{ slices meat} \times \frac{1 \text{ sandwich}}{3 \text{ slices meat}} = 8 \text{ sandwiches}$$

Cheese:

$$12 \text{ slices cheese} \times \frac{1 \text{ sandwich}}{1 \text{ slice cheese}} = 12 \text{ sandwiches}$$

How many sandwiches can you make? The answer is 8. Once you run out of meat, you must stop making sandwiches. The meat is the limiting ingredient.

268   Chapter 9   Chemical Quantities

What do you have left over? Making 8 sandwiches requires 16 pieces of bread. You started with 20 pieces, so you have 4 pieces of bread left. You also used 8 pieces of cheese for the 8 sandwiches, so you have $12 - 8 = 4$ pieces of cheese left.

In this example, the ingredient present in the largest number (the meat) was actually the component that limited the number of sandwiches you could make. This situation arose because each sandwich required 3 slices of meat—more than the quantity required of any other ingredient.

When molecules react with each other to form products, considerations very similar to those involved in making sandwiches arise. We can illustrate these ideas with the reaction of $N_2(g)$ and $H_2(g)$ to form $NH_3(g)$:

$$N_2(g) + 3H_2(g) \rightarrow 2NH_3(g)$$

Consider the following container of $N_2(g)$ and $H_2(g)$:

What will this container look like if the reaction between N_2 and H_2 proceeds to completion? To answer this question you need to remember that each N_2 requires 3 H_2 molecules to form 2 NH_3. To make things clear we will circle groups of reactants:

Before the reaction   After the reaction

In this case the mixture of N_2 and H_2 contained just the number of molecules needed to form NH_3 with nothing left over. That is, the ratio of the number of H_2 molecules to N_2 molecules was

$$\frac{15\ H_2}{5\ N_2} = \frac{3\ H_2}{1\ N_2}$$

9.6   The Concept of Limiting Reactants   **269**

This ratio exactly matches the numbers in the balanced equation $3H_2(g) + N_2(g) \rightarrow 2NH_3(g)$.

This type of mixture is called a *stoichiometric mixture*—one that contains the relative amounts of reactants that matches the numbers in the balanced equation. In this case all reactants will be consumed to form products.

Now consider another container of $N_2(g)$ and $H_2(g)$:

What will the container look like if the reaction between $N_2(g)$ and $H_2(g)$ proceeds to completion? Remember that each N_2 requires 3 H_2. Circling groups of reactants we have

Before the reaction   After the reaction

In this case the hydrogen (H_2) is limiting. That is, the H_2 molecules are used up before all of the N_2 molecules are consumed. In this situation the amount of hydrogen limits the amount of product (ammonia) that can form—hydrogen is the limiting reactant. Some N_2 molecules are left over in this case because the reaction runs out of H_2 molecules first.

To determine how much product can be formed from a given mixture of reactants, we have to look for the reactant that is limiting—the one that runs out first and thus limits the amount of product that can form. In some cases the mixture of reactants might be stoichiometric—that is, all reactants run out at the same time. In general, however, you cannot assume that a given mixture of reactants is a stoichiometric mixture, so you must determine whether one of the reactants is limiting. The reactant that runs out first and

270   Chapter 9   Chemical Quantities

thus limits the amounts of products that can form is called the **limiting reactant (limiting reagent).**

To this point we have considered examples where the numbers of reactant molecules could be counted. In "real life" you can't count the molecules directly—you can't see them and, even if you could, there would be far too many to count. Instead you must count by weighing. We must therefore explore how to find the limiting reactant, given the masses of the reactants. We will do so in the next section.

9.7 Calculations Involving a Limiting Reactant

Objectives: *To learn to recognize the limiting reactant in a reaction.*
To learn to use the limiting reactant to do stoichiometric calculations.

Manufacturers of cars, bicycles, and appliances order parts in the same proportion as they are used in their products. For example, auto manufacturers order four times as many wheels as engines and bicycle manufacturers order twice as many pedals as seats. Likewise, when chemicals are mixed together so that they can undergo a reaction, they are often mixed in stoichiometric quantities—that is, in exactly the correct amounts so that all reactants "run out" (are used up) at the same time.

Let's consider the production of hydrogen for use in the manufacture of ammonia. Ammonia, a very important fertilizer itself and a starting material for other fertilizers, is made by combining nitrogen from the air with hydrogen. The hydrogen for this process is produced by the reaction of methane with water according to the balanced equation

$$CH_4(g) + H_2O(g) \rightarrow 3H_2(g) + CO(g)$$

Ammonia being dissolved in irrigation water to provide fertilizer for a field of corn.

Let's consider the question, *What mass of water is required to react exactly with 249 g of methane?* That is, how much water will just use up all of the 249 g of methane, leaving no methane or water remaining?

This problem requires the same strategies we developed in Section 9.5. Again, drawing a map of the problem is helpful.

$$CH_4(g) \quad + \quad H_2O(g) \quad \rightarrow \quad 3H_2(g) \quad + \quad CO(g)$$

249 g CH₄		Grams of H₂O

Use molar mass of CH_4 Use molar mass of H_2O

Moles of CH₄	Use mole ratio from balanced equation	Moles of H₂O

portant to explain to them that the water is added to the test tubes to keep the volumes of the solutions constant. Ask students what is changing in the test tubes. Which reactant is the limiting reactant? How could the students tell for sure? Since we have not yet discussed molarity, they cannot calculate the amounts of products unless you tell them the mass of each reactant in each test tube.

 Section 9.7

Themes
Patterns of Change

Skills
Applying concepts, interpreting diagrams, making comparisons, making predictions, calculating

Laboratory
Experiment 37:
Stoichiometry, In Text

Laboratory
Experiment 38:
Temperature and Limiting Reactants, CBL

TEACHING TIPS

- It may be useful to begin this section by introducing several examples that include simple equations and starting with moles rather than masses. A good example for beginning the discussion is

  $$2Na + Cl_2 \rightarrow 2NaCl$$

- Have students consider what occurs if we add 2 mol Na to 1 mol Cl_2 and the reaction goes to completion. The result is 0 mol Na, 0 mol Cl_2, and 2 mol NaCl. Next, ask what will be the result of mixing 0.5 mol Cl_2 and 2 mol Na. The students must now consider the limit that the 0.5 mol Cl_2 places on the system. They should find that the result would now be 1 mol NaCl, 0 mol Cl_2, and 1 mol Na. Once this idea is clear, move on to solving problems with more complex equations or beginning with mass.

- Another way of presenting a limiting reactant problem is presented below:

  Sulfur and oxygen react to form sulfur trioxide:

  $$2S + 3O_2 \rightarrow 2SO_3$$

  Calculate the number of moles of SO_3 formed when 6.0 moles of each reactant is present initially and the reaction goes to completion.

  Set up a table that includes all of the known information:

	2S	+ 3O₂ →	2SO₃
Initial	6	6	0
Change	−?	−?	+?
End	?	?	?

(continued)

(continued)

Six moles of each reactant (and no product) are shown in the "Initial" row. The "Change" row shows the change in moles for each chemical. The "End" row shows the final reaction mixture. Because the reaction is complete, one (or possibly both) of the end values for sulfur or oxygen must be zero. But which one? We can decide by realizing a crucial point: *The ratio of the numbers in the "Change" row must be the same as the ratio of the coefficients in the balanced equation.* Consider the two possibilities:

	2S	+	3O$_2$	→	2SO$_3$
Initial	6		6		0
Change	−6		−9		+6
End	0		−3		6

	2S	+	3O$_2$	→	2SO$_3$
Initial	6		6		0
Change	−4		−6		+4
End	2		0		4

In the first table, we assume that all of the sulfur reacts. In the second table, we assume that all of the oxygen is consumed. We can see why sulfur is not limiting by looking at the first table—we need 3 more moles of oxygen than we actually have.

These tables give us all the needed information: which reactant is limiting, how much of the excess reactant is left over, and how much product is formed.

- Students have a great deal of trouble understanding that we cannot find the limiting reactant using mass. They should understand that comparisons in chemical reactions must be done using moles, not mass.

TEACHING TIP

Point out the clues that indicate a problem in which students should consider a limiting reactant. These clues include problems in which masses are given for two or more reactants and cases where one reactant is in excess (so the other becomes limiting).

We first convert the mass of CH$_4$ to moles, using the molar mass of CH$_4$ (16.04 g/mol).

$$249 \text{ g CH}_4 \times \frac{1 \text{ mol CH}_4}{16.04 \text{ g CH}_4} = 15.5 \text{ mol CH}_4$$

Because in the balanced equation 1 mol of CH$_4$ reacts with 1 mol of H$_2$O, we have

$$15.5 \text{ mol CH}_4 \times \frac{1 \text{ mol H}_2\text{O}}{1 \text{ mol CH}_4} = 15.5 \text{ mol H}_2\text{O}$$

Therefore, 15.5 mol of H$_2$O will react exactly with the given mass of CH$_4$. Converting 15.5 mol of H$_2$O to grams of H$_2$O (molar mass = 18.02 g/mol) gives

$$15.5 \text{ mol H}_2\text{O} \times \frac{18.02 \text{ g H}_2\text{O}}{1 \text{ mol H}_2\text{O}} = 279 \text{ g H}_2\text{O}$$

This result means that if 249 g of methane is mixed with 279 g of water, both reactants will "run out" at the same time. The reactants have been mixed in stoichiometric quantities.

If, on the other hand, 249 g of methane is mixed with 300 g of water, the methane will be consumed before the water runs out. The water will be in *excess*. In this case, the quantity of products formed will be determined by the quantity of methane present. Once the methane is consumed, no more products can be formed, even though some water still remains. In this situation, the amount of methane *limits* the amount of products that can be formed, and it is the limiting reactant. In any stoichiometry problem, where reactants are not mixed in stoichiometric quantities, it is essential to determine which reactant is limiting to calculate correctly the amounts of products that will be formed. This concept is illustrated in **Figure 9.1.** Note from this figure that because there are fewer water molecules than CH$_4$ molecules, the water is consumed first. After the water molecules are gone, no more products can form. So in this case water is the limiting reactant.

CHEMISTRY

The reactant that is consumed first limits the amounts of products that can form.

Figure 9.1
A mixture of 5CH$_4$ and 3H$_2$O molecules undergoes the reaction CH$_4$(g) + H$_2$O(g) → 3H$_2$(g) + CO(g). Note that the H$_2$O molecules are used up first, leaving two CH$_4$ molecules unreacted.

272   Chapter 9   Chemical Quantities

USING TECHNOLOGY

 Figure 9.1

Example 9.7

Stoichiometric Calculations: Identifying the Limiting Reactant

Suppose 25.0 kg (2.50×10^4 g) of nitrogen gas and 5.00 kg (5.00×10^3 g) of hydrogen gas are mixed and reacted to form ammonia. Calculate the mass of ammonia produced when this reaction is run to completion.

Solution

The balanced equation for this reaction is

$$N_2(g) + 3H_2(g) \rightarrow 2NH_3(g)$$

This problem is different from the others we have done so far in that we are mixing *specified amounts of two reactants* together. To know how much product forms, we must determine which reactant is consumed first. That is, we must determine which is the limiting reactant in this experiment. To do so we must add a step to our normal procedure. We can map this process as follows:

We will use the moles of the limiting reactant to calculate the moles and then the grams of the product.

(continued)

Aluminum reacts with chlorine gas to form aluminum chloride according to the balanced equation

$$2Al(s) + 3Cl_2(g) \rightarrow 2AlCl_3(s)$$

In a certain experiment, 10.0 g of aluminum is reacted with 35.0 g of chlorine gas.

1. What mass of aluminum chloride will be produced, assuming a complete reaction? **43.9 g AlCl$_3$(s)**

2. What mass of which reactant is left after the reaction? **1.1 g Al(s)**

(continued)

We first calculate the moles of the two reactants present:

$$2.50 \times 10^4 \ \cancel{g \ N_2} \times \frac{1 \ mol \ N_2}{28.02 \ \cancel{g \ N_2}} = 8.92 \times 10^2 \ mol \ N_2$$

$$5.00 \times 10^3 \ \cancel{g \ H_2} \times \frac{1 \ mol \ H_2}{2.016 \ \cancel{g \ H_2}} = 2.48 \times 10^3 \ mol \ H_2$$

Now we must determine which reactant is limiting (will be consumed first). We have 8.92×10^2 mol of N_2. Let's determine *how many moles of H_2 are required to react with this much N_2*. Because 1 mol of N_2 reacts with 3 mol of H_2, the number of moles of H_2 we need to react completely with 8.92×10^2 mol of N_2 is determined as follows:

$$8.92 \times 10^2 \ \cancel{mol \ N_2} \times \frac{3 \ mol \ H_2}{1 \ \cancel{mol \ N_2}} = 2.68 \times 10^3 \ mol \ H_2$$

Is N_2 or H_2 the limiting reactant? The answer comes from the comparison

Moles of H_2 available	less than	Moles of H_2 required
2.48×10^3		2.68×10^3

We see that 8.92×10^2 mol of N_2 requires 2.68×10^3 mol of H_2 to react completely. However, only 2.48×10^3 mol of H_2 is present. This means that the hydrogen will be consumed before the nitrogen runs out, so hydrogen is the *limiting reactant* in this particular situation.

Note that in our effort to determine the limiting reactant, we could have started instead with the given amount of hydrogen and calculated the moles of nitrogen required.

$$2.48 \times 10^3 \ \cancel{mol \ H_2} \times \frac{1 \ mol \ N_2}{3 \ \cancel{mol \ H_2}} = 8.27 \times 10^2 \ mol \ N_2$$

Thus 2.48×10^3 mol of H_2 requires 8.27×10^2 mol of N_2. Because 8.92×10^2 mol of N_2 is actually present, the nitrogen is in excess.

PROBLEM SOLVING

Always check to see which, if any, reactant is limiting when you are given the amounts of two or more reactants.

Moles of N_2 available	greater than	Moles of N_2 required
8.92×10^2		8.27×10^2

If nitrogen is in excess, hydrogen will "run out" first; again we find that hydrogen limits the amount of ammonia formed.

Because the moles of H_2 present are limiting, we must use this quantity to determine the moles of NH_3 that can form.

$$2.48 \times 10^3 \; \cancel{\text{mol } H_2} \times \frac{2 \text{ mol } NH_3}{3 \; \cancel{\text{mol } H_2}} = 1.65 \times 10^3 \text{ mol } NH_3$$

Next we convert moles of NH_3 to mass of NH_3.

$$1.65 \times 10^3 \; \cancel{\text{mol } NH_3} \times \frac{17.03 \text{ g } NH_3}{1 \; \cancel{\text{mol } NH_3}} = 2.81 \times 10^4 \text{ g } NH_3$$
$$= 28.1 \text{ kg } NH_3$$

Therefore, 25.0 kg of N_2 and 5.00 kg of H_2 can form 28.1 kg of NH_3. The strategy used in Example 9.7 is summarized in **Figure 9.2**.

Figure 9.2
A map of the procedure used in Example 9.7.

The following list summarizes the steps to take in solving stoichiometry problems in which the amounts of two (or more) reactants are given.

> ### Steps for Solving Stoichiometry Problems Involving Limiting Reactants
>
> **STEP 1** Write and balance the equation for the reaction.
> **STEP 2** Convert known masses of reactants to moles.
> **STEP 3** Using the numbers of moles of reactants and the appropriate mole ratios, determine which reactant is limiting.
> **STEP 4** Using the amount of the limiting reactant and the appropriate mole ratios, compute the number of moles of the desired product.
> **STEP 5** Convert from moles of product to grams of product, using the molar mass (if this is required by the problem).

Example 9.8

Stoichiometric Calculations: Reactions Involving the Masses of Two Reactants

Nitrogen gas can be prepared by passing gaseous ammonia over solid copper(II) oxide at high temperatures. The other products of the reaction are solid copper and water vapor. How many grams of N_2 are formed when 18.1 g of NH_3 is reacted with 90.4 g of CuO?

(continued)

9.7   Calculations Involving a Limiting Reactant   **275**

USING TECHNOLOGY

Steps for Solving Stoichiometry Problems Involving Limiting Reactants

Animation and Video
Video, Gravimetric Analysis

Additional Examples

Iron(III) oxide reacts with carbon monoxide to form iron metal and carbon dioxide gas:

$$Fe_2O_3(s) + 3CO(g) \rightarrow$$
$$2Fe(s) + 3CO_2(g)$$

In a certain experiment, 5.0 g of iron(III) oxide is reacted with 5.0 g of carbon monoxide gas.

1. What mass of iron will be produced, assuming a complete reaction?
3.5 g Fe(s)

2. What mass of carbon dioxide will be produced, assuming a complete reaction?
4.1 g CO_2(g)

(continued)

Step 1 The balanced equation for the reaction is

$$6Li(s) + N_2(g) \rightarrow 2Li_3N(s)$$

Step 2 To determine the limiting reactant, we must convert the masses of lithium (atomic mass = 6.941 g) and nitrogen (molar mass = 28.02 g) to moles.

$$56.0 \text{ g Li} \times \frac{1 \text{ mol Li}}{6.941 \text{ g Li}}$$
$$= 8.07 \text{ mol Li}$$

$$56.0 \text{ g N}_2 \times \frac{1 \text{ mol N}_2}{28.02 \text{ g N}_2}$$
$$= 2.00 \text{ mol N}_2$$

Step 3 Using the mole ratio from the balanced equation, we can calculate the moles of lithium required to react with 2.00 mol of nitrogen.

$$2.00 \text{ mol N}_2 \times \frac{6 \text{ mol Li}}{1 \text{ mol N}_2}$$
$$= 12.0 \text{ mol Li}$$

Therefore, 12.0 mol of Li is required to react with 2.00 mol of N_2. However, we have only 8.07 mol of Li, so lithium is limiting. It will be consumed before the nitrogen runs out.

Step 4 Because lithium is the limiting reactant, we must use the 8.07 mol of Li to determine how many moles of Li_3N can be formed.

$$8.07 \text{ mol Li} \times \frac{2 \text{ mol Li}_3\text{N}}{6 \text{ mol Li}}$$
$$= 2.69 \text{ mol Li}_3\text{N}$$

Step 5 We can now use the molar mass of Li_3N (34.83 g) to calculate the mass of Li_3N formed.

$$2.69 \text{ mol Li}_3\text{N}$$
$$\times \frac{34.83 \text{ g Li}_3\text{N}}{1 \text{ mol Li}_3\text{N}}$$
$$= 93.7 \text{ g Li}_3\text{N}$$

Copper(II) oxide reacting with ammonia in a heated tube.

Solution

Step 1   From the description of the problem, we obtain the following balanced equation:

$$2NH_3(g) + 3CuO(s) \rightarrow N_2(g) + 3Cu(s) + 3H_2O(g)$$

Step 2   From the masses of reactants available, we must compute the moles of NH_3 (molar mass = 17.03 g) and of CuO (molar mass = 79.55 g).

$$18.1 \text{ g NH}_3 \times \frac{1 \text{ mol NH}_3}{17.03 \text{ g NH}_3} = 1.06 \text{ mol NH}_3$$

$$90.4 \text{ g CuO} \times \frac{1 \text{ mol CuO}}{79.55 \text{ g CuO}} = 1.14 \text{ mol CuO}$$

Step 3   To determine which reactant is limiting, we use the mole ratio between CuO and NH_3.

$$1.06 \text{ mol NH}_3 \times \frac{3 \text{ mol CuO}}{2 \text{ mol NH}_3} = 1.59 \text{ mol CuO}$$

Then we compare how much CuO we have with how much of it we need.

Moles of CuO available	less than	Moles of CuO needed to react with all the NH_3
1.14		1.59

Therefore, 1.59 mol of CuO is required to react with 1.06 mol of NH_3, but only 1.14 mol of CuO is actually present. So the amount of CuO is limiting; CuO will run out before NH_3 does.

Note that CuO is limiting even though the original mass of CuO was much greater than the original mass of NH_3.

Step 4   CuO is the limiting reactant, so we must use the amount of CuO in calculating the amount of N_2 formed. Using the mole ratio between CuO and N_2 from the balanced equation, we have

$$1.14 \text{ mol CuO} \times \frac{1 \text{ mol N}_2}{3 \text{ mol CuO}} = 0.380 \text{ mol N}_2$$

Step 5   Using the molar mass of N_2 (28.02), we can now calculate the mass of N_2 produced.

$$0.380 \text{ mol N}_2 \times \frac{28.02 \text{ g N}_2}{1 \text{ mol N}_2} = 10.6 \text{ g N}_{24}$$

 Self-Check Exercise 9.7

Lithium nitride, an ionic compound containing the Li^+ and N^{3-} ions, is prepared by the reaction of lithium metal and nitrogen gas. Calculate the mass of lithium nitride formed from 56.0 g of nitrogen gas and 56.0 g of lithium in the unbalanced reaction

$$Li(s) + N_2(g) \rightarrow Li_3N(s)$$

9.8 Percent Yield

Objective: *To learn to calculate actual yield as a percentage of theoretical yield.*

In the previous section we calculated the amount of products formed when specified amounts of reactants were mixed together. In doing these calculations, we used the fact that the amount of product is controlled by the limiting reactant. Products stop forming when one reactant runs out.

The amount of product calculated in this way is called the **theoretical yield** of that product. It is the amount of product predicted from the amounts of reactants used. For instance, in Example 9.8, 10.6 g of nitrogen represents the theoretical yield. This is the *maximum amount* of nitrogen that can be produced from the quantities of reactants used. Actually, however, the amount of product predicted (the theoretical yield) is seldom obtained. One reason

Themes
Patterns of Change

Skills
Applying concepts, making comparisons, calculating

Laboratory
Experiment 39:
Synthesis of Manganese(II) Chloride, Microscale

TEACHING TIPS

- Students may find it difficult to understand that the answers to stoichiometry problems are actually theoretical yields. It is useful to draw a clear distinction between theoretical yield and actual yield. Point out that an actual yield must be determined by someone in the laboratory, whereas a theoretical yield can be determined by solving limiting reactant problems.

- Now is an excellent time to review the concept of percent composition. You may want to have students do some percent composition problems from Chapter 7 as part of the review.

Integrating the CHEMICAL IMPACT

The "Golden" Dollar

"The 'Golden' Dollar" can be used to lead to a discussion of U.S. coins. The Chemical Impact "U.S. Coins" in Chapter 18 contains a table of the coins and their compositions. If you do not plan to cover Chapter 18 for your course, now would be a good time to discuss the alloys used for the various U.S. coins. You could also use this table to review the percent composition ideas from Chapter 7.

Most likely some water remains in the product and it must be dried (for example, when students collect insoluble ionic solids from aqueous solutions). The result could also point to side reactions that give rise to greater than expected masses, but you probably do not want to offer this idea spontaneously.

Additional Examples

1. In a certain experiment, the expected yield is 1.352 g. The actual yield was 1.279 g. Determine the percent yield. **94.60%**

2. Urea is formed by the reaction of ammonia and carbon dioxide:

$$2NH_3(g) + CO_2(g) \rightarrow CN_2H_4O(s) + H_2O(l)$$

In a certain experiment 100.0 g of ammonia is reacted with 100.0 g of carbon dioxide, and 120.0 g of urea is produced. Determine the percent yield for this reaction. **88.23%**

Answer to Self-Check Exercise 9.8

a. Step 1 The balanced equation is

$$TiCl_4(g) + O_2(g) \rightarrow TiO_2(s) + 2Cl_2(g)$$

Step 2 The numbers of moles of reactants are

$$6.71 \times 10^3 \text{ g } TiCl_4$$
$$\times \frac{1 \text{ mol } TiCl_4}{189.68 \text{ g } TiCl_4}$$
$$= 3.54 \times 10^1 \text{ mol } TiCl_4$$

$$2.45 \times 10^3 \text{ g } O_2$$
$$\times \frac{1 \text{ mol } O_2}{32.00 \text{ g } O_2}$$
$$= 7.66 \times 10^1 \text{ mol } O_2$$

Step 3 In the balanced equation both $TiCl_4$ and O_2 have coefficients of 1, so

$$1 \text{ mol } TiCl_4 = 1 \text{ mol } O_2$$

and

$$3.54 \times 10^1 \text{ mol } TiCl_4$$
$$\times \frac{1 \text{ mol } O_2}{1 \text{ mol } TiCl_4}$$
$$= 3.54 \times 10^1 \text{ mol } O_2$$
$$\text{required}$$

CHEMISTRY

Percent yield is important as an indicator of the efficiency of a particular reaction.

Example 9.9

MATH

Remember

$$\text{Percent} = \frac{\text{Part}}{\text{Whole}} \times 100\%$$

WHAT IF?

In lab you always read the balance correctly and do all of your calculations correctly.

What if you still come up with a percent yield greater than 100%? How could this result happen?

---

for this is the presence of side reactions (other reactions that consume one or more of the reactants or products).

The *actual yield* of product, which is the amount of product *actually obtained*, is often compared to the theoretical yield. This comparison, usually expressed as a percent, is called the **percent yield.**

$$\frac{\text{Actual yield}}{\text{Theoretical yield}} \times 100\% = \text{percent yield}$$

For example, *if* the reaction considered in Example 9.8 *actually* gave 6.63 g of nitrogen instead of the *predicted* 10.6 g, the percent yield of nitrogen would be

$$\frac{6.63 \text{ g } N_2}{10.6 \text{ g } N_2} \times 100\% = 62.5\%$$

Stoichiometric Calculations: Determining Percent Yield

In the "Chemical Impact" on page 265, we stated that methanol can be produced by the reaction between carbon monoxide and hydrogen. Let's consider this process again. Suppose 68.5 kg (6.85×10^4 g) of $CO(g)$ is reacted with 8.60 kg (8.60×10^3 g) of $H_2(g)$.

a. Calculate the theoretical yield of methanol.

b. If 3.57×10^4 g of CH_3OH is actually produced, what is the percent yield of methanol?

Solution (a)

Step 1 The balanced equation is

$$2H_2(g) + CO(g) \rightarrow CH_3OH(l).$$

Step 2 Next we calculate the moles of reactants.

$$6.85 \times 10^4 \text{ g } CO \times \frac{1 \text{ mol } CO}{28.01 \text{ g } CO} = 2.45 \times 10^3 \text{ mol } CO$$

$$8.60 \times 10^3 \text{ g } H_2 \times \frac{1 \text{ mol } H_2}{2.016 \text{ g } H_2} = 4.27 \times 10^3 \text{ mol } H_2$$

Step 3 Now we determine which reactant is limiting. Using the mole ratio between CO and H_2 from the balanced equation, we have

$$2.45 \times 10^3 \text{ mol } CO \times \frac{2 \text{ mol } H_2}{1 \text{ mol } CO} = 4.90 \times 10^3 \text{ mol } H_2$$

We see that 2.45×10^3 mol of CO requires 4.90×10^3 mol of H_2. Because only 4.27×10^3 mol of H_2 is actually present, H_2 *is limiting.*

We have 7.66×10^1 mol of O_2, so the O_2 is in excess and the $TiCl_4$ is limiting. This makes sense. $TiCl_4$ and O_2 react in a 1:1 mole ratio, so the $TiCl_4$ is limiting because fewer moles of $TiCl_4$ are present than moles of O_2.

Step 4 We will now use the moles of $TiCl_4$ (the limiting reactant) to determine the moles of TiO_2 that would form if the reaction produced 100% of the expected yield (the theoretical yield).

$$3.54 \times 10^1 \text{ mol } TiCl_4$$
$$\times \frac{1 \text{ mol } TiO_2}{1 \text{ mol } TiCl_4}$$
$$= 3.54 \times 10^1 \text{ mol } TiO_2$$

The mass of TiO_2 expected for 100% yield is

$$3.54 \times 10^1 \text{ mol } TiO_2$$
$$\times \frac{79.88 \text{ g } TiO_2}{\text{mol } TiO_2}$$
$$= 2.83 \times 10^3 \text{ g } TiO_2$$

This amount represents the theoretical yield.

Step 4 We must therefore use the amount of H_2 and the mole ratio between H_2 and CH_3OH to determine the maximum amount of methanol that can be produced in the reaction.

$$4.27 \times 10^3 \text{ mol } H_2 \times \frac{1 \text{ mol } CH_3OH}{2 \text{ mol } H_2} = 2.14 \times 10^3 \text{ mol } CH_3OH$$

This represents the theoretical yield in moles.

Step 5 Using the molar mass of CH_3OH (32.04 g), we can calculate the theoretical yield in grams.

$$2.14 \times 10^3 \text{ mol } CH_3OH \times \frac{32.04 \text{ g } CH_3OH}{1 \text{ mol } CH_3OH} = 6.86 \times 10^4 \text{ g } CH_3OH$$

So, from the amounts of reactants given, the maximum amount of CH_3OH that can be formed is 6.85×10^4 g. This is the *theoretical yield*.

Solution (b)

The percent yield is

$$\frac{\text{Actual yield (grams)}}{\text{Theoretical yield (grams)}} \times 100\% = \frac{3.57 \times 10^4 \text{ g } CH_3OH}{6.86 \times 10^4 \text{ g } CH_3OH} \times 100\%$$
$$= 52.0\%$$

 Self-Check Exercise 9.8

Titanium(IV) oxide is a white compound used as a coloring pigment. In fact, the page you are now reading is white because of the presence of this compound in the paper. Solid titanium(IV) oxide can be prepared by reacting gaseous titanium(IV) chloride with oxygen gas. A second product of this reaction is chlorine gas.

$$TiCl_4(g) + O_2(g) \rightarrow TiO_2(s) + Cl_2(g)$$

a. Suppose 6.71×10^3 g of titanium(IV) chloride is reacted with 2.45×10^3 g of oxygen. Calculate the maximum mass of titanium(IV) oxide that can form.

b. If the percent yield of TiO_2 is 75%, what mass is actually formed?

 Answers to Focus Questions

Focus Questions

Sections 9.6–9.8

1. How do you recognize a stoichiometric mixture in a chemical reaction?

2. Suppose a lemonade recipe calls for 1 cup of sugar for every 6 lemons. You have 12 lemons and 3 cups of sugar. Which ingredient is limiting? Why?

3. How is a limiting reactant problem different from other stoichiometry problems? (What is your clue that the problem involves a limiting reactant?)

4. What is the difference between theoretical yield and actual yield? Why might a difference occur?

1. A stoichiometric mixture contains relative moles of reactants that just match the numbers in the balanced equation. It is recognizable because none of any reactant is left when the reaction is complete.

2. The lemons are limiting because they will all be used with 2 cups of sugar. One cup of sugar will be left.

3. A limiting reactant problem usually gives masses of more than one reactant. The other possible clue is that one reactant is given in excess. The other reactant is then the limiting reactant.

4. The theoretical yield is the maximum amount of product that can be produced in the reaction. The actual yield is the actual amount of product that is obtained in the laboratory. Differences occur between the theoretical and actual yields because side reactions may occur or the reaction conditions may not be optimal.

b. Because the reaction is said to give only a 75.0% yield of TiO_2, we use the definition of percent yield,

$$\frac{\text{Actual yield}}{\text{Theoretical yield}} \times 100\% = \% \text{ yield}$$

to write the equation

$$\frac{\text{Actual yield}}{2.83 \times 10^3 \text{ g } TiO_2} \times 100\% = 75.0\% \text{ yield}$$

We now want to solve for the actual yield. First we divide both sides by 100%.

$$\frac{\text{Actual yield}}{2.83 \times 10^3 \text{ g } TiO_2} \times \frac{100\%}{100\%}$$
$$= \frac{75.0}{100} = 0.750$$

Then we multiply both sides by 2.83×10^3 g TiO_2.

$$2.83 \times 10^3 \text{ g } TiO_2$$
$$\times \frac{\text{Actual yield}}{2.83 \times 10^3 \text{ g } TiO_2}$$
$$= 0.750 \times 2.83 \times 10^3 \text{ g } TiO_2$$

Actual yield = $0.750 \times 2.83 \times 10^3$ g $TiO_2 = 2.12 \times 10^3$ g TiO_2

Thus 2.12×10^3 g of $TiO_2(s)$ is actually obtained in this reaction.

Stoichiometry

Objectives

1. To determine the mass of copper formed in a reaction

2. To use this information to identify one of the products

Skills

Applying concepts, interpreting data, calculating

Materials

Goggles	Balance
Apron	Stirring rod
250-mL	Matches
beakers (2)	Copper(II)
Ringstand	sulfate
Ring	(anhydrous)
Wire gauze	Water
Bunsen burner	

Preparation Hints

Place containers of copper(II) sulfate throughout the lab for easy access.

Prelab Discussion

Students must wear safety goggles and lab aprons while in the lab.

Students should tie back their hair and loose clothing whenever they work with a flame in the lab. Students will often deposit matches in the sink. Let them know to dispose of burned matches in the trashcan after they are cool.

Remind students of the locations of eyewashes. If they come in contact with any solution, they should wash the contacted area thoroughly.

You may wish to demonstrate to students how to pour a solution down a stirring rod.

Procedure Hints

See the *Teacher's Guide* for the Laboratory

Disposal

Collect all solutions from the students and dispose of them properly.

Sample Data/Answers

Prelab Assignment

2. $CuSO_4(aq) + Fe(s) \rightarrow$
$\qquad Cu(s) + FeSO_4(aq)$

$3CuSO_4(aq) + 2Fe(s) \rightarrow$
$\qquad 3Cu(s) + Fe_2(SO_4)_3(aq)$

3. 3.41 g Cu

4. 2.28 g Cu

Problem

What is the formula for the iron-containing compound formed when copper(II) sulfate reacts with pure iron?

Introduction

We learned in Chapter 4 that iron can form more than one type of ion. The possible reactions are

copper(II) sulfate (aq) + iron (s) →
$\qquad$ copper (s) + iron(II) sulfate (aq)

copper(II) sulfate (aq) + iron (s) →
$\qquad$ copper (s) + iron(III) sulfate (aq)

In this lab you will measure the amount of product formed when measured amounts of reactants are mixed. From this information, you will determine which equation applies to the reaction you run in this experiment.

Prelab Assignment

1. Read the entire lab experiment before you begin.

2. Write and balance each of the equations given in the Introduction.

3. If iron(III) sulfate were formed, what mass of copper would be expected?

4. If iron(II) sulfate were formed, what mass of copper would be expected?

Materials

Goggles
Apron
Two 250-mL beakers
Ring stand
Ring
Wire gauze
Bunsen burner
Balance
Stirring rod
Matches
Copper(II) sulfate (anhydrous)
Water

Safety

1. If you come in contact with any solution, wash the contacted area thoroughly.

2. You will work with a flame in this lab. Tie back hair and loose clothing.

3. Do not drop matches into the sink. Dispose of burned matches in the trashcan after they are cool.

Procedure

1. Place 7.00 g of copper(II) sulfate in a beaker.

Setup to heat copper(II) sulfate solution.

2. Add about 50 mL of water to the beaker.

3. Arrange the beaker and ring stand as shown in the figure.

4. Light the Bunsen burner and place it under the beaker. Adjust the burner so that the hottest part of the flame touches the bottom of the beaker.

5. Carefully heat and stir the mixture in the beaker. The solution should be hot, but not boiling. After all of the crystals have dissolved, remove the beaker from the heat.

6. Add 2.00 g of iron filings slowly to the hot copper sulfate solution while stirring. Record your observations.

7. Allow the beaker to cool for 10–15 minutes.

8. Pour off (decant) the solution into a different beaker. Pouring the solution down a stirring rod is recommended. Make sure not to disturb the copper in the beaker.

9. Add a small amount of water (10–15 mL) to the copper and stir.

10. Let the copper settle to the bottom of the beaker and decant again.

11. Dry the copper as your teacher directs and determine its mass.

Data/Observations

1. Answers will vary. Answers might include the color of the solution changed slightly (to a lighter blue) and a new material was formed.

2. Answers will vary (but should be around 2.28 g).

Analysis and Conclusions

1. The iron was limiting, as can be seen because the solution remained light blue after the reaction was complete. Students should also show that if iron(II) sulfate is formed, only 5.71 g of copper(II) sulfate is required. If iron(III) sulfate is formed, 8.57 g of copper(II) sulfate is required.

2. If the copper(II) sulfate were limiting, iron would be left over. It would be difficult to separate the iron and copper metal to get the mass of the copper.

3. The water is used to wash the copper(II) sulfate or iron(II) sulfate from the copper.

4. The water provided the medium for the reaction. It did not take part in the reaction.

5. The formula is $FeSO_4$. Evidence for this conclusion includes the mass of copper produced and the identity of the limiting reactant.

Something Extra

The solution turns light yellow because the iron(II) sulfate solution is oxidized to iron(III) sulfate.

Cleaning Up

Clean up all materials and wash your hands thoroughly.

Data/Observations

1. Table 7.1 lists clues that a chemical reaction has occurred. Which of the observations you made support the idea that a chemical reaction has occurred in the experiment?

2. What mass of copper was produced?

Analysis and Conclusions

1. Which reactant was limiting? What observations support this? Use the chemical equation for the reaction that occurred in this lab and stoichiometric calculations to support your answer as well.

2. Why were the amounts chosen so this reactant was limiting? What would be a problem with having the other reactant as the limiting reactant?

3. Why was the copper washed with water (step 9 of the procedure)?

4. Why didn't the water added to the copper(II) sulfate have to be measured exactly?

5. What is the formula for the iron-containing compound that is formed when copper(II) sulfate and iron react?

Something Extra

Remove the copper metal and let the solution stand for a few days. What happens? Explain.

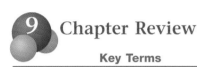

Chapter Review

Key Terms

mole ratio (9.2)
stoichiometry (9.4)
limiting reactant (limiting reagent) (9.6)
theoretical yield (9.8)
percent yield (9.8)

Summary

1. A balanced equation relates the numbers of molecules of reactants and products. It can also be expressed in terms of the numbers of moles of reactants and products.

2. The process of using a chemical equation to calculate the relative amounts of reactants and products involved in the reaction is called doing stoichiometric calculations. To convert between moles of reactants and moles of products, we use mole ratios derived from the balanced equation.

3. Often reactants are not mixed in stoichiometric quantities (they do not "run out" at the same time). In that case, we must use the limiting reactant to calculate the amounts of products formed.

4. The actual yield of a reaction is usually less than its theoretical yield. The actual yield is often expressed as a percentage of the theoretical yield, which is called the percent yield.

Questions and Problems

All exercises with blue numbers have answers in the back of this book.

9.1 Information Given by Chemical Equations

Questions

1. Although *mass* is a property of matter we can conveniently measure in the laboratory, the coefficients of a balanced chemical equation are *not* directly interpreted on the basis of mass. Explain why.

2. Explain why, in the balanced chemical equation $C + O_2 \rightarrow CO_2$, we know that 1 g of C will *not* react exactly with 1 g of O_2.

Problems

3. For each of the following reactions, give the balanced equation for the reaction and state the meaning of

Chapter Review
Assign the students to work individually on the Chapter 9 Review Worksheet at the appropriate level (Basic, Standard, or Challenge). Answers are found in the *Teacher Resources*.

Assessment
Chapter 9 Test is found in the *Teacher Resources*, along with the answers for the test.

 Computerized Test Bank for Chapter 9

Answers to End of Chapter Problems

1. Atoms and molecules react on a particle-by-particle basis. We have to "count" these particles (by weighing) when doing chemical calculations.

2. Balanced chemical equations tell us in what proportions on a mole basis substances combine; as the molar masses of $C(s)$ and $O_2(g)$ are different, 1 g of each reactant cannot represent the same number of moles of each reactant.

3. (a) $2NO(g) + O_2(g) \rightarrow 2NO_2(g)$. Two molecules (or two moles) of nitrogen monoxide gas combine with one molecule (or one mole) of oxygen gas, producing two molecules (or two moles) of nitrogen dioxide gas. (b) $2AgC_2H_3O_2(aq) + CuSO_4(aq) \rightarrow Ag_2SO_4(s) + Cu(C_2H_3O_2)_2(aq)$. Two formula units (or two moles) of silver acetate react with one

(continued)

(continued)

formula unit (or one mole) of copper(II) sulfate, precipitating one formula unit (or one mole) of silver sulfate and leaving one formula unit (or one mole) of copper(II) acetate in solution. (c) $PCl_3(l) + 3H_2O(l) \rightarrow H_3PO_3(l) + 3HCl(g)$. One molecule (or one mole) of phosphorus trichloride reacts with three molecules (or three moles) of water, producing one molecule (or one mole) of phosphorous acid and three molecules (or three moles) of hydrogen chloride. (d) $C_2H_6(g) + Cl_2(g) \rightarrow C_2H_5Cl(g) + HCl(g)$. One molecule (or one mole) of ethane (C_2H_6) reacts with one molecule (or one mole) of chlorine, producing one molecule (or one mole) of chloroethane (C_2H_5Cl) and one molecule (or one mole) of hydrogen chloride.

4. (a) $3MnO_2(s) + 4Al(s) \rightarrow 3Mn(s) + 2Al_2O_3(s)$. Three formula units (or three moles) of manganese(IV) oxide react with four atoms (or four moles) of aluminum, producing three atoms (or three moles) of manganese and two formula units (or two moles) of aluminum oxide. (b) $B_2O_3(s) + 3CaF_2(s) \rightarrow 2BF_3(g) + 3CaO(s)$. One molecule (or one mole) of diboron trioxide reacts with three formula units (or three moles) of calcium fluoride, producing two molecules (or two moles) of boron trifluoride. (c) $3NO_2(g) + H_2O(l) \rightarrow 2HNO_3(aq) + NO(g)$. Three molecules (or three moles) of nitrogen dioxide react with one molecule (or one mole) of water, producing two molecules (or two moles) of nitric acid and one molecule (or one mole) of nitrogen monoxide. (d) $C_6H_6(g) + 3H_2(g) \rightarrow C_6H_{12}(g)$. One molecule (or one mole) of benzene (C_6H_6) reacts with three molecules (or three moles) of hydrogen gas, producing one molecule (or one mole) of cyclohexane (C_6H_{12}).

5. False; the coefficients represent the mole ratio, not the mass ratio.

6. 2 mol O_2/1 mol CH_4; 1 mol CO_2/1 mol CH_4; 2 mol H_2O/1 mol CH_4

7. $2Ag(s) + H_2S(g) \rightarrow Ag_2S(s) + H_2(g)$. For Ag_2S: 1 mol Ag_2S/2 mol Ag;

---

the equation in terms of numbers of *individual molecules* and in terms of *moles* of molecules.
  a. $NO(g) + O_2(g) \rightarrow NO_2(g)$
  b. $AgC_2H_3O_2(aq) + CuSO_4(aq) \rightarrow Ag_2SO_4(s) + Cu(C_2H_3O_2)_2(aq)$
  c. $PCl_3(l) + H_2O(l) \rightarrow H_3PO_3(l) + HCl(g)$
  d. $C_2H_6(g) + Cl_2(g) \rightarrow C_2H_5Cl(g) + HCl(g)$

4. For each of the following reactions, give the balanced chemical equation for the reaction and state the meaning of the equation in terms of *individual molecules* and in terms of *moles* of molecules.
  a. $MnO_2(s) + Al(s) \rightarrow Mn(s) + Al_2O_3(s)$
  b. $B_2O_3(s) + CaF_2(s) \rightarrow BF_3(g) + CaO(s)$
  c. $NO_2(g) + H_2O(l) \rightarrow HNO_3(aq) + NO(g)$
  d. $C_6H_6(g) + H_2(g) \rightarrow C_6H_{12}(g)$

9.2 Mole–Mole Relationships

Questions

5. True or false? For the reaction represented by the chemical equation

$$2H_2O_2(aq) \rightarrow 2H_2O(l) + O_2(g)$$

if 2.0 g of hydrogen peroxide decomposes, then 2.0 g of water and 1.0 g of oxygen gas will be produced.

6. Consider the balanced equation

$$CH_4(g) + 2O_2(g) \rightarrow CO_2(g) + 2H_2O(g)$$

What is the mole ratio that would enable you to calculate the number of moles of oxygen needed to react exactly with a given number of moles of $CH_4(g)$? What mole ratios would you use to calculate how many moles of each product form from a given number of moles of CH_4?

7. Consider the unbalanced chemical equation

$$Ag(s) + H_2S(g) \rightarrow Ag_2S(s) + H_2(g)$$

Balance the equation. Identify the mole ratios that you would use to calculate the number of moles of each product that would form for a given number of moles of silver reacting.

Problems

8. For each of the following *unbalanced* chemical equations, calculate how many *moles of each product* would be produced by the complete conversion of 0.125 mol of the reactant indicated in boldface. State clearly the mole ratio used for the conversion.
  a. **FeO**(s) + C(s) $\rightarrow$ Fe(l) + $CO_2(g)$
  b. $Cl_2(g)$ + **KI**(aq) $\rightarrow$ KCl(aq) + $I_2(s)$
  c. **Na$_2$B$_4$O$_7$**(s) + $H_2SO_4(aq) \rightarrow H_3BO_3(s) + Na_2SO_4(aq)$
  d. **CaC$_2$**(s) + $H_2O(l) \rightarrow Ca(OH)_2(s) + C_2H_2(g)$

---

for H_2: 1 mol H_2/2 mol Ag

8. (a) 0.125 mol Fe; 0.0625 mol CO_2; (b) 0.125 mol KCl; 0.0625 mol I_2; (c) 0.500 mol H_3BO_3; 0.125 mol Na_2SO_4; (d) 0.125 mol $Ca(OH)_2$; 0.125 mol C_2H_2

9. (a) 0.50 mol NH_4Cl (27 g); (b) 0.125 mol CS_2 (9.5 g); 0.25 mol H_2S (8.5 g); (c) 0.50 mol H_3PO_3 (41 g); 1.5 mol HCl (55 g); (d) 0.50 mol $NaHCO_3$ (42 g)

10. (a) 0.469 mol O_2; (b) 0.938 mol Se; (c) 0.625 mol CH_3CHO; (d) 1.25 mol Fe

---

9. For each of the following balanced chemical equations, calculate how many *moles* and how many *grams* of each product would be produced by the complete conversion of 0.50 mol of the reactant indicated in boldface. State clearly the mole ratio used for each conversion.
  a. **NH$_3$**(g) + HCl(g) $\rightarrow$ $NH_4Cl(s)$
  b. $CH_4(g)$ + **4S**(s) $\rightarrow$ $CS_2(l)$ + $2H_2S(g)$
  c. **PCl$_3$**(l) + $3H_2O(l) \rightarrow H_3PO_3(aq) + 3HCl(aq)$
  d. **NaOH**(s) + $CO_2(g) \rightarrow NaHCO_3(s)$

10. For each of the following *unbalanced* equations, indicate how many *moles* of the *first product* are produced if *0.625 mol* of the *second product* forms. State clearly the mole ratio used for each conversion.
  a. $KO_2(s) + H_2O(l) \rightarrow O_2(g) + KOH(s)$
  b. $SeO_2(g) + H_2Se(g) \rightarrow Se(s) + H_2O(g)$
  c. $CH_3CH_2OH(l) + O_2(g) \rightarrow CH_3CHO(aq) + H_2O(l)$
  d. $Fe_2O_3(s) + Al(s) \rightarrow Fe(l) + Al_2O_3(s)$

9.3 Mass Calculations

Questions

11. What quantity serves as the conversion factor between the mass of a sample and the number of moles the sample contains?

12. What does it mean to say that the balanced chemical equation for a reaction describes the *stoichiometry* of the reaction?

Problems

13. Using the average atomic masses given inside the front cover of the text, calculate the number of *moles* of each substance contained in the following *masses*.
  a. 2.01×10^{-2} g of silver
  b. 45.2 mg of ammonium sulfide
  c. 61.7 μg of uranium
  d. 5.23 kg of sulfur dioxide
  e. 272 g of iron(III) nitrate
  f. 12.7 mg of iron(II) sulfate
  g. 6.91×10^3 g of lithium hydroxide

14. Using the average atomic masses given inside the front cover of the text, calculate the *mass in grams* of each of the following samples.
  a. 2.21×10^{-4} mol of calcium carbonate
  b. 2.75 mol of helium
  c. 0.00975 mol of oxygen gas
  d. 7.21×10^{-3} mol of carbon dioxide
  e. 0.835 mol of iron(II) sulfide
  f. 4.01 mol of potassium hydroxide
  g. 0.0219 mol of hydrogen gas

---

282 Chapter 9 Chemical Quantities

---

11. the molar mass of the substance

12. Stoichiometry is the process of using a chemical equation to calculate the relative masses of reactants and products involved in a reaction.

13. (a) 1.86×10^{-4} mol Ag; (b) 6.63×10^{-4} mol $(NH_4)_2S$; (c) 2.59×10^{-7} mol U; (d) 81.6 mol SO_2; (e) 1.12 mol $Fe(NO_3)_3$; (f) 8.36×10^{-5} mol $FeSO_4$; (g) 289 mol LiOH

14. (a) 0.0221 g $CaCO_3$;

(b) 11.0 g He; (c) 0.312 g O_2; (d) 0.317 g CO_2; (e) 73.4 g FeS; (f) 225 g KOH; (g) 0.0442 g H_2

15. (a) 1.03 mol $CuCl_2$; (b) 0.0735 mol $NiCl_2$; (c) 0.240 mol NaOH; (d) 0.250 mol HCl

16. (a) 7.36 mg $FeCO_3$; 11.5 mg K_2SO_4; (b) 30.4 mg $CrCl_3$; 17.1 mg Sn; (c) 21.6 mg Fe_2S_3; (d) 20.3 mg $AgNO_3$; 1.43 mg H_2O; 1.19 mg NO

17. 500. g H_2O

15. For each of the following *unbalanced* equations, calculate how many moles of the *second* reactant would be required to react completely with exactly *25.0 g* of the *first* reactant. Indicate clearly the mole ratio used for each conversion.

   a. $Mg(s) + CuCl_2(aq) \rightarrow MgCl_2(aq) + Cu(s)$
   b. $AgNO_3(aq) + NiCl_2(aq) \rightarrow AgCl(s) + Ni(NO_3)_2(aq)$
   c. $NaHSO_3(aq) + NaOH(aq) \rightarrow Na_2SO_3(aq) + H_2O(l)$
   d. $KHCO_3(aq) + HCl(aq) \rightarrow KCl(aq) + H_2O(l) + CO_2(g)$

16. For each of the following *unbalanced* equations, calculate how many *milligrams of each product* would be produced by complete reaction of *10.0 mg* of the reactant indicated in boldface. Indicate clearly the mole ratio used for the conversion.

   a. **$FeSO_4$**$(aq) + K_2CO_3(aq) \rightarrow FeCO_3(s) + K_2SO_4(aq)$
   b. **Cr**$(s) + SnCl_4(l) \rightarrow CrCl_3(s) + Sn(s)$
   c. $Fe(s) +$ **S_8**$(s) \rightarrow Fe_2S_3(s)$
   d. $Ag(s) +$ **HNO_3**$(aq) \rightarrow AgNO_3(aq) + H_2O(l) + NO(g)$

17. Although mixtures of hydrogen and oxygen are highly explosive, pure elemental hydrogen gas itself burns quietly in air with a pale blue flame, producing water vapor.

$$2H_2(g) + O_2(g) \rightarrow 2H_2O(g)$$

Calculate the mass (in grams) of water vapor produced when 56.0 g of pure hydrogen gas burns in air.

18. Given the information in Problem 17, calculate the mass of oxygen gas that would be necessary to burn 0.0275 mol of hydrogen gas.

19. When elemental carbon is burned in the open atmosphere, with plenty of oxygen gas present, the product is carbon dioxide.

$$C(s) + O_2(g) \rightarrow CO_2(g)$$

However, when the amount of oxygen present during the burning of the carbon is restricted, carbon monoxide is more likely to result.

$$2C(s) + O_2(g) \rightarrow 2CO(g)$$

What mass of each product is expected when a 5.00-g sample of pure carbon is burned under each of these conditions?

20. Although we usually think of substances as "burning" only in oxygen gas, the process of rapid oxidation to produce a flame may also take place in other strongly oxidizing gases. For example, when iron is heated and placed in pure chlorine gas, the iron "burns" according to the following (unbalanced) reaction:

$$Fe(s) + Cl_2(g) \rightarrow FeCl_3(s)$$

How many milligrams of iron(III) chloride result when 15.5 mg of iron is reacted with an excess of chlorine gas?

21. Small quantities of oxygen gas can be generated in the laboratory by the decomposition of hydrogen peroxide. The unbalanced equation for the reaction is

$$H_2O_2(aq) \rightarrow H_2O(l) + O_2(g)$$

Calculate the mass of oxygen produced when 10.00 g of hydrogen peroxide decomposes.

22. A tried-and-true introductory chemistry experiment involves heating finely divided copper metal with sulfur to determine the proportions in which the elements react to form copper(II) sulfide. The experiment works well, because any excess sulfur beyond that required to react with the copper may be simply boiled away from the reaction container.

$$Cu(s) + S(s) \rightarrow CuS(s)$$

If 1.25 g of copper is heated with an excess of sulfur, how many grams of sulfur will react?

23. Ammonium nitrate has been used as a high explosive because it is unstable and decomposes into several gaseous substances. The rapid expansion of the gaseous substances produces the explosive force.

$$NH_4NO_3(s) \rightarrow N_2(g) + O_2(g) + H_2O(g)$$

Calculate the mass of each product gas if 1.25 g of ammonium nitrate reacts.

24. Magnesium metal, which burns in oxygen with an intensely bright white flame, has been used in photographic flash units. The balanced equation for this reaction is

$$2Mg(s) + O_2(g) \rightarrow 2MgO(s)$$

How many grams of $MgO(s)$ are produced by complete reaction of 1.25 g of magnesium metal?

9.4 Mass Calculations Using Scientific Notation

Problems

25. If chlorine gas is bubbled through a potassium iodide solution, elemental iodine is produced. The *unbalanced* equation is

$$Cl_2(g) + KI(aq) \rightarrow I_2(s) + KCl(aq)$$

Calculate the mass of iodine produced when 4.50×10^3 g of chlorine gas is bubbled through an excess amount of potassium iodide solution.

26. Elemental fluorine and chlorine gases are very reactive. For example, they react with each other to form

---

18. 0.44 g O_2

19. 18.3 g CO_2; 11.7 g CO

20. 45.0 mg $FeCl_3$

21. 4.704 g O_2

22. 0.631 g S

23. 0.437 g N_2; 0.250 g O_2; 0.562 g H_2O

24. 2.07 g MgO

25. 1.61×10^4 g I_2

26. 3.26×10^{-3} g Cl_2

27. The propane (C_3H_8) will re-

quire more oxygen.

28. 1.42 g NH_3

29. The limiting reactant is the reactant that limits the amounts of products that can form in a chemical reaction. All reactants are necessary for a reaction to continue.

30. The representation should have four molecules of N_2 and four molecules of NH_3.

31. First use the masses given to calculate the number of moles of each reactant present. Then use

the mole ratio in the balanced equation to decide which reactant is limiting.

32. Once the limiting reactant is consumed, the reaction can no longer proceed and no more product can be formed.

33. A reactant is present in excess if more of that reactant is present than is required to react with the limiting reactant. The limiting reactant, by definition, cannot be present in excess. No.

34. (a) HCl is the limiting reactant; 18.3 g $AlCl_3$; 0.415 g H_2; (b) NaOH is the limiting reactant; 19.9 g Na_2CO_3; 3.38 g H_2O; (c) $Pb(NO_3)_2$ is the limiting reactant; 12.6 g $PbCl_2$; 5.71 g HNO_3; (d) I_2 is the limiting reactant; 19.6 g KI

35. (a) Na is the limiting reactant; 84.9 g $NaNH_2$; (b) $BaCl_2$ is the limiting reactant; 56.0 g $BaSO_4$; (c) NaOH is the limiting reactant; 78.8 g Na_2SO_3; (d) H_2SO_4 is the limiting reactant; 58.2 g $Al_2(SO_4)_3$

36. (a) CO is the limiting reactant; 11.4 mg CH_3OH; (b) I_2 is the limiting reactant; 10.7 mg AlI_3; (c) HBr is the limiting reactant; 12.4 mg $CaBr_2$; 2.23 mg H_2O; (d) H_3PO_4 is the limiting reactant; 15.0 mg $CrPO_4$; 0.309 mg H_2

37. 17.9 g I_2; 7.94 g I_2

38. 1.79 g Fe_2O_3

39. Not enough sodium oxalate has been added to precipitate all of the calcium ions in the sample.

40. The actual yield is the quantity of product actually isolated from the reaction vessel. The theoretical yield represents the maximum quantity of product possible if the reaction proceeds to completion. The percent yield represents the ratio of actual yield to theoretical yield.

41. If the reaction occurs in a solvent, the product may have a substantial solubility in the solvent; the reaction may come to equilibrium before the full yield of product is achieved (see Chapter 17); loss of product may occur to error.

42. 85.4%

43. 25.2 g $Na_2S_2O_3 \cdot 5H_2O$; 20.9% yield

44. $2LiOH(s) + CO_2(g) \rightarrow Li_2CO_3(s) + H_2O(g)$. 142 g of CO_2 can be ultimately absorbed; 102 g is 71.8% of the cannister's capacity.

45. 205 g XeF_4; 70.7% yield

46. 82.6%

47. 28.6 g $NaHCO_3$

48. 8.26 g FeS

49. $C_6H_{12}O_6(s) + 6O_2(g) \rightarrow 6CO_2(g) + 6H_2O(g)$; 1.47 g CO_2

50. 0.520 g $AgNO_3$ required, 0.439 g AgCl produced

51. for O_2, 5 mol O_2/1 mol C_3H_8; for CO_2, 3 mol CO_2/1 mol C_3H_8; for H_2O, 4 mol H_2O/1 mol C_3H_8

52. (a) 0.50 mol H_2O, 0.25 mol O_2; (b) 0.50 mol KCl, 0.75 mol O_2; (c) 0.50 mol $AlCl_3$, 0.75 mol H_2; (d) 1.5 mol CO_2, 2.0 mol H_2O

53. (a) 0.0587 mol NH_4Cl; $\frac{1NH_4Cl}{1NH_3}$ (b) 0.0178 mol $CaCO_3$; $\frac{1CaCO_3}{1CaO}$ (c) 0.0217 mol Na_2O; $\frac{2Na_2O}{4Na}$ (d) 0.0323 mol PCl_3 $\frac{2PCl_3}{2P}$

54. 0.667 g O_2

55. 4.6×10^2 g O_2

56. (a) 22.9 g CO_2; (b) 46.9 g NO; (c) 16.2 g NaCl; (d) 30.4 g NH_3

57. 0.624 mol N_2, 17.5 g N_2; 1.25 mol H_2O, 22.5 g H_2O

58. 5.0 g

59. $X_4 + 12HCl \rightarrow 4XCl_3 + 6H_2$; X is phosphorus

60. X = 20 g/mol; Z = 40 g/mol

61. 54.4 g H_3PO_4

---

chlorine monofluoride.

$$Cl_2(g) + F_2(g) \rightarrow 2ClF(g)$$

Calculate the mass of chlorine gas required to produce 5.00×10^{-3} g of chlorine monofluoride given an excess of fluorine gas.

9.5 Mass Calculations: Comparing Two Reactions

Problems

27. Both propane (C_3H_8) and butane (C_4H_{10}) react with oxygen gas to form carbon dioxide and water. If you have equal masses of each, which will require a greater mass of oxygen to react?

28. Methane (CH_4) reacts with oxygen in the air to produce carbon dioxide and water. Ammonia (NH_3) reacts with oxygen in the air to produce nitrogen monoxide and water. What mass of ammonia is needed to react with excess oxygen to produce the same amount of water as 1.00 g of methane reacting with excess oxygen?

9.6 The Concept of Limiting Reactants

Questions

29. What is the *limiting reactant* for a process? Why does a reaction stop when the limiting reactant is consumed, even though there may be plenty of the other reactants present?

30. Nitrogen (N_2) and hydrogen (H_2) react to form ammonia (NH_3). Consider the mixture of N_2 (⬤⬤) and H_2 (◯◯) in a closed container as illustrated below:

Assuming the reaction goes to completion, draw a representation of the product mixture. Explain how you arrived at this representation.

9.7 Calculations Involving a Limiting Reactant

Questions

31. Explain how one determines which reactant in a process is the limiting reactant. Does this depend only on the masses of the reactant present? Is the mole ratio in which the reactants combine involved?

32. How does the maximum *yield* of products for a reaction depend on the limiting reactant?

33. What does it mean to say a reactant is present "in excess" in a process? Can the *limiting reactant* be present in excess? Does the presence of an excess of a reactant affect the mass of products expected for a reaction?

Problems

34. For each of the following *unbalanced* chemical equations, suppose that exactly 15.0 g of *each* reactant is taken. Determine which reactant is limiting, and calculate what mass of each product is expected. (Assume that the limiting reactant is completely consumed.)

  a. $Al(s) + HCl(aq) \rightarrow AlCl_3(aq) + H_2(g)$

  b. $NaOH(aq) + CO_2(g) \rightarrow Na_2CO_3(aq) + H_2O(l)$

  c. $Pb(NO_3)_2(aq) + HCl(aq) \rightarrow PbCl_2(s) + HNO_3(aq)$

  d. $K(s) + I_2(s) \rightarrow KI(s)$

35. For each of the following *unbalanced* chemical equations, suppose that exactly 50.0 g of *each* reactant is taken. Determine which reactant is limiting, and calculate what mass of the product in boldface is expected. (Assume that the limiting reactant is completely consumed.)

  a. $NH_3(g) + Na(s) \rightarrow \mathbf{NaNH_2}(s) + H_2(g)$

  b. $BaCl_2(aq) + Na_2SO_4(aq) \rightarrow \mathbf{BaSO_4}(s) + H_2O(aq)$

  c. $SO_2(g) + NaOH(s) \rightarrow \mathbf{Na_2SO_3}(s) + H_2O(l)$

  d. $Al(s) + H_2SO_4(aq) \rightarrow \mathbf{Al_2(SO_4)_3}(s) + H_2(g)$

36. For each of the following *unbalanced* chemical equations, suppose 10.0 mg of *each* reactant is taken. Show by calculation which reactant is limiting. Calculate the mass of each product that is expected.

  a. $CO(g) + H_2(g) \rightarrow CH_3OH(l)$

  b. $Al(s) + I_2(s) \rightarrow AlI_3(s)$

  c. $Ca(OH)_2(aq) + HBr(aq) \rightarrow CaBr_2(aq) + H_2O(l)$

  d. $Cr(s) + H_3PO_4(aq) \rightarrow CrPO_4(s) + H_2(g)$

37. The more reactive halogen elements are able to replace the less reactive halogens from their compounds.

$$Cl_2(g) + NaI(aq) \rightarrow NaCl(aq) + I_2(s)$$
$$Br_2(l) + NaI(aq) \rightarrow NaBr(aq) + I_2(s)$$

Suppose separate solutions, each containing 25.0 g of NaI, are available. If 5.00 g of Cl_2 gas is bubbled into one NaI solution, and 5.00 g of liquid bromine is added to the other, calculate the number of grams of elemental iodine produced in each case.

38. If steel wool (iron) is heated until it glows and is placed in a bottle containing pure oxygen, the iron reacts spectacularly to produce iron(III) oxide.

$$Fe(s) + O_2(g) \rightarrow Fe_2O_3(s)$$

If 1.25 g of iron is heated and placed in a bottle containing 0.0204 mol of oxygen gas, what mass of iron(III) oxide is produced?

39. One method for chemical analysis involves finding some reagent that will precipitate the species of interest. The mass of the precipitate is then used to determine what mass of the species of interest was present in the original sample. For example, calcium ion can be precipitated from solution by addition of sodium oxalate. The balanced equation is

$$Ca^{2+}(aq) + Na_2C_2O_4(aq) \rightarrow CaC_2O_4(s) + 2Na^+(aq)$$

Suppose a solution is known to contain approximately 15 g of calcium ion. Show by calculation whether the addition of a solution containing 15 g of sodium oxalate will precipitate all of the calcium from the sample.

9.8 Percent Yield

Questions

40. What is the *actual yield* of a reaction? What is the *percent yield* of a reaction? How do the actual yield and the percent yield differ from the theoretical yield?

41. The text explains that one reason why the actual yield for a reaction may be less than the theoretical yield is side reactions. Suggest some other reasons why the percent yield for a reaction might not be 100%.

42. According to his prelaboratory theoretical yield calculations, a student's experiment should have produced 1.44 g of magnesium oxide. When he weighed his product after reaction, only 1.23 g of magnesium oxide was present. What is the student's percent yield?

Problems

43. The compound sodium thiosulfate pentahydrate, $Na_2S_2O_3 \cdot 5H_2O$, is important commercially to the photography business as "hypo," because it has the ability to dissolve unreacted silver salts from photographic film during development. Sodium thiosulfate pentahydrate can be produced by boiling elemental sulfur in an aqueous solution of sodium sulfite.

$$S_8(s) + Na_2SO_3(aq) + H_2O(l) \rightarrow Na_2S_2O_3 \cdot 5H_2O(s)$$
$$\text{(unbalanced)}$$

What is the theoretical yield of sodium thiosulfate pentahydrate when 3.25 g of sulfur is boiled with 13.1 g of sodium sulfite? Sodium thiosulfate pentahydrate is very soluble in water. What is the percent yield of the synthesis if a student doing this experiment is able to isolate (collect) only 5.26 g of the product?

44. Alkali metal hydroxides are sometimes used to "scrub" excess carbon dioxide from the air in closed spaces (such as submarines and spacecraft). For example, lithium hydroxide reacts with carbon dioxide according to the unbalanced chemical equation

$$LiOH(s) + CO_2(g) \rightarrow Li_2CO_3(s) + H_2O(g)$$

Suppose a lithium hydroxide cannister contains 155 g of $LiOH(s)$. What mass of $CO_2(g)$ will the cannister be able to absorb? If it is found that after 24 hours of use the cannister has absorbed 102 g of carbon dioxide, what percentage of its capacity has been reached?

45. Although they were formerly called the inert gases, at least the heavier elements of Group 8 do form relatively stable compounds. For example, xenon combines directly with elemental fluorine at elevated temperatures in the presence of a nickel catalyst.

$$Xe(g) + 2F_2(g) \rightarrow XeF_4(s)$$

What is the theoretical mass of xenon tetrafluoride that should form when 130. g of xenon is reacted with 100. g of F_2? What is the percent yield if only 145 g of XeF_4 is actually isolated?

46. Anhydrous calcium chloride, $CaCl_2$, is frequently used in the laboratory as a drying agent for solvents, because it absorbs 6 mol of water molecules for every mole of $CaCl_2$ used (forming a stable solid hydrated salt, $CaCl_2 \cdot 6H_2O$). Calcium chloride is typically prepared by treating calcium carbonate with hydrogen chloride gas.

$$CaCO_3(s) + 2HCl(g) \rightarrow CaCl_2(s) + CO_2(g) + H_2O(g)$$

A large amount of heat is generated by this reaction, so the water produced from the reaction is usually driven off as steam. Some liquid water may remain, however, and it may dissolve some of the desired calcium chloride. What is the percent yield if 155 g of calcium carbonate is treated with 250. g of anhydrous hydrogen chloride and only 142 g of $CaCl_2$ is obtained?

Critical Thinking

47. One process for the commercial production of baking soda (sodium hydrogen carbonate) involves the following reaction, in which the carbon dioxide is used in its solid form ("dry ice") both to serve as a source of reactant and to cool the reaction system to a temperature low enough for the sodium hydrogen carbonate to precipitate:

$$NaCl(aq) + NH_3(aq) + H_2O(l) + CO_2(s) \rightarrow$$
$$NH_4Cl(aq) + NaHCO_3(s)$$

Because they are relatively cheap, sodium chloride

and water are typically present in excess. What is the expected yield of $NaHCO_3$ when one performs such a synthesis using 10.0 g of ammonia and 15.0 g of dry ice, with an excess of NaCl and water?

48. A favorite demonstration among chemistry teachers, performed to show that the properties of a compound differ from those of its constituent elements, involves iron filings and powdered sulfur. If the teacher takes samples of iron and sulfur and just mixes them together, the two elements can be separated from one another with a magnet (iron is attracted to a magnet, sulfur is not). If the teacher then combines and *heats* the mixture of iron and sulfur, a reaction takes place and the elements combine to form iron(II) sulfide (which is not attracted by a magnet).

$$Fe(s) + S(s) \rightarrow FeS(s)$$

Suppose 5.25 g of iron filings is combined with 12.7 g of sulfur. What is the theoretical yield of iron(II) sulfide?

49. When the sugar glucose, $C_6H_{12}O_6$, is burned in air, carbon dioxide and water vapor are produced. Write the balanced chemical equation for this process, and calculate the theoretical yield of carbon dioxide when 1.00 g of glucose is burned completely.

50. The traditional method of analyzing the amount of chloride ion present in a sample was to dissolve the sample in water and then slowly add a solution of silver nitrate. Silver chloride is very insoluble in water, and by adding a slight excess of silver nitrate, it is possible effectively to remove all chloride ion from the sample.

$$Ag^+(aq) + Cl^-(aq) \rightarrow AgCl(s)$$

Suppose a 1.054-g sample is known to contain 10.3% chloride ion by mass. What mass of silver nitrate must be used to completely precipitate the chloride ion from the sample? What mass of silver chloride will be obtained?

51. Consider the balanced equation

$$C_3H_8(g) + 5O_2(g) \rightarrow 3CO_2(g) + 4H_2O(g)$$

What mole ratio enables you to calculate the number of moles of oxygen needed to react exactly with a given number of moles of $C_3H_8(g)$? What mole ratios enable you to calculate how many moles of each product form from a given number of moles of C_3H_8?

52. For each of the following balanced reactions, calculate how many *moles of each product* would be produced by complete conversion of *0.50 mol* of the reactant indicated in boldface. Indicate clearly the mole ratio used for the conversion.
   a. $\mathbf{2H_2O_2}(l) \rightarrow 2H_2O(l) + O_2(g)$
   b. $\mathbf{2KClO_3}(s) \rightarrow 2KCl(s) + 3O_2(g)$

   c. $\mathbf{2Al}(s) + 6HCl(aq) \rightarrow 2AlCl_3(aq) + 3H_2(g)$
   d. $\mathbf{C_3H_8}(g) + 5O_2(g) \rightarrow 3CO_2(g) + 4H_2O(g)$

53. For each of the following balanced equations, indicate how many *moles of the product* could be produced by complete reaction of *1.00 g* of the reactant indicated in boldface. Indicate clearly the mole ratio used for the conversion.
   a. $\mathbf{NH_3}(g) + HCl(g) \rightarrow NH_4Cl(s)$
   b. $\mathbf{CaO}(s) + CO_2(g) \rightarrow CaCO_3(s)$
   c. $\mathbf{4Na}(s) + O_2(g) \rightarrow 2Na_2O(s)$
   d. $\mathbf{2P}(s) + 3Cl_2(g) \rightarrow 2PCl_3(l)$

54. If sodium peroxide is added to water, elemental oxygen gas is generated:

$$Na_2O_2(s) + H_2O(l) \rightarrow NaOH(aq) + O_2(g)$$

Suppose 3.25 g of sodium peroxide is added to a large excess of water. What mass of oxygen gas will be produced?

55. The gaseous hydrocarbon acetylene, C_2H_2, is used in welders' torches because of the large amount of heat released when acetylene burns with oxygen.

$$2C_2H_2(g) + 5O_2(g) \rightarrow 4CO_2(g) + 2H_2O(g)$$

How many grams of oxygen gas are needed for the complete combustion of 150 g of acetylene?

56. For each of the following *unbalanced* chemical equations, suppose 25.0 g of each reactant is taken. Show by calculation which reactant is limiting. Calculate the theoretical yield in grams of the product in boldface.
   a. $C_2H_5OH(l) + O_2(g) \rightarrow \mathbf{CO_2}(g) + H_2O(l)$
   b. $N_2(g) + O_2(g) \rightarrow \mathbf{NO}(g)$
   c. $NaClO_2(aq) + Cl_2(g) \rightarrow ClO_2(g) + \mathbf{NaCl}(aq)$
   d. $H_2(g) + N_2(g) \rightarrow \mathbf{NH_3}(g)$

57. Hydrazine, N_2H_4, emits a large quantity of energy when it reacts with oxygen, which has led to hydrazine's use as a fuel for rockets:

$$N_2H_4(l) + O_2(g) \rightarrow N_2(g) + 2H_2O(g)$$

How many moles of each of the gaseous products are produced when 20.0 g of pure hydrazine is ignited in the presence of 20.0 g of pure oxygen? How many grams of each product are produced?

58. Before going to lab, a student read in her lab manual that the percent yield for a difficult reaction to be studied was likely to be only 40.% of the theoretical yield. The student's prelab stoichiometric calculations predict that the theoretical yield should be 12.5 g. What is the student's actual yield likely to be?

59. When a certain element whose formula is X_4 combines with HCl, the results are XCl_3 and hydrogen gas. Write a balanced equation for the reaction. When

24.0 g of hydrogen gas results from such a reaction, it is noted that 248 g of X_4 are consumed. Identify element X.

60. When a 5.00-g sample of element X reacts completely with a 15.0-g sample of element Y, compound XY is formed. When a 3.00-g sample of element X reacts with an 18.0-g sample of element Z, compound XZ_3 is formed. The molar mass of Y is 60.0 g/mol. Find the molar masses of X and Z.

61. Phosphoric acid, H_3PO_4, can be synthesized from phosphorus, oxygen, and water according to the following reactions:

$$P_4(s) + O_2(g) \rightarrow P_4O_{10}(s)$$

$$P_4O_{10}(s) + H_2O(l) \rightarrow H_3PO_4(l)$$

If you start with 20.0 g of phosphorus, 30.0 g of oxygen gas, and 15.0 g of water, what is the maximum mass of phosphoric acid that can be formed?

10 Energy

	Section	Text Features & Components	Labs, Demonstrations & Activities
Teaching Segment 10A **1 block** **pp. 289–293**	10.1 The Nature of Energy	**LP** Lesson Plans (Sec 10.1–10.3)	**TE** Teaching Support Demonstration *pp. 289–291* **TE** Mini Demo *pp. 289–290*
	10.2 Temperature and Heat	**SE** Top Ten Lowest Temperature Recorded by State *p. 292*	
	10.3 Exothermic and Endothermic Processes		**TE** Teaching Support: Demonstration *pp. 292–293*
Teaching Segment 10B **1 block** **pp. 293–301**	10.4 Thermodynamics	**LP** Lesson Plans (Sec 10.4–10.5)	
	10.5 Measuring Energy Changes	**SE** Chemical Impact: Nature Has Hot Plants *p. 297* **SE** Chemical Impact: Firewalking: Magic or Science *p. 301*	**TE** Teaching Support: Demonstration *pp. 294, 296–297, 300–301* **TE** Mini Demo *p. 297* **LM** Experiment 40: Energy Value of Nuts Lab Manual Report Sheets Teacher's Lab Guide
Teaching Segment 10C **3 blocks** **pp. 301–305**	10.6 Thermochemistry **2** (Enthalpy)	**LP** Lesson Plans (Sec 10.6–10.7) **SE** Celebrity Chemical: Methane *p. 303*	**SE** Chemistry in the Laboratory: Which is Your Metal *pp. 316–317* **TE** Mini Demo *p. 302* **LM** Experiment 41–43 Lab Manual Report Sheets Teacher's Lab Guide
	10.7 Hess's Law **2**	**TE** Teaching Support: Background Information *p. 304*	**LM** Experiment 44–45 Lab Manual Report Sheets Teacher's Lab Guide
	continued on next page		

continued on next page

Key **SE** Student Edition **TE** Teacher Edition **RP** Teacher Resource Package **LM** Lab Materials
LP Lesson Plans **AR** Additional Resources ● Florida Specific

Chapter Planning Guide

All Learners	Review & Assessment	Standards
(TE) Active Learning *p. 289* (TE) Teaching Tips *p. 289* (AR) Less Proficient Students *p. 18*	(SE) What if . . . *p. 290* (SE) Key Terms *p. 317* (SE) Questions and Problems *p. 318*	(TE) NSES A1, A2, B5, B6, C5 (SSS) SC.A.1.4.3, SC.B.1.4.7
(TE) Using the Top Ten *p. 292* (animation) Animation: Kinetic–Molecular Theory/Heat Theory (AR) Less Proficient Students *p. 18*	(SE) Key Terms *p. 317* (SE) Questions and Problems *p. 318*	
(video) Chemistry in Motion (9), (11), (18), (21) (TE) Teaching Tips *p. 292* (RP) Team Learning Worksheets (Section 10.1–10.3) *pp. 45–46* (AR) Less Proficient Students *p. 18*	(SE) Focus Questions (Sec 10. 1–10.3) *p. 293* (SE) Key Terms *p. 317* (SE) Questions and Problems *p. 318*	
(TE) Active Learning *p. 293* (TE) Teaching Tips *p. 294* (AR) Less Proficient Students *p. 18*	(SE) Key Terms *p. 317* (SE) Questions and Problems *pp. 318–319*	(TE) NSES A1, A2, B5, B6, C5 (SSS) SC.B.1.4.6, SC.B.1.4.7
(TE) Teaching Tips *pp. 294–295* (RP) Classroom Activities and Projects *pp. 17–19* (RP) Team Learning Worksheets (Sec 10.4–10.5) *pp. 47–48* (AR) Less Proficient Students *p. 18*	(TE) Additional Examples *pp. 295, 298–299* (SE) Self Check *pp. 295–296, 299–300* (SE) Focus Questions (Sec 10.4–10.5) *p. 300* (SE) Key Terms *p. 317* (SE) Questions and Problems *p. 319*	
(TE) Active Learning *p. 301* (transparency) Transparency: Figure 10.6 *p. 302* (video) Video: Coffee Cup Calorimeter Measuring Heat of Neutralization *p. 302* (AR) Less Proficient Students *p. 18*	(TE) Additional Examples *p. 302* (SE) Self Check *p. 302* (SE) Key Terms *p. 317* (SE) Questions and Problems *p. 319*	(TE) NSES A1, A2, B5, B6, C6, D2, F3, F4, F6 (SSS) SC.B.1.4.7
(TE) Teaching Tips *p. 303* (animation) Animation: Hess's Law *p. 304* (RP) Team Learning Worksheets (Sec 10.6–10.7) *pp. 49–50* (AR) Less Proficient Students *p. 19*	(TE) Additional Examples *p. 305* (SE) Self Check *p. 305* (SE) Focus Questions (Sec 10.6–10.7) *p. 305* (SE) Key Terms *p. 317* (SE) Questions and Problems *p. 319*	

10 Energy

Section	Text Features & Components	Labs, Demonstrations & Activities
Teaching Segment 10D 0.5 block pp. 306–315 10.8 **Quality Versus Quantity of Energy**	**LP** Lesson Plans (Sec 10.8–10.10)	
10.9 **Energy and Our World**	**SE** Chemical Impact: Veggie Gasoline *p. 311*	**TE** Additional Activity *p. 307*
10.10 **Energy as a Driving Force**		**SE** Chemistry in Action: Distribution of Wealth *pp. 314–315*

Key

SE Student Edition
TE Teacher Edition
RP Teacher Resource Package
LM Lab Materials
LP Lesson Plans
AR Additional Resources
 Florida Specific

Technology and Media

 Transparencies
Figure 10.6, 10.7, 10.8

PowerPoint Slides

 Animation Kinetic-Molecular Theory/Heat Transfer

 Video Coffee–Cup Calorimeter • Fireworks
Chemistry in Motion
(9) Ammonium Chloride . . . • (11) Thermite Reactions • (18) Dry Ice and Magnesium • (21) Sugar, . . . Sulfuric Acid • Hess's Law

eEdition CD-ROM
Easy Planner CD-ROM
English Summaries CD
Spanish Summaries CD

 Web Site classzone.com
McDougal Littell Test Generator

Chapter Planning Guide

All Learners	Review & Assessment	Standards
TE Active Learning *p. 306* **AR** Less Proficient Students *p. 19*	**SE** Questions and Problems *p. 320*	**TE** NSES A1, A2, B5, B6, E1, E2, F1, F3, F4, F6 **SSS** SC.H.1.4.1, SC.H.1.4.2, SC.A.1.4.3, SC.B.1.4.1, SC.G.2.4.1, SC.B.1.4.5, SC.H.3.4.6
TE Teaching Tip *p. 307* **Transparency:** Figure 10.7, 10.8 **AR** Less Proficient Students *p. 19*	**SE** What if . . . *p. 310* **SE** Key Terms *p. 317* **SE** Questions and Problems *p. 320*	
RP Classroom Activities and Projects *pp. 21– 24* **RP** Team Learning Worksheets (Sec 10.8–10.10) *pp. 51–52* **AR** Less Proficient Students *p. 19*	**SE** What if . . . *p. 315* **SE** Focus Questions (Sec 10.8–10.10) *p. 315* **SE** Key Terms *p. 317* **SE** Questions and Problems *p. 320*	

Chapter Materials

TE Reading Strategy **AR** English/Spanish Summaries *pp. 14–15* **AR** Challenge Projects/Problems *pp. 18–19* **AR** Less Proficient Students *p. 19* English Summary Audio Spanish Summary Audio **RP** Chapter Review Worksheets (Basic, Review, Challenge)	**SE** Chapter Summary *pp. 317–318* **SE** Critical Thinking *pp. 320–321* **RP** Solutions Guide **RP** Chapter Tests **RP** Test Bank McDougal Littell Test Generator **AR** Standardized Test Practice FCAT Test 5

288d

Integrating Reading Strategies and Chemistry Concepts

Chapter 10: Vocabulary

Advise the students that learning vocabulary is a crucial part of any subject, but it is especially important in the sciences. Explain that scientific terminology is course-specific; for example most of the key words in this text apply to chemistry and are not likely to be found in other subject areas, or even in other science courses. Tell the students that they will need to spend some time learning the new vocabulary.

Point out that vocabulary words are usually presented in boldface type, italics, or in a color different than the standard text. Encourage the students to review the vocabulary words in a section before reading that section. This review will reduce frustration and increase their reading comprehension.

Vocabulary words (presented in boldface blue text) are usually preceded or followed by a definition. If the students cannot define a vocabulary word by interpreting context clues, refer them to the glossary in the back of the textbook.

Vocabulary Review

Have the students turn to page 317 and look at the first portion of the **Chapter Review**. Ask the students what they notice about these terms. [They are the same as the vocabulary terms found throughout the chapter.] Point out that the number of the section in which the word is first introduced appears after each word. This reference allows students to locate the words more easily when they are reviewing.

---

10 Chapter Review

Key Terms

energy (10.1)	internal energy (10.4)
law of conservation of energy (10.1)	calorie (10.5)
	joule (10.5)
potential energy (10.1)	specific heat capacity (10.5)
kinetic energy (10.1)	
work (10.1)	enthalpy (10.6)
state function (10.1)	calorimeter (10.6)
temperature (10.2)	Hess's law (10.7)
heat (10.2)	fossil fuels (10.9)
system (10.3)	petroleum (10.9)
surroundings (10.3)	natural gas (10.9)
exothermic (10.3)	coal (10.9)
endothermic (10.3)	greenhouse effect (10.9)
thermodynamics (10.4)	energy spread (10.10)
first law of thermodynamics (10.4)	matter spread (10.10)

Emphasize that understanding the vocabulary is essential to thorough comprehension of the material. Let the students know that this chapter contains 28 new terms, and although it may take a significant amount of time to learn them all, it will be worth their effort.

How to Learn Vocabulary

Tell the students that there are several different strategies for learning vocabulary. Most of these strategies involve memorization. Emphasize that different people memorize material in different ways and that no one method is necessarily best. Point out that it may take a while for each student to discover which method works best and that they may want to try each of the methods described below before settling on any particular one. Keep in mind that some of the students may already have a memorization technique that is conducive to their learning style.

Method 1: Flashcards

Explain that writing information stores the material in the brain in a different way than only reading the information does. Encourage the students to write new vocabulary words on index cards. For each card, have the students write one vocabulary word on the front and its definition on the back. Advise the students to include the chapter and section number on each card as well.

Encourage the students to review all of the vocabulary cards for a given chapter each time they add new cards. Before a quiz or test, advise the students to study their vocabulary words by looking at the word on the front of the card, saying the definition aloud, and then flipping the card over to check accuracy.

Method 2: Notebook Vocabulary Pages

Some students prefer to keep all of their notes in a notebook. Encourage these students to keep a separate section for vocabulary. Point out that writing the words in a different color from the rest of their notes will allow them to find a particular word more easily.

Also encourage the students to write the vocabulary word to the left of the page margin and the definitions to the right. This practice will simplify studying for quizzes and tests. Tell the students to cover the right side of the page, recite a definition, and then uncover the definition in their notes to check their accuracy.

Vocabulary Page	
Word (Section Reference)	**Definition**
energy (10.1)	the capacity to do work or to cause the flow of heat
potential energy (10.1)	energy due to position or composition
kinetic energy (10.1)	energy due to the motion of an object

Chapter 10

Overview

In this Chapter our goals are for the students to:

- Understand the general properties of energy
- Understand the concepts of temperature and heat
- Consider the direction of energy flow as heat
- Understand how energy flow affects internal energy
- Understand how heat is measured
- Consider the heat (enthalpy) of chemical reactions
- Understand Hess's Law
- See how the quality of energy changes as it is used
- Consider the energy resources of our world
- Understand energy as a driving force for natural processes

10 Energy

Solar eruptions are large bursts of energy from the surface of the sun.

288

E nergy is the essence of our very existence as individuals and as a society. The food that we eat furnishes the energy to live, work, and play, just as the coal and oil consumed by manufacturing and transportation systems power our modern industrialized civilization.

Huge quantities of carbon-based fossil fuels have been available for the taking. This abundance of fuels has led to a world society with a voracious appetite for energy, consuming millions of barrels of petroleum every day. We are now dangerously dependent on the dwindling supplies of oil, and this dependence is an important source of tension among nations in today's world. In an incredibly short time we have moved from a period of ample and cheap supplies of petroleum to one of high prices and uncertain supplies. If our present standard of living is to be maintained, we must find alternatives to petroleum. To do this, we need to know the relationship between chemistry and energy, which we explore in this chapter.

10.1 The Nature of Energy

Objective: *To understand the general properties of energy.*

A lthough energy is a familiar concept, it is difficult to define precisely. For our purposes we will define **energy** as *the ability to do work or produce heat.* We will define these terms below.

Energy can be classified as either potential or kinetic energy. **Potential energy** is energy due to position or composition. For example, water behind a dam has potential energy that can be converted to work when the water flows down through turbines, thereby creating electricity. Attractive and repulsive forces also lead to potential energy. The energy released when gasoline is burned results from differences in attractive forces between the nuclei and electrons in the reactants and products. The **kinetic energy** of an object is energy due to the motion of the object and depends on the mass of the object *m* and its velocity *v*: $KE = \frac{1}{2}mv^2$.

One of the most important characteristics of energy is that it is conserved. The **law of conservation of energy** states *that energy can be converted from one form to another but can be neither created nor destroyed.* That is, the energy of the universe is constant.

Although the energy of the universe is constant, it can be converted from one form to another. Consider the two balls in **Figure 10.1a.** Ball A, because of its initially higher position, has more potential energy than ball B.

When ball A is released, it moves down the hill and strikes ball B. Eventually, the arrangement shown in **Figure 10.1b** is achieved. What has happened in going from the initial to the final arrangement? The potential energy of A has decreased because its position was lowered. However, this energy cannot disappear. Where is the energy lost by A?

—Held in place

(a) Initial

(b) Final

Figure 10.1
(a) In the initial positions, ball A has a higher potential energy than ball B. (b) After A has rolled down the hill, the potential energy lost by A has been converted to random motions of the components of the hill (frictional heating) and to an increase in the potential energy of B.

10.1 The Nature of Energy **289**

Chapter 10 Energy **289**

(which it has as it falls). As the object gets closer to the ground, the potential energy decreases and the kinetic energy increases. The object transfers this energy to the ground.

One outcome is that perpetual motion machines could be developed (that is, we could get "energy from nowhere"). This may seem like a good thing, but it could lead to tragic heat or cold spells. If energy is not conserved, we could "lose" it all.

TEACHING TIP

Another example of a state function is displacement. For example, if two students go from the chemistry room to the school cafeteria, they are both the same distance away from you. They may have taken different routes—one student may have traveled a greater distance—but they end up with the same displacement from you.

Initially, the potential energy of A is changed to kinetic energy as the ball rolls down the hill. Part of this energy is transferred to B, causing it to be raised to a higher final position. Thus the potential energy of B has been increased, which means that **work** (force acting over a distance) has been performed on B. Because the final position of B is lower than the original position of A, however, some of the energy is still unaccounted for. Both balls in their final positions are at rest, so the missing energy cannot be attributed to their motions. What has happened to the remaining energy?

The answer lies in the interaction between the hill's surface and the ball. As ball A rolls down the hill, some of its kinetic energy is transferred to the surface of the hill as heat. This transfer of energy is called *frictional heating*. The temperature of the hill increases very slightly as the ball rolls down. Thus the energy stored in A in its original position (potential energy) is distributed to B through work and to the surface of the hill by heat.

Imagine that we perform this same experiment several times, varying the surface of the hill from very smooth to very rough. In rolling to the bottom of the hill (see Figure 10.1), A always loses the same amount of energy because its position always changes by exactly the same amount. The way that this energy transfer is divided between work and heat, however, depends on the specific conditions—the *pathway*. For example, the surface of the hill might be so rough that the energy of A is expended completely through frictional heating: A is moving so slowly when it hits B that it cannot move B to the next level. In this case, no work is done. Regardless of the condition of the hill's surface, the *total energy* transferred will be constant, although the amounts of heat and work will differ. Energy change is independent of the pathway, whereas work and heat are both dependent on the pathway.

This brings us to a very important idea, the state function. A **state function** is a property of the system that changes independently of its pathway. Let's consider a nonchemical example. Suppose you are traveling from Chicago to Denver. Which of the following are state functions?

Distance traveled

Change in elevation

Because the distance traveled depends on the route taken (that is, the *pathway* between Chicago and Denver), it is *not* a state function. On the other hand, the change in elevation depends only on the difference between Denver's elevation (5280 ft) and Chicago's elevation (580 ft). The change in elevation is always 5280 ft − 580 ft = 4700 ft; it does not depend on the route taken between the two cities.

We can also learn about state functions from the example illustrated in Figure 10.1. Because ball A always goes from its initial position on the hill to the bottom of the hill, its energy change is always the same, regardless of whether the hill is smooth or bumpy. This energy is a state function—a given change in energy is independent of the pathway of the process. In contrast, work and heat are *not* state functions. For a given change in the position of A, a smooth hill produces more work and less heat than a rough hill does. That is, for a given change in the position of A, the change in energy is always the same (state function) but the way the resulting energy is distributed as heat or work depends on the nature of the hill's surface (heat and work are not state functions).

same manner to make a longer demonstration.

Presentation Discuss different forms of energy with the students. We most often "see" energy changes in chemical reactions as heat. Light is another form of energy that is observed in some chemical reactions. Show an unactivated lightstick, noting the noise that the small vial of hydrogen peroxide makes when the vial is shaken gently. Bend the lightstick to break the vial of hydrogen peroxide and observe the production of light from the chemical reaction. Pass the lighted stick around the class to have the students observe whether heat is also a product of the reaction. Dim the lights and pour the contents of the previously dissected lightstick into the funnel and follow it with the hydrogen peroxide solution from the film cannister. The solution should begin to glow as it passes through the tubing.

Teaching Notes More discussion of chemiluminescence can be accomplished after the students have an understanding of the role that electrons play in atoms. This demonstration can be done again in Chapter 11 with a more detailed explanation of the source of the energy.

10.2 Temperature and Heat

Objective: *To understand the concepts of temperature and heat.*

Figure 10.2
Equal masses of hot water and cold water separated by a thin metal wall in an insulated box.

What does the temperature of a substance tell us about that substance? Put another way, how is warm water different from cold water? The answer lies in the motions of the water molecules. **Temperature** is a *measure of the random motions of the components of a substance.* That is, the H_2O molecules in warm water are moving around more rapidly than the H_2O molecules in cold water.

Consider an experiment in which we place 1.00 kg of hot water (90. °C) next to 1.00 kg of cold water (10. °C) in an insulated box. The water samples are separated from each other by a thin metal plate (see **Figure 10.2**). You already know what will happen: the hot water will cool down and the cold water will warm up.

Assuming that no energy is lost to the air, can we determine the final temperature of the two samples of water? Let's consider how to think about this problem.

First picture what is happening. Remember that the H_2O molecules in the hot water are moving faster than those in the cold water (see **Figure 10.3**). As a result, energy will be transferred through the metal wall from the hot water to the cold water. This energy transfer will cause the H_2O molecules in the hot water to slow down and the H_2O molecules in the cold water to speed up.

Thus we have a transfer of energy from the hot water to the cold water. This flow of energy is called heat. **Heat** can be defined as a *flow of energy due to a temperature difference.* What will eventually happen? The two water samples will reach the same temperature (see **Figure 10.4**). At this point, how does the energy lost by the hot water compare to the energy gained by the cold water? They must be the same (remember that energy is conserved).

We conclude that the final temperature is the average of the original temperatures:

$$T_{\text{final}} = \frac{T_{\text{initial}}^{\text{hot}} + T_{\text{initial}}^{\text{cold}}}{2} = \frac{90\ °C + 10\ °C}{2} = 50\ °C$$

Figure 10.3
The H_2O molecules in hot water have much greater random motions than the H_2O molecules in cold water.

Figure 10.4
The water samples now have the same temperature (50 °C) and have the same random motions.

10.2   Temperature and Heat   **291**

Themes
Energy

Skills
Observing, making comparisons

TEACHING TIPS

- Some students have difficulty distinguishing between temperature and heat. It is important to talk about heat as a flow of energy and temperature as a measure of the "vigor" of the random motions of the components of a substance. Thermal energy is the energy that a substance contains due to the random motions of its components. Heat is the way that thermal energy is transferred from one object to another. Use Figures 10.2 through 10.4 to illustrate this point. Have students focus on the motion of the molecules in the compartments. Note that the molecules never mix, yet energy is transferred from one compartment to the other. The temperature in one compartment goes down and the temperature in the other compartment goes up. The energy flows from the higher-temperature compartment to the lower-temperature compartment.

- We take a molecular perspective to discuss temperature and heat. This approach allows students to have a better understanding of the difference between these concepts.

USING TECHNOLOGY

 Animation and Video

Animation, Kinetic–Molecular Theory/Heat Transfer

Section
10.3

Themes
Energy

Skills
Observing, making comparisons

TEACHING TIPS

To check the understanding of your students, ask them to label the following as endothermic or exothermic.

1. Your hand gets cold when you touch ice. (exothermic)

2. The ice melts when you touch it. (endothermic)

3. Ice cream melts. (endothermic)

4. Propane is burning in a propane torch. (exothermic)

5. Water drops on your skin after swimming evaporate. (endothermic)

6. Two chemicals mixing in a beaker give off heat. (exothermic)

TOP TEN

Lowest Temperature Recorded by State

Temperature (°C)	State	Date
1. −62.2	Alaska	1/23/71
2. −56.7	Montana	1/20/54
3. −56.1	Utah	2/1/85
4. −54.4	Wyoming	2/9/33
5. −51.7	Colorado	2/1/85
6. −51.1	Idaho	1/18/43
−51.1	North Dakota	2/15/36
−51.1	Minnesota	2/2/96
7. −50.0	South Dakota	2/17/36
8. −47.8	Oregon	2/10/33

For the hot water, the temperature change is

$$\text{Change in temperature (hot)} = \Delta T_{hot} = 90.\ °C - 50.\ °C = 40.\ °C$$

The temperature change for the cold water is

$$\text{Change in temperature (cold)} = \Delta T_{cold} = 50.\ °C - 10.\ °C = 40.\ °C$$

In this example, the masses of hot water and cold water are equal. If they were unequal, this problem would be more complicated.

Let's summarize the ideas we have introduced in this section. Temperature is a measure of the random motions of the components of an object. Heat is a *flow* of energy due to a temperature difference. We say that the random motions of the components of an object constitute the *thermal energy* of that object. The flow of energy called heat is the way in which thermal energy is transferred from a hot object to a colder object.

10.3 Exothermic and Endothermic Processes

Objective: *To consider the direction of energy flow as heat.*

In this section we will consider the energy changes that accompany chemical reactions. To explore this idea, let's consider the striking and burning of a match. Energy is clearly released through heat as the match burns. To discuss this reaction, we divide the universe into two parts: the system and the surroundings. The **system** is the part of the universe on which we wish to focus attention; the **surroundings** include everything else in the universe. In this case we define the system as the reactants and products of the reaction. The surroundings consist of the air in the room and anything else other than the reactants and products.

When a process results in the evolution of heat, it is said to be **exothermic** (*exo-* is a prefix meaning "out of"); that is, energy flows *out of the system.* For example, in the combustion of a match, energy flows out of the system as heat. Processes that absorb energy from the surroundings are said to be **endothermic.** When the heat flow moves *into a system,* the process is endothermic. Boiling water to form steam is a common endothermic process.

Where does the energy, released as heat, come from in an exothermic reaction? The answer lies in the difference in potential energies between the products and the reactants. Which has lower potential energy, the reactants or the products? We know that total energy is conserved and that energy flows from the system into the surroundings in an exothermic reaction. Thus *the energy gained by the surroundings must be equal to the energy lost by the system.* In the combustion of a match, the burned match has lost potential energy (in this case potential energy stored in the bonds of the reactants),

A burning match releases energy.

TEACHING SUPPORT
Demonstration

An Endothermic Reaction

Materials
250-mL beaker
Second smaller beaker
Wooden splint or tongue depressor
Wooden board
Wash bottle and water
Barium hydroxide hydrate
Ammonium thiocyanate

Preparation Measure about 20 g of $Ba(OH)_2 \cdot 8H_2O$ crystals into the 250-mL beaker. Place about 10 g of ammonium thiocyanate in the smaller beaker.

Presentation Place a small pool of water on the board. Place the 250-mL beaker on the board. Add the ammonium thiocyanate to the barium hydroxide in the 250-mL beaker. Stir the two solids together with the wooden splint. After 2–3 minutes the substances will be liquid and the beaker will be frozen to the board. You can lift the beaker and the board will stick to the bottom of it quite tightly.

Teaching Notes Ammonium chloride (7 g) or ammonium nitrate (10 g) can be substituted for the ammonium thiocyanate. The smell of ammonia is evident during the reaction. The reaction is unusual because two

---

Figure 10.5
The energy changes accompanying the burning of a match.

Animation and Video

Chemistry in Motion
Illustrates endothermic reactions in

Demonstration 9, Ammonium Chloride and Barium Hydroxide (not on CD); Demonstration 21, Sugar, Potassium Chlorate, and Sulfuric Acid; Demonstration 11, Thermite Reaction; and Demonstration 18, Dry Ice and Magnesium.

which was transferred through heat to the surroundings (see **Figure 10.5**). The heat flow into the surroundings results from a lowering of the potential energy of the reaction system. *In any exothermic reaction, some of the potential energy stored in the chemical bonds is converted to thermal energy (random kinetic energy) via heat.*

 Answers to Focus Questions

1. Energy is a state function because the amount of energy transferred in a chemical reaction is independent of the pathway. Heat and work are not state functions because they change depending on the pathway. The energy change is always independent of the pathway.

2. The most important characteristic of energy is the ability to do work.

3. Heat is a flow of energy; temperature is a measure of the random motions of the particles in the system.

4. See Figure 10.5.

Focus Questions

Sections 10.1–10.3

1. Explain why energy is a state function but heat and work are not.
2. What is probably the most important characteristic of energy?
3. What is the difference between temperature and heat?
4. Draw a picture of an endothermic reaction similar to the one for an exothermic reaction shown in Figure 10.5.

10.4 Thermodynamics

Objective: *To understand how energy flow affects internal energy.*

The study of energy is called **thermodynamics.** The law of conservation of energy is often called the **first law of thermodynamics** and is stated as follows:

The energy of the universe is constant.

The **internal energy**, *E*, of a system can be defined most precisely as the sum of the kinetic and potential energies of all "particles" in the system. The internal energy of a system can be changed by a flow of work, heat, or both.

 Section 10.4

Themes
Energy

Skills
Observing, applying concepts, making comparisons

Student Preparation
Assign the students to read Sections 10.4 and 10.5 and to answer the Focus Questions at the end of Section 10.5 before coming to class.

Active Learning
After introducing the material in Sections 10.4 and 10.5 in class, place the students in groups and have them work together on Sections 10.4–10.5: Team Learning Worksheet. Answers and/or discussion of these questions are located in the *Teacher Resources.*

10.4 Thermodynamics **293**

solids actually react without being dissolved in a solvent.

If you do not have access to these chemicals, you can use the following chemicals to create a demonstration of endothermic and exothermic reactions. For an endothermic process, dissolve about 15 g of ammonium nitrate in about 100 mL of water (many ammonium compounds dissolve endothermically). For an exothermic process, dissolve calcium chloride or sodium hydroxide. Allow the students to touch the beaker before and after dissolution.

TEACHING TIPS

- It is important that students think of energy from the system's point of view. Now is an excellent time to reinforce the idea that numbers representing thermodynamic quantities have two parts: the magnitude and the sign. It will be a new idea for many students to think about sign as a representation of direction. This idea is the key concept on which to focus attention.

- Emphasize that the sign convention is arbitrary. That is, because chemists chose to take the system's point of view, all signs are determined relative to the system.

Section 10.5

Themes
Energy

Skills
Observing, making comparisons, applying concepts

Laboratory
Experiment 40:
Energy Value of Nuts, Traditional

TEACHING TIPS

- In this section students learn the difference between calories in real life and calories for the chemist. It offers an opportunity to talk about the differences in the way scientists use language and the way we use language in our daily lives.

- This section also provides an excellent opportunity to review the process of unit conversion and to remind students that units should always be part of the calculations and the answers in chemistry.

294

That is,

$$\Delta E = q + w$$

where

Δ ("delta") means a change in the function that follows
q represents heat
w represents work

Thermodynamic quantities always consist of two parts: a *number*, giving the magnitude of the change, and a *sign*, indicating the direction of the flow. *The sign reflects the system's point of view.* For example, if a quantity of energy flows *into* the system via heat (an endothermic process), q is equal to $+x$, where the *positive* sign indicates that the *system's energy is increasing*. On the other hand, when energy flows *out of* the system via heat (an exothermic process), q is equal to $-x$, where the *negative* sign indicates that the *system's energy is decreasing*.

In this text the same conventions apply to the flow of work. If the system does work on the surroundings (energy flows out of the system), w is negative. If the surroundings do work on the system (energy flows into the system), w is positive. We define work from the system's point of view to be consistent for all thermodynamic quantities. That is, in this convention the signs of both q and w reflect what happens to the system; thus we use $\Delta E = q + w$.

10.5 Measuring Energy Changes

Objective: *To understand how heat is measured.*

Earlier in this chapter we saw that when we heat a substance to a higher temperature, we increase the motions of the components of the substance—that is, we increase the thermal energy of the substance. Different materials respond differently to being heated. To explore this idea we need to introduce the common units of energy: the *calorie* and the *joule* (pronounced "jewel").

In the metric system the **calorie** is defined as the amount of energy (heat) required to raise the temperature of one gram of water by one Celsius degree.

294 Chapter 10 Energy

TEACHING SUPPORT
Demonstration

Spontaneous Combustion

Materials
Potassium permanganate
Fireproof pad or evaporating dish
Glycerine
Spatula

Presentation Pile 5.0 g of potassium permanganate on the fireproof pad or in the evaporating dish. With a spatula form a depression in the center of the pile. Add about 1 mL of glycerine to the pile and step back. After a few seconds a white puff of smoke is produced, followed by a purplish flame.

Diet drinks are now labeled as "low joule" instead of "low calorie" in European countries.

The "calorie" with which you are probably familiar is used to measure the energy content of food and is actually a kilocalorie (1000 calories), written with a capital C (Calorie) to distinguish it from the calorie used in chemistry. The **joule** (an SI unit) can be most conveniently defined in terms of the calorie:

1 calorie = 4.184 joules

or using the normal abbreviations

1 cal = 4.184 J

You need to be able to convert between calories and joules. We will consider that conversion process in Example 10.1.

Example 10.1

Converting Calories to Joules

Express 60.1 cal of energy in units of joules.

Solution

By definition 1 cal = 4.184 J, so the conversion factor needed is $\frac{4.184\ J}{1\ cal}$, and the result is

$$60.1\ \cancel{cal} \times \frac{4.184\ J}{1\ \cancel{cal}} = 251\ J$$

Note that the 1 in the denominator is an exact number by definition and so does not limit the number of significant figures.

 Self-Check Exercise 10.1

How many calories of energy correspond to 28.4 J?

Now think about heating a substance from one temperature to another. How does the amount of substance heated affect the energy required? In 2 g of water there are twice as many molecules as in 1 g of water. It takes twice as much energy to change the temperature of 2 g of water by 1 °C, because we must change the motions of twice as many molecules in a 2-g sample as in a 1-g sample. Also, as we would expect, it takes twice as much energy to raise the temperature of a given sample of water by 2 degrees as it does to raise the temperature by 1 degree.

Example 10.2

Calculating Energy Requirements

Determine the amount of energy (heat) in joules required to raise the temperature of 7.40 g water from 29.0 °C to 46.0 °C.

(continued)

(continued)

Solution

In solving any kind of problem, it is often useful to draw a diagram that represents the situation. In this case, we have 7.40 g of water that is to be heated from 29.0 °C to 46.0 °C.

7.40 g water	⇨	7.40 g water
T = 29.0 °C	? energy	T = 46.0 °C

Our task is to determine how much energy is required to accomplish this task.

From the discussion in the text, we know that 4.184 J of energy is required to raise the temperature of *one* gram of water by *one* Celsius degree.

1.00 g water	⇨	1.00 g water
T = 29.0 °C	4.184 J	T = 30.0 °C

Because in our case we have 7.40 g of water instead of 1.00 g, it will take 7.40 × 4.184 J to raise the temperature by one degree.

7.40 g water	⇨	7.40 g water
T = 29.0 °C	7.40 × 4.184 J	T = 30.0 °C

However, we want to raise the temperature of our sample of water by more than 1 °C. In fact, the temperature change required is from 29.0 °C to 46.0 °C. This is change of 17.0 °C (46.0 °C − 29.0 °C = 17.0 °C). Thus we will have to supply 17.0 times the energy necessary to raise the temperature of 7.40 g of water by 1 °C.

7.40 g water	⇨	7.40 g water
T = 29.0 °C	17.0 × 7.40 × 4.184 J	T = 46.0 °C

This calculation is summarized as follows:

$$4.184 \frac{J}{g\,°C} \quad\times\quad 7.40\ g \quad\times\quad 17.0\ °C \quad=\quad 526\ J$$

| Energy per gram of water per degree of temperature | × | Actual grams of water | × | Actual temperature change | = | Energy required |

We have shown that 526 J of energy (as heat) is required to raise the temperature of 7.40 g of water from 29.0 °C to 46.0 °C. Note that because 4.184 J of energy is required to heat 1 g of water by 1 °C, the units are J/g °C (joules per gram per Celsius degree).

MATH
The result you will get on your calculator is 4.184 × 7.40 × 17.0 = 526.3472, which rounds off to 526.

Self-Check Exercise 10.2

Calculate the joules of energy required to heat 454 g of water from 5.4 °C to 98.6 °C.

Answer to Self-Check Exercise 10.2

We know that it takes 4.184 J of energy to change the temperature of each gram of water by 1 °C, so we must multiply 4.184 by the mass of water (454 g) and the temperature change (98.6 °C − 5.4 °C = 93.2 °C).

$$4.184\ \frac{J}{g\,°C} \times 454\ g$$
$$\times\ 93.2\ °C = 1.77 \times 10^5\ J$$

TEACHING SUPPORT
Demonstration

Heat Up or Chill Out?

Materials
Ammonium chloride (50 g)
Calcium chloride
Anhydrous (30 g)
2 small zip-lock storage bags
Graduated cylinder
Water

Preparation Measure 30 g calcium chloride and place it in a small zip-lock bag, label it "hot," and seal it. Measure 50 g ammonium chloride and place it into a second zip-lock bag, label it "cold," and seal it.

Presentation Introduce the idea that dissolving a solid can be an exothermic or endothermic process. Explain that common hot or cold packs used to relieve sore muscles are often based on this idea. Measure about 25 mL of water into the graduated cylinder. Open one of the plastic bags and pour in the water. Rezip the bag closed and shake it to mix the contents well. Repeat the process with the other plastic bag. Pass both bags around the class so that students can directly observe the temperature change associated with dissolving the solids.

Nature Has Hot Plants

Titan Arum is reputedly the largest flower in the world.

The voodoo lily is a beautiful and seductive plant. The exotic-looking lily features an elaborate reproductive mechanism—a purple spike that can reach nearly 3 feet in length and is cloaked by a hoodlike leaf. But approach to the plant reveals bad news—it smells terrible!

Despite its antisocial odor, this putrid plant has fascinated biologists for many years because of its ability to generate heat. At the peak of its metabolic activity, the plant's blossom can be as much as 15 °C above its surrounding temperature. To generate this much heat, the metabolic rate of the plant must be close to that of a flying hummingbird!

What's the purpose of this intense heat production? For a plant faced with limited food supplies in the very competitive tropical climate where it grows, heat production seems like a great waste of energy. The answer to this mystery is that the voodoo lily is pollinated mainly by carrion-loving insects. Thus the lily prepares a malodorous mixture of chemicals characteristic of rotting meat, which it then "cooks" off into the surrounding air to attract flesh-feeding beetles and flies. Then, once the insects enter the pollination chamber, the high temperatures there (as high as 110 °F) cause the insects to remain very active to better carry out their pollination duties.

The voodoo lily is only one of many thermogenic (heat-producing) plants. These plants are of special interest to biologists because they provide opportunities to study metabolic reactions that are quite subtle in "normal" plants.

Nature Has Hot Plants

"Nature Has Hot Plants" points out how sophisticated plants are in using chemistry to enhance their existence. Some plants, such as walnut trees, produce a natural herbicide to kill grass around their roots to lower the competition for water. Others produce insect alarm pheromones to scare off invaders. Still others, such as the voodoo lily, produce a mixture of chemicals that attract insects to aid in pollination. Some plants produce chemicals that attract predators, such as wasps, that kill caterpillars attacking the plant. Many other examples exist as well. This topic would be a good choice for a student paper that would nicely connect chemistry and biology.

TEACHING TIP

Students often do many problems involving water. Be sure to include some examples in which the specific heat capacities for other substances are needed.

MINI-DEMO

Use a heat conductivity apparatus (the apparatus looks like a star with a central circle of metal and spokes emanating from it) to demonstrate the specific heat capacities for various metals. Different metal spheres (shot) are attached to the ends of the spokes with paraffin. The apparatus is then heated at the center with a Bunsen burner. The heat travels out the spokes and the paraffin melts, causing the metal spheres to drop off at different times according to their specific heat capacities.

CHEMISTRY

Each state of a substance has a different specific heat.

So far we have seen that the energy (heat) required to change the temperature of a substance depends on

1. The amount of substance being heated (number of grams)

2. The temperature change (number of degrees)

There is, however, another important factor: the identity of the substance. Different substances respond differently to being heated. We have seen that 4.184 J of energy raises the temperature of 1 g of water 1 °C. In contrast, this same amount of energy applied to 1 g of gold raises its temperature by approximately 32 °C! The point is that some substances require relatively large amounts of energy to change their temperatures, whereas others require relatively little. Chemists describe this difference by saying that substances have different heat capacities. *The amount of energy required to change the temperature of one gram of a substance by one Celsius degree* is called its **specific heat capacity** or, more commonly, its *specific heat*. The specific heat capacities for several substances are listed in **Table 10.1.** You can see from the table that the specific heat capacity for water is very high compared to those of the other substances listed. This is why lakes and seas are much slower to respond to cooling or heating than are the surrounding land masses.

TABLE 10.1

The Specific Heat Capacities of Some Common Substances

Substance	Specific Heat Capacity (J/g °C)
water (*l*)* (liquid)	4.184
water (*s*) (ice)	2.03
water (*g*) (steam)	2.0
aluminum (*s*)	0.89
iron (*s*)	0.45
mercury (*l*)	0.14
carbon (*s*)	0.71
silver (*s*)	0.24
gold (*s*)	0.13

*The symbols (*s*), (*l*), and (*g*) indicate the solid, liquid, and gaseous states, respectively.

10.5 Measuring Energy Changes **297**

Teaching Notes The heats of dissolution for the packs are

$$NH_4Cl(s) \rightarrow NH_4^+(aq) + Cl^-(aq)$$
$$\Delta H = 15.2 \text{ kJ}$$

$$CaCl_2(s) \rightarrow Ca^{2+}(aq) + 2Cl^-(aq)$$
$$\Delta H = -82.8 \text{ kJ}$$

Be sure that students don't hold the hot pack too long—it generates enough heat to produce discomfort. Dispose of the contents according to regulations. You may also want to bring in commercial hot and cold packs to demonstrate their use.

Example 10.3

Additional Examples

1. Determine the apmount of energy as heat that is required to raise the temperature of a 10.0-g sample of aluminum from 25 °C to 58 °C. Answer in joules and calories.
   294 J; 70. cal

2. If 294 J of heat is transferred to a 10.0-g sample of silver at 25 °C, what is the final temperature of the silver?
   148 °C

Calculations Involving Specific Heat Capacity

a. What quantity of energy (in joules) is required to heat a piece of iron weighing 1.3 g from 25 °C to 46 °C?

b. What is the answer in calories?

Solution

a. It is helpful to draw the following diagram to represent the problem.

| 1.3 g iron $T = 25$ °C | ⇨ | 1.3 g iron $T = 46$ °C |

? joules

From Table 10.1 we see that the specific heat capacity of iron is 0.45 J/g °C. That is, it takes 0.45 J to raise the temperature of a 1-g piece of iron by 1 °C.

| 1.0 g iron $T = 25$ °C | ⇨ | 1.0 g iron $T = 26$ °C |

0.45 J

In this case our sample is 1.3 g, so 1.3×0.45 J is required for *each* degree of temperature increase.

| 1.3 g iron $T = 25$ °C | ⇨ | 1.3 g iron $T = 26$ °C |

1.3 × 0.45 J

Because the temperature increase is 21 °C (46 °C − 25 °C = 21 °C), the total amount of energy required is

$$0.45 \, \frac{J}{g \, °C} \times 1.3 \, g \times 21 \, °C = 12 \, J$$

| 1.3 g iron $T = 25$ °C | ⇨ | 1.3 g iron $T = 46$ °C |

21 × 1.3 × 0.45 J

Note that the final units are joules, as they should be.

b. To calculate this energy in calories, we can use the definition 1 cal = 4.184 J to construct the appropriate conversion factor. We want to change from joules to calories, so cal must be in the numerator and J in the denominator, where it cancels:

$$12 \, \cancel{J} \times \frac{1 \, cal}{4.184 \, \cancel{J}} = 2.9 \, cal$$

Remember that 1 in this case is an exact number by definition and therefore does not limit the number of significant figures (the number 12 is limiting here).

MATH

The result you will get on your calculator is 0.45 × 1.3 × 21 = 12.285, which rounds off to 12.

A 5.63-g sample of solid gold is heated from 21 °C to 32 °C. How much energy (in joules and calories) is required?

Note that in Example 10.3, to calculate the energy (heat) required, we took the product of the specific heat capacity, the sample size in grams, and the change in temperature in Celsius degrees.

$$
\begin{array}{c}
\boxed{\begin{array}{c}\text{Energy (heat)}\\\text{required } (Q)\end{array}} = \boxed{\begin{array}{c}\text{Specific heat}\\\text{capacity } (s)\end{array}} \times \boxed{\begin{array}{c}\text{Mass } (m)\\\text{in grams}\\\text{of sample}\end{array}} \times \boxed{\begin{array}{c}\text{Change in}\\\text{temperature}\\(\Delta T) \text{ in °C}\end{array}}
\end{array}
$$

MATH

The symbol Δ (the Greek letter delta) is shorthand for "change in."

We can represent this by the following equation:

$$Q = s \times m \times \Delta T$$

where

Q = energy (heat) required
s = specific heat capacity
m = mass of the sample in grams
ΔT = change in temperature in Celsius degrees

This equation always applies when a substance is being heated (or cooled) and no change of state occurs. Before you begin to use this equation, however, make sure you understand what it means.

Example 10.4

Specific Heat Capacity Calculations: Using the Equation

A 1.6-g sample of a metal that has the appearance of gold requires 5.8 J of energy to change its temperature from 23 °C to 41 °C. Is the metal pure gold?

Solution

We can represent the data given in this problem by the following diagram:

$$
\boxed{\begin{array}{c}1.6\text{ g metal}\\T = 23\text{ °C}\end{array}} \xrightarrow{\;5.8\text{ J}\;} \boxed{\begin{array}{c}1.6\text{ g metal}\\T = 41\text{ °C}\end{array}}
$$

$$\Delta T = 41\text{ °C} - 23\text{ °C} = 18\text{ °C}$$

Using the data given, we can calculate the value of the specific heat

(continued)

10.5 Measuring Energy Changes   **299**

Answer to Self-Check Exercise 10.4

Table 10.1 lists the specific heat capacities of several metals. We want to calculate the specific heat capacity (s) for this metal and then use Table 10.1 to identify the metal. Using the equation

$$Q = s \times m \times \Delta T$$

we can solve for s by dividing both sides by m (the mass of the sample) and by ΔT:

$$\frac{Q}{m \times \Delta T} = s$$

In this case,

Q = energy (heat)
required = 10.1 J
m = 2.8 g
ΔT = temperature change
= 36 °C − 21 °C = 15 °C

so

$$s = \frac{Q}{m \times \Delta T}$$
$$= \frac{10.1 \text{ J}}{(2.8 \text{ g})(15 \text{ °C})}$$
$$= 0.24 \text{ J/g °C}$$

Table 10.1 shows that silver has a specific heat capacity of 0.24 J/g °C. The metal is silver.

Answers to Focus Questions

1. Thermodynamic quantities consist of a number and a sign. We take the system's point of view because then all thermodynamic quantities are consistent.

2. A food calorie is 1000 times larger than the calorie we use in chemistry.

3. 1.9×10^2 cal or 7.8×10^4 J

4. We use the specific heat capacity for the substance instead of the specific heat capacity for water.

(continued)

capacity for the metal and compare this value to the one for gold given in Table 10.1. We know that

$$Q = s \times m \times \Delta T$$

or, pictorially,

| 1.6 g metal |
| $T = 23$ °C |

⟹ 5.8 J = ? × 1.6 × 18

| 1.6 g metal |
| $T = 41$ °C |

When we divide both sides of the equation

$$Q = s \times m \times \Delta T$$

by $m \times \Delta T$, we get

$$\frac{Q}{m \times \Delta T} = s$$

Thus, using the data given, we can calculate the value of s. In this case,

Q = energy (heat) required = 5.8 J

m = mass of the sample = 1.6 g

ΔT = change in temperature = 18 °C (41 °C − 23 °C = 18 °C)

Thus

$$s = \frac{Q}{m \times \Delta T} = \frac{5.8 \text{ J}}{(1.6 \text{ g})(18 \text{ °C})} = 0.20 \text{ J/g °C}$$

From Table 10.1, the specific heat capacity for gold is 0.13 J/g °C. Thus the metal must not be pure gold.

 MATH
The result you will get on your calculator is 5.8/(1.6) × 18 = 0.2013889, which rounds off to 0.20.

 Self-Check Exercise 10.4

A 2.8-g sample of pure metal requires 10.1 J of energy to change its temperature from 21 °C to 36 °C. What is this metal? (Use Table 10.1.)

Focus Questions

Sections 10.4–10.5

1. In our study of thermodynamics, we look at changes in the internal energy of systems. To do so, we consider thermodynamic quantities to consist of two parts. What are they? Why do we take the system's point of view?

2. How is a food calorie different from the calorie we use in chemistry?

3. Suppose you wanted to heat a mug of water (250 mL) from room temperature, 25 °C, to 100 °C to make a cup of tea. How much energy would you need from your microwave?

4. When calculating energy changes for substances other than water, how do we account for the differences in their abilities to absorb or release heat?

300 Chapter 10 Energy

TEACHING SUPPORT
Demonstration

The Fireproof Balloon

Materials
Black balloons (9-in. diameter)
Candle
Medium-size beaker or plastic cup

Preparation Place approximately 25 mL of water into one balloon. Place it along with sev-eral additional balloons into the cup or beaker, making sure that the water balloon is easy to remove.

Presentation Place a lighted candle on a flat, level surface. Ask for a volunteer. Have the volunteer take a balloon, blow it up, and tie it off with a knot. Demonstrate the process yourself by picking up the water balloon and blowing it up. (*Note:* As you do so be careful to keep your hand in front of the balloon to conceal the mass of water in the balloon.) Now hold your balloon over the flame (making sure that the flame is over the bottom of the balloon where the water is). Ask the volunteer to repeat the experiment with his/her balloon. At the end of the demonstration heat the balloon containing the water on its side while holding it over

Firewalking: Magic or Science?

For millennia people have been amazed at the ability of Eastern mystics to walk across beds of glowing coals without any apparent discomfort. Even in the United States, thousands of people have performed feats of firewalking as part of motivational seminars. How can this be possible? Do firewalkers have supernatural powers?

Actually, there are good scientific explanations of why firewalking is possible. First, human tissue is mainly composed of water, which has a relatively large specific heat capacity. This means that a large amount of energy must be transferred from the coals to change significantly the temperature of the feet. During the brief contact between feet and coals involved in firewalking, there is relatively little time for energy flow, so the feet do not reach a high enough temperature to cause damage.

Also, although the surface of the coals has a very high temperature, the red-hot layer is very thin. Therefore, the quantity of energy available to heat the feet is smaller than might be expected.

Thus, although firewalking is impressive, there are several scientific reasons why anyone with the proper training should be able to do it on a properly prepared bed of coals. (Don't try this on your own!)

A group of firewalkers in Japan.

10.6 Thermochemistry (Enthalpy)

Objective: *To consider the heat (enthalpy) of chemical reactions.*

We have seen that some reactions are exothermic (produce heat energy) and other reactions are endothermic (absorb heat energy). Chemists also like to know exactly how much energy is produced or absorbed by a given reaction. To make that process more convenient, we have invented a special energy function called **enthalpy**, which is designated by H. For a reaction occurring under conditions of constant pressure, the change in enthalpy (ΔH) is equal to the energy that flows as heat. That is,

$$\Delta H_p = \text{heat}$$

where the subscript "p" indicates that the process has occurred under conditions of constant pressure and Δ means "a change in." Thus the enthalpy change for a reaction (that occurs at constant pressure) is the same as the heat for that reaction.

10.6 Thermochemistry (Enthalpy) **301**

 Integrating the CHEMICAL IMPACT

Firewalking: Magic or Science?

"Firewalking: Magic or Science?" illustrates some important points about energy transfer and the special ability of water to absorb large amounts of heat energy with a relatively small change in temperature. One of water's most useful properties is its ability to act as a coolant. Automobiles use an aqueous solution of ethylene glycol to absorb the heat produced by the engine. Likewise, many industries use water from nearby lakes and rivers as a coolant. Also, nuclear power plants use vast quantities of water to carry away the excess heat of the nuclear fission process.

This Chemical Impact also points out that phenomena that appear to be "magical" have logical explanations. Magicians' tricks are just that—clever manipulations of our senses that never violate the laws of nature.

10.6 Section 10.6

Themes
Energy

Skills
Applying concepts, interpreting diagrams, making comparisons, calculating

Student Preparation
Assign the students to read Sections 10.6 and 10.7 and to answer the Focus Questions at the end of Section 10.7 before coming to class.

Active Learning
After introducing the material in Sections 10.6 and 10.7 in class, place the students in groups and have them work together on Sections 10.6–10.7: Team Learning Worksheet. Answers and/or discussion of these questions are located in the *Teacher Resources*.

Laboratory
Experiment 41: Specific Heat of a Metal, CBL

Laboratory
Experiment 42: Which Is Your Metal?, In Text

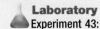
Additional Examples

1. When 1 mol of sulfur dioxide reacts with excess oxygen to form sulfur trioxide at constant pressure, 198.2 kJ of energy is released as heat. Calculate ΔH for a process in which a 12.8-g sample of sulfur dioxide reacts with excess oxygen at constant pressure. **39.6 kJ**

2. When 1 mol of hydrogen gas reacts with excess oxygen to form water at constant pressure, 241.8 kJ of energy is released as heat. Calculate ΔH for a process in which a 15.0-g sample of hydrogen gas reacts with excess oxygen at constant pressure. **1.80×10^3 kJ**

Answer to Self-Check Exercise 10.5

We are told that 1652 kJ of energy is *released* when 4 mol of Fe reacts. We first need to determine what number of moles the 1.00 g of Fe represents.

$$1.00 \text{ g Fe} \times \frac{1 \text{ mol}}{55.85 \text{ g}}$$
$$= 1.79 \times 10^{-2} \text{ mol Fe}$$

$$1.79 \times 10^{-2} \text{ mol Fe}$$
$$\times \frac{1652 \text{ kJ}}{4 \text{ mol Fe}} = 7.39 \text{ kJ}$$

Thus 7.39 kJ of energy (as heat) is released when 1.00 g of iron reacts.

MINI-DEMO

Lighting a Cheeto or a nut can bring the concept of calorimetry into the real world. Discuss the fact that to obtain the nutrition information on food someone has to determine the calorie value for the food. Using a calorimeter is one way to do so.

302

Example 10.5

Enthalpy

When 1 mol of methane (CH_4) is burned at constant pressure, 890 kJ of energy is released as heat. Calculate ΔH for a process in which a 5.8-g sample of methane is burned at constant pressure.

Solution

At constant pressure, 890 kJ of energy per mole of CH_4, is produced as heat:

$$q_p = \Delta H = -890 \text{ kJ/mol } CH_4$$

Note that the minus sign indicates an exothermic process. In this case, a 5.8-g sample of CH_4 (molar mass = 16.0 g/mol) is burned. Since this amount is smaller than 1 mol, less than 890 kJ will be released as heat. The actual value can be calculated as follows:

$$5.8 \text{ g } CH_4 \times \frac{1 \text{ mol } CH_4}{16.0 \text{ g } CH_4} = 0.36 \text{ mol } CH_4$$

and

$$0.36 \text{ mol } CH_4 \times \frac{-890 \text{ kJ}}{\text{mol } CH_4} = -320 \text{ kJ}$$

Thus, when a 5.8-g sample of CH_4 is burned at constant pressure,

$$\Delta H = \text{heat flow} = -320 \text{ kJ}$$

Self-Check Exercise 10.5

The reaction that occurs in the heat packs used to treat sports injuries is

$$4Fe(s) + 3O_2(g) \rightarrow 2Fe_2O_3(s) \qquad \Delta H = -1652 \text{ kJ}$$

How much heat is released when 1.00 g of Fe(s) is reacted with excess $O_2(g)$?

Calorimetry

A **calorimeter** (see **Figure 10.6**) is a device used to determine the heat associated with a chemical reaction. The reaction is run in the calorimeter and the temperature change of the calorimeter is observed. Knowing the temperature change that occurs in the calorimeter and the heat capacity of the calorimeter enables us to calculate the heat energy released or absorbed by the reaction. Thus we can determine ΔH for the reaction.

Once we have measured the ΔH values for various reactions, we can use these data to *calculate* the ΔH values of other reactions. We will see how to carry out these calculations in the next section.

Figure 10.6
A coffee-cup calorimeter made of two Styrofoam cups.

Thermometer

Styrofoam cover

Styrofoam cups

Stirrer

USING TECHNOLOGY

 Animation and Video

The "Coffee Cup Calorimeter Measuring Heat of Neutralization" video from the CD is a good way of showing the students how calorimetry is done in the lab.

 Figure 10.6
The Coffee Cup Calorimeter allows you to point out the essential features of a calorimeter.

Methane (CH₄)

Methane is the main component of natural gas, a valuable fossil fuel. It is such a good fuel because the combustion of methane with oxygen

$$CH_4(g) + 2O_2(g) \rightarrow CO_2(g) + 2H_2O(g)$$

produces 55 kJ of energy per gram of methane. Natural gas, which is associated with petroleum deposits and contains as much as 97% methane, originated from the decomposition of plants in ancient forests that became buried in natural geological processes.

Although the methane in natural gas represents a tremendous source of energy for our civilization, an even more abundant source of methane lies in the depths of the ocean. The U.S. Geological Survey estimates that 320,000 trillion cubic feet of methane is trapped in the deep ocean near the United States. This amount is 200 times the amount of methane contained in the natural gas deposits in the United States. In the ocean, the methane is trapped in cavities formed by water molecules that are arranged very much like the water molecules in ice. These structures are called methane hydrates.

Although extraction of methane from the ocean floor offers tremendous potential benefits, it also carries risks. Methane is a "greenhouse gas"—its presence in the atmosphere helps to trap the heat from the sun. As a result, any accidental release of the methane from the ocean could produce serious warming of the earth's climate. As usual, environmental trade-offs accompany human activities.

Flaming pieces of methane hydrate.

10.7 Hess's Law

Objective: *To understand Hess's law.*

One of the most important characteristics of enthalpy is that it is a state function. That is, the change in enthalpy for a given process is independent of the pathway for the process. Consequently, *in going from a particular set of reactants to a particular set of products, the change in enthalpy is the same whether the reaction takes place in one step or in a series of steps*. This principle, which is known as **Hess's law,** can be illustrated by examining the oxidation of nitrogen to produce nitrogen dioxide. The overall reaction can be written in one step, where the enthalpy change is represented by ΔH_1.

$$N_2(g) + 2O_2(g) \rightarrow 2NO_2(g) \qquad \Delta H_1 = 68 \text{ kJ}$$

CELEBRITY CHEMICAL

Methane (CH₄)

In connection with your discussion of methane, a good student project would be to explore the topic of methane hydrates, the huge quantity of methane in the deep ocean trapped in "shells" of water molecules. Several articles about this topic have appeared recently, and it would make a particularly good web-based research project.

Themes
Energy

Skills
Applying concepts, making comparisons, making predictions, calculating

Laboratory
Experiment 44:
Heat of Reaction, Traditional

Laboratory
Experiment 45:
Hess's Law, CBL

TEACHING TIPS

• Once students understand that energy changes can be measured in a calorimeter, the next logical question is, How can anyone measure all of the energy changes in the world? What if the reaction is unpleasant, or is an explosion, or is very complex—how can we measure the energy change then? To answer this question, Hess's law is useful. It provides an excellent example of how a chemist can extend knowledge by applying information gathered from simple systems to more complex systems.

• Hess's law problems relate well to the mathematics of equations. As students are already familiar with manipulating algebraic equations, this section is a good place to show the overlap of math and science. The two characteristics of enthalpy changes are easily related to algebraic concepts.

• An analogy you can use with Hess's law is paying for something at a store. If the net result is to pay the store $8, this goal can be achieved in many ways. For example, you can give the store one $5 bill and three $1 bills, or you can pay with a $10 bill and get $2 in change. No matter how many steps are involved in the process, the payment is the same.

This reaction can also be carried out in two distinct steps, with the enthalpy changes being designated as ΔH_2 and ΔH_3:

$$N_2(g) + O_2(g) \rightarrow 2NO(g) \qquad \Delta H_2 = 180 \text{ kJ}$$

$$2NO(g) + O_2(g) \rightarrow 2NO_2(g) \qquad \Delta H_3 = -112 \text{ kJ}$$

$$\text{Net reaction: } N_2(g) + 2O_2(g) \rightarrow 2NO_2(g) \qquad \Delta H_2 + \Delta H_3 = 68 \text{ kJ}$$

Note that the sum of the two steps gives the net, or overall, reaction and that

$$\Delta H_1 = \Delta H_2 + \Delta H_3 = 68 \text{ kJ}$$

The importance of Hess's law is that it allows us to *calculate* heats of reaction that might be difficult or inconvenient to measure directly in a calorimeter.

Characteristics of Enthalpy Changes

To use Hess's law to compute enthalpy changes for reactions, it is important to understand two characteristics of ΔH for a reaction:

1. If a reaction is reversed, the sign of ΔH is also reversed.

2. The magnitude of ΔH is directly proportional to the quantities of reactants and products in a reaction. If the coefficients in a balanced reaction are multiplied by an integer, the value of ΔH is multiplied by the same integer.

Both these rules follow in a straightforward way from the properties of enthalpy changes. The first rule can be explained by recalling that the *sign* of ΔH indicates the *direction* of the heat flow at constant pressure. If the direction of the reaction is reversed, the direction of the heat flow also will be reversed. To see this, consider the preparation of xenon tetrafluoride, which was the first binary compound made from a noble gas:

$$Xe(g) + 2F_2(g) \rightarrow XeF_4(s) \qquad \Delta H = -251 \text{ kJ}$$

This reaction is exothermic, and 251 kJ of energy flows into the surroundings as heat. On the other hand, if the colorless XeF_4 crystals are decomposed into the elements, according to the equation

$$XeF_4(s) \rightarrow Xe(g) + 2F_2(g)$$

the opposite energy flow occurs because 251 kJ of energy must be added to the system to produce this endothermic reaction. Thus, for this reaction, $\Delta H = +251$ kJ.

The second rule comes from the fact that ΔH is an extensive property, depending on the amount of substances reacting. For example, since 251 kJ of energy is evolved for the reaction

$$Xe(g) + 2F_2(g) \rightarrow XeF_4(s)$$

then for a preparation involving twice the quantities of reactants and products, or

$$2Xe(g) + 4F_2(g) \rightarrow 2XeF_4(s)$$

twice as much heat would be evolved:

$$\Delta H = 2(-251 \text{ kJ}) = -502 \text{ kJ}$$

CHEMISTRY

Reversing the direction of a reaction changes the sign of ΔH.

Crystals of xenon tetrafluoride, the first reported binary compound containing a noble gas element.

USING TECHNOLOGY

Animation and Video

Animation, Hess's Law

TEACHING SUPPORT
Background Information

The bombadier beetle (see the Chemical Impact, "The Beetle That Shoots Straight," in Chapter 7) is an amazing insect "knowledgeable" about thermochemistry and Hess's law. The beetle protects itself from predators by mixing chemicals within its abdomen and spraying its enemy with the resulting concoction. The chemicals are hydroquinone [$C_6H_4(OH)_2(aq)$] and hydrogen peroxide (H_2O_2). As these chemicals are mixed with a catalyst (enzyme), a fast exothermic reaction takes place that produces quinone ($C_6H_4O_2$) and water. The heat of reaction for this process is -204 kJ. This heat raises the entire solution to its boiling point and the resulting vapor is shot out in spurts (up to 30) as a hot mist with appropriate sound effects!

The appropriate steps for illustrating Hess's law follow.

$$C_6H_4(OH)_2(aq) \rightarrow C_6H_4O_2(aq) + H_2(g)$$
$$\Delta H = 177 \text{ kJ}$$

$$H_2O_2(aq) \rightarrow H_2O(l) + \tfrac{1}{2}O_2(g)$$
$$\Delta H = -95 \text{ kJ}$$

$$H_2(g) + \tfrac{1}{2}O_2(g) \rightarrow H_2O(l)$$
$$\Delta H = -286 \text{ kJ}$$

$$C_6H_4(OH)_2(aq) + H_2O_2(aq)$$
$$\rightarrow C_6H_4O_2(aq) + 2H_2O(l) \quad \Delta H = -204 \text{ kJ}$$

Example 10.6

Hess's Law

Two forms of carbon are graphite, the soft, black, slippery material used in "lead" pencils and as a lubricant for locks, and diamond, the brilliant, hard gemstone. Using the enthalpies of combustion for graphite (–394 kJ/mol) and diamond (–396 kJ/mol), calculate ΔH for the conversion of graphite to diamond:

$$C_{graphite}(s) \rightarrow C_{diamond}(s)$$

Solution

The combustion reactions are

$$C_{graphite}(s) + O_2(g) \rightarrow CO_2(g) \qquad \Delta H = -394 \text{ kJ}$$
$$C_{diamond}(s) + O_2(g) \rightarrow CO_2(g) \qquad \Delta H = -396 \text{ kJ}$$

Note that if we reverse the second reaction (which means we must change the sign of ΔH) and sum the two reactions, we obtain the desired reaction:

$$C_{graphite}(s) + O_2(g) \rightarrow CO_2(g) \qquad\qquad \Delta H = -394 \text{ kJ}$$
$$CO_2(g) \rightarrow C_{diamond}(s) + O_2(g) \qquad\qquad \Delta H = -(-396 \text{ kJ})$$

$$\overline{C_{graphite}(s) \rightarrow C_{diamond}(s) \qquad\qquad\qquad \Delta H = 2 \text{ kJ}}$$

Thus 2 kJ of energy is required to change 1 mol graphite to diamond. This process is endothermic.

 Self-Check Exercise 10.6

From the following information

$$S(s) + \tfrac{3}{2}O_2(g) \rightarrow SO_3(g) \qquad \Delta H = -395.2 \text{ kJ}$$

$$2SO_2(g) + O_2(g) \rightarrow 2SO_3(g) \qquad \Delta H = -198.2 \text{ kJ}$$

calculate ΔH for the reaction

$$S(s) + O_2(g) \rightarrow SO_2(g)$$

 Focus Questions ⃝ **Sections 10.6–10.7**

1. If enthalpy is the heat for a reaction, it must have a sign as well as a magnitude. What sign should the enthalpy for an exothermic reaction have? Why?

2. Suppose you ran a chemical reaction in the calorimeter shown in Figure 10.6. If the temperature of the solution goes from 27 °C to 36 °C for a 5.0-g sample, how would you determine the energy produced by the reaction?

3. What is Hess's law and why is it useful?

4. The enthalpy of combustion of solid carbon to form carbon dioxide is −393.7 kJ/mol C, and the enthalpy of combustion of carbon monoxide to form carbon dioxide is −283.3 kJ/mol CO. Using these data, calculate the change in enthalpy for the reaction

$$2C(s) + O_2(g) \rightarrow 2CO(g)$$

Focus Questions **305**

Additional Example

Given the following data

$$4CuO(s) \rightarrow 2Cu_2O(s) + O_2(g)$$
$$\Delta H = 288 \text{ kJ}$$

$$Cu_2O(s) \rightarrow Cu(s) + CuO(s)$$
$$\Delta H = 11 \text{ kJ}$$

calculate ΔH for the following reaction:

$$2Cu(s) + O_2(g) \rightarrow 2CuO(s)$$
$$-310. \text{ kJ}$$

✓ Answer to Self-Check Exercise 10.6

Noting the reactants and products in the desired reaction

$$S(s) + O_2(g) \rightarrow SO_2(g)$$

we need to reverse the second equation and multiply it by $\tfrac{1}{2}$. This action reverses the sign and cuts the amount of energy by a factor of 2:

$$\tfrac{1}{2}[2SO_3(g) \rightarrow 2SO_2(g) + O_2(g)]$$
$$\Delta H = \frac{198.2 \text{ KJ}}{2}$$

or

$$SO_3(g) \rightarrow SO_2(g) + \tfrac{1}{2}O_2(g)$$
$$\Delta H = 99.1 \text{ kJ}$$

Now we add this reaction to the first reaction:

$$S(s) + \tfrac{3}{2}O_2(g) \rightarrow SO_3(g)$$
$$\Delta H = -395.2 \text{ kJ}$$
$$+ \quad SO_3(g) \rightarrow SO_2(g) + \tfrac{1}{2}O_2(g)$$
$$\Delta H = 99.1 \text{ kJ}$$
$$\overline{S(s) + O_2(g) \rightarrow SO_2(g)}$$
$$\Delta H = -296.1 \text{ kJ}$$

⃝ Answers to Focus Questions

1. The sign for enthalpy in an exothermic reaction is negative because from the system's point of view, energy as heat is leaving the system.

2. To find the heat of reaction the mass (5.0 g) must be multiplied by the specific heat capacity and the result multiplied by the change in temperature (9 °C).

3. Hess's law states that the change in enthalpy for a reaction is the same whether the reaction occurs in one step or in a series of steps. It is important because it allows us to calculate heats of reaction that are difficult or inconvenient to measure in a calorimeter.

4. −220.81 kJ

Student Preparation
Assign the students to read Sections 10.8 and 10.10 and to answer the Focus Questions at the end of Section 10.10 before coming to class.

Active Learning
After introducing the material in Sections 10.8 to 10.10 in class, place the students in groups and have them work together on Sections 10.8–10.10: Team Learning Worksheet. Answers and/or discussion of these questions are located in the *Teacher Resources*.

TEACHING TIP

This section introduces the concept that energy naturally changes from useful forms to less useful forms. Each energy transformation results in the same amount of energy but in a less useful form. The focus on the quality of energy, rather than the quantity of energy, is the key idea to present here.

10.8 Quality Versus Quantity of Energy

Objective: *To see how the quality of energy changes as it is used.*

One of the most important characteristics of energy is that it is conserved. Thus the total energy content of the universe will always be what it is now. If that is the case, why are we concerned about energy? For example, why should we worry about conserving our petroleum supply? Surprisingly, the "energy crisis" is not about the *quantity* of energy, but rather about the *quality* of energy. To understand this idea, consider an automobile trip from Chicago to Denver. Along the way you would put gasoline into the car to get to Denver. What happens to that energy? The energy stored in the bonds of the gasoline and of the oxygen that reacts with it is changed to thermal energy, which is spread along the highway to Denver. The total quantity of energy remains the same as before the trip but the energy concentrated in the gasoline becomes widely distributed in the environment:

$$\text{gasoline}(l) + O_2(g) \rightarrow CO_2(g) + H_2O(l) + \text{energy}$$

C_8H_{18} and other similar compounds

Spread along the highway, heating the road and the air

Which energy is easier to use to do work: the concentrated energy in the gasoline or the thermal energy spread from Chicago to Denver? Of course, the energy concentrated in the gasoline is more convenient to use.

This example illustrates a very important general principle: when we utilize energy to do work, we degrade its usefulness. In other words, when we use energy the *quality* of that energy (its ease of use) is lowered.

In summary,

Concentrated energy → Use the energy to do work → Spread energy

You may have heard someone mention the "heat death" of the universe. Eventually (many eons from now), all energy will be spread evenly throughout the universe and everything will be at the same temperature. At this point it will no longer be possible to do any work. The universe will be "dead."

We don't have to worry about the heat death of the universe anytime soon, of course, but we do need to think about conserving "quality" energy supplies. The energy stored in petroleum molecules got there over millions of years through plants and simple animals absorbing energy from the sun and using this energy to construct molecules. As these organisms died and became buried, natural processes changed them into the petroleum deposits we now access for our supplies of gasoline and natural gas.

Petroleum is highly valuable because it furnishes a convenient, concentrated source of energy. Unfortunately, we are using this fuel at a much faster rate than natural processes can replace it, so we are looking for new sources of energy. The most logical energy source is the sun. *Solar energy* refers to using the sun's energy directly to do productive work in our society. We will discuss energy supplies in the next section.

306 Chapter 10 Energy

10.9 Energy and Our World

Objective: *To consider the energy resources of our world.*

Woody plants, coal, petroleum, and natural gas provide a vast resource of energy that originally came from the sun. By the process of photosynthesis, plants store energy that can be claimed by burning the plants themselves or the decay products that have been converted over millions of years to **fossil fuels.** Although the United States currently depends heavily on petroleum for energy, this dependency is a relatively recent phenomenon, as shown in **Figure 10.7.** In this section we discuss some sources of energy and their effects on the environment.

Figure 10.7
Energy sources used in the United States.

Petroleum and Natural Gas

Although how they were produced is not completely understood, petroleum and natural gas were most likely formed from the remains of marine organisms that lived approximately 500 million years ago. **Petroleum** is a thick, dark liquid composed mostly of compounds called *hydrocarbons* that contain carbon and hydrogen. (Carbon is unique among elements in the extent to which it can bond to itself to form chains of various lengths.) **Table 10.2** gives the formulas and names for several common hydrocarbons. **Natural gas,** usually associated with petroleum deposits, consists mostly of methane, but it also contains significant amounts of ethane, propane, and butane.

The composition of petroleum varies somewhat, but it includes mostly hydrocarbons having chains that contain from 5 to more than 25 carbons. To be used efficiently, the petroleum must be separated into fractions by boiling. The lighter molecules (having the lowest boiling points) can be boiled off, leaving the heavier ones behind. The commercial uses of various petroleum fractions are shown in **Table 10.3.**

The petroleum era began when the demand for lamp oil during the Industrial Revolution outstripped the traditional sources: animal fats

TABLE 10.2

Names and Formulas for Some Common Hydrocarbons

Formula	Name
CH_4	Methane
C_2H_6	Ethane
C_3H_8	Propane
C_4H_{10}	Butane
C_5H_{12}	Pentane
C_6H_{14}	Hexane
C_7H_{16}	Heptane
C_8H_{18}	Octane

TABLE 10.3

Uses of the Various Petroleum Fractions

Petroleum Fraction in Terms of Numbers of Carbon Atoms	Major Uses
C_5–C_{10}	Gasoline
C_{10}–C_{18}	Kerosene
	Jet fuel
C_{15}–C_{25}	Diesel fuel
	Heating oil
	Lubricating oil
>C_{25}	Asphalt

10.9 Energy and Our World

10.9 Energy and Our World **307**

Themes
Energy

Skills
Applying concepts, interpreting data, making comparisons, making predictions

TEACHING TIP

This section offers an excellent opportunity for students to work on a cross-curricular project with the Social Science department. Have them research energy resources in the news and on the web. They can make classroom presentations on alternative resources, have a debate about the advantages and disadvantages of different fuels, or discuss the implications of our energy use for the future.

USING TECHNOLOGY

 Figure 10.7

Additional Activity

Have students determine energy use inking with fuel and electric bills. Estimate an average yearly consumption of

Electricity in kilowatt hours (1 kWh = 3595 J)
Natural gas in therms or BTUs (1 therm = 1054 kJ)
Oil in gallons

Once this exercise is complete, find the annual class average. Then determine the annual city average, state average, and country average.

A similar exercise can be done using gasoline. Determine the weekly consumption of gasoline by an individual. Next determine the average consumption of gasoline in your school. Finally determine the cost of this fuel.

and whale oil. In response to this increased demand, Edwin Drake drilled the first oil well in 1859 at Titusville, Pennsylvania. The petroleum from this well was refined to produce *kerosene* (fraction $C_{10}–C_{18}$), which served as an excellent lamp oil. *Gasoline* (fraction $C_5–C_{10}$) had limited use and was often discarded. This situation soon changed. The development of the electric light decreased the need for kerosene, and the advent of the "horseless carriage" with its gasoline-powered engine signaled the birth of the gasoline age.

As gasoline became more important, new ways were sought to increase the yield of gasoline obtained from each barrel of petroleum. William Burton invented a process at Standard Oil of Indiana called *pyrolytic (high-temperature) cracking.* In this process, the heavier molecules of the kerosene fraction are heated to about 700 °C, causing them to break (crack) into the smaller molecules of hydrocarbons in the gasoline fraction. As cars became larger, more efficient internal combustion engines were designed. Because of the uneven burning of the gasoline then available, these engines "knocked," producing unwanted noise and even engine damage. Intensive research to find additives that would promote smoother burning produced tetraethyl lead, $(C_2H_5)_4Pb$, a very effective "antiknock" agent.

The addition of tetraethyl lead to gasoline became a common practice, and by 1960, gasoline contained as much as 3g of lead per gallon. As we have discovered so often in recent years, technological advances can produce environmental problems. To prevent air pollution from automobile exhaust, catalytic converters have been added to car exhaust systems. The effectiveness of these converters, however, is destroyed by lead. The use of leaded gasoline also greatly increased the amount of lead in the environment, where it can be ingested by animals and humans. For these reasons, the use of lead in gasoline has been phased out, requiring extensive (and expensive) modifications of engines and of the gasoline refining process.

CHEMISTRY

Coal has variable composition depending on both its age and location.

Coal

Coal was formed from the remains of plants that were buried and subjected to high pressure and heat over long periods of time. Plant materials have a high content of cellulose, a complex molecule whose empirical formula is CH_2O but whose molar mass is approximately 500,000 g/mol. After the plants and trees that grew on the earth at various times and places died and were buried, chemical changes gradually lowered the oxygen and hydrogen content of the cellulose molecules. Coal "matures" through four stages: lignite, subbituminous, bituminous, and anthracite. Each stage has a higher carbon-to-oxygen and carbon-to-hydrogen ratio; that is, the relative carbon content gradually increases. Typical elemental compositions of the various coals are given in **Table 10.4.** The energy available from the combustion of a given mass of coal increases as the carbon content increases. Anthracite is the most valuable coal, and lignite is the least valuable.

Coal is an important and plentiful fuel in the United States, currently furnishing ap-

TABLE 10.4

Element Composition of Various Types of Coal

Type of Coal	Mass Percent of Each Element				
	C	H	O	N	S
Lignite	71	4	23	1	1
Subbituminous	77	5	16	1	1
Bituminous	80	6	8	1	5
Anthracite	92	3	3	1	1

Coal being strip-mined.

proximately 20% of our energy. As the supply of petroleum decreases, the share of the energy supply from coal could eventually increase to as high as 30%. However, coal is expensive and dangerous to mine underground, and the strip mining of fertile farmland in the Midwest or of scenic land in the West causes obvious problems. In addition, the burning of coal, especially high-sulfur coal, yields air pollutants such as sulfur dioxide, which, in turn, can lead to acid rain. However, even if coal were pure carbon, the carbon dioxide produced when it was burned would still have significant effects on the earth's climate.

Effects of Carbon Dioxide on Climate

The earth receives a tremendous quantity of radiant energy from the sun, about 30% of which is reflected back into space by the earth's atmosphere. The remaining energy passes through the atmosphere to the earth's surface. Some of this energy is absorbed by plants for photosynthesis and some by the oceans to evaporate water, but most of it is absorbed by soil, rocks, and water, increasing the temperature of the earth's surface. This energy is, in turn, radiated from the heated surface mainly as *infrared radiation*, often called *heat radiation*.

The atmosphere, like window glass, is transparent to visible light but does not allow all the infrared radiation to pass back into space. Molecules in the atmosphere, principally H_2O and CO_2, strongly absorb infrared radiation and radiate it back toward the earth, as shown in **Figure 10.8.** A net amount of thermal energy is retained by the earth's atmosphere, causing the earth to be much warmer than it would be without its atmosphere. In a

CHEMISTRY

The average temperature of the earth's surface is 298 K. It would be 255 K without the "greenhouse gases."

Figure 10.8
The earth's atmosphere is transparent to visible light from the sun. This visible light strikes the earth, and part of it is changed to infrared radiation. The infrared radiation from the earth's surface is strongly absorbed by CO_2, H_2O, and other molecules present in smaller amounts (for example, CH_4 and N_2O) in the atmosphere. In effect, the atmosphere traps some of the energy, acting like the glass in a greenhouse and keeping the earth warmer than it would otherwise be.

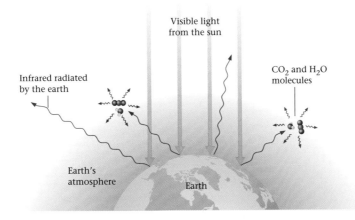

Visible light from the sun

Infrared radiated by the earth

CO_2 and H_2O molecules

Earth's atmosphere

Earth

10.9 Energy and Our World **309**

This resolution would not solve all of our pollution problems. Most likely it would just shift the pollution to where the batteries are produced. Energy is required to make batteries and electricity is required to charge them, so the pollution would be concentrated there.

A government study concludes that burning fossil fuels to power our automobiles causes too much pollution.

What if Congress decided that all cars and trucks must be powered by batteries? Would this change solve the air pollution problems caused by transportation?

way, the atmosphere acts like the glass of a greenhouse, which is transparent to visible light but absorbs infrared radiation, thus raising the temperature inside the building. This **greenhouse effect** is seen even more spectacularly on Venus, where the dense atmosphere is thought to be responsible for the high surface temperature of that planet.

Thus the temperature of the earth's surface is controlled to a significant extent by the carbon dioxide and water content of the atmosphere. The effect of atmospheric moisture (humidity) is readily apparent in the Midwest, for example. In summer, when the humidity is high, the heat of the sun is retained well into the night, giving very high nighttime temperatures. In winter, the coldest temperatures always occur on clear nights, when the low humidity allows efficient radiation of energy back into space.

The atmosphere's water content is controlled by the water cycle (evaporation and precipitation), and the average has remained constant over the years. However, as fossil fuels have been used more extensively, the carbon dioxide concentration has increased—up about 20% from 1880 to the present. Projections indicate that the carbon dioxide content of the atmosphere may be double in the twenty-first century what it was in 1880. This trend *could* increase the earth's average temperature by as much as 10 °C, causing dramatic changes in climate and greatly affecting the growth of food crops.

How well can we predict the long-term effects of carbon dioxide? Because weather has been studied for a period of time that is minuscule compared with the age of the earth, the factors that control the earth's climate in the long range are not clearly understood. For example, we do not understand what causes the earth's periodic ice ages. So it is difficult to estimate the effects of the increasing carbon dioxide levels.

In fact, the variation in the earth's average temperature over the past century is somewhat confusing. In the northern latitudes during the past century, the average temperature rose by 0.8 °C over a period of 60 years, then cooled by 0.5 °C during the next 25 years, and finally warmed by 0.2 °C in the succeeding 15 years. Such fluctuations do not match the steady increase in carbon dioxide. However, in southern latitudes and near the equator during the past century, the average temperature showed a steady rise totaling 0.4 °C. This figure is in reasonable agreement with the predicted effect of the increasing carbon dioxide concentration over that period. Another significant fact is that the last 10 years of the twentieth century have been the warmest decade on record.

Although the exact relationship between the carbon dioxide concentration in the atmosphere and the earth's temperature is not known at present, one thing is clear: The increase in the atmospheric concentration of carbon dioxide is quite dramatic (see **Figure 10.9**). We must consider the implications of this increase as we consider our future energy needs.

Figure 10.9
The atmospheric CO_2 concentration over the past 1000 years, based on ice core data and direct readings (since 1958). Note the dramatic increase in the past 100 years.

Veggie Gasoline?

Gasoline usage is as high as ever, and world petroleum supplies will eventually run out. One possible alternative to petroleum as a source of fuels and lubricants is vegetable oil—the same vegetable oil we now use to cook french fries. Researchers believe that the oils from soybeans, corn, canola, and sunflowers all have the potential to be used in cars as well as on salads.

The use of vegetable oil for fuel is not a new idea. Rudolf Diesel reportedly used peanut oil to run one of his engines at the Paris Exposition in 1900. In addition, ethyl alcohol has been used widely as a fuel in South America and as a fuel additive in the United States.

Biodiesel, a fuel made from the fatty acids found in vegetable oil, has some real advantages over regular diesel fuel. Biodiesel produces fewer pollutants such as particulates, carbon monoxide, and complex organic molecules. Also, because vegetable oils have no sulfur, there is no noxious sulfur dioxide in the exhaust gases. Biodiesel can run in existing engines with little modification. In addition, it is much more biodegradable than petroleum-based fuels, so spills cause less environmental damage.

Of course, biodiesel has some serious drawbacks. The main one is that it costs about three times as much as regular diesel fuel. Biodiesel also produces more nitrogen oxides in the exhaust

than conventional diesel fuel and is less stable in storage. It can leave more gummy deposits in engines and must be "winterized" by removing components that tend to solidify at low temperatures.

The best solution may be to use biodiesel as an additive to regular diesel fuel. One such fuel is known as B20 because it is 20% biodiesel and 80% conventional diesel fuel. B20 is especially attractive because of the higher lubricating ability of vegetable oils, which reduces diesel engine wear.

Vegetable oils are also being considered as replacements for motor oils and hydraulic fluids. Tests of a sunflower seed–based engine lubricant manufactured by Renewable Lubricants of Hartville, Ohio, have shown satisfactory lubricating ability and lower particle emissions. In addition, Lou Honary and his colleagues at the University of Northern Iowa have developed BioSOY, a vegetable oil–based hydraulic fluid for use in heavy machinery.

Veggie oil fuels and lubricants seem to have a growing market as petroleum supplies wane and as environmental laws become more stringent. In Germany's Black Forest region, for example, environmental protection laws require that farm equipment use only vegetable oil fuels and lubricants. In the near future there may be veggie oil in your garage as well as in your kitchen.

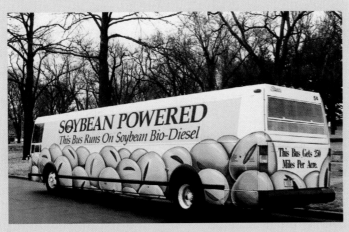

This promotion bus both advertises biodiesel and demonstrates its usefulness.

Adapted from "Fill 'Er Up . . . with Veggie Oil," by Corinna Wu, as appeared in *Science News*, Vol 154, December 5, 1998, p. 364.

10.9 Energy and Our World **311**

Veggie Gasoline?

"Veggie Gasoline?" brings up the research into alternative fuels meant to supplement or replace the increasingly expensive supplies of petroleum. Although the "energy crisis" has not seemed very acute for the last 25 years, the problem of limited petroleum supplies in the hands of relatively few countries is an ongoing issue that is in the news again because of the high prices of gasoline and heating oil. Now would be a good time to discuss with your students the "petroleum story"—the fact that petroleum was formed from plants and primitive animals that stored energy from the sun through photosynthesis. Because this process took millions of years, petroleum is not a renewable energy resource; there is a limited amount. As the supply dwindles, the price will become very high. Thus we need to develop energy sources that are truly renewable, such as the oil described in the Chemical Impact.

This chapter also presents the opportunity to discuss the true nature of the "energy crisis." It's really not about supplies of energy. Because energy is conserved, we always have the same amount. The energy crisis is about the *quality* of energy, not the *quantity* of energy. As we "use" energy, we degrade its quality. For example, petroleum is high-quality energy because it contains lots of stored energy in a very compact form. It took millions of years to form. When we burn petroleum to power our cars and heat our houses, we spread this energy throughout the environment via heat. This spread energy is much lower quality—it is much more difficult to use. To power our society we need concentrated sources of energy such as petroleum, coal, alcohol from corn, and oil from plants. Of course, the eventual hope is that we will learn to harness solar energy directly. Much research is being done to find devices that can transform solar polar directly into electrical power.

New Energy Sources

As we search for the energy sources of the future, we need to consider economic, climatic, and supply factors. There are several potential energy sources: the sun (solar), nuclear processes (fission and fusion), biomass (plants), and synthetic fuels. Direct use of the sun's radiant energy to heat our homes and run our factories and transportation systems seems a sensible long-term goal. But what do we do now? Conservation of fossil fuels is one obvious step, but substitutes for fossil fuels also must be found. There is much research going on now to solve this problem.

TEACHING TIP

In this section we discuss the "why" of energy. As in previous chapters, we emphasize that scientists want to know not only the "what" about a particular topic but also the "why." Energy is a driving force in chemical reactions. In this section we discuss why this driving force arises and use the "why" as a basis for introducing the concept of entropy on a qualitative level.

 10.10 Energy as a Driving Force

Objective: *To understand energy as a driving force for natural processes.*

A major goal of science is to understand why things happen as they do. In particular, we are interested in the driving forces of nature. Why do things occur in a particular direction? For example, consider a log that has burned in a fireplace, producing ashes and heat energy. If you are sitting in front of the fireplace, you would be very surprised to see the ashes begin to absorb heat from the air and reconstruct themselves into the log. It just doesn't happen. That is, the process that always occurs is

$$\text{log} + O_2(g) \rightarrow CO_2(g) + H_2O(g) + \text{ashes} + \text{energy}$$

The reverse of this process

$$CO_2(g) + H_2O(g) + \text{ashes} + \text{heat} \rightarrow \text{log} + O_2(g)$$

never happens.

Consider another example. A gas is trapped in one end of a vessel as shown below.

Ideal gas — — Vacuum

When the valve is opened, what always happens? The gas spreads evenly throughout the entire container.

You would be very surprised to see the following process occur spontaneously:

So, why does this process

occur spontaneously but the reverse process

never occur?

In many years of analyzing these and many other processes, scientists have discovered two very important driving forces:

- Energy spread
- Matter spread

Energy spread means that in a given process, concentrated energy is dispersed widely. This distribution happens every time an exothermic process occurs. For example, when a Bunsen burner burns, the energy stored in the fuel (natural gas—mostly methane) is dispersed into the surrounding air:

The energy that flows into the surroundings through heat increases the thermal motions of the molecules in the surroundings. In other words, this process increases the random motions of the molecules in the surroundings. *This always happens in every exothermic process.*

Matter spread means exactly what it says: the molecules of a substance are spread out and occupy a larger volume.

10.10 Energy as a Driving Force **313**

After looking at thousands of processes, scientists have concluded that these two factors are the important driving forces that cause events to occur. That is, processes are favored if they involve energy spread and matter spread.

Do these driving forces ever occur in opposition? Yes, they do—in many, many processes.

For example, consider ordinary table salt dissolving in water.

This process occurs spontaneously. You observe it every time you add salt to water to cook potatoes or pasta. Surprisingly, dissolving salt in water is *endothermic*. This process seems to go in the wrong direction—it involves energy concentration, not energy spread. Why does the salt dissolve? Because of matter spread. The Na^+ and Cl^- that are closely packed in the solid NaCl become spread around randomly in a much larger volume in the resulting solution. Salt dissolves in water because the favorable matter spread overcomes an unfavorable energy change.

Entropy

Entropy is a function we have invented to keep track of the natural tendency for the components of the universe to become disordered—entropy (designated by the letter S) is a measure of disorder or randomness. As randomness increases, S increases. Which has lower entropy, solid water (ice) or gaseous water (steam)? Remember that ice contains closely packed, ordered H_2O molecules, and steam has widely dispersed, randomly moving H_2O molecules (see **Figure 10.10**). Thus ice has more order and a lower value of S.

Figure 10.10
Comparing the entropies of ice and steam.

Solid (Ice)   Gas (Steam)

314   Chapter 10   Energy

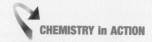

CHEMISTRY in ACTION

Distribution of Wealth

Materials Each student/group will need 20 pennies.

Purpose Students will better understand the concept of a distribution.

Discussion While individual groups may have graphs that look different from a typical Boltzmann distribution (bell curve), the data from the entire class should begin to give a rather

What do you suppose happens to the disorder of the universe as energy spread and matter spread occur during a process?

 Energy spread → Faster random motions of the molecules in surroundings

Matter spread → Components of matter are dispersed—they occupy a larger volume

It seems clear that both energy spread and matter spread lead to greater entropy (greater disorder) in the universe. This idea leads to a very important conclusion that is summarized in the second law of thermodynamics:

The entropy of the universe is always increasing.

That is, all processes that occur in the universe lead to a net increase in the disorder of the universe. As the universe "runs," it is always heading toward more disorder. We are plunging slowly but inevitably toward total randomness—the heat death of the universe. But don't despair, it will not happen soon.

WHAT IF?

What if the first law of thermodynamics is true, but the second law is not? How would the world be different?

Focus Questions

Sections 10.8–10.10

1. If energy is conserved, how can there be an "energy crisis"?
2. What is "cracking" of petroleum products? How did it help increase production of gasoline?
3. What is the greenhouse effect and what are the key molecules that cause it?
4. What driving force must be predominant for an endothermic reaction to occur? Why?

CHEMISTRY in ACTION

Distribution of Wealth

1. Obtain 20 pennies. Flip all of them and record the number of heads (head count). Do this 30 times.
2. Determine the frequency of each head count by counting the number of times each different head count appears. Construct a bar graph of frequency versus head count.
3. Obtain data from the other groups in your class and make a bar graph of frequency versus head count for all of the data.
4. How can these graphs be related to probability?

Focus Questions   **315**

WHAT IF Comments

The first law of thermodynamics tells us that energy is conserved. The second law gives us some indication of the natural direction of energy flows (the second law is often described as "time's arrow"). For example, the first law cannot explain why we could not "uncook" an egg by putting a cooked egg in the refrigerator, or why a ball that has just rolled down a hill (and has transferred energy to the hill) could not roll up the hill by spontaneously gathering the newly transferred energy from the hill. The second law informs us that these phenomena are impossible.

 Answers to Focus Questions

1. The amount of *useful* energy in the world is changing. As energy is used it is transformed into less useful forms. This situation creates the energy crisis—a constant quantity of energy is available but of lower quality.

2. Cracking is the high-temperature breaking of large petroleum molecules into the smaller hydrocarbon molecules that are found in the gasoline fraction of petroleum. It increases the amount of gasoline from each barrel of petroleum.

3. The greenhouse effect is the trapping of infrared radiation by molecules within the atmosphere, which raises the temperature of the earth. The key molecules in this process are water and carbon dioxide.

4. The driving force of matter spread must be predominant for an endothermic reaction to occur. The matter spread must overcome an energy change that occurs in opposition to it (energy concentration).

0	1	2	3	4	5	6	7	8	9	10	11	12	13	14	15	16	17	18	19	20
0	0	0	0	0	0	1	2	4	5	5	5	4	2	1	0	0	0	0	0	0

0	1	2	3	4	5	6	7	8	9	10	11	12	13	14	15	16	17	18	19	20
0	0	0	0	2	7	17	33	54	72	79	72	54	33	17	7	2	0	0	0	0

smooth distribution. This activity shows students that anything could happen (there may even be one trial in which all pennies are heads or all are tails) but that there is also a most likely, expected configuration (10 heads and 10 tails). This idea is the main point in understanding entropy—from a probability perspective, there is a driving force in the way matter (and energy) spreads. For example, a sample of a gas will spread to fill its container because this state has the greatest number of configurations. It is not impossible for all of the gas molecules to gather into one corner of the room, just very improbable (so improbable we will never see it).

With 20 coins and 30 repetitions (flipping all 20 coins each time), you can expect the following (approximate) distribution (the top row is number of heads). The bottom row is the number of times that this number of heads will likely occur in the 30 repetitions.

With 15 groups (450 repetitions), we can expect the following (approximate) distribution (the top row is number of heads).

Which Is Your Metal?

Objectives

1. To determine the specific heat capacity of a metal

2. To use this determination of specific heat capacity to identify the metal

Skills

Applying concepts, interpreting data, calculating

Materials

Goggles	Water
Apron	"Unknown"
2 foam cups	metal
Lid for foam cup	Graduated
(2 holes)	cylinder
Ringstand	Bunsen burner
Ring	Tongs
Wire gauze	Stirrer
Matches	Thermometer

Preparation Hints

Provide the students with as many different metal samples as possible.

Prelab Discussion

Students must wear safety goggles and lab aprons while in the lab.

Students should tie back their hair and loose clothing whenever they work with a flame in the lab. Students will often deposit matches in the sink. Tell them to dispose of burned matches in the trashcan after they are cool.

Procedure Hints

Make sure that students quickly transfer the metal from the boiling water to the water in the calorimeter. Most of the errors in this lab occur during this step.

Sample Data/Answers

Prelab Assignment

2. The final temperature of the metal is the same as the final temperature of the water.

3. The boiling water will reach a final constant temperature (this temperature will be close to 100 °C but should be measured).

4. We can assume that the density of water is 1.0 g/mL.

Data/Observations

The sample data provided are for aluminum.

Problem

What is the identity of the metal you are given?

Preparation

The specific heat capacity is the amount of energy required to change the temperature of one gram of a substance by one Celsius degree. Each substance has a unique specific heat capacity. In this lab you will use a determination of the specific heat capacity to identify an "unknown" metal.

Specific Heat Capacities (J/g °C)

water: 4.183
  Zn: 0.3882
  Al: 0.8910
  Sn: 0.2271
  Pb: 0.1280
  Cu: 0.3844

Prelab Assignment

1. Read the entire lab experiment before you begin.
2. How do you know the final temperature of the metal?
3. Why do you use a hot water bath to heat the metal?
4. Why do you measure the *volume* of the water in the calorimeter when we need to know the *mass* of the water for the calculations?

Materials

Goggles
Apron
2 Styrofoam cups
Lid for foam cup (2 holes)
Ring stand
Ring
Wire gauze
Matches
Water
"Unknown" metal
Graduated cylinder
Bunsen burner
Tongs
Stirrer
Thermometer

Safety

1. You will work with a flame in this lab. Tie back hair and loose clothing.
2. Do not drop matches into the sink. Dispose of burned matches in the trashcan after they are cool.

Procedure

1. Find the mass of your metal sample.
2. Place one foam cup into the other. This is your calorimeter.
3. Measure 75.0 mL of water and place it in your calorimeter. Record the temperature of the water.
4. Set up the ring and ring stand and place the 250-mL beaker on the wire gauze as shown in the figure.

Setup to boil water.

5. Add about 100 mL of water to the beaker and place the metal in the water.
6. Use a Bunsen burner to heat the water to boiling. Allow the metal to remain in the boiling water for at least three minutes. Record the temperature of the boiling water.
7. Using the tongs, quickly transfer the metal from the boiling water to the calorimeter. Cover the calorimeter.
8. Gently stir the water in the calorimeter for several seconds (do **not** use the thermometer).
9. Record the highest temperature reached.
10. Repeat these steps two more times.

Cleaning Up

Clean all materials and wash your hands thoroughly.

	Trial 1	Trial 2	Trial 3
Mass of metal	12.8 g	12.8 g	12.7 g
Mass of water (calorimeter)	75.0 g	75.0 g	75.0 g
Initial temperature of metal	100.0 °C	99.8 °C	100.0 °C
Initial temperature of water	24.2 °C	24.1 °C	24.2 °C
Final temperature of water	26.9 °C	26.7 °C	26.9 °C

Analysis and Conclusions

1. Trial 1: 847 J; Trial 2: 815 J; Trial 3: 847 J

2. It is the same (disregarding heat transferred to the surroundings).

3. Trial 1: 0.905 J/g °C; Trial 2: 0.872 J/g °C; Trial 3: 0.912 J/g °C

4. Average = 0.896 J/g °C

5. The metal is aluminum.

6. 0.561% error

7. a. The hot water will raise the final temperature. This change

Data/Observations

Fill in a table similar to the one shown.

	Trial #1	Trial #2	Trial #3
Mass of metal			
Mass of water (calorimeter)			
Initial temperature of metal			
Initial temperature of water			
Final temperature of water			

Analysis and Conclusions

1. Calculate the heat transferred to the water in the calorimeter in each trial.

2. How does the heat transferred to the water in the calorimeter compare to the heat transferred from the metal in the calorimeter?

3. Calculate the specific heat capacity of your metal in each trial.

4. Calculate the average specific heat capacity of your metal.

5. What is the identity of your metal?

6. Assuming that you identified your metal correctly, what is your percent error in the specific heat capacity?

7. Both of the following errors would cause a change in the calculated specific heat capacity for your metal. Would each change raise or lower your calculated value of the specific heat capacity? Explain.

   a. A significant amount of water is transferred with the hot metal.

   b. The metal "cools off" as you transfer it from the hot water to the calorimeter.

8. Suppose that in the procedure you added metal at room temperature to hot water. How do you think it would affect your percent error (higher, lower, or the same)? Explain your reasoning.

Something Extra

Will you get similar results if you use a beaker instead of nested foam cups? What about a paper cup? Try it.

10 Chapter Review

Key Terms

energy (10.1)
law of conservation of energy (10.1)
potential energy (10.1)
kinetic energy (10.1)
work (10.1)
state function (10.1)
temperature (10.2)
heat (10.2)
system (10.3)
surroundings (10.3)
exothermic (10.3)
endothermic (10.3)
thermodynamics (10.4)
first law of thermodynamics (10.4)

internal energy (10.4)
calorie (10.5)
joule (10.5)
specific heat capacity (10.5)
enthalpy (10.6)
calorimeter (10.6)
Hess's law (10.7)
fossil fuels (10.9)
petroleum (10.9)
natural gas (10.9)
coal (10.9)
greenhouse effect (10.9)
energy spread (10.10)
matter spread (10.10)

Summary

1. One of the fundamental characteristics of energy is that it is conserved. Energy is changed in form but it is not produced or consumed in a process. Thermodynamics is the study of energy and its changes.

2. In a process some functions—called state functions—depend only on the beginning and final states of the system, not on the specific pathway followed. Energy is a state function. Other functions, such as heat and work, depend on the specific pathway followed and are not state functions.

3. The temperature of a substance indicates the vigor of the random motions of the components of that substance. The thermal energy of an object is the energy content of the object as produced by its random motions.

Chapter Review   **317**

---

will make it seem as if the metal did not change its temperature as much, so the specific heat capacity will be calculated at a higher value.

b. If the metal enters the water at a lower temperature, the final temperature of the water will be lower. It will seem as if the metal changed its temperature by a greater amount, so the specific heat capacity will be calculated at a lower value.

8. The percent error will be greater. It will not be obvious when to take the final temperature of the water because the hot water will be cooled by the metal. Even though the foam cups are thermal insulators, the water will eventually cool to the same temperature as the room. We add hot metal to cool water because we can then measure the highest temperature of the water.

Something Extra
More heat will be transferred to the surroundings. The percent error will be larger.

Chapter Review
Assign the students to work individually on the Chapter 10 Review Worksheet at the appropriate level (Basic, Standard, or Challenge). Answers are found in the *Teacher Resources*.

Assessment
Chapter 10 Test is found in the *Teacher Resources*, along with the answers for the test.

 Computerized Test Bank for Chapter 10

Answers to End of Chapter Problems

1. Kinetic energy is energy of motion. Potential energy is energy of position.

2. Some energy is given off in other forms such as heat or light.

3. A state function is a function that is not dependent on the pathway. Energy is an example of a state function; heat and work are not state functions.

4. Ball A has higher potential energy in Figure 10.1a because of its higher position initially. In Figure 10.1b, ball B has the higher potential energy.

5. Because energy is conserved in any process, the pathway of the process does not matter. Thus energy is a

state function.

6. Heat is a flow of energy due to a temperature difference; temperature is a measure of the average kinetic energy of a substance; thermal energy comes from the random motion of the components of the substance.

7. (a) No; temperature is a measure of average kinetic energy. (b) Yes; the thermal energy is from the random motions of the components of an object.

8. The particles in the hot coffee are moving faster than the particles in the cold soft drink. Because they are in the same room, they are both in contact with air at the same temperature. The particles in the coffee will slow down (a decrease in temperature) and the particles in the soft drink will speed up (an increase in temperature). Eventually the kinetic energy of the two samples will be the same.

9. There is more heat involved in mixing 100.0-g samples of 60 °C and 10 °C water because there is a larger temperature difference.

10. The final temperature should be less than 90 °C and greater than 50 °C. If the water samples had equal mass, the final temperature would be the average of the two (50 °C). Because we have more of the warmer water, the final temperature will be higher than the average of the two temperatures. (*Note:* The actual temperature would be 63 °C).

11. The potential energy is the energy available to do work. Potential energy in a chemical reaction is stored in the chemical bonds.

12. The chemical is stable; the bonds holding the atoms in the molecule are strong.

13. the reactants

14. (a) endothermic; (b) exothermic; (c) exothermic; (d) endothermic

15. the process is exothermic; the process is endothermic

16. the system does work on the surroundings; the surroundings do work on the system

17. The chemist chooses the sign based on whether energy

4. Heat is a flow of energy between two objects due to a temperature difference in the two objects. In an exothermic reaction, energy as heat flows out of the system into its surroundings. In an endothermic process, energy as heat flows from the surroundings into the system.

5. The internal energy of an object is the sum of the kinetic (due to motion) and potential (due to position) energies of the object. Internal energy can be changed by two types of energy flows, work (w) and heat (q): $\Delta E = q + w$.

6. A calorimeter is used to measure the heats of chemical reactions. The common units for heat are joules and calories.

7. The specific heat capacity of a substance (the energy required to change the temperature of one gram of the substance by one Celsius degree) is used to calculate temperature changes when a substance is heated.

8. The change in enthalpy for a process is equal to the heat for that process run at constant pressure.

9. Hess's law allows the calculation of the heat of a given reaction from known heats of related reactions.

10. Although energy is conserved in every process, the quality (usefulness) of the energy decreases with each use.

11. Our world has many sources of energy. The use of these sources affects the environment in various ways.

12. Natural processes occur in the direction that leads to an increase in the disorder (entropy) of the universe. The principal driving forces for processes are energy spread and matter spread.

Questions and Problems

All exercises with blue numbers have answers in the back of this book.

10.1 The Nature of Energy

Questions

1. Explain the difference between kinetic and potential energy.

2. Why isn't all energy available for work?

3. Explain what is meant by the term "state function." Provide examples of state functions.

4. In Figure 10.1a, which ball has the higher potential energy? Explain. What about in Figure 10.1b?

5. The law of conservation of energy means that energy is a state function. Explain why.

10.2 Temperature and Heat

Questions

6. Explain the differences among heat, temperature, and thermal energy.

7. Do each of the following depend on the amount of substance you have? Explain.
   a. temperature
   b. thermal energy

8. Provide a molecular-level explanation of why the temperatures of a cold soft drink and hot coffee in the same room will eventually be the same.

9. In which case is more heat involved: mixing 100.0-g samples of 90 °C water and 80 °C water or mixing 100.0-g samples of 60 °C water and 10 °C water? Assume no heat is lost to the environment.

10. If 100.0 g of water at 90 °C is added to 50.0 g of water at 10 °C, estimate the final temperature of the water. Explain your reasoning.

10.3 Exothermic and Endothermic Processes

Questions

11. What is meant by potential energy in a chemical reaction? Where is it located?

12. What does it mean for a chemical to have a low potential energy?

13. Do the reactants or the products have the lower potential energy in an endothermic reaction?

14. Are the following processes exothermic or endothermic?
   a. When solid KBr is dissolved in water, the solution gets colder.
   b. Natural gas (CH_4) is burned in a furnace.
   c. When concentrated sulfuric acid is added to water, the solution gets very hot.
   d. Water is boiled in a tea kettle.

10.4 Thermodynamics

Questions

15. What does it mean when energy is reported with a negative sign? A positive sign?

16. What does it mean when work is reported with a negative sign? A positive sign?

17. In thermodynamics the chemist takes the system's point of view. What does this statement mean?

flows from the system (negative sign) or into the system (positive sign).

18. Engineers make machines that do work (the machine is the system and work is done on the surroundings). Thus they define work from the surroundings' point of view. Work done by the system has a positive sign (which is the opposite of that of the chemist).

19. (a) 36 kJ; (b) 35 kJ; (c) –85 kJ

20. 16 kJ

21. –21 kJ

22. In ice, the water molecules are held together rigidly in fixed positions. As the sample is heated, the molecules vibrate but stay in their positions until the melting point is reached. Once the melting point is reached, the molecules move around much more freely (although they are still held together). As more heat is applied, the molecules move more quickly and freely until the boiling point is reached. When the individual

molecules are moving quickly enough to overcome the forces holding them together, they escape from the liquid. As the molecules of the vapor are heated, they move more and more quickly.

23. lower

24. 1.70×10^3 J

25. (a) 32,820 J; 32.82 kJ; (b) 1.90×10^5 J; 190. kJ; (c) 2.600×10^5 J; 260. kJ; (d) 1.80×10^5 J; 180. kJ

26. 7.11 J/g °C

18. How do engineers define energy and work differently from chemists? Why do engineers take this approach?

Problems

19. Calculate ΔE for each of the following cases.
    a. $q = +51$ kJ, $w = -15$ kJ
    b. $q = +100.$ kJ, $w = -65$ kJ
    c. $q = -65$ kJ, $w = -20.$ kJ

20. A gas absorbs 45 kJ of heat and does 29 kJ of work. Calculate ΔE.

21. A system releases 125 kJ of heat, and 104 kJ of work is done on it. Calculate ΔE.

10.5 Measuring Energy Changes

Questions

22. Describe what happens to the molecules in a sample of ice as the sample is slowly heated until it liquefies and then vaporizes.

23. Metallic substances tend to have (lower/higher) specific heat capacities than nonmetallic substances.

Problems

24. If it takes 526 J of energy to warm 7.40 g of water by 17 °C, how much energy would be needed to warm 7.40 g of water by 55 °C?

25. Convert the following numbers of calories or kilocalories into joules or kilojoules.
    a. 7845 cal   c. 62.142 kcal
    b. 4.55×10^4 cal   d. 43,024 cal

26. If 72.4 kJ of heat is applied to a 952-g block of metal, the temperature increases by 10.7 °C. Calculate the specific heat capacity of the metal in J/g °C.

27. Three 75.0-g samples of copper, silver, and gold are available. Each of these samples is initially at 24.0 °C, and then 2.00 kJ of heat is applied to each sample. Which sample will end up at the highest temperature?

28. A 35.2-g sample of metal X requires 1251 J of energy to heat the sample by 25.0 °C. Calculate the specific heat capacity of this metal.

10.6 Thermochemistry (Enthalpy)

Questions

29. The equation for the fermentation of glucose to alcohol and carbon dioxide is

    $$C_6H_{12}O_6(aq) \rightarrow 2C_2H_5OH(aq) + 2CO_2(g)$$

    The enthalpy change for the reaction is −67 kJ. Is the reaction endothermic or exothermic? Is energy, in the form of heat, absorbed or released as the reaction occurs?

Problems

30. For the reaction

    $$S(s) + O_2(g) \rightarrow SO_2(g) \qquad \Delta H = -296 \text{ kJ/mol}$$

    a. How much heat is released when 275 g of sulfur is burned in excess oxygen?
    b. How much heat is released when 25 mol of sulfur is burned in excess oxygen?
    c. How much heat is released when 150. g of sulfur dioxide is produced?

31. Calculate the enthalpy change when 1.00 g of methane is burned in excess oxygen according to the reaction

    $$CH_4(g) + 2O_2(g) \rightarrow CO_2(g) + H_2O(l)$$
    $$\Delta H = -891 \text{ kJ/mol}$$

10.7 Hess's Law

Problems

32. Given the following data:

    $$S(s) + \tfrac{3}{2}O_2(g) \rightarrow SO_3(g) \qquad \Delta H = -395.2 \text{ kJ}$$
    $$2SO_2(g) + O_2(g) \rightarrow 2SO_3(g) \qquad \Delta H = -198.2 \text{ kJ}$$

    calculate ΔH for the reaction

    $$S(s) + O_2(g) \rightarrow SO_2(g)$$

33. Given the following data:

    $$C_2H_2(g) + \tfrac{5}{2}O_2(g) \rightarrow 2CO_2(g) + H_2O(l)$$
    $$\Delta H = -1300. \text{ kJ}$$
    $$C(s) + O_2(g) \rightarrow CO_2(g) \quad \Delta H = -394 \text{ kJ}$$
    $$H_2(g) + \tfrac{1}{2}O_2(g) \rightarrow H_2O(l) \quad \Delta H = -286 \text{ kJ}$$

    calculate ΔH for the reaction

    $$2C(s) + H_2(g) \rightarrow C_2H_2(g)$$

34. Given the following data:

    $$2O_3(g) \rightarrow 3O_2(g) \qquad \Delta H = -427 \text{ kJ}$$
    $$O_2(g) \rightarrow 2O(g) \qquad \Delta H = +495 \text{ kJ}$$
    $$NO(g) + O_3(g) \rightarrow NO_2(g) + O_2(g) \qquad \Delta H = -199 \text{ kJ}$$

    calculate ΔH for the reaction

    $$NO(g) + O(g) \rightarrow NO_2(g)$$

35. Given the following data:

    $$Fe_2O_3(s) + 3CO(g) \rightarrow 2Fe(s) + 3CO_2(g)$$
    $$\Delta H° = -23 \text{ kJ}$$
    $$3Fe_2O_3(s) + CO(g) \rightarrow 2Fe_3O_4(s) + CO_2(g)$$
    $$\Delta H° = -39 \text{ kJ}$$
    $$Fe_3O_4(s) + CO(g) \rightarrow 3FeO(s) + CO_2(g)$$
    $$\Delta H° = +18 \text{ kJ}$$

    calculate $\Delta H°$ for the reaction

    $$FeO(s) + CO(g) \rightarrow Fe(s) + CO_2(g)$$

have increased the most (see Figure 10.7).

41. The first law of thermodynamics tells us that the total amount of energy is constant. It does not tell us anything about direction or energy transfer.

42. A driving force tends to make a process occur. For example, when we open a pressurized tank of gas, the gas will move from the tank to the surroundings. Moving from high to low pressure is a driving force for a gas.

43. The driving force of an exothermic reaction is energy spread. In an exothermic reaction energy is transferred from the system to the surroundings.

44. The energy of the surroundings is used to melt solid water. The temperature of the water will eventually reach that of the room, and room temperature is higher than the melting point of water. In addition, liquid water has greater entropy than solid water, so entropy is the driving force in this process.

45. As the steam is cooled, the molecules of vapor gradually slow down (decrease in kinetic energy). At 100 °C, the vapor condenses into a liquid (the temperature is constant during this process). As the liquid water cools, the molecules move more slowly and are interacting. At 0 °C the liquid water freezes.

46. (a) 110.5 kcal; (b) 4.369 kcal; (c) 0.2424 kcal; (d) 45.53 kcal

47. (a) 190.9 kJ; (b) 17.43 kJ; (c) 657.5 cal; (d) 2.394×10^4 J

48. 7.64×10^3 cal

49. 1.6×10^3 g silver

50. 11 °C

51. 0.031 cal/g °C

52. 3.8×10^5 J

53. For a given mass of substance, the substance with the smallest specific heat capacity (gold, 0.13 J/g °C) will undergo the largest increase in temperature. Conversely, the substance with the largest specific heat capacity (water, 4.184 J/g °C) will undergo the smallest increase in temperature.

54. 63 °C

27. Gold (it has the smallest specific heat capacity)

28. 1.42 J/g °C

29. The reaction is exothermic; energy (in the form of heat) is released.

30. (a) 2.54×10^3 kJ; (b) 7.4×10^3 kJ; (c) 693 kJ

31. −55.5 kJ

32. −296.1 J

33. 226 kJ

34. −233 J

35. −11 kJ

36. The quality of energy tells us the form of the energy (potential or kinetic). The quantity of energy tells us how much is present. The total amount (or quantity) is conserved. When potential energy is converted to kinetic energy, we say that the quality is decreasing.

37. If there is no temperature difference, there can be no flow of energy.

38. Tetraethyl lead reduces engine

"knocking." It also lowers the effectiveness of catalytic converters (which lower air pollution) and increases the amount of lead in the environment.

39. If it were not for greenhouse gases, the surface temperature of the earth would be much colder. Having too large a quantity of greenhouse gases may cause the surface temperature of the earth to rise to dangerous levels.

40. Wood has decreased the most. Nuclear and petroleum/natural gas

55. 22 °C

56. 9.0 J

57.

Substance	Heat Required
water (*l*)	7.03×10^3 J
water (*s*)	3.41×10^3 J
water (*g*)	3.4×10^3 J
aluminum	1.5×10^3 J
iron	7.6×10^3 J
mercury	2.4×10^3 J
carbon	1.2×10^3 J
silver	4.0×10^3 J
gold	2.2×10^3 J

58.

Substance	Temperature Change
water (*l*)	23.9 °C
water (*s*)	49.3 °C
water (*g*)	50. °C
aluminum	1.1×10^2 °C
iron	2.2×10^2 °C
mercury	7.1×10^2 °C
carbon	1.4×10^2 °C
silver	4.2×10^2 °C
gold	7.7×10^2 °C

59. (a) 41 kJ; (b) 129 kJ; (c) 47 kJ; (d) a and b

60. (a) exothermic;
(b) exothermic;
(c) endothermic;
(d) endothermic

61. (a) 1652 kJ released (1650 kJ with 3 significant figures); (b) 826 kJ released; (c) 7.39 kJ released; (d) 34.4 kJ released

62. $(\frac{1}{2})C \rightarrow A + B + D + F$; 47 kJ/mol

63. 4.9×10^3 g, 4.9 L

64. About 9 hours at 4.0 mi/h

10.8 Quality Versus Quantity of Energy

Questions

36. What is the difference between the quality of energy and the quantity of energy? Which is decreasing?

37. Why can no work be done when everything in the universe is at the same temperature?

10.9 Energy and Our World

Questions

38. What was the advantage of using tetraethyl lead in gasoline? What were two disadvantages?

39. Why do we need some "greenhouse gases"? What is the problem with having too much of the greenhouse gases?

40. Which energy sources used in the United States have declined the most in the last 150 years? Which have increased the most?

10.10 Energy as a Driving Force

Questions

41. Why can't the first law of thermodynamics explain why a ball doesn't spontaneously roll up a hill?

42. What is meant by the term "driving force"?

43. What is the driving force of an exothermic reaction—matter spread or energy spread? Explain.

44. Exothermic reactions have a driving force. Nevertheless, water melting into a liquid is endothermic and this process occurs at room conditions. Explain why.

Critical Thinking

45. Consider a sample of *steam* (water in the gaseous state) at 150 °C. Describe what happens to the molecules in the sample as the sample is slowly cooled until it liquefies and then solidifies.

46. Convert the following numbers of kilojoules into kilocalories. (Remember: kilo means 1000.)
   a. 462.4 kJ
   b. 18.28 kJ
   c. 1.014 kJ
   d. 190.5 kJ

47. Perform the indicated conversions.
   a. 45.62 kcal into kilojoules
   b. 72.94 kJ into kilocalories
   c. 2.751 kJ into calories
   d. 5.721 kcal into joules

48. Calculate the amount of energy required (in calories) to heat 145 g of water from 22.3 °C to 75.0 °C.

49. It takes 1.25 kJ of energy to heat a certain sample of pure silver from 12.0 °C to 15.2 °C. Calculate the mass of the sample of silver.

50. If 50. J of heat is applied to 10. g of iron, by how much will the temperature of the iron increase? (See Table 10.1.)

51. The specific heat capacity of gold is 0.13 J/g °C. Calculate the specific heat capacity of gold in cal/g °C.

52. Calculate the amount of energy required (in joules) to heat 2.5 kg of water from 18.5 °C to 55.0 °C.

53. If 10. J of heat is applied to 5.0-g samples of each of the substances listed in Table 10.1, which substance's temperature will increase the most? Which substance's temperature will increase the least?

54. A 50.0-g sample of water at 100. °C is poured into a 50.0-g sample of water at 25 °C. What will be the final temperature of the water?

55. A 25.0-g sample of pure iron at 85 °C is dropped into 75 g of water at 20. °C. What is the final temperature of the water–iron mixture?

56. If it takes 4.5 J of energy to warm 5.0 g of aluminum from 25 °C to a certain higher temperature, then it will take _____ J to warm 10. g of aluminum over the same temperature interval.

57. For each of the substances listed in Table 10.1, calculate the quantity of heat required to heat 150. g of the substance by 11.2 °C.

58. Suppose you had 10.0-g samples of each of the substances listed in Table 10.1 and that 1.00 kJ of heat is applied to each of these samples. By what amount would the temperature of each sample be raised?

59. Calculate ΔE for each of the following.
   a. $q = -47$ kJ, $w = +88$ kJ
   b. $q = +82$ kJ, $w = +47$ kJ
   c. $q = +47$ kJ, $w = 0$
   d. In which of these cases do the surroundings do work on the system?

60. Are the following processes exothermic or endothermic?
   a. the combustion of gasoline in a car engine
   b. water condensing on a cold pipe
   c. $CO_2(s) \rightarrow CO_2(g)$
   d. $F_2(g) \rightarrow 2F(g)$

61. The overall reaction in commercial heat packs can be represented as
   $$4Fe(s) + 3O_2(g) \rightarrow 2Fe_2O_3(s) \qquad \Delta H = -1652 \text{ kJ}$$
   a. How much heat is released when 4.00 mol iron is reacted with excess O_2?
   b. How much heat is released when 1.00 mol Fe_2O_3 is produced?
   c. How much heat is released when 1.00 g iron is reacted with excess O_2?
   d. How much heat is released when 10.0 g Fe and 2.00 g O_2 are reacted?

62. Consider the following equations:

$$3A + 6B \rightarrow + 3D \qquad \Delta H = -403 \text{ kJ/mol}$$
$$E + 2F \rightarrow A \qquad \Delta H = -105.2 \text{ kJ/mol}$$
$$C \rightarrow E + 3D \qquad \Delta H = +64.8 \text{ kJ/mol}$$

Suppose the first equation is reversed and multiplied by $\frac{1}{6}$, the second and third equations are divided by 2, and the three adjusted equations are added. What is the net reaction and what is the overall heat of this reaction?

63. It has been determined that the body can generate 5500 kJ of energy during one hour of strenuous exercise. Perspiration is the body's mechanism for eliminating this heat. How many grams and how many liters of water would have to be evaporated through perspiration to rid the body of the heat generated during two hours of exercise? (The heat of vaporization of water is 40.6 kJ/mol.)

64. One way to lose weight is to exercise! Walking briskly at 4.0 miles per hour for an hour consumes about 400 kcal of energy. How many miles would you have to walk at 4.0 miles per hour to lose one pound of body fat? One gram of body fat is equivalent to 7.7 kcal of energy. There are 454 g in 1 lb.

11 Modern Atomic Theory

	Section	Text Features & Components	Labs, Demonstrations & Activities
Teaching Segment 11A **1.5 blocks** pp. 323–327	11.1 Rutherford's Atom	**LP** Lesson Plans (Sec 11.1–11.3)	
	11.2 Energy and Light		**TE** Mini Demo *p. 324* **SE** Chemistry in Action: Making Waves *p. 324* **LM** Experiment 46: Sunprint Paper Lab Manual Report Sheets Teacher's Lab Guide
	11.3 Emission of Energy by Atoms	**SE** Chemical Impact: Plants Seeing Red *p. 327*	**TE** Teaching Support: Demonstration *pp. 326–327* **LM** Experiment 47: Flame Tests Lab Manual Report Sheets Teacher's Lab Guide
Teaching Segment 11B **1 block** pp. 328–332	11.4–11.5 The Energy Levels of Hydrogen The Bohr Model of the Atom	**LP** Lesson Plans (Sec 11.4–11.6)	**TE** Teaching Support: Demonstration *pp. 328–329*
	11.6 The Wave Mechanical Model of the Atom		**SE** Chemistry in the Laboratory: Electron Probability *p. 353* **LM** Experiment 48: Electron Probability Lab Manual Report Sheets Teacher's Lab Guide
Teaching Segment 11C **0.5 block** pp. 333–339	11.7–11.8 The Hydrogen Orbitals The Wave Mechanical Model: Further Development	**LP** Lesson Plans (Sec 11.7–11.8) **SE** Celebrity Chemical: Hydrogen *p. 333* **TE** Teaching Support: Background Information *pp. 337–340*	**TE** Mini Demo *p. 337*
	continued on next page		

Key **SE** Student Edition **TE** Teacher Edition **RP** Teacher Resource Package **LM** Lab Materials
LP Lesson Plans **AR** Additional Resources **●** Florida Specific

Chapter Planning Guide

All Learners	Review & Assessment	Standards
TE Active Learning *p. 323* Animation: Scattering of Alpha Particles by Gold Foil *p. 323* **AR** Less Proficient Students *p. 20*	**SE** Questions and Problems *p. 354*	**TE** **NSES** UCP1, UCP2, A1, A2, B1, B2, B6, E1, E2, F6, G1, G2 **SSS** SC.H.1.4.1, SC.H.1.4.2, SC.H.1.4.3, SC.A.2.4.6, SC.A.2.4.5
TE Teaching Tips *p. 324* Transparency: Figure 11.4 *p. 325* Animation: Electromagnetic Wave • Refraction of White Light *p. 325* **AR** Less Proficient Students *p. 20*	**SE** Key Terms *p. 354* **SE** Questions and Problems *p. 354*	
Transparency: Figure 11.8 *p. 326* Video: Fireworks *p. 326* **RP** Team Learning Worksheets (Sec 11.1–11.3) *p. 53* **AR** Less Proficient Students *p. 20*	**SE** Focus Questions (Sec 11.1–11.3) *p. 327* **SE** Questions and Problems *p. 355*	
TE Active Learning *p. 328* **TE** Teaching Tips *pp. 328–329* Chemistry in Motion (12), (13) Transparency: Figure 11.11, 11.14, 11.15 Animation: Hydrogen Line Spectrum • Orbital Energies *p. 330* **AR** Less Proficient Students *p. 20*	**SE** Key Terms *p. 354* **SE** Questions and Problems *p. 355*	**TE** **NSES** UCP2, A1, A2, B6, G1, G2, G3 **SSS** SC.H.1.4.2, SC.H.1.4.3, SC.H.1.4.5, SC.H.1.4.6, SC.A.2.4.6
TE Teaching Tips *p. 332* **RP** Team Learning Worksheets (Sec 11.4–11.6) *pp. 55–56* **AR** Less Proficient Students *p. 21*	**TE** What if . . . *p. 331* **SE** Focus Questions (Sec 11.4–11.6) *p. 332* **SE** Key Terms *p. 354* **SE** Questions and Problems *p. 355*	
TE Active Learning *p. 333* **TE** Teaching Tips *pp. 333, 337* Chemistry in Motion (10) *p. 333* Transparency: Figures 11.20, 11.22, 11.26, 11.28 Animation: Orbitals • Shapes of *d* Orbitals **RP** Team Learning Worksheets (Sec 11.7–11.8) *p. 57* **AR** Less Proficient Students *p. 21*	**TE** Additional Examples *p. 338* **SE** Self Check *p. 339* **SE** Focus Questions (Sec 11.7–11.8) *p. 339* **SE** Key Terms *p. 354* **SE** Questions and Problems *p. 355*	**TE** **NSES** UCP1, UCP2, A1, A2, B6, E1, E2, F3, F4, F6 **SSS** SC.H.1.4.1, SC.H.1.4.2, SC.A.2.4.6

11 Modern Atomic Theory

Section	Text Features & Components	Labs, Demonstrations & Activities
Teaching Segment 11D **0.5 block** **pp. 339–352**	11.9 Electron Arrangements in the First Eighteen Atoms on the Periodic Table	(LP) Lesson Plans (Sec 11.9– 11.11) (TE) Teaching Support: Historical Background *pp. 340–341* (SE) Chemical Impact: A Magnetic Moment *p. 342*	
	11.10–11.11 Electron Configurations and the Periodic Table The Atomic Properties of the Periodic Table	(TE) Teaching Support: Background Information *pp. 344–346, 349–352* (SE) Chemical Impact: Fireworks *p. 351*	(TE) Mini Demo *p. 343* (TE) Teaching Support: Demonstration *pp. 347–348* (SE) Chemistry in Action: Whose Element Is It? *p. 348*

Key
(SE) Student Edition
(TE) Teacher Edition
(RP) Teacher Resource Package
(LM) Lab Materials
(LP) Lesson Plans
(AR) Additional Resources
(♦) Florida Specific

Technology and Media

 Transparencies
Figure 11.4, 11.8, 11.11, 11.14, 11.15, 11.20, 11.22, 11.26, 11.28, 11.29, 11.31, 11.34, 11.36

PowerPoint Slides

Video Fireworks
Chemistry in Motion
Flame Tests • Pickle Light

Animation Scattering of Alpha Particles by Gold Foil • Electromagnetic Wave • Refraction of White Light • Hydrogen Line Spectrum • Orbital Energies • 2s . . . orbitals • Shapes of *d* orbitals • Aufbau Principle

 eEdition CD-ROM
Easy Planner CD-ROM
English Summaries CD
Spanish Summaries CD

Web Site classzone.com
McDougal Littell Test Generator

Chapter Planning Guide

All Learners	Review & Assessment	Standards
TE Active Learning *p. 340*	**TE** Additional Examples *p. 342*	**TE** **NSES** UCP1, UCP3, A1, A2, B2, B6, E1, E2, G1, G2, G3
TE Teaching Tips *pp. 340, 343*	**SE** Self Check *p. 342*	**SSS** SC.A.1.4.1, SC.A.2.4.1, SC.A.2.4.6, SC.A.2.4.5, SC.H.3.4.6
Transparency: Figure 11.29 *p. 341*	**SE** Key Terms *p. 354*	
TE Integrating the Chemical Impact *pp. 342–343*	**SE** Questions and Problems *pp. 355–356*	
AR Less Proficient Students *p. 21*		

TE Teaching Tips *p. 343*	**TE** Additional Examples *p. 345*	
Animation: Aufbau Principle *p. 344*	**SE** Self Check *p. 346*	
Transparency: Figure 11.31, 11.34, 11.36	**SE** What if . . . *p. 346*	
Video: Fireworks *p. 351*	**SE** Focus Questions (Sec 11. 9–11.11) *p. 352*	
RP Team Learning Worksheets (Sec 11.9–11.11) *pp. 59–60*	**SE** Key Terms *p. 354*	
AR Less Proficient Students *pp. 21–22*	**SE** Questions and Problems *p. 356*	

Chapter Materials

TE Reading Strategy	**SE** Chapter Summary *p. 354*
AR English/Spanish Summaries *pp. 16–17*	**SE** Critical Thinking *p. 357*
RP Classroom Activities and Projects *pp. 25–26*	**RP** Solutions Guide
AR Challenge Projects/Problems *pp. 20–21*	**RP** Chapter Tests
AR Less Proficient Students *p. 22*	**RP** Test Bank
English Summary Audio	McDougal Littell Test Generator
Spanish Summary Audio	**AR** Standardized Test Practice
RP Chapter Review Worksheets (Basic, Review, Challenge)	**FCAT Test 6**

Integrating Reading Strategies and Chemistry Concepts

Chapter 11: Making a Sketch

Tell the students that visual models help all students, not just those who are visual learners. Some of the material presented in this course requires the use of visual models. Explain that one particular model is the sketch, a tool that can help the students organize, study, review and remember important concepts and complex material.

To demonstrate the value of a sketch, have the students review **Figure 11.10** on page 328. Point out that this simple sketch presents a complex concept. Instruct the students to begin at the left side of the sketch, travel up the "energy line," and then read the steps in the process shown from top to bottom. Then ask the students to explain the steps in their own words.

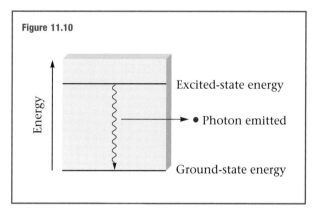

Figure 11.10

Energy

Excited-state energy

Photon emitted

Ground-state energy

The students' interpretations should be similar to this explanation:

"As an atom absorbs energy, it enters an excited state. The atom can then emit, or release, a photon to move back to a lower energy state. The lowest possible energy state of an atom is called its ground state."

Point out that making a sketch can help the students break down a complex scenario into relatively simple steps. Emphasize that difficult concepts, particularly those that involve complex structures, are more manageable when considered one piece at a time.

How to Make a Sketch

Reasons to Make a Sketch

1. To see the material more clearly.

2. To break down complex material into more manageable pieces.

3. To retain information by the use of a visual picture.

4. To represent physical structures.

5. To create an effective study tool for quizzes and tests. (Students can review the sketches and verbally summarize the material the sketch depicts.)

Remind the students to read the material carefully before they begin a sketch. Point out that they must know how the pieces of the information are connected before they can produce an effective model.

As a practice exercise, have the students consider **Figure 11.22** on page 334. Point out that **Figure 11.23** on the same page provides more detailed information for the first two principal energy levels of a hydrogen atom. Tell the students that they will use the information provided on page 336 to complete this sketch for the third and fourth principal energy levels.

Have the students draw a large inverted triangle on one sheet of paper in their notebooks and label the sketch "Energy Levels of a Hydrogen Atom." The students should then copy the overall structure shown in **Figure 11.22** to provide a general framework for the information that they will be adding. Next, instruct the students to copy the information provided in **Figure 11.23** onto the first two principal levels in their own sketches. Then have them add the *s*- and *p*- sublevels to the third and fourth principal energy levels.

Now, have the students read the first and second paragraphs on page 336 in the *Hydrogen Orbitals* section. Tell them to use the information in these paragraphs to add the appropriate sublevels of the third principal energy level to their sketches. Before they begin, ask the students what the labels should be and how many will be used. [3*d*, five] Point out that the students need not include the subscripts with the labels.

Finally, have the students read the remainder of the *Hydrogen Orbitals* section and complete the fourth principal energy level. Before they begin, ask the students what the labels should be and how many they will use. [4*f*, seven] Ask a volunteer to draw his or her sketch on the board so that the students can compare their sketches. If some of the students used different methods of labeling the sketch, make sure that the labels are correct. Then point out that the students can use any method that produces accurate results. Also point out that the students may include additional information (such as the shape of the orbital) on the sketch if they wish to do so.

As you continue through the chapter, have the students refer to and make use of their sketches whenever possible.

Energy Levels of a Hydrogen Atom

Overview

In this Chapter our goals are for the students to:

- Describe Rutherford's model of the atom

- Explore the nature of electromagnetic radiation

- See how atoms emit light

- Understand how the emission spectrum of hydrogen demonstrates the quantized nature of energy

- Learn about Bohr's model of the hydrogen atom

- Understand how the electron's position is represented in the wave mechanical model

- Learn about the shapes of orbitals designated by s, p and d.

- Learn about electron spin

- Understand how the principal energy levels fill with electrons in atoms beyond hydrogen

- Learn about valence electrons and core electrons

- Learn about the electron configurations of atoms with Z greater than 18

- Understand the general trends in atomic properties in the periodic table

The atomium in Brussels, Belgium is a giant-sized model of a crystal of solid iron.

322

The concept of atoms is a very useful one. It explains many important observations, such as why compounds always have the same composition (a specific compound always contains the same types and numbers of atoms) and how chemical reactions occur (they involve a rearrangement of atoms).

Once chemists came to "believe" in atoms, logical questions followed: What are atoms like? What is the structure of an atom? In Chapter 3 we learned to picture the atom with a positively charged nucleus composed of protons and neutrons at its center and electrons moving around the nucleus in a space very large compared to the size of the nucleus.

In this chapter we will look at atomic structure in more detail. In particular, we will develop a picture of the electron arrangements in atoms—a picture that allows us to account for the chemistry of the various elements. Recall from our discussion of the periodic table in Chapter 3 that, although atoms exhibit a great variety of characteristics, certain elements can be grouped together because they behave similarly. For example, fluorine, chlorine, bromine, and iodine (the halogens) show great chemical similarities. Likewise lithium, sodium, potassium, rubidium, and cesium (the alkali metals) exhibit many similar properties, and helium, neon, argon, krypton, xenon, and radon (the noble gases) are all very nonreactive. Although the members of each of these groups of elements show great similarity *within* the group, the differences in behavior *between* groups are striking. In this chapter we will see that it is the way the electrons are arranged in various atoms that accounts for these facts. However, before we examine atomic structure, we must consider the nature of electromagnetic radiation, which plays a central role in the study of the atom's behavior.

Alkali metals Halogens Noble gases

Neon signmaker and artist Jess Baird shows off a few of the items he has made in his Weatherford, Texas, shop.

11.1 Rutherford's Atom

Objective: *To describe Rutherford's model of the atom.*

Remember that in Chapter 3 we discussed the idea that an atom has a small positive core (called the nucleus) with negatively charged electrons moving around the nucleus in some way **(Figure 11.1).** This concept of a *nuclear atom* resulted from Ernest Rutherford's experiments in which he bombarded metal foil with α particles (see Section 3.5). Rutherford and his coworkers were able to show that the nucleus of the atom is composed of positively charged particles called *protons* and neutral particles called *neutrons*. Rutherford also found that the nucleus is apparently very small compared to the size of the entire atom. The electrons account for the rest of the atom.

A major question left unanswered by Rutherford's work was, What are the electrons doing? That is, how are the electrons arranged and how do they move? Rutherford suggested that electrons might revolve around the nucleus like the planets revolve around the sun in our solar system. He couldn't explain, however, why the negative electrons aren't attracted into the positive nucleus, causing the atom to collapse.

Figure 11.1
The Rutherford atom. The nuclear charge (n +) is balanced by the presence of n electrons moving in some way around the nucleus.

11.1 Rutherford's Atom **323**

USING TECHNOLOGY

Animation and Video

Animation, Scattering of ∝-Particles by Gold Foil

Section 11.1

Themes
Models, Systems

Skills
Applying concepts, interpreting diagrams

Student Preparation
Assign the students to read Sections 11.1 to 11.3 and to answer the Focus Questions at the end of Section 11.3 before coming to class.

Active Learning
After introducing the material in Sections 11.1 to 11.3 in class, place the students in groups and have them work together on Sections 11.1–11.3: Team Learning Worksheet. Answers and/or discussion of these questions are located in the *Teacher Resources.*

TEACHING TIP

This section is a review of the basic components of the atom. It offers an opportunity to reteach these components and to emphasize models and how they change over time.

At this point it became clear that more observations of the properties of atoms were needed to understand the structure of the atom more fully. To help us understand these observations, we need to discuss the nature of light and how it transmits energy.

Section 11.2

Themes
Energy

Skills
Observing, making comparisons

Laboratory
Experiment 46:
Sunprint Paper, Traditional

TEACHING TIPS

• Students often consider the forms of electromagnetic radiation outside the visible range (radio, X rays, infrared, microwaves) to be entirely different from light. Use a transparency of the electromagnetic spectrum to show the range of frequencies for each type of radiation.

• A popular way to remember the colors of light in the visible spectrum is the name Roy G. Biv. The letters in the name correspond to the colors in the spectrum from red to violet (long to short wavelength).

• Some insects use other forms of electromagnetic radiation to navigate. Students can investigate the travels of bees and migratory birds to find out how other animals perceive the electromagnetic spectrum.

MINI-DEMO

A long Slinky can be used to demonstrate the properties of waves. The physics teacher may have one you can borrow. Have a student volunteer hold one end of the Slinky. You can hold the other end and move it back and forth to make a wave. From this motion you can discuss wavelength, frequency, and amplitude. You can tie a ribbon to one point on the Slinky and show that it does not traverse along the length of the Slinky. The ribbon simply moves back and forth in the same place. The energy actually seems to move through the point, rather than carrying it along the wave.

324

Figure 11.2
A seagull floating on the ocean moves up and down as waves pass.

Figure 11.3
The wavelength of a wave is the distance between peaks.

11.2 Energy and Light

Objective: *To explore the nature of electromagnetic radiation.*

If you hold your hand a few inches from a brightly glowing light bulb, what do you feel? Your hand gets warm. The "light" from the bulb somehow transmits energy to your hand. The same thing happens if you move close to the glowing embers of wood in a fireplace—you receive energy that makes you feel warm. The energy you feel from the sun is a similar example.

In all three of these instances, energy is being transmitted from one place to another by light—more properly called **electromagnetic radiation.** Many kinds of electromagnetic radiation exist, including the X rays used to make images of bones, the "white" light from a light bulb, the microwaves used to cook hot dogs and other food, and the radio waves that transmit voices and music. How do these various types of electromagnetic radiation differ from one another? To answer this question we need to talk about waves. To explore the characteristics of waves, let's think about ocean waves. In **Figure 11.2** a seagull is shown floating on the ocean and being raised and lowered by the motion of the water surface as waves pass by. Notice that the gull just moves up and down as the waves pass—it is not moved forward. A particular wave is characterized by three properties: *wavelength, frequency,* and *speed.*

The **wavelength** (symbolized by the Greek letter lambda, λ) is the distance between two consecutive wave peaks (see **Figure 11.3**). The **frequency** of the wave (symbolized by the Greek letter nu, ν) indicates how many wave peaks pass a certain point per given time period. This idea can best be understood by thinking about how many times the seagull in Figure 11.2 goes up and down per minute. The *speed* of a wave indicates how fast a given peak travels through the water.

CHEMISTRY in ACTION
Making Waves

1. On a sheet of graph paper, draw three waves with wavelengths of *x*, 2*x*, and 4*x*.
2. Order the wavelengths from lowest to highest frequency and explain your answer.
3. Order the wavelengths from lowest to highest energy and explain your answer.

324   Chapter 11   Modern Atomic Theory

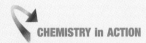
CHEMISTRY in ACTION

Making Waves

Materials Each student/group will need a sheet of graph paper.

Purpose Students will better understand the relationships among wavelength, frequency, and energy.

Discussion By drawing waves and comparing them with each other, students understand why a wave with a short wavelength has a higher frequency (and higher energy) than a wave with a longer wavelength. Have students imagine an object being hit by each of the three waves and have them decide which object would be affected the most. In this way the concept becomes more concrete. By having students draw the waves, you also get a better feeling for their understanding of wavelength.

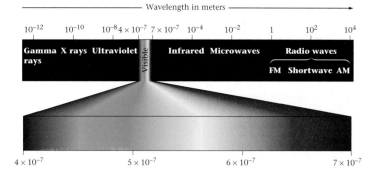

Figure 11.4
The different wavelengths of electromagnetic radiation.

Figure 11.4

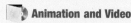

Animation and Video

Animation, Electromagnetic Wave, Refraction of White Light

Light as a wave

Light as a stream of photons (packets of energy)

Figure 11.5
Electromagnetic radiation (a beam of light) can be pictured in two ways: as a wave and as a stream of individual packets of energy called photons.

Although it is more difficult to picture than water waves, light (electromagnetic radiation) also travels as waves. The various types of electromagnetic radiation (X rays, microwaves, and so on) differ in their wavelengths. The classes of electromagnetic radiation are shown in **Figure 11.4**. Notice that X rays have very short wavelengths, whereas radiowaves have very long wavelengths.

Radiation provides an important means of energy transfer. For example, the energy from the sun reaches the earth mainly in the forms of visible and ultraviolet radiation. The glowing coals of a fireplace transmit heat energy by infrared radiation. In a microwave oven, the water molecules in food absorb microwave radiation, which increases their motions; this energy is then transferred to other types of molecules by collisions, thus increasing the food's temperature.

Thus we visualize electromagnetic radiation ("light") as a wave that carries energy through space. Sometimes, however, light doesn't behave as though it were a wave. That is, electromagnetic radiation can sometimes have properties that are characteristic of particles. (You will learn more about this idea in a physics course.) Another way to think of a beam of light traveling through space, then, is as a stream of tiny packets of energy called **photons.**

What is the exact nature of light? Does it consist of waves or is it a stream of particles of energy? It seems to be both (see **Figure 11.5**). This situation is often referred to as the wave–particle nature of light.

Different wavelengths of electromagnetic radiation carry different amounts of energy. For example, the photons that correspond to red light carry less energy than the photons that correspond to blue light. In general, the longer the wavelength of light, the lower the energy of its photons (see **Figure 11.6**).

Figure 11.6
A photon of red light (relatively long wavelength) carries less energy than a photon of blue light (relatively short wavelength) does.

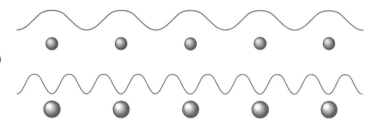

11.2   Energy and Light   **325**

Section 11.3

Themes
Energy

Skills
Observing, developing models

▲ **Laboratory**
Experiment 47:
Flame Tests, Traditional

11.3 Emission of Energy by Atoms

Objective: *To see how atoms emit light.*

Consider the results of the experiment shown in **Figure 11.7.** This experiment is run by dissolving compounds containing the Li^+ ion, the Cu^{2+} ion, and the Na^+ ion in separate dishes containing methyl alcohol (with a little water added to help dissolve the compounds). The solutions are then set on fire. Notice the brilliant colors that result. The solution containing Li^+ gives a beautiful, deep-red color, while the Cu^{2+} solution burns green. Notice that the Na^+ solution burns with a yellow–orange color, a color that should look familiar to you from the lights used in many parking lots. The color of these "sodium vapor lights" arises from the same source (the sodium atom) as the color of the burning solution containing Na^+ ions.

As we will see in more detail in the next section, the colors of these flames result from atoms in these solutions releasing energy by emitting visible light of specific wavelengths (that is, specific colors). The heat from the flame causes the atoms to absorb energy—we say that the atoms become *excited*. Some of this excess energy is then released in the form of light. The atom moves to a lower energy state as it emits a photon of light.

Figure 11.7
When salts containing Li^+, Cu^{2+}, and Na^+ dissolved in methyl alcohol are set on fire, brilliant colors result: Li^+, red; Cu^{2+}, green; and Na^+, yellow.

Lithium emits red light because its energy change corresponds to photons of red light (see **Figure 11.8**). Copper emits green light because it undergoes a different energy change than lithium; the energy change for copper corresponds to the energy of a photon of green light. Likewise, the energy change for sodium corresponds to a photon with a yellow–orange color.

To summarize, we have the following situation. When atoms receive energy from some source—they become excited—they can release this energy by emitting light. The emitted energy is carried away by a photon. Thus the energy of the photon corresponds exactly to the energy change experienced by the emitting atom. High-energy photons correspond to short-wavelength light and low-energy photons correspond to long-wavelength light. The photons of red light therefore carry less energy than the photons of blue light because red light has a longer wavelength than blue light does.

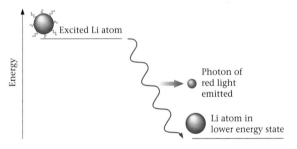

Figure 11.8
An excited lithium atom emitting a photon of red light to drop to a lower energy state.

326   Chapter 11   Modern Atomic Theory

TEACHING SUPPORT
Demonstration

Burning Rainbows

Materials
Several evaporating dishes
Nitrate salts of various metals
   (Li, Sr, Cu, Ba, K, Na)
Stirring rods
Methanol in a labeled wash
   bottle
Water in a wash bottle
Matches

Presentation Place a pea-sized amount of each salt in separate evaporating dishes. Add a small amount of water to just begin dissolution. Add about 10 mL of methanol using the wash bottle. Stir each mixture with a separate stirring rod. Light each dish with a match and dim the lights.

Teaching Notes The amount of methanol added will determine how long each dish burns.

Be careful to plan for this variation. Initially the methanol will burn as blue to colorless. Stirring may be necessary to produce color.

Variation Build a trough ½″ × ½″ × 10″ from aluminum foil. Make sure that the narrow ends are folded up and are leakproof. Add about 1.0 g of the metal salts in the order Sr, Li, Na, boric acid, Cu, K. Add a drop of water to each salt pile to aid

Plants Seeing Red

Vegetable growers have long used plastic sheeting (mulch) in the rows between plants to retain moisture, retard weeds, and provide warmth for the roots of young plants. It is now becoming apparent that the color of the plastic used has a significant effect on the plants. How can this be? Why does the color of their mulch matter to plants?

Michael J. Kasperbauer of the Department of Agriculture's Coastal Plains Soil, Water, and Plant Research Laboratory in Florence, South Carolina, has spent most of his 40-year career studying the responses of plants to various colors of light. Plants use proteins called phytochromes to sense light in the red (640–670 nm) and the far red (700–750 nm) ranges. Although far red light is not photosynthetically active—it does not provide energy for plant growth—this light gives plants important information about their environment. For example, green leaves reflect a lot of light in the far red region. Therefore, when a given plant's phytochromes sense a high ratio of far red to red light wavelengths, the plant knows that it has many neighbors—many other plants around it are reflecting red light. Because these neighbors are competitors for the lifegiving light from the sun—their leaves will shade neighboring plants—a plant sensing this situation tends to direct its growth above ground, producing a taller, thinner structure that can compete more successfully for sunlight. In fact, Kasperbauer and his colleagues have found that by using a red plastic mulch they can fool tomatoes into "thinking" they are crowded, leading to faster seedling growth and eventually producing earlier, larger fruit.

Since the opposite effect should benefit root crops, the Department of Agriculture scientists have

Red plastic mulch being used in an experimental plot.

grown turnips in soil covered by an orange mulch. These turnips proved much bigger than those mulched with black or red plastic, presumably because of increased reflection of red light by the orange plastic. The increased red light signaled no significant competition for light from other plants, encouraging growth of roots rather than above-ground foliage.

Besides affecting the plant's structure, the type of reflected light influences the nature of the waxy coating on the leaves and the taste of the plant product. Surprisingly, the color of the reflected light also seems to affect the plant's response to insect damage.

This research shows that plants are very sensitive to the type of red light that bathes them. Our plants may benefit from rose-colored glasses as much as we do.

Focus Questions

Sections 11.1–11.3

1. What was wrong with Rutherford's model of the atom? Why did it need to be modified?

2. What is the difference between the frequency of a wave and its speed?

3. What is the relationship between the wavelength of light and the energy of its photons?

4. How can red light improve germination and production in tomato crops?

Focus Questions **327**

in dissolution. Add enough methanol to cover the salts. Light the trough with a match.

Integrating the **CHEMICAL IMPACT**

Plants Seeing Red

Students may have studied the effect of light in connection with photosynthesis in biology. Have them research the effect of the wavelength of light on photosynthesis. One experiment that is often performed in biology classes involves growing plants in small cartons. Once the seedlings are growing, different ones are covered (that is, the top of the carton is covered) with various colors of cellophane. Observations of the condition of the plants over time give an excellent indication of the light required for photosynthesis.

Depending on your location, students may also have an interest in why leaves change color in autumn. *ChemMatters*, October 1986, has an excellent article on this process.

As days get shorter and temperatures drop, the production of chlorophyll in leaves stops. Once the chlorophyll disappears, the yellow pigments—carotene and xanthophylls—become visible, making the leaves appear yellow. The beautiful reds and purples are the result of bright light and cool nights. The bright daylight promotes sugar production in the leaves and the cool nights trap the sugar there, creating a red pigment called anthocyanin. Orange leaves result from combinations of the red and yellow pigments in the leaves. The best fall colors are observed when the days are sunny, nights are cool, and plenty of moisture is available.

Answers to Focus Questions

1. Rutherford's model of the atom did not explain how electrons are arranged or how they move. He could not explain why atoms do not collapse if the negative electrons revolve about the nucleus. Modifications were needed in Rutherford's model to clear up these flaws and to better elucidate the structure of the atom.

2. The frequency of a wave is the number of waves passing a

(continued)

(continued)

particular point in a given time. The speed of a wave is how fast the wave travels through the medium.

3. The relationship between energy and wavelength is inverse. The longer the wavelength, the less energy in its photons.

4. Plants see red light as meaning that many other plants are competing for sunlight. This perception causes the plant to direct its energy into growth above ground, resulting in faster seedling growth and earlier, larger fruit.

 Section 11.4

Themes
Energy, Models

Skills
Applying concepts, developing models, making comparisons

Student Preparation
Assign the students to read Sections 11.4 to 11.6 and to answer the Focus Questions at the end of Section 11.6 before coming to class.

Active Learning
After introducing the material in Sections 11.4 to 11.6 in class, place the students in groups and have them work together on Sections 11.4–11.6: Team Learning Worksheet. Answers and/or discussion of these questions are located in the *Teacher Resources.*

TEACHING TIPS

• This discussion is very significant. Discuss the ramifications of seeing only certain colors. Also consider discussing white light.

• A commonly used analogy for the energy levels within an atom is a staircase. A person can move from one step to another or even move up two or three steps and down a similar number of steps. It is not possible, however, to move up or down part of a step. Within atoms electron energies are quantized—the energy levels are like stair-steps. Electrons can change only be-
             (continued)

11.4 The Energy Levels of Hydrogen

Objective: *To understand how the emission spectrum of hydrogen demonstrates the quantized nature of energy.*

CHEMISTRY
An atom can lose energy by *emitting* a photon.

Each photon of blue light carries a larger quantity of energy than a photon of red light.

CHEMISTRY
A particular color (wavelength) of light carries a particular amount of energy per photon.

As we learned in the last section, an atom with excess energy is said to be in an *excited state*. An excited atom can release some or all of its excess energy by emitting a photon (a "particle" of electromagnetic radiation) and thus move to a lower energy state. The lowest possible energy state of an atom is called its *ground state.*

We can learn a great deal about the energy states of hydrogen atoms by observing the photons they emit. To understand the significance of this, you need to remember that the *different wavelengths of light carry different amounts of energy per photon*. Recall that a beam of red light has lower-energy photons than a beam of blue light.

When a hydrogen atom absorbs energy from some outside source, it uses this energy to enter an excited state. It can release this excess energy (go back to a lower state) by emitting a photon of light **(Figure 11.9)**. We can picture this process in terms of the energy-level diagram shown in **Figure 11.10**. The important point here is that *the energy contained in the photon corresponds to the change in energy that the atom experiences* in going from the excited state to the lower state.

Consider the following experiment. Suppose we take a sample of H atoms and put a lot of energy into the system (as represented in Figure 11.9). When

Figure 11.9
(a) A sample of H atoms receives energy from an external source, which causes some of the atoms to become excited (to possess excess energy). (b) The excited atoms (H) can release the excess energy by emitting photons. The energy of each emitted photon corresponds exactly to the energy lost by each excited atom.

Energy

Some H atoms absorb energy and become excited.

The excited atoms emit photons of light and return to the ground state.

Photon

Photon
Photon

○ H atom

Excited state H atom

(a)

(b)

Energy

Excited-state energy

Photon emitted

Ground-state energy

Figure 11.10
When an excited H atom returns to a lower energy level, it emits a photon that contains the energy released by the atom. Thus the energy of the photon corresponds to the difference in energy between the two states.

328 Chapter 11 Modern Atomic Theory

---

410 nm 434 nm 486 nm   656 nm

Figure 11.11
When excited hydrogen atoms return to lower energy states, they emit photons of certain energies, and thus certain colors. Shown here are the colors and wavelengths (in nanometers) of the photons in the visible region that are emitted by excited hydrogen atoms.

we study the photons of visible light emitted, we see only certain colors **(Figure 11.11)**. That is, *only certain types of photons* are produced. We don't see all colors, which would add up to give "white light;" we see only selected colors. This is a very significant result. Let's discuss carefully what it means.

Because only certain photons are emitted, we know that only certain energy changes are occurring **(Figure 11.12)**. This means that the hydrogen atom must have *certain discrete energy levels* **(Figure 11.13)**. Excited hydrogen atoms *always* emit photons with the same discrete colors (wavelengths)— those shown in Figure 11.11. They *never* emit photons with energies (colors) in between those shown. So we can conclude that all hydrogen atoms have the same set of discrete energy levels. We say the energy levels of hydrogen are **quantized.** That is, only *certain values are allowed.* Scientists have found that the energy levels of *all* atoms are quantized.

The quantized nature of the energy levels in atoms was a surprise when scientists discovered it. It had been assumed previously that an atom could

Figure 11.12
Hydrogen atoms have several excited-state energy levels. The color of the photon emitted depends on the energy change that produces it. A larger energy change may correspond to a blue photon, whereas a smaller change may produce a red photon.

Figure 11.13
Each photon emitted by an excited hydrogen atom corresponds to a particular energy change in the hydrogen atom. In this diagram the horizontal lines represent discrete energy levels present in the hydrogen atom. A given H atom can exist in any of these energy states and can undergo energy changes to the ground state as well as to other excited states.

11.4   The Energy Levels of Hydrogen   **329**

tween established energy levels, not in between those levels. Compare this situation to using a ramp, which is like continuous energies.

• Be careful to distinguish between an emission spectrum for an atom and light emitted by an atom. To see an emission spectrum the light must be separated into its component parts. This separation is accomplished by using a prism or a diffraction grating.

• Discuss how hydrogen can have multiple lines even though it has only one electron. Students often forget that they are observing many thousands of atoms simultaneously when observing a line emission spectrum.

• Point out that the quantized nature of atoms is a surprise and nonintuitive. It is comforting to students to realize that this topic is complicated even to people who have been studying it for a long time.

• Now is an excellent time to discuss the colors of streetlights. Mercury vapor lights have a blue cast, sodium lights are yellow, and neon lights are more orange. You may also want to discuss the difference between an incandescent light and a vapor light. Many students think that all lights are the same. They do not realize that an incandescent lamp produces a continuous spectrum because the tiny filament is radiating all wavelengths of visible light, whereas vapor lamps (like many street lights) are similar to gas discharge tubes in their operation.

USING TECHNOLOGY

Animation and Video

Chemistry in Motion
Demonstration 12, Pickle Light
This demonstration shows the characteristic color of sodium in the lighted pickle.

incandescent light and find the rainbow on either side of the slit in the tube. (*Note:* Students often look through the wrong end of the spectroscope. They should look through the end containing the diffraction grating, not the slit end.) You can also have students observe the fluorescent lights in the classroom with the spectroscopes. Once students are proficient at using the spectroscopes, place a gas discharge

tube at the front of the room. Darken the room and have the students observe the spectrum from the tube. They should see a line emission spectrum such as the one shown for hydrogen in Figure 11.11. Change the gas discharge tube to a different element and repeat the process. (*Note:* The gas discharge apparatus uses high voltage; be sure to unplug it before changing the tube.) Have the students com-

pare the emission spectra from different elements.

Variation If you do not have access to a gas discharge apparatus and tubes, you can use the solutions from the Burning Rainbows demonstration to do the same thing. Be sure to use only one evaporating dish at a time and add a little extra salt to obtain good color.

Figure 11.14
(a) Continuous energy levels. Any energy value is allowed. (b) Discrete (quantized) energy levels. Only certain energy states are allowed.

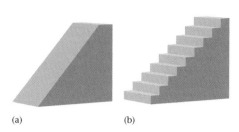

Figure 11.15
The difference between continuous and quantized energy levels can be illustrated by comparing a flight of stairs with a ramp. (a) A ramp varies continuously in elevation. (b) A flight of stairs allows only certain elevations; the elevations are quantized.

exist at any energy level. That is, everyone had assumed that atoms could have a continuous set of energy levels rather than only certain discrete values **(Figure 11.14)**. A useful analogy here is the contrast between the elevations allowed by a ramp, which vary continuously, and those allowed by a set of steps, which are discrete **(Figure 11.15)**. The discovery of the quantized nature of energy has radically changed our view of the atom, as we will see in the next few sections.

11.5 The Bohr Model of the Atom

Objective: *To learn about Bohr's model of the hydrogen atom.*

In 1911 at the age of twenty-five, Niels Bohr **(Figure 11.16)** received his Ph.D. in physics. He was convinced that the atom could be pictured as a small positive nucleus with electrons orbiting around it like the planets orbit the sun.

Over the next two years, Bohr constructed a model of the hydrogen atom with quantized energy levels that agreed with the hydrogen emission results we have just discussed. He pictured the electron moving in circular orbits corresponding to the various allowed energy levels. Bohr suggested that the electron could jump to a different orbit by absorbing or emitting a photon of light with exactly the correct energy content. Thus, in the Bohr atom, the energy levels in the hydrogen atom represented certain allowed circular orbits **(Figure 11.17)**.

At first Bohr's model appeared very promising. It fit the hydrogen atom very well. However, when this model was applied to atoms other than hydrogen, it did not work. In fact, further experiments showed that the Bohr model is fundamentally incorrect. Although the Bohr model paved the way for later theories, it is important to realize that the current theory of atomic

CHEMISTRY
Although Bohr's model is consistent with the energy levels for hydrogen, it is fundamentally incorrect.

330   Chapter 11   Modern Atomic Theory

330

Figure 11.17
The Bohr model of the hydrogen atom represented the electron as restricted to certain circular orbits around the nucleus.

structure is not the same as the Bohr model. Electrons do *not* move around the nucleus in circular orbits like planets orbiting the sun. Surprisingly, as we shall see later in this chapter, we do not know exactly how the electrons move in an atom.

11.6 The Wave Mechanical Model of the Atom

Objective: *To understand how the electron's position is represented in the wave mechanical model.*

CHEMISTRY

There is now much experimental evidence suggesting that all matter exhibits both wave and particle properties.

WHAT IF?

We now have evidence that electron energy levels in atoms are quantized.

What if energy levels in atoms were not quantized? What are some differences we would notice?

By the mid-1920s it had become apparent that the Bohr model was incorrect. Scientists needed to pursue a totally new approach. Two young physicists, Louis Victor de Broglie from France and Erwin Schrödinger from Austria, suggested that because light seems to have both wave and particle characteristics (it behaves simultaneously as a wave and as a stream of particles), the electron might also exhibit both of these characteristics. Although everyone had assumed that the electron was a tiny particle, these scientists said it might be useful to find out whether it could be described as a wave.

When Schrödinger carried out a mathematical analysis based on this idea, he found that it led to a new model for the hydrogen atom that seemed to apply equally well to other atoms—something Bohr's model failed to do. We will now explore a general picture of this model, which is called the **wave mechanical model** of the atom.

In the Bohr model, the electron was assumed to move in circular orbits. In the wave mechanical model, on the other hand, the electron states are described by orbitals. *Orbitals are nothing like orbits.* To approximate the idea of an orbital, picture a single male firefly in a room in the center of which is suspended an open vial of nectar, which fireflies eat. The room is extremely dark and there is a camera in one corner with its shutter open. Every time

11.6 The Wave Mechanical Model of the Atom **331**

- In this section the idea of probability as a model for understanding nature is introduced. This concept will be new to all students and most will find it confusing. Students tend to think of orbitals as physical structures and find it difficult to think of them as probability distributions. In Section 11.7 we describe the orbital as a *potential space* for an electron. This idea is a good way for the students to think about it initially.

- The firefly experiment offers a way for students to understand the difference between an orbit and an orbital. Many students confuse orbitals and orbits. An orbit describes a particular path that an object follows as it travels around another object. For example, the moon has an orbit about the earth. Electrons do not follow a particular path around the nucleus. Instead, an orbital describes the areas around the nucleus where an electron is likely to be found. The exact path of an electron in this area is not known, in the same way that the exact path of a firefly is not known.

Answers to Focus Questions

1. The lines produced in an emission spectrum are the lines from thousands of atoms of hydrogen. Each line represents a single electron transition. Because we are observing thousands of transitions simultaneously, however, we see multiple lines corresponding to the allowed transitions in the visible spectrum.

2. The Bohr model of the atom cannot adequately explain the energy levels in any multielectron atoms and incorrectly assumes that the hydrogen electron travels in fixed orbits.

3. In the wave mechanical model of the atom, the paths of the electrons are unknown. The electron motions

Louis Victor de Broglie

Figure 11.18
A representation of the photo of the firefly experiment. Remember that a picture is brightest where the film has been exposed to the most light. Thus the intensity of the color reflects how often the firefly visited a given point in the room. Notice that the brightest area is in the center of the room near the source of the nectar.

the firefly "flashes," the camera records a pinpoint of light and thus the firefly's position in the room at that particular moment. The firefly senses the nectar and, as you can imagine, it spends a lot of time at or close to it. However, now and then the insect flies randomly around the room.

When the film is taken out of the camera and developed, the picture will probably look like **Figure 11.18.** Because a picture is brightest where the film has been exposed to the most light, the color intensity at any given point tells us how often the firefly visited that point in the room. Notice that, as we might expect, the firefly spent the most time near the room's center.

Now suppose you are watching the firefly in the dark room. You see it flash at a given point far from the center of the room. Where do you expect to see it next? There is really no way to be sure. The firefly's flight path is not precisely predictable. However, if you had seen the time-exposure picture of the firefly's activities (Figure 11.18), you would have some idea where to look next. Your best chance would be to look more toward the center of the room. Figure 11.18 suggests there is the highest probability (the highest odds, the greatest likelihood) of finding the firefly at any particular moment near the center of the room. You *can't be sure* the firefly will fly toward the center of the room, but it *probably* will. So the time-exposure picture is a kind of "probability map" of the firefly's flight pattern.

According to the wave mechanical model, the electron in the hydrogen atom can be pictured as being something like this firefly. Schrödinger found that he could not precisely describe the electron's path. His mathematics enabled him only to predict the probabilities of finding the electron at given points in space around the nucleus. In its ground state the hydrogen electron has a probability map like that shown in **Figure 11.19.** The more intense the color at a particular point, the more probable it is that the electron will be found at that point at a given instant. The model gives *no information about when* the electron occupies a certain point in space or *how it moves.* In fact, we have good reasons to believe that we can *never know* the details of electron motion, no matter how sophisticated our models may become. But we do feel confident that the electron *does not* orbit the nucleus in circles as Bohr suggested.

Figure 11.19
The probability map, or orbital, that describes the hydrogen electron in its lowest possible energy state. The more intense the color of a given dot, the more likely it is that the electron will be found at that point. We have no information about when the electron will be at a particular point or about how it moves. Note that the probability of the electron's presence is highest closest to the positive nucleus (located at the center of this diagram), as might be expected.

Focus Questions

Sections 11.4–11.6

1. Figure 11.11 contains four colored lines. You already know that hydrogen has only one electron. How can we get four lines from one electron?

2. What is wrong with the Bohr model of the atom?

3. How does the wave mechanical model of the atom differ from Bohr's model?

332 Chapter 11 Modern Atomic Theory

are described by orbitals that give a probability map of the electron position. The electrons do not travel in orbits around the nucleus of the atom.

11.7 The Hydrogen Orbitals

Objective: *To learn about the shapes of orbitals designated by* s, p, *and* d.

(a)   (b)

Figure 11.20
The hydrogen 1s orbital. (a) The size of the orbital is defined by a sphere that contains 90% of the total electron probability. That is, the electron can be found *inside* this sphere 90% of the time.
(b) The 1s orbital is often represented simply as a sphere. However, the most accurate picture of the orbital is the probability map represented in (a).

The probability map for the hydrogen electron shown in Figure 11.19 is called an **orbital**. Although the probability of finding the electron decreases at greater distances from the nucleus, the probability of finding it even at great distances from the nucleus never becomes exactly zero. A useful analogy might be the lack of a sharp boundary between the earth's atmosphere and "outer space." The atmosphere fades away gradually, but there are always a few molecules present. Because the edge of an orbital is "fuzzy," an orbital does not have an exactly defined size. Chemists arbitrarily define its size as the sphere that contains 90% of the total electron probability **(Figure 11.20a).** This definition means that the electron spends 90% of the time inside this surface and 10% somewhere outside this surface. (Note that we are *not* saying the electron travels only on the *surface* of the sphere.) The orbital represented in **Figure 11.20b** is named the 1s orbital, and it describes the hydrogen electron's lowest energy state (the ground state).

In Section 11.4 we saw that the hydrogen atom can absorb energy to transfer the electron to a higher energy state (an excited state). In terms of the obsolete Bohr model, this meant the electron was transferred to an orbit with a larger radius. In the wave mechanical model, these higher energy states correspond to different kinds of orbitals with different shapes.

CELEBRITY CHEMICAL

Hydrogen (H₂)

Hydrogen is the most abundant element in the universe, being the major constituent of all stars. Most of the hydrogen found on earth is in the combined state—in compounds with other elements. The amount of elemental hydrogen (H_2) found on earth is actually very small. The atmosphere contains only 0.00005% H_2 gas. Therefore, when H_2 gas is required to produce a substance such as NH_3 in the reaction

$$N_2(g) + 3\,H_2(g) \rightarrow 2NH_3(g)$$

the H_2 must be obtained by decomposing a compound such as water.

Hydrogen is a colorless, odorless, and tasteless gas that reacts explosively with oxygen gas. In fact, the energetic reaction of $H_2(g)$ with $O_2(g)$ makes it a good candidate as a fuel. Hydrogen actually delivers four times as much energy per gram as does gasoline. The other advantage to using hydrogen as a fuel is that the combustion product is water, which is not harmful to the environment. Currently, hydrogen is too expensive to produce to be competitive as a fuel compared to gasoline or natural

gas. However, if cheaper ways are found to produce it, hydrogen could prove a valuable fuel in the future.

Liquid hydrogen is used to power the space shuttle.

CELEBRITY CHEMICAL

Hydrogen (H₂)

Animation and Video

Chemistry in Motion
**Demonstration 10,
Soap Bubbles**
This demonstration shows very effectively the difference between bubbles of pure hydrogen, pure oxygen, and a mixture of hydrogen and oxy-

gen. It can lead to a discussion of the use of hydrogen in dirigibles and hydrogen's safety and environmental friendliness as an alternative fuel for cars.

In many ways hydrogen seems like an ideal fuel. Because of its low molar mass, it provides lots of energy per gram and it gives only H_2O as a combustion product instead of the CO_2 and H_2O produced by fossil fuels. However, there are two major problems with using hydrogen as a fuel. First, virtually no free hydrogen exists, so energy

must be expended to free it from compounds such as water. Second, hydrogen has a very low boiling point and requires very low temperatures and very high pressures to store as a liquid. Some metals, such as palladium, absorb large amounts of hydrogen; attempts have been made to use such systems for hydrogen storage in hydrogen-powered automobiles.

Also, researchers are attempting to adapt H_2/O_2 fuel cells similar to those used in the U.S. space program for use in automobiles. The major stum-

bling block in these efforts has been H_2 storage problems. Several automobile companies are now studying fuel cells that use "reformers" to break down gasoline into hydrogen as it is needed.

Themes
Models

Skills
Applying concepts, interpreting diagrams, developing models

Student Preparation
Assign the students to read Sections 11.7 to 11.8 and to answer the Focus Questions at the end of Section 11.8 before coming to class.

Active Learning
After introducing the material in Sections 11.7 to 11.8 in class, place the students in groups and have them work together on Sections 11.7–11.8: Team Learning Worksheet. Answers and/or discussion of these questions are located in the *Teacher Resources*.

TEACHING TIP

You can use solid models (usually foam) to demonstrate the shapes of the *s, p*, and *d* orbitals. Remind students that the electron probability is high within the shape but the electron does not follow a set path.

USING TECHNOLOGY

 Figure 11.20

TEACHING TIP

Students can easily become confused about the meanings of the following terms: principal energy level, sublevel, and orbital. Point out that the *principal energy level* gives the region of energy for the electrons. It also turns out that a given principal quantum number indicates the number of *sublevels* available for that energy level. The sublevels are lettered *s*, *p*, *d*, and *f* based on the shapes of the orbitals within them. An *orbital* represents a specific region of probability that can contain at most two electrons.

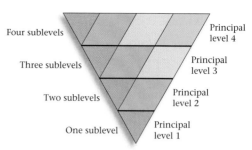

Figure 11.21
The first four principal energy levels in the hydrogen atom. Each level is assigned an integer, *n*.

Figure 11.22
An illustration of how principal levels can be divided into sublevels.

Hydrogen Energy Levels

At this point we need to stop and consider how the hydrogen atom is organized. Remember, we showed earlier that the hydrogen atom has discrete energy levels. We call these levels **principal energy levels** and label them with integers **(Figure 11.21).** Next we find that each of these levels is subdivided into **sublevels.** The following analogy should help you understand this. Picture an inverted triangle **(Figure 11.22).** We divide the principal levels into various numbers of sublevels. Principal level 1 consists of one sublevel, principal level 2 has two sublevels, principal level 3 has three sublevels, and principal level 4 has four sublevels.

Like our triangle, the principal energy levels in the hydrogen atom contain sublevels. As we will see presently, these sublevels contain spaces for the electron that we call orbitals. Principal energy level 1 consists of just one sublevel, or one type of orbital. The spherical shape of this orbital is shown in Figure 11.20. We label this orbital 1*s*. The number 1 is for the principal energy level, and *s* is a shorthand way to label a particular sublevel (type of orbital).

Figure 11.23
Principal level 2 shown divided into the 2*s* and 2*p* sublevels.

Figure 11.24
The relative sizes of the 1*s* and 2*s* orbitals of hydrogen.

Principal energy level 2 has two sublevels. (Note the correspondence between the principal energy level number and the number of sublevels.) These sublevels are labeled 2*s* and 2*p*. The 2*s* sublevel consists of one orbital (called the 2*s*), and the 2*p* sublevel consists of three orbitals (called 2*p_x*, 2*p_y*, and 2*p_z*). Let's return to the inverted triangle to illustrate this. **Figure 11.23** shows principal level 2 divided into the sublevels 2*s* and 2*p* (which is subdivided into 2*p_x*, 2*p_y*, and 2*p_z*). The orbitals have the shapes shown in **Figures 11.24** and **11.25.** The 2*s* orbital is spherical like the 1*s* orbital but larger in size (see Figure 11.24). The three 2*p* orbitals are not spherical but have two "lobes." These orbitals are shown in Figure 11.25 both as electron probability maps and as surfaces that contain 90% of the total electron probability. Notice that the label *x*, *y*, or *z* on a given 2*p* orbital tells along which axis the lobes of that orbital are directed.

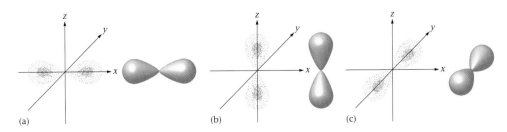

Figure 11.25
The three 2p orbitals: (a) $2p_x$, (b) $2p_z$, (c) $2p_y$.
The *x*, *y*, or *z* label indicates along which axis the two lobes are directed. Each orbital is
shown both as a probability map and as a surface that encloses 90% of the electron probability.

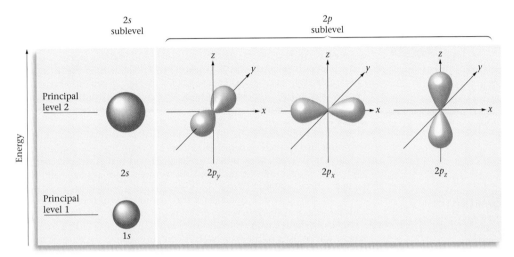

Figure 11.26
A diagram of principal energy levels 1 and 2 showing the shapes of orbitals that compose the sublevels.

**USING
TECHNOLOGY**

Figure 11.26

Animation and Video

Animation, *2s*, *$2p_x$*, *$2p_y$*, *$2p_z$* orbitals

What we have learned so far about the hydrogen atom is summarized in
Figure 11.26. Principal energy level 1 has one sublevel, which contains the
1*s* orbital. Principal energy level 2 contains two sublevels, one of which contains the 2*s* orbital and one of which contains the 2*p* orbitals (three of them).
Note that each orbital is designated by a symbol or label. We summarize the
information given by this label as follows:

Orbital Labels

1. The number tells the principal energy level.
2. The letter tells the shape. The letter *s* means a spherical orbital; the
   letter *p* means a two-lobed orbital. The *x*, *y*, or *z* subscript on a *p* orbital label tells along which of the coordinate axes the two lobes lie.

11.7 The Hydrogen Orbitals **335**

One important characteristic of orbitals is that as the level number increases, the average distance of the electron in that orbital from the nucleus also increases. That is, when the hydrogen electron is in the 1s orbital (the ground state), it spends most of its time much closer to the nucleus than when it occupies the 2s orbital (an excited state).

Hydrogen Orbitals

You may be wondering at this point why hydrogen, which has only one electron, has more than one orbital. It is best to think of an orbital as a *potential space* for an electron. The hydrogen electron can occupy only a single orbital at a time, but the other orbitals are still available should the electron be transferred into one of them. For example, when a hydrogen atom is in its ground state (lowest possible energy state), the electron is in the 1s orbital. By adding the correct amount of energy (for example, a specific photon of light), we can excite the electron to the 2s orbital or to one of the 2p orbitals.

So far we have discussed only two of hydrogen's energy levels. There are many others. For example, level 3 has three sublevels (see Figure 11.22), which we label 3s, 3p, and 3d. The 3s sublevel contains a single 3s orbital, a spherical orbital larger than 1s and 2s **(Figure 11.27).** Sublevel 3p contains three orbitals: $3p_x$, $3p_y$, and $3p_z$, which are shaped like the 2p orbitals except that they are larger. The 3d sublevel contains five 3d orbitals with the shapes and labels shown in **Figure 11.28.** (You do not need to memorize the 3d orbital shapes and labels. They are shown for completeness.)

Notice as you compare levels 1, 2, and 3 that a new type of orbital (sublevel) is added in each principal energy level. (Recall that the p orbitals are added in level 2 and the d orbitals in level 3.) This makes sense because in going farther out from the nucleus, there is more space available and thus room for more orbitals.

It might help you to understand that the number of orbitals increases with the principal energy level if you think of a theater in the round. Picture a round stage with circular rows of seats surrounding it. The farther from the stage a row of seats is, the more seats it contains because the circle is larger. Orbitals divide up the space around a nucleus somewhat like the seats in this circular theater. The greater the distance from the nucleus, the more space there is and the more orbitals we find.

The pattern of increasing numbers of orbitals continues with level 4. Level 4 has four sublevels labeled 4s, 4p, 4d, and 4f. The 4s sublevel has a single 4s orbital. The 4p sublevel contains three orbitals ($4p_x$, $4p_y$, and $4p_z$). The 4d sublevel has five 4d orbitals. The 4f sublevel has seven 4f orbitals.

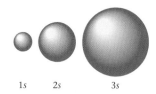

1s   2s   3s

Figure 11.27
The relative sizes of the spherical 1s, 2s, and 3s orbitals of hydrogen.

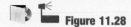

CHEMISTRY

Think of orbitals as ways of dividing up the space around a nucleus.

Figure 11.28
The shapes and labels of the five 3d orbitals.

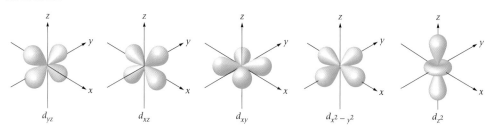

d_{yz} d_{xz} d_{xy} $d_{x^2-y^2}$ d_{z^2}

336   Chapter 11   Modern Atomic Theory

The 4s, 4p, and 4d orbitals have the same shapes as the earlier s, p, and d orbitals, respectively, but are larger. We will not be concerned here with the shapes of the f orbitals.

11.8 The Wave Mechanical Model: Further Development

Objectives: *To review the energy levels and orbitals of the wave mechanical model of the atom.*
To learn about electron spin.

A model for the atom is of little use if it does not apply to all atoms. The Bohr model was discarded because it could be applied only to hydrogen. The wave mechanical model can be applied to all atoms in basically the same form as we have just used it for hydrogen. In fact, the major triumph of this model is its ability to explain the periodic table of the elements. Recall that the elements on the periodic table are arranged in vertical groups, which contain elements that typically show similar chemical properties. The wave mechanical model of the atom allows us to explain, based on electron arrangements, why these similarities occur. We will see later how this is done.

Remember that an atom has as many electrons as it has protons to give it a zero overall charge. Therefore, all atoms beyond hydrogen have more than one electron. Before we can consider the atoms beyond hydrogen, we must describe one more property of electrons that determines how they can be arranged in an atom's orbitals. This property is spin. Each electron appears to be spinning as a top spins on its axis. Like the top, an electron can spin in only one of two directions. We often represent spin with an arrow: ↑ or ↓. One arrow represents the electron spinning in the one direction, and the other represents the electron spinning in the opposite direction. For our purposes, what is most important about electron spin is that two electrons must have *opposite* spins to occupy the same orbital. That is, two electrons that have the same spin cannot occupy the same orbital. This leads to the **Pauli exclusion principle:** An atomic orbital can hold a maximum of two electrons, and those two electrons must have opposite spins.

Before we apply the wave mechanical model to atoms beyond hydrogen, we will summarize the model for convenient reference.

Principal Components of the Wave Mechanical Model of the Atom

1. Atoms have a series of energy levels called **principal energy levels,** which are designated by whole numbers symbolized by n; n can equal 1, 2, 3, 4, . . . Level 1 corresponds to $n = 1$, level 2 corresponds to $n = 2$, and so on.

2. The energy of the level increases as the value of n increases.

3. Each principal energy level contains one or more *types* of orbitals, called **sublevels.**

(continued)

11.8   The Wave Mechanical Model: Further Development   **337**

Themes
Models, Organization

Skills
Applying concepts, interpreting diagrams, developing models

TEACHING TIP

The idea of electron spin is abstract and difficult for many students to grasp. Focus your discussion on the important point that for two electrons to occupy the same orbital, they must have opposite spins. An analogy to a magnet is often useful.

MINI-DEMO

Use two bar magnets or cow magnets (available from Educational Innovations or local farm supply resources) to illustrate electron spin. Suspend both magnets with separate pieces of fishing line wrapped around their middles. Bring the magnets together and illustrate how they twist apart when the same poles are close to each other. Explain that electrons with the same spin repel each other in a similar manner, so electrons in the same orbital have opposite spins.

TEACHING SUPPORT
Background Information

Polyelectronic Atoms
The quantum mechanical model gives a description of the hydrogen atom that agrees very well with experimental data. However, it would not be very useful if it did not account for the properties of all other atoms as well.

To see how the model applies to **polyelectronic atoms**—that is, atoms with more than one electron—let's consider helium, which has two protons in its nucleus and two electrons. Three energy contributions must be considered in the description of the helium atom: (1) the kinetic energy of the electrons as they move around the nucleus; (2) the potential energy of attraction between the nucleus and

the electrons; and (3) the potential energy of repulsion between the two electrons.

Although the helium atom can be readily described in terms of the quantum mechanical model, the resulting Schrödinger equation cannot be solved exactly. The difficulty arises in dealing with the repulsions between the electrons. Because the electron pathways are un-
(continued)

(continued)

4. The number of sublevels present in a given principal energy level equals *n*. For example, level 1 contains one sublevel (1*s*); level 2 contains two sublevels (two types of orbitals), the 2*s* orbital and the three 2*p* orbitals; and so on. These are summarized in the following table. The number of each type of orbital is shown in parentheses.

n	Sublevels (Types of Orbitals) Present			
1	1*s*(1)			
2	2*s*(1)	2*p*(3)		
3	3*s*(1)	3*p*(3)	3*d*(5)	
4	4*s*(1)	4*p*(3)	4*d*(5)	4*f*(7)

5. The *n* value is always used to label the orbitals of a given principal level and is followed by a letter that indicates the type (shape) of the orbital. For example, the designation 3*p* means an orbital in level 3 that has two lobes (a *p* orbital always has two lobes).

6. An orbital can be empty or it can contain one or two electrons, but never more than two. If two electrons occupy the same orbital, they must have opposite spins.

7. The shape of an orbital does not indicate the details of electron movement. It indicates the probability distribution for an electron residing in that orbital.

Example 11.1

Understanding the Wave Mechanical Model of the Atom

Indicate whether each of the following statements about atomic structure is true or false.

a. An *s* orbital is always spherical in shape.

b. The 2*s* orbital is the same size as the 3*s* orbital.

c. The number of lobes on a *p* orbital increases as *n* increases. That is, a 3*p* orbital has more lobes than a 2*p* orbital.

d. Level 1 has one *s* orbital, level 2 has two *s* orbitals, level 3 has three *s* orbitals, and so on.

e. The electron path is indicated by the surface of the orbital.

Solution

a. True. The size of the sphere increases as *n* increases, but the shape is always spherical.

b. False. The 3*s* orbital is larger (the electron is farther from the nucleus on average) than the 2*s* orbital.

c. False. A *p* orbital always has two lobes.

338 Chapter 11 Modern Atomic Theory

(continued)
known, the electron repulsions cannot be calculated exactly. This issue is called the *electron correlation problem*.

The electron correlation problem occurs with all polyelectronic atoms. To treat these systems using the quantum mechanical model, we must make approximations. Most commonly, the approximation used to treat each electron assumes that the electron is moving in a *field of charge that is the net result of the nuclear attraction and the average repulsions of all other electrons*.

Let's single out the outermost electron and consider the forces that this electron feels. Clearly, the electron is attracted to the highly charged nucleus. It also feels the repulsions caused by the other 10 electrons. The net effect is that the electron is not bound nearly as tightly to the nucleus as it would be if the other electrons were not present. We say that the electron is *screened* or *shielded* from the nuclear charge by the repulsions of the other electrons.

This picture leads to *hydrogen-like orbitals* for polyelectronic atoms. They have the same general shapes as the orbitals for hydrogen, but their sizes and energies are different. The

d. False. Each principal energy level has only one *s* orbital.

e. False. The electron is *somewhere inside* the orbital surface 90% of the time. The electron does not move around *on* this surface.

 Self-Check Exercise 11.1

Define the following terms.

a. Bohr orbits

b. orbitals

c. orbital size

d. sublevel

Focus Questions **Sections 11.7–11.8**

1. What is the difference between an orbit and an orbital in atomic theory?

2. Draw Figure 11.22 and fill in the different types of sublevels for each principal energy level.

3. Tell how many orbitals are found in each type of sublevel: *s, p, d, f*.

4. What is the Pauli exclusion principle and how does it help us determine where an electron is found within the atom?

11.9 Electron Arrangements in the First Eighteen Atoms on the Periodic Table

Objectives: *To understand how the principal energy levels fill with electrons in atoms beyond hydrogen.*
To learn about valence electrons and core electrons.

CHEMISTRY

H	($Z = 1$)
He	($Z = 2$)
Li	($Z = 3$)
Be	($Z = 4$)
B	($Z = 5$)
C	($Z = 6$)
N	($Z = 7$)
O	($Z = 8$)
F	($Z = 9$)
Ne	($Z = 10$)

We will now describe the electron arrangements in atoms with $Z = 1$ to $Z = 18$ by placing electrons in the various orbitals in the principal energy levels, starting with $n = 1$, and then continuing with $n = 2$, $n = 3$, and so on. For the first eighteen elements, the individual sublevels fill in the following order: $1s$, then $2s$, then $2p$, then $3s$, then $3p$.

The most attractive orbital to an electron in an atom is always the $1s$, because in this orbital the negatively charged electron is closer to the positively charged nucleus than in any other orbital. That is, the $1s$ orbital involves the space around the nucleus that is closest to the nucleus. As n increases, the orbital becomes larger—the electron, on average, occupies space farther from the nucleus.

So in its ground state hydrogen has its lone electron in the $1s$ orbital. This is commonly represented in two ways. First, we say that hydrogen has the electron arrangement, or **electron configuration**, $1s^1$. This just means

11.9 Electron Arrangements in the First Eighteen Atoms on the Periodic Table   **339**

---

differences occur because of the interplay between the nuclear attraction and the electron repulsions.

One especially important difference between polyelectronic atoms and the hydrogen atom is that for hydrogen all orbitals in a given principal quantum level have the same energy (they are said to be *degenerate*). This is not the case for polyelectronic atoms. In these

atoms, for a given principal level the orbitals vary in energy as follows:

$$E_{ns} < E_{np} < E_{nd} < E_{nf}$$

In other words, when electrons are placed in a particular quantum level, they "prefer" the orbitals in the order *s, p, d, f*. Why does this preference arise? Although an electron in the $2s$ orbital spends most of its time a little farther from the nucleus

than does an electron in the $2p$ orbital, it spends a small but very significant amount of time very near the nucleus. We say that the $2s$ electron *penetrates* to the nucleus more than the electron in the $2p$ orbital does. This *penetration effect* causes an electron in a $2s$ orbital to be attracted to the nucleus more strongly than an electron in a

(continued)

CHEMISTRY

Number of electrons in the orbital

→ 1s¹

Value of *n* ⌐ Type (shape) of orbital
(principal energy level)

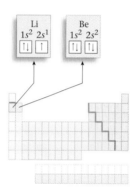

CHEMISTRY

Since electrons have the same charge, they repel each other.

there is one electron in the 1s orbital. We can also represent this configuration by using an **orbital diagram**, also called a **box diagram**, in which orbitals are represented by boxes grouped by sublevel with small arrows indicating the electrons. For *hydrogen*, the electron configuration and box diagram are

$$1s$$

H: $1s^1$ ↑

Configuration   Orbital diagram

The arrow represents an electron spinning in a particular direction. The next element is *helium*, $Z = 2$. It has two protons in its nucleus and so has two electrons. Because the 1s orbital is the most desirable, both electrons go there but with opposite spins. For helium, the electron configuration and box diagram are

Two electrons in 1s orbital

$$1s$$

He: $1s^2$ ↑↓

The opposite electron spins are shown by the opposing arrows in the box.

Lithium ($Z = 3$) has three electrons, two of which go into the 1s orbital. That is, two electrons fill that orbital. The 1s orbital is the only orbital for $n = 1$, so the third electron must occupy an orbital with $n = 2$—in this case the 2s orbital. This gives a $1s^2 2s^1$ configuration. The electron configuration and box diagram are

$$1s \quad 2s$$

Li: $1s^2 2s^1$ ↑↓ ↑

The next element, *beryllium*, has four electrons, which occupy the 1s and 2s orbitals with opposite spins.

$$1s \quad 2s$$

Be: $1s^2 2s^2$ ↑↓ ↑↓

Boron has five electrons, four of which occupy the 1s and 2s orbitals. The fifth electron goes into the second type of orbital with $n = 2$, one of the 2p orbitals.

$$1s \quad 2s \quad 2p$$

B: $1s^2 2s^2 2p^1$ ↑↓ ↑↓ ↑

Because all the 2p orbitals have the same energy, it does not matter which 2p orbital the electron occupies.

Carbon, the next element, has six electrons: two electrons occupy the 1s orbital, two occupy the 2s orbital, and two occupy 2p orbitals. There are three 2p orbitals, so each of the mutually repulsive electrons occupies a different 2p orbital. For reasons we will not consider, in the separate 2p orbitals the electrons have the same spin.

The configuration for carbon could be written $1s^2 2s^2 2p^1 2p^1$ to indicate that the electrons occupy separate 2p orbitals. However, the configuration is usually given as $1s^2 2s^2 2p^2$, and it is understood that the electrons are in different 2p orbitals.

$$1s \quad 2s \quad 2p$$

C: $1s^2 2s^2 2p^2$ ↑↓ ↑↓ ↑ ↑

340 Chapter 11 Modern Atomic Theory

(continued)

2p orbital is. That is, the 2s orbital is lower in energy than the 2p orbitals in a polyelectronic atom. The same thing happens in the other principal quantum levels.

Note the like spins for the unpaired electrons in the 2p orbitals.

The configuration for *nitrogen,* which has seven electrons, is $1s^22s^22p^3$. The three electrons in 2p orbitals occupy separate orbitals and have like spins.

N: $\quad 1s^22s^22p^3 \qquad$ 1s $\quad$ 2s $\quad$ 2p
$\qquad\qquad\qquad$ [↑↓] [↑↓] [↑|↑|↑]

The configuration for *oxygen,* which has eight electrons, is $1s^22s^22p^4$. One of the 2p orbitals is now occupied by a pair of electrons with opposite spins, as required by the Pauli exclusion principle.

O: $\quad 1s^22s^22p^4 \qquad$ 1s $\quad$ 2s $\quad$ 2p
$\qquad\qquad\qquad$ [↑↓] [↑↓] [↑↓|↑|↑]

The electron configurations and orbital diagrams for *fluorine* (nine electrons) and *neon* (ten electrons) are

$\qquad\qquad\qquad\qquad$ 1s $\quad$ 2s $\quad$ 2p

F: $\quad 1s^22s^22p^5 \qquad$ [↑↓] [↑↓] [↑↓|↑↓|↑]

Ne: $\quad 1s^22s^22p^6 \qquad$ [↑↓] [↑↓] [↑↓|↑↓|↑↓]

With neon, the orbitals with $n = 1$ and $n = 2$ are completely filled.

For *sodium,* which has eleven electrons, the first ten electrons occupy the 1s, 2s, and 2p orbitals, and the eleventh electron must occupy the first orbital with $n = 3$, the 3s orbital. The electron configuration for sodium is $1s^22s^22p^63s^1$. To avoid writing the inner-level electrons, we often abbreviate the configuration $1s^22s^22p^63s^1$ as [Ne]$3s^1$, where [Ne] represents the electron configuration of neon, $1s^22s^22p^6$.

The orbital diagram for sodium is

1s $\quad$ 2s $\quad$ 2p $\qquad$ 3s
[↑↓] [↑↓] [↑↓|↑↓|↑↓] [↑]

CHEMISTRY

[Ne] is shorthand for $1s^22s^22p^6$.

The next element, *magnesium,* $Z = 12$, has the electron configuration $1s^22s^22p^63s^2$, or [Ne]$3s^2$.

The next six elements, *aluminum* through *argon,* have electron configurations obtained by filling the 3p orbitals one electron at a time. **Figure 11.29** summarizes the electron configurations of the first eighteen elements by giving the number of electrons in the type of orbital (sublevel) occupied last.

H 1s^1								He 1s^2
Li 2s^1	Be 2s^2			B 2p^1	C 2p^2	N 2p^3	O 2p^4	F 2p^5	Ne 2p^6
Na 3s^1	Mg 3s^2			Al 3p^1	Si 3p^2	P 3p^3	S 3p^4	Cl 3p^5	Ar 3p^6

Figure 11.29
The electron configurations in the sublevel last occupied for the first eighteen elements.

11.9 Electron Arrangements in the First Eighteen Atoms on the Periodic Table $\quad$ **341**

opment paved the way for Mendeleev's own brilliant contribution to chemistry—the periodic table. In 1861 Mendeleev returned to St. Petersburg, where he wrote a book on organic chemistry. Later, when he wrote a book on inorganic chemistry, he was struck by the fact that the systematic approach for characterizing organic chemistry was lacking in inorganic chemistry. In at-tempting to systematize inorganic chemistry, Mendeleev eventually arranged the elements in the form of the periodic table.

Mendeleev was a versatile genius who was interested in many fields of science. He worked on many problems associated with Russia's natural resources, such as coal, salt, and various metals. Being particularly interested in the petroleum industry, he visited the United States in 1876 to study the Pennsylvania oil fields. His interests also included meteorology and hot-air balloons. In 1887 he made an ascent in a balloon to study a total eclipse of the sun.

Integrating the CHEMICAL IMPACT

A Magnetic Moment

Magnets have a useful application in human medicine in the form of MRI. A magnetic resonance imaging (MRI) scanner consists of a magnet large enough to accommodate an entire patient, along with additional coils (to excite hydrogen atoms, modify the magnetic field, and receive signals). Different tissues in the body give off different signals. These signals are separated into components that are then attributed to the site of origin in the body. A cross-sectional image of a patient can then be constructed on the screen. Most of the signals in an MRI scan originate from the hydrogen atoms in water. The difference in the way water is bound in different tissues produces the signal variations between healthy and diseased tissue.

MRI has become an important diagnostic tool for several reasons. An MRI scan does not expose the patient to X rays. Also, the image can be constructed irrespective of the patient's position in the machine. Diseased tissue produces a distinctive MRI image. MRI can also produce clear images of blood vessels.

Your students may want to investigate the use of magnetic fields in alternative medicine to

(continued)

Example 11.2

Writing Orbital Diagrams

Write the orbital diagram for magnesium.

Solution

Magnesium ($Z = 12$) has twelve electrons that are placed successively in the 1s, 2s, 2p, and 3s orbitals to give the electron configuration $1s^2 2s^2 2p^6 3s^2$. The orbital diagram is

1s	2s	2p	3s
↑↓	↑↓	↑↓ ↑↓ ↑↓	↑↓

Only occupied orbitals are shown here.

 Self-Check Exercise 11.2

Write the complete electron configuration and the orbital diagram for each of the elements aluminum through argon.

CHEMICAL IMPACT
Science, Technology, and Society

A Magnetic Moment

An anesthetized frog lies in the hollow core of an electromagnet. As the current in the coils of the magnet is increased, the frog magically rises and floats in midair (see photo). How can this happen? Is the electromagnet an antigravity machine? In fact, there is no magic going on here. This phenomenon demonstrates the magnetic properties of all matter. We know that iron magnets attract and repel each other depending on their relative orientations. Is a frog magnetic like a piece of iron? If a frog lands on a steel manhole cover, will it be trapped there by magnetic attractions? Of course not. The magnetism of the frog, as with most objects, shows up only in the presence of a strong inducing magnetic field. In other words, the powerful electromagnet surrounding the frog in the experiment described above *induces* a magnetic field in the frog that opposes the inducing field. The opposing magnetic field in the frog repels the inducing field, and the frog lifts up until the magnetic force is balanced by the gravitational pull on its body. The frog then "floats" in air.

How can a frog be magnetic if it is not made of iron? It's the electrons. Frogs are composed of cells containing many kinds of molecules. Of course, these molecules are made of atoms—carbon atoms, nitrogen atoms, oxygen atoms, and other types.

Each of these atoms contains electrons that are moving around the atomic nuclei. When these electrons sense a strong magnetic field, they respond by moving in a fashion that produces magnetic fields aligned to oppose the inducing field. This phenomenon is called *diamagnetism*.

All substances, animate and inanimate, because they are made of atoms, exhibit diamagnetism. Andre Geim and his colleagues at the University of Nijmegan, the Netherlands, have levitated frogs, grasshoppers, plants, and water droplets, among other objects. Geim says that, given a large enough electromagnet, even humans can be levitated. He notes, however, that constructing a magnet strong enough to float a human would be very expensive, and he sees no point in it. Geim does point out that inducing weightlessness with magnetic fields may be a good way to pretest experiments on weightlessness intended as research for future space flights—to see if the ideas fly as well as the objects.

A live frog being levitated in a magnetic field.

 Answers to Self-Check Exercise 11.2

Element	Electron Configuration	Orbital Diagram				
		1s	2s	2p	3s	3p
Al	$1s^2 2s^2 2p^6 3s^2 3p^1$ [Ne]$3s^2 3p^1$	↑↓	↑↓	↑↓ ↑↓ ↑↓	↑↓	↑ _ _
Si	[Ne]$3s^2 3p^2$	↑↓	↑↓	↑↓ ↑↓ ↑↓	↑↓	↑ ↑ _

Element	Electron Configuration	Orbital Diagram				
		1s	2s	2p	3s	3p
P	[Ne]$3s^2 3p^3$	↑↓	↑↓	↑↓ ↑↓ ↑↓	↑↓	↑ ↑ ↑
S	[Ne]$3s^2 3p^4$	↑↓	↑↓	↑↓ ↑↓ ↑↓	↑↓	↑↓ ↑ ↑
Cl	[Ne]$3s^2 3p^5$	↑↓	↑↓	↑↓ ↑↓ ↑↓	↑↓	↑↓ ↑↓ ↑
Ar	[Ne]$3s^2 3p^6$	↑↓	↑↓	↑↓ ↑↓ ↑↓	↑↓	↑↓ ↑↓ ↑↓

At this point it is useful to introduce the concept of **valence electrons**—that is, *the electrons in the outermost (highest) principal energy level of an atom.* For example, nitrogen, which has the electron configuration $1s^2 2s^2 2p^3$, has electrons in principal levels 1 and 2. Therefore, level 2 (which has $2s$ and $2p$ sublevels) is the valence level of nitrogen, and the $2s$ and $2p$ electrons are the valence electrons. For the sodium atom (electron configuration $1s^2 2s^2 2p^6 3s^1$, or $[\text{Ne}]3s^1$) the valence electron is the electron in the $3s$ orbital, because in this case principal energy level 3 is the outermost level that contains an electron. The valence electrons are the most important electrons to chemists because, being the outermost electrons, they are the ones involved when atoms attach to each other (form bonds), as we will see in the next chapter. The inner electrons, which are known as **core electrons,** are not involved in bonding atoms to each other.

Note in Figure 11.29 that a very important pattern is developing: except for helium, *the atoms of elements in the same group (vertical column of the periodic table) have the same number of electrons in a given type of orbital* (sublevel), except that the orbitals are in different principal energy levels. Remember that the elements were originally organized into groups on the periodic table on the basis of similarities in chemical properties. Now we understand the reason behind these groupings. Elements with the same valence electron arrangement show very similar chemical behavior.

11.10   Electron Configurations and the Periodic Table

Objective: *To learn about the electron configurations of atoms with Z greater than 18.*

In the previous section we saw that we can describe the atoms beyond hydrogen by simply filling the atomic orbitals starting with level $n = 1$ and working outward in order. This works fine until we reach the element *potassium* ($Z = 19$), which is the next element after argon. Because the $3p$ orbitals are fully occupied in argon, we might expect the next electron to go into a $3d$ orbital (recall that for $n = 3$ the sublevels are $3s$, $3p$, and $3d$). However, experiments show that the chemical properties of potassium are very similar to those of lithium and sodium. Because we have learned to associate similar chemical properties with similar valence-electron arrangements, we predict that the valence-electron configuration for potassium is $4s^1$, resembling sodium ($3s^1$) and lithium ($2s^1$). That is, we expect the last electron in potassium to occupy the $4s$ orbital instead of one of the $3d$ orbitals. This means that the principal energy level 4 begins to fill before level 3 has been completed. This conclusion is confirmed by many types of experiments. So the electron configuration of potassium is

K: $1s^2 2s^2 2p^6 3s^2 3p^6 4s^1$, or $[\text{Ar}]4s^1$

The next element is *calcium,* with an additional electron that also occupies the $4s$ orbital.

Ca: $1s^2 2s^2 2p^6 3s^2 3p^6 4s^2$, or $[\text{Ar}]4s^2$

The $4s$ orbital is now full.

CHEMISTRY

[Ar] is shorthand for $1s^2 2s^2 2p^6 3s^2 3p^6$.

treat sports injuries or arthritis. This topic would be an excellent choice for a web-based research project.

TEACHING TIPS

- Students are often confused about using core notation for writing electron configurations. It may be easier to have them use only the long form for electron configurations until Chapter 12, when an explanation of bonding makes core notation a useful form for writing the configurations. The major advantage of core notation is the emphasis it places on the outer electrons used in bonding. Be sure that students understand that in core notation, the last noble gas is used and the outer electrons are written after it.

- Point out that the periodic table (developed by considering the chemical properties of the elements) was created before the discovery of electrons. The wave mechanical model is consistent with the positions on the periodic table. This consistency presents strong support for the model.

 Section 11.10

Themes
Organization, Patterns of Change

Skills
Applying concepts, interpreting diagrams, making predictions

TEACHING TIP

Encourage students to use the periodic table as a guide in writing electron configurations. Understanding the structure of the table can be much more useful to students than memorizing an order of filling. Each row guides them through an energy level; each block guides them through a sublevel. Use the transparency for Figure 11.31 to discuss this process.

MINI-DEMO

Place two Petri dishes on an overhead projector. Cover the bottom of each dish to a depth of 1 cm with water. Cut **small** samples of Na and K metals. Dry each with a paper towel. Add the Na to one dish and the K to the other. Observe the results and compare the reactions. Both metals skate around on the surface of the water, and they may burst into flames or smoke.

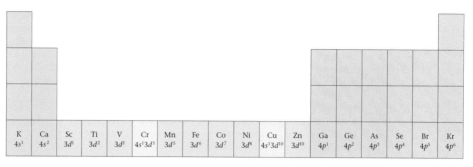

| K $4s^1$ | Ca $4s^2$ | Sc $3d^1$ | Ti $3d^2$ | V $3d^3$ | Cr $4s^13d^5$ | Mn $3d^5$ | Fe $3d^6$ | Co $3d^7$ | Ni $3d^8$ | Cu $4s^13d^{10}$ | Zn $3d^{10}$ | Ga $4p^1$ | Ge $4p^2$ | As $4p^3$ | Se $4p^4$ | Br $4p^5$ | Kr $4p^6$ |

Figure 11.30
Partial electron configurations for the elements potassium through krypton. The transition metals shown in green (scandium through zinc) have the general configuration [Ar]$4s^23d^n$, except for chromium and copper.

After calcium the next electrons go into the 3d orbitals to complete principal energy level 3. The elements that correspond to filling the 3d orbitals are called transition metals. Then the 4p orbitals fill. **Figure 11.30** gives partial electron configurations for the elements potassium through krypton.

Note from Figure 11.30 that all of the transition metals have the general configuration [Ar]$4s^23d^n$ except chromium ($4s^13d^5$) and copper ($4s^13d^{10}$). The reasons for these exceptions are complex and will not be discussed here.

Instead of continuing to consider the elements individually, we will now look at the overall relationship between the periodic table and orbital filling. **Figure 11.31** shows which type of orbital is filling in each area of the periodic table. Note the points in the box below.

To help you further understand the connection between orbital filling and the periodic table, **Figure 11.32** shows the orbitals in the order in which they fill.

A periodic table is almost always available to you. If you understand the relationship between the electron configuration of an element and its position on the periodic table, you can figure out the expected electron configuration of any atom.

CHEMISTRY

The $(n + 1)s$ orbital fills before the nd orbitals fill.

CHEMISTRY

Lanthanides are elements in which the 4f orbitals are being filled.

CHEMISTRY

Actinides are elements in which the 5f orbitals are being filled.

Orbital Filling

1. In a principal energy level that has d orbitals, the s orbital from the *next* level fills before the d orbitals in the current level. That is, the $(n + 1)s$ orbitals always fill before the nd orbitals. For example, the 5s orbitals fill for rubidium and strontium before the 4d orbitals fill for the second row of transition metals (yttrium through cadmium).

2. After lanthanum, which has the electron configuration [Xe]$6s^25d^1$, a group of fourteen elements called the **lanthanide series**, or the lanthanides, occurs. This series of elements corresponds to the filling of the seven 4f orbitals.

3. After actinium, which has the configuration [Rn]$7s^26d^1$, a group of fourteen elements called the **actinide series**, or the actinides, occurs. This series corresponds to the filling of the seven 5f orbitals.

4. Except for helium, the group numbers indicate the sum of electrons in the ns and np orbitals in the highest principal energy level that contains electrons (where n is the number that indicates a particular principal energy level). These electrons are the valence electrons, the electrons in the outermost principal energy level of a given atom.

344

Figure 11.31
The orbitals being filled for elements in various parts of the periodic table. Note that in going along a horizontal row (a period), the $(n + 1)s$ orbital fills before the nd orbital. The group label indicates the number of valence electrons (the number of s plus the number of p electrons in the highest occupied principal energy level) for the elements in each group.

Figure 11.32
A box diagram showing the order in which orbitals fill to produce the atoms in the periodic table. Each box can hold two electrons.

---

*After the $6s$ orbital is full, one electron goes into a $5d$ orbital. This corresponds to the element lanthanum ($[Xe]6s^25d^1$). After lanthanum, the $4f$ orbitals fill with electrons.

**After the $7s$ orbital is full, one electron goes into $6d$. This is actinium ($[Rn]7s^26d^1$). The $5f$ orbitals then fill.

Example 11.3

Determining Electron Configurations

Using the periodic table inside the back cover of the text, give the electron configurations for sulfur (S), gallium (Ga), hafnium (Hf), and radium (Ra).

Solution

Sulfur is element 16 and resides in Period 3, where the $3p$ orbitals are being filled (see **Figure 11.33**). Because sulfur is the fourth among the "$3p$ elements," it must have four $3p$ electrons. Sulfur's electron configuration is

S: $1s^22s^22p^63s^23p^4$, or $[Ne]3s^23p^4$

Figure 11.33
The positions of the elements considered in Example 11.3.

(continued) **345**

Additional Examples

Give the electron configuration for the following elements:

1. Bromine (Br)
$1s^22s^22p^63s^23p^64s^23d^{10}4p^5$
or $[Ar]4s^23d^{10}4p^5$

2. Tin (Sn)
$1s^22s^22p^63s^23p^64s^23d^{10}4p^6$ $5s^2 4d^{10}5p^2$ or
$[Kr]5s^24d^{10}5p^2$

3. Pollonium (Po)
$1s^22s^22p^63s^23p^64s^23d^{10}$ $4p^65s^24d^{10}5p^66s^24f^{14}5d^{10}$ $6p^4$ or $[Xe]6s^24f^{14}5d^{10}6p^4$

---

be arranged in *octaves*, based on the idea that certain properties seemed to repeat for every eighth tone. Although this model managed to group several elements with similar properties, it was not completely successful.

The present form of the periodic table was conceived independently by two chemists: the German Julius Lothar Meyer (1830–1895) and Dmitri

Ivanovich Mendeleev (1834–1907), a Russian. Mendeleev is usually given most of the credit, because it was he who emphasized how useful the table could be in predicting the existence and properties of still unknown elements. For example, when Mendeleev first published his table in 1872, the elements gallium, scandium, and germanium were unknown. Mendeleev correctly predicted the existence and properties of these

elements from gaps in his periodic table.

Using the table, Mendeleev also was able to correct several values for atomic masses. For example, the original atomic mass of 76 for indium was based on the assumption that indium oxide had the formula InO. This atomic mass placed indium, which has metallic properties, among the nonmetals. Mendeleev assumed that the atomic
(continued)

Answers to Self-Check Exercise 11.3

Fluorine (F): In Group 7 and Period 2, it is the fifth "2p element." The configuration is $1s^22s^22p^5$, or $[He]2s^22p^5$.

Silicon (Si): In Group 4 and Period 3, it is the second of the "3p elements." The configuration is $1s^22s^22p^63s^23p^2$, or $[Ne]3s^23p^2$.

Cesium (Cs): In Group 1 and Period 6, it is the first of the "6s elements." The configuration is $1s^22s^22p^63s^23p^6$ $4s^23d^{10}4p^65s^24d^{10}5p^66s^1$, or $[Xe]6s^1$.

Lead (Pb): In Group 4 and Period 6, it is the second of the "6p elements." The configuration is $[Xe]6s^24f^{14}$ $5d^{10}6p^2$.

Iodine (I): In Group 7 and Period 5, it is the fifth of the "5p elements." The configuration is $[Kr]5s^24d^{10}5p^5$.

WHAT IF Comments

There would be 3 elements in the "s block," 9 elements in the "p block," 15 elements in the "d block," and 21 elements in the "f block." The first few noble gases would have atomic numbers 3, 15, 27, and 54.

(continued)

Molten lead being poured into a mold to make toy soldiers.

Gallium is element 31 in Period 4 just after the transition metals (see Figure 11.33). It is the first element in the "4p series" and has a $4p^1$ arrangement. Gallium's electron configuration is

Ga: $1s^22s^22p^63s^23p^64s^23d^{10}4p^1$, or $[Ar]4s^23d^{10}4p^1$

Hafnium is element 72 and is found in Period 6, as shown in Figure 11.33. Note that it occurs just after the lanthanide series (see Figure 11.31). Thus the 4f orbitals are already filled. Hafnium is the second member of the 5d transition series and has two 5d electrons. Its electron configuration is

Hf: $1s^22s^22p^63s^23p^64s^23d^{10}4p^65s^24d^{10}5p^66s^24f^{14}5d^2$,

or $[Xe]6s^24f^{14}5d^2$

Radium is element 88 and is in Period 7 (and Group 2), as shown in Figure 11.33. Thus radium has two electrons in the 7s orbital, and its electron configuration is

Ra: $1s^22s^22p^63s^23p^64s^23d^{10}4p^65s^24d^{10}5p^66s^24f^{14}5d^{10}6p^67s^2$,

or $[Rn]7s^2$

 Self-Check Exercise 11.3

Using the periodic table inside the back cover of the text, predict the electron configurations for fluorine, silicon, cesium, lead, and iodine. If you have trouble, use Figure 11.31.

WHAT IF?

You have learned that each orbital can hold two electrons and this pattern is evident in the periodic table.

What if each orbital could hold three electrons? How would it change the appearance of the periodic table? For example, what would be the atomic numbers of the noble gases?

CHEMISTRY

The group label gives the total number of valence electrons for that group.

Summary of the Wave Mechanical Model and Valence-Electron Configurations

The concepts we have discussed in this chapter are very important. They allow us to make sense of a good deal of chemistry. When it was first observed that elements with similar properties occur periodically as the atomic number increases, chemists wondered why. Now we have an explanation. The wave mechanical model pictures the electrons in an atom as arranged in orbitals, with each orbital capable of holding two electrons. As we build up the atoms, the same types of orbitals recur in going from one principal energy level to another. This means that particular valence-electron configurations recur periodically. For reasons we will explore in the next chapter, elements with a particular type of valence configuration all show very similar chemical behavior. Thus groups of elements, such as the alkali metals, show similar chemistry because all the elements in that group have the same type of valence-electron arrangement. This concept, which explains so much chemistry, is the greatest contribution of the wave mechanical model to modern chemistry.

(continued)
mass was probably incorrect and proposed that the formula of indium oxide was really In_2O_3. Based on this correct formula, indium has an atomic mass of approximately 113, placing it among the metals. Mendeleev also corrected the atomic masses of beryllium and uranium. Because of its obvious usefulness, Mendeleev's periodic table was almost univer-

sally adopted, and it remains one of the most valuable tools at the chemist's disposal.

Representative Elements | d-Transition Elements | Representative Elements | Noble Gases

Period number, highest occupied electron level

1A ns^1	2A ns^2											3A ns^2np^1	4A ns^2np^2	5A ns^2np^3	6A ns^2np^4	7A ns^2np^5	8A ns^2np^6
1 H $1s^1$																	2 He $1s^2$
3 Li $2s^1$	4 Be $2s^2$											5 B $2s^22p^1$	6 C $2s^22p^2$	7 N $2s^22p^3$	8 O $2s^22p^4$	9 F $2s^22p^5$	10 Ne $2s^22p^6$
11 Na $3s^1$	12 Mg $3s^2$											13 Al $3s^23p^1$	14 Si $3s^23p^2$	15 P $3s^23p^3$	16 S $3s^23p^4$	17 Cl $3s^23p^5$	18 Ar $3s^23p^6$
19 K $4s^1$	20 Ca $4s^2$	21 Sc $4s^23d^1$	22 Ti $4s^23d^2$	23 V $4s^23d^3$	24 Cr $4s^13d^5$	25 Mn $4s^23d^5$	26 Fe $4s^23d^6$	27 Co $4s^23d^7$	28 Ni $4s^23d^8$	29 Cu $4s^13d^{10}$	30 Zn $4s^23d^{10}$	31 Ga $4s^24p^1$	32 Ge $4s^24p^2$	33 As $4s^24p^3$	34 Se $4s^24p^4$	35 Br $4s^24p^5$	36 Kr $4s^24p^6$
37 Rb $5s^1$	38 Sr $5s^2$	39 Y $5s^24d^1$	40 Zr $5s^24d^2$	41 Nb $5s^14d^4$	42 Mo $5s^14d^5$	43 Tc $5s^24d^5$	44 Ru $5s^14d^7$	45 Rh $5s^14d^8$	46 Pd $5s^14d^{10}$	47 Ag $5s^14d^{10}$	48 Cd $5s^24d^{10}$	49 In $5s^25p^1$	50 Sn $5s^25p^2$	51 Sb $5s^25p^3$	52 Te $5s^25p^4$	53 I $5s^25p^5$	54 Xe $5s^25p^6$
55 Cs $6s^1$	56 Ba $6s^2$	57 La* $6s^25d^1$	72 Hf $6s^25d^2$	73 Ta $6s^25d^3$	74 W $6s^25d^4$	75 Re $6s^25d^5$	76 Os $6s^25d^6$	77 Ir $6s^25d^7$	78 Pt $6s^15d^9$	79 Au $6s^15d^{10}$	80 Hg $6s^25d^{10}$	81 Tl $6s^26p^1$	82 Pb $6s^26p^2$	83 Bi $6s^26p^3$	84 Po $6s^26p^4$	85 At $6s^26p^5$	86 Rn $6s^26p^6$
87 Fr $7s^1$	88 Ra $7s^2$	89 Ac** $7s^26d^1$	104 Rf $7s^26d^2$	105 Db $7s^26d^3$	106 Sg $7s^26d^4$	107 Bh $7s^26d^5$	108 Hs $7s^26d^6$	109 Mt $7s^26d^7$	110 Ds $7s^26d^8$	111 Rg $7s^16d^{10}$	112 Uub $7s^26d^{10}$	113 Uut $7s^27p^1$	114 Uuq $7s^27p^2$	115 Uup $7s^27p^3$			

f-Transition Elements

*Lanthanides

58 Ce $6s^24f^15d^1$	59 Pr $6s^24f^35d^0$	60 Nd $6s^24f^45d^0$	61 Pm $6s^24f^55d^0$	62 Sm $6s^24f^65d^0$	63 Eu $6s^24f^75d^0$	64 Gd $6s^24f^75d^1$	65 Tb $6s^24f^95d^0$	66 Dy $6s^24f^{10}5d^0$	67 Ho $6s^24f^{11}5d^0$	68 Er $6s^24f^{12}5d^0$	69 Tm $6s^24f^{13}5d^0$	70 Yb $6s^24f^{14}5d^0$	71 Lu $6s^24f^{14}5d^1$

**Actinides

90 Th $7s^25f^06d^2$	91 Pa $7s^25f^26d^1$	92 U $7s^25f^36d^1$	93 Np $7s^25f^46d^1$	94 Pu $7s^25f^66d^0$	95 Am $7s^25f^76d^0$	96 Cm $7s^25f^76d^1$	97 Bk $7s^25f^96d^0$	98 Cf $7s^25f^{10}6d^0$	99 Es $7s^25f^{11}6d^0$	100 Fm $7s^25f^{12}6d^0$	101 Md $7s^25f^{13}6d^0$	102 No $7s^25f^{14}6d^0$	103 Lr $7s^25f^{14}6d^1$

Figure 11.34
The periodic table with atomic symbols, atomic numbers, and partial electron configurations.

For reference, the valence-electron configurations for all the elements are shown on the periodic table in **Figure 11.34.** Note the following points:

1. The group labels for Groups 1, 2, 3, 4, 5, 6, 7, and 8 indicate the *total number* of valence electrons for the atoms in these groups. For example, all the elements in Group 5 have the configuration ns^2np^3. (Any *d* electrons present are always in the next lower principal energy level than the valence electrons and so are not counted as valence electrons.)

2. The elements in Groups 1, 2, 3, 4, 5, 6, 7, and 8 are often called the **main-group elements,** or **representative elements.** Remember that every member of a given group (except for helium) has the same valence-electron configuration, except that the electrons are in different principal energy levels.

11.10 Electron Configurations and the Periodic Table **347**

TEACHING SUPPORT
Demonstration

Roman Candle

Materials
Test tube (200 × 24 cm)
600-mL beaker
Sand
Dropper
Copper(II) chloride
Potassium chlorate
Granulated sugar
Powdered iron

Strontium nitrate
Sulfuric acid (concentrated)

Preparation Measure 35.0 g potassium chlorate and 10.00 g granulated sugar separately and then mix them uniformly. **Caution:** Do not grind this mixture together. An explosion may result. Prepare a fresh mixture for each demonstration. Do not store the mixture.

Starting at the bottom, prepare four zones of chemicals in the

test tube as follows: (1) mixture of 3.0 g strontium nitrate and 9.0 g potassium chlorate/sugar **(red color)**; (2) mixture of 2.0 g copper(II) chloride and 10.0 g potassium chlorate/sugar **(blue color)**; (3) mixture of 3.0 g powdered iron and 9.0 g potassium chlorate/sugar **(yellow sparks)**; (4) 12.0 g potassium chlorate/sugar **(white color)**. Imbed the test tube upright in the beaker containing the sand. *(continued)*

Themes
Patterns of Change

Skills
Applying concepts, interpreting diagrams, making predictions, evaluating

CHEMISTRY in ACTION

Which Element Is It?

Materials Each group will need a periodic table and a textbook.

Purpose Students will better understand that chemical properties are similar in elements in the same period of the periodic table.

Discussion Questions asked should focus on the properties of the elements (not, for example, "Does the name of the element begin with a *C*?"). Questions should resemble the following: "Does the element have a higher electronegativity than bromine?" or "Is the element the smallest in its group?" You may wish to change the number of questions that each student is allowed to ask once students become more adept at answering questions. After a couple of rounds, they should see that asking about the properties narrows down their choices considerably.

11.11 Atomic Properties and the Periodic Table

Objective: *To understand the general trends in atomic properties in the periodic table.*

With all of this talk about electron probability and orbitals, we must not lose sight of the fact that chemistry is still fundamentally a science based on the observed properties of substances. We know that wood burns, steel rusts, plants grow, sugar tastes sweet, and so on because we *observe* these phenomena. The atomic theory is an attempt to help us understand why these things occur. If we understand why, we can hope to better control the chemical events that are so crucial in our daily lives.

In the next chapter we will see how our ideas about atomic structure help us understand how and why atoms combine to form compounds. As we explore this topic, and as we use theories to explain other types of chemical behavior later in the text, it is important that we distinguish the observation (steel rusts) from the attempts to explain why the observed event occurs (theories). The observations remain the same over the decades, but the theories (our explanations) change as we gain a clearer understanding of how nature operates. A good example of this is the replacement of the Bohr model for atoms by the wave mechanical model.

Because the observed behavior of matter lies at the heart of chemistry, you need to understand thoroughly the characteristic properties of the various elements and the trends (systematic variations) that occur in those properties. To that end, we will now consider some especially important properties of atoms and see how they vary, horizontally and vertically, on the periodic table.

Gold leaf being applied to the dome of the courthouse in Huntington, West Virginia.

CHEMISTRY in ACTION
Which Element Is It?

1. Work in a group of three or four students.
2. Have one person write down one of the representative elements without showing it to the other group members.
3. Take turns asking this person "yes/no" questions about the element. The person who chose the element must answer these questions (he or she can use Chapter 3 or 11 for information).
4. If the element is not identified after each person has asked three questions, the person choosing the element "wins" and identifies the element.
5. Continue until each group member has chosen an element.
6. Think about which questions were most helpful in identifying the element. Why were they so informative?

(continued)

Performance Note:
This demonstration produces lots of smoke. Perform it in a well-ventilated area or outside. Use a safety shield to protect the audience. When ready add 1 or 2 drops of concentrated sulfuric acid to the test tube and *step back.* The test tube sometimes begins to melt in this demonstration. Be careful to wait for it to cool after the

demonstration. The test tube can be discarded.

Teaching Notes You can use this demonstration as a review of the colors produced in the flame test. Ask students what chemical produces each color.

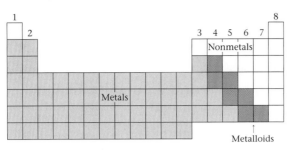

Figure 11.35
The classification of elements as metals, nonmetals, and metalloids.

Metals and Nonmetals

The most fundamental classification of the chemical elements is into metals and nonmetals. **Metals** typically have the following physical properties: a lustrous appearance, the ability to change shape without breaking (they can be pulled into a wire or pounded into a thin sheet), and excellent conductivity of heat and electricity. **Nonmetals** typically do not have these physical properties, although there are some exceptions. (For example, solid iodine is lustrous; the graphite form of carbon is an excellent conductor of electricity; and the diamond form of carbon is an excellent conductor of heat.) However, it is the *chemical* differences between metals and nonmetals that interest us the most: *metals tend to lose electrons to form positive ions, and nonmetals tend to gain electrons to form negative ions.* When a metal and a nonmetal react, a transfer of one or more electrons from the metal to the nonmetal often occurs.

Most of the elements are classed as metals, as is shown in **Figure 11.35.** Note that the metals are found on the left-hand side and at the center of the periodic table. The relatively few nonmetals are in the upper right-hand corner of the table. A few elements exhibit both metallic and nonmetallic behavior; they are classed as **metalloids** or semimetals.

It is important to understand that simply being classified as a metal does not mean that an element behaves exactly like all other metals. For example, some metals can lose one or more electrons much more easily than others. In particular, cesium can give up its outermost electron (a 6s electron) more easily than can lithium (a 2s electron). In fact, for the alkali metals (Group 1) the ease of giving up an electron varies as follows:

$$Cs \quad > \quad Rb \quad > \quad K \quad > \quad Na \quad > \quad Li$$

Loses an electron most easily   Least likely to lose an electron

Note that as we go down the group, the metals become more likely to lose an electron. This makes sense because as we go down the group, the electron being removed resides, on average, farther and farther from the nucleus. That is, the 6s electron lost from Cs is much farther from the attractive positive nucleus—and so is easier to remove—than the 2s electron that must be removed from a lithium atom.

11.11   Atomic Properties and the Periodic Table   **349**

- Students should understand the reasons for periodic trends. Focus on why a trend occurs and not simply on what the trend is.

- Students can easily understand why atomic size increases as we move down the periodic table. It is much more difficult for them to understand why it decreases as we move from left to right. Focus students' attention on the trend of adding electrons at approximately the same distance from the nucleus while simultaneously increasing the nuclear charge.

- Make sure that students understand the trends for atomic size across rows and down groups in the periodic table. If they understand these trends, the trends for ionization energy are much easier to grasp. Students should be able to see that the trends for atomic size and ionization energy are consistent with one another.

USING
TECHNOLOGY

Figure 11.36

Group 2

The same trend is also seen in the Group 2 metals (alkaline earth metals): the farther down in the group the metal resides, the more likely it is to lose an electron.

Just as metals vary somewhat in their properties, so do nonmetals. In general, the elements that can most effectively pull electrons from metals occur in the upper right-hand corner of the periodic table.

As a general rule, we can say that the most chemically active metals appear in the lower left-hand region of the periodic table, whereas the most chemically active nonmetals appear in the upper right-hand region. The properties of the semimetals, or metalloids, lie between the metals and the nonmetals, as might be expected.

Atomic Size

The sizes of atoms vary as shown in **Figure 11.36.** Notice that atoms get larger as we go down a group on the periodic table and that they get smaller as we go from left to right across a period.

We can understand the increase in size that we observe as we go down a group by remembering that as the principal energy level increases, the average distance of the electrons from the nucleus also increases. So atoms get bigger as electrons are added to larger principal energy levels.

Explaining the decrease in **atomic size** across a period requires a little thought about the atoms in a given row (period) of the periodic table. Recall that the atoms in a particular period all have their outermost electrons in a given principal energy level. That is, the atoms in Period 1 have their outer electrons in the 1s orbital (principal energy level 1), the atoms in Period 2 have their outermost electrons in principal energy level 2 (2s and 2p orbitals),

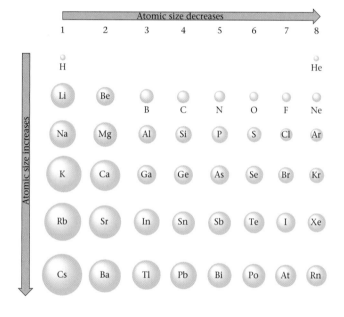

Figure 11.36
Relative atomic sizes for selected atoms. Note that atomic size increases down a group and decreases across a period.

350 Chapter 11 Modern Atomic Theory

(continued)
these values are significantly smaller than might be expected from the 90% electron density volumes of isolated atoms, because when atoms form bonds, their electron "clouds" penetrate one another. Nevertheless, these values form a self-consistent data set that can be used to discuss the trends in atomic radii.

Note from Figure 11.36 that atomic radii decrease in going

from left to right across a period. This decrease can be explained in terms of the increasing effective nuclear charge (decreasing shielding) in going from left to right. As a result, the valence electrons are drawn closer to the nucleus, decreasing the size of the atom.

Atomic radius increases down a group because of the increases in the orbital sizes in successive principal quantum levels.

Fireworks

The art of using mixtures of chemicals to produce explosives is an ancient one. Black powder—a mixture of potassium nitrate, charcoal, and sulfur—was being used in China well before A.D. 1000, and it has been used through the centuries in military explosives, in construction blasting, and for fireworks.

Brightly colored fireworks explode above the city lights.

Before the nineteenth century, fireworks were confined mainly to rockets and loud bangs. Orange and yellow colors came from the presence of charcoal and iron filings. However, with the great advances in chemistry in the nineteenth century, new compounds found their way into fireworks. Salts of copper, strontium, and barium added brilliant colors. Magnesium and aluminum metals gave a dazzling white light.

How do fireworks produce their brilliant colors and loud bangs? Actually, only a handful of different chemicals are responsible for most of the spectacular effects. To produce the noise and flashes, an oxidizer (something with a strong affinity for electrons) is reacted with a metal such as magnesium or aluminum mixed with sulfur. The resulting reaction produces a brilliant flash, which is due to the aluminum or magnesium burning, and a loud report is produced by the rapidly expanding gases. For a color effect, an element with a colored flame is included.

Yellow colors in fireworks are due to sodium. Strontium salts give the red color familiar from highway safety flares. Barium salts give a green color.

Although you might think that the chemistry of fireworks is simple, achieving the vivid white flashes and the brilliant colors requires complex combinations of chemicals. For example, because the white flashes produce high flame temperatures, the colors tend to wash out. Another problem arises from the use of sodium salts. Because sodium produces an extremely bright yellow color, sodium salts cannot be used when other colors are desired. In short, the manufacture of fireworks that produce the desired effects and are also safe to handle requires very careful selection of chemicals.*

*The chemical mixtures in fireworks are very dangerous. *Do not* experiment with chemicals on your own.

and so on (see Figure 11.31). Because all the orbitals in a given principal energy level are expected to be the same size, we might expect the atoms in a given period to be the same size. However, remember that the number of protons in the nucleus increases as we move from atom to atom in the period. The resulting increase in positive charge on the nucleus tends to pull the electrons closer to the nucleus. So instead of remaining the same size across a period as electrons are added in a given principal energy level, the atoms get smaller as the electron "cloud" is drawn in by the increasing nuclear charge.

11.11 Atomic Properties and the Periodic Table **351**

**Answers to
Focus Questions**

1.

	1s	2s	2p	2p	2p	3s
Li	↑↓	↑				
C	↑↓	↑↓	↑	↑		
Mg	↑↓	↑↓	↑↓	↑↓	↑↓	↑↓

2. A valence electron is in the outermost level for the atom; a core electron is in one of the inner levels for the atom.

Ca: $1s^2 2s 2p^6$ core $3s^2$ valence

3. The valence electron config-urations of atoms in the same families are the same but on different energy levels.

4. a. Hf, $6s^2 4f^{14} 5d^2$

   b. Ra, $7s^2$

   c. Sb, $5s^2 4d^{10} 5p^3$

   d. Pb, $6s^2 4f^{14} 5d^{10} 6p^2$

5. Metals tend to lose electrons; nonmetals tend to gain elec-trons in chemical reactions.

6. Metals have relatively few valence electrons located in the outer shell. In contrast, nonmetals have a large num-ber of electrons in the outer shell and a small size, mak-ing the attractive forces higher in these elements. It is therefore easier to remove an electron from a metal and to gain an electron for a non-metal.

Ionization Energies

The **ionization energy** of an atom is the energy required to remove an elec-tron from an individual atom in the gas phase:

As we have noted, the most characteristic chemical property of a metal atom is losing electrons to nonmetals. Another way of saying this is to say that *metals have relatively low ionization energies*—a relatively small amount of energy is needed to remove an electron from a typical metal.

Recall that metals at the bottom of a group lose electrons more easily than those at the top. In other words, ionization energies tend to decrease in going from the top to the bottom of a group.

In contrast to metals, nonmetals have relatively large ionization energies. Nonmetals tend to gain, not lose, electrons. Recall that metals appear on the left-hand side of the periodic table and nonmetals appear on the right-hand side. Thus it is not surprising that ionization energies tend to increase from left to right across a given period on the periodic table.

In general, the elements that appear in the lower left-hand region of the periodic table have the lowest ionization energies (and are therefore the most chemically active metals). On the other hand, the elements with the highest ionization energies (the most chemically active nonmetals) occur in the up-per right-hand region of the periodic table.

Focus Questions

Sections 11.9–11.11

1. Write the orbital diagram for the elements listed below:

Li $1s^2 2s^1$ C $1s^2 2s^2 2p^2$ Mg $1s^2 2s^2 2p^6 3s^2$

2. What is the difference between a valence electron and a core electron? Select an element from row 3 and label both using its electron configuration.

3. Elements in vertical columns (families) show similar chemical behavior. How are their electron configurations similar?

4. Using their positions on the periodic table, write the valence-electron configurations for the following elements.

   a. hafnium, $Z = 72$ **c.** antimony, $Z = 51$
   b. radium, $Z = 88$ **d.** lead, $Z = 82$

5. What chemical property distinguishes a metal from a nonmetal?

6. How can the property in question 5 be explained using ionization energy trends?

(continued)
Some discontinuities in ioniza-tion energy appear in going across a period. For example, in Period 2, boron has a lower ion-ization energy than beryllium and oxygen has a lower value than nitrogen. These excep-tions can be explained in terms of electron repulsions. The de-crease in ionization energy in going from beryllium to boron reflects the fact that the elec-trons in the filled 2s orbital shield electrons in the 2p orbital from the nuclear charge to some extent. The decrease in ionization energy in going from nitrogen to oxygen reflects the extra electron repulsions in the doubly occupied oxygen 2p or-bital.

Problem

How well can we model an orbital with a dartboard and a dart?

Introduction

According to modern atomic theory, we cannot be sure of the exact location of electrons in an atom. We predict that electrons will be relatively close to the nucleus (because the electrons are negatively charged and the nucleus is positively charged). However, we must discuss the "location" of an electron in terms of probability instead of an exact position.

In this activity you will construct and analyze a probability map using a dart and dartboard.

Prelab Assignment

Read the entire lab experiment before you begin.

Materials

Goggles
Apron
Darts
Graph paper
Target
Cardboard

Safety

Be careful to drop the darts toward the target on the floor. No one should ever be in the path of a dart.

Procedure

1. Tape the target to the center of the cardboard, place the cardboard on the floor, and tape the cardboard to the floor.
2. Drop the dart from shoulder height, trying to hit the center of the target. Your partner should retrieve the dart and mark the position of the hit with a small X (don't count drops that fall outside the largest circle).
3. Repeat this procedure 99 times for a total of 100 drops.
4. Count the number of hits in each ring and record this number.

Cleaning Up

Clean all materials and wash your hands thoroughly.

Data/Observations

Fill in a table similar to the following

Ring Number	Average Distance from Target Center (cm)	Area of Ring (cm²)	Number of Hits in the Ring	Number of Hits per Unit Area (hits/cm²)
1	0.5	3.1		
2	1.5	9.4		
3	2.5	16		
4	3.5	22		
5	4.5	28		
6	5.5	35		
7	6.5	41		
8	7.5	47		
9	8.5	53		
10	9.5	60		

Analysis and Conclusions

1. Which is the ring with the highest probability of finding a hit?
2. Which is the ring with the lowest probability of finding a hit?
3. Construct a graph of the number of hits versus average distance from the center.
4. Construct a graph of hits per unit area versus average distance from the center.
5. What does the graph of the number of hits versus average distance represent? Account for its shape.
6. What does the graph of the hits per unit area versus average distance represent? Account for its shape.
7. Is the maximum of each graph the same? Explain.
8. How well can we model an orbital with a dartboard and a dart? Specifically, focus on the following:
   a. Compare your target with Figure 11.19. How is it similar? How is it different?
   b. Why do we predict that an electron should be near the nucleus? Why do we expect the dart to land in the center of the target?

Something Extra

How would changing the number of drops affect your results? Do the experiment with 10 drops and with 500 drops, and compare your results.

353

get to look like after 100 drops. Can they predict with great certainty exactly where a specific dropped dart will land?

Procedure Hints

Make sure that the students' arms are stretched horizontally and that they simply drop the darts toward the target.

Post-Lab Discussion

Have students compare their targets and graphs. They should understand that orbitals are probability distributions that are similar conceptually to the probability distributions of the darts.

The graph of the number of hits versus distance shows that there is a most probable distance from the center of the target. Interestingly, when such a plot is made for the hydrogen atom, the most probable distance for the electron is the radius determined by Bohr. Of course, Bohr assumed that the electron was always at this distance, which is not true.

Data/Observations

Sample data are found in the *Teacher's Guide* for the Laboratory.

Analysis and Conclusions

1. Answers may vary, but should be ring 1. While there may be six times as many hits in ring 4 (from the sample data), the area of ring 4 is more than six times larger than the area of ring 1.

2. Answers may vary, but should be ring 10.

3. Graph depends on data. This graph should have a maximum around ring 4.

4. Graph depends on data. The maximum should be at ring 1 and the value should slowly approach zero.

5. This graph represents the total probability of finding a hit at a particular distance. The maximum at ring 4 (from the sample data) reflects the two opposing forces. The probability of finding a hit is highest closer to the center. Of course, the area of the rings increases as we get farther from the center.

6. This graph depicts the probability of finding a hit versus distance from the center of the target. Because students
(continued)

CHEMISTRY in the LABORATORY

Electron Probability

Objectives

To use darts to hit a dartboard that serves as a model of electron probability

Skills

Observing, applying concepts, interpreting data, drawing conclusions, developing models

Materials

Goggles	Graph paper
Apron	Target
Darts	Cardboard

Preparation Hints

Use upside-down lids from large cardboard boxes (such as paper boxes) to elevate the cardboard and targets. This setup allows the darts to penetrate the target and leave better marks. You can also make platforms by gluing small strips of wood to the back of the cardboard at two ends.

Prelab Discussion

Students should understand that they are not to throw the darts (at the target or at people).

Discuss the difference between predicting a pattern and predicting an event. We have a fairly good idea of where an electron will be in general (relatively close to the nucleus) but we never know exactly where it will be at any given instant. The same is true with the darts. Have students think about what they expect the tar-were aiming for the center, there is a greater chance that a dart will hit nearer to the center of the graph. The farther from the center, the less likely it will be to find a hit.

7. No. The highest probability is close to the center. The highest total probability is a little farther away from the center.

8. Answers will vary, but we can develop a fairly accurate electron probability distribution model.

   a. The targets should look similar to Figure 11.19, although with only 100 drops there could be some variation.

   b. Electrons are negatively charged and the nucleus is positively charged; therefore electrons are attracted to the nucleus and we expect the electron to be near the nucleus. We expect the dart to land near the center of the target because we are aiming for the center.

Something Extra
The more drops, the more closely the final targets should resemble Figure 11.19.

Chapter Review
Assign the students to work individually on the Chapter 11 Review Worksheet at the appropriate level (Basic, Standard, or Challenge). Answers are found in the *Teacher Resources*.

Assessment
Chapter 11 Test is found in the *Teacher Resources*, along with the answers for the test.

 Computerized Test Bank for Chapter 11

Answers to End of Chapter Problems

1. This experiment is explained in Chapter 3.

2. See Figure 11.1 for a sketch of Rutherford's atom. Rutherford could not answer questions such as, "Why are the negative electrons not attracted into the positive nucleus, causing atoms to collapse?"

3. Electromagnetic radiation is radiant energy that travels through space with wavelike behavior. Examples include visible light, radio and television signals, microwaves, infrared, and X rays.

11 Chapter Review

Key Terms

electromagnetic radiation (11.2)
wavelength (11.2)
frequency (11.2)
photon (11.2)
quantized energy levels (11.4)
wave mechanical model (11.6)
orbital (11.7)
principal energy levels (11.7)
sublevels (11.7)
Pauli exclusion principle (11.8)

electron configuration (11.9)
orbital (box) diagram (11.9)
valence electrons (11.9)
core electrons (11.9)
lanthanide series (11.10)
actinide series (11.10)
main-group (representative) elements (11.10)
metals (11.11)
nonmetals (11.11)
metalloids (11.11)
atomic size (11.11)
ionization energy (11.11)

Summary

1. Energy travels through space by electromagnetic radiation ("light"), which can be characterized by the wavelength and frequency of the waves. Light can also be thought of as packets of energy called photons. Atoms can gain energy by absorbing a photon and can lose energy by emitting a photon.

2. The emissions of energy from hydrogen atoms produce only certain energies as hydrogen changes from a higher to a lower energy. This shows that the energy levels of hydrogen are quantized.

3. The Bohr model of the hydrogen atom postulated that an electron moves in circular orbits corresponding to the various allowed energy levels. Though it worked well for hydrogen, the Bohr model did not work for other atoms.

4. The wave mechanical model explains atoms by postulating that the electron has both wave and particle characteristics. Electron states are described by orbitals, which are probability maps indicating how likely it is to find the electron at a given point in space. The orbital size can be thought of as a surface containing 90% of the total electron probability.

5. According to the Pauli exclusion principle, an atomic orbital can hold a maximum of two electrons, and those electrons must have opposite spins.

6. Atoms have a series of energy levels, called principal energy levels (n), which contain one or more sublevels (types of orbitals). The number of sublevels increases with increasing n.

354　Chapter 11　Modern Atomic Theory

7. Valence electrons are the *s* and *p* electrons in the outermost principal energy level of an atom. Core electrons are the inner electrons of an atom.

8. Metals are found at the left and center of the periodic table. The most chemically active metals are found in the lower left-hand corner of the periodic table. The most chemically active nonmetals are located in the upper right-hand corner.

9. For the representative elements, atomic size increases going down a group but decreases going from left to right across a period.

10. Ionization energy, the energy required to remove an electron from a gaseous atom, decreases going down a group and increases going from left to right across a period.

Questions and Problems

All exercises with blue numbers have answers in the back of this book.

11.1 Rutherford's Atom

Questions

1. Describe the experiment that allowed Rutherford to conclude that the atom consists of a relatively heavy positively charged nucleus surrounded by electrons.

2. Sketch a picture of the model of the atom that Rutherford developed. What questions were left unanswered by Rutherford's model?

11.2 Energy and Light

Questions

3. What do we mean by *electromagnetic radiation?* Give several examples of different sorts of electromagnetic radiation.

4. How are the different types of electromagnetic radiation similar? How do they differ?

5. What does the *wavelength* of electromagnetic radiation represent? Sketch a representation of a wave and indicate the *wavelength* on your graph. How does the *wavelength* of electromagnetic radiation differ from its *frequency?*

6. What do we mean by the *speed* of electromagnetic radiation? How do the *frequency* and the *speed* of electromagnetic radiation differ?

7. What is a "packet" of electromagnetic energy called?

8. What is meant by the *wave–particle* nature of light?

---

4. The different forms of electromagnetic radiation all exhibit the same wavelike behavior and move through space at the same speed (the speed of light). The types of electromagnetic radiation differ in their frequency and wavelength and in the resulting amount of energy carried per photon.

5. The wavelength represents the distance between two corresponding points on successive cycles of a wave (see Figure 11.3). The frequency represents the number of complete cycles of the wave that pass a given point per second.

6. The speed of electromagnetic radiation represents how fast energy is transferred through space; the frequency of the radiation tells us how many waves pass a given point in a certain amount of time.

7. photon

8. The wave–particle nature of light refers to the fact that a beam of electromagnetic energy can be considered not only as a continuous wave, but also as a stream of discrete packets of energy moving through space.

9. The colors are due to the release of energy.

10. Higher-energy photons are released with Cu^{2+} because green light is emitted (red light is emitted from Li^+). Green light is of higher energy than red light.

11. An atom is in an excited state when it possesses more than its minimum energy (ground state energy).

11.3 Emission of Energy by Atoms

Questions

9. Are the colors of flame tests due to taking in energy or releasing energy?

10. In which case are higher-energy photons released, with Li^+ or with Cu^{2+}? How do you know?

11.4 The Energy Levels of Hydrogen

Questions

11. What does it mean to say that an atom is in an "excited state"?

12. When an atom in an excited state returns to its ground state, what happens to the excess energy of the atom?

13. Describe briefly why the study of electromagnetic radiation has been important to our understanding of the arrangement of electrons in atoms.

14. What does it mean to say that the hydrogen atom has *discrete energy levels*? How is this fact reflected in the radiation that excited hydrogen atoms emit?

15. What experimental evidence do scientists have that the energy levels of hydrogen are *quantized*?

16. What is meant by the *ground state* of an atom?

11.5 The Bohr Model of the Atom

Questions

17. What are the essential points of Bohr's theory of the structure of the hydrogen atom?

18. According to Bohr, what types of motions do electrons have in an atom, and what happens when energy is applied to the atom?

19. How does the Bohr theory account for the observed phenomenon of the emission of discrete wavelengths of light by excited atoms?

20. Why was Bohr's theory for the hydrogen atom initially accepted, and why was it ultimately discarded?

11.6 The Wave Mechanical Model of the Atom

Questions

21. What major assumption (that was analogous to what had already been demonstrated for electromagnetic radiation) did de Broglie and Schrödinger make about the motion of tiny particles?

22. Discuss briefly the difference between an orbit (as described by Bohr for hydrogen) and an orbital (as described by the more modern, wave mechanical picture of the atom).

23. Explain why we cannot *exactly* specify the location of an electron in an atom but can discuss only where an electron is *most likely* to be at any given time.

11.7 The Hydrogen Orbitals

Questions

24. Why are the orbitals of the hydrogen atom described as "probability maps"? Why are the edges of the hydrogen orbitals sometimes drawn to appear "fuzzy?"

25. When we draw a picture of an orbital, we are indicating that the probability of finding the electron within this region of space is greater than 90%. Why is this probability never 100%?

26. What are the differences between the 2s orbital and the 1s orbital of hydrogen? How are they similar?

27. How is the *distance* of an electron from the nucleus related to the *principal energy level*? Does a *higher* principal energy level mean that the electron is *closer* to or *farther* away from the nucleus?

28. If an electron moves from the 1s orbital to the 2s orbital, its energy (increases/decreases).

29. Although a hydrogen atom has only one electron, the hydrogen atom possesses a complete set of available orbitals. What purpose do these additional orbitals serve?

11.8 The Wave Mechanical Model: Further Development

Questions

30. What is the *Pauli exclusion principle?* How many electrons can occupy an orbital, according to this principle? Why?

31. How does the *energy* of a principal energy level depend on the value of *n*? Does a higher value of *n* mean a higher or lower energy?

32. The number of sublevels in a principal energy level (increases/decreases) as *n* increases.

33. Which of the following orbital designations is (are) not correct?
   a. 2p   c. 3f
   b. 1d   d. 4s

11.9 Electron Arrangements in the First Eighteen Atoms on the Periodic Table

Questions

34. Which orbital is the *first* to be filled in any atom? Why?

35. Which electrons of an atom are the *valence* electrons? Why are these electrons especially important?

36. How are the electron arrangements in a given group (vertical column) of the periodic table related? How is this relationship manifested in the properties of the elements in the given group?

12. It is emitted as a photon.

13. Excited atoms emit light (which we can measure) because of changes in their microscopic structure. By studying emissions of atoms, we can trace back to what happened inside the atom.

14. When excited hydrogen atoms emit their excess energy, the photons of radiation released always have exactly the same wavelength and energy. Thus the hydrogen atom possesses only certain allowed energy states.

15. Hydrogen always transmits light at exactly the same wavelengths, which correspond to transitions of the electron between the fixed energy states of the atom.

16. The ground state of an atom is its lowest possible energy state.

17. Bohr pictured electrons moving in circular orbits that corresponded to the various allowed energy levels. He suggested that the electrons could jump to a different orbit by absorbing or emitting a photon of light with exactly the correct energy content (corresponding to the difference in energy between the orbits).

18. According to Bohr, electrons move in fixed circular orbits around the nucleus. An electron can move to a larger orbit if a photon of applied energy equals the difference in energy between the two orbits.

19. According to Bohr, the energy levels were definite and fixed, so the atom should always emit energy at the same wavelength.

20. Bohr's theory explained the line spectrum of hydrogen exactly. It did not explain measurements made for atoms other than hydrogen.

21. As light has both wave and particle characteristics, then perhaps the electron might exhibit both of these characteristics. Thus perhaps an electron has wavelike properties along with particle-like properties.

22. An orbit refers to an exact circular pathway for the electron around the nucleus. An orbital represents a region in space in which there is a high probability of finding an electron.

23. Trying to measure the exact location of an electron (for example, by shooting a beam of light at it) would cause the electron to move. Measurement requires an energy change, which moves the electron.

24. Chemists arbitrarily define an orbital as representing 90% of the probability of finding an electron in this region. Orbitals represent mathematical functions and have no distinct outer edge (so they are drawn to appear fuzzy). They represent the most likely region where an electron might be found.

25. Pictures representing orbitals are probability maps. They do not imply that the electron moves on the surface of, or within, the region of the picture. The mathematical probability of finding an electron never becomes zero moving out from the nucleus (the electron could be "anywhere").

26. The 2s orbital is similar in shape to the 1s orbital, but the 2s orbital is larger.

27. The higher the principal energy level (*n*), the farther from the nucleus (on average) the electron will be.

28. increases

29. The other orbitals serve as the excited states of the hydrogen atom. When energy of the appropriate frequency is applied to the hydrogen atom, the electron can move from its ground state to an excited state. The electron can move back if it releases the absorbed energy.

30. The Pauli exclusion principle states that an orbital can hold a maximum of two electrons, and those two electrons must have opposite spin.

31. The higher the value of the principal quantum number (n), the higher the energy of the principal energy level.

32. increases

33. b and c are incorrect; a and d are correct

34. The 1s orbital is closest to the nucleus and lowest in energy, so it is always filled first.

35. Valence electrons are those electrons in the outermost energy level. These electrons can interact with the (valence) electrons of another atom in a chemical reaction.

36. The elements in a given column of the periodic table have the same valence electron configuration. Having the same valence electron configuration causes the elements in a given group to have similar chemical properties.

37. (a) $1s^22s^22p^63s^23p^64s^2$ $3d^{10}4p^65s^2$; (b) $1s^22s^22p^63s^2$ $3p^64s^23d^{10}$; (c) $1s^2$; (d)$1s^22s^2$ $2p^63s^23p^64s^23d^{10}4p^5$

38. (a) $1s^22s^22p^63s^23p^64s^2$; (b) $1s^22s^22p^63s^23p^64s^1$; (c) $1s^22s^22p^5$; (d) $1s^22s^22p^6$ $3s^23p^64s^23d^{10}4p^6$

39. (a) (↑↓) (↑↓) (↑↓)(↑↓)(↑↓) (↑↓)
　　 1s　2s　　2p　　　3s
　　 (↑)( )( );
　　　3p

(b) (↑↓) (↑↓) (↑↓)(↑↓)(↑↓) (↑↓)
　　 1s　2s　　2p　　　3s
　　 (↑)(↑)(↑);
　　　3p

(c) (↑↓) (↑↓) (↑↓)(↑↓)(↑↓) (↑↓)
　　 1s　2s　　2p　　　3s
　　 (↑↓)(↑↓)(↑↓) (↑↓)
　　　3p　　　4s
　　 (↑↓)(↑↓)(↑↓)(↑↓)(↑↓) (↑↓)(↑↓)(↑);
　　　3d　　　　　4p

(d) (↑↓) (↑↓) (↑↓)(↑↓)(↑↓) (↑↓);
　　 1s　2s　　2p　　　3s
　　 (↑↓)(↑↓)(↑↓)
　　　3p

40. (a) 1; (b) 2; (c) 7; (d) 5

41. The physical and chemical properties of potassium are like those of the other Group 1 elements; calcium's properties are similar to those of the other Group 2 elements.

42. The properties of Rb and Sr suggest that they are members of Groups 1 and 2, respectively. Thus the outer electrons are filling the 5s orbital. The 5s orbital, then, must be lower in energy and fills before the 4d orbitals.

Problems

37. Write the full electron configuration ($1s^22s^2$, etc.) for each of the following elements.
  a. strontium, $Z = 38$
  b. zinc, $Z = 30$
  c. helium, $Z = 2$
  d. bromine, $Z = 35$

38. Write the full electron configuration ($1s^22s^2$, etc.) for each of the following elements.
  a. calcium, $Z = 20$
  b. potassium, $Z = 19$
  c. fluorine, $Z = 9$
  d. krypton, $Z = 36$

39. Write the complete orbital diagram for each of the following elements, using boxes to represent orbitals and arrows to represent electrons.
  a. aluminum, $Z = 13$
  b. phosphorus, $Z = 15$
  c. bromine, $Z = 35$
  d. argon, $Z = 18$

40. How many valence electrons does each of the following atoms possess?
  a. sodium, $Z = 11$
  b. calcium, $Z = 20$
  c. iodine, $Z = 53$
  d. nitrogen, $Z = 7$

11.10 Electron Configurations and the Periodic Table

Questions

41. Why do we believe that the valence electrons of calcium and potassium reside in the 4s orbital rather than in the 3d orbital?

42. Would you expect the valence electrons of rubidium and strontium to reside in the 5s or the 4d orbitals? Why?

Problems

43. Using the symbol of the previous noble gas to indicate the core electrons, write the valence-electron configuration for each of the following elements.
  a. calcium, $Z = 20$
  b. francium, $Z = 87$
  c. yttrium, $Z = 39$
  d. cerium, $Z = 58$

44. Using the symbol of the previous noble gas to indicate the core electrons, write the valence-electron configuration for each of the following elements.
  a. phosphorus, $Z = 15$
  b. chlorine, $Z = 17$
  c. magnesium, $Z = 12$
  d. zinc, $Z = 30$

45. How many 4d electrons are found in each of the following elements?
  a. yttrium, $Z = 39$
  b. zirconium, $Z = 40$
  c. strontium, $Z = 38$
  d. cadmium, $Z = 48$

46. For each of the following elements, indicate which set of orbitals is being filled last.
  a. plutonium, $Z = 94$
  b. nobelium, $Z = 102$

  c. praeseodymium, $Z = 59$
  d. radon, $Z = 86$

47. Write the shorthand valence-electron configuration of each of the following elements, basing your answer on the element's location on the periodic table.
  a. uranium, $Z = 92$
  b. manganese, $Z = 25$
  c. mercury, $Z = 80$
  d. francium, $Z = 87$

11.11 Atomic Properties and the Periodic Table

Questions

48. What types of ions do the metals and the nonmetallic elements form? Do the metals lose or gain electrons in doing this? Do the nonmetallic elements gain or lose electrons in doing this?

49. Give some similarities that exist among the elements of Group 1.

50. Give some similarities that exist among the elements of Group 7.

51. Where are the most nonmetallic elements located on the periodic table? Why do these elements pull electrons from metallic elements so effectively during a reaction?

52. Why do the metallic elements of a given period (horizontal row) typically have much lower ionization energies than do the nonmetallic elements of the same period?

53. Explain why the atoms of the elements at the bottom of a given group (vertical column) of the periodic table are *larger* than the atoms of the elements at the top of the same group.

54. Though all the elements in a given period (horizontal row) of the periodic table have their valence electrons in the same types of orbitals, the sizes of the atoms decrease from left to right within a period. Explain why.

Problems

55. In each of the following sets of elements, which element shows the least active chemical behavior?
  a. Cs, Rb, Na
  b. Ba, Ca, Be
  c. F, Cl, Br
  d. O, Te, S

56. In each of the following sets of elements, which element would be expected to have the highest ionization energy?
  a. Cs, K, Li
  b. Ba, Sr, Ca
  c. I, Br, Cl
  d. Mg, Si, S

57. Arrange the following sets of elements in order of increasing atomic size.
  a. Sn, Xe, Rb, Sr
  b. Rn, He, Xe, Kr
  c. Pb, Ba, Cs, At

43. (a) $[Ar]4s^2$; (b) $[Rn]7s^1$; (c) $[Kr]5s^24d^1$; (d) $[Xe]6s^24f^1\,5d^1$

44. (a) $[Ne]3s^23p^3$; (b) $[Ne]3s^23p^5$; (c) $[Ne]3s^2$; (d) $[Ar]4s^23d^{10}$

45. (a) 1; (b) 2; (c) 0; (d) 10

46. (a) 5f; (b) 5f; (c) 4f; (d) 6p

47. (a) $[Rn]7s^26d^15f^3$; (b) $[Ar]4s^23d^5$; (c) $[Xe]6s^24f^{14}5d^{10}$; (d) $[Rn]7s^1$

48. The metallic elements lose electrons and form positive ions (cations); the nonmetallic elements gain electrons and form negative ions (anions).

49. Group 1 metals are highly reactive, and all form 1+ ions almost exclusively when they react. Physically these metals are all soft and relatively low in density. They tend to be found with a layer of metal oxide coating, but appear shiny if a fresh surface is exposed.

50. All exist as diatomic molecules; all are nonmetals; all have relatively high electronegativities; all form 1– ions in reacting with metallic elements.

51. The nonmetallic elements are found in the upper-right corner of the periodic table. They tend to be small in size, so the electrons are held in tightly by the nucleus.

52. The elements of a given period (horizontal row) have valence electrons in the same subshells. Nuclear charge increases across a period going from left to right. Atoms at the left side have smaller

58. The distance in meters between two consecutive peaks (or troughs) in a wave is called the _____.

59. The speed at which electromagnetic radiation moves through a vacuum is called the _____.

60. The energy levels of hydrogen (and other atoms) are _____, which means that only certain values of energy are allowed.

61. In the modern theory of the atom, a(n) _____ represents a region of space in which there is a high probability of finding an electron.

62. Without referring to your textbook or a periodic table, write the full electron configuration, the orbital box diagram, and the noble gas shorthand configuration for the elements with the following atomic numbers.

a. $Z = 19$ d. $Z = 26$
b. $Z = 22$ e. $Z = 30$
c. $Z = 14$

63. Write the general valence configuration (for example, ns^1 for Group 1) for the group in which each of the following elements is found.

a. barium, $Z = 56$ d. potassium, $Z = 19$
b. bromine, $Z = 35$ e. sulfur, $Z = 16$
c. tellurium, $Z = 52$

64. How many valence electrons does each of the following atoms have?

a. titanium, $Z = 22$ c. radium, $Z = 88$
b. iodine, $Z = 53$ d. manganese, $Z = 25$

65. How do we know that the energy levels of the hydrogen atom are not *continuous*, as physicists originally assumed?

66. Why do the two electrons in the $2p$ sublevel of carbon occupy *different* $2p$ orbitals?

67. Write the full electron configuration ($1s^22s^2$, etc.) for each of the following elements.

a. bromine, $Z = 35$ c. barium, $Z = 56$
b. xenon, $Z = 54$ d. selenium, $Z = 34$

68. Metals have relatively (low/high) ionization energies, whereas nonmetals have relatively (high/low) ionization energies.

69. In each of the following sets of elements, indicate which element has the smallest atomic size.

a. Ba, Ca, Ra
b. P, Si, Al
c. Rb, Cs, K

70. A 2+ ion of a particular element has an atomic mass of 203 and 123 neutrons in its nucleus.

a. What is the nuclear charge in this element?
b. What are the symbol and name of this element?

c. How many valence electrons does a neutral atom of this element have?
d. How many levels of electrons are occupied when this element is in its ground state?

71. Given elements with the following electron configurations

i. $1s^22s^22p^63s^2$
ii. $1s^22s^22p^63s^1$
iii. $1s^22s^22p^6$
iv. $1s^22s^22p^4$
v. $1s^22s^22p^3$
vi. $1s^22s^22p^1$

specify which meet the following conditions.

a. Which will normally form a negative ion in solution?
b. Which will have the lowest ionization energy?
c. Which would be the most reactive metal?
d. Which has the greatest number of unpaired electrons?
e. Which metal would combine with oxygen in a one-to-one ratio?
f. Predict the formula for the compound that would form between (ii) and (v).
g. Predict the formula for the compound that would form between (i) and (v).
h. List the six elements in order of increasing ionization energy.

72. Identify the following elements.

a. the most reactive nonmetal (not a noble gas) on the periodic table
b. the smallest lanthanide
c. the largest metalloid
d. the metal with the lowest ionization energy
e. the least reactive halogen
f. the least reactive member of the fifth period
g. the actinide with the highest nuclear charge

73. Suppose that element 120 has just been discovered. Identify four chemical or physical properties expected of this element.

74. Suppose that in another universe there is a completely different set of elements from the ones we know. The inhabitants assign symbols of A, B, C, and so on in order of increasing atomic number, using all of the letters of the alphabet. They find that the following elements closely resemble one another in terms of their properties:

A, C, G, K, Q, and Y

B, F, J, P, and X

V is its own family

Sketch a periodic table, similar to ours, using this information.

---

nuclear charges and bind their valence electrons less tightly.

53. All atoms within a given group have the same number of valence electrons, and these valence electrons occur in the same type of subshell. At the bottom of the group, however, the valence electrons are in a higher principal energy level.

54. The nuclear charge increases from left to right within a period. The greater the nuclear charge, the more tightly the valence electrons

are "pulled."

55. (a) Na; (b) Be; (c) Br; (d) Te

56. (a) Li; (b) Ca; (c) Cl; (d) S

57. (a) Xe < Sn < Sr < Rb;
(b) He < Kr < Xe < Rn; (c) At < Pb < Ba < Cs

58. wavelength

59. speed of light

60. quantized

61. orbital

62. (a) (↑↓)(↑↓)(↑↓)(↑↓)(↑↓)
        1s   2s   2p   3s

(↑↓)(↑↓)(↑↓) (↑);
3p   4s
$1s^22s^22p^63s^23p^64s^1$; [Ar]$4s^1$;

(b) (↑↓) (↑↓) (↑↓)(↑↓)(↑↓)
    1s   2s   2p   3s
(↑↓)(↑↓)(↑↓) (↑↓)
      3p   4s
(↑)(↑)( )( )( );
      3d
$1s^22s^22p^63s^23p^64s^23d^2$; [Ar]$4s^23d^2$;

(c) (↑↓) (↑↓) (↑↓)(↑↓)(↑↓) (↑↓)
   1s   2s   2p   3s
(↑)(↑)( );
   3p
$1s^22s^22p^63s^23p^2$; [Ne]$3s^23p^2$;

(d) (↑↓) (↑↓) (↑↓)(↑↓)(↑↓)
    1s   2s   2p   3s
(↑↓)(↑↓)(↑↓) (↑↓)
     3p   4s
(↑↓)( )( )( )( );
     3d
$1s^22s^22p^63s^23p^64s^23d^6$;
[Ar]$4s^23d^6$;

(e) (↑↓) (↑↓) (↑↓)(↑↓)(↑↓)
   1s   2s   2p   3s
(↑↓)(↑↓)(↑↓) (↑↓)
    3p   4s
(↑↓)(↑↓)(↑↓)(↑↓)(↑↓);
    3d
$1s^22s^22p^63s^23p^64s^23d^{10}$;
[Ar]$4s^23d^{10}$

63. (a) ns^2; (b) ns^2np^5;
(c) ns^2np^4; (d) ns^1; (e) ns^2np^4

64. (a) 2 (d electrons are not counted as valence electrons); (b) 7; (c) 2; (d) 2 (d electrons are not counted as valence electrons)

65. Light is emitted from the hydrogen atom only at certain wavelengths. If the energy levels of hydrogen were continuous, a hydrogen atom would emit energy at all possible wavelengths.

66. The three $2p$ orbitals of the carbon atoms are of the same energy; by occupying different orbitals of the same energy, repulsion between electrons is minimized.

67. (a) $1s^22s^22p^63s^23p^64s^2$ $3d^{10}4p^5$; (b) $1s^22s^22p^63s^23p^6$ $4s^23d^{10}4p^65s^24d^{10}5p^6$; (c) $1s^2$ $2s^22p^63s^23p^64s^23d^{10}4p^65s^24d^{10}$ $5p^66s^2$; (d) $1s^22s^22p^63s^23p^64s^2$ $3d^{10}4p^4$

68. low; high

69. (a) Ca; (b) P; (c) K

70. (a) 80; (b) Hg, mercury; (c) 2; (d) 6

71. (a) iv; (b) ii; (c) ii; (d) v; (e) i; (f) NaN_3; (g) Mg_2N_3; (h) ii < i < vi < iv < v < iii

72. (a) F; (b) Lu; (c) Po; (d) Fr; (e) At; (f) Xe; (g) Lr

73. Element 120 would be a solid and a metal. It would be highly reactive with water and have a tendency to form ions with a 2+ charge.

74. Answers may vary. See the *Solutions Guide* for more detail.

12 Chemical Bonding

Section	Text Features & Components	Labs, Demonstrations & Activities
Teaching Segment 12A **1 block** **pp. 359–365** 12.1 Types of Chemical Bonds	**LP** Lesson Plans (Sec 12.1–12.3) **TE** Teaching Support: Background Information *pp. 360–361*	
12.2 Electronegativity		
12.3 Bond Polarity and Dipole Moments		**LM** Experiment 49: Dyes and Dying Lab Manual Report Sheets Teacher's Lab Guide
Teaching Segment 12B **0.5 block** **pp. 365–371** 12.4–12.5 Stable Electron Configurations and Charges on Ions Ionic Bonding and Structures of Ionic Compounds	**LP** Lesson Plans (Sec 12.4–12.5) **SE** Chemical Impact: Composite Cars *p. 368* **TE** Teaching Support: Background Information *pp. 368–369*	
Teaching Segment 12C **0.5 block** **pp. 371–381** 12.6 Lewis Structures	**LP** Lesson Plans (Sec 12.6–12.7) **TE** Teaching Support: Background Information *p. 372* **TE** Teaching Tips *p. 374*	
12.7 Lewis Structures of Molecules with Multiple Bonds	**SE** Celebrity Chemical: Capsaicin *p. 377* **TE** Teaching Support: Background Information *pp. 380–381*	
continued on next page		

continued on next page

Key **SE** Student Edition **TE** Teacher Edition **RP** Teacher Resource Package **LM** Lab Materials
LP Lesson Plans **AR** Additional Resources ◆ Florida Specific

    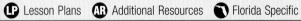

Chapter Planning Guide

All Learners	Review & Assessment	Standards
(TE) Active Learning *p. 359* (T) Transparency: Figure 12.1 *p. 360* (AR) Less Proficient Learners *p. 23*	(SE) Key Terms *p. 394* (SE) Questions and Problems *p. 394*	(TE) **NSES** UCP2, UCP5, A1, A2, B1, B2 (SSS) **SSS** SC.A.1.4.2, SC.A.1.4.5, SC.C.2.4.2, SC.C.2.4.5
(T) Transparency: Figure 12.3 *p. 362* (T) Transparency: Table 12.1 *p. 362* (T) Transparency: Figure 12.4 *p. 363* (AR) Less Proficient Students *p. 23*	(SE) What if . . . *p. 362* (TE) Additional Examples *p. 363* (SE) Self Check *p. 363* (SE) Key Terms *p. 394* (SE) Questions and Problems *pp. 394–395*	
(T) Transparency: Figure 12.5 *p. 364* (RP) Team Learning Worksheets (Sec 12.1–12.3) *pp. 61–62* (AR) Less Proficient Students *p. 23*	(SE) Focus Questions (Sec 12.1–12.3) *p. 365* (SE) Key Terms *p. 394* (SE) Questions and Problems *p. 395*	
(TE) Active Learning *p. 365* (T) Transparency: Table 12.2 *p. 365* (T) Transparency: Table 12.3 *p. 368* (T) Transparency: Figure 12.9 *p. 370* (RP) Team Learning Worksheets (Sec 12.4–12.5) *pp. 63–64* (AR) Less Proficient Students *p. 23*	(SE) What if . . . *p. 369* (SE) Focus Questions (Sec 12.4–12.5) *p. 371* (SE) Questions and Problems *pp. 395–396*	(TE) **NSES** UCP1, UCP2, UCP3, UCP5, A1, A2, B1, B2, E1, E2, F6 (SSS) **SSS** SC.H.1.4.1, SC.H.1.4.2, SC.H.1.4.7, SC.H.2.4.1, SC.A.1.4.1, SC.A.2.4.1, SC.A.1.4.2, SC.B.1.4.5, SC.H.3.4.1, SC.H.3.4.2
(TE) Active Learning *p. 371* (TE) Teaching Tips *p. 371* (AR) Less Proficient Students *p. 23*	(TE) Additional Examples *p. 374* (SE) Self Check *p. 375* (SE) Key Terms *p. 394* (SE) Questions and Problems *p. 396*	(TE) **NSES** UCP2, UCP5, A1, A2, B1, B2, E1, E2, F6, G1, G2, G3 (SSS) **SSS** SC.H.1.4.1, SC.H.1.4.3, SC.H.1.4.7, SC.A.2.4.1, SC.A.1.4.5
(TE) Teaching Tips *pp. 375–376* (□) Chemistry in Motion (16) (RP) Team Learning Worksheets (Sec 12.6–12.7) *p. 65* (AR) Less Proficient Students *p. 24*	(TE) Additional Examples *p. 378* (SE) Self Check *pp. 378–379* (SE) Focus Questions (Sec 12.6–12.7) *p. 381* (SE) Key Terms *p. 394* (SE) Questions and Problems *p. 396*	

12 Chemical Bonding

Teaching Segment 12D
1 block
pp. 381–392

Section	Text Features & Components	Labs, Demonstrations & Activities
12.8 Molecular Structures	Lesson Plans (Sec 12.8–12.10)	
12.9 Molecular Structure: The VSEPR Model	Chemical Impact: Taste—It's the Structure That Counts *p. 383*	**SE** Chemistry in Action: Geometric Balloons *p. 385*
12.10 Molecular Structure: Molecules with Double Bonds		**SE** Chemistry in the Laboratory: Models of Molecules *p. 393* **LM** Experiment 50: Models of Molecules Lab Manual Report Sheets Teacher's Lab Guide

Key

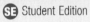

- **SE** Student Edition
- **TE** Teacher Edition
- **RP** Teacher Resource Package
- **LM** Lab Materials
- **LP** Lesson Plans
- **AR** Additional Resources
- **Florida Specific**

Technology and Media

 Transparencies
Table 12.1, 12.2, 12.3, 12.4
Figure 12.1, 12.3, 12.4, 12.5, 12.9

PowerPoint Slides

 Animation
Electron Pair Repulsion 2 pairs • 3 pairs
• 4 pairs

Chemistry in Motion
(16) Magnetic Properties of Liquid

eEdition CD-ROM
Easy Planner CD-ROM
English Summaries CD
Spanish Summaries CD

Web Site classzone.com
McDougal Littell Test Generator

Chapter Planning Guide

All Learners	Review & Assessment	Standards
(TE) Active Learning *p. 381* (TE) Teaching Tips *p. 382* (AR) Less Proficient Students *p. 24*	(SE) Key Terms *p. 394* (SE) Questions and Problems *p. 396*	(TE) **NSES** UCP2, UCP5, A1, A2, B1, B2, E1, E2, F6 (⚓) **SSS** SC.A.1.4.2, SC.A.1.4.5
Animation: Electron Pairs Repulsion 2 pairs • 3 pairs • 4 pairs *p. 384* Transparency: Table 12.4 *p. 389* (AR) Less Proficient Students *p. 24*	(SE) What if . . . *p. 385* (TE) Additional Examples *pp. 386–387* (SE) Self Check *p. 388* (SE) Key Terms *p. 394* (SE) Questions and Problems *pp. 396–397*	
(RP) Team Learning Worksheets (Sec 12.8–12.10) *pp. 67–68* (AR) Less Proficient Students *p. 24*	(TE) Additional Examples *p. 392* (SE) Focus Questions (Sec 12.8–12.10) *p. 392*	

Chapter Materials

- (TE) Reading Strategy
- (AR) English/Spanish Summaries *pp. 18–19*
- (RP) Classroom Activities and Projects *pp. 25–26*
- (AR) Challenge Projects/Problems *pp. 22–23*
- (AR) Less Proficient Students *p. 24*
- English Summary Audio
- Spanish Summary Audio
- (RP) Chapter Review Worksheets (Basic, Review, Challenge)

- (SE) Chapter Summary *p. 394*
- (SE) Critical Thinking *p. 397*
- (RP) Solutions Guide
- (RP) Chapter Tests
- (RP) Test Bank
- McDougal Littell Test Generator
- (AR) Standardized Test Practice
- (⚓) **FCAT Test 6**

12 Integrating Reading Strategies and Chemistry Concepts

Chapter 12: Reading a Diagram

Remind the students that diagrams are key to the study of chemistry, particularly in regard to the structure of atoms and how they bond to form various substances. Explain that different types of diagrams are meant to illustrate how something works or to show the relationship between two or more objects or processes. Diagrams include drawings, charts, tables, and other graphic representations. The method of reading a diagram depends on the type of diagram that is under consideration.

Tell the students to examine the various types of diagrams in Chapter 12. Discuss with the students these types of diagrams:

- **Figure 12.1**, p. 360, is a drawing that depicts the formation of a bond between two hydrogen atoms.

- **Figure 12.3**, p. 362, is a table (the Periodic Table) with a key that indicates the electronegativity values and trends for selected elements.

- **Table 12.1**, p. 362, is a table that describes the relationship between electronegativity and bond type.

- **Figure 12.4**, p. 363, is a drawing of the three possible types of bonds.

- **Figures 12.5** and **12.6**, p. 364, are graphic representations of water molecules.

Examples of Diagrams and How to Read Them—Tables Showing Trends

Draw the students' attention to **Table 12.1** on page 362. Point out that the diagram description, its title, and nearby text usually provide sufficient information to allow the students to read the diagram easily. Show the students that diagrams are usually arranged from left to right or from top to bottom, depending on the type of information shown. Explain that the first step in reading a diagram is identifying the content and determining how the information is arranged.

Ask the students to explain how they know what information is presented in the table. [by reading the table title] Ask the students how the information is arranged. [in rows and columns, or table form] Point out that each column is related to all of the other columns. Draw the students' attention to the first and fourth columns of the table. Ask the students to make a conjecture regarding the relationship between these two columns. [As the electronegativity difference between the bonding atoms increases from zero to a large number, the ionic character of the bond also increases.] Point out that arrows pointing in the same direction illustrate this fact. Then ask the students to make a similar statement using the relationship between columns 1 and 3. You may wish to caution the students that the arrows are not pointing in the same direction.

To confirm that the students are reading the diagram correctly, ask them to compare several pairs of substances and make statements about the substances' bond type, covalent character, and ionic character.

> For example: If substance *A* has an electronegativity difference of 0.3 and substance *B* has an electronegativity difference of 3.8, which substance is more likely to have a covalent bond type? Which substance has more ionic characteristics?

How to Read Graphic Representations

Explain that to read graphic representations correctly, the students must recognize the symbols and notations used. Tell the students that this textbook explains the meanings of various symbols and notations. Remind the students that each chapter builds on information presented in the preceding chapters, so the students should review the material frequently.

To demonstrate an effective way to review, ask the students to consider the diagram near the bottom of page 366, which depicts how oxygen and hydrogen bond to form water.

The diagram has no title, so instruct the students to read the text immediately preceding the diagram. The text explains that the oxygen atom combines with two hydrogen atoms to form water. However, to apply this concept to other types of atoms, the students must be able to read the diagram. Ask the following questions, and remind the students that they will need to recall symbols learned in previous chapters.

- What does the O represent? [the oxygen atom]

- What does the [He] represent? [the electron configuration of helium, the noble gas that comes before oxygen in the Periodic Table]

- What do the 2*s*, 2*p* and boxes with arrows represent? [the orbital diagram of the valence electrons for oxygen]

- What do the red arrows and the H's represent? [two hydrogen atoms, each of which shares one electron with the oxygen atom, filling the valence orbital]

Ask a volunteer to read the diagram aloud. Provide hints if necessary. [Oxygen, which has six electrons in its valence orbital, shares two electrons with two hydrogen atoms (one electron from each atom) to complete its valence orbital and achieve an (Ne) configuration.]

Chapter 12

12 Chemical Bonding

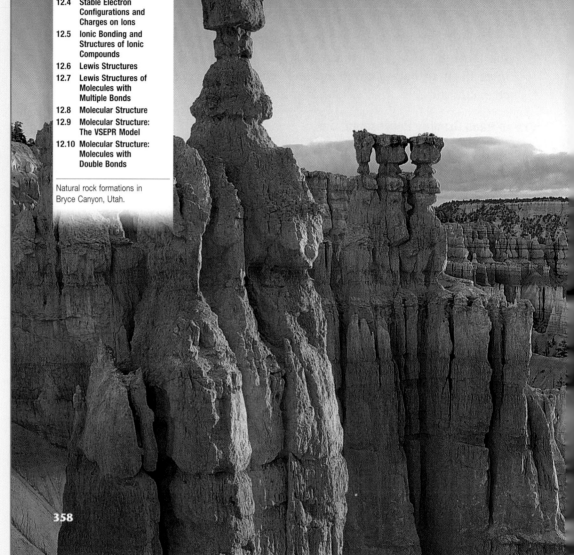

Natural rock formations in Bryce Canyon, Utah.

The world around us is composed almost entirely of compounds and mixtures of compounds. Rocks, coal, soil, petroleum, trees, and human beings are all complex mixtures of chemical compounds in which different kinds of atoms are bound together. Most of the pure elements found in the earth's crust also contain many atoms bound together. In a gold nugget each gold atom is bound to many other gold atoms, and in a diamond many carbon atoms are bonded very strongly to each other. Substances composed of unbound atoms do exist in nature, but they are very rare. (Examples include the argon atoms in the atmosphere and the helium atoms found in natural gas reserves.)

The manner in which atoms are bound together has a profound effect on the chemical and physical properties of substances. For example, both graphite and diamond are composed solely of carbon atoms. However, graphite is a soft, slippery material used as a lubricant in locks, and diamond is one of the hardest materials known, valuable both as a gemstone and in industrial cutting tools. Why do these materials, both composed solely of carbon atoms, have such different properties? The answer lies in the different ways in which the carbon atoms are bound to each other in these substances.

Diamond, composed of carbon atoms bonded together to produce one of the hardest materials known, makes a beautiful gemstone.

Molecular bonding and structure play the central role in determining the course of chemical reactions, many of which are vital to our survival. Most reactions in biological systems are very sensitive to the structures of the participating molecules; in fact, very subtle differences in shape sometimes serve to channel the chemical reaction one way rather than another. Molecules that act as drugs must have exactly the right structure to perform their functions correctly. Structure also plays a central role in our senses of smell and taste. Substances have a particular odor because they fit into the specially shaped receptors in our nasal passages. Taste is also dependent on molecular shape, as we discuss in the "Chemical Impact" on page 383.

To understand the behavior of natural materials, we must understand the nature of chemical bonding and the factors that control the structures of compounds. In this chapter, we will present various classes of compounds that illustrate the different types of bonds. We will then develop models to describe the structure and bonding that characterize the materials found in nature.

12.1 Types of Chemical Bonds

Objectives: *To learn about ionic and covalent bonds and explain how they are formed.*
To learn about the polar covalent bond.

A water molecule.

What is a chemical bond? Although there are several possible ways to answer this question, we will define a **bond** as a force that holds groups of two or more atoms together and makes them function as a unit. For example, in water the fundamental unit is the H—O—H molecule, which we describe as being held together by the two O—H bonds. We can obtain information about the strength of a bond by measuring the energy required to break the bond, the **bond energy**.

12.1   Types of Chemical Bonds   **359**

Themes
Models, Form and Function

Skills
Making comparisons, classifying, developing models

Student Preparation
Assign the students to read Sections 12.1 to 12.3 and to answer the Focus Questions at the end of Section 12.3 before coming to class.

Active Learning
After introducing the material in Sections 12.1 to 12.3 in class, place the students in groups and have them work together on Sections 12.1–12.3: Team Learning Worksheet. Answers and/or discussion of these questions are located in the *Teacher Resources*.

TEACHING TIPS

• Ionic and covalent bonding are the extremes of types of bonding. Students should understand that attractive forces in molecules lie on a continuum.

• Many of the terms used in bonding, such as "sharing," "unequal sharing," and "transfer," can be related to human experience. This helps students begin to understand bonding at the molecular level.

• Focus students' attention on where the electrons spend more time. Are they equally shared between two atoms or do they spend more time closer to one atom in the bond? This focus will help students understand bond polarity.

Atoms can interact with one another in several ways to form aggregates. We will consider specific examples to illustrate the various types of chemical bonds.

In Chapter 8 we saw that when solid sodium chloride is dissolved in water, the resulting solution conducts electricity, a fact that convinces chemists that sodium chloride is composed of Na^+ and Cl^- ions. Thus, when sodium and chlorine react to form sodium chloride, electrons are transferred from the sodium atoms to the chlorine atoms to form Na^+ and Cl^- ions, which then aggregate to form solid sodium chloride. The resulting solid sodium chloride is a very sturdy material; it has a melting point of approximately 800 °C. The strong bonding forces present in sodium chloride result from the attractions among the closely packed, oppositely charged ions. This is an example of **ionic bonding.** Ionic substances are formed when an atom that loses electrons relatively easily reacts with an atom that has a high affinity for electrons. In other words, an **ionic compound** results when a metal reacts with a nonmetal.

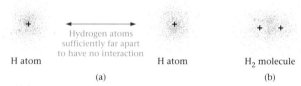

We have seen that a bonding force develops when two very different types of atoms react to form oppositely charged ions. But how does a bonding force develop between two identical atoms? Let's explore this situation by considering what happens when two hydrogen atoms are brought close together, as shown in **Figure 12.1.** When hydrogen atoms are close together, the two electrons are simultaneously attracted to both nuclei. Note in Figure 12.1b how the electron probability increases between the two nuclei, indicating that the electrons are shared by the two nuclei.

The type of bonding we encounter in the hydrogen molecule and in many other molecules where *electrons are shared by nuclei* is called **covalent bonding.** Note that in the H_2 molecule the electrons reside primarily in the space between the two nuclei, where they are attracted simultaneously by both protons. Although we will not go into detail about it here, the increased attractive forces in this area lead to the formation of the H_2 molecule from the two separated hydrogen atoms. When we say that a bond is formed between the hydrogen atoms, we mean that the H_2 molecule is more stable than two separated hydrogen atoms by a certain quantity of energy (the bond energy).

Figure 12.1
The formation of a bond between two hydrogen atoms. (a) Two separate hydrogen atoms. (b) When two hydrogen atoms come close together, the two electrons are attracted simultaneously by both nuclei. This produces the bond. Note the relatively large electron probability between the nuclei, indicating sharing of the electrons.

δ⁺   δ⁻

(a)   (b)

Figure 12.2
Probability representations of the electron sharing in HF. (a) What the probability map would look like if the two electrons in the H—F bond were shared equally. (b) The actual situation, where the shared pair spends more time close to the fluorine atom than to the hydrogen atom. This gives fluorine a slight excess of negative charge and the hydrogen a slight deficit of negative charge (a slight positive charge).

So far we have considered two extreme types of bonding. In ionic bonding, the participating atoms are so different that one or more electrons are transferred to form oppositely charged ions. The bonding results from the attractions between these ions. In covalent bonding, two identical atoms share electrons equally. The bonding results from the mutual attraction of the two nuclei for the shared electrons. Between these extremes are intermediate cases in which the atoms are not so different that electrons are completely transferred but are different enough so that unequal sharing of electrons results, forming what is called a **polar covalent bond.** The hydrogen fluoride (HF) molecule contains this type of bond, which produces the charge distribution

H—F
δ^+ δ^-

where δ (delta) is used to indicate a partial or fractional charge.

The most logical explanation for the development of *bond polarity* (the partial positive and negative charges on the atoms in such molecules as HF) is that the electrons in the bonds are not shared equally. For example, we can account for the polarity of the HF molecule by assuming that the fluorine atom has a stronger attraction than the hydrogen atom for the shared electrons **(Figure 12.2).** Because bond polarity has important chemical implications, we find it useful to assign a number that indicates an atom's ability to attract shared electrons. In the next section we show how this is done.

Electronegativity

Objective: *To understand the nature of bonds and their relationship to electronegativity.*

We saw in the previous section that when a metal and a nonmetal react, one or more electrons are transferred from the metal to the nonmetal to give ionic bonding. On the other hand, two identical atoms react to form a covalent bond in which electrons are shared equally. When *different* nonmetals react, a bond forms in which electrons are shared *unequally,* giving a polar covalent bond. The unequal sharing of electrons between two atoms is described by a property called **electronegativity:** *the relative ability of an atom in a molecule to attract shared electrons to itself.*

12.2   Electronegativity   **361**

complex. However, if we think of a protein as constructed of individual bonds, such as C—C, C—H, C—N, C—O, and N—H, it helps tremendously in predicting and understanding the protein's behavior. The essential idea is that we expect a given bond to behave in roughly the same way in any molecular environment. This model of the chemical bond has helped chemists to systematize the re- actions of the millions of existing compounds.

 Section 12.2

Themes
Models, Form and Function

Skills
Making comparisons, interpreting data, classifying, making predictions

TEACHING TIPS

- This section develops the concept of electronegativity and its trends on the periodic table. Focus students' attention on how electronegativity relates to ionization energy.

- Students can memorize electronegativity trends, but it is important that they understand the reasons behind these trends (just as they should understand trends for atomic radius and ionization energy).

- Students should be able to compare the electronegativities of two elements in the same group or same period. They should not memorize the actual electronegativity numbers but rather be able to predict which is greater.

Increasing electronegativity →

Decreasing electronegativity ↓

						H 2.1											
Li 1.0	Be 1.5											B 2.0	C 2.5	N 3.0	O 3.5	F 4.0
Na 0.9	Mg 1.2											Al 1.5	Si 1.8	P 2.1	S 2.5	Cl 3.0
K 0.8	Ca 1.0	Sc 1.3	Ti 1.5	V 1.6	Cr 1.6	Mn 1.5	Fe 1.8	Co 1.9	Ni 1.9	Cu 1.9	Zn 1.6	Ga 1.6	Ge 1.8	As 2.0	Se 2.4	Br 2.8
Rb 0.8	Sr 1.0	Y 1.2	Zr 1.4	Nb 1.6	Mo 1.8	Tc 1.9	Ru 2.2	Rh 2.2	Pd 2.2	Ag 1.9	Cd 1.7	In 1.7	Sn 1.8	Sb 1.9	Te 2.1	I 2.5
Cs 0.7	Ba 0.9	La-Lu 1.0-1.2	Hf 1.3	Ta 1.5	W 1.7	Re 1.9	Os 2.2	Ir 2.2	Pt 2.2	Au 2.4	Hg 1.9	Tl 1.8	Pb 1.9	Bi 1.9	Po 2.0	At 2.2
Fr 0.7	Ra 0.9	Ac 1.1	Th 1.3	Pa 1.4	U 1.4	Np-No 1.4-1.3										

Key

☐ < 1.5

☐ 1.5–1.9

☐ 2.0–2.9

☐ 3.0–4.0

Figure 12.3
Electronegativity values for selected elements. Note that electronegativity generally increases across a period and decreases down a group. Note also that metals have relatively low electronegativity values and that nonmetals have relatively high values.

Chemists determine electronegativity values for the elements **(Figure 12.3)** by measuring the polarities of the bonds between various atoms. Note that electronegativity generally increases going from left to right across a period and decreases going down a group for the representative elements. The range of electronegativity values goes from 4.0 for fluorine to 0.7 for cesium and francium. Remember, the higher the atom's electronegativity value, the closer the shared electrons tend to be to that atom when it forms a bond.

The polarity of a bond depends on the *difference* between the electronegativity values of the atoms forming the bond. If the atoms have very similar electronegativities, the electrons are shared almost equally and the bond shows little polarity. If the atoms have very different electronegativity values, a very polar bond is formed. In extreme cases one or more electrons are actually transferred, forming ions and an ionic bond. For example, when an element from Group 1 (electronegativity values of about 0.8) reacts with an element from Group 7 (electronegativity values of about 3), ions are formed and an ionic substance results. In general, if the *difference* between the electronegativities of two elements is about 2.0 or greater, the bond is considered to be ionic.

The relationship between electronegativity and bond type is shown in **Table 12.1.** The various types of bonds are summarized in **Figure 12.4.**

TABLE 12.1

The Relationship Between Electronegativity and Bond Type

Electronegativity Difference Between the Bonding Atoms	Bond Type	Covalent Character	Ionic Character
Zero	Covalent		
↓	↓	↑ Increase	⬇ Increases
Intermediate	Polar covalent		
↓	↓		
Large	Ionic		

(a)   (b)   (c)

Figure 12.4
The three possible types of bonds: (a) a covalent bond formed between identical atoms; (b) a polar covalent bond, with both ionic and covalent components; and (c) an ionic bond, with no electron sharing.

Example 12.1

Using Electronegativity to Determine Bond Polarity

Using the electronegativity values given in Figure 12.3, arrange the following bonds in order of increasing polarity: H—H, O—H, Cl—H, S—H, and F—H.

Solution

The polarity of the bond increases as the difference in electronegativity increases. From the electronegativity values in Figure 12.3, the following variation in bond polarity is expected (the electronegativity value appears in parentheses below each element).

Bond	Electronegativity Value	Difference in Electronegativity Values	Bond Type	Polarity
H—H	(2.1)(2.1)	2.1 − 2.1 = 0	Covalent	
S—H	(2.5)(2.1)	2.5 − 2.1 = 0.4	Polar covalent	Increasing
Cl—H	(3.0)(2.1)	3.0 − 2.1 = 0.9	Polar covalent	
O—H	(3.5)(2.1)	3.5 − 2.1 = 1.4	Polar covalent	
F—H	(4.0)(2.1)	4.0 − 2.1 = 1.9	Polar covalent	

Therefore, in order of increasing polarity, we have

    H—H   S—H   Cl—H   O—H   F—H

Least polar   Most polar

 Self-Check Exercise 12.1

For each of the following pairs of bonds, choose the bond that will be more polar.

    a. H—P, H—C   **c.** N—O, S—O
    b. O—F, O—I   **d.** N—H, Si—H

12.2 Electronegativity   **363**

Additional Examples

On the basis of the electronegativity values given in Figure 12.3, indicate which is the more polar bond in each of the following pairs.

1. H—S or H—F
    H—F

2. O—S or O—F
    O—S

3. N—S or N—Cl
    N—Cl

4. C—S or C—Cl
    C—Cl

 Answers to Self-Check Exercise 12.1

Using the electronegativity values given in Figure 12.3, we choose the bond in which the atoms exhibit the largest difference in electronegativity. (Electronegativity values are shown in parentheses.)

a. H—C > H—P
  (2.1)(2.5)   (2.1)(2.1)

b. O—I > O—F
  (3.5)(2.5)   (3.5)(4.0)

c. S—O > N—O
  (2.5)(3.5)   (3.0)(3.5)

d. N—H > Si—H
  (3.0)(2.1)   (1.8)(2.1)

12.3 Bond Polarity and Dipole Moments

Objective: *To understand bond polarity and how it is related to molecular polarity.*

We saw in Section 12.1 that hydrogen fluoride has a positive end and a negative end. A molecule such as HF that has a center of positive charge and a center of negative charge is said to have a **dipole moment.** The dipolar character of a molecule is often represented by an arrow. This arrow points toward the negative charge center, and its tail indicates the positive center of charge:

Any diatomic (two-atom) molecule that has a polar bond has a dipole moment. Some polyatomic (more than two atoms) molecules also have dipole moments. For example, because the oxygen atom in the water molecule has a greater electronegativity than the hydrogen atoms, the electrons are not shared equally. This results in a charge distribution **(Figure 12.5a)** that causes the molecule to behave as though it had two centers of charge—one positive and one negative **(Figure 12.5b).** So the water molecule has a dipole moment.

The fact that the water molecule is polar (has a dipole moment) has a profound effect on its properties. In fact, it is not overly dramatic to state that the polarity of the water molecule is crucial to life as we know it on earth. Because water molecules are polar, they can surround and attract both positive and negative ions **(Figure 12.6).** These attractions allow ionic materials to dissolve in water. Also, the polarity of water molecules causes them to attract each other strongly **(Figure 12.7).** This means that much energy

(a)

(b)

Figure 12.5
(a) The charge distribution in the water molecule. The oxygen has a charge of $2\delta^-$ because it pulls δ^- of charge from each hydrogen atom $(\delta^- + \delta^- = 2\delta^-)$.
(b) The water molecule behaves as if it has a positive end and a negative end, as indicated by the arrow.

(a)   (b)

Figure 12.6
(a) Polar water molecules are strongly attracted to positive ions by their negative ends. (b) They are also strongly attracted to negative ions by their positive ends.

Figure 12.7
Polar water molecules are strongly attracted to each other.

364 Chapter 12 Chemical Bonding

is required to change water from a liquid to a gas (the molecules must be separated from each other to undergo this change of state). Therefore, it is the polarity of the water molecule that causes water to remain a liquid at the temperatures on the earth's surface. If it were nonpolar, water would be a gas and the oceans would be empty.

Focus Questions **Sections 12.1–12.3**

1. How are ionic bonds and covalent bonds different?

2. How does a polar covalent bond differ from a nonpolar covalent bond?

3. How do electronegativity values help us to determine the polarity of a bond?

4. For each of the following binary molecules, draw an arrow under the molecule showing its dipole moment. If it has none, write "none."

   a. H—Cl   d. Br—Br
   b. H—H   e. CO
   c. H—I

1. An ionic bond involves a transfer of electrons from one atom to another; in a covalent bond, two atoms share a pair of electrons.

2. In a polar covalent bond, the electrons spend more time closer to one atom than to the other. In a nonpolar covalent bond, the electrons are shared equally between the atoms.

3. The polarity of a bond depends on the difference between the electronegativity values of the atoms forming the bond. If the atoms have similar electronegativities, the electrons are shared almost equally and the bond shows little polarity. If the atoms have very different electronegativity values, a very polar bond is formed.

4. a. H—Cl   d. Br—Br
   $\longmapsto$ none

   b. H—H   e. CO
   none $\leftrightarrow$

   c. H—I
   $\longmapsto$

12.4 Stable Electron Configurations and Charges on Ions

Objectives: *To learn about stable electron configurations.*
To learn to predict the formulas of ionic compounds.

We have seen many times that when a metal and a nonmetal react to form an ionic compound, the metal atom loses one or more electrons to the nonmetal. In Chapter 4, where binary ionic compounds were introduced, we saw that in these reactions, Group 1 metals always form 1+ cations, Group 2 metals always form 2+ cations, and aluminum in Group 3 always forms a 3+ cation. For the nonmetals, the Group 7 elements always form 1− anions, and the Group 6 elements always form 2− anions. This is further illustrated in **Table 12.2**.

TABLE 12.2

The Formation of Ions by Metals and Nonmetals

Group	Ion Formation	Electron Configuration	
		Atom	Ion
1	$Na \rightarrow Na^+ + e^-$	$[Ne]3s^1 \xrightarrow{\; e^- \text{ lost} \;}$	$[Ne]$
2	$Mg \rightarrow Mg^{2+} + 2e^-$	$[Ne]3s^2 \xrightarrow{\; 2e^- \text{ lost} \;}$	$[Ne]$
3	$Al \rightarrow Al^{3+} + 3e^-$	$[Ne]3s^23p^1 \xrightarrow{\; 3e^- \text{ lost} \;}$	$[Ne]$
6	$O + 2e^- \rightarrow O^{2-}$	$[He]2s^22p^4 + 2e^- \rightarrow [He]2s^22p^6 = [Ne]$	
7	$F + e^- \rightarrow F^-$	$[He]2s^22p^5 + e^- \rightarrow [He]2s^22p^6 = [Ne]$	

12.4   Stable Electron Configurations and Charges on Ions   **365**

- Now is an excellent time to review the electron configurations for atoms and write electron configurations for ions. Emphasize that the ion formed from a particular atom arises because of the stability associated with a noble gas electron configuration.

- This section also gives students an opportunity to understand why certain atoms are more likely to form negative ions and others to form positive ions. Use the electron configurations to discuss this point.

- The concept that atoms have a strong tendency to adopt a noble gas configuration is central to understanding the electronic structure of ions and the Lewis structures of molecules. This concept is emphasized in this chapter and should be stressed in class discussions.

- Science focuses on observing patterns (laws) and developing explanations (theories or models). The fact that the atoms in a compound have a tendency to achieve a noble gas electron configuration is an observation, not an explanation. Knowing this tendency helps us to make predictions, but does not answer the "why?" question. With this observation in mind, students should be able to predict, for example, that a sodium atom will lose only one electron when becoming an ion, and that a calcium atom will lose two electrons.

- You may want to begin a discussion of bonding by using a simple example of ionic bonding and another of covalent bonding to illustrate how atoms attain electron configurations of noble gases. One possibility is NaCl, in which Na loses an electron to Cl so that the sodium ion has the same electron configuration as Ne and the chloride ion has the same electron configuration as Ar. In the case of H_2, each hydrogen shares an electron with the other so that both

Notice something very interesting about the ions in Table 12.2: they all have the electron configuration of neon, a noble gas. That is, sodium loses its one valence electron (the 3s) to form Na^+, which has a [Ne] electron configuration. Likewise Mg loses its two valence electrons to form Mg^{2+}, which also has a [Ne] electron configuration. On the other hand, the nonmetal atoms gain just the number of electrons needed for them to achieve the noble gas electron configuration. The O atom gains two electrons and the F atom gains one electron to give O^{2-} and F^-, respectively, both of which have the [Ne] electron configuration. We can summarize these observations as follows:

Electron Configurations of Ions

1. Representative (main-group) metals form ions by losing enough electrons to achieve the configuration of the previous noble gas (that is, the noble gas that occurs before the metal in question on the periodic table). For example, note from the periodic table inside the back cover of this book that neon is the noble gas before sodium and magnesium. Similarly, helium is the noble gas before lithium and beryllium.

2. Nonmetals form ions by gaining enough electrons to achieve the configuration of the next noble gas (that is, the noble gas that follows the element in question on the periodic table). For example, note that neon is the noble gas that follows oxygen and fluorine, and argon is the noble gas that follows sulfur and chlorine.

This brings us to an important general principle. In observing millions of stable compounds, chemists have learned that **in almost all stable chemical compounds of the representative elements, all of the atoms have achieved a noble gas electron configuration.** The importance of this observation cannot be overstated. It forms the basis for all of our fundamental ideas about why and how atoms bond to each other.

We have already seen this principle operating in the formation of ions (see Table 12.2). We can summarize this behavior as follows: when representative metals and nonmetals react, they transfer electrons in such a way that both the cation and the anion have noble gas electron configurations.

On the other hand, when nonmetals react with each other, they share electrons in ways that lead to a noble gas electron configuration for each atom in the resulting molecule. For example, oxygen ($[He]2s^2 2p^4$), which needs two more electrons to achieve an [Ne] configuration, can get these electrons by combining with two H atoms (each of which has one electron),

to form water, H_2O. This fills the valence orbitals of oxygen.

In addition, each H shares two electrons with the oxygen atom,

which fills the H 1s orbital, giving it a $1s^2$ or [He] electron configuration. We will have much more to say about covalent bonding in Section 12.6.

hydrogens have the same electron configuration as He.

At this point let's summarize the ideas we have introduced so far.

Electron Configurations and Bonding

1. When a *nonmetal and a Group 1, 2, or 3 metal* react to form a binary ionic compound, the ions form in such a way that the valence-electron configuration of the *nonmetal* is *completed* to achieve the configuration of the *next* noble gas, and the valence orbitals of the *metal* are *emptied* to achieve the configuration of the *previous* noble gas. In this way both ions achieve noble gas electron configurations.

2. When *two nonmetals* react to form a covalent bond, they share electrons in a way that completes the valence-electron configurations of both atoms. That is, both nonmetals attain noble gas electron configurations by sharing electrons.

Predicting Formulas of Ionic Compounds

To show how to predict which ions form when a metal reacts with a nonmetal, we will consider the formation of an ionic compound from calcium and oxygen. We can predict what compound will form by considering the valence electron configurations of the two atoms.

Ca: $[Ar]4s^2$
O: $[He]2s^22p^4$

From Figure 12.3 we see that the electronegativity of oxygen (3.5) is much greater than that of calcium (1.0), giving a difference of 2.5. Because of this large difference, electrons are transferred from calcium to oxygen to form an oxygen anion and a calcium cation. How many electrons are transferred? We can base our prediction on the observation that noble gas configurations are the most stable. Note that oxygen needs two electrons to fill its valence orbitals (2s and 2p) and achieve the configuration of neon ($1s^22s^22p^6$), which is the next noble gas.

$$O + 2e^- \rightarrow O^{2-}$$
$$[He]2s^22p^4 + 2e^- \rightarrow [He]2s^22p^6, \text{ or } [Ne]$$

By losing two electrons, calcium can achieve the configuration of argon (the previous noble gas).

$$Ca \rightarrow Ca^{2+} + 2e^-$$
$$[Ar]4s^2 \rightarrow [Ar] \quad + 2e^-$$

Two electrons are therefore transferred as follows:

$$Ca + O \rightarrow Ca^{2+} + O^{2-}$$
$$\underset{2e^-}{\curvearrowright}$$

To predict the formula of the ionic compound, we use the fact that chemical compounds are always electrically neutral—they have the same total quantities of positive and negative charges. In this case we must have equal numbers of Ca^{2+} and O^{2-} ions, and the empirical formula of the compound is CaO.

The same principles can be applied to many other cases. For example, consider the compound formed from aluminum and oxygen. Aluminum has

12.4   Stable Electron Configurations and Charges on Ions   **367**

TEACHING TIP

Students should already know how to predict the charge on an ion from the group number on the periodic table. Now is a good time to review this issue and to point out that students can also predict the charge on an ion by looking at the valence electron configuration.

TEACHING TIP

Now is a good time to review predicting the products in chemical reactions between elements. Students can now predict the correct product by using the valence electron configurations for each atom. Once they have determined the number of electrons that are lost or gained to achieve the core electron configuration of a noble gas, they will be able to determine the charge on the ion and hence the formula for the product in the reaction.

Have students investigate other situations in which new materials are being used to replace older ones. Examples might include the use of steel in place of wood in framing houses, the use of foam insulation in houses and buildings in place of fiberglass, the use of plastic for automotive bumpers in place of metals, and so on. Ask students to consider the reason behind each change in materials. For example, in composite cars Al foam was used to save weight and thereby increase fuel economy.

USING TECHNOLOGY

Table 12.3
Common Ions with Noble Gas Configurations in Ionic Compounds, can be used in a team activity. Student teams can be assigned one row of the table. Each team must show how each element in its group gains or loses electrons to attain the electron configuration of the nearest noble gas. Students do not need to know the term *isoelectronic* to see that the electron configuration of each element's ion is the same. This activity also reinforces the concept that negative ions are formed by adding electrons and positive ions are formed by losing electrons.

Composite Cars

In designing fuel-efficient vehicles, weight is the enemy. The more mass a vehicle contains, the more energy will be required to move it. The problem is that saving weight almost always means higher cost. When the latest version of "America's Sportscar" (called the C5 by autophiles) was being developed, chief engineer Dave Hill used a $10 per kilogram rule: spending an extra $10 for a part was acceptable if it saved a kilogram of mass.

A new material that is likely to be a boon to auto designers is aluminum metal foam. Metal foams are a new class of material, consisting of a sandwich of porous foamed metal between metal skins. They are 50% lighter and ten times stiffer than the same part made from steel. They are also fireproof, good thermal insulators, and excellent energy absorbers, crushing progressively on impact.

Aluminum metal foam was developed by the German automotive supplier Wilhelm Karmann. The material starts as two aluminum sheets sandwiching an aluminum powder containing a titanium hydride propellant. This assembly is crushed at high pressures into a single flat sheet that, like regular sheet metal, can be formed into a variety of three-dimensional shapes. After shaping, the part is placed in an 1150 °F oven for two minutes, where the aluminum powder melts, releasing hydrogen gas from the titanium hydride. The foaming caused by the $H_2(g)$ increases the material's thickness by a factor of 6, producing an aluminum foam between the aluminum skins. The resulting material has such a low density that it floats on water, but it is ten times stiffer than steel. The material is ideal for automotive floorpans, firewalls, roof panels, and luggage compartment walls. It is projected that as much as 20% of a typical auto could be constructed from the new metal foam. Besides being lightweight and stiff, the new foam also increases the crash-worthiness of a car due to its energy-absorbing abilities. Aluminum foam sounds like a miracle.

An aluminum foam part with its mold.

MATH

$3 \times (2-)$ balances $2 \times (3+)$.

the electron configuration $[Ne]3s^23p^1$. To achieve the neon configuration, aluminum must lose three electrons, forming the Al^{3+} ion.

$$Al \rightarrow Al^{3+} + 3e^-$$
$$[Ne]3s^23p^1 \rightarrow [Ne] + 3e^-$$

Therefore, the ions will be Al^{3+} and O^{2-}. Because the compound must be electrically neutral, there will be three O^{2-} ions for every two Al^{3+} ions, and the compound has the empirical formula Al_2O_3.

Table 12.3 shows common elements that form ions with noble gas electron configurations in ionic compounds.

TABLE 12.3

Common Ions with Noble Gas Configurations in Ionic Compounds

Group 1	Group 2	Group 3	Group 6	Group 7	Electron Configuration
Li^+	Be^{2+}				[He]
Na^+	Mg^{2+}	Al^{3+}	O^{2-}	F^-	[Ne]
K^+	Ca^{2+}		S^{2-}	Cl^-	[Ar]
Rb^+	Sr^{2+}		Se^{2-}	Br^-	[Kr]
Cs^+	Ba^{2+}		Te^{2-}	I^-	[Xe]

TEACHING SUPPORT
Background Information

Ionic Compounds
At the beginning of this discussion emphasize that when chemists use the term *ionic compound,* they are usually referring to the solid state of that compound. In the solid state the ions are close together. That is, solid ionic compounds contain a large collection of positive and negative ions packed together in a way that minimizes the $-\cdots-$ and $+\cdots+$ repulsions and maximizes the $+\cdots-$ attractions. This situation stands in contrast to the gas phase of an ionic substance, where the ions are generally quite far apart. In the gas phase, a pair of ions may get close enough to interact, but large collections of ions do not exist. Thus, when we speak of the stability of an ionic compound, we are referring to the solid state, where the large attractive forces present among oppositely charged ions tend to stabilize (favor the formation of) the ions. For example, the O^{2-} ion is not stable as an isolated, gas-phase species but, of course, is very stable in many solid ionic compounds. That is, MgO(s), which contains Mg^{2+}

Notice that our discussion in this section refers to metals in Groups 1, 2, and 3 (the representative metals). The transition metals exhibit more complicated behavior (they form a variety of ions), which we will not consider in this text.

12.5 Ionic Bonding and Structures of Ionic Compounds

Objectives: *To learn about ionic structures.*
To understand factors governing ionic size.

WHAT IF?

Ions have different sizes than their parent atoms.

What if ions stayed the same sizes as their parent atoms? How would it change the structures of ionic compounds?

When metals and nonmetals react, the resulting ionic compounds are very stable; large amounts of energy are required to "take them apart." For example, the melting point of sodium chloride is approximately 800 °C. The strong bonding in these ionic compounds results from the attractions between the oppositely charged cations and anions.

We write the formula of an ionic compound such as lithium fluoride simply as LiF, but this is really the empirical, or simplest, formula. The actual solid contains huge and equal numbers of Li^+ and F^- ions packed together in a way that maximizes the attractions of the oppositely charged ions. A representative part of the lithium fluoride structure is shown in **Figure 12.8a.** In this structure the larger F^- ions are packed together like hard spheres, and the much smaller Li^+ ions are placed regularly among the F^- ions. The structure shown in **Figure 12.8b** represents only a tiny part of the actual structure, which continues in all three dimensions with the same pattern as that shown.

The structures of virtually all binary ionic compounds can be explained by a model that involves packing the ions as though they were hard spheres. The larger spheres (usually the anions) are packed together, and the small ions occupy the interstices (spaces or holes) among them.

To understand the packing of ions it helps to realize that *a cation is always smaller than the parent atom, and an anion is always larger than the parent*

CHEMISTRY

When spheres are packed together, they do not fill up all of the space. The spaces (holes) that are left can be occupied by smaller spheres.

(a) (b)

Figure 12.8
The structure of lithium fluoride. (a) This structure represents the ions as packed spheres. (b) This structure shows the positions (centers) of the ions. The spherical ions are packed in the way that maximizes the ionic attractions.

12.5 Ionic Bonding and Structures of Ionic Compounds **369**

Section 12.5

Themes
Form and Function, Models

Skills
Classifying, making comparisons, developing models

WHAT IF Comments

The structure of ionic compounds results from the packing of ions as hard spheres. Because the anions are usually larger than the cations, the solids consist of a matrix of anions in which the cations fill the holes among the anions. In this way not only do the ions achieve close packing, but an attraction of oppositely charged ions (called the lattice energy) also occurs. Without the size differences, the packing would not be as close and the compounds would not be as stable.

and O^{2-} ions, is very stable, but the isolated, gas-phase ion pair $Mg^{2+}..O^{2-}$ is not energetically favorable in comparison with the separate neutral gaseous atoms. In this section, and in most other cases where we are describing the nature of ionic compounds, the discussion refers to the solid state, where many ions are simultaneously interacting.

When *two nonmetals* react to form a covalent bond, they share electrons in a way that completes the valence electron configurations of both atoms. That is, both nonmetals attain noble gas electron configurations.

When a *nonmetal and a representative-group metal* react to form a binary ionic compound, the ions form such that the valence electron configuration of the nonmetal achieves the electron configuration of the next noble gas atom and the valence orbitals of the metal are emptied. In this way both ions achieve noble gas electron configurations.

Figure 12.9
Relative sizes of some ions and their parent atoms. Note that cations are smaller and anions are larger than their parent atoms. The sizes (radii) are given in units of picometers (1 pm = 10^{-12} m).

	Atom	Cation		Atom	Anion	
Li 152		Li$^+$ 60	F 72			F$^-$ 136
Na 186		Na$^+$ 95	Cl 99			Cl$^-$ 181
K 227		K$^+$ 133	Br 114			Br$^-$ 195
Rb 248		Rb$^+$ 148	I 133			I$^-$ 216
Cs 265		Cs$^+$ 169				

atom. This makes sense because when a metal loses all of its valence electrons to form a cation, it gets much smaller. On the other hand, in forming an anion, a nonmetal gains enough electrons to achieve the next noble gas electron configuration and so becomes much larger. The relative sizes of the Group 1 and Group 7 atoms and their ions are shown in **Figure 12.9.**

Ionic Compounds Containing Polyatomic Ions

So far in this chapter we have discussed only binary ionic compounds, which contain ions derived from single atoms. However, many compounds contain polyatomic ions: charged species composed of several atoms. For example, ammonium nitrate contains the NH_4^+ and NO_3^- ions. These ions with their opposite charges attract each other in the same way as do the simple ions in binary ionic compounds. However, the *individual* polyatomic ions are held together by covalent bonds, with all of the atoms behaving as a unit. For example, in the ammonium ion, NH_4^+, there are four N—H covalent bonds. Likewise, the nitrate ion, NO_3^-, contains three covalent N—O bonds. Thus, although ammonium nitrate is an ionic compound because it contains the NH_4^+ and NO_3^- ions, it also contains covalent bonds in the individual polyatomic ions. When ammonium nitrate is dissolved in water, it behaves as a strong electrolyte like the binary ionic compounds sodium chloride and

TEACHING TIP

Students have difficulty understanding polyatomic ions. It is difficult for them to see that these atoms are bonded together covalently and will not break up into atoms or simple ions. For example, when sodium sulfate dissolves in water, sodium and sulfate ions are formed, but the sulfate ion cannot break into sulfur and oxygen ions since these ions are covalently bonded together.

potassium bromide. As we saw in Chapter 8, this occurs because when an ionic solid dissolves, the ions are freed to move independently and can conduct an electric current.

The common polyatomic ions, which are listed in Table 4.4, are all held together by covalent bonds.

Focus Questions

Sections 12.4–12.5

1. Why do metals lose electrons to form ions? When does a metal stop losing ions?
2. Why does oxygen form an O^{2-} ion and not an O^{3-} ion?
3. Write the electron configurations for the pairs of atoms given below. Use them to predict the formula for an ionic compound formed from these elements.
   a. Mg, S   c. Cs, F
   b. K, Cl   d. Ba, Br
4. Why is aluminum foam useful in making cars more fuel-efficient?
5. Why are cations smaller than their parent atoms? Why are anions larger?
6. How do polyatomic anions differ from simple anions?

12.6 Lewis Structures

Objective: *To learn to write Lewis structures.*

*B*onding involves just the valence electrons of atoms. Valence electrons are transferred when a metal and a nonmetal react to form an ionic compound. Valence electrons are shared between nonmetals in covalent bonds.

The **Lewis structure** is a representation of a molecule that shows how the valence electrons are arranged among the atoms in the molecule. These representations are named after G. N. Lewis, who conceived the idea while lecturing to a class of general chemistry students in 1902. The rules for writing Lewis structures are based on observations of many molecules from which chemists have learned that the *most important requirement for the formation of a stable compound is that the atoms achieve noble gas electron configurations.*

We have already seen this rule operate in the reaction of metals and nonmetals to form binary ionic compounds. An example is the formation of KBr, where the K^+ ion has the [Ar] electron configuration and the Br^- ion has the [Kr] electron configuration. In writing Lewis structures, *we include only the valence electrons.* Using dots to represent valence electrons, we write the Lewis structure for KBr as follows:

CHEMISTRY
Remember that the electrons in the highest principal energy level of an atom are called the valence electrons.

$$K^+ \qquad [\,:\!\ddot{B}\!r\!:\,]^-$$

Noble gas configuration [Ar]   Noble gas configuration [Kr]

No dots are shown on the K^+ ion because it has lost its only valence electron (the $4s$ electron). The Br^- ion is shown with eight electrons because it has a filled valence shell.

12.6 Lewis Structures **371**

---

ions are larger than their parent atoms because electron(s) are added, increasing the electron–electron repulsions and causing the electron "cloud" to be larger than the parent atom.

6. Polyatomic ions contain covalently bonded atoms within the group of atoms that carry the charge. Simple ions are single atoms with electrons added or taken away.

 Section 12.6

Themes
Models, Form and Function

Skills
Applying concepts, interpreting diagrams

Student Preparation
Assign the students to read Sections 12.6 and 12.7 and to answer the Focus Questions at the end of Section 12.7 before coming to class.

Active Learning
After introducing the material in Sections 12.6 and 12.7 in class, place the students in groups and have them work together on Sections 12.6–12.7: Team Learning Worksheet. Answers and/or discussion of these questions are located in the *Teacher Resources.*

TEACHING TIPS
- Drawing Lewis structures provides a way for the students to use their knowledge about electron configurations to predict bonding in covalent molecules.
- You can show why noble gases do not generally form compounds by drawing the Lewis structures for several noble gases.

Answers to Focus Questions

1. Metals have just a few electrons in their valence level. These electrons are relatively easy to remove to form a positive ion. A metal stops losing electrons easily when it reaches the electron configuration of the previous noble gas.

2. Once oxygen has gained two electrons, it has the same electron configuration as neon. This config-

uration is favored and oxygen will not easily gain another electron.

3. a. Mg: $[Ne]3s^2$
      S: $[Ne]3s^23p^4$
      Formula for compound: MgS

   b. K: $[Ar]4s^1$
      Cl: $[Ne]3s^23p^5$
      Formula for compound: KCl

   c. Cs: $[Xe]6s^1$
      F: $[He]2s^22p^5$
      Formula for compound: CsF

   d. Ba: $[Xe]6s^2$

   Br: $[Ar]4s^24p^5$
   Formula for compound: BaBr₂

4. Aluminum foam is lighter and stronger than steel. The weight of a car is directly related to its fuel economy. The lighter the car, the better the fuel efficiency.

5. Cations are smaller than their parent atoms because the electrons in the valence level are removed and the remaining electrons are pulled closer to the cation's nucleus by the positive charge imbalance. An-

Lewis structures show only valence electrons.

Next we will consider Lewis structures for molecules with covalent bonds, involving nonmetals in the first and second periods. The principle of achieving a noble gas electron configuration applies to these elements as follows:

1. Hydrogen forms stable molecules where it shares two electrons. That is, it follows a **duet rule.** For example, when two hydrogen atoms, each with one electron, combine to form the H_2 molecule, we have

By sharing electrons, each hydrogen in H_2 has, in effect, two electrons; that is, each hydrogen has a filled valence shell.

2. Helium does not form bonds because its valence orbital is already filled; it is a noble gas. Helium has the electron configuration $1s^2$ and can be represented by the following Lewis structure:

He:

[He] configuration

CHEMISTRY

Carbon, nitrogen, oxygen, and fluorine almost always obey the octet rule in stable molecules.

3. The second-row nonmetals carbon through fluorine form stable molecules when they are surrounded by enough electrons to fill the valence orbitals—that is, the one $2s$ and the three $2p$ orbitals. Eight electrons are required to fill these orbitals, so these elements typically obey the **octet rule;** they are surrounded by eight electrons. An example is the F_2 molecule, which has the following Lewis structure:

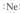

F atom with seven valence electrons F_2 molecule   F atom with seven valence electrons

Note that each fluorine atom in F_2 is, in effect, surrounded by eight valence electrons, two of which are shared with the other atom. This is a **bonding pair** of electrons, as we discussed earlier. Each fluorine atom also has three pairs of electrons that are not involved in bonding. These are called **lone pairs** or **unshared pairs.**

4. Neon does not form bonds because it already has an octet of valence electrons (it is a noble gas). The Lewis structure is

:Ne:

Note that only the valence electrons $(2s^2 2p^6)$ of the neon atom are represented by the Lewis structure. The $1s^2$ electrons are core electrons and are not shown.

Next we want to develop some general procedures for writing Lewis structures for molecules. Remember that Lewis structures involve only the valence electrons on atoms, so before we proceed, we will review the relationship of

G. N. Lewis in his lab.

372   Chapter 12   Chemical Bonding

an element's position on the periodic table to the number of valence electrons it has. Recall that the group number gives the total number of valence electrons. For example, all Group 6 elements have six valence electrons (valence configuration ns^2np^4).

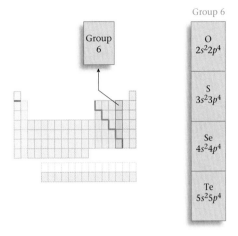

Similarly, all Group 7 elements have seven valence electrons (valence configuration ns^2np^5).

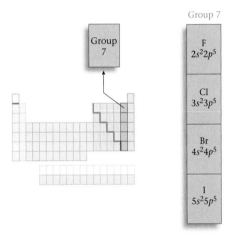

In writing the Lewis structure for a molecule, we need to keep the following things in mind:

1. We must include all the valence electrons from all atoms. The total number of electrons available is the sum of all the valence electrons from all the atoms in the molecule.

2. Atoms that are bonded to each other share one or more pairs of electrons.

12.6 Lewis Structures   **373**

TEACHING TIPS

- The rules for writing Lewis structures help students consistently write correct Lewis structures. Students who do not follow these rules will be less successful in drawing correct Lewis structures, especially for more complex molecules.

- Emphasize that to write correct structures for molecules it is necessary to sum all the valence electrons from all the atoms. Be sure that students do not attach valence electrons to individual atoms and then try to write a Lewis structure. This method can sometimes produce a correct structure, but often does not for molecules containing multiple bonds and for complex molecules.

Additional Examples

Write Lewis structures for each of the following molecules.

1. CCl_4 2. PH_3

(Lewis structure of CCl_4 with a central C bonded to four Cl atoms each with three lone pairs)

(Lewis structure of PH_3: H—P—H with H below and a lone pair on P)

3. The electrons are arranged so that each atom is surrounded by enough electrons to fill the valence orbitals of that atom. This means two electrons for hydrogen and eight electrons for second-row nonmetals.

The best way to make sure we arrive at the correct Lewis structure for a molecule is to use a systematic approach. We will use the approach summarized by the following rules.

Steps for Writing Lewis Structures

STEP 1 Obtain the sum of the valence electrons from all of the atoms. Do not worry about keeping track of which electrons come from which atoms. It is the *total* number of valence electrons that is important.

STEP 2 Use one pair of electrons to form a bond between each pair of bound atoms. For convenience, a line (instead of a pair of dots) is often used to indicate each pair of bonding electrons.

STEP 3 Arrange the remaining electrons to satisfy the duet rule for hydrogen and the octet rule for each second-row element.

To see how these rules are applied, we will write the Lewis structures of several molecules.

Example 12.2

CHEMISTRY
The number of valence electrons in an atom is the same as the group number on the periodic table for representative elements.

Writing Lewis Structures: Simple Molecules

Write the Lewis structure of the water molecule.

Solution

We will follow the steps listed above.

Step 1   Find the sum of the *valence* electrons for H_2O:

$$1 + 1 + 6 = 8 \text{ valence electrons}$$

H (Group 1)   H (Group 1)   O (Group 6)

Step 2   Using a pair of electrons per bond, we draw in the two O—H bonds, using a line to indicate each pair of bonding electrons.

H—O—H

Note that

H—O—H   represents   H : O : H

Step 3   We arrange the remaining electrons around the atoms to achieve a noble gas electron configuration for each atom. Four electrons have been used in forming the two bonds, so four electrons (8 − 4) remain to be distributed. Each hydrogen is satisfied with two electrons (duet rule), but oxygen needs eight electrons to have a noble gas electron configuration. So the remaining four electrons are added to oxygen as two lone pairs. Dots are used to represent the lone pairs.

This is the correct Lewis structure for the water molecule. Each hydrogen shares two electrons, and the oxygen has four electrons and shares four to give a total of eight.

Note that a line is used to represent a shared pair of electrons (bonding electrons) and dots are used to represent unshared pairs.

✓ **Self-Check Exercise 12.2**

Write the Lewis structure for HCl.

12.7 Lewis Structures of Molecules with Multiple Bonds

Objective: *To learn how to write Lewis structures for molecules with multiple bonds.*

Now let's write the Lewis structure for carbon dioxide. Summing the valence electrons gives

$$4 \quad + \quad 6 \quad + \quad 6 \quad = \quad 16$$
$$\begin{array}{ccc} \uparrow & \uparrow & \uparrow \\ C & O & O \\ \text{(Group 4)} & \text{(Group 6)} & \text{(Group 6)} \end{array}$$

O—C—O
represents
O:C:O

After forming a bond between the carbon and each oxygen,

O—C—O

we distribute the remaining electrons to achieve noble gas electron configurations on each atom. In this case twelve electrons ($16 - 4$) remain after the bonds are drawn. The distribution of these electrons is determined by a trial-and-error process. We have six pairs of electrons to distribute. Suppose we try three pairs on each oxygen to give

:Ö—C—Ö:
represents
:Ö:C:Ö:

:Ö—C—Ö:

Is this correct? To answer this question we need to check two things:

1. The total number of electrons. There are sixteen valence electrons in this structure, which is the correct number.

12.7 Lewis Structures of Molecules with Multiple Bonds **375**

2. The octet rule for each atom. Each oxygen has eight electrons around it, but the carbon has only four. This cannot be the correct Lewis structure.

How can we arrange the sixteen available electrons to achieve an octet for each atom? Suppose we place two shared pairs between the carbon and each oxygen:

$$\ddot{O}=C=\ddot{O}$$

represents

$$\ddot{O}::C::\ddot{O}$$

Now each atom is surrounded by eight electrons, and the total number of electrons is sixteen, as required. This is the correct Lewis structure for carbon dioxide, which has two *double* bonds. A **single bond** involves two atoms sharing one electron pair. A **double bond** involves two atoms sharing two pairs of electrons.

In considering the Lewis structure for CO_2, you may have come up with

$$:O\equiv C-\ddot{O}: \quad\text{or}\quad :\ddot{O}-C\equiv O:$$

Note that both of these structures have the required sixteen electrons and that both have octets of electrons around each atom (verify this for yourself). Both of these structures have a **triple bond** in which three electron pairs are shared. Are these valid Lewis structures for CO_2? Yes. So there really are three Lewis structures for CO_2:

$$:\ddot{O}-C\equiv O: \quad \ddot{O}=C=\ddot{O} \quad :O\equiv C-\ddot{O}:$$

This brings us to a new term, **resonance**. A molecule shows resonance when *more than one Lewis structure can be drawn for the molecule*. In such a case we call the various Lewis structures *resonance structures*.

Of the three resonance structures for CO_2 shown above, the one in the center with two double bonds most closely fits our experimental information about the CO_2 molecule. In this text we will not be concerned about how to choose which resonance structure for a molecule gives the "best" description of that molecule's properties.

Next let's consider the Lewis structure of the CN^- (cyanide) ion. Summing the valence electrons, we have

$$\underset{4 + 5 + 1 = 10}{CN^-}$$

Note that the negative charge means an extra electron must be added. After first drawing a single bond (C—N), we distribute the remaining electrons to achieve a noble gas configuration for each atom. Eight electrons remain to be distributed. We can try various possibilities, such as

$$\ddot{C}-\ddot{N} \quad\text{or}\quad :\ddot{C}-N: \quad\text{or}\quad :C-\ddot{N}:$$

These structures are incorrect. To show why none is a valid Lewis structure, count the electrons around the C and N atoms. In the left structure, neither atom satisfies the octet rule. In the center structure, C has eight electrons but N has only four. In the right structure, the opposite is true. Remember that both atoms must simultaneously satisfy the octet rule. Therefore, the correct arrangement is

$$:C\equiv N:$$

:O≡C—Ö:

represents

:O:::C:Ö:

:C≡N:

represents

:C:::N:

- Stress that resonance structures must all be correct Lewis structures. Students may think they can draw one correct structure and other resonance structures that are incorrect Lewis structures.

- The concept of resonance offers an opportunity to discuss the limitations of the bonding model we have developed.

- Students often have more trouble writing Lewis structures for ions than writing them for molecules. They are not sure what to do with the charge and how many electrons are available for the Lewis structure.

- Students often look at a species that has a negative charge and think that an electron has been removed.

Capsaicin

Capsaicin

Encourage students to search the Internet to find out more about the sources of capsaicin and its use. One interesting idea is to research the production of Tabasco sauce in the United States.

Consider having students use the molecular structure to practice identifying bonding concepts. Ask them to fill in any lone pairs of electrons that are not shown in the drawing.

When covering Sections 12.8–12.10, capsaicin can be used to discuss shape. Students can identify the shape at each carbon or nitrogen in the chain. This activity provides an excellent opportunity to review resonance using the benzene ring as an example. Finally, you can ask students to identify atoms that have shapes that differ from their electron pair arrangements.

Challenge your students to build a model of capsaicin.

Can you imagine why someone might add pepper to things like paint and fiber-optic cables? It's certainly not to flavor them so we can eat them! In fact, it's just the opposite. The idea is to use pepper as an environmentally safe animal deterrent.

The compound that gives pepper its characteristic "hot" taste is called capsaicin. Burlington Biomedical and Scientific Corporation in Farmingdale, New York, has found a way to manufacture a compound closely related to capsaicin that tastes painfully spicy and intensely bitter. One application for this compound is to add it to paint used for boats to prevent barnacles from sticking to the surface. Other applications include adding it to fiber-optic cables to prevent rodents from gnawing on them and using it to coat sutures employed in animal surgery to prevent pets from disturbing a healing wound.

A shipwright stands in the basket of a cherry-picker and paints the side of a ship.

(Satisfy yourself that both carbon and nitrogen have eight electrons.) In this case we have a triple bond between C and N, in which three electron pairs are shared. Because this is an anion, we indicate the charge outside of square brackets around the Lewis structure.

$$[:C\equiv N:]^-$$

In summary, sometimes we need double or triple bonds to satisfy the octet rule. Writing Lewis structures is a trial-and-error process. Start with single bonds between the bonded atoms and add multiple bonds as needed.

We will write the Lewis structure for NO_2^- in Example 12.3 to make sure the procedures for writing Lewis structures are clear.

12.7   Lewis Structures of Molecules with Multiple Bonds   **377**

Example 12.3

Example 12.4

Additional Examples

Write Lewis structures for each of the following molecules.

1. O_3

2. CO_3

$$\left[\begin{array}{c} :\ddot{O}: \\ \ddot{O}{\Large:}\overset{C}{}{\Large:}\ddot{O} \end{array}\right]^{2-} \leftrightarrow \left[\begin{array}{c} :\ddot{O}: \\ \ddot{O}{\Large:}\overset{C}{}{\Large:}\ddot{O} \end{array}\right]^{2-} \leftrightarrow$$

$$\left[\begin{array}{c} :O: \\ \| \\ C \\ :\ddot{O}\quad\ddot{O}: \end{array}\right]^{2-}$$

✓ **Answer to Self-Check Exercise 12.3**

Step 1 O_3: $3(6) = 18$ valence electrons

Step 2 O—O—O

Step 3

$$O{=}O{-}\ddot{O}:\quad \text{and} \quad :\ddot{O}{-}O{=}O$$

This molecule shows resonance (it has two valid Lewis structures).

Additional Examples

1. NI_3 **3.** PO_4^{3-}

$$:\ddot{I}{-}\overset{\textstyle N}{\underset{\textstyle |}{}}{-}\ddot{I}: \qquad \left[\begin{array}{c} :\ddot{O}: \\ | \\ :\ddot{O}{-}P{-}\ddot{O}: \\ | \\ :\ddot{O}: \end{array}\right]^{3-}$$
$$:\ddot{I}:$$

2. NO^+ **4.** SCN^- (C is the central atom)

$$:N{\equiv}O:$$

$$\left[:\ddot{S}{-}C{\equiv}N:\right]^-$$

Writing Lewis Structures: Resonance Structures

Write the Lewis structure for the NO_2^- anion.

Solution

Step 1 Sum the valence electrons for NO_2^-.

Valence electrons: $6 + 5 + 6 + 1 = 18$ electrons
$$\underset{O}{}\quad\underset{N}{}\quad\underset{O}{}\quad\underset{\substack{-1 \\ \text{charge}}}{}$$

Step 2 Put in single bonds.

O—N—O

Step 3 Satisfy the octet rule. In placing the electrons, we find there are two Lewis structures that satisfy the octet rule:

$$[O{=}N{-}\ddot{O}:]^- \quad \text{and} \quad [:\ddot{O}{-}N{=}\ddot{O}]^-$$

Verify that each atom in these structures is surrounded by an octet of electrons. Try some other arrangements to see whether other structures exist in which the eighteen electrons can be used to satisfy the octet rule. It turns out that these are the only two that work. Note that this is another case where resonance occurs; there are two valid Lewis structures.

✓ **Self-Check Exercise 12.3**

Ozone is a very important constituent of the atmosphere. At upper levels it protects us by absorbing high-energy radiation from the sun. Near the earth's surface it produces harmful air pollution. Write the Lewis structure for ozone, O_3.

Now let's consider a few more cases in Example 12.4.

Writing Lewis Structures: Summary

Give the Lewis structure for each of the following:

a. HF   **e.** CF_4
b. N_2 **f.** NO^+
c. NH_3 **g.** NO_3^-
d. CH_4

Solution

In each case we apply the three steps for writing Lewis structures. Recall that lines are used to indicate shared electron pairs and that dots are used to indicate nonbonding pairs (lone pairs). The table on page 379 summarizes our results.

Molecule or Ion	Total Valence Electrons	Draw Single Bonds	Calculate Number of Electrons Remaining	Use Remaining Electrons to Achieve Noble Gas Configurations	Check Atom	Check Electrons
a. HF	$1 + 7 = 8$	H—F	$8 - 2 = 6$	H—$\ddot{\underset{..}{F}}$:	H	2
					F	8
b. N_2	$5 + 5 = 10$	N—N	$10 - 2 = 8$	:N≡N:	N	8
c. NH_3	$5 + 3(1) = 8$	H—N—H | H	$8 - 6 = 2$	H—$\ddot{N}$—H | H	H	2
					N	8
d. CH_4	$4 + 4(1) = 8$	H | H—C—H | H	$8 - 8 = 0$	H | H—C—H | H	H	2
					C	8
e. CF_4	$4 + 4(7) = 32$	F | F—C—F | F	$32 - 8 = 24$	:$\ddot{F}$: | :$\ddot{F}$—C—$\ddot{F}$: | :$\ddot{F}$:	F	8
					C	8
f. NO^+	$5 + 6 - 1 = 10$	N—O	$10 - 2 = 8$	[:N≡O:]$^+$	N	8
					O	8
g. NO_3^-	$5 + 3(6) + 1 = 24$	$\left[\begin{array}{c} O \\ \| \\ N \\ / \quad \backslash \\ O \quad\quad O \end{array}\right]^-$	$24 - 6 = 18$	$\left[\begin{array}{c} :\ddot{O}: \\ \| \\ N \\ / \quad \backslash \\ :\ddot{O} \quad\quad \ddot{O}: \end{array}\right]^-$	N	8
					O	8
				$\left[\begin{array}{c} :\ddot{O}: \\ \| \\ N \\ / \quad \backslash \\ :\ddot{O} \quad\quad \ddot{O}: \end{array}\right]^-$	N	8
				NO_3^- shows resonance	O	8
				$\left[\begin{array}{c} :\ddot{O}: \\ \| \\ N \\ / \quad \backslash \\ :\ddot{O} \quad\quad \ddot{O}: \end{array}\right]^-$	N	8
					O	8

Self-Check Exercise 12.4

Write the Lewis structures for the following molecules:

a. NF_3 g. NH_4^+

b. O_2 h. ClO_3^-

c. CO i. SO_2

d. PH_3

e. H_2S

f. SO_4^{2-}

Answer to Self-Check Exercise 12.4

See table on page 382.

PROBLEM SOLVING

How do you decide which atom is the central atom in molecules of binary compounds? Where there is one atom of a given element and several atoms of a second element, the single atom is almost always the central atom of the molecule.

Remember, when writing Lewis structures, you don't have to worry about which electrons come from which atoms in a molecule. It is best to think of a molecule as a new entity that uses all of the available valence electrons from the various atoms to achieve the strongest possible bonds. Think of the

12.7 Lewis Structures of Molecules with Multiple Bonds **379**

Figure 12.10
When liquid oxygen is poured between the poles of a magnet, it "sticks" until it boils away. This shows that the O_2 molecule has unpaired electrons (is paramagnetic).

valence electrons as belonging to the molecule, rather than to the individual atoms. Simply distribute the valence electrons so that noble gas electron configurations are obtained for each atom, without regard to the origin of each particular electron.

Some Exceptions to the Octet Rule

The idea that covalent bonding can be predicted by achieving noble gas electron configurations for all atoms is a simple and very successful idea. The rules we have used for Lewis structures describe correctly the bonding in most molecules. However, with such a simple model, some exceptions are inevitable. Boron, for example, tends to form compounds in which the boron atom has fewer than eight electrons around it—that is, it does not have a complete octet. Boron trifluoride, BF_3, a gas at normal temperatures and pressures, reacts very energetically with molecules such as water and ammonia that have unshared electron pairs (lone pairs).

The violent reactivity of BF_3 with electron-rich molecules arises because the boron atom is electron-deficient. The Lewis structure that seems most consistent with the properties of BF_3 (twenty-four valence electrons) is

Note that in this structure the boron atom has only six electrons around it. The octet rule for boron could be satisfied by drawing a structure with a double bond between the boron and one of the fluorines. However, experiments indicate that each B—F bond is a single bond in accordance with the above Lewis structure. This structure is also consistent with the reactivity of BF_3 with electron-rich molecules. For example, BF_3 reacts vigorously with NH_3 to form H_3NBF_3.

Note that in the product H_3NBF_3, which is very stable, boron has an octet of electrons.

It is also characteristic of beryllium to form molecules where the beryllium atom is electron-deficient.

The elements carbon, nitrogen, oxygen, and fluorine obey the octet rule in the vast majority of their compounds. However, even these elements show a few exceptions. One important example is the oxygen molecule, O_2. The following Lewis structure that satisfies the octet rule can be drawn for O_2 (see Self-Check Exercise 12.4).

However, this structure does not agree with the *observed behavior* of oxygen. For example, the photo in **Figure 12.10** shows that when liquid oxygen is

380   Chapter 12   Chemical Bonding

poured between the poles of a strong magnet, it "sticks" there until it boils away. This provides clear evidence that oxygen is paramagnetic—that is, it contains unpaired electrons. However, the above Lewis structure shows only pairs of electrons. That is, no unpaired electrons are shown. There is no simple Lewis structure that satisfactorily explains the paramagnetism of the O_2 molecule.

Any molecule that contains an odd number of electrons does not conform to our rules for Lewis structures. For example, NO and NO_2 have eleven and seventeen valence electrons, respectively, and conventional Lewis structures cannot be drawn for these cases.

Even though there are exceptions, most molecules can be described by Lewis structures in which all the atoms have noble gas electron configurations, and this is a very useful model for chemists.

Focus Questions

Sections 12.6–12.7

1. Why is bonding based primarily on the octet rule? Why not a sextet rule?

2. What is the difference between a bonding pair of electrons and a lone pair of electrons?

3. Why do pairs of atoms share pairs (or multiples of pairs) of electrons? Why not share odd numbers?

4. For each molecule below:
    i. Give the sum of the valence electrons for all atoms.
    ii. Draw the Lewis structure.
    iii. Circle the octet (or duet) for each atom in the structure.
        a. ClF
        b. Br_2
        c. H_2O
        d. O_2

12.8 Molecular Structure

Objective: *To understand molecular structure and bond angles.*

So far in this chapter we have considered the Lewis structures of molecules. These structures represent the arrangement of the *valence electrons* in a molecule. We use the word *structure* in another way when we talk about the **molecular structure** or **geometric structure** of a molecule. These terms refer to the three-dimensional arrangement of the *atoms* in a molecule. For example, the water molecule is known to have the molecular structure

which is often called "bent" or "V-shaped." To describe the structure more precisely, we often specify the *bond angle*. For the H_2O molecule the bond angle is about 105°.

12.8   Molecular Structure   **381**

Answers to Focus Questions

1. The octet rule forms the basis for bonding because eight electrons are required to complete the *s* and *p* orbitals. The rule is not a sextet rule because the *s* and *p* orbitals must both be complete to form a stable atom within a molecule.

2. A bonding pair of electrons is involved in bonding and a lone pair of electrons is not. Otherwise, there is no difference between the two.

3. Only two electrons fit into an orbital. When orbitals overlap, atoms share the electrons in them, which results in shared pairs or multiples of pairs.

4. See the table on page 382.

Section 12.8

Themes
Models, Form and Function

Skills
Applying concepts, interpreting diagrams, developing models

Student Preparation
Assign the students to read Sections 12.8 to 12.10 and to answer the Focus Questions at the end of Section 12.10 before coming to class.

Active Learning
After introducing the material in Sections 12.8 to 12.10 in class, place the students in groups and have them work together on Sections 12.8–12.10: Team Learning Worksheet. Answers and/or discussion of these questions are located in the *Teacher Resources.*

---

and ask only appropriate questions. An illustration of this point involves the simple Aufbau principle, which is used to account for the electron configurations of the elements. Although this model correctly predicts the configurations for most atoms, chromium and copper do not agree with its predictions. Detailed studies show that the configurations of

chromium and copper result from complex electron interactions that are not taken into account in the simple model. This disagreement does not mean that we should discard the simple model that is so useful for most atoms. Instead, we must apply it with caution and not expect it to be correct in every case.

• When a model is wrong, we often learn much more than when it is right. If a model makes a wrong prediction, it usually means we do not understand some fundamental characteristic of nature. We often learn by making mistakes.

(a)   (b)   (c)

Computer graphics of (a) a linear molecule containing three atoms, (b) a trigonal planar molecule, and (c) a tetrahedral molecule.

On the other hand, some molecules exhibit a **linear structure** (all atoms in a line). An example is the CO_2 molecule.

Note that a linear molecule has a 180° bond angle.

A third type of molecular structure is illustrated by BF_3, which is planar or flat (all four atoms in the same plane) with 120° bond angles.

The name usually given to this structure is **trigonal planar**, although triangular might seem to make more sense.

Another type of molecular structure is illustrated by methane, CH_4. This molecule has the molecular structure shown in **Figure 12.11,** which is called a **tetrahedral structure** or a *tetrahedron*. The dashed lines shown connecting the H atoms define the four identical triangular faces of the tetrahedron.

In the next section we will discuss these various molecular structures in more detail. In that section we will learn how to predict the molecular structure of a molecule by looking at the molecule's Lewis structure.

Figure 12.11
The tetrahedral molecular structure of methane. This representation is called a ball-and-stick model; the atoms are represented by balls and the bonds by sticks. The dashed lines show the outline of the tetrahedron.

Focus Question 4 Answer (p. 381)

Molecule	Sum of valence electrons	Lewis structure
ClF	14	
Br_2	14	
H_2O	8	
O_2	12	

12.9 Molecular Structure: The VSEPR Model

Objective: To learn to predict molecular geometry from the number of electron pairs.

The structures of molecules play a very important role in determining their properties. For example, as we can see in the "Chemical Impact" below, taste is directly related to molecular structure. Structure is particularly important for biological molecules; a slight change in the structure of a large

Section 12.9

Themes
Models, Form and Function

Skills
Applying concepts, interpreting diagrams, developing models

Integrating the CHEMICAL IMPACT

Taste—It's the Structure That Counts

The three most common artificial sweeteners were all discovered by accident. Saccharin was discovered in 1879 at Johns Hopkins University in the laboratory of noted nineteenth-century chemist Ira Remsen. An associate of Remsen, Mr. Fahlberg, noticed that a substance he had prepared and spilled on his hands tasted unusually sweet. Fahlberg perfected a commercial synthesis process and took out a patent on the substance he named saccharin after *saccharum*, the Latin word for sugar.

In 1937, Michael Sveda, a graduate student working with Professor L. F. Andrieth at the University of Illinois, was preparing a series of sulfamate compounds because they were thought to have interesting pharmacological properties. Sveda noticed a markedly sweet taste on a cigarette he was smoking and was able to trace the taste to the sodium cyclohexylsulfamate (sodium cyclamate) compound he had prepared. The corresponding calcium salt was also sweet, and both compounds were widely used in artificial sweeteners (often mixed with saccharin) until 1970, when the U.S. FDA banned cyclamates on the basis of tetrogenic effects in animals. Cyclamates are still used in many other countries as artificial sweeteners.

Aspartame was discovered by accident by chemist James L. Schlatter while working at G. D. Searle in 1965. Schlatter had prepared aspartame as an intermediate. A methanol solution of the material bumped onto the outside of its flask, and Schlatter accidently got some of

(continued)

CHEMICAL IMPACT

Science, Technology, and Society

Taste—It's the Structure That Counts

Why do certain substances taste sweet, sour, bitter, or salty? Of course, it has to do with the taste buds on our tongues. But how do these taste buds work? For example, why does sugar taste sweet to us? The answer to this question remains elusive, but it does seem clear that sweet taste depends on how certain molecules fit the "sweet receptors" in our taste buds.

One of the mysteries of the sweet taste sensation is the wide variety of molecules that tastes sweet. For example, the many types of sugars include glucose and sucrose (table sugar). The first artificial sweetener was probably the Romans' sapa (see "Chemical Impact: Sugar of Lead" in Chapter 4), made by boiling wine in lead vessels to produce a syrup that contained lead acetate, $Pb(C_2H_3O_2)_2$, called sugar of lead because of its sweet taste. Other widely used modern artificial sweeteners include saccharin, cyclamate, and aspartame, whose structures are shown in this box. Note the great difference in of structures for these sweet-tasting molecules. It's certainly not obvious which structural features trigger a sweet sensation when these molecules interact with the taste buds.

The pioneers in relating structure to sweet taste were two chemists, Robert S. Shallenberger and

Terry E. Acree of Cornell University, who almost thirty years ago proposed that all sweet-tasting substances must contain a common feature they called a glycophore. They suggested that a glycophore always contains an atom or group of atoms that have available electrons located near a hydrogen atom attached to a relatively electronegative atom. Murray Goodman, a chemist at the University of California at San Diego, expanded the definition of a glycophore to include a hydrophobic ("water-hating") region. Goodman finds that a "sweet molecule" tends to be L-shaped with positively and negatively charged regions on the upright of the L and a hydrophobic region on the base of the L. To be sweet the L must be planar. If it is twisted in one direction, it gives a bitter taste. Twisting it in the other direction makes it tasteless. Goodman reports that by using his model he can design sweeteners, but these molecules remain too expensive for commercial use.

So the search goes on for a better artificial sweetener. One thing for sure, it all has to do with molecular structure.

Saccharin

Sodium cyclamate

Aspartame
(Nutra-Sweet)

12.9 Molecular Structure: The VSEPR Model **383**

(continued)

it on his hands. When he subsequently licked his finger to pick up a piece of paper, Schlatter noticed an extremely sweet taste. He traced this taste to the dipeptide, which eventually became the basis for a multibillion-dollar business.

TEACHING TIPS

- When teaching the VSEPR model, stress the difference between the arrangement of the electron pairs and the molecular structure. Students can easily confuse the two.

- Point out the differences between $BeCl_2$ and water. This distinction will help the students see the difference between electron pair structure and molecular shape. Many students do not understand why water has a bent shape and $BeCl_2$ is linear.

USING TECHNOLOGY

Animation, Electron Pair Repulsion, 2 pairs

Animation, Electron Pair Repulsion, 3 pairs

Animation, Electron Pair Repulsion, 4 pairs

---

biomolecule can completely destroy its usefulness to a cell and may even change the cell from a normal one to a cancerous one.

Many experimental methods now exist for determining the molecular structure of a molecule—that is, the three-dimensional arrangement of the atoms. These methods must be used when accurate information about the structure is required. However, it is often useful to be able to predict the *approximate* molecular structure of a molecule. In this section we consider a simple model that allows us to do this. The **valence shell electron pair repulsion (VSEPR) model** is useful for predicting the molecular structures of molecules formed from nonmetals. The main idea of this model is that *the structure around a given atom is determined by minimizing repulsions between electron pairs*. This means that the bonding and nonbonding electron pairs (lone pairs) around a given atom are positioned *as far apart as possible*. To see how this model works, we will first consider the molecule $BeCl_2$, which has the following Lewis structure (it is an exception to the octet rule):

$$:\ddot{C}l — Be — \ddot{C}l:$$

Note that there are two pairs of electrons around the beryllium atom. What arrangement of these electron pairs allows them to be as far apart as possible to minimize the repulsions? The best arrangement places the pairs on opposite sides of the beryllium atom at 180° from each other.

$$—Be—$$
$$180°$$

This is the maximum possible separation for two electron pairs. Now that we have determined the optimal arrangement of the electron pairs around the central atom, we can specify the molecular structure of $BeCl_2$—that is, the positions of the atoms. Because each electron pair on beryllium is shared with a chlorine atom, the molecule has a *linear structure* with a 180° bond angle.

$$:\ddot{C}l — Be — \ddot{C}l:$$
$$180°$$

Whenever two pairs of electrons are present around an atom, they should always be placed at an angle of 180° to each other to give a linear arrangement.

Next let's consider BF_3, which has the following Lewis structure (it is another exception to the octet rule):

$$:\ddot{F}:$$
$$|$$
$$:\ddot{F} — B — \ddot{F}:$$

Here the boron atom is surrounded by three pairs of electrons. What arrangement minimizes the repulsions among the three pairs of electrons? Here the greatest distance between the electron pairs is achieved by angles of 120°.

$$120° \diagup B \diagdown 120°$$
$$120°$$

Because each of the electron pairs is shared with a fluorine atom, the molecular structure is

$$120° \diagup B \diagdown 120° \quad \text{or} \quad$$

---

384 Chapter 12 Chemical Bonding

This is a planar (flat) molecule with a triangular arrangement of F atoms, commonly described as a trigonal planar structure. *Whenever three pairs of electrons are present around an atom, they should always be placed at the corners of a triangle (in a plane at an angle of 120° to each other).*

Next let's consider the methane molecule, which has the Lewis structure

There are four pairs of electrons around the central carbon atom. What arrangement of these electron pairs best minimizes the repulsions? First we try a square planar arrangement:

The carbon atom and the electron pairs are all in a plane represented by the surface of the paper, and the angles between the pairs are all 90°.

Is there another arrangement with angles greater than 90° that would put the electron pairs even farther away from each other? The answer is yes. We can get larger angles than 90° by using the following three-dimensional structure, which has angles of approximately 109.5°.

In this drawing the wedge indicates a position above the surface of the paper and the dashed lines indicate positions behind that surface. The solid line

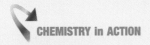

CHEMISTRY in ACTION
Geometric Balloons

1. Obtain nine round balloons.
2. Blow up all of the balloons to approximately the same size and tie each one.
3. Tie two of the balloons together. Then tie three of the remaining balloons together. Tie the final four balloons together.
4. Observe the geometry of each of the balloon clusters. What are the angles between each pair of balloons in each cluster?
5. Relate your findings to VSEPR theory. What does the knot in the center of each cluster represent? What does each balloon represent? Why do these geometries occur naturally?
6. Consider the cluster with three balloons. What is the arrangement of atoms (shape) if one balloon represents a lone pair of electrons? What if there were two lone pairs of electrons?
7. Consider the cluster with four balloons. What is the arrangement of atoms (shape) if one balloon represents a lone pair of electrons? What if there were two lone pairs of electrons? What if there were three lone pairs of electrons?

12.9 Molecular Structure: The VSEPR Model **385**

cause the balloons cannot occupy the same space. This is analogous to saying that electrons repel each other and electron pairs try to get as far apart from one another as possible. Thus the knot represents the center atom and each balloon represents an electron pair.

In the case of three balloons, if one is a lone pair, the shape is bent or V-shaped (like SO_2); if there are two lone pairs, it is linear (like CO_2). With four balloons, if there is one lone pair, the shape is trigonal pyramidal (like NH_3); with two lone pairs, the shape is bent or V-shaped (like H_2O); with three lone pairs, the shape is linear (like HCl).

Many students initially believe that a central atom with four other atoms around it will naturally form a square planar geometry. This activity can be used to confront this misconception. Once the tetrahedral geometry is naturally formed, you can show that it requires an input of energy to make a square planar geometry. Thus the square planar geometry is higher in energy and therefore less stable. In addition, if you drop the square planar geometry on the floor, it naturally converts back to the tetrahedral geometry.

If you wish, have students do five balloons (trigonal bipyramid, like PCl_5) or six balloons (octahedral, like SF_6). These geometries are not in the text. It is probably best to focus only on molecules that do not exceed the octet rule at this point. The oft-cited reason for molecules exceeding the octet rule (the *d* orbitals are involved) is considered to be wrong by many chemists and it is not necessary to introduce this issue here.

Many students can readily see that an octahedral geometry with a 90° bond angle gives the largest separations between the electron pairs when 6 pairs are present. The trigonal bipyramidal geometry (with five electron pairs) is much more difficult to see and should be avoided at this time. Five or six electron pairs around the central atom are possible because some atoms can exceed the octet rule. The reasons for this possibility are complicated (the oft-cited reason that the empty *d* orbitals are involved is, at best, incomplete). It is probably a good idea to inform students that the octet rule can be broken and leave it at that.

CHEMISTRY in ACTION

Geometric Balloons

Materials Each student/group will need nine uninflated balloons. You can decrease the number of balloons used by not having each group make each geometry.

Purpose Students will see three-dimensional models of simple molecules.

Discussion This activity is especially good for understanding tetrahedral geometry because this geometry is now seen to be "natural." While model kits are helpful, the angles are predetermined. In this exercise, students see that the geometries discussed in the book occur simply be-

A tetrahedron has four equal triangular faces.

indicates a position on the surface of the page. The figure formed by connecting the lines is called a tetrahedron, so we call this arrangement of electron pairs the *tetrahedral arrangement*.

This is the maximum possible separation of four pairs around a given atom. *Whenever four pairs of electrons are present around an atom, they should always be placed at the corners of a tetrahedron (the tetrahedral arrangement).*

Now that we have the arrangement of electron pairs that gives the least repulsion, we can determine the positions of the atoms and thus the molecular structure of CH_4. In methane each of the four electron pairs is shared between the carbon atom and a hydrogen atom. Thus the hydrogen atoms are placed as shown in **Figure 12.12,** and the molecule has a tetrahedral structure with the carbon atom at the center.

Recall that the main idea of the VSEPR model is to find the arrangement of electron pairs around the central atom that minimizes the repulsions. Then we can determine the *molecular structure* by knowing how the electron pairs are shared with the peripheral atoms. A systematic procedure for using the VSEPR model to predict the structure of a molecule is outlined here.

Figure 12.12
The molecular structure of methane. The tetrahedral arrangement of electron pairs produces a tetrahedral arrangement of hydrogen atoms.

Steps for Predicting Molecular Structure Using the VSEPR Model

STEP 1 Draw the Lewis structure for the molecule.

STEP 2 Count the electron pairs and arrange them in the way that minimizes repulsions (that is, put the pairs as far apart as possible).

STEP 3 Determine the positions of the atoms from the way the electron pairs are shared.

STEP 4 Determine the name of the molecular structure from the positions of the *atoms*.

Additional Examples

Describe the molecular structure (shape) of the following molecules using the VSEPR model.

1. Cl_2O
   Bent (V-shaped)

2. N_2O (N is a central atom)
   Linear

Example 12.5

Predicting Molecular Structure Using the VSEPR Model, I

Ammonia, NH_3, is used as a fertilizer (injected into the soil) and as a household cleaner (in aqueous solution). Predict the structure of ammonia using the VSEPR model.

Solution

Step 1 Draw the Lewis structure.

$$H—\overset{..}{N}—H$$
$$|$$
$$H$$

386 Chapter 12 Chemical Bonding

(a) (b) (c)

Figure 12.13
(a) The tetrahedral arrangement of electron pairs around the nitrogen atom in the ammonia molecule. (b) Three of the electron pairs around nitrogen are shared with hydrogen atoms as shown, and one is a lone pair. Although the arrangement of *electron pairs* is tetrahedral, as in the methane molecule, the hydrogen atoms in the ammonia molecule occupy only three corners of the tetrahedron. A lone pair occupies the fourth corner. (c) The NH_3 molecule has the trigonal pyramid structure (a pyramid with a triangle as a base).

Step 2 Count the pairs of electrons and arrange them to minimize repulsions. The NH_3 molecule has four pairs of electrons around the N atom: three bonding pairs and one nonbonding pair. From the discussion of the methane molecule, we know that the best arrangement of four electron pairs is the tetrahedral structure shown in **Figure 12.13a**.

Step 3 Determine the positions of the atoms. The three H atoms share electron pairs as shown in **Figure 12.13b**.

Step 4 Name the molecular structure. It is very important to recognize that the name of the molecular structure is always based on the *positions of the atoms. The placement of the electron pairs determines the structure, but the name is based on the positions of the atoms.* Thus it is incorrect to say that the NH_3 molecule is tetrahedral. It has a tetrahedral arrangement of electron pairs but *not* a tetrahedral arrangement of atoms. The molecular structure of ammonia is a **trigonal pyramid** (one side is different from the other three) rather than a tetrahedron.

Example 12.6

Predicting Molecular Structure Using the VSEPR Model, II

Describe the molecular structure of the water molecule.

Solution

Step 1 The Lewis structure for water is

H—Ö—H

(continued)

Additional Examples

Describe the molecular structure (shape) of the following molecules using the VSEPR model.

1. H_2Se
   Bent (V-shaped)

2. ClO_4^-
   Tetrahedral

Answers to Self-Check Exercise 12.5

a. NH_4^+
The Lewis structure is

$$\left[\begin{array}{c} H \\ | \\ H-N-H \\ | \\ H \end{array} \right]^+$$

There are four pairs of electrons around the nitrogen. This requires a tetrahedral arrangement of electron pairs. The NH_4^+ ion has a tetrahedral molecular structure (case 3 in Table 12.4), because all electron pairs are shared.

b. SO_4^{2-}
The Lewis structure is

$$\left[\begin{array}{c} :\ddot{O}: \\ | \\ :\ddot{O}-S-\ddot{O}: \\ | \\ :\ddot{O}: \end{array} \right]^{2-}$$

The four electron pairs around the sulfur require a tetrahedral arrangement. The SO_4^{2-} has a tetrahedral molecular structure (case 3 in Table 12.4).

c. NF_3
The Lewis structure is

The four pairs of electrons on the nitrogen require a tetrahedral arrangement. In this case only three of the pairs are shared with the fluorine atoms, leaving one lone pair. Thus the molecular structure is a trigonal pyramid (case 4 in Table 12.4).

d. H_2S
The Lewis structure is

$$H-\ddot{S}-H$$

The four pairs of electrons around the sulfur require a tetrahedral arrangement. In this case two pairs are shared with hydrogen atoms, leaving two lone pairs. Thus the molecular structure is bent or V-shaped (case 5 in Table 12.4).

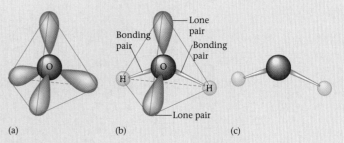

(a)   (b)   (c)

Figure 12.14
(a) The tetrahedral arrangement of the four electron pairs around oxygen in the water molecule. (b) Two of the electron pairs are shared between oxygen and the hydrogen atoms, and two are lone pairs. (c) The V-shaped molecular structure of the water molecule.

Step 2 There are four pairs of electrons: two bonding pairs and two non-bonding pairs. To minimize repulsions, these are best arranged in a tetrahedral structure as shown in **Figure 12.14a.**

Step 3 Although H_2O has a tetrahedral arrangement of *electron pairs*, it is *not a tetrahedral molecule.* The *atoms* in the H_2O molecule form a V shape, as shown in **Figure 12.14b and c.**

Step 4 The molecular structure is called V-shaped or bent.

 Self-Check Exercise 12.5

Predict the arrangement of electron pairs around the central atom. Then sketch and name the molecular structure for each of the following molecules or ions.

   a. NH_4^+ **d.** H_2S
   b. SO_4^{2-} **e.** ClO_3^-
   c. NF_3 **f.** BeF_2

The various cases we have considered are summarized in **Table 12.4** on the following page. Note the following general rules.

Rules for Predicting Molecular Structure Using the VSEPR Model

1. Two pairs of electrons on a central atom in a molecule are always placed 180° apart. This is a linear arrangement of pairs.
2. Three pairs of electrons on a central atom in a molecule are always placed 120° apart in the same plane as the central atom. This is a trigonal planar (triangular) arrangement of pairs.
3. Four pairs of electrons on a central atom in a molecule are always placed 109.5° apart. This is a tetrahedral arrangement of electron pairs.

---

388   Chapter 12   Chemical Bonding

e. ClO_3^-
The Lewis structure is

$$\left[\begin{array}{c} :\ddot{O}-Cl-\ddot{O}: \\ | \\ :\ddot{O}: \end{array} \right]^-$$

The four pairs of electrons require a tetrahedral arrangement. In this case, three pairs are shared with oxygen atoms, leaving one lone pair. Thus the molecular structure is a trigonal pyramid (case 4 in Table 12.4).

f. BeF_2
The Lewis structure is

$$:\ddot{F}-Be-\ddot{F}:$$

The two electron pairs on beryllium require a linear arrangement. Because both pairs are shared by fluorine atoms, the molecular structure is also linear (case 1 in Table 12.4).

4. When *every pair* of electrons on the central atom is *shared* with another atom, the molecular structure has the same name as the arrangement of electron pairs.

Number of Pairs	Name of Arrangement
2	linear
3	trigonal planar
4	tetrahedral

5. When one or more of the electron pairs around a central atom are unshared (lone pairs), the name for the molecular structure is *different* from that for the arrangement of electron pairs (see cases 4 and 5 in Table 12.4).

USING TECHNOLOGY

 Table 12.4

Arrangement of Electron Pairs and the Resulting Molecular Structures for Two, Three, and Four Electron Pairs, can be used when having students predict molecular structures in class.

TABLE 12.4

Arrangements of Electron Pairs and the Resulting Molecular Structures for Two, Three, and Four Electron Pairs

Case	Number of Electron Pairs	Bonds	Electron Pair Arrangement	Partial Lewis Structure	Molecular Structure	Example
1	2	2	180° Linear	A — B — A	Linear	F — Be — F BeF_2
2	3	3	120° Trigonal planar (triangular)	A, B, A A	Trigonal planar (triangular)	F, B, F F BF_3
3	4	4	109.5° Tetrahedral	A — B — A, A	Tetrahedral	H, C, H H H CH_4
4	4	3	109.5° Tetrahedral	A — B — A, A	Trigonal pyramid	H, N, H H NH_3
5	4	2	109.5° Tetrahedral	A — B — A	Bent or V-shaped	H, O, H H_2O

Section 12.10

Themes
Models, Form and Function

Skills
Applying concepts, interpreting diagrams, making predictions

Laboratory
Experiment 50:
Models of Molecules, In Text

12.10 Molecular Structure: Molecules with Double Bonds

Objective: *To learn to apply the VSEPR model to molecules with double bonds.*

Up to this point we have applied the VSEPR model only to molecules (and ions) that contain single bonds. In this section we will show that this model applies equally well to species with one or more double bonds. We will develop the procedures for dealing with molecules with double bonds by considering examples whose structures are known.

First we will examine the structure of carbon dioxide, a substance that may be contributing to the warming of the earth. The carbon dioxide molecule has the Lewis structure

$$\ddot{O}=C=\ddot{O}$$

as discussed in Section 12.7. Carbon dioxide is known by experiment to be a linear molecule. That is, it has a 180° bond angle.

Recall from Section 12.9 that two electron pairs around a central atom can minimize their mutual repulsions by taking positions on opposite sides of the atom (at 180° from each other). This causes a molecule like $BeCl_2$, which has the Lewis structure

$$:\ddot{Cl}—Be—\ddot{Cl}:$$

to have a linear structure. Now recall that CO_2 has two double bonds and is known to be linear, so the double bonds must be at 180° from each other. Therefore, we conclude that each double bond in this molecule acts *effectively* as one repulsive unit. This conclusion makes sense if we think of a bond in terms of an electron density "cloud" between two atoms. For example, we can picture the single bonds in $BeCl_2$ as follows:

The minimum repulsion between these two electron density clouds occurs when they are on opposite sides of the Be atom (180° angle between them).

Each double bond in CO_2 involves the sharing of four electrons between the carbon atom and an oxygen atom. Thus we might expect the bonding cloud to be "fatter" than for a single bond:

However, the repulsive effects of these two clouds produce the same result as for single bonds; the bonding clouds have minimum repulsions when they are positioned on opposite sides of the carbon. The bond angle is 180°, and so the molecule is linear:

In summary, examination of CO_2 leads us to the conclusion that in using the VSEPR model for molecules with double bonds, each double bond should be treated the same as a single bond. In other words, although a double bond involves four electrons, these electrons are restricted to the space between a given pair of atoms. Therefore, these four electrons do not function as two independent pairs but are "tied together" to form one effective repulsive unit.

We reach this same conclusion by considering the known structures of other molecules that contain double bonds. For example, consider the ozone molecule, which has eighteen valence electrons and exhibits two resonance structures:

$$:\ddot{O}-\ddot{O}=\ddot{O}: \longleftrightarrow :\ddot{O}=\ddot{O}-\ddot{O}:$$

The ozone molecule is known to have a bond angle close to 120°. Recall that 120° angles represent the minimum repulsion for three pairs of electrons.

This indicates that the double bond in the ozone molecule is behaving as one effective repulsive unit:

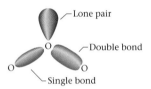

These and other examples lead us to the following rule: *When using the VSEPR model to predict the molecular geometry of a molecule, a double bond is counted the same as a single electron pair.*

Thus CO_2 has two "effective pairs" that lead to its linear structure, whereas O_3 has three "effective pairs" that lead to its bent structure with a 120° bond angle. Therefore, to use the VSEPR model for molecules (or ions) that have double bonds, we use the same steps as those given in Section 12.9, but we count any double bond the same as a single electron pair. Although we have not shown it here, triple bonds also count as one repulsive unit in applying the VSEPR model.

12.10   Molecular Structure: Molecules with Double Bonds   **391**

Describe the molecular structure (shape) of the following molecules using the VSEPR model.

1. C_2H_2
   Linear

2. CO_3^{2-}
   Trigonal planar

Answers to Focus Questions

1. The Lewis structure shows how many electron pairs surround each atom in the molecule. It enables you to determine the molecular structure by counting the number of bonding pairs and lone pairs for each atom.

2. The molecular structure is the same as the arrangement of electron pairs when there are no lone pairs on the central atom in the structure.

3. The name for the molecular structure differs from that for the electron pair arrangement when there are lone pairs around the central atom.

4. The electrons in a double bond are restricted to the space between the two atoms and so cannot operate as independent pairs.

Example 12.7

Predicting Molecular Structure Using the VSEPR Model, III

Predict the structure of the nitrate ion.

Solution

Step 1   The Lewis structures for NO_3^- are

$$\left[\begin{array}{c} :\ddot{O}: \\ N \\ :\ddot{O} \quad \ddot{O}: \end{array}\right]^{-} \leftrightarrow \left[\begin{array}{c} :\ddot{O}: \\ N \\ :\ddot{O} \quad \ddot{O}: \end{array}\right]^{-} \leftrightarrow \left[\begin{array}{c} :\ddot{O}: \\ N \\ :\ddot{O} \quad \ddot{O}\cdot \end{array}\right]^{-}$$

Step 2   In each resonance structure there are effectively three pairs of electrons: the two single bonds and the double bond (which counts as one pair). These three "effective pairs" will require a trigonal planar arrangement (120° angles).

Step 3   The atoms are all in a plane, with the nitrogen at the center and the three oxygens at the corners of a triangle (trigonal planar arrangement).

Step 4   The NO_3^- ion has a trigonal planar structure.

Focus Questions

Sections 12.8–12.10

1. How does drawing a Lewis structure for a molecule help in determining its molecular shape?

2. When is the molecular structure for a molecule the same as the arrangement of electron pairs?

3. What causes the name for the molecular structure to be different from the name for the arrangement of electron pairs?

4. If double bonds contain four electrons instead of two, why should they be treated as if they were the same as single bonds when determining molecular structure?

CHEMISTRY in the LABORATORY
Models of Molecules

Problem

Can we use the molecular formula to predict the shapes of small molecules?

Introduction

The shape of a molecule greatly affects its properties. In this activity you will use clay and toothpicks to determine the shapes of small molecules. You will use toothpicks to represent both bonding pairs and lone pairs of electrons.

Prelab Assignment

1. Read the entire lab experiment before you begin.
2. Draw Lewis structures for each of the molecules given below. (*Note:* In all of the molecules containing carbon, the carbon atom is the central atom.)

   HCN

   O_3

   H_2CO

   H_2S

   CCl_2H_2

   PH_3

Materials

Ruler
Protractor
Toothpicks
Modeling clay

Procedure

1. Use toothpicks and modeling clay to make models for each of the molecules given in the Prelab assignment. Make sure the toothpicks stick out an equal distance from the center clay ball (make sure this distance is the same for all molecules; in this way we can compare measurements for different molecules). Use toothpicks for both bonding pairs and lone pairs.
2. Use the ruler to make sure the ends of the toothpicks are as far apart from each other as possible. Measure this distance.
3. Measure the bond angles between the toothpicks.

Cleaning Up

Clean all materials and wash your hands thoroughly.

Analysis and Conclusions

1. Which shape has the longest distance between the ends of the toothpicks? Which shape has the shortest distance between the ends of the toothpicks?

2. Group together molecules that have the same number of atoms coming off the central atom. Do these molecules have the same geometry? The same shape?
3. Group together models that have the same number of toothpicks coming off the central atom. Do these molecules have the same geometry? The same shape?
4. What do the toothpicks represent?
5. Why do we position the ends of the toothpicks as far apart as possible?
6. Can we use the molecular formula to predict the shape of a small molecule? Explain.

Summary Table

Include in your lab report a summary table similar to the one below.

Molecule	Distance Between Ends of Toothpicks	Bond Angles	Electron Pair Geometry	Shape
HCN				
O_3				
CCl_2H_2				
H_2CO				
H_2S				
PH_3				

Something Extra

In this activity the greatest number of toothpicks coming off the central atom was four. Make models with five and six toothpicks coming off the central atom. Show these to your teacher.

The lone pairs affect the actual bond angles. For example, if a molecule has a tetrahedral geometry but a bent shape, the angle is smaller than 109.5° (close to 105°). It is up to you whether you wish to introduce this complication.

Sample Data/Answers

Prelab Assignment

HCN
$H—C≡N:$

H_2CO

O_3

CCl_2H_2

H_2S

PH_3

Analysis and Conclusions

1. The linear shape has the longest distance between the ends of the toothpicks. The tetrahedral shape has the shortest distance between the ends of the toothpicks.

2. 2 atoms off the central atom: HCN, O_3, H_2S; 3 atoms: H_2CO, PH_3; 4 atoms: CCl_2H_2. In a given group the molecules do not necessarily have the same geometry or the same shape.

3. 2 toothpicks: HCN; 3 toothpicks: O_3, H_2CO; 4 toothpicks: H_2S, CCl_2H_2, PH_3. In a given group the molecules have the same arrangement of electron pairs but not necessarily the same shape.

4. The toothpicks represent electron pairs (bonding pairs and lone pairs).

5. The toothpicks represent electron pairs, and electrons are negatively charged and therefore repel each other. To minimize electron pair interactions, we position the toothpicks as far apart as possible.

(continued)

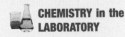

CHEMISTRY in the LABORATORY

Models of Molecules

Objectives

1. To use clay and toothpicks to make models of simple molecules
2. To use these models to better understand shapes of molecules

Skills

Applying concepts, making models, making comparisons

Materials

Ruler   Toothpicks
Protractor   Modeling clay

Preparation Hints

Ideally, you should have enough toothpicks and clay available so that students can construct all of the models and compare them to each other.

Prelab Discussion

Students should use their Lewis structures as a guide to make the models. One toothpick should be used to represent a single bond, double bond, or triple bond.

Procedure Hints

Make sure that students are inserting the toothpicks in the clay to the same depth.

Post-Lab Discussion

Encourage students to compare their results. The distances between the ends of the toothpicks will differ. The HCN model will have the longest distance. The molecules with tetrahedral arrangements of electrons will have the shortest distances.

(continued)

6. We cannot use the molecular formula to predict the shape of a small molecule. We need to know how many lone pairs of electrons are present (from the Lewis structure) to determine the shape.

Chapter Review

Assign the students to work individually on the Chapter 12 Review Worksheet at the appropriate level (Basic, Standard, or Challenge). Worksheets and answers are found in the *Teacher Resources*.

Assessment

Chapter 12 Test is found in the *Teacher Resources*, along with the answers for the test.

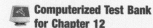 **Computerized Test Bank for Chapter 12**

Answers to End of Chapter Problems

1. A chemical bond represents a force that holds groups of two or more atoms together and makes them function as a unit.

2. An ionic compound results when a metallic element reacts with a nonmetallic element. An example is $2Na(s) + Cl_2(g) \rightarrow 2Na^{(+)}Cl^{(-)}(s)$.

3. ionic; covalent

4. When two hydrogen atoms are brought close together, each hydrogen atom contributes its electron to the formation of a covalent bond. The pair of electrons is shared equally by the two hydrogen atoms.

5. By bonding with each other, the atoms (H and F) share a pair of valence electrons. Because the atoms have different attractions for the electrons, this sharing is not equal. The bonding in HF is polar covalent.

6. Electronegativity is the ability of an atom to attract a shared pair of electrons toward itself in forming a chemical bond. The larger the electronegativity, the greater the attraction for a shared electron.

7. A bond is polar if the shared electron pair is attracted more strongly by one of the bonded atoms than the other due to differences in electronegativity

---

12 Chapter Review

Key Terms

bond (12.1)
bond energy (12.1)
ionic bonding (12.1)
ionic compound (12.1)
covalent bonding (12.1)
polar covalent bond (12.1)
electronegativity (12.2)
dipole moment (12.3)
Lewis structure (12.6)
duet rule (12.6)
octet rule (12.6)
bonding pair (12.6)
lone (unshared) pair (12.6)
single bond (12.7)

double bond (12.7)
triple bond (12.7)
resonance (12.7)
molecular (geometric) structure (12.8)
linear structure (12.8)
trigonal planar structure (12.8)
tetrahedral structure (12.8)
valence shell electron pair repulsion (VSEPR) model (12.9)
trigonal pyramid (12.9)

Summary

1. Chemical bonds hold groups of atoms together. They can be classified into several types. An ionic bond is formed when a transfer of electrons occurs to form ions; in a purely covalent bond, electrons are shared equally between identical atoms. Between these extremes lies the polar covalent bond, in which electrons are shared unequally between atoms with different electronegativities.

2. Electronegativity is defined as the relative ability of an atom in a molecule to attract the electrons shared in a bond. The difference in electronegativity values between the atoms involved in a bond determines the polarity of that bond.

3. In stable chemical compounds, the atoms tend to achieve a noble gas electron configuration. In the formation of a binary ionic compound involving representative elements, the valence-electron configuration of the nonmetal is completed: it achieves the configuration of the next noble gas. The valence orbitals of the metal are emptied to give the electron configuration of the previous noble gas. Two nonmetals share the valence electrons so that both atoms have completed valence-electron configurations (noble gas configurations).

4. Lewis structures are drawn to represent the arrangement of the valence electrons in a molecule. The rules for drawing Lewis structures are based on the observation that nonmetal atoms tend to achieve noble gas electron configurations by sharing electrons. This leads to a duet rule for hydrogen and to an octet rule for many other atoms.

5. Some molecules have more than one valid Lewis structure, a property called resonance. Although Lewis structures in which the atoms have noble gas electron configurations correctly describe most molecules, there are some notable exceptions, including O_2, NO, NO_2, and the molecules that contain Be and B.

6. The molecular structure of a molecule describes how the atoms are arranged in space.

7. The molecular structure of a molecule can be predicted by using the valence shell electron pair repulsion (VSEPR) model. This model bases its prediction on minimum repulsions among the electron pairs around an atom, which means arranging the electron pairs as far apart as possible.

Questions and Problems

All exercises with blue numbers have answers in the back of this book.

12.1 Types of Chemical Bonds

Questions

1. Define a chemical bond.

2. What types of elements react to form *ionic* compounds? Give an example of the formation of an ionic compound from its elements.

3. What type of bonding requires the complete *transfer* of an electron from one atom to another? What type of bonding involves the sharing (either equally or unequally) of electrons between atoms?

4. Describe the type of chemical bonding that exists between the atoms in the hydrogen molecule, H_2.

5. Describe the type of chemical bonding that exists between the atoms in the hydrogen fluoride molecule, HF.

12.2 Electronegativity

Questions

6. What do chemists mean by the term *electronegativity*? What does its electronegativity tell us about the atom?

7. What does it mean to say that a bond is *polar*? What are the conditions that give rise to a bond's being polar? Does the fact that a molecule possesses polar bonds necessarily mean that the molecule itself will also be polar?

Problems

8. For each of the following sets of elements, identify the element expected to be most electronegative and that expected to be least electronegative.
   a. K, Sc, Ca   **b.** Br, F, At   **c.** C, O, N

---

values. A molecule may have polar bonds but not necessarily be a polar molecule. To determine the polarity of a molecule, its overall shape must be considered.

8. (a) K < Ca < Sc; (b) At < Br < F; (c) C < N < O

9. (a) covalent; (b) polar covalent; (c) polar covalent; (d) ionic

10. (a) no polar covalent bonds; (b) no polar covalent bonds; (c) no polar covalent bonds; (d) polar covalent bonds

11. (a) H—O; (b) H—F; (c) H—F; (d) H—O

12. (a) Na—O; (b) K—S; (c) K—Cl; (d) Na—Cl

13. A dipole moment occurs in a molecule that has separate centers of positive and negative charge. Examples include $^{\delta+}C \rightarrow O^{\delta-}$; $^{\delta+}N \rightarrow O^{\delta-}$; $^{\delta+}Cl \rightarrow F^{\delta-}$; $^{\delta+}Br \rightarrow Cl^{\delta-}$.

14. The presence of strong dipoles and a large overall dipole moment makes water a very polar substance. Properties of water that are dependent on its dipole moment

include its freezing point, melting point, vapor pressure, and ability to dissolve many substances.

15. (a) H; (b) Cl; (c) I

16. (a) $^{\delta+}P \rightarrow F^{\delta-}$; (b) $^{\delta+}P \rightarrow O^{\delta-}$; (c) $^{\delta+}P \rightarrow C^{\delta-}$; (d) P and H have similar electronegativities

17. (a) $^{\delta+}P \rightarrow S^{\delta-}$; (b) $^{\delta+}S \rightarrow O^{\delta-}$; (c) $^{\delta+}S \rightarrow N^{\delta-}$; (d) $^{\delta+}S \rightarrow Cl^{\delta-}$

18. gaining

9. On the basis of the electronegativity values given in Figure 12.3, indicate whether each of the following bonds would be expected to be ionic, covalent, or polar covalent.
   a. S—S
   b. S—O
   c. S—H
   d. S—K

10. Which of the following molecules contain polar covalent bonds?
   a. phosphorus, P_4
   b. oxygen, O_2
   c. ozone, O_3
   d. hydrogen fluoride, HF

11. On the basis of the electronegativity values given in Figure 12.3, indicate which is the more polar bond in each of the following pairs.
   a. H—O or H—N
   b. H—N or H—F
   c. H—O or H—F
   d. H—O or H—Cl

12. On the basis of the electronegativity values given in Figure 12.3, indicate which bond of the following pairs has a more ionic character.
   a. Na—O or Na—N
   b. K—S or K—P
   c. Na—Cl or K—Cl
   d. Na—Cl or Mg—Cl

12.3 Bond Polarity and Dipole Moments

Questions

13. What is a *dipole moment?* Give four examples of molecules that possess dipole moments, and draw the direction of the dipole as shown in this section.

14. Why is the presence of a dipole moment in the water molecule so important? What are some properties of water that are determined by its polarity?

Problems

15. In each of the following diatomic molecules, which end of the molecule is positive relative to the other end?
   a. hydrogen fluoride, HF
   b. chlorine monofluoride, ClF
   c. iodine monochloride, ICl

16. For each of the following bonds, draw a figure indicating the direction of the bond dipole, including which end of the bond is positive and which is negative.
   a. P—F
   b. P—O
   c. P—C
   d. P—H

17. For each of the following bonds, draw a figure indicating the direction of the bond dipole, including which end of the bond is positive and which is negative.
   a. S—P
   b. S—O
   c. S—N
   d. S—Cl

12.4 Stable Electron Configurations and Charges on Ions

Questions

18. Nonmetals form negative ions by (losing/gaining) enough electrons to achieve the electron configuration of the next noble gas.

19. Explain how the atoms in *covalent* molecules achieve configurations similar to those of the noble gases. How does this differ from the situation in ionic compounds?

Problems

20. Write the electron configuration for each of the following atoms and for the simple ion that the element most commonly forms. In each case, indicate which noble gas has the same electron configuration as the ion.
   a. lithium, $Z = 3$
   b. bromine, $Z = 35$
   c. cesium, $Z = 55$
   d. sulfur, $Z = 16$
   e. magnesium, $Z = 12$

21. What simple ion does each of the following elements most commonly form?
   a. calcium, $Z = 20$
   b. nitrogen, $Z = 7$
   c. bromine, $Z = 35$
   d. magnesium, $Z = 12$

22. On the basis of their electron configurations, predict the formula of the simple binary ionic compound likely to form when the following pairs of elements react with each other.
   a. sodium, Na, and sulfur, S
   b. barium, Ba, and selenium, Se
   c. magnesium, Mg, and bromine, Br
   d. lithium, Li, and nitrogen, N
   e. potassium, K, and hydrogen, H

23. Name the noble gas atom that has the same electron configuration as each of the ions in the following compounds.
   a. aluminum sulfide, Al_2S_3
   b. magnesium nitride, Mg_3N_2
   c. rubidium oxide, Rb_2O
   d. cesium iodide, CsI

12.5 Ionic Bonding and Structures of Ionic Compounds

Questions

24. Is the formula we write for an ionic compound the *molecular* formula or the *empirical* formula? Why?

25. Describe in general terms the structure of ionic solids such as NaCl. How are the ions packed in the crystal?

26. Why are cations always smaller than the atoms from which they are formed?

27. Why are anions always larger than the atoms from which they are formed?

a filled $n = 3$ shell. A sodium atom has lost the electron from the $n = 3$ shell, leaving $n = 2$ as its outermost shell. (c) Ca is larger than Ca^{2+}. The calcium ion has $n = 3$ as its outer shell, and the calcium atom has $n = 4$ as its outer shell. (d) I^- is larger than Cs^+. The I^- ion has a filled $n = 5$ shell. A cesium atom has lost the electron from the $n = 6$ shell, leaving $n = 5$ as its outermost shell. However, cesium has a greater nuclear charge than iodine, so the electrons are drawn in closer.

29. (a) I^-; (b) Cl^-; (c) Cl^-; (d) S^{2-}

30. The valence electrons effectively represent the outside edge of the atom. These electrons are most likely influenced by the electrons of another atom.

31. When atoms form covalent bonds, they try to attain a valence electron configuration similar to that of the nearest noble gas element. Thus hydrogen in a bond would have two electrons (like helium; the duet rule) and others would have eight electrons (like neon and argon; the octet rule).

32. 4 electrons; an example is O_2.
$$:\!\overset{..}{O}\!=\!\overset{..}{O}\!:$$

33. (a) 32; (b) 17; (c) 30; (d) 14

34. (a) NH_3

H—N—H
|
H

(c) NCl_3

:Cl—N—Cl:
|
:Cl:

(b) CI_4

(d) $SiBr_4$

35. (a) H_2S (c) C_2H_4

(b) SiF_4 (d) C_3H_8

---

19. See *Solutions Guide.*

20. (a) Li: $[He]2s^1$; Li^+: [He];
(b) Br: $[Ar]4s^23d^{10}4p^5$; Br^-: [Kr];
(c) Cs: $[Xe]6s^1$; Cs^+: [Xe];
(d) S: $[Ne]3s^23p^4$; S^{2-}: [Ar];
(e) Mg: $[Ne]3s^2$; Mg^{2+}: [Ne]

21. (a) Ca^{2+}; (b) N^{3-}; (c) Br^-; (d) Mg^{2+}

22. (a) Na_2S; (b) BaSe; (c) $MgBr_2$; (d) Li_3N; (e) KH

23. (a) Al^{3+}, [Ne]; S^{2-}, [Ar]; (b) Mg^{2+}, [Ne]; N^{3-}, [Ne]; (c) Rb^+, [Kr]; O^{2-}, [Ne]; (d) Cs^+, [Xe]; I^-, [Xe]

24. The formula of an ionic compound is the empirical formula (the smallest whole-number ratio of the positive and negative ions present).

25. An ionic solid such as NaCl consists of an array of alternating positively and negatively charged ions. In most ionic solids, the ions are packed as tightly as possible.

26. In forming the cation, the electrons in the valence electron shell are removed from the atom. The valence shell of the cation is the next lowest energy level compared with the parent atom.

27. In forming an anion, an atom gains additional electrons in its outermost (valence) shell. Having additional electrons in the valence shell increases the repulsive forces between electrons, and the outermost shell becomes larger to accommodate this increase.

28. (a) F^- is larger than Li^+. The F^- ion has a filled $n = 2$ shell. A lithium atom has lost the electron from the $n = 2$ shell, leaving $n = 1$ as its outermost shell. (b) Cl^- is larger than Na^+. The Cl^- ion has

36. (a) Cl_2O (b) CO_2

(c) SO_3

(Lewis structure of SO_3 shown)

37. (a) SO_4^{2-} (b) PO_4^{3-}

(Lewis structures shown)

(c) SO_3^{2-}

(Resonance Lewis structures shown)

38. (a) HPO_4^{2-}

(Lewis structure shown)

(b) $H_2PO_4^-$

(Lewis structure shown)

(c) PO_4^{3-}

(Lewis structure shown)

39. Water is a bent (or V-shaped) molecule. There are four pairs of valence electrons on the oxygen atom (two lone pairs and two bonding pairs). The expected bond angle is approximately 109.5° (for water, the angle is closer to 105° due to the lone pair repulsions).

40. Trigonal pyramidal structure with four electron pairs (three bonding pairs and one lone pair). The bond angle is somewhat less than 109.5° (due to the lone pair).

41. BF_3 is a trigonal planar

Problems

28. For each of the following pairs, indicate which species is larger. Explain your reasoning in terms of the electron structure of each species.
   a. Li^+ or F^- c. Ca^{2+} or Ca
   b. Na^+ or Cl^- d. Cs^+ or I^-

29. For each of the following pairs, indicate which is larger.
   a. Cl^- or I^- c. Cl^- or Cl
   b. Cl^- or Na^+ d. Cl^- or S^{2-}

12.6 and 12.7 Lewis Structures

Questions

30. Why are the *valence* electrons of an atom the only electrons likely to be involved in bonding to other atoms?

31. Explain what the "duet" and "octet" rules are and how they are used to describe the arrangement of electrons in a molecule.

Problems

32. How many electrons are involved when two atoms in a molecule are connected by a "double bond"? Write the Lewis structure of a molecule containing a double bond.

33. Give the *total* number of *valence* electrons in each of the following molecules.
   a. CBr_4 c. C_6H_6
   b. NO_2 d. H_2O_2

34. Write a Lewis structure for each of the following simple molecules. Show all bonding valence electron pairs as lines and all nonbonding valence electron pairs as dots.
   a. NH_3 c. NCl_3
   b. Cl_4 d. $SiBr_4$

35. Write a Lewis structure for each of the following simple molecules. Show all bonding valence electron pairs as lines and all nonbonding valence electron pairs as dots.
   a. H_2S c. C_2H_4
   b. SiF_4 d. C_3H_8

36. Write a Lewis structure for each of the following simple molecules. Show all bonding valence electron pairs as lines and all nonbonding valence electron pairs as dots. For those molecules that exhibit resonance, draw the various possible resonance forms.
   a. Cl_2O b. CO_2 c. SO_3

37. Write a Lewis structure for each of the following polyatomic ions. Show all bonding valence electron pairs as lines and all nonbonding valence electron pairs as dots. For those ions that exhibit resonance, draw the various possible resonance forms.
   a. sulfate ion, SO_4^{2-}
   b. phosphate ion, PO_4^{3-}
   c. sulfite ion, SO_3^{2-}

38. Write a Lewis structure for each of the following polyatomic ions. Show all bonding valence electron pairs as lines and all nonbonding valence electron pairs as dots. For those ions that exhibit resonance, draw the possible resonance forms.
   a. hydrogen phosphate ion, HPO_4^{2-}
   b. dihydrogen phosphate ion, $H_2PO_4^-$
   c. phosphate ion, PO_4^{3-}

12.8 Molecular Structure

Questions

39. What is the geometric structure of the water molecule? How many pairs of valence electrons are there on the oxygen atom in the water molecule? What is the approximate H—O—H bond angle in water?

40. What is the geometric structure of the ammonia molecule? How many pairs of electrons surround the nitrogen atom in NH_3? What is the approximate H—N—H bond angle in ammonia?

41. What is the geometric structure of the boron trifluoride molecule, BF_3? How many pairs of valence electrons are present on the boron atom in BF_3? What are the approximate F—B—F bond angles in BF_3?

42. What is the geometric structure of the CH_4 molecule? How many pairs of valence electrons are present on the carbon atom of CH_4? Refer to Figure 12.11 and estimate the H—C—H bond angles in CH_4.

12.9 Molecular Structure: The VSEPR Model

Questions

43. Why is the geometric structure of a molecule important, especially for biological molecules?

44. What general principles determine the molecular structure (shape) of a molecule?

45. Although the valence electron pairs in ammonia have a tetrahedral arrangement, the overall geometric structure of the ammonia molecule is *not* described as being tetrahedral. Explain.

46. Although both the BF_3 and NF_3 molecules contain the same number of atoms, the BF_3 molecule is flat, whereas the NF_3 molecule is trigonal pyramidal. Explain.

Problems

47. For the indicated atom in each of the following molecules or ions, give the number and arrangement of the electron pairs around that atom.
   a. P in PH_3
   b. Cl in ClO_4^-
   c. O in H_2O

48. Using the VSEPR theory, predict the molecular structure of each of the following molecules.
   a. CCl_4 b. H_2S c. GeI_4

molecule. Boron is surrounded by three bonding pairs of electrons and no lone pairs. The F—B—F bond angle is 120°.

42. Tetrahedral structure with four bonding electron pairs. The bond angle is 109.5°.

43. For biological molecules, a slight change in the geometric structure can completely destroy the molecule's usefulness to a cell or cause a destructive change in the cell.

44. The general molecular structure is determined by the number of electron pairs around the central atom (bonding and lone pairs).

45. One of the four pairs of valence electrons surrounding the nitrogen is a lone pair of electrons. This lone pair does not enter into the description of the molecule's overall shape. While the lone pair does influence the geometry, we name the shape by considering only the atoms in the molecule.

46. In NF_3 the nitrogen is surrounded by four electron pairs (tetrahedral geometry); in BF_3 the boron is surrounded by three electron pairs (trigonal planar).

47. (a) four electron pairs (tetrahedral geometry); (b) four electron pairs (tetrahedral geometry); (c) four electron pairs (tetrahedral geometry)

48. (a) tetrahedral; (b) bent (V-shaped); (c) tetrahedral

49. (a) tetrahedral; (b) tetrahedral; (c) trigonal pyramidal

49. Using the VSEPR theory, predict the molecular structure of each of the following polyatomic ions.
   a. dihydrogen phosphate ion. $H_2PO_4^-$
   b. perchlorate ion, ClO_4^-
   c. sulfite ion, SO_3^{2-}

50. For each of the following molecules or ions, indicate the bond angle expected between the central atom and any two adjacent hydrogen atoms.
   a. H_2O c. NH_4^+
   b. NH_3 d. CH_4

51. Predict the geometric structure of the carbonate ion, CO_3^{2-}. What are the bond angles in this molecule?

52. Predict the geometric structure of the acetylene molecule, C_2H_2. What are the bond angles in this molecule?

Critical Thinking

53. What is *resonance?* Give three examples of molecules or ions that exhibit resonance, and draw Lewis structures for each of the possible resonance forms.

54. In each case, which of the following pairs of bonded elements forms the more polar bond?
   a. S—F or S—Cl
   b. N—O or P—O
   c. C—H or Si—H

55. What do we mean by the *bond energy* of a chemical bond?

56. For each of the following pairs of elements, identify which element would be expected to be more electronegative. It should not be necessary to look at a table of actual electronegativity values.
   a. Be or Ba
   b. N or P
   c. F or Cl

57. In each of the following molecules, which end of the molecule is negative relative to the other end?
   a. carbon monoxide, CO
   b. iodine monobromide, IBr
   c. hydrogen iodide, HI

58. What simple ion does each of the following elements most commonly form?
   a. sodium   e. sulfur
   b. iodine   f. magnesium
   c. potassium   g. aluminum
   d. calcium   h. nitrogen

59. Using the VSEPR theory, predict the molecular structure of each of the following molecules or ions containing multiple bonds.
   a. SO_2
   b. SO_3
   c. HCO_3^- (hydrogen is bonded to oxygen)
   d. HCN

60. Explain the difference between a covalent bond formed between two atoms of the same element and a covalent bond formed between atoms of two different elements.

50. (a) $< 109.5°$; (b) $< 109.5°$; (c) $109.5°$; (d) $109.5°$

51. Trigonal planar, $120°$ bond angles

52. The acetylene molecule is linear, with bond angles of $180°$, because of the presence of the triple bond between carbon atoms.

53. See *Solutions Guide.*

54. (a) S—F; (b) P—O; (c) C—H

55. The energy required to break the bond

56. (a) Be; (b) N; (c) F

57. (a) O; (b) Br; (c) I

58. (a) Na^+; (b) I^-; (c) K^+; (d) Ca^{2+}; (e) S^{2-}; (f) Mg^{2+}; (g) Al^{3+}; (h) N^{3-}

59. (a) bent (or V-shaped); (b) trigonal planar; (c) trigonal planar; (d) linear

60. In a covalent bond formed between two atoms of the same element, the electron pair is shared equally and the bond is nonpolar; in a bond between atoms of different elements, the electron pair is shared unequally and the bond is polar (unless the different elements happen to have the same electronegativity values).

13 Gases

Section	Text Features & Components	Labs, Demonstrations & Activities
Teaching Segment 13A **3 blocks** **pp. 398–415**	**13.1 Pressure** ●	**(LP)** Lesson Plans (Sec 13.1–13.4)	**(TE)** Teaching Support: Demonstration *pp. 400–401* **(TE)** Mini Demo *p. 401* **(SE)** Chemistry in the Laboratory: Gas Laws and Drinking Straws *p. 434* **(LM)** Experiment 51: Gas Laws and Drinking Straws Lab Manual Report Sheets Teacher's Lab Guide
	13.2 Pressure and Boyle's Law ◗	**(TE)** Teaching Support: Historical Background *pp. 404–405*	**(TE)** Mini Demo *p. 403* **(SE)** Chemistry in Action: The Cartesian Diver *p. 404*
	13.3 Volume and Temperature: Charles's Law ● ◗		**(TE)** Teaching Support: Demonstration *pp. 408–409* **(LM)** Experiment 52: Determining Absolute Zero Lab Manual Report Sheets Teacher's Lab Guide
	13.4 Volumes and Moles: Avogadro's Law ● ◗		**(TE)** Mini Demo *p. 412* **(SE)** Chemistry in Action: The Candle and the Tumbler *p. 413* **(LM)** Experiment 53: The P-n Relationship of Gases Lab Manual Report Sheets Teacher's Lab Guide
	continued on next page		

continued on next page

Key **(SE)** Student Edition   **(TE)** Teacher Edition   **(RP)** Teacher Resource Package   **(LM)** Lab Materials
(LP) Lesson Plans   **(AR)** Additional Resources   **⬤** Florida Specific

Chapter Planning Guide

All Learners

- Teaching Tips *pp. 399–400*
- Animation: Single Molecule in a Box *p. 399*
- Chemistry in Motion (6) *p. 400*
- Transparency: Figures 13.2, 13.3 *p. 401*
- Less Proficient Students *p. 25*

- Teaching Tips *p. 403*
- Transparency: Figure 13.4, Table 13.1 *p. 403*
- Animation: Boyles Law • Microscopic Illustration of Boyles Law *p. 403*
- Transparency: Figure 13.6 *p. 405*
- Teaching Tips *pp. 405–406*
- Less Proficient Students *p. 25*

- Transparency: Figure 13.7 *p. 407*
- Teaching Tips *p. 408*
- Animation: Balloon Submersion in Nitrogen • Charles's Law • Microscopic Illustration of Charles's Law *pp. 408–409*
- Chemistry in Motion (7) *p. 408*
- Transparency: Figure 13.8 *p. 408*
- Less Proficient Students *p. 25*

- Teaching Tips *p. 412*
- Transparency: Figure 13.9 *p. 413*
- Team Learning Worksheets (Sec 12.1–12.4) *pp. 69–70*
- Less Proficient Students *p. 25*

Review & Assessment

- Additional Examples *p. 402*
- Self Check *p. 403*
- Questions and Problems *p. 435*
- Key Terms *p. 435*

- Additional Examples *pp. 406–407*
- Self Check *p. 406*
- Key Terms *p. 435*
- Questions and Problems *pp. 435–436*

- What if . . . *p. 409*
- Additional Examples *pp. 409–411*
- Self Check *p. 411*
- Key Terms *p. 435*
- Questions and Problems *p. 436*

- Additional Examples *p. 414*
- Self Check *p. 414*
- Focus Questions (Sec 13.1–13.4) *pp. 414–415*
- Key Terms *p. 435*
- Questions and Problems *p. 436*

Standards

- **NSES** UCP1, UCP3, A1, A2, B2, B4, G1, G2, G3
- **SSS** SC.H.1.4.1

13 Gases

	Section	Text Features & Components	Labs, Demonstrations & Activities
Teaching Segment 13B **2 blocks** **pp. 415–425**	13.5 The Ideal Gas Law ● ◐	**LP** Lesson Plans (Sec 13.5–13.6) **SE** Chemical Impact: Snacks Need Chemistry, Too! *p. 420*	**TE** Teaching Support: Demonstration *pp. 416–417, 420–421* **LM** Experiment 54: Molar Volume and the Universal Gas Constant Lab Manual Report Sheets Teacher's Lab Guide
	13.6 Dalton's Law of Partial Pressures ● ◐	**SE** Top Ten Components of Air *p. 421*	**TE** Teaching Support: Demonstration *pp. 422–423*
Teaching Segment 13C **1 block** **pp. 425–433**	13.7 Laws and Models: A Review ◐	**LP** Lesson Plans (Sec 13.7–13.11)	**TE** Mini Demo *p. 426*
	13.8–13.9 ◐ The Implications of the Kinetic Molecular Theory of Gases The Implicatios of the Kinetic Molecular Theory	**SE** Celebrity Chemical: Carbon Monoxide *p. 427* **SE** Chemical Impact: Signs of Pollution *p. 429*	**TE** Mini Demos *pp. 427–428*
	13.10–13.11 ◐ Real Gases Gas Stoichiometry	**TE** Teaching Tips *p. 430* **SE** Chemical Impact: The Chemistry of Air Bags *p. 432*	**TE** Teaching Support: Demonstration *pp. 430, 432–433*

Key

SE Student Edition

TE Teacher Edition

RP Teacher Resource Package

LM Lab Materials

LP Lesson Plans

AR Additional Resources

⬤ Florida Specific

Technology and Media

 Transparencies
Table 13.1 • Figures 13.2, 13.3, 13.4, 13.6, 13.7, 13.8, 13.9, 13.11, 13.12
Postulates of Kinetic Energy

PowerPoint Slides

 Chemistry in Motion
(6) Collapsing Can
(7) Liquid Nitrogen and Balloons

 Animation Single Molecule in a Box • Boyle's Law • Illustration of Boyles' Law • Balloon Submersion in Nitrogen • Charles's Law • Illustration of Charles's Law • Ideal Gas Law • Visualizing Molecular Motion

⬤ **eEdition CD-ROM**
Easy Planner CD-ROM
English Summaries CD
Spanish Summaries CD

⬤ **Web Site** classzone.com
McDougal Littell Test Generator

Chapter Planning Guide

All Learners	Review & Assessment	Standards
(TE) Active Learning *p. 415* **(Animation)** Animation: Ideal Gas Law *p. 415* **(TE)** Teaching Tips *p. 416, 418* **(TE)** Integrating the Chemical Impact *p. 420* **(AR)** Less Proficient Students *p. 25*	**(TE)** Additional Examples *pp. 416–417, 419* **(SE)** Self Check *pp. 416–419* **(SE)** Key Terms *p. 435* **(SE)** Questions and Problems *pp. 436–437*	**(TE)** NSES UCP1, UCP3, A1, A2, B2, B4 **(SSS)** SSS SC.H.1.4.1
(Transparency) Transparency: Figures 13.11, 13.12 **(RP)** Team Learning Worksheets (Sec 13.5–13.6) *pp. 71–72* **(AR)** Less Proficient Students *p. 25*	**(TE)** Additional Examples *pp. 422, 424* **(SE)** Self Check *p. 423, 425* **(SE)** Focus Questions (Sec 13.5–13.6) *p. 425* **(SE)** Key Terms *p. 435* **(SE)** Questions and Problems *p. 437*	
(TE) Active Learning *p. 425* **(TE)** Teaching Tips *p. 426* **(AR)** Less Proficient Students *p. 25*	**(SE)** Questions and Problems *p. 437*	**(TE)** NSES UCP2, UCP3, A1, A2, B2, B4, E1, E2, F1, F4, F5, F6, G3 **(SSS)** SSS SC.B.1.4.3, SC.G.2.4.1, SC.H.3.4.2, SC.H.3.4.3, SC.H.3.4.6
(TE) Teaching Tips *pp. 426, 427* **(Transparency)** Transparency: Postulates of Kinetic Energy *p. 426* **(Animation)** Animation: Visualizing Molecular Motion *p. 428* **(TE)** Integrating the Chemical Impact *p. 429* **(AR)** Less Proficient Students *p. 26*	**(SE)** Additional Examples *p. 428* **(SE)** Key Terms *p. 435* **(SE)** Questions and Problems *p. 437*	
(TE) Teaching Tips *p. 429* **(RP)** Team Learning Worksheets (Sec 13.7–13.11) *pp. 73–74* **(AR)** Less Proficient Students *p. 26*	**(SE)** What if . . . *p. 430* **(TE)** Additional Examples *pp. 430, 432–433* **(SE)** Self Check *pp. 43–432* **(SE)** Focus Questions (Sec 13.7–13.11) *p. 433* **(SE)** Key Terms *p. 435* **(SE)** Questions and Problems *pp. 437–438*	

Chapter Materials

(TE) Reading Strategy
(AR) English/Spanish Summaries *pp. 20–21*
(AR) Challenge Projects/Problems *pp. 24–25*
(AR) Less Proficient Students *p. 26*
(🔘) English Summary Audio
(🔘) Spanish Summary Audio
(RP) Chapter Review Worksheets (Basic, Review, Challenge)

(SE) Chapter Summary *p. 435*
(SE) Critical Thinking *p. 438–439*
(RP) Solutions Guide
(RP) Chapter Tests
(RP) Test Bank
(🖥) McDougal Littell Test Generator
(AR) Standardized Test Practice
(🔘) FCAT Test 7

Chapter 13: Summarizing in your Journal

Journal writing is an effective reading strategy but may be a challenge to some of the students. When you introduce the concept of summarizing in a journal, you may need to grade each entry so that the students complete them. Then, as the students become more and more involved in writing in their journals, you can occasionally spot-check to be sure that they are keeping up with their summaries.

Explain to the students that a journal is not a place to take notes, but a place to reflect on what they have read or what has been discussed in class. Summarizing material in a journal helps the students organize their thoughts, ideas and questions about the material. Point out that a journal can be formal or informal, and that the goal is to develop ideas in such a way that the student can easily review the material in preparation for a quiz or test.

Point out the following benefits of summarizing in a journal:

• Requires the student to organize thoughts and ideas.

• Provides an opportunity for the students to react to what they are reading or being taught.

• Allows the students to process readings and think through material that might otherwise be forgotten.

• Provides a method of elaborating on notes taken during class or on a reading assignment.

• Clarifies thinking and allows space for the students to shape, add to, or edit their thoughts at a later time if they wish.

• Serves as an effective study tool.

How to Assign Journal Summaries

Journal assignments should be varied so that the students stay interested in the strategy and do not use the same writing technique repeatedly. Require the students to summarize textbook readings one week, class notes one week, a lab experiment one week, and an assigned topic one week. Each weekly assignment will encourage the students to think differently, although there are certain questions that they should ask themselves in each case. Provide the students with the questions shown here to help them write their summaries. Emphasize that they do not have to answer the questions directly, but that they should think about them as they write.

> **Questions to Consider When Summarizing in a Journal**
>
> 1. What points in the material strike you as important?
>
> 2. Have you learned anything new? If so, what did you learn?
>
> 3. Do you have any questions about what you learned?
>
> 4. How does what you learned relate to other information that you have learned in this course?
>
> 5. How did the reading (class/lab) stimulate your thinking?

Techniques for Summarizing a Reading Assignment in a Journal

Encourage the students to keep their journals separate from their notebooks. When they write in the journal, they should write on only one side of the page. They can use the facing page to add to their thoughts or to clarify concepts at a later time.

Require one summary for each chapter section rather than one summary per chapter. Although the students should experiment to find the style that works best for them, recommend that they follow the steps described below for the first few assignments.

Journal Writing Steps

Step 1: Skim the assigned section and take note of whether the section contains vocabulary words and/or formulas.

Step 2: Use an entire page for each summary. If the section contains vocabulary words and formulas, divide the page into three areas: the first half for your own sentences; the next quarter for vocabulary words; and the final quarter for formulas.

Step 3: As you read the section, write one sentence in your own words that summarizes each paragraph. If graphs, tables, or other diagrams in the section present main ideas, write one sentence explaining how they are related to the text. When you finish the section, write a single sentence that summarizes the entire section.

Step 4: Jot down vocabulary words in the middle section of the page and formulas in the bottom section. You can go back and add definitions and examples.

Step 5: Jot down any concepts that you do not understand and leave a few blank lines beneath each concept. Ask your teacher to explain these concepts, and then add a one-sentence summary of each to your journal page.

Step 6: Add anything that you believe is pertinent to your summary at any time—as soon as you finish writing it, the first time you review it, or even three weeks later as you are studying for a test.

Demonstrating Journal Summaries

The best way to demonstrate journal summaries is to provide several examples. Before beginning this chapter, write your own journal summaries for the first four sections. After presenting the *Questions to Consider* and *Journal Writing Steps* provided on these pages, give the students copies of your journal summaries and instruct them to read the summaries after they read the first three sections of the chapter.

For homework, assign journal summaries for the next two teaching segments of the chapter and inform the students that they will be exchanging journals during the next class period. Initially, have the students read one another's journals to better define summarizing in a journal. Emphasize that no two journal summaries will the same, nor should they be. Remind the students that journal writing is intended to be a personal experience for each student—an opportunity for each student to record his or her thoughts about the material being presented.

Chapter 13

Overview

In this Chapter our goals are for the students to:

- Learn about atmospheric pressure and how barometers work

- Learn the various units of pressure

- Understand Boyles Law

- Learn about Charles's Law and absolute zero

- Understand Avogadro's Law

- Understand the ideal gas law and use it in calculations

- Understand the relationship between the partial and total pressures of a gas mixture

- Understand the relationship between laws and models

- Understand the basic postulates of the kinetic molecular theory

- Understand the meaning of temperature

- Describe the properties of real gasses

- Learn about the molar volume of an ideal gas and the definition of STP

13 Gases

Hoop of steam being ejected from the Bocca Nuova crater on Mount Etna in Sicily.

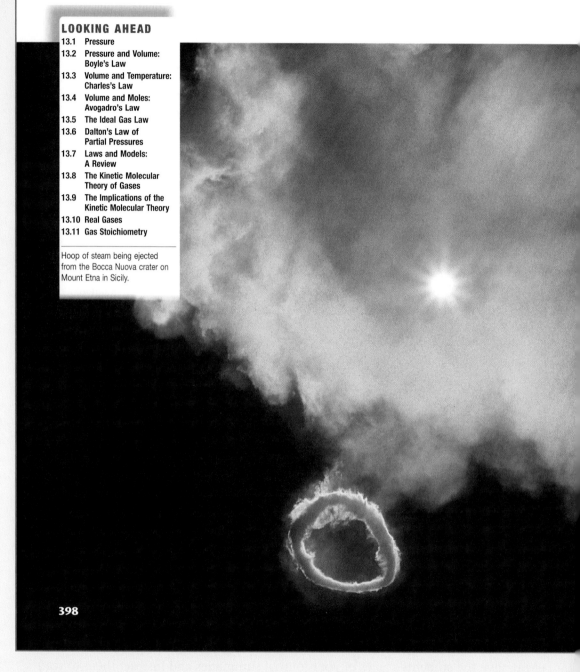

398

We are all familiar with gases. In fact, we live immersed in a gaseous "sea"—a mixture of nitrogen [$N_2(g)$], oxygen [$O_2(g)$], water vapor [$H_2O(g)$], and small amounts of other gases. So it is important from a practical point of view for us to understand the properties of gases. But gases are also important because they provide a nice illustration of the scientific method that we first considered in Chapter 1. Recall that scientists study matter by making *observations* that are then formulated into *laws*. We try to explain the observed behavior by hypothesizing what the components—atoms or molecules—of the substance are doing. This explanation based in the microscopic world is called a *model* or *theory*.

To explore these ideas further, let's consider some observations from daily life. For example, you know that blowing air into a balloon causes it to expand—the volume of the balloon increases as you put more air into it. On the other hand, when you add more air to an inflated basketball, the ball doesn't expand—it gets "harder." In this case the added air increases the pressure inside the ball rather than causing an increase in volume. Although you probably have never tried this, can you guess what happens when an inflated balloon is placed in a freezer? The balloon gets smaller—its volume decreases. (You can easily do this experiment at home.) Thus, when we cool a gas, its volume decreases.

Observations such as these show us that when we make a change in a property of a gas, other properties change in a predictable way. In this chapter we will discuss relationships among the characteristics of gases such as pressure, volume, temperature, and amount of gas. These relationships were discovered by making observations as simple as seeing that a balloon expands when you blow into it, or that a sealed balloon will shrink if you put it in the freezer. These facts lead us to formulate the laws that describe gas behavior. But we also want to explain these observations. Why do gases behave the way they do? To explain gas behavior we will propose a model called the kinetic molecular theory. Because we have taken a microscopic view throughout this text, you probably can predict many aspects of this model already.

The Breitling Orbiter 3, shown over the Swiss Alps, recently completed a nonstop trip around the world.

13.1 Pressure

Objectives: *To learn about atmospheric pressure and the way in which barometers work.*
To learn the various units of pressure.

A gas uniformly fills any container, is easily compressed, and mixes completely with any other gas (see Section 2.3). One of the most obvious properties of a gas is that it exerts pressure on its surroundings. For example, when you blow up a balloon, the air inside pushes against the elastic sides of the balloon and keeps it firm.

The gases most familiar to us form the earth's atmosphere. The pressure exerted by this gaseous mixture that we call air can be dramatically demonstrated by the experiment shown in **Figure 13.1.** A small volume of water is

Themes
Systems, Energy

Skills
Observing, interpreting data, converting

Student Preparation
Assign the students to read Sections 13.1 to 13.4 and to answer the Focus Questions at the end of Section 13.4 before coming to class.

Active Learning
After introducing the material in Sections 13.1 to 13.4 in class, place the students in groups and have them work together on Sections 13.1–13.4: Team Learning Worksheet. Answers and/or discussion of these questions are located in the *Teacher Resources*.

Laboratory
Experiment 51:
Gas Laws and Drinking Straws, In Text

USING TECHNOLOGY

Animation and Video
Animation, Single Molecule in a Box

TEACHING TIPS

- Students have many ideas about gases before they learn about them. This point offers a good opportunity to ask students about their conceptions of how a gas behaves. If you are doing portfolios, they are an excellent place to have students write down their ideas and put them away for later review.

- Use real-world examples to introduce the concept of pressure.

Good examples include automobile tires, basketballs, balloons, and soda bottles.

- This chapter emphasizes the scientific method in action. Focus on the way that observations lead to natural laws and our attempts to explain these laws with theories or models.

- Students should understand that while laws are based on observations, laws do not explain *why* the observed behavior occurs. Laws can help us make predictions, but

they are not explanations. Knowing the law of gravity, for example, allows us to predict that if we drop a pen it will fall to the ground. It does not explain why the pen fell, what gravity is, or how gravity "works."

- To explain our observations, we develop models or theories. A model should be as simple as possible and still answer the desired questions.

- We have taken an atomic/molecular-level perspective throughout

the text, so our model for understanding the behavior of gases is based on looking at a gas as a collection of individual particles.

Figure 13.1
The pressure exerted by the gases in the atmosphere can be demonstrated by boiling water in a can (a), and then turning off the heat and sealing the can. As the can cools, the water vapor condenses, lowering the gas pressure inside the can. This causes the can to crumple (b).

(a)   (b)

Dry air (air from which the water vapor has been removed) is 78.1% N_2 molecules, 20.9% O_2 molecules, 0.9% Ar atoms, and 0.03% CO_2 molecules, along with smaller amounts of Ne, He, CH_4, Kr, and other trace components.

As a gas, water occupies 1300 times as much space as it does as a liquid at 25 °C and atmospheric pressure.

Soon after Torricelli died, a German physicist named Otto von Guericke invented an air pump. In a famous demonstration for the King of Prussia in 1683, Guericke placed two hemispheres together, pumped the air out of the resulting sphere through a valve, and showed that teams of horses could not pull the hemispheres apart. Then, after secretly opening the air valve, Guericke easily separated the hemispheres by hand. The King of Prussia was so impressed that he awarded Guericke a lifetime pension!

placed in a metal can and the water is boiled, which fills the can with steam. The can is then sealed and allowed to cool. Why does the can collapse as it cools? It is the atmospheric pressure that crumples the can. When the can is cooled after being sealed so that no air can flow in, the water vapor (steam) inside the can condenses to a very small volume of liquid water. As a gas, the water vapor filled the can, but when it is condensed to a liquid, the liquid does not come close to filling the can. The H_2O molecules formerly present as a gas are now collected in a much smaller volume of liquid, and there are very few molecules of gas left to exert pressure outward and counteract the air pressure. As a result, the pressure exerted by the gas molecules in the atmosphere smashes the can.

A device that measures atmospheric pressure, the **barometer,** was invented in 1643 by an Italian scientist named Evangelista Torricelli (1608–1647), who had been a student of the famous astronomer Galileo. Torricelli's barometer is constructed by filling a glass tube with liquid mercury and inverting it in a dish of mercury, as shown in **Figure 13.2.** Notice that a large quantity of mercury stays in the tube. In fact, at sea level the height of this column of mercury averages 760 mm. Why does this mercury stay in the tube, seemingly in defiance of gravity? The pressure exerted by the atmospheric gases on the surface of the mercury in the dish keeps the mercury in the tube.

Atmospheric pressure results from the mass of the air being pulled toward the center of the earth by gravity—in other words, it results from the weight of the air. Changing weather conditions cause the atmospheric pressure to vary, so the height of the column of Hg supported by the atmosphere at sea level varies; it is not always 760 mm. The meteorologist who says a "low" is approaching means that the atmospheric pressure is going to decrease. This condition often occurs in conjunction with a storm.

Atmospheric pressure also varies with altitude. For example, when Torricelli's experiment is done in Breckenridge, Colorado (elevation 9600 feet), the atmosphere supports a column of mercury only about 520 mm high because the air is "thinner." That is, there is less air pushing down on the earth's surface at Breckenridge than at sea level.

400   Chapter 13   Gases

Figure 13.2
When a glass tube is filled with mercury and inverted in a dish of mercury at sea level, the mercury flows out of the tube until a column approximately 760 mm high remains (the height varies with atmospheric conditions). The pressure of the atmosphere balances the weight of the column of mercury in the tube.

Empty space (a vacuum)

Hg

Weight of the mercury in the column

760 mm

Weight of the atmosphere (atmospheric pressure)

Units of Pressure

Mercury is used to measure pressure because of its high density. The column of water required to measure a given pressure would be 13.6 times as high as a mercury column.

Because instruments used for measuring pressure (see **Figure 13.3**) often contain mercury, the most commonly used units for pressure are based on the height of the mercury column (in millimeters) that the gas pressure can support. The unit **mm Hg** (millimeters of mercury) is often called the **torr** in honor of Torricelli. The terms *torr* and *mm Hg* are used interchangeably by chemists. A related unit for pressure is the **standard atmosphere** (abbreviated atm).

1 standard atmosphere = 1.000 atm = 760.0 mm Hg = 760.0 torr

Figure 13.3
A device called a manometer is used for measuring the pressure of a gas in a container. The pressure of the gas is equal to *h* (the difference in mercury levels) in units of torr (equivalent to mm Hg). (a) Gas pressure = atmospheric pressure − *h*. (b) Gas pressure = atmospheric pressure + *h*.

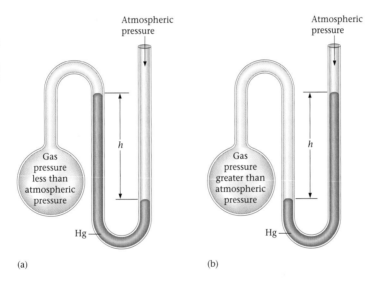

Atmospheric pressure

Atmospheric pressure

h

h

Gas pressure less than atmospheric pressure

Gas pressure greater than atmospheric pressure

Hg

Hg

(a)

(b)

The SI unit for pressure is the **pascal** (abbreviated Pa).

1 standard atmosphere = 101,325 Pa

Thus 1 atmosphere is about 100,000 or 10^5 pascals. Because the pascal is so small we will use it sparingly in this book. A unit of pressure that is employed in the engineering sciences and that we use for measuring tire pressure is pounds per square inch, abbreviated psi.

1.000 atm = 14.69 psi

Sometimes we need to convert from one unit of pressure to another. We do this by using conversion factors. The process is illustrated in Example 13.1.

Example 13.1

Pressure Unit Conversions

The pressure of the air in a tire is measured to be 28 psi. Represent this pressure in atmospheres, torr, and pascals.

Checking the air pressure in a tire.

Solution

To convert from pounds per square inch to atmospheres, we need the equivalence statement

1.000 atm = 14.69 psi

which leads to the conversion factor

$$\frac{1.000 \text{ atm}}{14.69 \text{ psi}}$$

$$28 \text{ psi} \times \frac{1.000 \text{ atm}}{14.69 \text{ psi}} = 1.9 \text{ atm}$$

To convert from atmospheres to torr, we use the equivalence statement

1.000 atm = 760.0 torr

which leads to the conversion factor

$$\frac{760.0 \text{ torr}}{1.000 \text{ atm}}$$

$$1.9 \text{ atm} \times \frac{760.0 \text{ torr}}{1.000 \text{ atm}} = 1.4 \times 10^3 \text{ torr}$$

To change from torr to pascals, we need the equivalence statement

1.000 atm = 101,325 Pa

which leads to the conversion factor

$$\frac{101,325 \text{ Pa}}{1.000 \text{ atm}}$$

$$1.9 \text{ atm} \times \frac{101,325 \text{ Pa}}{1.000 \text{ atm}} = 1.9 \times 10^5 \text{ Pa}$$

MATH

$1.9 \times 760.0 = 1444$

$1444 \Rightarrow 1400 = 1.4 \times 10^3$
Round off

MATH

$1.9 \times 101,325 = 192,517.5$

$192,517.5 \Rightarrow 190,000$
Round off

$190,000 = 1.9 \times 10^5$

Note: The best way to check a problem like this one is to make sure the final units are the ones required.

 Self-Check Exercise 13.1

On a summer day in Breckenridge, Colorado, the atmospheric pressure is 525 mm Hg. What is this air pressure in atmospheres?

13.2 Pressure and Volume: Boyle's Law

Objectives: *To understand the law that relates the pressure and volume of a gas.*
To do calculations involving this law.

Mercury added

Gas   Gas

h

h

Hg

Figure 13.4
A J-tube similar to the one used by Boyle. The pressure on the trapped gas can be changed by adding or withdrawing mercury.

The fact that the constant is sometimes 1.40×10^3 instead of 1.41×10^3 is due to experimental error (uncertainties in measuring the values of *P* and *V*).

The first careful experiments on gases were performed by the Irish scientist Robert Boyle (1627–1691). Using a J-shaped tube closed at one end **(Figure 13.4)**, which he reportedly set up in the multistory entryway of his house, Boyle studied the relationship between the pressure of the trapped gas and its volume. Representative values from Boyle's experiments are given in **Table 13.1**. The units given for the volume (cubic inches) and pressure (inches of mercury) are the ones Boyle used. Keep in mind that the metric system was not in use at this time.

First let's examine Boyle's observations (Table 13.1) for general trends. Note that as the pressure increases, the volume of the trapped gas decreases. In fact, if you compare the data from experiments 1 and 4, you can see that as the pressure is doubled (from 29.1 to 58.2), the volume of the gas is halved (from 48.0 to 24.0). The same relationship can be seen in experiments 2 and 5 and in experiments 3 and 6 (approximately).

TABLE 13.1

A Sample of Boyle's Observations (moles of gas and temperature both constant)

Experiment	Pressure (in. Hg)	Volume (in.^{3})	Pressure × Volume (in. Hg) × (in.^{3})	
			Actual	Rounded*
1	29.1	48.0	1396.8	1.40×10^3
2	35.3	40.0	1412.0	1.41×10^3
3	44.2	32.0	1414.4	1.41×10^3
4	58.2	24.0	1396.8	1.40×10^3
5	70.7	20.0	1414.0	1.41×10^3
6	87.2	16.0	1395.2	1.40×10^3
7	117.5	12.0	1410.0	1.41×10^3

*Three significant figures are allowed in the product because both of the numbers that are multiplied together have three significant figures.

13.2 Pressure and Volume: Boyle's Law **403**

 Answer to Self-Check Exercise 13.1

We know that 1.000 atm = 760.0 mm Hg. So

$$525 \text{ mm Hg} \times \frac{1.000 \text{ atm}}{760.0 \text{ mm Hg}}$$
$$= 0.691 \text{ atm}$$

13.2 Section 13.2

Themes
Systems, Patterns of Change

Skills
Making comparisons, converting, evaluating

TEACHING TIPS

- Boyle's law provides an excellent example of an inverse relationship as well as an opportunity to use graphing to illustrate the application of a math concept. Have students plot the data from Table 13.1 and observe the shape of the graph. This shape (half a hyperbola) is indicative of an inverse relationship, and students should learn to recognize that the equation for an inverse relationship is $xy = k$ or, in this case, $PV = k$. Table 13.1 shows the constant for the data graphed.

- You cannot overemphasize that for Boyle's law to hold true, the temperature and the amount of gas must be held constant. Certain activities, such as filling a tire or a basketball with air, seem on the surface to be at odds with Boyle's law. Students often reason this way: "If I add more gas to a container such as a basketball, the volume and pressure both increase. Thus, as pressure increases, so does volume." Because of this reasoning, students may believe that pressure and volume are directly related.

USING TECHNOLOGY

 Animation and Video

Animation, Boyles Law

Animation, Microscopic Illustration of Boyles Law

MINI-DEMO

For a qualitative demonstration of pressure volume relationships, you can use a syringe that is mounted between two blocks of wood (4″ × 4″ × ½″). The top of the plunger of the syringe is attached to one block and the base of the syringe (with a plastic cap glued to the needle opening to prevent the escape of air) is attached to the other. The apparatus should stand unsupported with air trapped in the syringe. Attach the apparatus to a ringstand to ensure stability during the demonstration. Show students the apparatus and ask what will happen when a chemistry text is added to the top of the apparatus. Add one. Repeat the process, showing students that the volume of gas decreases with increasing "book" pressure.

Chapter 13 Gases **403**

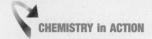

The Cartesian Diver

Materials Each student/group will need a diver and plastic soft-drink bottle. The diver can be made from either a plastic pipet that is cut and fitted with a nut, an inverted test tube, or an eye-dropper that just floats in a plastic soft-drink bottle filled with water. The divers should contain just enough water to float.

To make a diver with the plastic pipet, cut off most of the tip (leave enough of it to fit a hex nut). Fill the pipet about halfway with water and place it in a beaker of water. If the diver sinks, remove a bit of water until the diver just floats. Place the diver in a plastic soft-drink bottle that is filled with water and cap the bottle. The diver should sink easily when the bottle is squeezed. If the diver does not sink easily, remove the diver and add more water to it.

A glass eyedropper can be used as a diver as well (no hex nut is required). See the preceding instructions. In addition, an inverted test tube can function as a diver. Fill a test tube halfway with water, cover the opening with your fingers, invert the tube, and place it in a filled plastic soft-drink bottle.

To expand this activity to a closed diver, you can use condiment packets from fast-food restaurants.

Purpose Students will investigate Boyle's law and density/buoyancy relationships and develop and test their own ideas.

Discussion When you squeeze the soft-drink bottle, water enters the diver. The gas (air) in the diver is compressible, whereas the water is relatively noncompressible. When water enters the diver, the volume of the gas is decreased (due to the increased pressure caused by squeezing the bottle). The diver now has more mass but the same volume (overall volume of the diver—some students will find this distinction confusing). The density of the diver is increased and the diver will sink. When you release the bottle, the pressure on the trapped air decreases. The volume of the air therefore increases, which pushes water out of the diver. The diver then rises.

CHEMISTRY in ACTION

The Cartesian Diver

1. Obtain a Cartesian diver from your teacher.
2. Squeeze the diver. What happens? Make careful observations.
3. Explain your observations. Feel free to experiment with the diver. It is a good idea to take the diver apart and experiment with variables (for example, what happens if the bottle is not completely filled with water?). Be sure to reconstruct the diver so that it works again—this effort will help you to better understand it.

CHEMISTRY

For Boyle's law to hold, the amount of gas (moles) must not be changed. The temperature must also be constant.

Figure 13.5
A plot of P versus V from Boyle's data in Table 13.1.

We can see the relationship between the volume of a gas and its pressure more clearly by looking at the product of the values of these two properties ($P \times V$) using Boyle's observations. This product is shown in the last column of Table 13.1. Note that for all the experiments,

$$P \times V = 1.4 \times 10^3 \text{ (in Hg)} \times \text{in.}^3$$

with only a slight variation due to experimental error. Other similar measurements on gases show the same behavior. This means that the relationship of the pressure and volume of a gas can be expressed in words as

pressure times volume equals a constant

or in terms of an equation as

$$PV = k$$

which is called **Boyle's law**, where k is a constant at a specific temperature for a given amount of gas. For the data we used from Boyle's experiment, $k = 1.41 \times 10^3$ (in Hg) $\times$ in.^{3}

It is often easier to visualize the relationships between two properties if we make a graph. **Figure 13.5** uses the data given in Table 13.1 to show how pressure is related to volume. This relationship, called a plot or a graph, shows that V decreases as P increases. When this type of relationship exists, we say that volume and pressure are inversely related or *inversely proportional;* when one increases, the other decreases. Boyle's law is illustrated by the gas samples in **Figure 13.6**.

Figure 13.6
Illustration of Boyle's law. These three flasks contain the same number of molecules. At 298 K, $P \times V = 1$ L atm in all three flasks.

$P = 1$ atm $\qquad$ $P = 2$ atm $\qquad$ $P = 4$ atm

$V = 1$ L $\qquad$ $V = 0.50$ L $\qquad$ $V = 0.25$ L
$T = 298$ K $\qquad$ $T = 298$ K $\qquad$ $T = 298$ K

404 Chapter 13 Gases

TEACHING SUPPORT
Historical Background

Robert Boyle
Robert Boyle, the fourteenth child of the Earl of Cork, was born at Lismore Castle, Ireland, on January 25, 1627. Boyle was a true child prodigy who began studies at Eton at age eight (he was already speaking Greek and Latin) and traveled through Europe with a tutor at age eleven.

On his travels he observed demonstrations by the German Otto von Guericke, who had developed an air pump. Guericke's favorite "trick" was to seal two hemispheres together and then remove the air from inside. The difference in pressure between the atmosphere and the inside of the sphere was so great that teams of horses pulling in opposite directions could not separate them. Guericke would then discreetly let the air back in and separate the hemispheres himself. Boyle was intrigued by this act and proceeded to develop an even better air pump. Using this pump he evacuated a chamber and demonstrated that a feather and a lump of coal both fall at the same rate. He also showed that sound could not travel in a vacuum. Eventually Boyle carried out his famous experiments in which he dis-

Boyle's law means that if we know the volume of a gas at a given pressure, we can predict the new volume if the pressure is changed, *provided that neither the temperature nor the amount of gas is changed.* For example, if we represent the original pressure and volumes as P_1 and V_1 and the final values as P_2 and V_2, using Boyle's law we can write

$$P_1 V_1 = k$$

and

$$P_2 V_2 = k$$

We can also say

$$P_1 V_1 = k = P_2 V_2$$

or simply

$$P_1 V_1 = P_2 V_2$$

This is really another way to write Boyle's law. We can solve for the final volume (V_2) by dividing both sides of the equation by P_2.

$$\frac{P_1 V_1}{P_2} = \frac{P_2 V_2}{P_2}$$

Canceling the P_2 terms on the right gives

$$\frac{P_1}{P_2} \times V_1 = V_2$$

or

$$V_2 = V_1 \times \frac{P_1}{P_2}$$

This equation tells us that we can calculate the new gas volume (V_2) by multiplying the original volume (V_1) by the ratio of the original pressure to the final pressure (P_1/P_2), as illustrated in Example 13.2.

Example 13.2

Calculating Volume Using Boyle's Law

Freon-12 (the common name for the compound CCl_2F_2) was once widely used in refrigeration systems, but has now been replaced by other compounds that do not lead to the breakdown of the protective ozone in the upper atmosphere. Consider a 1.5-L sample of gaseous CCl_2F_2 at a pressure of 56 torr. If pressure is changed to 150 torr at a constant temperature,

a. Will the volume of the gas increase or decrease?

b. What will be the new volume of the gas?

Solution

a. As the first step in a gas law problem, always write down the information given, in the form of a table showing the initial and final conditions.

(continued)

13.2   Pressure and Volume: Boyle's Law   **405**

USING TECHNOLOGY

 Figure 13.6

TEACHING TIPS

- Emphasize to students that in Boyle's law the temperature and the amount of gas are both constant. This idea is important in working through the initial laws toward the ideal gas equation.

- Many beginning students have trouble with the algebra required to rearrange the law to solve for the variable. Remind them that mathematics and chemistry work together and that this resolution is the same as solving an algebra problem.

- Students sometimes confuse the idea of an inverse relationship with that of a line having a negative slope. A linear graph with a negative slope represents a direct relationship between the variables. To make this distinction clear, focus on the idea that *inverse* means the relationship varies with the reciprocal (1/x). Have students examine the shape of the graph in Figure 13.5. Ask them to tell you what will happen to the pressure as the volume becomes extremely large (the pressure approaches zero, but will never reach zero). As the volume gets smaller, the pressure increases (as the volume goes to zero, the pressure goes to infinity). Thus the graph must not touch the axes—it is a hyperbola, not a straight line.

covered the inverse relationship between gas volume and pressure.

In 1661 Boyle published *The Sceptical Chymist,* in which he abandoned the ancient view of the four elements and took the position that an element must be defined by experiment.

Boyle died in London on December 30, 1691.

1. A sample of helium gas has a pressure of 3.54 atm in a container with a volume of 23.1 L. This sample is transferred to a new container and the pressure is measured to be 1.87 atm. What is the volume of the new container? Assume constant temperature. **43.7 L**

2. A steel tank of argon gas has a pressure of 34.6 atm. If all of the argon is transferred to a new tank with a volume of 456 L, the pressure is measured to be 2.94 atm. What is the volume of the original container? Assume constant temperature. **38.7 L**

TEACHING TIP

Remind students that they should check their answers to make sure that they "make sense." Go through an example and show students how to predict in advance whether volume and pressure should increase or decrease. Then show them that this check allows them to see whether the answer makes sense.

 Answer to Self-Check Exercise 13.2

Initial Conditions	Final Conditions
P_1 = 635 torr	P_2 = 785 torr
V_1 = 1.51 L	V_2 = ?

Solving Boyle's law ($P_1V_1 = P_2V_2$) for V_2 gives

$$V_2 = V_1 \times P_1/P_2$$

$$= 1.51 \text{ L} \times \frac{635 \text{ torr}}{785 \text{ torr}}$$

$$= 1.22 \text{ L}$$

Note that the volume decreased, as the increase in pressure led us to expect.

(continued)

Initial Conditions	Final Conditions
P_1 = 56 torr	P_2 = 150 torr
V_1 = 1.5 L	V_2 = ?

Drawing a picture also is often helpful. Notice that the pressure is increased from 56 torr to 150 torr, so the volume must decrease:

We can verify this by using Boyle's law in the form

$$V_2 = V_1 \times \frac{P_1}{P_2}$$

Note that V_2 is obtained by "correcting" V_1 using the ratio P_1/P_2. Because P_1 is less than P_2, the ratio P_1/P_2 is a fraction that is less than 1. Thus V_2 must be a fraction of (smaller than) V_1; the volume decreases.

b. We calculate V_2 as follows:

$$V_2 = V_1 \times \frac{P_1}{P_2} = 1.5 \text{ L} \times \frac{56 \text{ torr}}{150 \text{ torr}} = 0.56 \text{ L}$$

The volume of the gas decreases from 1.5 to 0.56 L. This change is in the expected direction.

 Self-Check Exercise 13.2

A sample of neon to be used in a neon sign has a volume of 1.51 L at a pressure of 635 torr. Calculate the volume of the gas after it is pumped into the glass tubes of the sign, where it shows a pressure of 785 torr.

$P_1V_1 \Rightarrow P_2V_2$

PROBLEM SOLVING

The fact that the volume decreases in Example 13.2 makes sense because the pressure was increased. *To help catch errors, make it a habit to check whether an answer to a problem makes physical sense.*

Neon signs in Hong Kong.

Example 13.3

Calculating Pressure Using Boyle's Law

In an automobile engine the gaseous fuel–air mixture enters the cylinder and is compressed by a moving piston before it is ignited. In a certain engine the initial cylinder volume is 0.725 L. After the piston moves up, the volume is 0.075 L. The fuel–air mixture initially has a pressure of 1.00 atm. Calculate the pressure of the compressed fuel–air mixture, assuming that both the temperature and the amount of gas remain constant.

MATH

$$P_1 V_1 = P_2 V_2$$
$$\frac{P_1 V_1}{V_2} = \frac{P_2 \cancel{V_2}}{\cancel{V_2}}$$
$$P_1 \times \frac{V_1}{V_2} = P_2$$

MATH

$$\frac{0.725}{0.075} = 9.666\ldots$$

$9.666 \Rightarrow 9.7$

Round off

Solution

We summarize the given information in the following table:

Initial Conditions	Final Conditions
$P_1 = 1.00$ atm	$P_2 = ?$
$V_1 = 0.725$ L	$V_2 = 0.075$ L

Then we solve Boyle's law in the form $P_1 V_1 = P_2 V_2$ for P_2 by dividing both sides by V_2 to give the equation

$$P_2 = P_1 \times \frac{V_1}{V_2} = 1.00 \text{ atm} \times \frac{0.725 \cancel{L}}{0.075 \cancel{L}} = 9.7 \text{ atm}$$

Note that the pressure must increase because the volume gets smaller. Pressure and volume are inversely related.

13.3 Volume and Temperature: Charles's Law

Objectives: *To learn about absolute zero.*
To learn about the law relating the volume and temperature of a sample of gas at constant moles and pressure, and to do calculations involving that law.

In the century following Boyle's findings, scientists continued to study the properties of gases. The French physicist Jacques Charles (1746–1823), who was the first person to fill a balloon with hydrogen gas and who made the first solo balloon flight, showed that the volume of a given amount of gas (at constant pressure) increases with the temperature of the gas. That is, the volume increases when the temperature increases. A plot of the volume of a given sample of gas (at constant pressure) versus its temperature (in Celsius degrees) gives a straight line. This type of relationship is called *linear*, and this behavior is shown for several gases in **Figure 13.7**.

The solid lines in Figure 13.7 are based on actual measurements of temperature and volume for the gases listed. As we cool the gases

Figure 13.7
Plots of V (L) versus T (°C) for several gases.
Note that each sample of gas contains a different number of moles to spread out the plots.

13.3 Volume and Temperature: Charles's Law **407**

The air in a balloon expands when it is heated. This means that some of the air escapes from the balloon, lowering the air density inside and thus making the balloon buoyant.

CHEMISTRY

Temperatures such as 0.00000002 K have been obtained in the laboratory, but 0 K has never been reached.

From Figure 13.8 for Helium

V (L)	T (K)	b
0.7	73	0.01
1.7	173	0.01
2.7	273	0.01
3.7	373	0.01
5.7	573	0.01

they eventually liquefy, so we cannot determine any experimental points below this temperature. However, when we extend each straight line (which is called *extrapolation* and is shown here by a dashed line), something very interesting happens. *All* of the lines extrapolate to zero volume at the same temperature: −273 °C. This suggests that −273 °C is the lowest possible temperature, because a negative volume is physically impossible. In fact, experiments have shown that matter cannot be cooled to temperatures lower than −273 °C. Therefore, this temperature is defined as **absolute zero** on the Kelvin scale.

When the volumes of the gases shown in Figure 13.7 are plotted against temperature on the Kelvin scale rather than the Celsius scale, the plots shown in **Figure 13.8** result. These plots show that the volume of each gas is *directly proportional to the temperature* (in kelvins) and extrapolates to zero when the temperature is 0 K. Let's illustrate this statement with an example. Suppose we have 1 L of gas at 300 K. When we double the temperature of this gas to 600 K (without changing its pressure), the volume also doubles, to 2 L. Verify this type of behavior by looking carefully at the lines for various gases shown in Figure 13.8.

The direct proportionality between volume and temperature (in kelvins) is represented by the equation known as **Charles's law:**

$$V = bT$$

where *T* is in kelvins and *b* is the proportionality constant. Charles's law holds for a given sample of gas at constant pressure. It tells us that (for a given amount of gas at a given pressure) the volume of the gas is directly proportional to the temperature on the Kelvin scale:

$$V = bT \quad \text{or} \quad \frac{V}{T} = b = \text{constant}$$

Figure 13.8
Plots of *V* versus *T* as in Figure 13.7, except that here the Kelvin scale is used for temperature.

408   Chapter 13   Gases

Notice that in the second form, this equation states that the *ratio* of V to T (in kelvins) must be constant. (This is shown for helium in the margin.) Thus, when we triple the temperature (in kelvins) of a sample of gas, the volume of the gas triples also.

$$\frac{V}{T} = \frac{3 \times V}{3 \times T} = b = \text{constant}$$

We can also write Charles's law in terms of V_1 and T_1 (the initial conditions) and V_2 and T_2 (the final conditions).

$$\frac{V_1}{T_1} = b \quad \text{and} \quad \frac{V_2}{T_2} = b$$

Thus

$$\frac{V_1}{T_1} = \frac{V_2}{T_2}$$

We will illustrate the use of this equation in Examples 13.4 and 13.5.

Example 13.4

Calculating Volume Using Charles's Law, I

A 2.0-L sample of air is collected at 298 K and then cooled to 278 K. The pressure is held constant at 1.0 atm.

a. Does the volume increase or decrease?

b. Calculate the volume of the air at 278 K.

Solution

PROBLEM SOLVING

$\frac{V_1}{T_1} \Rightarrow \frac{V_2}{T_2}$

Temperature smaller, volume smaller

a. Because the gas is cooled, the volume of the gas must decrease:

$$\frac{V}{T} = \text{constant}$$

T is decreased, so *V* must decrease to maintain a constant ratio

b. To calculate the new volume, V_2, we will use Charles's law in the form

$$\frac{V_1}{T_1} = \frac{V_2}{T_2}$$

We are given the following information:

Initial Conditions	Final Conditions
$T_1 = 298$ K	$T_2 = 278$ K
$V_1 = 2.0$ L	$V_2 = ?$

(continued)

13.3 Volume and Temperature: Charles's Law **409**

(continued)

We want to solve the equation

$$\frac{V_1}{T_1} = \frac{V_2}{T_2}$$

for V_2. We can do this by multiplying both sides by T_2 and canceling.

$$T_2 \times \frac{V_1}{T_1} = \frac{V_2}{\cancel{T_2}} \times \cancel{T_2} = V_2$$

Thus

$$V_2 = T_2 \times \frac{V_1}{T_1} = 278\ \cancel{K} \times \frac{2.0\ \text{L}}{298\ \cancel{K}} = 1.9\ \text{L}$$

Note that the volume gets smaller when the temperature decreases, just as we predicted.

Additional Examples

1. A sample of oxygen gas has a volume of 4.55 L at 25 °C. Calculate the volume of the oxygen gas when the temperature is raised to 45 °C. Assume constant pressure. **4.86 L**

2. A sample of hydrogen gas is collected at 34 °C and heated to 68 °C. At 68 °C the volume of hydrogen is 26.0 L. Calculate the volume of the hydrogen sample at 34 °C. **23.4 L**

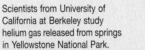

Example 13.5

Calculating Volume Using Charles's Law, II

A sample of gas at 15 °C (at 1 atm) has a volume of 2.58 L. The temperature is then raised to 38 °C (at 1 atm).

a. Does the volume of the gas increase or decrease?

b. Calculate the new volume.

Solution

a. In this case we have a given sample (constant amount) of gas that is heated from 15 °C to 38 °C *while the pressure is held constant*. We know from Charles's law that the volume of a given sample of gas is directly proportional to the temperature (at constant pressure). So the increase in temperature will *increase* the volume; the new volume will be greater than 2.58 L.

Scientists from University of California at Berkeley study helium gas released from springs in Yellowstone National Park.

b. To calculate the new volume, we use Charles's law in the form

$$\frac{V_1}{T_1} = \frac{V_2}{T_2}$$

We are given the following information:

Initial Conditions	Final Conditions
$T_1 = 15\ °C$	$T_2 = 38\ °C$
$V_1 = 2.58\ \text{L}$	$V_2 = ?$

As is often the case, the temperatures are given in Celsius degrees. However, for us to use Charles's law, the temperature *must be in kelvins*. Thus we must convert by adding 273 to each temperature.

Initial Conditions | Final Conditions
$T_1 = 15\ °C = 15 + 273$ | $T_2 = 38\ °C = 38 + 273$
$= 288\ K$ | $= 311\ K$
$V_1 = 2.58\ L$ | $V_2 = ?$

Solving for V_2 gives

$$V_2 = V_1 \times \frac{T_2}{T_1} = 2.58\ L\left(\frac{311\ \cancel{K}}{288\ \cancel{K}}\right) = 2.79\ L$$

The new volume (2.79 L) is greater than the initial volume (2.58 L), as we expected.

 Self-Check Exercise 13.3

A child blows a bubble that contains air at 28 °C and has a volume of 23 cm³ at 1 atm. As the bubble rises, it encounters a pocket of cold air (temperature 18 °C). If there is no change in pressure, will the bubble get larger or smaller as the air inside cools to 18 °C? Calculate the new volume of the bubble.

Notice from Example 13.5 that we adjust the volume of a gas for a temperature change by multiplying the original volume by the ratio of the Kelvin temperatures—final (T_2) over initial (T_1). Remember to check whether your answer makes sense. When the temperature increases (at constant pressure), the volume must increase, and vice versa.

Example 13.6

Calculating Temperature Using Charles's Law

In former times, gas volume was used as a way to measure temperature using devices called gas thermometers. Consider a gas that has a volume of 0.675 L at 35 °C and 1 atm pressure. What is the temperature (in units of °C) of a room where this gas has a volume of 0.535 L at 1 atm pressure?

Solution

The information given in the problem is

Initial Conditions | Final Conditions
$T_1 = 35\ °C = 35 + 273 = 308\ K$ | $T_2 = ?$
$V_1 = 0.0675\ L$ | $V_2 = 0.535\ L$
$P_1 = 1\ atm$ | $P_2 = 1\ atm$

The pressure remains constant, so we can use Charles's law in the form

$$\frac{V_1}{T_1} = \frac{V_2}{T_2}$$

and solve for T_2. First we multiply both sides by T_2.

(continued)

Because the temperature of the gas inside the bubble decreases (at constant pressure), the bubble gets smaller. The conditions are

Initial Conditions
$T_1 = 28\ °C = 28 + 273 = 301\ K$
$V_1 = 23\ cm^3$

Final Conditions
$T_2 = 18\ °C = 18 + 273 = 291\ K$
$V_2 = ?$

Solving Charles's law,

$$\frac{V_1}{T_1} = \frac{V_2}{T_2}$$

for V_2 gives

$$V_2 = V_1 \times \frac{T_2}{T_1} = 23\ cm^3$$
$$\times \frac{291\ \cancel{K}}{301\ \cancel{K}} = 22\ cm^3$$

Additional Examples

1. Consider a gas with a volume of 5.65 L at 27 °C and 1 atm pressure. At what temperature will this gas have a volume of 6.69 L and 1 atm pressure?
   82 °C (355 K)

2. Consider a gas with a volume of 9.25 L at 47 °C and 1 atm pressure. At what temperature does this gas have a volume of 3.50 L and 1 atm pressure?
   −152 °C (121 K)

(continued)

$$T_2 \times \frac{V_1}{T_1} = \frac{V_2}{\cancel{P_2}} \times \cancel{P_2} = V_2$$

Next we multiply both sides by T_1.

$$\cancel{P_1} \times T_2 \times \frac{V_1}{\cancel{P_1}} = T_1 \times V_2$$

This gives

$$T_2 \times V_1 = T_1 \times V_2$$

Now we divide both sides by V_1 (multiply by $1/V_1$),

$$\frac{1}{\cancel{V_1}} \times T_2 \times \cancel{V_1} = \frac{1}{V_1} \times T_1 \times V_2$$

and obtain

$$T_2 = T_1 \times \frac{V_2}{V_1}$$

We have now isolated T_2 on one side of the equation, and we can do the calculation.

$$T_2 = T_1 \times \frac{V_2}{V_1} = (308 \text{ K}) \times \frac{0.535 \cancel{L}}{0.675 \cancel{L}} = 244 \text{ K}$$

To convert from units of K to units of °C, we subtract 273 from the Kelvin temperature.

$$T_{°C} = T_K - 273 = 244 - 273 = -29 \text{ °C}$$

The room is very cold; the temperature is −29 °C.

13.4 Volume and Moles: Avogadro's Law

Objective: *To understand the law relating the volume and the number of moles of a sample of gas at constant temperature and pressure, and to do calculations involving this law.*

What is the relationship between the volume of a gas and the number of molecules present in the gas sample? Experiments show that when the number of moles of gas is doubled (at constant temperature and pressure), the volume doubles. In other words, the volume of a gas is directly proportional to the number of moles if temperature and pressure remain constant. **Figure 13.9** illustrates this relationship, which can also be represented by the equation

$$V = an \qquad \text{or} \qquad \frac{V}{n} = a$$

where V is the volume of the gas, n is the number of moles, and a is the proportionality constant. Note that this equation means that the ratio of V to n is constant as long as the temperature and pressure remain constant. Thus,

---

Section 13.4

Themes
Systems, Patterns of Change

Skills
Making comparisons, evaluating

Laboratory
Experiment 53:
The P-n Relationship of Gases, CBL

TEACHING TIP

At this point all four variables (P, V, T, and n) have been used in gas law problems. Now is an excellent time to focus on problem-solving skills. Have students write down what they know from the problem, what they are looking for, and what they need to know to find it.

MINI-DEMO

As a qualitative demonstration of Avogadro's law, you can blow up a balloon. Discuss about why this scenario is a constant-pressure situation (since the balloon is very flexible, the pressure inside the balloon is essentially always equal to the atmospheric pressure). You can also place a small piece of dry ice in an inflated balloon and tie it. As the dry ice sublimes (and the moles of gas increase), the volume of the balloon will increase.

Figure 13.9
The relationship between
volume V and number of moles
n. As the number of moles is
increased from 1 to 2 (a to b),
the volume doubles. When the
number of moles is tripled
(c), the volume is also tripled.
The temperature and pressure
remain the same in these cases.

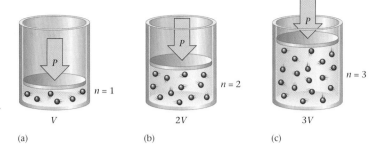

when the number of moles of gas is increased by a factor of 5, the volume also increases by a factor of 5,

$$\frac{V}{n} = \frac{5 \times V}{5 \times n} = a = \text{constant}$$

and so on. In words, this equation means that *for a gas at constant temperature and pressure, the volume is directly proportional to the number of moles of gas*. This relationship is called **Avogadro's law** after the Italian scientist Amadeo Avogadro, who first postulated it in 1811.

For cases where the number of moles of gas is changed from an initial amount to another amount (at constant T and P), we can represent Avogadro's law as

$$\frac{V_1}{n_1} = a = \frac{V_2}{n_2}$$

Initial   Final
amount   amount

or

$$\frac{V_1}{n_1} = \frac{V_2}{n_2}$$

We will illustrate the use of this equation in Example 13.7.

CHEMISTRY in ACTION

The Candle and the Tumbler

1. Light a candle and let some wax drip onto the bottom of a glass that is taller than the candle. Blow out the candle and fix the candle to the glass before the wax solidifies.

2. Add water to the glass until the candle is about half-submerged. Do not get the wick of the candle wet.

3. Light the candle. Take a test tube that is wider than the candle and quickly place it over the candle, submerging the opening of the test tube. What happens? Make careful observations.

4. Explain your results.

13.4   Volume and Moles: Avogadro's Law   **413**

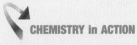

CHEMISTRY in ACTION

The Candle and the Tumbler

Materials Each student/group will need a candle, a glass, a test tube that fits over the candle, clay, and matches.

Purpose Students will better understand the gas laws and the kinetic molecular theory.

Discussion This experiment involves a complex system. As the test tube is placed over the flame, the air inside the test tube is heated, causing the air to expand and allowing some to escape the test tube (this release can sometimes be evidenced by the bubbling of air through the water if the test tube is placed over the candle and into the water with the correct speed). The reaction consumes oxygen (and generates carbon dioxide and water) and eventually the flame goes out. Once the flame is out, the air cools. The amount of gas inside the test tube remains constant, but a decrease in temperature gives rise to a lower pressure. Atmospheric pressure pushes water into the test tube until the pressure inside the tube and the weight of the water equal the atmospheric pressure. Of course, oxygen is consumed in the reaction, but carbon dioxide and water are generated. While this reaction gives rise to a net decrease in moles of gas, the decrease is not enough to account for the amount of water that enters the test tube.

Many students initially claim that the fire uses up oxygen, and therefore the amount of gas inside the tube is less after the reaction than before it takes place. Because of this change, they will say, the pressure is decreased and atmospheric pressure will push the water into the tube.

Although this explanation is incorrect, it involves good thinking on the part of students. First, they know that oxygen is used up in the process of burning. Second, they understand that a decrease in the amount of gas will cause a decrease in pressure. Third, they know that atmospheric pressure will force water into the tube. In fact, this idea is so attractive that many texts (usually at the middle school level) use this activity as a demonstration that air is about 20% oxygen by volume; having the volume change by about 15%–25% is common.

Ultimately, the idea that oxygen being used up is the sole cause of the rise in water level fails for several reasons. Most importantly, it disregards the fact that another gas (carbon dioxide) is a product of the reaction. It also neglects any effect resulting from a temperature difference. In addition, careful observation will show students that the water level doesn't start rising significantly until the flame goes out. If oxygen being "used up" was the sole cause, the water level would increase smoothly over the course of the reaction. The fact that the water level rises dramatically only after the flame is very low or out suggests that the heat has a great deal to do with this phenomenon.

USING TECHNOLOGY

 Figure 13.9

Additional Examples

1. If 2.55 mol of helium gas occupies a volume of 59.5 L at a particular temperature and pressure, what volume does 7.83 mol of helium occupy under the same conditions?
183 L

2. If 4.35 g of neon gas occupies a volume of 15.0 L at a particular temperature and pressure, what volume does 2.00 g of neon gas occupy under the same conditions?
6.90 L

 Answer to Self-Check Exercise 13.4

Because the temperature and pressure of the two samples are the same, we can use Avogadro's law in the form

$$\frac{V_1}{n_1} = \frac{V_2}{n_2}$$

The following information is given:

Sample 1	Sample 2
$V_1 = 36.7$ L	$V_2 = 16.5$ L
$n_1 = 1.5$ mol	$n_2 = ?$

We can now solve Avogadro's law for the value of n_2 (the moles of N_2 in Sample 2):

$$n_2 = n_1 \times \frac{V_2}{V_1}$$

$$= 1.5 \text{ mol} \times \frac{16.5 \,\cancel{L}}{36.7 \,\cancel{L}}$$

$$= 0.67 \text{ mol}$$

Here n_2 is smaller than n_1, which makes sense in view of the fact that V_2 is smaller than V_1.

Note: We isolate n_2 from Avogadro's law as given above by multiplying both sides of the equation by n_2 and then by n_1/V_1,

$$\left(n_2 \times \frac{n_1}{V_1} \right) \frac{V_1}{n_1}$$

$$= \left(n_2 \times \frac{n_1}{V_1} \right) \frac{V_2}{n_2}$$

to give $n_2 = n_1 \times V_2/V_1$.

 Answer to Focus Questions

1. Mercury is used because of its density. The volume (height) needed is inversely proportional to the density of the substance. The column of mercury is much shorter than that of other liquids at the same pressure.

Example 13.7

Using Avogadro's Law in Calculations

Suppose we have a 12.2-L sample containing 0.50 mol of oxygen gas, O_2, at a pressure of 1 atm and a temperature of 25 °C. If all of this O_2 is converted to ozone, O_3, at the same temperature and pressure, what will be the volume of the ozone formed?

Solution

To do this problem we need to compare the moles of gas originally present to the moles of gas present after the reaction. We know that 0.50 mol of O_2 is present initially. To find out how many moles of O_3 will be present after the reaction, we need to use the balanced equation for the reaction.

$$3O_2(g) \rightarrow 2O_3(g)$$

We calculate the moles of O_3 produced by using the appropriate mole ratio from the balanced equation.

$$0.50 \,\cancel{\text{mol } O_2} \times \frac{2 \text{ mol } O_3}{3 \,\cancel{\text{mol } O_2}} = 0.33 \text{ mol } O_3$$

Avogadro's law states that

$$\frac{V_1}{n_1} = \frac{V_2}{n_2}$$

where V_1 is the volume of n_1 moles of O_2 gas and V_2 is the volume of n_2 moles of O_3 gas. In this case we have

 MATH

$$\frac{V_1}{n_1} = \frac{V_2}{n_2}$$

$$n_2 \times \frac{V_1}{n_1} = \frac{V_2}{\cancel{n_2}} \times \cancel{n_2}$$

$$V_1 \times \frac{n_2}{n_1} = V_2$$

Initial Conditions	Final Conditions
$n_1 = 0.50$ mol	$n_2 = 0.33$ mol
$V_1 = 12.2$ L	$V_2 = ?$

Solving Avogadro's law for V_2 gives

$$V_2 = V_1 \times \frac{n_2}{n_1} = 12.2 \text{ L} \left(\frac{0.33 \,\cancel{\text{mol}}}{0.50 \,\cancel{\text{mol}}} \right) = 8.1 \text{ L}$$

Note that the volume decreases, as it should, because fewer molecules are present in the gas after O_2 is converted to O_3.

✓ **Self-Check Exercise 13.4**

Consider two samples of nitrogen gas (composed of N_2 molecules). Sample 1 contains 1.5 mol of N_2 and has a volume of 36.7 L at 25 °C and 1 atm. Sample 2 has a volume of 16.5 L at 25 °C and 1 atm. Calculate the number of moles of N_2 in Sample 2.

Focus Questions ⭕   Sections 13.1–13.4

1. Mercury is a very toxic substance. Why is it used in barometers and manometers instead of water?
2. What is the SI unit for pressure? What is the unit commonly used in chemistry for pressure? Why aren't they the same?

---

2. The SI unit for pressure is the pascal. In chemistry the most common unit for pressure is the torr or the atmosphere. The pascal is a very small unit, so the numbers would be very large. In chemistry using atm keeps the numbers small.

3.

		Boyle	Charles	Avogadro
a.	constant parameters	T, n	P, n	T, P
b.	variables	P, V	V, T	V, n
c.	graphs	inverse (hyperbola)	direct (line)	direct (line)
d.	laws	$V = k/P$ inverse	$V = kT$ direct	$V = kn$ direct

4. 352 mm Hg

5. 569 mL

3. Compare Boyle's law, Charles's law, and Avogadro's law.
   a. What remains constant?
   b. What are the variables?
   c. What do the graphs for these laws look like?
   d. Write the laws with V isolated. Using these equations and the graphs from part c, which law(s) show a directly proportional relationship? How can you tell?

4. A 1.04-L sample of gas at 759 mm Hg pressure is expanded until its volume is 2.24 L. What is the pressure in the expanded gas sample (at constant temperature)?

5. If 525 mL of gas at 25 °C is heated to 50. °C, at constant pressure, calculate the new volume of the sample.

13.5 The Ideal Gas Law

Objective: *To understand the ideal gas law and use it in calculations.*

We have considered three laws that describe the behavior of gases as it is revealed by experimental observations.

CHEMISTRY
Constant n means a constant number of moles of gas.

$$\text{Boyle's law:} \quad PV = k \quad \text{or} \quad V = \frac{k}{P} \quad \text{(at constant } T \text{ and } n\text{)}$$

$$\text{Charles's law:} \qquad\qquad V = bT \quad \text{(at constant } P \text{ and } n\text{)}$$

$$\text{Avogadro's law:} \qquad\qquad V = an \quad \text{(at constant } T \text{ and } P\text{)}$$

These relationships, which show how the volume of a gas depends on pressure, temperature, and number of moles of gas present, can be combined as follows:

$$V = R\left(\frac{Tn}{P}\right)$$

where R is the combined proportionality constant and is called the **universal gas constant.** When the pressure is expressed in atmospheres and the volume is in liters, R always has the value 0.08206 L atm/K mol. We can rearrange the above equation by multiplying both sides by P,

$$R = 0.08206 \, \frac{\text{L atm}}{\text{K mol}}$$

$$P \times V = \cancel{P} \times R\left(\frac{Tn}{\cancel{P}}\right)$$

to obtain the **ideal gas law** written in its usual form,

$$PV = nRT$$

The ideal gas law involves all the important characteristics of a gas: its pressure (P), volume (V), number of moles (n), and temperature (T). Knowledge of any three of these properties is enough to define completely the condition of the gas, because the fourth property can be determined from the ideal gas law.

It is important to recognize that the ideal gas law is based on experimental measurements of the properties of gases. A gas that obeys this equation is

13.5   The Ideal Gas Law   **415**

13.5 Section 13.5

Themes
Systems, Patterns of Change

Skills
Applying concepts, making comparisons, solving problems

Student Preparation
Assign the students to read Sections 13.5 and 13.6 and to answer the Focus Questions at the end of Section 13.6 before coming to class.

Active Learning
After introducing the material in Sections 13.5 and 13.6 in class, place the students in groups and have them work together on Sections 13.5–13.6: Team Learning Worksheet. Answers and/or discussion of these questions are located in the *Teacher Resources.*

USING TECHNOLOGY

 Animation and Video
Animation, Ideal Gas Law

 Laboratory
Experiment 54:
Molar Volume and the Universal Gas Constant, Microscale

- Remind students that when
they solve problems using
the ideal gas law, all units
for variables must be the
same as those in the gas
constant *R*. Show students
that the units of *R* (except
those for the variable) cancel
with units on numbers given
in the problem.

- Here is another opportunity to
help students improve their
problem-solving skills. Remind them to write down the
information from the problem, decide what they are
solving for, decide what they
need to solve for that variable, and finally solve the
problem. Students should
then consider the answer and
check whether it makes
sense given what they predict should happen.

- Emphasize how the ideal gas
law can be used to derive all
of the other gas laws.

Additional Examples

1. A 2.50-mol sample of nitrogen gas has a volume of 5.50
L at a temperature of 27 °C.
Calculate the pressure of the
nitrogen gas.
11.2 atm

2. A 5.00-mol sample of oxygen
gas has a pressure of 1.25
atm at 22 °C. What volume
does this gas occupy?
96.8 L

 **Answer to Self-Check
Exercise 13.5**

We are given the following information:

$P = 1.00$ atm
$V = 2.70 \times 10^6$ L
$n = 1.10 \times 10^5$ mol

We solve for *T* by dividing both
sides of the ideal gas law by *nR*:

$$\frac{PV}{nR} = \frac{nRT}{nR}$$

to give

$$T = \frac{PV}{nR}$$

$$= \frac{(1.00 \text{ atm})(2.70 \times 10^6 \text{ L})}{(1.10 \times 10^5 \text{ mol})\left(0.08206 \frac{\text{L atm}}{\text{K mol}}\right)}$$

$$= 299 \text{ K}$$

The temperature of the helium is
299 K, or $299 - 273 = 26$ °C.

---

said to behave *ideally*. That is, this equation defines the behavior of an **ideal
gas.** Most gases obey this equation closely at pressures of approximately 1 atm
or lower, when the temperature is approximately 0 °C or higher. You should
assume ideal gas behavior when working problems involving gases in this
text.

The ideal gas law can be used to solve a variety of problems. Example
13.8 demonstrates one type in which you are asked to find one property characterizing the condition of a gas given the other three properties.

Example 13.8

Using the Ideal Gas Law in Calculations

A sample of hydrogen gas, H_2, has a volume of 8.56 L at a temperature of
0 °C and a pressure of 1.5 atm. Calculate the number of moles of H_2 present in this gas sample. (Assume that the gas behaves ideally.)

Solution

In this problem we are given the pressure, volume, and temperature of the
gas: $P = 1.5$ atm, $V = 8.56$ L, and $T = 0$ °C. Remember that the temperature must be changed to the Kelvin scale.

$$T = 0 \text{ °C} = 0 + 273 = 273 \text{ K}$$

We can calculate the number of moles of gas present by using the ideal
gas law, $PV = nRT$. We solve for *n* by dividing both sides by RT:

$$\frac{PV}{RT} = n\frac{RT}{RT}$$

to give

$$\frac{PV}{RT} = n$$

Thus

$$n = \frac{PV}{RT} = \frac{(1.5 \text{ atm})(8.56 \text{ L})}{\left(0.08206 \frac{\text{L atm}}{\text{K mol}}\right)(273 \text{ K})} = 0.57 \text{ mol}$$

 Self-Check Exercise 13.5

A weather balloon contains 1.10×10^5 mol of helium and has a volume
of 2.70×10^6 L at 1.00 atm pressure. Calculate the temperature of the helium in the balloon in kelvins and in Celsius degrees.

Example 13.9

Ideal Gas Law Calculations Involving
Conversion of Units

What volume is occupied by 0.250 mol of carbon dioxide gas at 25 °C and
371 torr?

416 Chapter 13 Gases

Marshmallow Man

Materials
Bag of large marshmallows
Toothpicks
Vacuum pump
Vacuum chamber

Preparation Assemble a marshmallow man from marshmal-
lows and toothpicks. Use a pen

to give him a face. Seat him on
the platform of the vacuum
chamber (you may need to
prop him up with a small
beaker).

Presentation Place the vacuum chamber over the marshmallow man. Attach the vacuum pump and turn it on.
Observe the marshmallow man
getting larger as the pressure
decreases. When the pressure is
released, the marshmallow man

deflates, never to inflate the
same way again.

Teaching Notes A marshmallow has a large amount of air
trapped in the tiny cells in its
structure. As the surrounding
pressure decreases, the cells
swell. If the pump is very
strong, the marshmallow man
may suddenly deflate (the cells
burst).

Variation If you do not have

Solution

We can use the ideal gas law to calculate the volume, but we must first convert pressure to atmospheres and temperature to the Kelvin scale.

$$P = 371 \text{ torr} = 371 \text{ torr} \times \frac{1.000 \text{ atm}}{760.0 \text{ torr}} = 0.488 \text{ atm}$$

$$T = 25 \text{ °C} = 25 + 273 = 298 \text{ K}$$

MATH

$PV = nRT$

$\dfrac{PV}{P} = \dfrac{nRT}{P}$

$V = \dfrac{nRT}{P}$

We solve for V by dividing both sides of the ideal gas law ($PV = nRT$) by P.

$$V = \frac{nRT}{P} = \frac{(0.250 \text{ mol})\left(0.08206 \dfrac{\text{L atm}}{\text{K mol}}\right)(298 \text{ K})}{0.488 \text{ atm}} = 12.5 \text{ L}$$

The volume of the sample of CO_2 is 12.5 L.

✔ Self-Check Exercise 13.6

Radon, a radioactive gas formed naturally in the soil, can cause lung cancer. It can pose a hazard to humans by seeping into houses, and there is concern about this problem in many areas. A 1.5-mol sample of radon gas has a volume of 21.0 L at 33 °C. What is the pressure of the gas?

Note that R has units of L atm/K mol. Accordingly, whenever we use the ideal gas law, we must express the volume in units of liters, the temperature in kelvins, and the pressure in atmospheres. When we are given data in other units, we must first convert to the appropriate units.

The ideal gas law can also be used to calculate the changes that will occur when the conditions of the gas are changed as illustrated in Example 13.10.

Example 13.10

Using the Ideal Gas Law Under Changing Conditions

Suppose we have a 0.240-mol sample of ammonia gas at 25 °C with a volume of 3.5 L at a pressure of 1.68 atm. The gas is compressed to a volume of 1.35 L at 25 °C. Use the ideal gas law to calculate the final pressure.

Solution

In this case we have a sample of ammonia gas in which the conditions are changed. We are given the following information:

Initial Conditions	Final Conditions
$V_1 = 3.5$ L	$V_2 = 1.35$ L
$P_1 = 1.68$ atm	$P_2 = ?$
$T_1 = 25 \text{ °C} = 25 + 273 = 298 \text{ K}$	$T_2 = 25 \text{ °C} = 25 + 273 = 298 \text{ K}$
$n_1 = 0.240$ mol	$n_2 = 0.240$ mol

(continued)

1. A sample of neon gas has a volume of 3.45 L at 25 °C and a pressure of 565 torr. Calculate the number of moles of neon present in this gas sample.
0.105 mol

2. A 0.250-mol sample of argon gas has a volume of 9.00 L at a pressure of 875 mm Hg. What is the temperature (in °C) of the gas?
232 °C

✔ Answer to Self-Check Exercise 13.6

We are given the following information about the radon sample:

$n = 1.5$ mol
$V = 21.0$ L
$T = 33 \text{ °C} = 33 + 273$
$\quad = 306 \text{ K}$
$P = ?$

We solve the ideal gas law ($PV = nRT$) for P by dividing both sides of the equation by V:

$$P = \frac{nRT}{V} =$$

$$\frac{(1.5 \text{ mol})\left(0.08206 \dfrac{\text{L atm}}{\text{K mol}}\right)(306 \text{ K})}{21.0 \text{ L}}$$

$$= 1.8 \text{ atm}$$

Additional Examples

1. Consider a sample of helium gas at 23 °C with a volume of 5.60 L at a pressure of 2.45 atm. The pressure is changed to 8.75 atm and the gas is cooled to 15 °C. Calculate the new volume of the gas using the ideal gas law equation.
1.53 L

2. Consider a sample of helium gas at 28 °C with a volume of 3.80 L at a pressure of 3.15 atm. The gas expands to a volume of 9.50 L and the gas is heated to 43 °C. Calculate the new pressure of the gas using the ideal gas law equation.
1.32 atm

access to a vacuum pump, you can place a single large marshmallow in an Erlenmeyer flask and stopper the flask tightly. Insert the needle of a large plastic syringe through the stopper and remove the air from the flask with one quick pull of the plunger. (Veterinary supply houses carry large syringes.)

TEACHING TIPS

- Encourage students to use the ideal gas law to solve most gas law problems, even when some conditions are not changing. All of the other gas laws can be derived from the ideal gas law. If students understand how to perform this derivation, they need not memorize all the other gas laws. Encourage the use of finesse and understanding to replace the brute force method of memorizing formulas and plugging numbers into them.

- An almost infinite number of gas law problems exist. Expose your students to many different types. Ask them to find mass instead of moles, density, or molar mass for a gas. These types of problems bring together information that students learned earlier in the course and create a more challenging environment.

- By asking different types of questions, you also encourage students to work toward understanding the concepts instead of memorizing formulas and equations.

Answer to Self-Check Exercise 13.7

To solve this problem we take the ideal gas law and separate those quantities that change from those that remain constant (on opposite sides of the equation). In this case volume and temperature change, and number of moles and pressure (and, of course, R) remain constant. So $PV = nRT$ becomes $V/T = nR/P$, which leads to

$$\frac{V_1}{T_1} = \frac{nR}{P} \quad \text{and} \quad \frac{V_2}{T_2} = \frac{nR}{P}$$

Combining these gives

$$\frac{V_1}{T_1} = \frac{nR}{P} = \frac{V_2}{T_2} \quad \text{or}$$

$$\frac{V_1}{T_1} = \frac{V_2}{T_2}$$

We are given

Initial Conditions
$T_1 = 5\,°C = 5 + 273 = 278\ K$
$V_1 = 3.8\ L$

Final Conditions
$T_2 = 86\,°C = 86 + 273 = 359\ K$
$V_2 = ?$

418

Note that both n and T remain constant—only P and V change. Thus we could simply use Boyle's law ($P_1V_1 = P_2V_2$) to solve for P_2. However, we will use the ideal gas law to solve this problem to introduce the idea that one equation—the ideal gas equation—can be used to do almost any gas problem. The key idea here is that in using the ideal gas law to describe a change in conditions for a gas, we always *solve the ideal gas equation in such a way that the variables that change are on one side of the equals sign and the constant terms are on the other side.* That is, we start with the ideal gas equation in the conventional form ($PV = nRT$) and rearrange it so that all the terms that change are moved to one side and all the terms that do not change are moved to the other side. In this case the pressure and volume change, and the temperature and number of moles remain constant (as does R, by definition). So we write the ideal gas law as

$$\underset{\text{Change}}{PV} = \underset{\text{Remain constant}}{nRT}$$

 PROBLEM SOLVING

Does this answer make sense? The volume was decreased (at constant temperature and constant number of moles), which means that the pressure should increase, as the calculation indicates.

Because n, R, and T remain the same in this case, we can write $P_1V_1 = nRT$ and $P_2V_2 = nRT$. Combining these gives

$$P_1V_1 = nRT = P_2V_2 \quad \text{or} \quad P_1V_1 = P_2V_2$$

and

$$P_2 = P_1 \times \frac{V_1}{V_2} = (1.68\ \text{atm})\left(\frac{3.5\ \cancel{L}}{1.35\ \cancel{L}}\right) = 4.4\ \text{atm}$$

✔️ **Self-Check Exercise 13.7**

A sample of methane gas that has a volume of 3.8 L at 5 °C is heated to 86 °C at constant pressure. Calculate its new volume.

Note that in solving Example 13.10, we actually obtained Boyle's law ($P_1V_1 = P_2V_2$) from the ideal gas equation. You might well ask, "Why go to all this trouble?" The idea is to learn to use the ideal gas equation to solve all types of gas law problems. This way you will never have to ask yourself, "Is this a Boyle's law problem or a Charles's law problem?"

We continue to practice using the ideal gas law in Example 13.11. Remember, the key idea is to rearrange the equation so that the quantities that change are moved to one side of the equation and those that remain constant are moved to the other.

Example 13.11

Calculating Volume Changes Using the Ideal Gas Law

A sample of diborane gas, B_2H_6, a substance that bursts into flames when exposed to air, has a pressure of 0.454 atm at a temperature of $-15\,°C$ and a volume of 3.48 L. If conditions are changed so that the temperature is 36 °C and the pressure is 0.616 atm, what will be the new volume of the sample?

Thus

$$V_2 = \frac{T_2 V_1}{T_1}$$

$$= \frac{(359\ \cancel{K})(3.8\ L)}{278\ \cancel{K}} = 4.9\ L$$

Check: Is the answer sensible? In this case the temperature was increased (at constant pressure), so the volume should increase. The answer makes sense.

Note that this problem could be described as a "Charles's law problem." The real advantage of using the ideal gas law is that you need to remember only *one* equation to do virtually any problem involving gases.

Solution

We are given the following information:

Initial Conditions	Final Conditions
$P_1 = 0.454$ atm	$P_2 = 0.616$ atm
$V_1 = 3.48$ L	$V_2 = ?$
$T_1 = -15\ °C = 273 - 15 = 258$ K	$T_2 = 36\ °C = 273 + 36 = 309$ K

Note that the value of n is not given. However, we know that n is constant (that is, $n_1 = n_2$) because no diborane gas is added or taken away. Thus, in this experiment, n is constant and P, V, and T change. Therefore, we rearrange the ideal gas equation ($PV = nRT$) by dividing both sides by T,

$$\frac{PV}{T} = nR$$

Change   Constant

which leads to the equation

$$\frac{P_1V_1}{T_1} = nR = \frac{P_2V_2}{T_2}$$

or

$$\frac{P_1V_1}{T_1} = \frac{P_2V_2}{T_2}$$

We can now solve for V_2 by dividing both sides by P_2 and multiplying both sides by T_2.

$$\frac{1}{P_2} \times \frac{P_1V_1}{T_1} = \frac{P_2V_2}{T_2} \times \frac{1}{P_2} = \frac{V_2}{T_2}$$

$$T_2 \times \frac{P_1V_1}{P_2T_1} = \frac{V_2}{P_2} \times P_2 = V_2$$

That is,

$$\frac{T_2P_1V_1}{P_2T_1} = V_2$$

It is sometimes convenient to think in terms of the ratios of the initial temperature and pressure and the final temperature and pressure. That is,

$$V_2 = \frac{T_2P_1V_1}{T_1P_2} = V_1 \times \frac{T_2}{T_1} \times \frac{P_1}{P_2}$$

Substituting the information given yields

$$V_2 = \frac{309\ K}{258\ K} \times \frac{0.454\ atm}{0.616\ atm} \times 3.48\ L = 3.07\ L$$

MATH

$$PV = nRT$$
$$\frac{PV}{T} = \frac{nRT}{T}$$
$$\frac{PV}{T} = nR$$

💡 **PROBLEM SOLVING**

Always convert the temperature to the Kelvin scale and the pressure to atmospheres when applying the ideal gas law.

✔ **Self-Check Exercise 13.8**

A sample of argon gas with a volume of 11.0 L at a temperature of 13 °C and a pressure of 0.747 atm is heated to 56 °C and a pressure of 1.18 atm. Calculate the final volume.

---

1. Consider a sample of hydrogen gas at 63 °C with a volume of 3.65 L at a pressure of 4.55 atm. The pressure is changed to 2.75 atm and the gas is cooled to -35 °C. Calculate the new volume of the gas.
   4.28 L

2. Consider a sample of oxygen gas at 27 °C with a volume of 9.55 L at a pressure of 2.97 atm. The pressure is changed to 8.25 atm and the gas is heated to 125 °C. Calculate the new volume of the gas using the ideal gas law equation.
   4.56 L

✔ **Answer to Self-Check Exercise 13.8**

We are given the following information:

Initial Conditions
$P_1 = 0.747$ atm
$T_1 = 13\ °C = 13 + 273$
   $= 286$ K
$V_1 = 11.0$ L

Final Conditions
$P_2 = 1.18$ atm
$T_2 = 56\ °C = 56 + 273$
   $= 329$ K
$V_2 = ?$

In this case the number of moles remains constant. Thus we can say

$$\frac{P_1V_1}{T_1} = nR \text{ and } \frac{P_2V_2}{T_2} = nR$$

or

$$\frac{P_1V_1}{T_1} = \frac{P_2V_2}{T_2}$$

Solving for V_2 gives

$$V_2 = V_1 \times \frac{T_2}{T_1} \times \frac{P_1}{P_2} =$$

$$(11.0\ L)\left(\frac{329\ K}{286\ K}\right)\left(\frac{0.747\ atm}{1.18\ atm}\right)$$

$$= 8.01\ L$$

Popcorn is a cereal grain composed mainly of starch and water. Water inside the kernel turns to steam as the kernel is heated. The pressure builds up inside the kernel to approximately 9 atm, then the pericarp splits open and the popcorn pops. During this process the starch expands to form the white portion of the popped corn.

To investigate some of the factors affecting the popping of corn, use the Demonstration given at the bottom of this page.

Student Activity Assign teams of students to bring in a variety of brands of popcorn. Each team will test-pop 20 kernels of its brand and the data will be pooled to determine the percent water in each brand. Have each team determine the mass and volume of 20 kernels of popcorn. Place the kernels into a 250-mL flask and add just enough vegetable oil to cover the kernels. Make a cover for the flask from aluminum foil. Find the mass of the system before popping. Heat the flask until all kernels pop. Remove the foil and allow the steam to escape. After the flask cools, recover it and find the mass of the system after popping. Determine the mass of the water lost and measure the volume of the popped corn. Determine the percent moisture for each brand by finding the ratio of the mass of water lost to the mass of the unpopped corn. Collect the information from all teams, including volume of the unpopped corn, volume of the popped corn, and percent moisture. Compare the data for the different brands of popcorn.

Section 13.6

Themes
Systems, Patterns of Change

Skills
Applying concepts, interpreting diagrams, making comparisons, solving problems

---

CHEMICAL IMPACT

Snacks Need Chemistry, Too!

Have you ever wondered what makes popcorn pop? The popping is linked with the properties of gases. What happens when a gas is heated? Charles's law tells us that if the pressure is held constant, the volume of the gas must increase as the temperature is increased. But what happens if the gas being heated is trapped at a constant volume? We can see what happens by rearranging the ideal gas law ($PV = nRT$) as follows:

$$P = \left(\frac{nR}{V}\right)T$$

When n, R, and V are held constant, the pressure of a gas is directly proportional to the temperature. Thus, as the temperature of the trapped gas increases, its pressure also increases. This is exactly what happens inside a kernel of popcorn as it is heated. The moisture inside the kernel vaporized by the heat produces increasing pressure. The pressure finally becomes so great that the kernel breaks open, allowing the starch inside to expand to about 40 times its original size.

What's special about popcorn? Why does it pop while "regular" corn doesn't? William da Silva, a biologist at the University of Campinas in Brazil, has traced the "popability" of popcorn to its outer casing, called the pericarp. The molecules in the pericarp of popcorn, which are packed in a much more orderly way than in regular corn, transfer heat unusually quickly, producing a very fast pressure jump that pops the kernel. In addition, because the pericarp of popcorn is much thicker and stronger than that of regular corn, it can withstand more pressure, leading to a more explosive pop when the moment finally comes.

Popcorn popping.

The equation obtained in Example 13.11,

$$\frac{P_1V_1}{T_1} = \frac{P_2V_2}{T_2}$$

is often called the **combined gas law** equation. It holds when the amount of gas (moles) is held constant. While it may be convenient to remember this equation, it is not necessary because you can always use the ideal gas equation.

13.6 Dalton's Law of Partial Pressures

Objective: *To understand the relationship between the partial and total pressures of a gas mixture, and to use this relationship in calculations.*

Many important gases contain a mixture of components. One notable example is air. Scuba divers who are going deeper than 150 feet use another important mixture, helium and oxygen. Normal air is not used because the nitrogen present dissolves in the blood in large quantities as a result of the high pressures experienced by the diver under several hundred feet of water. When the diver returns too quickly to the surface, the nitrogen bubbles out of the blood just as soda fizzes when it's opened, and the diver gets

---

TEACHING SUPPORT
Demonstration

The Scoop on the Pop in Popcorn

Materials
2 cups popcorn
Hot-air popcorn popper
2-cup graduated measuring cup

Preparation The day before the demonstration, dry $\frac{1}{3}$ cup popcorn kernels in a 200 °F oven for 8–10 hours. Soak $\frac{1}{3}$ cup popcorn kernels in water for 2–3 hours and pat dry. Break the hulls of $\frac{1}{3}$ cup popcorn kernels by using a knife or poking several holes in each kernel (student volunteers in class can handle this task during the first two popping experiments).

Presentation Explain that you are planning to investigate some factors that might affect the popping of popcorn. Measure $\frac{1}{3}$ cup popcorn and determine its volume. Pop this corn in the hot-air popper and record the popped volume. Ask students to predict what will happen if the popcorn is dried before popping. Repeat your experiment using $\frac{1}{3}$ cup of dried popcorn. Next, ask the students to predict what will happen if the popcorn is wet. Repeat your experiment

Components of Air (dry air at sea level)	
Component	Volume Percent
1. N_2	78
2. O_2	21
3. Ar	0.93
4. CO_2	0.01–0.10
5. Ne	0.0018
6. He	5.2×10^{-4}
7. CH_4	2.0×10^{-4}
8. Kr	1.1×10^{-4}
9. H_2, N_2O	5.0×10^{-5}

MATH

$$PV = nRT$$

$$\frac{PV}{V} = \frac{nRT}{V}$$

$$P = \frac{nRT}{V}$$

"the bends"— a very painful and potentially fatal condition. Because helium gas is only sparingly soluble in blood, it does not cause this problem.

Studies of gaseous mixtures show that each component behaves independently of the others. In other words, a given amount of oxygen exerts the same pressure in a 1.0-L vessel whether it is alone or in the presence of nitrogen (as in the air) or helium.

Among the first scientists to study mixtures of gases was John Dalton. In 1803 Dalton summarized his observations in this statement: *For a mixture of gases in a container, the total pressure exerted is the sum of the partial pressures of the gases present. The* **partial pressure** *of a gas is the pressure that the gas would exert if it were alone in the container.* This statement, known as **Dalton's law of partial pressures,** can be expressed as follows for a mixture containing three gases:

$$P_{total} = P_1 + P_2 + P_3$$

where the subscripts refer to the individual gases (gas 1, gas 2, and gas 3). The pressures P_1, P_2, and P_3 are the partial pressures; that is, each gas is responsible for only part of the total pressure **(Figure 13.10).**

Assuming that each gas behaves ideally, we can calculate the partial pressure of each gas from the ideal gas law:

$$P_1 = \frac{n_1RT}{V}, \ P_2 = \frac{n_2RT}{V}, \ P_3 = \frac{n_3RT}{V}$$

The total pressure of the mixture, P_{total}, can be represented as

$$P_{total} = P_1 + P_2 + P_3 = \frac{n_1RT}{V} + \frac{n_2RT}{V} + \frac{n_3RT}{V}$$

$$= n_1\left(\frac{RT}{V}\right) + n_2\left(\frac{RT}{V}\right) + n_3\left(\frac{RT}{V}\right)$$

$$= (n_1 + n_2 + n_3)\left(\frac{RT}{V}\right)$$

$$= n_{total}\left(\frac{RT}{V}\right)$$

where n_{total} is the sum of the numbers of moles of the gases in the mixture. Thus, for a mixture of ideal gases, it is the *total number of moles of particles*

Figure 13.10
When two gases are present, the total pressure is the sum of the partial pressures of the gases.

2.4 atm

0.50 mol H_2

5.0 L at 20 °C
P_{H_2} = 2.4 atm

6.0 atm

1.25 mol He

5.0 L at 20 °C
P_{He} = 6.0 atm

8.4 atm

1.25 mol He
+ 0.50 mol H_2
_____
1.75 mol gas

5.0 L at 20 °C

$P_{total} = P_{H_2} + P_{He}$
= 2.4 atm + 6.0 atm
= 8.4 atm

13.6   Dalton's Law of Partial Pressures   **421**

8.4 atm

1.75 mol He

5.0 L at 20 °C
P_{total} = 8.4 atm

8.4 atm

0.75 mol H_2
0.75 mol He
0.25 mol Ne

1.75 mol

5.0 L at 20 °C
P_{total} = 8.4 atm

8.4 atm

1.00 mol N_2
0.50 mol O_2
0.25 mol Ar

1.75 mol

5.0 L at 20 °C
P_{total} = 8.4 atm

Figure 13.11
The total pressure of a mixture of gases depends on the number of moles of gas particles (atoms or molecules) present, not on the identities of the particles. Note that these three samples show the same total pressure because each contains 1.75 mol of gas. The detailed nature of the mixture is unimportant.

that is important, not the *identity* of the individual gas particles. This idea is illustrated in **Figure 13.11.**

The fact that the pressure exerted by an ideal gas is affected by the *number* of gas particles and is independent of the *nature* of the gas particles tells us two important things about ideal gases:

1. The volume of the individual gas particle (atom or molecule) must not be very important.

2. The forces among the particles must not be very important.

If these factors were important, the pressure of the gas would depend on the nature of the individual particles. For example, an argon atom is much larger than a helium atom. Yet 1.75 mol of argon gas in a 5.0-L container at 20 °C exerts the same pressure as 1.75 mol of helium gas in a 5.0-L container at 20 °C.

The same idea applies to the forces among the particles. Although the forces among gas particles depend on the nature of the particles, this seems to have little influence on the behavior of an ideal gas. We will see that these observations strongly influence the model that we will construct to explain ideal gas behavior.

Example 13.12

Using Dalton's Law of Partial Pressures, I

Mixtures of helium and oxygen are used in the "air" tanks of underwater divers for deep dives. For a particular dive, 12 L of O_2 at 25 °C and 1.0 atm and 46 L of He at 25 °C and 1.0 atm were both pumped into a 5.0-L tank. Calculate the partial pressure of each gas and the total pressure in the tank at 25 °C.

Solution

Because the partial pressure of each gas depends on the moles of that gas present, we must first calculate the number of moles of each gas by using the ideal gas law in the form

422 Chapter 13 Gases

MATH

$$PV = nRT$$
$$\frac{PV}{RT} = \frac{nRT}{RT}$$
$$\frac{PV}{RT} = n$$

Divers use a mixture of oxygen and helium in their breathing tanks when diving to depths greater than 150 feet.

$$n = \frac{PV}{RT}$$

From the above description we know that $P = 1.0$ atm, $V = 12$ L for O_2 and 46 L for He, and $T = 25 + 273 = 298$ K. Also, $R = 0.08206$ L atm/K mol (as always).

$$\text{Moles of } O_2 = n_{O_2} = \frac{(1.0 \text{ atm})(12 \text{ L})}{(0.08206 \text{ L atm/K mol})(298 \text{ K})} = 0.49 \text{ mol}$$

$$\text{Moles of He} = n_{He} = \frac{(1.0 \text{ atm})(46 \text{ L})}{(0.08206 \text{ L atm/K mol})(298 \text{ K})} = 1.9 \text{ mol}$$

The tank containing the mixture has a volume of 5.0 L, and the temperature is 25 °C (298 K). We can use these data and the ideal gas law to calculate the partial pressure of each gas.

$$P = \frac{nRT}{V}$$

$$P_{O_2} = \frac{(0.49 \text{ mol})(0.08206 \text{ L atm/K mol})(298 \text{ K})}{5.0 \text{ L}} = 2.4 \text{ atm}$$

$$P_{He} = \frac{(1.9 \text{ mol})(0.08206 \text{ L atm/K mol})(298 \text{ K})}{5.0 \text{ L}} = 9.3 \text{ atm}$$

The total pressure is the sum of the partial pressures.

$$P_{total} = P_{O_2} + P_{He} = 2.4 \text{ atm} + 9.3 \text{ atm} = 11.7 \text{ atm}$$

Self-Check Exercise 13.9

A 2.0-L flask contains a mixture of nitrogen gas and oxygen gas at 25 °C. The total pressure of the gaseous mixture is 0.91 atm, and the mixture is known to contain 0.050 mol N_2. Calculate the partial pressure of oxygen and the moles of oxygen present.

A mixture of gases always occurs when a gas is collected by displacement of water. For example, **Figure 13.12** shows the collection of the oxygen gas that was produced by the decomposition of solid potassium chlorate. The gas is collected by bubbling it into a bottle initially filled with water. Thus the

Figure 13.12
The production of oxygen by thermal decomposition of $KClO_3$. MnO_2 is mixed with the $KClO_3$ to make the reaction proceed at a more rapid rate.

KClO₃ (with a small amount of MnO₂)

Oxygen plus water vapor

13.6 Dalton's Law of Partial Pressures **423**

into your mouth!

Teaching Notes You can use a small coffee stirrer to open the egg valve slightly and make removing the egg by blowing slightly easier. You can also use a quart milk bottle or any other quart bottle with an opening of the correct size. Remember that these bottles are not Pyrex and must be heated slowly. Fill the bottle with hot water and empty it. Then fill the bottle with almost boiling water, let it sit 5–10 seconds, and empty it, immediately placing the egg on the opening. Place the small end of the egg on the opening, or the egg may split as it enters the bottle.

USING TECHNOLOGY

 Figure 13.12

TABLE 13.2	
The Vapor Pressure of Water as a Function of Temperature	
T (°C)	P (torr)
0.0	4.579
10.0	9.209
20.0	17.535
25.0	23.756
30.0	31.824
40.0	55.324
60.0	149.4
70.0	233.7
90.0	525.8

gas in the bottle is really a mixture of water vapor and oxygen. (Water vapor is present because molecules of water escape from the surface of the liquid and collect as a gas in the space above the liquid.) Therefore, the total pressure exerted by this mixture is the sum of the partial pressure of the gas being collected and the partial pressure of the water vapor. The partial pressure of the water vapor is called the *vapor pressure of water*. Because water molecules are more likely to escape from hot water than from cold water, the *vapor pressure* of water increases with temperature. This is shown by the values of water vapor pressure at various temperatures shown in **Table 13.2.**

Example 13.13

Using Dalton's Law of Partial Pressures, II

A sample of solid potassium chlorate, $KClO_3$, was heated in a test tube (see Figure 13.12) and decomposed according to the reaction

$$2KClO_3(s) \rightarrow 2KCl(s) + 3O_2(g)$$

The oxygen produced was collected by displacement of water at 22 °C. The resulting mixture of O_2 and H_2O vapor had a total pressure of 754 torr and a volume of 0.650 L. Calculate the partial pressure of O_2 in the gas collected and the number of moles of O_2 present. The vapor pressure of water at 22 °C is 21 torr.

Solution

We know the total pressure (754 torr) and the partial pressure of water (vapor pressure = 21 torr). We can find the partial pressure of O_2 from Dalton's law of partial pressures:

$$P_{\text{total}} = P_{O_2} + P_{H_2O} = P_{O_2} + 21 \text{ torr} = 754 \text{ torr}$$

or

$$P_{O_2} + 21 \text{ torr} = 754 \text{ torr}$$

We can solve for P_{O_2} by subtracting 21 torr from both sides of the equation.

$$P_{O_2} = 754 \text{ torr} - 21 \text{ torr} = 733 \text{ torr}$$

Next we solve the ideal gas law for the number of moles of O_2.

$$n_{O_2} = \frac{P_{O_2}V}{RT}$$

In this case, $P_{O_2} = 733$ torr. We change the pressure to atmospheres as follows:

$$\frac{733 \text{ torr}}{760 \text{ torr/atm}} = 0.964 \text{ atm}$$

MATH

$$PV = nRT$$
$$\frac{PV}{RT} = \frac{nRT}{RT}$$
$$\frac{PV}{RT} = n$$

Then,

$$V = 0.650 \text{ L}$$

$$T = 22 \text{ °C} = 22 + 273 = 295 \text{ K}$$

$$R = 0.08206 \text{ L atm/K mol}$$

so

$$n_{O_2} = \frac{(0.964 \text{ atm})(0.650 \text{ L})}{(0.08206 \text{ L atm/K mol})(295 \text{ K})} = 2.59 \times 10^{-2} \text{ mol}$$

 Self-Check Exercise 13.10

Consider a sample of hydrogen gas collected over water at 25 °C where the vapor pressure of water is 24 torr. The volume occupied by the gaseous mixture is 0.500 L, and the total pressure is 0.950 atm. Calculate the partial pressure of H_2 and the number of moles of H_2 present.

Focus Questions **Sections 13.5–13.6**

1. When solving gas problems, you can use the ideal gas equation even when some of the variables remain constant. Explain how you could do this.

2. At what temperature will 6.21 g of oxygen gas exert a pressure of 5.00 atm in a 10.0-L container?

3. The pressure of a gas is affected by the number of particles and not affected by the kind of gas it is. What does this fact tell us about ideal gases?

4. A tank contains a mixture of 3.0 mol N_2, 2.0 mol O_2, and 1.0 mol CO_2 at 25 °C and a total pressure of 10.0 atm. Calculate the partial pressure (in torr) of each gas in the mixture.

5. In Figure 13.12 oxygen gas is being collected over water. Assume that this experiment is being done at 25 °C. Write an equation for it, and find the pressure of the oxygen gas (assume the pressure in the bottle is P_T).

13.7 Laws and Models: A Review

Objective: *To understand the relationship between laws and models (theories).*

In this chapter we have considered several properties of gases and have seen how the relationships among these properties can be expressed by various laws written in the form of mathematical equations. The most useful of these is the ideal gas equation, which relates all the important gas properties. However, under certain conditions gases do not obey the ideal gas equation. For example, at high pressures and/or low temperatures, the properties of gases deviate significantly from the predictions of the ideal gas equation. On the other hand, as the pressure is lowered and/or the temperature is increased,

13.7 Laws and Models: A Review **425**

 Answer to Self-Check Exercise 13.10

The volume is 0.500 L, the temperature is 25 °C (or 25 + 273 = 298 K), and the total pressure is given as 0.950 atm. Of this total pressure, 24 torr is due to the water vapor. We can calculate the partial pressure of the H_2 because we know that

$$P_{total} = P_{H_2} + P_{H_2O} = 0.950 \text{ atm}$$
$$\underset{\uparrow}{\phantom{P_{total} = P_{H_2} + }} $$
24 torr

Before we carry out the calculation,

however, we must convert the pressures to the same units. Converting P_{H_2O} to atmospheres gives

$$24 \text{ torr} \times \frac{1.000 \text{ atm}}{760.0 \text{ torr}}$$
$$= 0.032 \text{ atm}$$

Thus

$$P_{total} = P_{H_2} + P_{H_2O}$$
$$= 0.950 \text{ atm}$$
$$= P_{H_2} + 0.032 \text{ atm}$$

and

$$P_{H_2} = 0.950 \text{ atm} - 0.032 \text{ atm}$$
$$= 0.918 \text{ atm}$$

Now that we know the partial pressure of the hydrogen gas, we can use the ideal gas equation to calculate the moles of H_2.

$$n_{H_2} = \frac{P_{H_2}V}{RT}$$

$$= \frac{(0.918 \text{ atm})(0.500 \text{ L})}{\left(0.08206 \dfrac{\text{L atm}}{\text{K mol}}\right)(298 \text{ K})}$$

$$= 0.0188 \text{ mol} = 1.88 \times 10^{-2} \text{ mol}$$

almost all gases show close agreement with the ideal gas equation. This means that an ideal gas is really a hypothetical substance. At low pressures and/or high temperatures, real gases *approach* the behavior expected for an ideal gas.

At this point we want to build a model (a theory) to explain *why* a gas behaves as it does. We want to answer the question, *What are the characteristics of the individual gas particles that cause a gas to behave as it does?* However, before we do this let's briefly review the scientific method. Recall that a law is a generalization about behavior that has been observed in many experiments. Laws are very useful; they allow us to predict the behavior of similar systems. For example, a chemist who prepares a new gaseous compound can assume that that substance will obey the ideal gas equation (at least at low *P* and/or high *T*).

However, laws do not tell us *why* nature behaves the way it does. Scientists try to answer this question by constructing theories (building models). The models in chemistry are speculations about how individual atoms or molecules (microscopic particles) cause the behavior of macroscopic systems (collections of atoms and molecules in large enough numbers so that we can observe them).

A model is considered successful if it explains known behavior and predicts correctly the results of future experiments. But a model can never be proved absolutely true. In fact, by its very nature *any model is an approximation* and is destined to be modified, at least in part. Models range from the simple (to predict approximate behavior) to the extraordinarily complex (to account precisely for observed behavior). In this text, we use relatively simple models that fit most experimental results.

13.8 The Kinetic Molecular Theory of Gases

Objective: *To understand the basic postulates of the kinetic molecular theory.*

A relatively simple model that attempts to explain the behavior of an ideal gas is the **kinetic molecular theory.** This model is based on speculations about the behavior of the individual particles (atoms or molecules) in a gas. The assumptions (postulates) of the kinetic molecular theory can be stated as follows:

Postulates of the Kinetic Molecular Theory of Gases

1. Gases consist of tiny particles (atoms or molecules).

2. These particles are so small, compared with the distances between them, that the volume (size) of the individual particles can be assumed to be negligible (zero).

3. The particles are in constant random motion, colliding with the walls of the container. These collisions with the walls cause the pressure exerted by the gas.

4. The particles are assumed not to attract or to repel each other.

5. The average kinetic energy of the gas particles is directly proportional to the Kelvin temperature of the gas.

Carbon Monoxide (CO)

arbon monoxide is a colorless, odorless gas originally discovered in the United States by Joseph Priestley in 1799. It is formed in the combustion of fossil fuels (carbon-based molecules formed by the decay of ancient life forms) when the oxygen supply is limited.

Carbon monoxide is quite toxic, because it binds to hemoglobin 200 times more strongly than oxygen does. Thus, when carbon monoxide is present in inhaled air, it preferentially binds to the hemo-globin and excludes the oxygen needed for human survival. This gas is especially dangerous because it has no taste or odor. The most common type of carbon monoxide poisonings occur in homes where the flow of oxygen to the furnace has become restricted, often due to squirrels or birds building nests in intake air flues. Today carbon monoxide detectors are available that automatically sound an alarm when the carbon monoxide levels become unsafe.

Section 13.9

Themes
Energy, Models, Stability

Skills
Applying concepts, making comparisons, developing models

The kinetic energy referred to in postulate 5 is the energy associated with the motion of a particle. Kinetic energy (KE) is given by the equation $KE = \frac{1}{2}mv^2$, where m is the mass of the particle and v is the velocity (speed) of the particle. The greater the mass or velocity of a particle, the greater its kinetic energy. Postulate 5 means that if a gas is heated to higher temperatures, the average speed of the particles increases; therefore, their kinetic energy increases.

Although real gases do not conform exactly to the five assumptions listed above, we will see in the next section that these postulates do indeed explain *ideal* gas behavior—behavior shown by real gases at high temperatures and/or low pressures.

13.9 The Implications of the Kinetic Molecular Theory

Objectives: *To understand the term* temperature.
To learn how the kinetic molecular theory explains the gas laws.

In this section we will discuss the *qualitative* relationships between the kinetic molecular (KM) theory and the properties of gases. That is, without going into the mathematical details, we will show how the kinetic molecular theory explains some of the observed properties of gases.

The Meaning of Temperature

Recall from Section 10.2 that the temperature of a substance reflects the vigor of the motions of the components that make up the substance. Thus the temperature of a gas reflects how rapidly, on average, its individual particles are moving. At high temperatures the particles move very fast and hit the walls of the container frequently, and at low temperatures the particles' motions

13.9   The Implications of the Kinetic Molecular Theory   **427**

Carbon Monoxide (CO)

Carbon forms several oxides, including CO, CO_2, C_2O_3, C_5O_2, $C_{12}O_9$, and C_2O, most of which are quite unstable. Tricarbon dioxide, C_3O_2, which is often called carbon suboxide, is a foul-smelling gas obtained by dehydrating malonic acid using P_4O_{10}. C_3O_2 is a linear molecule with the Lewis structure

:O=C=C=C=O:

It has a melting point of -112.5 °C and a boiling point of 6.7 °C, and it polymerizes at room temperature to a yellow solid.

Carbon monoxide, CO, which has a melting point of -205 °C and a boiling point of -192 °C, is a colorless, odorless, flammable gas. It is widely used as a fuel in the form of producer gas (25% CO, 4% CO_2, 70% N_2) or water gas (50% H_2, 40% CO, 5% CO_2, and 5% N_2 and CH_4); the latter fuel is made by the reaction of steam and hot coke. Because of its toxicity, carbon monoxide in the atmosphere creates a real concern. Of course, automobiles are the most common source of carbon monoxide, but the introduction of catalytic converters on cars has greatly diminished the amount of CO in exhaust gases. Although the number of cars in the United States approximately doubled between 1970 and 1990, the average concentration of CO decreased by 40% over the same period.

TEACHING TIPS

- Begin this section with a review of temperature and its meaning. Apply this concept to students' mental movie of the molecular level of gases so that they can understand how things change at that level as the temperature changes. Encourage students to think about the model for gases at the molecular level.

- Once students see the molecular-level action of gases with changing temperature, begin to investigate and develop models for the molecular level to illustrate the *P*, *T* and *V*, *T* relationships. Now is an opportune time for students to begin to think as chemists. Observing gases at the macroscopic level allows us to predict behavior, whereas developing a model at the microscopic level allows us to understand why gases behave as they do.

MINI-DEMO

Add 100 mL of water (and a few drops of food coloring if desired) to a 250-mL beaker and place a 50-mL beaker upside down in the water. Place this apparatus on a hot plate and heat the water to boiling (the smaller beaker will "bounce" in the larger beaker). Allow the water to boil for a few minutes and then remove it from the heat. Water will rise in the 50-mL beaker. As the water boils, steam enters the 50-mL beaker and pushes the air out (which is why the beaker "bounces"). After a few minutes, the small beaker is filled with steam (with very little air). As this system is cooled, the steam condenses, which lowers the pressure in the 50-mL beaker. Atmospheric pressure pushes the water up into the 50-mL beaker.

Chapter 13   Gases   **427**

are slower and they collide with the walls of the container much less often. As postulate 5 of the KM theory states, the Kelvin temperature of a gas is directly proportional to the *average kinetic energy* of the gas particles.

The Relationship Between Pressure and Temperature

To see how the meaning of temperature given above helps to explain gas behavior, picture a gas in a rigid container. As the gas is heated to a higher temperature, the particles move faster, hitting the walls more often. And, of course, the impacts become more forceful as the particles move faster. If the pressure is due to collisions with the walls, the gas pressure should increase as temperature is increased.

Is this what we observe when we measure the pressure of a gas as it is heated? Yes. A given sample of gas in a rigid container (if the volume is not changed) shows an increase in pressure as its temperature is increased.

The Relationship Between Volume and Temperature

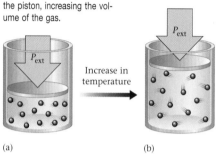

Figure 13.13
(a) A gas confined in a cylinder with a movable piston. The gas pressure P_{gas} is just balanced by the external pressure P_{ext}. That is, $P_{gas} = P_{ext}$. (b) The temperature of the gas is increased at constant pressure P_{ext}. The increased particle motions at the higher temperature push back the piston, increasing the volume of the gas.

Now picture the gas in a container with a movable piston. As shown in **Figure 13.13a**, the gas pressure P_{gas} is just balanced by an external pressure P_{ext}. What happens when we heat the gas to a higher temperature? As the temperature increases, the particles move faster, causing the gas pressure to increase. As soon as the gas pressure P_{gas} becomes greater than P_{ext} (the pressure holding the piston), the piston moves up until $P_{gas} = P_{ext}$. Therefore, the KM model predicts that the volume of the gas will increase as we raise its temperature at a constant pressure. This agrees with experimental observations (as summarized by Charles's law).

Example 13.14

Using the Kinetic Molecular Theory to Explain Gas Law Observations

Use the KM theory to predict what will happen to the pressure of a gas when its volume is decreased (*n* and *T* constant). Does this prediction agree with the experimental observations?

Solution

When we decrease the gas's volume (make the container smaller), the particles hit the walls more often because they do not have to travel so far between the walls. This would suggest an increase in pressure. This prediction on the basis of the model is in agreement with experimental observations of gas behavior (as summarized by Boyle's law).

In this section we have seen that the predictions of the kinetic molecular theory generally fit the behavior observed for gases. This makes it a useful and successful model.

428 Chapter 13 Gases

Signs of Pollution

About 6% of the cars on the road produce 50% of auto-based air pollution. However, finding these offenders can be difficult. Scientists at the University of Denver in Colorado have developed a system that can measure the pollution produced by individual cars as they pass the roadside detector. This information is then transmitted to a billboard display. When the emissions are within acceptable lim-

its, a smiling car is displayed. When the emissions are too high, a frowning car is displayed with the message that the problem is "costing you money." This "smart sign" operates reliably even with traffic flows exceeding 1,000 vehicles per hour. The system has given millions of readings at a cost of about 2 cents each. Approximately 2% of the passing vehicles see the "frowning car."

Signs of Pollution

Student Project Have students design a road sign to encourage people to reduce pollution. Teams of students could create an ad campaign to focus on reducing pollution in the local community.

13.10 Real Gases

Objective: *To describe the properties of real gases.*

So far in our discussion of gases, we have assumed that we are dealing with an ideal gas—one that exactly obeys the equation $PV = nRT$. Of course, there is no such thing as an ideal gas. An ideal gas is a hypothetical substance consisting of particles with zero volumes and no attractions for one another. All is not lost, however, because real gases behave very much like ideal gases under many conditions. For example, in a sample of helium gas at 25 °C and

Figure 13.14
A gas sample is compressed (the volume is decreased).

(a)   (b)

1 atm pressure, the He atoms are so far apart that the tiny volume of each atom has no importance. Also, because the He atoms are moving so rapidly and have very little attraction for one another, the ideal gas assumption that there are no attractions is virtually true. Thus a sample of helium at 25 °C and 1 atm pressure very closely obeys the ideal gas law.

As real gases are compressed into smaller and smaller volumes (see **Figure 13.14**), the particles of the gas begin to occupy a significant fraction of the available volume. That is, in a very small container the space taken up by the particles

13.10   Real Gases   **429**

Section 13.10

Themes
Models, Patterns of Change

Skills
Developing models, evaluating

TEACHING TIP

Students should understand that, although our model for gases assumes ideal behavior and gases are not ideal, we can nevertheless use the model to predict behavior and understand gases. The difficulties with real gases surface when we have small volumes and large pressures. The ideal gas law still allows us to predict the behavior of gases under most everyday conditions.

TEACHING TIPS

- Discussing the relationship between volume and temperature at constant pressure is complex because for the pressure to remain constant, the volume must change. When the temperature increases, the volume increases due to an instantaneous increase in pressure (the volume increase then brings the pressure back to its original value).

- Consider discussing a semi-quantitative relationship between pressure and volume for mathematically inclined students. Imagine a sample of gas in a cubic container with sides of 1 ft. If we transfer this sample to a cube with sides of 2 ft, the gas particles will have to travel (on average) twice as far from one wall to the next, and half as many collisions will occur (decreasing the pressure by a factor of 2). In ad-

dition, the area of each wall will be four times as large (4 ft² versus 1 ft²). Because pressure is a measure of force per area, this change will cause the pressure to decrease by a factor of 4. Thus the pressure should be reduced overall by a factor of 8 (2 × 4). This finding is consistent with Boyle's law, as the second container has a volume 8 times larger than the first container's volume.

Section 13.11

Themes
Models, Patterns of Change

Skills
Applying concepts, solving problems, evaluating

becomes important. Also, as the volume of the container gets smaller, the particles move much closer together and are more likely to attract one another. Thus, in a highly compressed state (small V, high P), the facts that real gas molecules take up space and have attractions for one another become important. Under these conditions a real gas does not obey the equation $PV = nRT$ very well. In other words, under conditions of high pressure (small volume), real gases act differently from the ideal gas behavior.

Because we typically deal with gases that have pressures near 1 atm, however, we can safely assume ideal gas behavior in our calculations.

13.11 Gas Stoichiometry

Objectives: *To understand the molar volume of an ideal gas.*
To learn the definition of STP.
To use these concepts and the ideal gas equation.

We have seen repeatedly in this chapter just how useful the ideal gas equation is. For example, if we know the pressure, volume, and temperature for a given sample of gas, we can calculate the number of moles present: $n = PV/RT$. This fact makes it possible to do stoichiometric calculations for reactions involving gases. We will illustrate this process in Example 13.15.

Example 13.15

Gas Stoichiometry: Calculating Volume

Calculate the volume of oxygen gas produced at 1.00 atm and 25 °C by the complete decomposition of 10.5 g of potassium chlorate. The balanced equation for the reaction is

$$2KClO_3(s) \rightarrow 2KCl(s) + 3O_2(g)$$

Solution

This is a stoichiometry problem very much like the type we considered in Chapter 9. The only difference is that in this case, we want to calculate the volume of a gaseous product rather than the number of grams. To do so, we can use the relationship between moles and volume given by the ideal gas law.

We'll summarize the steps required to do this problem in the following schematic:

Grams of KClO$_3$	→①	Moles of KClO$_3$	→②	Moles of O$_2$	→③	Volume of O$_2$

MATH

$\frac{10.5}{122.6} = 0.085644$

$0.085644 \Rightarrow 0.0856$
Round off
$0.0856 = 8.56 \times 10^{-2}$

Step 1 To find the moles of $KClO_3$ in 10.5 g, we use the molar mass of $KClO_3$ (122.6 g).

$$10.5 \text{ g KClO}_3 \times \frac{1 \text{ mol KClO}_3}{122.6 \text{ g KClO}_3} = 8.56 \times 10^{-2} \text{ mol KClO}_3$$

Step 2 To find the moles of O_2 produced, we use the mole ratio of O_2 to $KClO_3$ derived from the balanced equation.

$$8.56 \times 10^{-2} \text{ mol KClO}_3 \times \frac{3 \text{ mol O}_2}{2 \text{ mol KClO}_3} = 1.28 \times 10^{-1} \text{ mol O}_2$$

Step 3 To find the volume of oxygen produced, we use the ideal gas law $PV = nRT$, where

$P = 1.00$ atm

$V = ?$

$n = 1.28 \times 10^{-1}$ mol, the moles of O_2 we calculated

$R = 0.08206$ L atm/K mol

$T = 25\ °C = 25 + 273 = 298$ K

Solving the ideal gas law for V gives

$$V = \frac{nRT}{P} = \frac{(1.28 \times 10^{-1} \text{ mol})\left(0.08206 \frac{\text{L atm}}{\text{K mol}}\right)(298 \text{ K})}{1.00 \text{ atm}} = 3.13 \text{ L}$$

Thus 3.13 L of O_2 will be produced.

 Self-Check Exercise 13.11

Calculate the volume of hydrogen produced at 1.50 atm and 19 °C by the reaction of 26.5 g of zinc with excess hydrochloric acid according to the balanced equation

$$Zn(s) + 2HCl(aq) \rightarrow ZnCl_2(aq) + H_2(g)$$

In dealing with the stoichiometry of reactions involving gases, it is useful to define the volume occupied by 1 mol of a gas under certain specified conditions. For 1 mol of an ideal gas at 0 °C (273 K) and 1 atm, the volume of the gas given by the ideal gas law is

$$V = \frac{nRT}{P} = \frac{(1.00 \text{ mol})(0.08206 \text{ L atm/K mol})(273 \text{ K})}{1.00 \text{ atm}} = 22.4 \text{ L}$$

This volume of 22.4 L is called the **molar volume** of an ideal gas.

The conditions 0 °C and 1 atm are called **standard temperature and pressure** (abbreviated **STP**). Properties of gases are often given under these conditions. Remember, the molar volume of an ideal gas is 22.4 L *at STP*. That is, 22.4 L contains 1 mol of an ideal gas at STP.

CHEMISTRY

STP: 0 °C and 1 atm

Answer to Self-Check Exercise 13.11

We will solve this problem by taking the following steps:

| Grams of zinc | ➡ | Moles of zinc | ➡ | Moles of H_2 | ➡ | Volume of H_2 |

Step 1 Using the atomic mass of zinc (65.38 g), we calculate the moles of zinc in 26.5 g.

$$26.5 \text{ g Zn} \times \frac{1 \text{ mol Zn}}{65.38 \text{ g Zn}}$$

$$= 0.405 \text{ mol Zn}$$

Step 2 Using the balanced equation, we next calculate the moles of H_2 produced.

$$0.405 \text{ mol Zn} \times \frac{1 \text{ mol H}_2}{1 \text{ mol Zn}}$$

$$= 0.405 \text{ mol H}_2$$

Step 3 Now that we know the moles of H_2, we can compute the volume of H_2 by using the ideal gas law, where

$P = 1.50$ atm
$V = ?$
$n = 0.405$ mol
$R = 0.08206$ L atm/K mol
$T = 19\ °C = 19 + 273 = 292$ K

$$V = \frac{nRT}{P}$$

$$= \frac{(0.405 \text{ mol})\left(0.08206 \frac{\text{L atm}}{\text{K mol}}\right)(292 \text{ K})}{1.50 \text{ atm}}$$

$$= 6.47 \text{ L of H}_2$$

Integrating the CHEMICAL IMPACT

The Chemistry of Air Bags

This application involving sodium azide (NaN_3) provides a good opportunity to reteach Lewis structures. The azide ion N_3^- has 16 electrons and has the Lewis structure $:\ddot{N}{=}N{=}\ddot{N}:$. Notice that this ion is isoelectronic with CO_2, which also has a linear structure.

HN_3 (hydrazoic acid) can be formed by careful addition of H_2SO_4 to NaN_3. However, HN_3 is very toxic and highly explosive and has a repulsive, intensely irritating odor. The Lewis structure of HN_3 is H $\overset{\displaystyle :\ddot{N}{=}N{=}\ddot{N}:}{}$ and the H—N—N angle is 112°, a little smaller than the angle of 120° predicted by VSEPR theory.

You can use this Chemical Impact to review stoichiometry if desired. NaN_3 reacts with water to form hydrozoic acid:

$$NaN_3 + H_2O \rightarrow HN_3 + NaOH$$

Since most air bags are not used during a car's lifetime, they could begin piling up in junkyards. If a typical airbag contains 150 g sodium azide, how much hydrazoic acid could be released if water leaked into the sodium azide? This problem of toxic air bags can be solved by igniting the air bag or by using recyclable modules that contain sodium azide pellets in a reusable form.

Additional Examples

1. A sample of argon gas has a volume of 3.45 L at STP. What is the mass of the argon?
   6.15 g

2. A sample of hydrogen gas occupies a volume of 15.0 L at STP. What volume will this sample occupy at 22 °C and 2.50 atm?
   6.48 L

CHEMICAL IMPACT

The Chemistry of Air Bags

Most experts agree that air bags represent a very important advance in automobile safety. These bags, which are stored in the auto's steering wheel or dash, are designed to inflate rapidly (within about 40 ms) in the event of a crash, cushioning the front seat occupants against impact. The bags than deflate immediately to allow vision and movement after the crash. Air bags are activated when a severe deceleration (an impact) causes a steel ball to compress a spring and electrically ignite a detonator cap, which, in turn, causes sodium azide (NaN_3) to decompose explosively, forming sodium and nitrogen gas:

$$2NaN_3(s) \rightarrow 2Na(s) + 3N_2(g)$$

This system works very well and requires a relatively small amount of sodium azide (100 g yields 56 L $N_2(g)$ at 25 °C and 1.0 atm).

When a vehicle containing air bags reaches the end of its useful life, the sodium azide present in the activators must be given proper disposal. Sodium azide, besides being explosive, has a toxicity roughly equal to that of sodium cyanide. It also forms hydrazoic acid (HN_3), a toxic and explosive liquid, when treated with acid.

The air bag represents an application of chemistry that has already saved thousands of lives.

Inflated air bags.

Example 13.16

Gas Stoichiometry: Calculations Involving Gases at STP

A sample of nitrogen gas has a volume of 1.75 L at STP. How many moles of N_2 are present?

Solution

We could solve this problem by using the ideal gas equation, but we can take a shortcut by using the molar volume of an ideal gas at STP. Because 1 mol of an ideal gas at STP has a volume of 22.4 L, a 1.75-L sample of N_2 at STP contains considerably less than 1 mol. We can find how many moles by using the equivalence statement

$$1.000 \text{ mol} = 22.4 \text{ L (STP)}$$

which leads to the conversion factor we need:

$$1.75 \text{ L } N_2 \times \frac{1.000 \text{ mol } N_2}{22.4 \text{ L } N_2} = 7.81 \times 10^{-2} \text{ mol } N_2$$

 Self-Check Exercise 13.12

Ammonia is commonly used as a fertilizer to provide a source of nitrogen for plants. A sample of $NH_3(g)$ occupies 5.00 L at 25 °C and 15.0 atm. What volume will this sample occupy at STP?

432 Chapter 13 Gases

TEACHING SUPPORT
Demonstration

Density of Gases

Materials
Balloons filled with a variety of gases (helium, methane, carbon dioxide, air)
Ribbons or string

Preparation Fill the balloons to about equal volume. It is helpful to use a different color balloon for each type of gas. You can generate CO_2 by using dry ice. If you have lecture bottles of any gases, they may be used to fill the balloons. Tie a ribbon or string to each balloon. Be sure that the string is at least 1 m long. Gather the balloons together, holding them together at the necks so students cannot observe the densities before the demonstration.

Presentation Find a volunteer for each balloon. Give the volunteer the balloon, having him or her hold it by the neck with the end of the string in the volunteer's other hand. Have all volunteers hold the balloons about 6 feet from the floor. Ask all volunteers to drop the balloons at the same time. Observe the order in which the balloons fall (or rise). You will need to repeat the demonstration to actu-

432

Standard conditions (STP) and molar volume are also useful in carrying out stoichiometric calculations on reactions involving gases, as shown in Example 13.17.

Example 13.17

Gas Stoichiometry: Reactions Involving Gases at STP

Quicklime, CaO, is produced by heating calcium carbonate, $CaCO_3$. Calculate the volume of CO_2 produced at STP from the decomposition of 152 g of $CaCO_3$ according to the reaction

$$CaCO_3(s) \rightarrow CaO(s) + CO_2(g)$$

Solution

The strategy for solving this problem is summarized by the following schematic:

Grams of $CaCO_3$ ⇨① Moles of $CaCO_3$ ⇨② Moles of CO_2 ⇨③ Volume of CO_2

Step 1 Using the molar mass of $CaCO_3$ (100.1 g), we calculate the number of moles of $CaCO_3$.

$$152 \text{ g } CaCO_3 \times \frac{1 \text{ mol } CaCO_3}{100.0 \text{ g } CaCO_3} = 1.52 \text{ mol } CaCO_3$$

Step 2 Each mole of $CaCO_3$ produces 1 mol of CO_2, so 1.52 mol of CO_2 will be formed.

Step 3 We can convert the moles of CO_2 to volume by using the molar volume of an ideal gas, because the conditions are STP.

$$1.52 \text{ mol } CO_2 \times \frac{22.4 \text{ L } CO_2}{1 \text{ mol } CO_2} = 34.1 \text{ L } CO_2$$

Thus the decomposition of 152 g of $CaCO_3$ produces 34.1 L of CO_2 at STP.

CHEMISTRY

Remember that the molar volume of an ideal gas is 22.4 L at STP.

Note that the final step in Example 13.17 involves calculating the volume of gas from the number of moles. Because the conditions were specified as STP, we were able to use the molar volume of a gas at STP. If the conditions of a problem are different from STP, we must use the ideal gas law to compute the volume, as we did in Section 13.5.

Focus Questions ○

Sections 13.7–13.11

1. When do real gases behave as ideal gases?
2. Draw a molecular-level picture of a gas using kinetic molecular theory. Briefly describe the motion of the gas particles.
3. What is the most useful thing to know about gases at STP?

Focus Questions **433**

The most convenient method of solution involves using the molar volume at STP. First we use the ideal gas equation to calculate the moles of NH_3 present:

$$n = \frac{PV}{RT}$$

where $P = 15.0$ atm, $V = 5.00$ L, and $T = 25 \text{ °C} + 273 = 298$ K.

$$n = \frac{(15.0 \text{ atm})(5.00 \text{ L})}{\left(0.08206 \frac{\text{L atm}}{\text{K mol}}\right)(298 \text{ K})} = 3.07 \text{ mol}$$

At STP each mole of gas occupies 22.4 L. Therefore, 3.07 mol has the volume

$$3.07 \text{ mol} \times \frac{22.4 \text{ L}}{1 \text{ mol}} = 68.8 \text{ L}$$

Additional Examples

1. When magnesium reacts with hydrochloric acid, hydrogen gas is produced: $Mg(s) + 2HCl(aq) \rightarrow MgCl_2 (aq) + H_2(g)$. Calculate the volume of hydrogen gas produced at STP by reacting 5.00 g Mg and an excess of $HCl(aq)$.
4.61 L

2. When subjected to an electric current, water decomposes to hydrogen and oxygen gas: $2H_2O(l) \rightarrow 2H_2(g) + O_2(g)$. If 25.0 g of water is decomposed, what volume of oxygen gas is produced at STP?
15.5 L

Answers to Focus Questions

1. Real gases behave as ideal gases under normal, everyday conditions and under many other conditions as long as the volume is not very small or the pressure very large.

2. Drawings may look like Figure 13.14. The particles are in constant random motion, colliding with the walls of the container. The vigor of the particles' motion is directly proportional to the temperature of the gas.

3. One mole of any gas at STP occupies 22.4 L assuming ideal behavior.

---

ally have the students observe the order—the first time they just see what happens. (It is important to have the strings so that volunteers do not lose the balloons.)

Teaching Notes Write the gases on the board. Have students match the balloon colors with the gases and explain how they arrived at their conclusions. You can also use this activity to review many concepts by asking

students to order the balloons from largest to smallest: pressure, volume, temperature, number of particles, mass of gas, density, average kinetic energy, average speed of particles.

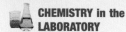

Gas Laws and Drinking Straws

Objectives

1. To investigate the science behind drinking straws

2. To better understand atmospheric pressure

Skills

Observing, applying concepts, drawing conclusions, making inferences, developing hypotheses

Materials

Preform   Modeling clay
Cup   Straws
Transparent
    tape

Preparation Hints

Preforms can be ordered from Educational Innovations (see *Teacher Resources*). However, any rigid container with a relatively small mouth will work.

Procedure Hints

When performing Part III, make sure that students check the connections between the straws. If there are any gaps, they will not be able to drink through the straws. Students should be able to drink through a straw that is longer than 8 feet. Consider allowing students to carry out this part of the experiment in a stairway (if available).

Remind students to make careful observations in Part IV. Because most of them are familiar with this phenomenon, they will tend to overlook crucial observations.

Post-Lab Discussion

Allow for a lengthy discussion of Part IV. Most students have seen this phenomenon, but many have probably not made careful observations or thought about the science involved. Pay careful attention to the students as they discuss this part—you may be surprised to hear many interesting theories (that the finger blocks gravity is one of the most interesting ideas we have heard—and it was from a college student). Ask students about the pressure inside the straw ("Is it higher, lower, or equal to atmospheric pressure?"). It is likely that you will get all three responses back.

Some students will believe that the pressure is higher in the straw. Many of these students will use Boyle's law as justifica-

Problem

Why can we drink through a straw?

Introduction

You have probably used drinking straws many times, but have you ever wondered how they work? In this lab we will investigate the science behind the drinking straw.

Prelab Assignment

Read the entire lab experiment before you begin.

Materials

Preform
Cup
Transparent tape
Modeling clay
Straws

Procedure

Part I

1. Fill a "preform" with water. Put a drinking straw into the preform and use clay to seal the opening.
2. Try to drink the water. Record your observations.

Part II

1. Half-fill a cup with water. Place the ends of two drinking straws in your mouth.
2. Submerge the other end of one straw into the water, and leave the other straw out of the water (on the side of the cup).
3. Try to drink the water. Record your observations.

Part III

1. Determine the maximum number of straws you can connect together end-to-end and still drink water. (*Note:* you may have to tape the straws together.)
2. Measure the height.

Part IV

Place a drinking straw vertically into a cup that is half-filled with water. Place your finger over the opening of the straw and take the straw out of the water. What happens? Make careful observations.

Cleaning Up

Clean all materials and wash your hands thoroughly.

Data/Observations

1. Were you able to drink the water in Part I?
2. Were you able to drink the water in Part II?
3. How many drinking straws could you drink through in Part III? What was the limiting height?
4. What happens to the water in the straw in Part IV (careful observations are required)?

Analysis and Conclusions

1. Explain your results from Part I.
2. Explain your results from Part II.
3. Compare your number of straws and heights from Part III with those of other groups.
4. Why is there a limit to the number of straws through which you can drink?
5. What is the maximum theoretical height through which you can drink? Why can't you drink from this height?
6. Explain your results from Part IV.
7. Why can we drink through a straw?

Something Extra

Does the diameter of a drinking straw affect the results? Carry out an experiment to answer this question.

tion—the top of the straw is open to the atmosphere; when you place your finger on it, the volume is decreased. Because the volume is decreased, the pressure must increase. This theory at least shows that students remember Boyle's law and are justifying their answers with something they have seen in class; however, the volume inside the straw is not changing.

Some students will believe that the pressure is lower in the straw. Two reasons are commonly cited to justify

this theory. First, because there is less air in the straw than in the room, there must be less pressure (it could be argued that students are using Avogadro's law, even though it doesn't apply here because the volume is lower in the straw as well). Also, don't be surprised if some students state that the finger blocks air pressure. This theory is an interesting argument because it comes close to being correct. Once the water level falls, the pressure does drop. And because the finger covers the opening of the

straw, air cannot enter to keep the pressure in the straw at atmospheric pressure. Not all students who argue that "the finger blocks air pressure" mean this, so it is worth having students elaborate on this theory. It is best if you can salvage some of the students' ideas as they head toward a scientifically accepted answer.

Some students will come to the incorrect conclusion that the pressure inside the straw must equal atmospheric pressure to create a balance

Chapter Review

Key Terms

barometer (13.1)
mm Hg (13.1)
torr (13.1)
standard atmosphere (13.1)
pascal (13.1)
Boyle's law (13.2)
absolute zero (13.3)
Charles's law (13.3)
Avogadro's law (13.4)
universal gas constant (13.5)
ideal gas law (13.5)
ideal gas (13.5)
combined gas law (13.5)
partial pressure (13.6)
Dalton's law of partial pressures (13.6)
kinetic molecular theory (13.8)
molar volume (13.11)
standard temperature and pressure (STP) (13.11)

Summary

1. Atmospheric pressure is measured with a barometer. The most commonly used units of pressure are mm Hg (torr), atmosphere, and pascal (the SI unit).

2. Boyle's law states that the volume of a given amount of gas is inversely proportional to its pressure (at constant temperature): $PV = k$ or $P = k/V$. That is, as pressure increases, volume decreases.

3. Charles's law states that, for a given amount of gas at constant pressure, the volume is directly proportional to the temperature (in kelvins): $V = bT$. At $-273\ °C$ (0 K), the volume of a gas extrapolates to zero, and this temperature is called absolute zero.

4. Avogadro's law states that for a gas at constant temperature and pressure, the volume is directly proportional to the number of moles of gas: $V = an$.

5. These three laws can be combined into the ideal gas law, $PV = nRT$, where R is called the universal gas constant. This equation makes it possible to calculate any one of the properties—volume, pressure, temperature, or moles of gas present—given the other three. A gas that obeys this equation is said to behave ideally.

6. From the ideal gas equation we can derive the combined gas law,

$$\frac{P_1 V_1}{T_1} = \frac{P_2 V_2}{T_2}$$

which holds when the amount of gas (moles) remains constant.

7. The pressure of a gas mixture is described by Dalton's law of partial pressures, which states that the total pressure of the mixture of gases in a container is the sum of the partial pressures of the gases that make up the mixture.

8. The kinetic molecular theory of gases is a model that accounts for ideal gas behavior. This model assumes that a gas consists of tiny particles with negligible volumes, that there are no interactions among particles, and that the particles are in constant motion, colliding with the container walls to produce pressure.

Questions and Problems

All exercises with blue numbers have answers in the back of this book.

13.1 Pressure

Questions

1. How are the three states of matter similar, and how do they differ?

2. What is meant by "the pressure of the atmosphere"? What causes this pressure?

3. Describe a simple mercury barometer. How is such a barometer used to measure the pressure of the atmosphere?

Problems

4. Convert the following pressures into *atmospheres*.
   a. 105.2 kPa
   b. 75.2 cm Hg
   c. 752 mm Hg
   d. 767 torr

5. Convert the following pressures into units of *mm Hg*.
   a. 0.9975 atm
   b. 225,400 Pa
   c. 99.7 kPa
   d. 1.078 atm

6. Convert the following pressures into pascals.
   a. 774 torr
   b. 0.965 atm
   c. 112.5 kPa
   d. 801 mm Hg

13.2 Pressure and Volume: Boyle's Law

Problems

7. For each of the following sets of pressure/volume data, calculate the missing quantity. Assume that the temperature and the amount of gas remain constant.

Chapter Review **435**

Sample Data/Answers

Data/Observations

1. The students cannot drink the water.

2. The students cannot drink the water.

3. Answers will vary. Expect the average number to be about 15, which is a height of about 8 feet.

4. Most of the water stays in the straw, but either a drop or so will fall out of the straw or the water

will bulge a bit out of the bottom of the straw. This observation is very important.

Analysis and Conclusions

Answers to these questions are found in the *Teacher's Guide* to the Laboratory.

Answers to End of Chapter Problems

1. Solids are rigid and incompressible and have definite shapes and volumes. Liquids are less rigid than solids; although they have definite volumes, liquids take the shape of their containers. Gases have no fixed volume or shape; they take the volume and shape of their container, and are affected more by changes in their pressure and temperature than are liquids and solids.

2. The pressure of the atmosphere represents the weight of the several-mile-thick layer of gases pressing down on the earth. Pressure represents a force exerted over an area.

3. Figure 13.2 shows a simple barometer. A tube filled with mercury is inverted in a pool of mercury that is open to the atmosphere. The mercury in the tube falls to a level at which the pressure of the atmosphere is sufficient to support the column of mercury.

4. (a) 1.038 atm; (b) 0.989 atm; (c) 0.989 atm; (d) 1.01 atm

5. (a) 758.1 mm Hg; (b) 1691 mm Hg; (c) 748 mm Hg; (d) 819.3 mm Hg

6. (a) 1.03×10^5 Pa; (b) 9.78×10^4 Pa; (c) 1.125×10^5 Pa; (d) 1.07×10^5 Pa

7. (a) 59.7 mL; (b) 1.88 atm; (c) 3.40 L

8. (a) 146 mL; (b) 0.354 L; (c) 687 mm Hg

9. The volume will increase by a factor of 1.80.

10. 20.0 atm

11. Absolute zero is the temperature at which the volume of an ideal gas sample is pre-

Chapter 13   Gases   **435**

12. Measure the volume of a gas at several different temperatures (keep pressure and moles of gas constant). Plot these data and extrapolate the line (continue past the points you have measured). The temperature at which the gas has zero volume is absolute zero.

13. 49.2 mL

14. (a) 273 °C; (b) 35 °C; (c) 298 mL

15. (a) −238 °C; (b) 0 mL; (c) 40.5 mL

16. 0.02 L (20 mL)

17. The volume of the neon gas would become half the initial value at 149 K. The volume would double at 596 K.

18. 548 mL

19. 1.14 L

20. 10.8 L

21. Real gases behave most ideally at relatively high temperatures and low pressures.

22. $PV = nRT$; If n, R, and T are all constant, then $PV =$ constant, or $P_1V_1 = P_2V_2$.

23. (a) 5.02 L; (b) 3.56 atm; (c) 334 K

24. (a) 0.201 L; (b) 0.338 atm; (c) 2.48×10^{-2} mol

25. 2.01 L

26. 4440 g He; 2240 g H_2

27. 655 K

28. 340 atm

29. 85.2 mL

30. 464 mL

31. This is Dalton's law of partial pressures: $P_{total} = P_1 + P_2 + \ldots P_n$. We assume that the gas particles themselves take up no space and do not interact with one another. Under these conditions, there is no difference in the bulk behavior of different gases.

32. The pressure of the water vapor must be subtracted from the total pressure.

33. $P_{oxygen} = 0.693$ atm; $P_{helium} = 5.54$ atm; $P_{total} = 6.233$ atm (6.2 atm considering significant figures)

34. 5.0 atm N_2; 3.3 atm O_2; 1.7 atm CO_2

35. 745 torr

a. $V = 53.2$ mL at 785 mm Hg; $V = ?$ at 700 mm Hg
b. $V = 2.25$ L at 1.67 atm; $V = 2.00$ L at ? atm
c. $V = 5.62$ L at 695 mm Hg; $V = ?$ at 1.51 atm

8. For each of the following sets of pressure/volume data, calculate the missing quantity. Assume that the temperature and the amount of gas remain the same.
   a. $V = 291$ mL at 1.07 atm; $V = ?$ at 2.14 atm
   b. $V = 1.25$ L at 755 mm Hg; $V = ?$ at 3.51 atm
   c. $V = 2.71$ at 101.4 kPa; $V = 3.00$ L at ? mm Hg

9. If the pressure exerted on the gas in a weather balloon decreases from 1.01 atm to 0.562 atm as it rises, by what factor will the volume of the gas in the balloon increase as it rises?

10. What pressure (in atmospheres) is required to compress 1.00 L of gas at 760. mm Hg pressure to a volume of 50.0 mL?

13.3 Volume and Temperature: Charles's Law

Questions

11. What is meant by the *absolute zero* of temperature?

12. How can Charles's law be used to determine absolute zero?

Problems

13. If a 45.0-mL sample of gas at 26.5 °C is heated to 55.2 °C, what is the new volume of the gas sample (at constant pressure)?

14. For each of the following sets of volume/temperature data, calculate the missing quantity. Assume that the pressure and the mass of gas remain constant.
    a. $V = 25.0$ L at 0 °C; $V = 50.0$ L at ? °C
    b. $V = 247$ mL at 25 °C; $V = 255$ mL at ? °C
    c. $V = 1.00$ mL at −272 °C; $V = ?$ at 25 °C

15. For each of the following sets of volume/temperature data, calculate the missing quantity. Assume that the pressure and mass of gas remain constant.
    a. $V = 2.01 \times 10^2$ L at 1150 °C; $V = 5.00$ L at ? °C
    b. $V = 44.2$ mL at 298 K; $V = ?$ at 0 K
    c. $V = 44.2$ mL at 298 K; $V = ?$ at 0 °C

16. If 5.00 L of an ideal gas is cooled from 24 °C to −272 °C, what will the volume of the gas become?

17. A sample of neon gas occupies 266 mL at 25.2 °C. At what temperature would the volume of this sample of neon be reduced to half its initial size (at constant pressure)? At what temperature would the volume of this sample of neon be doubled (at constant pressure)?

18. The label on an aerosol spray can contains a warning that the can should not be heated to over 130 °F because of the danger of explosion due to the pressure

increase as it is heated. Calculate the potential volume of the gas contained in a 500.-mL aerosol can when it is heated from 25 °C to 54 °C (approximately 130 °F), assuming a constant pressure.

13.4 Volume and Moles: Avogadro's Law

Problems

19. If 0.214 mol of argon gas occupies a volume of 652 mL at a particular temperature and pressure, what volume would 0.375 mol of argon occupy under the same conditions?

20. If 46.2 g of oxygen gas occupies a volume of 100. L at a particular temperature and pressure, what volume will 5.00 g of oxygen gas occupy under the same conditions?

13.5 The Ideal Gas Law

Questions

21. Under what conditions do *real* gases behave most ideally?

22. Show how Boyle's law can be derived from the ideal gas law.

Problems

23. Given each of the following sets of values for an ideal gas, calculate the unknown quantity.
    a. $P = 782$ mm Hg; $V = ?$; $n = 0.210$ mol; $T = 27$ °C
    b. $P = ?$ mm Hg; $V = 644$ mL; $n = 0.0921$ mol; $T = 303$ K
    c. $P = 745$ mm Hg; $V = 11.2$ L; $n = 0.401$ mol; $T = ?$ K

24. Given each of the following sets of values for an ideal gas, calculate the unknown quantity.
    a. $P = 1.01$ atm; $V = ?$; $n = 0.00831$ mol; $T = 25$ °C
    b. $P = ?$ atm; $V = 602$ mL; $n = 8.01 \times 10^{-3}$ mol; $T = 310$ K
    c. $P = 0.998$ atm; $V = 629$ mL; $n = ?$ mol; $T = 35$ °C

25. What volume does 4.24 g of nitrogen gas occupy at 58.2 °C and 2.04 atm?

26. Suppose two 200.0-L tanks are to be filled separately with the gases helium and hydrogen. What mass of each gas is needed to produce a pressure of 135 atm in its respective tank at 24 °C?

27. At what temperature does 16.3 g of nitrogen gas have a pressure of 1.25 atm in a 25.0-L tank?

28. Determine the pressure in a 125-L tank containing 56.2 kg of oxygen gas at 21 °C.

29. What will be the new volume if 125 mL of He gas at 100 °C and 0.981 atm is cooled to 25 °C and the pressure is increased to 1.15 atm?

436   Chapter 13   Gases

36. 1.98×10^{-2} mol O_2, 732 torr

37. A law is a statement that precisely expresses generally observed behavior. A theory consists of a set of assumptions/hypotheses that is put forth to explain the law.

38. A theory is successful if it explains known experimental observations; no.

39. We assume that the volume of the particles themselves in a gas sample is negligible compared to the volume of their container. This idea helps us explain observations

such as the compressibility of gases.

40. Pressure is due to the atoms or molecules of a gas colliding with the walls of the container.

41. kinetic energy

42. Temperature is a measure of the average kinetic energy of a sample. The speed of the particles depends on the temperature of the sample and the mass of the particles. So, for a given gas, the temperature reflects how rapidly the particles are moving.

43. As the temperature of a gas increases, the average kinetic energy of the gas particles increases; the particles will therefore move faster. By moving at a higher speed, the particles will collide with the wall more often (and with more force) and the pressure will increase.

44. Any gas that does not follow the ideal gas law is not behaving ideally. In addition, if there are reasons to believe that the assumptions of the kinetic molecular theory are poor assumptions, the gas sample is not behaving ideally. The

30. What will the volume of the sample become if 459 mL of an ideal gas at 27 °C and 1.05 atm is cooled to 15 °C and 0.997 atm?

13.6 Dalton's Law of Partial Pressures

Questions

31. Explain why the measured properties of a mixture of gases depend only on the total number of moles of particles, not on the identities of the individual gas particles. How is this observation summarized as a law?

32. We often collect small samples of gases in the laboratory by bubbling the gas into a bottle or flask containing water. Explain why the gas becomes saturated with water vapor and how we must take the presence of water vapor into account when calculating the properties of the gas sample.

Problems

33. If 4.0 g of $O_2(g)$ and 4.0 g of $He(g)$ are placed in a 5.0-L vessel at 65 °C, what will be the partial pressure of each gas and the total pressure in the vessel?

34. A tank contains a mixture of 3.0 mol N_2, 2.0 mol O_2, and 1.0 mol CO_2 at 25 °C and a total pressure of 10.0 atm. Calculate the partial pressure (in torr) of each gas in the mixture.

35. A sample of oxygen gas is saturated with water vapor at 27 °C. The total pressure of the mixture is 772 torr, and the vapor pressure of water is 26.7 torr at 27 °C. What is the partial pressure of the oxygen gas?

36. A 500.-mL sample of O_2 gas at 24 °C was prepared by decomposing a 3% aqueous solution of hydrogen peroxide, H_2O_2, in the presence of a small amount of manganese catalyst by the reaction

$$2H_2O_2(aq) \rightarrow 2H_2O(g) + O_2(g)$$

The oxygen thus prepared was collected by displacement of water. The total pressure of gas collected was 755 mm Hg. What is the partial pressure of O_2 in the mixture? How many moles of O_2 are in the mixture? (The vapor pressure of water at 24 °C is 23 mm Hg.)

13.7 Laws and Models: A Review

Questions

37. What is a scientific *law*? What is a *theory*? How do these concepts differ? Does a law explain a theory, or does a theory attempt to explain a law?

38. When is a scientific theory considered to be successful? Are all theories successful? Will a theory that has been successful in the past necessarily be successful in the future?

13.8 The Kinetic Molecular Theory of Gases

Questions

39. What do we assume about the volume of the actual molecules themselves in a sample of gas, compared to the bulk volume of the gas overall? Why?

40. How do chemists explain on a molecular basis the fact that gases in containers exert pressure on the walls of the container?

41. Temperature is a measure of the average _____ of the molecules in a sample of gas.

13.9 The Implications of the Kinetic Molecular Theory

Questions

42. How is the phenomenon of temperature explained on the basis of the kinetic molecular theory? What microscopic property of gas molecules is reflected in the temperature measured?

43. Explain, in terms of the kinetic molecular theory, how an increase in the temperature of a gas confined to a rigid container causes an increase in the pressure of the gas.

13.10 Real Gases

Questions

44. What does it mean for a gas to behave nonideally? How do we know that real gases behave nonideally?

45. Why does decreasing the volume of a gas cause nonideal behavior?

13.11 Gas Stoichiometry

Problems

46. When calcium carbonate is heated strongly, carbon dioxide gas is released

$$CaCO_3(s) \rightarrow CaO(s) + CO_2(g)$$

What volume of $CO_2(g)$, measured at STP, is produced if 15.2 g of $CaCO_3(s)$ is heated?

47. Consider the following *unbalanced* chemical equation for the combustion of propane.

$$C_3H_8(g) + O_2(g) \rightarrow CO_2(g) + H_2O(g)$$

What volume of oxygen gas at 25 °C and 1.04 atm is needed for the complete combustion of 5.53 g of propane?

48. Ammonia and gaseous hydrogen chloride combine to form ammonium chloride.

$$NH_3(g) + HCl(g) \rightarrow NH_4Cl(s)$$

60. 2.8 L

61. 5.8 L O_2; 3.9 L SO_2

62. 32 L; $P_{He} = 0.86$ atm; $P_{Ar} = 0.017$ atm; $P_{Ne} = 0.12$ atm

63. 442 mL

64. 508 °C

65. 2.26×10^7 K

66. Boron

67. 0.0228 mol; 2.75×10^{21} molecules

68. $C_3H_6O_2$; draw two possible Lewis structures

Chapter Review **437**

fact that gases condense into liquids, for example, shows nonideal behavior.

45. When the volume of a gas is decreased, the gas particles take up a greater percentage of the volume of the container. The assumption of the kinetic molecular theory that gas particles take up a negligible volume is less correct.

46. 3.41 L CO_2

47. 14.7 L O_2

48. 9.31 g of NH_4Cl is produced.

NH_3 is the limiting reactant, so HCl is in excess.

49. 5.03 L (dry volume)

50. 359 L

51. 184 mL

52. 15.6 L; $P_{oxygen} = 0.225$ atm; $P_{nitrogen} = 0.256$ atm; $P_{carbon\ dioxide} = 0.163$ atm; $P_{neon} = 0.356$ atm

53. 2.34 L Cl_2

54. 0.709 L Cl_2

55. 125 balloons

56. A decrease in temperature would tend to make the volume of the weather balloon decrease. Since the overall volume of the weather balloon increases when it rises to a higher altitude, the decrease in pressure must be more important than the decrease in temperature.

57. 2.28 L O_2

58. The volume would be 3.0 L, so the balloon will burst.

59. 922 mL

If 4.21 L of $NH_3(g)$ at 27 °C and 1.02 atm is combined with 5.35 L of $HCl(g)$ at 26 °C and 0.998 atm, what mass of $NH_4Cl(s)$ will be produced? Which gas is the limiting reactant? Which gas is present in excess?

49. If water is added to magnesium nitride, ammonia gas is produced when the mixture is heated.

$$Mg_3N_2(s) + 3H_2O(l) \rightarrow 3MgO(s) + 2NH_3(g)$$

If 10.3 g of magnesium nitride is treated with water, what volume of ammonia gas would be collected at 24 °C and 752 mm Hg?

50. What volume does a mixture of 14.2 g of He and 21.6 g of H_2 occupy at 28 °C and 0.985 atm?

51. A sample of hydrogen gas has a volume of 145 mL when measured at 44 °C and 1.47 atm. What volume would the hydrogen sample occupy at STP?

52. A mixture contains 5.00 g *each* of O_2, N_2, CO_2, and Ne gas. Calculate the volume of this mixture at STP. Calculate the partial pressure of each gas in the mixture at STP.

53. Given the following *unbalanced* chemical equation for the combination reaction of sodium metal and chlorine gas

$$Na(s) + Cl_2(g) \rightarrow NaCl(s)$$

what volume of chlorine gas, measured at STP, is necessary for the complete reaction of 4.81 g of sodium metal?

54. Potassium permanganate, $KMnO_4$, is produced commercially by oxidizing aqueous potassium manganate, K_2MnO_4, with chlorine gas. The *unbalanced* chemical equation is

$$K_2MnO_4(aq) + Cl_2(g) \rightarrow KMnO_4(s) + KCl(aq)$$

What volume of $Cl_2(g)$, measured at STP, is needed to produce 10.0 g of $KMnO_4$?

Critical Thinking

55. A helium tank contains 25.2 L of helium at 8.40 atm pressure. Determine how many 1.50-L balloons at 755 mm Hg can be inflated with the gas in the tank, assuming that the tank will also have to contain He at 755 mm Hg after the balloons are filled (that is, it is not possible to empty the tank completely). The temperature is 25 °C in all cases.

56. As weather balloons rise from the earth's surface, the pressure of the atmosphere becomes less, tending to cause the volume of the balloons to expand. However, the temperature is much lower in the upper atmosphere than at sea level. Would this temperature effect tend to make such a balloon expand or contract?

Weather balloons do, in fact, expand as they rise. What does this tell you?

57. Sulfur trioxide, SO_3, is produced in enormous quantities each year for use in the synthesis of sulfuric acid.

$$S(s) + O_2(g) \rightarrow SO_2(g)$$
$$2SO_2(g) + O_2(g) \rightarrow 2SO_3(g)$$

What volume of $O_2(g)$ at 350. °C and a pressure of 5.25 atm is needed to completely convert 5.00 g of sulfur to sulfur trioxide?

58. A particular balloon is designed by its manufacturer to be inflated to a volume of no more than 2.5 L. If the balloon is filled with 2.0 L of helium at sea level, is released, and rises to an altitude at which the atmospheric pressure is only 500. mm Hg, will the balloon burst?

59. An expandable vessel contains 729 mL of gas at 22 °C. What volume will the gas sample in the vessel have if it is placed in a boiling water bath (100. °C)?

60. A weather balloon is filled with 1.0 L of helium at 23 °C and 1.0 atm. What volume does the balloon have when it has risen to a point in the atmosphere where the pressure is 220 torr and the temperature is −31 °C?

61. Consider the following *unbalanced* chemical equation:

$$Cu_2S(s) + O_2(g) \rightarrow Cu_2O(s) + SO_2(g)$$

What volume of oxygen gas, measured at 27.5 °C and 0.998 atm, is required to react with 25 g of copper(I) sulfide? What volume of sulfur dioxide gas is produced under the same conditions?

62. A mixture contains 5.0 g of He, 1.0 g of Ar, and 3.5 g of Ne. Calculate the volume of this mixture at STP. Calculate the partial pressure of each gas in the mixture at STP.

63. In an experiment 350.0 mL of hydrogen gas was collected over water at 27 °C and 72 cm Hg. Then the absolute temperature doubled, the total pressure changed to 1.00 atm, and one-third of the gas leaked out of the container. What would the final volume be?

64. A balloon will burst at a volume of 2.00 L. If it is partially filled at a temperature of 20 °C and a pressure of 775 mm Hg to a volume of 0.750 L, what is the temperature at which it will burst?

65. One method for estimating the temperature at the center of the sun is based on the ideal gas law. If the center of the sun is assumed to be a mass of gases with average molar mass of 2.00 g and if the density and pressure are 1.4 g/cm^3 and 1.3×10^9 atm, respectively, calculate the temperature.

66. A 0.0712-g sample of X_4H_{10} has a volume of 30.0 cm^3 at 801 mm Hg and 20.0 °C. What is the element X?

67. A certain German sportscar engine has a cylinder volume of 618 cm^3. The cylinder is full of air at 75 °C and 802 mm Hg. How many moles of gas are in the cylinder? If air is 20.0% oxygen by volume, how many molecules of oxygen are present?

68. A certain compound contains 48.6% carbon, 8.18% hydrogen, and 43.2% oxygen by mass. The gas at 150.0 °C and 1.00 atm has a density of 2.13 g/L. Suggest two possible Lewis structures for the compound.

14 Liquids and Solids

	Section	Text Features & Components	Labs, Demonstrations & Activities
Teaching Segment 14A **3 blocks** **pp. 442–449**	14.1 Intermolecular ● Forces	**LP** Lesson Plans (Sec 14.1–14.3)	**LM** Experiment 55: Magic Sand Lab Manual Report Sheets Teacher's Lab Guide
	14.2 Water and Its Phase ◕ Changes		**LM** Experiment 56–57 Lab Manual Report Sheets Teacher's Lab Guide
	14.3 Energy Requirements ● for the Changes of ◔ State	**SE** Top Ten Lowest Melting Points *p. 447* **SE** Chemical Impact: Whales Need Changes of State *p. 448*	**SE** Chemistry in the Laboratory: Heat of Fusion of Ice *p. 462* **LM** Experiment 58–59 Lab Manual Report Sheets Teacher's Lab Guide
Teaching Segment 14B **1.5 blocks** **pp. 449–453**	14.4 Evaporation and ● Vapor Pressure ◑	**LP** Lesson Plans (Sec 14.4–14.5)	**TE** Mini Demo *pp. 449–450* **TE** Teaching Support: Demonstration *pp. 450–451* **LM** Experiment 60: Vapor Pressure of Water Lab Manual Report Sheets Teacher's Lab Guide
	14.5 Boiling Point and ◔ Vapor Pressure		**TE** Mini Demo *p. 452* **TE** Teaching Support: Demonstration *pp. 452–453* **SE** Chemistry in Action: Hot Molecules *p. 453*
Teaching Segment 14C **0.5 block** **pp. 454–461**	14.6–14.7 ◔ The Solid State: Types of Solids Bonding in Solids	**LP** Lesson Plans (Sec 14.6–14.7) **SE** Celebrity Chemical: Titanium *p. 454* **SE** Chemical Impact: Reducing Friction *p. 458* **SE** Chemical Impact: Metal with a Memory *p. 460*	

Key

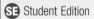 Student Edition
TE Teacher Edition
RP Teacher Resource Package
LM Lab Materials
LP Lesson Plans
AR Additional Resources
 Florida Specific

Technology and Media

 Transparencies
Figure 14.4, 14.6, 14.7, 14.13, 14.14, 14.17, 14.18
PowerPoint Slides

 Animation Polar Molecules • Hydrogen Bonding • London Forces I • London Forces II

 Video Vapor Pressure
Chemistry in Motion (19) Boiling Water with Ice

 eEdition CD-ROM
Easy Planner CD-ROM
English Summaries CD
Spanish Summaries CD

Web Site classzone.com
McDougal Littell Test Generator

Chapter Planning Guide

All Learners	Review & Assessment	Standards
TE Active Learning *p. 442* ▗ Transparency: Figure 14.4, 14.6 **TE** Teaching Tips *p. 443* ▗ Animation: Polar Molecules • Hydrogen Bonding • London Forces I and II **AR** Less Proficient Students *p. 27*	**SE** What if . . . *p. 443* **SE** Key Terms *p. 462* **SE** Questions and Problems *p. 463*	**TE** **NSES** UCP1, UCP3, UCP5, A1, A2, B2, B4, B5, C5, C6 ◗ **SSS** SC.A.1.4.3, SC.A.1.4.2, SC.B.1.4.1
TE Teaching Tip *p. 444* ▗ Transparency: Figure 14.7 **AR** Less Proficient Students *p. 27*	**SE** Key Terms *p. 462* **SE** Questions and Problems *p. 463*	
TE Teaching Tip *p. 447* **TE** Integrating the Chemical Impact *p. 448* **RP** Team Learning Worksheets (Sec 4.1–4.3) *pp. 75–76* **AR** Less Proficient Students *p. 27*	**TE** Additional Examples *pp. 446–447* **SE** Self Check *p. 448* **SE** Focus Questions (Sec 14.1–14.3) *p. 449* **SE** Key Terms *p. 462* **SE** Questions and Problems *p. 464*	
TE Active Learning *p. 449* ▣ Video: Vapor Pressure *p. 449* **AR** Less Proficient Students *p. 27*	**TE** Additional Examples *p. 451* **SE** Key Terms *p. 462* **SE** Questions and Problems *p. 464*	**TE** **NSES** UCP3, UCP5, A1, A2, B2, B4, B5 ◗ **SSS** SC.A.1.4.3, SC.B.1.4.3
▗ Transparency: Figures 14.13, 14.14 ▣ Chemistry in Motion (19) *p. 452* **TE** Misconceptions *p. 452* **RP** Team Learning Worksheets (Sec 14.4–14.5) *pp. 77–78* **AR** Less Proficient Students *p. 28*	**SE** What if . . . *p. 453* **SE** Focus Questions (Sec 14.4–14.5) *p. 453* **SE** Questions and Problems *p. 464*	
TE Active Learning *p. 454* **TE** Teaching Tip *pp. 455, 456, 459* ▗ Transparency: Figure 14.17, 14.18 **RP** Team Learning Worksheets (Sec 14.6–14.7) *p. 79* **AR** Less Proficient Students *p. 28*	**TE** Additional Examples *p. 461* **SE** Self Check *p. 461* **SE** Focus Questions (Sec 14.6–14.7) *p. 461* **SE** Key Terms *p. 462* **SE** Questions and Problems *pp. 464–465*	**TE** **NSES** UCP2, UCP5, A1, A2, B2, B5, E1, E2, F1, F6, G2 ◗ **SSS** SC.H.1.4.1, SC.H.1.4.2, SC.H.1.4.3, SC.H.1.4.6, SC.A.2.4.5, SC.A.1.4.2, SC.H.3.4.2, SC.H.3.4.3, SC.H.3.4.5, SC.H.3.4.6

Chapter Materials

TE Reading Strategy **AR** English/Spanish Summaries *pp. 22–23* **AR** Challenge Projects/Problems *pp. 26–27* **AR** Less Proficient Students *p. 28* ◎ English Summary Audio ◎ Spanish Summary Audio **RP** Chapter Review Worksheets (Basic, Review, Challenge)	**SE** Chapter Summary *p. 463* **SE** Critical Thinking *p. 465* **RP** Solutions Guide **RP** Chapter Tests **RP** Test Bank ▤ McDougal Littell Test Generator **AR** Standardized Test Practice ◗ **FCAT Test 7**

Chapter 14: Reading Graphs and Tables

Many students may be familiar with reading graphs and tables in mathematics class, but they may struggle with reading them in this course because of the complexity of the material. Explain that graphs and tables summarize information and show relationships, comparisons, and changes. Emphasize that these visual displays have to be read and then interpreted correctly for a complete understanding of the material.

How to Read Graphs

Remind the students that a graph is a visual representation of a relationship between two variables. A graph always has a horizontal axis and a vertical axis, each of which represents one of the two variables. Have students examine **Figure 14.5** on page 443.

Figure 14.5

In many cases, the title or the description of the graph provides valuable information. Point out that the first step in reading and understanding a graph is identifying the two variables that are being compared. Tell the students to read the labels on the axes.

Discuss with the students the two variables represented in the graph in **Figure 14.5**. According to the label, the vertical axis represents the boiling point, in Celsius degrees, of several compounds. This fact requires little interpretation by the reader. The horizontal axis label, however, may require some thought. The label reads "Period of X (H_2X)." Have the students look at the four points that are labeled on the graph and make conjectures about what the horizontal axis represents. Provide hints if necessary until the students arrive at the correct answer. [The horizontal axis represents the period (horizontal row) in the Periodic Table of an element (X) that is bonded to the hydrogen atom (H).] Provide this example if necessary:

> The number 2 on the horizontal axis represents the fact that oxygen (O) is in the second period of the Group 6 elements in the Periodic Table.

Have students use the Periodic Table on the inside back cover of their texts to check this.

Ask four of the students to read the boiling points of the four compounds plotted on the graph. Then have these students identify the period to which the element bonded to the hydrogen atom in each compound belongs. Make sure that each student understands before moving on.

Interpreting Graphs

Have the students look at **Figure 14.5** again. Point out that graphs are used not only to organize data, but also to show relationships, comparisons, and trends. To make use of this information, however, the students must study the data and make conjectures about any patterns they observe.

Ask the students to look at the relationship between the boiling points of H_2S, H_2Se, and H_2Te. What do they notice? [The boiling point increases as the period in the Periodic Table increases.]

Next, ask the students to consider the boiling point of water as presented in the graph. Without reading the text near the graph, have the students make a statement about the boiling point of water compared to the trend shown by the other Group 6 elements. [It is much higher than the trend suggests.] Point out that although the text explains this phenomenon in terms of the electronegativity of the oxygen atom, the graph effectively presents the fact that water has some special properties that cause the hydrogen and oxygen atoms to bond more strongly. Therefore, water has a much higher boiling point than the other compounds shown. This visual display will likely help the students to recall this information.

How to Read Tables

Tell the students that tables are another way of organizing data, particularly when there is a large range of numbers to consider. The information is organized in two or more columns and rows. Point out that columns (and sometimes rows) have headings to explain information being presented.

Have the students examine **Table 14.2** on page 444. Explain that by reading the title, the students can determine that the table presents the freezing points of the elements in Group 8 of the Periodic Table. Ask five of the students to use **Table 14.2** to determine the freezing point of each of the five elements listed in the table.

Keep in mind that even though reading tables may be easier for some of the students than reading graphs, the trends are not always as evident. Point out that in this particular table, the elements are arranged from top to bottom by their periods, just as they were in **Figure 14.5**. Given that fact, it can be determined that the freezing points of Group 8 elements increase as the period of the element increases. Ask the students to rearrange the elements alphabetically and it will not be as easy to see the trend.

TABLE 14.2

The Freezing Points of the Group 8 Elements

Element	Freezing Point (°C)
helium*	−272.0 (25 atm)
neon	−248.6
argon	−189.4
krypton	−157.3
xenon	−111.9

*Helium will not freeze unless the pressure is increased above 1 atm.

To make sure the students understand how to read graphs and tables, assign this exercise: Have the students take the information provided in **Figure 14.5** (page 443) and arrange it in a table as shown in **Table 14.2** (page 444). Then, have the students take the information provided in **Table 14.2** and arrange it in a graph as shown in **Figure 14.5**.

Chapter 14

Overview

In this Chapter our goals are for the students to:

- Learn about dipole–dipole attraction, hydrogen bonding and London dispersion forces

- Understand the effect of intermolecular forces on the properties of liquids

- Explore some important properties of water

- Understand and use heat of fusion and heat of vaporization

- Understand the relationship among vaporization, condensation and vapor pressure

- Relate the boiling point of water to its vapor pressure

- Learn about the various types of crystalline solids

- Learn about bonding in crystalline solids

14 Liquids and Solids

Ice, the solid form of water, provides recreation for this ice climber.

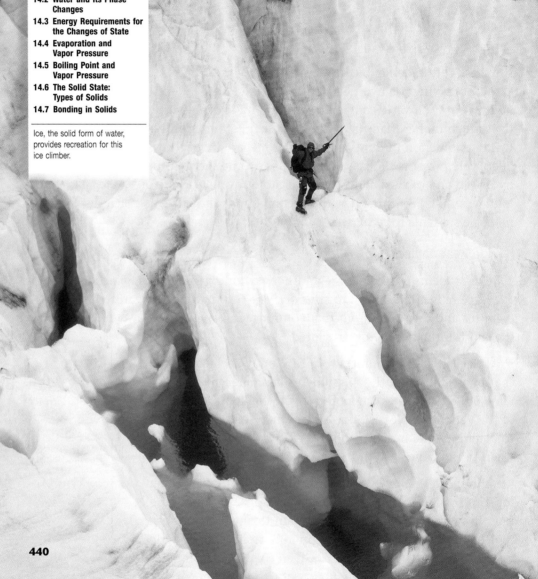

440

You have only to think about water to appreciate how different the three states of matter are. Flying, swimming, and ice skating are all done in contact with water in its various states. We swim in liquid water and skate on water in its solid form (ice). Airplanes fly in an atmosphere containing water in the gaseous state (water vapor). To allow these various activities, the arrangements of the water molecules must be significantly different in their gas, liquid, and solid forms.

In Chapter 13 we saw that the particles of a gas are far apart, are in rapid random motion, and have little effect on each other. Solids are obviously very different from gases. Gases have low densities, have high compressibilities, and completely fill a container. Solids have much greater densities than gases, are compressible only to a very slight extent, and are rigid; a solid maintains its shape regardless of its container. These properties indicate that the components of a solid are close together and exert large attractive forces on each other.

The properties of liquids lie somewhere between those of solids and of gases—but not midway between, as can be seen from some of the properties of the three states of water. For example, it takes about seven times more energy to change liquid water to steam (a gas) at 100 °C than to melt ice to form liquid water at 0 °C.

$$H_2O(s) \rightarrow H_2O(l) \qquad \text{energy required} \cong 6 \text{ kJ/mol}$$

$$H_2O(l) \rightarrow H_2O(g) \qquad \text{energy required} \cong 41 \text{ kJ/mol}$$

These values indicate that going from the liquid to the gaseous state involves a much greater change than going from the solid to the liquid. Therefore, we can conclude that the solid and liquid states are more similar than the liquid and gaseous states. This is also demonstrated by the densities of the three states of water **(Table 14.1).** Note that water in its gaseous state is about 2000 times less dense than in the solid and liquid states and that the latter two states have very similar densities.

We find in general that the liquid and solid states show many similarities and are strikingly different from the gaseous state (see **Figure 14.1**). The best way to picture the solid state is in terms of closely packed, highly ordered particles in contrast to the widely spaced, randomly arranged particles of a gas. The liquid state lies in between, but its properties indicate that it much more closely resembles the solid than the gaseous state. It is useful to picture a liquid in terms of particles that are generally quite close together, but with a more disordered arrangement than for the solid state and with some empty spaces. For most substances, the solid state has a higher density than the liquid, as Figure 14.1 suggests. However, water is an exception to this rule. Ice has an unusual amount of empty space and so is less dense than liquid water, as indicated in Table 14.1.

In this chapter we will explore the important properties of liquids and solids. We will illustrate many of these properties by considering one of the earth's most important substances: water.

A swimmer in water, one of the earth's most important substances.

TABLE 14.1

Densities of the Three States of Water

State	Density (g/cm³)
solid (0 °C, 1 atm)	0.9168
liquid (25 °C, 1 atm)	0.9971
gas (100 °C, 1 atm)	5.88×10^{-4}

Figure 14.1
Representations of the gas, liquid, and solid states.

Gas

Liquid

Solid

441

14.1 Intermolecular Forces

Objectives: *To learn about dipole–dipole attraction, hydrogen bonding, and London dispersion forces.*
To understand the effect of these forces on the properties of liquids.

Most substances consisting of small molecules are gases at normal temperatures and pressures. Examples are oxygen gas (contains O_2), nitrogen gas (contains N_2), methane gas (contains CH_4), and carbon dioxide gas (contains CO_2). A notable exception to this rule is water. Given the small size of its molecules we might expect water to be a gas at normal temperatures and pressures. Think about how different the world would be if water were a gas at 25 °C and 1 atm pressure. The oceans would be empty chasms, the Mississippi River would be a big, dry ditch, and it would never rain! Life on earth as we know it would be impossible if water were a gas under normal conditions.

So why is water a liquid rather than a gas at normal temperatures and pressures? The answer has to do with something called **intermolecular forces**—forces that occur between molecules. We can better understand this concept by referring to **Figure 14.2.** Notice that molecules are held together by bonds (sometimes called **intramolecular forces**) that occur inside the molecules. Intermolecular forces exist *between* molecules. We have seen that covalent bonding forces within molecules arise from the sharing of electrons, but how do intermolecular forces arise? Actually several types of intermolecular forces exist. To illustrate one type, we will consider the forces that exist among water molecules.

As we saw in Chapter 12, water is a polar molecule—it has a dipole moment. When molecules with dipole moments are put together, they orient themselves to take advantage of their charge distributions. Molecules with dipole moments can attract each other by lining up so that the positive and negative ends are close to each other, as shown in **Figure 14.3a.** This is called a **dipole–dipole attraction.** In the liquid, the dipoles find the best compromise between attraction and repulsion, as shown in **Figure 14.3b.**

Dipole–dipole forces are typically only about 1% as strong as covalent or ionic bonds, and they become weaker as the distance between the dipoles increases. In the gas phase, where the molecules are usually very far apart, these forces are relatively unimportant.

A plant physiologist is lowering a container of seeds into liquid nitrogen (77K) to preserve them.

Figure 14.2
Intermolecular forces exist *between* molecules. Bonds exist *within* molecules.

Figure 14.3
(a) The interaction of two polar molecules.
(b) The interaction of many dipoles in a liquid.

Attraction ----------
Repulsion ----------

(a)   (b)

Hydrogen Bonding

Particularly strong dipole–dipole forces occur between molecules in which hydrogen is bound to a highly electronegative atom, such as nitrogen, oxygen, or fluorine. Two factors account for the strengths of these interactions: the great polarity of the bond and the close approach of the dipoles, which is made possible by the very small size of the hydrogen atom. Because dipole–dipole attractions of this type are so unusually strong, they are given a special name—**hydrogen bonding. Figure 14.4** illustrates hydrogen bonding among water molecules.

Figure 14.4
(a) The polar water molecule. (b) Hydrogen bonding among water molecules. The small size of the hydrogen atoms allows the molecules to get very close and thus to produce strong interactions.

(a)   (b)

Hydrogen bonding has a very important effect on various physical properties. For example, the boiling points for the covalent compounds of hydrogen with the elements in Group 6 are given in **Figure 14.5.** Note that the boiling point of water is much higher than would be expected from the trend shown by the other members of the series. Why? Because the especially large electronegativity value of the oxygen atom compared with that of other group members causes the O—H bonds to be much more polar than the S—H, Se—H, or Te—H bonds. This leads to very strong hydrogen-bonding forces among the water molecules. An unusually large quantity of energy is required to overcome these interactions and separate the molecules to produce the gaseous state. That is, water molecules tend to remain together in the liquid state even at relatively high temperatures—hence the very high boiling point of water.

Figure 14.5
The boiling points of the covalent hydrides of elements in Group 6.

London Dispersion Forces

However, even molecules without dipole moments must exert forces on each other. We know this because all substances—even the noble gases—exist in the liquid and solid states at very low temperatures. There must be forces to hold the atoms or molecules as close together as they are in these condensed states. The forces that exist among noble gas atoms and nonpolar molecules are called **London dispersion forces.** To understand the origin of these

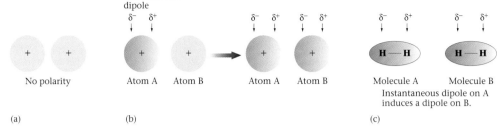

Instantaneous dipole

No polarity (a)

Atom A   Atom B (b)

Atom A   Atom B

Molecule A   Molecule B
Instantaneous dipole on A induces a dipole on B. (c)

Figure 14.6
(a) Two atoms with spherical electron probability. These atoms have no polarity. (b) The atom on the left develops an instantaneous dipole when more electrons happen to congregate on the left than on the right. (c) Nonpolar molecules also interact by developing instantaneous dipoles.

TABLE 14.2

The Freezing Points of the Group 8 Elements

Element	Freezing Point (°C)
helium*	−272.0 (25 atm)
neon	−248.6
argon	−189.4
krypton	−157.3
xenon	−111.9

*Helium will not freeze unless the pressure is increased above 1 atm.

forces, consider a pair of noble gas atoms. Although we usually assume that the electrons of an atom are uniformly distributed about the nucleus (see **Figure 14.6a**), this is apparently not true at every instant. Atoms can develop a temporary dipolar arrangement of charge as the electrons move around the nucleus. This *instantaneous dipole* can then *induce* a similar dipole in a neighboring atom, as shown in **Figure 14.6b.** The interatomic attraction thus formed is both weak and short-lived, but it can be very significant for large atoms and large molecules, as we will see.

The motions of the atoms must be greatly slowed down before the weak London dispersion forces can lock the atoms into place to produce a solid. This explains, for instance, why the noble gas elements have such low freezing points (see **Table 14.2**).

Nonpolar molecules such as H_2, N_2, and I_2, none of which has a permanent dipole moment, also attract each other by London dispersion forces (see **Figure 14.6c**). London forces become more significant as the sizes of atoms or molecules increase. Larger size means there are more electrons available to form the dipoles.

14.2 Water and Its Phase Changes

Objective: *To learn some of the important features of water.*

In the world around us we see many solids (soil, rocks, trees, concrete, and so on), and we are immersed in the gases of the atmosphere. But the liquid we most commonly see is water; it is virtually everywhere, covering about 70% of the earth's surface. Approximately 97% of the earth's water is found in the oceans, which are actually mixtures of water and huge quantities of dissolved salts.

Water is one of the most important substances on earth. It is crucial for sustaining the reactions within our bodies that keep us alive, but it also affects our lives in many indirect ways. The oceans help moderate the earth's temperature. Water cools automobile engines and nuclear power plants. Water provides a means of transportation on the earth's surface and acts as a medium for the growth of many of the creatures we use as food, and much more.

Section 14.2

Themes
Form and Function

Skills
Applying concepts, interpreting diagrams, making inferences

Laboratory
Experiment 56:
Freezing Point—A Physical Property, Traditional

Laboratory
Experiment 57:
Heating and Cooling Behavior of a Pure Substance, Traditional

TEACHING TIPS

- This section provides an opportunity to review calorimetry and the specific heat capacity for water.

- Because water is such a common substance, many interesting phenomena related to it can be discussed in class. For example, you might discuss why ice floats (its density), why pipes burst when they freeze (and why human tissue does not be-

have in the same way after freezing), why potholes form in road surfaces in the winter, and how water can crack large rocks and cause them to fall. If students are familiar with pressure cookers, this section offers an excellent opportunity to explain why foods cook faster in them.

CHEMISTRY

Remember that temperature is a measure of the random motions (average kinetic energy) of the particles in a substance.

Pure water is a colorless, tasteless substance that at 1 atm pressure freezes to form a solid at 0 °C and vaporizes completely to form a gas at 100 °C. This means that (at 1 atm pressure) the liquid range of water occurs between the temperatures 0 °C and 100 °C.

What happens when we heat liquid water? First the temperature of the water rises. Just as with gas molecules, the motions of the water molecules increase as it is heated. Eventually the temperature of the water reaches 100 °C; now bubbles develop in the interior of the liquid, float to the surface, and burst—the boiling point has been reached. An interesting thing happens at the boiling point: even though heating continues, the temperature stays at 100 °C until all the water has changed to vapor. Only when all of the water has changed to the gaseous state does the temperature begin to rise again. (We are now heating the vapor.) At 1 atm pressure, liquid water always changes to gaseous water at 100 °C, the **normal boiling point** for water.

The experiment just described is represented in **Figure 14.7**, which is called the **heating/cooling curve** for water. Going from left to right on this graph means energy is being added (heating). Going from right to left on the graph means that energy is being removed (cooling).

Figure 14.7
The heating/cooling curve for water heated or cooled at a constant rate. The plateau at the boiling point is longer than the plateau at the melting point, because it takes almost seven times as much energy (and thus seven times the heating time) to vaporize liquid water as to melt ice.

When liquid water is cooled, the temperature decreases until it reaches 0 °C, where the liquid begins to freeze (see Figure 14.7). The temperature remains at 0 °C until all the liquid water has changed to ice and then begins to drop again as cooling continues. At 1 atm pressure, water freezes (or, in the opposite process, ice melts) at 0 °C. This is called the **normal freezing point** of water. Liquid and solid water can co-exist indefinitely if the temperature is held at 0 °C. However, at temperatures below 0 °C liquid water freezes, while at temperatures above 0 °C ice melts.

Interestingly, water expands when it freezes. That is, one gram of ice at 0 °C has a greater volume than one gram of liquid water at 0 °C. This has very important practical implications. For instance, water in a confined space can break its container when it freezes and expands. This accounts for the bursting of water pipes and engine blocks that are left unprotected in freezing weather.

The expansion of water when it freezes also explains why ice cubes float. Recall that density is defined as mass/volume. When one gram of liquid water freezes, its volume becomes greater (it expands). Therefore, the *density* of one gram of ice is less than the density of one gram of water, because in the case of ice we divide by a slightly larger volume. For example, at 0 °C the density of liquid water is

$$\frac{1.00 \text{ g}}{1.00 \text{ mL}} = 1.00 \text{ g/mL}$$

and the density of ice is

$$\frac{1.00 \text{ g}}{1.09 \text{ mL}} = 0.917 \text{ g/mL}$$

The lower density of ice also means that ice floats on the surface of lakes as they freeze, providing a layer of insulation that helps to prevent lakes and rivers from freezing solid in the winter. This means that aquatic life continues to have liquid water available through the winter.

USING TECHNOLOGY

Figure 14.7

14.2 Water and Its Phase Changes **445**

Themes
Form and Function, Systems

Skills
Applying concepts, interpreting diagrams, solving problems

Laboratory
Experiment 58:
Heat of Fusion of Ice, In Text

Laboratory
Experiment 59:
Energy and Changes of State, CBL

TEACHING TIPS

• Remind students that energy is required for a phase change, even though the temperature is not changing during that time. The energy applied to the system is used to overcome the intermolecular forces.

• Remind students that during a phase change, no temperature change occurs, and that no change of phase occurs when the temperature is changing.

Additional Examples

1. Calculate the energy released when 15.5 g of ice freezes at 0 °C. The molar heat of fusion of ice is 6.02 kJ/mol.
5.18 kJ

2. Calculate the energy required to melt 12.5 g of ice at 0 °C and change it to water at 25 °C. The specific heat capacity of liquid water is 4.18 J/g °C and the molar heat of fusion of ice is 6.02 kJ/mol.
5.48 kJ

14.3 Energy Requirements for the Changes of State

Objectives: *To learn about interactions among water molecules.*
To understand and use heat of fusion and heat of vaporization.

It is important to recognize that changes of state from solid to liquid and from liquid to gas are *physical* changes. No *chemical* bonds are broken in these processes. Ice, water, and steam all contain H_2O molecules. When water is boiled to form steam, water molecules are separated from each other (see **Figure 14.8**) but the individual molecules remain intact.

It takes energy to melt ice and to vaporize water, because intermolecular forces between water molecules must be overcome. In ice the molecules are virtually locked in place, although they can vibrate about their positions. When energy is added, the vibrational motions increase, and the molecules eventually achieve the greater movement and disorder characteristic of liquid water. The ice has melted. As still more energy is added, the gaseous state is eventually reached, in which the individual molecules are far apart and interact relatively little. However, the gas still consists of water molecules. It would take *much* more energy to overcome the covalent bonds and decompose the water molecules into their component atoms.

The energy required to melt 1 mol of a substance is called the **molar heat of fusion**. For ice, the molar heat of fusion is 6.02 kJ/mol. The energy required to change 1 mol of liquid to its vapor is called the **molar heat of vaporization**. For water, the molar heat of vaporization is 40.6 kJ/mol at 100 °C. Notice in Figure 14.7 that the plateau that corresponds to the vaporization of water is much longer than that for the melting of ice. This occurs because it takes much more energy (almost seven times as much) to vaporize a mole of water than to melt a mole of ice. This is consistent with our models of solids, liquids, and gases (see Figure 14.1). In liquids, the particles (molecules) are relatively close together, so most of the intermolecular forces are still present. However, when the molecules go from the liquid to the gaseous state, they must be moved far apart. To separate the molecules enough to form a gas, virtually all of the intermolecular forces must be overcome, and this requires large quantities of energy.

Figure 14.8
Both liquid water and gaseous water contain H_2O molecules. In liquid water the H_2O molecules are close together, whereas in the gaseous state the molecules are widely separated. The bubbles contain gaseous water.

Example 14.1

Calculating Energy Changes: Solid to Liquid

Calculate the energy required to melt 8.5 g of ice at 0 °C. The molar heat of fusion for ice is 6.02 kJ/mol.

Solution

The molar heat of fusion is the energy required to melt *1 mol* of ice. In this problem we have 8.5 g of solid water. We must find out how many moles of ice this mass represents. Because the molar mass of water is 16 + 2(1) = 18, we know that 1 mol of water has a mass of 18 g, so we can convert 8.5 g of H_2O to moles of H_2O.

$$8.5 \text{ g } H_2O \times \frac{1 \text{ mol } H_2O}{18 \text{ g } H_2O} = 0.47 \text{ mol } H_2O$$

Because 6.02 kJ of energy is required to melt a mole of solid water, our sample will take about half this amount (we have approximately half a mole of ice). To calculate the exact amount of energy required, we will use the equivalence statement

6.02 kJ required for 1 mol of H_2O

which leads to the conversion factor we need:

$$0.47 \; \cancel{mol \; H_2O} \times \frac{6.02 \; kJ}{\cancel{mol \; H_2O}} = 2.8 \; kJ$$

This can be represented symbolically as

0.47 mol ice		2.8 kJ required
	⇨ $\frac{6.02 \; kJ}{mol}$	

Example 14.2

Calculating Energy Changes: Liquid to Gas

Calculate the energy (in kJ) required to heat 25 g of liquid water from 25 °C to 100. °C and change it to steam at 100. °C. The specific heat capacity of liquid water is 4.18 J/g °C, and the molar heat of vaporization of water is 40.6 kJ/mol.

Specific heat capacity was discussed in Section 10.5.

TOP TEN
Lowest Melting Points

Element	Melting Point (°C)
1. Helium	−270.
2. Hydrogen	−259
3. Neon	−249
4. Fluorine	−220.
5. Oxygen	−218
6. Nitrogen	−210.
7. Argon	−189
8. Krypton	−157
9. Xenon	−112
10. Chlorine	−101

MATH

When possible, try to break a large problem into a series of smaller problems.

Solution

This problem can be split into two parts: (1) heating the water to its boiling point and (2) converting the liquid water to vapor at the boiling point.

Step 1: Heating to Boiling We must first supply energy to heat the liquid water from 25 °C to 100. °C. Because 4.18 J is required to heat one gram of water by one Celsius degree, we must multiply by both the mass of water (25 g) and the temperature change (100. °C 2 25 °C 5 75 °C),

Energy required (Q)	=	Specific heat capacity (s)	×	Mass of water (m)	×	Temperature change (ΔT)

which we can represent by the equation

$$Q = s \times m \times \Delta T$$

Thus

$$Q = 4.18 \frac{J}{g \, °C} \times 25 \; g \times 75 \; °C = 7.8 \times 10^3 \; J$$

Energy required to heat 25 g of water from 25 °C to 100. °C · Specific heat capacity · Mass of water · Temperature change

$$= 7.8 \times 10^3 \; \cancel{J} \times \frac{1 \; kJ}{1000 \; \cancel{J}} = 7.8 \; kJ$$

(continued)

14.3   Energy Requirements for the Changes of State   **447**

Step 2: Vaporization Now we must use the molar heat of vaporization to calculate the energy required to vaporize the 25 g of water at 100. °C. The heat of vaporization is given per mole rather than per gram, so we must first convert the 25 g of water to moles.

$$25 \text{ g H}_2\text{O} \times \frac{1 \text{ mol H}_2\text{O}}{18 \text{ g H}_2\text{O}} = 1.4 \text{ mol H}_2\text{O}$$

We can now calculate the energy required to vaporize the water.

$$\underbrace{\frac{40.6 \text{ kJ}}{\text{mol H}_2\text{O}}}_{\substack{\text{Molar heat of} \\ \text{vaporization}}} \times \underbrace{1.4 \text{ mol H}_2\text{O}}_{\substack{\text{Moles of water}}} = 57 \text{ kJ}$$

The total energy is the sum of the two steps.

$$\underbrace{7.8 \text{ kJ}}_{\substack{\text{Heat from} \\ 25 \text{ °C to} \\ 100. \text{ °C}}} + \underbrace{57 \text{ kJ}}_{\substack{\text{Change to} \\ \text{vapor}}} = 65 \text{ kJ}$$

 Self-Check Exercise 14.1

Calculate the total energy required to melt 15 g of ice at 0 °C, heat the water to 100. °C, and vaporize it to steam at 100. °C.

Hint: Break the process into three steps and then take the sum.

CHEMICAL IMPACT   Connection to Biology

Whales Need Changes of State

Sperm whales are prodigious divers. They commonly dive a mile or more into the ocean, hovering at that depth in search of schools of squid or fish. To remain motionless at a given depth, the whale must have the same density as the surrounding water. Because the density of seawater increases with depth, the sperm whale has a system that automatically increases its density as it dives. This system involves the spermaceti organ found in the whale's head. Spermaceti is a waxy substance with the formula

$$\text{CH}_3\text{--(CH}_2)_{15}\text{--O--C--(CH}_2)_{14}\text{--CH}_3$$
$$\overset{\|}{\underset{\text{O}}{}}$$

which is a liquid above 30 °C. At the ocean surface the spermaceti in the whale's head is a liquid, warmed by the flow of blood through the spermaceti organ. When the whale dives, this blood flow decreases and the colder water causes the spermaceti to begin freezing. Because solid spermaceti is more dense than the liquid state, the sperm whale's density increases as it dives, matching the increase in the water's density.* When the whale wants to resurface, blood flow through the spermaceti organ increases, remelting the spermaceti and making the whale more buoyant. So the sperm whale's sophisticated density-regulating mechanism is based on a simple change of state.

A sperm whale.

*For most substances, the solid state is more dense than the liquid state. Water is an important exception.

448   Chapter 14   Liquids and Solids

Sections 14.1–14.3

1. What is the difference between intermolecular forces and intramolecular forces?

2. Is a hydrogen bond a true chemical bond? Explain.

3. How can molecules without dipoles condense to form liquids or solids?

4. Draw a cooling curve for a sample of steam (120 °C) that condenses to liquid water and cools to eventually form ice (0 °C).

5. Why are changes of state considered to be physical changes and not chemical changes?

6. Why doesn't the temperature of a substance (such as ice) change during melting? What is happening to the energy being added to the system?

Themes
Energy, Stability

Skills
Applying concepts, interpreting diagrams, making inferences

Student Preparation
Assign the students to read Sections 14.4 and 14.5 and to answer the Focus Questions at the end of Section 14.5 before coming to class.

Active Learning
After introducing the material in Sections 14.4 and 14.5 in class, place the students in groups and have them work together on Sections 14.4–14.5: Team Learning Worksheet (located in the *Teacher Resources*). Answers and/or discussion of these questions are located in the *Teacher Resources*.

14.4 Evaporation and Vapor Pressure

Objective: *To understand the relationship among vaporization, condensation, and vapor pressure.*

We all know that a liquid can evaporate from an open container. This is clear evidence that the molecules of a liquid can escape the liquid's surface and form a gas. This process, which is called **vaporization** or **evaporation,** requires energy to overcome the relatively strong intermolecular forces in the liquid.

To help you understand the energy changes that accompany evaporation, consider the microscopic view of a liquid shown in **Figure 14.9.** Remember that the temperature of a substance reflects the *average* kinetic energy of the components of that substance. Not all components have this average value of the kinetic energy, however. In fact, some components have a relatively small kinetic energy (are moving relatively slowly), whereas other components may have a kinetic energy much higher than the average (are moving much faster than the "average component"). To escape into the vapor phase a given component must have sufficient speed to overcome the intermolecular forces of the liquid. Thus only the fastest-moving components can escape the surface of the liquid.

The high energy molecules escape the surface.

Figure 14.9
The microscopic view of a liquid near its surface.

Now consider what will happen if the evaporation process is taking place from an insulated container (no energy can flow in or out as heat). What will happen to the temperature of the liquid as evaporation occurs? Because the higher-energy components escape as evaporation occurs, the *average* energy of the remaining components will decrease. As the average kinetic energy of the components of the liquid drops, the temperature decreases. Thus evaporation is a cooling process—it is endothermic.

On the other hand, if a liquid evaporates from a container that is not insulated, energy will flow in (heat) as evaporation occurs to keep the temperature constant. Again, this process shows that evaporation is endothermic.

14.4 Evaporation and Vapor Pressure **449**

TEACHING TIPS

• The idea that evaporation is an endothermic process is difficult for many students to grasp. Take time to explain that the temperature of the liquid drops because the molecules with higher kinetic energy are going into the gas phase. Energy flows in if the container is not insulated; the temperature of the liquid will then remain constant.

• The familiar scents of fingernail polish remover and rubbing alcohol tell us that these liquids evaporate relatively easily.

MINI-DEMO

You will need a beaker of room-temperature water, a thermometer, and an electric fan. Have a student come to the front of the room and read the thermometer. Then ask students to tell you what will happen when you *(continued)*

1. Intermolecular forces occur between molecules; intramolecular forces occur within molecules.

2. A hydrogen bond is an example of an attractive force that occurs between molecules. In that sense, it is not a true chemical bond, which we consider to be formed within a molecule.

3. Molecules without dipoles can condense to form liquids as a result of London dispersion forces. These forces provide enough attraction when nonpolar molecules are moving slowly to cause the molecules to condense into the next state.

4. See Figure 14.7 drawn from steam downward.

5. A change of state does not change the molecules of the substance in any way. Their motion simply increases or decreases. A chemical change requires that the molecule be changed to a different chemical.

6. The temperature of a substance doesn't change when it is melting because the energy being added to the system is used to overcome the attractive forces holding the molecules together in the solid state.

(continued)

place the thermometer in front of the running fan. Many will believe that the thermometer will show a cooler temperature. It does not (the fan does not cool the air, although some students believe that it does). Then put the tip of the thermometer in the water and have a student read the temperature. Place the wet thermometer in front of the fan. The temperature will decrease significantly. Use this demonstration to explain the cooling effect of evaporation. We feel cooler in front of a fan because sweat evaporates from our skin. *Note:* You can also perform this demonstration without the fan to prove that the evaporation of water lowers the temperature. The fan merely serves to remove the warmer air more quickly from around the bulb of the thermometer.

Water is used to absorb heat from nuclear reactors. The water is then cooled in cooling towers before it is returned to the environment.

Figure 14.10
Behavior of a liquid in a closed container. (a) Net evaporation occurs at first, so the amount of liquid decreases slightly. (b) As the number of vapor molecules increases, the rate of condensation increases. Finally the rate of condensation equals the rate of evaporation. The system is at equilibrium.

A system at equilibrium is dynamic on the molecular level, but shows no visible changes.

CHEMISTRY

Vapor, not *gas,* is the term we customarily use for the gaseous state of a substance that exists naturally as a solid or liquid at 25 °C and 1 atm.

The fact that vaporization requires energy has great practical significance; in fact, one of the most important roles that water plays in our world is to act as a coolant. Because of the strong hydrogen bonding among its molecules in the liquid state, water has an unusually large heat of vaporization (41 kJ/mol). A significant portion of the sun's energy is spent evaporating water from the oceans, lakes, and rivers rather than warming the earth. The vaporization of water is also crucial to our body's temperature-control system, which relies on the evaporation of perspiration.

Vapor Pressure

When we place a given amount of liquid in a container and then close it, we observe that the amount of liquid at first decreases slightly but eventually becomes constant. The decrease occurs because there is a transfer of molecules from the liquid to the vapor phase **(Figure 14.10)**. However, as the number of vapor molecules increases, it becomes more and more likely that some of them will return to the liquid. The process by which vapor molecules form a liquid is called **condensation.** Eventually, the same number of molecules are leaving the liquid as are returning to it: the rate of condensation equals the rate of evaporation. *At this point no further change occurs in the amounts of liquid or vapor, because the two opposite processes exactly balance each other;* the system is at *equilibrium.* Note that this system is highly *dynamic* on the molecular level—molecules are constantly escaping from and entering the liquid. However, there is no *net* change because the two opposite processes just *balance* each other.

As an analogy, consider two island cities connected by a bridge. Suppose the traffic flow on the bridge is the same in both directions. There is motion—we can see the cars traveling across the bridge—but the number of cars in each city is not changing because an equal number enter and leave each one. The result is no *net* change in the number of autos in each city: an equilibrium exists.

The pressure of the vapor present at equilibrium with its liquid is called the *equilibrium vapor pressure* or, more commonly, the **vapor pressure** of the liquid. A simple barometer can be used to measure the vapor pressure of a liquid, as shown in **Figure 14.11.** Because mercury is so dense, any common liquid injected at the bottom of the column of mercury floats to the top, where it produces a vapor, and the pressure of this vapor pushes some mercury out of the tube. When the system reaches equilibrium, the vapor pressure can be determined from the change in the height of the mercury column.

In effect, we are using the space above the mercury in the tube as a closed container for each liquid. However, in this case as the liquid vaporizes, the vapor formed creates a pressure that pushes some mercury out of the tube and lowers the mercury level. The mercury level stops changing when the excess liquid floating on the mercury comes to equilibrium with the vapor. The change in the mercury level (in millimeters) from its initial position (before the liquid was injected) to its final position is equal to the vapor pressure of the liquid.

450   Chapter 14   Liquids and Solids

Figure 14.11
(a) It is easy to measure the vapor pressure of a liquid by using a simple barometer of the type shown here.
(b) The water vapor pushed the mercury level down 24 mm (760 − 736), so the vapor pressure of water is 24 mm Hg at this temperature.
(c) Diethyl ether is much more volatile than water and thus shows a higher vapor pressure. In this case, the mercury level has been pushed down 545 mm (760 − 215), so the vapor pressure of diethyl ether is 545 mm Hg at this temperature.

CHEMISTRY
Heavy molecules move at lower speeds than light ones and so produce a lower vapor pressure.

The vapor pressures of liquids vary widely (see Figure 14.11). Liquids with high vapor pressures are said to be *volatile*—they evaporate rapidly.

The vapor pressure of a liquid at a given temperature is determined by the *intermolecular forces* that act among the molecules. Liquids in which the intermolecular forces are large have relatively low vapor pressures, because such molecules need high energies to escape to the vapor phase. For example, although water is a much smaller molecule than diethyl ether, C_2H_5—O—C_2H_5, the strong hydrogen-bonding forces in water cause its vapor pressure to be much lower than that of ether (see Figure 14.11).

Example 14.3

Using Knowledge of Intermolecular Forces to Predict Vapor Pressure

Predict which substance in each of the following pairs will show the largest vapor pressure at a given temperature.

   a. $H_2O(l)$, $CH_3OH(l)$
   b. $CH_3OH(l)$, $CH_3CH_2CH_2CH_2OH(l)$

Solution

   a. Water contains two polar O—H bonds; methanol (CH_3OH) has only one. Therefore, the hydrogen bonding among H_2O molecules is expected to be much stronger than that among CH_3OH molecules. This gives water a lower vapor pressure than methanol.

   b. Each of these molecules has one polar O—H bond. However, because $CH_3CH_2CH_2CH_2OH$ is a much larger molecule than CH_3OH, it has much greater London forces and thus is less likely to escape from its liquid. Thus $CH_3CH_2CH_2CH_2OH(l)$ has a lower vapor pressure than $CH_3OH(l)$.

14.4   Evaporation and Vapor Pressure   **451**

temperature for each liquid on a table on the board. While the students are waiting to find the lowest temperature for each substance, use reference materials to have other students find the boiling point of each substance. Record this information on the board.

Teaching Notes Ask students to explain why the temperatures drop when the thermometers covered with wet filter paper are exposed to the air. On the basis of the observations of the behavior of the four liquids, what is the relationship between the normal boiling point and the effectiveness of the liquids in cooling by evaporation? You can relate this issue to the technique by giving a person with a high fever a sponge bath or a rubdown with alcohol to reduce the fever.

Section 14.5

Themes
Form and Function, Energy

Skills
Observing, interpreting data, making inferences

MISCONCEPTIONS

Ask students what they think is inside the bubbles formed when water boils. Students often have some interesting misconceptions about the phenomenon of boiling. Sometimes they will say that air or hydrogen and oxygen is in the bubbles. This answer clearly indicates how difficult it is for students to understand that boiling is a change of state that is a physical, not chemical, process. Spend time here discussing the ideas presented in the early part of this section to clear up confusion on this point.

MINI-DEMO

When discussing boiling, keep a boiling beaker of water in front of the class so you can refer to it. If possible, get some liquid nitrogen (hospital supply stores will sometimes sell small quantities of it). By having both a hot liquid and a cold liquid boiling visibly, you can dispel misconceptions that all boiling occurs at high temperatures.

USING TECHNOLOGY

 Figure 14.13

 Figure 14.14

Animation and Video
If you prefer, you can use the *Chemistry in Motion,* Demonstration 19, instead of the demonstration at the right.

452

Boiling Point and Vapor Pressure

Objective: *To relate the boiling point of water to its vapor pressure.*

Look at the photo in **Figure 14.12** of water boiling and recall your own experiences with boiling water. When water boils, bubbles form in the interior of the liquid, then rise to the surface where they "pop." What causes these bubbles to form at the boiling point and not at a lower temperature?

Figure 14.12
Water rapidly boiling on a stove.

CHEMISTRY

As you heat water, notice that tiny bubbles form well below the boiling point. These bubbles result from dissolved air being expelled from the water.

Figure 14.13
An air bubble acts as a "birth place" for a bubble growing in the interior of water as high-energy H_2O (●) molecules enter. ●● represent N_2 molecules; ◌ represent O_2 molecules.

Figure 14.13 depicts the formation of an interior bubble. Assume we start with a tiny air bubble in the water. This bubble expands when high-energy water molecules enter the bubble and produce enough internal pressure to push back the water surrounding the bubble. The formation of a bubble can happen only when the average kinetic energy of the water molecules is great enough to produce a pressure inside the bubble that can oppose the atmospheric pressure pushing down on the surface of the water (see **Figure 14.14**). That is, the vapor pressure of the water must be equal to atmospheric pressure before boiling can occur. This explains why the boiling of water occurs at 100 °C at an atmospheric pressure of 1 atm and not at a lower temperature. Only when the water temperature reaches 100 °C are bubbles able to form in the interior of the liquid because the water molecules are energetic enough to sustain a pressure of 1 atm inside the bubbles. At temperatures below 100 °C the external pressure (1 atm) pushing on the surface

Figure 14.14
The formation of the bubble in the interior of water is opposed by atmospheric pressure.

452   Chapter 14   Liquids and Solids

TEACHING SUPPORT
Demonstration

Boiling Water at Reduced Temperatures

Materials
1-L round-bottom flask (do not use a flat-bottom flask—it may implode due to the low pressure)
Ice (in a small zip-lock bag)
Thermometer

One-hole stopper to fit the flask
Ringstand
Clamp for round-bottom flask
Oven mitt
Burner

Preparation Carefully insert the thermometer through the one-hole stopper. (Use glycerin to lubricate the stopper and protect your hand during the process.) Half-fill the flask with tap water.

Presentation Clamp the flask to the ringstand. Heat the water until it boils and the vapor fills the flask. (*Note:* It is best to start this process and then do something else in class until the water is hot, as the time required could be as long as 10 minutes.) Remove the heat source and firmly insert the stopper assembly into the flask. Carefully invert the flask assembly, taking care not to break the thermometer.

TABLE 14.3

Boiling Point of Water at Various Locations

Location	Feet Above Sea Level	P_{atm} (atm)	Boiling Point (°C)
Top of Mt. Everest, Tibet	29,028	0.32	70
Top of Mt. McKinley, Alaska	20,320	0.45	79
Top of Mt. Whitney, California	14,494	0.57	85
Top of Mt. Washington, New Hampshire	6293	0.78	93
Boulder, Colorado	5430	0.80	94
Madison, Wisconsin	900	0.96	99
New York City, New York	10	1.00	100
Death Valley, California	−282	1.01	100.3

WHAT IF?

You have seen that the water molecule has a bent shape and is therefore a polar molecule. This characteristic accounts for many of water's interesting properties.

What if the water molecule were linear? How would it affect the properties of water? How would life be different?

of the water prevents bubbles formation. So water boils at 100 °C (1 atm atmospheric pressure) because its vapor pressure is 1 atm at 100 °C.

Given this information, why do you suppose that water boils at 90 °C in Leadville, Colorado (elevation 10,000 ft)? Because Leadville is located at a high elevation where the atmospheric pressure is much less than 1 atm, the pressure pushing on the surface of water there is much less than at sea level. Thus you do not have to heat water to as high a temperature in Leadville to enable bubbles to form in the interior of the water. As a consequence, water can boil at a lower temperature in Leadville than in Los Angeles.

We have seen that the boiling point of water changes with atmospheric pressure. **Table 14.3** shows the boiling point of water at various locations around the world.

CHEMISTRY in ACTION

Hot Molecules

1. Obtain a molecular model kit from your teacher.
2. Build models for each pair of molecules.
   a. H_2O, CH_4
   b. C_2H_6, C_6H_{14}
   c. C_8H_{18}, C_8H_{18} (make one molecule with all the carbons connected in a line and one other molecule)
   d. C_2H_6O, C_2H_6O (make two different molecules)
3. Use your models to decide which of the molecules in each pair has the highest boiling point. Explain your reasoning.

Focus Questions

Sections 14.4–14.5

1. Use your knowledge of evaporation to explain why perspiration cools you on a warm, dry day.
2. Would you expect your hand to feel cooler if you dipped it into water and removed it to the air, or if you dipped your hand into methyl alcohol and removed it to the air? Explain.
3. What is the difference between boiling and evaporation?

Focus Questions **453**

CHEMISTRY in ACTION

Hot Molecules

Materials Each student/group will need a model kit (alternatively, they can use toothpicks and clay).

Purpose Students will explore the relationships between the shape of a molecule and the physical property of boiling point. In addition, they will review Lewis structures and the VSEPR theory.

Discussion The stronger the intermolecular attractions, the higher the boiling point. For small molecules, dipole–dipole interactions (of which hydrogen bonding is a special case) are stronger than London forces. When comparing two molecules with only London forces, the larger molecule (with more electrons) has a greater probability of a momentary dipole and, therefore, has stronger attractions (and a higher boiling point).

a. H_2O has a higher boiling point than CH_4 (100 °C versus −164 °C). Water is polar and methane is not (water also exhibits hydrogen bonding).

b. C_6H_{14} (have the students make the straight chain) has a higher boiling point than C_2H_6 (69 °C versus −88.6 °C). Hexane and ethane are both nonpolar, but hexane is a larger molecule.

c. The straight chain (*n*-octane) has a higher boiling point. For example, the boiling point

(continued)

Place the zip-lock bag of ice on top of the inverted flask. It will cool the gas within the flask. Have a student volunteer read the temperature on the thermometer every minute or so as the flask continues to cool and the water continues to boil.

Teaching Notes Condensing water vapor reduces the pressure inside the flask. Boiling occurs whenever the vapor pressure of the water equals the atmospheric pressure, so boiling will occur below the "normal" boiling point. Do not let the temperature go below 20 °C. The flask may implode at such a low pressure.

(continued)

of iso-octane (used in gasoline; also called 2,2,4-trimethylpentane) is 99.2 °C and the boiling point of *n*-octane is 125.7 °C. The *n*-octane molecules have more regions of attraction.

d. Ethanol (CH_3CH_2OH, 78.5 °C) has a higher boiling point than dimethyl ether (CH_3OCH_3, −25 °C). Both molecules are polar, but ethanol exhibits hydrogen bonding.

Answers to Focus Questions

1. Perspiration cools you on a warm day because the perspiration on your skin evaporates. The evaporation process is endothermic. The energy to change the state of the perspiration comes from your body, which causes your skin to feel cool.

2. Your hand would feel cooler if you dipped it into methyl alcohol and removed it to the air. At the same temperature, the vapor pressure of methyl alcohol is higher than the vapor pressure of water. Thus more molecules of methyl alcohol would leave the surface of your skin, each requiring energy to change state, thereby making your skin feel cool.

3. Evaporation occurs at temperatures below the boiling point. The phase change occurs at the surface of the liquid. At the boiling point the vapor pressure of the liquid is equal to the atmospheric pressure, so the change of state can take place anywhere within the liquid. Boiling is a much faster process than evaporation for this reason.

14.6 The Solid State: Types of Solids

Objective: *To learn about the various types of crystalline solids.*

Solids play a very important role in our lives. The concrete we drive on, the trees that shade us, the windows we look through, the paper that holds this print, the diamond in an engagement ring, and the plastic lenses in eyeglasses are all important solids. Most solids, such as wood, paper, and glass, contain mixtures of various components. However, some natural solids, such as diamonds and table salt, are nearly pure substances.

Many substances form **crystalline solids**—those with a regular arrangement of their components. This is illustrated by the partial structure of sodium chloride shown in **Figure 14.15**. The highly ordered arrangement of the components in a crystalline solid produces beautiful, regularly shaped crystals such as those shown in **Figure 14.16**.

$\bigcirc$ = Cl^-
$\bigcirc$ = Na^+

Figure 14.15
The regular arrangement of sodium and chloride ions in sodium chloride, a crystalline solid.

(a) (b) (c)

Figure 14.16
Several crystalline solids: (a) quartz, SiO_2; (b) rock salt, NaCl; and (c) red beryl, $Be_3AL_2Si_6O_{18}$.

CELEBRITY CHEMICAL

Titanium (Ti)

Titanium is a wonderful structural material. It is 43% less dense than steel but has 30% greater yield strength than steel when alloyed with metals such as aluminum and tin. Titanium also has excellent resistance to fatigue and corrosion. Titanium is especially well suited for making bicycle frames. After their first ride on a bicycle with a titanium frame, most experienced cyclists find themselves searching for the right words to describe the "magic" of titanium. In fact, the magic of titanium results from its combination of toughness, stretchability, and resilience. It resists deforming under

pedaling loads but does not transmit road shocks to the rider nearly as much as steel.

Titanium, a lustrous metal with a melting point of 1667 °C, is quite abundant in the earth's crust, ranking ninth of among the elements. Unfortunately, it is difficult to obtain from its ores in pure form. Titanium becomes very brittle when trace impurities such as C, N, and O are present, and it must be processed with great care. Its stretchability also makes it difficult to machine on a lathe to make specific parts. The resulting bicycle makes all these troubles worthwhile, however.

Titanium is used to make artificial hip joints.

454 Chapter 14 Liquids and Solids

Section 14.6

Themes
Models, Form and Function

Skills
Applying concepts, interpreting diagrams, making comparisons

Student Preparation
Assign the students to read Sections 14.6 and 14.7 and to answer the Focus Questions at the end of Section 14.7 before coming to class.

Active Learning
After introducing the material in Sections 14.6 and 14.7 in class, place the students in groups and have them work together on Sections 14.6–14.7: Team Learning Worksheet. Answers and/or discussion of these questions are located in the *Teacher Resources*.

CELEBRITY CHEMICAL
Titanium (Ti)
Ask students to research other uses for titanium.

Figure 14.17
The classes of crystalline solids.

Figure 14.18
Examples of three types of
crystalline solids. Only part of
the structure is shown in each
case. The structures continue in
three dimensions with the same
patterns. (a) An atomic solid.
Each sphere represents a
carbon atom in diamond.
(b) An ionic solid. The spheres
represent alternating Na⁺ and
Cl⁻ ions in solid sodium chloride.
(c) A molecular solid. Each unit
of three spheres represents an
H₂O molecule in ice. The dashed
lines show the hydrogen bonding
among the polar water molecules.

Figure 14.18

Examples of three types of crystalline solids. Only part of the structure is shown in each case. The structures continue in three dimensions with the same patterns. (a) An atomic solid. Each sphere represents a carbon atom in diamond. (b) An ionic solid. The spheres represent alternating Na^+ and Cl^- ions in solid sodium chloride. (c) A molecular solid. Each unit of three spheres represents an H_2O molecule in ice. The dashed lines show the hydrogen bonding among the polar water molecules.

There are many different types of crystalline solids. For example, both sugar and salt have beautiful crystals that we can easily see. However, although both dissolve readily in water, the properties of the resulting solutions are quite different. The salt solution readily conducts an electric current; the sugar solution does not. This behavior arises from the different natures of the components in these two solids. Common salt, NaCl, is an ionic solid that contains Na^+ and Cl^- ions. When solid sodium chloride dissolves in water, sodium ions and chloride ions are distributed throughout the resulting solution. These ions are free to move through the solution to conduct an electric current. Table sugar (sucrose), on the other hand, is composed of neutral molecules that are dispersed throughout the water when the solid dissolves. No ions are present, and the resulting solution does not conduct electricity. These examples illustrate two important types of crystalline solids: **ionic solids**, represented by sodium chloride; and **molecular solids**, represented by sucrose.

A third type of crystalline solid is represented by elements such as graphite and diamond (both pure carbon), boron, silicon, and all metals. These substances, which contain atoms of only one element covalently bonded to each other, are called **atomic solids.**

We have seen that crystalline solids can be grouped conveniently into three classes as shown in **Figure 14.17**. Notice that the names of the three classes come from the components of the solid. An ionic solid contains ions, a molecular solid contains molecules, and an atomic solid contains atoms. Examples of the three types of solids are shown in **Figure 14.18.**

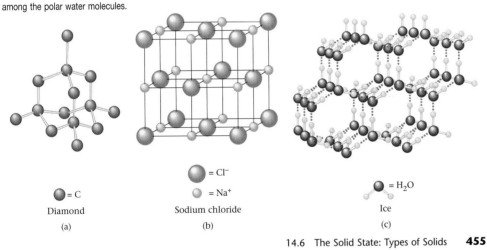

= C

Diamond

(a)

= Cl^-

= Na^+

Sodium chloride

(b)

= H_2O

Ice

(c)

USING TECHNOLOGY

 Figure 14.17

 Figure 14.18

The properties of a solid are determined primarily by the nature of the forces that hold the solid together. For example, although argon, copper, and diamond are all atomic solids (their components are atoms), they have strikingly different properties. Argon has a very low melting point (−189 °C), whereas diamond and copper melt at high temperatures (about 3500 °C and 1083 °C, respectively). Copper is an excellent conductor of electricity (it is widely used for electrical wires), whereas both argon and diamond are insulators. The shape of copper can easily be changed; it is both malleable (will form thin sheets) and ductile (can be pulled into a wire). Diamond, on the other hand, is the hardest natural substance known. The marked differences in properties among these three atomic solids are due to differences in bonding. We will explore the bonding in solids in the next section.

> The internal forces in a solid determine many of the properties of the solid.

Section 14.7

Themes
Form and Function

Skills
Applying concepts, interpreting diagrams, making comparisons

TEACHING TIPS

- Models of different crystal structures can be used very effectively to discuss the different types of solids.

- Remind students that the formulas for ionic solids are actually empirical formulas, not molecular formulas.

14.7 Bonding in Solids

Objectives: *To understand the interparticle forces in crystalline solids.*
To learn about how the bonding in metals determines metallic properties.

We have seen that crystalline solids can be divided into three classes, depending on the fundamental particle or unit of the solid. Ionic solids consist of oppositely charged ions packed together, molecular solids contain molecules, and atomic solids have atoms as their fundamental particles. Examples of the various types of solids are given in **Table 14.4.**

TABLE 14.4

Examples of the Various Types of Solids

Type of Solid	Examples	Fundamental Unit(s)
ionic	sodium chloride, $NaCl(s)$	Na^+, Cl^- ions
ionic	ammonium nitrate, $NH_4NO_3(s)$	NH_4^+, NO_3^- ions
molecular	dry ice, $CO_2(s)$	CO_2 molecules
molecular	ice, $H_2O(s)$	H_2O molecules
atomic	diamond, $C(s)$	C atoms
atomic	iron, $Fe(s)$	Fe atoms
atomic	argon, $Ar(s)$	Ar atoms

Ionic Solids

Ionic solids are stable substances with high melting points that are held together by the strong forces that exist between oppositely charged ions. The structures of ionic solids can be visualized best by thinking of the ions as spheres packed together as efficiently as possible. For example, in NaCl the larger Cl^- ions are packed together much like one would pack balls in a box. The smaller Na^+ ions occupy the small spaces ("holes") left among the spherical Cl^- ions, as represented in **Figure 14.19.**

> When spheres are packed together, there are many small empty spaces (holes) left among the spheres.

$\bigcirc$ = Cl^- $\bigcirc$ = Na^+

Figure 14.19
The packing of Cl^- and Na^+ ions in solid sodium chloride.

Molecular Solids

In a molecular solid the fundamental particle is a molecule. Examples of molecular solids include ice (contains H_2O molecules), dry ice (contains CO_2 molecules), sulfur (contains S_8 molecules), and white phosphorus (contains P_4 molecules). The latter two substances are shown in **Figure 14.20**.

Molecular solids tend to melt at relatively low temperatures because the intermolecular forces that exist among the molecules are relatively weak. If the molecule has a dipole moment, dipole–dipole forces hold the solid together. In solids with nonpolar molecules, London dispersion forces hold the solid together.

Part of the structure of solid phosphorus is represented in **Figure 14.21**. Note that the distances between P atoms in a given molecule are much shorter than the distances between the P_4 molecules. This is because the covalent bonds *between atoms* in the molecule are so much stronger than the London dispersion forces *between molecules*.

Figure 14.21
A representation of part of the structure of solid phosphorus, a molecular solid that contains P_4 molecules.

Covalent bonding forces

= London dispersion forces

= P

Atomic Solids

The properties of atomic solids vary greatly because of the different ways in which the fundamental particles, the atoms, can interact with each other. For example, the solids of the Group 8 elements have very low melting points (see Table 14.2), because these atoms, having filled valence orbitals, cannot form covalent bonds with each other. So the forces in these solids are the relatively weak London dispersion forces.

On the other hand, diamond, a form of solid carbon, is one of the hardest substances known and has an extremely high melting point (about 3500 °C). The incredible hardness of diamond arises from the very strong covalent carbon–carbon bonds in the crystal, which lead to a giant molecule. In fact, the entire crystal can be viewed as one huge molecule. A small part of the diamond structure is represented in Figure 14.18. In diamond each carbon atom is bound covalently to four other carbon atoms to produce a very stable solid. Several other elements also form solids whereby the atoms join together covalently to form giant molecules. Silicon and boron are examples.

At this point you might be asking yourself, "Why aren't solids such as a crystal of diamond, which is a 'giant molecule,' classified as molecular solids?" The answer is that, by convention, a solid is classified as a molecular solid only if (like ice, dry ice, sulfur, and phosphorus) it contains small molecules. Substances like diamond that contain giant molecules are called network solids.

Integrating the CHEMICAL IMPACT

Reducing Friction

Ask students to investigate uses for solid lubricants. Some students may have used graphite to lubricate the wheels of pinewood derby cars or locks.

CHEMICAL IMPACT

Science, Technology, and Society

Reducing Friction

Undoubtedly, you know about the ability of oil to reduce friction between moving parts. But did you know that some of the best industrial lubricants are solids? For example, graphite—you can feel its slipperiness by rubbing the "lead" in a pencil—is often used to lubricate locks, a place where oil would draw unwanted dirt. One of the best lubricants in industry today is powdered tungsten disulfide (WS_2), which exists as flat platelets about 500 nm in width. A team of scientists from the Weizmann Institute of Science in Rehovot, Israel, led by Keshef Tenne, has produced a new form of WS_2 that exists as spherical particles approximately 120 nm in diameter. The researchers hope that the spherical particles will act like miniature ball bearings and thus provide even more effective lubrication than the irregularly shaped particles in the WS_2 powders. Although thorough testing of the new lubricant has been hampered by difficulties in making the spher-

A single nanoparticle of WS_2.

ically shaped WS_2 particles, initial results indicate that this form provides a modest improvement in lubricating ability relative to the WS_2 powders.

Interestingly, other research has shown that just because something is spherical and rolls does not mean it will effectively lower friction. For example, spherical C_{60} molecules (buckyballs) are not very good lubricants by themselves, although they show some promise as additives to traditional liquid lubricants.

Tenne maintains that spherical WS_2 might work better than the buckyballs, because the much larger size of the WS_2 spheres should keep surfaces farther apart. Also, because the WS_2 particles are constructed of up to 20 concentric layers, like onions, they tend to maintain their spherical shape even as they wear away. Only time will tell whether the spherical WS_2 can beat the already outstanding lubricating properties of WS_2 powders.

Figure 14.22
Two types of alloys.

copper
Brass   zinc

(a) Brass is a substitutional alloy in which copper atoms in the host crystal are replaced by the similarly sized zinc atoms.

iron
Steel   carbon

(b) Steel is an interstitial alloy in which carbon atoms occupy interstices (holes) among the closely packed iron atoms.

A steel sculpture in Chicago.

Bonding in Metals

Metals represent another type of atomic solid. Metals have familiar physical properties: they can be pulled into wires, they can be hammered into sheets, and they are efficient conductors of heat and electricity. However, although the shapes of most pure metals can be changed relatively easily, metals are also durable and have high melting points. These facts indicate that it is difficult to separate metal atoms but relatively easy to slide them past each other. In other words, the bonding in most metals is *strong* but *nondirectional*.

The simplest picture that explains these observations is the **electron sea model,** which pictures a regular array of metal atoms in a "sea" of valence electrons that are shared among the atoms in a nondirectional way and that are quite mobile in the metal crystal. The mobile electrons can conduct heat and electricity, and the atoms can be moved rather easily, as, for example, when the metal is hammered into a sheet or pulled into a wire.

Because of the nature of the metallic crystal, other elements can be introduced relatively easily to produce substances called alloys. An **alloy** is best defined as *a substance that contains a mixture of elements and has metallic properties*. There are two common types of alloys.

In a **substitutional alloy** some of the host metal atoms are *replaced* by other metal atoms of similar sizes. For example, in brass approximately one-third of the atoms in the host copper metal have been replaced by zinc atoms, as shown in **Figure 14.22a.** Sterling silver (93% silver and 7% copper) and pewter (85% tin, 7% copper, 6% bismuth, and 2% antimony) are other examples of substitutional alloys.

An **interstitial alloy** is formed when some of the interstices (holes) among the closely packed metal atoms are occupied by atoms much smaller than the host atoms, as shown in **Figure 14.22b.** Steel, the best-known interstitial alloy, contains carbon atoms in the "holes" of an iron crystal. The presence of interstitial atoms changes the properties of the host metal. Pure iron is relatively soft, ductile, and malleable because of the absence of strong directional bonding. The spherical metal atoms can be moved rather easily with respect to each other. However, when carbon, which forms strong directional bonds, is introduced into an iron crystal, the presence of the directional carbon–iron bonds makes the resulting alloy harder, stronger, and less ductile than pure iron. The amount of carbon directly affects the properties of steel. *Mild steels* (containing less than 0.2% carbon) are still ductile and malleable and are used for nails, cables, and chains. *Medium steels* (containing 0.2–0.6% carbon) are harder than mild steels and are used in rails and structural steel beams. *High-carbon steels* (containing 0.6–1.5% carbon) are tough and hard and are used for springs, tools, and cutlery.

Many types of steel also contain elements in addition to iron and carbon. Such steels are often called *alloy steels* and can be viewed as being mixed interstitial (carbon) and substitutional (other metals) alloys. An example is stainless steel, which has chromium and nickel atoms substituted for some of the iron atoms. The addition of these metals greatly increases the steel's resistance to corrosion.

14.7 Bonding in Solids   **459**

You can perform the demonstration illustrated in this Chemical Impact by ordering memory metal from a supplier. The Institute for Chemical Education at the University of Wisconsin has Memory Metal kits that include the *ICE* sample, an explanation of how it works, and transparency masters for class. Both Flinn Scientific and Educational Innovations (see *Teacher Resources*) carry memory metal as well.

Students can also find more information on memory metal in *ChemMatters* magazine and on the Internet. Ask them to research other uses for this amazing substance.

Metal with a Memory

A distraught mother walks into the optical shop carrying her mangled pair of $400 eyeglasses. Her child had gotten into her purse, found her glasses, and twisted them into a pretzel. She hands them to the optometrist with little hope that they can be salvaged. The optometrist says not to worry and drops the glasses into a dish of warm water where the glasses magically spring back to their original shape. The optometrist hands the restored glasses to the woman and says there is no charge for repairing them.

How can the frames "remember" their original shape when placed in warm water? The answer is a nickel–titanium alloy called Nitinol that was developed in the late 1950s and early 1960s at the Naval Ordnance Laboratory in White Oak, Maryland, by William J. Buehler. (The name Nitinol comes from *Ni*ckel *Ti*tanium *Na*val *O*rdnance *L*aboratory.)

Nitinol has the amazing ability to remember a shape originally impressed in it. For example, note the accompanying photos. What causes Nitinol to behave this way? Although the details are too complicated to describe here, this phenomenon results from two different forms of solid Nitinol. When Nitinol is heated to a sufficiently high temperature, the Ni and Ti atoms arrange themselves in a way that leads to the most compact and regular pattern of the atoms—a form called austenite (A). When the alloy is cooled, its atoms rearrange slightly to a form called martensite (M). The shape desired (for example, the word *ICE*) is set into the alloy at a high temperature (A form), then the metal is cooled, causing it to assume the M form. In this process no visible change is noted. Then, if the image is deformed, it will magically return if the alloy is heated (hot water works fine) to a temperature that changes it back to the A form.

Nitinol has many medical applications, including hooks used by orthopedic surgeons to attach ligaments and tendons to bone and "baskets" to catch blood clots. In the latter case a length of Nitinol wire is shaped into a tiny basket and this shape is set at a high temperature. The wires forming the basket are then straightened so they can be inserted as a small bundle through a catheter. When the wires warm up in the blood, the basket shape springs back and acts as a filter to stop blood clots from moving to the heart.

One of the most promising consumer uses of Nitinol is for eyeglass frames. It's handy to have frames that remember their original shape. Nitinol is also now being used for braces to straighten crooked teeth.

The word *ICE* is formed from Nitinol wire.

The wire is stretched to obliterate the word *ICE*.

The wire pops back to *ICE* when immersed in warm water.

Example 14.4

Identifying Types of Crystalline Solids

Name the type of crystalline solid formed by each of the following substances:

    a. ammonia

    b. iron

    c. cesium fluoride

    d. argon

    e. sulfur

Solution

    a. Solid ammonia contains NH_3 molecules, so it is a molecular solid.

    b. Solid iron contains iron atoms as the fundamental particles. It is an atomic solid.

    c. Solid cesium fluoride contains the Cs^+ and F^- ions. It is an ionic solid.

    d. Solid argon contains argon atoms, which cannot form covalent bonds to each other. It is an atomic solid.

    e. Sulfur contains S_8 molecules, so it is a molecular solid.

 Self-Check Exercise 14.2

Name the type of crystalline solid formed by each of the following substances:

    a. sulfur trioxide

    b. barium oxide

    c. gold

 Focus Questions

Sections 14.6–14.7

1. Salt and sugar are both crystalline solids. How are they different?

2. What are the forces holding each type of crystalline solid together? Predict which type would have the lowest boiling point. Explain your choice.

3. How are metals different from an atomic solid such as diamond?

Focus Questions   **461**

Additional Examples

Name the type of crystalline solid formed by each of the following substances:

1. water
   molecular solid

2. calcium oxide
   ionic solid

3. krypton
   atomic solid

 Answers to Self-Check Exercise 14.2

a. Contains SO_3 molecules—a molecular solid.

b. Contains Ba^{2+} and O^{2-} ions—an ionic solid.

c. Contains Au atoms—an atomic solid.

Answers to Focus Questions

1. Salt is an ionic solid and sugar is a molecular solid.

2. molecular: dipole–dipole forces and London dispersion forces
ionic: electrostatic
atomic: covalent
The lowest boiling point would be molecular, because the intermolecular forces are weakest in these crystals.

3. Diamond has directed covalent bonds. In metals, the bonding is nondirectional.

CHEMISTRY in the LABORATORY

Heat of Fusion of Ice

Objectives

1. To carry out an experiment to determine the heat of fusion of ice

2. To compare the results to the accepted value and determine a percent error

Skills

Observing, applying concepts, evaluating, calculating

Materials

Goggles · Ice chips
Apron · (or small
Styrofoam · cubes) at 0 °C
cups (2) · Water
Lid for cup · Stirrer
(with 2 holes) · Thermometer
Plastic spoon

Preparation Hints

Have several coolers filled with ice placed around the lab.

Prelab Discussion

Remind students that thermometers are fragile. They must be careful in handling them and should never use a thermometer as a stirring rod.

Procedure Hints

The three major sources of error are (1) adding cold water along with the ice; (2) stirring the ice–water mixture too vigorously; and (3) removing water along with the excess ice at the end of the experiment. Watch for these errors as you circulate around the lab.

Post-Lab Discussion

This lab generally provides an accurate value for the heat of fusion of ice. Have students compare their values and discuss sources of errors.

Sample Data/Answers

Prelab Assignment

2. The density of water is dependent on the temperature of the water.

3. We are interested in determining the heat required to melt ice. As long as we add excess ice and keep the mixture at 0 °C, we are assured that the heat from the original water will be used solely to melt the ice and not to heat the newly formed liquid water.

Data/Observations

1. Answers will vary. This value depends on the temperature

CHEMISTRY in the LABORATORY
Heat of Fusion of Ice

Problem

How much heat is required to melt a gram of ice?

Introduction

Ice and water can coexist at the freezing point. To melt the ice, energy must be added. In this lab you will determine the amount of heat required to melt a gram of ice.

Prelab Assignment

1. Read the entire lab experiment before you begin.

2. You could have made volume measurements of the water and used the density of water as 1.0 g/mL to make your calculations. Why would this choice introduce error?

3. Why must excess ice be added? What problems might occur if this ice were not in excess?

Materials

Goggles · Ice chips (or small cubes)
Apron · at 0 °C
Styrofoam cups (2) · Water
Lid for cup (with 2 holes) · Stirrer
Plastic spoon · Thermometer

Safety

Thermometers are fragile. Be careful in handling them and never use a thermometer as a stirring rod.

Procedure

1. Place one Styrofoam cup into the other. This device is your calorimeter.

2. Place 75.0 g of water at room temperature in the calorimeter. Record the temperature of the water.

3. Using a paper towel, remove the residual water from several ice chips and add them to the water in the calorimeter. Cover the calorimeter.

---

4. Gently stir the water as the ice melts. Do not stir too vigorously or you will affect the temperature of the water. Add ice if necessary (there should always be ice present).

5. When the temperature of the ice–water mixture is 0 °C, use a plastic spoon to remove any excess ice in the calorimeter. Be careful not to take any water.

6. Measure the final mass of the water.

Cleaning Up

Clean all materials and wash your hands thoroughly.

Data/Observations

1. What was the change in temperature of the water?

2. What was the mass of ice that melted?

Analysis and Conclusions

1. Determine the heat transferred from the water to the ice.

2. According to your results, how much heat is required to melt a gram of ice?

3. The actual value for the heat of fusion of ice is about 330 J/g. Determine the percent error in your value.

4. Would each of the following scenarios cause you to calculate a heat of fusion higher or lower than the accepted answer? Explain your answer.
   a. The ice you add to the calorimeter has a significant amount of water on it.
   b. The ice is initially colder than 0 °C.
   c. A significant amount of water is taken when the excess ice is removed from the calorimeter.

Something Extra

We assume that all of the heat transfer in the calorimeter is from the water to the ice. Design an experiment to determine the heat transferred to the environment surrounding the calorimeter.

Key Terms

intermolecular forces (14.1)
intramolecular forces (14.1)
dipole–dipole attraction (14.1)
hydrogen bonding (14.1)
London dispersion

forces (14.1)
normal boiling point (14.2)
heating/cooling curve (14.2)
normal freezing point (14.2)
molar heat of fusion (14.3)
molar heat of vaporization (14.3)

vaporization (evaporation) (14.4)
condensation (14.4)
vapor pressure (14.4)
crystalline solid (14.6)
ionic solid (14.6)

molecular solid (14.6)
atomic solid (14.6)
electron sea model (14.7)
alloy (14.7)
substitutional alloy (14.7)
interstitial alloy (14.7)

(14) **Chapter Review**

---

of the water—if the water is 22 °C, for example, the change is 22 °C, since the final temperature is 0 °C.

2. Answers will vary (assume 21.2 g for the analysis below).

Analysis and Conclusions

1. If the water was at 22 °C, the heat transferred is 6.90 kJ.

2. From the results given above, the energy required to melt 1 g of ice is 325 J/g.

3. Given the above values, the percent error is 1.5%.

4. a. If there is a significant amount of water on the ice, less energy is required to achieve a final temperature of 0 °C (the water on the ice is at or above 0 °C). If less energy is required, we would expect an answer that is lower than the accepted answer.

b. If the ice is initially colder than 0 °C, the temperature of the ice must first be raised to 0 °C be-

fore it is melted. Thus it would require more energy to bring the final mixture up to 0 °C, and the answer would be higher than expected.

c. If a significant amount of water is taken out when the excess ice is removed from the calorimeter, our value for the mass of ice melted would be too low. In this case, our value for the heat of fusion of ice would be higher than expected.

Summary

1. Liquids and solids exhibit some similarities and are very different from the gaseous state.

2. The temperature at which a liquid changes its state to a gas (at 1 atm pressure) is called the normal boiling point of that liquid. Similarly, the temperature at which a liquid freezes (at 1 atm pressure) is the normal freezing point. Changes of state are physical changes, not chemical changes.

3. To convert a substance from the solid to the liquid and then to the gaseous state requires the addition of energy. Forces among the molecules in a solid or a liquid must be overcome by the input of energy. The energy required to melt 1 mol of a substance is called the molar heat of fusion, and the energy required to change 1 mol of liquid to the gaseous state is called the molar heat of vaporization.

4. There are several types of intermolecular forces. Dipole–dipole interactions occur when molecules with dipole moments attract each other. A particularly strong dipole–dipole interaction called hydrogen bonding occurs in molecules that contain hydrogen bonded to a very electronegative element such as N, O, or F. London dispersion forces occur when instantaneous dipoles in atoms or nonpolar molecules lead to relatively weak attractions.

5. The change of a liquid to its vapor is called vaporization or evaporation. The process whereby vapor molecules form a liquid is called condensation. In a closed container, the pressure of the vapor over its liquid reaches a constant value called the vapor pressure of the liquid.

6. Many solids are crystalline (contain highly regular arrangements of their components). The three types of crystalline solids are ionic, molecular, and atomic solids. In ionic solids, the ions are packed together in a way that maximizes the attractions of oppositely charged ions and minimizes the repulsions among identically charged ions. Molecular solids are held together by dipole–dipole attractions if the molecules are polar and by London dispersion forces if the molecules are nonpolar. Atomic solids are held together by covalent bonding forces or London dispersion forces, depending on the atoms present.

Questions and Problems

All exercises with blue numbers have answers in the back of this book.

14.1 Intermolecular Forces

Questions

1. What is a *dipole–dipole* attraction? Give three examples of liquid substances in which you would expect dipole–dipole attractions to be large.

2. How is the strength of dipole–dipole interactions related to the *distance* between polar molecules? Are dipole–dipole forces short-range or long-range forces?

3. What is meant by *hydrogen bonding*? Give three examples of substances that would be expected to exhibit hydrogen bonding in the liquid state.

4. The normal boiling point of water is unusually high, compared to the boiling points of H_2S, H_2Se, and H_2Te. Explain this observation in terms of the *hydrogen bonding* that exists in water, but that does not exist in the other compounds.

5. Why are the dipole–dipole interactions between polar molecules *not* important in the vapor phase?

6. Although the noble gas elements are monatomic and could not give rise to dipole–dipole forces or hydrogen bonding, these elements still can be liquefied and solidified. Explain.

Problems

7. Discuss the types of intermolecular forces acting in the liquid state of each of the following substances.
   - a. Kr
   - b. S_8
   - c. NF_3
   - d. H_2O

8. The boiling points of the noble gas elements are listed below. Comment on the trend in the boiling points. Why do the boiling points vary in this manner?

He	−272 °C	Kr	−152.3 °C
Ne	245.9 °C	Xe	−107.1 °C
Ar	−185.7 °C	Rn	−61.8 °C

9. When 50 mL of liquid water at 25 °C is added to 50 mL of ethanol (ethyl alcohol), also at 25 °C, the combined volume of the mixture is considerably *less* than 100 mL. Give a possible explanation.

14.2 Water and Its Phase Changes

Questions

10. What are some important physical properties of water? How do these properties of water help to moderate the earth's environment?

11. Describe some uses, both in nature and in industry, of water as a *cooling* agent.

12. We all have observed that ice *floats* on liquid water. Why? What is unusual about this?

13. Discuss some implications of the fact that, unlike most substances, water *expands* in volume when it freezes.

14. Describe, on both a microscopic and a macroscopic basis, what happens to a sample of water as it is heated from room temperature to 50 °C above its normal boiling point.

15. Figure 14.7 presents the *cooling curve* for water. Discuss the meaning of the different portions of this curve (for example, explain what each flat section and each sloping section represents).

Chapter Review   **463**

Computerized Test Bank for Chapter 14

Answers to End of Chapter Problems

1. Dipole–dipole interactions occur when molecules possessing dipole moments orient themselves so that the positive and negative ends of the adjacent molecules attract each other. Any three polar liquids will possess dipole–dipole forces among their molecules [e.g., $CHCl_3(l)$, $SO_2\,(l)$, $NO_2\,(l)$].

2. Dipole–dipole forces are stronger at shorter distances; they are relatively short range forces.

3. Hydrogen bonding is a special case of dipole–dipole forces that can come into play in molecules in which hydrogen atoms are directly bonded to highly electronegative atoms (such as nitrogen, oxygen, or fluorine). Three examples of substances exhibiting hydrogen bonding are water, ammonia, and ethyl alcohol (CH_3CH_2OH).

4. Hydrogen bonding can exist when H is bonded to O, N, or F. This additional intermolecular force requires more energy to separate the molecules for boiling.

5. The magnitude of the dipole–dipole interactions is strongly dependent on the distance between the dipoles. In the vapor phase the molecules are too far apart for these interactions to be very strong.

6. All atoms and molecules exhibit London dispersion forces among each other.

7. (a) London dispersion forces; (b) London dispersion forces; (c) dipole–dipole forces and London dispersion forces; (d) hydrogen bonding and London dispersion forces

8. The boiling points increase with an increase in the molar mass of the noble gas. The valence electrons of a larger atom will be farther from the nucleus. At a greater distance from the nucleus, the electron clouds are easier to distort so as to give a momentary dipole moment. Thus, as the size of the noble gas atoms increases, so does the magnitude of the London dispersion forces.

9. Strong hydrogen bonding occurs in both ethanol and water. Thus the molecules have great attraction for one another and are able to approach each other very closely; in fact, they must approach each other more closely in the mixture than either can approach a like molecule in the separate liquids.

10. Pure water is a colorless, tasteless substance that has a normal freezing point of 0 °C and a normal boiling point of 100 °C. It has a relatively large specific heat capacity and is able to absorb massive amounts of energy from the sun, preventing rapid or unusually large changes in temperature in the environment.

11. Water, as perspiration, helps cool the human body. Nuclear power plants use water to cool the reactor core.

12. Ice floats because it is less dense than liquid water. Generally a solid is more dense than a liquid, but water is an exception to this rule.

13. Water pipes can be bro-

ken during cold weather. Also, ice can float on water, which is crucial for aquatic life (and ultimately for humans).

14. From room temperature to 100 °C, adding energy as heat to water raises the temperature of the water (and the molecules of water move more quickly). At 100 °C, water molecules possess enough kinetic energy to escape readily from the liquid's surface (the temperature remains constant during this process). If heated above 100 °C, steam molecules absorb additional kinetic energy and the temperature of the steam increases.

15. The sloped portions represent changes in temperature. The flat portions represent phase changes.

16. As heat energy is added to a solid, the vibrational motions of the particles increase. Eventually the particles are vibrating so strongly that they come apart and begin to move in the more random manner of particles of a liquid.

17. As a liquid reaches its boiling point, bubbles of vapor begin to form in the liquid. These rise to the surface and burst. As the liquid remains at its boiling point, the energy added is used to overcome attractive forces among particles.

18. Intramolecular forces are forces within a molecule (for example, a covalent bond is an intramolecular force). Intermolecular forces are forces between or among different molecules.

19. intermolecular

20. In ice, water molecules are in more or less regular fixed positions in the ice crystal. In liquid water, the molecules are in less fixed positions and move freely. In both solid and liquid water, strong hydrogen bonds exist between water molecules. In steam, the water molecules are far apart and move randomly. The water molecules in the vapor phase exert minimal force on each other and act relatively independently.

21. Refer to the *Solutions Guide.*

22. 8.35 kJ; 84.4 kJ; 23.1 kJ

23. 33.1 kJ

14.3 Energy Requirements for the Changes of State

Questions

16. Describe in detail the microscopic processes that take place when a solid melts.

17. Describe in detail the microscopic processes that take place when a liquid boils.

18. Explain the difference between *intra*molecular and *inter*molecular forces.

19. Which type of forces (*intra*molecular or *inter*molecular) must be overcome to melt a solid or vaporize a liquid?

20. Discuss the similarities and differences between the arrangements of molecules and the forces between molecules in liquid water versus steam, and in liquid water versus ice.

Problems

21. The following data have been collected for substance X. Construct a heating curve for substance X. (The drawing does not need to be absolutely to scale, but it should clearly show relative differences.)

normal melting point	−15 °C
molar heat of fusion	2.5 kJ/mol
normal boiling point	134 °C
molar heat of vaporization	55.3 kJ/mol

22. The molar heats of fusion and vaporization for water are 6.02 kJ/mol and 40.6 kJ/mol, respectively, and the specific heat capacity of liquid water is 4.18 J/g °C. What quantity of heat energy is required to melt 25.0 g of ice at 0 °C? What quantity of heat is required to vaporize 37.5 g of liquid water at 100 °C? What quantity of heat is required to warm 55.2 g of liquid water from 0 °C to 100 °C?

23. Given that the specific heat capacities of ice and steam are 2.06 J/g °C and 2.03 J/g °C, respectively, and considering the information about water given in Problem 22, calculate the total quantity of heat evolved when 10.0 g of steam at 200. °C is condensed, cooled, and frozen to ice at −50. °C.

14.4 Evaporation and Vapor Pressure

Questions

24. Describe, on a microscopic basis, the processes of *evaporation* and *condensation*. Which process requires the input of energy?

25. What is *vapor pressure?* On a microscopic basis, how does a vapor pressure develop in a closed flask containing a small amount of liquid? What processes are going on in the flask?

26. What do we mean by a *dynamic equilibrium?* Describe how the development of a vapor pressure above a liquid represents such an equilibrium.

27. Describe an experimental method that could be used to determine the vapor pressure of a volatile liquid.

Problems

28. Which substance in each pair would be expected to be more volatile at a particular temperature? Explain your reasoning.
   a. $H_2O(l)$ or $H_2S(l)$
   b. $H_2O(l)$ or $CH_3OH(l)$
   c. $CH_3OH(l)$ or $CH_3CH_2OH(l)$

29. Although water and ammonia differ in molar mass by only one unit, the boiling point of water is over 100 °C higher than that of ammonia. What forces in liquid water that do *not* exist in liquid ammonia could account for this observation?

30. Two molecules that contain the same number of each kind of atom but that have different molecular structures are said to be *isomers* of each other. For example, both ethyl alcohol and dimethyl ether (shown below) have the formula C_2H_6O and are isomers. Based on considerations of intermolecular forces, which substance would you expect to be more volatile? Which would you expect to have the higher boiling point? Explain.

dimethyl ether	ethyl alcohol
CH_3—O—CH_3	CH_3—CH_2—OH

14.5 Boiling Point and Vapor Pressure

Questions

31. Cake mixes and other packaged foods that require cooking often contain special directions for use at high elevations. Typically these directions indicate that the food should be cooked longer at elevations above 5000 ft. Explain why it takes longer to cook something at higher elevations.

32. Why is the boiling temperature of water less than 100 °C at high altitudes?

14.6 The Solid State: Types of Solids

Questions

33. What are crystalline solids? What kind of microscopic structure do such solids have? How is this microscopic structure reflected in the macroscopic appearance of such solids?

34. On the basis of the smaller units that make up the crystals, cite three types of crystalline solids. For each type of crystalline solid, give an example of a substance that forms that type of solid.

14.7 Bonding in Solids

Questions

35. How do *ionic* solids differ in structure from *molecular* solids? What are the fundamental particles in each? Give two examples of each type of solid and indicate

24. Evaporation represents molecules of a liquid entering the vapor phase; condensation is the reverse process. Evaporation requires an input of energy so that the molecules have enough energy to escape the bulk liquid.

25. Vapor pressure is the pressure of vapor at equilibrium above a liquid in a sealed container at a given temperature. Molecules in the liquid evaporate, but as the number of molecules in the vapor state increases, some of these molecules rejoin (condense). Eventually dynamic equilibrium is reached between evaporation and condensation.

26. A dynamic equilibrium is a situation in which two opposite processes are occurring at the same speed; there is no net change in the system. As a liquid evaporates into the empty space above it, molecules accumulate in the vapor state. Eventually condensation will occur at the same rate as evaporation. At this point, a fixed pressure of vapor has developed and there will be no further net change in the amount of liquid present.

27. See Figure 14.10 and the corresponding explanation.

28. (a) H_2S. H_2O exhibits hydrogen bonding, and H_2S does not. (b) CH_3OH. H_2O exhibits stronger hydrogen bonding than CH_3OH because there are two locations where hydrogen bonding is possible on water. (c) CH_3OH. Both are capable of hydrogen bonding, but generally lighter molecules are more volatile the individual particles that make up the solids in each of your examples.

36. How do the physical properties of ionic solids, in general, differ from the properties of molecular solids? Give an example of each to illustrate your discussion.

37. Ionic solids are generally considerably harder than most molecular solids. Explain.

38. Ionic solids typically have melting points hundreds of degrees higher than the melting points of molecular solids. Explain.

39. What types of forces exist between the individual particles in an ionic solid? Are these forces relatively strong or relatively weak?

40. Explain and compare the intermolecular forces that exist in a sample of solid krypton, Kr, with those that exist in diamond, C.

41. What is an *alloy*? Explain the differences in structure between substitutional and interstitial alloys. Give an example of each type.

42. Explain how the properties of a metal may be modified by alloying the metal with some other substance. Discuss, in particular, how the properties of iron are modified in producing the various types of steel.

Critical Thinking

Matching

For exercises 43–52 choose one of the following terms to match the definition or description given.

   a. alloy
   b. specific heat
   c. crystalline solid
   d. dipole–dipole attraction
   e. equilibrium vapor pressure
   f. intermolecular
   g. intramolecular
   h. ionic solids
   i. London dispersion forces
   j. molar heat of fusion
   k. molar heat of vaporization
   l. molecular solids
   m. normal boiling point
   n. semiconductor

43. boiling point at pressure of 1 atm

44. energy required to melt 1 mol of a substance

45. forces between atoms in a molecule

46. forces between molecules in a solid

47. instantaneous dipole forces for nonpolar molecules

48. lining up of opposite charges on adjacent polar molecules

49. maximum pressure of vapor that builds up in a closed container

50. mixture of elements having metallic properties overall

51. repeating arrangement of component species in a solid

52. solids that melt at relatively low temperatures

53. In carbon compounds a given group of atoms can often be arranged in more than one way. This means that more than one structure may be possible for the same atoms. For example, both the molecules diethyl ether and 1-butanol have the same number of each type of atom, but they have different structures and are said to be *isomers* of one another.

   diethyl ether $CH_3-CH_2-O-CH_2-CH_3$
   1-butanol $CH_3-CH_2-CH_2-CH_2-OH$

Which substance would you expect to have the larger vapor pressure? Why?

54. Which of the substances in each of the following sets would be expected to have the highest boiling point? Explain why.
   a. Ga, KBr, O_2
   b. Hg, NaCl, He
   c. H_2, O_2, H_2O

55. When a person has a severe fever, one therapy to reduce the fever is an "alcohol rub." Explain how the evaporation of alcohol from the person's skin removes heat energy from the body.

56. What is steel? How do the properties of steel differ from the properties of its constituents?

57. Which is stronger, a dipole–dipole attraction between two molecules or a covalent bond between two atoms within the same molecule? Explain.

58. What are *London dispersion forces* and how do they arise in a nonpolar molecule? Are London forces typically stronger or weaker than dipole–dipole attractions between polar molecules? Are London forces stronger or weaker than covalent bonds? Explain.

59. Discuss the types of intermolecular forces acting in the liquid state of each of the following substances.
   a. N_2
   b. NH_3
   c. He
   d. CO_2 (linear, nonpolar)

60. What do we mean when we say a liquid is *volatile*? Do volatile liquids have large or small vapor pressures? What types of intermolecular forces occur in highly volatile liquids?

61. Although methane, CH_4, and ammonia, NH_3, differ in molar mass by only one unit, the boiling point of ammonia is over 100 °C higher than that of methane (a nonpolar molecule). Explain.

an alternating regular array of Na^+ and Cl^- ions. An ionic solid such as calcium bromide consists of a regular array of Ca^{2+} and Br^- ions. In ionic crystals, each ion is surrounded by and attracted to a group of oppositely charged ions. The fundamental units of molecular solids are molecules (two examples are the sugars glucose, $C_6H_{12}O_6$, and sucrose, $C_{12}H_{22}O_{11}$). These molecules are held together by relatively weaker forces, leading to lower melting points for molecular solids as compared to ionic solids.

36. Ionic solids tend to be harder and have higher melting and boiling points. Compare table salt (NaCl) to table sugar (sucrose), for example.

37. The strong electrostatic forces make it very difficult to move or displace ions from one another; the solid is therefore perceived as hard. Molecular solids are held together by dipole–dipole forces, which are weaker than electrostatic forces. Thus the molecular solid is more easily deformed.

38. Ionic solids have strong electrostatic forces (due to the attraction of positively and negatively charged ions). These forces require a great deal of energy to be overcome.

39. Strong electrostatic forces exist between oppositely charged ions in ionic solids.

40. In solid Kr, the only forces that exist are the very weak London dispersion forces. In diamond, however, each carbon atom is held to its four nearest neighbors by strong covalent bonds.

41. An alloy represents a mixture of elements that, as a whole, show metallic properties. In a substitutional alloy some of the host metal atoms are replaced by (substituted with) other atoms (brass, for example). In an interstitial alloy, other small atoms occupy the spaces between the larger host metal atoms (carbon steel, for example).

(Please refer to page A13 in the back of this book to find answers to problems 42–61.)

---

than heavier molecules.

29. The polarity of the O—H bond in water is greater than the polarity of the N—H bond in ammonia (oxygen is more electronegative than nitrogen).

30. Hydrogen bonding can exist in ethyl alcohol but not dimethyl ether. Therefore ethyl alcohol would be less volatile (higher boiling point).

31. At higher altitudes the boiling temperatures of liquids are lower because less atmospheric pressure exists above the liquid. The temperature at which food cooks is determined by the temperature to which water in the food can be heated before it escapes as steam. By boiling at a lower temperature, the food must cook longer.

32. The boiling point is the point at which the vapor pressure of the liquid is equal to the atmospheric pressure. At higher altitudes, the atmospheric pressure is lower, so the boiling temperature is lower.

33. A crystalline solid is a solid with a regular, repeating microscopic arrangement of its components (atoms, molecules, or ions). This highly ordered microscopic arrangement is frequently reflected macroscopically in beautiful, regularly shaped crystals.

34. ionic solids (NaCl); molecular solids (ice); atomic solids (copper)

35. The fundamental particles in ionic solids are positive and negative ions. For example, the ionic solid sodium chloride consists of

15 Solutions

Section	Text Features & Components	Labs, Demonstrations & Activities
Teaching Segment 15A 2.5 blocks pp. 467–473	15.1 Solubility ❷	**LP** Lesson Plans (Sec 15.1–15.3) **SE** Chemical Impact: Green Chemistry *p. 471*	**TE** Teaching Support: Demonstration *pp. 468–469, 470–471* **TE** Mini Demo *pp. 470, 471* **SE** Chemistry in Action: Colors in Motion *p. 470* **LM** Experiment 61–62 Lab Manual Report Sheets Teacher's Lab Guide
	15.2–15.3 ◐ Solution Composition: An Introduction Factors Affecting the Rate of Dissolution		**TE** Mini Demos *pp. 472–473* **LM** Experiment 63: Temperature and Solubility Lab Manual Report Sheets Teacher's Lab Guide
Teaching Segment 15B 1 block pp. 474–485	15.4 ◔ Solution Composition: Mass Percent	**LP** Lesson Plans (Sec 15.4–15.6)	**SE** Chemistry in Action: Rainbow in a Straw *p. 475*
	15.5 ◔ Solution Composition: Molarity	**SE** Top Ten Elements in Sea Water *p. 479*	**TE** Chemistry in Action: Can We Add Concentrations? *p. 476* **TE** Mini Demo *pp. 478, 480* **SE** Chemistry in the Laboratory: Chloride in Water *pp. 497–498* **LM** Experiment 64: Chloride in Water Lab Manual Report Sheets Teacher's Lab Guide
	15.6 Dilution ◑		**TE** Mini Demo *p. 481* **SE** Chemistry in Action: Good to the Last Drop! *p. 482*
	continued on next page		

continued on next page

Key **SE** Student Edition **TE** Teacher Edition **RP** Teacher Resource Package **LM** Lab Materials
 LP Lesson Plans **AR** Additional Resources ◕ Florida Specific

Chapter Planning Guide

All Learners	Review & Assessment	Standards
TE Active Learning *p. 467* **TE** Teaching Tips *p. 467* Transparency: Figure 15.2, 15.3 Animation: Dissolution of a Solid in a Liquid Video: Ammonia Fountain *pp. 468–469* **TE** Teaching Tips *p. 472* **AR** Less Proficient Learners *p. 29*	**SE** Key Terms *p. 498* **SE** Questions and Problems *p. 499*	**TE** **NSES** UCP1, A1, A2, B2, F1, F3, F4, F5, F6 **SSS** SC.H.1.4.7, SC.A.1.4.4, SC.B.1.4.5, SC.H.3.4.2, SC.H.3.4.3, SC.H.3.4.4
Chemistry in Motion (20) *p. 472* **RP** Team Learning Worksheets (Sec 15.1–15.3) *pp. 81–82* **AR** Less Proficient Students *p. 29*	**SE** What if . . . *p. 472* **SE** Focus Questions (Sec 15.1–15.3) *p. 473* **SE** Key Terms *p. 498* **SE** Questions and Problems *p. 499*	
TE Active Learning *p. 474* **TE** Teaching Tips *p. 474* **AR** Less Proficient Students *p. 29*	**TE** Additional Examples *pp. 474–475* **SE** Self Check *pp. 474, 476* **SE** Key Terms *p. 498* **SE** Questions and Problems *p. 499*	**TE** **NSES** UCP1, UCP3, A1, A2, B2 **SSS** SC.A.1.4.4
TE Teaching Tips *pp. 478–479* **AR** Less Proficient Students *p. 29*	**TE** Additional Exercises *pp. 477–478, 480–481* **SE** Self Check *pp. 478–481* **SE** Key Terms *p. 498* **SE** Questions and Problems *pp. 499–500*	
TE Teaching Tip *p. 483* **RP** Team Learning Worksheets (Sec 15.4–15.6) *pp. 83–84* **AR** Less Proficient Students *p. 30*	**TE** Additional Examples *p. 484* **SE** Self Check *p. 485* **SE** Focus Questions (Sec 15.4–15.6) *p. 485* **SE** Key Terms *p. 498* **SE** Questions and Problems *p. 500*	

15 Solutions

	Section	Text Features & Components	Labs, Demonstrations & Activities
Teaching Segment 15C **1 block** **pp. 485–491**	15.7 ● Stoichiometry of Solution Reactions	**LP** Lesson Plans (Sec 15.7–15.8)	**TE** Mini Demo *p. 486* **LM** Experiment 65: Hard Water Analysis Lab Manual Report Sheets Teacher's Lab Guide
	15.8 ◐ Neutralization Reactions	**SE** Celebrity Chemical: Mercury *p. 490*	
Teaching Segment 15D **1 block** **pp. 491–496**	15.9 ◐ Solution Composition: Normality	**LP** Lesson Plans (Sec 15.9–15.10)	
	15.10 ● The Properties of Solutions: Boiling Point and Freezing Point		**TE** Teaching Support: Demonstration *pp. 496–497*

Key

- **SE** Student Edition
- **TE** Teacher Edition
- **RP** Teacher Resource Package
- **LM** Lab Materials
- **LP** Lesson Plans
- **AR** Additional Resources
- ⬤ Florida Specific

Technology and Media

 Transparencies
Figure 15.2
Figure 15.3

PowerPoint Slides

 Animation
Dissolution of a Solid in a Liquid

 Video Ammonia Fountain
Chemistry in Motion
(20) Supersaturated Sodium Acetate

 eEdition CD-ROM
Easy Planner CD-ROM
English Summaries CD
Spanish Summaries CD

Web Site classzone.com
McDougal Littell Test Generator

Chapter Planning Guide

All Learners	Review & Assessment	Standards
(TE) Active Learning *p. 485* (AR) Less Proficient Students *p. 30*	(SE) What if . . . *p. 485* (TE) Additional Examples *pp. 486–487* (SE) Self Check *p. 488* (SE) Questions and Problems *p. 500*	(TE) **NSES** UCP3, A1, A2, B2, B3, F5, G3 (◐) **SSS** SC.B.1.4.2
(TE) Teaching Tips *p. 488* (RP) Team Learning Worksheets (Sec 15.7–15.8) *pp. 85–86* (AR) Less Proficient Students *p. 30*	(TE) Additional Examples *p. 489* (SE) Self Check *p. 490* (SE) Focus Questions (Sec 15.7–15.8) *p. 491* (SE) Key Terms *p. 498* (SE) Questions and Problems *p. 501*	
(TE) Active Learning *p. 491* (TE) Teaching Tips *p. 491* (AR) Less Proficient Students *p. 30*	(TE) Additional Examples *pp. 492–493, 495* (SE) Self Check *pp. 494–495* (SE) Key Terms *p. 498* (SE) Questions and Problems *p. 501*	(TE) **NSES** UCP1, UCP3, A1, A2, B2
(TE) Teaching Tips *p. 495* (RP) Team Learning Worksheets (Sec 15.9–15.10) *pp. 87–88* (AR) Less Proficient Students *p. 30*	(SE) Focus Questions (Sec 15.9–15.10) *p. 496* (SE) Key Terms *p. 498* (SE) Questions and Problems *p. 501*	

Chapter Materials

(TE) Reading Strategy
(AR) English/Spanish Summaries *pp. 24–25*
(AR) Challenge Projects/Problems *pp. 28–29*
(AR) Less Proficient Students *p. 30*
(◉) English Summary Audio
(◉) Spanish Summary Audio
(RP) Chapter Review Worksheets (Basic, Review, Challenge)

(SE) Chapter Summary *pp. 498–499*
(SE) Critical Thinking *p. 501*
(RP) Solutions Guide
(RP) Chapter Tests
(RP) Test Bank
(▣) McDougal Littell Test Generator
(AR) Standardized Test Practice
(◐) **FCAT Test 4**

15 Integrating Reading Strategies and Chemistry Concepts

Chapter 15: SQ3R

Explain to the students that reading to learn is slightly different than reading for enjoyment. Some of the students read material in a textbook without comprehending it and, as a result, they forget the material as soon as they put the book away. Inform the students that there are a number of reading strategies that will help them remember what they read, many of which have been presented throughout this course. Point out that one particularly effective strategy is known as the SQ3R system of reading.

First, explain the acronym SQ3R to the students (see box at right). Next, provide the students with examples of how to perform each step of the SQ3R system.

S	= Survey
Q	= Question
R1	= Read
R2	= Recite
R3	= Review

Survey—10 minutes

Purpose: To gather general information that will allow the students to focus on the material being presented.

How to: Tell the students to skim the chapter, taking note of the chapter title, major headings, subheadings, boldface vocabulary words, and diagrams. Point out that the **Looking Ahead** box on the first page of each chapter is a good place to start. The authors also include an introduction to each chapter, which highlights information that will be presented in the chapter. Explain to the students that they should skim the introduction as well as the chapter summary provided in the **Chapter Review**.

Question—5 minutes per section

Purpose: To engage the students in active reading.

How to: Instruct the students to divide a sheet of paper in their notebooks in half lengthwise. They should begin with the first section of the chapter. One section at a time, they should write questions about each section on the left side of the paper. The students should use the headings, subheadings, and objectives in each section to prompt their questions. Encourage the students to put thought into their questions; the better the questions, the better their comprehension is likely to be.

R1: Read—length of time depends on the length of chapter and the complexity of the material

Purpose: To answer the questions that the students have prepared.

How to: Instruct the students to read the chapter, one section at a time, with their questions in mind. As they read, they should write the answers to their questions on the right side of their notebook pages. Encourage the students to add additional questions and answers if they discover that they have left out an important topic.

R2: Recite—2–3 minutes per section

Purpose: To check recollection and comprehension of key points presented in the reading.

How to: After the students have read each section and answered all of their questions, they should recite the information. Tell them to cover the right side of the paper, read the question on the left side, and verbally answer the question.

R3: Review—15 minutes

Purpose: To better define students' mental organization and begin building long-term memory.

How to: Tell the students that within 24 hours after reading the entire assignment using steps *S* through *R2*, they should review all of their questions and answers. Point out that typical learners forget more than half of what they have learned if they do not review the material within a day's time. Encourage the students to review their notes on a weekly basis until exam time.

Getting Started with SQ3R—Chapter 15, Sections 15.1–15.3

Instruct the students to use the SQ3R system to survey and question Sections 15.1 through 15.3. After they have completed the assignment, have them compare their questions with those of the other students. Stress that the students are likely to have written different questions. Then have the students compare their questions to the ones below. As a homework assignment, instruct the students to complete the 3*R*s for these sections.

Chapter 15: Solutions	
Introduction What is a solution? What is a solvent? What is a solute? What are aqueous solutions? *15.1 Solubility* What is solubility? What happens when ionic substances dissolve? What happens when polar substances dissolve? What substances are not soluble in water? How do substances dissolve? *15.2 Solution Composition: An Introduction* What does it mean for a solution to be saturated? What does it mean for a solution to be unsaturated? What does it mean for a solution to be supersaturated? What is a concentrated solution? What is a dilute solution? *15.3 Affecting the Rate of Dissolution* What are the factors that affect the rate at which a solute dissolves and how does each one affect the rate?	

Chapter 15

Solutions

Overview

In this Chapter our goals are for the students to:

- Understand the process of dissolving and why certain substances dissolve in water

- Understand qualitative descriptions of the concentration of a solution

- Understand the factors that affect the rate at which a solid dissolves

- Understand and use the concentration terms: mass percent and molarity

- Learn to calculate the concentration of a solution made by dilution

- Understand the strategy for solving problems in solution reactions

- Learn to do calculations for acid-base reactions

- Learn about normality and equivalent weight

- Understand the effect of a solute on solution properties

Bubbles on the surface of a soap solution.

466

Most of the important chemistry that keeps plants, animals, and humans functioning occurs in aqueous solutions. Even the water that comes out of a tap is not pure water but a solution of various materials in water. For example, tap water may contain dissolved chlorine to disinfect it, dissolved minerals that make it "hard," and traces of many other substances that result from natural and human-initiated pollution. We encounter many other chemical solutions in our daily lives: air, shampoo, orange soda, coffee, gasoline, cough syrup, and many others.

A **solution** is a homogeneous mixture, a mixture in which the components are uniformly intermingled. This means that a sample from one part is the same as a sample from any other part. For example, the first sip of coffee is the same as the last sip.

The atmosphere that surrounds us is a gaseous solution containing $O_2(g)$, $N_2(g)$, and other gases randomly dispersed. Solutions can also be solids. For example, brass is a homogeneous mixture—a solution—of copper and zinc. These examples illustrate that a solution can be a gas, a liquid, or a solid (see **Table 15.1**). The substance present in the largest amount is called the **solvent**, and the other substance or substances are called **solutes**. For example, when we dissolve a teaspoon of sugar in a glass of water, the sugar is the solute and the water is the solvent.

Aqueous solutions are solutions with water as the solvent. Because they are so important, in this chapter we will concentrate on the properties of aqueous solutions.

Brass, a solid solution of copper and zinc, is used to make musical instruments and many other objects.

TABLE 15.1
Various Types of Solutions

Example	State of Solution	Original State of Solute	State of Solvent
air, natural gas	gas	gas	gas
antifreeze in water	liquid	liquid	liquid
brass	solid	solid	solid
carbonated water (soda)	liquid	gas	liquid
seawater, sugar solution	liquid	solid	liquid

 Solubility

Objectives: *To understand the process of dissolving.*
To learn why certain substances dissolve in water.

What happens when you put a teaspoon of sugar in your iced tea and stir it, or when you add salt to water for cooking vegetables? Why do the sugar and salt "disappear" into the water? What does it mean when something dissolves—that is, when a solution forms?

Solubility of Ionic Substances

We saw in Chapter 8 that when sodium chloride dissolves in water, the resulting solution conducts an electric current. This convinces us that the solution contains *ions* that can move (this is how the electric current is

15.1 Solubility **467**

 Section 15.1

Themes
Systems

Skills
Observing, applying concepts, developing models, interpreting diagrams

Student Preparation
Assign the students to read Sections 15.1 to 15.3 and to answer the Focus Questions at the end of Section 15.3 before coming to class.

Active Learning
After introducing the material in Sections 15.1 to 15.3 in class, place the students in groups and have them work together on Sections 15.1–15.3: Team Learning Worksheet. Answers and/or discussion of these questions are located in the *Teacher Resources*.

Laboratory
Experiment 61:
Solution Properties, Traditional

Laboratory
Experiment 62:
Polar and Nonpolar Solvents, Microscale

TEACHING TIPS

- Introduce the topic of solubility by using examples from daily life, then move to the molecular level to help students understand how a substance dissolves.

- Entropy is also a driving force for dissolving. If you have already discussed entropy (Chapter 10), you may wish to remind the students of entropy here.

- This section offers an excellent opportunity to repeat the conductivity demonstration used in earlier chapters. It will remind students that we can tell whether a solution contains ions by its conductivity.

Figure 15.1
When solid sodium chloride dissolves, the ions are dispersed randomly throughout the solution.

conducted). The dissolving of solid sodium chloride in water is represented in **Figure 15.1**. Notice that in the solid state the ions are packed closely together. However, when the solid dissolves, the ions are separated and dispersed throughout the solution. The strong ionic forces that hold the sodium chloride crystal together are overcome by the strong attractions between the ions and the polar water molecules. This process is represented in **Figure 15.2**. Notice that each polar water molecule orients itself in a way to maximize its attraction with a Cl^- or Na^+ ion. The negative end of a water molecule is attracted to a Na^+ ion, while the positive end is attracted to a Cl^- ion. The strong forces holding the positive and negative ions in the solid are replaced by strong water–ion interactions, and the solid dissolves (the ions disperse).

It is important to remember that when an ionic substance (such as a salt) dissolves in water, it breaks up into *individual* cations and anions, which are

CHEMISTRY
Cations are positive ions. Anions are negative ions.

USING TECHNOLOGY

 Figure 15.2

Animation and Video

Animation, Dissolution of a Solid in a Liquid

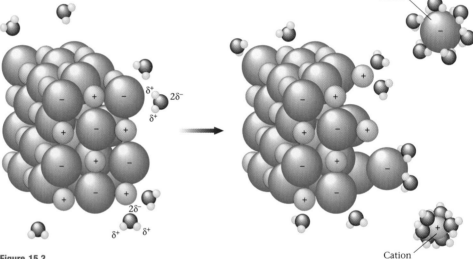

Figure 15.2
Polar water molecules interact with the positive and negative ions of a salt. These interactions replace the strong ionic forces holding the ions together in the undissolved solid, thus assisting in the dissolving process.

468   Chapter 15   Solutions

---

dispersed in the water. For instance, when ammonium nitrate, NH_4NO_3, dissolves in water, the resulting solution contains NH_4^+ and NO_3^- ions, which move around independently. This process can be represented as

$$NH_4NO_3(s) \xrightarrow{H_2O(l)} NH_4^+(aq) + NO_3^-(aq)$$

where (aq) indicates that the ions are surrounded by water molecules.

Solubility of Polar Substances

Water also dissolves many nonionic substances. Sugar is one example of a nonionic solute that is very soluble in water. Another example is ethanol, C_2H_5OH. Alcoholic beverages are aqueous solutions of ethanol (and other substances). Why is ethanol so soluble in water? The answer lies in the structure of the ethanol molecule **(Figure 15.3a).** The molecule contains a polar O—H bond like those in water, which makes it very compatible with water. Just as hydrogen bonds form among water molecules in pure water (see Figure 14.4), ethanol molecules can form hydrogen bonds with water molecules in a solution of the two. This is shown in **Figure 15.3b.**

The sugar molecule (common table sugar has the chemical name sucrose) is shown in **Figure 15.4.** Notice that this molecule has many polar O—H groups, each of which can hydrogen-bond to a water molecule. Because of the attractions between sucrose and water molecules, solid sucrose is quite soluble in water.

(a)   (b)

Figure 15.3
(a) The ethanol molecule contains a polar O—H bond similar to those in the water molecule. (b) The polar water molecule interacts strongly with the polar O—H bond in ethanol.

Figure 15.4
The structure of common table sugar (called sucrose). The large number of polar O—H groups in the molecule causes sucrose to be very soluble in water.

15.1 Solubility   **469**

ume. Discuss why the volume is not 2.5 cups but still more than 2 cups.

Finally, ask what happens when liquids are mixed. Begin by measuring 50 mL of water into one 100-mL graduated cylinder. In a second graduated cylinder, measure 50 mL of water. Color one water sample blue with food coloring and the other yellow. Ask students to predict the final volume when the two water samples are mixed. Mix the two samples in one graduated cylinder. Record the volume. Discuss the color change. (Did a reaction occur? If not, why did the colors change? Did the volumes add?) Repeat the experiment, this time using 50 mL of water and 50 mL of alcohol. Mix the two samples and note the volume. Discuss why the volume is less than the sum of the individual volumes.

Teaching Notes Addition of sugar or alcohol interferes with the attractions between the water molecules. The molecules assume a more compact arrangement, which reduces the volume to less than the sums of the independent volumes.

Figure 15.5
A molecule typical of those found in petroleum. The bonds are not polar.

MINI-DEMO

You can show the immiscibility of oil and water by dissolving a little food coloring in 50 mL of water in a 25-mL flask and adding 50 mL of vegetable oil to the water. Stopper the flask and shake it. Allow the flask to stand, and two layers will separate out.

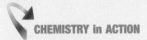

CHEMISTRY in ACTION

Colors in Motion

Materials Each student/group will need a large, clear container (a beaker works well, as does a 2-L soft-drink bottle cut in half), filter paper, water-soluble markers (at least one primary color and one non-primary color), and water.

Purpose Students will apply the concept of solubility to paper chromatography.

Discussion Paper chromatography is a procedure that separates a mixture into its individual components. The components that are not soluble in the solvent (water, in this case) are left on the original dot. The components that are completely soluble move with the water as it travels up the filter paper. Components that are partially soluble are brought to different levels up the filter paper. The distance traveled reflects the solubility (this property can be quantified by the retention factor, or Rf, which is a ratio of the distance traveled by a particular component to the distance traveled by the solvent; it is not necessary to calculate this value here).

Some colors will separate if they are made of two or more fundamental colors (for example, green is made of blue and yellow). The colors that move the farthest with the water consist of components that are the most soluble in water. Since water is polar, the colors that move the greatest distance consist of the most polar components.

An emergency worker uses a vacuum to clean up oil from a spill in Sydney Harbor, Australia. The orange booms in the water help contain the spilled oil.

Figure 15.6
An oil layer floating on water. For a substance to dissolve, the water–water hydrogen bonds must be broken to make a "hole" for each solute particle. However, the water–water interactions will break only if they are replaced by similar strong interactions with the solute.

Substances Insoluble in Water

Many substances do not dissolve in water. For example, when petroleum leaks from a damaged tanker, it does not disperse uniformly in the water (does not dissolve) but rather floats on the surface because its density is less than that of water. Petroleum is a mixture of molecules like the one shown in **Figure 15.5**. Since carbon and hydrogen have very similar electronegativities, the bonding electrons are shared almost equally and the bonds are essentially nonpolar. The resulting molecule with its nonpolar bonds is not compatible with the polar water molecules, which prevents it from being soluble in water. This situation is represented in **Figure 15.6**.

CHEMISTRY in ACTION
Colors in Motion

1. Add water to a large clear container so that it covers the bottom of the container to a depth of about ¼". Cover the container.
2. Obtain a piece of filter paper and use water-soluble markers to place four dots at least ½" apart and ½" from the bottom of the paper.
3. Place the filter paper in the container so that the bottom of the paper is underwater. The dots should not be submerged.
4. Make observations for the next several minutes.
5. Why do some colors separate but others do not?
6. Why do some colors move farther than others up the paper?
7. How do the separation of the colors and their rate of movement relate to solubility and intermolecular forces?

470   Chapter 15   Solutions

TEACHING SUPPORT
Demonstration

Supersaturation

Materials
Heating unit
500-mL Erlenmeyer flask
100-mL beaker
Sodium acetate trihydrate
Baking dish (8" × 8" glass pan or smaller)

Preparation Measure out 175 g of sodium acetate trihydrate. Place it in a 500-mL flask containing 50 mL of water. Heat the flask slowly on a heating unit (a water bath makes it easier to heat), swirling the flask occasionally until a clear, homogeneous solution is obtained. Remove the flask from the heat and invert a 100-mL beaker over the mouth of the flask. Allow the solution to cool undisturbed until it reaches room temperature (1–3 hours). (*Note:* Be careful not to jar the solution or it will crystallize out.) Cover the solution with parafilm until needed. Place one or two crystals of sodium acetate trihydrate in the baking dish.

Presentation Slowly pour the solution of supersaturated sodium acetate trihydrate on the crystals in the baking dish.

How Substances Dissolve

Notice in Figure 15.6 that the water molecules in liquid water are associated with each other by hydrogen-bonding interactions. For a solute to dissolve in water, a "hole" must be made in the water structure for each solute particle. This will occur only if the lost water–water interactions are replaced by similar water–solute interactions. In the case of sodium chloride, strong interactions occur between the polar water molecules and the Na^+ and Cl^- ions. This allows the sodium chloride to dissolve. In the case of ethanol or sucrose, hydrogen-bonding interactions can occur between the O—H groups on these molecules and water molecules, making these substances soluble as well. But oil molecules are not soluble in water, because the many water–water interactions that would have to be broken to make "holes" for these large molecules are not replaced by favorable water–solute interactions.

CHEMICAL IMPACT

Consumer Connection

Green Chemistry

Although some chemical industries have been culprits in the past for fouling the earth's environment, that situation is rapidly changing. In fact, a quiet revolution is sweeping through chemistry from academic labs to *Fortune* 500 companies. Chemistry is going green. *Green chemistry* means minimizing hazardous wastes, substituting water and other environmentally friendlier substances for traditional organic solvents, and manufacturing products out of recyclable materials.

A good example of green chemistry is the increasing use of carbon dioxide, one of the by-products of the combustion of fossil fuels. For example, CO_2 is now being used rather than chlorofluorocarbons (CFCs; substances known to catalyze the decomposition of protective stratospheric ozone) to put the "sponginess" into polystyrene egg cartons, meat trays, and burger boxes. The CO_2 used for this process typically comes from waste gases captured from various other manufacturing processes.

Another very promising use of carbon dioxide is to replace the solvent perchloroethylene (PERC),

The dry-cleaning agent PERC is a health concern for workers in the dry-cleaning industry.

$$Cl_2C=CCl_2$$

now used by about 80% of dry cleaners in the United States. Chronic exposure to PERC has been linked to kidney and liver damage and cancer. Although PERC is not a hazard to the general public (little PERC adheres to dry-cleaned garments), it represents a major concern for employees in the drycleaning industry. At high pressures CO_2 is a liquid that, when used with appropriate detergents, is a very effective solvent for the soil found on dry-clean-only fabrics. When the pressure is lowered, the CO_2 immediately changes to its gaseous form, quickly drying the clothes without the need for added heat. The gas can then be condensed and reused for the next batch of clothes.

The good news is that green chemistry makes sense economically. When all of the costs are taken into account, green chemistry is usually cheaper chemistry as well. Everybody wins.

15.1 Solubility **471**

Crystallization occurs immediately, forming a tower of solid sodium acetate.

Teaching Notes After the demonstration you can cut up the solid with a spatula and return it to the flask. The supersaturated solution is restored by heating as in the preparation. The mixture can be used repeatedly if it is not contaminated. You may need to add small amounts of water to compensate for evaporation losses.

These considerations account for the observed behavior that *"like dissolves like."* In other words, we observe that a given solvent usually dissolves solutes that have polarities similar to its own. For example, water dissolves most polar solutes, because the solute–solvent interactions formed in the solution are similar to the water–water interactions present in the pure solvent. Likewise, nonpolar solvents dissolve nonpolar solutes. For example, drycleaning solvents used for removing grease stains from clothes are nonpolar liquids. "Grease" is composed of nonpolar molecules, so a nonpolar solvent is needed to remove a grease stain.

15.2 Solution Composition: An Introduction

Objective: *To learn qualitative terms associated with the concentration of a solution.*

Even for very soluble substances, there is a limit to how much solute can be dissolved in a given amount of solvent. For example, when you add sugar to a glass of water, the sugar rapidly disappears at first. However, as you continue to add more sugar, at some point the solid no longer dissolves but collects at the bottom of the glass. When a solution contains as much solute as will dissolve at that temperature, we say it is **saturated.** If a solid solute is added to a solution already saturated with that solute, the added solid does not dissolve. A solution that has *not* reached the limit of solute that will dissolve in it is said to be **unsaturated.** When more solute is added to an unsaturated solution, it dissolves.

Sometimes when a solid is dissolved to the saturation limit at an elevated temperature and then allowed to cool, all of the solid may remain dissolved. This type of solution is called a **supersaturated** solution—it contains more dissolved solid than a saturated solution will hold at that temperature. A supersaturated solution is very unstable. Adding a crystal of the solid will cause immediate precipitation of solid until the solution reaches the saturation point.

Although a chemical compound always has the same composition, a solution is a mixture and the amounts of the substances present can vary in different solutions. For example, coffee can be strong or weak. Strong coffee has more coffee dissolved in a given amount of water than weak coffee. To describe a solution completely, we must specify the amounts of solvent and solute. We sometimes use the qualitative terms *concentrated* and *dilute* to describe a solution. A relatively large amount of solute is dissolved in a **concentrated** solution (strong coffee is concentrated). A relatively small amount of solute is dissolved in a **dilute** solution (weak coffee is diluted).

Although these qualitative terms serve a useful purpose, we often need to know the exact amount of solute present in a given amount of solution. In the next several sections, we will consider various ways to describe the composition of a solution.

Sodium acetate crystallizing from a saturated solution.

15.3 Factors Affecting the Rate of Dissolution

Objective: *To understand the factors that affect the rate at which a solute dissolves.*

When a solid is being dissolved in a liquid to form a solution, the dissolution (dissolving) process may occur rapidly or slowly. Three factors affect the speed of the dissolving process: *surface area, stirring,* and *temperature.*

Because the dissolving process occurs at the surface of the solid being dissolved, the greater the amount of surface area exposed to the solvent, the faster the dissolving will occur. For example, if we want to dissolve a cube of sugar in water, how can we speed up the process? The answer is to grind up the cube into tiny crystals. Because the crystals from the ground-up cube expose much more surface area to the water than the original cube did, the sugar dissolves much more quickly.

The dissolution process is also increased by stirring the solution. Stirring removes newly dissolved particles from the solid surface and continuously exposes the surface to fresh solvent.

Finally, dissolving occurs more rapidly at higher temperatures. (Sugar dissolves much more rapidly in hot tea than iced tea.) Higher temperatures cause the solvent molecules to move more rapidly, thus increasing the rate of the dissolving process.

Tea dissolves much faster in the hot water on the left than in the cold water on the right.

In addition to dissolving faster at higher temperatures, most solids are more soluble at higher temperatures. That is, in most cases more solid will dissolve in water at 90 °C than in water at 25 °C. The opposite is true for gases dissolved in water. The solubility of a gas in water typically decreases as the temperature increases.

Focus Questions

Sections 15.1–15.3

1. Draw a molecular-level picture to show how salt and sugar look when dissolved in water.

2. Chemists often say "like dissolves like." What does this statement mean?

3. Can a dilute solution also be saturated? Explain.

4. Increasing the number of collisions between solid and solvent particles increases the rate at which a solid dissolves. Explain how stirring, increased surface area, and higher temperature increase the number of collisions that take place.

Focus Questions **473**

(continued)

ing the particles and increasing their rate of collision. The availability of an increased surface area increases the rate of dissolving because more particles on the surface come in contact with the solvent. This factor results in increased collisions with the solvent. At a higher temperature the particles are moving faster, increasing the number of collisions that occur within the container and so increasing the rate of dissolving.

Section 15.4

Themes
Systems

Skills
Applying concepts, solving problems, evaluating

Student Preparation
Assign the students to read Sections 15.4 to 15.6 and to answer the Focus Questions at the end of Section 15.6 before coming to class.

Active Learning
After introducing the material in Sections 15.4 to 15.6 in class, place the students in groups and have them work together on Sections 15.4–15.6: Team Learning Worksheet. Answers and/or discussion of these questions are located in the *Teacher Resources.*

TEACHING TIPS

- Now is a good time to review the math concept of "percent." Students often forget to calculate the mass of the entire solution, instead using the mass of the solvent and leaving out the mass of the solute. Be sure they understand that a percentage is the amount as a portion of the total (in this case, the sum of the masses of the solvent and solute).

- Review the rules for determining significant figures.

- A common example of a solution with a concentration expressed in mass percent is vinegar. You may want to bring a bottle to class that has a label giving the mass percent.

474

15.4 Solution Composition: Mass Percent

Objective: *To understand the concentration term* mass percent *and learn how to calculate it.*

One way of describing a solution's composition is **mass percent** (sometimes called *weight percent*), which expresses the mass of solute present in a given mass of solution. The definition of mass percent follows:

$$\text{Mass percent} = \frac{\text{mass of solute}}{\text{mass of solution}} \times 100\%$$

$$= \frac{\text{grams of solute}}{\text{grams of solute} + \text{grams of solvent}} \times 100\%$$

The mass of the solution is the sum of the masses of the solute and the solvent.

For example, suppose a solution is prepared by dissolving 1.0 g of sodium chloride in 48 g of water. The solution has a mass of 49 g (48 g of H_2O plus 1.0 g of NaCl), and there is 1.0 g of solute (NaCl) present. The mass percent of solute, then, is

$$\frac{1.0 \text{ g solute}}{49 \text{ g solution}} \times 100\% = 0.020 \times 100\% = 2.0\% \text{ NaCl}$$

Example 15.1

Solution Composition: Calculating Mass Percent

A solution is prepared by mixing 1.00 g of ethanol, C_2H_5OH, with 100.0 g of water. Calculate the mass percent of ethanol in this solution.

Solution

In this case we have 1.00 g of solute (ethanol) and 100.0 g of solvent (water). We now apply the definition of mass percent.

$$\text{Mass percent } C_2H_5OH = \left(\frac{\text{grams of } C_2H_5OH}{\text{grams of solution}}\right) \times 100\%$$

$$= \left(\frac{1.00 \text{ g } C_2H_5OH}{100.0 \text{ g } H_2O + 1.00 \text{ g } C_2H_5OH}\right) \times 100\%$$

$$= \frac{1.00 \text{ g}}{101.0 \text{ g}} \times 100\%$$

$$= 0.990\% \text{ } C_2H_5OH$$

 Self-Check Exercise 15.1

A 135-g sample of seawater is evaporated to dryness, leaving 4.73 g of solid residue (the salts formerly dissolved in the seawater). Calculate the mass percent of solute present in the original seawater.

Additional Examples

1. A solution is prepared by mixing 2.50 g of calcium chloride with 50.0 g of water. Calculate the mass percent of calcium chloride in this solution.
4.76% CaCl₂

2. A 75.0-g sample of a solution is known to contain 23.8 g of glucose. Calculate the mass percent of glucose in this solution.
31.7% glucose

Answer to Self-Check Exercise 15.1

$$\text{Mass percent} = \frac{\text{mass of solute}}{\text{mass of solution}} \times 100\%$$

For this sample, the mass of solution is 135 g and the mass of the solute is 4.73 g, so

$$\text{Mass percent} = \frac{4.73 \text{ g solute}}{135 \text{ g solution}} \times 100\%$$

$$= 3.50\%$$

Example 15.2

Solution Composition: Determining Mass of Solute

Although milk is not a true solution (it is really a suspension of tiny globules of fat, protein, and other substrates in water), it does contain a dissolved sugar called lactose. Cow's milk typically contains 4.5% by mass of lactose, $C_{12}H_{22}O_{11}$. Calculate the mass of lactose present in 175 g of milk.

Solution

We are given the following information:

Mass of solution (milk) = 175 g
Mass percent of solute (lactose) = 4.5%

We need to calculate the mass of solute (lactose) present in 175 g of milk. Using the definition of mass percent, we have

$$\text{Mass percent} = \frac{\text{grams of solute}}{\text{grams of solution}} \times 100\%$$

We now substitute the quantities we know:

$$\text{Mass percent} = \frac{\overbrace{\text{grams of solute}}^{\text{Mass of lactose}}}{\underbrace{175 \text{ g}}_{\text{Mass of milk}}} \times 100\% = \overset{\text{Mass percent}}{4.5\%}$$

We now solve for grams of solute by multiplying both sides by 175 g,

$$\cancel{175 \text{ g}} \times \frac{\text{grams of solute}}{\cancel{175 \text{ g}}} \times 100\% = 4.5\% \times 175 \text{ g}$$

and then dividing both sides by 100%,

$$\text{Grams of solute} \times \frac{\cancel{100\%}}{\cancel{100\%}} = \frac{4.5\%}{100\%} \times 175 \text{ g}$$

to give

$$\text{Grams of solute} = 0.045 \times 175 \text{ g} = 7.9 \text{ g lactose}$$

(continued)

Additional Examples

1. Vinegar is a solution of acetic acid in water and typically contains 5.00% acetic acid by mass. Calculate the mass of acetic acid in a 250.0-g sample of vinegar.
12.5 g

2. Concentrated hydrochloric acid solution contains 37.2% by mass HCl. What mass of HCl is contained in 35.5 g of concentrated HCl?
13.2 g

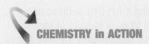

CHEMISTRY in ACTION

Rainbow in a Straw

Materials Each student/group will need five cups, a clear colorless plastic straw, and five colored salt solutions. The salt solutions should vary from 0% (just water) to 20% (20 g salt in 100 g total solution) by 5% increments, and each should be a different color.

Purpose Students will better understand what is meant by *concentration*. They should also see how the density of a solution is related to its concentration.

Discussion The higher the salt concentration, the more dense the solution. Each student should first place one end of the straw in a solution and then place a finger over the top opening. Next, the student should remove the straw from the solution and, keeping the finger over the opening, put the straw into another solution. Releasing the finger then allows the next solution to enter the straw. The finger is placed over the opening again and this process is continued. As long as the salt solutions become successively more concentrated, the solutions (and therefore colors) will not mix. Once all five unmixed colors are in the straw, the student should know which solution is which.

Allow students time to experiment with this activity. If some students have a difficult time getting started, discuss the relationship between density and concentration with them.

Answer to Self-Check Exercise 15.2

Using the definition of mass percent, we have

$$\frac{\text{Mass of solute}}{\text{Mass of solution}}$$

$$= \frac{\text{grams of solute}}{\text{grams of solute} + \text{grams of solvent}} \times 100\% = 40.0\%$$

There are 425 g of solute (formaldehyde). Substituting, we have

$$\frac{425\ g}{425\ g + \text{grams of solvent}} \times 100\% = 40.0\%$$

We must now solve for grams of solvent (water). This will take some patience, but we can do it if we proceed step by step. First we divide both sides by 100%.

$$\frac{425\ g}{425\ g + \text{grams of solvent}}$$
$$\times \frac{\cancel{100\%}}{\cancel{100\%}} = \frac{40.0\%}{100\%} = 0.400$$

Now we have

$$\frac{425\ g}{425\ g + \text{grams of solvent}} = 0.400$$

Next we multiply both sides by (425 g + grams of solvent).

$$(\cancel{425\ g + \text{grams of solvent}})$$
$$\times \frac{425\ g}{\cancel{425\ g + \text{grams of solvent}}}$$
$$= 0.400 \times (425\ g + \text{grams of solvent})$$

This gives

$$425\ g = 0.400 \times (425\ g + \text{grams of solvent})$$

Carrying out the multiplication gives

$$425\ g = 170.\ g + 0.400$$
$$(\text{grams of solvent})$$

Now we subtract 170. g from both sides,

$$425\ g - 170.\ g = \cancel{170.\ g} -$$
$$\cancel{170.\ g} + 0.400\ (\text{grams of solvent})$$
$$255\ g = 0.400\ (\text{grams of solvent})$$

and divide both sides by 0.400.

$$\frac{255\ g}{0.400} = \frac{\cancel{0.400}}{\cancel{0.400}}\ (\text{grams of solvent})$$

We finally have the answer:

$$\frac{255\ g}{0.400} = 638\ g = \text{grams of solvent}$$
$$= \text{mass of water needed}$$

(continued)

 Self-Check Exercise 15.2

What mass of water must be added to 425 g of formaldehyde to prepare a 40.0% (by mass) solution of formaldehyde? This solution, called formalin, is used to preserve biological specimens.

Hint: Substitute the known quantities into the definition for mass percent, and then solve for the unknown quantity (mass of solvent).

15.5 Solution Composition: Molarity

Objectives: *To understand molarity.*
To learn to use molarity to calculate the number of moles of solute present.

When a solution is described in terms of mass percent, the amount of solution is given in terms of its mass. However, it is often more convenient to measure the volume of a solution than to measure its mass. Because of this, chemists often describe a solution in terms of concentration. We define the *concentration* of a solution as the amount of solute in a *given volume* of solution. The most commonly used expression of concentration is **molarity (M).** Molarity describes the amount of solute in moles and the volume of the solution in liters. Molarity is *the number of moles of solute per volume of solution in liters*. That is

$$M = \text{molarity} = \frac{\text{moles of solute}}{\text{liters of solution}} = \frac{\text{mol}}{\text{L}}$$

A solution that is 1.0 molar (written as 1.0 *M*) contains 1.0 mol of solute per liter of solution.

CHEMISTRY in ACTION
Can We Add Concentrations?

1. Place 10.0 mL of water in a cup and add 10 drops of food coloring. Label the concentration of this solution 1.0 *D* (where *D* has units of drops/mL). This is solution A.

2. Add 10.0 mL of water to another cup and add 5 drops of food coloring. What is the concentration of this solution in units of *D*? This is solution B.

3. Add half of solution A and half of solution B to a third cup to make solution C. How does the color of solution C compare to the colors of solution A and solution B?

4. Calculate the concentration of solution C in units of *D*.

5. Can you add the concentrations of solution A and solution B to get the concentration of solution C? Why or why not? How does your observation in step 3 help you answer this question?

476 Chapter 15 Solutions

 Section 15.5

Themes
Systems

Skills
Applying concepts, solving problems, evaluating

Laboratory
Experiment 64:
Chloride in Water, In Text

TEACHING TIPS

• Students need to understand the importance of calculations involving molarity. This concept will be used in solution stoichiometry, titration, and acid–base calculations.

• Emphasize that *molarity* is an important term because we are often interested in moles of reactants or products. Let students know that we will be performing stoichiometric calculations with solutions, and

remind them that to do so we need to work in units of moles. Stress that molarity involves two amounts: the number of moles of solute and the volume of solution.

CHEMISTRY in ACTION

Can We Add Concentrations?

Materials Each student/group will need water, food coloring, and three clear, colorless cups of equal diameter.

Example 15.3

Solution Composition: Calculating Molarity, I

Calculate the molarity of a solution prepared by dissolving 11.5 g of solid NaOH in enough water to make 1.50 L of solution.

Solution

We are given the following information:

Mass of solute = 11.5 g NaOH
Volume of solution = 1.50 L

Because we are asked to calculate the molarity of the solution, we start by writing the definition of molarity.

$$M = \frac{\text{moles of solute}}{\text{liters of solution}}$$

We have the mass (in grams) of solute, so we need to convert the mass of solute to moles (using the molar mass of NaOH). Then we can divide the number of moles by the volume in liters.

We compute the number of moles of solute, using the molar mass of NaOH (40.0 g).

$$11.5 \text{ g NaOH} \times \frac{1 \text{ mol NaOH}}{40.0 \text{ g NaOH}} = 0.288 \text{ mol NaOH}$$

Then we divide by the volume of the solution in liters.

$$\text{Molarity} = \frac{\text{moles of solute}}{\text{liters of solution}} = \frac{0.288 \text{ mol NaOH}}{1.50 \text{ L solution}} = 0.192 \, M \text{ NaOH}$$

Example 15.4

Solution Composition: Calculating Molarity, II

Calculate the molarity of a solution prepared by dissolving 1.56 g of gaseous HCl into enough water to make 26.8 mL of solution.

Solution

We are given

Mass of solute (HCl) = 1.56 g
Volume of solution = 26.8 mL

Molarity is defined as

$$\frac{\text{Moles of solute}}{\text{Liters of solution}}$$

(continued)

---

of the solution is still 1.0 D. This fact may not be obvious to some students, who may claim that the concentration is 0.5 D because only half of the solution is present.

Consider having students carry out a more complicated calculation. For example, what if they added 3.0 mL of solution A to 7.0 mL of solution B? In this case, the final solution contains 6.5 drops of food coloring (3.0 drops from solution A and 3.5 drops from solution B) in 10.0 mL of solution. The concentration is 0.65 D. In doing such a calculation, students see that by mixing two solutions, the new concentration is not always an average of the two initial concentrations.

Additional Examples

1. Calculate the molarity of a solution prepared by dissolving 15.6 g of solid KBr in enough water to make 1.25 L of solution.
   0.105 *M*

2. Calculate the molarity of a solution prepared by dissolving 250.0 g of solid $Ca(NO_3)_2$ in enough water to make 2.50 L of solution.
   0.609 *M*

Additional Examples

1. Calculate the molarity of a solution prepared by dissolving 2.80 g of solid NaCl in enough water to make 135 mL of solution.
   0.355 *M*

2. Calculate the molarity of a solution prepared by dissolving 8.55 g of $MgCl_2$ in enough water to make 65.0 L of solution.
   1.38 *M*

TEACHING TIPS

- Students may need to be reminded to change mL to L when completing molarity calculations.

- This point is an excellent place to review the conversions between grams and moles. Students may have forgotten that they know how to calculate moles if given grams.

Purpose Students will achieve a better understanding of the concept of concentration (including the realization that we cannot add concentrations of solutions). In addition, they will practice doing calculations by adding different volumes of solutions with different concentrations.

Discussion The concentration of solution A is 1.0 D, the concentration of solution B is 0.5 D, and the concentration of solution C is 0.75 D.

There will be 5 drops of food coloring from half (5.0 mL) of solution A and 2.5 drops of food coloring from solution B (this statement assumes homogeneous solutions, something that the students may not assume). Therefore, there are 7.5 drops of food coloring in 10 mL of solution, giving a concentration of 0.75 D. The coloring of the solution should lie between the colors of solutions A and B, indicating that this calculation makes sense. If we could add concentra-

tions, solution C would be the darkest of the three.

In comparing the colors, the students should compare equal volumes of each solution (which requires that they remove half of solution C). They should place all three cups on a sheet of white paper and look into the cups from above.

A misconception may come to light when students pour half of solution A into the third cup. The concentration

Left column

Answer to Self-Check Exercise 15.3

The moles of ethanol can be obtained from its molar mass (46.1).

$$1.00 \text{ g } C_2H_5OH \times \frac{1 \text{ mol } C_2H_5OH}{46.1 \text{ g } C_2H_5OH}$$

$$= 2.17 \times 10^{-2} \text{ mol } C_2H_5OH$$

Volume in liters = 101 mL

$$\times \frac{1 \text{ L}}{1000 \text{ mL}} = 0.101 \text{ L}$$

Molarity of C_2H_5OH

$$= \frac{\text{moles of } C_2H_5OH}{\text{liters of solution}}$$

$$= \frac{2.17 \times 10^{-2} \text{ mol}}{0.101 \text{ L}}$$

$$= 0.215 \text{ } M$$

TEACHING TIP

Beginning students may struggle when asked to determine the concentration of ions in a solution. Emphasize that students should write an equation for the dissociation of the ions in solution and use the mole ratios in the balanced equation to determine the concentrations of the ions. For example, a 1 M solution of $CaCl_2$ contains Ca^{2+} ions in a concentration of 1 M and Cl^- ions in a concentration of 2 M— 2 mol of chloride ion are found in the solution for each 1 mol of calcium ion.

Additional Examples

Give the concentrations of all ions in each of the following solutions.

1. 1.20 M Na_2SO_4
 2.40 M Na^+ , 1.20 M SO_4^{2-}

2. 0.750 M K_2CrO_4
 1.50 M K^+, 0.750 M CrO_4^{2-}

Right column

so we must change 1.56 g of HCl to moles of HCl, and then we must change 26.8 mL to liters (because molarity is defined in terms of liters). First we calculate the number of moles of HCl (molar mass = 36.5 g).

$$1.56 \text{ g HCl} \times \frac{1 \text{ mol HCl}}{36.5 \text{ g HCl}} = 0.0427 \text{ mol HCl}$$

$$= 4.27 \times 10^{-2} \text{ mol HCl}$$

Next we change the volume of the solution from milliliters to liters, using the equivalence statement 1 L = 1000 mL, which gives the appropriate conversion factor.

$$26.8 \text{ mL} \times \frac{1 \text{ L}}{1000 \text{ mL}} = 0.0268 \text{ L}$$

$$= 2.68 \times 10^{-2} \text{ L}$$

Finally, we divide the moles of solute by the liters of solution.

$$\text{Molarity} = \frac{4.27 \times 10^{-2} \text{ mol HCl}}{2.68 \times 10^{-2} \text{ L solution}} = 1.59 \text{ } M \text{ HCl}$$

 Self-Check Exercise 15.3

Calculate the molarity of a solution prepared by dissolving 1.00 g of ethanol, C_2H_5OH, in enough water to give a final volume of 101 mL.

It is important to realize that the description of a solution's composition may not accurately reflect the true chemical nature of the solute as it is present in the dissolved state. Solute concentration is always written in terms of the form of the solute *before* it dissolves. For example, describing a solution as 1.0 M NaCl means that the solution was prepared by dissolving 1.0 mol of solid NaCl in enough water to make 1.0 L of solution; it does not mean that the solution contains 1.0 mol of NaCl units. Actually the solution contains 1.0 mole of Na^+ ions and 1.0 mole of Cl^- ions. That is, it contains 1.0 M Na^+ and 1.0 M Cl^-.

Example 15.5

CHEMISTRY

Remember, ionic compounds separate into the component ions when they dissolve in water.

$Co(NO_3)_2$

↓

Co^{2+}
NO_3^- NO_3^-

Solution Composition: Calculating Ion Concentration from Molarity

Give the concentrations of all the ions in each of the following solutions:

a. 0.50 M $Co(NO_3)_2$
b. 1 M $FeCl_3$

Solution

a. When solid $Co(NO_3)_2$ dissolves, it produces ions as follows:

$$Co(NO_3)_2(s) \xrightarrow{H_2O(l)} Co^{2+}(aq) + 2NO_3^-(aq)$$

CHEMISTRY

$FeCl_3$

$\Downarrow$

Fe^{3+}
Cl^- Cl^- Cl^-

TOP TEN

Elements in Sea Water

Element	Amount (kg/mi³)
1. Oxygen	3.9×10^{12}
2. Hydrogen	5.0×10^{11}
3. Chlorine	9.2×10^{10}
4. Sodium	5.3×10^{10}
5. Magnesium	6.1×10^{9}
6. Sulfur	4.3×10^{9}
7. Calcium	1.9×10^{9}
8. Potassium	1.9×10^{9}
9. Bromine	3.1×10^{8}
10. Carbon	1.3×10^{8}

which we can represent as

$$1 \text{ mol } Co(NO_3)_2(s) \xrightarrow{H_2O(l)} 1 \text{ mol } Co^{2+}(aq) + 2 \text{ mol } NO_3^-(aq)$$

Therefore, a solution that is $0.50 \ M \ Co(NO_3)_2$ contains $0.50 \ M \ Co^{2+}$ and $(2 \times 0.50) \ M \ NO_3^-$, or $1.0 \ M \ NO_3^-$.

b. When solid $FeCl_3$ dissolves, it produces ions as follows:

$$FeCl_3(s) \xrightarrow{H_2O(l)} Fe^{3+}(aq) + 3Cl^-(aq)$$

or

$$1 \text{ mol } FeCl_3(s) \xrightarrow{H_2O(l)} 1 \text{ mol } Fe^{3+}(aq) + 3 \text{ mol } Cl^-(aq)$$

A solution that is $1 \ M \ FeCl_3$ contains $1 \ M \ Fe^{3+}$ ions and $3 \ M \ Cl^-$ ions.

A solution of cobalt(II) nitrate.

Self-Check Exercise 15.4

Give the concentrations of the ions in each of the following solutions:

a. $0.10 \ M \ Na_2CO_3$

b. $0.010 \ M \ Al_2(SO_4)_3$

MATH

$$M = \frac{\text{moles of solute}}{\text{liters of solution}}$$

Liters $\times M \Rightarrow$ Moles of solute

Often we need to determine the number of moles of solute present in a given volume of a solution of known molarity. To do this, we use the definition of molarity. When we multiply the molarity of a solution by the volume (in liters), we get the moles of solute present in that sample:

$$\text{Liters of solution} \times \text{molarity} = \cancel{\text{liters of solution}} \times \frac{\text{moles of solute}}{\cancel{\text{liters of solution}}}$$

$$= \text{moles of solute}$$

15.5   Solution Composition: Molarity   **479**

Example 15.6

Solution Composition: Calculating Number of Moles from Molarity

How many moles of Ag^+ ions are present in 25 mL of a 0.75 M $AgNO_3$ solution?

Solution

In this problem we know

Molarity of the solution = 0.75 M

Volume of the solution = 25 mL

We need to calculate the moles of Ag^+ present. To solve this problem, we must first recognize that a 0.75 M $AgNO_3$ solution contains 0.75 M Ag^+ ions and 0.75 M NO_3^- ions. Next we must express the volume in liters. That is, we must convert from mL to L.

$$25 \; \cancel{mL} \times \frac{1 \; L}{1000 \; \cancel{mL}} = 0.025 \; L = 2.5 \times 10^{-2} \; L$$

Now we multiply the volume times the molarity.

$$2.5 \times 10^{-2} \; \cancel{L \; solution} \times \frac{0.75 \; mol \; Ag^+}{\cancel{L \; solution}} = 1.9 \times 10^{-2} \; mol \; Ag^+$$

✓ Self-Check Exercise 15.5

Calculate the number of moles of Cl^- ions in 1.75 L of 1.0×10^{-3} M $AlCl_3$.

A **standard solution** is a solution whose *concentration is accurately known*. When the appropriate solute is available in pure form, a standard solution can be prepared by weighing out a sample of solute, transferring it completely to a *volumetric flask* (a flask of accurately known volume), and adding enough solvent to bring the volume up to the mark on the neck of the flask. This procedure is illustrated in **Figure 15.7.**

Figure 15.7
Steps involved in the preparation of a standard aqueous solution.
(a) Put a weighed amount of a substance (the solute) into the volumetric flask, and add a small quantity of water. (b) Dissolve the solid in the water by gently swirling the flask *(with the stopper in place)*. (c) Add more water (with gentle swirling) until the level of the solution just reaches the mark etched on the neck of the flask. Then mix the solution thoroughly by inverting the flask several times.

Example 15.7

Solution Composition: Calculating Mass from Molarity

To analyze the alcohol content of a certain substance, a chemist needs 1.00 L of an aqueous 0.200 M $K_2Cr_2O_7$ (potassium dichromate) solution. How much solid $K_2Cr_2O_7$ (molar mass = 294.2 g) must be weighed out to make this solution?

Solution

We know the following:

Molarity of the solution = 0.200 M

Volume of the solution = 1.00 L

We need to calculate the number of grams of solute ($K_2Cr_2O_7$) present (and thus the mass needed to make the solution). First we determine the number of moles of $K_2Cr_2O_7$ present by multiplying the volume (in liters) by the molarity.

MATH

Liters $\times$ M Moles of solute

$$1.00 \text{ L solution} \times \frac{0.200 \text{ mol } K_2Cr_2O_7}{\text{L solution}} = 0.200 \text{ mol } K_2Cr_2O_7$$

Then we convert the moles of $K_2Cr_2O_7$ to grams, using the molar mass of $K_2Cr_2O_7$ (294.2 g).

$$0.200 \text{ mol } K_2Cr_2O_7 \times \frac{294.2 \text{ g } K_2Cr_2O_7}{\text{mol } K_2Cr_2O_7} = 58.8 \text{ g } K_2Cr_2O_7$$

Therefore, to make 1.00 L of 0.200 M $K_2Cr_2O_7$, the chemist must weigh out 58.8 g of $K_2Cr_2O_7$ and dissolve it in enough water to make 1.00 L of solution. This is most easily done by using a 1.00-L volumetric flask (see Figure 15.7).

✓ Self-Check Exercise 15.6

Formalin is an aqueous solution of formaldehyde, HCHO, used as a preservative for biological specimens. How many grams of formaldehyde must be used to prepare 2.5 L of 12.3 M formalin?

15.6 Dilution

Objective: *To learn to calculate the concentration of a solution made by diluting a stock solution.*

The molarities of stock solutions of the common concentrated acids are:

Sulfuric (H_2SO_4)	18 M
Nitric (HNO_3)	16 M
Hydrochloric (HCl)	12 M

To save time and space in the laboratory, solutions that are routinely used are often purchased or prepared in concentrated form (called *stock solutions*). Water (or another solvent) is then added to achieve the molarity desired for a particular solution. The process of adding more solvent to a solution is called **dilution**. For example, the common laboratory acids are purchased as concentrated solutions and diluted with water as they are

15.6 Dilution **481**

CHEMISTRY

Dilution with water doesn't alter the number of moles of solute present.

needed. A typical dilution calculation involves determining how much water must be added to an amount of stock solution to achieve a solution of the desired concentration. The key to doing these calculations is to remember that *only water is added in the dilution*. The amount of solute in the final, more dilute, solution is the *same* as the amount of solute in the original concentrated stock solution. That is,

Moles of solute after dilution = moles of solute before dilution

The number of moles of solute stays the same but more water is added, increasing the volume, so the molarity decreases.

$$M = \frac{\text{moles of solute}}{\text{volume (L)}}$$

Decreases — Remains constant / Increases (water added)

For example, suppose we want to prepare 500. mL of 1.00 *M* acetic acid, $HC_2H_3O_2$, from a 17.5 *M* stock solution of acetic acid. What volume of the stock solution is required?

The first step is to determine the number of moles of acetic acid needed in the final solution. We do this by multiplying the volume of the solution by its molarity.

$$\frac{\text{Volume of dilute}}{\text{solution (liters)}} \times \frac{\text{molarity of}}{\text{dilute solution}} = \frac{\text{moles of solute}}{\text{present}}$$

The number of moles of solute present in the more dilute solution equals the number of moles of solute that must be present in the more concentrated (stock) solution, because this is the only source of acetic acid.

Because molarity is defined in terms of liters, we must first change 500. mL to liters and then multiply the volume (in liters) by the molarity.

$$500. \text{ mL solution} \times \frac{1 \text{ L solution}}{1000 \text{ mL solution}} = 0.500 \text{ L solution}$$

$V_{\text{dilute solution}}$ (in mL) — Convert mL to L

CHEMISTRY in ACTION

Good to the Last Drop!

1. Place 10.0 mL of water in a cup and add 20 drops of food coloring to the water. Label the concentration of this solution 2.0 *D* (where *D* has units of drops/mL). This is solution A.

2. Take 1.0 mL of solution A and place it in an empty cup. Add 9.0 mL of water. What is the concentration of this solution in units of *D*? This is solution B.

3. Take 1.0 mL of solution B and place it in an empty cup. Add 9.0 mL of water. What is the concentration of this solution in units of *D*? This is solution C.

4. Continue this successive dilution until you can no longer see any color. What is the concentration of the last solution in units of *D*?

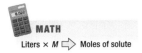
$$0.500 \; \cancel{\text{L solution}} \times \underbrace{\frac{1.00 \; \text{mol HC}_2\text{H}_3\text{O}_2}{\cancel{\text{L solution}}}}_{M_{\text{dilute solution}}} = 0.500 \; \text{mol HC}_2\text{H}_3\text{O}_2$$

Now we need to find the volume of 17.5 *M* acetic acid that contains 0.500 mol of $HC_2H_3O_2$. We will call this unknown volume *V*. Because volume × molarity = moles, we have

$$V \; (\text{in liters}) \times \frac{17.5 \; \text{mol HC}_2\text{H}_3\text{O}_2}{\text{L solution}} = 0.500 \; \text{mol HC}_2\text{H}_3\text{O}_2$$

Solving for *V* $\left(\text{by dividing both sides by } \dfrac{17.5 \; \text{mol}}{\text{L solution}}\right)$ gives

$$V = \frac{0.500 \; \cancel{\text{mol HC}_2\text{H}_3\text{O}_2}}{\dfrac{17.5 \; \cancel{\text{mol HC}_2\text{H}_3\text{O}_2}}{\text{L solution}}} = 0.0286 \; \text{L, or } 28.6 \; \text{mL, of solution}$$

Therefore, to make 500. mL of a 1.00 *M* acetic acid solution, we take 28.6 mL of 17.5 *M* acetic acid and dilute it to a total volume of 500. mL. This process is illustrated in **Figure 15.8.** Because the moles of solute remain the same before and after dilution, we can write

Initial conditions   Final conditions

$$M_1 \quad \times \quad V_1 \quad = \quad \text{moles of solute} \quad = \quad M_2 \quad \times \quad V_2$$

Molarity before dilution   Volume before dilution   Molarity after dilution   Volume after dilution

(a)   (b)   (c)

Figure 15.8
(a) 28.6 mL of 17.5 *M* acetic acid solution is transferred to a volumetric flask that already contains some water. (b) Water is added to the flask (with swirling) to bring the volume to the calibration mark, and the solution is mixed by inverting the flask several times. (c) The resulting solution is 1.00 *M* acetic acid.

15.6 Dilution   **483**

- Understanding the process of dilution is important for most students intending to work in quantitative fields. Using this formula can help them only if they understand what is happening. Be sure that students focus on the idea that the number of moles of solute remains constant: $M \times V = \text{mol}$.

- The formula $M_1V_1 = M_2V_2$ works well but some students memorize it without understanding *why* it works. Emphasize what each variable means and explain that the formula works only because the moles of solute are the same before and after dilution. Consider asking students to solve for the volume of water that must be added to achieve a dilution (see the second example problem given for Example 15.8). In this way, students learn to think about what they are solving for, instead of just plugging numbers into an equation.

- Be sure that students answer the question being asked. Students often give the volume of concentrated solution when the question asks for the volume of water needed to make the dilution.

We can check our calculations on acetic acid by showing that $M_1 \times V_1 = M_2 \times V_2$. In the above example, $M_1 = 17.5$ M, $V_1 = 0.0286$ L, $V_2 = 0.500$ L, and $M_2 = 1.00$ M, so

$$M_1 \times V_1 = 17.5 \frac{\text{mol}}{\text{L}} \times 0.0286 \text{ L} = 0.500 \text{ mol}$$

$$M_2 \times V_2 = 1.00 \frac{\text{mol}}{\text{L}} \times 0.500 \text{ L} = 0.500 \text{ mol}$$

and therefore

$$M_1 \times V_1 = M_2 \times V_2$$

This shows that the volume (V_2) we calculated is correct.

Additional Examples

1. What volume of 19 M NaOH must be used to prepare 1.0 L of a 0.15 M NaOH solution?
7.9 mL

2. What volume of water is needed to prepare 500.0 mL of a 0.250 M Ca(NO$_3$)$_2$ solution from a 5.00 M Ca(NO$_3$)$_2$ solution?
475 mL

Example 15.8

Approximate dilutions can be carried out using a calibrated beaker. Here concentrated sulfuric acid is being added to water to make a dilute solution.

Calculating Concentrations of Diluted Solutions

What volume of 16 M sulfuric acid must be used to prepare 1.5 L of a 0.10 M H$_2$SO$_4$ solution?

Solution

We can summarize what we are given as follows:

Initial Conditions (concentrated)	*Final Conditions (dilute)*
$M_1 = 16 \frac{\text{mol}}{\text{L}}$	$M_2 = 0.10 \frac{\text{mol}}{\text{L}}$
$V_1 = ?$	$V_2 = 1.5$ L

We know that

$$\text{Moles of solute} = M_1 \times V_1 = M_2 \times V_2$$

and we can solve the equation

$$M_1 \times V_1 = M_2 \times V_2$$

for V_1 by dividing both sides by M_1

$$\frac{\cancel{M_1} \times V_1}{\cancel{M_1}} = \frac{M_2 \times V_2}{M_1}$$

to give

$$V_1 = \frac{M_2 \times V_2}{M_1}$$

Now we substitute the known values of M_2, V_2, and M_1.

$$V_1 = \frac{\left(0.10 \frac{\text{mol}}{\cancel{L}}\right)(1.5 \text{ L})}{16 \frac{\text{mol}}{\cancel{L}}} = 9.4 \times 10^{-3} \text{ L}$$

$$9.4 \times 10^{-3} \cancel{L} \times \frac{1000 \text{ mL}}{1 \cancel{L}} = 9.4 \text{ mL}$$

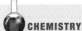
CHEMISTRY

It is always best to add concentrated acid to water, not water to the acid. That way, if any splashing occurs accidentally, it is dilute acid that splashes.

Therefore, $V_1 = 9.4 \times 10^{-3}$ L, or 9.4 mL. To make 1.5 L of 0.10 M H_2SO_4 using 16 M H_2SO_4, we must take 9.4 mL of the concentrated acid and dilute it with water to a final volume of 1.5 L. The correct way to do this is to add the 9.4 mL of acid to about 1 L of water and then dilute to 1.5 L by adding more water.

 Self-Check Exercise 15.7

What volume of 12 M HCl must be taken to prepare 0.75 L of 0.25 M HCl?

Focus Questions **Sections 15.4–15.6**

1. A solution is labeled "0.450 M magnesium nitrate." Calculate the concentration of each ion present in solution.
2. Calculate the number of moles of KOH in 150.0 mL of a 0.500 M solution.
3. If 4.25 g of $CaBr_2$ is dissolved in enough water to make 125 mL of solution, what is the molarity of the solution?
4. What is the key idea to remember when considering the dilution of a solution?
5. Why is it important to add concentrated acid to water rather than water to the acid?

 15.7 **Stoichiometry of Solution Reactions**

Objective: *To understand the strategy for solving stoichiometric problems for solution reactions.*

Because so many important reactions occur in solution, it is important to be able to do stoichiometric calculations for solution reactions. The principles needed to perform these calculations are very similar to those developed in Chapter 9. It is helpful to think in terms of the following steps:

> **Steps for Solving Stoichiometric Problems Involving Solutions**
>
> **STEP 1** Write the balanced equation for the reaction. For reactions involving ions, it is best to write the net ionic equation.
> **STEP 2** Calculate the moles of reactants.
> **STEP 3** Determine which reactant is limiting.
> **STEP 4** Calculate the moles of other reactants or products, as required.
> **STEP 5** Convert to grams or other units, if required.

See Section 8.3 for a discussion of net ionic equations.

WHAT IF?

What if all ionic solids were soluble in water? How would it affect reactions in aqueous solution?

Themes
Patterns of Change, Scale and Structure

Skills
Applying concepts, interpreting data, making comparisons, solving problems

Student Preparation
Assign the students to read Sections 15.7 and 15.8 and to answer the Focus Questions at the end of Section 15.8 before coming to class.

Active Learning
After introducing the material in Sections 15.7 and 15.8 in class, place the students in groups and have them work together on Sections 15.7–15.8: Team Learning Worksheet. Answers and/or discussion of these questions are located in the *Teacher Resources.*

Laboratory
Experiment 65:
Hard Water Analysis, Microscale

TEACHING TIPS

- Begin this section with a review of basic stoichiometry. The steps outlined in the text form the basis for a review of the principles for solving stoichiometry problems.

- Remind students to balance all chemical equations before beginning a problem.

- Now is a good time to review writing net ionic equations. Using a net ionic equation simplifies the work done in solving solution problems. It also focuses students' attention on the species reacting and, therefore, on the question being asked.

WHAT IF Comments

This question is the reverse of the "What If . . . ?" from Chapter 8 (What if no ionic solids were soluble in water?). The answer is basically the same—we would get no reactions in aqueous solutions—but the reason is different. We can write the equation $KCl(aq) + NaNO_3(aq) \rightarrow KNO_3(aq) + NaCl(aq)$, but it isn't
(continued)

 Answer to Self-Check Exercise 15.7

We are given the following information:

$M_1 = 12\ \dfrac{mol}{L}$ $M_2 = 0.25\ \dfrac{mol}{L}$

$V_1 = ?$ (what we need to find) $V_2 = 0.75\ L$

Using the fact that the moles of solute do not change upon dilution, we know that

$M_1 \times V_1 = M_2 \times V_2$

Solving for V_1 by dividing both sides by M_1 gives

$V_1 = \dfrac{M_2 \times V_2}{M_1}$

$= \dfrac{0.25\ \frac{mol}{L} \times 0.75\ L}{12\ \frac{mol}{L}}$

and

$V_1 = 0.016\ L = 16\ mL$

 Answers to Focus Questions

1. Mg^{2+} concentration = 0.450 M;
NO_3^- concentration = 0.900 M
2. mol KOH = 0.075 mol
3. 0.170 M
4. The key idea in working with dilution is to remember that the moles of solute remain the same.
5. If any splashing occurs during the addition, it is dilute acid that splashes.

a chemical reaction, because all of the ions are spectator ions; there is no net ionic equation. This case demonstrates the importance of having students think about what a reaction "looks" like at a molecular level.

Additional Examples

1. Calculate the mass of solid sodium sulfate that must be added to 250.0 mL of a 0.200 M solution of barium nitrate to precipitate all of the barium ions in the form of barium sulfate. Also calculate the mass of barium sulfate formed.

   7.10 g Na_2SO_4 required; 11.7 g $BaSO_4$ produced

2. Calculate the mass of NaI that must be added to 425.0 mL of a 0.100 M $Pb(NO_3)_2$ solution to precipitate all of the Pb^{2+} ions as PbI_2. Also calculate the mass of PbI_2 formed.

   12.7 g NaI required; 19.6 g PbI_2 produced

MINI-DEMO

When working problems in solution stoichiometry, it is more interesting to students if you can show them the reaction in class. Before class, make dilute solutions of the reactants for the examples you plan to present. Then for each example, after you write the reactants on the board, stop and mix the chemicals together. Have students name the products and complete the equation. Balance the equation and proceed with the solution stoichiometry problem. This approach allows students to be actively involved in a review of earlier topics while solving a new problem.

Example 15.9

Solution Stoichiometry: Calculating Mass of Reactants and Products

Calculate the mass of solid NaCl that must be added to 1.50 L of a 0.100 M $AgNO_3$ solution to precipitate all of the Ag^+ ions in the form of AgCl. Calculate the mass of AgCl formed.

Solution

Step 1 *Write the balanced equation for the reaction.*
When added to the $AgNO_3$ solution (which contains Ag^+ and NO_3^- ions), the solid NaCl dissolves to yield Na^+ and Cl^- ions. Solid AgCl forms according to the following balanced net ionic reaction:

$$Ag^+(aq) + Cl^-(aq) \rightarrow AgCl(s)$$

Step 2 *Calculate the moles of reactants.*
In this case we must add enough Cl^- ions to just react with all the Ag^+ ions present, so we must calculate the moles of Ag^+ ions present in 1.50 L of a 0.100 M $AgNO_3$ solution. (Remember that a 0.100 M $AgNO_3$ solution contains 0.100 M Ag^+ ions and 0.100 M NO_3^- ions.)

MATH

Liters × M ⇒ Moles of solute

$$1.50 \, \cancel{L} \times \frac{0.100 \text{ mol Ag}^+}{\cancel{L}} = 0.150 \text{ mol Ag}^+$$

Moles of Ag^+ present in 1.5 L of 0.100 M $AgNO_3$

Step 3 *Determine which reactant is limiting.*
In this situation we want to add just enough Cl^- to react with the Ag^+ present. That is, we want to precipitate *all* the Ag^+ in the solution. Thus the Ag^+ present determines the amount of Cl^- needed.

Step 4 *Calculate the moles of Cl^- required.*
We have 0.150 mol of Ag^+ ions and, because one Ag^+ ion reacts with one Cl^- ion, we need 0.150 mol of Cl^-,

$$0.150 \, \cancel{\text{mol Ag}^+} \times \frac{1 \text{ mol Cl}^-}{1 \, \cancel{\text{mol Ag}^+}} = 0.150 \text{ mol Cl}^-$$

so 0.150 mol of AgCl will be formed.

$$0.150 \text{ mol Ag}^+ + 0.150 \text{ mol Cl}^- \rightarrow 0.150 \text{ mol AgCl}$$

When aqueous sodium chloride is added to a solution of silver nitrate, a white silver chloride precipitate forms.

Step 5 *Convert to grams of NaCl required.*
To produce 0.150 mol Cl^-, we need 0.150 mol NaCl. We calculate the mass of NaCl required as follows:

$$0.150 \, \cancel{\text{mol NaCl}} \times \frac{58.4 \text{ g NaCl}}{\cancel{\text{mol NaCl}}} = 8.76 \text{ g NaCl}$$

| Moles | ⇒ | Mass |

Times molar mass

The mass of AgCl formed is

$$0.150 \, \cancel{\text{mol AgCl}} \times \frac{143.3 \text{ g AgCl}}{\cancel{\text{mol AgCl}}} = 21.5 \text{ g AgCl}$$

486   Chapter 15   Solutions

Example 15.10

See Section 8.2 for a discussion of this reaction.

Solution Stoichiometry: Determining Limiting Reactants and Calculating Mass of Products

When $Ba(NO_3)_2$ and K_2CrO_4 react in aqueous solution, the yellow solid $BaCrO_4$ is formed. Calculate the mass of $BaCrO_4$ that forms when 3.50×10^{-3} mole of solid $Ba(NO_3)_2$ is dissolved in 265 mL of 0.0100 M K_2CrO_4 solution.

Solution

Step 1 The original K_2CrO_4 solution contains the ions K^+ and CrO_4^{2-}. When the $Ba(NO_3)_2$ is dissolved in this solution, Ba^{2+} and NO_3^- ions are added. The Ba^{2+} and CrO_4^{2-} ions react to form solid $BaCrO_4$. The balanced net ionic equation is

$$Ba^{2+}(aq) + CrO_4^{2-}(aq) \rightarrow BaCrO_4(s)$$

Step 2 Next we determine the moles of reactants. We are told that 3.50×10^{-3} mol of $Ba(NO_3)_2$ is added to the K_2CrO_4 solution. Each formula unit of $Ba(NO_3)_2$ contains one Ba^{2+} ion, so 3.50×10^{-3} mole of $Ba(NO_3)_2$ gives 3.50×10^{-3} mole of Ba^{2+} ions in solution.

3.50×10^{-3} mol $Ba(NO_3)_2$	$\Rightarrow$ (dissolves to give)	3.50×10^{-3} mol Ba^{2+}

Because $V \times M$ = moles of solute, we can compute the moles of K_2CrO_4 in the solution from the volume and molarity of the original solution. First we must convert the volume of the solution (265 mL) to liters.

$$265 \text{ mL} \times \frac{1 \text{ L}}{1000 \text{ mL}} = 0.265 \text{ L}$$

Next we determine the number of moles of K_2CrO_4, using the molarity of the K_2CrO_4 solution (0.0100 M).

$$0.265 \text{ L} \times \frac{0.0100 \text{ mol } K_2CrO_4}{\text{L}} = 2.65 \times 10^{-3} \text{ mol } K_2CrO_4$$

We know that

2.65×10^{-3} mol K_2CrO_4	$\Rightarrow$ (dissolves to give)	2.65×10^{-3} mol CrO_4^{2-}

so the solution contains 2.65×10^{-3} mole of CrO_4^{2-} ions.

Step 3 The balanced equation tells us that one Ba^{2+} ion reacts with one CrO_4^{2-}. Because the number of moles of CrO_4^{2-} ions (2.65×10^{-3}) is smaller than the number of moles of Ba^{2+} ions (3.50×10^{-3}), the CrO_4^{2-} will run out first.

$$Ba^{2+}(aq) + CrO_4^{2-}(aq) \rightarrow BaCrO_4(s)$$

3.50×10^{-3} mol	2.65×10^{-3} mol
	Smaller (runs out first)

(continued)

Barium chromate precipitating.

Additional Examples

1. Calculate the mass of the white solid $CaCO_3$ that forms when 25.0 mL of a 0.100 M $Ca(NO_3)_2$ solution is mixed with 20.0 mL of a 0.150 M Na_2CO_3 solution. **0.250 g $CaCO_3$**

2. Calculate the mass of the blood-red solid Ag_2CrO_4 that forms when 50.0 mL of a 0.250 M $AgNO_3$ solution is mixed with 30.0 mL of a 0.250 M K_2CrO_4 solution. **2.07 g Ag_2CrO_4**

TEACHING TIP

Include some examples in class in which a salt dissolves to produce multiple moles of an ion per mole of compound. Such an example illustrates the need for writing net ionic equations when solving solution stoichiometry problems.

(continued)

Therefore, the CrO_4^{2-} is limiting.

| Moles of CrO_4^{2-} | $\Rightarrow$ limits | Moles of $BaCrO_4$ |

Step 4 The 2.65×10^{-3} mole of CrO_4^{2-} ions will react with 2.65×10^{-3} mole of Ba^{2+} ions to form 2.65×10^{-3} mole of $BaCrO_4$.

| 2.65×10^{-3} mol Ba^{2+} | + | 2.65×10^{-3} mol CrO_4^{2-} | $\Rightarrow$ | 2.65×10^{-3} mol $BaCrO_4(s)$ |

Step 5 The mass of $BaCrO_4$ formed is obtained from its molar mass (253.3 g) as follows:

$$2.65 \times 10^{-3} \text{ mol BaCrO}_4 \times \frac{253.3 \text{ g BaCrO}_4}{\text{mol BaCrO}_4} = 0.671 \text{ g BaCrO}_4$$

 Self-Check Exercise 15.8

When aqueous solutions of Na_2SO_4 and $Pb(NO_3)_2$ are mixed, $PbSO_4$ precipitates. Calculate the mass of $PbSO_4$ formed when 1.25 L of 0.0500 M $Pb(NO_3)_2$ and 2.00 L of 0.0250 M Na_2SO_4 are mixed.

Hint: Calculate the moles of Pb^{2+} and SO_4^{2-} in the mixed solution, decide which ion is limiting, and calculate the moles of $PbSO_4$ formed.

15.8 Neutralization Reactions

Objective: *To learn how to do calculations involved in acid–base reactions.*

So far we have considered the stoichiometry of reactions in solution that result in the formation of a precipitate. Another common type of solution reaction occurs between an acid and a base. We introduced these reactions in Section 8.4. Recall from that discussion that an acid is a substance that furnishes H^+ ions. A strong acid, such as hydrochloric acid, HCl, dissociates (ionizes) completely in water.

$$HCl(aq) \rightarrow H^+(aq) + Cl^-(aq)$$

Strong bases are water-soluble metal hydroxides, which are completely dissociated in water. An example is NaOH, which dissolves in water to give Na^+ and OH^- ions.

$$NaOH(s) \xrightarrow{H_2O(l)} Na^+(aq) + OH^-(aq)$$

When a strong acid and strong base react, the net ionic reaction is

$$H^+(aq) + OH^-(aq) \rightarrow H_2O(l)$$

An acid–base reaction is often called a **neutralization reaction.** When just enough strong base is added to react exactly with the strong acid in a solution, we say the acid has been *neutralized.* One product of this reaction is always water. The steps in dealing with the stoichiometry of any neutralization reaction are the same as those we followed in the previous section.

488 Chapter 15 Solutions

 Answer to Self-Check Exercise 15.8

Step 1 When the aqueous solutions of Na_2SO_4 (containing Na^+ and SO_4^{2-} ions) and $Pb(NO_3)_2$ (containing Pb^{2+} and NO_3^- ions) are mixed, solid $PbSO_4$ is formed.

$$Pb^{2+}(aq) + SO_4^{2-}(aq) \rightarrow PbSO_4(s)$$

Step 2 We must first determine whether Pb^{2+} or SO_4^{2-} is the limiting reactant by calculating the moles of Pb^{2+} and SO_4^{2-} ions present. Because 0.0500 M $Pb(NO_3)_2$ contains 0.0500 M Pb^{2+} ions, we can calculate the moles of Pb^{2+} ions in 1.25 L of this solution as follows:

$$1.25 \text{ L} \times \frac{0.0500 \text{ mol Pb}^{2+}}{\text{L}}$$
$$= 0.0625 \text{ mol Pb}^{2+}$$

The 0.0250 M Na_2SO_4 solution contains 0.0250 M SO_4^{2-} ions, and the number of moles of SO_4^{2-} ions in 2.00 L of this solution is

$$2.00 \text{ L} \times \frac{0.0250 \text{ mol SO}_4^{2-}}{\text{L}}$$
$$= 0.0500 \text{ mol SO}_4^{2-}$$

Step 3 Pb^{2+} and SO_4^{2-} react in a 1:1 ratio, so the amount of SO_4^{2-} ions is limiting because a smaller number of SO_4^{2-} moles is present.

Step 4 The Pb^{2+} ions are present in excess, and only 0.0500 mol of solid $PbSO_4$ will be formed.

Step 5 We calculate the mass of $PbSO_4$ by using the molar mass of $PbSO_4$ (303.3 g).

$$0.0500 \text{ mol PbSO}_4 \times \frac{303.3 \text{ g PbSO}_4}{1 \text{ mol PbSO}_4}$$
$$= 15.2 \text{ g PbSO}_4$$

 Section 15.8

Themes
Patterns of Change, Scale and Structure

Skills
Applying concepts, interpreting data, solving problems

TEACHING TIPS

- This section presents an opportunity to help students learn to approach solving problems by thinking through the problem. These problems are applications of material that students have seen previously. Focus students' attention on the basic requirements for solving problems in chemistry: writing down what is known, writing a balanced equation, determining what is being asked for, deciding what needs to be found to get what is asked for, and then solving the problem.

- Neutralization reaction problems often ask for volume, which is a new variable for students. In stoichiometry we tend to ask for moles or mass.

Example 15.11

Solution Stoichiometry: Calculating Volume in Neutralization Reactions

What volume of a 0.100 M HCl solution is needed to neutralize 25.0 mL of a 0.350 M NaOH solution?

Solution

Step 1 *Write the balanced equation for the reaction.*
Hydrochloric acid is a strong acid, so all the HCl molecules dissociate to produce H^+ and Cl^- ions. Also, when the strong base NaOH dissolves, the solution contains Na^+ and OH^- ions. When these two solutions are mixed, the H^+ ions from the hydrochloric acid react with the OH^- ions from the sodium hydroxide solution to form water. The balanced net ionic equation for the reaction is

$$H^+(aq) + OH^-(aq) \rightarrow H_2O(l)$$

Step 2 *Calculate the moles of reactants.*
In this problem we are given a volume (25.0 mL) of 0.350 M NaOH, and we want to add just enough 0.100 M HCl to provide just enough H^+ ions to react with all the OH^-. Therefore, we must calculate the number of moles of OH^- ions in the 25.0-mL sample of 0.350 M NaOH. To do this, we first change the volume to liters and multiply by the molarity.

$$25.0 \text{ mL NaOH} \times \frac{1 \text{ L}}{1000 \text{ mL}} \times \frac{0.350 \text{ mol } OH^-}{\text{L NaOH}} = 8.75 \times 10^{-3} \text{ mol } OH^-$$

Moles of OH^- present
in 25.0 mL of
0.350 M NaOH

Step 3 *Determine which reactant is limiting.*
This problem requires the addition of just enough H^+ ions to react exactly with the OH^- ions present, so the number of moles of OH^- ions present determines the number of moles of H^+ that must be added. The OH^- ions are limiting.

Step 4 *Calculate the moles of H^+ required.*
The balanced equation tells us that the H^+ and OH^- ions react in a 1:1 ratio, so 8.75×10^{-3} mole of H^+ ions is required to neutralize (exactly react with) the 8.75×10^{-3} mole of OH^- ions present.

Step 5 *Calculate the volume of 0.100 M HCl required.*
Next we must find the volume (V) of 0.100 M HCl required to furnish this amount of H^+ ions. Because the volume (in liters) times the molarity gives the number of moles, we have

$$V \times \frac{0.100 \text{ mol } H^+}{\text{L}} = 8.75 \times 10^{-3} \text{ mol } H^+$$

Unknown volume (in liters)　　　Moles of H^+ needed

Now we must solve for V by dividing both sides of the equation by 0.100.

$$V \times \frac{0.100 \text{ mol } H^+}{0.100 \text{ L}} = \frac{8.75 \times 10^{-3} \text{ mol } H^+}{0.100}$$

$$V = 8.75 \times 10^{-2} \text{ L}$$

(continued)

15.8 Neutralization Reactions **489**

Additional Examples

1. What volume of 0.150 M HNO_3 solution is needed to neutralize 45.0 mL of a 0.550 M KOH solution?
   165 mL

2. What volume of 1.00×10^{-2} M HCl solution is needed to neutralize 35.0 mL of a 5.00×10^{-3} M $Ba(OH)_2$ solution?
   35.0 mL

Changing liters to milliliters, we have

$$V = 8.75 \times 10^{-2} \, \cancel{L} \times \frac{1000 \text{ mL}}{\cancel{L}} = 87.5 \text{ mL}$$

Therefore, 87.5 mL of 0.100 M HCl is required to neutralize 25.0 mL of 0.350 M NaOH.

 Self-Check Exercise 15.9

Calculate the volume of 0.10 M HNO_3 needed to neutralize 125 mL of 0.050 M KOH.

 Answer to Self-Check Exercise 15.9

Step 1 Because nitric acid is a strong acid, the nitric acid solution contains H^+ and NO_3^- ions. The KOH solution contains K^+ and OH^- ions. When these solutions are mixed, the H^+ and OH^- react to form water.

$$H^+ (aq) + OH^- (aq) \rightarrow H_2O(l)$$

Step 2 The number of moles of OH^- present in 125 mL of 0.050 M KOH is

$$125 \, \cancel{\text{mL}} \times \frac{1 \, \cancel{L}}{1000 \, \cancel{\text{mL}}}$$
$$\times \frac{0.050 \text{ mol } OH^-}{\cancel{L}}$$
$$= 6.3 \times 10^{-3} \text{ mol } OH^-$$

Step 3 H^+ and OH^- react in a 1:1 ratio, so we need 6.3×10^{-3} mol of H^+ from the 0.100 M HNO_3.

Step 4 6.3×10^{-3} mol of OH^- requires 6.3×10^{-3} mol of H^+ to form 6.3×10^{-3} mol of H_2O. Therefore,

$$V \times \frac{0.100 \text{ mol } H^+}{L}$$
$$= 6.3 \times 10^{-3} \text{ mol } H^+$$

where V represents the volume in liters of 0.100 M HNO_3 required. Solving for V, we have

$$V = \frac{6.3 \times 10^{-3} \, \cancel{\text{mol } H^+}}{\frac{0.100 \, \cancel{\text{mol } H^+}}{L}}$$
$$= 6.3 \times 10^{-2} \text{ L}$$
$$= 6.3 \times 10^{-2} \, \cancel{L} \times \frac{1000 \text{ mL}}{\cancel{L}}$$
$$= 63 \text{ mL}$$

CELEBRITY CHEMICAL

Mercury (Hg)

ercury was isolated from its principal ore, cinnabar (HgS), as early as 500 B.C. Cinnabar was widely used in the ancient world as a red pigment (vermilion). Mercury, whose mobility inspired its naming after the messenger of the gods in Roman mythology, was of special interest to alchemists. Alchemists hoped to find a way to change cheap metals into gold, and it was generally thought that mercury, which easily forms alloys with many metals, was the key to this process. Mercury has a common name of quicksilver.

Mercury is a very dense (13.5 times denser than water), shiny liquid that has a surprisingly high vapor pressure for a heavy metal. Because mercury vapor is quite toxic, it must be stored in stoppered containers and handled in well-ventilated areas. Many instances of suspected mercury poisoning occurred in the days before its hazards were understood.

For example, it is very possible that Sir Isaac Newton, the renowned physicist, suffered from mercury poisoning at one time in his career and had to "retire" to the country away from his laboratory to regain his strength. Some have speculated that Mozart, the famous composer, may have died of mercury poisoning due to the mercury salts that were used to treat an illness. Also, the "mad hatters" of *Alice in Wonderland* fame have a historical connection to mercury. Apparently, the mercury salts used by workers in London to treat felt used in hats caused the hatters to become "mad" over the years. It turns out that a change in personality is a characteristic of heavy metal poisoning.

The Mad Hatter's Tea Party, an illustration by Sir John Tenniel, from *Alice's Adventures in Wonderland*.

CELEBRITY CHEMICAL

Mercury (Hg)

Paracelsus introduced the use of mercury as a treatment for syphilis. In 1799 Howard used mercury fulminate as a detonator for explosives. Mercury has many uses in daily life, such as in mercury-vapor lamps, electrical switches, thermometers, and barometers.

With the notable exception of iron, almost all metals can form alloys with mercury. These alloys are called amalgams. Sodium amalgams form in electrolytic cells used to produce chlorine. Dental amalgam is also prepared with mercury. The key to creating dental amalgam is for it to form a smooth paste within 90 seconds. It must then set within 3–5 minutes and within 2 hours it must be hard enough to withstand biting and chewing stresses. Standard dental alloy is generally composed of silver (67%–74%), tin (25%–27%), copper (0–6%), and zinc (0–2%). This alloy is mixed with mercury (1:1 mass ratio) just before use.

1. How does mixing solutions instead of reacting solids, liquids, or gases change your problem-solving approach for stoichiometry problems?

2. How many milliliters of 0.10 M $Pb(NO_3)_2$ solution are required to precipitate all of the lead, as PbI_2, from 125.0 mL of 0.10 M NaI solution?

3. What is the net ionic equation found in a neutralization reaction?

4. Once you have determined the number of moles of H^+ or OH^- in a neutralization reaction, how can you find the volume of the substance? What is the critical information you need to determine volume?

Answers to Focus Questions

1. When solutions are mixed, the number of moles must be determined before proceeding with the problem. Also, a net ionic equation must be written for the reaction to determine the concentrations of the ions present.

2. 62.5 mL

3. $H^+(aq) + OH^-(aq) \rightarrow H_2O(l)$

4. The volume can be determined by dividing the number of moles by the molarity of the solution. The critical information needed to find the volume is the molarity of the solution.

15.9 Solution Composition: Normality

Objectives: *To learn about normality and equivalent weight.*
To learn to use these concepts in stoichiometric calculations.

Normality is another unit of concentration that is sometimes used, especially when dealing with acids and bases. The use of normality focuses mainly on the H^+ and OH^- available in an acid–base reaction. Before we discuss normality, however, we need to define some terms. One **equivalent of an acid** is the *amount of that acid that can furnish 1 mol of H^+ ions*. Similarly, one **equivalent of a base** is defined as the *amount of that base that can furnish 1 mol of OH^- ions*. The **equivalent weight** of an acid or a base is the mass in grams of 1 equivalent (equiv) of that acid or base.

The common strong acids are HCl, HNO_3, and H_2SO_4. For HCl and HNO_3 each molecule of acid furnishes one H^+ ion, so 1 mol of HCl can furnish 1 mol of H^+ ions. This means that

Furnishes 1 mol of H^+
↓
1 mol HCl = 1 equiv HCl
Molar mass (HCl) = equivalent weight (HCl)

Likewise, for HNO_3,

1 mol HNO_3 = 1 equiv HNO_3
Molar mass (HNO_3) = equivalent weight (HNO_3)

However, H_2SO_4 can furnish *two* H^+ ions per molecule, so 1 mol of H_2SO_4 can furnish *two* mol of H^+. This means that

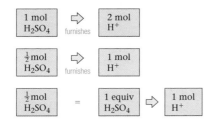

15.9   Solution Composition: Normality   **491**

 Section 15.9

Themes
Systems, Patterns of Change

Skills
Applying concepts, making comparisons, solving problems

Student Preparation
Assign the students to read Sections 15.9 and 15.10 and to answer the Focus Questions at the end of Section 15.10 before coming to class.

Active Learning
After introducing the material in Sections 15.9 and 15.10 in class, place the students in groups and have them work together on Sections 15.9–15.10: Team Learning Worksheet. Answers and/or discussion of these questions are located in the *Teacher Resources*.

TEACHING TIP

It may help to introduce the idea of equivalents from the standpoint of equivalence statements. Since the chapter on measurement, students have been using equivalence statements to convert from one system to another. In this section an equivalence exists between moles of hydrogen (or hydroxide) ions and an equivalent. If students can view this process as a conversion, it will simplify their thinking about normality.

TABLE 15.2

The Molar Masses and Equivalent Weights of the Common Strong Acids and Bases

	Molar Mass (g)	Equivalent Weight (g)
Acid		
HCl	36.5	36.5
HNO_3	63.0	63.0
H_2SO_4	98.0	$49.0 = \dfrac{98.0}{2}$
Base		
NaOH	40.0	40.0
KOH	56.1	56.1

TEACHING TIP

Students should begin solving these problems by writing an equation for the dissociation of one mole of the acid or base. This step will help them see the number of hydrogen ions or hydroxide ions that are produced.

Additional Examples

1. Arsenic acid, H_3AsO_4, can furnish three H^+ ions per molecule. Calculate the equivalent weight of H_3AsO_4.
   47.31 g

2. Calculate the equivalent weight of HBr.
   80.91 g

Because each mole of H_2SO_4 can furnish 2 mol of H^+, we need to take only $\frac{1}{2}$ mol of H_2SO_4 to get 1 equiv of H_2SO_4. Therefore,

$$\tfrac{1}{2} \text{ mol } H_2SO_4 = 1 \text{ equiv } H_2SO_4$$

and

$$\text{Equivalent weight } (H_2SO_4) = \tfrac{1}{2} \text{ molar mass } (H_2SO_4)$$
$$= \tfrac{1}{2} \, (98 \text{ g}) = 49 \text{ g}$$

The equivalent weight of H_2SO_4 is 49 g.

The common strong bases are NaOH and KOH. For NaOH and KOH, each formula unit furnishes one OH^- ion, so we can say

1 mol NaOH = 1 equiv NaOH
Molar mass (NaOH) = equivalent weight (NaOH)

1 mol KOH = 1 equiv KOH
Molar mass (KOH) = equivalent weight (KOH)

These ideas are summarized in **Table 15.2**.

Example 15.12

Solution Stoichiometry: Calculating Equivalent Weight

Phosphoric acid, H_3PO_4, can furnish three H^+ ions per molecule. Calculate the equivalent weight of H_3PO_4.

Solution

The key point here involves how many protons (H^+ ions) each molecule of H_3PO_4 can furnish.

Because each H_3PO_4 can furnish three H^+ ions, 1 mol of H_3PO_4 can furnish 3 mol of H^+ ions:

$$\boxed{\begin{array}{c} 1 \text{ mol} \\ H_3PO_4 \end{array}} \xrightarrow[\text{furnishes}]{} \boxed{\begin{array}{c} 3 \text{ mol} \\ H^+ \end{array}}$$

So 1 equiv of H_3PO_4 (the amount that can furnish 1 mol of H^+) is one-third of a mole.

$$\boxed{\begin{array}{c} \frac{1}{3}\text{mol} \\ H_3PO_4 \end{array}} \xrightarrow[\text{furnishes}]{} \boxed{\begin{array}{c} 1 \text{ mol} \\ H^+ \end{array}}$$

This means the equivalent weight of H_3PO_4 is one-third its molar mass.

$$\boxed{\begin{array}{c} \text{Equivalent} \\ \text{weight} \end{array}} = \boxed{\dfrac{\text{Molar mass}}{3}}$$

$$\text{Equivalent weight }(H_3PO_4) = \frac{\text{molar mass }(H_3PO_4)}{3} = \frac{98.0 \text{ g}}{3} = 32.7 \text{ g}$$

Normality (N) is defined as the number of equivalents of solute per liter of solution.

$$\text{Normality} = N = \frac{\text{number of equivalents}}{1 \text{ liter of solution}} = \frac{\text{equivalents}}{\text{liter}} = \frac{\text{equiv}}{L}$$

This means that a 1 N solution contains 1 equivalent of solute per liter of solution. Notice that when we multiply the volume of a solution in liters by the normality, we get the number of equivalents.

MATH

L × Normality ⇨ Equiv

$$N \times V = \frac{\text{equiv}}{\cancel{L}} \times \cancel{L} = \text{equiv}$$

Example 15.13

Solution Stoichiometry: Calculating Normality

A solution of sulfuric acid contains 86 g of H_2SO_4 per liter of solution. Calculate the normality of this solution.

PROBLEM SOLVING

Whenever you need to calculate the concentration of a solution, first write the appropriate definition. Then decide how to calculate the quantities shown in the definition.

Solution

We want to calculate the normality of this solution, so we focus on the definition of normality, the number of equivalents per liter:

$$N = \frac{\text{equiv}}{L}$$

This definition leads to two questions we need to answer:

1. What is the number of equivalents?

2. What is the volume?

(continued)

15.9   Solution Composition: Normality   **493**

The key idea in understanding normality is to determine equivalents. In these problems this step is analogous to determining moles in other solution problems.

Additional Examples

1. A solution of phosphoric acid contains 50.0 g of H_3PO_4 per liter of solution. Calculate the normality of this solution. **1.53 N**

2. A solution of hydrochloric acid contains 25.0 g of HCl per liter of solution. Calculate the normality of this solution. **0.686 N**

(continued)

We know the volume; it is 1.0 L. To find the number of equivalents present, we must calculate the number of equivalents represented by 86 g of H_2SO_4. To do this calculation, we focus on the definition of the equivalent: it is the amount of acid that furnishes 1 mol of H^+. Because H_2SO_4 can furnish two H^+ ions per molecule, 1 equiv of H_2SO_4 is $\frac{1}{2}$ mol of H_2SO_4, so

$$\text{Equivalent weight } (H_2SO_4) = \frac{\text{molar mass } (H_2SO_4)}{2}$$

$$= \frac{98.0 \text{ g}}{2} = 49.0 \text{ g}$$

We have 86 g of H_2SO_4.

$$86 \text{ g } H_2SO_4 \times \frac{1 \text{ equiv } H_2SO_4}{49.0 \text{ g } H_2SO_4} = 1.8 \text{ equiv } H_2SO_4$$

$$N = \frac{\text{equiv}}{L} = \frac{1.8 \text{ equiv } H_2SO_4}{1.0 \text{ L}} = 1.8 \; N \; H_2SO_4$$

We know that 86 g is more than 1 equiv of H_2SO_4 (49 g), so this answer makes sense.

 Self-Check Exercise 15.10

Calculate the normality of a solution containing 23.6 g of KOH in 755 mL of solution.

Answer to Self-Check Exercise 15.10

From the definition of normality, $N = \text{equiv}/L$, we need to calculate (1) the equivalents of KOH and (2) the volume of the solution in liters. To find the number of equivalents, we use the equivalent weight of KOH, which is 56.1 g (see Table 15.2).

$$23.6 \text{ g KOH} \times \frac{1 \text{ equiv KOH}}{56.1 \text{ g KOH}}$$
$$= 0.421 \text{ equiv KOH}$$

Next we convert the volume to liters.

$$755 \text{ mL} \times \frac{1 \text{ L}}{1000 \text{ mL}}$$
$$= 0.755 \text{ L}$$

Finally, we substitute these values into the equation that defines normality.

$$\text{Normality} = \frac{\text{equiv}}{L}$$
$$= \frac{0.421 \text{ equiv}}{0.755 \text{ L}}$$
$$= 0.558 \; N$$

The main advantage of using equivalents is that 1 equiv of acid contains the same number of available H^+ ions as the number of OH^- ions present in 1 equiv of base. That is,

0.75 equiv (base) will react exactly with 0.75 equiv (acid).

0.23 equiv (base) will react exactly with 0.23 equiv (acid).

And so on.

In each of these cases, the *number of* H^+ ions furnished by the sample of acid is the same as the *number of* OH^- ions furnished by the sample of base. The point is that n *equivalents of any acid will exactly neutralize* n *equivalents of any base.*

| *n* equiv acid | ← reacts exactly with → | *n* equiv base |

Because we know that equal equivalents of acid and base are required for neutralization, we can say that

equiv (acid) = equiv (base)

That is,

$$N_{acid} \times V_{acid} = \text{equiv (acid)} = \text{equiv (base)} = N_{base} \times V_{base}$$

Therefore, for any neutralization reaction, the following relationship holds:

$$N_{acid} \times V_{acid} = N_{base} \times V_{base}$$

Example 15.14

Solution Stoichiometry: Using Normality in Calculations

What volume of a 0.075 N KOH solution is required to react exactly with 0.135 L of 0.45 N H_3PO_4?

Solution

We know that for neutralization, equiv (acid) = equiv (base), or

$$N_{acid} \times V_{acid} = N_{base} \times V_{base}$$

We want to calculate for the volume of base, V_{base}, so we solve for V_{base} by dividing both sides by N_{base}.

$$\frac{N_{acid} \times V_{acid}}{N_{base}} = \frac{\cancel{N_{base}} \times V_{base}}{\cancel{N_{base}}} = V_{base}$$

Now we can substitute the given values $N_{acid} = 0.45$ N, $V_{acid} = 0.135$ L, and $N_{base} = 0.075$ N into the equation.

$$V_{base} = \frac{N_{acid} \times V_{acid}}{N_{base}} = \frac{\left(0.45 \; \frac{equiv}{\cancel{L}}\right)(0.135 \; L)}{0.075 \; \frac{equiv}{\cancel{L}}} = 0.81 \; L$$

This gives $V_{base} = 0.81$ L, so 0.81 L of 0.075 N KOH is required to react exactly with 0.135 L of 0.45 N H_3PO_4.

 Self-Check Exercise 15.11

What volume of 0.50 N H_2SO_4 is required to react exactly with 0.250 L of 0.80 N KOH?

15.10 The Properties of Solutions: Boiling Point and Freezing Point

Objective: *To understand the effect of a solute on solution properties.*

We saw in Chapter 14 that at an atmospheric pressure of 1 atm water freezes at 0 °C and boils at 100 °C. If we dissolve a solute such as NaCl in water, does the presence of the solute affect the freezing point of the water? Yes. A 1.0 M NaCl solution freezes at about −1 °C and boils at about 104 °C. The presence of solute "particles" in the water extends the liquid range of water—that is, water containing a solute exists as a liquid over a wider temperature range than does pure water.

Why does this happen? For example, what effect do the particles have that causes the boiling point of water to increase? To answer this question we need to reconsider the boiling process described in Section 14.5. Recall that for water to boil, bubbles must be able to form in the interior of the liquid. That is, energetic water molecules in the bubble must be able to exert an internal pressure large enough to push back the atmospheric pressure.

15.10   The Properties of Solutions: Boiling Point and Freezing Point   **495**

Additional Examples

1. What volume of 0.500 N NaOH is required to react exactly with 125 mL of 0.500 N H_2SO_4?
   125 mL

2. What volume of 1.00 N H_3PO_4 is required to react exactly with 25.0 mL of 0.500 N NaOH?
   12.5 mL

 Answer to Self-Check Exercise 15.11

To solve this problem, we use the relationship

$$N_{acid} \times V_{acid} = N_{base} \times V_{base}$$

where

$$N_{acid} = 0.50 \; \frac{equiv}{L}$$

$$V_{acid} = ?$$

$$N_{base} = 0.80 \; \frac{equiv}{L}$$

$$V_{base} = 0.250 \; L$$

We solve the equation

$$N_{acid} \times V_{acid} = N_{base} \times V_{base}$$

for V_{acid} by dividing both sides by N_{acid}.

$$\frac{N_{acid} \times V_{acid}}{N_{acid}} = \frac{N_{base} \times V_{base}}{N_{acid}}$$

$$V_{acid} = \frac{N_{base} \times V_{base}}{N_{acid}}$$

$$= \frac{\left(0.80 \; \frac{equiv}{\cancel{L}}\right) \times (0.250 \; L)}{0.50 \; \frac{equiv}{\cancel{L}}}$$

$$V_{acid} = 0.40 \; L$$

Therefore, 0.40 L of 0.50 N H_2SO_4 is required to neutralize 0.250 L of 0.80 N KOH.

15.10 Section 15.10

Themes
Patterns of Change, Systems

Skills
Applying concepts, interpreting diagrams, making predictions, evaluating

TEACHING TIPS

• This section ties the properties of solutions to the properties of liquids learned in the preceding chapter. Students can now think about how a solution behaves as compared with a pure liquid.

• Now is an excellent time to bring real-world examples, such as high-altitude cooking and melting ice on winter roads, into the classroom.

• The goal in this section is to have students understand why the boiling point is elevated and the freezing point is lowered in solutions. We do not expect beginning students to calculate the quantitative effects of these occurrences. The point that colligative properties depend on the number of particles in solution is key to this section.

Figure 15.9
A bubble in the interior of an aqueous solution surrounded by solute particles and water molecules.

(a) Pure water

(b) Solution (contains solute)

Figure 15.10
(a) In pure water more H₂O molecules surround the bubble and thus more enter the bubble. (b) In a solution fewer H₂O molecules can enter the bubble.

Now consider the situation in a solution that contains a solute **(Figure 15.9)**. The forming bubble is now surrounded by solute particles as well as water molecules. As a result, solute particles may block the pathway of some of the water molecules trying to enter the bubble. Because fewer H_2O molecules can enter the bubble, the molecules that do get inside it must have relatively high energies to produce the internal pressure necessary to maintain the bubble. Compare the situation with and without a solute shown in **Figure 15.10.** To produce the same pressure, the smaller number of molecules found in Figure 15.10 b must have higher energies (speeds) than those in the bubble in pure water.

Thus, to cause the water in the solution to boil, we must heat the water to a temperature higher than 100 °C to produce the higher-energy water molecules needed. In other words, the boiling point of the solution occurs at a higher temperature than does the boiling point of pure water. The presence of the solute increases the boiling point of water. The more solute present, the higher the boiling point, because the smaller number of H_2O molecules able to enter the bubble must have increasing energies. Note that the raising of the boiling point depends on the number and not the specific identity of the solute particles. It's the number that matters—the more particles present, the more those particles block water molecules from entering the bubble. A solution property that depends on the *number* of solute particles present is called a **colligative property.** Raising of the boiling point by a solute is one of the colligative properties of solutions.

Another colligative property of solutions is the lowering of the freezing point. (As mentioned before, a 1 *M* NaCl solution freezes at approximately −1 °C.) This property is particularly important in cold areas of the world where salt is applied to icy roads. When the applied salt dissolves in the thin layer of water on the surface of ice, forming a very concentrated solution, it causes the ice to melt (it lowers the freezing point of water). The same property is also used to protect automobile engines. The coolant used in engines is a

solution containing ethylene glycol $\left(\begin{matrix} & H & H \\ & | & | \\ H-&C-&C-H \\ & | & | \\ & OH & OH \end{matrix}\right)$ dissolved in water. The

solute (ethylene glycol) raises the boiling point and lowers the freezing point of the water, thereby protecting the engine from overheating and freezing.

Focus Questions **Sections 15.9–15.10**

1. How is normality different from molarity?
2. Is a 1 *M* H₂SO₄ solution the same as a 1 *N* H₂SO₄ solution? Explain.
3. Other than for taste reasons, why is salt added to water when cooking pasta?

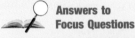

Answers to Focus Questions

1. Molarity is based on the number of moles of solute per liter of solution; normality is based on the number of equivalents of solute per liter of solution.

2. These solutions are not the same. A 1 *M* solution contains 2 mol hydrogen ions per liter of solution, whereas a 1 *N* solution contains 1 equivalent of hydrogen ions per liter of solution. Since an equivalent of hydrogen ions is the same as 1 mol of hydrogen ions, the 1 *M* solution contains twice as many hydrogen ions as the 1 *N* solution.

3. The salt added to water when cooking pasta raises the boiling point of the water, which increases the speed of cooking by a small amount. The main reason for adding salt is flavoring.

TEACHING SUPPORT
Demonstration

Making Ice Cream Freeze

Materials Each group will need the following: 1-quart zip-lock plastic bag, 1-gallon zip-lock plastic bag, 1–2 L crushed ice, ½ cup rock salt, 1 cup milk mixture (any combination of whole or low-fat milk, half and half, or cream), ¼ cup sugar, 1 tea-spoon vanilla extract, small paper cups, and plastic spoons.

Preparation Make the ice cream mixture the night before in quantities large enough for the entire class. Alternatively, you can bring all ingredients to school along with the appropriate measuring spoons.

Presentation Place about 1 cup of the mixture into the small plastic bag. (If you haven't already mixed in the sugar and vanilla, do so at this time.) Seal the plastic bag securely and make sure all of the substances are well mixed (the sugar is all dissolved). Place the small plastic bag and its contents into the larger plastic bag. Add crushed ice and rock salt. Seal the larger bag. Shake or roll it until the ice cream hardens. Remove the small bag from the larger one. Carefully wipe off the outside of

Problem

What is the chloride ion concentration in your water?

Introduction

Water samples—even bottled water—naturally contain chloride ions. In this lab you will determine the concentration of the chloride ions in various samples of water. You will be able to estimate the accuracy of your technique by testing solutions with known concentrations of chloride ions.

The technique you will use is called a titration. It involves adding a measured volume of a solution of known concentration to a measured volume of a solution of unknown concentration. The two solutions react with each other.

You will use aqueous silver nitrate to titrate your water sample. The silver ion reacts with chloride ion to form the white solid silver chloride. This solid is insoluble in water, so a cloudy solution indicates the presence of chloride ions in your water. The indicator for the titration is fluorescein. The end of the titration is indicated by a color change from light green to pink. Because of the presence of silver chloride, the solution will resemble strawberry milk.

Prelab Assignment

1. Read the entire lab experiment before you begin.
2. Provide balanced net ionic equations for all chemical reactions in this lab.
3. What is the purpose of titrating solutions of potassium chloride with known concentrations?
4. What is the purpose of diluting the potassium chloride solutions and titrating them?
5. Provide calculations for all dilutions to be made in this lab.

Materials

Goggles	Bottled water
Lab apron	Water sample
Graduated cylinder	Fluorescein
Ring stand	Dextrin
250-mL beaker	Potassium chloride
Buret clamp	$(5.00 \times 10^{-3} M)$
Buret	Silver nitrate $(5.00 \times 10^{-3} M)$

Safety

If you come in contact with any solution, wash the contacted area thoroughly.

Procedure

Part I: Determining Accuracy of the Titration

1. Fill the buret with $5.00 \times 10^{-3} M$ silver nitrate. Record the initial reading.
2. Use the graduated cylinder to measure about 10.0 mL of the $5.00 \times 10^{-3} M$ potassium chloride solution and place it in the 250-mL beaker. Record the actual volume.
3. Add 2–3 drops of the fluorescein and a small amount of dextrin. The dextrin is an anti-coagulating agent that gives the silver chloride small particles with maximum surface area.
4. Slowly add the silver nitrate solution until the solution turns pale pink. Record the final volume reading on the buret.
5. Make 50.0 mL of $5.00 \times 10^{-4} M$ silver nitrate and 50.0 mL of $5.00 \times 10^{-4} M$ potassium chloride solutions from the given $5.00 \times 10^{-3} M$ solutions. Titrate the potassium chloride solution as before (use 10.0 mL of potassium chloride). Record the initial and final volume readings on the buret.
6. Make 50.0 mL of $5.00 \times 10^{-5} M$ potassium chloride solution from the $5.00 \times 10^{-4} M$ solution and titrate 30.0 mL of this solution with the $5.00 \times 10^{-4} M$ silver nitrate solution. Record the initial and final volume readings on the buret.

Part II: Testing Water Samples

1. Bring in a sample of water from your home faucet or from a local lake, river, or stream.
2. Titrate 10.0 mL of your water sample twice, once with $5.00 \times 10^{-3} M$ silver nitrate solution and once with $5.00 \times 10^{-4} M$ silver nitrate solution. Record the initial and final volume readings on the buret for each titration.
3. Titrate two 10.0-mL samples of water from the nearest drinking fountain in your school. Do one titration with $5.00 \times 10^{-3} M$ silver nitrate solution and another titration with $5.00 \times 10^{-4} M$ silver nitrate solution. Record the initial and final volume readings on the buret for each titration.
4. Titrate 10.0-mL samples of bottled water. Do one titration with $5.00 \times 10^{-3} M$ silver nitrate solution and another titration with $5.00 \times 10^{-4} M$ silver nitrate solution. Record the initial and final volume readings on the buret for each titration.

Cleaning Up

Clean up all materials and wash your hands thoroughly. Dispose of all chemicals as instructed by your teacher.

(continued)   **497**

CHEMISTRY in the LABORATORY
Chloride in Water (FIELD)

Objectives

1. To make dilutions
2. To carry out titrations
3. To determine the chloride ion concentrations of several water samples

Skills

Applying concepts, making dilutions, performing titrations, calculating

Materials

Goggles	Water sample
Apron	Fluorescein
Graduated	Dextrin
cylinder	Potassium
Ringstand	chloride
250-mL beaker	$(5.00 \times 10^{-3} M)$
Buret clamp	Silver nitrate
Buret	$(5.00 \times 10^{-3} M)$
Bottled water	

Preparation Hints

Prepare the fluorescein indicator by adding 0.10 g of dichlorofluorescein to 100.0 g of a 65% ethanol/35% water mixture.

Tell students several days in advance to bring in water samples. You may also wish to take the class to a nearby stream or lake to collect the water.

Prelab Discussion

You may decide to perform a sample titration for students in front of the class to let them see what the endpoint looks like.

Procedure Hints

Watch the students as they perform the titrations. The most common mistake is overshooting the endpoint.

Average water samples have chloride ion concentrations around $1.0 \times 10^{-4} M$. If the concentration is significantly lower, students may need to make further dilutions of the silver nitrate solution.

Disposal

Collect all solutions from the students and dispose of them properly.

Post-Lab Discussion

Have students bring all of the data together. Use this information to discuss chloride ion concentration differences in various locations around your town.

the small bag. Scoop out the ice cream into paper cups and enjoy the results of freezing-point depression!

Teaching Notes Be sure to complete this experiment away from all chemicals. Students can do this experiment in the classroom instead of the lab. Do not use any chemistry glassware for this demonstration.

Prelab Assignment

2. The net ionic equation is Ag^+ (aq) $+ Cl^-$ (aq) $\rightarrow$ AgCl(s).

3. We titrate known solutions so that we can estimate the percent error of the titration.

4. By diluting and titrating known solutions, we see how the percent error changes for more dilute solutions.

5. To make 50.0 mL of a solution with a concentration of 5.00×10^{-4} M from a 5.00×10^{-3} M solution, take 5.0 mL of the 5.00×10^{-3} M solution and add 45.0 mL of water. To make 50.0 mL of a solution with a concentration of 5.00×10^{-5} M from a 5.00×10^{-4} M solution, take 5.0 mL of the 5.00×10^{-4} M solution and add 45.0 mL of water.

Analysis and Conclusions

1. Answers will vary. For the sample results given in the Summary Tables, the percent errors are 0.300%, 0.500%, and 1.00%.

2. The higher the concentration, the smaller the percent error should be. All titrations have a slight inherent error. With a larger initial concentration, the percent error is lower. In addition, larger concentrations lead to more clear endpoints (color changes).

3. Answers will vary. Water samples taken from the same school site or the same bottled-water company should be similar.

Summary Tables

Sample data are found in the *Teacher's Guide* to the Laboratory.

Analysis and Conclusions

1. Determine the percent error for each of the three titrations in Part I by comparing the known chloride concentrations to those you found by titration.

2. Which known concentration of potassium chloride gave the smallest percent error? Was this result expected? Explain.

3. Compare your school sample and bottled water results with those of your classmates. Are they similar?

Summary Tables

Part I: Determining Accuracy of the Titration

Fill in tables like the following (there should be three tables for Part I):

	10.0 mL __ M KCl (aq)
Initial buret reading	
Final buret reading	
Volume __ M AgNO$_3$ added	

Part II: Testing Water Samples

Fill in tables like the following (there should be six tables for Part II):

	10.0 mL (sample)
Initial buret reading	
Final buret reading	
Volume __ M AgNO$_3$ added	

Calculate the chloride ion concentration for the home sample, school sample, and bottled water sample.

	Using 5.00×10^{-3} M silver nitrate	Using 5.00×10^{-4} M silver nitrate
Home sample		
School sample		
Bottled water		

Something Extra

Contact your local water company and the bottled water distributor and obtain data on their chloride ion concentrations. Do these data agree with your results?

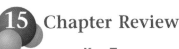

15 Chapter Review

Key Terms

solution (p. 467)
solvent (p. 467)
solute (p. 467)
aqueous solutions (p. 467)
saturated (15.2)
unsaturated (15.2)
supersaturated (15.2)
concentrated (15.2)
dilute (15.2)
mass percent (15.4)

molarity (M) (15.5)
standard solution (15.5)
dilution (15.6)
neutralization reaction (15.8)
equivalent of an acid (15.9)
equivalent of a base (15.9)
equivalent weight (15.9)
normality (N) (15.9)
colligative property (15.10)

Summary

1. A solution is a homogeneous mixture. The solubility of a solute in a given solvent depends on the interactions between the solvent and solute particles. Water dissolves many ionic compounds and compounds with polar molecules, because strong forces occur between the solute and the polar water molecules. Nonpolar solvents tend to dissolve nonpolar solutes. "Like dissolves like."

2. Solution composition can be described in many ways. Two of the most important are in terms of mass percent of solute:

498 Chapter 15 Solutions

$$\text{Mass percent} = \frac{\text{mass of solute}}{\text{mass of solution}} \times 100\%$$

and molarity:

$$\text{Molarity} = \frac{\text{moles of solute}}{\text{liters of solution}}$$

3. A standard solution is one whose concentration is accurately known. Solutions are often made from a stock solution by dilution. When a solution is diluted, only solvent is added, which means that

Moles of solute after dilution
= moles of solute before dilution

4. Normality is defined as the number of equivalents per liter of solution. One equivalent of acid is the amount of acid that furnishes 1 mol of H^+ ions. One equivalent of base is the amount of base that furnishes 1 mol of OH^- ions.

5. The colligative properties of solutions refer to properties that depend on the number of solute particles present. Examples of colligative properties include boiling point raising and freezing point lowering.

Questions and Problems

All exercises with blue numbers have answers in the back of this book.

15.1 Solubility

Questions

1. What does it mean that a solution is a *homogeneous* mixture? Give two examples of homogeneous mixtures.

2. In a solution, the substance present in the largest amount is called the _____, whereas the other substances present are called the _____.

3. Discuss how an *ionic* solute dissolves in water. How are the strong interionic forces in the solid overcome to permit the solid to dissolve? How are the dissolved positive and negative ions shielded from one another, preventing them from recombining to form the solid?

4. Why are some molecular solids (such as sugar or ethyl alcohol) soluble in water, while other molecular solids (such as petroleum) are insoluble in water? What structural features(s) of *some* molecular solids may tend to make them soluble in water?

15.2 Solution Composition: An Introduction

Questions

5. A solution that contains as much solute as will dissolve at a given temperature is said to be _____.

6. A solution that has not reached its limit of dissolved solute is said to be _____.

7. A solution is a homogeneous mixture and, unlike a compound, has _____ composition.

8. The label "concentrated H_2SO_4" on a bottle means that there is a relatively _____ amount of H_2SO_4 present in the solution.

15.3 Factors Affecting the Rate of Dissolution

Questions

9. What does it mean to increase the surface area of a solid? Explain why this change causes an increase in the rate of dissolving.

10. Use a molecular explanation to explain why increasing the temperature speeds up the rate of dissolving a solid in a liquid.

11. Explain why the solubility of a gas generally decreases with an increase in temperature.

15.4 Solution Composition: Mass Percent

Problems

12. Calculate the mass percent of calcium chloride in each of the following solutions.
   a. 5.00 g of calcium chloride in 95.0 g of water
   b. 1.00 g of calcium chloride in 19.0 g of water
   c. 15.0 g of calcium chloride in 285 g of water
   d. 2.00 mg of calcium chloride in 0.0380 g of water

13. Calculate the mass, in grams, of NaCl present in each of the following solutions.
   a. 11.5 g of 6.25% NaCl solution
   b. 6.25 g of 11.5% NaCl solution
   c. 54.3 g of 0.91% NaCl solution
   d. 452 g of 12.3% NaCl solution

14. A laboratory assistant prepared a potassium chloride solution for her class by dissolving 5.34 g of KCl in 152 g of water. What is the mass percent of the solution she prepared?

15. If 67.1 g of $CaCl_2$ is added to 275 g of water, calculate the mass percent of $CaCl_2$ in the solution.

16. What mass of each solute is present in 285 g of a solution that contains 5.00% by mass NaCl and 7.50% by mass Na_2CO_3?

17. A hexane solution contains as impurities 5.2% (by mass) heptane and 2.9% (by mass) pentane. Calculate the mass of each component present in 93 g of the solution.

15.5 Solution Composition: Molarity

Questions

18. A solution that is labeled "0.105 *M* NaOH" would contain _____ mol of NaOH per liter of solution.

Chapter Review **499**

1. A homogeneous mixture is a combination of two (or more) pure substances that is uniform in composition and appearance throughout. Examples of homogeneous mixtures include rubbing alcohol (70% isopropyl alcohol and 30% water) and gasoline (a mixture of hydrocarbons).

2. solvent; solute

3. When an ionic solute dissolves in water, a given ion is pulled into solution by the attractive ion–dipole forces exerted by several water molecules. Although the ionic forces in the crystal are stronger than the ion–dipole forces, entropy is also a driving force for an ionic solid to dissolve, because the solution is more disordered than the pure water and solid ionic crystal. After entering the solution, the dissolved ion is surrounded completely by water molecules, which tends to prevent the ion from reentering the crystal.

4. The intermolecular forces must be similar in the two substances for them to mix. Polar and ionic solids may dissolve in water.

5. saturated

6. unsaturated

7. variable

8. large

9. Increasing the surface area of a solid increases the amount of solid that comes into contact with the solvent.

10. An increase in temperature means an increase in the average kinetic energy. Thus, in a warmer solution, the particles of the liquid solvent are moving more rapidly. As a result, there is an increased rate of solute–solvent interactions, which increases the rate of dissolving.

11. An increase in temperature means an increase in the average kinetic energy. In a warmer solution, the solvent and solute particles are moving more rapidly. If the solute particles are gaseous, faster-moving particles are more likely to have enough energy to escape from the liquid.

12. (a) 5.00% $CaCl_2$; (b) 5.00% $CaCl_2$; (c) 5.00% $CaCl_2$; (d) 5.00% $CaCl_2$

13. (a) 0.719 g NaCl; (b) 0.719 g NaCl; (c) 0.49 g NaCl; (d) 55.6 g NaCl

14. 3.39% KCl

15. 19.6% $CaCl_2$

16. 14.3 g NaCl

17. 4.8 g heptane; 2.7 g pentane; 86 g hexane

18. 0.105

19. 0.221 mol Ca^{2+}; 0.442 mol Cl^-

20. A 5.00 M solution means there are 5.00 moles of solute per 1.00 L of solution (not water). To make such a solution, we would add enough water to 5.00 moles of solute so that the total volume of the solution is 1.00 L.

21. (a) 2.0 M; (b) 1.0 M; (c) 0.67 M; (d) 0.50 M

22. (a) 0.253 M; (b) 0.106 M; (c) 0.434 M; (d) 1.7 × 10^{-3} M

23. 1.99 M

24. 0.0902 M

25. 0.623 M Fe^{3+}; 1.87 M Cl^-

26. 0.619 M

27. (a) 0.0133 mol; 0.838 g; (b) 2.34 mol; 39.9 g; (c) 0.00505 mol; 0.490 g; (d) 0.0299 mol; 1.09 g

28. 6.04 g NH_4Cl

29. (a) 4.60 × 10^{-3} mol Al^{3+}; 1.38 × 10^{-2} mol Cl^-; (b) 1.70 mol Na^+; 0.568 mol PO_4^{3-}; (c) 2.19 × 10^{-3} mol Cu; 4.38 × 10^{-3} mol Cl^-; (d) 3.96 × 10^{-5} mol Ca^{2+}; 7.91 × 10^{-5} mol OH^-

30. 4.25 g

31. (a) 0.0837 M; (b) 0.320 M; (c) 0.0964 M; (d) 0.622 M

32. 56 mL HCl; 42 mL HNO_3; 38 mL H_2SO_4; 39 mL $H_2H_3O_2$; 45 mL H_3PO_4

33. Transfer 6.21 mL of the 3.02 M solution to a 125-mL volumetric flask and add water to the calibration mark.

34. 167 mL

35. 0.113 M

36. 7.5 mL

37. 0.560 g $CaCO_3$

38. 0.976 g $PbCrO_4$

39. 18.8 mL

---

19. How many moles of each ion are present, per liter, in a solution that is labeled "0.221 M $CaCl_2$"?

20. If you were to prepare exactly 1.00 L of a 5 M NaCl solution, you would *not* need exactly 1.00 L of water. Explain.

Problems

21. For each of the following solutions, the number of moles of solute is given, followed by the total volume of solution prepared. Calculate the molarity.
  a. 0.50 mol KBr; 250 mL
  b. 0.50 mol KBr; 500. mL
  c. 0.50 mol KBr; 750 mL
  d. 0.50 mol KBr; 1.0 L

22. For each of the following solutions the mass of the solute is given, followed by the total volume of the solution prepared. Calculate the molarity.
  a. 4.25 g $CuCl_2$; 125 mL
  b. 0.101 g $NaHCO_3$; 11.3 mL
  c. 52.9 g Na_2CO_3; 1.15 L
  d. 0.14 mg KOH; 1.5 mL

23. If a 45.3-g sample of potassium nitrate is dissolved in enough water to make 225 mL of solution, what will be the molarity?

24. An alcoholic iodine solution ("tincture" of iodine) is prepared by dissolving 5.15 g of iodine crystals in enough alcohol to make a volume of 225 mL. Calculate the molarity of iodine in the solution.

25. Suppose 1.01 g of $FeCl_3$ is placed in a 10.0-mL volumetric flask, water is added, the mixture is shaken to dissolve the solid, and then water is added to the calibration mark of the flask. Calculate the molarity of each ion present in the solution.

26. If 495 g of NaOH is dissolved to a final total volume of 20.0 L, what is the molarity of the solution?

27. Calculate the number of *moles* and the number of *grams* of the indicated solutes present in each of the following solution samples.
  a. 127 mL of 0.105 M HNO_3
  b. 155 mL of 15.1 M NH_3
  c. 2.51 L of 2.01 × 10^{-3} M KSCN
  d. 12.2 mL of 2.45 M HCl

28. What mass (in grams) of NH_4Cl is needed to prepare 450. mL of 0.251 M NH_4Cl solution?

29. Calculate the number of moles of *each* ion present in each of the following solutions.
  a. 10.2 mL of 0.451 M $AlCl_3$ solution
  b. 5.51 L of 0.103 M Na_3PO_4 solution
  c. 1.75 mL of 1.25 M $CuCl_2$ solution
  d. 25.2 mL of 0.00157 M $Ca(OH)_2$ solution

30. Standard silver nitrate solutions are used in the analysis of samples containing chloride ion. How many grams of silver nitrate are needed to prepare 250. mL of a 0.100 M $AgNO_3$ solution?

15.6 Dilution

Problems

31. Calculate the new molarity that results when 250. mL of water is added to each of the following solutions.
  a. 125 mL of 0.251 M HCl
  b. 445 mL of 0.499 M H_2SO_4
  c. 5.25 L of 0.101 M HNO_3
  d. 11.2 mL of 14.5 M $HC_2H_3O_2$

32. Many laboratories keep bottles of 3.0 M solutions of the common acids on hand. Given the following molarities of the concentrated acids, determine how many milliliters of each concentrated acid would be required to prepare 225 mL of a 3.0 M solution of the acid.

Acid	*Molarity of Concentrated Reagent*
HCl	12.1 M
HNO_3	15.9 M
H_2SO_4	18.0 M
$HC_2H_3O_2$	17.5 M
H_3PO_4	14.9 M

33. A chemistry student needs 125 mL of 0.150 M NaOH solution for her experiment, but the only solution available in the laboratory is 3.02 M. Describe how the student could prepare the solution she needs.

34. How much *water* must be added to 500. mL of 0.200 M HCl to produce a 0.150 M solution? (Assume that the volumes are additive.)

15.7 Stoichiometry of Solution Reactions

Problems

35. One way to determine the amount of chloride ion in a water sample is to titrate the sample with standard $AgNO_3$ solution to produce solid AgCl.

$$Ag^+(aq) + Cl^-(aq) \rightarrow AgCl(s)$$

If a 25.0-mL water sample requires 27.2 mL of 0.104 M $AgNO_3$ in such a titration, what is the concentration of Cl^- in the sample?

36. What volume (in mL) of 0.25 M Na_2SO_4 solution is needed to precipitate all the barium, as $BaSO_4(s)$, from 12.5 mL of 0.15 M $Ba(NO_3)_2$ solution?

$$Ba(NO_3)_2(aq) + Na_2SO_4(aq) \rightarrow$$
$$BaSO_4(s) + 2NaNO_3(aq)$$

37. If 36.2 mL of 0.158 M $CaCl_2$ solution is added to 37.5 mL of 0.149 M Na_2CO_3, what mass of calcium carbonate, $CaCO_3$, will be precipitated? The reaction is

$$CaCl_2(aq) + Na_2CO_3(aq) \rightarrow CaCO_3(s) + 2NaCl(aq)$$

38. When aqueous solutions of lead(II) ion are treated with potassium chromate solution, a bright yellow precipitate of lead(II) chromate, $PbCrO_4$, forms. How many grams of lead chromate form when a 1.00-g sample of $Pb(NO_3)_2$ is added to 25.0 mL of 1.00 M K_2CrO_4 solution?

---

40. 0.107 M NaOH

41. (a) 3.85 mL NaOH; (b) 3.57 mL NaOH; (c) 4.29 mL NaOH; (d) 15.4 mL NaOH

42. Each mole of H_2SO_4 provides two moles of H^+ ions. Thus it is necessary to take only half a mole of H_2SO_4 to provide 1 mole of H^+ ions. The equivalent weight is therefore half the molar mass.

43. 1.53 equivalents OH^- ion. By definition, one equivalent of OH^- ion exactly neutralizes one equiv-

alent of H^+ ion.

44. (a) 0.277 N; (b) 3.37 × 10^{-3} N; (c) 1.63 N

45. (a) 0.134 N; (b) 0.0104 N; (c) 13.3 N

46. 0.359 M; 1.08 N

47. 47.4 mL

48. 20.0 mL; 39.9 mL

49. Colligative properties are properties of a solution that depend only on the number—not the identity—of the solute particles.

50. For a solution to boil, bubbles must form in the solution. Solute particles block water from entering these bubbles. It is not the nature of these particles that matters, but the number of the particles. Thus the increase in boiling point is a colligative property.

51. Antifreeze solution is a concentrated aqueous solution that has a lower freezing point than water. It will also have a higher boiling point than water (a solute in water both lowers the freezing

15.8 Neutralization Reactions

Problems

39. What volume of 0.200 M HCl solution is needed to neutralize 25.0 mL of 0.150 M NaOH solution?

40. The concentration of a sodium hydroxide solution is to be determined. A 50.0-mL sample of 0.104 M HCl solution requires 48.7 mL of the sodium hydroxide solution to reach the point of neutralization. Calculate the molarity of the NaOH solution.

41. What volume of 1.00 M NaOH is required to neutralize each of the following solutions?
    a. 25.0 mL of 0.154 M acetic acid, $HC_2H_3O_2$
    b. 35.0 mL of 0.102 M hydrofluoric acid, HF
    c. 10.0 mL of 0.143 M phosphoric acid, H_3PO_4
    d. 35.0 mL of 0.220 M sulfuric acid, H_2SO_4

15.9 Solution Composition: Normality

Questions

42. Explain why the equivalent weight of H_2SO_4 is half the molar mass of this substance. How many hydrogen ions does each H_2SO_4 molecule produce when reacting with an excess of OH^- ions?

43. How many equivalents of hydroxide ion are needed to react with 1.53 equivalents of hydrogen ion? How did you know this when no balanced chemical equation was provided for the reaction?

Problems

44. For each of the following solutions, the mass of solute taken is indicated, along with the total volume of solution prepared. Calculate the normality of each solution.
    a. 0.113 g NaOH; 10.2 mL
    b. 12.5 mg $Ca(OH)_2$; 100. mL
    c. 12.4 g H_2SO_4; 155 mL

45. Calculate the normality of each of the following solutions.
    a. 0.134 M NaOH
    b. 0.00521 M $Ca(OH)_2$
    c. 4.42 M H_3PO_4

46. A solution of phosphoric acid, H_3PO_4, is found to contain 35.2 g of H_3PO_4 per liter of solution. Calculate the molarity and normality of the solution.

47. What volume of 0.172 N H_2SO_4 is required to neutralize 56.2 mL of 0.145 M NaOH?

48. What volume of 0.151 N NaOH is required to neutralize 24.2 mL of 0.125 N H_2SO_4? What volume of 0.151 N NaOH is required to neutralize 24.1 mL of 0.125 M H_2SO_4?

15.10 The Properties of Solutions: Boiling Point and Freezing Point

Questions

49. What is meant by the term "colligative property"?

50. Explain on a molecular level why the increase in boiling point is a colligative property.

51. Antifreeze that you use in your car could also be called "antiboil." Explain why.

Critical Thinking

52. Suppose 50.0 mL of 0.250 M $CoCl_2$ solution is added to 25.0 mL of 0.350 M $NiCl_2$ solution. Calculate the concentration, in moles per liter, of each of the ions present after mixing. Assume that the volumes are additive.

53. Calculate the mass of AgCl formed, and the concentration of silver ion remaining in solution, when 10.0 g of solid $AgNO_3$ is added to 50. mL of 1.0×10^{-2} M NaCl solution. Assume there is no volume change upon addition of the solid.

54. What mass of $BaSO_4$ will be precipitated from a large container of concentrated $Ba(NO_3)_2$ solution if 37.5 mL of 0.221 M H_2SO_4 is added?

55. Strictly speaking, the solvent is the component of a solution that is present in the largest amount on a *mole* basis. For solutions involving water, water is almost always the solvent because there tend to be many more water molecules present than molecules of any conceivable solute. To see why this is so, calculate the number of moles of water present in 1.0 L of water. Recall that the density of water is very nearly 1.0 g/mL under most conditions.

56. If 14.2 g of $CaCl_2$ is added to a 50.0-mL volumetric flask, and after dissolving the salt, water is added to the calibration mark of the flask, calculate the molarity of the solution.

57. Calculate the new molarity when 150. mL of water is added to each of the following solutions.
    a. 125 mL of 0.200 M HBr
    b. 155 mL of 0.250 M $Ca(C_2H_3O_2)_2$
    c. 0.500 L of 0.250 M H_3PO_4
    d. 15 mL of 18.0 M H_2SO_4

58. Calculate the normality of each of the following solutions.
    a. 0.50 M acetic acid, $HC_2H_3O_2$
    b. 0.00250 M sulfuric acid, H_2SO_4
    c. 0.10 M potassium hydroxide, KOH

59. If 27.5 mL of 3.5×10^{-2} N $Ca(OH)_2$ solution is needed to neutralize 10.0 mL of nitric acid solution of unknown concentration, what is the normality of the nitric acid?

---

point and raises the boiling point). **59.** 9.6×10^{-2} N

52. 0.167 M Co^{3+}; 0.117 M Ni^{2+}; 0.567 M Cl^-

53. 0.072 g AgCl; 1.2 M Ag^+

54. 1.93 g

55. 56 mol water

56. 2.56 M

57. (a) 0.0909 M; (b) 0.127 M; (c) 0.192 M; (d) 1.6 M

58. (a) 0.50 N $HC_2H_3O_2$; (b) 5.00×10^{-3} N H_2SO_4; (c) 0.10 N KOH

16 Acids and Bases

Section	Text Features & Components	Labs, Demonstrations & Activities
Teaching Segment 16A **1 block** **pp. 503–513**	**16.1–16.2** ● **Acids and Bases** **Acid Strength**	**LP** Lesson Plans (Sec 16.1–16.3) **SE** Top Ten Fruit Crops in the World *p. 504* **SE** Chemical Impact: Gum That Foams *p. 505* **SE** Chemical Impact: Plants Fight Back *p. 510* **TE** Teaching Tips *pp. 504, 506*	**TE** Mini Demo *p. 506* **LM** Experiment 66: Acids and Bases Lab Manual Report Sheets Teacher's Lab Guide
	16.3 Water as an Acid ◐ **and a Base**	**SE** What if . . . *p. 510*	**TE** Mini Demo *p. 510*
Teaching Segment 16B **2 blocks** **pp. 513–524**	**16.4 The pH Scale** ● ◔	**LP** Lesson Plans (Sec 16.4–16.6) **SE** Chemical Impact: Airplane Rash *p. 516*	**TE** Class Activity *p. 515* • Mini Demo *p. 515* **TE** Teaching Support: Demonstration *pp. 520–522* **SE** Chemistry in the Laboratory *pp. 530–531* **LM** Experiment 67: Acid Rain Lab Manual Report Sheets Teacher's Lab Guide
	16.5–16.6 ● **Measuring pH** ◑ **Calculating the pH of Strong Acid Solutions**	**SE** Chemical Impact: Arnold Beckman, Man of Science *p. 523*	**TE** Class Activity *p. 521* **SE** Chemistry in Action: Cabbage Juice *p. 522* **LM** Experiment 68: Indicators Lab Manual Report Sheets Teacher's Lab Guide
Teaching Segment 16C **3 blocks** **pp. 524–529**	**16.7 Acid-Base Titrations** ❸	**LP** Lesson Plans (Sec 16.7–16. 8) **SE** Celebrity Chemical: Sulfur Dioxide *p. 525* **TE** Teaching Tips *pp. 524, 527*	**LM** Experiments 69–71 Lab Manual Report Sheets Teacher's Lab Guide
	16.8 Acid-Base Titrations ● ◐	**SE** Chemical Impact: The Heart of the Matter *p. 529* **TE** Teaching Tips *p. 528*	**TE** Mini Demo *p. 528* **LM** Experiment 72: Acids, Bases, and Buffers Lab Manual Report Sheets Teacher's Lab Guide

Key

SE Student Edition
TE Teacher Edition
RP Teacher Resource Package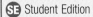
LM Lab Materials
LP Lesson Plans
AR Additional Resources
◆ Florida Specific

Technology and Media

Transparencies
Figures 16.1, 16.3, 16.8

PowerPoint Slides

 Video Cabbage Juice Indicator Part A–D
Chemistry in Motion
(2) Conductivities of Aqueous Solutions
(26) Buffering

Animation Bronsted-Lowery Reaction • Weak Acid Dissolved in Water • Self-ionization of Water • Acid Ionization • Neutralization Strong Acid/Base

eEdition CD-ROM
Easy Planner CD-ROM
English Summaries CD
Spanish Summaries CD

Web Site classzone.com
McDougal Littell Test Generator

Chapter Planning Guide

All Learners	Review & Assessment	Standards
(TE) Active Learning *p. 503* **(animation)** Animation: Bronsted-Lowry Reaction • Weak Acid Dissolved in Water • Acid Ionization **(transparency)** Transparency: Figure 16.1 *p. 508* **(video)** Chemistry in Motion (2) *p. 508* **(AR)** Less Proficient Students *p. 31*	**(TE)** Additional Examples *pp. 505–506* **(SE)** Self Check *p. 506* **(SE)** What if . . . *p. 507* **(SE)** Key Terms *p. 531* **(SE)** Questions and Problems *p. 532*	**(TE) NSES** UCP1, UCP2, UCP5, A1, A2, B2, B3, C4, C6, E1 **SSS** SC.H.1.4.1, SC.H.1.4.2, SC.H.1.4.3, SC.H.1.4.5, SC.H.1.4.6, SC.A.1.4.1, SC.A.1.4.5, SC.C.2.4.2, SC.C.2.4.5
(animation) Animation: Self Ionization of Water *p. 510* **(RP)** Team Learning Worksheets (Section 16.1–16.3) *pp. 89–90* **(AR)** Less Proficient Students *p. 31*	**(TE)** Additional Examples *pp. 511–512* **(SE)** Self Check *p. 512* **(SE)** Focus Questions (Sec 16. 1–16.3) *p. 513* **(SE)** Key Terms *p. 531* **(SE)** Questions and Problems *p. 533*	
(TE) Active Learning *p. 513* **(TE)** Teaching Tips *pp. 513–514, 518* **(transparency)** Transparency: Figure 16.3 *p. 515* **(AR)** Less Proficient Students *p. 32*	**(SE)** What if . . . *p. 514* **(TE)** Additional Examples *pp. 514, 516-517, 519* **(SE)** Self Check *pp. 515, 517, 519* **(SE)** Key Terms *p. 531* **(SE)** Questions and Problems *p. 533*	**(TE) NSES** UCP1, UCP2, UCP3, A1, A2, B2, E1, E2, F6, G1, G2, G3 **SSS** SC.H.1.4.1, SC.H.3.4.1, SC.H.3.4.2, SC.H.3.4.4, SC.H.3.4.5, SC.H.3.4.6
(video) Video: Cabbage Juice Indicator *p. 521* **(TE)** Teaching Tips *pp. 521, 523* **(TE)** Integrating the Chemical Impact *p. 523* **(RP)** Team Learning Worksheets (Sec 16.4–16.6) *pp. 91–92* **(AR)** Less Proficient Students *p. 32*	**(TE)** Additional Examples *p. 523* **(SE)** Self Check *p. 523* **(SE)** Focus Questions (Sec 16.4–16.6) *p. 524* **(SE)** Key Terms *p. 531* **(SE)** Questions and Problems *p. 534*	
(TE) Active Learning *p. 524* **(transparency)** Transparency Figure 16.8 *p. 526* **(animation)** Animation: Neutralization Strong Acid/Base *p. 526* **(AR)** Less Proficient Students *p. 32*	**(TE)** Additional Examples *p. 526* **(SE)** Self Check *p. 527* **(SE)** Key Terms *p. 531* **(SE)** Questions and Problems *p. 534*	**(TE) NSES** UCP2, UCP3, UCP5, A1, A2, B2, B3, F1, F4, F5, F6 **SSS** SC.H.1.4.1, SC.H.1.4.7, SC.H.3.4.1, SC.H.3.4.3, SC.H.3.4.5, SC.H.3.4.6
(video) Chemistry in Motion (26) *p. 528* **(RP)** Team Learning Worksheets (Sec 16.7–16.8) *pp. 93–94* **(AR)** Less Proficient Students *p. 32*	**(SE)** Focus Questions (Sec 16.7–16.8) *p. 529* **(SE)** Key Terms *p. 531* **(SE)** Questions and Problems *p. 534*	

Chapter Materials

(TE) Reading Strategy
(AR) English/Spanish Summaries *pp. 25–26*
(AR) Challenge Projects/Problems *pp. 30–31*
(AR) Less Proficient Students *p. 32*
(audio) English Summary Audio
(audio) Spanish Summary Audio
(RP) Chapter Review Worksheets (Basic, Review, Challenge)

(SE) Chapter Summary *pp. 531–532*
(SE) Critical Thinking *pp. 534–535*
(RP) Solutions Guide
(RP) Chapter Tests
(RP) Test Bank
(software) McDougal Littell Test Generator
(AR) Standardized Test Practice
(globe) FCAT Test 8

16 Integrating Reading Strategies and Chemistry Concepts

Chapter 16: Choosing Supplemental Reading Materials

Emphasize that the students can supplement their textbook reading with outside materials. Often, such supplemental materials can clarify a topic or explain it in greater detail. At the same time, point out that one of the primary goals of the textbook authors is to present sufficient information to allow readers a thorough understanding of the subject. Some of that information is explanatory, some provides examples, and some is meant to stimulate reader interest in the subject.

Explain that a variety of relevant reading materials are available that will complement the information in the text. Encourage the students to do additional reading whenever they need or want more information about a topic. Remind the students that there are several sources of additional material. Ask the students to suggest sources for some of these. List their suggestions on the board and use the guide below to complete the list.

Where to Find Relevant Chemistry Reading Materials	
• Internet	• Encyclopedia
• Library	• Dictionary
• Bookstore	• Teacher

What to Look for When Choosing Supplemental Reading Materials

The first place that the students are likely to look for additional reading material is the Internet. Many students are already familiar with entering search terms and looking for particular Web sites. Remind the students that information on the Web may not always be accurate. Choosing a trusted site for information is important. Point out that the students can search the Internet in a number of ways. The most direct approach is to identify the topic and use it as a keyword in an applicable search engine. For example, this chapter focuses on acids and bases. The students can search for "acid and base," or they may use more specific topics, such as diprotic or organic acids. Explain that in addition to using search terms, the students may want to look for general chemistry Web sites. Many high schools and colleges maintain such Web sites, which cover most major topics. Finally, point out that the students can search for additional materials written by the authors of the text used in class. Have the students turn to page vi of the text and note that the first author, Steven Zumdahl, is the author of several chemistry textbooks.

Remind the students that the library is an excellent resource for locating relevant supplemental reading materials. Many libraries have a textbook section in which the students can find chemistry textbooks written by various authors. A different perspective or additional textbook features can help students with certain learning styles.

Encourage the students to use other textbooks, but remind them to choose wisely. Ask the students to suggest how a copyright date of 1970 might affect the reliability of the information. [The information is likely to be out of date because new scientific discoveries occur frequently.] Point out that public libraries also have catalogues or computer applications that allow the students to search for materials.

Remind the students that current encyclopedias and dictionaries are reliable sources of general information. Point out that many computers come with encyclopedias and dictionaries either already installed or on a CD. In addition, libraries often have scientific dictionaries that contain information about a specific topic. Remind the students to check the copyright date of each resource they use.

Another source of additional information for the students is the teacher. Emphasize that most teachers also maintain a library of supplementary materials and are often happy to share these with the students. In addition, many science teachers keep multiple editions of scientific journals and other publications that contain detailed articles about various topics.

Suggestions for Supplemental Reading

Use these ideas to encourage the students to find additional reading material for these subjects. Instruct the students to write a summary about what they learn from their reading.

- *Teacher's Edition,* Using the Top Ten feature, page 504: Have the students read about acids and bases found in fruit.

- *Teacher's Edition,* Integrating the Chemical Impact feature, page 505: Have the students investigate other candies or treats that produce unexpected reactions. (Ideas: pop rocks, super-sour candy, etc.)

- *Student Edition,* Chemical Impact feature, page 510: Have the students read current research involving plant communication.

- *Student Edition,* Chemical Impact feature, page 516: Have the students read about the current findings involving paint for airplanes.

- *Teacher's Edition,* Integrating the Chemical Impact feature, page 523: Have the students read about a current Nobel Prize winner, for example 2004 winners Aaron Ciechanover, Avram Hershko, or Irwin Rose.

- *Teacher's Edition,* Celebrity Chemical feature, page 525: Have the students read about the effects of acid rain or sulfur dioxide and current related studies and findings.

- *Teacher's Edition,* Chemical Impact feature, page 529: Have the students read about the medical advancements made in the study of diabetes.

- Have the students read about one of the scientists mentioned in the chapter: Svante Arrhenius, Johannes Bronsted, or Thomas Lowry.

CHEMICAL IMPACT

Mad Dawg chewing gum is a practical joker's dream come true. It is noticeably sour when someone first starts to chew it, but the big surprise comes about ten chews later when brightly colored foam oozes from the person's mouth. Although the effect is dramatic, the cause is simple acid–base chemistry.

Chemical Impact feature, page 505

Chapter 16

Overview

In this Chapter our goals are for the students to:

- Understand the Arrhenius and Brønsted–Lowry models for acids and bases

- Understand acid strength

- Understand the relationship between acid strength and strength of the conjugate base

- Learn about the ionization of water

- Understand and use the terms pH and POH

- Learn methods for measuring the pH of a solution

- Learn to calculate the pH of solutions of strong acids

- Learn about acid-base titration

- Understand the general characteristics of buffered solutions

16 Acids and Bases

Fruits contain various amounts of citric acid.

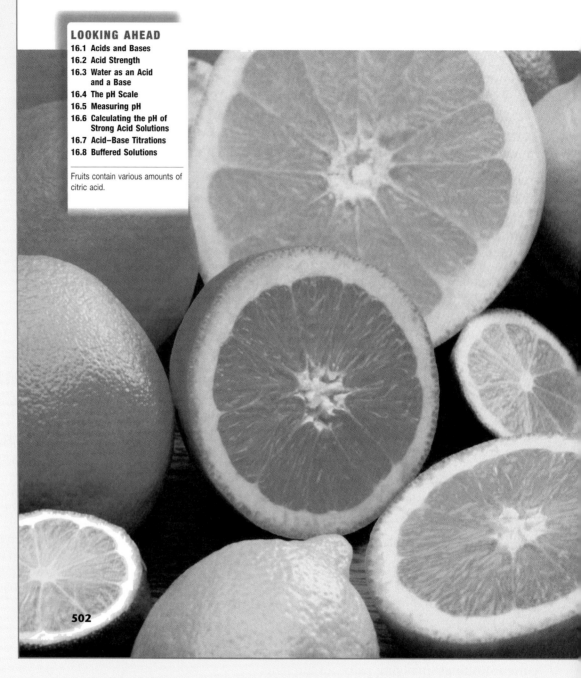

502

A cids are very important substances. They cause lemons to be sour, digest food in the stomach (and sometimes cause heartburn), dissolve rock to make fertilizer, dissolve your tooth enamel to form cavities, and clean the deposits out of your coffee maker. Acids are essential industrial chemicals. In fact, the chemical in first place in terms of the amount manufactured in the United States is sulfuric acid, H_2SO_4. Eighty *billion* pounds of this material are used every year in the manufacture of fertilizers, detergents, plastics, pharmaceuticals, storage batteries, and metals. The acid–base properties of substances also can be used to make interesting novelties such as the foaming chewing gum described on page 505.

In this chapter we will consider the most important properties of acids and of their opposites, the bases.

Red cabbage juice can be used as an indicator of acidity.

16.1 Acids and Bases

Objective: *To learn about two models of acids and bases and the relationship of conjugate acid–base pairs.*

CHEMISTRY

Don't taste chemical reagents!

A cids were first recognized as substances that taste sour. Vinegar tastes sour because it is a dilute solution of acetic acid; citric acid is responsible for the sour taste of a lemon. Bases, sometimes called *alkalis*, are characterized by their bitter taste and slippery feel. Most hand soaps and commercial preparations for unclogging drains are highly basic.

The Arrhenius Model

The first person to recognize the essential nature of acids and bases was Svante Arrhenius. On the basis of his experiments with electrolytes, Arrhenius postulated that **acids** *produce hydrogen ions in aqueous solution,* whereas **bases** *produce hydroxide ions* (review Section 8.4).

For example, when hydrogen chloride gas is dissolved in water each molecule produces ions as follows:

$$HCl(g) \xrightarrow{H_2O} H^+(aq) + Cl^-(aq)$$

This solution is the strong acid known as hydrochloric acid. On the other hand, when solid sodium hydroxide is dissolved in water, its ions separate producing a solution containing Na^+ and OH^- ions.

$$NaOH(s) \xrightarrow{H_2O} Na^+(aq) + OH^-(aq)$$

This solution is called a strong base.

The label on a bottle of concentrated hydrochloric acid.

16.1 Acids and Bases **503**

Section
16.1

Themes
Models, Form and Function

Skills
Making comparisons, classifying, developing models

Student Preparation
Assign the students to read Sections 16.1 to 16.3 and to answer the Focus Questions at the end of Section 16.3 before coming to class.

Active Learning
After introducing the material in Sections 16.1 to 16.3 in class, place the students in groups and have them work together on Sections 16.1–16.3: Team Learning Worksheet. Answers and/or discussion of these questions are located in the *Teacher Resources.*

Using the TOP TEN

Have students choose a fruit from the Top Ten and find out what acids and/or bases are found in the fruit.

TEACHING TIPS

- Spend time developing the model for acid–base pairs in this section. Students need to be able to look at a chemical equation and identify these pairs.

- The Brønsted–Lowry definition of acids and bases is preferable because it emphasizes that for one reactant to act like an acid, the other reactant must act like a base.

- It is important to show students that acidic and basic substances work together. A proton donor must have a substance to accept the proton. The idea that water can act as both an acid and a base can be developed here.

- This occasion marks the first time that students have seen the hydronium ion. Make sure that they understand how it forms from the donation of a proton to water.

USING TECHNOLOGY

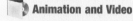 **Animation and Video**

Use the Brønsted–Lowry Reaction animation here. The self-ionization of water to form H^+ and OH^- can also be used here.

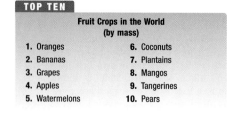

TOP TEN

**Fruit Crops in the World
(by mass)**

1. Oranges		6. Coconuts
2. Bananas		7. Plantains
3. Grapes		8. Mangos
4. Apples		9. Tangerines
5. Watermelons		10. Pears

CHEMISTRY

Recall that (*aq*) means the substance is hydrated—it has water molecules clustered around it.

The Brønsted–Lowry Model

Although the **Arrhenius concept of acids and bases** was a major step forward in understanding acid–base chemistry, this concept is limited because it allows for only one kind of base—the hydroxide ion. A more general definition of acids and bases was suggested by the Danish chemist Johannes Brønsted and the English chemist Thomas Lowry. In the **Brønsted–Lowry model**, *an acid is a proton (H⁺) donor, and a base is a proton acceptor.* According to the Brønsted–Lowry model, the general reaction that occurs when an acid is dissolved in water can best be represented as an acid (HA) donating a proton to a water molecule to form a new acid (the **conjugate acid**) and a new base (the **conjugate base**).

$$HA(aq) + H_2O(l) \rightarrow H_3O^+(aq) + A^-(aq)$$

Acid   Base   Conjugate acid   Conjugate base

This model emphasizes the significant role of the polar water molecule in pulling the proton from the acid. Note that the conjugate base is everything that remains of the acid molecule after a proton is lost. The conjugate acid is formed when the proton is transferred to the base. A **conjugate acid–base pair** consists of two substances related to each other by the donating and accepting of a *single proton*. In the above equation there are two conjugate acid–base pairs: HA (acid) and A⁻ (base), and H₂O (base) and H₃O⁺ (acid). For example, when hydrogen chloride is dissolved in water it behaves as an acid.

Acid–conjugate base pair

$$HCl(aq) + H_2O(l) \rightarrow H_3O^+(aq) + Cl^-(aq)$$

Base–conjugate acid pair

In this case HCl is the acid that loses an H⁺ ion to form Cl⁻, its conjugate base. On the other hand, H₂O (behaving as a base) gains an H⁺ ion to form H₃O⁺ (the conjugate acid).

How can water act as a base? Remember that the oxygen of the water molecule has two unshared electron pairs, either of which can form a covalent bond with an H⁺ ion. When gaseous HCl dissolves in water, the following reaction occurs.

$$H\!-\!\ddot{O}\!: + H\!-\!Cl \rightarrow \left[H\!-\!\ddot{O}\!-\!H \right]^+ + Cl^-$$

$$\quad\quad |\quad\quad \delta^+ \;\; \delta^- \quad\quad\quad |$$

$$\quad\quad H \quad\quad\quad\quad\quad\quad\quad\quad H$$

Note that an H⁺ ion is transferred from the HCl molecule to the water molecule to form H₃O⁺, which is called the **hydronium ion.**

504   Chapter 16   Acids and Bases

Example 16.1

Identifying Conjugate Acid–Base Pairs

Which of the following represent conjugate acid–base pairs?

    a. HF, F^-

    b. NH_4^+, NH_3

    c. HCl, H_2O

Solution

    a and **b.** HF, F^- and NH_4^+, NH_3 are conjugate acid–base pairs because the two species differ by one H^+.

$$HF \rightarrow H^+ + F^-$$

$$NH_4^+ \rightarrow H^+ + NH_3$$

    c. HCl and H_2O are not a conjugate acid–base pair because they are not related by the removal or addition of one H^+. The conjugate base of HCl is Cl^-. The conjugate acid of H_2O is H_3O^+.

CHEMICAL IMPACT

Science, Technology, and Society

Gum That Foams

Mad Dawg chewing gum is a practical joker's dream come true. It is noticeably sour when someone first starts to chew it, but the big surprise comes about ten chews later when brightly colored foam oozes from the person's mouth. Although the effect is dramatic, the cause is simple acid–base chemistry.

The foam consists of sugar and saliva churned into a bubbling mess by carbon dioxide released from the gum. The carbon dioxide is formed when sodium bicarbonate (NaHCO₃) present in the gum is mixed with citric acid and malic acid (also present in the gum) in the moist environment of the mouth. As NaHCO₃ dissolves in the water of the saliva, it separates into its ions:

Chewing Mad Dawg gum.

The acids present in the gum also cause it to be sour, stimulating extra salivation and thus extra foam.

Although the chemistry behind Mad Dawg is well understood, the development of the gum into a safe, but fun, product was not so easy. In fact, early versions of the gum exploded because the acids and the sodium bicarbonate mixed prematurely. As solids, citric and malic acids and sodium bicarbonate do not react with each other. However, the presence of water frees the ions to move and react. In the manufacture of the gum, colorings and flavorings are applied as aqueous solutions. The water caused the gum to explode in early attempts to manufacture it. The makers of Mad Dawg obviously solved the problem.

$$NaHCO_3(s) \xrightarrow{H_2O} Na^+(aq) + HCO_3^-(aq)$$

The bicarbonate ion, when exposed to H^+ ions from acids, decomposes to carbon dioxide and water.*

$$H^+(aq) + HCO_3^-(aq) \rightarrow H_2O(l) + CO_2(g)$$

*This reaction is often used to power "bottle rockets" by adding vinegar (dilute acetic acid) to baking soda (sodium bicarbonate).

16.1 Acids and Bases **505**

Additional Examples

Which of the following represent conjugate acid–base pairs?

a. $HClO_4$, ClO_4^-

b. HCl, ClO^-

c. $H_2PO_4^-$, HPO_4^{2-}

d. HNO_3, NO_3^-

    a, c, and d

Integrating the CHEMICAL IMPACT

Gum That Foams

Have students investigate other candies or treats that produce unexpected reactions. Are these materials other examples of acid–base chemistry at work? Pop Rocks and other candies that fizz are excellent possibilities. Also have students investigate how jelly beans or jawbreakers are made. In both cases, a number of layers are applied to produce the finished candy.

You might have students make CO_2 rockets. Use 2-L soft-drink bottles (empty) fitted with corks in place of the screw caps. Place 50.0 mL of vinegar in the bottle. Place 2 teaspoons of baking soda in a paper tissue. Roll the tissue into a "cigar" and stuff it into the bottle. Cork the bottle immediately, point it away from other people, and shake the bottle. As the pressure builds, the cork will be launched from the bottle.

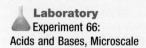
506

Example 16.2

Writing Conjugate Bases

Write the conjugate base for each of the following:

a. $HClO_4$

b. H_3PO_4

c. $CH_3NH_3^+$

Solution

To get the conjugate base for an acid, we must remove an H^+ ion.

a. $HClO_4 \rightarrow H^+ + ClO_4^-$
   Acid   Conjugate base

b. $H_3PO_4 \rightarrow H^+ + H_2PO_4^-$
   Acid   Conjugate base

c. $CH_3NH_3^+ \rightarrow H^+ + CH_3NH_2$
   Acid   Conjugate base

 Self-Check Exercise 16.1

Which of the following represent conjugate acid–base pairs?

a. H_2O, H_3O^+

b. OH^-, HNO_3

c. H_2SO_4, SO_4^{2-}

d. $HC_2H_3O_2$, $C_2H_3O_2^-$

 16.2 Acid Strength

Objectives: *To understand what acid strength means.*
To understand the relationship between acid strength and the strength of the conjugate base.

We have seen that when an acid dissolves in water, a proton is transferred from the acid to water:

$$HA(aq) + H_2O(l) \rightarrow H_3O^+(aq) + A^-(aq)$$

In this reaction a new acid, H_3O^+ (called the conjugate acid), and a new base, A^- (the conjugate base), are formed. The conjugate acid and base can react with one another,

$$H_3O^+(aq) + A^-(aq) \rightarrow HA(aq) + H_2O(l)$$

to re-form the parent acid and a water molecule. Therefore, this reaction can occur "in both directions." The forward reaction is

$$HA(aq) + H_2O(l) \rightarrow H_3O^+(aq) + A^-(aq)$$

506   Chapter 16   Acids and Bases

and the reverse reaction is

$$H_3O^+(aq) + A^-(aq) \rightarrow HA(aq) + H_2O(l)$$

Note that the products in the forward reaction are the reactants in the reverse reaction. We usually represent the situation in which the reaction can occur in both directions by double arrows:

$$HA(aq) + H_2O(l) \rightleftharpoons H_3O^+(aq) + A^-(aq)$$

This situation represents a competition for the H^+ ion between H_2O (in the forward reaction) and A^- (in the reverse reaction). If H_2O "wins" this competition—that is, if H_2O has a very high attraction for H^+ compared to A^-—then the solution will contain mostly H_3O^+ and A^-. We describe this situation by saying that the H_2O molecule is a much stronger base (more attraction for H^+) than A^-. In this case the forward reaction predominates:

$$HA(aq) + H_2O(l) \implies H_3O^+(aq) + A^-(aq)$$

We say that the acid HA is **completely ionized** or **completely dissociated**. This situation represents a **strong acid.**

The opposite situation can also occur. Sometimes A^- "wins" the competition for the H^+ ion. In this case A^- is a much stronger base than H_2O and the reverse reaction predominates:

$$HA(aq) + H_2O(l) \impliedby H_3O^+(aq) + A^-(aq)$$

Here A^- has a much larger attraction for H^+ than does H_2O, and most of the HA molecules remain intact. This situation represents a **weak acid.**

We can determine what is actually going on in a solution by measuring its ability to conduct an electric current. Recall from Chapter 8 that a solution can conduct a current in proportion to the number of ions that are present (see Figure 8.2). When 1 mole of solid sodium chloride is dissolved in 1 L of water, the resulting solution is an excellent conductor of an electric current because the Na^+ and Cl^- ions separate completely. We call NaCl a strong electrolyte. Similarly, when 1 mole of hydrogen chloride is dissolved in 1 L of water, the resulting solution is an excellent conductor. Therefore, hydrogen chloride is also a strong electrolyte, which means that each HCl molecule must produce H^+ and Cl^- ions. This tells us that the forward reaction predominates:

$$HCl(aq) + H_2O(l) \rightleftharpoons H_3O^+(aq) + Cl^-(aq)$$

(Accordingly, the arrow pointing right is longer than the arrow pointing left.) In solution there are virtually no HCl molecules, only H^+ and Cl^- ions. This shows that Cl^- is a very poor base compared to the H_2O molecule; it has virtually no ability to attract H^+ ions in water. This aqueous solution of hydrogen chloride (called *hydrochloric acid*) is a strong acid.

In general, the strength of an acid is defined by the position of its ionization (dissociation) reaction:

$$HA(aq) + H_2O(l) \rightleftharpoons H_3O^+(aq) + A^-(aq)$$

WHAT IF?

Vinegar contains acetic acid and is used in salad dressings.

What if acetic acid was a strong acid instead of a weak acid? Would it be safe to use vinegar as a salad dressing?

A hydrochloric acid solution readily conducts electric current, as shown by the brightness of the bulb.

TEACHING TIP

We use the terms "ionized" and "dissociated" interchangeably when discussing acids.

WHAT IF Comments

Whether an acid is harmful to human tissue reflects the concentration of H^+ ions in solution. A weak acid, such as vinegar, has a much lower concentration of H^+ ions than a strong acid such as HCl. For example, a 1.0 *M* solution of HCl has more than 200 times as many H^+ ions as an equal volume of a 1.0 *M* solution of acetic acid (vinegar is only about 5% acetic acid). If acetic acid were a strong acid, it would not be safe as a salad dressing because the high concentration of H^+ ions would damage human tissues.

USING TECHNOLOGY

 Animation and Video

Animation, Weak Acid Dissolved in Water

Animation, Acid Ionization

Figure 16.2
The relationship of acid strength and conjugate base strength for the dissociation reaction

$$HA(aq) + H_2O(l) \rightleftharpoons H_3O^+(aq) + A^-(aq)$$
Acid   Conjugate base

 CHEMISTRY
A strong acid is completely dissociated in water. No HA molecules remain. Only H_3O^+ and A^- are present.

A strong acid has a weak conjugate base.

 CHEMISTRY
A weak acid is mostly undissociated in water.

Figure 16.1
Graphical representation of the behavior of acids of different strengths in aqueous solution. A strong acid is completely dissociated. In contrast, only a small fraction of the molecules of a weak acid are dissociated.

A strong acid is one for which *the forward reaction predominates*. This means that almost all the original HA is dissociated (ionized) (see **Figure 16.1**). There is an important connection between the strength of an acid and that of its conjugate base. *A strong acid contains a relatively weak conjugate base*—one that has a low attraction for protons. A strong acid can be described as an acid whose conjugate base is a much weaker base than water **(Figure 16.2).** In this case the water molecules win the competition for the H^+ ions.

In contrast to hydrochloric acid, when acetic acid, $HC_2H_3O_2$, is dissolved in water, the resulting solution conducts an electric current only weakly. That is, acetic acid is a weak electrolyte, which means that only a few ions are present. In other words, for the reaction

$$HC_2H_3O_2(aq) + H_2O(l) \rightleftharpoons H_3O^+(aq) + C_2H_3O_2^-(aq)$$

the reverse reaction predominates (thus the arrow pointing left is longer). In fact, measurements show that only about one in one hundred (1%) of the $HC_2H_3O_2$ molecules is dissociated (ionized) in a 0.1 M solution of acetic acid. Thus acetic acid is a weak acid. When acetic acid molecules are placed in water, almost all of the molecules remain undissociated. This tells us that the acetate ion, $C_2H_3O_2^-$, is an effective base—it very successfully attracts H^+ ions in water. This means that acetic acid remains largely in the form of $HC_2H_3O_2$ molecules in solution. A weak acid is one for which the *reverse reaction*

$$HA(aq) + H_2O(l) \quad \Longleftarrow \quad H_3O^+(aq) + A^-(aq)$$

predominates. Most of the acid originally placed in the solution is still present as HA at equilibrium. That is, a weak acid dissociates (ionizes) only to a very small extent in aqueous solution (see **Figure 16.1**). In contrast to a strong acid, a weak acid has a conjugate base that is a much stronger base than water. In this case a water molecule is not very successful in pulling an

An acetic acid solution conducts only a small amount of current as shown by the dimly lit bulb.

Perchloric acid can explode when handled improperly.

Phosphoric acid   Acetic acid

Nitrous acid   Hypochlorous acid

H^+ ion away from the conjugate base. A *weak acid contains a relatively strong conjugate base* (Figure 16.2).

The various ways of describing the strength of an acid are summarized in **Table 16.1.**

The common strong acids are sulfuric acid, $H_2SO_4(aq)$; hydrochloric acid, $HCl(aq)$; nitric acid, $HNO_3(aq)$; and perchloric acid, $HClO_4(aq)$. Sulfuric acid is actually a **diprotic acid**, an acid that can furnish two protons. The acid H_2SO_4 is a strong acid that is virtually 100% dissociated in water:

$$H_2SO_4(aq) \rightarrow H^+(aq) + HSO_4^-(aq)$$

The HSO_4^- ion is also an acid but it is a weak acid:

$$HSO_4^-(aq) \rightleftharpoons H^+(aq) + SO_4^{2-}(aq)$$

Most of the HSO_4^- ions remain undissociated.

Most acids are **oxyacids,** in which the acidic hydrogen is attached to an oxygen atom (several oxyacids are shown in the margin). The strong acids we have mentioned, except hydrochloric acid, are typical examples. **Organic acids,** those with a carbon-atom backbone, commonly contain the **carboxyl group:**

Acids of this type are usually weak. An example is acetic acid, CH_3COOH, which is often written as $HC_2H_3O_2$.

There are some important acids in which the acidic proton is attached to an atom other than oxygen. The most significant of these are the hydrohalic acids HX, where X represents a halogen atom. Examples are $HCl(aq)$, a strong acid, and $HF(aq)$, a weak acid.

TABLE 16.1

Ways to Describe Acid Strength

Property	Strong Acid	Weak Acid
the acid ionization (dissociation) reaction	forward reaction predominates	reverse reaction predominates
strength of the conjugate base compared with that of water	A^- a much weaker base than H_2O	A^- a much stronger base than H_2O

16.2 Acid Strength   **509**

Plants Fight Back

Salicylic acid is a chemical closely related in structure to aspirin. Have students compare the structures of salicylic acid and aspirin (acetylsalicylic acid). How does the chemical structure compare to methyl salicylate?

If you have advanced students, you might have them synthesize aspirin for a student project. You may find a procedure for this synthesis in beginning college laboratory manuals.

CHEMICAL IMPACT

Plants Fight Back

Plants sometimes do not seem to get much respect. We often think of them as rather dull life forms. We are used to animals communicating with each other, but we think of plants as mute. However, this perception is changing. It is now becoming clear that plants communicate with other plants and also with insects. Ilya Roskin and his colleagues at Rutgers University, for example, have found that tobacco plants under attack by disease signal distress using the chemical salicylic acid, a precursor of aspirin. When a tobacco plant is infected with tobacco mosaic virus (TMV), which forms dark blisters on leaves and causes them to pucker and yellow, the sick plant produces large amounts of salicylic acid to alert its immune system to fight the virus. In addition, some of the salicylic acid is converted to methyl salicylate, a volatile compound that evaporates from the sick plant. Neighboring plants absorb this chemical and turn it back to salicylic acid, thus triggering their immune systems to protect them against the impending attack by TMV. Thus, as a tobacco plant gears up to fight an attack by TMV, it also warns its neighbors to be ready for this virus.

In another example of plant communication, a tobacco leaf under attack by a caterpillar emits a chemical signal that attracts a parasitic wasp that stings and kills the insect. Even more impressive is the ability of the plant to customize the emitted signal so that the wasp attracted will be the one that specializes in killing the particular caterpiller involved in the attack. The plant does this by changing the proportions of two chemicals emitted when a caterpillar chews on a leaf. Studies have shown that other plants, such as corn and cotton, also emit wasp-attracting chemicals when they face attack by caterpillars.

This research shows that plants can "speak up" to protect themselves. Scientists hope to learn to help them do this even more effectively.

A wasp lays its eggs on a gypsy moth caterpillar on the leaf of a corn plant.

Salicylic acid   Methyl salicylate

Themes
Models, Form and Function

Skills
Making comparisons, interpreting data, evaluating

WHAT IF Comments

If K for the auto-ionization of water were 1×10^{14} (a very large number), water would be a strong acid. That is, all of the water molecules would be dissociated into H^+ and OH^- ions. Water would therefore be a highly corrosive liquid incapable of sustaining life. In fact, it would decompose virtually anything that came in contact with it. The value of 10^{14} for K_w would be mathematically impossible even if all of the water molecules were dissociated, however. Pure water is 55.6 M, which means that the maximum value of K_w would be $(55.6)^2 = 3.1 \times 10^3$.

TEACHING TIP

Use an equation with two water molecules on the reactant side to show students that water acts as an acid and as a base. In this way, students can see that a proton is donated from one water molecule and accepted by the other molecule. This choice of equation allows students to correctly identify acid–base pairs.

MINI-DEMO

A conductivity tester can be used to demonstrate that pure water does not conduct a current. Thus, in the auto-ionization of water, the reverse reaction must dominate—very few ions are present.

16.3 Water as an Acid and a Base

Objective: *To learn about the ionization of water.*

WHAT IF?

What if the K for the auto-ionization of water were 1×10^{14} instead of 1×10^{-14}?

A substance is said to be *amphoteric* if it can behave either as an acid or as a base. Water is the most common **amphoteric substance.** We can see this clearly in the **ionization of water,** which involves the transfer of a proton from one water molecule to another to produce a hydroxide ion and a hydronium ion.

$$H_2O(l) + H_2O(l) \rightleftharpoons H_3O^+(aq) + OH^-(aq)$$

In this reaction one water molecule acts as an acid by furnishing a proton, and the other acts as a base by accepting the proton. The forward reaction for this process does not occur to a very great extent. That is, in pure water only a tiny amount of H_3O^+ and OH^- exist. At 25 °C the actual concentrations are

$$[H_3O^+] = [OH^-] = 1.0 \times 10^{-7} \, M$$

510   Chapter 16   Acids and Bases

USING TECHNOLOGY

Animation and Video
Animation, Self-ionization of Water

Notice that in pure water the concentrations of $[H_3O^+]$ and $[OH^-]$ are equal because they are produced in equal numbers in the ionization reaction.

One of the most interesting and important things about water is that the mathematical *product* of the H_3O^+ and OH^- concentrations is always constant. We can find this constant by multiplying the concentrations of H_3O^+ and OH^- at 25 °C:

$$[H_3O^+][OH^-] = (1.0 \times 10^{-7})(1.0 \times 10^{-7}) = 1.0 \times 10^{-14}$$

We call this constant K_w. Thus at 25 °C

$$[H_3O^+][OH^-] = 1.0 \times 10^{-14} = K_w$$

To simplify the notation we often write H_3O^+ as just H^+. Thus we would write the K_w expression as follows:

$$[H^+][OH^-] = 1.0 \times 10^{-14} = K_w$$

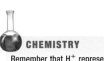

CHEMISTRY

$K_w = [H^+][OH^-]$
$= 1.0 \times 10^{-14}$

K_w is called the **ion-product constant** for water. The units are customarily omitted when the value of the constant is given and used.

It is important to recognize the meaning of K_w. In any aqueous solution at 25 °C, *no matter what it contains*, the product of $[H^+]$ and $[OH^-]$ must always equal 1.0×10^{-14}. This means that if the $[H^+]$ goes up, the $[OH^-]$ must go down so that the product of the two is still 1.0×10^{-14}. For example, if HCl gas is dissolved in water, increasing the $[H^+]$, the $[OH^-]$ must decrease.

There are three possible situations we might encounter in an aqueous solution. If we add an acid to water (an H^+ donor), we get an *acidic solution*. In this case, because we have added a source of H^+, the $[H^+]$ will be greater than the $[OH^-]$. On the other hand, if we add a base (a source of OH^-) to water, the $[OH^-]$ will be greater than the $[H^+]$. This is a *basic solution*. Finally, we might have a situation in which $[H^+] = [OH^-]$. This is called a *neutral solution*. Pure water is automatically neutral but we can also obtain a neutral solution by adding equal amounts of H^+ and OH^-. It is very important that you understand the definitions of neutral, acidic, and basic solutions. In summary:

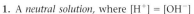

CHEMISTRY

Remember that H^+ represents H_3O^+.

1. A *neutral solution*, where $[H^+] = [OH^-]$

2. An *acidic solution*, where $[H^+] > [OH^-]$

3. A *basic solution*, where $[OH^-] > [H^+]$

In each case, however, $K_w = [H^+][OH^-] = 1.0 \times 10^{-14}$.

Example 16.3

Calculating Ion Concentrations in Water

Calculate $[H^+]$ or $[OH^-]$ as required for each of the following solutions at 25 °C, and state whether the solution is neutral, acidic, or basic.

    a. $1.0 \times 10^{-5}\ M\ OH^-$

    b. $1.0 \times 10^{-7}\ M\ OH^-$

    c. $10.0\ M\ H^+$

(continued)

16.3   Water as an Acid and a Base   **511**

TEACHING TIPS

- At this point, students have no experience with the concept of an equilibrium constant. When you discuss the idea that K_w is a constant, be prepared for students who reason that "Pure water contains $1.0 \times 10^{-7}\ M\ H^+$ and $1.0 \times 10^{-7}\ M\ OH^-$. If we add 1.0 mol of HCl to a liter of water, the concentration of H^+ is about 1.0 M. So isn't $K_w = [H^+][OH^-] = [1.0\ M][1.0 \times 10^{-7}\ M] = 1.0 \times 10^{-7}$?" These students do not understand that added H^+ will react with OH^-, thereby lowering the concentration of OH^-. If 1.0 mol of H^+ is added to a liter of water, the OH^- concentration would be $1.0 \times 10^{-14}\ M$. This relationship will not be obvious to students at this point.

- Emphasize the definitions of acidic, basic, and neutral solutions. Note, however, that the emphasis should be on the relationship of the concentrations of the ions, not on the pH of the solution.

Additional Examples

Calculate $[H^+]$ or $[OH^-]$ as required for each of the following at 25 °C and state whether the solution is neutral, acidic, or basic.

a. $[H^+] = 3.4 \times 10^{-4}\ M$
    $[OH^-] = 2.9 \times 10^{-11}\ M$;
    acidic

b. $[H^+] = 2.6 \times 10^{-8}\ M$
    $[OH^-] = 3.9 \times 10^{-7}\ M$;
    basic

c. $[OH^-] = 6.2 \times 10^{-9}\ M$
    $[H^+] = 1.6 \times 10^{-6}\ M$; acidic

d. $[OH^-] = 8.1 \times 10^{-3}\ M$
    $[H^+] = 1.2 \times 10^{-12}\ M$; basic

(continued)

MATH

$$K_w = [H^+][OH^-]$$
$$\frac{K_w}{[OH^-]} = [H^+]$$

Solution

a. We know that $K_w = [H^+][OH^-] = 1.0 \times 10^{-14}$. We need to calculate the $[H^+]$. However, the $[OH^-]$ is given—it is 1.0×10^{-5} M—so we will solve for $[H^+]$ by dividing both sides by $[OH^-]$.

$$[H^+] = \frac{1.0 \times 10^{-14}}{[OH^-]} = \frac{1.0 \times 10^{-14}}{1.0 \times 10^{-5}} = 1.0 \times 10^{-9} \ M$$

Because $[OH^-] = 1.0 \times 10^{-5}$ M is greater than $[H^+] = 1.0 \times 10^{-9}$ M, the solution is basic. (Remember: the more negative the exponent, the smaller the number.)

b. Again the $[OH^-]$ is given, so we solve the K_w expression for $[H^+]$.

$$[H^+] = \frac{1.0 \times 10^{-14}}{[OH^-]} = \frac{1.0 \times 10^{-14}}{1.0 \times 10^{-7}} = 1.0 \times 10^{-7} \ M$$

Here $[H^+] = [OH^-] = 1.0 \times 10^{-7}$ M, so the solution is neutral.

c. In this case the $[H^+]$ is given, so we solve for $[OH^-]$.

MATH

$$K_w = [H^+][OH^-]$$
$$\frac{K_w}{[H^+]} = [OH^-]$$

$$[OH^-] = \frac{1.0 \times 10^{-14}}{[H^+]} = \frac{1.0 \times 10^{-14}}{10.0} = 1.0 \times 10^{-15} \ M$$

Now we compare $[H^+] = 10.0$ M with $[OH^-] = 1.0 \times 10^{-15}$ M. Because $[H^+]$ is greater than $[OH^-]$, the solution is acidic.

 Self-Check Exercise 16.2

Calculate $[H^+]$ in a solution in which $[OH^-] = 2.0 \times 10^{-2}$ M. Is this solution acidic, neutral, or basic?

Answer to Self-Check Exercise 16.2

Because $[H^+][OH^-] = 1.0 \times 10^{-14}$, we can solve for $[H^+]$.

$$[H^+] = \frac{1.0 \times 10^{-14}}{[OH^-]}$$

$$= \frac{1.0 \times 10^{-14}}{2.0 \times 10^{-2}}$$

$$= 5.0 \times 10^{-13} \ M$$

This solution is basic: $[OH^-] = 2.0 \times 10^{-2}$ M is greater than $[H^+] = 5.0 \times 10^{-13}$ M.

Additional Examples

1. Which is greater, $[OH^-]$ or $[H^+]$, if $[H^+] = 2.8 \times 10^{-5}$ M in an aqueous solution at 25 °C?

$[H^+]$ is greater than $[OH^-]$.

2. How many times greater is $[OH^-]$ than $[H^+]$ if $[H^+] = 1.0 \times 10^{-9}$ M in an aqueous solution at 25 °C?

1.0×10^5 times greater

Example 16.4

Using the Ion-Product Constant in Calculations

Is it possible for an aqueous solution at 25 °C to have $[H^+] = 0.010$ M and $[OH^-] = 0.010$ M?

Solution

The concentration 0.010 M can also be expressed as 1.0×10^{-2} M. Thus, if $[H^+] = [OH^-] = 1.0 \times 10^{-2}$ M, the product

$$[H^+][OH^-] = (1.0 \times 10^{-2})(1.0 \times 10^{-2}) = 1.0 \times 10^{-4}$$

This is not possible. The product of $[H^+]$ and $[OH^-]$ must always be 1.0×10^{-14} in water at 25 °C, so a solution could not have $[H^+] = [OH^-] = 0.010$ M. If H^+ and OH^- are added to water in these amounts, they will react with each other to form H_2O,

$$H^+ + OH^- \rightarrow H_2O$$

until the product $[H^+][OH^-] = 1.0 \times 10^{-14}$.

This is a general result. When H^+ and OH^- are added to water in amounts such that the product of their concentrations is greater than 1.0×10^{-14}, they will react to form water until enough H^+ and OH^- are consumed (until $[H^+][OH^-] = 1.0 \times 10^{-14}$).

1. How is the Arrhenius concept of an acid different from the Brønsted–Lowry model of an acid?

2. Which of the following represent conjugate acid–base pairs? For those pairs that are not conjugates, write the correct conjugate acid or base for each species in the pair.

   a. HSO_4^-, SO_4^{2-} **c.** $H_2PO_4^-$, PO_4^{3-}
   b. HBr, BrO^- **d.** HNO_3, NO_2^-

3. Draw a molecular-level view of an aqueous solution of the strong acid HCl.

4. Draw a molecular-level view of an aqueous solution of the weak acid HF.

5. Use the Brønsted–Lowry model to label the acid–base pairs in the following equation for the ionization of water:

$$H_2O(l) + H_2O(l) \rightleftharpoons H_3O^+(aq) + OH^-(aq)$$

16.4 The pH Scale

Objectives: *To understand pH and pOH.*
To learn to find pOH and pH for various solutions.
To learn to use a calculator in these calculations.

To express small numbers conveniently, chemists often use the "p scale," which is based on common logarithms (base 10 logs). In this system, if N represents some number, then

$$pN = -\log N = (-1) \times \log N$$

That is, the p means to take the log of the number that follows and multiply the result by -1. For example, to express the number 1.0×10^{-7} on the p scale, we first take the log of 1.0×10^{-7}. On most calculators this means entering the number and then pressing the log key.

1. Enter 1.0×10^{-7}.

2. Press the $\boxed{\log}$ key.

Now the calculator shows the log of the number 1.0×10^{-7}, which is

$$-7.00$$

Next we must multiply by -1. On most calculators this is done by using the $+/-$ key (the $+/-$ key just reverses the sign, which is what multiplying by -1 really does). In this case we get the result

$$7.00$$

So

$$p(1.0 \times 10^{-7}) = -\log(1.0 \times 10^{-7}) = 7.00$$

Because the $[H^+]$ in an aqueous solution is typically quite small, using the p scale in the form of the **pH scale** provides a convenient way to represent solution acidity. The pH is defined as

$$pH = -\log[H^+]$$

CHEMISTRY
The pH scale provides a compact way to represent solution acidity.

16.4   The pH Scale   **513**

Students may be surprised to learn than most of the products they buy have a pH outside the 6–8 range. Fruits and their juices and soft drinks all have pH values lower than 6. In fact, many food products are acidic. Also, many household cleaners (such as ammonia) are basic, as are antacid tablets. Students could buy bottled water (which is usually slightly basic due to bicarbonates) and milk (which is slightly acidic).

TEACHING TIP

Significant figures in logs are especially difficult for students to determine. Because logs are taught on calculators instead of using log tables, students often do not understand the characteristic and the mantissa. The easiest way to teach students to use the proper number of significant figures in logs is to explain that the number of significant figures in the original number is equal to the number of places to the right of the decimal in the log of the number.

Additional Examples

Calculate the pH value for each of the following aqueous solutions at 25 °C.

a. a solution in which $[H^+] = 2.1 \times 10^{-5}\ M$
pH = 4.68

b. a solution in which $[OH^-] = 5.9 \times 10^{-8}\ M$
pH = 6.77

What if an elected official decided to ban all products with a pH outside of the 6–8 range? How would it affect the products you could buy? Give some examples of products that would no longer be available.

To obtain the pH value of a solution, we must compute the negative log of the $[H^+]$. On a typical calculator, this involves the following steps:

Steps for Calculating pH on a Calculator

STEP 1 Enter the $[H^+]$.
STEP 2 Press the $\boxed{\log}$ key.
STEP 3 Press the $\boxed{+/-}$ (change-of-sign) key.

In the case where $[H^+] = 1.0 \times 10^{-5}\ M$, following the above steps gives a pH value of 5.00.

To represent pH to the appropriate number of significant figures, you need to know the following rule for logarithms: *the number of decimal places for a log must be equal to the number of significant figures in the original number.* Thus

2 significant figures

$$[H^+] = 1.0 \times 10^{-5}\ M$$

and

$$pH = 5.00$$

2 decimal places

Example 16.5

Calculating pH

Calculate the pH value for each of the following solutions at 25 °C.

a. A solution in which $[H^+] = 1.0 \times 10^{-9}\ M$
b. A solution in which $[OH^-] = 1.0 \times 10^{-6}\ M$

Solution (a)

For this solution $[H^+] = 1.0 \times 10^{-9}$.

Step 1 Enter the number.

Step 2 Push the $\boxed{\log}$ key to give −9.00.

Step 3 Push the $\boxed{+/-}$ key to give 9.00.

$$pH = 9.00$$

Solution (b)

In this case we are given the $[OH^-]$. Thus we must first calculate $[H^+]$ from the K_w expression. We solve

$$K_w = [H^+][OH^-] = 1.0 \times 10^{-14}$$

for $[H^+]$ by dividing both sides by $[OH^-]$.

$$[H^+] = \frac{1.0 \times 10^{-14}}{[OH^-]} = \frac{1.0 \times 10^{-14}}{1.0 \times 10^{-6}} = 1.0 \times 10^{-8}$$

Now that we know the $[H^+]$, we can calculate the pH by taking the three steps listed above. Doing so yields pH = 8.00.

 Self-Check Exercise 16.3

Calculate the pH value for each of the following solutions at 25 °C.

    a. A solution in which $[H^+] = 1.0 \times 10^{-3}\ M$

    b. A solution in which $[OH^-] = 5.0 \times 10^{-5}\ M$

PROBLEM SOLVING

The pH decreases as $[H^+]$ increases, and vice versa.

Because the pH scale is a log scale based on 10, *the pH changes by 1 for every power-of-10 change in the $[H^+]$.* For example, a solution of pH 3 has an H^+ concentration of $10^{-3}\ M$, which is 10 times that of a solution of pH 4 ($[H^+] = 10^{-4}\ M$) and 100 times that of a solution of pH 5. This is illustrated in **Table 16.2**. Also note from Table 16.2 that *the pH decreases as the $[H^+]$ increases.* That is, a lower pH means a more acidic solution. The pH scale and the pH values for several common substances are shown in **Figure 16.3**.

TABLE 16.2

The Relationship of the H^+ Concentration of a Solution to Its pH

$[H^+]$	pH
1.0×10^{-1}	1.00
1.0×10^{-2}	2.00
1.0×10^{-3}	3.00
1.0×10^{-4}	4.00
1.0×10^{-5}	5.00
1.0×10^{-6}	6.00
1.0×10^{-7}	7.00

Figure 16.3
The pH scale and pH values of some common substances.

 Answers to Self-Check Exercise 16.3

a. Because $[H^+] = 1.0 \times 10^{-3}\ M$, we get pH = 3.00 by using the regular steps.

b. Because $[OH^-] = 5.0 \times 10^{-5}\ M$, we can find $[H^+]$ from the K_w expression.

$$[H^+] = \frac{K_w}{[OH^-]} = \frac{1.0 \times 10^{-14}}{5.0 \times 10^{-5}}$$
$$= 2.0 \times 10^{-10}\ M$$

Then we follow the regular steps to get pH from $[H^+]$.

1. Enter 2.0×10^{-10}.

2. Push $\boxed{\text{log}}$.

3. Push $\boxed{+/-}$.

    pH = 9.70

TEACHING TIP

Point out to students that a change of 1 in pH represents a change of 10 in hydrogen ion concentration.

CLASS ACTIVITY

To emphasize that each pH unit corresponds to a tenfold change in $[H^+]$, consider the following class project.

1. Obtain a 4-foot-long piece of butcher paper.

2. Hang the paper on the wall so that the 4-foot length lies in a horizontal direction.

3. Near the left edge of the paper, use a black marker to draw a vertical line. This line will be the beginning reference for the remainder

---

of the activity. Always begin your marks from this reference line. Using a colored marker, make a 1-mm horizontal mark near the bottom of the butcher paper beginning at the vertical reference line. Label this mark "pH = 7.00."

4. Discuss how you can represent other pH values on this paper. If a 1-mm mark corresponds to a pH of 7.00 or $[H^+] = 1.0 \times 10^{-7}\ M$, a 10-mm mark is required for pH = 6.00, a 100-mm mark for pH = 5.00, and so on. Since 1000 mm is just under 3.5 feet, a pH of 4.00 is the lowest pH that can be represented on the butcher paper.

5. Calculate how large the paper would have to be to represent additional pH values. For example, to show a pH of 0.00 ($[H^+] = 1\ M$), you would need a line almost 33,000 feet long.

6. Refer to this chart as you discuss pH values to remind students that the pH scale is a log scale.

Expressing integer pH values greater than 7.00 on this scale would require lines that start at 10 times smaller than the beginning 1-mm line. These lines would not be useful for class visualization. You can discuss this effect and explain why you are not representing these values.

MINI-DEMO

Use pH paper or a pH meter (if one is available) to show the pH of various solutions. Some possible solutions are vinegar, HCl, NaOH, liquid drain cleaner, salt water, lemon juice, other fruit juices, and soap solutions. You may want to bring in samples of household items for pH testing. As you show students each item and find its pH, have students classify the item as acidic, basic, or neutral.

USING TECHNOLOGY

 Figure 16.3

CHEMICAL IMPACT   **Science, Technology, and Society**

Airplane Rash

Because airplanes remain in service for many years, it is important to spot corrosion that might weaken the structure at an early stage. In the past, looking for minute signs of corrosion has been very tedious and labor-intensive, especially for large planes. This situation is about to change, however, thanks to a new paint system developed by Gerald S. Frankel and Jian Zhang of Ohio State University. The paint they created turns pink in areas that are beginning to corrode, making these areas easy to spot.

The secret to the paint's magic is phenolphthalein, the common acid–base indicator that turns pink in a basic solution. The corrosion of the aluminum skin of the airplane involves a reaction that forms OH^- ions, producing a basic area at the site of the corrosion that turns the phenolphthalein pink. Because this system is highly sensitive, corrosion can be corrected before it damages the plane.

Next time you fly, if the plane has pink spots you might want to wait for a later flight!

Log scales similar to the pH scale are used for representing other quantities. For example,

The symbol p means −log.

$$pOH = -\log[OH^-]$$

Therefore, in a solution in which

$$[OH^-] = 1.0 \times 10^{-12} \, M$$

the pOH is

$$-\log[OH^-] = -\log(1.0 \times 10^{-12}) = 12.00$$

Additional Examples

Calculate the pH and pOH values for each of the following aqueous solutions at 25 °C.

a. a solution in which $[H^+] = 3.6 \times 10^{-9} \, M$
pH = 8.44; pOH = 5.56

b. a solution in which $[OH^-] = 9.2 \times 10^{-2} \, M$
pOH = 1.04; pH = 12.96

Example 16.6

Calculating pH and pOH

Calculate the pH and pOH for each of the following solutions at 25 °C.

a. $1.0 \times 10^{-3} \, M \, OH^-$

b. $1.0 \, M \, H^+$

Solution

a. We are given the $[OH^-]$, so we can calculate the pOH value by taking $-\log[OH^-]$.

$$pOH = -\log[OH^-] = -\log(1.0 \times 10^{-3}) = 3.00$$

To calculate the pH, we must first solve the K_w expression for $[H^+]$.

$$[H^+] = \frac{K_w}{[OH^-]} = \frac{1.0 \times 10^{-14}}{1.0 \times 10^{-3}} = 1.0 \times 10^{-11} \, M$$

Now we compute the pH.

$$pH = -\log[H^+] = -\log(1.0 \times 10^{-11}) = 11.00$$

516   Chapter 16   Acids and Bases

b. In this case we are given the $[H^+]$ and we can compute the pH.

$$pH = -\log[H^+] = -\log(1.0) = 0$$

We next solve the K_w expression for $[OH^-]$.

$$[OH^-] = \frac{K_w}{[H^+]} = \frac{1.0 \times 10^{-14}}{1.0} = 1.0 \times 10^{-14} \, M$$

Now we compute the pOH.

$$pOH = -\log[OH^-] = -\log(1.0 \times 10^{-14}) = 14.00$$

We can obtain a convenient relationship between pH and pOH by starting with the K_w expression $[H^+][OH^-] = 1.0 \times 10^{-14}$ and taking the negative log of both sides.

$$-\log([H^+][OH^-]) = -\log(1.0 \times 10^{-14})$$

Because the log of a product equals the sum of the logs of the terms—that is, $\log(A \times B) = \log A + \log B$—we have

$$\underbrace{-\log[H^+]}_{pH} \; \underbrace{-\log[OH^-]}_{pOH} = -\log(1.0 \times 10^{-14}) = 14.00$$

which gives the equation

$$pH + pOH = 14.00$$

This means that once we know either the pH or the pOH for a solution, we can calculate the other. For example, if a solution has a pH of 6.00, the pOH is calculated as follows:

$$pH + pOH = 14.00$$
$$pOH = 14.00 - pH$$
$$pOH = 14.00 - 6.00 = 8.00$$

Example 16.7

Red blood cells can exist only over a narrow range of pH.

Calculating pOH from pH

The pH of blood is about 7.4. What is the pOH of blood?

Solution

$$pH + pOH = 14.00$$
$$pOH = 14.00 - pH$$
$$= 14.00 - 7.4$$
$$= 6.6$$

The pOH of blood is 6.6.

Self-Check Exercise 16.4

A sample of rain in an area with severe air pollution has a pH of 3.5. What is the pOH of this rainwater?

16.4   The pH Scale   **517**

Additional Examples

1. The pH of a solution is 5.67. What is the pOH of the solution?
   pOH = 8.33

2. The pH of a solution is 9.23. What is the pOH of the solution?
   pOH = 4.77

☑ **Answer to Self-Check Exercise 16.4**

$$pOH + pH = 14.00$$
$$pOH = 14.00 - pH$$
$$= 14.00 - 3.5$$
$$pOH = 10.5$$

- Some calculators have an inverse log key; others use 10^x for the inverse log function. This discrepancy can cause difficulties for students. Make sure they understand how to use their calculators to find inverse logs.

- This discussion represents another opportunity for a review of significant figures. Students may become confused over how many significant figures to put in the inverse log concentration. Remind them that the correct number of significant figures will be the same as the number of digits to the right of the decimal in the log number.

MATH

This operation may involve a 10^x key on some calculators.

It is also possible to find the $[H^+]$ or $[OH^-]$ from the pH or pOH. To find the $[H^+]$ from the pH, we must go back to the definition of pH:

$$pH = -\log[H^+]$$

or

$$-pH = \log[H^+]$$

To arrive at $[H^+]$ on the right-hand side of this equation we must "undo" the log operation. This is called taking the *antilog* or the *inverse* log.

$$\text{Inverse log } (-pH) = \text{inverse log } (\log[H^+])$$
$$\text{Inverse log } (-pH) = [H^+]$$

There are different methods for carrying out the inverse log operation on various calculators. One common method is the two-key $\boxed{inv}$ $\boxed{log}$ sequence. (Consult the user's manual for your calculator to find out how to do the antilog or inverse log operation.) The steps in going from pH to $[H^+]$ are as follows:

Steps for Calculating $[H^+]$ from pH

STEP 1 Enter the pH.

STEP 2 Change the sign of the pH by using the $\boxed{+/-}$ key.

STEP 3 Take the inverse log (antilog) of $-pH$ to give $[H^+]$ by using the $\boxed{inv}$ $\boxed{log}$ keys in that order. (Your calculator may require different keys for this operation.)

For practice, we will convert pH = 7.0 to $[H^+]$.

Step 1   pH = 7.0

Step 2 $-pH = -7.0$

Step 3 $\boxed{inv}$ $\boxed{log}$ -7.0 gives 1×10^{-7}

$$[H^+] = 1 \times 10^{-7} \, M$$

This process is illustrated further in Example 16.8.

Measuring the pH of the water in a river.

Example 16.8

Calculating [H⁺] from pH

The pH of a human blood sample was measured to be 7.41. What is the [H⁺] in this blood?

Solution

Step 1   pH = 7.41

Step 2   −pH = −7.41

Step 3   [H⁺] = inverse log of −7.41

$\boxed{\text{inv}}$ $\boxed{\text{log}}$ $-7.41 = 3.9 \times 10^{-8}$

[H⁺] = 3.9×10^{-8} *M*

Notice that because the pH has two decimal places, we need two significant figures for [H⁺].

 Self-Check Exercise 16.5

The pH of rainwater in a polluted area was found to be 3.50. What is the [H⁺] for this rainwater?

A similar procedure is used to change from pOH to [OH⁻], as shown in Example 16.9.

Example 16.9

Calculating [OH⁻] from pOH

The pOH of the water in a fish tank is found to be 6.59. What is the [OH⁻] for this water?

Solution

We use the same steps as for converting pH to [H⁺], except that we use the pOH[OH⁻].

Step 1   pOH = 6.59

Step 2   −pOH = −6.59

Step 3 $\boxed{\text{inv}}$ $\boxed{\text{log}}$ $-6.59 = 2.6 \times 10^{-7}$

[OH⁻] = 2.6×10^{-7} *M*

Note that two significant figures are required.

 Self-Check Exercise 16.6

The pOH of a liquid drain cleaner was found to be 10.50. What is the [OH⁻] for this cleaner?

16.4   The pH Scale   **519**

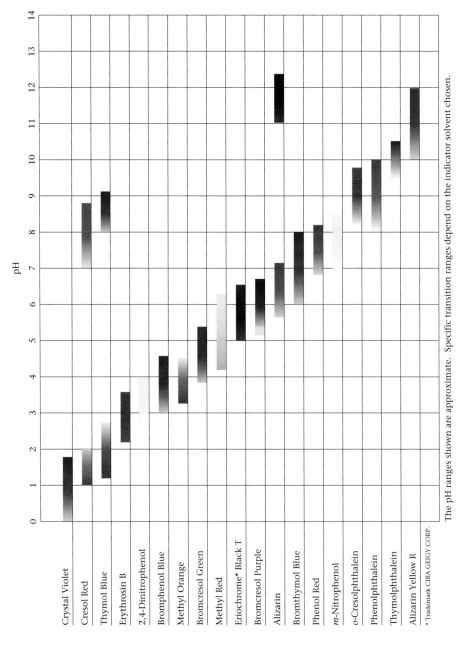

The pH ranges shown are approximate. Specific transition ranges depend on the indicator solvent chosen. Note that most indicators have a useful range of about two pH units.

pH

Crystal Violet
Cresol Red
Thymol Blue
Erythrosin B
2,4-Dinitrophenol
Bromphenol Blue
Methyl Orange
Bromcresol Green
Methyl Red
Eriochrome* Black T
Bromcresol Purple
Alizarin
Bromthymol Blue
Phenol Red
m-Nitrophenol
o-Cresolphthalein
Phenolphthalein
Thymolphthalein
Alizarin Yellow R

* Trademark CIBA GEIGY CORP.

Figure 16.4
The useful pH ranges for several common indicators.

Objective: *To learn methods for measuring the pH of a solution.*

The traditional way of determining the pH of a solution is by using **indicators**—substances that exhibit different colors in acidic and basic solutions. We can represent a generic indicator as a weak acid HIn. Let's assume that for a particular indicator HIn is red and the anion In^- is blue. Thus, in a solution containing lots of H^+, the indicator will be red (the HIn form). In a basic solution, the H^+ will be removed from HIn to form the blue In^- ion and the solution will be blue. In intermediate pH regions, significant amounts of both HIn and In^- will be present and the solution will be some shade of purple (red plus blue).

Many substances exist that turn different colors when H^+ is present (HIn) than when H^+ is absent (In^-). Some of these indicators are shown in **Figure 16.4** along with the colors of their HIn and In^- forms. Note that different indicators change at different pH values depending on the acid strength of HIn for a particular indicator.

A convenient way to measure the approximate pH of a solution is by using **indicator paper**—a strip of paper coated with a combination of indicators. Indicator paper turns a specific color for each pH value (see **Figure 16.5**).

The pH value of a solution can be measured electronically using a **pH meter (Figure 16.6)**. A pH meter contains a probe that is very sensitive to the $[H^+]$ in a solution. When the probe is inserted into a solution, the $[H^+]$ in the solution produces a voltage that appears as a pH reading on the meter. Because a pH meter can determine the pH value of a solution so quickly and accurately, these devices are now used almost universally.

Figure 16.5
Indicator paper being used to measure the pH of a solution. The pH is determined by comparing the color that the solution turns the paper to the color chart.

Figure 16.6
A pH meter. The electrode on the right is placed in the solution with unknown pH. The difference between the $[H^+]$ in the solution sealed into the electrode and the $[H^+]$ in the solution being analyzed is translated into an electrical potential and registered on the meter as a pH reading.

16.5   Measuring pH   **521**

Section 16.5

Themes
Models, Systems

Skills
Developing mod els, evaluating, solving problems

Laboratory
Experiment 68: Indicators, Traditional

TEACHING TIPS

- Students are probably not aware of the use of indicators for determining acidity. As many of these substances are found in nature, now is a good time to show several of them to the students.

- The Chemistry in Action, "Cabbage Juice Indicator," uses cabbage juice as an indicator. You can also use grape juice or tea as indicators.

CLASS ACTIVITY

An Indicator Challenge Puzzle
Display three 500-mL beakers but do not discuss their contents with the students (beaker 1: 100 mL water and 3 drops phenolphthalein indicator; beaker 2: 100 mL of 0.20 *M* NaOH; beaker 3: 100 mL of 0.10 *M* HCl). Pour the contents of the first beaker into the second beaker (the solution turns pink because the phenolphthalein is now in a basic solution). Pour this solution into the third beaker (the solution becomes colorless as it enters the beaker because the acid neutralizes the base, but eventually the solution turns pink because there is more basic solution than acidic solution). Challenge students to explain these observations.

USING TECHNOLOGY

 Animation and Video

Video, Cabbage Juice Indicator

Cut the tops off the water bottles to form tall cylinders. Fill each one three-fourths full of distilled water and arrange the cylinders in pairs. Add the indicators (1–2 mL) to the pairs in the following sequence: pair 1: thymolphthalein; pair 2: phenolphthalein; pair 3: phenol red; pair 4: bromothymol blue; pair 5: methyl red and methylene blue; pair 6: Yamada's universal indicator. Pour 0.1 *M* NaOH into a graduated cylinder. Add just enough to the first pair of cylinders to produce a blue color. Note the amount added to each cylinder and add the same amount to each of the other cylinders.

Presentation Explain that you have made a solution of pH 11 in each cylinder. Explain that each pair of cylinders contains a different indicator. One cylinder in each pair will act as a control; nothing will be added to it. Next, place a chunk of dry ice in one cylinder of each pair and note the color changes.

Teaching Notes
Discuss how dry ice can change the pH of a solution. It dissolves to form carbonic acid (H_2CO_3), which then reacts with water. Write the reaction equations on the board. Use Figure 16.4 to

CHEMISTRY in ACTION

Cabbage Juice Indicator

Materials Each student/group will need cabbage juice indicator and at least one solution from home (film cannisters can be given to students to hold their samples). They may also need some water and reference solutions. To make these reference solutions, add a few drops of cabbage juice indicator to solutions of HCl and NaOH ranging in concentration from 0.10 M to $1.0 \times 10^{-6} M$ and to pure water (which will give you solutions with pH values ranging from 1.00 to 14.00). Be careful to boil the water when making these solutions to remove dissolved CO_2. The dissolved carbon dioxide in the water will change the pH of the water and cause inconsistent results, especially with pHs in the 5–9 range. To make the indicator, place red cabbage leaves in a small amount of water and boil the water for several minutes. Let the indicator cool before using it.

Purpose Students can identify some of the acids and bases in everyday life.

Discussion Many cleaning supplies are basic. Fruits, fruit juices, and soft drinks are acidic. Unless the student brings boiled distilled water, it is doubtful that any sample will be neutral. This activity can be used as a starting point for emphasizing that acids and bases are not "bad" chemicals.

 Section 16.6

Themes
Models, Patterns of Change

Skills
Applying concepts, solving problems

TEACHING TIP

Focus students' attention on the molecular view of a strong acid. Once they understand that the acid ionizes completely in solution, they are ready to find the hydrogen ion concentration and the pH.

CHEMISTRY in ACTION

Cabbage Juice Indicator

1. Bring some samples from home to test for pH levels. If they are liquids, the samples should be clear, white, or light-colored. If they are solids, they should be at least a little soluble in water.
2. Obtain cabbage juice indicator from your teacher. This pH indicator is made by boiling red cabbage leaves in water.
3. Take a small amount of your sample (about 5 mL of the liquid or a small amount of solid dissolved in 5 mL of water) and add a few drops of cabbage juice indicator to the sample.
4. Use the reference solutions provided by your teacher to determine the approximate pH of each of your samples.
5. Compare your results with those of your classmates.
6. Do you see any patterns in pH values? For example, are most cleaning supplies acidic, basic, or neutral? What about most foods?
7. Do any of the pH values surprise you? Why?

16.6 Calculating the pH of Strong Acid Solutions

Objective: *To learn to calculate the pH of solutions of strong acids.*

In this section we will learn to calculate the pH for a solution containing a strong acid of known concentration. For example, if we know a solution contains 1.0 M HCl, how can we find the pH of the solution? To answer this question we must know that when HCl dissolves in water, each molecule dissociates (ionizes) into H^+ and Cl^- ions. That is, we must know that HCl is a strong acid. Thus, although the label on the bottle says 1.0 M HCl, the solution contains virtually no HCl molecules. A 1.0 M HCl solution contains H^+ and Cl^- ions rather than HCl molecules. Typically, container labels indicate the substance(s) used to make up the solution but do not necessarily describe the solution components after dissolution. In this case,

$$1.0 \ M \ HCl \rightarrow 1.0 \ M \ H^+ \text{ and } 1.0 \ M \ Cl^-$$

Therefore, the $[H^+]$ in the solution is 1.0 M. The pH is then

$$pH = -\log[H^+] = -\log(1.0) = 0$$

Example 16.10

Calculating the pH of Strong Acid Solutions

Calculate the pH of 0.10 M HNO_3.

Solution

HNO_3 is a strong acid, so the ions in solution are H^+ and NO_3^-. In this case,

$$0.10 \ M \ HNO_3 \rightarrow 0.10 \ M \ H^+ \text{ and } 0.10 \ M \ NO_3^-$$

522 Chapter 16 Acids and Bases

find the pH ranges for the indicators. Neutralize the solutions and dispose them properly. You may wish to save the Yamada's pair of cylinders to use alone after you have discussed the rest of the indicators. When you place the dry ice in this pair, the colors will change one after another through the pH range. If you add a little 0.1 M HCl at the end of the color changes, you

may be able to produce one last color at the lowest pH.

Arnold Beckman, Man of Science

Arnold Beckman turned 100 years old on April 10, 2000. Beckman's leadership of science and business spans virtually the entire twentieth century. He was born in 1900 in Cullom, Illinois, a town of 500 people that had no electricity or telephones. Beckman says, "In Cullom we were forced to improvise. I think it was a good thing."

The son of a blacksmith, Beckman had his interest in science awakened at age nine. At that time, in the attic of his house he discovered *J. Dorman Steele's Fourteen Weeks in Chemistry*, a book containing instructions for doing chemistry experiments. Beckman became so fascinated with chemistry that his father built him a small "chemistry shed" in the back yard for his tenth birthday.

Beckman's interest in chemistry was fostered by his high school teachers, and he eventually attended the University of Illinois, Urbana–Champaign. He graduated with a bachelor's degree in chemical engineering in 1922 and stayed one more year to get a master's degree. He then went to Caltech where he earned a Ph.D. and became a faculty member.

Beckman was always known for his inventiveness. As a youth he designed a pressurized fuel system for his Model T Ford to overcome problems with its normal gravity feed fuel system—you had to *back* it up steep hills to keep it from starving for fuel. In 1927 he applied for his first patent: a buzzer to alert drivers that they were speeding.

In 1935 Beckman invented something that would cause a revolution in scientific instrumentation. A college friend who worked in a laboratory in the California citrus industry needed an accurate, convenient way to measure the acidity of orange juice. In response, Beckman invented the pH meter, which he initially called the acidimeter. This compact, sturdy device was an immediate hit. In fact, business was so good that Beckman left Caltech to head his own company.

Arnold Beckman

Over the years Beckman invented many other devices, including an improved potentiometer and an instrument for measuring the light absorbed by molecules. At age 65 he retired as president of Beckman Instruments (headquartered in Fullerton, California). After a merger the company became Beckman Coulter; it had sales of $1.8 billion in 1999.

After stepping down as president of Beckman Instruments, Beckman began a new career—donating his wealth for the improvement of science. In 1984 he and Mabel, his wife of 58 years, donated $40 million to his alma mater—the University of Illinois—to fund the Beckman Institute. The Beckmans have also funded many other research institutes, including one at Caltech, and formed a foundation that currently gives $20 million each year to various scientific endeavors.

Arnold Beckman was a man known for his incredible creativity but even more he was recognized as a man of absolute integrity. Mr. Beckman has important words for us: "Whatever you do, be enthusiastic about it." Mr. Beckman passed away on May 18, 2004, at age 104 years.

Note: You can see Arnold Beckman's biography at the Chemical Heritage Foundation Website (http://www.chemheritage.org).

Thus

$$[H^+] = 0.10 \ M \quad \text{and} \quad pH = -\log(0.10) = 1.00$$

 Self-Check Exercise 16.7

Calculate the pH of a solution of $5.0 \times 10^{-3} \ M$ HCl.

 Answer to Self-Check Exercise 16.7

Because HCl is a strong acid, it is completely dissociated:

$$5.0 \times 10^{-3} \ M \ \text{HCl} \rightarrow$$
$$5.0 \times 10^{-3} \ M \ \text{H}^+$$
$$\text{and} \ 5.0 \times 10^{-3} \ M \ \text{Cl}^-$$

so $[H^+] = 5.0 \times 10^{-3} \ M$.

$$pH = -\log(5.0 \times 10^{-3})$$
$$= 2.30$$

TEACHING TIP

If you have excellent mathematics students looking for additional challenges, ask them to try to calculate the pH of 1.0 L of water after 1.0×10^{-7} mol of HCl is added. The answer 7.00 is not correct, because H^+ is coming from both the water and HCl; thus the pH is lower than 7.00. The students might decide to add the H^+ from the HCl ($1.0 \times 10^{-7} \ M$) to that in pure water ($1.0 \times 10^{-7} \ M$) to give $2.0 \times 10^{-7} \ M$, which leads to a pH of 6.70 [$-\log(2.0 \times 10^{-7})$]. However, the added H^+ from the HCl shifts the water equilibrium to the left, using up some H^+. Thus the pH must be higher than 6.70 but lower than 7.00.

Additional Examples

1. Calculate the pH of 0.025 M $HClO_4$.
   pH = 1.60

2. Calculate the pH of $1.2 \times 10^{-5} \ M$ HBr.
   pH = 4.92

Integrating the CHEMICAL IMPACT

Arnold Beckman, Man of Science

This Chemical Impact provides an opportunity for students to write papers on current scientists and engineers. Have them choose a scientist born in the last 150 years to investigate. The student papers can include information on the scientist's personal history as well as scientific discoveries. Many scientists have interesting personal histories. For possible subjects for these reports, try a Nobel Prize winner or use the Internet to find the inventors of products or machines that have changed our lives. The chemical heritage web site found at *www. chemheritage.org* can also provide possibilities for investigation.

Answers to Focus Questions

1. The pH scale represents a convenient way to express a solution's acidity. It allows us to represent small numbers without using exponents.

2. a. 3.638

   b. 10.363

3. a. 4.0×10^{-4}

   b. 6.3×10^{-10}

4. yellow

5. 0.824

Section 16.7

Themes
Models, Patterns of Change

Skills
Applying concepts, interpreting diagrams, solving problems, making predictions

Student Preparation
Assign the students to read Sections 16.7 and 16.8 and to answer the Focus Questions at the end of Section 16.8 before coming to class.

Active Learning
After introducing the material in Sections 16.7 and 16.8 in class, place the students in groups and have them work together on Sections 16.7–16.8: Team Learning Worksheet. Answers and/or discussion of these questions are located in the *Teacher Resources*.

Laboratory
Experiment 69:
Analysis of Vinegar, Microscale

Laboratory
Experiment 70:
Quantitative Titration, Traditional

Laboratory
Experiment 71:
Conductivity Titration, CBL

TEACHING TIPS

- It is helpful to demonstrate a titration as you discuss it in class. You can carry out a titration of HCl with NaOH relatively easily as you discuss the process of titration. Stop along the way during the titration and calculate the volume of base needed to

524

Focus Questions

Sections 16.4–16.6

1. What is the importance of pH?
2. Calculate the pH of an aqueous solution that has a concentration of H^+ equal to the following.
   a. $2.30 \times 10^{-4}\ M$ **b.** $4.37 \times 10^{-11}\ M$
3. Calculate the concentration of H^+ in an aqueous solution with the following pH.
   a. 3.40   **b.** 9.20
4. If you placed phenol red in an acidic solution, what color would the solution turn?
5. Calculate the pH of 100.0 mL of a 0.150 M aqueous solution of HNO_3.

16.7 Acid–Base Titrations

Objective: *To learn about acid–base titrations.*

By this time you know that a strong acid solution contains H^+ ions and a solution of strong base contains OH^- ions. As we saw in Section 8.4, when a strong acid and a strong base are mixed, the H^+ and OH^- react to form H_2O:

$$H^+(aq) + OH^-(aq) \rightarrow H_2O(l)$$

This reaction is called a **neutralization reaction** because if equal amounts of H^+ and OH^- are available for reaction, a neutral solution (pH = 7) will result.

To analyze the acid or base content of a solution, chemists often perform a titration. A **titration** involves the delivery of a measured volume of a solution of known concentration (the *titrant*) into the solution being analyzed (the *analyte*). The titrant contains a substance that reacts in a known way with the analyte. For example, if the analyte contains a base, the titrant would be a **standard solution** (a solution of known concentration) of a strong acid. To run the titration the standard solution of titrant is loaded into a buret. A **buret** is a cylindrical device with a stopcock at the bottom that allows accurate measurement of the delivery of a given volume of liquid (see **Figure 16.7**). The titrant is added slowly to the analyte until exactly enough has been added to just react with all of the analyte. This point is called the **stoichiometric point** or **equivalence point** for the titration. For an acid–base titration the equivalence point can be determined by using a pH meter or indicator. In the titration of a strong acid and a strong base, the equivalence point occurs when an equal amount of H^+ and OH^- have reacted so that the solution is neutral (pH = 7). Thus the titration would stop when the pH meter shows pH = 7. Alternatively, an indicator could be used that changes color near pH = 7.

Figure 16.7 shows three steps in the titration of a solution of strong acid (the analyte) with a solution of sodium hydroxide (the titrant). The titration is stopped (equivalence point reached) after the drop of NaOH(*aq*) that first changes the indicator permanently from colorless to red.

524 Chapter 16 Acids and Bases

---

titrate the acid. Point out that this exercise is just a stoichiometry problem like many that students have encountered previously.

- Have students draw molecular-level pictures of the solution before titration, at the equivalence point, and beyond the equivalence point. Many students know that equal numbers of ions are present at the equivalence point but do not form water molecules with them. Also, many students forget the spectator ions in solution.

- Some students may realize that for phenolphthalein to turn pink, an excess of NaOH must be added to the acid. Thus the endpoint of the titration is not exactly at the stoichiometric point of the reaction. Discuss the titration curve (Figure 16.9) and show these students that a very small excess of NaOH is required to change the color of the indicator. If we use about 20 mL of NaOH to reach the equivalence point, we have added approximately 400 drops. An excess

of one or two drops is less than 0.5% error.

(a)   (b)   (c)

Figure 16.7
The titration of an acid with a base. (a) The titrant (the base) is in the buret, and the flask contains the acid solution along with a small amount of indicator. (b) As base is added drop by drop to the acid solution in the flask during the titration, the indicator changes color, but the color disappears on mixing. (c) The stoichiometric (equivalence) point is marked by a permanent indicator color change. The volume of base added is the difference between the final and initial buret readings.

CELEBRITY CHEMICAL

Sulfur Dioxide (SO₂)

If you have a hood in your classroom, you can demonstrate the solubility of sulfur dioxide in water and show its effect on the acidity of the water. Prepare three Evian or 1-L water bottles by cutting off the tops to form cylinders. Add about 100 mL of water to each. Add enough universal indicator to make the solutions green (neutral). The first container will act as a control. Nothing will be added to it. To the second container add a few drops of acid (HCl works well) to show the color change associated with an acid. Now move to the hood. Place a pea-sized piece of sulfur in a deflagrating spoon and ignite it in a Bunsen burner flame. (It should burn with a blue color.) Lower the deflagrating spoon into the third container to a level just above the water. Note the gas given off by the sulfur. Swirl the container to dissolve the gas in the water. Observe the color change as the gas dissolves in the water. The universal indicator should change to the acid color of the second container.

Since sulfur dioxide is the primary air pollutant from burning coal for power, the air near coal-powered plants contains plenty of sulfur dioxide that can be returned to the ground as acid rain. Ask students to investigate the effects of acid rain. Information on this topic is readily available in the library or on the Internet. The Institute for Chemical Education also has a monograph on this topic (91-009) available from the Institute for Chemical Education, Department of Chemistry, University of Wisconsin–Madison, 1101 University Avenue, Madison, WI 53706.

CELEBRITY CHEMICAL

Sulfur Dioxide (SO₂)

Sulfur dioxide (SO₂) is a mixed blessing to our society. It is quite useful as a preservative for fruits, vegetables, and juices, and it is employed as a disinfectant in food factories. Sulfur dioxide is also used to manufacture sulfuric acid (H_2SO_4), the compound produced in larger quantities than any other in the United States, as in the following reaction:

$$SO_2(g) + \frac{1}{2}O_2(g) \rightarrow SO_3(g)$$

$$SO_3(g) + H_2O(l) \rightarrow H_2SO_4(l)$$

Unfortunately, it is just this reaction to form sulfuric acid that makes SO₂ an environmentally damaging substance. When coal or petroleum that contains sulfur is burned in a power plant, SO₂ is a by-product. If released into the air, it can be converted to sulfuric acid droplets (acid rain). Acid rain damages structures and trees and can damage human health. To prevent these problems either sulfur must be removed before the fuel is burned or the SO₂ in the exhaust gases must be removed in a process called "scrubbing."

Trees damaged by acid rain.

16.7   Acid–Base Titrations   **525**

Example 16.11

Additional Examples

1. Determine the volume of 0.250 *M* KOH required to titrate 25.0 mL of 0.150 *M* HCl.
   15.0 mL of 0.250 *M* KOH

2. Determine the volume of 0.200 *M* NaOH required to titrate 75.0 mL of 0.250 *M* HNO$_3$.
   93.8 mL of 0.200 *M* NaOH

USING TECHNOLOGY

 Figure 16.8

 Animation and Video

Animation, Neutralization of a Strong Acid by a Strong Base

The Titration of a Strong Acid with a Strong Base

Determine the volume of 0.100 *M* NaOH needed to titrate 50.0 mL of 0.200 *M* HNO$_3$.

Solution

Nitric acid (HNO$_3$) is a strong acid so the 0.200 *M* HNO$_3$ solution actually contains H$^+$ and NO$_3^-$ ions. Likewise, sodium hydroxide is a strong base so the 0.100 *M* NaOH solution contains Na$^+$ and OH$^-$ ions. We show this titration schematically in **Figure 16.8**. When the NaOH(*aq*) solution is added to the HNO$_3$(*aq*) solution, the following neutralization reaction occurs:

$$H^+(aq) + OH^-(aq) \rightarrow H_2O(l)$$

To reach the equivalence point we must add enough OH$^-$ ions to just react with the H$^+$ ions originally present in the HNO$_3$(*aq*) solution.

That is, at the equivalence point:

$$\text{moles OH}^- \text{ added} = \text{moles H}^+ \text{ originally present}$$

From 0.100 *M* NaOH   From 50.0 mL 0.200 *M* HNO$_3$

We can determine the moles of H$^+$ originally present in the 50.0-mL sample of 0.200 *M* HNO$_3$ by multiplying the volume (in L) times the molarity:

$$50.0 \text{ mL} \times \frac{1 \text{ L}}{1000 \text{ mL}} \times 0.200 \frac{\text{mol H}^+}{\text{L}} =$$

$$0.0500 \text{ L} \times 0.200 \frac{\text{mol H}^+}{\text{L}} = 1.00 \times 10^{-2} \text{ mol H}^+$$

Thus, to complete the titration (give a neutral solution), we must add 1.00×10^{-2} mol OH$^-$. What volume of 0.100 *M* NaOH contains 1.00×10^{-2} mol OH$^-$?

$$? \text{ vol} \times 0.100 \frac{\text{mol H}^+}{\text{L}} = 1.00 \times 10^{-2} \text{ mol OH}^-$$

Figure 16.8
A molecular-level representation of the solutions in the titration of 0.200 *M* HNO$_3$ with 0.100 *M* NaOH. Note that the solutions contain ions because HNO$_3$ is a strong acid and NaOH is a strong base.

Rearranging the preceding equation gives

$$? \text{ vol} = \frac{1.00 \times 10^{-2}}{0.100} \text{ L} = 1.00 \times 10^{-1} \text{ L}$$

Thus

$$? \text{ vol} = 0.100 \text{ L} = 100. \text{ mL}$$

Thus it takes 100. mL of 0.100 M NaOH to neutralize 50.0 mL of 0.200 M HNO_3.

 Self-Check Exercise 16.8

Calculate the volume of 0.3000 M HCl needed to titrate 75.00 mL of 0.1500 M KOH(aq).

In a modern acid–base titration, typically the probe of a pH meter is inserted in the solution being analyzed and the pH is monitored during the entire titration. A plot of the resulting data (pH versus volume of titrant added) is called the **titration curve** (or **pH curve**). The pH curve for the titration of 0.200 M HNO_3 with 0.100 M NaOH (see Example 16.11) is shown in **Figure 16.9.** Notice from this pH curve that the pH changes very rapidly when the titration nears the equivalence point.

So far we have discussed the titration of a strong acid with a strong base such as NaOH(aq). Weak acids can also be titrated with NaOH(aq). For example, acetic acid ($HC_2H_3O_2$), the weak acid found in vinegar, can be titrated according to the following reaction:

$$OH^-(aq) + HC_2H_3O_2(aq) \rightarrow H_2O(l) + C_2H_3O_2^-(aq)$$

Here the formula for the entire acid is written in the neutralization reaction instead of just H^+, as is the case for strong acids. This is done because acetic acid is a weak acid and retains its H^+ in water. In contrast, OH^- is such a strong base that it can easily extract the H^+ from $HC_2H_3O_2$.

Figure 16.9
The pH curve for the titration of 50.0 mL of 0.200 M HNO_3 with 0.100 M NaOH. Note that the equivalence point occurs at 100.0 mL of NaOH added, the point where exactly enough OH^- has been added to react with all the H^+ originally present. The pH of 7 at the equivalence point is characteristic of a strong acid–strong base titration.

16.7 Acid–Base Titrations **527**

Skills
Applying concepts, making comparisons, making predictions

Laboratory
Experiment 72:
Acids, Bases, and Buffers, CBL

TEACHING TIP

The concept of a buffer is one of the more complex ideas covered up to this point. It is important to go slowly through the explanation of how a buffer works. Students need to see each of the possibilities and understand what happens at each step.

MINI-DEMO

Show the effects of a buffer by making an acetic acid/sodium acetate buffer solution (0.1 *M* for each) in one flask. In another flask place the same amount of distilled water. Measure the pH of each (using paper or a meter). Then add a drop of a solution containing H⁺ or OH⁻ to each flask and check the pH. Repeat the process several times.

USING TECHNOLOGY

 Animation and Video

Chemistry in Motion,
Demonstration 26
This demonstration, Buffering, shows the effects of adding a strong acid to a buffered solution.

16.8 Buffered Solutions

Objective: *To understand the general characteristics of buffered solutions.*

Water: pH = 7
0.01 *M* HCl : pH = 2

A buffered solution is one that resists a change in its pH even when a strong acid or base is added to it. For example, when 0.01 mol of HCl is added to 1 L of pure water, the pH changes from its initial value of 7 to a final value of 2, a change of 5 pH units. However, when 0.01 mol of HCl is added to a solution containing both 0.1 *M* acetic acid ($HC_2H_3O_2$) and 0.1 *M* sodium acetate ($NaC_2H_3O_2$), the pH changes from an initial value of 4.74 to a final value of 4.66, a change of only 0.08 pH units. The latter solution is buffered—it undergoes only a very slight change in pH when a strong acid or base is added to it.

Buffered solutions are vitally important to living organisms whose cells can survive only in a very narrow pH range. Many goldfish have died because their owners did not realize the importance of buffering the aquarium water at an appropriate pH. For humans to survive, the pH of the blood must be maintained between 7.35 and 7.45. This narrow range is maintained by several different buffering systems.

A solution is **buffered** by the *presence of a weak acid and its conjugate base.* An example of a buffered solution is an aqueous solution that contains acetic acid and sodium acetate. The sodium acetate is a salt that furnishes acetate ions (the conjugate base of acetic acid) when it dissolves. To see how this system acts as a buffer, we must recognize that the species present in this solution are

$$HC_2H_3O_2, \quad Na^+, \quad C_2H_3O_2^-$$

When $NaC_2H_3O_2$ is
dissolved, it produces
the separated ions

What happens in this solution when a strong acid such as HCl is added? In pure water, the H⁺ ions from the HCl accumulate, thus lowering the pH.

$$HCl \xrightarrow{100\%} H^+ + Cl^-$$

However, this buffered solution contains $C_2H_3O_2^-$ ions, which are basic. That is, $C_2H_3O_2^-$ has a strong affinity for H^+, as evidenced by the fact that $HC_2H_3O_2$ is a weak acid. This means that the $C_2H_3O_2^-$ and H^+ ions do not exist together in large numbers. Because the $C_2H_3O_2^-$ ion has a high affinity for H^+, these two combine to form $HC_2H_3O_2$ molecules. Thus the H^+ from the added HCl does not accumulate in solution but reacts with the $C_2H_3O_2^-$ as follows:

$$H^+(aq) + C_2H_3O_2^-(aq) \rightarrow HC_2H_3O_2(aq)$$

Next consider what happens when a strong base such as sodium hydroxide is added to the buffered solution. If this base were added to pure water, the OH^- ions from the solid would accumulate and greatly change (raise) the pH.

$$NaOH \xrightarrow{100\%} Na^+ + OH^-$$

However, in the buffered solution the OH^- ion, which has a *very strong* affinity for H^+, reacts with $HC_2H_3O_2$ molecules as follows:

$$HC_2H_3O_2(aq) + OH^-(aq) \rightarrow H_2O(l) + C_2H_3O_2^-(aq)$$

For goldfish to survive, the pH of the water must be carefully controlled.

TABLE 16.3
The Characteristics of a Buffer

1. The solution contains a weak acid HA and its conjugate base A^-.
2. The buffer resists changes in pH by reacting with any added H^+ or OH^- so that these ions do not accumulate.
3. Any added H^+ reacts with the base A^-.

$$H^+(aq) + A^-(aq) \rightarrow HA(aq)$$

4. Any added OH^- reacts with the weak acid HA.

$$OH^-(aq) + HA(aq) \rightarrow H_2O(l) + A^-(aq)$$

This happens because, although $C_2H_3O_2^-$ has a strong affinity for H^+, OH^- has a much stronger affinity for H^+ and thus can remove H^+ ions from acetic acid molecules.

Note that the buffering materials dissolved in the solution prevent added H^+ or OH^- from building up in the solution. Any added H^+ is trapped by $C_2H_3O_2^-$ to form $HC_2H_3O_2$. Any added OH^- reacts with $HC_2H_3O_2$ to form H_2O and $C_2H_3O_2^-$.

The general properties of a buffered solution are summarized in **Table 16.3.**

Focus Questions

Sections 16.7–16.8

1. What is true about the amounts of H^+ and OH^- at the stoichiometric point in a titration?
2. At the equivalence point in a titration you know the volume (x mL) of a standard solution of acid (2.5 M) that has been added to a known volume of base (y mL). Show how you can determine the concentration of the base.
3. List two ways to identify the equivalence point in a titration.
4. What is the importance of a buffer?
5. How does a buffer keep the pH from changing greatly when an acid is added to the solution?

CHEMICAL IMPACT

Consumer Connection

The Heart of the Matter

Doctors use many tests to measure how well someone's heart is functioning. One such test involves taking the pH of the blood and tissues in the heart. When you consider how you measure the pH of solutions in the laboratory, you can see that measuring the pH of a heart inside a living person is not easy. Scientists at the University of North Carolina at Chapel Hill have developed a tiny pH probe that can be placed on the end of a catheter that is then threaded through a vein to reach the heart. The pH sensor, which is only 1 mm in diameter, is made by plating iridium oxide onto a platinum wire.

Measuring the pH inside the heart can reveal a great deal about the patient's condition. For example, a lowering of the pH might indicate the formation of lactic acid due to a low supply of oxygen. This new pH sensor is just another example of how science can help us deal more effectively with disease.

Focus Questions **529**

TEACHING TIP

Discuss the chemical properties that are necessary to produce a buffer. Why is it important to use a weak acid and its salt?

Answers to Focus Questions

1. The amounts of H^+ and OH^- are equal at the stoichiometric point in a titration (they react to form water).
2. (2.5 M) (x mL) = B(y mL) where B is the molarity of the base.
3. The equivalence point can be identified by using a pH meter or by using an indicator that changes color at the appropriate pH.
4. Buffers keep the acidity of a solution relatively constant in the face of additions of either acid or base.
5. When an acid is added to a buffer, the salt anion in the buffer reacts with the acid to produce a weak acid, thus removing the hydrogen ions from the solution.

Integrating the CHEMICAL IMPACT

The Heart of the Matter

Many of the tests now used to detect disease in humans are either chemical tests or tests that rely on instruments originally constructed for chemical research. The test for diabetes involves sugar analysis, the test for anemia looks at iron levels, susceptibility to heart disease is detected by analysis of cholesterol levels, and so on. In addition, instrumental techniques such as MRI (magnetic resonance imaging) are based on methods—in this case, nuclear magnetic resonance (nmr)—developed to further chemical research. Another example is positron emission tomography (PET), which is used to monitor metabolic processes in various organs of the body.

The field of chemistry has had a tremendous effect on diagnostic medicine.

Acid Rain (FIELD)
Objectives

1. To collect rainwater

2. To perform titrations

3. To determine the acidity level of the rainwater

4. To examine the effect of soil on the acidity of rainwater

Skills

Applying concepts, interpreting data, making comparisons, evaluating, computing

Materials

Goggles	Collecting
Apron	bottle
Buret	Funnels (2)
Buret clamp	Rainwater
Ringstand	Soil
250-mL	Calcium
beaker	carbonate
500-mL	NaOH
beaker	(0.100 *M*)
Filter paper	Phenolph-
	thalein

Preparation Hints

While it is preferable for students to collect the rainwater, it may not be feasible; therefore, you may wish to collect the rainwater for them.

You may want to perform a titration before class to estimate the concentration of NaOH that students will need to use (see the discussion in the Procedure Hints). In this way the students will not need to make dilutions of the NaOH you provide them.

Place several bottles of 0.100 *M* NaOH throughout the lab for easy access.

Prelab Discussion

Discuss the successive dilutions needed to make the 1.00×10^{-4} *M* NaOH solutions.

If this activity is the first time that students will perform titrations, it is a good idea to demonstrate a titration in front of the class. Emphasize how to read the buret and how to look for an endpoint.

Procedure Hints

Watch students as they perform the titrations. Students often overshoot the endpoint.

The pH value of rainwater varies. If it is 5 or greater, students will have to dilute the given NaOH solution by a factor of 10 or

Problem

What is the normal range of pH for rainwater? Can soil neutralize the rainwater?

Introduction

At 25 °C a pH of 7.00 indicates that a solution is neutral. Very few substances are neutral (pure water is, but pure water is not found in nature). Rainwater is naturally acidic due to dissolved carbon dioxide from the air.

In this lab you will determine a range of pH values of rainwater in your area. You will also determine the effect of soil on the acidity of rainwater.

Prelab Assignment

1. Read the entire lab experiment before you begin.

2. Provide calculations for all dilutions to be made in this lab.

Materials

Goggles	Collecting bottle
Apron	Funnels (2)
Buret	Rainwater
Buret clamp	Soil
Ring stand	Calcium carbonate
250-mL beaker	NaOH (0.100 *M*)
500-mL beaker	Phenolphthalein
Filter paper	

Safety

If you come in contact with any solution, wash the contacted area thoroughly.

Procedure

Part I: Determining the pH of Rainwater

1. Obtain a sample of rainwater by placing a funnel in the mouth of a collecting bottle and placing the bottle and funnel outside while it is raining.

2. Make 200.0 mL of 1.00×10^{-4} *M* NaOH from the 0.100 *M* NaOH provided by your teacher.

3. Titrate 50.0 mL of rainwater with 1.00×10^{-4} *M* NaOH. Use phenolphthalein indicator.

4. If the titration requires less than 5 mL of the 1.00×10^{-4} *M* NaOH, dilute the NaOH solution so that the titration of 50.00 mL of rainwater will require about 20 mL of aqueous NaOH (you will need to calculate the exact concentration of the NaOH). Titrate a new sample of rainwater with the new NaOH and record the volume.

Part II: Determining the Effect of Soil

1. Obtain a soil sample from home or outside your school. Collect about 200 mL of soil in a 500-mL beaker.

2. Place the soil in a funnel fitted with filter paper.

3. Pour the rainwater through the soil and collect it into a 250-mL beaker.

4. Collect the rainwater that has been poured through the soil (filter it again if soil remains in the sample).

5. Titrate 50.0 mL of rainwater with NaOH of the same concentration used in Part I (either step 3 or step 4, if that step is necessary). Use phenolphthalein indicator.

Part III: Increasing Soil Capacity

1. Crush and powder 5 g of calcium carbonate. Mix it with the same amount of soil as in Part II (until homogeneous).

2. Place the soil in a filter.

3. Pour the rainwater through the soil and collect it into a 250-mL beaker.

4. Collect the rainwater that has been poured through the soil (filter it again if soil remains in the sample).

5. Titrate 50.0 mL of this rainwater with NaOH of the same concentration in Part I (either step 3 or step 4, if that step is necessary). Use phenolphthalein indicator.

Cleaning Up

Clean all materials and wash your hands thoroughly. Dispose of all solutions and soil as instructed by your teacher.

Data/Observations

For each part, fill in a table similar to the one provided below.

	(Sample)
Initial buret reading	
Final buret reading	
Volume of NaOH	

Analysis and Conclusions
Part I

1. What is the number of moles of NaOH used in the titration?

2. What is the number of moles of acid in your rainwater sample?

---

more. If the pH is less than 4, students will need to use approximately 1×10^{-3} *M* NaOH.

Disposal

Collect all solutions from students and dispose of them properly.

Post-Lab Discussion

Have students pool all of their data.

Sample Data/Answers

Prelab Assignment

To make 200.0 mL of 1.00×10^{-4} *M* NaOH from 0.100 *M* NaOH requires

adding 199.8 mL water to 0.2 mL of 0.100 *M* NaOH. This is not practical. Have students successively dilute the NaOH (take 20.0 mL of 0.100 *M* NaOH and add 180.0 mL water to make 1.00×10^{-2} *M* NaOH; take 20.0 mL of 1.00×10^{-2} NaOH and add 180.0 mL water to make 1.00×10^{-3} *M* NaOH; take 20.0 mL of 1.00×10^{-3} NaOH and add 180.0 mL water to make 1.00×10^{-4} *M* NaOH). This way students also have NaOH available at higher concentrations in case they need it.

If the titration of 50.0 mL of rainwater requires less than 5 mL of NaOH, students will need to dilute the NaOH so that the titration takes about 20 mL.

3. Determine the concentration of H⁺ in your rainwater sample.
4. Calculate the pH of your rainwater sample
5. Collect class data.

Parts II and III

1. Determine the pH of rainwater after it flows through untreated soil.
2. Determine the pH of rainwater after it flows through soil mixed with calcium carbonate.
3. What is the normal range of pH for rainwater? Use class data.
4. Does the untreated soil neutralize the rainwater?

5. Does soil mixed with calcium carbonate neutralize the rainwater?
6. Which soil (untreated or mixed with calcium carbonate) neutralized the rainwater better?

Something Extra

1. Does boiling affect the pH of rainwater? Boil and cool rainwater and test it. Explain your results.
2. Does potting soil have an effect on the pH of rainwater? Test it and compare your results to the soil you gathered.

 Chapter Review

Key Terms

acid (16.1)
base (16.1)
Arrhenius concept of acids and bases (16.1)
Brønsted–Lowry model (16.1)
conjugate acid (16.1)
conjugate base (16.1)
conjugate acid–base pair (16.1)
hydronium ion (16.1)
completely ionized (dissociated) (16.2)
strong acid (16.2)
weak acid (16.2)
diprotic acid (16.2)
oxyacid (16.2)
organic acid (16.2)
carboxyl group (16.2)
amphoteric substance (16.3)
ionization of water (16.3)
ion-product constant, K_w (16.3)
pH scale (16.4)
indicator (16.5)
indicator paper (16.5)
pH meter (16.5)
neutralization reaction (16.7)
titration (16.7)
standard solution (16.7)
buret (16.7)
equivalence (stoichiometric) point (16.7)
titration (pH) curve (16.7)
buffered solution (16.8)
buffered (16.8)

Summary

1. Acids and bases in water are commonly described by two different models. Arrhenius postulated that acids produce H⁺ ions in aqueous solutions and that bases produce OH⁻ ions. The Brønsted–Lowry model is more general: an acid is a proton donor, and a base is a proton acceptor. Water acts as a Brønsted-Lowry base when it accepts a proton from an acid to form a hydronium ion:

$$HA(aq) + H_2O(l) \rightleftharpoons H_3O^+(aq) + A^-(aq)$$

Acid   Base   Conjugate acid   Conjugate Base

A conjugate base is everything that remains of the acid molecule after the proton is lost. A conjugate acid is formed when a proton is transferred to the base. Two substances related in this way are called a conjugate acid–base pair.

2. A strong acid or base is one that is completely ionized (dissociated). A weak acid is one that is ionized (dissociated) only to a slight extent. Strong acids have weak conjugate bases. Weak acids have relatively strong conjugate bases.

3. Water is an amphoteric substance—it can behave either as an acid or as a base. The ionization of water reveals this property; one water molecule transfers a proton to another water molecule to produce a hydronium ion and a hydroxide ion.

$$H_2O(l) + H_2O(l) \rightleftharpoons H_3O^+(aq) + OH^-(aq)$$

Chapter Review   **531**

Analysis and Conclusions

Part I

1. 2.35×10^{-6} mol NaOH
2. 2.35×10^{-6} mol H⁺ (in 50.0 mL)
3. $[H^+] = 4.70 \times 10^{-5}$ M
4. pH = 4.33
5. Answers will vary.

Parts II and III

1. pH = 4.43
2. pH = 5.37
3. Answers will vary.
4. The untreated soil slightly neutralizes the rainwater (the rainwater is less acidic but not neutral).
5. The soil mixed with calcium carbonate neutralizes the rainwater somewhat (the rainwater is less acidic but not neutral).
6. The soil mixed with calcium carbonate neutralized the rainwater better than the untreated soil.

Something Extra

1. Boiling the rainwater will remove dissolved CO_2. The dissolved CO_2 in the water will lower the pH of the water, so removing it will make the rainwater less acidic.
2. Most potting soil is treated to reduce the acidity level of rainwater.

Chapter Review

Assign the students to work individually on the Chapter 16 Review Worksheet at the appropriate level (Basic, Standard, or Challenge). Answers are found in the *Teacher Resources*.

Assessment

Chapter 16 Test is found in the *Teacher Resources*, along with the answers for the test.

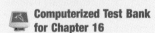 **Computerized Test Bank for Chapter 16**

Data/Observations

Sample Data

Part I

	50.0 mL Rainwater
Initial buret reading	0.00 mL
Final buret reading	23.50 mL
Volume of NaOH	23.50 mL

Part II

	50.0 mL Rainwater Through Soil
Initial buret reading	1.23 mL
Final buret reading	19.73 mL
Volume of NaOH	18.50 mL

Part III

	50.0 mL Rainwater Through Treated Soil
Initial buret reading	0.00 mL
Final buret reading	2.15 mL
Volume of NaOH	2.15 mL

1. Acids were recognized primarily from their sour taste. Bases were recognized from their bitter taste and slippery feel on the skin.

2. In the Arrhenius definition, an acid is a substance that produces hydrogen ions (H^+) when dissolved in water. An Arrhenius base produces hydroxide ions (OH^-) when dissolved in water. These definitions are not complete because they limit bases to compounds with a hydroxide ion, and the only allowable solvent is water.

3. A Brønsted–Lowry acid is a molecule or ion capable of providing a proton to some other species; acids are proton donors. A Brønsted–Lowry base is a molecule or ion capable of receiving a proton from some other species; bases are proton acceptors.

4. A conjugate acid–base pair differs by one hydrogen ion, H^+. For example, $HC_2H_3O_2$ (acetic acid) differs from its conjugate base, $C_2H_3O_2^-$ (acetate ion), by a single hydrogen ion.

5. The portion of the original acid molecule or ion that remains after the proton leaves is the conjugate base. In this model, water behaves as the base since it receives the proton from the acid.

6. When an acid is dissolved in water, the hydronium ion (H_3O^+) is formed. The hydronium ion is the conjugate acid of water.

7. (a) The conjugate base of H_2SO_4 is the HSO_4^- ion. The conjugate acid of SO_4^{2-} is also the HSO_4^- ion. (b) These constitute a conjugate acid–base pair. (c) The conjugate base of $HClO_4$ is the ClO_4^- ion. The conjugate acid of Cl^- is HCl. (d) The conjugate base of NH_4^+ is NH_3. The conjugate acid of NH_2^- is also NH_3.

8. (a) NH_3 (base), NH_4^+ (acid); H_2O (acid), OH^- (base); (b) PO_4^{3-} (base), H_2O (acid), HPO_4^{2-} (acid), OH^- (base); (c) $C_2H_3O_2^-$ (base), H_2O (acid), $HC_2H_3O_2$ (acid), OH^- (base)

9. (a) H_2SO_4; (b) HSO_3^-; (c) $HClO_4$; (d) H_3PO_4

The expression

$$K_w = [H_3O^+][OH^-] = [H^+][OH^-]$$

is called the ion-product constant. It has been shown experimentally that at 25 °C,

$$[H^+] = [OH^-] = 1.0 \times 10^{-7}\ M$$

so $K_w = 1.0 \times 10^{-14}$.

4. In an acidic solution, $[H^+]$ is greater than $[OH^-]$. In a basic solution, $[OH^-]$ is greater than $[H^+]$. In a neutral solution, $[H^+] = [OH^-]$.

5. To describe $[H^+]$ in aqueous solutions, we use the pH scale.

$$pH = -\log[H^+]$$

Note that the pH decreases as $[H^+]$ (acidity) increases.

6. The pH of strong acid solutions can be calculated directly from the concentration of the acid, because 100% dissociation occurs in aqueous solution.

7. A buffered solution is one that resists a change in its pH even when a strong acid or base is added to it. A buffered solution contains a weak acid and its conjugate base.

Questions and Problems

All exercises with blue numbers have answers in the back of this book.

16.1 Acids and Bases

Questions

1. What are some physical properties that historically led chemists to classify various substances as acids and bases?

2. In the Arrhenius definition, what characterizes an acid? What characterizes a base? Why are the Arrhenius definitions too restrictive?

3. What is an acid in the Brønsted–Lowry model? What is a base?

4. How do the components of a conjugate acid–base pair differ from one another? Give an example of a conjugate acid–base pair to illustrate your answer.

5. How does a Brønsted–Lowry acid form its conjugate base when dissolved in water? How is the water involved in this process?

6. When an acid is dissolved in water, what ion does the water form? What is the relationship of this ion to water itself?

Problems

7. Which of the following represent conjugate acid–base pairs? For those pairs that are not conjugates, write the correct conjugate acid or base for each species in the pair.
   a. H_2SO_4, SO_4^{2-}
   b. $H_2PO_4^-$, HPO_4^{2-}
   c. $HClO_4$, Cl^-
   d. NH_4^+, NH_2^-

8. In each of the following chemical equations, identify the conjugate acid–base pairs.
   a. $NH_3 + H_2O \rightleftharpoons NH_4^+ + OH^-$
   b. $PO_4^{3-} + H_2O \rightleftharpoons HPO_4^{2-} + OH^-$
   c. $C_2H_3O_2^- + H_2O \rightleftharpoons HC_2H_3O_2 + OH^-$

9. Write the conjugate *acid* for each of the following:
   a. HSO_4^-
   b. SO_3^{2-}
   c. ClO_4^-
   d. $H_2PO_4^-$

10. Write the conjugate *base* for each the following:
   a. HCO_3^-
   b. $H_2PO_4^-$
   c. HCl
   d. HSO_4^-

11. Write a chemical equation showing how each of the following species behaves as a *base* when dissolved in water.
   a. NH_3
   b. NH_2^-
   c. O^{2-}
   d. F^-

12. Write a chemical equation showing how each of the following species behaves as an *acid* when dissolved in water.
   a. $HClO_4$
   b. $HC_2H_3O_2$
   c. HSO_3^-
   d. HBr

16.2 Acid Strength

Questions

13. What does it mean to say that an acid is strong in aqueous solution? What does this reveal about the ability of the acid's anion to attract protons?

14. What does it mean to say that an acid is weak in aqueous solution? What does this reveal about the ability of the acid's anion to attract protons?

15. A strong acid has a weak conjugate base, whereas a weak acid has a relatively strong conjugate base. Explain.

16. Name four strong acids. For each acid, write the equation showing the acid dissociating in water.

17. Which of the following acids have relatively strong conjugate bases?
   a. $CH_3COOH(HC_2H_3O_2)$
   b. HF
   c. H_2S
   d. HCl

18. Which of the following bases have relatively strong conjugate acids?
   a. SO_4^{2-}
   b. Br^-
   c. CN^-
   d. $CH_3COO^-(C_2H_3O_2^-)$

10. (a) CO_3^{2-}; (b) HPO_4^{2-}; (c) Cl^-; (d) SO_4^{2-}

11. (a) $NH_3 + H_2O \rightleftharpoons NH_4^+ + OH^-$; (b) $NH_2^- + H_2O \rightleftharpoons NH_3 + OH^-$; (c) $O^{2-} + H_2O \rightleftharpoons OH^- + OH^-$; (d) $F^- + H_2O \rightleftharpoons HF + OH^-$

12. (a) $HClO_4 + H_2O \rightarrow ClO_4^- + H_3O^+$; (b) $HC_2H_3O_2 + H_2O \rightleftharpoons C_2H_3O_2^- + H_3O^+$; (c) $HSO_3^- + H_2O \rightleftharpoons SO_3^{2-} + H_3O^+$; (d) $HBr + H_2O \rightarrow Br^- + H_3O^+$

13. A strong acid is one for which the equilibrium in water lies far to the right. A strong acid is completely converted to its conjugate base when dissolved in water. The conjugate base must therefore be poor at attracting or holding onto protons.

14. If an acid is weak in aqueous solution, it does not easily transfer protons to water (and does not fully ionize). Thus the anion of the acid must attract protons rather strongly.

15. A strong acid loses its protons easily and fully ionizes in water. Thus the acid's conjugate base is poor at attracting protons (that is, a very weak base). A weak acid does not ionize fully, so its conjugate base must have a rather strong attraction for a proton (that is, it must be a relatively strong base).

16. sulfuric: $H_2SO_4 + H_2O \rightarrow HSO_4^- + H_3O^+$; hydrochloric: $HCl + H_2O \rightarrow Cl^- + H_3O^+$;

16.3 Water as an Acid and a Base

Questions

19. Anions containing hydrogen (for example, HCO_3^- and $H_2PO_4^{2-}$) show amphoteric behaviour when reacting with other acids or bases. Write equations illustrating the amphoterism of these anions.

20. Write an equation showing the auto-ionization of water. Write the expression for the ion-product constant, K_w, for water.

21. What happens to the hydroxide ion concentration in aqueous solutions when we increase the hydrogen ion concentration by adding an acid? What happens to the hydrogen ion concentration in aqueous solutions when we increase the hydroxide ion concentration by adding a base? Explain.

Problems

22. Calculate the $[H^+]$ in each of the following solutions, and indicate whether the solution is acidic, basic, or neutral.
    a. $[OH^-] = 3.99 \times 10^{-5}\ M$
    b. $[OH^-] = 2.91 \times 10^{-9}\ M$
    c. $[OH^-] = 7.23 \times 10^{-2}\ M$
    d. $[OH^-] = 9.11 \times 10^{-7}\ M$

23. Calculate the $[OH^-]$ in each of the following solutions, and indicate whether the solution is acidic, basic, or neutral.
    a. $[H^+] = 1.00 \times 10^{-7}\ M$
    b. $[H^+] = 7.00 \times 10^{-7}\ M$
    c. $[H^+] = 7.00 \times 10^{-1}\ M$
    d. $[H^+] = 5.99 \times 10^{-6}\ M$

24. For each pair of concentrations, tell which represents the more acidic solution.
    a. $[H^+] = 1.2 \times 10^{-3}\ M$ or $[H^+] = 4.5 \times 10^{-4}\ M$
    b. $[H^+] = 2.6 \times 10^{-6}\ M$ or $[H^+] = 4.3 \times 10^{-8}\ M$
    c. $[H^+] = 0.000010\ M$ or $[H^+] = 0.0000010\ M$

25. For each pair of concentrations, tell which represents the more basic solution.
    a. $[H^+] = 1.59 \times 10^{-7}\ M$ or $[H^+] = 1.04 \times 10^{-8}\ M$
    b. $[H^+] = 5.69 \times 10^{-8}\ M$ or $[OH^-] = 4.49 \times 10^{-6}\ M$
    c. $[H^+] = 5.99 \times 10^{-8}\ M$ or $[OH^-] = 6.01 \times 10^{-7}\ M$

16.4 The pH Scale

Questions

26. Why do scientists tend to express the acidity of a solution in terms of its pH, rather than in terms of the molarity of hydrogen ion present? How is pH defined mathematically?

27. Using Figure 16.3, list the approximate pH of five "everyday" solutions. How do the familiar properties (such as sour taste for acids) of these solutions correspond to their pH?

28. For a hydrogen ion concentration of $2.33 \times 10^{-6}\ M$, how many *decimal places* should we give when expressing the pH of the solution?

29. As the hydrogen ion concentration of a solution *increases*, does the pH of the solution increase or decrease? Explain.

Problems

30. Calculate the pH corresponding to each of the hydrogen ion concentrations given below. Tell whether each solution is acidic, basic, or neutral.
    a. $[H^+] = 0.00100\ M$
    b. $[H^+] = 2.19 \times 10^{-4}\ M$
    c. $[H^+] = 9.18 \times 10^{-11}\ M$
    d. $[H^+] = 4.71 \times 10^{-7}\ M$

31. Calculate the pH corresponding to each of the hydroxide ion concentrations given below. Tell whether each solution is acidic, basic, or neutral.
    a. $[OH^-] = 1.00 \times 10^{-7}\ M$
    b. $[OH^-] = 4.59 \times 10^{-13}\ M$
    c. $[OH^-] = 1.04 \times 10^{-4}\ M$
    d. $[OH^-] = 7.00 \times 10^{-1}\ M$

32. Calculate the pH corresponding to each of the pOH values listed, and indicate whether each solution is acidic, basic, or neutral.
    a. pOH = 4.32
    b. pOH = 8.90
    c. pOH = 1.81
    d. pOH = 13.1

33. For each hydrogen or hydroxide ion concentration listed, calculate the concentration of the complementary ion and the pH and pOH of the solution.
    a. $[H^+] = 1.00 \times 10^{-7}\ M$
    b. $[OH^-] = 4.39 \times 10^{-5}\ M$
    c. $[H^+] = 4.29 \times 10^{-11}\ M$
    d. $[OH^-] = 7.36 \times 10^{-2}\ M$

34. Calculate the hydrogen ion concentration, in moles per liter, for solutions with each of the following pH values.
    a. pH = 1.04
    b. pH = 13.1
    c. pH = 5.99
    d. pH = 8.62

35. Calculate the hydrogen ion concentration, in moles per liter, for solutions with each of the following pOH values.
    a. pOH = 3.91   c. pOH = 1.15
    b. pOH = 12.56   d. pOH = 8.77

36. Calculate the hydrogen ion and hydroxide ion concentrations, in moles per liter, for solutions with each of the following pH or pOH values.
    a. pH = 5.12   c. pH = 7.00
    b. pOH = 5.12   d. pOH = 13.00

nitric: $HNO_3 + H_2O \rightarrow NO_3^- + H_3O^+$;

hydrobromic: $HBr + H_2O \rightarrow Br^- + H_3O^+$

17. (a) CH_3COO^- is a relatively strong base; (b) F^- is a relatively strong base; (c) HS^- is a relatively strong base; (d) Cl^- is a very weak base

18. (a) HSO_4^- is a moderately strong acid; (b) HBr is a strong acid; (c) HCN is a weak acid; (d) CH_3COOH is a weak acid

19. $HCO_3^-(aq) + OH^-(aq) \rightarrow CO_3^{2-}(aq) + H_2O(l)$; $HCO_3^-(aq) + H^+(aq) \rightarrow H_2CO_3(aq)$; $H_2PO_4^-(aq) + OH^-(aq) \rightarrow HPO_4^{2-}(aq) + H_2O(l)$; $H_2PO_4^-(aq) + H^+(aq) \rightarrow H_3PO_4(aq)$

20. $H_2O + H_2O \rightleftharpoons H_3O^+ + OH^-$; $K_w = [H_3O^+][OH^-]$

21. The hydrogen ion concentration and hydroxide ion concentration are inversely related in aqueous solutions. That is, as the hydrogen ion concentration increases, the hydroxide ion concentration decreases, and vice versa. This is because $K_w = [H^+][OH^-] = 1.0 \times 10^{-14}$ at 25 °C. This value is a constant, so if H^+ or OH^- is added to the solution, the other ion must decrease.

22. (a) $[H^+] = 2.5 \times 10^{-10}\ M$; basic; (b) $[H^+] = 3.4 \times 10^{-6}\ M$; acidic; (c) $[H^+] = 1.4 \times 10^{-13}\ M$; basic; (d) $[H^+] = 1.1 \times 10^{-8}\ M$; basic

23. (a) $[OH^-] = 1.00 \times 10^{-7}\ M$; neutral; (b) $[OH^-] = 1.4 \times 10^{-8}\ M$; acidic; (c) $[OH^-] = 1.4 \times 10^{-14}\ M$; acidic; (d) $[OH^-] = 1.7 \times 10^{-9}\ M$; acidic

24. (a) $[H^+] = 1.2 \times 10^{-3}\ M$ is more acidic; (b) $[H^+] = 2.6 \times 10^{-6}\ M$ is more acidic; (c) $[H^+] = 0.000010\ M$ is more acidic

25. (a) $[H^+] = 1.04 \times 10^{-8}\ M$ is more basic; (b) $[OH^-] = 4.49 \times 10^{-6}\ M$ is more basic; (c) $[OH^-] = 6.01 \times 10^{-7}\ M$ is more basic

26. The concentrations of hydrogen ion present are generally quite small and are best expressed in scientific notation. The pH scale converts these numbers to numbers that are easier to compare. The pH of a solution is defined as the negative of the base 10 logarithm of the hydrogen ion concentration; that is, pH = $-\log[H^+]$.

27. household ammonia (pH 12); blood (pH 7–8); milk (pH 6–7); vinegar (pH 3); lemon juice (pH 2–3); stomach acid (pH 2)

28. The number 2.33×10^{-6} has three significant figures, so the pH must have three significant figures. However, the number in front of the decimal place is not significant (it comes from the exponent). Thus the pH should be reported to the third decimal place (5.633).

29. The pH of a solution is defined as the negative logarithm of the hydrogen ion concentration; that is, pH = $-\log[H^+]$. Mathematically, as $[H^+]$ increases, pH must decrease.

30. (a) 3.000 (acidic); (b) 3.660 (acidic); (c) 10.037 (basic); (d) 6.327 (acidic)

31. (a) 7.00 (neutral); (b) 1.662 (acidic); (c) 10.017 (basic); (d) 13.845 (basic)

32. (a) 9.68 (basic); (b) 5.10 (acidic); (c) 12.19 (basic); (d) 0.9 (acidic)

33. (a) $[OH^-] = 1.0 \times 10^{-7}\ M$; pH = 7.00; pOH = 7.00; (b) $[H^+] = 2.3 \times 10^{-10}\ M$; pH = 9.64; pOH = 4.36; (c) $[OH^-] = 2.33 \times 10^{-4}\ M$; pH = 10.37; pOH = 3.63; (d) $[H^+] = 1.4 \times 10^{-13}\ M$; pH = 12.87; pOH = 1.13

34. (a) 0.0912 M; (b) 8×10^{-14} M; (c) 1.0×10^{-6} M; (d) 2.4×10^{-9} M

35. (a) $[H^+] = 8.1 \times 10^{-11}$ M; (b) $[H^+] = 3.6 \times 10^{-2}$ M; (c) $[H^+] = 1.4 \times 10^{-13}$ M; (d) $[H^+] = 5.9 \times 10^{-6}$ M

36. (a) $[H^+] = 7.6 \times 10^{-6}$ M; $[OH^-] = 1.3 \times 10^{-9}$ M; (b) $[H^+] = 1.3 \times 10^{-9}$ M; $[OH^-] = 7.6 \times 10^{-6}$ M; (c) $[H^+] = [OH^-] = 1.0 \times 10^{-7}$ M; (d) $[H^+] = 1.0 \times 10^{-1}$ M; $[OH^-] = 1.0 \times 10^{-13}$ M

37. We can measure the pH of a solution with a pH meter, pH paper, and indicators. The pH meter is the most accurate.

38. Indicators are substances that turn a different color when H^+ is present than when H^+ is absent. Consider the equation $HIn \rightleftharpoons H^+ + In^-$. The substance HIn is a different color from the substance In^-.

39. Essentially no molecules of HCl are present because HCl is a strong acid for which the equilibrium with water lies far to the right.

40. The solution contains water molecules, H_3O^+ ions (protons), and NO_3^- ions. No HNO_3 molecules are present because HNO_3 is a strong acid.

41. (a) $[H^+] = 1.04 \times 10^{-4}$ M; pH = 3.983; (b) $[H^+] = 0.00301$ M; pH = 2.521; (c) $[H^+] = 5.41 \times 10^{-4}$ M; pH = 3.267; (d) $[H^+] = 6.42 \times 10^{-2}$ M; pH = 1.192

42. (a) $[H^+] = 0.00010$ M; pH = 4.00; (b) $[H^+] = 0.0050$ M; pH = 2.30; (c) $[H^+] = 4.21 \times 10^{-5}$ M; pH = 4.376; (d) $[H^+] = 6.33 \times 10^{-3}$ M; pH = 2.199

43. 5.0×10^2 mL

44. 0.11 M

45. A buffered solution is one that resists a change in its pH even when a strong acid or base is added to it. A solution is buffered by the presence of the combination of a weak acid and its conjugate base.

46. A buffered solution consists of a mixture of a weak acid and its conjugate base; one example of a buffered solution is a mixture of acetic acid ($HC_2H_3O_2$) and sodium acetate ($NaC_2H_3O_2$).

47. The conjugate base com-

16.5 Measuring pH

Questions

37. Name three ways we can measure the pH of a solution. Which is the most accurate? Explain.

38. Describe how an indicator works. Use a chemical equation in your explanation.

16.6 Calculating the pH of Strong Acid Solutions

Questions

39. When 1 mol of gaseous hydrogen chloride is dissolved in enough water to make 1 L of solution, approximately how many HCl molecules remain in the solution? Explain.

40. A bottle of acid solution is labeled "3 M HNO_3." What are the substances that are actually present in the solution? Are any HNO_3 molecules present? Why or why not?

Problems

41. Calculate the hydrogen ion concentration and the pH of each of the following solutions of strong acids.
   a. 1.04×10^{-4} M HCl
   b. 0.00301 M HNO_3
   c. 5.41×10^{-4} M $HClO_4$
   d. 6.42×10^{-2} M HNO_3

42. Calculate the hydrogen ion concentration and the pH of each of the following solutions of strong acids.
   a. 0.00010 M HCl
   b. 0.0050 M HNO_3
   c. 4.21×10^{-5} M $HClO_4$
   d. 6.33×10^{-3} M HNO_3

16.7 Acid–Base Titrations

Problems

43. A 100.0-mL sample of 0.50 M HCl(aq) is titrated with 0.10 M NaOH(aq). What volume of the NaOH solution is required to reach the endpoint of the titration?

44. If 26.5 mL of a 0.20 M aqueous solution of NaOH is required to titrate 50.0 mL of an aqueous solution of HNO_3, what is the concentration of the HNO_3 solution?

16.8 Buffered Solutions

Questions

45. What characteristic properties do buffered solutions possess?

46. What two components make up a buffered solution? Give an example of a combination that would serve as a buffered solution.

---

47. Which component of a buffered solution is capable of combining with an added strong acid? Using your example from Question 46, show how this component would react with added HCl.

48. Which component of a buffered solution consumes added strong base? Using your example from Question 46, show how this component would react with added NaOH.

Problems

49. Which of the following combinations would act as buffered solutions?
   a. HCl and NaCl
   b. CH_3COOH and KCH_3COO
   c. H_2S and NaHS
   d. H_2S and Na_2S

50. For those combinations in Question 49 that behave as buffered solutions, write equations showing how the components of the buffer consume added strong acid (HCl) or strong base (NaOH).

Critical Thinking

51. The concepts of acid–base equilibria were developed in this chapter for aqueous solutions (in aqueous solutions, water is the solvent and is intimately involved in the equilibria). However, the Brønsted–Lowry acid–base theory can be extended easily to other solvents. One such solvent that has been investigated in depth is liquid ammonia, NH_3.
   a. Write a chemical equation indicating how HCl behaves as an acid in liquid ammonia.
   b. Write a chemical equation indicating how OH^- behaves as a base in liquid ammonia.

52. Which of the following conditions indicate an acidic solution?
   a. pH < 7.0   c. $[H^+] > [OH^-]$
   b. pOH < 7.0   d. $[H^+] > 1.0 \times 10^{-7}$ M

53. Which of the following conditions indicate a basic solution?
   a. pOH < 7.0   c. $[OH^-] < [H^+]$
   b. pH > 7.0   d. $[H^+] < 1.0 \times 10^{-7}$ M

54. Which of the following acids are classified as strong acids?
   a. HNO_3 d. HF
   b. CH_3COOH ($HC_2H_3O_2$) e. $HClO_4$
   c. HCl

55. Which of the following represent conjugate acid–base pairs? For those pairs that are not conjugates, write the correct conjugate acid or base for each species in the pair.
   a. H_2O, OH^- c. H_3PO_4, $H_2PO_4^-$
   b. H_2SO_4, SO_4^{2-} d. $HC_2H_3O_2$, $C_2H_3O_2^-$

---

ponent of the buffered solution is capable of combining with any strong acid that might be added to the buffered solution. For the example from Question 46, we would have $H^+ + C_2H_3O_2^- \rightarrow HC_2H_3O_2$.

48. The weak acid component of the buffered solution reacts with the strong base. For example, hydroxide reacts with the acetic acid as follows: $OH^- + HC_2H_3O_2 \rightarrow H_2O + C_2H_3O_2^-$.

49. (a) not a buffer; (b) a buffer; (c) a buffer; (d) not a buffer

50. added OH^-: $OH^- + HC_2H_3O_2 \rightarrow H_2O + C_2H_3O_2^-$; added H^+: $H^+ + C_2H_3O_2^- \rightarrow HC_2H_3O_2$; added OH^-: $OH^- + H_2S \rightarrow H_2O + HS^-$; added H^+: $H^+ + HS^- \rightarrow H_2S$

51. (a) $HCl + NH_3 \rightarrow Cl^- + NH_4^+$; (b) $OH^- + NH_3 \rightarrow H_2O + NH_2^-$

52. (a) acidic; (b) basic; (c) acidic; (d) acidic

53. (a) basic; (b) basic; (c) acidic; (d) basic

54. (a) strong acid; (b) weak acid; (c) strong acid; (d) weak acid; (e) strong acid

55. (a) a conjugate acid–base pair; (b) not a conjugate acid–base pair; (c) a conjugate acid–base pair; (d) a conjugate acid–base pair

56. (a) CH_3NH_2 (base), $CH_3NH_3^+$ (acid); H_2O (acid), OH^- (base); (b) CH_3COOH (acid), CH_3COO^- (base); NH_3 (base), NH_4^+ (acid); (c) HF (acid), F^- (base); NH_3 (base), NH_4^+ (acid)

56. In each of the following chemical equations, identify the conjugate acid–base pairs.
 a. $CH_3NH_2 + H_2O \rightleftharpoons CH_3NH_3^+ + OH^-$
 b. $CH_3COOH + NH_3 \rightleftharpoons CH_3COO^- + NH_4^+$
 c. $HF + NH_3 \rightleftharpoons F^- + NH_4^+$

57. Which of the following bases have relatively strong conjugate acids?
 a. F^-
 b. Cl^-
 c. HSO_4^-
 d. NO_3^-

58. For each pair of concentrations, tell which represents the more basic solution.
 a. $[H^+] = 0.000013\ M$ or $[OH^-] = 0.0000032\ M$
 b. $[H^+] = 1.03 \times 10^{-6}\ M$ or $[OH^-] = 1.54 \times 10^{-8}\ M$
 c. $[OH^-] = 4.02 \times 10^{-7}\ M$ or $[OH^-] = 0.0000001\ M$

59. A poor, misguided chemistry student is working on a laboratory experiment. He has 90.0 mL of a strong base, 0.400 M NaOH. To this he adds 30.0 mL of a 1.75 M solution of HNO_3. He then adds 240.0 mL of water. Will the resulting solution be neutral? What will the $[H^+]$ and pH be? What is the pOH? Would the solution turn litmus pink?

60. An eyedropper is calibrated by counting the number of drops required to deliver exactly 1.00 mL. Twenty drops are required. What is the volume of one drop? Suppose one such drop of 0.200 M HCl is added to 1.00 mL of water. What is the $[H^+]$? By what factor did the $[H^+]$ change when the one drop was added?

61. Determine the pH of 100.0 mL of a 1.00 M HCl solution. Suppose you double the volume of the solution by adding water. What is the new pH? You double the volume once more with water. What is the new pH? If you continue to add more water, what is the maximum pH that can be reached? Explain your answer.

57. (a) HF is a weak acid; (b) HCl is a strong acid; (c) H_2SO_4 is a strong acid; (d) HNO_3 is a strong acid

58. (a) $[OH^-] = 0.000320\ M$; (b) $[OH^-] = 1.54 \times 10^{-8}\ M$; (c) $[OH^-] = 4.02 \times 10^{-7}\ M$

59. The solution will be acidic, with $[H^+] = 0.0458\ M$ and a pH of 1.339; $[OH^-] = 2.18 \times 10^{-13}\ M$

60. $[H^+] = 9.52 \times 10^{-3}\ M$; changed by a factor of 95,200

61. pH = 0.000; pH = 0.301; pH = 0.602; maximum pH = 7.000, since water contributes $1.00 \times 10^{-7}\ M\ H^+$

17 Equilibrium

	Section	Text Features & Components	Labs, Demonstrations & Activities
Teaching Segment 17A **1 block** **pp. 537–547**	17.1–17.2 How Chemical Reactions Occur Conditions That Affect Reaction Rates	**LP** Lesson Plans (Sec 17.1–17.5) **SE** Chemical Impact: Protecting the Ozone *p. 541*	**TE** Student Activity *pp. 538–539* **TE** Teaching Support: Demonstration *pp. 538–540* **LM** Experiment 73: Iodine Clock Reaction Lab Manual Report Sheets Teacher's Lab Guide
	17.3–17.4 Heterogeneous Reactions The Equilibrium Condition	**SE** Chemical Impact: Some Like It Hot: The Top Ten Spices *p. 543* **SE** Top Ten Antimicrobial Spices *p. 543*	**TE** Teaching Support: Demonstration *p. 541* **TE** Mini Demos *p. 542*
	17.5 Chemical Equilibrium: A Dynamic Condition		**SE** Chemistry in Action: Reaching Equilibrium: Are We There Yet? *p. 547* **SE** Chemistry in the Laboratory: Equilibrium Beads *pp. 568–569* **LM** Experiment 74: Equilibrium Beads Lab Manual Report Sheets Teacher's Lab Guide
Teaching Segment 17B **0.5 block** **pp. 548–554**	17.6–17.7 The Equilibrium Constant: An Introduction Heterogeneous Equilibria	**LP** Lesson Plans (Sec 17.6–17.7)	
	continued on next page		

continued on next page

Key **SE** Student Edition **TE** Teacher Edition **RP** Teacher Resource Package **LM** Lab Materials
LP Lesson Plans **AR** Additional Resources ◆ Florida Specific

Chapter Planning Guide

All Learners	Review & Assessment	Standards
TE Active Learning *p. 537* **TE** Teaching Tips *pp. 537, 538* Animation: The Gas Phase Reaction *p. 537* Transparency: Figures 17.2, 17.3, 17.4 Chemistry in Motion (14), (23) *p. 539* Video: Coffee Creamer Flammability • Iodine Clock Reaction *p. 539* **AR** Less Proficient Students *p. 33*	**SE** What if . . . *pp. 538–539* **SE** Key Terms *p. 569* **SE** Questions and Problems *p. 570*	**TE** **NSES** UCP1, UCP2, UCP3, A1, A2, B3, B6, E1, E2, F4, F6, G3 **SSS** SC.H.1.4.1, SC.H.1.4.4, SC.A.1.4.4, SC.G.2.4.2, SC.B.1.4.5, SC.H.3.4.2, SC.H.3.4.3, SC.H.3.4.4, SC.H.3.4.6
Chemistry in Motion (3), (14), (23) **TE** Using the Top Ten *p. 543* Animation: Equilibrium Decomposition of N_2O_4 *p. 544* **AR** Less Proficient Students *p. 33*	**SE** Key Terms *p. 569* **SE** Questions and Problems *p. 570*	
TE Teaching Tips *p. 545* **RP** Team Learning Worksheets (Section 17.1–17.5) *pp. 95–96* **AR** Less Proficient Students *p. 33*	**SE** Focus Questions (Sec 17.1–17.5) *p. 547* **SE** Questions and Problems *p. 570*	
TE Active Learning *p. 548* **TE** Teaching Tips *p. 549* **RP** Team Learning Worksheets (Sec 17.6–17.7) *pp. 97–98* **AR** Less Proficient Students *p. 33*	**TE** Additional Examples *pp. 548, 550, 553* **TE** Self Check *pp. 549, 554* **SE** Focus Questions (Sec 17.6–17.7) *p. 554* **SE** Key Terms *p. 569* **SE** Questions and Problems *pp. 570–571*	**TE** **NSES** UCP1, UCP2, UCP3, A1, A2, B3 **SSS** SC.C.2.4.2, SC.G.2.4.2

17 Equilibrium

Section	Text Features & Components	Labs, Demonstrations & Activities
Teaching Segment 17C **2 blocks** pp. 554–567 17.8 Le Châtelier's Principle ●	**LP** Lesson Plans (Sec 17.8–17. 10) **SE** Celebrity Chemical: Carbon Dioxide p. 555	**TE** Teaching Support: Demonstration pp. 554–555 **TE** Mini Demo pp. 556, 558, 560 **LM** Experiment 75: Le Chatelier's Principle Lab Manual Report Sheets Teacher's Lab Guide
17.9 Applications Involving the Equilibrium Constant ● ◗		**LM** Experiments 76–77 Lab Manual Report Sheets Teacher's Lab Guide
17.10 Solubility Equilibria ◗		

Key

SE Student Edition
TE Teacher Edition
RP Teacher Resource Package
LM Lab Materials
LP Lesson Plans
AR Additional Resources
◐ Florida Specific

Technology and Media

Transparencies
Figure 17.2, 17.3, 17.4

PowerPoint Slides

Animation
The Gas Phase Reactions of NO and Cl_2
Equilibrium Decomposition of N_2O_4

Video Coffee Creamer and Flammability Parts A–B • Iodine Clock Reaction • Gaseous Equilibrium of NO_2 and N_2O_4 and Temperature; and Pressure
Chemistry in Motion (3) Reactions of Metals with Acids • (14) Flammability of Powder • (23) Reaction Rate and Concentration

eEdition CD-ROM
Easy Planner CD-ROM
English Summaries CD
Spanish Summaries CD

Web Site classzone.com
McDougal Littell Test Generator

Chapter Planning Guide

All Learners	Review & Assessment	Standards
TE Active Learning *p. 554*	**TE** Additional Examples *pp. 557, 560–561*	**TE** **NSES** UCP1, UCP3, A1, A2, B3, C4, C5, E1, E2, F1, F4, F5
TE Teaching Tips *pp. 555, 559*	**SE** Self Check *pp. 558, 560, 562*	**SSS** SC.H.1.4.1, SC.H.1.4.3, SC.A.1.4.3, SC.A.1.4.4, SC.G.2.4.2, SC.H.3.4.3
▶ Video: Gaseous Equilibrium of NO_2 and N_2O_4 and Temperature *p. 561*	**SE** Key Terms *p. 569*	
AR Less Proficient Students *p. 33*	**SE** Questions and Problems *pp. 571–572*	
AR Less Proficient Students *p. 34*	**TE** Additional Examples *p. 563*	
	SE Questions and Problems *p. 572*	
RP Team Learning Worksheets (Sec 17.8–17.10) *pp. 99–100*	**TE** Additional Examples *pp. 565–566*	
AR Less Proficient Students *p. 34*	**SE** Self Check *pp. 565–567*	
	SE Focus Questions (Sec 17.8–17.10) *p. 567*	
	SE Key Terms *p. 569*	
	SE Questions and Problems *p. 572*	

Chapter Materials

TE Reading Strategy
AR English/Spanish Summaries *pp. 29–30*
RP Classroom Activities and Projects
AR Challenge Projects/Problems *p. 34*
AR Less Proficient Students *p. 34*
💿 English Summary Audio
💿 Spanish Summary Audio
RP Chapter Review Worksheets (Basic, Review, Challenge)

SE Chapter Summary *pp. 569–570*
SE Critical Thinking *p. 573*
RP Solutions Guide
RP Chapter Tests
RP Test Bank
🖥 McDougal Littell Test Generator
AR Standardized Test Practice
🌐 FCAT Test 5

17 Integrating Reading Strategies and Chemistry Concepts

Chapter 17: Critical Reading Skills

Discuss the importance of evaluating reading material by familiarizing the students with critical reading skills. Tell the students that responsible readers actively participate in the reading process and must determine the purpose and the credibility of the materials they are reading.

Evaluating Reading Materials

As an initial activity, distribute newspaper or magazine articles. As the students skim their articles, ask them to respond to the following.

- What is the main idea?
- What points support the main idea?
- Highlight the facts, examples, and details that the writer uses to support each point.
- What is the writer's purpose in writing the material?
- What conclusion does the writer want the reader to draw?

Discuss the ways that a writer can use words to influence the audience. Point out how a statement can be written in a way that is influential. Encourage the students to find articles that discuss the same topic, but that support opposing points of view. Have the students compare and contrast these related articles. Tell them to look for likenesses and differences in the approach to the claim and to the argument. You may wish to review that a claim is an opinion, a point of view, or an idea that is supported by examples, facts, or statistics. Emphasize that the examples, facts, or statistics provide the basis for reaching a particular conclusion.

Determining Credibility

Ask the students to choose which of the articles is most credible and to provide support for their choice. Stress the importance of evaluating the source of an article and caution the students against accepting a claim and an argument before they obtain this information. Encourage the students to note the credentials of the writer(s) of the material as well as the date on which the material was published. Tell the students that this information can be helpful when determining whether the material is outdated or biased. Allow time for the students to find this information about the writers of their articles. Ask whether anyone changed his or her mind about the credibility of the articles.

Scientific Journals, Textbooks, Research Papers

Distribute copies of an article from a scientific journal or research paper. Tell the students that just as they must evaluate the source and context of newspaper and magazine articles or advertisements, they must also do the same for a textbook, a technical article, or a research paper. Emphasize that although unsubstantiated claims and arguments are not expected in these types of materials, such items should be critically read, analyzed, and evaluated.

Show the students how to determine the publication date of the scientific article or paper, and discuss ways to find information about its author(s). Point out the reference section following the article, and encourage the students to refer to this section when analyzing the article's content. Explain that reading critically involves being aware of an author's purpose and style, rather than simply reading for facts and information. Caution the students to evaluate scientific materials carefully before using them as a reference.

Discuss with the students how our society relies on the knowledge of experts in many fields. Explore what actually qualifies a person as an expert in a particular field. Explain the basis for choosing the materials for this chemistry course. Point out the qualifications of the authors of this textbook. Show the students where they can find author and publication information in a textbook.

Internet Sources

Discuss ways of determining the credibility of Internet material. Warn the students that anybody can post information on the Internet and that no system is in place to verify that the information is reliable or that the author is an expert. Advise the students that information obtained from the Internet must be critically evaluated for source, point of view, and content.

Tell the students to use these tips to evaluate online sources.

- Consider the source of the information on the page you are viewing.
  - Look at the URL, or Web site address, as one way of considering where or how this information is provided. Material hosted by businesses or individuals will often end in ".com". Sites hosted by governmental organizations will often end in ".gov". Sites hosted by schools, colleges or universities often end in ".edu".
  - Follow links to other Web pages on the site to learn what is associated with the material.
  - Because all domain names must be registered, learn who registered the site and the name and address of the organization the site supports. Also note contact and server information.
  - Identify the host domain of the Web site by reducing the Web site address to the host's domain name, and evaluate the credibility of the host site. For example: here is a Web site about greenhouse gases: http://www.usda.gov/wps/portal/!ut/p/_s.7_0_A/7_0_1OB?contentidonly=true&contentid=event_11.xml. The host domain is http://www.usda.gov.
- Find out who wrote the material.
  - Conduct a search of the author's name. Enter the name in quotation marks in the search line of a familiar search engine.
  - Review the search results (other Web sites, articles, or books) for credibility.
  - Learn about the author's educational background and experience.
- Determine the purpose of the Web site.
  - What is the Web site trying to accomplish?
  - Why was the Web site created?

Project Ideas

Many students may find it challenging to evaluate textbooks, journals or newspapers for credibility and point of view. To help the students understand the process, consider assigning research projects in which the students research and present opposing points of view on scientific topics. For example, students can research opposing perspectives on global warming, elimination of chlorofluorocarbons, energy exploration in environmentally sensitive areas, or wildlife preservation policy.

Overview

In this Chapter our goals are for the students to:

- Understand the collision model of how chemical reactions occur

- Understand activation energy and how a catalyst speeds up a reaction

- Consider reactions with reactants and products in different phases

- Learn how equilibrium is established

- Learn about the characteristics of chemical equilibrium

- Understand the law of chemical equilibrium and how to calculate values for equilibrium constants

- Understand the role that liquids and solids play in constructing the equilibrium expression

- Learn to predict the changes that occur when a system at equilibrium is disturbed

- Learn to calculate equilibrium concentrations from equilibrium constants

- Learn to calculate the solubility product of a salt given its solubility, and vice versa

17 Equilibrium

Equilibrium can be analogous to traffic flowing both ways on the George Washington bridge between New Jersey and New York.

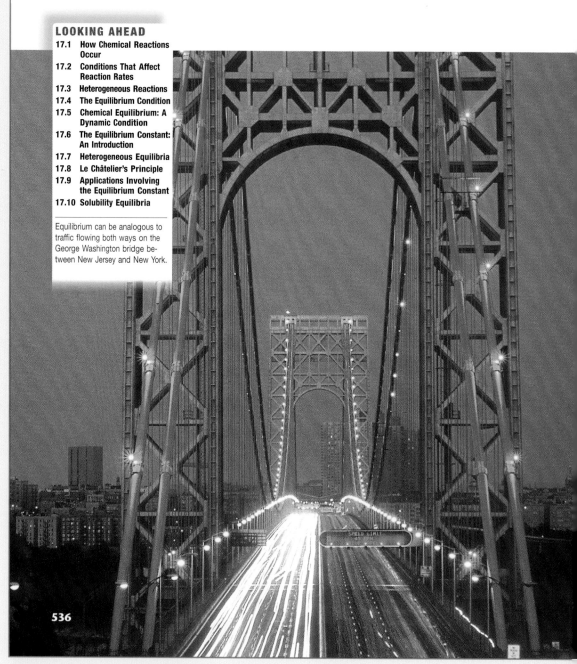

536

C hemistry is mostly about reactions—processes in which groups of atoms are reorganized. So far we have learned to describe chemical reactions by using balanced equations and to calculate amounts of reactants and products. However, there are many important characteristics of reactions that we have not yet considered.

For example, why do refrigerators prevent food from spoiling? That is, why do the chemical reactions that cause food to decompose occur more slowly at lower temperatures? On the other hand, how can a chemical manufacturer speed up a chemical reaction that runs too slowly to be economical?

Another question that arises is why chemical reactions carried out in a closed vessel appear to stop at a certain point. For example, when the reaction of reddish-brown nitrogen dioxide to form colorless dinitrogen tetroxide,

$$2NO_2(g) \rightarrow N_2O_4(g)$$
Reddish-brown   Colorless

is carried out in a closed container, the reddish-brown color at first fades but stops changing after a time and then stays the same color indefinitely if left undisturbed (see **Figure 17.1**). We will account for all of these important observations about reactions in this chapter.

Refrigeration prevents food spoilage.

(a)   (b)   (c)

Figure 17.1
(a) A sample containing a large quantity of reddish-brown NO_2 gas. (b) As the reaction to form colorless N_2O_4 occurs, the sample becomes lighter brown. (c) After equilibrium is reached [$2NO_2(g) \rightleftharpoons N_2O_4(g)$], the color remains the same.

 ## 17.1 How Chemical Reactions Occur

Objective: *To understand the collision model of how chemical reactions occur.*

I n writing the equation for a chemical reaction, we put the reactants on the left and the products on the right with an arrow between them. But how do the atoms in the reactants reorganize to form the products?

Chemists believe that molecules react by colliding with each other. Some collisions are violent enough to break bonds, allowing the reactants to rearrange to form the products. For example, consider the reaction

$$2BrNO(g) \rightleftharpoons 2NO(g) + Br_2(g)$$

17.1   How Chemical Reactions Occur   **537**

Themes
Models

Skills
Developing models, interpreting diagrams

Student Preparation
Assign the students to read Sections 17.1 to 17.5 and to answer the Focus Questions at the end of Section 17.5 before coming to class.

Active Learning
After introducing the material in Sections 17.1 to 17.5 in class, place the students in groups and have them work together on Sections 17.1–17.5: Team Learning Worksheet. Answers and/or discussion of these questions are located in the *Teacher Resources*.

TEACHING TIP

Use the molecular-level view of molecules to show students what is happening during a molecular collision. Figure 17.2 shows how a collision results in a chemical reaction.

USING TECHNOLOGY

 Animation and Video

Animation, The Gas Phase Reaction of NO and Cl_2

Figure 17.2
Visualizing the reaction 2BrNO(g) → 2NO(g) + Br₂(g). (a) Two BrNO molecules approach each other at high speeds. (b) The collision occurs. (c) The energy of the collision causes the Br—N bonds to break and allows the Br—Br bond to form. (d) The products: one Br₂ and two NO molecules.

USING TECHNOLOGY

  Figure 17.2

17.2 Section 17.2

Themes
Models

Skills
Developing models, making comparisons

Laboratory
Experiment 73:
Iodine Clock Reaction, Traditional

TEACHING TIPS

• Use Figure 17.3 to illustrate the energy changes that occur when the two BrNO molecules from Figure 17.2 interact.

• Compare the reaction curves from Figures 17.3 and 17.4. Emphasize the similarities between them. Also, point out that Figure 17.3 represents an exothermic reaction and Figure 17.4 represents an endothermic reaction. Discuss how we can tell from the graph whether the reaction is exothermic or endothermic.

WHAT IF Comments

Most collisions do not result in a chemical reaction because of the energy requirements and positioning of the molecules. If all collisions resulted in a chemical reaction, life would be extremely unstable. Virtually everything would happen at a much higher speed (including our aging). Students should appreciate the vast number and types of chemical reactions that are occurring all around them (especially in an atmosphere rich in oxygen).

STUDENT ACTIVITY

Kinetics of Lightsticks
Have students work in teams for this activity. Each team will need three lightsticks. Students should prepare a warm water bath (not to exceed 60 °C) and an ice bath. Once the baths are ready, each team should activate one lightstick (the control). The

which we think occurs as shown in **Figure 17.2.** Notice that the Br—N bonds in the two BrNO molecules must be broken and a new Br—Br bond must be formed during a collision for the reactants to become products.

The idea that reactions occur during molecular collisions, which is called the **collision model,** explains many characteristics of chemical reactions. For example, it explains why a reaction proceeds faster if the concentrations of the reacting molecules are increased (higher concentrations lead to more collisions and therefore to more reaction events). The collision model also explains why reactions go faster at higher temperatures, as we will see in the next section.

17.2 Conditions That Affect Reaction Rates

Objectives: *To understand activation energy.*
To understand how a catalyst speeds up a reaction.

It is easy to see why reactions speed up when the *concentrations* of reacting molecules are increased: higher concentrations (more molecules per unit volume) lead to more collisions and so to more reaction events. But reactions also speed up when the *temperature* is increased. Why? The answer lies in the fact that not all collisions possess enough energy to break bonds. A minimum energy called the **activation energy** (E_a) is needed for a reaction to occur (see **Figure 17.3**). If a given collision possesses an energy greater than E_a, that collision can result in a reaction. If a collision has an energy less than E_a, the molecules will bounce apart unchanged.

The reason that a reaction occurs faster as the temperature is increased is that the speeds of the molecules increase with temperature. So at higher temperatures, the average collision is more energetic. This makes it more likely that a given collision will possess enough energy to break bonds and to produce the molecular rearrangements needed for a reaction to occur.

| Higher temperatures | Higher speeds | More high-energy collisions | More collisions that break bonds | Faster reaction |

Is it possible to speed up a reaction without changing the temperature or the reactant concentrations? Yes, by using something called a **catalyst,** *a*

538 Chapter 17 Equilibrium

TEACHING SUPPORT
Demonstration

Temperature and Reaction Rate

Materials
0.005 *M* KMnO₄
0.75 *M* H₂C₂O₄ (saturated)
12 test tubes
2 thermometers
Water bath (at least a 600-mL beaker, one-third full of water)

Hot plate

Preparation Place 20 mL KMnO₄ in each of six test tubes. Place 20 mL H₂C₂O₄ in each of six additional test tubes. Set up the water bath. Place all test tubes in an empty large beaker.

Procedure Ask a student to determine room temperature. Record this temperature on the board. Place 10 test tubes (5 of each solution) in the water bath and begin heating the water.

Assign one student to keep track of the temperature of the water bath. The student should tell you when the temperature of the water reaches 10 degrees above room temperature. While waiting for the water bath to heat, run the reaction at room temperature. Using the remaining test tube of KMnO₄ and the remaining test tube of H₂C₂O₄, explain that you will mix the solutions and students

Figure 17.3
When molecules collide, a certain minimum energy called the activation energy (E_a) is needed for a reaction to occur. If the energy contained in a collision of two BrNO molecules is greater than E_a, the reaction can go "over the hump" to form products. If the collision energy is less than E_a, the colliding molecules bounce apart unchanged.

WHAT IF?

Most modern refrigerators have an internal temperature of 45 °F.

What if refrigerators were set at 55 °F in the factory? How would this change affect our lives?

Cutaways of catalytic converters used in automobiles.

substance that speeds up a reaction without being consumed. This may sound too good to be true, but it is a very common occurrence. In fact, you would not be alive now if your body did not contain thousands of catalysts called **enzymes.** Enzymes allow our bodies to speed up complicated reactions that would be too slow to sustain life at normal body temperatures. For example, the enzyme carbonic anhydrase speeds up the reaction between carbon dioxide and water

$$CO_2(g) + H_2O(l) \rightleftharpoons H^+(aq) + HCO_3^-(aq)$$

to help prevent an excess accumulation of carbon dioxide in our blood.

Although we cannot consider the details here, a catalyst works because it provides a new pathway for the reaction—a pathway that has a lower activation energy than the original pathway, as illustrated in **Figure 17.4.** Because of the lower activation energy, more collisions will have enough energy to allow a reaction. This in turn leads to a faster reaction.

A very important example of a reaction involving a catalyst occurs in our atmosphere; it is the breakdown of ozone, O_3, which is catalyzed by chlorine atoms. Ozone is one constituent of the earth's upper atmosphere that is especially crucial, because it absorbs harmful high-energy radiation from the sun. There are natural processes that result in both the formation and the destruction of ozone in the upper atmosphere. The natural balance of all these opposing processes has resulted in an amount of ozone that has

Figure 17.4
Comparison of the activation energies for an uncatalyzed reaction (E_a) and for the same reaction with a catalyst present (E'_a). Note that a catalyst works by lowering the activation energy for a reaction.

17.2 Conditions That Affect Reaction Rates   **539**

will time the reaction until the color has changed to pale yellow with no remaining purple. The timer should begin as soon as the solutions make contact. Pour the oxalic acid into the potassium permanganate solution. To mix pour the solutions back and forth twice. Be consistent in all trials. Record the time of reaction on the board. Place the reacted test tube back in the empty large beaker. Re-

peat this procedure with a second pair of test tubes when the temperature of the water bath is 10 degrees higher than room temperature. Record both the temperature and the time on the board. Continue to repeat the procedure at 10-degree intervals until all test tubes are reacted.

Teaching Notes You can graph time versus temperature for this reaction on the board as you do

the demonstration. Ask students to determine what is happening to the rate of the reaction as the temperature increases. This reaction occurs at times that are halved for every 10-degree increase in temperature. It is actually a study in complex kinetics, but can be used to illustrate the effect of temperature on reaction rate for beginning classes. The Mn^{2+} ion catalyzes the reac-
(continued)

team should then activate the other lightsticks, placing one in the warm water and one in the ice bath. Have students compare the different lightsticks. Which is glowing the brightest? What does this brighter light mean? Which is dimmest? Why? Which should stop glowing first? Why?

TEACHING TIP

Remind students that the kinetic energy of a collection of molecules is directly proportional to the temperature (K).

USING TECHNOLOGY

 Figure 17.3

 Figure 17.4

WHAT IF Comments

At 55 °F reactions will occur at a much faster rate than they do at 45 °F. The spoiling of food is a chemical reaction, so food would spoil more quickly. This problem would require us to buy a smaller amount of perishable food at one time.

USING TECHNOLOGY

Animation and Video
Video, *Chemistry in Motion*, Demonstration 14, The Flammability of Powder;
Video, *Chemistry in Motion*, Demonstration 23, Reaction Rate and Concentration

Animation and Video
Video, Coffee Creamer Flammability;
Video, Iodine Clock Reaction

Figure 17.5
Data from the Total Ozone Mapping Spectrometer (TOMS) Earth Probe for the month of October, 1999. Areas of depleted ozone over the Antarctic are shown in blue.

October 1999

Although O atoms are too reactive to exist near the earth's surface, they do exist in the upper atmosphere.

been relatively constant over the years. However, the ozone level now seems to be decreasing, especially over Antarctica **(Figure 17.5)**, apparently because chlorine atoms act as catalysts for the decomposition of ozone to oxygen by the following pair of reactions:

$$Cl + O_3 \rightarrow ClO + O_2$$
$$O + ClO \rightarrow Cl + O_2$$
$$\overline{\text{Sum: } Cl + O_3 + O + ClO \rightarrow ClO + O_2 + Cl + O_2}$$

When species that appear on both sides of the equation are canceled, the end result is the reaction

$$O + O_3 \rightarrow 2O_2$$

Notice that a chlorine atom is used up in the first reaction but a chlorine atom is formed again by the second reaction. Therefore, the amount of chlorine does not change as the overall process occurs. This means that the chlorine atom is a true catalyst: it participates in the process but is not consumed. Estimates show that *one chlorine atom can catalyze the destruction of about one million ozone molecules per second.*

The chlorine atoms that promote this damage to the ozone layer are present because of pollution. Specifically, they come from the decomposition of compounds called Freons, such as CF_2Cl_2, which have been widely used in refrigerators and air conditioners. The Freons have leaked into the atmosphere, where they are decomposed by light to produce chlorine atoms and other substances. As a result, the manufacture of Freons was banned by agreement among the nations of the world as of the end of 1996. Substitute compounds are now being used in most countries in newly manufactured refrigerators and air conditioners.

540 Chapter 17 Equilibrium

TEACHING TIPS

Now is an excellent time to discuss the use of catalysts. Catalytic converters in automobiles use metals such as palladium and platinum to convert uncombusted hydrocarbons into carbon dioxide and water. The metals are used repeatedly in these processes. In the human body, enzymes act as catalysts, thereby speeding up reactions that would take hours in the laboratory to fractions of a second in the body.

(continued)
tion, which contributes to the increase in rate. This fact does not need to be discussed to effectively perform the demonstration. Times for the reaction will vary from about 4 minutes at room temperature to about 5 seconds at the highest temperature.

540

CHEMICAL IMPACT

Science, Technology, and Society

Protecting the Ozone

Chlorofluorocarbons (CFCs) are ideal compounds for refrigerators and air conditioners because they are nontoxic and noncorrosive. However, the chemical inertness of these substances, once thought to be their major virtue, turns out to be their fatal flaw. When these compounds leak into the atmosphere, as they inevitably do, they are so unreactive they persist there for decades. Eventually these CFCs reach altitudes where ultraviolet light causes them to decompose, producing chlorine atoms that promote the destruction of the ozone in the stratosphere (see discussion in Section 17.2). Because of this problem, the world's industrialized nations have signed an agreement (called the Montreal Protocol) that banned CFCs in 1996 (with a 10-year grace period for developing nations). So we must find substitutes for the CFCs—and fast.

In fact, the search for substitutes is now well under way. Worldwide production of CFCs has already decreased to half of

A modern refrigerator, one of many appliances that now use HFC-134a. This compound is replacing CFCs, which lead to the destruction of the atmospheric ozone.

the 1986 level of 1.13 million metric tons. One strategy for replacing the CFCs has been to switch to similar compounds that contain carbon and hydrogen atoms substituted for chlorine atoms. For example, the United States appliance industry has switched from Freon-12 (CF_2Cl_2) to the compound CH_2FCH_3 (called HFC-134a) for home refrigerators, and most of the new cars and trucks sold in the United States have air conditioners that employ HFC-134a. Converting the 140 million autos currently on the road in the United States that use CF_2Cl_2 will pose a major headache, but experience suggests that replacement of Freon-12 with HFC-134a is less expensive than was originally feared.

A related environmental issue involves replacing the halons for fire-fighting applications. In particular, scientists are seeking an effective replacement for CF_3Br (halon-1301), the nontoxic "magic gas" used to flood enclosed spaces such as offices, aircraft, race cars, and military tanks in case of fire. The compound CF_3I, which appears to have a lifetime in the atmosphere of only a few days, looks like a promising candidate. Much more research on the toxicology and ozone-depleting properties of CF_3I will be required, however, before it receives government approval as a halon substitute.

The chemical industry has responded amazingly fast to the ozone depletion emergency. It is encouraging that we can act rapidly when an environmental crisis occurs. Now we need to get better at keeping the environment at a higher priority as we plan for the future.

Use this Chemical Impact as an opportunity to interact with the earth science department. Have students research the hole in the ozone layer to determine its effects on plant and animal life. Is the hole in the ozone continuing to grow? Have students find out what products in our society still contain chlorofluorocarbons. Ask them to explain why using these products in the United States causes problems in Antarctica. This discussion provides an opportunity to integrate the gases chapter with this chapter.

17.3 Heterogeneous Reactions

Objective: *To consider reactions with reactants or products in different phases.*

Most of the reactions we have considered in this text occur in one phase. That is, the reactants and products are all gases or the reaction occurs with all reactants and products dissolved in a solution. Reactions involving only one phase are called **homogeneous reactions.**

Many other important reactions involve reactants in two phases. These reactions are **heterogeneous reactions.** An example of a heterogeneous reaction is zinc metal reacting with hydrochloric acid to produce hydrogen gas and aqueous zinc chloride:

$$Zn(s) + 2HCl(aq) \rightarrow H_2(g) + ZnCl_2(aq)$$

17.3 Heterogeneous Reactions **541**

Section 17.3

Themes
Organization, Patterns of Change

Skills
Making comparisons, making predictions

USING TECHNOLOGY

Animation and Video

Chemistry in Motion, **Demonstration 3, Reactions of Metals with Acids.** This demonstration illustrates several heterogeneous reactions.

TEACHING SUPPORT
Demonstration

Visualizing a Reaction

Materials
$KNaC_4H_4O_6$ crystals
$CoCl_2$ crystals
400-mL beaker
6% hydrogen peroxide
Hot plate
Teaspoon

Preparation Place 6 g of

$KNaC_4H_4O_6$ crystals in the beaker. Add 100 mL distilled water and dissolve the crystals.

Procedure Warm the solution of $KNaC_4H_4O_6$ to about 60 °C. Add 40 mL of hydrogen peroxide. Add a few crystals ($\frac{1}{2}$ teaspoon) of $CoCl_2$ crystals to the solution. A vigorous reaction occurs, and the solution turns green with lots of bubbling. Eventually the solution will return to its original pink color.

Teaching Notes This reaction involves the oxidation of tartrate by the peroxide to form $CO_2(g)$, $O_2(g)$ and oxalic acid. The green color occurs because of the activated complex for the reaction. The cobalt(II) ion is the catalyst for the reaction. The pink color at the beginning and end of the reaction indicates the presence of the catalyst [$Co^{2+}(aq)$].

Figure 17.6
(a) The reaction between Zn and HCl(*aq*). (b) Molecular-level picture of the reaction.

(a)   (b)

This reaction is shown in **Figure 17.6.** The speed of this reaction depends on the surface area of the Zn available to react with H⁺ ions from the solution. Large pieces of zinc are associated with a relatively slow reaction; if the zinc is ground up, however, the reaction is greatly accelerated by the increased surface area of the zinc.

Another example of the effect of surface area on the rate of a heterogeneous reaction is the explosive combustion of grain dust. Although grains of wheat will burn, the combustion reaction is relatively slow and controlled. In a storage silo, however, the tiny bits of dry plant materials ("grain dust") that become airborne as grain is poured into the silo can combust explosively if a spark occurs. The force of these explosions is quite devastating (see **Figure 17.7**). The reaction of grain dust occurs explosively because the tiny sizes of the dust particles expose a tremendous amount of surface area to the oxygen in the air.

Figure 17.7
A grain elevator near Haysville, Kansas was severely damaged by a grain dust explosion.

542   Chapter 17   Equilibrium

Factors That Affect Reaction Rates

Nature of Reactants: Substances vary greatly in their tendency to react depending on their bond strengths and structures.

Concentration (Pressure): The rate of a homogeneous reaction depends on the number of collisions that occur between reactants. Reaction rates typically increase as concentration (solution reactions) or pressure (gaseous reactions) increases.

Temperature: Because increased temperature accelerates reactant speeds, and thus increases the number of high-energy collisions, reaction rates increase with an increase in temperature.

Surface Area: For heterogeneous reactions, reaction rates increase with increased surface area.

CHEMICAL IMPACT

Consumer Connection

Some Like It Hot: The Top Ten Spices

Have you ever noticed that a direct relationship exists between the temperature of a place and the spiciness of its food? That is, the closer a country is to the equator, the spicier its food tends to be. Think about the difference between Scandinavian food, which uses relatively few spices, and Thai food, which often is extremely "hot." An extensive study headed by biologist Paul Sherman of Cornell University has actually confirmed this relationship. Sherman and his students reviewed 4600 recipes from more than 90 cookbooks of traditional food from 36 countries and found that the amount of spicing is directly proportional to the warmth of the country's climate.

What's responsible for this interesting correlation? Kinetics. Food spoils by chemical reactions, and chemical reactions occur much more rapidly at higher temperatures. That's why we have refrigerators. Keeping food cold makes it last much longer because the bacteria that cause food to spoil grow much more slowly at low temperatures. In ancient times before refrigeration existed, people had to find other ways to preserve their food. Obviously, this issue would be a much greater problem near the equator than near the Arctic Circle. People discovered that certain spices are very effective at killing bacteria. The Top Ten table lists the top ten spices in order of their antimicrobial (bacteria-killing) ability. It seems clear that "hot" spices protect food against hot temperatures.

Garlic is the most popular spice.

TOP TEN
Antimicrobial Spices
1. Garlic
2. Onion
3. Allspice
4. Oregano
5. Thyme
6. Cinnamon
7. Tarragon
8. Cumin
9. Cloves
10. Lemon grass

17.4 The Equilibrium Condition

Objective: *To learn how equilibrium is established.*

*E*quilibrium is a word that implies balance or steadiness. When we say that someone is maintaining his or her equilibrium, we are describing a state of balance among various opposing forces. The term is used in a similar but more specific way in chemistry. Chemists define **equilibrium** as the *exact balancing of two processes, one of which is the opposite of the other.*

17.4   The Equilibrium Condition   **543**

USING TECHNOLOGY

Animation and Video

Chemistry in Motion, Demonstration 14, Flammability of a Powder. This demonstration shows the difference in reaction speed of a fine dust and a solid chunk.

Chemistry in Motion, Demonstration 23, Reaction Rate and Concentration. This demonstration shows the effect of concentration on the rate of a reaction.

Integrating the CHEMICAL IMPACT

Some Like It Hot: The Top Ten Spices

Have students research methods for preserving food without refrigeration. This project could be done in connection with a social science study.

Students could also undertake a project to determine the effectiveness of refrigeration in controlling the growth of microbes. This project could be used as a connection to biology. Have students obtain two samples of fresh food. One should be covered and refrigerated, the other covered but not refrigerated. Test each sample for microbes daily by using biological techniques for culturing microbes.

Using the TOP TEN

Students could choose a spice and write its autobiography, including its source, chemical structure, favorite recipe, uses in alternative medicine, and other relevant information.

If you are ready for a classroom adventure, students could bring in samples of different foods containing the spices for taste comparisons.

Section 17.4

Themes
Organization, Patterns of Change

Skills
Applying concepts, making comparisons

Chapter 17   Equilibrium   **543**

Evaporation

Condensation

We first encountered the concept of equilibrium in Section 14.4, when we described the way vapor pressure develops over a liquid in a closed container (see Figure 14.10). This equilibrium process is summarized in **Figure 17.8.** The *equilibrium state* occurs when the rate of evaporation exactly equals the rate of condensation.

So far in this textbook we have usually assumed that reactions proceed to completion—that is, until one of the reactants "runs out." Indeed, many reactions *do* proceed essentially to completion. For such reactions we can assume that the reactants are converted to products until the limiting reactant is completely consumed. On the other hand, there are many chemical reactions that "stop" far short of completion when they are allowed to take place in a closed container. An example is the reaction of nitrogen dioxide to form dinitrogen tetroxide.

$$NO_2(g) + NO_2(g) \rightarrow N_2O_4(g)$$
Reddish-brown   Colorless

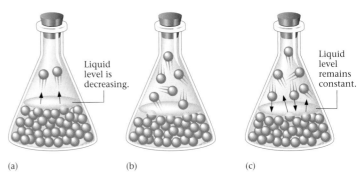

Liquid level is decreasing.

Liquid level remains constant.

(a)   (b)   (c)

Figure 17.8
The establishment of the equilibrium vapor pressure over a liquid in a closed container.
(a) At first there is a net transfer of molecules from the liquid state to the vapor state.
(b) After a while, the amount of the substance in the vapor state becomes constant—both the pressure of the vapor and the level of the liquid stay the same. This is the equilibrium state. (c) The equilibrium state is very dynamic. The vapor pressure and liquid level remain constant because exactly the same number of molecules escape the liquid as return to it.

TEACHING TIPS

• Point out that equilibrium can be reached only in closed systems. Such systems include gases in closed containers and ions in solution (since the ions cannot escape). In industry processes rarely reach equilibrium. Instead, they are designed to maximize the amount of product formed (and avoid the limitation of equilibrium) by removing the product as it is formed.

• Students often think that equilibrium is a static condition. Emphasize that, although at the macroscopic level things appear to be constant at equilibrium, at the molecular level chemical reactions continue to occur. The rates of the forward and reverse reactions are equal.

• Emphasize that equilibrium is *not* a condition in which the reactants and products are present in equal amounts. The balance is between the rates of the forward and reverse reactions.

USING TECHNOLOGY

Animation and Video
Animation, Equilibrium Decompositin of N_2O_4

The reactant NO_2 is a reddish-brown gas, and the product N_2O_4 is a colorless gas. Imagine an experiment where pure NO_2 is placed in an empty, sealed glass vessel at 25 °C. The initial dark brown color will decrease in intensity as the NO_2 is converted to colorless N_2O_4 (see Figure 17.1). However, even over a long period of time, the contents of the reaction vessel do not become colorless. Instead, the intensity of the brown color eventually becomes constant, which means that the concentration of NO_2 is no longer changing. This simple observation is a clear indication that the reaction has "stopped" short of completion. In fact, the reaction has not stopped. Rather, the system has reached **chemical equilibrium,** *a dynamic state where the concentrations of all reactants and products remain constant.*

This situation is similar to the one where a liquid in a closed container develops a constant vapor pressure, except that in this case two opposite chemical reactions are involved. When pure NO_2 is first placed in the closed flask, there is no N_2O_4 present. As collisions between NO_2 molecules occur, N_2O_4 is formed and the concentration of N_2O_4 in the container increases. However, the reverse reaction can also occur. A given N_2O_4 molecule can decompose into two NO_2 molecules.

$$N_2O_4(g) \rightarrow NO_2(g) + NO_2(g)$$

That is, chemical reactions are *reversible;* they can occur in either direction. We usually indicate this fact by using double arrows.

$$2NO_2(g) \underset{\text{Reverse}}{\overset{\text{Forward}}{\rightleftharpoons}} N_2O_4(g)$$

In this case the double arrows mean that either two NO_2 molecules can combine to form an N_2O_4 molecule (the *forward* reaction) or an N_2O_4 molecule can decompose to give two NO_2 molecules (the *reverse* reaction).

Equilibrium is reached whether pure NO_2, pure N_2O_4, or a mixture of NO_2 and N_2O_4 is initially placed in a closed container. In any of these cases, conditions will eventually be reached in the container such that N_2O_4 is being formed and is decomposing at exactly the same rate. This leads to chemical equilibrium, a dynamic situation where the concentrations of reactants and products remain the same indefinitely, as long as the conditions are not changed.

17.5 Chemical Equilibrium: A Dynamic Condition

Objective: *To learn about the characteristics of chemical equilibrium.*

Equilibrium is a dynamic situation.

Because no changes occur in the concentrations of reactants or products in a reaction system at equilibrium, it may appear that everything has stopped. However, this is not the case. On the molecular level there is frantic activity. Equilibrium is not static but is a highly *dynamic* situation. Consider again the analogy between chemical equilibrium and two island cities connected by a single bridge. Suppose the traffic flow on the bridge is the same in both directions. It is obvious that there is motion (we can see the cars traveling across the bridge), but the number of cars in each city does not change because there is an equal flow of cars entering and leaving. The result is no *net* change in the number of cars in each of the two cities.

Section 17.5

Themes
Organization, Patterns of Change

Skills
Making predictions, interpreting data, drawing conclusions

Laboratory
Experiment 74:
Equilibrium Beads, In Text

TEACHING TIP

The concept of equilibrium is one of the most difficult for students to understand. Proceed slowly and use many examples in this chapter.

(a)   (b)   (c)   (d)

Key:

CO_2

CO

H_2

H_2O

Figure 17.9
The reaction of H_2O and CO to form CO_2 and H_2 as time passes. (a) Equal numbers of moles of H_2O and CO are mixed in a closed container. (b) The reaction begins to occur, and some products (H_2 and CO_2) are formed. (c) The reaction continues as time passes and more reactants are changed to products. (d) Although time continues to pass, the numbers of reactant and product molecules are the same as in (c). No further changes are seen as time continues to pass. The system has reached equilibrium.

CHEMISTRY

A double arrow ($\rightleftharpoons$) is used to show that a reaction is occurring in both directions.

To see how this concept applies to chemical reactions, let's consider the reaction between steam and carbon monoxide in a closed vessel at a high temperature where the reaction takes place rapidly.

$$H_2O(g) + CO(g) \rightleftharpoons H_2(g) + CO_2(g)$$

Assume that the same number of moles of gaseous CO and gaseous H_2O are placed in a closed vessel and allowed to react **(Figure 17.9a).**

When CO and H_2O, the reactants, are mixed, they immediately begin to react to form the products, H_2 and CO_2. This leads to a decrease in the concentrations of the reactants, but the concentrations of the products, which were initially at zero, are increasing **(Figure 17.9b).** After a certain period of time, the concentrations of reactants and products no longer change at all—equilibrium has been reached **(Figure 17.9c and d).** Unless the system is somehow disturbed, no further changes in the concentrations will occur.

Why does equilibrium occur? We saw earlier in this chapter that molecules react by colliding with one another, and that the more collisions, the faster the reaction. This is why the speed of a reaction depends on concentrations. In this case the concentrations of H_2O and CO are lowered as the forward reaction occurs—that is, as products are formed.

$$H_2O + CO \rightarrow H_2 + CO_2$$

As the concentrations of the reactants decrease, the forward reaction slows down **(Figure 17.10).** But as in the traffic-on-the-bridge analogy, there is also movement in the reverse direction.

$$H_2 + CO_2 \rightarrow H_2O + CO$$

Initially in this experiment, no H_2 and CO_2 are present, so this reverse reaction cannot occur. However, as the forward reaction proceeds, the concentrations of H_2 and CO_2 build up and the speed (or rate) of the reverse reaction increases (Figure 17.10) as the forward reaction slows down. Eventually the concentrations reach levels at which *the rate of the forward reaction equals the rate of the reverse reaction*. The system has reached equilibrium.

546 Chapter 17 Equilibrium

Figure 17.10
The changes with time in the rates of the forward and reverse reactions for $H_2O(g) + CO(g) \rightleftharpoons H_2(g) + CO_2(g)$ when equal numbers of moles of $H_2O(g)$ and $CO(g)$ are mixed. At first, the rate of the forward reaction decreases and the rate of the reverse reaction increases. Equilibrium is reached when the forward rate and the reverse rate become the same.

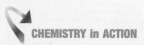
Reaching Equilibrium: Are We There Yet?

Materials Each student/group will need two large containers (plastic milk jugs cut in half work well), a large cup (15 oz), a small cup (5 oz), water, and a marker.

Purpose Students will better understand that chemical equilibrium is a dynamic process even when it appears to be static (it is microscopically dynamic and macroscopically static).

Discussion Students sometimes have difficulty grasping the idea that chemical equilibrium is a dynamic condition. This confusion makes sense because we usually think of equilibrium as a balance, and something that is balanced is not moving. This discussion reveals the benefits of taking a microscopic approach to studying chemistry; that is, a system at equilibrium may appear to the human eye to be unmoving, but at a molecular level it is dynamic. The balance is between the rates of the forward and reverse reactions.

The number of transfers will vary, although equilibrium should be achieved within several minutes.

Focus Questions

Sections 17.1–17.5

1. How does a catalyst speed up a chemical reaction?

2. Use collision theory to explain why reactions should occur more slowly at lower temperatures.

3. Explain how grinding a solid in a heterogeneous reaction can speed up the reaction. Use collision theory in your answer.

4. What is equal at equilibrium?

5. At the macroscopic level a system at equilibrium appears to be unchanging. Is it also unchanging at the molecular level? Explain.

CHEMISTRY in ACTION

Reaching Equilibrium: Are We There Yet?

1. Fill two large containers with different amounts of water. (Plastic milk jugs cut in half horizontally work well.) You will also need a large cup, a small cup, a marker, and a partner.

2. Mark the level of water on the outside of each container.

3. Each person should do the following using his or her container:
   a. Fill the cup as much as possible by dipping it into the container.
   b. Pour the cup of water into your partner's container.

4. Repeat step 3 until the level of water in each container is no longer changing. It is important that the same number of transfers occur in each direction.

5. Make five additional transfers as you did in step 3. Observe what happens to the water levels.

6. How many transfers were required until the water levels stopped changing?

7. Why does the level of water in each container stop changing? How is this situation similar to chemical equilibrium?

8. Even after the volume of water in each container stopped changing, water was still being transferred from one container to another. How is this situation similar to chemical equilibrium?

Focus Questions   **547**

Answers to Focus Questions

1. A catalyst provides a new pathway with a lower activation energy for a chemical reaction. Thus, at a given temperature, more molecules have enough energy to react. This catalysis speeds up the chemical reaction.

2. At lower temperatures molecules have a lower average kinetic energy. Thus fewer molecules will have the necessary activation energy for the chemical reaction. Since only molecules having this energy actually react, the chemical reaction will proceed at a slower rate.

3. Grinding a solid increases its surface area. Since a chemical reaction can occur only when the molecules collide, increasing the surface area of a reactant increases the number of collisions that this substance has with other molecules (because more of these molecules are on the surface). More collisions increase the chemical reaction.

4. The rates of the forward and the reverse reactions are equal at equilibrium.

5. At the microscopic level chemical reactions continue to occur at equilibrium. The rates of the forward and reverse reactions are equal but both are still occurring. The system continues to change (the molecules continue to interact) at a molecular level.

TEACHING TIPS

- Be sure to use balanced chemical equations, including states for each chemical species, in this section. In the next section we discuss heterogeneous equilibria and students will need to distinguish among the states of the chemicals.

- Once students understand how to set up the equilibrium expression for a reaction, you can begin to talk about calculations involving the expression. It is important to distinguish between initial conditions and equilibrium conditions when students begin calculations.

Additional Examples

Write the equilibrium expression for the following reactions.

1. $CH_3OH(g) \rightleftharpoons$
$CH_2O(g) + H_2(g)$
$K = [CH_2O(g)][H_2(g)] / [CH_3OH(g)]$

2. $4NH_3(g) + 5O_2(g) \rightleftharpoons$
$4NO(g) + 6H_2O(g)$
$K = [NO(g)]^4[H_2O(g)]^6 / [NH_3(g)]^4[O_2(g)]^5$

17.6 The Equilibrium Constant: An Introduction

Objective: *To understand the law of chemical equilibrium and to learn how to calculate values for the equilibrium constant.*

Science is based on the results of experiments. The development of the equilibrium concept is typical. On the basis of their observations of many chemical reactions, two Norwegian chemists, Cato Maximilian Guldberg and Peter Waage, proposed in 1864 the **law of chemical equilibrium** (originally called the *law of mass action*) as a general description of the equilibrium condition. Guldberg and Waage postulated that for a reaction of the type

$$aA + bB \rightleftharpoons cC + dD$$

where A, B, C, and D represent chemical species and *a*, *b*, *c*, and *d* are their coefficients in the balanced equation, the law of chemical equilibrium is represented by the following **equilibrium expression:**

$$K = \frac{[C]^c[D]^d}{[A]^a[B]^b}$$

CHEMISTRY
Square brackets, [ ], indicate concentration units of mol/L.

The square brackets indicate the concentrations of the chemical species *at equilibrium* (in units of mol/L), and K is a constant called the **equilibrium constant.** Note that the equilibrium expression is a special ratio of the concentrations of the products to the concentrations of the reactants. Each concentration is raised to a power corresponding to its coefficient in the balanced equation.

The law of chemical equilibrium as proposed by Guldberg and Waage is based on experimental observations. Experiments on many reactions showed that the equilibrium condition could always be described by this special ratio, called the equilibrium expression.

To see how to construct an equilibrium expression, consider the reaction where ozone changes to oxygen:

$$\underset{\text{Reactant}}{\overset{\text{Coefficient}}{2O_3(g)}} \rightleftharpoons \underset{\text{Product}}{\overset{\text{Coefficient}}{3O_2(g)}}$$

To obtain the equilibrium expression, we place the concentration of the product in the numerator and the concentration of the reactant in the denominator.

$$\frac{[O_2]}{[O_3]} \quad \begin{array}{l} \leftarrow \text{Product} \\ \leftarrow \text{Reactant} \end{array}$$

Then we use the coefficients as powers.

$$K = \frac{[O_2]^3}{[O_3]^2} \quad \text{Coefficients become powers}$$

Example 17.1

Writing Equilibrium Expressions

Write the equilibrium expression for the following reactions.

a. $H_2(g) + F_2(g) \rightleftharpoons 2HF(g)$ **b.** $N_2(g) + 3H_2(g) \rightleftharpoons 2NH_3(g)$

548   Chapter 17   Equilibrium

Applying the law of chemical equilibrium, we place products over reactants (using square brackets to denote concentrations in units of moles per liter) and raise each concentration to the power that corresponds to the coefficient in the balanced chemical equation.

MATH

A number raised to a power of 1 shows no exponent:

$$x^1 = x$$

a. $K = \dfrac{[HF]^2}{[H_2][F_2]}$ ← Product (coefficient of 2 becomes power of 2)
← Reactants (coefficients of 1 become powers of 1)

Note that when a coefficient (power) of 1 occurs, it is not written but is understood.

b. $K = \dfrac{[NH_3]^2}{[N_2][H_2]^3}$

✓ **Self-Check Exercise 17.1**

Write the equilibrium expression for the following reaction.

$$4NH_3(g) + 7O_2(g) \rightleftharpoons 4NO_2(g) + 6H_2O(g)$$

What does the equilibrium expression mean? It means that, for a given reaction at a given temperature, the special ratio of the concentrations of the products to reactants defined by the equilibrium expression will always be equal to the same number—namely, the equilibrium constant K. For example, consider a series of experiments on the ammonia synthesis reaction

$$N_2(g) + 3H_2(g) \rightleftharpoons 2NH_3(g)$$

carried out at 500 °C to measure the concentrations of N_2, H_2, and NH_3 present at equilibrium. The results of these experiments are shown in **Table 17.1**. In this table, subscript zeros next to square brackets are used to indicate *initial concentrations:* the concentrations of reactants and products originally mixed together before any reaction has occurred.

Consider the results of experiment I. One mole each of N_2 and H_2 were sealed into a 1-L vessel at 500 °C and allowed to reach chemical equilibrium.

TABLE 17.1

Results of Three Experiments for the Reaction $N_2(g) + 3H_2(g) \rightleftharpoons 2NH_3(g)$ at 500 °C

Experiment	Initial Concentrations			Equilibrium Concentrations			$\dfrac{[NH_3]^2}{[N_2][H_2]^3} = K^*$
	$[N_2]_0$	$[H_2]_0$	$[NH_3]_0$	$[N_2]$	$[H_2]$	$[NH_3]$	
I	1.000 M	1.000 M	0	0.921 M	0.763 M	0.157 M	$\dfrac{(0.157)^2}{(0.921)(0.763)^3} = 0.0602$
II	0	0	1.000 M	0.399 M	1.197 M	0.203 M	$\dfrac{(0.203)^2}{(0.399)(1.197)^3} = 0.0602$
III	2.00 M	1.00 M	3.00 M	2.59 M	2.77 M	1.82 M	$\dfrac{(1.82)^2}{(2.59)(2.77)^3} = 0.0602$

*The units for K are customarily omitted.

17.6   The Equilibrium Constant: An Introduction   **549**

✓ **Answer to Self-Check Exercise 17.1**

Applying the law of chemical equilibrium gives

Coefficient of NO_2 Coefficient of H_2O

$$K = \dfrac{[NO_2]^4[H_2O]^6}{[NH_3]^4[O_2]^7}$$ ←Coefficient of O_2

↑
Coefficient of NH_3

TEACHING TIPS

- Have students calculate the change in concentrations for each of the species in Table 17.1. Make sure they understand that the ratio of concentration changes is the same ratio as the ratio of the coefficients in the balanced equation.

- Use the results in Table 17.1 to emphasize the difference between "equilibrium position" and "equilibrium constant."

- When calculating K from concentrations of reactants and products, emphasize both initial and equilibrium concentrations so that students can distinguish between the two sets of data. These concentrations can be a major source of confusion for beginning students when working these problems.

At equilibrium the concentrations in the flask were found to be $[N_2] = 0.921$ M, $[H_2] = 0.763$ M, and $[NH_3] = 0.157$ M. The equilibrium expression for the reaction

$$N_2(g) + 3H_2(g) \rightleftharpoons 2NH_3(g)$$

is

$$K = \frac{[NH_3]^2}{[N_2][H_2]^3} = \frac{(0.157)^2}{(0.921)(0.763)^3}$$
$$= 0.0602 = 6.02 \times 10^{-2}$$

Similarly, as shown in Table 17.1, we can calculate for experiments II and III that K, the equilibrium constant, has the value 6.02×10^{-2}. In fact, whenever N_2, H_2, and NH_3 are mixed together at this temperature, the system *always* comes to an equilibrium position such that

$$K = 6.02 \times 10^{-2}$$

regardless of the amounts of the reactants and products that are mixed together initially.

It is important to see from Table 17.1 that the *equilibrium concentrations are not always the same.* However, even though the individual sets of equilibrium concentrations are quite different for the different situations, the *equilibrium constant, which depends on the ratio of the concentrations, remains the same.*

Each *set of equilibrium concentrations* is called an **equilibrium position.** It is essential to distinguish between the equilibrium constant and the equilibrium positions for a given reaction system. There is only *one* equilibrium constant for a particular system at a particular temperature, but there is an *infinite* number of equilibrium positions. The specific equilibrium position adopted by a system depends on the initial concentrations; the equilibrium constant does not.

Note that in the preceding discussion, the equilibrium constant was given without units. In certain cases the units are included when the values of equilibrium constants are given, and in other cases they are omitted. We will not discuss the reasons for this. We will omit the units in this text.

CHEMISTRY

For a reaction at a given temperature, there are many equilibrium positions but only one value for K.

Example 17.2

Calculating Equilibrium Constants

The reaction of sulfur dioxide with oxygen in the atmosphere to form sulfur trioxide has important environmental implications because SO_3 combines with moisture to form sulfuric acid droplets, an important component of acid rain. The following results were collected for two experiments involving the reaction at 600 °C between gaseous sulfur dioxide and oxygen to form gaseous sulfur trioxide:

$$2SO_2(g) + O_2(g) \rightleftharpoons 2SO_3(g)$$

The law of chemical equilibrium predicts that the value of K should be the same for both experiments. Verify this by calculating the equilibrium constant observed for each experiment.

Additional Examples

1. For the reaction

$$2NBr_3(g) \rightleftharpoons$$
$$N_2(g) + 3Br_2(g)$$

the system at equilibrium at a particular temperature is analyzed and the following concentrations are found: $[NBr_3] = 2.07 \times 10^{-3}$ M; $[N_2] = 4.11 \times 10^{-2}$ M; $[Br_2] = 1.06 \times 10^{-3}$ M. Calculate the value of K for the reaction at this temperature. **1.14×10^{-5}**

2. At high temperatures, elemental bromine, Br_2, dissociates into individual bromine atoms:

$$Br_2(g) \rightleftharpoons 2Br(g)$$

This system at equilibrium at a particular temperature is analyzed and the following concentrations are found: $[Br_2] = 0.97$ M; $[Br] = 3.4 \times 10^{-2}$ M. Calculate the value of K for the reaction at this temperature. **1.2×10^{-3}**

	Initial	Equilibrium
Experiment I	$[SO_2]_0 = 2.00\ M$	$[SO_2] = 1.50\ M$
	$[O_2]_0 = 1.50\ M$	$[O_2] = 1.25\ M$
	$[SO_3]_0 = 3.00\ M$	$[SO_3] = 3.50\ M$
Experiment II	$[SO_2]_0 = 0.500\ M$	$[SO_2] = 0.590\ M$
	$[O_2]_0 = 0$	$[O_2] = 0.045\ M$
	$[SO_3]_0 = 0.350\ M$	$[SO_3] = 0.260\ M$

Solution

The balanced equation for the reaction is

$$2SO_2(g) + O_2(g) \rightleftharpoons 2SO_3(g)$$

From the law of chemical equilibrium, we can write the equilibrium expression

$$K = \frac{[SO_3]^2}{[SO_2]^2[O_2]}$$

For experiment I we calculate the value of K by substituting the observed *equilibrium* concentrations,

$$[SO_3] = 3.50\ M$$
$$[SO_2] = 1.50\ M$$
$$[O_2] = 1.25\ M$$

into the equilibrium expression:

$$K_I = \frac{(3.50)^2}{(1.50)^2(1.25)} = 4.36$$

For experiment II at equilibrium

$$[SO_3] = 0.260\ M$$
$$[SO_2] = 0.590\ M$$
$$[O_2] = 0.045\ M$$

and

$$K_{II} = \frac{(0.260)^2}{(0.590)^2(0.045)} = 4.32$$

Notice that the values calculated for K_I and K_{II} are nearly the same, as we expected. That is, the value of K is constant, within differences due to rounding off and due to experimental error. These experiments show *two different equilibrium positions* for this system, but K, the equilibrium constant, is, indeed, constant.

17.6   The Equilibrium Constant: An Introduction   **551**

Themes

Organization, Patterns of Change

Skills

Applying concepts, interpreting data, solving problems

17.7 Heterogeneous Equilibria

Objective: *To understand the role that liquids and solids play in constructing the equilibrium expression.*

S o far we have discussed equilibria only for systems in the gaseous state, where all reactants and products are gases. These are examples of **homogeneous equilibria**, in which all substances are in the same state. However, many equilibria involve more than one state and are called **heterogeneous equilibria.** For example, the thermal decomposition of calcium carbonate in the commercial preparation of lime occurs by a reaction involving solids and gases.

In terms of amount produced, lime is among the top ten chemicals manufactured in the United States.

$$CaCO_3(s) \rightleftharpoons CaO(s) + CO_2(g)$$
$$\text{Lime}$$

Straightforward application of the law of equilibrium leads to the equilibrium expression

$$K = \frac{[CO_2][CaO]}{[CaCO_3]}$$

CHEMISTRY

The concentrations of pure liquids and solids are constant.

However, experimental results show that the *position of a heterogeneous equilibrium does not depend on the amounts of pure solids or liquids present.* The fundamental reason for this behavior is that the concentrations of pure solids and liquids cannot change. In other words, we might say that the concentrations of pure solids and liquids are constants. Therefore, we can write the equilibrium expression for the decomposition of solid calcium carbonate as

$$K' = \frac{[CO_2]C_1}{C_2}$$

where C_1 and C_2 are constants representing the concentrations of the solids CaO and $CaCO_3$, respectively. This expression can be rearranged to give

$$\frac{C_2 K'}{C_1} = K = [CO_2]$$

where the constants C_2, K', and C_1 are combined into a single constant K. This leads us to the following general statement: the concentrations of pure solids or pure liquids involved in a chemical reaction *are not included in the equilibrium expression* for the reaction. This applies *only* to pure solids or liquids. It does not apply to solutions or gases, because their concentrations can vary.

For example, consider the decomposition of liquid water to gaseous hydrogen and oxygen:

$$2H_2O(l) \rightleftharpoons 2H_2(g) + O_2(g)$$

where

$$K = [H_2]^2[O_2]$$

Water is not included in the equilibrium expression because it is a pure liquid. However, when the reaction is carried out under conditions where the water is a gas rather than a liquid,

$$2H_2O(g) \rightleftharpoons 2H_2(g) + O_2(g)$$

552   Chapter 17   Equilibrium

we have

$$K = \frac{[H_2]^2[O_2]}{[H_2O]^2}$$

because the concentration of water vapor can change.

Example 17.3

Writing Equilibrium Expressions for Heterogeneous Equilibria

Write the expressions for K for the following processes.

   a. Solid phosphorus pentachloride is decomposed to liquid phosphorus trichloride and chlorine gas.

   b. Deep-blue solid copper(II) sulfate pentahydrate is heated to drive off water vapor to form white solid copper(II) sulfate.

Solution

   a. The reaction is

$$PCl_5(s) \rightleftharpoons PCl_3(l) + Cl_2(g)$$

In this case, neither the pure solid PCl_5 nor the pure liquid PCl_3 is included in the equilibrium expression. The equilibrium expression is

$$K = [Cl_2]$$

   b. The reaction is

$$CuSO_4 \cdot 5H_2O(s) \rightleftharpoons CuSO_4(s) + 5H_2O(g)$$

The two solids are not included. The equilibrium expression is

$$K = [H_2O]^5$$

As solid copper(II) sulfate pentahydrate, $CuSO_4 \cdot 5H_2O$, is heated, it loses H_2O, eventually forming white $CuSO_4$.

(continued)

Additional Examples

Write the expression for K for the following processes.

1. $CO_2(g) + H_2O(l) \rightleftharpoons$
                     $H_2CO_3(l)$
   $K = 1/[SO_3(g)]$

2. $ZrI_4(s) \rightleftharpoons Zr(s) + 2I_2(g)$
   $K = [I_2(g)]^2$

Answers to Self-Check Exercise 17.2

a. $K = [O_2]^3$ The solids are not included.

b. $K = [N_2O][H_2O]^2$ The solid is not included. Water is gaseous in this reaction, so it is included.

c. $K = \dfrac{1}{[CO_2]}$ The solids are not included.

d. $K = \dfrac{1}{[SO_3]}$ Water and H_2SO_4 are pure liquids and so are not included.

 Answers to Focus Questions

1. $K = \dfrac{[NO_2]^2}{[NO]^2[O_2]}$

2. 2.35×10^{13}

3. The concentrations of pure liquids and pure solids cannot change. For this reason they are not included in the equilibrium expression.

4. $K = 1/[NH_3][HCl]$

 Section 17.8

Themes
Organization, Patterns of Change

Skills
Applying concepts, making predictions

Student Preparation
Assign the students to read Sections 17.8 to 17.10 and to answer the Focus Questions at the end of Section 17.10 before coming to class.

Active Learning
After introducing the material in Sections 17.8 to 17.10 in class, place the students in groups and have them work together on Sections 17.8–17.10: Team Learning Worksheet. Answers and/or discussion of these questions are located in the *Teacher Resources*.

Laboratory
Experiment 75:
Le Châtelier's Principle, Microscale

 Self-Check Exercise 17.2

Write the equilibrium expression for each of the following reactions.

   a. $2KClO_3(s) \rightleftharpoons 2KCl(s) + 3O_2(g)$
     This reaction is often used to produce oxygen gas in the laboratory.
   b. $NH_4NO_3(s) \rightleftharpoons N_2O(g) + 2H_2O(g)$
   c. $CO_2(g) + MgO(s) \rightleftharpoons MgCO_3(s)$
   d. $SO_3(g) + H_2O(l) \rightleftharpoons H_2SO_4(l)$

Focus Questions   **Sections 17.6–17.7**

1. Write the equilibrium expression for

$$2NO(g) + O_2(g) \rightleftharpoons 2NO_2(g)$$

2. Suppose that for the reaction

$$N_2(g) + 3Cl_2(g) \rightleftharpoons 2NCl_3(g)$$

it is determined that, at a particular temperature, the equilibrium concentrations are $[N_2(g)] = 0.000104\ M$, $[Cl_2(g)] = 0.000201\ M$, and $[NCl_3(g)] = 0.141\ M$. Calculate the value of K for the reaction at this temperature.

3. Why are solids and liquids not included in the equilibrium expression?

4. Write the equilibrium expression for

$$NH_3(g) + HCl(g) \rightleftharpoons NH_4Cl(s)$$

 17.8   Le Châtelier's Principle

Objective: *To learn to predict the changes that occur when a system at equilibrium is disturbed.*

It is important to understand the factors that control the *position* of a chemical equilibrium. For example, when a chemical is manufactured, the chemists and chemical engineers in charge of production want to choose conditions that favor the desired product as much as possible. That is, they want the equilibrium to lie far to the right (toward products). When the process for the synthesis of ammonia was being developed, extensive studies were carried out to determine how the equilibrium concentration of ammonia depended on the conditions of temperature and pressure.

In this section we will explore how various changes in conditions affect the equilibrium position of a reaction system. We can predict the effects of changes in concentration, pressure, and temperature on a system at equilibrium by using **Le Châtelier's principle**, which states that *when a change is imposed on a system at equilibrium, the position of the equilibrium shifts in a direction that tends to reduce the effect of that change.*

554   Chapter 17   Equilibrium

TEACHING SUPPORT
Demonstration

FeSCN²⁺ and Le Châtelier's Principle

Materials
0.20 M $Fe(NO_3)_2$
Na_2HPO_4 crystals
0.2 M HCl
0.002 M KSCN
Solid KSCN
0.20 M $AgNO_3$

3 Petri dishes
Eyedroppers
Overhead projector

Procedure Cover the bottom of a Petri dish with the KSCN solution and place it on the overhead projector. Add several drops of $Fe(NO_3)_3$ to the Petri dish and swirl gently to mix well. The reaction is

$$Fe^{3+} + SCN^- \Leftrightarrow FeSCN^{2+}$$
Yellow   Colorless   Red

Now divide the solution about equally among three Petri dishes. Place all three on the overhead projector. The third Petri dish will act as a standard for comparison. Add a small amount of solid KSCN to the first Petri dish. Notice that the solution becomes more colored, which indicates that more $FeSCN^{2+}$ is forming. Add several drops of $Fe(NO_3)_3$ solution to the second Petri dish. Once

Carbon Dioxide (CO₂)

Carbon dioxide is a very familiar molecule that is the product of human respiration and of the combustion of fossil fuels. This gas also puts the "fizz" in soda pop. It turns out that the simple, familiar CO_2 molecule has profound implications for our continued existence on this planet.

The concentration of carbon dioxide in the earth's atmosphere has risen steadily since the beginning of the Industrial Revolution and is expected to double from today's levels in the next 50 years. This change will have important effects on our environment. Consider the case of global warming. Many scientists feel that the increased CO_2 levels will trap more of the sun's energy near the earth, significantly increasing the earth's average temperature. Some evidence suggests that this is already occurring, although scientists disagree about the contribution of CO_2 to the changes. One thing that everyone does agree on is that the increased CO_2 levels will make plants grow faster.

On the surface the increase in plant growth due to increased CO_2 might seem like a good thing. Surprisingly, this situation could spell disaster for plant eaters, from caterpillars to antelopes, and for the animals that eat these herbivores. Faster plant growth often leads to lower nutritional value. As the plants increase their rate of photosynthesis and use the carbon in CO_2 to build more fiber and starch, the amount of nitrogen—which indicates the amount of proteins present—declines. Studies show that new leaves on plants grown in a CO_2-rich atmosphere are starchy, but protein-poor. This is bad news for caterpillars, which need to bulk up before they pupate. Studies have indicated that caterpillars eat 40% more of the starchy, protein-poor leaves but grow 10% slower and produce smaller than normal adult butterflies.

Studies on larger herbivores, such as cows and sheep, have been more difficult to carry out. Nevertheless, indications are that plants grown in a CO_2-enriched environment provide less protein and produce slower growth in these species as well.

Research is continuing to try to assess the effects of the increasing CO_2 levels on the food chain.

A Monarch butterfly caterpillar eating a leaf.

The Effect of a Change in Concentration

Let us consider the ammonia synthesis reaction. Suppose there is an equilibrium position described by these concentrations:

$$[N_2] = 0.399\ M \qquad [H_2] = 1.197\ M \qquad [NH_3] = 0.203\ M$$

What will happen if 1.000 mol/L of N_2 is suddenly injected into the system? We can begin to answer this question by remembering that for the system at equilibrium, the rates of the forward and reverse reactions exactly balance,

$$N_2(g) + 3H_2(g) \rightleftharpoons 2NH_3(g)$$

as indicated here by arrows of the same length. When the N_2 is added, there are suddenly more collisions between N_2 and H_2 molecules. This increases

17.8 Le Châtelier's Principle **555**

---

again, the solution color intensifies, which indicates further formation of $FeSCN^{2+}$.

To shift the equilibrium again, add a few crystals of solid Na_2HPO_4 to the first Petri dish. The HPO_4^{2-} reacts with the iron ions to form $FeHPO_4^+$. The red color disappears, because the equilibrium of the initial reaction shifts to the left as iron ions are removed from the solution. Add a few drops of $AgNO_3$ solution to the second Petri dish. Once again, the red color disappears. In this case the silver ions react with the SCN^- ions to form $AgSCN$. Finally, add a few drops of HCl to the second Petri dish. The chloride ions react with the silver ions to form the white precipitate $AgCl$, but the red color returns because the SCN^- ions are released from the $AgSCN$ and interact with the iron ions in solution once again to re-form $FeSCN^{2+}$.

Teaching Notes During this demonstration, discuss each addition by using the initial reaction to illustrate how the equilibrium is changing. Students need to be able to think about these changes as they occur.

TEACHING TIP

Proceed slowly through this section, giving lots of examples. Students often have a difficult time with these questions. Think through each example with students and be sure they understand how concentrations change each time.

CELEBRITY CHEMICAL

Carbon Dioxide (CO₂)

You can investigate the chemical composition of a variety of minerals and rocks by testing for the formation of carbon dioxide when the samples are treated with HCl. Use the overhead projector and small beakers for sample testing. Obtain samples of several rocks and minerals. Your earth science teacher will probably have samples that you can use for this activity. Good samples include calcite, marble, limestone, quartz, chalk, coral, and clam shells. You will need 3 M HCl to test the materials. Place enough HCl in each of the small beakers to cover the bottom of the beaker. Place the beakers on an overhead projector on top of a transparency. Place a rock or mineral sample in each beaker, labeling the transparency as you proceed. Use small pieces of rock or mineral, but not powder. Look for bubbles of CO_2, which indicate the presence of carbonate in the sample.

You can integrate this activity with the earth science curriculum even further by discussing the origins of these samples. For example, limestone is sedimentary rock and marble is metamorphic rock. Both have the same chemical composition, although their appearances are quite different because of the manner in which they were formed.

You could also use this activity as an opportunity to demonstrate some of the features of solid carbon dioxide (dry ice). You can purchase dry ice at your local ice company or sometimes at the local hospital or ice cream store. Be careful to protect your hand whenever handling dry ice. Place a piece of dry ice in a beaker of water to observe the

(continued)

(continued)

formation of fog and the bubbling of the CO_2. Dry ice slides very easily on the lab demonstration bench. You can pulverize a sample of dry ice and place it in a balloon (use a funnel). Tie the balloon and wait. As the dry ice sublimes, the balloon will expand. If you add too much, it will pop!

MINI-DEMO

Concentration Effects
To illustrate the effect of a change in concentration on equilibrium, place about 20 mL of 0.2 M $CoCl_2$ in a 250-mL flask. Observe the pink color of the solution. Add about 50 mL of concentrated HCl and show students the color change from pink to blue. This change results from the formation of a cobalt complex:

$Co^{2+}(aq) + 4Cl^-(aq) \Leftrightarrow CoCl_4^{2-}$
Pink   Blue

Divide the solution into two equal parts in two 250-mL flasks. Add water to one of the flasks until the solution turns pink. This activity illustrates Le Châtelier's principle, because the water dilutes the chloride concentration and pulls the equilibrium to the left.

---

the rate of the forward reaction (shown here by the greater length of the arrow pointing in that direction),

$$N_2(g) + 3H_2(g) \longrightarrow 2NH_3(g)$$

and the reaction produces more NH_3. As the concentration of NH_3 increases, the reverse reaction also speeds up (as more collisions between NH_3 molecules occur) and the system again comes to equilibrium. However, the new equilibrium position has more NH_3 than was present in the original position. We say that the equilibrium has shifted to the *right*—toward the products. The original and new equilibrium positions are shown below.

Equilibrium Position I		*Equilibrium Position II*
$[N_2] = 0.399\ M$	$\Rightarrow$	$[N_2] = 1.348\ M$
$[H_2] = 1.197\ M$	1.000 mol/L	$[H_2] = 1.044\ M$
$[NH_3] = 0.203\ M$	of N_2 added	$[NH_3] = 0.304\ M$

Note that the equilibrium does in fact shift to the right; the concentration of H_2 decreases (from 1.197 M to 1.044 M), the concentration of NH_3 increases (from 0.203 M to 0.304 M), and, of course, because nitrogen was added, the concentration of N_2 shows an increase relative to the original amount present.

It is important to note at this point that, although the equilibrium shifted to a new position, the *value of* K *did not change*. We can demonstrate this by inserting the equilibrium concentrations from positions I and II into the equilibrium expression.

- Position I: $K = \dfrac{[NH_3]^2}{[N_2][H_2]^3} = \dfrac{(0.203)^2}{(0.399)(1.197)^3} = 0.0602$

- Position II: $K = \dfrac{[NH_3]^2}{[N_2][H_2]^3} = \dfrac{(0.304)^2}{(1.348)(1.044)^3} = 0.0602$

These values of K are the same. Therefore, although the *equilibrium position* shifted when we added more N_2, the *equilibrium constant* K remained the same.

Could we have predicted this shift by using Le Châtelier's principle? Because the change in this case was to add nitrogen, Le Châtelier's principle predicts that the system will shift in a direction that *consumes* nitrogen. This tends to offset the original change—the addition of N_2. Therefore, Le Châtelier's principle correctly predicts that adding nitrogen will cause the equilibrium to shift to the right **(Figure 17.11)** as some of the added nitrogen is consumed.

Figure 17.11
(a) The initial equilibrium mixture of N_2, H_2, and NH_3. (b) Addition of N_2. (c) The new equilibrium position for the system containing more N_2 (because of the addition of N_2), less H_2, and more NH_3 than in (a).

(a)   (b)   (c)

556   Chapter 17   Equilibrium

PROBLEM SOLVING

A system at equilibrium shifts in the direction that compensates for any imposed change.

If ammonia had been added instead of nitrogen, the system would have shifted to the left, consuming ammonia. Another way of stating Le Châtelier's principle, then, is to say that *when a reactant or product is added to a system at equilibrium, the system shifts away from the added component.* On the other hand, if *a reactant or product is removed, the system shifts toward the removed component.* For example, if we had removed nitrogen, the system would have shifted to the left and the amount of ammonia present would have been reduced.

A real-life example that shows the importance of Le Châtelier's principle is the effect of high elevations on the oxygen supply to the body. If you have ever traveled to the mountains on vacation, you may have noticed that you felt "light-headed" and especially tired during the first few days of your visit. These feelings resulted from a decreased supply of oxygen to your body because of the lower air pressure that exists at higher elevations. For example, the oxygen supply in Leadville, Colorado (elevation ~ 10,000 ft), is only about two-thirds that found at sea level. We can understand the effects of diminished oxygen supply in terms of the following equilibrium:

$$Hb(aq) + 4O_2(g) \rightleftharpoons Hb(O_2)_4(aq)$$

where Hb represents hemoglobin, the iron-containing protein that transports O_2 from your lungs to your tissues, where it is used to support metabolism. The coefficient 4 in the equation signifies that each hemoglobin molecule picks up four O_2 molecules in the lungs. Note by Le Châtelier's principle that a lower oxygen pressure will cause this equilibrium to shift to the left, away from oxygenated hemoglobin. This leads to an inadequate oxygen supply at the tissues, which in turn results in fatigue and a "woozy" feeling.

This problem can be solved in extreme cases, such as when climbing Mt. Everest or flying in a plane at high altitudes, by supplying extra oxygen from a tank. This extra oxygen pushes the equilibrium to its normal position. However, lugging around an oxygen tank would not be very practical for people who live in the mountains. In fact, nature solves this problem in a very interesting way. The body adapts to living at high elevations by producing additional hemoglobin—the other way to shift this equilibrium to the right. Thus people who live at high elevations have significantly higher hemoglobin levels than those living at sea level. For example, the Sherpas who live in Nepal can function in the rarefied air at the top of Mt. Everest without an auxiliary oxygen supply.

Example 17.4

An ore sample containing arsenic.

Using Le Châtelier's Principle: Changes in Concentration

Arsenic, As_4, is obtained from nature by first reacting its ore with oxygen (called *roasting*) to form solid As_4O_6. (As_4O_6, a toxic compound fatal in doses of 0.1 g or more, is the "arsenic" made famous in detective stories.) The As_4O_6 is then reduced using carbon:

$$As_4O_6(s) + 6C(s) \rightleftharpoons As_4(g) + 6CO(g)$$

(continued)

17.8 Le Châtelier's Principle **557**

Additional Examples

Suppose the reaction system

$$2SO_2(g) + O_2(g) \rightleftharpoons 2SO_3(g)$$

has reached equilibrium. Predict the effect of each of the following changes on the position of the equilibrium.

1. $SO_2(g)$ is added to the system.
Shifts to the right.

2. The $SO_3(g)$ present is liquefied and removed from the system.
Shifts to the right.

3. Some of the $O_2(g)$ is removed from the system.
Shifts to the left.

(continued)

Predict the direction of the shift in the equilibrium position for this reaction that occurs in response to each of the following changes in conditions.

  a. Addition of carbon monoxide
  b. Addition or removal of C(s) or $As_4O_6(s)$
  c. Removal of $As_4(g)$

Solution

  a. Le Châtelier's principle predicts a shift away from the substance whose concentration is increased. The equilibrium position will shift to the left when carbon monoxide is added.
  b. Because the amount of a pure solid has no effect on the equilibrium position, changing the amount of carbon or tetraarsenic hexoxide will have no effect.
  c. When gaseous arsenic is removed, the equilibrium position will shift to the right to form more products. In industrial processes, the desired product is often continuously removed from the reaction system to increase the yield.

 Self-Check Exercise 17.3

Novelty devices for predicting rain contain cobalt(II) chloride and are based on the following equilibrium:

$$CoCl_2(s) + 6H_2O(g) \rightleftharpoons CoCl_2 \cdot 6H_2O(s)$$
$$\text{Blue} \qquad\qquad\qquad \text{Pink}$$

What color will this indicator be when rain is likely due to increased water vapor in the air?

When blue anhydrous $CoCl_2$ reacts with water, pink $CoCl_2 \cdot 6H_2O$ is formed.

The Effect of a Change in Volume

When the volume of a gas is decreased (when a gas is compressed), the pressure increases. This occurs because the molecules present are now contained in a smaller space and they hit the walls of their container more often, giving a greater pressure. Therefore, when the volume of a gaseous reaction system at equilibrium is suddenly reduced, leading to a sudden increase in pressure, by Le Châtelier's principle the system will shift in the direction that reduces the pressure.

For example, consider the reaction

$$CaCO_3(s) \rightleftharpoons CaO(s) + CO_2(g)$$

in a container with a movable piston **(Figure 17.12).** If the volume is suddenly decreased by pushing in the piston, the pressure of the CO_2 gas initially increases. How can the system offset this pressure increase? By shifting to the left—the direction that reduces the amount of gas present. That is, a shift to the left will use up CO_2 molecules, thereby lowering the pressure. (There will be fewer molecules present to hit the walls, because more of the CO_2 molecules have combined with CaO and thus become part of the solid $CaCO_3$.)

Answer to Self-Check Exercise 17.3

When rain is imminent, the concentration of water vapor in the air increases. This shifts the equilibrium to the right, forming $CoCl_2 \cdot 6H_2O(s)$, which is pink.

MINI-DEMO

Two everyday examples of Le Châtelier's principle are the novelty barometers often found in gift shops and commercial desiccants (containing Drierite as the moisture indicator). In both cases $CoCl_2$ is used to indicate the level of moisture. A color change from blue to pink indicates a rise in the moisture content.

Figure 17.12
The reaction system $CaCO_3(s) \rightleftharpoons CaO(s) + CO_2(g)$. (a) The system is initially at equilibrium. (b) The piston is pushed in, decreasing the volume and increasing the pressure. The system shifts in the direction that consumes CO_2 molecules, lowering the pressure again.

CO$_2$

CaCO$_3$ — CaO

(a)   (b)

CHEMISTRY

Shifts in equilibrium brought about by volume changes also produce changes in pressure.

Therefore, when the volume of a gaseous reaction system at equilibrium is decreased (thus increasing the pressure), *the system shifts in the direction that gives the smaller number of gas molecules*. So a decrease in the system volume leads to a shift that decreases the total number of gaseous molecules in the system.

Suppose we are running the reaction

$$N_2(g) + 3H_2(g) \rightleftharpoons 2NH_3(g)$$

and we have a mixture of the gases nitrogen, hydrogen, and ammonia at equilibrium **(Figure 17.13a).** If we suddenly reduce the volume, what will happen to the equilibrium position? Because the decrease in volume initially increases the pressure, the system moves in the direction that lowers its pressure. The reaction system can reduce its pressure by reducing the number of gas molecules present. This means that the reaction

$$N_2(g) + 3H_2(g) \rightleftharpoons 2NH_3(g)$$
4 gaseous molecules   2 gaseous molecules

shifts to the right, because in this direction four molecules (one of nitrogen and three of hydrogen) react to produce two molecules (of ammonia), thus *reducing the total number of gaseous molecules present*. The equilibrium position shifts to the right—toward the side of the reaction that involves the smaller number of gaseous molecules in the balanced equation.

The opposite is also true. When the container volume is increased (which lowers the pressure of the system), the system shifts so as to increase its pressure. An increase in volume in the ammonia synthesis system produces a shift to the left to increase the total number of gaseous molecules present (to increase the pressure).

Figure 17.13
(a) A mixture of $NH_3(g)$, $N_2(g)$, and $H_2(g)$ at equilibrium. (b) The volume is suddenly decreased. (c) The new equilibrium position for the system containing more NH_3 and less N_2 and H_2. The reaction $N_2(g) + 3H_2(g) \rightleftharpoons 2NH_3(g)$ shifts to the right (toward the side with fewer molecules) when the container volume is decreased.

Key:
- N_2
- H_2
- NH_3

(a)   (b)   (c)

17.8 Le Châtelier's Principle **559**

560

Additional Examples

Predict the shift in equilibrium position that will occur for each of the following processes when the volume is increased.

1. $4NH_3(g) + 5O_2(g) \rightleftharpoons$
   $4NO(g) + 6H_2O(g)$
   Shift to the right.

2. $NH_4NO_3(s) \rightleftharpoons$
   $N_2O(g) + 2H_2O(g)$
   Shift to the right.

Answers to Self-Check Exercise 17.4

a. No change. Both sides of the equation contain the same number of gaseous components. The system cannot change its pressure by shifting its equilibrium position.

b. Shifts to the left. The system can increase the number of gaseous components present, and so increase the pressure, by shifting to the left.

c. Shifts to the right to increase the number of gaseous components and thus its pressure.

MINI-DEMO

Temperature Effect

To illustrate the effect of a change in temperature on equilibrium, place about 50 mL of 0.2 M $CoCl_2$ in a small beaker. Observe the pink color of the solution. Add concentrated HCl until the color of the solution changes from pink to blue. This change results from the formation of a cobalt complex:

$$\text{Heat} + Co^{2+}(aq) + 4Cl^-(aq) \Leftrightarrow CoCl_4^{2-}$$
$$\quad\quad\quad\quad\text{Pink}\quad\quad\quad\quad\quad\quad\text{Blue}$$

To observe the effect of temperature on the reaction, place the solution in a large test tube and immerse the test tube about halfway into a beaker containing crushed ice and salt. The solution in the bottom part of the test tube will turn pink after several minutes, because lowering the temperature pulls the endothermic reaction to the left.

Example 17.5

Using Le Châtelier's Principle: Changes in Volume

Predict the shift in equilibrium position that will occur for each of the following processes when the volume is reduced.

a. The preparation of liquid phosphorus trichloride by the reaction

$$P_4(s) + 6Cl_2(g) \rightleftharpoons 4PCl_3(l)$$
6 gaseous molecules   0 gaseous molecules

b. The preparation of gaseous phosphorus pentachloride according to the equation

$$PCl_3(g) + Cl_2(g) \rightleftharpoons PCl_5(g)$$
2 gaseous molecules   1 gaseous molecule

c. The reaction of phosphorus trichloride with ammonia:

$$PCl_3(g) + 3NH_3(g) \rightleftharpoons P(NH_2)_3(g) + 3HCl(g)$$
4 gaseous molecules   4 gaseous molecules

Solution

a. P_4 and PCl_3 are a pure solid and a pure liquid, respectively, so we need to consider only the effect on Cl_2. If the volume is decreased, the Cl_2 pressure will initially increase, so the position of the equilibrium will shift to the right, consuming gaseous Cl_2 and lowering the pressure (to counteract the original change).

b. Decreasing the volume (increasing the pressure) will shift this equilibrium to the right, because the product side contains only one gaseous molecule while the reactant side has two. That is, the system will respond to the decreased volume (increased pressure) by lowering the number of molecules present.

c. Both sides of the balanced reaction equation have four gaseous molecules. A change in volume will have no effect on the equilibrium position. There is no shift in this case, because the system cannot change the number of molecules present by shifting in either direction.

 Self-Check Exercise 17.4

For each of the following reactions, predict the direction in which the equilibrium will shift when the volume of the container is increased.

a. $H_2(g) + F_2(g) \rightleftharpoons 2HF(g)$

b. $CO(g) + 2H_2(g) \rightleftharpoons CH_3OH(g)$

c. $2SO_3(g) \rightleftharpoons 2SO_2(g) + O_2(g)$

The Effect of a Change in Temperature

It is important to remember that although the changes we have just discussed may alter the equilibrium *position,* they do not alter the equilibrium *constant.* For example, the addition of a reactant shifts the equilibrium position to the right but has no effect on the value of the equilibrium constant; the new equilibrium concentrations satisfy the original equilibrium constant. This was demonstrated earlier in this section for the addition of N_2 to the ammonia synthesis reaction.

The effect of temperature on equilibrium is different, however, because *the value of K changes with temperature*. We can use Le Châtelier's principle to predict the direction of the change in K.

To do this we need to classify reactions according to whether they produce heat or absorb heat. A reaction that produces heat (heat is a "product") is said to be *exothermic*. A reaction that absorbs heat is called *endothermic*. Because heat is needed for an endothermic reaction, energy (heat) can be regarded as a "reactant" in this case.

In an exothermic reaction, heat is treated as a product. For example, the synthesis of ammonia from nitrogen and hydrogen is exothermic (produces heat). We can represent this by treating energy as a product:

$$N_2(g) + 3H_2(g) \rightleftharpoons 2NH_3(g) + 92 \text{ kJ}$$
Energy released

Le Châtelier's principle predicts that when we add energy to this system at equilibrium by heating it, the shift will be in the direction that consumes energy—that is, to the left.

On the other hand, for an endothermic reaction (one that absorbs energy), such as the decomposition of calcium carbonate,

$$CaCO_3(s) + 556 \text{ kJ} \rightleftharpoons CaO(s) + CO_2(g)$$
Energy needed

energy is treated as a reactant. In this case an increase in temperature causes the equilibrium to shift to the right.

In summary, to use Le Châtelier's principle to describe the effect of a temperature change on a system at equilibrium, *simply treat energy as a reactant (in an endothermic process) or as a product (in an exothermic process),* and *predict the direction of the shift* in the same way you would if an actual reactant or product were being added or removed.

Example 17.6

Using Le Châtelier's Principle: Changes in Temperature

For each of the following reactions, predict how the equilibrium will shift as the temperature is increased.

a. $N_2(g) + O_2(g) \rightleftharpoons 2NO(g)$ (endothermic)
b. $2SO_2(g) + O_2(g) \rightleftharpoons 2SO_3(g)$ (exothermic)

Solution

a. This is an endothermic reaction, so energy can be viewed as a reactant.

$$N_2(g) + O_2(g) + \text{energy} \rightleftharpoons 2NO(g)$$

Thus the equilibrium will shift to the right as the temperature is increased (energy added).

(continued)

Animation and Video

Video, Gaseous Equilibrium of NO_2 and N_2O_4 and Temperature

Additional Examples

1. The reaction

$$C_2H_2(g) + 2Br_2(g) \rightleftharpoons C_2H_2Br_4(g)$$

is exothermic as written. Will an increase in temperature shift the position of equilibrium toward the reactants or the products?
reactants

2. The reaction

$$ZrI_4(s) \rightleftharpoons Zr(s) + 2I_2(g)$$

is endothermic as written. Will an increase in temperature shift the position of equilibrium toward the reactants or the products?
products

(continued)

b. This is an exothermic reaction, so energy can be regarded as a product.

$$2SO_2(g) + O_2(g) \rightleftharpoons 2SO_3(g) + \text{energy}$$

As the temperature is increased, the equilibrium will shift to the left.

 Self-Check Exercise 17.5

For the exothermic reaction

$$2SO_2(g) + O_2(g) \rightleftharpoons 2SO_3(g)$$

predict the equilibrium shift caused by each of the following changes.

a. SO_2 is added.   **c.** The volume is decreased.

b. SO_3 is removed.   **d.** The temperature is decreased.

TABLE 17.2

Shifts in the Equilibrium Position for the Reaction: Energy + $N_2O_4(g) \rightleftharpoons 2NO_2(g)$

Change	Shift
addition of $N_2O_4(g)$	right
addition of $NO_2(g)$	left
removal of $N_2O_4(g)$	left
removal of $NO_2(g)$	right
decrease in container volume	left
increase in container volume	right
increase in temperature	right
decrease in temperature	left

We have seen how Le Châtelier's principle can be used to predict the effects of several types of changes on a system at equilibrium. To summarize these ideas, **Table 17.2** shows how various changes affect the equilibrium position of the endothermic reaction $N_2O_4(g) \rightleftharpoons 2NO_2(g)$. The effect of a temperature change on this system is depicted in **Figure 17.14**.

Figure 17.14
Shifting the $N_2O_4(g) \rightleftharpoons 2NO_2(g)$ equilibrium by changing the temperature. (a) At 100 °C the flask is definitely reddish-brown due to a large amount of NO_2 present. (b) At 0 °C the equilibrium is shifted toward colorless $N_2O_4(g)$.

 Section 17.9

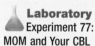 **17.9 Applications Involving the Equilibrium Constant**

Objective: *To learn to calculate equilibrium concentrations from equilibrium constants.*

Knowing the value of the equilibrium constant for a reaction allows us to do many things. For example, the size of K tells us the inherent tendency of the reaction to occur. A value of K much larger than 1 means that at equilibrium, the reaction system will consist of mostly products—the

Themes
Organization, Patterns of Change

Skills
Applying concepts, interpreting data, solving problems

Laboratory
Experiment 76:
Chemical Equilibrium, Traditional

Laboratory
Experiment 77:
MOM and Your CBL

TEACHING TIP

Now is an excellent time to explain the relationship between the value of K and the extent of the reaction. Discuss the meaning of a K value of 1, <1, and >1.

562 Chapter 17 Equilibrium

equilibrium lies to the right. For example, consider a general reaction of the type

$$A(g) \rightarrow B(g)$$

where

$$K = \frac{[B]}{[A]}$$

If K for this reaction is 10,000 (10^4), then at equilibrium,

$$\frac{[B]}{[A]} = 10,000 \quad \text{or} \quad \frac{[B]}{[A]} = \frac{10,000}{1}$$

That is, at equilibrium [B] is 10,000 times greater than [A]. This means that the reaction strongly favors the product B. Another way of saying this is that the reaction goes essentially to completion. That is, virtually all of A becomes B.

On the other hand, a small value of K means that the system at equilibrium consists largely of reactants—the equilibrium position is far to the left. The given reaction does not occur to any significant extent.

Another way we use the equilibrium constant is to calculate the equilibrium concentrations of reactants and products. For example, if we know the value of K and the concentrations of all the reactants and products except one, we can calculate the missing concentration. This is illustrated in Example 17.7 below.

Example 17.7

Calculating Equilibrium Concentration Using Equilibrium Expressions

Gaseous phosphorus pentachloride decomposes to chlorine gas and gaseous phosphorus trichloride. In a certain experiment, at a temperature where $K = 8.96 \times 10^{-2}$, the equilibrium concentrations of PCl_5 and PCl_3 were found to be 6.70×10^{-3} M and 0.300 M, respectively. Calculate the concentration of Cl_2 present at equilibrium.

Solution

For this reaction, the balanced equation is

$$PCl_5(g) \rightleftharpoons PCl_3(g) + Cl_2(g)$$

and the equilibrium expression is

$$K = \frac{[PCl_3][Cl_2]}{[PCl_5]} = 8.96 \times 10^{-2}$$

We know that

$$[PCl_5] = 6.70 \times 10^{-3} \ M$$
$$[PCl_3] = 0.300 \ M$$

We want to calculate $[Cl_2]$. We will rearrange the equilibrium expression to solve for the concentration of Cl_2. First we divide both sides of the expression

$$K = \frac{[PCl_3][Cl_2]}{[PCl_5]}$$

by $[PCl_3]$ to give

$$\frac{K}{[PCl_3]} = \frac{\cancel{[PCl_3]}[Cl_2]}{\cancel{[PCl_3]}[PCl_5]} = \frac{[Cl_2]}{[PCl_5]}$$

(continued)

Additional Examples

1. Assume the equilibrium constant for the reaction $H_2(g) + F_2(g) \rightleftharpoons 2HF(g)$ has the value 2.1×10^3 at a particular temperature. When the system is analyzed at equilibrium at this temperature, the concentrations of both $H_2(g)$ and $F_2(g)$ are 0.0021 M. What is the concentration of $HF(g)$ in the equilibrium system under these conditions? $[HF(g)] = 9.6 \times 10^{-2} \ M$

2. Assume the equilibrium constant for the reaction $2H_2O(g) \rightleftharpoons 2H_2(g) + O_2(g)$ has the value 2.4×10^{-3} at a particular temperature. When the system is analyzed at equilibrium at this temperature, it is found that $[H_2O(g)] = 1.1 \times 10^{-1} \ M$ and $[H_2(g)] = 1.9 \times 10^{-2} \ M$. What is the concentration of $O_2(g)$ in the equilibrium system under these conditions? $[O_2(g)] = 8.0 \times 10^{-2} \ M$

Next we multiply both sides by $[PCl_5]$.

$$\frac{K[PCl_5]}{[PCl_3]} = \frac{[Cl_2]\cancel{[PCl_5]}}{\cancel{[PCl_5]}} = [Cl_2]$$

Then we can calculate $[Cl_2]$ by substituting the known information.

$$[Cl_2] = K \times \frac{[PCl_5]}{[PCl_3]} = (8.96 \times 10^{-2})\frac{(6.70 \times 10^{-3})}{(0.300)}$$

$$[Cl_2] = 2.00 \times 10^{-3}$$

The equilibrium concentration of Cl_2 is 2.00×10^{-3} M.

Section 17.10

Themes
Organization, Patterns of Change

Skills
Applying concepts, interpreting data, solving problems, making predictions

---

TEACHING TIP

Now is an excellent time to review polyatomic ions and the procedure for writing and balancing chemical equations. Students must be able to break compounds into their component ions and write equations for the dissociation to work with solubility equilibria.

17.10 Solubility Equilibria

Objective: *To learn to calculate the solubility product of a salt given its solubility, and vice versa.*

Solubility is a very important phenomenon. Consider the following examples.

- Because sugar and table salt dissolve readily in water, we can flavor foods easily.

- Because calcium sulfate is less soluble in hot water than in cold water, it coats tubes in boilers, reducing thermal efficiency.

- When food lodges between teeth, acids form that dissolve tooth enamel, which contains the mineral hydroxyapatite, $Ca_5(PO_4)_3OH$. Tooth decay can be reduced by adding fluoride to toothpaste. Fluoride replaces the hydroxide in hydroxyapatite to produce the corresponding fluorapatite, $Ca_5(PO_4)_3F$, and calcium fluoride, CaF_2, both of which are less soluble in acids than the original enamel.

- The use of a suspension of barium sulfate improves the clarity of X rays of the digestive tract. Barium sulfate contains the toxic ion Ba^{2+}, but its very low solubility makes ingestion of solid $BaSO_4$ safe.

This X ray of the large intestine has been enhanced by the patient's consumption of barium sulfate.

In this section we will consider the equilibria associated with dissolving solids in water to form aqueous solutions. When a typical ionic solid dissolves in water, it dissociates completely into separate cations and anions. For example, calcium fluoride dissolves in water as follows:

$$CaF_2(s) \xrightarrow{\text{H}_2\text{O}(l)} Ca^{2+}(aq) + 2F^-(aq)$$

When the solid salt is first added to the water, no Ca^{2+} and F^- ions are present. However, as dissolving occurs, the concentrations of Ca^{2+} and F^- increase, and it becomes more and more likely that these ions will collide and re-form the solid. Thus two opposite (competing) processes are occurring—the dissolving reaction shown above and the reverse reaction to re-form the solid:

$$Ca^{2+}(aq) + 2F^-(aq) \rightarrow CaF_2(s)$$

564 Chapter 17 Equilibrium

Ultimately, equilibrium is reached. No more solid dissolves and the solution is said to be saturated.

We can write an equilibrium expression for this process according to the law of chemical equilibrium:

$$K_{sp} = [Ca^{2+}][F^-]^2$$

where $[Ca^{2+}]$ and $[F^-]$ are expressed in mol/L. The constant K_{sp} is called the **solubility product constant**, or simply the **solubility product.**

Because CaF_2 is a pure solid, it is not included in the equilibrium expression. It may seem strange at first that the amount of excess solid present does not affect the position of the solubility equilibrium. Surely more solid means more surface area exposed to the solvent, which would seem to result in greater solubility. This is not the case, however, because both dissolving and re-forming of the solid occur at the surface of the excess solid. When a solid dissolves, it is the ions at the surface that go into solution. And when the ions in solution re-form the solid, they do so on the surface of the solid. So doubling the surface area of the solid doubles not only the rate of dissolving but also the rate of re-formation of the solid. The amount of excess solid present therefore has no effect on the equilibrium position. Similarly, although either increasing the surface area by grinding up the solid or stirring the solution speeds up the attainment of equilibrium, neither procedure changes the *amount* of solid dissolved at equilibrium.

 PROBLEM SOLVING
Pure liquids and pure solids are never included in an equilibrium expression.

Example 17.8

Writing Solubility Product Expressions

Write the balanced equation describing the reaction for dissolving each of the following solids in water. Also write the K_{sp} expression for each solid.

   a. $PbCl_2(s)$ **b.** $Ag_2CrO_4(s)$ **c.** $Bi_2S_3(s)$

Solution

   a. $PbCl_2(s) \rightleftharpoons Pb^{2+}(aq) + 2Cl^-(aq)$; $K_{sp} = [Pb^{2+}][Cl^-]^2$
   b. $Ag_2CrO_4(s) \rightleftharpoons 2Ag^+(aq) + CrO_4^{2-}(aq)$; $K_{sp} = [Ag^+]^2[CrO_4^{2-}]$
   c. $Bi_2S_3(s) \rightleftharpoons 2Bi^{3+}(aq) + 3S^{2-}(aq)$; $K_{sp} = [Bi^{3+}]^2[S^{2-}]^3$

Self-Check Exercise 17.6

Write the balanced equation for the reaction describing the dissolving of each of the following solids in water. Also write the K_{sp} expression for each solid.

   a. $BaSO_4(s)$ **b.** $Fe(OH)_3(s)$ **c.** $Ag_3PO_4(s)$

Example 17.9

Calculating Solubility Products

Copper(I) bromide, CuBr, has a measured solubility of 2.0×10^{-4} mol/L at 25 °C. That is, when excess $CuBr(s)$ is placed in 1.0 L of water, we can determine that 2.0×10^{-4} mol of the solid dissolves to produce a saturated solution. Calculate the solid's K_{sp} value.

(continued)

Additional Examples

Write the balanced equation for dissolving each of the following solids in water. Also write the K_{sp} expression for each solid.

1. $Cr(OH)_3(s)$
   $Cr(OH)_3(s) \rightleftharpoons$
   $Cr^{3+}(aq) + 3OH^-(aq)$;
   $K_{sp} = [Cr^{3+}(aq)][OH^-(aq)]^3$

2. $Ca_3(PO_4)_2(s)$
   $Ca_3(PO_4)_2(s) \rightleftharpoons$
   $3Ca^{2+}(aq) + 2PO_4^{3-}(aq)$;
   $K_{sp} =$
   $[Ca^{2+}(aq)]^3[PO_4^{3-}(aq)]^2$

Answers to Self-Check Exercise 17.6

a. $BaSO_4(s) \rightleftharpoons Ba^{2+}(aq) + SO_4^{2-}(aq)$;
   $K_{sp} = [Ba^{2+}][SO_4^{2-}]$

b. $Fe(OH)_3(s) \rightleftharpoons Fe^{3+}(aq) + 3OH^-(aq)$;
   $K_{sp} = [Fe^{3+}][OH^-]^3$

c. $Ag_3PO_4(s) \rightleftharpoons 3Ag^+(aq) + PO_4^{3-}(aq)$;
   $K_{sp} = [Ag^+]^3[PO_4^{3-}]$

Additional Examples

1. Zinc carbonate, $ZnCO_3(s)$, dissolves in water to give a solution that is 1.7×10^{-5} M at 22 °C. Calculate K_{sp} for $ZnCO_3(s)$ at this temperature (ignoring the fact that CO_3^{2-} reacts with water).
   $K_{sp} = 2.9 \times 10^{-10}$

2. Copper(II) chromate, $CuCrO_4(s)$, dissolves in water to give a solution that contains 1.1×10^{-5} g $CuCrO_4$ per liter at 23 °C. Calculate K_{sp} for $CuCrO_4(s)$ at this temperature.
   $K_{sp} = 3.8 \times 10^{-15}$

(continued)

Solution

At first it is not obvious how to use the given information to solve the problem, but think about what happens when the solid dissolves. When the solid CuBr is placed in contact with water, it dissolves to form the separated Cu^+ and Br^- ions:

$$CuBr(s) \rightleftharpoons Cu^+(aq) + Br^-(aq)$$

where

$$K_{sp} = [Cu^+][Br^-]$$

PROBLEM SOLVING

Solubilities must be expressed in mol/L in K_{sp} calculations.

Therefore, we can calculate the value of K_{sp} if we know $[Cu^+]$ and $[Br^-]$, the equilibrium concentrations of the ions. We know that the measured solubility of CuBr is 2.0×10^{-4} mol/L. This means that 2.0×10^{-4} mol of solid CuBr dissolves per 1.0 L of solution to come to equilibrium. The reaction is

$$CuBr(s) \rightarrow Cu^+(aq) + Br^-(aq)$$

so

$$2.0 \times 10^{-4} \text{ mol/L CuBr}(s) \rightarrow$$
$$2.0 \times 10^{-4} \text{ mol/L Cu}^+(aq) + 2.0 \times 10^{-4} \text{ mol/L Br}^-(aq)$$

We can now write the equilibrium concentrations

$$[Cu^+] = 2.0 \times 10^{-4} \text{ mol/L}$$

and

$$[Br^-] = 2.0 \times 10^{-4} \text{ mol/L}$$

These equilibrium concentrations allow us to calculate the value of K_{sp} for CuBr.

$$K_{sp} = [Cu^+][Br^-] = (2.0 \times 10^{-4})(2.0 \times 10^{-4})$$
$$= 4.0 \times 10^{-8}$$

The units for K_{sp} values are omitted.

✔ **Self-Check Exercise 17.7**

Calculate the K_{sp} value for barium sulfate, $BaSO_4$, which has a solubility of 3.9×10^{-5} mol/L at 25 °C.

We have seen that the known solubility of an ionic solid can be used to calculate its K_{sp} value. The reverse is also possible: the solubility of an ionic solid can be calculated if its K_{sp} value is known.

Example 17.10

Calculating Solubility from K_{sp} Values

The K_{sp} value for solid AgI(s) is 1.5×10^{-16} at 25 °C. Calculate the solubility of AgI(s) in water at 25 °C.

Solution

The solid AgI dissolves according to the equation

$$AgI(s) \rightleftharpoons Ag^+(aq) + I^-(aq)$$

☑ **Answer to Self-Check Exercise 17.7**

$[Ba^{2+}] = [SO_4^{2-}]$
      $= 3.9 \times 10^{-5} M$

$K_{sp} = [Ba^{2+}][SO_4^{2-}]$

$K_{sp} = (3.9 \times 10^{-5})^2$
      $= 1.5 \times 10^{-9}$

Additional Examples

1. The K_{sp} value for $ZnCO_3(s)$ is 5.1×10^{-9}. Calculate the solubility of $ZnCO_3(s)$ in water in moles per liter.
   $7.1 \times 10^{-5} M$

2. The K_{sp} value for $CoCO_3(s)$ is 1.5×10^{-13}. Calculate the solubility of $CoCO_3(s)$ in water in moles per liter.
   $3.9 \times 10^{-7} M$

Note: These examples neglect the fact that CO_3^{2-} reacts with water.

and the corresponding equilibrium expression is

$$K_{sp} = 1.5 \times 10^{-16} = [Ag^+][I^-]$$

Because we do not know the solubility of this solid, we will assume that x moles per liter dissolves to reach equilibrium. Therefore,

$$x \ \frac{mol}{L} \ AgI(s) \rightarrow x \ \frac{mol}{L} \ Ag^+(aq) + x \ \frac{mol}{L} \ I^-(aq)$$

and at equilibrium,

$$[Ag^+] = x \ \frac{mol}{L}$$

$$[I^-] = x \ \frac{mol}{L}$$

Substituting these concentrations into the equilibrium expression gives

$$K_{sp} = 1.5 \times 10^{-16} = [Ag^+][I^-] = (x)(x) = x^2$$

Thus

$$x^2 = 1.5 \times 10^{-16}$$

$$x = \sqrt{1.5 \times 10^{-16}} = 1.2 \times 10^{-8} \ mol/L$$

The solubility of AgI(s) is 1.2×10^{-8} mol/L.

 Self-Check Exercise 17.8

The K_{sp} value for lead chromate, $PbCrO_4$, is 2.0×10^{-16} at 25 °C. Calculate its solubility at 25 °C.

 Focus Questions   **Sections 17.8–17.10**

1. Suppose the reaction system

$$UO_2(s) + 4HF(g) \rightleftharpoons UF_4(g) + 2H_2O(g)$$

has already reached equilibrium. Predict the effect of each of the following changes on the position of the equilibrium. Tell whether the equilibrium will shift to the right, will shift to the left, or will not be affected.
a. Additional $UO_2(s)$ is added to the system.
b. The reaction is performed in a glass reaction vessel; HF(g) attacks and reacts with glass.
c. Water vapor is removed.
d. The size of the reaction vessel is increased.

2. A reaction has a small value for K. At equilibrium what does this information tell you about each of the following:
a. amount of reactants
b. amount of products
c. extent of reaction

3. Write the equilibrium expression for

$$AgCl(s) \rightleftharpoons Ag^+(aq) + Cl^-(aq)$$

4. Why doesn't the solid appear in the K_{sp} expression?

 Answer to Self-Check Exercise 17.8

$$PbCrO_4(s) \rightleftharpoons$$
$$Pb^{2+}(aq) + CrO_4{}^{2-}(aq)$$
$$K_{sp} = [Pb^{2+}][CrO_4{}^{2-}]$$
$$= 2.0 \times 10^{-16}$$
Solubility $= x$ mol/L
$$= [Pb^{2+}]$$
$$= [CrO_4{}^{2-}]$$
$$K_{sp} = (x)(x) = x^2$$
$$= 2.0 \times 10^{-16}$$
$$x = 1.4 \times 10^{-8} \ mol/L$$

 Answers to Focus Questions

1. a. not affected
b. left
c. right
d. left

2. a. A small K means that the equilibrium position lies to the left. The reactants will predominate in the vessel.

b. The amount of products will be small since the equilibrium lies to the left.

c. The reaction does not proceed very far at all.

3. $K_{sp} = [Ag^+][Cl^-]$

4. The concentration of a solid never changes, so it is not included in the expression.

Equilibrium Beads

Objectives

1. To model dynamic chemical equilibrium

Skills

Applying concepts, interpreting data, drawing conclusions, making inferences, evaluating, computing

Materials

100 type A pop-it beads
50 type B pop-it beads
Cardboard box reaction vessel
Blindfolds (2)

Preparation Hints

Keep the different types of beads separated and in groups of 100 (type A) and 50 (type B) in sandwich baggies.

Prelab Discussion

Discuss Prelab question 1. Make sure that students understand how they will be able to tell when equilibrium is achieved and that they understand that the numbers after each reading will not be exactly the same for equilibrium. That is, there will always be a slight variation because we are dealing with such small numbers of "reactants." Once the variation seems to converge around one position, we can assume that equilibrium has been achieved.

The letter Q is introduced in the Summary Table. It stands for "reaction quotient" and the form of this expression is the same as that of K. The reaction quotient can be calculated at any condition and is equal to K at equilibrium.

Procedure Hints

Students should shake the box at a constant rate. In addition, they should double-check their counting (it is easy to miss a "product molecule" and, with relatively small numbers of products, this omission causes a large percentage difference).

Post-Lab Discussion

Have students take the "products" apart so the beads are ready for the next class.

Have students pool all of their results. Discuss the differences in K values for different parts of

Problem

How can we model dynamic chemical equilibrium?

Introduction

A chemical system at equilibrium appears to be unchanging because the rates of the forward and reverse reactions are equal. However, such a system is dynamic because at the molecular level the forward and reverse reactions are constantly taking place. In this activity you will model a system achieving equilibrium.

Prelab Assignment

1. Read the entire lab experiment before you begin.
2. How will you tell when equilibrium is established?
3. Why must the agitator be careful to always shake the box at the same rate?

Materials

100 type A pop-it beads
50 type B pop-it beads
Cardboard box reaction vessel
Blindfolds (2)

Procedure

Assign roles to the different members of your group:
1. Forward Reaction—the student finds two reactants and snaps them together to form a product molecule.
2. Reverse Reaction—the student searches for product molecules and unsnaps or breaks the bonds to form reactants.
3. Agitator—the student agitates or shakes the cardboard box reaction vessel to simulate the constant random kinetic motion of atoms and molecules.
4. Timer—the student times the reaction and starts and stops the activity.

Part I: A + A → A₂

1. Place 100 type A beads in the reaction vessel.
2. Blindfold the students representing the forward and reverse reactions.
3. The Agitator begins shaking the reaction vessel. *Caution:* The box needs to be shaken at a constant rate and care must be taken to not spill the beads.
4. The Timer signals the reactions to begin. The Timer stops the reaction after one minute.
5. Count the number of products (A_2) and determine the number of reactants. Record these numbers.
6. Leave all products intact and repeat the process until equilibrium is established.

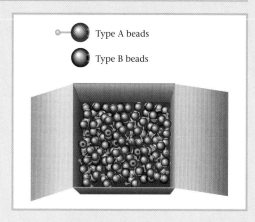

Type A beads

Type B beads

Part II: A + B → AB

1. All participants should switch roles.
2. Place 50 type A beads and 50 type B beads in the reaction vessel.
3. The Forward Reaction student forms only the product AB. Repeat the procedure used for Part I.

Cleaning Up

Put all materials away as directed by your teacher.

Data/Observations

Report the time to reach equilibrium in each part.

Analysis and Conclusions

1. Compare your times required to reach equilibrium with those of other groups.
2. Compare your values of K with those determined by other groups.
3. Should you expect the same value of K for Parts I and II? What causes differences in K values?
4. Should you expect the same value of K for each group in a given part? What causes differences in K values?
5. How does this activity show that equilibrium is microscopically dynamic but macroscopically static?
6. List some differences between this activity and a chemical system achieving equilibrium.

the experiment and between different groups.

Sample Data/Answers
Prelab Assignment

2. When the number of products (or reactants) is relatively constant for a few consecutive trials, then equilibrium is established.

3. Different rates of shaking the box will bring about different values for the equilibrium constant.

Shaking the box at different rates may make it easier or harder to find a "reactant" or a "product." Thus the number of "reactants" and "products" at equilibrium will vary, which will affect the value for the equilibrium constant.

Data/Observations

Answers will vary. Equilibrium should be reached within 10 minutes.

Analysis and Conclusions

1. Answers will vary.

2. Answers will vary.

3. No, we should not expect the same value of K. The value of the equilibrium constant is dependent on the nature of the reactants and products (and temperature). Since the "reactants" and "products" are different in these cases, we have no reason to

Summary Table

Fill in tables like the ones shown below.

Part I

Time	Number of "A" Particles	Number of "A₂" Particles	Value for K Expression
Initial			
1 minute			
2 minutes			
. . .			

Part II

Time	Number of "A" Particles	Number of "B" Particles	Number of "AB" Particles	Value for K Expression
Initial				
1 minute				
2 minutes				
. . .				

Something Extra

How would different numbers of beads affect the results? Carry out an experiment to answer this question.

17 Chapter Review

Key Terms

collision model (17.1)
activation energy (E_a) (17.2)
catalyst (17.2)
enzyme (17.2)
homogeneous reactions (17.3)
heterogeneous reactions (17.3)
equilibrium (17.4)
chemical equilibrium (17.4)
law of chemical equilibrium (17.6)
equilibrium expression (17.6)
equilibrium constant (17.6)
equilibrium position (17.6)
homogeneous equilibria (17.7)
heterogeneous equilibria (17.7)
Le Châtelier's principle (17.8)
solubility product (K_{sp}) (17.10)

Summary

1. Chemical reactions can be described by the collision model, which assumes that molecules must collide to react. In terms of this model, a certain threshold energy, called the activation energy (E_a), must be overcome for a collision to form products.

2. A catalyst is a substance that speeds up a reaction without being consumed. A catalyst operates by providing a lower-energy pathway for the reaction in question. Enzymes are biological catalysts.

3. When a chemical reaction is carried out in a closed vessel, the system achieves chemical equilibrium, the state where the concentrations of both reactants and products remain constant over time. Equilibrium is a highly dynamic state; reactants are converted continually into products, and vice versa, as molecules collide with each other. At equilibrium, the rates of the forward and reverse reactions are equal.

4. The law of chemical equilibrium is a general description of the equilibrium condition. It states that for a reaction of the type

$$aA + bB \rightleftharpoons cC + dD$$

the equilibrium expression is given by

$$K = \frac{[C]^c[D]^d}{[A]^a[B]^b}$$

where K is the equilibrium constant.

5. For each reaction system at a given temperature, there is only one value for the equilibrium constant, but there is an infinite number of possible equilibrium positions. An equilibrium position is defined as a particular set of equilibrium concentrations that satisfy the equilibrium expression. A specific equilibrium position depends on the initial concentrations. The amount of a pure liquid or a pure solid is never included in the equilibrium expression.

6. Le Châtelier's principle allows us to predict the effects of changes in concentration, volume, and temperature on a system at equilibrium. This principle states that when a change is imposed on a system at equilibrium,

Chapter Review   **569**

think that the value of K should be the same.

4. No. Agitators in each group will be shaking at different rates that may make it easier or harder to find a "reactant" or a "product." Consequently, the number of "reactants" and "products" at equilibrium will vary; this variation has an effect on the value of the equilibrium constant. In addition, different people will have differ-

ent abilities to find "reactants" and "products."

5. After several trials, the number of products is relatively constant (macroscopically static). However, products are being taken apart and re-formed constantly during the trials (microscopically dynamic).

6. Answers will vary. One difference is that with relatively small numbers of reactants and products,

we can expect some deviation in the numbers of products (even after reaching what we would consider to be equilibrium). Also, reaching equilibrium in this activity is dependent on students' consistency in making and taking apart products.

Summary Table

Sample data follow.

Part I

Time	Number of "A" Particles	Number of "A₂" Particles	Value for K Expression
Initial	100	0	0
1 minute	80	10	1.56×10^{-3}
2 minutes	70	15	3.06×10^{-3}
3 minutes	64	18	4.39×10^{-3}
4 minutes	60	20	5.56×10^{-3}
5 minutes	58	21	6.24×10^{-3}
6 minutes	56	22	7.02×10^{-3}
7 minutes	58	21	6.24×10^{-3}
8 minutes	58	21	6.24×10^{-3}

Part II

Time	Number of "A" Particles	Number of "B" Particles	Number of "AB" Particles	Value for K Expression
Initial	50	50	0	0
1 minute	45	45	5	2.47×10^{0}
2 minutes	42	42	8	4.54×10^{0}
3 minutes	40	40	10	6.25×10^{0}
4 minutes	38	38	12	8.31×10^{0}
5 minutes	39	39	11	7.23×10^{0}
6 minutes	38	38	12	8.31×10^{0}
7 minutes	38	38	12	8.31×10^{0}

Something Extra

Everything being equal, the number of beads should not affect the value of K. However, this activity is not completely analogous to chemical equilibrium, so answers will probably vary (plus it is difficult to keep everything else the same).

Chapter Review

Assign the students to work individually on the Chapter 17 Review Worksheet at the appropriate level (Basic, Standard, or Challenge). Answers are found in the *Teacher Resources*.

Assessment

Chapter 17 Test is found in the *Teacher Resources*, along with the answers for the test.

 Computerized Test Bank for Chapter 17

Answers to End of Chapter Problems

1. The hydrogen–hydrogen bond of H_2 and the bromine–bromine bond of Br_2 must break. Two hydrogen–bromine bonds (one in each of the HBr molecules) must form.

2. A nitrogen–nitrogen triple bond and three hydrogen–hydrogen bonds must be broken. Six nitrogen–hydrogen bonds must form.

3. The collision model pictures chemical reactions as taking place only when the reactant molecules physically collide with one another with enough energy to break the bonds in the reactant mole-

cules. A minimum energy (the activation energy) is needed for a collision to result in reaction. If molecules do not possess this minimum energy when they collide, they just bounce off one another without reacting.

4. The activation energy is the minimum energy required by two molecules for their collision to result in a reaction. If this energy requirement is not met, a collision will not result in a reaction.

5. A catalyst is a substance that speeds up a reaction without being consumed in the reaction. Catalysts work by providing an alternate pathway by which a reaction can take place; this alternate pathway has a lower activation energy.

6. The catalysts found in living cells are called enzymes. They are necessary for life because most of the cells' chemical processes would be too slow at room temperature without a catalyst.

7. In a heterogeneous reaction, reactants are in two phases. Reactions involving only one phase are homogeneous reactions.

8. For a chemical reaction to occur, the reactants must collide with one another. As the temperature increases, the average kinetic energy increases. The particles are moving faster and the collisions will occur more frequently.

9. Grain dust becomes airborne when grain is poured into a silo. This dust consists of tiny particles, which exposes a large amount of surface area to the oxygen in the air.

10. In an equilibrium system, two opposing processes are taking place at the same time and at the same speed. There is no net change in a system at equilibrium with time. Every time one process occurs, the opposite process occurs at the same time elsewhere in the system.

11. A state of equilibrium is reached when two opposing processes are exactly balanced. The development of a vapor pressure above a liquid in a closed container is an example of a physical equilibrium. Any chemical reaction

the equilibrium position will shift in a direction that tends to compensate for the imposed change.

7. The principle of equilibrium can also be applied when an excess of a solid is added to water to form a saturated solution. The solubility product (K_{sp}) is an equilibrium constant defined by the law of chemical equilibrium. Solubility is an equilibrium position, and the K_{sp} value of a solid can be determined by measuring its solubility. Conversely, the solubility of a solid can be determined if its K_{sp} value is known.

Questions and Problems

All exercises with blue numbers have answers in the back of this book.

17.1 How Chemical Reactions Occur

Questions

1. For the reaction $H_2(g) + Br_2(g) \rightarrow 2HBr(g)$, list the types of bonds that must be broken and the type of bond that must form for the chemical reaction to take place.

2. For the reaction $N_2(g) + 3H_2(g) \rightarrow 2NH_3(g)$, list the types of bonds that must be broken and the type of bond that must form for the chemical reaction to take place.

17.2 Conditions That Affect Reaction Rates

Questions

3. How do chemists envision reactions taking place in terms of the *collision model* for reactions? Give an example of a simple reaction and how you might envision the reaction taking place by means of a collision between the molecules.

4. What does the *activation energy* for a reaction represent? How is the activation energy related to whether a collision between molecules is successful?

5. What is a *catalyst*? How does a catalyst speed up a reaction?

6. What are the catalysts found in living cells called? Why are these biological catalysts necessary?

17.3 Heterogeneous Reactions

Questions

7. Explain the difference between a heterogeneous reaction and a homogeneous reaction.

8. Why does increasing the temperature speed up the rate of a chemical reaction?

9. Why is pouring grain into a silo a potentially explosive process? Use the collision theory in your explanation.

570   Chapter 17   Equilibrium

17.4 The Equilibrium Condition

Questions

10. How does *equilibrium* represent the balancing of opposing processes? Give an example of an "equilibrium" encountered in everyday life, showing how the processes involved oppose each other.

11. What do chemists mean by a state of *equilibrium?* Give an example of a *physical* equilibrium and of a *chemical* equilibrium.

12. What does it mean to say that chemical reactions are *reversible?* Are all chemical reactions, in principle, reversible? Are some reactions more likely to occur in one direction than in the other?

13. How do chemists recognize a system that has reached a state of chemical equilibrium? When writing chemical equations, how do we indicate reactions that come to a state of chemical equilibrium?

17.5 Chemical Equilibrium: A Dynamic Condition

Questions

14. When a reaction system has reached chemical equilibrium, the concentrations of the reactants and products no longer change with time. Why does the amount of product no longer increase, even though large concentrations of the reactants may still be present?

15. What does it mean to say that the condition of chemical equilibrium is a *dynamic* situation? Although the reaction overall may appear to have stopped, what is still going on in the system?

17.6 The Equilibrium Constant: An Introduction

Questions

16. In general terms, what does the equilibrium constant for a reaction represent? What is the algebraic form of the equilibrium constant for a typical reaction? What do square brackets indicate when we write an equilibrium constant?

17. There is only one value of the equilibrium constant for a particular system at a particular temperature, but there is an infinite number of equilibrium positions. Explain.

Problems

18. Write the equilibrium expression for each of the following reactions.
   a. $N_2(g) + 3Cl_2(g) \rightleftharpoons 2NCl_3(g)$
   b. $H_2(g) + I_2(g) \rightleftharpoons 2HI(g)$
   c. $N_2(g) + 2H_2(g) \rightleftharpoons N_2H_4(g)$

19. Write the equilibrium expression for each of the following reactions.
   a. $CO(g) + 2H_2(g) \rightleftharpoons CH_3OH(g)$
   b. $2NO_2(g) \rightleftharpoons 2NO(g) + O_2(g)$
   c. $P_4(g) + 6Br_2(g) \rightleftharpoons 4PBr_3(g)$

that appears to "stop" before completion is an example of chemical equilibrium.

12. Chemical reactions are reversible if they can occur in either direction (as written from left to right, or vice versa). In principle, all chemical reactions are microscopically reversible. In practice, many (but by no means all) reactions are favored in one direction over the other. This is especially true for open systems.

13. A system has reached equilibrium when the product concentrations no longer increase, even though significant amounts of all reactants are present. At that point, the reverse process is occurring at the same rate as the forward process. In other words, every time a product molecule is formed, another product molecule reacts to give back the reactants. Reactions that come to equilibrium are indicated by a double arrow.

14. Although we recognize a state of chemical equilibrium by the fact that the concentrations of reactants and products no longer change with time, the lack of change results from the fact that two opposing processes are going on at the same time at the same rate (not because the reaction has truly "stopped"). Further reaction in the forward direction is canceled out by an equal extent of reaction in the reverse direc-

20. Suppose that for the reaction

$$CH_3OH(g) \rightleftharpoons CH_2O(g) + H_2(g)$$

it is determined that, at a particular temperature, the equilibrium concentrations are $[CH_3OH(g)] = 0.00215$ M, $[CH_2O(g)] = 0.441\ M$, and $[H_2(g)] = 0.0331\ M$. Calculate the value of K for the reaction at this temperature.

21. Ammonia, a very important industrial chemical, is produced by the direct combination of the following elements under carefully controlled conditions:

$$N_2(g) + 3H_2(g) \rightleftharpoons 2NH_3(g)$$

Suppose, in an experiment, that the reaction mixture is analyzed after equilibrium is reached and it is found, at the particular temperature, that $[NH_3(g)] = 0.34\ M$, $[H_2(g)] = 2.1 \times 10^{-3}\ M$, and $[N_2(g)] = 4.9 \times 10^{-4}\ M$. Calculate the value of K at this temperature.

22. At high temperatures, elemental nitrogen and oxygen react with each other to form nitrogen monoxide.

$$N_2(g) + O_2(g) \rightleftharpoons 2NO(g)$$

Suppose the system is analyzed at a particular temperature, and the equilibrium concentrations are found to be $[N_2] = 0.041\ M$, $[O_2] = 0.0078\ M$, and $[NO] = 4.7 \times 10^{-4}\ M$. Calculate the value of K for the reaction.

17.7 Heterogeneous Equilibria

Questions

23. What is a *homogeneous* equilibrium system? Give an example of a homogeneous equilibrium reaction. What is a *heterogeneous* equilibrium system? Write two chemical equations that represent heterogeneous equilibria.

24. Explain why the position of a heterogeneous equilibrium does not depend on the amounts of pure solid or pure liquid reactants or products present.

Problems

25. Write the equilibrium expression for each of the following heterogeneous equilibria.
    a. $2LiHCO_3(s) \rightleftharpoons Li_2CO_3(s) + H_2O(g) + CO_2(g)$
    b. $PbCO_3(s) \rightleftharpoons PbO(s) + CO_2(g)$
    c. $4Al(s) + 3O_2(g) \rightleftharpoons 2Al_2O_3(s)$

26. Write the equilibrium expression for each of the following heterogeneous equilibria.
    a. $2NBr_3(s) \rightleftharpoons N_2(g) + 3Br_2(g)$
    b. $CuO(s) + H_2(g) \rightleftharpoons Cu(l) + H_2O(g)$
    c. $PbCO_3(s) \rightleftharpoons PbO(s) + CO_2(g)$

17.8 Le Châtelier's Principle

Questions

27. In your own words, describe what Le Châtelier's principle tells us about how we can change the position of a reaction system at equilibrium.

28. Discuss in general terms the effect on the net amount of product when an additional amount of one of the reactants is added to an equilibrium system. Does the value of the equilibrium constant change in this situation?

29. For an equilibrium involving gaseous substances, what effect, in general terms, is realized when the volume of the system is decreased?

30. What is the effect on the equilibrium position if an endothermic reaction is performed at a higher temperature? Does the net amount of product increase or decrease? Does the value of the equilibrium constant change if the temperature is increased?

Problems

31. For the reaction system

$$4NH_3(g) + 5O_2(g) \rightleftharpoons 4NO(g) + 6H_2O(g)$$

which has already reached a state of equilibrium, predict the effect that each of the following changes will have on the position of the equilibrium. Tell whether the equilibrium will shift to the right, will shift to the left, or will not be affected.
    a. The pressure of oxygen is increased by injecting one additional mole of oxygen into the reaction vessel.
    b. A desiccant (a material that absorbs water) is added to the system.
    c. The system is compressed and the ammonia liquefies.

32. Suppose the reaction system

$$CH_4(g) + 2O_2(g) \rightleftharpoons CO_2(g) + 2H_2O(l)$$

has already reached equilibrium. Predict the effect of each of the following changes on the position of the equilibrium. Tell whether the equilibrium will shift to the right, will shift to the left, or will not be affected.
    a. Any liquid water present is removed from the system.
    b. CO_2 is added to the system by dropping a chunk of dry ice into the reaction vessel.
    c. The reaction is performed in a metal cylinder fitted with a piston, and the piston is compressed to decrease the total volume of the system.
    d. Additional $O_2(g)$ is added to the system from a cylinder of pure O_2.

33. Old-fashioned "smelling salts" consist of ammonium carbonate, $(NH_4)_2CO_3$. The reaction for the decomposition of ammonium carbonate

$$(NH_4)_2CO_3(s) \rightleftharpoons 2NH_3(g) + CO_2(g) + H_2O(g)$$

is endothermic. What would be the effect on the position of this equilibrium if the reaction were performed at a lower temperature?

numbers, but each of these ratios is equal to 2.

18. (a) $K = [NCl_3(g)]^2 / [N_2(g)][Cl_2(g)]^3$;
    (b) $K = [HI(g)]^2 / [H_2(g)][I_2(g)]$;
    (c) $K = [N_2H_4(g)] / [N_2(g)][H_2(g)]^2$

19. (a) $K = [CH_3OH(g)] / [CO(g)][H_2(g)]^2$; (b) $K = [NO(g)]^2[O_2(g)] / [NO_2(g)]^2$;
    (c) $K = [PBr_3(g)]^4 / [P_4(g)][Br_2(g)]^6$

20. $K = 6.79$

21. $K = 2.5 \times 10^{10}$

22. $K = 6.9 \times 10^{-4}$

23. A homogeneous equilibrium system is a system in which all substances present are in the same physical state. An example is $N_2(g) + O_2(g) \rightleftharpoons 2NO(g)$. Heterogeneous equilibrium systems are those involving substances in more than one physical state—for example,
$BaCO_3(s) \rightleftharpoons BaO(s) + CO_2(g)$.

24. Equilibrium constants represent ratios of the concentrations of the products and reactants present at equilibrium. The concentration of a pure liquid or solid is constant and is determined by the density of the solid or liquid.

25. (a) $K = [H_2O(g)][CO_2(g)]$;
    (b) $K = [CO_2(g)]$;
    (c) $K = 1/[O_2(g)]^3$

26. (a) $K = [N_2(g)][Br_2(g)]^3$;
    (b) $K = [H_2O(g)]/[H_2(g)]$;
    (c) $K = [CO_2(g)]$

27. Le Châtelier's principle states that when a change is imposed on a system at equilibrium, the position of the equilibrium shifts in a direction that tends to reduce the effect of the change.

28. When more of one reactant is added to an equilibrium system, the system shifts to the right and adjusts to use up some of the added reactant. A net increase in the amount of product results, as compared with the equilibrium position before the additional reactant was added. The numerical value of the equilibrium constant does not change when a reactant is added. The concentrations of all reactants and products adjust until the ratios satisfy K.

29. When the volume decreases suddenly, the pressure in the container increases. The equilibrium shifts in the direction that gives the

tion. The reaction is still proceeding, but the opposite reaction is also proceeding at the same rate.

15. We recognize a state of chemical equilibrium by the fact that the concentrations of reactants and products no longer change with time. However, this lack of change does not mean the reaction has "stopped." The concentrations remain the same because the forward and reverse reactions are occurring at the same rate.

16. The equilibrium constant represents a ratio of the equilibrium concentration(s) of the product(s) present to the equilibrium concentration(s) of the reactant(s) present (with the concentration of each species raised to the power of its coefficient in the balanced equation). For a general reaction $aA + bB \rightleftharpoons cC + dD$, the equilibrium constant, K, has the form $[C]^c[D]^d / [A]^a[B]^b$.

The square brackets indicate the concentrations of the substances (in units of molarity, M).

17. Depending on the amounts of reactants that were present originally, differing amounts of products and reactants will be present at equilibrium. However, the ratio of the products to the reactants (which is represented by the equilibrium constant) will always be the same. For example, 4/2 and 6/3 involve different smaller number of gas molecules to reduce this increase in pressure.

30. If heat is applied (the temperature is raised) to an endothermic reaction, the equilibrium shifts to the right. More product (and less reactant) will be present at equilibrium than if the temperature had not been increased. The value of K increases.

31. (a) shifts right; (b) shifts right; (c) shifts left

32. (a) no change; (b) shifts left; (c) shifts right; (d) shifts right

33. For an endothermic reaction, a decrease in temperature will shift the position of equilibrium to the left (toward the reactants).

34. For an endothermic reaction, an increase in temperature will shift the position of equilibrium to the right (toward the products).

35. The production of dextrose will be favored.

36. A large equilibrium constant means that at equilibrium the concentration of the products is large compared with the concentration of the reactants. The position of the equilibrium lies far to the right. A reaction with a large equilibrium constant is therefore useful as a means of producing the products.

37. A small equilibrium constant means that at equilibrium the concentration of the products is small compared with the concentration of the reactants. The position of the equilibrium lies far to the left. A reaction with a small equilibrium constant is therefore not useful as a means of producing the products. To become useful, the equilibrium position would have to be shifted to the right.

38. $K = 3.2 \times 10^{11}$

39. $[O_3] = 1.8 \times 10^{-8}$ M

40. $K = 2.1 \times 10^{-3}$

41. $[NO] = 1.41 \times 10^{-3}$ M

42. $[N_2O_4] = 5.4 \times 10^{-4}$ M

43. When an ionic solid is placed in water, the crystal dissolves to produce ions. As the concentrations of the ions in the solutions increase, however, the likelihood of the oppositely charged ions colliding and re-forming the solid increases. Eventually, an

34. The reaction

$$4NO(g) + 6H_2O(g) \rightleftharpoons 4NH_3(g) + 5O_2(g)$$

is strongly endothermic. Will an increase in temperature shift the equilibrium position toward the products or toward the reactants?

35. Plants synthesize the sugar dextrose according to the following reaction by absorbing radiant energy from the sun (photosynthesis).

$$6CO_2(g) + 6H_2O(g) \rightleftharpoons C_6H_{12}O_6(s) + 6O_2(g)$$

Will an increase in temperature tend to favor or discourage the production of $C_6H_{12}O_6(s)$?

17.9 Applications Involving the Equilibrium Constant

Questions

36. Suppose a reaction has the equilibrium constant $K = 1.3 \times 10^8$. What does the magnitude of this constant tell you about the relative concentrations of products and reactants that will be present once equilibrium is reached? Is this reaction likely to be a good source of the products?

37. Suppose a reaction has the equilibrium constant $K = 4.5 \times 10^{-6}$ at a particular temperature. If an experiment is set up with this reaction, will there be large relative concentrations of products present at equilibrium? Is this reaction useful as a means of producing the products? How might the reaction be made more useful?

Problems

38. For the reaction

$$N_2(g) + 3Cl_2(g) \rightleftharpoons 2NCl_3(g)$$

an analysis of an equilibrium mixture is performed. It is found that $[NCl_3(g)] = 1.9 \times 10^{-1}$ M, $[N_2(g)] = 1.4 \times 10^{-3}$ M, and $[Cl_2(g)] = 4.3 \times 10^{-4}$ M. Calculate K for the reaction.

39. For the reaction

$$3O_2(g) \rightleftharpoons 2O_3(g)$$

$K = 1.8 \times 10^{-7}$ at a particular temperature. If the equilibrium system is analyzed and it is found that $[O_2] = 0.0012$ M, what is the concentration of O_3 in the system?

40. For the reaction

$$CaCO_3(s) \rightleftharpoons CaO(s) + CO_2(g)$$

it is found that at equilibrium $[CO_2] = 2.1 \times 10^{-3}$ M at a particular temperature. Calculate K for the reaction at this temperature.

41. For the reaction

$$N_2(g) + O_2(g) \rightleftharpoons 2NO(g)$$

the equilibrium constant K has the value 1.71×10^{-3} at a particular temperature. If the concentrations of both $N_2(g)$ and $O_2(g)$ are 0.0342 M in an equilibrium mixture at this temperature, what is the concentration of $NO(g)$ under these conditions?

42. For the reaction

$$N_2O_4(g) \rightleftharpoons 2NO_2(g)$$

the equilibrium constant K has the value 8.1×10^{-3} at a particular temperature. If the concentration of $NO_2(g)$ is found to be 0.0021 M in the equilibrium system, what is the concentration of $N_2O_4(g)$ under these conditions?

17.10 Solubility Equilibria

Questions

43. Explain how the dissolving of an ionic solute in water represents an equilibrium process.

44. Why does the amount of excess solid solute present in a solution not affect the amount of solute that ultimately dissolves in a given amount of solvent?

45. Why does neither stirring nor grinding a solute affect the amount of solute that ultimately dissolves in a given amount of solvent?

Problems

46. Write the balanced chemical equations describing the dissolving of the following solids in water. Write the expression for K_{sp} for each process.
   a. NiS(s)   c. $BaCrO_4(s)$
   b. $CuCO_3(s)$ d. $Ag_3PO_4(s)$

47. Write the balanced chemical equations describing the dissolving of the following solids in water. Write the expression for K_{sp} for each process.
   a. $PbBr_2(s)$ c. $PbCO_3(s)$
   b. $Ag_2S(s)$ d. $Sr_3(PO_4)_2(s)$

48. Zinc carbonate dissolves in water to the extent of 1.12×10^{-4} g/L at 25 °C. Calculate the solubility product K_{sp} for $ZnCO_3$ at 25 °C.

49. A saturated solution of nickel(II) sulfide contains approximately 3.6×10^{-4} g of dissolved NiS per liter at 20 °C. Calculate the solubility product K_{sp} for NiS at 20 °C.

50. The solubility product constant, K_{sp}, for calcium carbonate at room temperature is approximately 3.0×10^{-9}. Calculate the solubility of $CaCO_3$ in grams per liter under these conditions.

51. Chromate ion is used as a qualitative test for lead(II) ion, forming a bright yellow precipitate of lead chromate, $PbCrO_4(s)$. The K_{sp} for $PbCrO_4$ is 2.8×10^{-13} at 25 °C. Calculate the solubility of $PbCrO_4$ in grams per liter at 25 °C.

52. Lead(II) chloride, $PbCl_2(s)$, dissolves in water to the extent of approximately 3.6×10^{-2} M at 20 °C. Calculate the K_{sp} for $PbCl_2(s)$, and calculate its solubility in grams per liter.

53. Mercury(I) chloride, Hg_2Cl_2, was formerly administered orally to induce vomiting. Although we usually think of mercury compounds as highly toxic, the K_{sp} of mercury(I) chloride is small enough (1.3×10^{-18})

equilibrium is established in which the dissolving and re-forming of the solid occur at the same rate.

44. A given amount of solvent can "hold" only a certain amount of solute. Once this amount has been reached, adding more solid will not increase the concentration of dissolved solute in solution.

45. Stirring or grinding the solute increases the speed with which the solute dissolves. However, the amount of solute that

dissolves is set by the equilibrium constant for that process.

46. (a) NiS(s) $\rightleftharpoons$ $Ni^{2+}(aq)$ + $S^{2-}(aq)$; $K_{sp} = [Ni^{2+}(aq)]$ $[S^{2-}(aq)]$; (b) $CuCO_3(s) \rightleftharpoons$ $Cu^{2+}(aq) + CO_3^{2-}(aq)$; $K_{sp} = [Cu^{2+}(aq)][CO_3^{2-}(aq)]$; (c) $BaCrO_4(s) \rightleftharpoons Ba^{2+}(aq) +$ $CrO_4^{2-}(aq)$; $K_{sp} =$ $[Ba^{2+}(aq)][CrO_4^{2-}(aq)]$; (d) $Ag_3PO_4(s) \rightleftharpoons 3Ag^+(aq) +$ $PO_4^{3-}(aq)$; $K_{sp} = [Ag^+(aq)]^3[PO_4^{3-}(aq)]$

47. (a) $PbBr_2(s) \rightleftharpoons Pb^{2+}(aq) +$ $2Br^-(aq)$; $K_{sp} = [Pb^{2+}(aq)]$ $[Br^-(aq)]^2$; (b) $Ag_2S(s) \rightleftharpoons$ $2Ag^+(aq) + S^{2-}(aq)$; $K_{sp} =$ $[Ag^+(aq)]^2[S^{2-}(aq)]$; (c) $PbCO_3(s)$ $\rightleftharpoons Pb^{2+}(aq) + CO_3^{2-}(aq)$; $K_{sp} =$ $[Pb^{2+}(aq)][CO_3^{2-}(aq)]$; (d) $Sr_3(PO_4)_2(s) \rightleftharpoons 3Sr^{2+}(aq) +$ $2PO_4^{3-}(aq)$; $K_{sp} = [Sr^{2+}(aq)]^3[PO_4^{3-}(aq)]^2$

48. $K_{sp} = 7.98 \times 10^{-13}$

49. $K_{sp} = 1.6 \times 10^{-11}$

50. 5.5×10^{-3} g/L

51. 1.7×10^{-4} g/L

that the amount of mercury that dissolves and enters the bloodstream is tiny. Calculate the concentration of mercury(I) ion present in a saturated solution of Hg_2Cl_2.

Critical Thinking

54. Before two molecules can react, chemists envision that the molecules must first *collide* with each other. Is collision among molecules the only consideration for the molecules to react with one another?

55. Why does an increase in temperature favor an increase in the speed of a reaction?

56. What does it mean to say that all chemical reactions are, to one extent or another, *reversible*?

57. What does it mean to say that chemical equilibrium is a *dynamic* process?

58. Why does increasing the temperature for an exothermic process tend to favor the conversion of products back to reactants?

59. Suppose $K = 4.5 \times 10^{-3}$ at a certain temperature for the reaction

$$PCl_5(g) \rightleftharpoons PCl_3(g) + Cl_2(g)$$

If it is found that the concentration of PCl_5 is twice the concentration of PCl_3, what must be the concentration of Cl_2 under these conditions?

60. How does the collision model account for the fact that a reaction proceeds faster when the concentrations of the reactants are increased?

61. How does an increase in temperature result in an increase in the number of successful collisions between reactant molecules? What does an increase in temperature mean on a molecular basis?

62. Explain why the development of a vapor pressure above a liquid in a closed container represents an equilibrium. What are the opposing processes? How do we recognize when the system has reached a state of equilibrium?

63. Write the equilibrium expression for each of the following reactions.
   a. $H_2(g) + Br_2(g) \rightleftharpoons 2HBr(g)$
   b. $2H_2(g) + S_2(g) \rightleftharpoons 2H_2S(g)$
   c. $H_2(g) + C_2N_2(g) \rightleftharpoons 2HCN(g)$

64. Write the equilibrium expression for each of the following heterogeneous equilibria.
   a. $4Al(s) + 3O_2(g) \rightleftharpoons 2Al_2O_3(s)$
   b. $NH_3(g) + HCl(g) \rightleftharpoons NH_4Cl(s)$
   c. $2Mg(s) + O_2(g) \rightleftharpoons 2MgO(s)$

65. Suppose the reaction system

$$2NO(g) + O_2(g) \rightleftharpoons 2NO_2(g)$$

has already reached equilibrium. Predict the effect of each of the following changes on the position of the equilibrium. Tell whether the equilibrium will shift to the right, will shift to the left, or will not be affected.
   a. Additional oxygen is injected into the system.
   b. NO_2 is removed from the reaction vessel.
   c. 1.0 mol of helium is injected into the system.

66. Approximately 0.14 g of nickel(II) hydroxide, $Ni(OH)_2(s)$, dissolves per liter of water at 20 °C. Calculate the K_{sp} for $Ni(OH)_2(s)$ at this temperature.

61. At higher temperatures, the average kinetic energy of the reactant molecules is larger. Therefore, the probability that the molecules will have enough energy for a reaction to take place is greater. At the molecular level, a higher temperature means that a given molecule is moving faster.

62. The liquid begins to evaporate and produces molecules of vapor above the liquid. As the amount of vapor increases, the molecules collide and condense. Eventually, the opposite processes of evaporation and condensation occur at equal rates, and equilibrium is established.

63. (a) $K = [HBr(g)]^2/[H_2(g)][Br_2(g)]$; (b) $K = [H_2S(g)]^2/[H_2(g)]^2[S_2(g)]$; (c) $K = [HCN(g)]^2/[H_2(g)][C_2N_2(g)]$

64. (a) $K = 1/[O_2(g)]^3$; (b) $K = 1/[NH_3(g)][HCl(g)]$; (c) $K = 1/[O_2(g)]$

65. (a) shifts right; (b) shifts right; (c) no effect; although this change increases the total pressure, it does not change the pressures of any of the gases involved in the reaction and thus no shift will occur.

66. $K_{sp} = 1.4 \times 10^{-8}$

---

52. $K_{sp} = 1.9 \times 10^{-4}$; 10. g/L

53. 6.9×10^{-7} M

54. No. The molecules must also possess sufficient energy to react with one another and they must have the proper orientation in space for a reaction to occur.

55. An increase in temperature increases the fraction of molecules with energy greater than the activation energy.

56. To say a reaction is reversible means that it may occur in either direction.

57. Even though the reaction appears macroscopically to have stopped, on a microscopic basis the forward and reverse reactions are still taking place at the same speed.

58. In an exothermic process heat can be considered a product of the reaction. Adding heat (by increasing the temperature) therefore works against the forward process.

59. 9.0×10^{-3} M

60. A higher concentration means that more molecules are present in a given volume, which results in a greater frequency of collisions between molecules.

	Section	Text Features & Components	Labs, Demonstrations & Activities
Teaching Segment 18A 2.5 blocks pp. 575–584	18.1 Oxidation–Reduction Reactions	**LP** Lesson Plans (Sec 18.1–18.3) **TE** Teaching Support: Historical Background *p. 575*	**SE** Chemistry in the Laboratory: Activity Series *p. 601* **LM** Experiments 78–79 Lab Manual Report Sheets Teacher's Lab Guide
	18.2 Oxidation States		
	18.3 Oxidation–Reduction Reactions Between Nonmetals	**SE** Chemical Impact: U.S. Coins *p. 580* **SE** Celebrity Chemical: Hydrazine *p. 581*	**TE** Teaching Support: Demonstration *pp. 580–581* **LM** Experiment 80: Halogen Activity Series Lab Manual Report Sheets Teacher's Lab Guide
Teaching Segment 18B 2 blocks pp. 585–594	18.4 Balancing Oxidation–Reduction Reactions by the Half-Reaction Method	**LP** Lesson Plans (Sec 18.4–18.5) **SE** Chemical Impact: Real Gold *p. 590*	**TE** Teaching Support: Demonstration *pp. 590–591* **LM** Experiment 81: Analysis of Hydrogen Peroxide Lab Manual Report Sheets Teacher's Lab Guide
	18.5 Electrochemistry: An Introduction	**SE** Top Ten Most Active Metals *p. 591*	**TE** Teaching Support: Demonstration *pp. 592–593* **LM** Experiment 82: Galvanic Cells Lab Manual Report Sheets Teacher's Lab Guide
	continued on next page		

continued on next page

Key **SE** Student Edition   **TE** Teacher Edition   **RP** Teacher Resource Package   **LM** Lab Materials
LP Lesson Plans   **AR** Additional Resources   **◆** Florida Specific

Chapter Planning Guide

All Learners	Review & Assessment	Standards
TE Active Learning *p. 575* **TE** Teaching Tips *p. 575* **AR** Less Proficient Students *p. 35*	**TE** Additional Examples *p. 576* **SE** Self Check *p. 576* **SE** Key Terms *p. 602* **SE** Questions and Problems *p. 602*	**TE** NSES UCP1, A1, A2, B2, B3, E1, E2, G1, G2, G3 **SSS** SC.A.1.4.5, SC.C.2.4.2, SC.C.2.4.5, SC.B.1.4.5, SC.H.3.4.2, SC.H.3.4.3, SC.H.3.4.5, SC.H.3.4.6
AR Less Proficient Students *p. 35*	**TE** Additional Examples *p. 579* **SE** Self Check *p. 579* **SE** Key Terms *p. 602* **SE** Questions and Problems *pp. 602–603*	
TE Teaching Tips *pp. 580, 582* **TE** Integrating the Chemical Impact *p. 580* **Transparency: Rules for Assigning Oxidation Numbers** **RP** Team Learning Worksheets (Sec 18.1–18.3) *pp. 101–102* **AR** Less Proficient Students *p. 35*	**TE** Additional Examples *p. 583* **SE** Self Check *p. 584* **SE** Focus Questions (Sec 18. 1–18.3) *p. 584* **SE** Key Terms *p. 602* **SE** Questions and Problems *p. 603*	
TE Active Learning *p. 585* **AR** Less Proficient Students *p. 35*	**TE** Additional Examples *pp. 587, 589* **SE** Self Check *p. 590* **SE** Key Terms *p. 602* **SE** Questions and Problems *pp. 603–604*	**TE** NSES UCP1, UCP3, UCP5, A1, A2, B2, B3, E1, F3, G1, G2, G3 **SSS** SC.C.2.4.2, SC.C.2.4.5, SC.B.1.4.2, SC.H.3.4.5
Animation: Electrochemical Hall–Reactions • Anode Reaction • Cathode Reaction • Oxidation–Reduction Reaction Transparency: Figure 18.3, 18.4 *p. 592* Chemistry in Motion (29) *p. 592* **RP** Team Learning Worksheets (Sec 18.4–18.5) *pp. 103–104* **AR** Less Proficient Students *p. 35*	**SE** Focus Questions (Sec 18.4–18.5) *p. 594* **SE** Key Terms *p. 602* **SE** Questions and Problems *p. 604*	

18 Oxidation–Reduction Reactions and Electrochemistry

Section	Text Features & Components	Labs, Demonstrations & Activities

Teaching Segment 18C
1 block
pp. 595–600

18.6 Batteries	**LP** Lesson Plans (Sec 18.6–18.8) **SE** Chemical Impact: An Engine for the Twenty-First Century *p. 597*	
18.7 Corrosion		**SE** Chemistry in Action: Lemon Power *p. 599* **LM** Experiment 83: Corrosion of Iron Lab Manual Report Sheets Teacher's Lab Guide
18.8 Electrolysis		

Key

- **SE** Student Edition
- **TE** Teacher Edition
- **RP** Teacher Resource Package
- **LM** Lab Materials
- **LP** Lesson Plans
- **AR** Additional Resources
- Florida Specific

Technology and Media

 Transparencies
Rules for Assigning Oxidation Numbers, Figure 18.3, 1834, 18.6, 18.7, 18.8

PowerPoint Slides

 Animation Electrochemical Half Reactions • Anode Reaction • Cathode Reaction • Oxidation–Reduction Reaction

Video Lemon Battery
Chemistry in Motion (29) Galvanic Cells • (30) Electrolysis of Water

 eEdition CD-ROM
Easy Planner CD-ROM
English Summaries CD
Spanish Summaries CD

 Web Site classzone.com
McDougal Littell Test Generator

Chapter Planning Guide

All Learners	Review & Assessment	Standards
TE Active Learning *p. 595* **TE** Teaching Tips *p. 595* **(transparency)** Transparency: Figure 18.6, 18.7, 18.8 **(video)** Video: Lemon Battery *p. 595* **AR** Less Proficient Students *p. 36*	**SE** Key Terms *p. 602* **SE** Questions and Problems *p. 604*	**TE** **NSES** UCP3, UCP5, A1, A2, B2, B3, E1, E2, F3, F4, F6, G1, G2, G3 **SSS** SC.H.1.4.1, SC.H.1.4.2, SC.H.1.4.3, SC.H.1.4.4, SC.H.1.4.5, SC.H.1.4.6, SC.H.1.4.7, SC.C.2.4.2, SC.C.2.4.5, SC.B.1.4.5, SC.H.3.4.2, SC.H.3.4.3, SC.H.3.4.4, SC.H.3.4.5, SC.H.3.4.6
AR Less Proficient Students *p. 36*	**SE** Key Terms *p. 602* **SE** Questions and Problems *p. 604*	
(video) Chemistry in Motion (30) *p. 600* **RP** Team Learning Worksheets (Sec 18.6–18.8) *p. 105* **AR** Less Proficient Students *p. 36*	**SE** What if . . . *p. 599* **SE** Focus Questions (Sec 18.7–18.8) *p. 600* **SE** Questions and Problems *p. 604*	

Chapter Materials

TE Reading Strategy
AR English/Spanish Summaries *pp. 29–30*
AR Challenge Projects/Problems *p. 34*
AR Less Proficient Students *p. 36*
(audio) English Summary Audio
(audio) Spanish Summary Audio
RP Chapter Review Worksheets (Basic, Review, Challenge)

SE Chapter Summary *p. 602*
SE Critical Thinking *pp. 604–605*
RP Solutions Guide
RP Chapter Tests
RP Test Bank
(generator) McDougal Littell Test Generator
AR Standardized Test Practice
(globe) FCAT Test 9

18 Integrating Reading Strategies and Chemistry Concepts

Chapter 18: Reading Rules

Reading rules is a necessary part of most areas of study. Discuss the examples of rules below with the students.

English Grammar Rules
• Spelling Rules
• Capitalization Rules
• Punctuation Rules
• Subject-Verb Agreement Rules
• Verb Conjugation Rules

Mathematics
• Order of Operations
• Adding, Subtracting, Multiplying, and Dividing Signed Numbers
• Pythagorean Theorem
• Right Triangle Rules

Instruct the students to write a definition of *rule* and then ask for volunteers to read aloud their definition. List these definitions on the board. Many students will define a rule as a formula or equation. Discuss some of the more general definitions provided by the students.

Direct the students' attention to the box on page 582, "Rules for Assigning Oxidation States." Point out that the rules are numbered. Instruct the students to skim the rules. Then direct the students' attention to the box on page 586, "The Half-Reaction Method for Balancing Equations for Oxidation-Reduction Reactions Occurring in Acidic Solution." Ask the students how the presentation of this information is different from that found on page 582. [It is presented in steps rather than in numbered rules.] Instruct the students to skim the steps. Ask the students whether the compilation of the steps would also qualify as rules. [Yes] Have the students revise their definitions of *rule* if necessary.

Provide the following definition: **In chemistry, rules are generalizations that summarize chemical behavior.** Point out that sometimes these rules are purely chemical in nature, sometimes they are mathematical, and sometimes they are a combination of both. Stress that rules can be presented as rules, steps, principles or laws, or equations and formulas. An author may consider several formats before deciding which one is most appropriate for the goal and the complexity of the concept involved.

Reading Rules in Chemistry

Direct the students' attention back to page 582, "Rules for Assigning Oxidation States." Stress that before using a rule or set of rules, the user needs to:
• have a good understanding of what the rules are intended to accomplish.
• have a good understanding of the concepts and facts involved.
• know when to apply the rule.
• know whether there are any exceptions to the rule.

Explain that knowing when to apply a rule is particularly important because many sets of rules contain information designed to fit all circumstances; the particular circumstance that the students are working on might require use of only one or two of the rules.

As an exercise in reading rules and determining which ones apply, have the students consider each of the following examples. Point out that a good strategy is to read through all of the rules to determine which are applicable. Sometimes more than one rule is applicable, and the students can choose whichever rule is easier to apply. Walk through the first example with the students step by step.

Example 1: In the compound carbon monoxide (CO), carbon is assigned an oxidation state of $+2$ and oxygen is assigned an oxidation state of -2.

- Rule 1 does not apply because CO is not an uncombined element.
- Rule 2 does not apply because CO is not a monatomic ion.
- Rule 3 DOES apply because CO contains oxygen. The rule tells us that oxygen is assigned an oxidation state of -2. This is a simple rule and should be applied immediately. There is an exception to this rule, which the students should make note of, but it does not apply in this case.
- Rule 4 does not apply because CO does not contain hydrogen.
- Rule 5 is not needed because oxygen is already assigned an oxidation state of -2 from Rule 3.
- Rule 6 DOES apply because CO is an electrically neutral compound. The rule states that the sum of the oxidation states must be zero, and it is fairly simple to add -2 and $+2$ to get zero, so the students should apply this rule.
- Rule 7 does not apply because CO is not an ionic species.

> ### Rules for Assigning Oxidation States
>
> 1. The oxidation state of an atom in an uncombined element is 0.
> 2. The oxidation state of a monatomic ion is the same as its charge.
> 3. Oxygen is assigned an oxidation state of -2 in most of its covalent compounds. Important exception: peroxides (compounds containing the O_2^{2-} group), in which each oxygen is assigned an oxidation state of -1.
> 4. In its covalent compounds with nonmetals, hydrogen is assigned an oxidation state of $+1$.
> 5. In binary compounds, the element with the greater electronegativity is assigned a negative oxidation state equal to its charge as an anion in its ionic compounds.
> 6. For an electrically neutral compound, the sum of the oxidation states must be zero.
> 7. For an ionic species, the sum of the oxidation states must equal the overall charge.

Instruct the students to work through the next examples using the same process as above.

Example 2: In the compound ammonia (NH_3), hydrogen is assigned an oxidation state of $+1$ and nitrogen is assigned an oxidation state of -3.

Example 3: On the left side of the equation $2Na + Cl_2 \rightarrow 2NaCl$, sodium is assigned an oxidation state of 0 and chlorine is assigned an oxidation state of 0. On the right side of the equation, sodium is assigned an oxidation state of $+1$ and chlorine is assigned an oxidation state of -1.

Overview

In this Chapter our goals are for the students to:

- Learn about metal/nonmetal oxidation reduction reactions

- Learn to assign oxidation states

- Understand oxidation and reduction in terms of oxidation states

- Learn to identify oxidizing and reducing agents

- Learn to balance oxidation–reduction equations using half reactions

- Understand the term electrochemistry

- Learn to identify the components of an electrochemical cell

- Learn about the composition and operation of commonly used batteries

- Understand the electrochemical nature of corrosion and to learn ways of preventing it

- Understand the process of electrolysis and learn about the commercial preparation of aluminum

18 Oxidation–Reduction Reactions and Electrochemistry

A nickel electroplated with copper.

574

What do a forest fire, rusting steel, combustion in an automobile engine, and the metabolism of food in a human body have in common? All of these important processes involve oxidation–reduction reactions. In fact, virtually all of the processes that provide energy to heat buildings, power vehicles, and allow people to work and play depend on oxidation–reduction reactions. And every time you start your car, turn on your calculator, look at your digital watch, or listen to a radio at the beach, you are depending on an oxidation–reduction reaction to power the battery in each of these devices. In addition, because "pollution-free" vehicles have been mandated in California (and other states are soon to follow), battery-powered cars are about to become more common on U.S. roads (see "Chemical Impact: An Engine for the Twenty-First Century" on page 597). This will lead to increased reliance of our society on batteries and will spur the search for new, more efficient batteries.

In this chapter we will explore the properties of oxidation–reduction reactions, and we will see how these reactions are used to power batteries.

The power generated by an alkaline AA battery and a mercury battery results from oxidation–reduction reactions.

18.1 Oxidation–Reduction Reactions

Objective: *To learn about metal–nonmetal oxidation–reduction reactions.*

In Section 8.5 we discussed the chemical reactions between metals and non-metals. For example, sodium chloride is formed by the reaction of elemental sodium and chlorine.

$$2Na(s) + Cl_2(g) \rightarrow 2NaCl(s)$$

Because elemental sodium and chlorine contain uncharged atoms and because sodium chloride is known to contain Na^+ and Cl^- ions, this reaction must involve a transfer of electrons from sodium atoms to chlorine atoms.

Reactions like this one, in which one or more electrons are transferred, are called **oxidation–reduction reactions,** *or* **redox reactions. Oxidation** is defined as a *loss of electrons.* **Reduction** is defined as a *gain of electrons.* In

18.1 Oxidation–Reduction Reactions **575**

Chapter 18   Oxidation–Reduction Reactions and Electrochemistry   **575**

Additional Examples

For the following reactions, identify which element is oxidized and which element is reduced.

1. $Cl_2(g) + Cu(s) \rightarrow CuCl_2(s)$
   Copper is oxidized and chlorine is reduced.

2. $O_2(g) + 2Ni(s) \rightarrow 2NiO(s)$
   Nickel is oxidized and oxygen is reduced.

3. $S(s) + 2Hg(l) \rightarrow Hg_2S(s)$
   Mercury is oxidized and sulfur is reduced.

  Answers to Self-Check Exercise 18.1

a. CuO contains Cu^{2+} and O^{2-} ions, so copper is oxidized ($Cu \rightarrow Cu^{2+} + 2e^-$) and oxygen is reduced ($O + 2e^- \rightarrow O^{2-}$).

b. CsF contains Cs^+ and F^- ions. Thus cesium is oxidized ($Cs \rightarrow Cs^+ + e^-$) and fluorine is reduced ($F + e^- \rightarrow F^-$).

the reaction of elemental sodium and chlorine, each sodium atom loses one electron, forming a 1+ ion. Therefore, sodium is oxidized. Each chlorine atom gains one electron, forming a negative chloride ion, and is thus reduced. Whenever a metal reacts with a nonmetal to form an ionic compound, electrons are transferred from the metal to the nonmetal. So these reactions are always oxidation–reduction reactions where the metal is oxidized (loses electrons) and the nonmetal is reduced (gains electrons).

Example 18.1

Magnesium burns in air to give a bright, white flame.

Identifying Oxidation and Reduction in a Reaction

In the following reactions, identify which element is oxidized and which element is reduced.

    a. $2Mg(s) + O_2(g) \rightarrow 2MgO(s)$

    b. $2Al(s) + 3I_2(s) \rightarrow 2AlI_3(s)$

Solution

    a. We have learned that Group 2 metals form 2+ cations and that Group 6 nonmetals form 2− anions, so we can predict that magnesium oxide contains Mg^{2+} and O^{2-} ions. This means that in the reaction given, each Mg loses two electrons to form Mg^{2+} and so is oxidized. Also each O gains two electrons to form O^{2-} and so is reduced.

    b. Aluminum iodide contains the Al^{3+} and I^- ions. Thus aluminum atoms lose electrons (are oxidized). Iodine atoms gain electrons (are reduced).

  Self-Check Exercise 18.1

For the following reactions, identify the element oxidized and the element reduced.

    a. $2Cu(s) + O_2(g) \rightarrow 2CuO(s)$

    b. $2Cs(s) + F_2(g) \rightarrow 2CsF(s)$

       Although we can identify reactions between metals and nonmetals as redox reactions, it is more difficult to decide whether a given reaction between nonmetals is a redox reaction. In fact, many of the most significant redox reactions involve only nonmetals. For example, combustion reactions such as methane burning in oxygen,

$$CH_4(g) + 2O_2(g) \rightarrow CO_2(g) + 2H_2O(g) + energy$$

are oxidation–reduction reactions. Even though none of the reactants or products in this reaction is ionic, the reaction does involve a transfer of electrons from carbon to oxygen. To explain this, we must introduce the concept of oxidation states.

18.2 Oxidation States

Objective: *To learn how to assign oxidation states.*

The concept of **oxidation states** (sometimes called *oxidation numbers*) lets us keep track of electrons in oxidation–reduction reactions by assigning charges to the various atoms in a compound. Sometimes these charges are quite apparent. For example, in a binary ionic compound the ions have easily identified charges: in sodium chloride, sodium is +1 and chlorine is −1; in magnesium oxide, magnesium is +2 and oxygen is −2; and so on. In such binary ionic compounds the oxidation states are simply the charges of the ions.

Ion	Oxidation State
Na^+	+1
Cl^-	−1
Mg^{2+}	+2
O^{2-}	−2

In an uncombined element, all of the atoms are uncharged (neutral). For example, sodium metal contains neutral sodium atoms, and chlorine gas is made up of Cl_2 molecules, each of which contains two neutral chlorine atoms. Therefore, an atom in a pure element has no charge and is assigned an oxidation state of zero.

In a covalent compound such as water, although no ions are actually present, chemists find it useful to assign imaginary charges to the elements in the compound. The oxidation states of the elements in these compounds are equal to the imaginary charges we determine by assuming that the most electronegative atom (see Section 12.2) in a bond controls or possesses *both* of the shared electrons. For example, in the O—H bonds in water, it is assumed for purposes of assigning oxidation states that the much more electronegative oxygen atom controls both of the shared electrons in each bond. This gives the oxygen eight valence electrons.

$$
\begin{array}{c}
H \\
\ \ \ \diagdown \\
\ \ \ \ \ O\!: \longleftarrow 2e^- \\
\ \ \ \diagup \ \ \ \longleftarrow 2e^- \\
H
\end{array}
$$

In effect we say that each hydrogen has lost its single electron to the oxygen. This gives each hydrogen an oxidation state of +1 and the oxygen an oxidation state of −2 (the oxygen atom has formally gained two electrons). In virtually all covalent compounds, oxygen is assigned an oxidation state of −2 and hydrogen is assigned an oxidation state of +1.

Because fluorine is so electronegative, it is always assumed to control any shared electrons. So fluorine is always assumed to have a complete octet of electrons and is assigned an oxidation state of −1. That is, for purposes of assigning oxidation states, fluorine is always imagined to be F^- in its covalent compounds.

The most electronegative elements are F, O, N, and Cl. In general, we give each of these elements an oxidation state equal to its charge as an anion (fluorine is −1, chlorine is −1, oxygen is −2, and nitrogen is −3). When two of these elements are found in the same compound, we assign them in order of electronegativity, starting with the element that has the largest electronegativity.

18.2 Oxidation States **577**

$$F > O > N > Cl$$

Greatest   Least
electronegativity   electronegativity

For example, in the compound NO_2, because oxygen has a greater electronegativity than nitrogen, we assign each oxygen an oxidation state of -2. This gives a total "charge" of -4 (2×-2) on the two oxygen atoms. Because the NO_2 molecule has zero overall charge, the N must be $+4$ to exactly balance the -4 on the oxygens. In NO_2, then, the oxidation state of *each* oxygen is -2 and the oxidation state of the nitrogen is $+4$.

The rules for assigning oxidation states are given below and are illustrated in **Table 18.1.** Application of these rules allows us to assign oxidation states in most compounds. The principles are illustrated by Example 18.2.

TABLE 18.1

Examples of Oxidation States

Substance	Oxidation States	Comments
sodium metal, Na	Na, 0	rule 1
phosphorus, P	P, 0	rule 1
sodium fluoride, NaF	Na, +1	rule 2
	F, −1	rule 2
magnesium sulfide, MgS	Mg, +2	rule 2
	S, −2	rule 2
carbon monoxide, CO	C, +2	
	O, −2	rule 3
sulfur dioxide, SO_2	S, +4	
	O, −2	rule 3
hydrogen peroxide, H_2O_2	H, +1	
	O, −1	rule 3 (exception)
ammonia, NH_3	H, +1	rule 4
	N, −3	rule 5
hydrogen sulfide, H_2S	H, +1	rule 4
	S, −2	rule 5
hydrogen iodide, HI	H, + 1	rule 4
	I, −1	rule 5
sodium carbonate, Na_2CO_3	Na, +1	rule 2
	O, −2	rule 3
	C, +4	For $CO_3{}^{2-}$, the sum of the oxidation states is $+4 + 3(-2) = -2$. rule 7
ammonium chloride, NH_4Cl	N, −3	rule 5
	H, +1	rule 4
		For $NH_4{}^+$, the sum of the oxidation states is $-3 + 4(+1) = +1$. rule 7
	Cl, −1	rule 2

Hydrogen peroxide can be used to disinfect a wound.

Example 18.2

Assigning Oxidation States

Assign oxidation states to all atoms in the following molecules or ions.

    a. CO_2

    b. SF_6

    c. NO_3^-

Solution

a. Rule 3 takes precedence here: oxygen is assigned an oxidation state of -2. We determine the oxidation state for carbon by recognizing that because CO_2 has no charge, the sum of the oxidation states for oxygen and carbon must be 0 (rule 6). Each oxygen is -2 and there are two oxygen atoms, so the carbon atom must be assigned an oxidation state of $+4$.

$$CO_2$$
$$+4 \uparrow \uparrow \;\; -2 \text{ for } each \text{ oxygen}$$

Check: $+4 + 2(-2) = 0$

b. Because fluorine has the greater electronegativity, we assign its oxidation state first. Its charge as an anion is always -1, so we assign -1 as the oxidation state of each fluorine atom (rule 5). The sulfur must then be assigned an oxidation state of $+6$ to balance the total of -6 from the six fluorine atoms (rule 7).

$$SF_6$$
$$+6 \uparrow \uparrow \;\; -1 \text{ for } each \text{ fluorine}$$

Check: $+6 + 6(-1) = 0$

c. Oxygen has a greater electronegativity than nitrogen, so we assign its oxidation state of -2 first (rule 5). Because the overall charge on NO_3^- is -1 and because the sum of the oxidation states of the three oxygens is -6, the nitrogen must have an oxidation state of $+5$.

$$NO_3^-$$
$$+5 \uparrow \uparrow \;\; -2 \text{ for } each \text{ oxygen gives } -6 \text{ total}$$

Check: $+5 + 3(-2) = -1$

This is correct; NO_3^- has a -1 charge.

 Self-Check Exercise 18.2

Assign oxidation states to all atoms in the following molecules or ions.

    a. SO_3

    b. SO_4^{2-}

    c. N_2O_5

    d. PF_3

    e. C_2H_6

18.2   Oxidation States   **579**

c. N_2O_5

We assign oxygen before nitrogen because oxygen is more electronegative. Thus each O is assigned an oxidation state of -2, giving a total of $-10(5 \times -2)$ on the five oxygen atoms. Therefore, the oxidation states of the *two* nitrogen atoms must total $+10$, because N_2O_5 has no overall charge. Each N is assigned an oxidation state of $+5$.

Check: $2(+5) + 5(-2) = 0$

d. PF_3

First we assign the fluorine an oxidation state of -1, giving a total of -3 (3×-1) on the three fluorine atoms. Thus P must have an oxidation state of $+3$.

Check: $+3 + 3(-1) = 0$

e. C_2H_6

In this case it is best to recognize that hydrogen is always $+1$ in compounds with nonmetals. Thus each H is assigned an oxidation state of $+1$, which means that the six H atoms account for a total of $+6$ $(6 \times +1)$. Therefore, the *two* carbon atoms must account for -6, and each carbon is assigned an oxidation state of -3.

Check: $2(-3) + 6(+1) = 0$

Additional Examples

Assign oxidation states to all atoms in the following molecules or ions.

1. NF_3
   nitrogen, $+3$; fluorine, -1

2. $HOCl$
   hydrogen, $+1$; oxygen, -2; chlorine, $+1$

3. SO_4^{2-}
   sulfur, $+6$; oxygen, -2

Answers to Self-Check Exercise 18.2

a. SO_3
We assign oxygen first. Each O is assigned an oxidation state of -2, giving a total of -6 (3×-2) for the three oxygen atoms. Because the molecule has zero charge overall, the sulfur must have an oxidation state of $+6$.

Check: $+6 + 3(-2) = 0$

b. SO_4^{2-}
As in part a, each oxygen is assigned an oxidation state of -2, giving a total of -8 (4×-2) on the four oxygen atoms. The anion has a net charge of -2, so the sulfur must have an oxidation state of $+6$.

Check: $+6 + 4(-2) = -2$
SO_4^{2-} has a charge of -2, so this is correct.

Themes
Organization, Systems

Skills
Making comparisons, applying concepts, classifying

Laboratory
Experiment 80:
Halogen Activity Series, CBL

TEACHING TIPS

• Use examples from earlier chapters, including single-displacement, synthesis, and decomposition reactions, to show students how many oxidation–reduction reactions they already know. Assign oxidation states to all of the elements in the reactants and products of these reactions to illustrate that in an oxidation–reduction reaction one substance is oxidized at the same time that another substance is reduced.

• Students need to practice determining the number of electrons gained or lost in a reaction. This is important for balancing oxidation–reduction reactions correctly. Students sometimes have trouble applying the rules of oxidation states to compounds. For example, oxygen has a −2 oxidation state. A compound such as SO_2 contains two oxygen atoms, however, which means that four electrons must have been transferred in $S + O_2 \rightarrow SO_2$.

Integrating the CHEMICAL IMPACT

U.S. Coins

Have students research the history of the composition of U.S. coins. Ask them to determine when the composition of each coin changed. Was a copper penny ever really copper? What are the implications of changing the composition of coins? Will they still work in various machines (such as vending machines)?

For an interesting demonstration of the composition of a penny see the Teaching Support, "Floating Pennies."

18.3 Oxidation–Reduction Reactions Between Nonmetals

Objectives: *To understand oxidation and reduction in terms of oxidation states.*
To learn to identify oxidizing and reducing agents.

We have seen that oxidation–reduction reactions are characterized by a transfer of electrons. In some cases, the transfer literally occurs to form ions, such as in the reaction

$$2Na(s) + Cl_2(g) \rightarrow 2NaCl(s)$$

We can use oxidation states to verify that electron transfer has occurred.

$$2Na(s) + Cl_2(g) \rightarrow 2NaCl(s)$$

Oxidation state:	0	0	+1 −1
	(element)	(element)	(Na^+) (Cl^-)

Thus in this reaction, we represent the electron transfer as follows:

$$e \overset{Na}{\underset{Cl}{\big(}} \Rightarrow \overset{Na^+}{\underset{Cl^-}{}}$$

CHEMICAL IMPACT

Consumer Connections

U.S. Coins

We all use coins every day without thinking much about them. It turns out that some interesting chemistry is associated with the making of the coins used in the United States. For example, the "copper" penny is really mostly zinc with a coating of copper. The "nickel" coin contains much more copper than nickel—it's made of a copper/nickel alloy that is 75% copper and 25% nickel. All of the other coins used in the United States are clad—they have a pure copper core that is surrounded (sandwiched) by an alloy. The dime, the quarter, the half-dollar, and the Susan B. Anthony dollar all have a copper core sandwiched by a copper/nickel alloy. The new Sacagawea dollar* has a copper core surrounded by a special alloy containing copper, zinc, nickel, and manganese that gives it the same electromagnetic properties as the Anthony dollar so it will work in current vending machines.

The composition and physical properties of the coins are listed in the accompanying table.

Coin	Composition	Mass (g)	Diameter (mm)
Penny	Copper-plated zinc (97.5% Zn, 2.5% Cu)	2.5	19.1
Nickel	Copper/nickel alloy (75% Cu, 25% Zn)	5.0	21.2
Dime	Copper–nickel clad (91.7% Cu, 8.3% Ni)	2.3	17.9
Quarter	Copper–nickel clad (91.7% Cu, 8.3% Ni)	5.7	24.3
Half-dollar	Copper–nickel clad (91.7% Cu, 8.3% Ni)	11.3	30.6
Susan B. Anthony dollar	Copper–nickel clad (87.5% Cu, 12.5% Ni)	8.1	26.5
Sacagawea dollar	Manganese–brass clad (88.5% Cu, 6.0% Zn, 3.5% Mn, 2.0% Ni)	8.1	26.5

*See "The 'Golden' Dollar," page 277.

TEACHING SUPPORT
Demonstration

Floating Pennies

Materials
Post-1982 penny
File
6 *M* HCl
Large Erlenmeyer flask
Parafilm or watch glass

Presentation Place about 100 mL of HCl in the large flask. Using the file, make four or five notches in the edge of the penny, being sure to break through the copper covering on the penny. Carefully drop the penny into the acid. Cover the flask and allow it to remain undisturbed for several days (this activity is an excellent demonstration for a Friday). Eventually, the penny will float. Ask students to explain why.

Teaching Notes The penny floats because the zinc inside the copper plating reacts with the HCl to produce hydrogen gas, which is trapped inside the penny and causes it to float to the surface. You can carefully pour out the HCl and retrieve the penny after washing it gently with water to remove the acid. If the penny is placed on a paper towel, it becomes evident that most of the penny has

In other cases the electron transfer occurs in a different sense, such as in the combustion of methane (the oxidation state for each atom is given below each reactant and product).

$$CH_4(g) \ + \ 2O_2(g) \ \rightarrow \ CO_2(g) \ + \ 2H_2O(g)$$

Oxidation state: -4 $+1$ (each H)   0 $+4$ -2 (each O) $+1$ (each H) -2 (each O)

Note that the oxidation state of oxygen in O_2 is 0 because the oxygen is in elemental form. In this reaction there are no ionic compounds, but we can still describe the process in terms of the transfer of electrons. Note that carbon undergoes a change in oxidation state from -4 in CH_4 to $+4$ in CO_2. Such a change can be accounted for by a loss of eight electrons:

$$C \ (in \ CH_4) \quad \Rightarrow \quad C \ (in \ CO_2)$$

-4 Loss of 8e$^-$ $+4$

or, in equation form,

$$CH_4 \rightarrow CO_2 + 8e^-$$

-4 $+4$

On the other hand, each oxygen changes from an oxidation state of 0 in O_2 to -2 in H_2O and CO_2, signifying a gain of two electrons per atom. Four oxygen atoms are involved, so this is a gain of eight electrons:

$$4O \ atoms \ (in \ 2O_2) \quad \Rightarrow \quad 4O^{2-} \ (in \ 2H_2O \ and \ CO_2)$$

Gain of 8e$^-$

or, in equation form,

$$2O_2 + 8e^- \rightarrow CO_2 + 2H_2O$$

0                    $4(-2) = -8$

Note that eight electrons are required because four oxygen atoms are going from an oxidation state of 0 to -2. Each oxygen requires two electrons. No change occurs in the oxidation state of hydrogen, and it is not involved in the electron transfer process.

CELEBRITY CHEMICAL

Hydrazine (N_2H_4)

Hydrazine, N_2H_4, is a colorless liquid with an ammonia-like odor that freezes at 2 °C and boils at 114 °C. This powerful reducing agent reacts with oxygen in a highly exothermic reaction,

$$N_2H_4(l) + O_2(g) \rightarrow N_2(g) + 2H_2O(g)$$

which produces 622 kJ of energy per mole of N_2H_4. Substituted hydrazines, where one or more of the hydrogen atoms are replaced by other groups, are useful as rocket fuels. For example, methylhydrazine ($CH_3N_2H_3$) is used with the oxidizing agent N_2O_4

(dinitrogen tetroxide) to power the U.S. space shuttle orbiter. The reaction is

$$5N_2O_4(l) + 4CH_3N_2H_3(l)$$
$$\rightarrow 12H_2O(g) + 9N_2(g) + 4CO_2(g)$$

Because of the large number of gaseous molecules produced and the highly exothermic nature of this reaction, a very high value of thrust per gram of fuels is achieved. The reaction is also self-starting. That is, it begins immediately when the fuels are mixed—a useful characteristic for rocket engines that must be started and stopped frequently.

18.3 Oxidation–Reduction Reactions Between Nonmetals **581**

reacted, leaving only the "copper skin" of the penny. Have students write the oxidation–reduction equation for the reaction of zinc and HCl.

With this background, we can now define *oxidation* and *reduction* in terms of oxidation states. **Oxidation** is an *increase* in oxidation state (a loss of electrons). **Reduction** is a *decrease* in oxidation state (a gain of electrons). Thus in the reaction

$$2Na(s) + Cl_2(g) \rightarrow 2NaCl(s)$$

Oxidizing Agent:
  Accepts electrons
  Contains element reduced

Reducing Agent:
  Furnishes electrons
  Contains element oxidized

sodium is oxidized and chlorine is reduced. Cl_2 is called the **oxidizing agent (electron acceptor)** and Na is called the **reducing agent (electron donor)**. We can also define the *oxidizing agent* as the reactant containing the element that is reduced (gains electrons). The *reducing agent* can be defined similarly as the reactant containing the element that is oxidized (loses electrons).

Concerning the reaction

$$CH_4(g) + 2O_2(g) \rightarrow CO_2(g) + 2H_2O(g)$$
$$\underset{-4}{\uparrow} \underset{+1}{\uparrow} \qquad \underset{0}{\uparrow} \qquad \underset{+4}{\nearrow} \underset{-2}{\nwarrow} \qquad \underset{+1}{\nearrow} \underset{-2}{\nwarrow}$$

we can say the following:

1. Carbon is oxidized because there is an increase in its oxidation state (carbon has apparently lost electrons).

2. The reactant CH_4 contains the carbon that is oxidized, so CH_4 is the reducing agent. It is the reactant that furnishes the electrons (those lost by carbon).

3. Oxygen is reduced because there has been a decrease in its oxidation state (oxygen has apparently gained electrons).

4. The reactant that contains the oxygen atoms is O_2, so O_2 is the oxidizing agent. That is, O_2 accepts the electrons.

Note that when the oxidizing or reducing agent is named, the *whole compound* is specified, not just the element that undergoes the change in oxidation state.

Rules for Assigning Oxidation States

1. The oxidation state of an atom in an uncombined element is 0.

2. The oxidation state of a monatomic ion is the same as its charge.

3. Oxygen is assigned an oxidation state of -2 in most of its covalent compounds. Important exception: peroxides (compounds containing the O_2^{2-} group), in which each oxygen is assigned an oxidation state of -1.

4. In its covalent compounds with nonmetals, hydrogen is assigned an oxidation state of $+1$.

5. In binary compounds, the element with the greater electronegativity is assigned a negative oxidation state equal to its charge as an anion in its ionic compounds.

6. For an electrically neutral compound, the sum of the oxidation states must be zero.

7. For an ionic species, the sum of the oxidation states must equal the overall charge.

---

582   Chapter 18   Oxidation–Reduction Reactions and Electrochemistry

TEACHING TIPS

- Students need to learn the rules for assigning oxidation states. It is a good idea to give them a number of practice problems in which they must assign oxidation states to all of the elements in a compound.

- Students often become more concerned with the exceptions than with the compounds that follow the rules. For beginning students, focus on compounds that obey the rules. If students ask about exceptions, use examples such as H_2O_2 and NaH.

USING TECHNOLOGY

Rules for Assigning Oxidation Numbers

Example 18.3

Identifying Oxidizing and Reducing Agents, I

When powdered aluminum metal is mixed with pulverized iodine crystals and a drop of water is added, the resulting reaction produces a great deal of energy. The mixture bursts into flames, and a purple smoke of I_2 vapor is produced from the excess iodine. The equation for the reaction is

$$2Al(s) + 3I_2(s) \rightarrow 2AlI_3(s)$$

For this reaction, identify the atoms that are oxidized and those that are reduced, and specify the oxidizing and reducing agents.

Solution

The first step is to assign oxidation states.

$$2Al(s) + 3I_2(s) \rightarrow 2AlI_3(s)$$

0   0   +3 −1 (each I)
Free elements $AlI_3(s)$ is a salt that
contains Al^{3+} and I^- ions

Because each aluminum atom changes its oxidation state from 0 to +3 (an increase in oxidation state), aluminum is *oxidized* (loses electrons). On the other hand, the oxidation state of each iodine atom decreases from 0 to −1, and iodine is *reduced* (gains electrons). Because Al furnishes electrons for the reduction of iodine, it is the *reducing agent*. I_2 is the *oxidizing agent* (the reactant that accepts the electrons).

Example 18.4

Identifying Oxidizing and Reducing Agents, II

Metallurgy, the process of producing a metal from its ore, always involves oxidation–reduction reactions. In the metallurgy of galena (PbS), the principal lead-containing ore, the first step is the conversion of lead sulfide to its oxide (a process called *roasting*).

$$2PbS(s) + 3O_2(g) \rightarrow 2PbO(s) + 2SO_2(g)$$

The oxide is then treated with carbon monoxide to produce the free metal.

$$PbO(s) + CO(g) \rightarrow Pb(s) + CO_2(g)$$

For each reaction, identify the atoms that are oxidized and those that are reduced, and specify the oxidizing and reducing agents.

Solution

For the first reaction, we can assign the following oxidation states:

$$PbS(s) + 3O_2(g) \rightarrow 2PbO(s) + 2SO_2(g)$$

+2 −2   0   +2 −2   +4 −2 (each O)

(continued)

Additional Examples

For the following reaction, identify the atoms that are oxidized and those that are reduced, and specify the oxidizing and reducing agents.

$$Fe_2O_3(s) + 3CO(g) \rightarrow 2Fe(l) + 3CO_2(g)$$

Iron is reduced and carbon is oxidized. $Fe_2O_3(s)$ is the oxidizing agent and $CO(g)$ is the reducing agent.

Additional Examples

For the following reaction, identify the atoms that are oxidized and those that are reduced, and specify the oxidizing and reducing agents.

$$Cl_2(g) + 2NaBr(aq) \rightarrow 2NaCl(aq) + Br_2(l)$$

Chlorine is reduced and bromine is oxidized. $Cl_2(g)$ is the oxidizing agent and NaBr(aq) is the reducing agent.

18.3 Oxidation–Reduction Reactions Between Nonmetals   **583**

(continued)

The oxidation state for the sulfur atom increases from -2 to $+4$, so sulfur is oxidized (loses electrons). The oxidation state for each oxygen atom decreases from 0 to -2. Oxygen is reduced (gains electrons). The oxidizing agent (electron acceptor) is O_2, and the reducing agent (electron donor) is PbS.

For the second reaction, we have

$$PbO(s) \ + \ CO(g) \ \rightarrow \ Pb(s) \ + \ CO_2(g)$$
$$\quad \underset{+2}{\uparrow} \ \underset{-2}{\nwarrow} \qquad \underset{+2}{\uparrow} \ \underset{-2}{\nwarrow} \qquad \underset{0}{\uparrow} \qquad \underset{+4}{\uparrow} \ \underset{-2 \text{ (each O)}}{\nwarrow}$$

Lead is reduced (gains electrons; its oxidation state decreases from $+2$ to 0), and carbon is oxidized (loses electrons; its oxidation state increases from $+2$ to $+4$). PbO is the oxidizing agent (electron acceptor), and CO is the reducing agent (electron donor).

 Self-Check Exercise 18.3

Ammonia, NH_3, which is widely used as a fertilizer, is prepared by reaction of the elements:

$$N_2(g) + 3H_2(g) \rightarrow 2NH_3(g)$$

Is this an oxidation–reduction reaction? If so, specify the oxidizing agent and the reducing agent.

Focus Questions

Sections 18.1–18.3

1. In a reaction between a metal and a nonmetal, which substance tends to be oxidized? Reduced? Why?

2. How do oxidation states help us to decide if an oxidation–reduction reaction has occurred?

3. Assign oxidation states to all atoms in each of the following.
   a. O_2
   b. HSO_4^-
   c. Na_2HPO_4
   d. $CrCl_3$

4. For each of the following oxidation–reduction reactions of metals and nonmetals, identify which element is oxidized and which is reduced.
   a. $4Fe(s) + 3O_2(g) \rightarrow 2Fe_2O_3(s)$
   b. $Zn(s) + 2AgNO_3(g) \rightarrow Zn(NO_3)_2(aq) + 2Ag(s)$
   c. $2K(s) + Cl_2(g) \rightarrow 2KCl(s)$
   d. $2Ca(s) + O_2(g) \rightarrow 2CaO(s)$

584 Chapter 18 Oxidation–Reduction Reactions and Electrochemistry

---

 Answer to Self-Check Exercise 18.3

We can tell whether this is an oxidation–reduction reaction by comparing the oxidation states of the elements in the reactants and products:

$$N_2 + 3H_2 \rightarrow 2NH_3$$
$$\uparrow \qquad \uparrow \qquad \uparrow \ \nwarrow$$
Oxidation states: $\quad 0 \qquad 0 \qquad -3 \ +1 \text{ (each H)}$

Nitrogen goes from 0 to -3. Thus it gains three electrons and is reduced. Each hydrogen atom goes from 0 to $+1$ and is thus oxidized, so this is an oxidation–reduction reaction. The oxidizing agent is N_2 (it takes electrons from H_2). The reducing agent is H_2 (it gives electrons to N_2).

$$N_2 + 3H_2 \rightarrow 2NH_3$$
$$\underset{6e^-}{\curvearrowleft}$$

Answers to Focus Questions

1. The metal tends to be oxidized and the nonmetal tends to be reduced, because metals have relatively low ionization energies and fewer valence electrons than do nonmetals.

2. If the oxidation state of an element changes in a chemical reaction, an oxidation–reduction reaction has occurred.

3. a. 0, 0
   b. H, $+1$; S, $+6$; 0, -2
   c. Na, $+1$; H, $+1$; P, $+5$; 0, -2
   d. Cr, $+3$; Cl, -1

4.

	Oxidized	Reduced
a.	Fe	O
b.	Zn	Ag
c.	K	Cl
d.	Ca	O

18.4 Balancing Oxidation–Reduction Reactions by the Half-Reaction Method

Objective: *To learn to balance oxidation–reduction equations by using half-reactions.*

Section 18.4

Themes
Patterns of Change

Skills
Applying concepts, interpreting data

Student Preparation
Assign the students to read Sections 18.4 and 18.5 and to answer the Focus Questions at the end of Section 18.5 before coming to class.

Active Learning
After introducing the material in Sections 18.4 and 18.5 in class, place the students in groups and have them work together on Sections 18.4–18.5: Team Learning Worksheet. Answers and/or discussion of these questions are located in the *Teacher Resources.*

Laboratory
Experiment 81:
Analysis of Hydrogen Peroxide, Microscale

TEACHING TIPS

- Use the concept of half-reactions to emphasize that oxidation cannot occur without reduction, and vice versa.

- Students may need help to identify the half-reactions. Writing half-reactions correctly requires correctly assigning oxidation states in compounds.

Many oxidation–reduction reactions can be balanced readily by trial and error. That is, we use the procedure described in Chapter 7 to find a set of coefficients that give the same number of each type of atom on both sides of the equation.

However, the oxidation–reduction reactions that occur in aqueous solution are often so complicated that it becomes very tedious to balance them by trial and error. In this section we will develop a systematic approach for balancing the equations for these reactions.

To balance the equations for oxidation–reduction reactions that occur in aqueous solution, we separate the reaction into two half-reactions. **Half-reactions** are equations that have electrons as reactants or products. One half-reaction represents a reduction process and the other half-reaction represents an oxidation process. In a reduction half-reaction, electrons are shown on the reactant side (electrons are gained by a reactant in the equation). In an oxidation half-reaction, the electrons are shown on the product side (electrons are lost by a reactant in the equation).

For example, consider the unbalanced equation for the oxidation–reduction reaction between the cerium(IV) ion and the tin(II) ion.

$$Ce^{4+}(aq) + Sn^{2+}(aq) \rightarrow Ce^{3+}(aq) + Sn^{4+}(aq)$$

This reaction can be separated into a half-reaction involving the substance being *reduced*:

$$e^- + Ce^{4+}(aq) \rightarrow Ce^{3+}(aq) \quad \text{Reduction half-reaction}$$

and a half-reaction involving the substance being *oxidized*:

$$Sn^{2+}(aq) \rightarrow Sn^{4+}(aq) + 2e^- \quad \text{Oxidation half-reaction}$$

Notice that Ce^{4+} must gain one electron to become Ce^{3+}, so one electron is shown as a reactant along with Ce^{4+} in this half-reaction. On the other hand, for Sn^{2+} to become Sn^{4+}, it must lose two electrons. This means that two electrons must be shown as products in this half-reaction.

The key principle in balancing oxidation–reduction reactions is that the number of electrons lost (from the reactant that is oxidized) must equal the number of electrons gained (from the reactant that is reduced).

In the half-reaction shown above, one electron is gained by each Ce^{4+} while two electrons are lost by each Sn^{2+}. We must equalize the number of electrons gained and lost. To do this, we first multiply the reduction half-reaction by 2.

$$2e^- + 2Ce^{4+} \rightarrow 2Ce^{3+}$$

CHEMISTRY
Ce^{4+} gains $1e^-$ to form Ce^{3+} and is thus reduced.

CHEMISTRY
Sn^{2+} loses $2e^-$ to form Sn^{4+} and is thus oxidized.

18.4 Balancing Oxidation–Reduction Reactions by the Half-Reaction Method **585**

- Students should balance both atoms and charges in the half-reactions. A common error is for students to place the electrons on the wrong side of the half-reaction.

- Remind students that an equal number of electrons must be transferred. They often forget to equalize this number when they begin to work with these equations. Explain that the electrons are transferred and so must be accounted for. That is, the number gained must equal the number lost.

- It takes time and practice to learn to balance these reactions. Students need to pay close attention to the details of the balancing process. Learning to use the method of half-reactions on relatively easy equations makes it easier to balance more difficult equations later.

Then we add this half-reaction to the oxidation half-reaction.

$$2e^- + 2Ce^{4+} \rightarrow 2Ce^{3+}$$
$$\underline{Sn^{2+} \rightarrow Sn^{4+} + 2e^-}$$
$$2e^- + 2Ce^{4+} + Sn^{2+} \rightarrow 2Ce^{3+} + Sn^{4+} + 2e^-$$

Finally, we cancel the $2e^-$ on each side to give the overall balanced equation

$$\cancel{2e^-} + 2Ce^{4+} + Sn^{2+} \rightarrow 2Ce^{3+} + Sn^{4+} + \cancel{2e^-}$$
$$2Ce^{4+} + Sn^{2+} \rightarrow 2Ce^{3+} + Sn^{4+}$$

We can now summarize what we have said about the method for balancing oxidation–reduction reactions in aqueous solution:

1. Separate the reaction into an oxidation half-reaction and a reduction half-reaction.

2. Balance the half-reactions separately.

3. Equalize the number of electrons gained and lost.

4. Add the half-reactions together and cancel electrons to give the overall balanced equation.

It turns out that most oxidation–reduction reactions occur in solutions that are distinctly basic or distinctly acidic. We will cover only the acidic case in this text, because it is the most common. The detailed procedure for balancing the equations for oxidation–reduction reactions that occur in acidic solution is given below, and Example 18.5 illustrates the use of these steps.

The Half-Reaction Method for Balancing Equations for Oxidation–Reduction Reactions Occurring in Acidic Solution

STEP 1 Identify and write the equations for the oxidation and reduction half-reactions.

STEP 2 For each half-reaction:
 a. Balance all of the elements except hydrogen and oxygen.
 b. Balance oxygen using H_2O.
 c. Balance hydrogen using H^+.
 d. Balance the charge using electrons.

STEP 3 If necessary, multiply one or both balanced half-reactions by an integer to equalize the number of electrons transferred in the two half-reactions.

STEP 4 Add the half-reactions, and cancel identical species that appear on both sides.

STEP 5 Check to be sure the elements and charges balance.

Example 18.5

Balancing Oxidation–Reduction Reactions Using the Half-Reaction Method, I

Balance the equation for the reaction between permanganate and iron(II) ions in acidic solution. The net ionic equation for this reaction is

$$MnO_4^-(aq) + Fe^{2+}(aq) \xrightarrow{Acid} Fe^{3+}(aq) + Mn^{2+}(aq)$$

This reaction is used to analyze iron ore for its iron content.

H₂O and H⁺ will be added to this equation as we balance it. We do not have to worry about them now.

A solution containing MnO_4^- ions (*left*) and a solution containing Fe^{2+} ions (*right*).

CHEMISTRY

Note that the left side contains oxygen but the right side does not. This will be taken care of later when we add water.

Solution

Step 1 *Identify and write equations for the half-reactions.*
The oxidation states for the half-reaction involving the permanganate ion show that manganese is reduced.

$$MnO_4^- \rightarrow Mn^{2+}$$
$$\overset{\uparrow}{+7} \overset{\nwarrow}{-2} \qquad \overset{\uparrow}{+2}$$
$$\text{(each O)}$$

Because manganese changes from an oxidation state of +7 to +2, it is reduced. So this is the *reduction half-reaction*. It will have electrons as reactants, although we will not write them yet. The other half-reaction involves the oxidation of iron(II) to the iron(III) ion and is the *oxidation half-reaction*.

$$Fe^{2+} \rightarrow Fe^{3+}$$
$$\overset{\uparrow}{+2} \qquad \overset{\uparrow}{+3}$$

This reaction will have electrons as products, although we will not write them yet.

Step 2 *Balance each half-reaction.*
For the reduction reaction, we have

$$MnO_4^- \rightarrow Mn^{2+}$$

a. The manganese is already balanced.

b. We balance oxygen by adding $4H_2O$ to the right side of the equation.

$$MnO_4^- \rightarrow Mn^{2+} + 4H_2O$$

The H⁺ comes from the acidic solution in which the reaction is taking place.

c. Next we balance hydrogen by adding $8H^+$ to the left side.

$$8H^+ + MnO_4^- \rightarrow Mn^{2+} + 4H_2O$$

(continued)

Balance each of the following oxidation–reduction reactions using the half-reaction method.

1. $Ce^{4+}(aq) + H_3AsO_3(aq) \rightarrow Ce^{3+}(aq) + H_3AsO_4(aq)$
$2Ce^{4+}(aq) + H_3AsO_3(aq) + H_2O(l) \rightarrow 2Ce^{3+}(aq) + H_3AsO_4(aq) + 2H^+(aq)$

2. $MnO_4^-(aq) + I^-(aq) \rightarrow Mn^{2+}(aq) + I_2(s)$
$2MnO_4^-(aq) + 10I^-(aq) + 16H^+(aq) \rightarrow 2Mn^{2+}(aq) + 5I_2(s) + 8H_2O(l)$

(continued)

CHEMISTRY

Always add electrons to the side of the half-reaction with excess positive charge.

d. All of the elements have been balanced, but we need to balance the charge using electrons. At this point we have the following charges for reactants and products in the reduction half-reaction.

$$8H^+ + MnO_4^- \rightarrow Mn^{2+} + 4H_2O$$
$$\underbrace{8+ \quad + \quad 1-}_{7+} \qquad \underbrace{2+ \quad + \quad 0}_{2+}$$

We can equalize the charges by adding five electrons to the left side.

$$\underbrace{5e^- + 8H^+ + MnO_4^-}_{2+} \rightarrow \underbrace{Mn^{2+} + 4H_2O}_{2+}$$

Both the *elements* and the *charges* are now balanced, so this represents the balanced reduction half-reaction. The fact that five electrons appear on the reactant side of the equation makes sense, because five electrons are required to reduce MnO_4^- (in which Mn has an oxidation state of +7) to Mn^{2+} (in which Mn has an oxidation state of +2).

For the oxidation reaction,

$$Fe^{2+} \rightarrow Fe^{3+}$$

the elements are balanced, so all we have to do is balance the charge.

$$\underbrace{Fe^{2+}}_{2+} \rightarrow \underbrace{Fe^{3+}}_{3+}$$

One electron is needed on the right side to give a net 2+ charge on both sides.

$$\underbrace{Fe^{2+}}_{2+} \quad \rightarrow \quad \underbrace{Fe^{3+} + e^-}_{2+}$$

The number of electrons gained in the reduction half-reaction must equal the number of electrons lost in the oxidation half-reaction.

Step 3 *Equalize the number of electrons transferred in the two half-reactions.* Because the reduction half-reaction involves a transfer of five electrons and the oxidation half-reaction involves a transfer of only one electron, the oxidation half-reaction must be multiplied by 5.

$$5Fe^{2+} \rightarrow 5Fe^{3+} + 5e^-$$

Step 4 *Add the half-reactions and cancel identical species.*

$$5e^- + 8H^+ + MnO_4^- \rightarrow Mn^{2+} + 4H_2O$$
$$5Fe^{2+} \rightarrow 5Fe^{3+} + 5e^-$$

$$\overline{\cancel{5e^-} + 8H^+ + MnO_4^- + 5Fe^{2+} \rightarrow Mn^{2+} + 5Fe^{3+} + 4H_2O + \cancel{5e^-}}$$

Note that the electrons cancel (as they must) to give the final balanced equation

$$5Fe^{2+}(aq) + MnO_4^-(aq) + 8H^+(aq) \rightarrow 5Fe^{3+}(aq) + Mn^{2+}(aq) + 4H_2O(l)$$

Note that we show the physical states of the reactants and products—(*aq*) and (*l*) in this case—only in the final balanced equation.

Step 5 *Check to be sure that elements and charges balance.*

Elements $5Fe, 1Mn, 4O, 8H \rightarrow 5Fe, 1Mn, 4O, 8H$
Charges $17+ \rightarrow 17+$

The equation is balanced.

588   Chapter 18   Oxidation–Reduction Reactions and Electrochemistry

Example 18.6

Balancing Oxidation–Reduction Reactions Using the Half-Reaction Method, II

When an automobile engine is started, it uses the energy supplied by a lead storage battery. This battery uses an oxidation–reduction reaction between elemental lead (lead metal) and lead(IV) oxide to provide the power to start the engine. The unbalanced equation for a simplified version of the reaction is

$$Pb(s) + PbO_2(s) + H^+(aq) \rightarrow Pb^{2+}(aq) + H_2O(l)$$

Balance this equation using the half-reaction method.

Solution

Step 1   First we identify and write the two half-reactions. One half-reaction must be

$$Pb \rightarrow Pb^{2+}$$

and the other is

$$PbO_2 \rightarrow Pb^{2+}$$

The first reaction involves the oxidation of Pb to Pb^{2+}. The second reaction involves the reduction of Pb^{4+} (in PbO_2) to Pb^{2+}.

Step 2   Now we will balance each half-reaction separately.

The oxidation half-reaction

$$Pb \rightarrow Pb^{2+}$$

a–c. All the elements are balanced.

d. The charge on the left is zero and that on the right is 2+, so we must add $2e^-$ to the right to give zero overall charge.

$$Pb \rightarrow Pb^{2+} + 2e^-$$

This half-reaction is balanced.

The reduction half-reaction

$$PbO_2 \rightarrow Pb^{2+}$$

a. All elements are balanced except O.

b. The left side has two oxygen atoms and the right side has none, so we add $2H_2O$ to the right side.

$$PbO_2 \rightarrow Pb^{2+} + 2H_2O$$

c. Now we balance hydrogen by adding $4H^+$ to the left.

$$4H^+ + PbO_2 \rightarrow Pb^{2+} + 2H_2O$$

d. Because the left side has a 4+ overall charge and the right side has a 2+ charge, we must add $2e^-$ to the left side.

$$2e^- + 4H^+ + PbO_2 \rightarrow Pb^{2+} + 2H_2O$$

The half-reaction is balanced.

Step 3   Because each half-reaction involves $2e^-$, we can simply add the half-reactions as they are.

(continued)

Because Pb^{2+} is the only lead-containing product, it must be the product in both half-reactions.

18.4   Balancing Oxidation–Reduction Reactions by the Half-Reaction Method   **589**

---

1. The HNO_3 must be included in the oxidation half-reaction to supply NO_3^- in the product $Cu(NO_3)_2$.

2. Although water is a product in the overall reaction, it does not need to be included in either half-reaction at the beginning. It will appear later as we balance the equation.

Step 2 Balance the oxidation half-reaction.

$$Cu + HNO_3 \rightarrow Cu(NO_3)_2$$

a. Balance nitrogen first.

$$Cu + 2HNO_3 \rightarrow Cu(NO_3)_2$$

b. Balancing nitrogen also caused oxygen to balance.

c. Balance hydrogen using H^+.

$$Cu + 2HNO_3 \rightarrow Cu(NO_3)_2 + 2H^+$$

d. Balance the charge using e^-.

$$Cu + 2HNO_3 \rightarrow Cu(NO_3)_2 + 2H^+ + 2e^-$$

This is the balanced oxidation half-reaction.

Balance the reduction half-reaction.

$$HNO_3 \rightarrow NO$$

a. All elements are balanced except hydrogen and oxygen.

b. Balance oxygen using H_2O.

$$HNO_3 \rightarrow NO + 2H_2O$$

c. Balance hydrogen using H^+.

$$3H^+ + HNO_3 \rightarrow NO + 2H_2O$$

d. Balance the charge using e^-.

$$3e^- + 3H^+ + HNO_3 \rightarrow NO + 2H_2O$$

This is the balanced reduction half-reaction.

Step 3 We equalize electrons by multiplying the oxidation half-reaction by 3:

$$3 \times (Cu + 2HNO_3 \rightarrow Cu(NO_3)_2 + 2H^+ + 2e^-)$$

which gives

$$3Cu + 6HNO_3 \rightarrow 3Cu(NO_3)_2 + 6H^+ + 6e^-$$

Multiplying the reduction half-reaction by 2

$$2 \times (3e^- + 3H^+ + HNO_3 \rightarrow NO + 2H_2O)$$

gives

$$6e^- + 6H^+ + 2HNO_3 \rightarrow 2NO + 4H_2O$$

Additional Examples

1. $MnO_4^-(aq) + C_2O_4^{2-}(aq) \rightarrow Mn^{2+}(aq) + CO_2(g)$

   $2MnO_4^-(aq) + 5C_2O_4^{2-}(aq) + 16H^+(aq) \rightarrow 2Mn^{2+}(aq) + 10CO_2(g) + 8H_2O(l)$

2. $BiO_3^-(aq) + Mn^{2+}(aq) \rightarrow Bi^{3+}(aq) + MnO_4^-(aq)$

   $5BiO_3^-(aq) + 2Mn^{2+}(aq) + 14H^+(aq) \rightarrow 5Bi^{3+}(aq) + 2MnO_4^-(aq) + 7H_2O(l)$

Answer to Self-Check Exercise 18.4

The unbalanced equation for this reaction is

$$Cu(s) + HNO_3(aq) \rightarrow Cu(NO_3)_2(aq) + H_2O(l) + NO(g)$$

Copper metal   Nitric acid   Aqueous copper(II) nitrate (contains Cu^{2+})   Water   Nitrogen monoxide

Step 1 The oxidation half-reaction is

$$Cu + HNO_3 \rightarrow Cu(NO_3)_2$$

Oxidation states: 0   +1 +5 −2   +2   +5   −2
                                        (each 0)   (each 0)

The copper goes from 0 to +2 and thus is oxidized. This reduction reaction is

$$HNO_3 \rightarrow NO$$

Oxidation states: +1 +5 −2   +2 −2
                             (each 0)

In this case nitrogen goes from +5 in HNO_3 to +2 in NO and so is reduced. Notice two things about these reactions:

(continued)

Chapter 18   Oxidation–Reduction Reactions and Electrochemistry   **589**

Step 4 We can now add the balanced half-reactions, which both involve a six-electron change.

$$3Cu + 6HNO_3 \rightarrow 3Cu(NO_3)_2 \\ + 6H^+ + 6e^-$$
$$\underline{6e^- + 6H^+ + 2HNO_3 \rightarrow 2NO + 4H_2O}$$
$$\cancel{6e^-} + \cancel{6H^+} + 3Cu + 8HNO_3 \rightarrow \\ 3Cu(NO_3)_2 + 2NO + 4H_2O + \\ \cancel{6H^+} + \cancel{6e^-}$$

Canceling species common to both sides gives the balanced overall equation:

$$3Cu(s) + 8HNO_3(aq) \rightarrow \\ 3Cu(NO_3)_2(aq) + 2NO(g) + \\ 4H_2O(l)$$

Step 5 Check the elements and charges.

Elements 3Cu, 8H, 8N, 24O → 3Cu, 8H, 8N, 24O
Charges   0 → 0

Integrating the CHEMICAL IMPACT

Real Gold

Gold is so unreactive that it is most commonly found in its elemental form. This lack of reactivity is useful when creating jewelry that does not interact with the chemicals on the skin. The only natural compounds that gold forms are those in combination with tellurium. The most common oxidation states for gold are +1 and +3.

Gold has reflective properties similar to those of silver and copper. These substances can all be used to make mirrors by depositing the metal on the surface of a piece of glass. Silver is most commonly used for this purpose because it does not color the reflection. You can demonstrate the silvering process (discovered in 1835 by Justus von Liebig, a German chemist) in class by using the Teaching Support, "A Silver Mirror."

(continued)

Step 4

$$Pb \rightarrow Pb^{2+} + 2e^-$$
$$\underline{2e^- + 4H^+ + PbO_2 \rightarrow Pb^{2+} + 2H_2O}$$
$$2e^- + 4H^+ + Pb + PbO_2 \rightarrow 2Pb^{2+} + 2H_2O + 2e^-$$

Canceling electrons gives the balanced overall equation

$$Pb(s) + PbO_2(s) + 4H^+(aq) \rightarrow 2Pb^{2+}(aq) + 2H_2O(l)$$

where the appropriate states are also indicated.

Step 5 Both the elements and the charges balance.

Elements 2Pb, 2O, 4H → 2Pb, 2O, 4H
Charges   4+ → 4+

The equation is correctly balanced.

Self-Check Exercise 18.4

Copper metal reacts with dilute nitric acid, $HNO_3(aq)$, to give aqueous copper(II) nitrate, water, and nitrogen monoxide gas as products. Write and balance the equation for this reaction.

Copper metal reacting with concentrated nitric acid. The solution is colored by the presence of Cu^{2+} ions. The brown gas is NO_2.

CHEMICAL IMPACT

Science, Technology, and Society

Real Gold

Recently, a woman wrote to Annie's Mailbox complaining that the necklace her boyfriend had given her turned her neck green. Her concern was whether the necklace was "real gold." This leads to the question: What is "real gold"? To chemists, real gold is pure gold, called 24-carat gold by jewelers. Thus, when you see 24K (for "carat," which is also spelled "karat") on a piece of gold, it means that it is 100% gold. However, the woman's necklace was surely not 24K gold, because pure gold is too soft for making jewelry. Jewelry is usually made of 18K gold (which is 18/24 = 75% gold by mass) or 14K gold (14/24 = 58% gold). The carat system was invented by the British in about 1300 to provide a standard for the use of gold as currency.

Gold jewelry in a store in Thailand.

In the United States, the lowest carat designation for gold is 10K. Because a 0.5-carat error is allowed, 10K gold is actually 9.5K (39.6% gold by mass). So if 9.5K gold is only about 40% gold, what makes up the rest of the "gold" jewelry? The metals most commonly used to form gold alloys are copper, silver, zinc, and nickel, depending on the specific use and color desired. For example, "yellow gold" typically contains Au, Cu, Ag, and Zn, whereas "white gold" contains Au, Cu, Ni, and Zn.

Now back to the woman's original question. Was her necklace "real gold"? Not likely. The necklace was probably mostly copper with a thin layer of gold plated on the surface. The woman's necklace turned green because copper "leaked" through cracks in the gold plating. Alloys of 14K gold do not behave in this way. She was right to worry about her friend's honesty.

TEACHING SUPPORT
Demonstration

A Silver Mirror

Materials
100-mL graduated cylinder
250-mL Erlenmeyer flask
Small flask and stopper to fit
4 small beakers
Sodium hydroxide
Glucose
Fructose
Silver nitrate
Ammonium nitrate
Tartaric acid
Ethanol
Heating unit

Preparation Make the following solutions: To make solution A, dissolve 2.5 g glucose and 2.5 g fructose in 50 mL distilled water and add 0.6 g tartaric acid. Heat the solution to boiling; cool and then pour it into the 100-mL graduated cylinder. Add 10 mL of ethanol and dilute the solution to the 100-mL mark. Label it A. To make solution B, dissolve 4.0 g of silver nitrate in 50 mL water. Label it B. To make solution C, dissolve 6.0 g of ammonium nitrate in 50 mL water and label it C. To make solution D, dissolve 10 g NaOH in 50 mL water and label it D. Clean the small flask thoroughly with concentrated nitric acid.

18.5 Electrochemistry: An Introduction

Objectives: *To understand the term* electrochemistry.
To learn to identify the components of an electrochemical (galvanic) cell.

Our lives would be very different without batteries. We would have to crank the engines in our cars by hand, wind our watches, and buy very long extension cords if we wanted to listen to a radio on a picnic. Indeed, our society sometimes seems to run on batteries. In this section and the next, we will find out how these important devices produce electrical energy.

A battery uses the energy from an oxidation–reduction reaction to produce an electric current. This is an important illustration of **electrochemistry**, *the study of the interchange of chemical and electrical energy.*

Electrochemistry involves two types of processes:

1. The production of an electric current from a chemical (oxidation–reduction) reaction

2. The use of an electric current to produce a chemical change

To understand how a redox reaction can be used to generate a current, let's reconsider the aqueous reaction between MnO_4^- and Fe^{2+} that we worked with in Example 18.5. We can break this redox reaction into the following half-reactions:

$$8H^+ + MnO_4^- + 5e^- \rightarrow Mn^{2+} + 4H_2O \quad \text{Reduction}$$
$$Fe^{2+} \rightarrow Fe^{3+} + e^- \quad \text{Oxidation}$$

When the reaction between MnO_4^- and Fe^{2+} occurs in solution, electrons are transferred directly as the reactants collide. No useful work is obtained from the chemical energy involved in the reaction. How can we harness this energy? The key is to *separate the oxidizing agent (electron acceptor) from the reducing agent (electron donor)*, thus requiring the electron transfer to occur through a wire. That is, to get from the reducing agent to the oxidizing agent, the electrons must travel through a wire. The current produced in the wire by this electron flow can be directed through a device, such as an electric motor, to do useful work.

For example, consider the system illustrated in **Figure 18.1**. If our reasoning has been correct, electrons should flow through the wire from Fe^{2+} to MnO_4^-. However, when we construct the apparatus as shown, no flow of electrons occurs. Why? The problem is that if the electrons flowed from the

CHEMISTRY

The energy involved in a chemical reaction is customarily not shown in the balanced equation. In the reaction of MnO_4^- with Fe^{2+}, energy is released that can be used to do useful work.

TOP TEN

Most Active Metals (Best Reducing Agents in Water)

1. Li
2. K
3. Ba
4. Ca
5. Na
6. La
7. Mg
8. Al
9. Mn
10. Zn

Figure 18.1
Schematic of a method for separating the oxidizing and reducing agents in a redox reaction. (The solutions also contain other ions to balance the charge.) This cell is incomplete at this point.

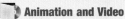

MnO₄⁻(aq)
H⁺(aq)

Fe²⁺(aq)

Oxidizing agent
(electron acceptor)

Reducing agent
(electron donor)

18.5 Electrochemistry: An Introduction **591**

Section 18.5

Themes
Organization, Form and Function

Skills
Classifying, making comparisons, evaluating

Laboratory
Experiment 82:
Galvanic Cells, CBL

Using the TOP TEN

Students can practice writing half-reactions and electrochemical equations by using the Top Ten. Have them write equations for the interaction of each element in the Top Ten with each of the other elements below it in the table. Students will need to know which metal is oxidized and which is reduced. They will then need to write the correct half-reactions and finally the chemical equation for the net reaction between the substances.

USING TECHNOLOGY

Animation and Video

Animation, Electrochemical Hall–Reactions in a Galvanic Cell

Animation, Anode Reaction

Animation, Cathode Reaction

Animation, Oxidation–Reduction Reaction

Presentation Place 30 mL of solution A into the clean flask. In a small beaker mix 15 mL of solution B with 15 mL of solution C. Add this solution to the flask. Quickly add 30 mL of solution D to the flask and mix the flask with quick but gentle swirling motions. Be sure to cover the inside surface of the glass evenly while swirling. Continue swirling until the silver mirror forms inside the flask.

Immediately pour out the remaining solution and deactivate the solution by adding lots of water. Rinse the silvered flask with distilled water.

Teaching Notes Do not mix solutions B and C until the demonstration is performed. They are potentially unstable after mixing. Metallic silver forms on the surface of the glass when the silver ions oxidize the aldehyde on the sugar molecule. If

the silver doesn't stick to the glass, it was not completely clean.

right to the left compartment, the left compartment would become negatively charged and the right compartment would experience a build-up of positive charge **(Figure 18.2)**. Creating a charge separation of this type would

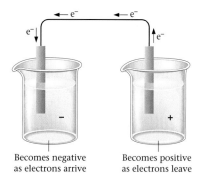

Figure 18.2
Electron flow under these conditions would lead to a build-up of negative charge on the left and positive charge on the right, which is not feasible without a huge input of energy.

Becomes negative as electrons arrive   Becomes positive as electrons leave

require large amounts of energy. Therefore, electron flow does not occur under these conditions.

We can, however, solve this problem very simply. The solutions must be connected (without allowing them to mix extensively) so that *ions* can also flow to keep the net charge in each compartment zero **(Figure 18.3)**. This can be accomplished by using a salt bridge (a U-shaped tube filled with

Figure 18.3
Here the ion flow between the two solutions keeps the charge neutral as electrons are transferred. This can be accomplished by having negative ions (anions) flow in the opposite direction to the electrons or by having positive ions (cations) flow in the same direction as the electrons. Both actually occur in a working battery.

Ions need to flow

a strong electrolyte) or a porous disk in a tube connecting the two solutions (see **Figure 18.4**). Either of these devices allows ion flow but prevents

Figure 18.4
A salt bridge or a porous-disk connection allows ions to flow, completing the electric circuit. (a) The salt bridge contains a strong electrolyte either as a gel or as a solution; both ends are covered with a membrane that allows only ions to pass. (b) The porous disk allows ion flow but does not permit overall mixing of the solutions in the two compartments.

Salt bridge

Porous disk

(a)   (b)

592   Chapter 18   Oxidation–Reduction Reactions and Electrochemistry

Alessandro Volta.

Anode: The electrode where oxidation occurs.

Cathode: The electrode where reduction occurs.

The name *galvanic cell* honors Luigi Galvani (1737–1798), an Italian scientist generally credited with the discovery of electricity. These cells are sometimes called *voltaic cells* after Alessandro Volta (1745–1827), another Italian, who first constructed cells of this type around 1800.

extensive mixing of the solutions. When we make a provision for ion flow, the circuit is complete. Electrons flow through the wire from reducing agent to oxidizing agent, and ions in the two aqueous solutions flow from one compartment to the other to keep the net charge zero.

Thus an **electrochemical battery,** also called a **galvanic cell,** is a device powered by an oxidation–reduction reaction where the oxidizing agent is separated from the reducing agent so that the electrons must travel through a wire from the reducing agent to the oxidizing agent **(Figure 18.5).**

Figure 18.5 Schematic of a battery (galvanic cell).

Notice that in a battery, the reducing agent loses electrons (which flow through the wire toward the oxidizing agent) and so is oxidized. The electrode where oxidation occurs is called the **anode.** At the other electrode, the oxidizing agent gains electrons and is thus reduced. The electrode where reduction occurs is called the **cathode.**

An electric car being charged.

"salt bridge." The voltmeter should register about 1 volt. Electrons can now flow through the wire because ions can flow through the "salt bridge."

Teaching Notes The solutions and electrodes can be safely stored and reused. If you don't have your own voltmeter, you may be able to borrow one from the electronics classroom or purchase one at a local elec-

tronics store. Ask students to write the half-reaction equations and identify the cathode and the anode.

We have seen that an oxidation–reduction reaction can be used to generate an electric current. In fact, this type of reaction is used to produce electric currents in many space vehicles. An oxidation–reduction reaction that can be used for this purpose is hydrogen and oxygen reacting to form water.

$$2H_2(g) \; + \; O_2(g) \; \rightarrow \; 2H_2O(l)$$

Oxidation states: 0   0   +1   −2
(each H)

Notice from the changes in oxidation states that in this reaction, hydrogen is oxidized and oxygen reduced. The opposite process can also occur. We can *force* a current through water to produce hydrogen and oxygen gas.

$$2H_2O(l) \xrightarrow[\text{energy}]{\text{Electrical}} 2H_2(g) + O_2(g)$$

This process, where *electrical energy is used to produce a chemical change,* is called **electrolysis.**

In the remainder of this chapter, we will discuss both types of electrochemical processes. In the next section we will concern ourselves with the practical galvanic cells we know as batteries.

Answers to Focus Questions

1. a. $Br_2(l) + 2e^- \rightarrow 2Br^-(aq)$

b. $Zn(s) \rightarrow Zn^{2+}(aq) + 2e^-$

2. a. $8H^+(aq) + 2NO_3^-(aq) + 6Br^-(aq) \rightarrow 2NO(g) + 3Br_2(l) + 4H_2O(l)$

b. $4H^+(aq) + Ni(s) + 2NO_3^-(aq) \rightarrow Ni^{2+}(aq) + 2NO_2(g) + 2H_2O(l)$

c. $2H^+(aq) + ClO_4^-(aq) + 2Cl^-(aq) \rightarrow ClO_3^-(aq) + Cl_2(g) + H_2O(l)$

3. In a galvanic cell, electric current is produced from an oxidation–reduction reaction. In an electrolytic cell, current is used to produce a chemical change.

4. a. The electrons (labeled as e) in the wire point from right to left.

b. The anode is the electrode in the right cell and the cathode is the electrode in the left cell.

c. Oxidation occurs in the right cell and reduction occurs in the left cell.

d. Current would cease to flow without the salt bridge.

Focus Questions

Sections 18.4–18.5

1. Write the balanced half-reactions corresponding to each of the following

   a. The reduction of $Br_2(l)$ to $Br^-(aq)$.

   b. The oxidation of $Zn(s)$ to $Zn^{2+}(aq)$.

2. Balance each of the following oxidation–reduction reactions, which take place in acidic solution, by using the half-reaction method.

   a. $NO_3^-(aq) + Br^-(aq) \rightarrow NO(g) + Br_2(l)$

   b. $Ni(s) + NO_3^-(aq) \rightarrow Ni^{2+}(aq) + NO_2(g)$

   c. $ClO_4^-(aq) + Cl^-(aq) \rightarrow ClO_3^-(aq) + Cl_2(g)$

3. What is the difference between a galvanic cell and an electrolytic cell?

4. Draw the galvanic cell shown in Figure 18.4.

   a. Label the electrons in the wire as flowing from right to left.

   b. Label the anode and the cathode.

   c. Show where oxidation occurs. Show where reduction occurs.

   d. What would happen to the cell if you removed the salt bridge?

18.6 Batteries

Objective: *To learn about the composition and operation of commonly used batteries.*

In the previous section we saw that a galvanic cell is a device that uses an oxidation–reduction reaction to generate an electric current by separating the oxidizing agent from the reducing agent. In this section we will consider several specific galvanic cells and their applications.

Lead Storage Battery

Since about 1915, when self-starters were first used in automobiles, the **lead storage battery** has been a major factor in making the automobile a practical means of transportation. This type of battery can function for several years under temperature extremes ranging from -30 °F to 100 °F and under incessant punishment from rough roads. The fact that this same type of battery has been in use for so many years in the face of all of the changes in science and technology over that span of time attests to how well it does its job.

In the lead storage battery, the reducing agent is lead metal, Pb, and the oxidizing agent is lead(IV) oxide, PbO_2. We have already considered a simplified version of this reaction in Example 18.6. In an actual lead storage battery, sulfuric acid, H_2SO_4, furnishes the H^+ needed in the reaction; it also furnishes SO_4^{2-} ions that react with the Pb^{2+} ions to form solid $PbSO_4$. A schematic of one cell of the lead storage battery is shown in **Figure 18.6**.

In this cell the anode is constructed of lead metal, which is oxidized. In the cell reaction, lead atoms lose two electrons each to form Pb^{2+} ions, which combine with SO_4^{2-} ions present in the solution to give solid $PbSO_4$.

The cathode of this battery has lead(IV) oxide coated onto lead grids. Lead atoms in the $+4$ oxidation state in PbO_2 accept two electrons each (are reduced) to give Pb^{2+} ions that also form solid $PbSO_4$.

In the cell the anode and cathode are separated (so that the electrons must flow through an external wire) and bathed in sulfuric acid. The half-reactions that occur at the two electrodes and the overall cell reaction are shown below.

Anode reaction:

$$Pb + H_2SO_4 \rightarrow PbSO_4 + 2H^+ + 2e^- \quad \text{Oxidation}$$

Cathode reaction:

$$PbO_2 + H_2SO_4 + 2e^- + 2H^+ \rightarrow PbSO_4 + 2H_2O \quad \text{Reduction}$$

Overall reaction:

$$Pb(s) + PbO_2(s) + 2H_2SO_4(aq) \rightarrow 2PbSO_4(s) + 2H_2O(l)$$

> **Remember:** The oxidizing agent accepts electrons and the reducing agent furnishes electrons.

e⁻ flow

H_2SO_4 electrolyte solution

Pb metal grid (anode)

PbO_2 coated onto a lead grid (cathode)

Figure 18.6
In a lead storage battery each cell consists of several lead grids that are connected by a metal bar. These lead grids furnish electrons (the lead atoms lose electrons to form Pb^{2+} ions, which combine with SO_4^{2-} ions to give solid $PbSO_4$). Because the lead is oxidized, it functions as the anode of the cell. The substance that gains electrons is PbO_2; it is coated onto lead grids, several of which are hooked together by a metal bar. The PbO_2 formally contains Pb^{4+}, which is reduced to Pb^{2+}, which in turn combines with SO_4^{2-} to form solid $PbSO_4$. The PbO_2 accepts electrons, so it functions as the cathode.

18.6 Batteries **595**

Section 18.6

Themes
Form and Function

Skills
Applying concepts, interpreting diagrams

Student Preparation
Assign the students to read Sections 18.6 to 18.8 and to answer the Focus Questions at the end of Section 18.8 before coming to class.

Active Learning
After introducing the material in Sections 18.6 to 18.8 in class, place the students in groups and have them work together on Sections 18.6–18.8: Team Learning Worksheet. Answers and/or discussion of these questions are located in the *Teacher Resources.*

TEACHING TIPS

• The remainder of this chapter explains practical applications of electrochemistry. Now is an excellent time for students to make connections between chemistry and their own lives.

• If you can obtain an old lead storage battery, drain it, and saw it in half, you can make a good model to use in class when explaining how lead storage batteries work. The model will serve as a permanent one for the classroom.

USING TECHNOLOGY

 Figure 18.6

Animation and Video

Video, The Lemon Battery

The tendency for electrons to flow from the anode to the cathode in a battery depends on the ability of the reducing agent to release electrons and on the ability of the oxidizing agent to capture electrons. If a battery consists of a reducing agent that releases electrons readily and an oxidizing agent with a high affinity for electrons, the electrons are driven through the connecting wire with great force and can provide much electrical energy. It is useful to think of the analogy of water flowing through a pipe. The greater the pressure on the water, the more vigorously the water flows. The "pressure" on electrons to flow from one electrode to the other in a battery is called the **potential** of the battery and is measured in volts. For example, each cell in a lead storage battery produces about 2 volts of potential. In an actual automobile battery, six of these cells are connected to produce about 12 volts of potential.

Dry Cell Batteries

The calculators, electronic watches, portable radios, and tape players that are so familiar to us are all powered by small, efficient **dry cell batteries.** They are called dry cells because they do not contain a liquid electrolyte. The common dry cell battery was invented more than 100 years ago by George Leclanché (1839–1882), a French chemist. In its *acid version,* the dry cell battery contains a zinc inner case that acts as the anode and a carbon (graphite) rod in contact with a moist paste of solid MnO_2, solid NH_4Cl, and carbon that acts as the cathode **(Figure 18.7).** The half-cell reactions are complex but can be approximated as follows:

Anode reaction:

$$Zn \rightarrow Zn^{2+} + 2e^- \quad \text{Oxidation}$$

Cathode reaction:

$$2NH_4^+ + 2MnO_2 + 2e^- \rightarrow Mn_2O_3 + 2NH_3 + H_2O \quad \text{Reduction}$$

This cell produces a potential of about 1.5 volts.

In the *alkaline version* of the dry cell battery, the NH_4Cl is replaced with KOH or NaOH. In this case the half-reactions can be approximated as follows:

Anode reaction:

$$Zn + 2OH^- \rightarrow ZnO(s) + H_2O + 2e^- \quad \text{Oxidation}$$

Cathode reaction:

$$2MnO_2 + H_2O + 2e^- \rightarrow Mn_2O_3 + 2OH^- \quad \text{Reduction}$$

The alkaline dry cell lasts longer, mainly because the zinc anode corrodes less rapidly under basic conditions than under acidic conditions.

Other types of dry cell batteries include the *silver cell,* which has a Zn anode and a cathode that employs Ag_2O as the oxidizing agent in a basic environment. *Mercury cells,* often used in calculators, have a Zn anode and a cathode involving HgO as the oxidizing agent in a basic medium (see **Figure 18.8**).

USING TECHNOLOGY

Figure 18.7

Figure 18.8

Cathode
(graphite rod)

Paste of MnO_2,
NH_4Cl, and carbon

Anode (zinc
inner case)

Figure 18.7
A common dry cell battery.

Cathode (steel)

Insulation

Anode (zinc container)

Paste of HgO (oxidizing
agent) in a basic medium
of KOH and $Zn(OH)_2$

Figure 18.8
A mercury battery of the type used in small calculators.

An especially important type of dry cell is the *nickel–cadmium battery,* in which the electrode reactions are

Anode reaction:

$$Cd + 2OH^- \rightarrow Cd(OH)_2 + 2e^- \quad \text{Oxidation}$$

Cathode reaction:

$$NiO_2 + 2H_2O + 2e^- \rightarrow Ni(OH)_2 + 2OH^- \quad \text{Reduction}$$

In this cell, as in the lead storage battery, the products adhere to the electrodes. Therefore, a nickel–cadmium battery can be recharged an indefinite number of times, because the products can be turned back into reactants by the use of an external source of current.

CHEMICAL IMPACT

Science, Technology, and Society

An Engine for the Twenty-First Century

Life in the United States has the personal automobile at its very center. To preserve this way of life into the twenty-first century requires that a new power plant be developed. The current internal combustion engine makes inefficient use of energy and causes significant air pollution. One strategy under consideration involves the use of electric cars powered by storage batteries. However, the storage batteries currently available and on the near horizon have very limited capacity and require frequent charging.

The Daimler-Benz Necar II uses hydrogen fuel stored in tanks on its roof.

The General Motors EV 1, currently being tested in selected cities in the United States, has a range of 80–100 miles at speeds of about 55 mph before requiring a full recharge of its lead storage batteries. Although other storage batteries are being developed, as yet none will give you anything close to the speed and range of a car powered by an internal combustion engine.

One inherent difficulty with a storage battery is that the supply of reactants is limited. When these reactants are consumed, the battery must be recharged. A different kind of battery, called a fuel cell, is one in which the reactants are continuously supplied from an external source. The best-known fuel cell is the H_2/O_2 unit used by NASA to provide electric power for the space shuttle. In this fuel cell, electric current is produced as the electrons flow from H_2 (the reducing agent) to O_2 (the oxidizing agent). This unit has never been applied to automobiles because of the difficulties in storing hydrogen.

New research, however, indicates that gasoline might serve as a good source of H_2 in an H_2/O_2 fuel cell for automobiles. Jeffrey Bentley, a mechanical engineer working for Arthur D. Little, Inc., in Cambridge, Massachusetts, found that careful heating of gasoline mixed with steam in an oxygen-poor environment results in a mixture of carbon dioxide, carbon monoxide, and hydrogen (contaminated with various sulfur compounds). Using metal catalysts developed by Nick Vanderborgh, a chemical engineer at Los Alamos National Laboratory, this mixture is then "cleaned up" to produce relatively pure H_2 that can be used in an H_2/O_2 fuel cell to produce electricity to run electric motors and power an automobile. The energy efficiency of this system is about twice that of a conventional internal combustion engine, so projected gas mileage should be about double that for current cars. In addition, the system can handle alternative fuels, such as natural gas and alcohol, without any major adjustments. As petroleum supplies dwindle, this consideration will become increasingly important. These new developments make H_2/O_2 fuel cells for automobiles much more likely in the twenty-first century.

Integrating the CHEMICAL IMPACT

An Engine for the Twenty-First Century

Have students use the Internet to research the types of electric/fuel cell cars available on the market. The technology of each vehicle can then be studied and its energy use discussed. This feature represents an excellent time to discuss the feasibility and efficiency of fuel cell use.

18.6 Batteries **597**

Section 18.7

Themes
Patterns of Change

Skills
Applying concepts, interpreting diagrams, making predictions

Laboratory
Experiment 83:
Corrosion of Iron, Traditional

18.7 Corrosion

Objective: *To understand the electrochemical nature of corrosion and to learn some ways of preventing it.*

Some metals, such as copper, gold, silver, and platinum, are relatively difficult to oxidize. They are often called noble metals.

A car rusting in a field.

An alloy is a mixture of elements with metallic properties.

Most metals are found in nature in compounds with nonmetals such as oxygen and sulfur. For example, iron exists as iron ore (which contains Fe_2O_3 and other oxides of iron).

Corrosion can be viewed as the process of returning metals to their natural state—the ores from which they were originally obtained. Corrosion involves oxidation of the metal. Because corroded metal often loses its strength and attractiveness, this process causes great economic loss. For example, approximately one-fifth of the iron and steel produced annually is used to replace rusted metal.

Because most metals react with O_2, we might expect them to corrode so fast in air that they wouldn't be useful. It is surprising, therefore, that the problem of corrosion does not virtually prevent the use of metals in air. Part of the explanation is that most metals develop a thin oxide coating, which tends to protect their internal atoms against further oxidation. The best example of this is aluminum. Aluminum readily loses electrons, so it should be very easily oxidized by O_2. Given this fact, why is aluminum so useful for building airplanes, bicycle frames, and so on? Aluminum is such a valuable structural material because it forms a thin adherent layer of aluminum oxide, Al_2O_3, which greatly inhibits further corrosion. Thus aluminum protects itself with this tough oxide coat. Many other metals, such as chromium, nickel, and tin, do the same thing.

Iron can also form a protective oxide coating. However, this oxide is not a very effective shield against corrosion, because it scales off easily, exposing new metal surfaces to oxidation. Under normal atmospheric conditions, copper forms an external layer of greenish copper sulfate or carbonate called *patina. Silver tarnish* is silver sulfide, Ag_2S, which in thin layers gives the silver surface a richer appearance. Gold shows no appreciable corrosion in air.

Preventing corrosion is an important way of conserving our natural supplies of metals and energy. The primary means of protection is the application of a coating—most often paint or metal plating—to protect the metal from oxygen and moisture. Chromium and tin are often used to plate steel because they oxidize to form a durable, effective oxide coating.

Alloying is also used to prevent corrosion. *Stainless steel* contains chromium and nickel, both of which form oxide coatings that protect the steel.

Cathodic protection is the method most often employed to protect steel in buried fuel tanks and pipelines. A metal that furnishes electrons more easily than iron, such as magnesium, is connected by a wire to the pipeline or tank that is to be protected **(Figure 18.9).** Because the magnesium is a better reducing agent than iron, electrons flow through the wire from the magnesium to the iron pipe.

Figure 18.9
Cathodic protection of an underground pipe.

Thus the electrons are furnished by the magnesium rather than by the iron, keeping the iron from being oxidized. As oxidation of the magnesium occurs, the magnesium dissolves, so it must be replaced periodically.

18.8 Electrolysis

Objective: *To understand the process of electrolysis and learn about the commercial preparation of aluminum.*

Unless it is recharged, a battery "runs down" because the substances in it that furnish and accept electrons (to produce the electron flow) are consumed. For example, in the lead storage battery (see Section 18.6), PbO_2 and Pb are consumed to form $PbSO_4$ as the battery runs.

$$PbO_2(s) + Pb(s) + 2H_2SO_4(aq) \rightarrow 2PbSO_4(s) + 2H_2O(l)$$

However, one of the most useful characteristics of the lead storage battery is that it can be recharged. *Forcing* current through the battery in the direction opposite to the normal direction reverses the oxidation–reduction reaction. That is, $PbSO_4$ is consumed and PbO_2 and Pb are formed in the charging process. This recharging is done continuously by the automobile's alternator, which is powered by the engine.

The process of **electrolysis** involves *forcing a current through a cell to produce a chemical change that would not otherwise occur.*

One important example of this type of process is the electrolysis of water. Water is a very stable substance that can be broken down into its elements by using an electric current **(Figure 18.10).**

$$2H_2O(l) \xrightarrow[\text{current}]{\text{Forced electric}} 2H_2(g) + O_2(g)$$

Figure 18.10
The electrolysis of water produces hydrogen gas at the cathode (on the left) and oxygen gas at the anode (on the right). A nonreacting strong electrolyte such as Na_2SO_4 is needed to furnish ions to allow the flow of current.

18.8 Electroysis **599**

Figure 18.11
Charles Martin Hall (1863–1914) was a student at Oberlin College in Ohio when he first became interested in aluminum. One of his professors commented that anyone who could find a way to manufacture aluminum cheaply would make a fortune, and Hall decided to give it a try. The 21-year-old worked in a wooden shed near his house with an iron frying pan as a container, a blacksmith's forge as a heat source, and galvanic cells constructed from fruit jars. Using these crude galvanic cells, Hall found that he could produce aluminum by passing a current through a molten mixture of Al_2O_3 and Na_3AlF_6. By a strange coincidence, Paul Heroult, a French chemist who was born and died in the same years as Hall, made the same discovery at about the same time.

The electrolysis of water to produce hydrogen and oxygen occurs whenever a current is forced through an aqueous solution. Thus, when the lead storage battery is charged, or "jumped," potentially explosive mixtures of H_2 and O_2 are produced by the current flow through the solution in the battery. This is why it is very important not to produce a spark near the battery during these operations.

Another important use of electrolysis is in the production of metals from their ores. The metal produced in the greatest quantities by electrolysis is aluminum.

Aluminum is one of the most abundant elements on earth, ranking third behind oxygen and silicon. Because aluminum is a very reactive metal, it is found in nature as its oxide in an ore called *bauxite* (named after Les Baux, France, where it was discovered in 1821). Production of aluminum metal from its ore proved to be more difficult than the production of most other metals. In 1782 Lavoisier, the pioneering French chemist, recognized aluminum as a metal "whose affinity for oxygen is so strong that it cannot be overcome by any known reducing agent." As a result, pure aluminum metal remained unknown. Finally, in 1854, a process was found for producing metallic aluminum by using sodium, but aluminum remained a very expensive rarity. In fact, it is said that Napoleon III served his most honored guests with aluminum forks and spoons, while the others had to settle for gold and silver utensils!

The breakthrough came in 1886 when two men, Charles M. Hall in the United States **(Figure 18.11)** and Paul Heroult in France, almost simultaneously discovered a practical electrolytic process for producing aluminum, which greatly increased the availability of aluminum for many purposes. **Table 18.2** shows how dramatically the price of aluminum dropped after this discovery. The effect of the electrolysis process is to reduce Al^{3+} ions to neutral Al atoms that form aluminum metal. The aluminum produced in this electrolytic process is 99.5% pure. To be useful as a structural material, aluminum is alloyed with metals such as zinc (for trailer and aircraft construction) and manganese (for cooking utensils, storage tanks, and highway signs). The production of aluminum consumes about 4.5% of all electricity used in the United States.

TABLE 18.2

The Price of Aluminum, 1855–1990

Date	Price of Aluminum ($/lb)*
1855	$100,000
1885	100
1890	2
1895	0.50
1970	0.30
1980	0.80
1990	0.74

*Note the precipitous drop in price after the discovery of the Hall–Heroult process in 1886.

An electrolytic cell uses electrical energy to produce a chemical change that would not otherwise occur.

Focus Questions

Sections 18.6–18.8

1. What is electrochemical potential?
2. Why does an alkaline battery (like those in the famous pink bunny commercials) keep going longer than an acid dry cell?
3. What are three ways to protect against corrosion?
4. What happens to a battery when it is "recharged"?

600   Chapter 18   Oxidation–Reduction Reactions and Electrochemistry

---

 CHEMISTRY in the LABORATORY

Activity Series

Objectives

1. To react several metals with several metal ions in aqueous solutions and observe changes
2. To use observations to develop an activity series for the metals

Skills

Making observations, applying concepts, drawing conclusions, making judgments

Materials

Goggles
Apron
Reaction wells
HCl (6.0 *M*)
Metal strips (Cu, Al, Zn, Fe, and MG)

0.10 *M* solutions of $CuCl_2$
$Fe(NO_3)_2$
$Zn(NO_3)_2$
$Mg(NO_3)_2$
$Al(NO_3)_3$

Preparation Hints

If possible, have each solution available in different bottles around the lab for easier access.

Prelab Discussion

Tell students that if they come in con-

tact with any solution, they need to wash the contacted area thoroughly. This point is especially crucial for the 6.0 *M* HCl. Make sure that students know the locations of eyewashes.

Remind students that they need only a small amount of each solution.

Disposal

Collect all solutions from the students and dispose of them properly.

Post-Lab Discussion

If you have enough time, you may

CHEMISTRY in the LABORATORY
Activity Series

Problem

Which metals are the most active? Which are the least active? How do we measure activity?

Introduction

In this lab you will react various metals with different solutions and rank the activities of the metals.

Prelab Assignment

Read the entire lab experiment before you begin.

Materials

Goggles
Apron
Reaction wells
HCl (6.0 M)

Metal strips (Cu, Al, Zn, Fe, and Mg)
0.10 M solutions of
CuCl$_2$,
Fe(NO$_3$)$_2$
Zn(NO$_3$)$_2$
Mg(NO$_3$)$_2$
Al(NO$_3$)$_3$

Safety

1. The 6.0 M HCl is corrosive. Handle it with extreme care.
2. If you come in contact with any solution, wash the contacted area thoroughly.

Procedure

Part I: Developing an Activity Series

1. Place a few drops of each solution in separate reaction wells.
2. Place a strip of each metal in each solution.
3. Record all changes observed in the metals and solutions.

Part II: Testing the Activity Series

1. Place a few drops of 6.0 M HCl in five separate reaction wells.
2. Place a strip of each metal in the separate solutions of 6.0 M HCl.
3. Record all changes observed in the metals and solutions.

Cleaning Up

Clean all materials and wash your hands thoroughly.

Data/Observations

Part I

Record your observations in a table like the one shown below.

	CuCl$_2$	Fe(NO$_3$)$_2$	Zn(NO$_3$)$_2$	Mg(NO$_3$)$_2$	Al(NO$_3$)$_3$
Cu					
Fe					
Zn					
Mg					
Al					

Part II

Record your observations in a table like the one shown below.

	Cu	Fe	Zn	Mg	Al
HCl					

Analysis and Conclusions

1. Suppose metal A reacts with a solution containing ions of metal B. Can we predict whether metal B will react with a solution containing ions of metal A?
2. Based on your results in Part I, order the metals from most active to least active. Explain your reasoning. This order is called the activity series.
3. Are your results in Part II consistent with the activity series you developed in Part I? Explain. Where would H$^+$ fit in this series?
4. Identify the oxidizing agent and reducing agent in each reaction.
5. Do metals react with solutions containing ions of the same metals? Explain the results when a metal was added to a solution containing the same metal.

Something Extra

Would changing the concentrations of the solutions affect your activity series? Try it.

3. The results in Part II do not contradict the results in Part I. In this case, copper is still seen to be nonreactive. The H$^+$ ion would fit between Fe and Cu in the series. Actually, because this series is an oxidation series, H$_2$ is between Fe and Cu (since H$^+$ is reduced to H$_2$ in the reaction).

4. In Part I, the oxidizing agent is the metal ion and the reducing agent is the metal. In Part II, the oxidizing agent is H$^+$ and the reducing agent is the metal.

5. No, metals do not react with solutions containing ions of the same metals. There would be no net reaction. For example, if Mg reacted with Mg^{2+}, we would have Mg + Mg^{2+} → Mg^{2+} + Mg, which is not a reaction.

Something Extra

Changing the concentrations will not affect the order of the activity series. This series depends only on the tendency of a metal to lose electrons.

601

wish to have students write and balance the oxidation–reduction reactions for all observed reactions in the lab. These equations follow:

Fe + Cu^{2+} → Fe^{2+} + Cu
Zn + Fe^{2+} → Zn^{2+} + Fe
Mg + Fe^{2+} → Mg^{2+} + Fe
3Mg + 2Al^{3+} → 3Mg^{2+} + 2Al
2Al + 3Fe^{2+} → 2Al^{3+} + 3Fe
Fe + 2H$^+$ → Fe^{2+} + H$_2$
Mg + 2H$^+$ → Mg^{2+} + H$_2$
Zn + Cu^{2+} → Zn^{2+} + Cu
Mg + Cu^{2+} → Mg^{2+} + Cu
Mg + Zn^{2+} → Mg^{2+} + Zn

2Al + 3Cu^{2+} → 2Al^{3+} + 3Cu
2Al + 3Zn$_2$$^+$ → 2Al^{3+} + 3Zn
Zn + 2H$^+$ → Zn^{2+} + H$_2$
2Al + 6H$^+$ → 2Al^{3+} + 3H$_2$

Sample Data/Answers
Data/Observations

See the *Teacher's Guide* to the Laboratory for sample data.

Analysis and Conclusions

1. Yes. If metal A reacts with a solution containing ions of metal B, then metal B will not react with a solution containing ions of metal A.

2. From most to least active: Mg > Al > Zn > Fe > Cu. Magnesium metal reacted with ions of all of the other metals. Aluminum metal reacted with Zn^{2+}, Fe^{2+}, and Cu^{2+} ions. Zinc metal reacted with Fe^{2+} and Cu^{2+} ions. Iron metal reacted with Cu^{2+} ions. Copper metal did not react with any of the other ions.

Answers to End of Chapter Problems

1. Oxidation can be defined as the loss of electrons by an atom, molecule, or ion. It may also be defined as an increase in oxidation state for an element. This increase occurs because of the loss of one or more electrons (thus the definitions are the same). The following equation shows the oxidation of copper:

$$Cu(s) \rightarrow Cu^{2+}(aq) + 2e^-$$

2. Reduction can be defined as the gain of electrons by an atom, molecule, or ion. It may also be defined as a decrease in oxidation state for an element. This decrease occurs because of the gain of one or more electrons (thus the definitions are the same). The following equation shows the reduction of sulfur:

$$S(s) + 2e^- \rightarrow S^{2-}(aq)$$

3. (a) sodium is oxidized, nitrogen is reduced; (b) magnesium is oxidized, chlorine is reduced; (c) aluminum is oxidized, bromine is reduced; (d) iron is oxidized, oxygen is reduced

4. (a) magnesium is oxidized, bromine is reduced; (b) sodium is oxidized, sulfur is reduced; (c) bromide ion is oxidized, chlorine is reduced; (d) potassium is oxidized, nitrogen is reduced

5. The assignment of oxidation states is a bookkeeping method by which charges are assigned to the various atoms in a compound. This method allows us to keep track of electrons transferred between species in oxidation–reduction reactions.

6. For very electronegative elements (such as oxygen), we assign each of these elements an oxidation state equal to its charge when the element

forms an anion. The most common exception to oxygen having an oxidation state of −2 occurs with the peroxide ion, in which each oxygen has an oxidation state of −1.

7. A neutral molecule has an overall charge of zero.

8. The sum of all the oxidation states of the atoms in a polyatomic ion must equal the overall charge on the ion.

9. (a) N, +3; Cl, −1; (b) S, +6; F, − 1; (c) P, +5; Cl, −1;

(d) Si, −4; H, +1

10. (a) H, +1; Br, −1; (b) H, +1; O, −2; Br, +1; (c) Br, 0; (d) H, +1; O, −2; Br, +7

11. (a) H, +1; O, −2; N, +5; (b) H, +1; O, −2; P, +5; (c) H, +1; O, −2; S, +6; (d) O, −1

12. (a) Cu, +2; Cl, −1; (b) Cr, +3; Cl, −1; (c) H, +1; O, −2; Cr, +6; (d) Cr, +3; O, −2

13. (a) H, +1; C, −4; (b) Na, +1; O, −2; C, +4; (c) K, +1; H, +1; C, +4; O, −2; (d) O, −2; C, +2

14. Consider the following simple oxidation reaction: Na → $Na^+ + e^-$. The sodium atom on the left side of the equation is losing an electron. Because electrons are negatively charged, the oxidation state is increasing (from 0 to +1).

15. When an atom gains an electron, it gains a negative charge, which will lower its oxidation state. For example, in the reaction $Cl + e^- \rightarrow Cl^-$, the oxidation state goes from 0 to −1.

Chapter Review

Key Terms

oxidation–reduction (redox) reactions (18.1)
oxidation (18.1)
reduction (18.1)
oxidation states (18.2)
oxidizing agent (electron acceptor) (18.3)
reducing agent (electron donor) (18.3)
half-reactions (18.4)
electrochemistry (18.5)

electrochemical battery (galvanic cell) (18.5)
anode (18.5)
cathode (18.5)
electrolysis (18.5)
lead storage battery (18.6)
potential (18.6)
dry cell battery (18.6)
corrosion (18.7)
cathodic protection (18.7)

Summary

1. Oxidation–reduction reactions involve a transfer of electrons. Oxidation states provide a way to keep track of electrons in these reactions. A set of rules is used to assign oxidation states.

2. Oxidation is an increase in oxidation state (a loss of electrons); reduction is a decrease in oxidation state (a gain of electrons). An oxidizing agent accepts electrons, and a reducing agent donates electrons. Oxidation and reduction always occur together.

3. Oxidation–reduction equations can be balanced by inspection or by the half-reaction method. This method involves splitting a reaction into two parts (the oxidation half-reaction and the reduction half-reaction).

4. Electrochemistry is the study of the interchange of chemical and electrical energy that occurs through oxidation–reduction reactions.

5. When an oxidation–reduction reaction occurs with the reactants in the same solution, the electrons are transferred directly, and no useful work can be obtained. However, when the oxidizing agent is separated from the reducing agent, so that the electrons must flow through a wire from one to the other, chemical energy is transformed into electrical energy. The opposite process, in which electrical energy is used to produce chemical change, is called electrolysis.

6. A galvanic (electrochemical) cell is a device in which chemical energy is transformed into useful electrical energy. Oxidation occurs at the anode of a cell; reduction occurs at the cathode.

7. A battery is a galvanic cell, or group of cells, that serves as a source of electric current. The lead storage battery has a lead anode and a cathode of lead coated with

PbO_2, both immersed in a solution of sulfuric acid. Dry cell batteries do not have liquid electrolytes but contain a moist paste instead.

8. Corrosion involves the oxidation of metals to form mainly oxides and sulfides. Some metals, such as aluminum, form a thin protective oxide coating that inhibits their further corrosion. Corrosion of iron can be prevented by a coating (such as paint), by alloying, and by cathodic protection.

Questions and Problems

All exercises with blue numbers have answers in the back of this book.

18.1 Oxidation–Reduction Reactions

Questions

1. How is *oxidation* defined? Write an equation showing an atom being *oxidized*.

2. How is *reduction* defined? Write an equation showing an atom being *reduced*.

3. For each of the following oxidation–reduction reactions of metals with nonmetals, identify which element is oxidized and which is reduced.
   a. $6Na(s) + N_2(g) \rightarrow 2Na_3N(s)$
   b. $Mg(s) + Cl_2(g) \rightarrow MgCl_2(s)$
   c. $2Al(s) + 3Br_2(l) \rightarrow 2AlBr_3(s)$
   d. $4Fe(s) + 3O_2(g) \rightarrow 2Fe_2O_3(s)$

4. For each of the following oxidation–reduction reactions, identify which element is oxidized and which is reduced.
   a. $Mg(s) + Br_2(l) \rightarrow MgBr_2(s)$
   b. $2Na(s) + S(s) \rightarrow Na_2S(s)$
   c. $Cl_2(g) + 2NaBr(aq) \rightarrow Br_2(l) + 2NaCl(aq)$
   d. $6K(s) + N_2(g) \rightarrow 2K_3N(s)$

18.2 Oxidation States

Questions

5. What is an oxidation state? Why do we define such a concept?

6. Explain why, although it is not an ionic compound, we still assign oxygen an oxidation state of −2 in water, H_2O. Give an example of a compound in which oxygen is *not* in the −2 oxidation state.

7. Why must the sum of all the oxidation states of the atoms in a neutral molecule be zero?

8. What must be the sum of the oxidation states of all the atoms in a polyatomic ion?

Problems

9. Assign oxidation states to all of the atoms in each of the following:
   a. NCl_3
   b. SF_6
   c. PCl_5
   d. SiH_4

10. Assign oxidation states to all of the atoms in each of the following:
    a. HBr
    b. $HOBr$
    c. Br_2
    d. $HBrO_4$

11. Assign oxidation states to all of the atoms in each of the following:
    a. HNO_3
    b. $HPO_4{}^{2-}$
    c. $HSO_4{}^-$
    d. $O_2{}^{2-}$

12. Assign oxidation states to all of the atoms in each of the following:
    a. $CuCl_2$
    b. $CrCl_3$
    c. $HCrO_4{}^-$
    d. Cr_2O_3

13. Assign oxidation states to all of the atoms in each of the following:
    a. CH_4
    b. Na_2CO_3
    c. $KHCO_3$
    d. CO

18.3 Oxidation–Reduction Reactions Between Nonmetals

Questions

14. Oxidation can be defined as a loss of electrons or as an increase in oxidation state. Explain why the two definitions mean the same thing, and give an example to support your explanation.

15. Reduction can be defined as a gain of electrons or as a decrease in oxidation state. Explain why the two definitions mean the same thing, and give an example to support your explanation.

16. Is an oxidizing agent itself oxidized or reduced? Is a reducing agent itself oxidized or reduced?

17. Does an oxidizing agent increase or decrease its own oxidation state when it acts on another atom? Does a reducing agent increase or decrease its own oxidation state when it acts on another substance?

Problems

18. In each of the following reactions, identify which element is oxidized and which is reduced by assigning oxidation numbers.
    a. $Zn(s) + 2HNO_3(aq) \rightarrow Zn(NO_3)_2(aq) + H_2(g)$
    b. $H_2(g) + CuSO_4(aq) \rightarrow Cu(s) + H_2SO_4(aq)$
    c. $N_2(g) + 3Br_2(l) \rightarrow 2NBr_3(g)$
    d. $2KBr(aq) + Cl_2(g) \rightarrow 2KCl(aq) + Br_2(l)$

19. In each of the following reactions, identify which element is oxidized and which is reduced by assigning oxidation states.
    a. $Cu(s) + 2AgNO_3(aq) \rightarrow 2Ag(s) + Cu(NO_3)_2(aq)$
    b. $N_2(g) + 3F_2(g) \rightarrow 2NF_3(g)$
    c. $2Fe_2O_3(s) + 3S \rightarrow 4Fe(s) + 3SO_2(g)$
    d. $2H_2O_2(l) \rightarrow 2H_2O(l) + O_2(g)$

20. In ordinary photography, the light-sensitive portion of the film is a thin coating of a silver halide (usually silver bromide). When the film is exposed to light, the reaction

    $$2AgBr(s) \rightarrow 2Ag(s) + Br_2(g)$$

    occurs. Identify which element is reduced and which is oxidized.

21. Although magnesium metal does not react with water at room temperature, it does react vigorously with steam at higher temperatures, releasing elemental hydrogen gas from the water.

    $$Mg(s) + 2H_2O(g) \rightarrow Mg(OH)_2(s) + H_2(g)$$

    Identify which element is being oxidized and which is being reduced.

18.4 Balancing Oxidation–Reduction Reactions by the Half-Reaction Method

Questions

22. In what *two* respects must oxidation–reduction reactions be balanced?

23. Why must the number of electrons lost in the oxidation equal the number of electrons gained in the reduction? Is it possible to have "leftover" electrons in a reaction?

Problems

24. Balance each of the following half-reactions.
    a. $N_2(g) \rightarrow N^{3-}(aq)$
    b. $O_2{}^{2-}(aq) \rightarrow O_2(g)$
    c. $Zn(s) \rightarrow Zn^{2+}(aq)$
    d. $F_2(g) \rightarrow F^-(aq)$

atom, ion, or molecule. Consequently, the total number of electrons lost by the species being oxidized must equal the total number of electrons gained by the species being reduced.

24. (a) $N_2(g) + 6e^- \rightarrow 2N^{3-}(aq)$; (b) $O_2{}^{2-}(aq) \rightarrow O_2(g) + 2e^-$; (c) $Zn(s) \rightarrow Zn^{2+}(aq) + 2e^-$; (d) $F_2(g) + 2e^- \rightarrow 2F^-(aq)$

25. (a) $4e^- + 4H^+(aq) + O_2(g) \rightarrow 2H_2O(l)$; (b) $10e^- + 12H^+(aq) + 2IO_3{}^-(aq) \rightarrow I_2(s) + 6H_2O(l)$; (c) $e^- + 2H^+(aq) + VO^{2+}(aq) \rightarrow V^{3+}(aq) + H_2O(l)$; (d) $3e^- + 2H^+(aq) + BiO^+(aq) \rightarrow Bi(s) + H_2O(l)$

26. (a) $2MnO_4{}^-(aq) + 16H^+(aq) + 5Zn(s) \rightarrow 2Mn^{2+}(aq) + 8H_2O(l) + 5Zn^{2+}(aq)$; (b) $H_2(g) + Sn^{4+}(aq) \rightarrow 2H^+(aq) + Sn^{2+}(aq)$; (c) $2NO_3{}^-(aq) + 4H^+(aq) + Zn(s) \rightarrow 2NO_2(g) + 2H_2O(l) + Zn^{2+}(aq)$; (d) $H_2S(g) + Br_2(l) \rightarrow S(s) + 2H^+(aq) + 2Br^-(aq)$

27. (a) $IO_3{}^-(aq) + 6H^+(aq) + 5I^-(aq) \rightarrow 3I_2(aq) + 3H_2O(l)$; (b) $6I^-(aq) + Cr_2O_7{}^{2-}(aq) + 14H^+(aq) \rightarrow 3I_2(aq) + 2Cr^{3+}(aq) + 7H_2O(l)$; (c) $2Cu^{2+}(aq) + 4I^-(aq) \rightarrow 2CuI(s) + I_2(aq)$

28. An oxidation–reduction reaction is made useful as a galvanic cell (battery) by physically separating the oxidation half-reaction from the reduction half-reaction and by causing the electrons to be transferred through a wire connecting the two. The passage of electrons through the wire represents an electrical current, which might be used to drive a motor or some other device.

29. A salt bridge completes the electrical circuit in a cell. It does so by allowing ion flow from one half of the cell to the other half without allowing bulk mixing of the solutions. It is typically a U-shaped tube filled with an electrolyte that is not involved in the oxidation–reduction reaction. Any method that allows ion flow without large-scale mixing of solutions (such as a porous cup or frit) can be used in place of a salt bridge.

30. In a galvanic cell, electrons flow from the anode

Chapter Review **603**

16. An oxidizing agent causes another species to be oxidized (to lose electrons). To do this, the oxidizing agent must take in electrons (be reduced). Thus an oxidizing agent is reduced (and a reducing agent is oxidized).

17. An oxidizing agent oxidizes another species by gaining the electrons lost by the other species. Therefore, the oxidizing agent itself decreases in oxidation state. A reducing agent increases its oxidation state when acting on another atom or molecule.

18. (a) zinc is oxidized (0 to +2); hydrogen is reduced (+1 to 0); (b) hydrogen is oxidized (0 to +1); copper is reduced (+2 to 0); (c) nitrogen is reduced (0 to −3); bromine is oxidized (0 to +1); (d) bromine is oxidized (−1 to 0); chlorine is reduced (0 to −1)

19. (a) copper is oxidized (0 to +2); silver is reduced (+1 to 0); (b) nitrogen is oxidized (0 to +3); fluorine is reduced (0 to −1); (c) sulfur is oxidized (0 to +4); iron is reduced (+3 to 0); oxygen is both oxidized (−1 to 0) and reduced (−1 to −2)

20. silver is reduced [+1 in $AgBr(s)$, 0 in $Ag(s)$]; bromine is oxidized [−1 in $AgBr(s)$, 0 in $Br_2(g)$]

21. magnesium is oxidized [0 in $Mg(s)$, +2 in $Mg(OH)_2(s)$]; hydrogen is reduced [+1 in $H_2O(l)$, 0 in $H_2(g)$]

22. Oxidation–reduction reactions must be balanced with respect to mass and charge.

23. Under ordinary conditions it is impossible to have "free" electrons that are not part of some (where oxidation occurs) to the cathode (where reduction occurs).

31. See the *Solutions Guide* for the drawing.

32. See the *Solutions Guide* for the drawing.

33. The overall reaction is $Pb(s) + PbO_2(s) + 2H_2SO_4(aq) \rightarrow 2PbSO_4(s) + 2H_2O(l)$, in which lead is both oxidized (0 to +2) and reduced (+4 to +2). The battery can be recharged because the reaction can be reversed by the electrolysis of the mixture of water and solid lead(II) sulfate.

34. Both normal and alkaline cells contain zinc as an electrode; zinc corrodes more slowly under alkaline (basic) conditions than in a normal dry cell (which is acidic). Anode: $Zn(s) + 2OH^-(aq) \rightarrow ZnO(s) + H_2O(l) + 2e^-$. Cathode: $2MnO_2(s) + H_2O(l) + 2e^- \rightarrow Mn_2O_3(s) + 2OH^-(aq)$.

35. Corrosion returns metals to their natural state (ore) and involves oxidation of the metal. It is undesirable because as the metal is converted to its oxide, the bulk of the metal loses strength, flexibility, and other metallic properties.

36. Aluminum reacts very quickly with the oxygen in air to form a thin coating of Al_2O_3 on its surface. This coating is transparent and clings tightly to the aluminum. In addition, the aluminum oxide is much less reactive than aluminum and protects the surface from further reaction.

37. Most steels contain additives such as chromium or nickel. These additives are able to form protective oxide coatings on the surface of the steel. These coatings tend to prevent further oxidation.

38. In the cathodic protection of steel tanks and pipes, a more reactive metal than iron is connected to the item to be protected. The active metal is then oxidized instead of the iron of the tank or pipe.

39. Electrolysis is the process of forcing an electrical current through a cell to produce a chemical change that would otherwise not occur on its own.

25. Balance each of the following half-reactions, which take place in acidic solution.
   a. $O_2(g) \rightarrow H_2O(l)$
   b. $IO_3^-(aq) \rightarrow I_2(s)$
   c. $VO^{2+}(aq) \rightarrow V^{3+}(aq)$
   d. $BiO^+(aq) \rightarrow Bi(s)$

26. Balance each of the following oxidation–reduction reactions, which take place in acidic solution, by using the half-reaction method.
   a. $MnO_4^-(aq) + Zn(s) \rightarrow Mn^{2+}(aq) + Zn^{2+}(aq)$
   b. $Sn^{4+}(aq) + H_2(g) \rightarrow Sn^{2+}(aq) + H^+(aq)$
   c. $Zn(s) + NO_3^-(aq) \rightarrow Zn^{2+}(aq) + NO_2(g)$
   d. $H_2S(g) + Br_2(l) \rightarrow S(s) + Br^-(aq)$

27. Iodide ion, I–, is one of the most easily oxidized species. Balance each of the following oxidation–reduction reactions, which take place in acidic solution, by using the half-reaction method.
   a. $IO_3^-(aq) + I^-(aq) \rightarrow I_2(aq)$
   b. $Cr_2O_7^{2-}(aq) + I^-(aq) \rightarrow Cr^{3+}(aq) + I_2(aq)$
   c. $Cu^{2+}(aq) + I^-(aq) \rightarrow CuI(s) + I_2(aq)$

18.5 Electrochemistry: An Introduction

Questions

28. How is an oxidation–reduction reaction set up as a galvanic cell (battery)? How is the transfer of electrons between reducing agent and oxidizing agent made useful?

29. What is a salt bridge? Why is a salt bridge necessary in a galvanic cell? Can some other method be used in place of the salt bridge?

30. In which direction do electrons flow in a galvanic cell, anode to cathode, or vice versa?

Problems

31. Consider the oxidation–reduction reaction

   $Al(s) + Ni^{2+}(aq) \rightarrow Al^{3+}(aq) + Ni(s)$

   Sketch a galvanic cell that makes use of this reaction. Which metal ion is reduced? Which metal is oxidized? What half-reaction takes place at the anode in the cell? What half-reaction takes place at the cathode in the cell?

32. Consider the oxidation–reduction reaction

   $Zn(s) + Pb^{2+}(aq) \rightarrow Zn^{2+}(aq) + Pb(s)$

   Sketch a galvanic cell that uses this reaction. Which metal ion is reduced? Which metal is oxidized? What half-reaction takes place at the anode in the cell? What half-reaction takes place at the cathode?

18.6 Batteries

Questions

33. Write the chemical equation for the overall cell reaction that occurs in a lead storage automobile battery. What species is oxidized in such a battery? What

species is reduced? Why can such a battery be "recharged"?

34. Why does an alkaline dry cell battery typically last longer than a normal dry cell? Write the chemical equation for the overall cell reaction in an alkaline dry cell.

18.7 Corrosion

Questions

35. What process is represented by the *corrosion* of a metal? Why is corrosion undesirable?

36. Explain how some metals, notably aluminum, naturally resist complete oxidation by the atmosphere.

37. Pure iron ordinarily rusts quickly, but steel does not corrode nearly as fast. How does steel resist corrosion?

38. What is *cathodic protection,* and how is it applied to prevent oxidation of steel tanks and pipes?

18.8 Electrolysis

Questions

39. What is *electrolysis?* What types of reactions is electrolysis capable of causing?

40. What reactions go on during the recharging of an automobile battery?

41. How is aluminum metal produced by electrolysis? Why can't simpler chemical reduction methods be used?

42. Jewelry is often manufactured by plating an expensive metal such as gold over a cheaper metal. How might such a process be set up as an electrolysis reaction?

Critical Thinking

43. An oxidizing agent causes the (oxidation/reduction) of another species, and the oxidizing agent itself is (oxidized/reduced).

44. To function as a good reducing agent, a species must _____ electrons easily.

45. "Jump-starting" a dead automobile battery can be dangerous if precautions are not taken, because of the production of an explosive mixture of _____ and _____ gases in the battery.

46. For each of the following unbalanced oxidation–reduction chemical equations, balance the equation by inspection, and identify which species is undergoing oxidation and which is undergoing reduction.
   a. $Fe(s) + O_2(g) \rightarrow Fe_2O_3(s)$
   b. $Al(s) + Cl_2(g) \rightarrow AlCl_3(s)$
   c. $Mg(s) + P_4(s) \rightarrow Mg_3P_2(s)$

40. The main recharging reaction for the lead storage battery is $2PbSO_4(s) + 2H_2O(l) \rightarrow Pb(s) + PbO_2(s) + 2H_2SO_4(aq)$. A major side reaction is the electrolysis of water, $2H_2O(l) \rightarrow 2H_2(g) + O_2(g)$.

41. Aluminum combines readily with oxygen, so it cannot be produced by electrolysis of aqueous solutions of an aluminum salt. Aluminum is most commonly prepared by the Hall process, which is the electrolysis of a molten mixture of Al_2O_3 and Na_3AlF_6.

42. The item to be plated should be made the cathode in a cell containing a solution of ions of the desired plating metal.

43. oxidation; reduced

44. lose

45. hydrogen; oxygen

46. (a) $4Fe(s) + 3O_2(g) \rightarrow 2Fe_2O_3(s)$; iron is oxidized, oxygen is reduced; (b) $2Al(s) + 3Cl_2(g) \rightarrow 2AlCl_3(s)$; aluminum is oxidized, chlorine is reduced; (c) $6Mg(s) + P_4(s) \rightarrow 2Mg_3P_2(s)$; magnesium is oxidized, phosphorus is reduced

47. (a) $2MnO_4^-(aq) + 6H^+(aq) + 5H_2O_2(aq) \rightarrow 2Mn^{2+}(aq) + 8H_2O(l) + 5O_2(g)$; (b) $6Cu^+(aq) + 6H^+(aq) + BrO_3^-(aq) \rightarrow 6Cu^{2+}(aq) + Br^-(aq) + 3H_2O(l)$; (c) $2HNO_2(aq) + 2H^+(aq) + 2I^-(aq) \rightarrow 2NO(g) + 2H_2O(l) + I_2(aq)$

48. (a) zinc is oxidized, nitrogen is reduced; (b) cobalt is oxidized, sulfur is reduced; (c) potassium is oxidized, oxygen is reduced; (d) silver is oxidized, oxygen is reduced

47. Balance each of the following oxidation–reduction reactions, which take place in acidic solution.
    a. $MnO_4^-(aq) + H_2O_2(aq) \rightarrow Mn^{2+}(aq) + O_2(g)$
    b. $BrO_3^-(aq) + Cu^+(aq) \rightarrow Br^-(aq) + Cu^{2+}(aq)$
    c. $HNO_2(aq) + I^-(aq) \rightarrow NO(g) + I_2(aq)$

48. For each of the following oxidation–reduction reactions of metals with nonmetals, identify which element is oxidized and which is reduced.
    a. $3Zn(s) + N_2(g) \rightarrow Zn_3N_2(s)$
    b. $Co(s) + S(s) \rightarrow CoS(s)$
    c. $4K(s) + O_2(g) \rightarrow 2K_2O(s)$
    d. $4Ag(s) + O_2(g) \rightarrow 2Ag_2O(s)$

49. Assign oxidation states to all of the atoms in each of the following:
    a. MnO_2
    b. $BaCrO_4$
    c. H_2SO_3
    d. $Ca_3(PO_4)_2$

50. In each of the following reactions, identify which element is oxidized and which is reduced by assigning oxidation states.
    a. $2B_2O_3(s) + 6Cl_2(g) \rightarrow 4BCl_3(l) + 3O_2(g)$
    b. $GeH_4(g) + O_2(g) \rightarrow Ge(s) + 2H_2O(g)$
    c. $C_2H_4(g) + Cl_2(g) \rightarrow C_2H_4Cl_2(l)$
    d. $O_2(g) + 2F_2(g) \rightarrow 2OF_2(g)$

51. Consider the oxidation–reduction reaction

    $$Mg(s) + Cu^{2+}(aq) \rightarrow Mg^{2+}(aq) + Cu(s)$$

    Sketch a galvanic cell that uses this reaction. Which metal ion is reduced? Which metal is oxidized? What half-reaction takes place at the anode in the cell? What half-reaction takes place at the cathode?

49. (a) Mn, +4; O, −2;
(b) Ba, +2; Cr, +6; O, −2;
(c) H, +1; S, +4; O, −2;
(d) Ca, +2; P, +5; O, −2

50. (a) oxygen is oxidized, chlorine is reduced; (b) germanium is oxidized, oxygen is reduced; (c) carbon is oxidized, chlorine is reduced; (d) oxygen is oxidized, fluorine is reduced

51. See the *Solutions Guide* for the drawing.

Section	Text Features & Components	Labs, Demonstrations & Activities
Teaching Segment 19A **1.5 blocks** **pp. 608–618** 19.1 Radioactive Decay	**LP** Lesson Plans (Sec 19.1–19.4)	**LM** Experiment 84: Investigating Radioactivity Lab Manual Report Sheets Teacher's Lab Guide
19.2–19.3 Nuclear Transformations Detection of Radioactivity and the Concept of Half-life	**SE** Chemical Impact: Making Elements *p. 613*	**TE** Mini Demo *p. 614* **SE** Chemistry in the Laboratory: The Half-life of Pennies *p. 628* **LM** Experiment 85: The Half-life of Pennies Lab Manual Report Sheets Teacher's Lab Guide
19.4 Dating by Radioactivity	**SE** Chemical Impact: Dating Diamonds *p. 617*	
continued on next page		

Chapter Planning Guide

All Learners	Review & Assessment	Standards
TE Active Learning *p. 608* **▣** Video: Radioactivity of Everyday Objects **TE** Teaching Tips *p. 608* **⬟** Transparency: Figure 19.1 *p. 610* **AR** Less Proficient Students *p. 37*	**TE** Additional Examples *pp. 610, 612* **SE** Self Check *pp. 611, 612* **SE** Key Terms *p. 629* **SE** Questions and Problems *pp. 629–630*	**TE** **NSES** UCP1, UCP3, A1, A2, B1, B2, D3, E1, E2, F1, F6, G1, G2, G3 **⬤** **SSS** SC.H.1.4.2, SC.H.1.4.3, SC.H.1.4.4, SC.H.1.4.5, SC.H.2.4.1, SC.H.2.4.2, SC.A.2.4.3, SC.B.1.4.2, SC.H.3.4.3
⬜ Animation: Geiger Counter in Operation *p. 614* **▣** Video: Radioactivity of Everyday Objects *p. 614* **TE** Teaching Tips *p. 615* **AR** Less Proficient Students *p. 37*	**TE** Additional Examples *p. 615* **SE** Self Check *p. 616* **SE** Key Terms *p. 629* **SE** Questions and Problems *p. 630*	
RP Team Learning Worksheets (Sec 19.1–19.4) *pp. 107–108* **AR** Less Proficient Students *p. 37*	**SE** Focus Questions (Sec 19.1–19.4) *p. 618* **SE** Key Terms *p. 629* **SE** Questions and Problems *p. 630*	

	Section	Text Features & Components	Labs, Demonstrations & Activities
Teaching Segment 19B **1 block** **pp. 618–627**	**19.5 Medical Applications of Radioactivity**	**LP** Lesson Plans (Sec 19.5–19.10)	
	19.6 Nuclear Energy	**SE** Top Ten Countries Producing Electricity by Nuclear Power *p. 619*	
	19.7 Nuclear Fission		
	19.8 Nuclear Reactors	**SE** Celebrity Chemical: Uranium *p. 622*	
	19.9 Nuclear Fusion	**SE** Chemical Impact: Stellar Nucleosynthesis *p. 624*	
	19.10 Effects of Radiation	**TE** Teaching Support: Historical Background *p. 625* **SE** Top Ten Elements in the Sun *p. 625* **SE** Chemical Impact: Nuclear Waste Disposal *p. 626*	

Key

SE Student Edition
TE Teacher Edition
RP Teacher Resource Package
LM Lab Materials
LP Lesson Plans
AR Additional Resources
Florida Specific

Technology and Media

 Transparencies
Figure 19.1, 19.6

PowerPoint Slides

 Animation Geiger Counter in Operation • Nuclear Fission • Nuclear Fusion

 Video Radioactivity of Everyday Objects

 eEdition CD-ROM
Easy Planner CD-ROM
English Summaries CD
Spanish Summaries CD

 Web Site classzone.com
McDougal Littell Test Generator

Chapter Planning Guide

All Learners	Review & Assessment	Standards
TE Active Learning *p. 618* **TE** Teaching Tips *p. 618* **AR** Less Proficient Students *p. 38*	**SE** Key Terms *p. 629* **SE** Questions and Problems *p. 630*	**TE** **NSES** UCP1, UCP3, UCP5, A1, A2, B1, B2, D3, D4, E1, E2, F3, F4, F6, G1, G2, G3
AR Less Proficient Students *p. 38*	**SE** Key Terms *p. 629* **SE** Questions and Problems *p. 630*	**SSS** SC.H.1.4.1, SC.H.1.4.2, SC.H.1.4.3, SC.H.1.4.4, SC.H.1.4.5, SC.H.1.4.6, SC.H.1.4.7, SC.H.2.4.1, SC.H.2.4.2, SC.A.2.4.4,
TE Teaching Tip *p. 620* **⏯** Animation: Nuclear Fission *p. 620* **AR** Less Proficient Students *p. 38*	**SE** What if . . . *p. 620* **SE** Key Terms *p. 629* **SE** Questions and Problems *p. 631*	SC.C.2.4.4, SC.B.1.4.5, SC.H.3.4.1, SC.H.3.4.2, SC.H.3.4.4, SC.H.3.4.6
⏚ Transparency: Figure 19.6 *p. 621* **AR** Less Proficient Students *p. 38*	**SE** Key Terms *p. 629* **SE** Questions and Problems *p. 631*	
⏯ Animation: Nuclear Fusion *p. 623* **AR** Less Proficient Students *p. 38*	**SE** Key Terms *p. 629* **SE** Questions and Problems *p. 631*	
TE Teaching Tips *pp. 625, 627* **RP** Team Learning Worksheets (Sec 19.5–19.10) *p. 109* **AR** Less Proficient Students *p. 38*	**SE** Focus Questions (Sec 19.5–19.10) *p. 627* **SE** Key Terms *p. 629* **SE** Questions and Problems *p. 631*	

Chapter Materials

TE Reading Strategy
AR English/Spanish Summaries *pp. 31–32*
AR Challenge Projects/Problems *p. 35*
AR Less Proficient Students *p. 38*
💿 English Summary Audio
💿 Spanish Summary Audio
RP Chapter Review Worksheets (Basic, Review, Challenge)

SE Chapter Summary *p. 629*
SE Critical Thinking *p. 631*
RP Solutions Guide
RP Chapter Tests
RP Test Bank
🖥 McDougal Littell Test Generator
AR Standardized Test Practice
🌐 FCAT Test 10

Integrating Reading Strategies and Chemistry Concepts

Chapter 19: Comparing and Contrasting the Effectiveness of Features

Identifying Textbook Features

Explain that this text includes a number of special features intended to stimulate student interest in chemistry and provide learning tools that will make studying easier. Have the students skim the chapter and list the different features that they find in the text. Provide a few examples before the students begin and explain that most of the features are accompanied by a small icon or appear in a colored box. After a few minutes, have individual students identify features found and write them on the board. Use the chapter features shown below to complete the list.

Chapter Features	
✳ Looking Ahead (p. 606)	🧪 Chemistry (p. 607)
✳ Chapter Introduction (p. 607)	✳ Focus Questions (p. 618)
✳ Section Objectives (p. 608)	✳ What If . . . (p. 620)
💡 Problem Solving (p. 608)	🔵 Chemical Impacts (p. 624)
✳ Example Problems (p. 610)	🔴 Celebrity Chemical (p. 622)
🧮 Math (p. 549)	🧪 Chemistry in the Laboratory (p. 628)
☑ Self-Check Exercises (p. 611)	⚗ Chapter Review: Key Terms, Summary, Questions and Problems, and Critical
🖋 Chemistry in Action (p. 599)	Thinking Problems (p. 629)

Understanding the Features

Discuss the general properties of the features. Is the feature a question? Does it provide additional information or give an example? Does it offer a hint or a technique for completing a task? Help the students group the features on the basis of their responses to these questions. The following are examples of categories you might suggest.

- Features that preview material that the students will find in the chapter, that indicate the authors' goals in presenting the information, and that show how the information might be applied in the real world. [Looking Ahead, Chapter Introduction, and Section Objectives]

- Features that explain in more detail or provide additional information about the material in the chapter. [Example Problems, Celebrity Chemical, and Chapter Summary]

- Features that provide additional questions that will help the students test, practice, and apply what they have learned. [Self-Check Exercises, Focus Questions, Chapter Review Questions and Problems, and Critical Thinking Problems]

- Features that provide prompts and clues that the students can use to solve problems and verify that their answers are reasonable. [Problem Solving, Math, and Chemistry]

- Features that provide real-world implications of chemistry and hands-on techniques for demonstrating or testing those implications. [Chemistry in Action, What If, Chemical Impact, and Chemistry in the Laboratory]

Which Features Are Most Effective?

Have the students to turn to page 6 and read the last paragraph.

> "Our sincere hope is that this text will motivate you to learn chemistry, make its concepts understandable to you, and demonstrate how interesting and vital the study of chemistry is."

Point out that the authors attempt to realize this hope by presenting tools that will meet the needs of all learning styles. Explain that because students can and do learn in different ways, particular features may be more effective for some of the students than for others.

As an example, point out that some students learn well by doing practice problems. Remind the students that each section's example problems provide a step-by-step explanation of how to solve certain types of problems. Because each Self-Check Exercise is associated with a specific example problem, most students find these exercises relatively easy to understand and complete. The same is not true for the problems found in the Chapter Review, which are divided by section but which are not illustrated by specific examples.

For Chapter Reviews, the student must first determine the type of problem to be solved, recall how similar problems were solved, and apply that technique. Keep in mind that some students who can solve the Self-Check Problems readily may have difficulty with similar problems in the Chapter Review because no model is provided.

Organize the students in groups of two or three. Have each group discuss how the features in each of the categories developed earlier are similar, how they are different, and whether they are effective learning tools. If the students consider a particular feature to be ineffective, ask them to suggest how the feature could be made more effective. Explain that these discussions will help the students discover their individual learning styles and discover which textbook features can help them learn most efficiently.

Chapter 19

Overview

In this Chapter our goals are for the students to:

- Learn the types of radioactive decay

- Learn to write nuclear equations

- Learn how one element can be changed into another by particle bombardment

- Learn about instruments for detecting radiation

- Understand half life

- Learn how objects can be dated by radioactivity

- Discuss the use of radiotracers in medicine

- Introduce fusion and fission as producers of nuclear energy

- Learn about nuclear fission

- Understand how a nuclear reactor works

- Learn about nuclear fusion

- See how radiation damages human tissue

19 Radioactivity and Nuclear Energy

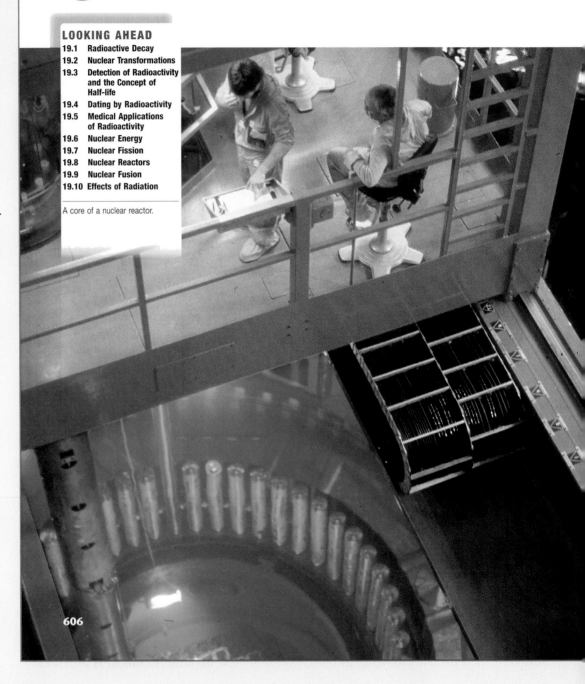

A core of a nuclear reactor.

606

Because the chemistry of an atom is determined by the number and arrangement of its electrons, the properties of the nucleus do not strongly affect the chemical behavior of an atom. Therefore, you might be wondering why there is a chapter on the nucleus in a chemistry textbook. The reason for this chapter is that the nucleus is very important to all of us—a quick reading of any daily newspaper will testify to that. Nuclear processes can be used to detect explosives in airline luggage (see "Chemical Impact: Measuring Changes," page 123), to generate electric power, and to establish the ages of very old objects such as human artifacts, rocks, and diamonds (see "Chemical Impact: Dating Diamonds," page 617). This chapter considers aspects of the nucleus and its properties that you should know about.

Several facts about the nucleus are immediately impressive: its very small size, its very large density, and the energy that holds it together. The radius of a typical nucleus is about 10^{-13} cm, only a hundred-thousandth the radius of a typical atom. In fact, if the nucleus of the hydrogen atom were the size of a ping-pong ball, the electron in the $1s$ orbital would be, on the average, 0.5 km (0.3 mile) away. The density of the nucleus is equally impressive; it is approximately 1.6×10^{14} g/cm³. A sphere of nuclear material the size of a ping-pong ball would have a mass of 2.5 *billion tons!* Finally, the energies involved in nuclear processes are typically millions of times larger than those associated with normal chemical reactions, a fact that makes nuclear processes potentially attractive for generating energy.

The nucleus is believed to be made of particles called **nucleons** (**neutrons** and **protons**). Recall from Chapter 3 that the number of protons in a nucleus is called the **atomic number (Z)** and that the sum of the numbers of neutrons and protons is the **mass number (A)**. Atoms that have identical atomic numbers but different mass numbers are called **isotopes.** The general term **nuclide** is applied to each unique atom, and we represent it as follows:

CHEMISTRY

The atomic number (Z) represents the number of protons in a nucleus; the mass number (A) represents the sum of the numbers of protons and neutrons in a nucleus.

Mass number
↓
$^{A}_{Z}X$ ← Element symbol
↑
Atomic number

where X represents the symbol for a particular element. For example, the following nuclides constitute the common isotopes of carbon: carbon-12, $^{12}_{6}C$; carbon-13, $^{13}_{6}C$; and carbon-14, $^{14}_{6}C$. Notice that all the carbon nuclides have six protons ($Z = 6$) and that they have six, seven, and eight neutrons, respectively.

Wooden artifacts from Easter Island can be dated by carbon-14 analysis.

Radioactivity and Nuclear Energy   **607**

Skills
Observing, applying concepts, making predictions

Student Preparation
Assign the students to read Sections 19.1 to 19.4 and to answer the Focus Questions at the end of Section 19.4 before coming to class.

Active Learning
After introducing the material in Sections 19.1 to 19.4 in class, place the students in groups and have them work together on Sections 19.1–19.4: Team Learning Worksheet. Answers and/or discussion of these questions are located in the *Teacher Resources*.

 Animation and Video

Video, Radioactivity of Everyday Objects

Laboratory
Experiment 84:
Investigating Radioactivity, CBL

TEACHING TIPS

- Balancing nuclear equations provides an excellent opportunity to review balancing by atoms and by charge and to review the meanings of the mass number and atomic number in element notation.

- Students should be aware that in a nuclear decay the product is a different element. Therefore we cannot balance the equation by balancing the atoms.

- Remind students that in forming ions the number of electrons changes but the number of protons (and therefore the type of atom) remains the same. In nuclear equations, if the number of protons changes, the atom's identity also changes.

19.1 Radioactive Decay

Objectives: *To learn the types of radioactive decay.*
To learn to write nuclear equations that describe radioactive decay.

Many nuclei are **radioactive**; that is, they spontaneously decompose, forming a different nucleus and producing one or more particles. An example is carbon-14, which decays as shown in the equation

$$^{14}_{6}\text{C} \rightarrow {}^{14}_{7}\text{N} + {}^{0}_{-1}\text{e}$$

where $^{0}_{-1}\text{e}$ represents an electron, which in nuclear terminology is called a **beta particle**, or β **particle**. This **nuclear equation**, which is typical of those representing radioactive decay, is quite different from the chemical equations we have written before. Recall that in a balanced chemical equation the atoms must be conserved. In a nuclear equation *both the atomic number (Z) and the mass number (A) must be conserved.* That is, the sums of the Z values on both sides of the arrow must be equal, and the same restriction applies to the A values. For example, in the above equation, the sum of the Z values is 6 on both sides of the arrow (6 and $7 - 1$), and the sum of the A values is 14 on both sides of the arrow (14 and $14 + 0$). Notice that the mass number for the β particle is zero; the mass of the electron is so small that it can be neglected here. Of the approximately 2000 known nuclides, only 279 do not undergo radioactive decay. Tin has the largest number of nonradioactive isotopes—ten.

Over 85% of all known nuclides are radioactive.

Types of Radioactive Decay

There are several different types of radioactive decay. One frequently observed decay process involves production of an **alpha (α) particle**, which is a helium nucleus ($^{4}_{2}\text{He}$). **Alpha-particle production** is a very common mode of decay for heavy radioactive nuclides. For example, $^{222}_{88}\text{Ra}$, radium-222, decays by α-particle production to give radon-218.

$$^{222}_{88}\text{Ra} \rightarrow {}^{4}_{2}\text{He} + {}^{218}_{86}\text{Rn}$$

Notice in this equation that the mass number is conserved ($222 = 4 + 218$) and the atomic number is conserved ($88 = 2 + 86$). Another α-particle producer is $^{230}_{90}\text{Th}$:

$$^{230}_{90}\text{Th} \rightarrow {}^{4}_{2}\text{He} + {}^{226}_{88}\text{Ra}$$

Notice that the production of an α particle results in a loss of 4 in mass number (A) and a loss of 2 in atomic number (Z).

β**-particle production** is another common decay process. For example, the thorium-234 nuclide produces a β particle as it changes to protactinium-234.

$$^{234}_{90}\text{Th} \rightarrow {}^{234}_{91}\text{Pa} + {}^{0}_{-1}\text{e}$$

Iodine-131 is also a β-particle producer.

$$^{131}_{53}\text{I} \rightarrow {}^{0}_{-1}\text{e} + {}^{131}_{54}\text{Xe}$$

Recall that the β particle is assigned mass number 0, because its mass is tiny compared to that of a proton or neutron. The value of Z is -1 for the β par-

PROBLEM SOLVING
Notice that both Z and A balance in each of these nuclear equations.

ticle, so the atomic number for the new nuclide is greater by 1 than the atomic number for the original nuclide. Therefore, *the net effect of β-particle production is to change a neutron to a proton.*

Production of a β particle results in no change in mass number (A), and an increase of 1 in atomic number (Z).

A **gamma ray**, or γ **ray**, is a high-energy photon of light. A nuclide in an excited nuclear energy state can release excess energy by producing a gamma ray, and γ-ray production often accompanies nuclear decays of various types. For example, in the α-particle decay of $^{238}_{92}\text{U}$,

$$^{238}_{92}\text{U} \rightarrow {}^{4}_{2}\text{He} + {}^{234}_{90}\text{Th} + 2{}^{0}_{0}\gamma$$

two γ rays of different energies are produced in addition to the α particle ($^{4}_{2}\text{He}$). Gamma rays are photons of light and so have zero charge and zero mass number.

Production of a γ ray results in no change in mass number (A), and no change in atomic number (Z).

The **positron** is a particle with the same mass as the electron but opposite charge. An example of a nuclide that decays by **positron production** is sodium-22.

$$^{22}_{11}\text{Na} \rightarrow {}^{0}_{1}\text{e} + {}^{22}_{10}\text{Ne}$$

Note that the production of a positron has the effect of changing a proton to a neutron.

Production of a positron results in no change in mass number (A), and a decrease of 1 in atomic number (Z).

Electron capture is a process in which one of the inner-orbital electrons is captured by the nucleus, as illustrated by the process

$$^{201}_{80}\text{Hg} + {}^{0}_{-1}\text{e} \rightarrow {}^{201}_{79}\text{Au} + {}^{0}_{0}\gamma$$

↑
Inner-orbital electron

This reaction would have been of great interest to the alchemists, but unfortunately it does not occur often enough to make it a practical means of changing mercury to gold. Gamma rays are always produced along with electron capture.

Table 19.1 lists the common types of radioactive decay, with examples.

Often a radioactive nucleus cannot achieve a stable (nonradioactive) state through a single decay process. In such a case, a **decay series** occurs until a

A gamma ray is a high-energy photon produced in connection with nuclear decay.

CHEMISTRY

The $^{0}_{0}\gamma$ notation indicates $Z = 0$ and $A = 0$ for a γ ray. A gamma ray is often simply indicated by γ.

Bone scintigraph of a patient's cranium following administration of the radiopharmaceutical technetium-99.

TABLE 19.1

Various Types of Radioactive Processes

Process	Example
β-particle (electron) production	$^{227}_{89}\text{Ac} \rightarrow {}^{227}_{90}\text{Th} + {}^{0}_{-1}\text{e}$
positron production	$^{13}_{7}\text{N} \rightarrow {}^{13}_{6}\text{C} + {}^{0}_{1}\text{e}$
electron capture	$^{73}_{33}\text{As} + {}^{0}_{-1}\text{e} \rightarrow {}^{73}_{32}\text{Ge}$
α-particle production	$^{210}_{84}\text{Po} \rightarrow {}^{206}_{82}\text{Pb} + {}^{4}_{2}\text{He}$
γ-ray production	excited nucleus → ground-state nucleus + $^{0}_{0}\gamma$
	excess energy lower energy

Alchemists attempted to convert base metals (such as lead) to precious metals (such as gold) by chemical means. We now know that this goal can be accomplished only by nuclear reactions, which is not practical.

Figure 19.1
The decay series from $^{238}_{92}$U to $^{206}_{82}$Pb. Each nuclide in the series except $^{206}_{82}$Pb is radioactive, and the successive transformations (shown by the arrows) continue until $^{238}_{82}$Pb is finally formed. The horizontal red arrows indicate β-particle production (Z increases by 1 and A is unchanged). The diagonal blue arrows signify α-particle production (both A and Z decrease).

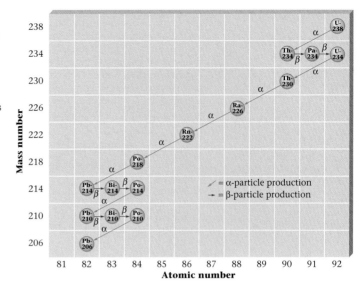

stable nuclide is formed. A well-known example is the decay series that starts with $^{238}_{92}$U and ends with $^{206}_{82}$Pb, as shown in **Figure 19.1.** Similar series exist for $^{235}_{92}$U:

$$^{235}_{92}\text{U} \xrightarrow[\text{decays}]{\text{Series of}} {}^{207}_{82}\text{Pb}$$

and for $^{232}_{90}$Th:

$$^{232}_{90}\text{Th} \xrightarrow[\text{decays}]{\text{Series of}} {}^{208}_{82}\text{Pb}$$

Additional Examples

Write balanced nuclear equations for each of the following processes.

1. $^{116}_{47}$Ag produces a beta particle.

$$^{116}_{47}\text{Ag} \rightarrow {}^{0}_{-1}\text{e} + {}^{116}_{48}\text{Cd}$$

2. $^{211}_{83}$Bi produces an alpha particle.

$$^{211}_{83}\text{Bi} \rightarrow {}^{4}_{2}\text{He} + {}^{207}_{81}\text{Tl}$$

Example 19.1

Writing Nuclear Equations, I

Write balanced nuclear equations for each of the following processes.

a. $^{11}_{6}$C produces a positron.

b. $^{214}_{83}$Bi produces a β particle.

c. $^{237}_{93}$Np produces an α particle.

Solution

a. We must find the product nuclide represented by $^{A}_{Z}$X in the following equation:

$$^{11}_{6}\text{C} \rightarrow \underset{\underset{\text{Positron}}{\uparrow}}{{}^{0}_{1}\text{e}} + {}^{A}_{Z}\text{X}$$

The key to solving this problem is to recognize that both A and Z must be conserved. That is, we can find the identity of $^A_Z X$ by recognizing that the sums of the Z and the A values must be the same on both sides of the equation. Thus for X, Z must be 5 because $Z + 1 = 6$. A must be 11 because $11 + 0 = 11$. Therefore, $^A_Z X$ is $^{11}_5 B$. (The fact that Z is 5 tells us that the nuclide is boron. See the periodic table on the inside back cover of the book.) So the balanced equation is $^{11}_6 C \rightarrow ^0_1 e + ^{11}_5 B$.

Check:

	Left Side	Right Side
	$Z = 6$	$Z = 5 + 1 = 6$
$\rightarrow$	$A = 11$	$A = 11 + 0 = 11$

b. Knowing that a β particle is represented by $_{-1}^0 e$, we can write

$$^{214}_{83} Bi \rightarrow ^0_{-1} e + ^A_Z X$$

where $Z - 1 = 83$ and $A + 0 = 214$. This means $Z = 84$ and $A = 214$. We can now write

$$^{214}_{83} Bi \rightarrow ^0_{-1} e + ^{214}_{84} X$$

Using the periodic table, we find that $Z = 84$ for the element polonium, so $^{214}_{84} X$ must be $^{214}_{84} Po$.

Check:

	Left Side	Right Side
	$Z = 83$	$Z = 84 - 1 = 83$
$\rightarrow$	$A = 214$	$A = 214 + 0 = 214$

c. Because an α particle is represented by $^4_2 He$, we can write

$$^{237}_{93} Np \rightarrow ^4_2 He + ^A_Z X$$

where $A + 4 = 237$ or $A = 237 - 4 = 233$, and $Z + 2 = 93$ or $Z = 93 - 2 = 91$. Thus $A = 233$, $Z = 91$, and the balanced equation must be

$$^{237}_{93} Np \rightarrow ^4_2 He + ^{233}_{91} Pa$$

Check:

	Left Side	Right Side
	$Z = 93$	$Z = 91 + 2 = 93$
$\rightarrow$	$A = 237$	$A = 233 + 4 = 237$

 Self-Check Exercise 19.1

The decay series for $^{238}_{92} U$ is represented in Figure 19.1. Write the balanced nuclear equation for each of the following radioactive decays.

a. Alpha-particle production by $^{226}_{88} Ra$

b. Beta-particle production by $^{214}_{82} Pb$

Answers to Self-Check Exercise 19.1

a. An alpha particle is a helium nucleus, $^4_2 He$. We can initially represent the production of an α particle by $^{226}_{88} Ra$ as follows:

$$^{226}_{88} Ra \rightarrow ^4_2 He + ^A_Z X$$

Because we know that both A and Z are conserved, we can write

$A + 4 = 226$ and
$Z + 2 = 88$

Solving for A gives 222 and for Z gives 86, so $^A_Z X$ is $^{222}_{86} X$. Because Rn has $Z = 86$, $^A_Z X$ is $^{222}_{86} Rn$. The overall balanced equation is

$$^{226}_{88} Ra \rightarrow ^4_2 He + ^{222}_{86} Rn$$

Check: $\begin{array}{l} Z = 88 \\ A = 226 \end{array} \rightarrow \begin{array}{l} Z = 86 + 2 = 88 \\ A = 222 + 4 = 226 \end{array}$

b. Using a similar strategy, we have

$$^{214}_{82} Pb \rightarrow ^0_{-1} e + ^A_Z X$$

Because $Z - 1 = 82$, $Z = 83$, and because $A + 0 = 214$, $A = 214$. Therefore, $^A_Z X = ^{214}_{83} Bi$. The balanced equation is

$$^{214}_{82} Pb \rightarrow ^0_{-1} e + ^{214}_{83} Bi$$

Check: $\begin{array}{l} Z = 82 \\ A = 214 \end{array} \rightarrow \begin{array}{l} Z = 83 - 1 = 82 \\ A = 214 + 0 = 214 \end{array}$

In each of the following nuclear reactions, supply the missing particle.

1. $^{210}_{89}\text{Ac} \rightarrow \, ^{4}_{2}\text{He} + \, ?$

$^{206}_{87}\text{Fr}$

2. $^{131}_{53}\text{I} \rightarrow \, ^{131}_{54}\text{Xe} + \, ?$

$^{0}_{-1}\text{e}$

3. $^{88}_{35}\text{Br} \rightarrow \, ^{87}_{35}\text{Br} + \, ?$

$^{1}_{0}\text{n}$

Answers to Self-Check Exercise 19.2

a. The missing particle must be $^{4}_{2}\text{H}$ (an α particle), because

$$^{222}_{86}\text{Rn} \rightarrow \, ^{218}_{84}\text{Po} + \, ^{4}_{2}\text{He}$$

is a balanced equation.

Check: $Z = 86 \quad \rightarrow \quad Z = 84 + 2 = 86$
$A = 222 \quad \quad A = 218 + 4 = 222$

b. The missing species must be $^{15}_{7}\text{X}$ or $^{15}_{7}\text{N}$, because the balanced equation is

$$^{15}_{8}\text{O} \rightarrow \, ^{15}_{7}\text{N} + \, ^{0}_{1}\text{e}$$

Check: $Z = 8 \quad \rightarrow \quad Z = 7 + 1 = 8$
$A = 15 \quad \quad A = 15 + 0 = 15$

Section 19.2

Themes
Stability, Patterns of Change

Skills
Making predictions, interpreting data, applying concepts

TEACHING TIPS

- Nuclear transformations are balanced in the same way as nuclear decay reactions.

- Radioisotopes are found in many household devices. Some examples are starters for fluorescent lamps and appliances (promethium-147, krypton-85, and thorium-232), antistatic devices (polonium-210), and smoke detectors (americium-241).

Example 19.2

Writing Nuclear Equations, II

In each of the following nuclear reactions, supply the missing particle.

a. $^{195}_{79}\text{Au} + \, ? \rightarrow \, ^{195}_{78}\text{Pt}$

b. $^{38}_{19}\text{K} \rightarrow \, ^{38}_{18}\text{Ar} + \, ?$

Solution

a. A does not change and Z for Pt is 1 lower than Z for Au, so the missing particle must be an electron.

$$^{195}_{79}\text{Au} + \, ^{0}_{-1}\text{e} \rightarrow \, ^{195}_{78}\text{Pt}$$

Check: | **Left Side** | **Right Side** |
| $Z = 79 - 1 = 78$ | $Z = 78$ |
| $A = 195 + 0 = 195$ $\rightarrow$ | $A = 195$ |

This is an example of electron capture.

b. For Z and A to be conserved, the missing particle must be a positron.

$$^{38}_{19}\text{K} \rightarrow \, ^{38}_{18}\text{Ar} + \, ^{0}_{1}\text{e}$$

Check: | **Left Side** | **Right Side** |
| $Z = 19$ | $Z = 18 + 1 = 19$ |
| $A = 38$ $\rightarrow$ | $A = 38 + 0 = 38$ |

Potassium-38 decays by positron production.

 Self-Check Exercise 19.2

Supply the missing species in each of the following nuclear equations.

a. $^{222}_{86}\text{Rn} \rightarrow \, ^{218}_{84}\text{Po} + \, ?$ **b.** $^{15}_{8}\text{O} \rightarrow \, ? + \, ^{0}_{1}\text{e}$

19.2 Nuclear Transformations

Objective: *To learn how one element may be changed into another by particle bombardment.*

In 1919 Lord Rutherford observed the first **nuclear transformation**, *the change of one element into another*. He found that bombarding $^{14}_{7}\text{N}$ with α particles produced the nuclide $^{17}_{8}\text{O}$,

$$^{14}_{7}\text{N} + \, ^{4}_{2}\text{He} \rightarrow \, ^{17}_{8}\text{O} + \, ^{1}_{1}\text{H}$$

with a proton ($^{1}_{1}\text{H}$) as another product. Fourteen years later, Irene Curie and her husband Frederick Joliot observed a similar transformation from aluminum to phosphorus:

$$^{27}_{13}\text{Al} + \, ^{4}_{2}\text{He} \rightarrow \, ^{30}_{15}\text{P} + \, ^{1}_{0}\text{n}$$

where $^{1}_{0}\text{n}$ represents a neutron that is produced in the process.

612   Chapter 19   Radioactivity and Nuclear Energy

Irene Curie and
Frederick Joliot.

Notice that in both of these cases the bombarding particle is a helium nucleus (an α particle). Other small nuclei, such as $^{12}_{6}C$ and $^{15}_{7}N$, can also be used to bombard heavier nuclei and cause transformations. However, because these positive bombarding ions are repelled by the positive charge of the target nucleus, the bombarding particle must be moving at a very high speed to penetrate the target. These high speeds are achieved in various types of *particle accelerators*.

Neutrons are also employed as bombarding particles to effect nuclear transformations. However, because neutrons are uncharged (and thus not repelled by a target nucleus), they are readily absorbed by many nuclei, producing new nuclides. The most common source of neutrons for this purpose is a fission reactor (see Section 19.8).

By using neutron and positive-ion bombardment, scientists have been able to extend the periodic table—that is, to produce chemical elements that are not present naturally. Prior to 1940, the heaviest known element was uranium ($Z = 92$), but in 1940, neptunium ($Z = 93$) was produced by neutron bombardment of $^{238}_{92}U$. The process initially gives $^{239}_{92}U$, which decays to $^{239}_{93}Np$ by β-particle production

$$^{238}_{92}U + {}^{1}_{0}n \rightarrow {}^{239}_{92}U \rightarrow {}^{239}_{93}Np + {}^{0}_{-1}e$$

CHEMICAL IMPACT

Science, Technology, and Society

Making Elements

In the last 75 years scientists have learned to be alchemists of a sort, making new types of atoms from naturally occurring atoms. These "synthetic" atoms are made in particle accelerators in which ions at great speeds hit target atoms. For example, in experiments conducted in Germany in 1999, atoms of the elements 114, 116, and 118 were made for the first time. During the ten-day experiment, a million trillion krypton ions were directed at high speeds at a lead target. During this time *three atoms* of element 118 formed, which then decomposed into elements 116 and 114. The re-

searchers hope that by using a bismuth target instead of lead they can form the new element 119, which would decompose into the as-yet-undiscovered elements 117, 115, and 113. Eventually scientists hope to reach the elements in the 120's, which are predicted to persist for much longer than the fleeting lifetimes of elements 114, 116, and 118. In previous experiments at Berkeley, California, element 116 lasted only 1.2 milliseconds and element 118 lasted only 200 microseconds. We will have to be very fast to study the chemical properties of these new elements!

19.2 Nuclear Transformations **613**

Integrating the
CHEMICAL
IMPACT

Making Elements

Why would elements discovered with atomic numbers in the 120s be expected to last longer than those with atomic numbers in the lower hundreds? Have students predict the properties of these elements based on their positions in the periodic table.

Students may also be interested in the way that elements are named. The discoverer of an element can propose a name for the element (within the IUPAC rules). The name does not become official, however, until the IUPAC votes on it. Elements are often named for the place of discovery or a well-known scientist in the field. Have students research the origins of the names of the latest elements.

TABLE 19.2

Syntheses of Some of the Transuranium Elements

Neutron Bombardment	neptunium ($Z = 93$)	$^{238}_{92}U + ^{1}_{0}n \rightarrow ^{239}_{92}U \rightarrow ^{239}_{93}Np + ^{0}_{-1}e$
	americium ($Z = 95$)	$^{239}_{94}Pu + 2\,^{1}_{0}n \rightarrow ^{241}_{94}Pu \rightarrow ^{241}_{95}Am + ^{0}_{-1}e$
Positive-Ion Bombardment	curium ($Z = 96$)	$^{239}_{94}Pu + ^{4}_{2}He \rightarrow ^{242}_{96}Cm + ^{1}_{0}n$
	californium ($Z = 98$)	$^{242}_{96}Cm + ^{4}_{2}He \rightarrow ^{245}_{98}Cf + ^{1}_{0}n$ or
		$^{238}_{92}U + ^{12}_{6}C \rightarrow ^{246}_{98}Cf + 4\,^{1}_{0}n$
	rutherfordium ($Z = 104$)	$^{249}_{98}Cf + ^{12}_{6}C \rightarrow ^{257}_{104}Rf + 4\,^{1}_{0}n$
	dubnium ($Z = 105$)	$^{249}_{98}Cf + ^{15}_{7}N \rightarrow ^{260}_{105}Db + 4\,^{1}_{0}n$
	seaborgium ($Z = 106$)	$^{249}_{98}Cf + ^{18}_{8}O \rightarrow ^{263}_{106}Sg + 4\,^{1}_{0}n$

In the years since 1940, the elements with atomic numbers 93 through 112, called the **transuranium elements**, have been synthesized. In addition, preliminary reports in 1999 indicated that elements 114, 116, and 118 have also been produced. **Table 19.2** gives some examples of these processes.

19.3 Detection of Radioactivity and the Concept of Half-life

Objectives: *To learn about radiation detection instruments.*
To understand half-life.

Geiger counters are commonly called survey meters.

The most familiar instrument for measuring radioactivity levels is the **Geiger–Müller counter**, or **Geiger counter (Figure 19.2)**. High-energy particles from radioactive decay produce ions when they travel through matter. The probe of the Geiger counter contains argon gas. The argon atoms have no charge, but they can be ionized by a rapidly moving particle.

$$Ar(g) \xrightarrow[\text{particle}]{\text{High-energy}} Ar^{+}(g) + e^{-}$$

That is, the fast-moving particle "knocks" electrons off some of the argon atoms. Although a sample of uncharged argon atoms does not conduct a current, the ions and electrons formed by the high-energy particle allow a current to flow momentarily, so a "pulse" of current flows every time a particle

Section 19.3

Themes
Systems, Stability

Skills
Making comparisons, applying concepts

 Laboratory
Experiment 85:
Half-life of Pennies, Traditional

MINI-DEMO

If you have access to a Geiger counter, bring it to class for demonstration. A typical mantle from a gas camping lantern or a piece of orange Fiestaware pottery can be used as a source of radioactive material.

USING TECHNOLOGY

Animation and Video

Animation, Geiger Counter in Operation

Video, Radioactivity of Everyday Objects

Figure 19.2
A schematic representation of a Geiger–Müller counter. The high-speed particle knocks electrons off argon atoms to form ions,

$$Ar \xrightarrow{\text{Particle}} Ar^{+} + e^{-}$$

and a pulse of current flows.

Speaker gives "click" for each particle

Window

Particle path

Argon atoms

enters the probe. The Geiger counter detects each pulse of current, and these events are counted.

A **scintillation counter** is another instrument often employed to detect radioactivity. This device uses a substance, such as sodium iodide, that gives off light when it is struck by a high-energy particle. A detector senses the flashes of light and thus counts the decay events.

One important characteristic of a given type of radioactive nuclide is its half-life. The **half-life** is the *time required for half of the original sample of nuclei to decay*. For example, if a certain radioactive sample contains 1000 nuclei at a given time and 500 nuclei (half of the original number) 7.5 days later, this radioactive nuclide has a half-life of 7.5 days.

A given type of radioactive nuclide always has the same half-life. However, the various radioactive nuclides have half-lives that cover a tremendous range. For example, $^{234}_{91}Pa$, protactinium-234, has a half-life of 1.2 minutes, and $^{238}_{92}U$, uranium-238, has a half-life of 4.5×10^9 (4.5 *billion*) years. This means that a sample containing 100 million $^{234}_{91}Pa$ nuclei will have only 50 million $^{234}_{91}Pa$ nuclei in it (half of 100 million) after 1.2 minutes have passed. In another 1.2 minutes, the number of nuclei will decrease to half of 50 million, or 25 million nuclei.

$$100 \text{ million } ^{234}_{91}Pa \xrightarrow[\text{minutes}]{1.2} 50 \text{ million } ^{234}_{91}Pa \xrightarrow[\text{minutes}]{1.2} 25 \text{ million } ^{234}_{91}Pa$$

(50 million decays)   (25 million decays)

This means that a sample of $^{234}_{91}Pa$ with 100 million nuclei will show 50 million decay events (50 million $^{234}_{91}Pa$ nuclei will decay) over a time of 1.2 minutes. By contrast, a sample containing 100 million $^{238}_{92}U$ nuclei will undergo 50 million decay events over 4.5 billion years. Therefore, $^{234}_{91}Pa$ shows much greater activity than $^{238}_{92}U$. We sometimes say that $^{234}_{91}Pa$ is "hotter" than $^{238}_{92}U$.

Thus, at a given moment, a radioactive nucleus with a short half-life is much more likely to decay than one with a long half-life.

Example 19.3

Understanding Half-life

Table 19.3 lists various radioactive nuclides of radium.

a. Order these nuclides in terms of activity (from most to least decays per day).

b. How long will it take for a sample containing 1.00 mol of $^{223}_{88}Ra$ to reach a point where it contains only 0.25 mol of $^{223}_{88}Ra$?

TABLE 19.3

The Half-lives for Some of the Radioactive Nuclides of Radium

Nuclide	Half-life
$^{223}_{88}Ra$	12 days
$^{224}_{88}Ra$	3.6 days
$^{225}_{88}Ra$	15 days
$^{226}_{88}Ra$	1600 years
$^{228}_{88}Ra$	6.7 years

Solution

a. The shortest half-life indicates the greatest activity (the most decays over a given period of time). Therefore, the order is

Most activity (shortest half-life)				Least activity (longest half-life)
$^{224}_{88}Ra$ >	$^{223}_{88}Ra$ >	$^{225}_{88}Ra$ >	$^{228}_{88}Ra$ >	$^{226}_{88}Ra$
3.6 days	12 days	15 days	6.7 years	1600 years

(continued)

TEACHING TIPS

- Students have difficulty with the concept of half-life. They often believe that after two half-lives, all of the material should be decayed. You may want to relate the story of the tortoise that always travels half the distance to the finish line in each minute. How long will it take for the turtle to reach the finish line?

- The Chemistry in the Laboratory feature in this chapter will allow students to get a better understanding of the concept of half-life.

- This section offers an excellent opportunity to connect to the math program. Ask students to find a function in math that operates in the same way that half-life does.

- Now is a good time to plot the amount of a radionuclide present versus time on the board to show students the progression of its decay over time. You can use data from Table 19.3 to do so.

Additional Examples

1. Gold-198, which has a half-life of 2.7 days, is used as an implant for cancer therapy. For an implant containing 50 μg of Au-198, approximately how much Au-198 remains after 1 week?
   Just over 6 μg. After 8.1 days, or 4 half-lives, 6.25 μg remains.

2. Krypton-76 has a half-life of 14.8 hr. About how long will it take to reach a point where a sample contains about 10% of its original Kr-76?
   About 2 days. After 3 half-lives (around 44 hours), approximately 12.5% of the Kr-76 will remain.

b. In one half-life (12 days), the sample will decay from 1.00 mol of $^{223}_{88}$Ra to 0.50 mol of $^{223}_{88}$Ra. In the next half-life (another 12 days), it will decay from 0.50 mol of $^{223}_{88}$Ra to 0.25 mol of $^{223}_{88}$Ra.

$$1.00 \text{ mol } ^{223}_{88}\text{Ra} \xrightarrow[\text{12 days}]{} 0.50 \text{ mol } ^{223}_{88}\text{Ra} \xrightarrow[\text{12 days}]{} 0.25 \text{ mol } ^{223}_{88}\text{Ra}$$

Therefore, it will take 24 days (two half-lives) for the sample to change from 1.00 mol of $^{223}_{88}$Ra to 0.25 mol of $^{223}_{88}$Ra.

Self-Check Exercise 19.3

Watches with numerals that "glow in the dark" were formerly made by including radioactive radium in the paint used to letter the watch faces. Assume that to make the numeral 3 on a given watch, a sample of paint containing 8.0×10^{-7} mol of $^{228}_{88}$Ra was used. This watch was then put in a drawer and forgotten. Many years later someone finds the watch and wishes to know when it was made. Analyzing the paint, this person finds 1.0×10^{-7} mol of $^{228}_{88}$Ra in the numeral 3. How much time elapsed between the making of the watch and the finding of the watch?

A watch dial with radium paint.   Hint: Use the half-life of $^{228}_{88}$Ra from Table 19.3.

19.4 Dating by Radioactivity

Objective: *To learn how objects can be dated by radioactivity.*

Archaeologists, geologists, and others involved in reconstructing the ancient history of the earth rely heavily on the half-lives of radioactive nuclei to provide accurate dates for artifacts and rocks. A method for dating ancient articles made from wood or cloth is **radiocarbon dating**, or **carbon-14 dating**, a technique originated in the 1940s by Willard Libby, an American chemist who received the Nobel Prize for his efforts.

Radiocarbon dating is based on the radioactivity of $^{14}_{6}$C, which decays by β-particle production.

$$^{14}_{6}\text{C} \rightarrow {}^{0}_{-1}\text{e} + {}^{14}_{7}\text{N}$$

Carbon-14 is continuously produced in the atmosphere when high-energy neutrons from space collide with nitrogen-14.

$$^{14}_{7}\text{N} + {}^{1}_{0}\text{n} \rightarrow {}^{14}_{6}\text{C} + {}^{1}_{1}\text{H}$$

Just as carbon-14 is continuously produced by this process, it continuously decomposes through β-particle production. Over the years, these two opposing processes have come into balance, causing the amount of $^{14}_{6}$C present in the atmosphere to remain approximately constant.

Carbon-14 can be used to date wood and cloth artifacts because the $^{14}_{6}$C, along with the other carbon isotopes in the atmosphere, reacts with oxygen to form carbon dioxide. A living plant consumes this carbon dioxide in the

---

Answer to Self-Check Exercise 19.3

Let's do this problem by thinking about the number of half-lives required to go from 8.0×10^{-7} mol to 1.0×10^{-7} mol of $^{228}_{88}$Ra.

$$8.0 \times 10^{-7} \text{ mol} \xrightarrow[\text{First half-life}]{} 4.0 \times 10^{-7} \text{ mol} \xrightarrow[\text{Second half-life}]{}$$

$$2.0 \times 10^{-7} \text{ mol} \xrightarrow[\text{Third half-life}]{} 1.0 \times 10^{-7} \text{ mol}$$

It takes three half-lives, then, for the sample to go from 8.0×10^{-7} mol of $^{228}_{88}$Ra to 1.0×10^{-7} mol of $^{228}_{88}$Ra. From Table 19.3, we know that the half-life of $^{228}_{88}$Ra is 6.7 years. Therefore, the elapsed time is 3(6.7 years) = 20.1 years, or 2.0×10^{1} years when we use the correct number of significant figures.

19.4 Section 19.4

Themes
Patterns of Change, Stability

Skills
Applying concepts, making predictions

TEACHING TIPS

- Radiocarbon dating is a practical application of the half-life concept.

- Carbon-14 is produced naturally in the environment. When it is incorporated into carbon dioxide, it can be fixed as a carbohydrate in plants. Carbon dioxide containing carbon-14 is an example of a natural source of radioactivity in the environment with which we regularly come in contact.

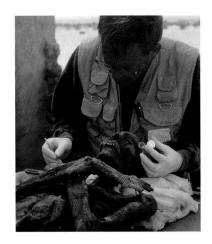

Brigham Young researcher Scott Woodward taking a bone sample for carbon-14 dating at an archeological site in Egypt.

photosynthesis process and incorporates the carbon, including $^{14}_{6}C$, into its molecules. As long as the plant lives, the $^{14}_{6}C$ content in its molecules remains the same as in the atmosphere because of the plant's continuous uptake of carbon. However, as soon as a tree is cut to make a wooden bowl or a flax plant is harvested to make linen, it stops taking in carbon. There is no longer a source of $^{14}_{6}C$ to replace that lost to radioactive decay, so the material's $^{14}_{6}C$ content begins to decrease.

Because the half-life of $^{14}_{6}C$ is known to be 5730 years, a wooden bowl found in an archaeological dig that shows a $^{14}_{6}C$ content of half that found in currently living trees is approximately 5730 years old. That is, because half of the $^{14}_{6}C$ present when the tree was cut has disappeared, the tree must have been cut one half-life of $^{14}_{6}C$ ago.

CHEMICAL IMPACT

Science, Technology, and Society

Dating Diamonds

While connoisseurs of gems value the clearest possible diamonds, geologists learn the most from impure diamonds. Diamonds are formed in the earth's crust at depths of about 200 kilometers, where the high pressures and temperatures favor the most dense form of carbon. As the diamond is formed, impurities are sometimes trapped and these can be used to determine the diamond's date of "birth." One valuable dating impurity is $^{238}_{92}U$, which is radioactive and decays in a series of steps to $^{206}_{82}Pb$, which is stable (nonradioactive). Because the rate at which $^{238}_{92}U$ decays is known, determining how much $^{238}_{92}U$ has been converted to $^{206}_{82}Pb$ tells scientists the amount of time that has elapsed since the $^{238}_{92}U$ was trapped in the diamond as it was formed.

Using these dating techniques, Peter D. Kinney of Curtin University of Technology in Perth, Australia, and Henry O. A. Meyer of Purdue University

The Hope Diamond.

in West Lafayette, Indiana, have recently identified the youngest diamond ever found. Discovered in Mbuji Mayi, Zaire, the diamond is 628 million years old, far younger than all previously dated diamonds, which range from 2.4 to 3.2 billion years old.

The great age of all previously dated diamonds had caused some geologists to speculate that all diamond formation occurred billions of years ago. However, this "youngster" suggests that diamonds have formed throughout geologic time and are probably being formed right now in the earth's crust. We won't see these diamonds for a long time, because diamonds typically remain deeply buried in the earth's crust for millions of years until they are brought to the surface by volcanic blasts called kimberlite eruptions.

It's good to know that eons from now there will be plenty of diamonds to mark the engagements of future couples.

Integrating the CHEMICAL IMPACT

Dating Diamonds

New techniques for distinguishing diamonds have recently been developed by the major diamond traders to maintain their control over the price and quality of diamonds. Students can investigate how this identification is made and learn more about the chemistry involved by using the Internet.

19.4   Dating by Radioactivity   **617**

1. Mass and charge must be conserved when balancing nuclear equations. In other chemistry equations, atoms and charge are conserved.

2. **a.** $^{28}_{13}\text{Al} \longrightarrow {}^{0}_{-1}\text{e} + {}^{28}_{14}\text{Si}$

   b. $^{56}_{24}\text{Cr} \longrightarrow {}^{0}_{-1}\text{e} + {}^{56}_{25}\text{Mn}$

   c. $^{72}_{30}\text{Zn} \longrightarrow {}^{0}_{-1}\text{e} + {}^{72}_{31}\text{Ga}$

3. In nuclear decay one particle emits smaller particles and becomes another element. In nuclear transformations an element is bombarded with a particle and is transformed into another element.

4. At the end of the first half-life, one half of the original sample remains. At the end of the second half-life, half of this sample still remains. This is one half of the half of the original sample, or one-fourth of the original sample.

5. Carbon dating is used to date objects that come from a once-living organic source. Once the object dies, the resource for carbon-14 is no longer available, and the carbon-14 content begins to decrease. In diamonds the source for carbon is not living tissue, so they cannot be dated using the carbon-14 method. Instead the decay of the uranium tells us when the diamond was formed.

 Section 19.5

Themes
Stability, Patterns of Change

Skills
Applying concepts, making judgments

Student Preparation
Assign the students to read Sections 19.5 to 19.10 and to answer the Focus Questions at the end of Section 19.10 before coming to class.

Active Learning
After introducing the material in Sections 19.5 to 19.10 in class, place the students in groups and have them work together on Sections 19.5–19.10: Team Learning Worksheet. Answers and/or discussion of these questions are located in the *Teacher Resources*.

Focus Questions **Sections 19.1–19.4**

1. When balancing a nuclear equation, what two quantities must be conserved? How is this process different from balancing other chemistry equations?

2. Complete each of the following nuclear equations by supplying the missing particle.

   a. $^{28}_{13}\text{Al} \rightarrow ? + {}^{28}_{14}\text{Si}$

   b. $^{56}_{24}\text{Cr} \rightarrow {}^{0}_{-1}\text{e} + ?$

   c. $^{72}_{30}\text{Zn} \rightarrow {}^{0}_{-1}\text{e} + ?$

3. What is the difference between nuclear decay and nuclear transformation reactions?

4. Explain why one-fourth of a given radioactive sample still remains at the end of two half-lives.

5. Diamonds are made of carbon. In "Chemical Impact: Dating Diamonds," however, uranium—and not carbon—is used to determine when a diamond was formed. Why don't scientists use carbon dating to determine this date?

19.5 Medical Applications of Radioactivity

Objective: *To discuss the use of radiotracers in medicine.*

Although we owe the rapid advances of the medical sciences in recent decades to many causes, one of the most important has been the discovery and use of **radiotracers**—radioactive nuclides that can be introduced into organisms in food or drugs and subsequently *traced* by monitoring their radioactivity. For example, the incorporation of nuclides such as $^{14}_{6}\text{C}$ and $^{32}_{15}\text{P}$ into nutrients has yielded important information about how these nutrients are used to provide energy for the body.

Iodine-131 has proved very useful in the diagnosis and treatment of illnesses of the thyroid gland. Patients drink a solution containing a small amount of NaI that includes ^{131}I, and the uptake of the iodine by the thyroid gland is monitored with a scanner **(Figure 19.3)**.

Nuclides used as radiotracers have short half-lives so that they disappear rapidly from the body.

Figure 19.3
After consumption of Na^{131}I, the patient's thyroid is scanned for radioactivity levels to determine the efficiency of iodine absorption. (a) Scan of radioactive iodine in a normal thyroid. (b) Scan of an enlarged thyroid.

(a)   (b)

618   Chapter 19   Radioactivity and Nuclear Energy

TEACHING TIPS

- Students could be assigned projects in which they learn more about the applications in Table 19.4. Their summaries could be shared with the class as oral reports.

- The useful properties of radiotracers depend on their half-lives. Have your students compare the half-lives of radiotracers with carbon-14.

TABLE 19.4

Some Radioactive Nuclides, Their Half-lives, and Their Medical Applications as Radiotracers*

Nuclide	Half-life	Area of the Body Studied
^{131}I	8.1 days	thyroid
^{59}Fe	45.1 days	red blood cells
^{99}Mo	67 hours	metabolism
^{32}P	14.3 days	eyes, liver, tumors
^{51}Cr	27.8 days	red blood cells
^{87}Sr	2.8 hours	bones
^{99}Tc	6.0 hours	heart, bones, liver, lungs
^{133}Xe	5.3 days	lungs
^{24}Na	14.8 hours	circulatory system

*Z is sometimes not written when listing nuclides.

Thallium-201 can be used to assess the damage to the heart muscle in a person who has suffered a heart attack, because thallium becomes concentrated in healthy muscle tissue. Technetium-99, which is also taken up by normal heart tissue, is used for damage assessment in a similar way.

Radiotracers provide sensitive and nonsurgical methods for learning about biological systems, for detecting disease, and for monitoring the action and effectiveness of drugs. Some useful radiotracers are listed in **Table 19.4.**

19.6 Nuclear Energy

Objective: *To introduce fusion and fission as producers of nuclear energy.*

The protons and the neutrons in atomic nuclei are bound together with forces that are much greater than the forces that bind atoms together to form molecules. In fact, the energies associated with nuclear processes are more than a million times those associated with chemical reactions. This potentially makes the nucleus a very attractive source of energy.

Because medium-sized nuclei contain the strongest binding forces ($^{56}_{26}Fe$ has the strongest binding forces of all), there are two types of nuclear processes that produce energy:

1. Combining two light nuclei to form a heavier nucleus. This process is called **fusion.**

2. Splitting a heavy nucleus into two nuclei with smaller mass numbers. This process is called **fission.**

As we will see in the next several sections, these two processes can supply amazing quantities of energy with relatively small masses of materials consumed.

TOP TEN

Countries Producing Electricity by Nuclear Power (in order of total nuclear output)

	Country	Percentage of Country's Total Power Production
1.	United States	21.9
2.	France	77.4
3.	Japan	34.0
4.	Germany	30.3
5.	Russia	13.1
6.	Canada	16.0
7.	Ukraine	43.8
8.	United Kingdom	26.0
9.	Sweden	52.4
10.	South Korea	35.8

Section 19.6

Themes
Patterns of Change, Form and Function, Stability

Skills
Applying concepts, interpreting diagrams, making comparisons, making predictions

Using the TOP TEN

Students can investigate the types of nuclear power plants in use in each country listed in the Top Ten. Have them research the safety records for each country and determine the environmental concerns that arise when using power generated by nuclear resources. It may also be possible to determine the cost-efficiency of nuclear power versus other types of power by using the Internet.

19.6 Nuclear Energy **619**

19.7 Nuclear Fission

Objective: *To learn about nuclear fission.*

Nuclear fission was discovered in the late 1930s when $^{235}_{92}U$ nuclides bombarded with neutrons were observed to split into two lighter elements.

$$^{1}_{0}n + ^{235}_{92}U \rightarrow ^{141}_{56}Ba + ^{92}_{36}Kr + 3\,^{1}_{0}n$$

This process, shown schematically in **Figure 19.4**, releases 2.1×10^{13} joules of energy per mole of $^{235}_{92}U$. Compared with what we get from typical fuels, this is a huge amount of energy. For example, the fission of 1 mol of $^{235}_{92}U$ produces about *26 million times* as much energy as the combustion of 1 mol of methane.

The process shown in Figure 19.4 is only one of the many fission reactions that $^{235}_{92}U$ can undergo. In fact, over 200 different isotopes of 35 different elements have been observed among the fission products of $^{235}_{92}U$.

In addition to the product nuclides, neutrons are produced in the fission reactions of $^{235}_{92}U$. As these neutrons fly through the solid sample of uranium, they may collide with other $^{235}_{92}U$ nuclei, producing additional fission events. Each of these fission events produces more neutrons that can, in turn, produce the fission of more $^{235}_{92}U$ nuclei. Because each fission event produces neutrons, the process can be self-sustaining. We call it a **chain reaction (Figure 19.5)**. For the fission process to be self-sustaining, at least one neutron from

Figure 19.4
Upon capturing a neutron, the $^{235}_{92}U$ nucleus undergoes fission to produce two lighter nuclides, more neutrons (typically three), and a large amount of energy.

Figure 19.5
Representation of a fission process in which each event produces two neutrons that can go on to split other nuclei, leading to a self-sustaining chain reaction.

620 Chapter 19 Radioactivity and Nuclear Energy

each fission event must go on to split another nucleus. If, on the average, *less than one* neutron causes another fission event, the process dies out. If *exactly one* neutron from each fission event causes another fission event, the process sustains itself at the same level and is said to be *critical*. If *more than one* neutron from each fission event causes another fission event, the process rapidly escalates and the heat build-up causes a violent explosion.

To achieve the critical state, a certain mass of fissionable material, called the **critical mass,** is needed. If the sample is too small, too many neutrons escape before they have a chance to cause a fission event, and the process stops.

During World War II, the United States carried out an intense research effort called the Manhattan Project to build a bomb based on the principles of nuclear fission. This program produced the fission bomb, which was used with devastating effect on the cities of Hiroshima and Nagasaki in 1945. Basically, a fission bomb operates by suddenly combining subcritical masses, which results in rapidly escalating fission events that produce an explosion of incredible intensity.

19.8 Nuclear Reactors

Objective: *To understand how a nuclear reactor works.*

Because of the tremendous energies involved, fission has been developed as an energy source to produce electricity in reactors where controlled fission can occur. The resulting energy is used to heat water to produce steam that runs turbine generators, in much the same way that a coal-burning power plant generates energy by heating water to produce steam. A schematic diagram of a nuclear power plant is shown in **Figure 19.6.**

19.8
Section 19.8

Themes
Organization, Patterns of Change, Form and Function

Skills
Applying concepts, interpreting diagrams, making comparisons, making predictions

USING TECHNOLOGY

 Figure 19.6

Figure 19.6
A schematic diagram of a nuclear power plant. The energy from the fission process is used to boil water, producing steam for use in a turbine-driven generator. Cooling water from a lake or river is used to condense the steam after it leaves the turbine.

19.8 Nuclear Reactors **621**

Natural uranium consists mostly of $^{238}_{92}$U.

→ Hot coolant

Control rods of neutron-absorbing substance

Uranium in fuel cylinders

Figure 19.7
A schematic of the reactor core.

Incoming coolant

In the reactor core **(Figure 19.7)**, uranium that has been enriched to approximately 3% $^{235}_{92}$U (natural uranium contains only 0.7% $^{235}_{92}$U) is housed in metal cylinders. A *moderator* surrounding the cylinders slows the neutrons down so that the uranium fuel can capture them more efficiently. *Control rods,* composed of substances (such as cadmium) that absorb neutrons, are used to regulate the power level of the reactor. The reactor is designed so that if a malfunction occurs, the control rods are automatically inserted into the core to absorb neutrons and stop the reaction. A liquid (usually water) is circulated through the core to extract the heat generated by the energy of fission. This heat energy is then used to change water to steam, which runs turbines that in turn run electrical generators.

Although the concentration of $^{235}_{92}$U in the fuel elements is not great enough to allow an explosion such as that which occurs in a fission bomb, a failure of the cooling system can lead to temperatures high enough to melt the reactor core. This means that the building housing the core must be designed to contain the core even in the event of such a "melt-down." A great deal of controversy now exists about the efficiency of the safety systems in nuclear power plants. Accidents such as the one at the Three Mile Island facility in

CELEBRITY CHEMICAL

Uranium (U)

Uranium was first discovered in 1789 as a component of pitchblende. Its name came from the planet Uranus, which had been discovered only shortly before. Uranium, which is not a rare element in the earth's crust (it is more abundant than tin), is widely scattered on earth. The most easily accessible deposits of uranium are found in the United States, Canada, South Africa, and Australia. Although uranium is used in small amounts as a coloring agent for glass and ceramics, its major use is as a nuclear fuel in fission reactors.

Uranium consists principally of $^{238}_{92}$U mixed with smaller amounts of $^{235}_{92}$U. Both isotopes are radioactive, although ^{235}U decays more rapidly than ^{238}U by about a factor of six. The ^{235}U isotope splits into two smaller nuclei (fission) when it is bombarded by neutrons, which makes it useful for producing energy in nuclear reactions.

Uranium-238 kernels for use in a reactor

Because fission of ^{235}U requires carefully controlled conditions, scientists were shocked to find that a natural nuclear reactor existed millions of years ago in Oklo, Gabon. Apparently, conditions were just right in a uranium deposit at Oklo to allow natural fission to occur. Water trapped in clay mixed with the ore acted as the moderator, slowing down the neutrons to promote efficient fission. As the "reactor" heated up, it apparently drove off some of the water. This loss caused the fission to slow down, thus preventing an explosion. As the area cooled down, the water returned, leading to an increase in fission again. This speeding up and slowing down of the natural reactor apparently occurred repeatedly over many years until conditions changed enough to cause the reactor to stop. It seems clear that nature invented the nuclear reactor millions of years before humans thought of the idea.

622 Chapter 19 Radioactivity and Nuclear Energy

Pennsylvania in 1979 and the one at Chernobyl in the Soviet Union in 1986 have led many people to question the wisdom of continuing to build fission-based power plants.

Breeder Reactors

One potential problem facing the nuclear power industry is the limited supply of $^{235}_{92}U$. Some scientists believe we have nearly depleted the uranium deposits that are rich enough in $^{235}_{92}U$ to make the production of fissionable fuel economically feasible. Because of this possibility, reactors have been developed in which fissionable fuel is actually produced while the reactor runs. In these **breeder reactors**, the major component of natural uranium, nonfissionable $^{238}_{92}U$, is changed to fissionable $^{239}_{94}Pu$. The reaction involves absorption of a neutron, followed by production of two β particles.

$$^1_0n + {}^{238}_{92}U \rightarrow {}^{239}_{92}U$$

$$^{239}_{92}U \rightarrow {}^{239}_{93}Np + {}^{0}_{-1}e$$

$$^{239}_{93}Np \rightarrow {}^{239}_{94}Pu + {}^{0}_{-1}e$$

As the reactor runs and $^{235}_{92}U$ is split, some of the excess neutrons are absorbed by $^{238}_{92}U$ to produce $^{239}_{94}Pu$. The $^{239}_{94}Pu$ is then separated out and used to fuel another reactor. Such a reactor thus "breeds" nuclear fuel as it operates.

Although breeder reactors are now used in Europe, the United States is proceeding slowly with their development because much controversy surrounds their use. One problem involves the hazards that arise in handling plutonium, which is very toxic and flames on contact with air.

19.9 Nuclear Fusion

Objective: *To learn about nuclear fusion.*

The process of combining two light nuclei—called **nuclear fusion**—produces even more energy per mole than does nuclear fission. In fact, stars produce their energy through nuclear fusion. Our sun, which presently consists of 73% hydrogen, 26% helium, and 1% other elements, gives off vast quantities of energy from the fusion of protons to form helium. One possible scheme for this process is

$$^1_1H + {}^1_1H \rightarrow {}^2_1H + {}^0_1e + \text{energy}$$

$$^1_1H + {}^2_1H \rightarrow {}^3_2He + \text{energy}$$

$$^3_2He + {}^3_2He \rightarrow {}^4_2He + 2\,{}^1_1H + \text{energy}$$

$$^3_2He + {}^1_1H \rightarrow {}^4_2He + {}^0_1e + \text{energy}$$

^2_1H particles are called deuterons.

Intense efforts are under way to develop a feasible fusion process because of the ready availability of many light nuclides (deuterium, ^2_1H, in seawater, for example) that can serve as fuel in fusion reactors. However, initiating the fusion process is much more difficult than initiating fission. The forces that bind nucleons together to form a nucleus become effective only at *very small* distances (approximately 10^{-13} cm), so for two protons to bind together and

Section 19.9

Themes
Patterns of Change, Form and Function, Stability

Skills
Applying concepts, interpreting diagrams, making comparisons

USING TECHNOLOGY

▶ **Animation and Video**

Animation, Nuclear Fusion

19.9 Nuclear Fusion   **623**

Integrating the
CHEMICAL
IMPACT

**Stellar
Nucleosynthesis**

Use this Chemical Impact to connect with astronomy. Have students investigate the connections between chemistry and the formation of the stars and other celestial objects.

CHEMICAL IMPACT

Connection to Astronomy

Stellar Nucleosynthesis

How did all the matter around us originate? One scientific answer to this question is a theory called *stellar nucleosynthesis*—the formation of nuclei in stars.

Many scientists believe that our universe originated as a cloud of neutrons that became unstable and produced an immense explosion, giving this model its name: *the big bang theory*. The model postulates that after the initial explosion, neutrons decomposed into protons and electrons,

$$_0^1n \rightarrow\ _1^1H +\ _{-1}^0e$$

which eventually combined to form clouds of hydrogen. Over the eons, gravitational forces caused many of these hydrogen clouds to contract and heat up sufficiently to reach temperatures at which proton fusion began to occur, releasing large quantities of energy. When the tendency to expand in response to the heat from fusion and the tendency to contract in response to the forces of gravity are balanced, a stable young star such as our sun can form.

Eventually, when the star's supply of hydrogen is exhausted, the core of the star again contracts, with further heating, until it reaches temperatures at which fusion of helium nuclei can occur, leading to the formation of $_6^{12}C$ and $_8^{16}O$ nuclei. In turn, when the supply of helium nuclei runs out, further contraction and heating occur, until the fusion of heavier nuclei takes place. This process occurs repeatedly, forming heavier and heavier nuclei, until iron nuclei are formed. Because the iron nucleus has the greatest binding forces of all, iron nuclei do not release excess energy when they fuse to form heavier nuclei. This means that there is no further fusion energy to sustain the star, and it cools to a small, dense *white dwarf*.

The evolution just described is characteristic of small and medium-sized stars. Much larger stars, however, become unstable at some time during their evolution and undergo a *supernova explosion*. In this explosion, nuclei with medium mass numbers are fused to produce heavy elements. Also in the explosion, light nuclei capture neutrons. These neutron-rich nuclei then produce β particles, increasing their atomic number with each β decay. This eventually leads to nuclei with large atomic numbers. In fact, almost all nuclei beyond iron are thought to originate in supernova explosions. The debris of such an explosion contains a wide variety of elements, and it is thought that this debris might eventually form a solar system such as our own.

A portion of the Cygnus Loop supernova remnant taken by the Hubble Space Telescope.

A solar flare erupts from the surface of the sun.

thereby release energy, they must get very close together. But protons, because they are identically charged, repel each other. This suggests that to get two protons (or two deuterons) close enough to bind together (the strong nuclear binding force is *not* related to charge), they must be "shot" at each other at speeds high enough to overcome their repulsion from each other. The repulsive forces between two $_1^2H$ nuclei are so great that temperatures of about 40 million K are thought to be necessary. Only at these temperatures are the nuclei moving fast enough to overcome the repulsions.

Currently, scientists are studying two types of systems to produce the extremely high temperatures required: high-powered lasers and heating by electric currents. At present many technical problems remain to be solved, and it is not clear whether either method will prove useful.

624   Chapter 19   Radioactivity and Nuclear Energy

624

19.10 Effects of Radiation

Objective: *To see how radiation damages human tissue.*

E veryone knows that being hit by a train is a catastrophic event. The energy transferred in such a collision is very large. In fact, any source of energy is potentially harmful to organisms. Energy transferred to cells can break chemical bonds and cause malfunctioning of the cell systems. This fact is behind our present concern about maintaining the ozone layer in the earth's upper atmosphere, which screens out high-energy ultraviolet radiation arriving from the sun. Radioactive elements, which are sources of high-energy particles, are also potentially hazardous. However, the effects are usually quite subtle, because even though high-energy particles are involved, the quantity of energy actually deposited in tissues *per decay event* is quite small. The resulting damage is no less real, but the effects may not be apparent for years.

Radiation damage to organisms can be classified as somatic or genetic damage. *Somatic damage* is damage to the organism itself, resulting in sickness or death. The effects may appear almost immediately if a massive dose of radiation is received; for smaller doses, damage may appear years later, usually in the form of cancer. *Genetic damage* is damage to the genetic machinery of reproductive cells, creating problems that often afflict the offspring of the organism.

The biological effects of a particular source of radiation depend on several factors:

1. *The energy of the radiation.* The higher the energy content of the radiation, the more damage it can cause.

2. *The penetrating ability of the radiation.* The particles and rays produced in radioactive processes vary in their ability to penetrate human tissue: γ rays are highly penetrating, β particles can penetrate approximately 1 cm, and α particles are stopped by the skin **(Figure 19.8).**

3. *The ionizing ability of the radiation.* Because ions behave quite differently from neutral molecules, radiation that removes electrons from molecules in living tissues seriously disturbs their functions. The ionizing ability of radiation varies dramatically. For example, γ rays penetrate very deeply but cause only occasional ionization. On the other hand, α particles, although they are not very penetrating, are very effective at causing ionization and produce serious damage. Therefore, the ingestion of a producer of α particles, such as plutonium, is particularly damaging.

4. *The chemical properties of the radiation source.* When a radioactive nuclide is ingested, its capacity to cause damage depends on how long it remains in the body. For example, both $^{85}_{36}Kr$ and $^{90}_{38}Sr$ are β-particle producers. Because krypton, being a noble gas, is chemically inert, it passes through the body quickly and does not have much time to do damage. Strontium, on the other hand, is chemically similar to calcium. It can collect in bones, where it may cause leukemia and bone cancer.

Because of the differences in the behavior of the particles and rays produced by radioactive decay, we have invented a unit called the **rem** that indicates the danger the radiation poses to humans.

Figure 19.8
Radioactive particles and rays vary greatly in penetrating power. Gamma rays are by far the most penetrating.

TOP TEN

Elements in the Sun (by mass)
1. Hydrogen
2. Helium
3. Oxygen
4. Carbon
5. Iron
6. Neon
7. Nitrogen
8. Silicon
9. Magnesium
10. Sulfur

TEACHING TIPS

- This section offers an opportunity to connect the study of chemistry to medicine and health. Many students do not understand the different effects of radiation on human tissue.

- The preservation of food by using gamma radiation was first approved by the U.S. Food and Drug Administration in 1963. The first foods approved for radiation preservation were wheat flour and potatoes. Not until 1986 could fruits and vegetables be preserved by radiation.

Using the TOP TEN

Use this Top Ten to review the properties of these elements with students. Have them locate each element on the periodic table and list the properties associated with each.

Compare the elements in the sun to those on earth (from Table 3.1 in Chapter 3, p. 48).

TEACHING SUPPORT
Historical Background

During the early days of nuclear chemistry scientists did not understand the hazards of radioactive substances. As a result, many of the early scientists were exposed to harmful radiation. Marie Curie is a well-known example; she suffered from radiation poisoning during her days of refining pitch-blende. When doctors first began using X rays for diagnosis, patients were burned by the radiations. In 1896 Elihu Thompson (a physicist) deliberately exposed his hand to X rays to determine the effect of X ray burns on the skin. One of Thomas Edison's assistants became fatally ill from X ray exposure. Henri Becquerel also experienced radiation burns when he carried a radioactive sample in his pocket.

Integrating the CHEMICAL IMPACT

Nuclear Waste Disposal

Have students investigate the waste products from nuclear reactors. How do we store our radioactive waste? How long will it take before the material is "safe"?

Nuclear Waste Disposal

Our society does not have a very impressive record for safe disposal of industrial wastes. We have polluted our water and air, and some land areas have become virtually uninhabitable because of the improper burial of chemical wastes. As a result, many people are wary about the radioactive wastes from nuclear reactors. The potential threats of cancer and genetic mutations make these materials especially frightening.

Because of its controversial nature, most of the nuclear waste generated over the past 50 years has been placed in temporary storage. However, in 1982 the U.S. Congress passed the Nuclear Waste Policy Act, which established a timetable for choosing and preparing sites for the deep underground disposal of radioactive materials.

The tentative disposal plan calls for incorporation of the spent nuclear fuel into blocks of glass that will be packed in corrosion-resistant metal containers and then buried in a deep, stable rock formation indicated by the rock layers in **Figure 19.9**.

There are indications that this method will isolate the waste until the radioactivity decays to safe levels. Some reassuring evidence comes from the natural fission "reactor" that was discovered at Oklo in Gabon, Africa (see "Celebrity Chemical: Uranium" on page 622). Spawned about 2 billion years ago when uranium in ore deposits there formed a critical mass, this "reactor" produced fission and fusion products for several thousand years. Although some of these products have migrated away from the site in the intervening 2 billion years, most have stayed in place.

Finally, more than 15 years after the Nuclear Waste Policty Act, it looks like some waste will soon be stored. In 1998 the Waste Isolation Pilot Plant (WIPP) in New Mexico was issued a license by the U.S. Environmental Protection Agency to begin receiving nuclear waste. This facility employs tunnels carved into the salt beds of an ancient ocean. Once a repository room becomes full, the salt will collapse around the waste, encapsulating it forever.

Another waste depository, under Yucca Mountain in Nevada, is being contemplated. For nearly two decades, this area has been studied to determine its suitability for storage of high-level radioactive wastes. At present it looks to be a long time before this issue is settled.

Figure 19.9
A schematic diagram for the tentative plan for deep underground isolation of nuclear waste. The disposal system would consist of a waste package buried in tunnels like the one shown above.

Table 19.5 shows the physical effects of short-term exposure to various doses of radiation, and **Table 19.6** gives the sources and amounts of the radiation to which a typical person in the United States is exposed each year. Note that natural sources contribute about twice as much as human activities do to the total exposure. However, although the nuclear industry con-

626   Chapter 19   Radioactivity and Nuclear Energy

TABLE 19.5

Effects of Short-Term Exposures to Radiation

Dose (rem)	Clinical Effect
0–25	nondetectable
25–50	temporary decrease in white blood cell counts
100–200	strong decrease in white blood cell counts
500	death of half the exposed population within 30 days after exposure

TABLE 19.6

Typical Radiation Exposures for a Person Living in the United States
(1 millirem = 10^{-3} rem)

Source	Exposure (millirems/year)
cosmic	50
from the earth	47
from building materials	3
in human tissues	21
inhalation of air	5
Total from natural sources	126
X-ray diagnosis	50
radiotherapy X rays, radioisotopes	10
internal diagnosis and therapy	1
nuclear power industry	0.2
luminous watch dials, TV tubes, industrial wastes	2
radioactive fallout	4
Total from human activities	67
Total	193 = 0.193 rems

tributes only a small percentage of the total exposure, controversy surrounds nuclear power plants because of their *potential* for creating radiation hazards. These hazards arise mainly from two sources: accidents allowing the release of radioactive materials, and improper disposal of the radioactive products in spent fuel elements.

Focus Questions

Sections 19.5–19.10

1. How do the half-lives of tracers compare to the half-life of carbon-14? Why would these nuclides be a better choice for medical applications than carbon-14?
2. What are the differences between fission and fusion?
3. If there is no danger of a nuclear power plant having a nuclear explosion (if the reaction got out of control), why do we need to build containment buildings for the core?
4. How is a typical nuclear power plant in the United States different from the breeder reactor commonly used in Europe?
5. What are the factors that determine the biological effects of radiation?

Focus Questions **627**

TEACHING TIPS

- Table 19.6 gives sources and amounts of radiation exposure for humans. This information can be used in a discussion of the natural sources of radioactivity and exposure to radioactivity expected in our lives.
- The use of nuclear imaging techniques is a good starting point for a discussion of the hazards and benefits of nuclear medicine.

 Answers to Focus Questions

1. Tracers have a much shorter half-life than carbon-14. When using a radioactive substance in medicine, the most common goal is to have the substance become inactive and "safe" within a short time.

2. Fission is the splitting of an atom into lighter atoms. Fusion is the formation of a heavier nucleus from smaller nuclei.

3. The containment buildings are designed to hold in the radioactive material and prevent it from leaking into the environment at large.

4. U.S. power plants do not make fuel in the course of the reaction. Breeder reactors make fuel that can then be used in the reactor.

5. The factors determining the effects of radiation are the energy of the radiation, its penetrating ability, its ionizing ability, and the chemical properties of the radiation source.

The Half-Life of Pennies

Objectives

1. To use flipping pennies to model the concept of half-life

Skills

Observing, applying concepts, making comparisons, graphing

Materials

100 pennies   Graph paper

Preparation Hints

You may wish to ask students several days in advance to bring in pennies so that you do not have to supply all of them.

Procedure Hints

You could have students flip the pennies in a container such as a box lid.

Post-Lab Discussion

Make sure students return all of the pennies to the lab station for the next group of students.

Have each group present its graph to the class and have students compare their individual graphs with a graph of the whole-class data.

Sample Data/Answers

Prelab Assignment

2. Pennies that land "heads" represent nuclides that have not yet decayed.

3. Pennies that land "tails" represent the nuclides that have decayed.

4. Each flip in this activity constitutes a half-life; after each flip, there will be about half as many pennies left (since we eliminate all of the pennies that land tails).

Data/Observations

1. Sample data follow.

Trial Number	Number of Pennies Flipped
0	100
1	52
2	25
3	13
4	7
5	4
6	2
7	1

2. Answers will vary. The average will be around 7. Thus, for a sample of 100 atoms, it will require about 7 half-lives

Problem

What does flipping pennies have to do with the concept of half-life?

Introduction

The half-life of a radioactive sample is the time required for half of the original sample of nuclei to decay. Knowing the half-life of carbon-14, for example, enables us to determine the age of wooden artifacts. This lab activity uses pennies to make a model of the behavior of radioactive nuclides.

Prelab Assignment

1. Read the entire lab experiment before you begin.
2. In this model, what do the pennies that land "heads" represent?
3. In this model, what do the pennies that land "tails" represent?
4. In this model, what does each flip represent?

Materials

100 pennies
Graph paper

Procedure

1. Flip 100 pennies and separate them according to which landed heads and which landed tails. Record the number of heads.
2. Flip only the pennies that landed heads, and then separate the pennies according to which landed heads and which landed tails. Record the number of heads. Repeat this process until you run out of pennies.

Cleaning Up

Leave the pennies on the lab bench. Wash your hands thoroughly.

Data/Observations

1. Fill in a table similar to the one provided.

Trial Number	Number of Pennies Flipped
0	100
1	
2	
. . .	

2. How many times did you flip the pennies until no pennies were left?

Analysis and Conclusions

1. Make a graph of the number of pennies you flipped versus the trial number.
2. Gather together all of the class data and make a second graph of the total number of pennies flipped versus the trial number.
3. Why is there a difference between the graph of your data and the graph of the class data?
4. Draw a graph that shows the decay of a 100.0-g sample of a radioactive nuclide with a half-life of 10 years. It should be a graph of mass versus time for the first four half-lives.
5. Compare the two graphs using your data and the class data to the graph of the 100.0-g sample. Does your graph or the graph of the class data look more like the graph of the 100.0-g sample? Why?
6. Approximately how many half-lives would it take for one mole of a radioactive nuclide to completely disappear?

Something Extra

Would the shape of the graph change if you used a different number of pennies? Try this activity again with a different number of pennies and comment on the results. Use a wide range (from 10 pennies to a few hundred pennies).

before the radioactive sample becomes too small to detect.

Analysis and Conclusions

1. The graph depends on the data.
2. The graph depends on the data. This graph should be much smoother than the graph from Question 1. It should look similar to the graph in Question 4.
3. The graph for each group may be rather rough. However, once all of the class data is taken into account, the graph should be quite

smooth. Discrepancies can arise because while there is the greatest chance that half of the pennies will land heads at any given throw, this will not always be exactly the case. With larger samples, we will get closer to having half of the pennies landing heads each time.

4. See the *Teacher's Guide for the Laboratory* for the graph.

5. The graph of the class data will look very similar to the graph from Question 4. Individual graphs will vary.

6. For a sample of 1 mole of radioactive atoms, about 80 half-lives are required before the entire sample disappears. You can have students verify this conclusion by dividing 6.022×10^{23} by 2 on their calculators until they reach a number less than 1. A more systematic solution that requires an understanding of logarithms follows.

We use the equation

$$(6.022 \times 10^{23})/2^x = 1$$

Key Terms

nucleons (neutrons and
  protons) (p. 607)
atomic number (Z) (p. 607)
mass number (A) (p. 607)
isotopes (p. 607)
nuclide (p. 607)
radioactive (19.1)
beta (β) particle (19.1)
nuclear equation (19.1)
alpha (α) particle (19.1)
alpha (α)-particle
  production (19.1)
beta (β)-particle
  production (19.1)
gamma (γ) ray (19.1)
positron (19.1)
electron capture (19.1)
decay series (19.1)

nuclear transformation
  (19.2)
transuranium elements
  (19.2)
Geiger–Müller counter
  (Geiger counter) (19.3)
scintillation counter (19.3)
half-life (19.3)
radiocarbon dating
  (carbon-14 dating) (19.4)
radiotracers (19.5)
fusion (19.6)
fission (19.6)
chain reaction (19.7)
critical mass (19.7)
breeder reactor (19.8)
nuclear fision (19.9)
rem (19.10)

Summary

1. Radioactivity is the spontaneous decomposition of a nucleus to form another nucleus and produce one or more particles. We can write a nuclear equation to represent radioactive decay, in which both A (mass number) and Z (atomic number) must be conserved.

2. There are several types of radioactive decay: alpha-particle production, in which an alpha particle (helium nucleus) is produced; beta-particle (or electron) production; the production of gamma rays (high-energy photons of light); and electron capture, in which one of the inner-orbital electrons is captured by the nucleus. Often a series of decays occurs before a radioactive nucleus attains a stable state.

3. The production of new elements by nuclear transformation (the change of one element into another) is carried out by bombarding various nuclei with particles in accelerators. The transuranium elements have been synthesized in this way.

4. The half-life of a radioactive nuclide is the time required for one-half of the original sample to decay. Radiocarbon dating is based on the radioactivity of carbon-14.

5. Radiotracers—radioactive nuclides that can be introduced into organisms in food or drugs and whose pathways can be traced by monitoring their radioactivity—are used diagnostically in medicine.

6. Nuclear fusion is the process of combining two light nuclei to form a heavier, more stable nucleus. Nuclear fission involves the splitting of a heavy nucleus into two (more stable) lighter nuclei. Current nuclear reactors employ controlled fission.

7. Radiation can cause either direct damage to living tissues or damage to reproductive cells that manifests itself in the organism's offspring. The biological effects of radiation depend on the energy of the radiation, the radiation's penetrating ability and ionizing ability, and the chemical properties of the source of the radiation.

Questions and Problems

All exercises with blue numbers have answers in the back of this book.

19.1 Radioactive Decay

Questions

1. Does the nucleus of an atom have much of an effect on the atom's chemical properties? Explain.

2. How large is a typical atomic nucleus, and how does the size of the nucleus of an atom compare with the overall size of the atom?

3. What do the *atomic number* and the *mass number* of a nucleus represent? Use a specific element as an example to illustrate your answer.

4. What are *isotopes*? Do the isotopes of an element have the same atomic number? Do they have the same mass number? Explain.

5. Using Z to represent the atomic number and A to represent the mass number, give the general symbol for a nuclide of element X. Give also a specific example of the use of such symbolism.

6. When an unstable nucleus produces an alpha particle, by how many units does the atomic number of the nucleus change? Does the atomic number increase or decrease?

7. When an unstable nucleus produces a beta particle, by how many units does the atomic number of the nucleus change? Does the atomic number increase or decrease?

8. What does a *gamma ray* represent? Is a gamma ray a particle? Is there a change in mass or atomic number when a nucleus produces only a gamma ray?

9. What is a *positron*? What are the mass number and charge of a positron? How do the mass number and atomic number of a nucleus change when the nucleus produces a positron?

10. What do we mean when we say a nucleus has undergone an *electron capture* process? What type of electron is captured by the nucleus in this process?

Chapter Review **629**

---

8. Gamma rays are high-energy photons of electromagnetic radiation; they are not normally considered to be particles. When a nucleus produces only gamma radiation, the atomic number and mass number are the same.

9. A positron is a particle with the same mass as an electron, but with the opposite charge (a positive charge). The mass number of a positron is zero. When an unstable nucleus produces a positron, the mass number of the original nucleus is unchanged, but the atomic number decreases by 1.

10. Electron capture occurs when one of the inner orbital electrons is pulled into, and becomes part of, the nucleus.

11. Each contains 12 protons. Magnesium-24 contains 12 neutrons, magnesium-25 contains 13 neutrons, and magnesium-26 contains 14 neutrons.

12. (a) $^{192}_{83}$Bi; (b) $^{204}_{82}$Pb; (c) $^{206}_{84}$Po

13. (a) $^{0}_{-1}$e; (b) $^{0}_{-1}$e; (c) $^{210}_{83}$Bi

14. (a) $^{136}_{53}$I → $^{0}_{-1}$e + $^{136}_{54}$Xe; (b) $^{133}_{51}$Sb → $^{0}_{-1}$e + $^{133}_{52}$Te; (c) $^{117}_{49}$In → $^{0}_{-1}$e + $^{117}_{50}$Sn

15. (a) $^{226}_{88}$Ra → $^{222}_{86}$Rn + $^{4}_{2}$He; (b) $^{222}_{86}$Rn → $^{218}_{84}$Po + $^{4}_{2}$He; (c) $^{239}_{94}$Pu → $^{235}_{92}$U + $^{4}_{2}$He; (d) $^{8}_{4}$Be → $^{4}_{2}$He + $^{4}_{2}$He

16. A nuclear transformation represents the change of one element into another. It is accomplished by bombardment of a target nucleus with some small energetic particle.

17. The target nucleus and the bombarding particles often repel each other greatly, especially when the bombarding particles are positively charged. Accelerators are needed to speed up the particles to overcome this repulsion.

18. The elements with atomic numbers greater than 92 are referred to as transuranium elements. The transuranium elements have been prepared by bombardment reactions of other nuclei.

19. $^{27}_{13}$Al + $^{4}_{2}$He → $^{30}_{15}$P + $^{1}_{0}$n

20. Geiger counters contain a probe that holds argon gas. The argon atoms have no charge but can be ionized by high-energy particles from a radioactive decay process. Ionized argon gas will conduct a current briefly. If an electrical field is applied to the argon gas probe, a brief pulse of electricity will be passed through the argon each time a high-energy particle strikes the argon gas probe (an ionization event). The Geiger counter detects each pulse of current, and these pulses are counted and displayed on the meter of the device. A scintillation counter uses a substance like sodium iodide, which emits light when struck by a high-energy particle from radioactive decay. A detector senses the flashes of light, which are counted and displayed on the meter of the device.

21. The half-life for a nucleus is the time required for one-half of the original sample of nuclei to decay. A given isotope of an element always has the same half-life. Different isotopes of the same element may have very different half-lives. Nuclei of different elements have different half-lives.

22. The "hot" nucleus undergoes more decay events per time period.

23. From highest to lowest activity: ^{24}Na > ^{131}I > ^{60}Co > ^{3}H > ^{14}C

24. From highest to lowest activity: ^{87}Sr > ^{99}Tc > ^{24}Na > ^{99}Mo > ^{133}Xe > ^{131}I > ^{32}P > ^{51}Cr > ^{59}Fe

25. For ^{223}Ra, approximately 125 mg (after 36 days or 3 half-lives); for ^{224}Ra, approximately 4 mg (after 29 days or 8 half-lives); for ^{225}Ra, approximately 250 mg (after 30 days, or 2 half-lives)

Problems

11. Naturally occurring magnesium consists primarily of three isotopes, of mass numbers 24, 25, and 26. How many protons does each of these nuclides contain? How many neutrons does each of these nuclides contain? Write nuclear symbols for each of these isotopes.

12. Complete each of the following nuclear equations by supplying the missing particle.
  a. $^{196}_{85}$At → $^{4}_{2}$He + ?   c. $^{210}_{86}$Rn → $^{4}_{2}$He + ?
  b. $^{208}_{84}$Po → $^{4}_{2}$He + ?

13. Complete each of the following nuclear equations by supplying the missing particle.
  a. $^{201}_{80}$Hg + ? → $^{201}_{79}$Au   c. ? → $^{210}_{84}$Po + $^{0}_{-1}$e
  b. $^{210}_{82}$Pb → $^{210}_{83}$Bi + ?

14. Write a balanced nuclear equation for the decay of each of the following nuclides to produce a beta particle.
  a. $^{136}_{53}$I   c. $^{117}_{49}$In
  b. $^{133}_{51}$Sb

15. Write a balanced nuclear equation for the decay of each of the following nuclides to produce an alpha particle.
  a. $^{226}_{88}$Ra   c. $^{239}_{94}$Pu
  b. $^{222}_{86}$Rn   d. $^{8}_{4}$Be

19.2 Nuclear Transformations

Questions

16. What does a *nuclear transformation* represent? How is a nuclear transformation performed?

17. Why are particle accelerators needed for bombardment processes?

18. What are the elements with atomic numbers greater than 92 called? How have these elements been prepared?

19. Write a balanced nuclear equation for the bombardment of $^{27}_{13}$Al with alpha particles to produce $^{30}_{15}$P and a neutron.

19.3 Detection of Radioactivity and the Concept of Half-life

Questions

20. Describe the operation of a Geiger counter. How does a Geiger counter detect radioactive particles? How does a scintillation counter differ from a Geiger counter?

21. What is the *half-life* of a radioactive nucleus? Does a given type of nucleus always have the same half-life? Do nuclei of different elements have the same half-life?

22. What do we mean when we say that one radioactive nucleus is "hotter" than another? Which element would have more decay events over a given period of time?

Problems

23. The following isotopes (listed with their half-lives) have been used in the medical and biological sciences. Arrange these isotopes in order of their relative decay activities: ^{3}H (12.2 years), ^{24}Na (15 hours), ^{131}I (8 days), ^{60}Co (5.3 years), ^{14}C (5730 years).

24. A list of several important radioactive nuclides is given in Table 19.4. Arrange these nuclides in order of their relative decay activities.

25. For the first three isotopes of radium listed in Table 19.3, given a starting amount of 1000 mg, *estimate* the approximate amount of each isotope remaining after 1 month.

26. Technetium-99 has been used as a radiographic agent in bone scans ($^{99}_{43}$Tc is absorbed by bones). If $^{99}_{43}$Tc has a half-life of 6.0 hours, what fraction of an administered dose of 100 μg of $^{99}_{43}$Tc remains in a patient's body after 2.0 days?

19.4 Dating by Radioactivity

Questions

27. What nuclide is commonly used in the dating of artifacts?

28. How is $^{14}_{6}$C produced in the atmosphere? Write a balanced equation for this process.

29. Why is it assumed that the amount of $^{14}_{6}$C in the atmosphere remains constant?

30. Why does an ancient wood or cloth artifact contain less $^{14}_{6}$C than contemporary or more recently fabricated articles made of similar materials?

19.5 Medical Applications of Radioactivity

Questions

31. What is a *radiotracer?* Which tracers have been used to study the conversion of nutrients into energy in living cells?

32. List four radioisotopes used in medical diagnosis or treatment, and give their nuclear symbols. Discuss why the isotopes you choose are particularly well suited to their uses.

19.6 Nuclear Energy

Questions

33. How do the forces that hold an atomic nucleus together compare in strength with the forces between atoms in a molecule?

34. Define the terms *nuclear fission* and *nuclear fusion.* Which process results in the production of a heavier nucleus? Which results in the production of smaller nuclei?

19.7 Nuclear Fission

Questions

35. How do the energies released by nuclear processes compare in magnitude with the energies of ordinary chemical processes?

36. Write an equation for the fission of $^{235}_{92}U$ by bombardment with neutrons.

37. How is it possible for the fission of $^{235}_{92}U$, once started, to lead to a chain reaction?

38. What does it mean to say that fissionable material possesses a *critical mass*? Can a chain reaction occur when a sample has less than the critical mass?

19.8 Nuclear Reactors

Questions

39. Describe the purpose of each of the major components of a nuclear reactor (moderator, control rods, containment, cooling liquid, and so on).

40. Can a nuclear explosion take place in a reactor? Is the concentration of fissionable material used in reactors large enough for this?

41. What is a *melt-down* and how can it occur? Most nuclear reactors use water as the cooling liquid. Is there any danger of a steam explosion if the reactor core becomes overheated?

42. In a *breeder* nuclear reactor, nonfissionable $^{238}_{92}U$ is converted to fissionable $^{239}_{94}Pu$. Write nuclear equations showing this transformation.

19.9 Nuclear Fusion

Questions

43. What is the nuclear *fusion* of small nuclei? How does the energy released by fusion compare in magnitude with that released by fission?

44. What are some reasons why no practical fusion reactor has yet been developed?

45. Why is the development of nuclear fusion reactors desirable?

19.10 Effects of Radiation

Questions

46. Although the energy transferred per event when a living creature is exposed to radiation is small, why is such exposure dangerous?

47. Explain the difference between *somatic* damage from radiation and *genetic* damage. Which type causes immediate damage to the exposed individual?

48. Describe the relative penetrating powers of alpha, beta, and gamma radiation.

49. Explain why, although gamma rays are far more penetrating than alpha particles, the latter are actually more likely to cause damage to an organism. Which radiation is more effective at causing ionization of biomolecules?

50. How do the *chemical properties* of radioactive nuclei (as opposed to the nuclear decay they undergo) influence the degree of damage they do to an organism?

51. Although radiation has been measured in many terms, the *rem* is most commonly used in discussions of the exposure of human beings to radiation. Using Table 19.6, discuss the sources of radiation to which humans are exposed naturally, and indicate how the total exposure compares with the "acceptable" (nondetectable clinical effect) level of exposure given in Table 19.5.

Critical Thinking

52. The decay series from uranium-238 to lead-206 is indicated in Figure 19.1. For each *step* of the process indicated in the figure, specify what type of particle is produced by the particular nucleus involved at that point in the series.

53. Each of the following isotopes has been used medically for the purpose indicated. Suggest reasons why the particular element might have been chosen for this purpose.
   a. cobalt-57, for study of the body's use of vitamin B$_{12}$
   b. calcium-47, for study of bone metabolism
   c. iron-59, for study of red blood cell function
   d. mercury-197, for brain scans before CAT scan became available

54. Discuss some of the problems associated with the storage and disposal of the waste products of the nuclear industry.

55. Aluminum exists in several isotopic forms, including $^{27}_{13}Al$, $^{28}_{13}Al$, and $^{29}_{13}Al$. Indicate the number of protons and the number of neutrons in each of these isotopes.

56. How have $^{131}_{53}I$ and $^{201}_{81}Tl$ been used in medical diagnosis? Why are these particular nuclides especially well suited for this purpose?

57. What is a *breeder* nuclear reactor? What difficulties with such reactors have led to their not yet being used in the United States for the generation of electricity?

26. On a percentage basis, less than 0.4% of the original radioisotope remains.

27. Carbon-14 ($^{14}_6C$) is most commonly used.

28. Carbon-14 is produced in the upper atmosphere by the bombardment of nitrogen with neutrons from space: $^{14}_7N + ^1_0n \rightarrow ^{14}_6C + ^1_1H$.

29. The quantity of $^{14}_6C$ in the atmosphere is assumed to remain constant because a balance exists between its production (from bombardment of nitrogen in the upper atmosphere by cosmic rays) and its decay through beta particle production.

30. When a plant dies, it no longer replenishes itself with carbon-14 from the atmosphere. As the carbon-14 in the plant undergoes decay, the amount decreases over time. This process assumes that the concentration of carbon-14 in the atmosphere remains constant over time.

31. A radiotracer is a radioactive nuclide that can be introduced into an organism via food or drugs, whose pathway through the body can then be traced by monitoring the radioactivity of the nuclide. Carbon-14 and phosphorus-32 have been used to study the conversion of nutrients into energy by living cells.

32. These isotopes are listed in Table 19.4.

33. The forces that hold protons and neutrons together in the nucleus are much greater than the forces that bind atoms together in molecules.

34. Nuclear fusion is the combining of two light nuclei to form a heavier, more stable nucleus. Splitting a heavy nucleus into nuclei with smaller mass numbers is nuclear fission.

35. The energies released by nuclear processes are on the order of 10^6 times more powerful than those associated with ordinary chemical reactions.

36. $^1_0n + ^{235}_{92}U \rightarrow ^{142}_{56}Ba + ^{91}_{36}Kr + 3\,^1_0n$

37. For every nucleus of $^{235}_{92}U$ that decays, three neutrons are produced. Once the reaction has been started (with neutrons from an outside source), the neutrons generated by the decay cause the reaction to continue.

38. A critical mass of fissionable material is the amount needed to sustain a chain reaction. Enough neutrons must be produced to cause a constant fission of more material. A sample with less than the critical mass is still radioactive, but cannot sustain a chain reaction.

39. The moderator surrounds the fuel rods and slows down the neutrons produced by the uranium decay process so that they can be absorbed more easily by other uranium atoms. The control rods absorb neutrons and are used to control the power level of the reactor. The containment is the building in which the reactor is located, which is designed to contain the radioactive core in case of a nuclear accident. A cooling liquid (usually water) is circulated throughout the reactor to draw off heat produced by the nuclear reaction; this heat energy is converted to electrical energy in the power plant's turbines.

40. The type of nuclear explosion produced by a nuclear weapon cannot occur in a nuclear reactor, because the concentration of fissionable materials is not sufficient to form a supercritical mass.

(Please refer to page A13 in the back of this book to find answers to problems 41–57.)

Section	Text Features & Components	Labs, Demonstrations & Activities
Teaching Segment 20A 1 block pp. 634–648	20.1 Carbon Bonding	**LP** Lesson Plans (Sec 20.1–20.4)	
	20.2–20.3 Alkanes Structural Formulas and Isomerism	**SE** Chemical Impact: Plastic Tasters *p. 637*	
	20.4 Naming Alkanes	**SE** Chemical Impact: www.Dot.Safety *p. 646*	
Teaching Segment 20B 0.5 block pp. 648–653	20.5–20.6 Petroleum Reactions of Alkanes	**LP** Lesson Plans (Sec 20.5–20.7) **SE** Top Ten Joule-Consuming Countries *p. 649*	**TE** Mini Demo *p. 649*
	20.7 Alkenes and Alkynes		**TE** Mini Demo *p. 653*
Teaching Segment 20C 0.5 block pp. 654–659	20.8–20.9 Aromatic Hydrocarbons Naming Aromatic Compounds	**LP** Lesson Plans (Sec 20.8–20.9) **SE** Chemical Impact: Termite Mothballing *p. 659*	
	continued on next page		

Key **SE** Student Edition **TE** Teacher Edition **RP** Teacher Resource Package **LM** Lab Materials
LP Lesson Plans **AR** Additional Resources **◆** Florida Specific

Chapter Planning Guide

All Learners	Review & Assessment	Standards
TE Active Learning *p. 634* **TE** Teaching Tips *p. 634* **AR** Less Proficient Students *p. 39*	**SE** Questions and Problems *p. 677*	**TE** NSES UCP1, UCP2, UCP5, A1, A2, B1, B2, B3, C5, E1, F1, F6, G1, G2, G3 SSS SC.H.1.4.1, SC.H.1.4.5, SC.A.1.4.5, SC.H.3.4.1, SC.H.3.4.4, SC.H.3.4.6
TE Teaching Tips *pp. 635, 638, 640* **AR** Less Proficient Students *p. 39*	**TE** Additional Examples *pp. 636–637, 639* **SE** Self Check *p. 636* **SE** Key Terms *p. 676* **SE** Questions and Problems *p. 677*	
TE Teaching Tips *pp. 641, 644* Transparency: Table 20.2 *p. 642* **RP** Team Learning Worksheets (Sec 20.1–20.4) *p. 111* **AR** Less Proficient Students *p. 39*	**TE** Additional Examples *pp. 644, 647* **SE** Self Check *pp. 646–647* **SE** Focus Questions (Sec 20.1–20.4) *p. 648* **SE** Questions and Problems *p. 677*	
TE Active Learning *p. 648* **TE** Teaching Tip *p. 650* **AR** Less Proficient Students *p. 39*	**SE** What if . . . *p. 648* **SE** Key Terms *p. 676* **SE** Questions and Problems *p. 678*	**TE** NSES UCP1, UCP2, UCP5, A1, A2, B2, B3, E1, E2, F3, F4, F5, F6 SSS SC.H.1.4.2, SC.H.1.4.3, SC.H.1.4.7, SC.A.1.4.5, SC.B.1.4.1, SC.G.2.4.1, SC.B.1.4.5, SC.H.3.4.2, SC.H.3.4.4
TE Teaching Tips *p. 651* **RP** Team Learning Worksheets (Sec 20.5–20.7) *pp. 113–114* **AR** Less Proficient Students *p. 40*	**TE** Additional Examples *p. 652* **SE** Self Check *p. 652* **SE** Focus Questions (Sec 20.5–20.7) *p. 653* **SE** Key Terms *p. 676* **SE** Questions and Problems *p. 678*	
TE Active Learning *p. 654* **TE** Teaching Tips *p. 654* **RP** Team Learning Worksheets (Sec 20.8–20.9) *p. 115* **AR** Less Proficient Students *p. 40*	**TE** Additional Examples *p. 658* **SE** Self Check *p. 658* **SE** Focus Questions (Sec 20.8–20.9) *p. 659* **SE** Key Terms *p. 676* **SE** Questions and Problems *p. 678*	**TE** NSES UCP1, UCP5, A1, A2, B2, B3, C6 SSS SC.H.1.4.1, SC.A.1.4.5

20 Organic Chemistry

Section	Text Features & Components	Labs, Demonstrations & Activities
Teaching Segment 20D — 0.5 block — pp. 660–664	20.10 Functional Groups	**LP** Lesson Plans (Sec 20.10–20.12)	**TE** Mini Demo *p. 660*
	20.11–20.12 Alcohols — Properties and Uses of Alcohols		**TE** Mini Demo *p. 660*
Teaching Segment 20E — 1 block — pp. 664–668	20.13 Aldehydes and Ketones	**LP** Lesson Plans (Sec 20.13–20.14)	**TE** Mini Demo *p. 665*
	20.14 Naming Aldehydes and Ketones	**SE** Celebrity Chemical: Polyhydroxyamide *p. 668*	
Teaching Segment 20F — 3 blocks — pp. 669–674	20.15 Carboxylic Acids and Esters	**LP** Lesson Plans (Sec 20.15–20.16)	**TE** Mini Demo *p. 670* **LM** Experiments 86–87 Lab Manual Report Sheets Teacher's Lab Guide
	20.16 Polymers	**SE** Chemical Impact: Polymers Are Tacky *p. 673*	**TE** Student Activity *p. 671* **TE** Teaching Support: Demonstration *pp. 672–673* **SE** Chemistry in Action: Guar Gum Slime *p. 674* **SE** Chemistry in the Laboratory *p. 675* **LM** Experiments 88–89 Lab Manual Report Sheets Teacher's Lab Guide

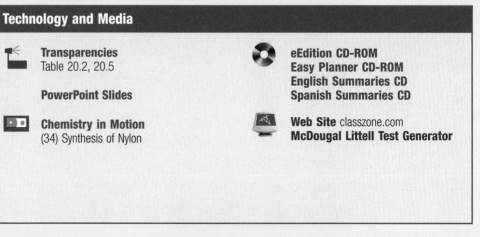

Key

SE Student Edition
TE Teacher Edition
RP Teacher Resource Package
LM Lab Materials
LP Lesson Plans
AR Additional Resources
⬤ Florida Specific

Technology and Media

Transparencies
Table 20.2, 20.5

PowerPoint Slides

Chemistry in Motion
(34) Synthesis of Nylon

eEdition CD-ROM
Easy Planner CD-ROM
English Summaries CD
Spanish Summaries CD

Web Site classzone.com
McDougal Littell Test Generator

Chapter Planning Guide

All Learners	Review & Assessment	Standards
(TE) Active Learning *p. 660* **(icon)** Transparency: Table 20.5 *p. 660* **(TE)** Teaching Tips *p. 660* **(AR)** Less Proficient Students *p. 40*	**(SE)** Key Terms *p. 676* **(SE)** Questions and Problems *p. 678*	**(TE)** **NSES** UCP2, UCP3, UCP5, A1, A2, B2, B3 **(icon)** **SSS** SC.A.1.4.2, SC.H.3.4.6
(RP) Team Learning Worksheets (Sec 20.10–20.12) *pp. 117–118* **(AR)** Less Proficient Students *p. 40*	**(TE)** Additional Examples *p. 661* **(SE)** Self Check *p. 662* **(SE)** Focus Questions (Sec 20.10–20.12) *p. 664* **(SE)** Key Terms *p. 676* **(SE)** Questions and Problems *p. 679*	
(TE) Active Learning *p. 664* **(AR)** Less Proficient Students *p. 41*	**(SE)** Key Terms *p. 676* **(SE)** Questions and Problems *p. 679*	**(TE)** **NSES** UCP1, UCP3, UCP5, A1, A2, B2, B3, E1, E2, F6 **(icon)** **SSS** SC.H.1.4.1, SC.H.1.4.5, SC.A.1.4.2, SC.A.1.4.5, SC.H.3.4.4
(TE) Teaching Tips *p. 665* **(RP)** Team Learning Worksheets (Sec 20.13–20.14) *p. 119* **(AR)** Less Proficient Students *p. 41*	**(TE)** Additional Examples *p. 667* **(SE)** Self Check *p. 667* **(SE)** Focus Questions (Sec 20.13–20.14) *p. 668* **(SE)** Questions and Problems *p. 679*	
(TE) Active Learning *p. 669* **(TE)** Teaching Tips *p. 670* **(AR)** Less Proficient Students *p. 41*	**(SE)** Key Terms *p. 676* **(SE)** Questions and Problems *p. 680*	**(TE)** **NSES** UCP1, UCP3, UCP5, A1, A2, B2, B3, E1, E2, F6, G1, G2, G3 **(icon)** **SSS** SC.H.1.4.1, SC.A.1.4.5, SC.H.3.4.4, SC.H.3.4.6
(TE) Teaching Tips *p. 671* **(icon)** Chemistry in Motion (34) *p. 673* **(RP)** Team Learning Worksheets (Sec 20.15–20.16) *pp. 121–122* **(AR)** Less Proficient Students *p. 41*	**(SE)** Focus Questions (Sec 20.15–20.16) *p. 674* **(SE)** Key Terms *p. 676* **(SE)** Questions and Problems *p. 680*	

Chapter Materials

(TE) Reading Strategy
(AR) English/Spanish Summaries *pp. 33–34*
(AR) Challenge Projects/Problems *p. 36*
(AR) Less Proficient Students *p. 41*
(icon) English Summary Audio
(icon) Spanish Summary Audio
(RP) Chapter Review Worksheets (Basic, Review, Challenge)

(SE) Chapter Summary *p. 676*
(SE) Critical Thinking *pp. 680–681*
(RP) Solutions Guide
(RP) Chapter Tests
(RP) Test Bank
(icon) McDougal Littell Test Generator
(AR) Standardized Test Practice
(icon) **FCAT Test 10**

20 Integrating Reading Strategies and Chemistry Concepts

Chapter 20: Using Graphic Organizers

To organize the material they are learning, the students can use graphic organizers to show relationships among concepts. Although much of the material presented in this chapter is given in table or list form, some of the students may benefit from creating and using another visual display.

When you introduce the strategy of graphic organizers, explain that the design of the organizer can vary. The students can be creative in their designs and include as much or as little detail as they find necessary. Direct the students' attention to **Figure 1.2** on page 16 and to **Figure 2.18** on page 41, and discuss the similarities and differences between these two graphic organizers. Ask the students how they could redesign one of these organizers to allow room for more detailed information.

Figure 1.2
Student-centered learning.

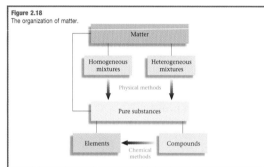

Figure 2.18
The organization of matter.

Reasons for Using Graphic Organizers

Point out the following benefits to creating and using a graphic organizer.

- Requires the students to find and organize important facts, structures, or formulas.
- Provides an opportunity for the students to rearrange the material presented in class or in the chapter.
- Allows the students to process readings and organize the material in a visually stimulating way.
- Provides a method of viewing the concepts as a whole, rather than in parts.
- Clarifies relationships among previously learned concepts.
- Helps summarize key concepts within a section or chapter.
- Serves as an effective study tool.

Creating a Graphic Organizer

Encourage the students to focus on the main objective of a section or chapter and determine the key points that support this objective. When the students determine what material to include in the organizers, they should design a graphic organizer format that is best suited for the material they are learning. The relationship among the ideas presented should be shown with connecting lines.

Show examples of graphic organizers and explain the benefit of each type.

Explain that the tree graphic organizer format (below left) is typically used for showing how items within a system are ordered.

Explain that the web graphic organizer format (above center) helps organize facts about a key concept.

Show how a chain graphic organizer format (above right) can be used to describe the steps of a process.

Using Graphic Organizers

The students may need help in creating an organizer for the information in this chapter. Before beginning the chapter, create your own graphic organizer for the first teaching segment (Sections 20.1–20.4), leaving several blank areas. After presenting this reading strategy, distribute copies of your graphic organizer. Instruct the students to complete the organizer by using their class notes and information from their reading assignment.

Next, organize the students in small groups and have each group create and fill out a graphic organizer format based on the chapter material. Students should not fill in information in the organizer yet. Suggest these topics for a graphic organizer.

- the formulas of the alkanes, alkenes, and alkynes
- the rules for naming alkanes, alkenes, and alkynes
- the functional groups and the corresponding general formulas
- the facts about hydrocarbons
- the relationship between alkanes and the other types of hydrocarbons
- the key terms or the chapter summary on page 676

When the students have completed this exercise, ask each group to display its organizer format. The groups should explain why they choose the design and the level of detail they used. Copy each group's organizer and distribute copies to the class. Encourage the students to personalize each organizer for use as a study tool.

Chapter 20

Overview

In this Chapter our goals are for the students to:

- Understand the types of bonds formed by the carbon atom

- Learn about alkanes

- Learn about structural isomers

- Learn the system of naming alkanes and substituted alkanes

- Learn about the composition and uses of petroleum

- Learn various types of chemical reactions that alkanes undergo

- Learn to name alkenes and alkynes

- Understand addition reaction

- Learn about aromatic hydrocarbons and how to name them

- Learn the common functional groups in organic molecules

- Learn how some alcohols are made and used

- Learn the general formulas for aldehydes and ketones and some of their uses

- Learn the system for naming aldehydes and ketones

- Learn the structures and names of the common carboxylic acids

- Learn about some common polymers

20 Organic Chemistry

The sail of this paraglider is made of nylon.

632

The study of carbon-containing compounds and their properties is called **organic chemistry.** The industries based on organic substances have truly revolutionized our lives. In particular, the development of polymers, such as nylon for fabrics; Velcro for fasteners; Kevlar for the composites used in exotic cars, airplanes, and bicycles; and polyvinyl chloride (PVC) for pipes, siding, and toys has produced a wondrous new world. Polymers are now even being considered for apprehension of criminals (see "Chemical Impact: Polymers Are Tacky," page 673).

Two Group 4 elements, carbon and silicon, form the basis of most natural substances. Silicon, with its great affinity for oxygen, forms chains and rings containing Si—O—Si bonds to produce the silica and silicates that form the basic structures for most rocks, sands, and soils. Therefore, silicon compounds are the fundamental inorganic materials of the earth. What silicon is to the geological world, carbon is to the organic or biological world. Carbon has the unusual ability of bonding strongly to itself, forming long chains or rings of carbon atoms. In addition, carbon forms strong bonds to other nonmetals such as hydrogen, nitrogen, oxygen, sulfur, and the halogens. Because of these bonding properties, an extraordinary number of carbon compounds exists; several million are now known, and the number continues to grow rapidly. Among these many compounds are the **biomolecules,** those molecules that make possible the maintenance and reproduction of life.

Although a few compounds of carbon, such as the oxides of carbon and carbonates, are considered to be inorganic substances, the vast majority of carbon compounds are designated as organic compounds—compounds that typically contain chains or rings of carbon atoms. Originally, the distinction between inorganic and organic substances was based on whether they were produced by living systems. For example, until the early nineteenth century, it was believed that organic compounds had some kind of "life force" and could be synthesized only by living organisms. This misconception was dispelled in 1828 when the German chemist Friedrich Wöhler (1800–1882) prepared urea from the inorganic salt ammonium cyanate by simple heating.

A close-up photo of Velcro, a synthetic organic material used for fasteners.

$$NH_4OCN \xrightarrow{\text{Heat}} N_2H—\overset{\displaystyle \|}{\underset{\displaystyle O}{C}}—NH_2$$

Ammonium cyanate   Urea

Urea is a component of urine, so it is clearly an organic material formed by living things, yet here was clear evidence that it could be produced in the laboratory as well.

Organic chemistry plays a vital role in our quest to understand living systems. Beyond that, the synthetic fibers, plastics, artificial sweeteners, and medicines that we take for granted are products of industrial organic chemistry. Finally, the energy which we rely so heavily on to power our civilization is based mostly on the combustion of organic materials found in coal and petroleum.

Because organic chemistry is such a vast subject, we can introduce it only briefly in this text. We will begin with the simplest class of organic compounds, the hydrocarbons, and then show how most other organic compounds can be considered to be derived from hydrocarbons.

633

Themes

Models, Form and Function

Skills

Making comparisons, developing models

Student Preparation

Assign the students to read Sections 20.1 to 20.4 and to answer the Focus Questions at the end of Section 20.4 before coming to class.

Active Learning

After introducing the material in Sections 20.1 to 20.4 in class, place the students in groups and have them work together on Sections 20.1–20.4: Team Learning Worksheet. Answers and/or discussion of these questions are located in the *Teacher Resources.*

TEACHING TIPS

• To introduce the topic of organic chemistry and its impact on our lives, ask students what the classroom would look like without carbon-containing compounds. You will need to assist them in figuring out which items contain carbon, but it will not be long before they appreciate how many of the objects surrounding us are organic compounds.

• You will find a good set of three-dimensional models very helpful in presenting this material. Use the models to illustrate the shapes of the molecules discussed in this section. The tetrahedral shape of methane, for instance, is difficult to visualize without a model.

• Inexpensive classroom-sized models can be built from painted Styrofoam balls and wooden dowels (or old Tinker Toys).

• This section provides an excellent opportunity to review the concept of covalent bonding.

20.1 Carbon Bonding

Objective: *To understand the types of bonds formed by the carbon atom.*

So many carbon-containing compounds exist because carbon forms strong bonds to itself and to many other elements. A carbon atom can form bonds to a maximum of four other atoms; these can be either carbon atoms or atoms of other elements. One of the hardest, toughest materials known is diamond, a form of pure carbon in which each carbon atom is bound to four other carbon atoms (see Figure 3.18).

One of the most familiar compounds of carbon is methane, CH_4, the main component of natural gas. The methane molecule consists of a carbon atom with four hydrogen atoms bound to it in a tetrahedral fashion. That is, as predicted by the VSEPR model (see Section 12.9), the four pairs of bonding electrons around the carbon have minimum repulsions when they are located at the corners of a tetrahedron.

Figure 20.1
Methane is a tetrahedral molecule.

CO₂ and CO are classed as inorganic substances.

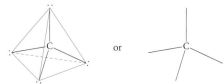

This leads to the structure for CH_4 shown in **Figure 20.1.** *When carbon has four atoms bound to it, these atoms will always have a tetrahedral arrangement about the carbon.*

Carbon can bond to fewer than four elements by forming one or more multiple bonds. Recall that a multiple bond involves the sharing of more than one pair of electrons. For example, a *double bond* involves sharing two pairs of electrons, as in carbon dioxide:

$$\ddot{O}=C=\ddot{O}$$

A *triple bond* involves sharing three pairs of electrons, as in carbon monoxide:

$$:C\equiv O:$$

Note that carbon is bound to two other atoms in CO_2 and to only one other atom in CO.

Multiple bonding also occurs in organic molecules. Ethylene, C_2H_4, has a double bond.

In this case each carbon is bound to three other atoms (one C atom and two H atoms). A molecule with a triple bond is acetylene, C_2H_2:

$$H-C\equiv C-H$$

Here each carbon is bound to two other atoms (one carbon atom and one hydrogen atom).

More than any other element, carbon has the ability to form chains of atoms, as illustrated by the structures of propane and butane shown in Figure 20.3. In these compounds each carbon atom is bound to four atoms in a tetrahedral fashion. We will discuss these molecules in detail in the next section.

634   Chapter 20   Organic Chemistry

20.2 Alkanes

Objective: *To learn about the alkanes—compounds that contain saturated carbon atoms.*

Hydrocarbons, as the name indicates, are compounds composed of carbon and hydrogen. Those whose carbon–carbon bonds are all single bonds are said to be **saturated**, because each carbon is bound to four atoms, the maximum number. Hydrocarbons containing carbon–carbon multiple bonds are described as being **unsaturated**, because the carbon atoms involved in a multiple bond can bond to one or more additional atoms. This is shown by the *addition* of hydrogen to ethylene.

Computer-generated model of ethane.

Note that each carbon in ethylene is bonded to three atoms (one carbon and two hydrogens) but can bond to one additional atom after one bond of the carbon–carbon double bond is broken. This leads to ethane, a saturated hydrocarbon (each carbon atom is bonded to four atoms).

Saturated hydrocarbons are called **alkanes.** The simplest alkane is *methane*, CH_4, which has a tetrahedral structure (Figure 20.1). The next alkane, the one containing two carbon atoms, is *ethane*, C_2H_6, shown in **Figure 20.2**. Note that each carbon atom in ethane is bonded to four atoms.

Figure 20.2
(a) The Lewis structure of ethane, C_2H_6. The molecular structure of ethane represented by (b) a space-filling model and (c) a ball-and-stick model.

(a)   (b)   (c)

(a) Propane   (b) Butane

The next two members of the series are *propane*, with three carbon atoms and the formula C_3H_8, and *butane*, with four carbon atoms and the formula C_4H_{10}. These molecules are shown in **Figure 20.3**. Again, these are saturated hydrocarbons (alkanes); each carbon is bonded to four atoms.

Figure 20.3
The structures of (a) propane and (b) butane.

20.2 Alkanes   **635**

Alkanes in which the carbon atoms form long "strings" or chains are called **normal, straight-chain,** or **unbranched hydrocarbons.** As Figure 20.3 illustrates, the chains in normal alkanes are not really straight but zigzag, because the tetrahedral C—C—C angle is 109.5°. The normal alkanes can be represented by the structure

where m is an integer. Note that each member is obtained from the previous one by insertion of a *methylene*, CH_2, group. We can condense the structural formulas by omitting some of the C—H bonds. For example, the general formula for normal alkanes shown above can be condensed to

$$CH_3—(CH_2)_m—CH_3$$

Additional Examples

Give the formulas for the normal (or straight-chain) alkanes with 5 and 12 carbons.
$CH_3CH_2CH_2CH_2CH_3$;
$C_5H_{12}CH_3CH_2CH_2CH_2CH_2CH_2CH_2$
$CH_2CH_2CH_2CH_2CH_3$;
$C_{12}H_{26}$

Example 20.1

Writing Formulas for Alkanes

Give the formulas for the normal (or straight-chain) alkanes with six and eight carbon atoms.

Solution

The alkane with six carbon atoms can be written as

$$CH_3CH_2CH_2CH_2CH_2CH_3$$

which can be condensed to

$$CH_3—(CH_2)_4—CH_3$$

Notice that the molecule contains fourteen hydrogen atoms in addition to the six carbon atoms. Therefore, the formula is C_6H_{14}.

The alkane with eight carbons is

$$CH_3CH_2CH_2CH_2CH_2CH_2CH_2CH_3$$
$$12345678$$

which can be written in condensed form as

$$CH_3—(CH_2)_6—CH_3$$

This molecule has eighteen hydrogens. The formula is C_8H_{18}.

 Self-Check Exercise 20.1

Give the molecular formulas for the alkanes with ten and fifteen carbon atoms.

 Answer to Self-Check Exercise 20.1

The alkane with 10 carbon atoms can be represented as $CH_3—(CH_2)_8—CH_3$ and its formula is $C_{10}H_{22}$. The alkane with 15 carbons,

$$CH_3—(CH_2)_{13}—CH_3$$

has the formula $C_{15}H_{32}$.

The first ten straight-chain alkanes are shown in **Table 20.1.** Note that all alkanes can be represented by the general formula C_nH_{2n+2}, where n represents the number of carbon atoms. For example, nonane, which has nine carbon atoms, is represented by $C_9H_{(2×9)+2}$, or C_9H_{20}. The formula C_nH_{2n+2} reflects the fact that each carbon in the chain has two hydrogen atoms except the two end carbons, which have three each. Thus the number of hydrogen atoms present is twice the number of carbon atoms plus two (for the extra two hydrogen atoms on the ends).

TABLE 20.1

Formulas of the First Ten Straight-Chain Alkanes

Name	Condensed Formula (C_nH_{2n+2})	Extended Formula
methane	CH_4	CH_4
ethane	C_2H_6	CH_3CH_3
propane	C_3H_8	$CH_3CH_2CH_3$
n-butane	C_4H_{10}	$CH_3CH_2CH_2CH_3$
n-pentane	C_5H_{12}	$CH_3CH_2CH_2CH_2CH_3$
n-hexane	C_6H_{14}	$CH_3CH_2CH_2CH_2CH_2CH_3$
n-heptane	C_7H_{16}	$CH_3CH_2CH_2CH_2CH_2CH_2CH_3$
n-octane	C_8H_{18}	$CH_3CH_2CH_2CH_2CH_2CH_2CH_2CH_3$
n-nonane	C_9H_{20}	$CH_3CH_2CH_2CH_2CH_2CH_2CH_2CH_2CH_3$
n-decane	$C_{10}H_{22}$	$CH_3CH_2CH_2CH_2CH_2CH_2CH_2CH_2CH_2CH_3$

Example 20.2

Using the General Formula for Alkanes

Show that the alkane with fifteen carbon atoms can be represented in terms of the general formula C_nH_{2n+2}.

Solution

In this case $n = 15$. The formula is $C_{15}H_{2(15)+2}$, or $C_{15}H_{32}$.

CHEMICAL IMPACT

Science, Technology, and Society

Plastic Tasters

The scene: A lab near Brussels, Belgium; room temperature 21 °C; humidity 60%. A woman in a white lab coat is sitting in a private cubicle in front of a row of glasses each filled with a liquid. The woman rinses out her mouth with pure water and then begins the tasting. Fine wines? Exotic coffees? Premium teas? No. The woman is tasting water that has had various plastics soaking in it.

What is going on here? This scene takes place every Tuesday through Friday at Exxon Chemicals' Machelen Research Center in Belgium, where trained tasters (called *organolepticians*) sniff and taste plastic-marinated water. Their job is to make sure that you never detect the taste or smell of plastic in your favorite cheese, meat, pizza, or other packaged foods. Today's shoppers expect clear plastic wrapping and plastic containers that keep food fresh, safe, and ready to use right out of the package. They also expect it to taste just like it came from the farm or from mom's kitchen.

Ensuring that plastic packaging does not impart a taste to the food stored inside is quite a challenge. That's where organoleptics—the art and science of tasting and smelling—comes in. To test a new type of plastic, the material is sealed into an aluminum bag with mineral water. After about a week the water is tasted by a panel of highly trained organolepticians. The sample is also checked for odors. Although highly sophisticated instruments are used to test the samples as well, the human nose and tongue have been found to be the most sensitive and reliable detectors of odors and tastes. For the plastic manufacturers, no taste means good business.

Produce wrapped in plastic.

Additional Examples

Determine the number of hydrogens on an alkane with

a. 8 carbons

18

b. 22 carbons

46

 Integrating the CHEMICAL IMPACT

Plastic Tasters

Discuss the effects of smell and taste on marketing a product. What products have "pleasing" smells added to them? Why? Should people with allergies have products available without smells? What colors are pleasing to people in foods? How do manufacturers determine the preferences of people for their products?

Section
20.3

Themes
Organization, Systems

Skills
Making comparisons, developing models, using the writing process

TEACHING TIPS

- Use the board to draw structural isomers with your students. Show them that structural isomers actually have a different order of atoms. Rotating a carbon to point up or down on the end of a chain, for instance, does not produce a new structure.

- Use strings of children's pop beads to illustrate that bending or twisting the string does not produce a change in the structure. To create a different order of beads, you must take the chain apart and put it together differently.

20.3 Structural Formulas and Isomerism

Objective: *To learn about structural isomers and how to draw their structural formulas.*

Butane and all succeeding alkanes exhibit structural isomerism. **Structural isomerism** occurs when two molecules have the same atoms but different bonds. That is, the molecules have the same formulas but different arrangements of the atoms. For example, butane can exist as a straight-chain molecule (normal butane, or *n*-butane) or with a branched-chain structure (called isobutane), as shown in **Figure 20.4.** Because of their different structures, these structural isomers have different properties.

	Ball-and-stick structure	Space-filling structure	Lewis structure
n-butane			
isobutane			

Figure 20.4
The structural isomers of C_4H_{10}. Each molecule is represented in three ways: a ball-and-stick structure, a space-filling structure, and a structure that shows the shared electrons as lines (a Lewis structure).

People wait to refill their butane gas canisters at a gas station in Belgrade.

638   Chapter 20   Organic Chemistry

Example 20.3

Drawing Structural Isomers of Alkanes

Draw the structural isomers of pentane, C_5H_{12}.

Solution

To find the isomeric structures for pentane, C_5H_{12}, we first write the straight carbon chain and then add the hydrogen atoms.

1. The straight-chain structure has the five carbon atoms in a row.

C—C—C—C—C

We can now add the H atoms.

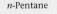

This can be written in shorthand form as

$CH_3—CH_2—CH_2—CH_2—CH_3$ or $CH_3—(CH_2)_3—CH_3$

and is called *n*-pentane.

2. Next we remove one C atom from the main chain and bond it to the second carbon in the chain.

Then we put on the H atoms, so that each carbon has four bonds.

This structure can be represented as

$$CH_3—\overset{\displaystyle CH_3}{\overset{|}{CH}}—CH_2—CH_3$$

and is called isopentane. *(continued)*

n-Pentane

Isopentane

20.3 Structural Formulas and Isomerism **639**

Draw three structural isomers of heptane, C_7H_{16}.

a.

b.

c.

d.

e.

f.

g.

(continued)

3. Finally, we take two carbons out of the chain to give the arrangement

```
        C
        |
    C—C—C
        |
        C
```

Adding the H atoms gives

```
              H
              |
          H—C—H
   H          |          H
   |          |          |
 H—C——————C——————C—H
   |          |          |
   H          |          H
          H—C—H
              |
              H
```

which can be written in shorthand form as

```
          CH₃
          |
  CH₃—C—CH₃
          |
          CH₃
```

Neopentane

This molecule is called neopentane.

The space-filling models for these molecules are shown in the margin. Note that all of these molecules have the formula C_5H_{12}, as required. Also note that the structures

```
                                CH₃
                                |
CH₃—CH₂—CH—CH₃    CH₃—CH—CH₂—CH₃    CH₃—CH₂—CH—CH₃
                                                     |                            |
                                                   CH₃                          CH₃
```

which might at first appear to be additional isomers, are actually identical to structure 2. All three of these structures have exactly the same skeleton of carbons as the structure shown in part 2. All of these structures have four carbons in the chain with one carbon on the side:

```
C—C—C—C
    |
    C
```

TEACHING TIP

This example is important for showing students that the three structures with four carbons in the chain and one branch are identical.

20.4 Naming Alkanes

Objective: *To learn the system for naming alkanes and substituted alkanes.*

Because there are literally millions of organic compounds, it would be impossible to remember common names for all of them. Just as we did in Chapter 4 for inorganic compounds, we must learn a systematic method for naming organic compounds. We will first consider the principles applied in naming alkanes and then summarize them as a set of rules.

1. The first four members of the alkane series are called methane, ethane, propane, and butane. The names of the alkanes beyond butane are obtained by adding the suffix *-ane* to the Greek root for the number of carbon atoms.

Number	Greek Root
5	*pent*
6	*hex*
7	*hept*
8	*oct*
9	*non*
10	*dec*

Therefore, the alkane

$$CH_3CH_2CH_2CH_2CH_2CH_2CH_2CH_3$$

which has eight carbons in the chain, is called octane.

(oct   –   ane)

Tells us there are eight carbons   Tells us it is an alkane

2. For a branched hydrocarbon, the longest continuous chain of carbon atoms gives the root name for the hydrocarbon. For example, in the alkane

$$
\begin{array}{c}
CH_3 \\
| \\
CH_2 \\
| \\
CH_2 \\
| \\
CH_3{-}CH_2{-}CH{-}CH_2{-}CH_3
\end{array}
$$

Six carbons

Five carbons

the longest continuous chain contains six carbon atoms. The specific name of this compound is not important at this point, but it will be named as a hexane (indicating a six-carbon chain).

3. Alkanes lacking one hydrogen atom can be attached to a hydrocarbon chain in place of one hydrogen atom. For example, the molecule

$$
\begin{array}{ccccccccc}
 & H & & H & & H & & H & & H \\
 & | & & | & & | & & | & & | \\
H{-} & C & {-} & C & {-} & C & {-} & C & {-} & C & {-}H \\
 & | & & | & & | & & | & & | \\
 & H & & H & & H & & (CH_3) & & H
\end{array}
$$

CH_3 substituted for H

20.4 Naming Alkanes   **641**

can be viewed as a pentane (five-carbon chain) in which one hydrogen atom has been replaced by a —CH₃ group, which is a methane, CH_4, molecule with a hydrogen removed. When a group is substituted for a hydrogen on an alkane chain, we call this group a *substituent*. To name the —CH₃ substituent, we start with the name of its parent alkane, drop the *-ane,* and add *-yl.* Therefore, —CH₃ is called *methyl.* Likewise, when we remove one hydrogen from ethane, CH_3CH_3, we get —CH₂CH₃. Dropping the *-ane* ending and adding *-yl* gives this group the name *ethyl.* Removal of a hydrogen from the end carbon of propane, $CH_3CH_2CH_3$, yields —CH₂CH₂CH₃, which is called the *propyl* group.

There are two ways in which the propyl group can be attached as a substituent. A hydrogen can be removed from an end carbon to give the propyl group or from the middle carbon to give the isopropyl group.

$$\begin{array}{c} | \\ CH_2 \\ | \\ CH_2 \\ | \\ CH_3 \end{array} \quad \text{or} \quad H_3C-\overset{\displaystyle |}{\underset{\displaystyle H}{C}}-CH_3$$

Name: Propyl   Isopropyl

When a hydrogen is removed from butane, $CH_3CH_2CH_2CH_3$, we get a butyl substituent. In the case of the butyl group, there are four ways in which the atoms can be arranged. These are shown, with their respective names, in **Table 20.2.**

The general name for an alkane when it functions as a substituent is *alkyl.* All of the common alkyl groups are shown in Table 20.2.

TABLE 20.2

The Most Common Alkyl Substituents and Their Names

Structure*	Name
—CH₃	methyl
—CH₂CH₃	ethyl
—CH₂CH₂CH₃	propyl
CH₃CHCH₃	isopropyl
—CH₂CH₂CH₂CH₃	butyl
CH₃CHCH₂CH₃	*sec*-butyl
—CH₂—C(H)—CH₃ with CH₃ below	isobutyl
—C(CH₃)—CH₃ with CH₃ above and below	*tert*-butyl

*The bond with one end open shows the point of attachment of the substituent.

4. We specify the positions of substituent groups by numbering sequentially the carbons in the longest chain of carbon atoms, starting at the end closest to the branching (the place where the first substituent occurs). For example, the compound

$$\underset{\text{Incorrect numbering} \quad 6 \qquad 5 \qquad 4 \qquad 3 \qquad 2 \qquad 1}{\underset{\text{Correct numbering} \quad 1 \qquad 2 \qquad 3 \qquad 4 \qquad 5 \qquad 6}{CH_3-CH_2-\overset{\overset{\displaystyle CH_3 \quad \text{Methyl substituent}}{|}}{CH}-CH_2-CH_2-CH_3}}$$

is called 3-methylhexane. Note that the top set of numbers is correct; the left end of the molecule is closest to the branching, and this gives the smallest number for the position of the substituent. Also note that a hyphen is written between the number and the name of the substituent.

5. When a given type of substituent occurs more than once, we indicate this by using a prefix. The prefix *di-* indicates two identical substituents, and *tri-* indicates three. For example, the compound

$$\overset{\overset{\displaystyle 1 \qquad 2 \qquad 3 \qquad 4 \qquad 5}{}}{CH_3-\underset{\underset{\displaystyle CH_3}{|}}{CH}-\underset{\underset{\displaystyle CH_3}{|}}{CH}-CH_2-CH_3}$$

has the root name pentane (five carbons in the longest chain). We use *di-* to indicate the two methyl substituents and use numbers to locate them on the chain. The name is 2,3-dimethylpentane.

The following rules summarize the principles we have just developed.

Rules for Naming Alkanes

1. Find the longest continuous chain of carbon atoms. This chain (called the parent chain) determines the base alkane name.

2. Number the carbons in the parent chain, starting at the end closest to any branching (the first alkyl substituent). When a substituent occurs the same number of carbons from each end, use the next substituent (if any) to determine from which end to start numbering.

3. Using the appropriate name for each alkyl group, specify its position on the parent chain with a number.

4. When a given type of alkyl group occurs more than once, attach the appropriate prefix (*di-* for two, *tri-* for three, and so on) to the alkyl name.

5. The alkyl groups are listed in alphabetical order, *disregarding any prefix.*

20.4 Naming Alkanes **643**

Name three structural isomers of heptane, C_7H_{16}.

n-heptane
2-methylhexane
3-methylhexane
2,3-dimethylpentane
2,4-dimethylpentane
2,2,3-trimethylbutane
2,2-dimethylpentane

TEACHING TIP

It is helpful to show students how to think about these isomer problems. An organized approach to drawing and naming isomers makes the process much simpler. Start with the longest carbon chain, remove one methyl group at a time, and try to place the group on as many new carbons as possible without producing duplicates. Naming each molecule will help to eliminate duplicates. If the names are the same, then the molecules are the same even if they look different in the drawing.

PROBLEM SOLVING

Note that placing the —CH_3 group on carbon 4 gives the same molecule as placing it on carbon 2.

Example 20.4

Naming Isomers of Alkanes

Draw the structural isomers for the alkane C_6H_{14}, and give the systematic name for each one.

Solution

We proceed systematically, starting with the longest chain and then rearranging the carbons to form the shorter, branched chains.

1. $CH_3CH_2CH_2CH_2CH_2CH_3$

   This alkane has six carbons all in the same continuous chain, so we call it hexane or, more properly, *n*-hexane, indicating that all of the carbon atoms are in the same chain.

2. We now take one carbon out of the main chain and make it a methyl substituent. This gives the molecule

   $$CH_3CHCH_2CH_2CH_3$$
   $$|$$
   $$CH_3$$

   The carbon skeleton is as follows:

   $$C-C-C-C-C$$
   $$|$$
   $$C$$

   Because the longest chain has five carbons, the base name is pentane. We have numbered the chain from the left, starting closest to the substituent, a methyl group. We indicate the position of the methyl group on the chain by the number 2, the number of the carbon to which it is attached. So the name is 2-methylpentane. Note that if we numbered the chain from the right end, the methyl group would be on carbon 4. We want the smallest possible number, so the numbering shown is correct.

3. The methyl substituent can also be on the number-3 carbon:

   $$CH_3CH_2CHCH_2CH_3$$
   $$|$$
   $$CH_3$$

   The name is 3-methylpentane. We have now exhausted all possibilities for placing a single methyl group on pentane.

4. Next we take two carbons out of the original six-member chain.

   $$CH_3CH-CHCH_3$$
   $$|\quad|$$
   $$CH_3\ CH_3$$

   The carbon skeleton is

   $$C-C-C-C$$
   $$|\ |$$
   $$C\ C$$

   The longest chain of this molecule has four carbons, so the root name is butane. Because there are two methyl groups (on carbons 2 and 3), we use the prefix *di-*. The name of the molecule is 2,3-dimethylbutane. Note that when two or more numbers are used, they are separated by a comma.

5. Two methyl groups can also be attached to the same carbon atom in the four-carbon chain to give the following molecule:

$$CH_3 - \underset{\underset{CH_3}{|}}{\overset{\overset{CH_3}{|}}{C}} - CH_2CH_3$$

The carbon skeleton is

$$\underset{\underset{C}{|}}{\overset{\overset{C}{|}}{\underset{1 \quad 2 \quad 3 \quad 4}{C - C - C - C}}}$$

The root name is butane, and there are two methyl groups on the number-2 carbon. The name is 2,2-dimethylbutane.

6. As we search for more isomers, we might try to place an ethyl substituent on the four-carbon chain to give the molecule

$$CH_3 - \underset{\underset{CH_3}{|}}{\overset{}{\underset{CH_2}{|}}}{CHCH_2CH_3}$$

The carbon skeleton is

$$\underset{\underset{C}{\overset{|}{\underset{C}{|}}}}{C - C - C - C}$$

We might be tempted to name this molecule 2-ethylbutane, but this is incorrect. Notice that there are five carbon atoms in the longest chain.

$$\underset{\underset{C}{\overset{|}{\underset{C}{\overset{|}{C}}}}_{1}}{C - C - C - C}{}^{3}_{4 \quad 5}$$

We can rearrange this carbon skeleton to give

$$\underset{1 \quad 2 \quad 3 \quad 4 \quad 5}{C - C - \overset{\overset{C}{|}}{C} - C - C}$$

This molecule is in fact a pentane (3-methylpentane), because the longest chain has five carbon atoms, so it is not a new isomer.

In searching for more isomers, we might try a structure such as

$$CH_3 - \underset{\underset{CH_2}{|}}{\overset{\overset{CH_3}{|}}{C}} - CH_3$$
$$\underset{CH_3}{|}$$

646

Answers to Self-Check Exercise 20.2

a.

This molecule is 5-ethyl-3-methyloctane.

b.

This molecule is 5-ethyl-3-methylheptane. Note that this chain could be numbered from the opposite direction to give the name 3-ethyl-5-methylheptane. These two names are equally correct.

Integrating the CHEMICAL IMPACT

www.Dot.Safety

Have students investigate the number of highways in your state that use these dots for safety. In some states a special blue dot is used to demark fire hydrants on the roadside. If the dots are not in use in your area, students could write their state representatives to urge their use. Look on the Internet to discover the safety records on roads using the dots versus the safety records on similar roads without the dots. The dots can also protect drivers from wandering into another lane at night or in poor visibility conditions.

(continued)

As we have drawn it, this molecule might appear to be a propane. However, the molecule has a longest chain of four atoms (look vertically), so the correct name is 2,2-dimethylbutane.

Thus there are five distinct structural isomers of C_6H_{14}: *n*-hexane, 2-methylpentane, 3-methylpentane, 2,3-dimethylbutane, and 2,2-dimethylbutane.

Self-Check Exercise 20.2

Name the following molecules.

So far we have learned how to name a compound by examining its structural formula. We must also be able to do the reverse: to write the structural formula from the name.

CHEMICAL IMPACT   **Consumer Connection**

www.Dot.Safety

Elbert Dysart Botts may have saved your life, even though you have probably never heard of him. Botts, who was born in rural Missouri in 1893, was a chemist who specialized in paints and who taught chemistry at San Jose State University in California. Eventually he went to work for the California Department of Transportation (Caltrans), where he tried unsuccessfully to find a paint for road stripes that would be both durable and visible even on rainy, gloomy nights. Discouraged by his failure, Botts decided that a reflective pavement marker might be a better solution. He and his team came up with a glass-and-ceramic marker that was visible at night for over 100 meters. The biggest problem was how to attach the markers to the pavement. Eventually Botts settled on a fast-setting epoxy developed by one of his former chemistry students, which would bond the reflectors to virtually any solid surface.

The first "Botts Dots" were put in service in California in 1966. Today, hundreds of millions of them all over the world protect drivers from straying out of their lanes.

"Botts Dots" highlight traffic lanes.

Example 20.5

Writing Structural Isomers from Names

Write the structural formula for each of the following compounds.

    a. 4-ethyl-3,5-dimethylnonane

    b. 4-*tert*-butylheptane

Solution

a. The root name nonane signifies a nine-carbon chain. Therefore, we have the following main chain of carbons:

$$\overset{1}{C}-\overset{2}{C}-\overset{3}{C}-\overset{4}{C}-\overset{5}{C}-\overset{6}{C}-\overset{7}{C}-\overset{8}{C}-\overset{9}{C}$$

The name indicates an ethyl group attached to carbon 4 and two methyl groups, one on carbon 3 and one on carbon 5. This gives the following carbon skeleton:

$$\overset{1}{C}-\overset{2}{C}-\overset{3}{C}-\overset{4}{C}-\overset{5}{C}-\overset{6}{C}-\overset{7}{C}-\overset{8}{C}-\overset{9}{C}$$
$$\qquad\quad C\ \ C\ \ C$$
$$\qquad\qquad C$$

When we add the hydrogen atoms, we get the final structure

$$\overset{1}{C}H\overset{2}{C}H_2\overset{3}{C}H-\overset{4}{C}H-\overset{5}{C}H\overset{6}{C}H_2\overset{7}{C}H_2\overset{8}{C}H_2\overset{9}{C}H_3$$

Methyl (CH₃) (CH₂) (CH₃) Methyl

CH₃

Ethyl

b. Heptane signifies a seven-carbon chain, and the *tert*-butyl group (see Table 20.2) is

$$H_3C-\overset{\displaystyle |}{\underset{\displaystyle CH_3}{C}}-CH_3$$

Thus we have the molecule

$$\overset{1}{C}H_3\overset{2}{C}H_2\overset{3}{C}H_2\overset{4}{C}H\overset{5}{C}H_2\overset{6}{C}H_2\overset{7}{C}H_3$$
$$H_3C-\overset{\displaystyle |}{\underset{\displaystyle CH_3}{C}}-CH_3$$

 Self-Check Exercise 20.3

Write the structural formula for 5-isopropyl-4-methyldecane.

Additional Examples

Draw the structural formula for each of the following compounds.

1. 3-methylheptane

2. 2,4-dimethylheptane

Answer to Self-Check Exercise 20.3

The root name decane indicates a ten-carbon chain. There is a methyl group at the number-4 position and an isopropyl group at the number-5 position. The structural formula is

Answers to Focus Questions

1. Carbon atoms form four bonds with other atoms and carbon can form molecules with long chains of carbon atoms.

2. **a.** tetrahedral

   b. trigonal planar

   c. linear

3. A saturated carbon compound contains only single bonds. An unsaturated compound contains both single and multiple bonds among the carbon atoms.

4. **a.** 3-methylheptane

   b. 2,3-dimethylbutane

   c. 2,3-dimethylbutane

   d. 2,3,4-trimethylheptane

5. Selected structural isomers follow:

   a. CH₃CH₂CH₂CH₂CH₂CH₂CH₂CH₃

   b. CH₃CHCH₂CH₂CH₂CH₂CH₃
            |
           CH₃

   c. CH₃CH₂CHCH₂CH₂CH₂CH₃
                |
               CH₃

   d. CH₃CH₂CH₂CHCH₂CH₂CH₃
                   |
                  CH₃

   e. CH₃CHCH₂CH₂CHCH₃
            | |
           CH₃   CH₃

   f. CH₃CH₂CHCHCH₂CH₃
                | |
               CH₃
               CH₃

   g. CH₃CHCH₂CHCH₂CH₃
            | |
           CH₃   CH₃

   h. CH₃CHCH—CHCH₃
            | | |
           CH₃ CH₃
           CH₃

   i.   CH₃
                 |
       CH₃—C—CH₂CHCH₃
            | |
           CH₃   CH₃

   j.   CH₃
            |
       CH₃—C—CH—CH₂CH₃
            | |
           CH₃ CH₃

   k.   CH₃
              |
       CH₃CHCHCH₂CH₂CH₃
              |
             CH₃

   l.   CH₃
                 |
       CH₃CHCCH₂CH₃
            |
           CH₃

   m.   CH₃ CH₃
             | |
       CH₃C—C—CH₃
             | |
            CH₃ CH₃

Sections 20.1–20.4

1. How are carbon and its bonding unusual compared to other elements?

2. Determine the shape of each of the following molecules (assume C is the central atom).

   a. CH₄

   b. H₂CO

   c. C₂H₂

3. How is a saturated carbon compound different from an unsaturated one?

4. Give the systematic name for each of the following alkanes.

   a. CH₃—CH—CH₂—CH₂—CH₂—CH₃
               |
              CH₂—CH₃

   b. CH₃—CH—CH—CH₃
               | |
              CH₃ CH₃

   c.   CH₃
                 |
       CH₃—CH—CH—CH₃
                 |
                CH₃

   d. CH₃—CH₂—CH₂—CH—CH—CH—CH₃
                       | | |
                      CH₃ CH₃ CH₃

5. Draw the structural formulas for at least five isomeric alkanes having the formula C₈H₁₈.

20.5 Petroleum

Objective: *To learn about the composition and uses of petroleum.*

Woody plants, coal, petroleum, and natural gas provide a vast resource of energy that originally came from the sun. By the process of photosynthesis, plants store energy that we can claim by burning the plants themselves or, more commonly, burning the decay products that have been converted to fossil fuels. Although the United States currently depends heavily on petroleum for energy, this dependency is a relatively recent phenomenon **(Figure 20.5).**

Figure 20.5
Energy sources used in the United States.

648 Chapter 20 Organic Chemistry

Active Learning

After introducing the material in Sections 20.5 to 20.7 in class, place the students in groups and have them work together on Sections 20.5–20.7: Team Learning Worksheet. Answers and/or discussion of these questions are located in the *Teacher Resources.*

Section 20.5

Themes
Form and Function, Models

Skills
Applying concepts, making comparisons

Student Preparation
Assign the students to read Sections 20.5 to 20.7 and to answer the Focus Questions at the end of Section 20.7 before coming to class.

Petroleum and natural gas deposits probably formed from the remains of marine organisms that lived approximately 500 million years ago. **Petroleum** is a thick, dark liquid composed largely of hydrocarbons containing from 5 to more than 25 carbon atoms. **Natural gas,** which is usually associated with petroleum deposits, consists mostly of methane but also contains significant amounts of ethane, propane, and butane.

To be used efficiently, petroleum must be separated by boiling into portions called fractions. The smaller hydrocarbons can be boiled off at relatively low temperatures; the larger molecules require successively higher temperatures. The major uses of various petroleum fractions are shown in **Table 20.3.**

The petroleum era began when the demand for lamp oil during the Industrial Revolution outstripped the traditional sources: animal fats and whale oil. In response to this increased demand, Edwin Drake drilled the first oil well in 1859 at Titusville, Pennsylvania. The petroleum from this well was refined to produce *kerosene* (fraction C_{10}—C_{18}), which served as an excellent lamp oil. *Gasoline* (fraction C_5—C_{12}) was of limited use and was often discarded. However, the importance of these fractions was reversed when the development of the electric light reduced the need for kerosene, and the advent of the "horseless carriage" signaled the birth of the gasoline age.

As gasoline became more important, new ways were sought to increase the yield of gasoline obtained from each barrel of petroleum. William Burton invented a process called *pyrolytic cracking* at Standard Oil of Indiana. In this process the heavier molecules of the kerosene fraction are heated to about 700 °C, which causes them to break (crack) into the smaller molecules characteristic of the gasoline fraction. As cars became larger, more efficient internal combustion engines were designed. Because of the uneven burning of the gasoline then available, these engines "knocked," producing unwanted noise and even engine damage. Intensive research to find additives that would promote smoother burning yielded tetraethyl lead, $(C_2H_5)_4Pb$, a very effective "antiknock" agent.

Adding tetraethyl lead to gasoline became a common practice, and by 1960 gasoline contained as much as 3 grams of lead per gallon. As we have discovered so often in recent years, technological advances can produce environmental problems. Lead in gasoline causes two important problems. First, it "poisons" the catalytic converters that have been added to exhaust systems to help prevent air pollution. Second, the use of leaded gasoline has greatly increased the amount of lead in the environment, where it can be ingested by animals and humans. For these reasons the use of lead in gasoline has been largely discontinued. This has required extensive (and expensive) modifications of engines and of the gasoline-refining process.

Distillation (separation by boiling) was discussed in Section 2.5.

Pumping unleaded gas.

TABLE 20.3

Uses of the Various Petroleum Fractions

Petroleum Fraction*	Major Uses
C_5—C_{12}	gasoline
C_{10}—C_{18}	kerosene jet fuel
C_{15}—C_{25}	diesel fuel heating oil lubricating oil
>C_{25}	asphalt

*Shows the chain lengths present in each fraction.

WHAT IF Comments

More than 90% of all petroleum currently produced is used for fuels. If we could not use petroleum for fuels, we would need to develop technologies that utilize resources such as the sun, wind, water, and nuclear fission.

Using the TOP TEN

Have the students find the population of each of the Top Ten countries. Then have them determine the amount of joules consumed by each country. How does this figure compare with the per-person energy consumption?

MINI-DEMO

If you can obtain a sample of crude oil, bring it to class along with a sample of gasoline to show students the differences between the two.

20.5 Petroleum **649**

Themes
Form and Function

Skills
Applying concepts, making comparisons, making predictions

TEACHING TIPS

- Classifying reactions is a new skill for students. It is important to help them practice classifying organic reactions. Explain how you think about each reaction so as to classify it.

- In substitution reactions, any one of the hydrogens can be substituted. Not all substitutions will produce different products. This idea may be confusing to students. Use three-dimensional models to illustrate this concept, one molecule at a time.

TEACHING TIP

For dehydrogenation reactions point out that a hydrogen is removed from each of two adjacent carbons and that these two carbons form a double bond.

20.6 Reactions of Alkanes

Objective: *To learn various types of chemical reactions that alkanes undergo.*

At low temperatures alkanes are not very reactive because the C—C and C—H bonds in alkanes are relatively strong. For example, at 25 °C alkanes do not react with acids, bases, or strong oxidizing agents. This chemical inertness makes alkanes valuable as lubricating materials and as the backbone for structural materials such as plastics.

At sufficiently high temperatures, however, alkanes *react vigorously with oxygen*. These **combustion reactions** are the basis for the alkanes' widespread use as fuels. For example, the combustion reaction of butane with oxygen is

$$2C_4H_{10}(g) + 13O_2(g) \rightarrow 8CO_2(g) + 10H_2O(g)$$

The alkanes can also undergo **substitution reactions**—reactions in which *one or more hydrogen atoms of the alkane are replaced* (substituted) *by different atoms*. We can represent the substitution reaction of an alkane with a halogen molecule as follows:

$$R—H + X_2 \rightarrow R—X + HX$$

where R represents an alkyl group and X represents a halogen atom. For example, methane can react successively with chlorine as follows:

The symbol *hv* signifies ultraviolet light used to furnish energy for the reaction.

$$CH_4 + Cl_2 \xrightarrow{hv} CH_3Cl + HCl$$
Chloromethane

$$CH_3Cl + Cl_2 \xrightarrow{hv} CH_2Cl_2 + HCl$$
Dichloromethane

$$CH_2Cl_2 + Cl_2 \xrightarrow{hv} CHCl_3 + HCl$$
Trichloromethane
(chloroform)

$$CHCl_3 + Cl_2 \xrightarrow{hv} CCl_4 + HCl$$
Tetrachloromethane
(carbon tetrachloride)

The *hv* above each arrow signifies that ultraviolet light is needed to furnish the energy to break the Cl—Cl bond to produce chlorine atoms:

$$Cl_2 \rightarrow Cl \cdot + Cl \cdot$$

A chlorine atom has an unpaired electron, indicated by the dot, which makes it very reactive and able to disrupt the C—H bond.

Notice that each step in the process involves replacement of a C—H bond by a C—Cl bond. That is, a chlorine atom *substitutes* for a hydrogen atom. The names of the products of these reactions use the term *chloro* for the chlorine substituents with a prefix that gives the number of chlorine atoms present: *di-* for two, *tri-* for three, and *tetra-* for four. No number is used to describe the chlorine positions in this case, because methane has only one carbon atom. Note that the products of the last two reactions have two names, the systematic name and the common name in parentheses.

Besides substitution reactions, alkanes can undergo **dehydrogenation reactions** in which *hydrogen atoms are removed* and the product is an unsaturated hydrocarbon. For example, in the presence of a catalyst (chromium(III) oxide) at high temperatures, ethane can be dehydrogenated, yielding ethylene, C_2H_4.

$$CH_3CH_3 \xrightarrow[500 \ °C]{Cr_2O_3} CH_2{=}CH_2 + H_2$$
Ethylene

20.7 Alkenes and Alkynes

Objectives: *To learn to name hydrocarbons with double bonds (alkenes) and triple bonds (alkynes).*
To understand addition reactions.

We have seen that alkanes are saturated hydrocarbons—each of the carbon atoms is bound to four atoms by single bonds. Hydrocarbons that contain carbon–carbon *double bonds*

$$\text{\Large$\diagdown$C}=\text{C}\diagup$$

are called **alkenes.** Hydrocarbons with carbon–carbon *triple bonds* are called **alkynes.** Alkenes and alkynes are unsaturated hydrocarbons.

Multiple carbon–carbon bonds result when hydrogen atoms are removed from alkanes. Alkenes that contain one carbon–carbon double bond have the general formula C_nH_{2n}. The simplest alkene, C_2H_4, commonly known as *ethylene,* has the Lewis structure

$$\begin{array}{c} H \qquad\quad H \\ \diagdown\;\;\diagup \\ C=C \\ \diagup\;\;\diagdown \\ H \qquad\quad H \end{array}$$

The ball-and-stick model of ethylene is shown in **Figure 20.6.**

The system for naming alkenes and alkynes is similar to the one we have used for alkanes. The following rules are useful.

Figure 20.6
The ball-and-stick model of ethylene (ethene).

Acetylene gas burning. The acetylene is formed by the reaction of calcium carbide, CaC_2, with water in the flask.

Rules for Naming Alkenes and Alkynes

1. Select the longest continuous chain of carbon atoms that contains the double or triple bond.

2. For an alkene, the root name of the carbon chain is the same as for the alkane, except that the *-ane* ending is replaced by *-ene*. For an alkyne, the *-ane* is replaced by *-yne*. For example, for a two-carbon chain we have

   $$CH_3CH_3 \qquad CH_2{=}CH_2 \qquad CH{\equiv}CH$$
   Ethane   Ethene   Ethyne

3. Number the parent chain, starting at the end closest to the double or triple bond. The location of the multiple bond is given by the lowest-numbered carbon involved in the bond. For example,

   $$\underset{\substack{1 \quad 2 \quad 3 \quad 4}}{CH_2{=}CHCH_2CH_3}$$

   is called 1-butene and

   $$\underset{\substack{1 \quad 2 \quad\; 3 \quad 4}}{CH_3CH{=}CHCH_3}$$

   is called 2-butene.

4. Substituents on the parent chain are treated the same way as in naming alkanes. For example, the molecule $ClCH{=}CHCH_2CH_3$ is called 1-chloro-1-butene.

20.7 Alkenes and Alkynes **651**

TEACHING TIP

Use models to show the shapes of the alkene and alkyne molecules around the single and multiple bonds.

Additional Examples

Name each of the following molecules.

1. $CH_3CH=CHCH_2CH_2CH_2-CH_2CH_2CH_3$
   2-decene

2. $CH_3CH_2C\equiv CCH_3$
   2-pentyne

TEACHING TIP

Molecules that have the same number of carbons and hydrogens but have double or triple bonds between different carbons are isomers. Students can identify which molecules are the same and which are structural isomers from the different locator numbers for the double and triple bonds in the names of the compounds.

 Answers to Self-Check Exercise 20.4

a. The longest chain has eight carbon atoms with a double bond, so the root name is octene. The double bond exists between carbons 3 and 4, so the name is 3-octene. There is a methyl group on the number-2 carbon. The name is 2-methyl-3-octene.

b. The carbon chain has five carbons with a triple bond between carbons 1 and 2. The name is 1-pentyne.

Example 20.6

Naming Alkenes and Alkynes

Name each of the following molecules.

   a. $CH_3CH_2CHCH=CHCH_3$
             |
             CH_3

   b. $CH_3CH_2C\equiv CCHCH_2CH_3$
                 CH_2
                 |
                 CH_3

Solution

a. The longest chain contains six carbon atoms, and we number the carbons starting from the end closest to the double bond.

    6   5   4 3   2 1
   $CH_3CH_2CHCH=CHCH_3$
             |
             CH_3

Thus the root name for the hydrocarbon is 2-hexene. Remember to use the lower number of the two carbon atoms involved in the double bond. There is a methyl group attached to the number-4 carbon. Therefore, the name of the compound is 4-methyl-2-hexene.

b. The longest chain of carbon atoms is seven carbons long, and the chain is numbered as shown (starting from the end closest to the triple bond).

    1 2   3   4 5 6   7
   $CH_3CH_2C\equiv CCHCH_2CH_3$
                CH_2
                |
                CH_3

The hydrocarbon is a 3-heptyne (we use the lowest-numbered carbon in the triple bond). Because there is an ethyl group on carbon number 5, the full name is 5-ethyl-3-heptyne.

 Self-Check Exercise 20.4

Name the following molecules.

   a. $CH_3CH_2CH_2CH_2CH=CHCHCH_3$
                       |
                       CH_3

   b. $CH_3CH_2CH_2C\equiv CH$

Reactions of Alkenes

Because alkenes and alkynes are unsaturated, their most important reactions are **addition reactions,** in which *new atoms form single bonds to the carbons formerly involved in the double or triple bonds.* An addition reaction for an alkene changes the carbon–carbon double bond to a single bond, giving a saturated hydrocarbon (each carbon bonded to four atoms). For example, **hydrogenation reactions,** which use H_2 as a reactant, lead to the addition of a hydrogen atom to each carbon formerly involved in the double bond.

$$CH_2{=}CHCH_3 + H_2 \xrightarrow{\text{Catalyst}} CH_3CH_2CH_3$$

1-Propene   Propane

Hydrogenation of molecules with double bonds is an important industrial process, particularly in the manufacture of solid shortenings. Unsaturated fats (fats containing double bonds) are generally liquids at room temperatures, whereas saturated fats (those containing C—C single bonds) are solids. The liquid unsaturated fats are converted to solid saturated fats by hydrogenation.

Halogenation of unsaturated hydrocarbons involves the addition of halogen atoms. Here is an example:

$$CH_2{=}CHCH_2CH_2CH_3 + Br_2 \rightarrow CH_2BrCHBrCH_2CH_2CH_3$$

1-Pentene   1,2-Dibromopentane

Another important reaction of certain unsaturated hydrocarbons is **polymerization,** a process in which many small molecules are joined together to form a large molecule. Polymerization will be discussed in Section 20.16.

Focus Questions

Sections 20.5–20.7

1. Write a balanced equation for the combustion of propane.

2. How is a substitution reaction in alkanes different from a dehydrogenation reaction, as both involve removing hydrogen atoms from the molecule?

3. Draw structural formulas for the following.
   a. 2,5-dimethyl-3-hexene
   b. 4-methyl-2-pentene
   c. iodoethyne
   d. 3-methylpentyne

4. Why do alkenes and alkynes react by addition reactions, whereas alkanes do not?

5. How is a halogenation reaction similar to a hydrogenation reaction?

Focus Questions   **653**

 Answers to Focus Questions

1. $C_3H_8(l) + 5O_2(g) \rightarrow 3CO_2(g) + 4H_2O(g)$

2. In a substitution reaction a hydrogen is replaced by another atom. In a dehydrogenation reaction hydrogen atoms are removed from adjacent carbons to create a double bond between carbon atoms.

3. a.
$$CH_3C\!-\!\overset{\overset{\textstyle H}{|}}{C}{=}C\!-\!\overset{\overset{\textstyle H}{|}}{C}\!-\!CH_3$$
$$\underset{CH_3}{|}\qquad\underset{H}{|}\quad\underset{CH_3}{|}$$

   b.
$$CH_3\!-\!C{=}\overset{\overset{\textstyle H}{|}}{C}\!-\!\overset{\overset{\textstyle H}{|}}{C}\!-\!CH_3$$
$$\qquad\underset{H}{|}\qquad\underset{CH_3}{|}$$

   c. $H\!-\!C{\equiv}C\!-\!I$

   d.
$$H\!-\!C{\equiv}C\!-\!CH\!-\!CH_2CH_3$$
$$\qquad\qquad\underset{CH_3}{|}$$

4. Alkanes contain only single bonds. For an addition reaction to occur, a double or triple bond must be present on which atoms can be added.

5. In both cases a diatomic molecule is added across a double or triple bond.

Themes
Organization, Form and Function

Skills
Applying concepts, interpreting diagrams, making comparisons, making predictions

Student Preparation
Assign the students to read Sections 20.8 and 20.9 and to answer the Focus Questions at the end of Section 20.9 before coming to class.

Active Learning
After introducing the material in Sections 20.8 and 20.9 in class, place the students in groups and have them work together on Sections 20.8–20.9: Team Learning Worksheet. Answers and/or discussion of these questions are located in the *Teacher Resources.*

TEACHING TIPS

• A model that shows the difference between cyclohexane (a puckered ring) and benzene (a flat ring) would be useful in helping students understand aromatic hydrocarbons.

• You may wish to discuss the delocalization of the electrons in the benzene ring as an example of a limitation of our bonding model. Drawing the benzene ring structure with the circle inside the hexagon reminds us that benzene behaves differently than a carbon molecule with a double bond.

20.8 Aromatic Hydrocarbons

Objective: *To learn about the aromatic hydrocarbons.*

When mixtures of hydrocarbons from natural sources, such as petroleum or coal, are separated, certain of the compounds that emerge have pleasant odors and are thus known as **aromatic hydrocarbons.** When these substances, which include wintergreen, cinnamon, and vanillin, are examined, they are all found to contain a common feature: a six-membered ring of carbon atoms called the benzene ring. **Benzene** has the formula C_6H_6 and a planar (flat) structure in which all of the bond angles are 120° **(Figure 20.7).**

When we examine the bonding in the benzene ring, we find that more than one Lewis structure can be drawn. That is, the double bonds can be located in different positions, as shown in **Figure 20.8.** Because the actual bonding is a combination of the structures represented in Figure 20.8, the benzene ring is usually shown with a circle **(Figure 20.9).**

Figure 20.7
Benzene, C_6H_6, consists of six carbon atoms bonded together to form a ring. Each carbon has one hydrogen atom bonded to it. All of the atoms in benzene lie in the same plane. This representation does not show all the bonds between the carbon atoms in the ring.

(a)

(b)

Figure 20.8
(a) Two Lewis structures for the benzene ring.
(b) As a shorthand notation, the rings are usually represented without labeling the carbon and hydrogen atoms.

Figure 20.9
To show that the bonding in the benzene ring is a combination of different Lewis structures, the ring is drawn with a circle inside.

Cinnamon is an aromatic hydrocarbon.

20.9 Naming Aromatic Compounds

Objective: *To learn the system for naming aromatic compounds.*

TEACHING TIPS

- Students need to learn the basic monosubstituted benzene molecule names, as they are used repeatedly.
- Many students forget that when benzene is a substituent the correct name for the group is *phenyl-*, not *benzyl-*.

Substituted benzene molecules are formed by replacing one or more of the H atoms on the benzene ring with other atoms or groups of atoms. We will consider benzene rings with one substituent (called monosubstituted benzenes) first.

Monosubstituted Benzenes

The systematic method for naming monosubstituted benzenes uses the substituent name as a prefix of benzene. For example, the molecule

is called chlorobenzene, and the molecule

is called ethylbenzene.

Sometimes monosubstituted benzene compounds have special names. For example, the molecule

has the systematic name methylbenzene. However, for convenience it is given the name toluene. Likewise, the molecule

which might be called hydroxybenzene, has the special name phenol. Several examples of monosubstituted benzenes are shown in **Figure 20.10**.

Sometimes it is more convenient to name compounds if we view the benzene ring itself as a substituent. For example, the compound

Mothballs used to contain naphthalene, composed of "fused" benzene rings, but now contain p-dichlorobenzene.

Figure 20.10
Names of some common monosubstituted benzenes.

is most easily named as a 1-butene with a benzene ring as a substituent on the number-3 carbon. When the benzene ring is used as a substituent, it is called the **phenyl** (pronounced fen'-ill) **group.** So the name of this compound is 3-phenyl-1-butene. As another example, the compound

$$\underset{1}{CH_3}\underset{2}{CH}\underset{3}{CH_2}\underset{4}{CH}\underset{5}{CH_2}\underset{6}{CH_3}$$

is named 4-chloro-2-phenylhexane. Remember, we start to number the chain from the end closest to the first substituent and name the substituents in alphabetical order (chloro before phenyl).

Disubstituted Benzenes

When there is more than one substituent on the benzene ring, numbers are used to indicate substituent position. For example, the compound

is named 1,2-dichlorobenzene. Another naming system uses the prefix *ortho-* (*o-*) for two adjacent substituents, *meta-* (*m-*) for two substituents with one carbon between them, and *para-* (*p-*) for two substituents opposite each other. This means that 1,2-dichlorobenzene can also be called *ortho*-dichlorobenzene or *o*-dichlorobenzene. Likewise, the compound

can be called 1,3-dichlorobenzene or *m*-dichlorobenzene. The compound

is named 1,4-dichlorobenzene or *p*-dichlorobenzene.

Benzenes that have two methyl substituents have the special name xylene. So the compound

which might be called 1,3-dimethylbenzene, is instead called *m*-xylene (*meta*-xylene).

TEACHING TIPS

• When naming disubstituted benzenes, give the names in both naming systems. Students tend to find the system using numbers a little easier than the older (*ortho-*, *meta-*, *para-*) system.

• Naming disubstituted benzenes can be complicated. When both substituents use the same two numbers as locators, but the substituents are different, only one number is used because we assume that the first substituent is on the number-1 carbon. You will need to help your students understand this distinction.

Ortho- (*o-*) means two adjacent substituents.

Para- (*p-*) means two substituents directly across the ring from each other.

Meta- (*m-*) means two substituents with one carbon between them.

When two different substituents are present on the benzene ring, one is always assumed to be at carbon number 1, and this number is not often specified in the name. For example, the compound

is named 2-bromochlorobenzene, not 2-bromo-1-chlorobenzene. Various examples of disubstituted benzenes are shown in **Figure 20.11.**

Benzene is the simplest aromatic molecule. More complex aromatic systems can be viewed as consisting of a number of "fused" benzene rings. Some examples are given in **Table 20.4.**

1,2-Dibromobenzene
(o-dibromobenzene)

1,3-Dibromobenzene
(m-dibromobenzene)

1,4-Dibromobenzene
(p-dibromobenzene)

1,4-Dimethylbenzene
(p-xylene)

1,2-Dimethylbenzene
(o-xylene)

1,3-Dimethylbenzene
(m-xylene)

2-Nitrotoluene
(o-nitrotoluene)

3-Bromonitrobenzene
(m-bromonitrobenzene)

3-Chlorotoluene
(m-chlorotoluene)

Figure 20.11
Some selected disubstituted benzenes and their names. Common names are given in parentheses.

TABLE 20.4

More Complex Aromatic Molecules

Structural Formula	Name	Use
	naphthalene	
	anthracene	dyes
	phenanthrene	dyes, explosives, and synthesis of drugs

20.9 Naming Aromatic Compounds **657**

Name the following compounds.

1.

CH$_3$
|
CH
|
CH$_3$

2-phenylpropane

2.

Cl

Br

3-bromochlorobenzene

✓ **Answers to Self-Check Exercise 20.5**

a. 2-chloronitrobenzene or *o*-chloronitrobenzene

b. 4-phenyl-2-hexene

Example 20.7

Naming Aromatic Compounds

Name the following compounds.

a. CH$_2$CH$_3$

CH$_2$CH$_3$

c. CH$_3$—CH—C≡CH

b. CH$_3$

Br

d. CH$_3$

O$_2$N   NO$_2$

NO$_2$

Solution

a. There are ethyl groups in the 1 and 3 (or *meta*-) positions, so the name is 1,3-diethylbenzene or *m*-diethylbenzene.

b. The

CH$_3$

group is called toluene. The bromine is in the 4 (or *para*-) position. The name is 4-bromotoluene or *p*-bromotoluene.

c. In this case we name the compound as a butyne with a phenyl substituent. The name is 3-phenyl-1-butyne.

d. We name this compound as a substituted toluene (with the —CH$_3$ group assumed to be on carbon number 1). So the name is 2,4,6-trinitrotoluene. This compound is more commonly known as TNT, a component of high explosives.

✓ **Self-Check Exercise 20.5**

Name the following compounds.

a. NO$_2$

Cl

b. CH$_3$CH$_2$CH—CH=CHCH$_3$

1. Draw the structures for the ring compounds with formulas C_6H_{12} and C_6H_6.
   a. Name each compound.
   b. How are they similar?
   c. How are they different?
   d. Would C_6H_{12} react by addition or substitution reactions? Why?
   e. Would C_6H_6 react by addition or substitution reactions? Why?

2. Name each of the following aromatic or substituted aromatic compounds.

   a.

   c.

   b.

   d.

CHEMICAL IMPACT

Science, Technology, and Society

Termite Mothballing

Termites typically do not get a lot of respect. They are regarded as lowly, destructive insects. However, termites are the first insects known to fumigate their nests with naphthalene, a chemical long used by humans to prevent moths from damaging wool garments. Although termites are not concerned about holes in their sweaters, they may use naphthalene to ward off microbes and predatory ants, among other pests.

Gregg Henderson and Jian Chen, of the Louisiana State University Agricultural Center in Baton Rouge, have observed that Formosan termites are unusually resistant to naphthalene. In fact these insects build their underground galleries from chewed wood glued together with saliva and excrement. This "glue" (called *carton*) contains significant amounts of naphthalene, which evaporates and permeates the air in the underground tunnels. The source of the naphthalene is unknown—it might be a metabolite from a food source of the termites or it might be produced from the carton by organisms present in the nest. Whatever the source of the

Formosan subterranean termites.

naphthalene, this interesting example shows how organisms use chemistry to protect themselves.

Naphthalene

1. The structures are

a. cyclohexane and benzene

b. Both molecules contain six carbons linked in a ring.

c. Cyclohexane contains no double bonds and twice the number of hydrogen atoms as benzene. Benzene contains three double bonds and half as many hydrogen atoms as cyclohexane.

d. This is a substitution reaction since there are no double bonds.

e. Although benzene looks like it should undergo addition reactions, the delocalization of electrons in the ring makes it behave like a saturated hydrocarbon. It undergoes substitution reactions to form the monosubstituted and disubstituted benzenes discussed in the text.

2. a. *ortho*-dimethylbenzene or 1,2-dimethylbenzene or 2-methyltoluene

   b. 1,3,5-tribromobenzene

   c. 2-chloronitrobenzene or 2-nitrochlorobenzene

   d. naphthalene

Integrating the CHEMICAL IMPACT

Termite Mothballing

Have students investigate other animals and plants that use chemical means to protect their environments. Many excellent biological examples of this phenomenon exist. This Chemical Impact makes an excellent connection to biology.

Section 20.10

Themes
Models, Patterns of Change, Form and Function

Skills
Applying concepts, interpreting diagrams, making comparisons, making predictions

Student Preparation
Assign the students to read Sections 20.10 to 20.12 and to answer the Focus Questions at the end of Section 20.12 before coming to class.

Active Learning
After introducing the material in Sections 20.10 to 20.12 in class, place the students in groups and have them work together on Sections 20.10–20.12: Team Learning Worksheet. Answers and/or discussion of these questions are located in the *Teacher Resources*.

MINI-DEMO

If you have samples of molecules containing the functional groups you plan to discuss, bring them to class. These chemicals have interesting odors and physical properties.

USING TECHNOLOGY

 Table 20.5
Functional Groups can be used in class to help students recognize the functional groups and learn to draw their structures correctly.

TEACHING TIP

You may wish to spend some time drawing organic molecules on the board or overhead projector, with students circling the functional groups. Learning to identify the functional group is the first step in being able to predict the organic reaction that occurs when chemicals are mixed.

20.10 Functional Groups

Objective: *To learn the common functional groups in organic molecules.*

The vast majority of organic molecules contain elements in addition to carbon and hydrogen. However, most of these substances can be viewed as **hydrocarbon derivatives,** molecules that are fundamentally hydrocarbons but that have additional atoms or groups of atoms called **functional groups.** The common functional groups are listed in **Table 20.5;** one example of a compound that contains that functional group is given for each. We will briefly describe some of these functional groups in the next few sections and learn to name the compounds that contain them.

TABLE 20.5
The Common Functional Groups

Class	Functional Group	General Formula*	Example
halohydrocarbons†	—X (F, Cl, Br, I)	R—X	CH_3I
alcohols	—OH	R—OH	CH_3OH
ethers	—O—	R—O—R'	$CH_3—O—CH_3$
aldehydes	—C(=O)H	R—C(=O)H	H—C(=O)H
ketones	—C(=O)—	R—C(=O)—R'	$CH_3—C(=O)—CH_3$
carboxylic acids	—C(=O)—OH	R—C(=O)—OH	$CH_3—C(=O)—OH$
esters	—C(=O)—O—	R—C(=O)—O—R'	$CH_3—C(=O)—OCH_2CH_3$
amines	—NH$_2$	R—NH$_2$	CH_3NH_2

*R and R' represent hydrocarbon fragments, which may be the same or different. †These substances are also called alkyl halides.

20.11 Alcohols

Objective: *To learn about simple alcohols and explain how to name them.*

Alcohols are characterized by the presence of the —OH group. Some common alcohols are listed in **Table 20.6.** The systematic name for an alcohol is obtained by replacing the final *-e* of the parent hydrocarbon name

TABLE 20.6
Some Common Alcohols

Formula	Systematic Name	Common Name
CH_3OH	methanol	methyl alcohol
CH_3CH_2OH	ethanol	ethyl alcohol
$CH_3CH_2CH_2OH$	1-propanol	*n*-propyl alcohol
CH_3CHCH_3 OH	2-propanol	isopropyl alcohol

660   Chapter 20   Organic Chemistry

Section 20.11

Themes
Patterns of Change, Form and Function

Skills
Applying concepts, interpreting diagrams, making predictions

MINI-DEMO

Bring samples of rubbing alcohol, methanol, and ethylene glycol (antifreeze) to class as examples of alcohols.

with -ol. The position of the —OH group is specified by a number (where necessary) chosen such that it is the smallest of the substituent numbers.

The rules for naming alcohols follow.

Rules for Naming Alcohols

1. Select the longest chain of carbon atoms containing the —OH group.
2. Number the chain such that the carbon with the —OH group gets the lowest possible number.
3. Obtain the root name from the name of the parent hydrocarbon chain by replacing the final -e with -ol.
4. Name any other substituents as usual.

For example, the compound

$$CH_3CHCH_2CH_2CH_3$$
$$|$$
$$OH$$

is called 2-pentanol because the parent carbon chain is pentane. The compound

$$CH_3CH_2CHCH_2CH_2CH_3$$
$$|$$
$$OH$$

is called 3-hexanol.

Alcohols are classified according to the number of hydrocarbon fragments (alkyl groups) bonded to the carbon where the —OH group is attached. Thus we have

$$R—CH_2OH$$

$$\underset{R'}{\overset{R}{\diagdown}}CHOH$$

$$R'—\underset{R''}{\overset{R}{\underset{|}{\overset{|}{C}}}}OH$$

Primary alcohol (one R group)
Secondary alcohol (two R groups)
Tertiary alcohol (three R groups)

where R, R', and R" (which may be the same or different) represent hydrocarbon fragments (alkyl groups).

Example 20.8

Naming Alcohols

Give the systematic name for each of the following alcohols, and specify whether the alcohol is primary, secondary, or tertiary.

a. $CH_3CHCH_2CH_3$
       $|$
       OH

b. $ClCH_2CH_2CH_2OH$

c. CH_3
       $|$
       $CH_3CCH_2CH_2CH_2CH_2Br$
       $|$
       OH

(continued)

20.11 Alcohols **661**

Additional Examples

Give the systematic names for each of the following alcohols, and specify whether the alcohol is primary, secondary, or tertiary.

1.   OH
           $|$
$CH_3—CCH_2CH_3$
           $|$
           CH_3

2-methyl-2-butanol; tertiary alcohol

2. $CH_3CH_2CH_2CHCH_2OH$
                   $|$
                   CH_3

2-methyl-1-pentanol; primary alcohol

Chapter 20 Organic Chemistry **661**

Solution

a. The chain is numbered as follows:

$$\overset{1}{C}H_3\overset{2}{C}H\overset{3}{C}H_2\overset{4}{C}H_3$$
$$\underset{OH}{|}$$

The compound is called 2-butanol, because the —OH group is located at the number-2 position of a four-carbon chain. Note that the carbon to which the —OH is attached also has two R groups (—CH₃ and —CH₂CH₃) attached. Therefore, this is a *secondary* alcohol.

$$\text{CH}_3 - \overset{\overset{H}{|}}{C} - \text{CH}_2\text{CH}_3$$
$$\underset{\text{R}}{} \quad \underset{\text{OH}}{|} \quad \underset{\text{R'}}{}$$

b. The chain is numbered as follows:

$$\overset{3}{Cl} - \overset{}{C}H_2 - \overset{2}{C}H_2 - \overset{1}{C}H_2 - OH$$

Remember that in naming an alcohol, we give the carbon with the —OH attached the lowest possible number. The name is 3-chloro-1-propanol. This is a *primary* alcohol.

$$\text{Cl} - \text{CH}_2\text{CH}_2 - \overset{\overset{H}{|}}{\underset{\underset{H}{|}}{C}} - \text{OH}$$

One R group
attached to the
carbon with the
—OH group

c. The chain is numbered as follows:

$$\overset{1}{CH_3} - \overset{2}{\underset{\underset{OH}{|}}{\overset{\overset{CH_3}{|}}{C}}} - \overset{3}{CH_2} - \overset{4}{CH_2} - \overset{5}{CH_2} - \overset{6}{CH_2Br}$$

The name is 6-bromo-2-methyl-2-hexanol. This is a tertiary alcohol, because the carbon where the —OH is attached also has three R groups attached.

 Self-Check Exercise 20.6

Name each of the following alcohols, and specify whether it is primary, secondary, or tertiary.

a. CH₃CH₂CH₂CH₂CH₂OH

b.
$$\text{CH}_3 - \overset{\overset{CH_3}{|}}{\underset{\underset{OH}{|}}{C}} - \text{CH}_3$$

c.
$$\text{CH}_3 - \text{CH} - \text{CH}_2\text{CH}_2\overset{\overset{Br}{|}}{C}\text{HCH}_3$$
$$\underset{OH}{|}$$

662   Chapter 20   Organic Chemistry

TEACHING TIP

When determining whether an alcohol is primary, secondary, or tertiary, focus on the carbon where the —OH is attached. Students often erroneously focus on the —OH group itself, which does not reveal anything about the classification.

 Answers to Self-Check Exercise 20.6

a. 1-pentanol; primary alcohol

b. 2-methyl-2-propanol (but this alcohol is usually called tertiary butyl alcohol); tertiary alcohol

c. 5-bromo-2-hexanol; secondary alcohol

20.12 Properties and Uses of Alcohols

Objective: *To learn about how some alcohols are made and used.*

TEACHING TIP

You may want to compare the toxicities of methanol, ethanol, and ethylene glycol.

Although there are many important alcohols, the simplest ones, methanol and ethanol, have the greatest commercial value. Methanol, also known as *wood alcohol* because it was formerly obtained by heating wood in the absence of air, is prepared industrially (over 20 million tons per year in the United States) by the hydrogenation of carbon monoxide (catalyzed by a ZnO/Cr_2O_3 mixture).

$$CO + 2H_2 \xrightarrow[ZnO/Cr_2O_3]{400\ ^\circ C} CH_3OH$$

Methanol is used as a starting material for the synthesis of acetic acid and many types of adhesives, fibers, and plastics. It also can be used as a motor fuel. In fact, pure methanol has been used for many years in the engines of the cars that are driven in the Indianapolis 500 and similar races. Methanol is especially useful in racing engines because of its resistance to knock. It is advantageous for regular cars because it produces less carbon monoxide (a toxic gas) in the exhaust than does gasoline. Methanol is highly toxic to humans, and swallowing it can lead to blindness and death.

Ethanol, which is used in the production of some beverages, is produced by the fermentation of the sugar glucose in corn, barley, grapes, and so on.

$$\underset{\text{Glucose}}{C_6H_{12}O_6} \xrightarrow{\text{Yeast}} \underset{\text{Ethanol}}{2CH_3CH_2OH} + 2CO_2$$

This reaction is catalyzed by the enzymes (biological catalysts) found in yeast, and it can proceed only until the alcohol content reaches approximately 13%, at which point the yeast can no longer survive. Beverages with higher alcohol content are made by distilling the fermentation mixture.

Ethanol, like methanol, can be burned in the internal combustion engines of automobiles and is now commonly added to gasoline to form gasohol. It is also used in industry as a solvent and for the preparation of acetic acid. The commercial production of ethanol (half a million tons per year in the United States) is carried out by reaction of water with ethylene.

$$CH_2{=}CH_2 + H_2O \xrightarrow[\text{Catalyst}]{\text{Acid}} CH_3CH_2OH$$

Many alcohols are known that contain more than one —OH group. The one that is the most important commercially is ethylene glycol,

$$\begin{array}{l} H_2C{-}OH \\ \ \ \ | \\ H_2C{-}OH \end{array}$$

a toxic substance that is the major constituent of most automobile antifreezes.

The simplest aromatic alcohol is

Ethylene glycol is a component of antifreeze, which is used to protect the cooling systems of automobiles.

Section 20.13

Themes
Organization, Patterns of Change, Form and Function

Skills
Applying concepts, interpreting diagrams, making comparisons

Student Preparation
Assign the students to read Sections 20.13 and 20.14 and to answer the Focus Questions at the end of Section 20.14 before coming to class.

Active Learning
After introducing the material in Sections 20.13 and 20.14 in class, place the students in groups and have them work together on Sections 20.13–20.14: Team Learning Worksheet. Answers and/or discussion of these questions are located in the *Teacher Resources*.

664

---

commonly called **phenol.** Most of the 1 million tons of phenol produced annually in the United States is used to produce polymers for adhesives and plastics.

Focus Questions   **Sections 20.10–20.12**

1. Name the following compounds:
   a. CH₃CH₂CH₂CH₂OH
   b. CH₃CH(OH)CH₃

                CH₃
                |
   c. HOCH₂CHCHCH₂CH₂OH
                     |
                     CH₃

2. Draw a structural formula for each of the following alcohols. Indicate whether the alcohol is primary, secondary, or tertiary.
   a. 2-propanol   **c.** 4-isopropyl-2-heptanol
   b. 2-methyl-2-propanol **d.** 2,3-dichloro-1-pentanol

3. Why is methanol important commercially?

20.13 Aldehydes and Ketones

Objective: *To learn the general formulas for aldehydes and ketones and some of their uses.*

Aldehydes and ketones contain the **carbonyl group**

   —C—
   ‖
   O

In **ketones** this group is bonded to two carbon atoms; an example is acetone:

   CH₃—C—CH₃
      ‖
      O

The general formula for a ketone is

   R—C—R′
      ‖
      O

where R and R′ are alkyl groups that may or may not be the same. In a ketone the carbonyl group is never at the end of the hydrocarbon chain. (If it were, it would be an aldehyde.)

   In **aldehydes** the carbonyl group always appears at the end of the hydrocarbon chain. There is always at least one hydrogen bonded to the

Vanillin

Cinnamaldehyde

$CH_3CH_2CH_2C\overset{O}{\underset{H}{\big\langle}}$

Butyraldehyde

Figure 20.12
Some common aldehydes.

$$R-OH \longrightarrow R-C\overset{O}{\underset{H}{\big\langle}}$$

carbonyl carbon atom. An example of an aldehyde is acetaldehyde:

$$CH_3-\underset{\underset{O}{\|}}{C}-H$$

The general formula for an aldehyde is

$$R-\underset{\underset{O}{\|}}{C}-H$$

We often use compact formulas for aldehydes and ketones. For example, formaldehyde (where R = H) and acetaldehyde (where R = CH₃) are usually represented as HCHO and CH_3CHO, respectively. Acetone is often written as CH_3COCH_3 or $(CH_3)_2CO$.

Many ketones have useful solvent properties (acetone is often found in nail polish remover, for example) and are frequently used in industry for this purpose. Aldehydes typically have strong odors. Vanillin is responsible for the pleasant odor of vanilla beans; cinnamaldehyde produces the characteristic odor of cinnamon. On the other hand, the unpleasant odor of rancid butter arises from the presence of butyraldehyde and butyric acid. (See **Figure 20.12** for the structures of these compounds.)

Aldehydes and ketones are most often produced commercially by the oxidation of alcohols. Oxidation of a *primary* alcohol gives the corresponding aldehyde, for example,

$$CH_3CH_2OH \xrightarrow{\text{Oxidation}} CH_3C\overset{O}{\underset{H}{\big\langle}}$$

Oxidation of a *secondary* alcohol results in a ketone:

$$CH_3\underset{\underset{OH}{|}}{C}HCH_3 \xrightarrow{\text{Oxidation}} CH_3\underset{\underset{O}{\|}}{C}CH_3$$

20.14 Naming Aldehydes and Ketones

Objective: To learn the systems for naming aldehydes and ketones.

We obtain the systematic name for an aldehyde from the parent alkane by removing the final *-e* and adding *-al*. For ketones the final *-e* is replaced by *-one*, and a number indicates the position of the carbonyl group where necessary. The carbon chain in ketones is numbered such that the

$$-\underset{\underset{O}{\|}}{C}-$$

carbon gets the lowest possible number. In aldehydes the

$$-\underset{\underset{O}{\|}}{C}-H$$

is always at the end of the chain and is always assumed to be carbon

20.14 Naming Aldehydes and Ketones **665**

number 1. The positions of other substituents are specified by numbers, as usual. The following examples illustrate these principles.

$$H-\overset{\overset{\displaystyle O}{\|}}{C}-H \qquad CH_3-\overset{\overset{\displaystyle O}{\|}}{C}-H \qquad CH_3-\overset{\overset{\displaystyle O}{\|}}{C}-CH_3$$

Methanal (formaldehyde) Ethanal (acetaldehyde) Propanone (acetone)

$$CH_3-\overset{\overset{\displaystyle O}{\|}}{C}-CH_2CH_2CH_3 \qquad CH_3\underset{\overset{\displaystyle |}{Cl}}{CH}CH_2\overset{\overset{\displaystyle O}{\|}}{C}-H$$

2-Pentanone   3-Chlorobutanal

The names in parentheses are common names that are used much more often than the systematic names.

Another common aldehyde is benzaldehyde (an aromatic aldehyde), which has the structure

Benzaldehyde

An alternative system for naming ketones specifies the substituents attached to the C=O group. For example, the compound

$$CH_3\overset{\overset{\displaystyle }{C}}{\underset{\overset{\displaystyle \|}{O}}{}}CH_2CH_3$$

is called 2-butanone when we use the system just described. However, this molecule can also be named methyl ethyl ketone and is commonly referred to in industry as MEK (*m*ethyl *e*thyl *k*etone):

Another example is the use of the name ketone for the compound

O
C
CH₃ Methyl

Phenyl

which is commonly called methyl phenyl ketone.

Example 20.9

Naming Aldehydes and Ketones

Name the following molecules.

a.

$$CH_3$$
$$CH_3C—CHCH_3 \quad \text{(Give two names.)}$$
$$\quad \| \quad$$
$$\quad O \quad$$

c. CH_3CH_2

b. H

NO_2

d. $CH_3CHCH_2CH_2CHO$
$\quad | \quad$
$\quad Cl \quad$

Solution

a. We can name this molecule as a 2-butanone because the longest chain has four carbon atoms (butane root) with the

$$\text{\Large $>$}C{=}O$$

group in the number 2 position (the lowest possible number). Because the methyl group is in the number 3 position, the name is 3-methyl-2-butanone. We can also name this compound methyl isopropyl ketone.

CH_3
(CH_3)   CH   Isopropyl
Methyl   CH_3
          C
          ‖
          O

b. We name this molecule as a substituted benzaldehyde (the nitro group is in the number 3 position): 3-nitrobenzaldehyde. It might also be named *m*-nitrobenzaldehyde.

c. We name this molecule as a ketone: ethyl phenyl ketone.

d. The name is 4-chloropentanal. Note that an aldehyde group is always at the end of the chain and is automatically assigned as the number 1 carbon.

 Self-Check Exercise 20.7

Name the following molecules.

a.
$$\quad\quad O$$
$$\quad\quad \|$$
$$CH_3CH_2CCHCH_2CH_3$$
$$\quad\quad\quad |$$
$$\quad\quad\quad CH_2CH_3$$

b. $CH_3CH_2CH_2CHCH_2CH_2CH_2CH_2CH_2CHO$
$$\quad\quad\quad\quad |$$
$$\quad\quad\quad\quad CH_3CHCH_3$$

Additional Examples

Name the following molecules.

1.
$$\quad H \quad O$$
$$\quad | \quad \|$$
$$CH_3C—C—CH_2CH_2CH_3$$
$$\quad |$$
$$\quad CH_3$$

2-methyl-3-hexanone

2.
$$\quad\quad\quad CH_3 \quad O$$
$$\quad\quad\quad | \quad\quad \|$$
$$CH_3CH_2—C—CH_2C—H$$
$$\quad\quad\quad |$$
$$\quad\quad\quad H$$

3-methylpentanal

 Answers to Self-Check Exercise 20.7

a. 4-ethyl-3-hexanone
Because the compound is named as a hexanone, the carbonyl group is assigned the lowest possible number.

b. 7-isopropyldecanal

1. The most important structural characteristic is the carbonyl group.

2. In ketones the carbonyl group is located between two other carbons; in aldehydes the carbonyl group is an end carbon.

3. a.

$$CH_3CH_2CCH_2C-H$$

with CH_3 and O (double bond) above, H below

b.

$$CH_3CH_2-C-C-CH_3$$

with CH_3 above, H and O below

c.

$$CH_3-C-\text{(phenyl ring)}$$

with O above

d.

$$CH_3C-C-C-H$$

with H, H, O above and H, OH below

e.

$$CH_3CH_2C-H$$

with O above

CELEBRITY CHEMICAL

Polyhydroxyamide (PHA)

Have students research other "smart chemicals." Another example of a smart molecule is memory metal, which was discussed in Chapter 14.

---

1. What is the most important structural characteristic of aldehydes or ketones?

2. How is a ketone different from an aldehyde?

3. Draw a structural formula for each of the following.
   a. 3-methylpentanal
   b. 3-methyl-2-pentanone
   c. methyl phenyl ketone
   d. 2-hydroxybutanal
   e. propanal

CELEBRITY CHEMICAL

Polyhydroxyamide (PHA)

When an airplane makes a crash landing, the major danger is fire. So the FAA (Federal Aviation Administration) is looking hard for fire-resistant materials for airplane interiors. One very promising material is a smart material called PHA (polyhydroxamide). PHA is "plastic" that can be molded into parts useful for airplane interiors, such as seats, overhead bins, and wall panels. The best news about PHA is that when it is heated, it changes chemically into a new material called PBO (polybenzoxazole), which has relatively low flammability:

Thus the "smart" PHA changes to fire-resistant PBO when it "senses" the heat of a fire.

The interior of an airliner contains a great deal of plastic.

20.15 Carboxylic Acids and Esters

Objective: *To learn the structures and names of the common carboxylic acids.*

Carboxylic acids are characterized by the presence of the **carboxyl group**, —COOH, which has the structure

$$-\overset{\displaystyle O}{\underset{\displaystyle O-H}{C}}$$

The general formula of a carboxylic acid is RCOOH, where R represents the hydrocarbon fragment. These molecules typically are weak acids in aqueous solution. That is, the dissociation (ionization) equilibrium

$$RCOOH(aq) + H_2O(l) \rightleftharpoons H_3O^+(aq) + RCOO^-(aq)$$

lies far to the left—only a small percentage of the RCOOH molecules are ionized.

We name carboxylic acids by dropping the final -*e* from the parent alkane (the longest chain containing the —COOH group) and adding -*oic*. Carboxylic acids are frequently known by their common names. For example, CH_3COOH, often written $HC_2H_3O_2$ and commonly called acetic acid, has the systematic name ethanoic acid because the parent alkane is ethane. Several carboxylic acids, their systematic names, and their common names are given in **Table 20.7.** Other examples of carboxylic acids are shown in **Figure 20.13.** Note that the —COOH group is always assigned the number 1 position in the chain.

Carboxylic acids can be produced by oxidizing primary alcohols with a strong oxidizing agent. For example, we can oxidize ethanol to acetic acid by using potassium permanganate.

$$CH_3CH_2OH \xrightarrow{\text{KMnO}_4(aq)} CH_3COOH$$

A carboxylic acid reacts with an alcohol to form an ester and a water molecule. For example, the reaction of acetic acid and ethanol produces the ester ethyl acetate and water.

$$CH_3\overset{\displaystyle O}{\overset{\|}{C}}-OH \quad H-OCH_2CH_3 \rightarrow CH_3\overset{\displaystyle O}{\overset{\|}{C}}-OCH_2CH_3 + H_2O$$

React to form water

COOH

Benzoic acid

COOH

NO$_2$

p-Nitrobenzoic acid

$CH_3CHCH_2CH_2COOH$
|
Br

4-Bromopentanoic acid

CH_2CH_2COOH
|
Cl

3-Chloropropanoic acid

Figure 20.13
Some carboxylic acids.

TABLE 20.7		
Several Carboxylic Acids, Their Systematic Names, and Their Common Names		
Formula	**Systematic Name**	**Common Name**
HCOOH	methanoic acid	formic acid
CH_3COOH	ethanoic acid	acetic acid
CH_3CH_2COOH	propanoic acid	propionic acid
$CH_3CH_2CH_2COOH$	butanoic acid	butyric acid
$CH_3CH_2CH_2CH_2COOH$	pentanoic acid	valeric acid

20.15 Carboxylic Acids and Esters **669**

 Section 20.15

Themes
Organization, Patterns of Change, Form and Function

Skills
Applying concepts, interpreting diagrams, making comparisons

Student Preparation
Assign the students to read Sections 20.15 and 20.16 and to answer the Focus Questions at the end of Section 20.16 before coming to class.

Active Learning
After introducing the material in Sections 20.15 and 20.16 in class, place the students in groups and have them work together on Sections 20.15–20.16: Team Learning Worksheet. Answers and/or discussion of these questions are located in the *Teacher Resources.*

Laboratory
Experiment 86:
Ester Synthesis, Microscale

Laboratory
Experiment 87:
Saponification, Traditional

The smell of bananas results from an aromatic ester.

Amyl is a common name for $CH_3CH_2CH_2CH_2CH_2-$.

Computer-generated space-filled model of acetylsalicylic acid (aspirin).

This reaction can be represented in general as follows:

$$RCOOH + R'OH \rightarrow RCOOR' + H_2O$$

Acid   Alcohol   Ester   Water

An **ester** has the following general formula:

$$R-C\overset{\displaystyle O}{\underset{\displaystyle O-R'}{\big\|}}$$

From the acid   From the alcohol

Esters often have a sweet, fruity odor that contrasts markedly with the often-pungent odors of the parent carboxylic acids. For example, the odor of bananas derives from *n*-amyl acetate:

$$CH_3C\overset{\displaystyle O}{\underset{\displaystyle OCH_2CH_2CH_2CH_2CH_3}{\big\|}}$$

and that of oranges from *n*-octyl acetate:

$$CH_3C-OC_8H_{17}$$
$$\underset{O}{\big\|}$$

Like carboxylic acids, esters are often referred to by their common names. The name consists of the alkyl name from the alcohol followed by the acid name, where the *-ic* ending is replaced by *-ate*. For example, the ester

$$CH_3C\overset{\displaystyle O}{\underset{\displaystyle O-CH}{\big\|}}\overset{\displaystyle CH_3}{\underset{\displaystyle CH_3}{}}$$

is made from acetic acid, CH_3COOH, and isopropyl alcohol,

$$CH_3CHCH_3$$
$$\underset{OH}{|}$$

and is called isopropyl acetate. The systematic name for this ester is isopropylethanoate (from ethanoic acid, the systematic name for acetic acid).

A very important ester is formed from the reaction of salicylic acid and acetic acid.

Salicylic acid   Acetic acid   Acetylsalicylic acid

The product is acetylsalicylic acid, commonly known as *aspirin*, which is manufactured in huge quantities and is widely used as an analgesic (painkiller).

670   Chapter 20   Organic Chemistry

20.16 Polymers

Objective: *To learn about some common polymers.*

Polymers are large, usually chain-like molecules that are built from small molecules called *monomers*. Polymers form the basis for synthetic fibers, rubbers, and plastics and have played a leading role in the revolution brought about in our lives by chemistry during the past 50 years. (Many important biomolecules are also polymers.)

The simplest and one of the best-known synthetic polymers is *polyethylene,* which is constructed from ethylene monomers. Its structure is

$$nCH_2{=}CH_2 \xrightarrow{\text{Catalyst}} \left(\begin{array}{c} \text{H} \quad \text{H} \\ | \quad \ | \\ \text{C}{-}\text{C} \\ | \quad \ | \\ \text{H} \quad \text{H} \end{array}\right)_n$$

Ethylene   Polyethylene

where *n* represents a large number (usually several thousand). Polyethylene is a tough, flexible plastic used for piping, bottles, electrical insulation, film for packaging, garbage bags, and many other purposes. Its properties can be varied by using substituted ethylene monomers. For example, when tetra-fluoroethylene is the monomer, the polymer Teflon is obtained.

$$n\left(\begin{array}{c} \text{F} \quad\quad \text{F} \\ \ \ \diagdown \quad\ \diagup \\ \ \ \text{C}{=}\text{C} \\ \ \ \diagup \quad\ \diagdown \\ \text{F} \quad\quad \text{F} \end{array}\right) \longrightarrow \left(\begin{array}{c} \text{F} \quad \text{F} \\ | \quad \ | \\ \text{C}{-}\text{C} \\ | \quad \ | \\ \text{F} \quad \text{F} \end{array}\right)_n$$

Tetrafluoroethylene   Teflon

Because of the resistance of the strong C—F bonds to chemical attack, Teflon is an inert, tough, and nonflammable material that is widely used for electrical insulation, nonstick coatings for cooking utensils, and bearings for low-temperature applications.

Other similar polyethylene-type polymers are made from monomers containing chloro, methyl, cyano, and phenyl substituents **(Table 20.8).** In each case, the carbon–carbon double bond in the substituted ethylene monomer becomes a single bond in the polymer. The different substituents lead to a wide variety of properties.

The polyethylene polymers illustrate one of the major types of polymerization reactions, called **addition polymerization,** in which the monomers simply "add together" to form the polymer and there are no other products.

Another common type of polymerization is **condensation polymerization,** in which a small molecule, such as water, is formed for each extension of the polymer chain. The most familiar polymer produced by condensation is *nylon.* Nylon is a **copolymer,** because two different types of monomers combine to form the chain (a **homopolymer,** by contrast, results from the polymerizing of a single type of monomer). One common form of nylon is produced when hexamethylenediamine and adipic acid react by splitting out a water molecule to form a C—N bond:

Nylon netting
magnified 62 times.

Hexamethylenediamine   Adipic acid

20.16   Polymers   **671**

Themes
Organization, Patterns of Change, Form and Function

Skills
Applying concepts, interpreting diagrams, making comparisons

Laboratory
Experiment 88:
Slime, Traditional

Laboratory
Experiment 89:
Gluep, In Text

TEACHING TIPS

- Do not expect students to be able to tell which functional groups should interact on monomers to form polymers.

- You can bring in common household items made from the polymers discussed in this section—for example, polyethylene bags and bottles, polystyrene toys, PVC pipe, and Teflon-coated pans.

STUDENT ACTIVITY

Have students bring in examples of plastics with a recycling code on the bottom. Have students investigate the meaning of these codes. Use the Internet to learn more about recycling plastics.

The molecule formed, which is called a **dimer** (two monomers joined), can undergo further condensation reactions because it has an amino group at one end and a carboxyl group at the other. Thus both ends are free to react with another monomer. Repetition of this process leads to a long chain of the type

$$\left(\begin{array}{c} \overset{H}{\underset{|}{N}} - (CH_2)_6 - \overset{H}{\underset{|}{N}} - \overset{O}{\underset{\|}{C}} - (CH_2)_4 - \overset{O}{\underset{\|}{C}} \end{array} \right)_n$$

TABLE 20.8

Some Common Synthetic Polymers, Their Monomers, and Applications

Monomer Name and Formula	Polymer Name and Formula	Applications
ethylene $H_2C{=}CH_2$	polyethylene $-(CH_2-CH_2)_n-$	plastic piping, bottles, electrical insulation, toys
propylene $H_2C{=}\overset{H}{\underset{\underset{CH_3}{\|}}{C}}$	polypropylene $-(CH-CH_2CH-CH_2)_n-$ with CH_3 groups	film for packaging, carpets, lab wares, toys
vinyl chloride $H_2C{=}\overset{H}{\underset{\underset{Cl}{\|}}{C}}$	polyvinyl chloride (PVC) $-(CH_2-CH)_n-$ with Cl	piping, siding, floor tile, clothing, toys
acrylonitrile $H_2C{=}\overset{H}{\underset{\underset{CN}{\|}}{C}}$	polyacrylonitrile (PAN) $-(CH_2-CH)_n-$ with CN	carpets, fabrics
tetrafluoroethylene $F_2C{=}CF_2$	Teflon $-(CF_2-CF_2)_n-$	coating for cooking utensils, electrical insulation, bearings
styrene $H_2C{=}\overset{H}{\underset{\underset{\phi}{\|}}{C}}$	polystyrene $-(CH_2CH)_n-$	containers, thermal insulation, toys
butadiene $H_2C{=}\overset{H}{\underset{}{C}}-\overset{H}{\underset{}{C}}{=}CH_2$	polybutadiene $-(CH_2CH{=}CHCH_2)_n-$	tire tread, coating resin
butadiene and styrene (see above)	styrene–butadiene rubber $(CH-CH_2-CH_2-CH{=}CH-CH_2)_n$	synthetic rubber

Figure 20.14
The reaction to form nylon can be carried out at the interface of two immiscible liquid layers in a beaker. The bottom layer contains adipoyl chloride,

dissolved in CCl_4, and the top layer contains hexamethylenediamine,

$$H_2N—(CH_2)_6—NH_2$$

dissolved in water. A molecule of HCl is formed as each C—N bond forms. This is a variation of the reaction to form nylon discussed in the text.

which is the general structure of nylon. The reaction to form nylon occurs quite readily and is often used as a classroom demonstration **(Figure 20.14).** The properties of nylon can be varied by changing the number of carbon atoms in the chain of the acid or amine monomers.

More than 1 million tons of nylon are produced annually in the United States for use in clothing, carpets, rope, and so on. Many other types of condensation polymers are also produced. For example, Dacron is a copolymer formed from the condensation reaction of ethylene glycol (a dialcohol) and *p*-terephthalic acid

CHEMICAL IMPACT

Polymers Are Tacky

Nonlethal means for dealing with violent situations constitute a problem for law enforcement officials worldwide. Water cannons and rubber bullets are two examples of nonfatal methods used for dealing with mob action. Now there is another way—sticky foam.

Although the "dummy" in the photo looks like an alien of the most fearsome type, it actually has been sprayed with a sticky polymer foam developed at Sandia National Laboratories. The sticky foam was originally developed in the 1960s for classified nuclear security operations, but in the past few years the Justice Department has asked Sandia to develop a portable sprayer for the foam to use for law enforcement purposes.

Tom Goolsby, a mechanical engineer working on the project, explains that the sprayer can shoot the material a distance of 30 feet in a stream about one-fourth inch in diameter. The foam quickly expands to 50 times its original size, however, creating snakes of glue that "stay sticky forever." In tests the foam has proved capable of immobilizing people by wrapping them with "snakes" or by sticking them to walls or floors. The foam is incredibly sticky. It can be cleaned off the skin with mineral oil but at the rate of only one square inch per minute. In the future criminals may have more than just sticky fingers.

A dummy that has been sprayed with a sticky polymer foam.

20.16 Polymers **673**

Integrating the CHEMICAL IMPACT

Polymers Are Tacky

You can make a fun and interesting polymer foam by purchasing Mountains in Minutes from your local hobby or model railroad store. Mix the two components in a plastic cup and pour them into a latex glove. When the foam swells the glove will fill up, forming a hand. As the foam sets, the hand will become hard. You can then give your students a hand!

Teaching Notes Be careful when handling the nylon, which is coated with HCl until it has been neutralized with $NaHCO_3(aq)$. Be sure to dispose of all excess chemicals as required.

USING TECHNOLOGY

Animation and Video

Chemistry in Motion, **Demonstration 34, Synthesis of Nylon**

Answers to Focus Questions

1. Organic chemists write the formula CH_3COOH because it tells us on sight that the compound is a carboxylic acid. The structure of the compound is given in the formula.

2.

3. propanoic acid + methanol yields methylpropanoate

4. All of the monomers in a polymer do not have to be the same. An example where they are not the same is synthetic rubber.

(a dicarboxylic acid).

$$HOCH_2CH_2O-H \quad HO-\underset{\text{Ethylene glycol}}{} \quad \underset{H_2O}{\downarrow} \quad \underset{p\text{-Terephthalic acid}}{}-O-H$$

The repeating unit of Dacron is

$$\left(\!\!-OCH_2CH_2-O-\overset{O}{\underset{\parallel}{C}}-\bigcirc-\overset{O}{\underset{\parallel}{C}}-\!\!\right)_{\!n}$$

Note that this polymerization involves a carboxylic acid and an alcohol to form an ester group,

$$-O-\overset{O}{\underset{\parallel}{C}}-$$

Thus Dacron is called a **polyester.** By itself or blended with cotton, Dacron is widely used in fibers for the manufacture of clothing.

Focus Questions

Sections 20.15–20.16

1. Why do organic chemists often write the formula for acetic acid as CH_3COOH (instead of $HC_2H_3O_2$)?

2. To make an ester, a carboxylic acid is reacted with an alcohol. Water is removed to form the new ester. Circle the water that is removed in the following reaction and draw the ester that results:

$$CH_3CH_2\overset{O}{\underset{\parallel}{C}}-OH + H-OCH_3$$

3. Name each of the compounds in your reaction for Question 2.

4. Do all of the monomers in a polymer have to be the same? Give examples to support your answer.

Problem

Can you make a cross-linked polymer from white glue?

Introduction

Polymers are large chain-like molecules that are built from small molecules called monomers. You have used polymers, such as Teflon and nylon, in everyday life. Polymers are also used in plastic bottles, carpets, clothing, and synthetic rubber.

Cross-linked polymers consist of polymer chains connected by chemical bonds. Substances such as Slime or Gak are cross-linked polymers. Cross-linking polyvinyl acetate (which is present in most white glues) with laundry borax can make a substance called gluep.

In this lab activity, you will make gluep from white glue and laundry borax. You will also test its properties.

Prelab Assignment

Read the entire lab experiment before you begin.

Materials

Goggles	Water
Apron	Borax solution
Plastic cups	White glue
Wax paper	Baking soda
Plastic spoons	Vinegar
Food coloring	

Safety

If you come in contact with any solution, wash the contacted area thoroughly.

Procedure

Part I: Making Gluep

1. Pour about 15 mL (one tablespoon) of white glue into a plastic cup.
2. Add about 15 mL of water to the white glue and stir. Add a drop or two of food coloring. Record your observations.
3. Add about 10 mL (two teaspoons) of borax solution (provided by your teacher) to the glue–water mixture and stir. Record your observations.
4. Use the plastic spoon to transfer the gluep onto wax paper. Use a paper towel to get rid of any excess liquid.
5. Squeeze out the excess liquid and roll the gluep into a ball.

Part II: Testing Gluep's Properties

1. Does a ball made from gluep bounce? Drop your ball from a height of 2 feet onto a noncarpeted floor and measure how high the ball bounces.
2. Some substances you can buy at a toy store can lift an image from the newspaper. Can gluep do this?

Part III: Reacting Gluep with Vinegar and Baking Soda

1. Place a small ball (1 cm in diameter) of gluep in a cup. Add about 20 drops of vinegar and stir. Record your observations.
2. Add about half a teaspoon of baking soda to this mixture and stir. Record your observations.

Cleaning Up

Clean up all materials and wash your hands thoroughly.

Data/Observations

1. Write a paragraph discussing your observations when making gluep.
2. How high could your gluep ball bounce?
3. Can gluep lift an image from the newspaper?
4. What happened when vinegar was added to gluep? What happened when baking soda was added?

Analysis and Conclusions

1. Write a paragraph summarizing the properties of gluep.
2. Explain your observations when gluep reacted with vinegar and baking soda.

Something Extra

Vary the proportions of water and borax solution in making gluep and retest its properties.

675

CHEMISTRY in the LABORATORY

Gluep
Objectives

1. To make a cross-linked polymer (gluep) from white glue and laundry borax
2. To test the properties of gluep

Skills

Making observations, applying concepts, drawing conclusions, using the writing process

Materials

Goggles	Water
Apron	Borax
Plastic cups	solution
Wax paper	White glue
Plastic spoons	Baking soda
Food coloring	Vinegar

Preparation Hints

The borax solution should be 4% by mass (add 4 g of borax to 96 mL of water).

Prelab Discussion

The materials in this lab are not hazardous, but students should wash their hands thoroughly after completing this lab.

Do not leave the gluep on clothes or wood surfaces because it will stain these materials.

Post-Lab Discussion

Have students compare their observations when making gluep and testing its properties.

Disposal

Gather all materials from the students and dispose of them properly.

Sample Data/Answers
Data/Observations

1. Answers will vary.
2. Answers will vary. The gluep balls should bounce well.
3. Yes, the gluep can lift an image from the newspaper.
4. When vinegar is added to gluep, the ball "falls apart." When baking soda is added to it, the cross-links reform and the gluep re-gels and bubbles.

Analysis and Conclusions

1. Responses will vary.
2. Vinegar is acidic and the cross-links break because the acid attracts the —OH groups of the borate ion. The baking soda is basic and neutralizes the acid. Carbon dioxide is a product.

Something Extra

Varying the amounts of water and borax solution will change the gluep (from "slimier" to more "rubber-like").

Chapter Review

Answers to End of Chapter Problems

1. Carbon has the unusual ability to bond strongly to itself, forming long chains or rings of carbon atoms. There are many possible arrangements for a long chain of carbon atoms, so there are many possible carbon compounds.

2. Four. Carbon atoms have four valence electrons. By making four bonds, carbon atoms complete their valence octet.

3. A double bond represents the sharing of an extra pair of electrons between two bonded atoms. Two examples are

$$
\begin{array}{cc}
\overset{\displaystyle H}{\underset{\displaystyle H}{\overset{|}{\underset{|}{C}}}}=\overset{\displaystyle H}{\underset{\displaystyle H}{\overset{|}{\underset{|}{C}}}} & \text{and} \quad \overset{\displaystyle H}{\underset{\displaystyle H}{\overset{|}{\underset{|}{C}}}}=\overset{\displaystyle H}{\underset{\displaystyle H}{\overset{|}{\underset{|}{C}}}}-\overset{\displaystyle H}{\underset{\displaystyle H}{\overset{|}{\underset{|}{C}}}}-H
\end{array}
$$

4. four; tetrahedral

5. A saturated hydrocarbon is one in which all carbon–carbon bonds are single bonds, with each carbon atom forming bonds to four other atoms. The saturated hydrocarbons are called alkanes.

6. The geometry around each carbon is a tetrahedral, making the angles 109.5°. To be "straight," the angles would have to be 180°.

7. (a)

heptane,
$CH_3CH_2CH_2CH_2CH_2CH_2CH_3$

(b)

nonane, $CH_3CH_2CH_2CH_2$ $CH_2CH_2CH_2CH_2CH_3$

Key Terms

organic chemistry (p. 633)
biomolecules (p. 633)
hydrocarbon (20.2)
saturated (20.2)
unsaturated (20.2)
alkane (20.2)
normal (straight-chain or unbranched) hydrocarbons (20.2)
structural isomerism (20.3)
petroleum (20.5)
natural gas (20.5)
combustion reaction (20.6)
substitution reaction (20.6)
dehydrogenation reaction (20.6)
alkene (20.7)
alkyne (20.7)
addition reaction (20.7)
hydrogenation reaction (20.7)
halogenation (20.7)
polymerization (20.7)

aromatic hydrocarbon (20.8)
benzene (20.8)
phenyl group (20.9)
hydrocarbon derivative (20.10)
functional group (20.10)
alcohol (20.11)
phenol (20.12)
carbonyl group (20.13)
ketone (20.13)
aldehyde (20.13)
carboxylic acid (20.15)
carboxyl group (20.15)
ester (20.15)
polymer (20.16)
addition polymerization (20.16)
condensation polymerization (20.16)
copolymer (20.16)
homopolymer (20.16)
dimer (20.16)
polyester (20.16)

Summary

1. The study of carbon-containing compounds and their properties is called organic chemistry. Most organic compounds contain chains or rings of carbon atoms. The organic molecules responsible for maintaining and reproducing life are called biomolecules.

2. Hydrocarbons are organic compounds composed of carbon and hydrogen. Those that contain only C—C single bonds are saturated and are called alkanes, and those with carbon–carbon multiple bonds are unsaturated. Unsaturated hydrocarbons can become saturated by the addition of hydrogen, halogens, and/or other substituents.

3. All alkanes can be represented by the general formula C_nH_{2n+2}. Methane, CH_4, is the simplest alkane, and the next three in the series are ethane, C_2H_6; propane, C_3H_8; and butane, C_4H_{10}. In a saturated hydrocarbon, each carbon atom is bonded to four other atoms. Al-kanes containing long chains of car-

bon atoms are called normal, or straight-chain, hydrocarbons.

4. Structural isomerism in alkanes involves the formation of branched structures. Specific rules for systematically naming alkanes indicate the point of attachment of any substituent group, the length of the root chain, and so on.

5. Alkanes can undergo combustion reactions to form carbon dioxide and water or substitution reactions in which hydrogen atoms are replaced by other atoms. Alkanes can also undergo dehydrogenation to form unsaturated hydrocarbons.

6. Hydrocarbons with carbon–carbon double bonds are called alkenes. The simplest alkene is ethylene, C_2H_4. Alkynes are unsaturated hydrocarbons with a carbon–carbon triple bond. The simplest in the series is acetylene, C_2H_2.

7. Unsaturated hydrocarbons undergo addition reactions such as hydrogenation (addition of hydrogen atoms) and halogenation (addition of halogen atoms). Ethylene and substituted ethylene molecules can undergo polymerization, a process by which many molecules (monomers) are joined together to form a large chain-like molecule.

8. Organic molecules that contain elements in addition to carbon and hydrogen can be viewed as hydrocarbon derivatives: hydrocarbons with functional groups. Each functional group exhibits characteristic chemical properties.

9. Alcohols contain the —OH functional group. Aldehydes and ketones contain the carbonyl functional group,

$$\overset{\diagdown}{\underset{\diagup}{C}}=O$$

In aldehydes this group is bonded to at least one hydrogen atom. Carboxylic acids are characterized by the carboxyl functional group,

$$-C\overset{\displaystyle O}{\underset{\displaystyle OH}{\diagup\diagdown}}$$

They can react with alcohols to form esters.

10. Polymers can be formed by addition polymerization, in which monomers add together, or by condensation polymerization, which involves the splitting out of small molecules (such as water) as the monomers react.

(c)

propane, $CH_3CH_2CH_3$

(d)

decane, $CH_3CH_2CH_2CH_2CH_2CH_2$ $CH_2CH_2CH_2CH_3$

8. (a)

(b)

(c)

(d)

9. Structural isomerism occurs when two molecules have the same atoms present, but those atoms are bonded differently. The molecules have the same formulas but different arrangements of the atoms. Butane and 2-methylpropane are examples.

$$CH_3CH_2CH_2CH_3 \qquad \overset{\displaystyle CH_3}{\underset{}{CH_3CHCH_3}}$$
Butane   2-Methylpropane

10. a branch or substituent

Questions and Problems

All exercises with blue numbers have answers in the back of this book.

20.1 Carbon Bonding

Questions

1. What makes carbon able to form so many different compounds?

2. What is the maximum number of other atoms to which a given carbon atom can be attached? Why?

3. What does a double bond represent? Give two examples of molecules in which double bonds occur, and draw the Lewis structures of those molecules.

4. Structural representations of the hydrocarbon ethane are shown in Figure 20.2. To how many other atoms is each carbon atom bonded in ethane? What is the geometry around each carbon atom in ethane?

20.2 Alkanes

Questions

5. What does it mean to say that a hydrocarbon is *saturated*? To how many other atoms is each carbon atom in a saturated hydrocarbon bonded? What name is given to the family of saturated hydrocarbons?

6. Figure 20.3 shows the structures of the hydrocarbons propane and butane. Alkanes that contain an unbranched chain of carbon atoms are often called "straight-chain" alkanes. Why is such an unbranched chain not really "straight"? What are the bond angles between the carbon atoms in propane and butane?

Problems

7. For each of the following straight-chain alkanes, draw the structural formula.
   a. heptane
   b. nonane
   c. propane
   d. decane

8. Draw the structural formula for each of the following straight-chain alkanes.
   a. butane
   b. octane
   c. pentane
   d. hexane

20.3 Structural Formulas and Isomerism

Questions

9. What are structural *isomers*? What is the smallest alkane that has a structural isomer? Draw structures to illustrate the isomers.

10. What is a small chain of carbon atoms called when it is attached to a longer chain of carbon atoms?

Problems

11. Draw structural formulas for at least *five* isomeric alkanes having the formula C_6H_{14}.

20.4 Naming Alkanes

Questions

12. Give the *root names* for the alkanes with five through ten carbon atoms.

13. To what does the root name for a *branched* hydrocarbon correspond?

14. How is the *position* of substituents along the longest chain of a hydrocarbon indicated?

15. In giving the name of a hydrocarbon with several substituents, in what order do we list the substituents?

Problems

16. Give the systematic name for each of the following alkanes.

   a. $CH_3-CH_2-CH-CH_2-CH_3$
      $\quad\quad\quad\quad\quad\quad | $
      $\quad\quad\quad\quad\quad CH_2-CH_3$

   b.
   $\quad\quad\quad CH_3$
   $\quad\quad\quad\quad | $
   CH_3-C-CH_3
   $\quad\quad\quad\quad | $
   $\quad\quad\quad CH_2-CH_3$

   c.
   $CH_3\quad\quad CH_3$
   $\quad\quad \diagdown\,/$
   $\quad\quad C$
   $\quad\quad /\,\diagdown$
   $CH_3\quad\quad CH_3$

   d. $CH_3-CH-CH-CH-CH_3$
      $\quad\quad\quad\quad | \quad\; | \quad\; | $
      $\quad\quad\quad CH_3\; CH_3\; CH_3$

17. Draw structural formulas for each of the following compounds.
   a. 2-methylhexane
   b. 3-methylhexane
   c. 2,2-dimethylhexane
   d. 2,3-dimethylhexane
   e. 3,3-dimethylhexane

(b)
$CH_3-CH_2-CH-CH_2-CH_2-CH_3$
$\quad\quad\quad\quad\quad\quad | $
$\quad\quad\quad\quad\quad\; CH_3$

(c)
$\quad\quad\quad CH_3$
$\quad\quad\quad\quad | $
$CH_3-C-CH_2-CH_2-CH_2-CH_3$
$\quad\quad\quad\quad | $
$\quad\quad\quad CH_3$

(d)
$CH_3-CH-CH-CH_2-CH_2-CH_3$
$\quad\quad\quad | \quad\; | $
$\quad\quad CH_3\; CH_3$

(e)
$\quad\quad\quad\quad\quad CH_3$
$\quad\quad\quad\quad\quad\quad | $
$CH_3-CH_2-C-CH_2-CH_2-CH_3$
$\quad\quad\quad\quad\quad\quad | $
$\quad\quad\quad\quad\quad CH_3$

18. Petroleum is a thick, dark liquid composed mainly of hydrocarbons containing from 5 to more than 25 carbon atoms. Natural gas consists mostly of methane, but may also contain significant amounts of ethane, propane, and butane. These substances were formed over the eons from the decay of living organisms.

19.
Number of Carbon Atoms	Use
5–12	gasoline
10–18	kerosene, jet fuel
15–25	diesel fuel, heating oil
>25	asphalt

20. In the pyrolytic cracking of petroleum, the more abundant kerosene fraction of petroleum is heated to about 700 °C, which causes the large molecules of the kerosene fraction to break into the smaller molecules characteristic of the gasoline fraction.

21. To prevent "knocking" of engines; it has been discontinued because of the danger of lead in the environment.

22. Alkanes are relatively unreactive because the C—C and C—H bonds that characterize these substances are relatively strong and difficult to break.

23. Combustion represents the vigorous reaction of a hydrocarbon (or other substance) with oxygen. Combustion has been used as a source of heat and light.

24. In a substitution reaction, one or more hydrogen atoms in an alkane are replaced by another type of atom. Because of the unreactivity of alkanes, only very vigorous reactants (such as the halogens) are able to substitute for the hydrogen atoms of alkanes.

11. With six carbon atoms, there are five isomers possible. Here are the carbon skeletons:

C—C—C—C—C—C

C—C—C—C—C
$\quad\quad | $
$\quad\quad C$

C—C—C—C—C
$\quad\quad\quad\quad | $
$\quad\quad\quad\quad C$

C—C—C—C
$\; | \quad\; | $
C\quad C

$\quad\quad C$
$\quad\quad | $
C—C—C—C
$\quad\quad | $
$\quad\quad C$

12.
Number of Carbons	Root Name
5	pentane (*pent-*)
6	hexane (*hex-*)
7	heptane (*hept-*)
8	octane (*oct-*)
9	nonane (*non-*)
10	decane (*dec-*)

13. The root name is derived from the number of carbon atoms in the longest continuous chain of carbon atoms.

14. The position of a substituent is indicated by a number that corresponds to the carbon atom in the longest chain to which the substituent is attached.

15. Multiple substituents are listed in alphabetical order, disregarding any prefix.

16. (a) 3-ethylpentane;
(b) 2,2-dimethylbutane;
(c) 2,2-dimethylpropane;
(d) 2,3,4-trimethylpentane

17. (a)
$CH_3-CH-CH_2-CH_2-CH_2-CH_3$
$\quad\quad\quad | $
$\quad\quad CH_3$

25. Dehydrogenation reactions involve the removal of hydrogen atoms from adjacent carbon atoms in an alkane (or other substance). When two hydrogen atoms are removed from an alkane, a double bond is formed.

26. (a) $2C_6H_{14}(l) + 19O_2(g)$ $\rightarrow 12CO_2(g) + 14H_2O(g)$;
(b) $CH_4(g) + Cl_2(g) \rightarrow$ $CH_3Cl(l) + HCl(g)$;
(c) $CHCl_3(l) + Cl_2(g) \rightarrow$ $CCl_4(l) + HCl(g)$

27. Alkenes are hydrocarbons that contain a carbon–carbon double bond. The general formula for alkenes is C_nH_{2n}, where n is the number of carbon atoms present.

28. An alkyne is a hydrocarbon containing a carbon–carbon triple bond. The general formula is C_nH_{2n-2}, where n is the number of carbon atoms present.

29. (a) $CH_3CH_2CH_3(g)$;
(b) $CH_3CHBrCHBrCH_3(g)$;
(c) $CO_2(g)$ and $H_2O(g)$ (coefficients of 8 and 6, respectively)

30. (a) 2-butene;
(b) 3-methyl-1-butene;
(c) 1-butyne; (d) 3-chloro-1-butene

31. The most obvious choices would be the *normal* alkenes with seven carbon atoms:

$CH_2{=}CH{-}CH_2{-}CH_2$
$\quad$ $-CH_2{-}CH_2{-}CH_3$ 1-Heptene
$CH_3{-}CH{=}CH{-}CH_2$
$\quad$ $-CH_2{-}CH_2{-}CH_3$ 2-Heptene
$CH_3{-}CH_2{-}CH{=}CH$
$\quad$ $-CH_2{-}CH_2{-}CH_3$ 3-Heptene

Additional choices are shorter-chain alkenes with branches, such as

$CH_2{=}C{-}CH_2{-}CH_2{-}CH_2{-}CH_3$
$\quad$ $|$
$\quad$ CH_3

2-Methyl-1-hexene

$CH_3{-}C{=}CH{-}CH_2{-}CH_2{-}CH_3$
$\quad$ $|$
$\quad$ CH_3

2-Methyl-2-hexene

32. Aromatic hydrocarbons all contain a benzene ring (phenyl group).

33. A set of equivalent Lewis structures can be drawn for benzene. Each structure differs only in the location of the three double bonds in the ring. Experimentally benzene does not have the chemical properties expected for molecules having double bonds.

34. The systematic method for naming monosubstituted ben-

20.5 Petroleum

Questions

18. What are the major constituents of crude petroleum? What is the major constituent of natural gas? How were these mixtures formed?

19. List several petroleum fractions and tell how each fraction is primarily used.

20. What is *pyrolytic cracking,* and why is the process applied to the kerosene fraction of petroleum?

21. Why was tetraethyl lead, $(C_2H_5)_4Pb$, added to gasoline in the past? Why is the use of this substance being phased out?

20.6 Reactions of Alkanes

Questions

22. Explain why alkanes are relatively unreactive.

23. What is a *combustion* reaction? How have we made use of the combustion reactions of alkanes?

24. What is a *substitution* reaction? Give an example of a reactive molecule that is able to replace the hydrogen atoms of an alkane.

25. What is a *dehydrogenation* reaction? What results when an alkane is dehydrogenated?

Problems

26. Complete and balance each of the following chemical equations.
   a. $C_6H_{14}(l) + O_2(g) \rightarrow$
   b. $CH_4(g) + Cl_2(g) \rightarrow$
   c. $CHCl_3(l) + Cl_2(g) \rightarrow$

20.7 Alkenes and Alkynes

Questions

27. What is an alkene? What structural feature characterizes alkenes? Give the general formula for alkenes.

28. What is an alkyne? What structural feature characterizes alkynes? Give the general formula for alkynes.

29. Complete each of the following chemical equations:
   a. $CH{\equiv}C{-}CH_3(g) + H_2(g) \rightarrow$
   b. $CH_3{-}CH{=}CH{-}CH_3(l) + Br_2(l) \rightarrow$
   c. $CH_3{-}C{\equiv}C{-}CH_3(l) + O_2(g) \rightarrow$

Problems

30. Give the systematic name for each of the following unsaturated hydrocarbons and substituted unsaturated compounds.
   a. $CH_3{-}CH{=}CH{-}CH_3$
   b. $CH_3{-}CH{-}CH{=}CH_2$
   $\quad\quad\quad\;\; |$
   $\quad\quad\quad\;\; CH_3$
   c. $CH{\equiv}C{-}CH_2{-}CH_3$
   d. $CH_2{=}CH{-}CH{-}CH_3$
   $\quad\quad\quad\quad\;\; |$
   $\quad\quad\quad\quad\;\; Cl$

---

31. Draw structural formulas, and give the systematic names, for at least *four* isomeric hydrocarbons containing seven carbon atoms and one double bond.

20.8 Aromatic Hydrocarbons

Questions

32. What structure do all aromatic hydrocarbons have in common?

33. Benzene exhibits resonance. Explain this statement in terms of the different Lewis structures that can be drawn for benzene.

20.9 Naming Aromatic Compounds

Questions

34. How is a monosubstituted benzene named? Give the structures and names of two examples. Also give two examples of monosubstituted benzenes that have special names.

35. What do the prefixes *ortho-*, *meta-*, and *para-* refer to in terms of the relative location of substituents in a disubstituted benzene?

Problems

36. Draw a structural formula for each of the following aromatic or substituted aromatic compounds.
   a. naphthalene
   b. 2-bromophenol
   c. 3-methylstyrene
   d. 4-nitrochlorobenzene
   e. 1,3-dinitrobenzene

37. Name each of the following aromatic or substituted aromatic compounds.
   a. [structure: benzene ring with two adjacent CH_3 groups]
   b. [structure: benzene ring with five Cl substituents]
   c. [structure: anthracene, three fused rings]
   d. [structure: benzene ring with CH_3 at top and two Cl at positions 3 and 5]

---

zenes uses the substituent name as a *prefix* for the word *benzene.* Examples are

[structure] Cl — Chlorobenzene [structure] CH_2CH_3 — Ethylbenzene

Two monosubstituted benzenes with their own special names are

[structure] CH_3 — Toluene (methylbenzene) [structure] OH — Phenol (hydroxybenzene)

35. *ortho-*: adjacent substituents (1,2-); *meta-*: two substituents with one unsubstituted carbon between them (1,3-); *para-*: two substituents with two unsubstituted carbon atoms between them (1,4-)

36. (a)

(b)

(c) [structure: benzene ring with $CH{=}CH_2$ and CH_3]

(d) [structure: benzene ring with Cl at top and NO_2 at bottom]

20.10 Functional Groups

Problems

38. On the basis of the functional groups listed in Table 20.5, identify the family of organic compounds to which each of the following belongs.

    a. $CH_3-CH_2-CH_2-CH_2-CH_2-OH$

    b. $CH_3-CH_2-\underset{\underset{\displaystyle CH_2-CH_3}{|}}{C}=O$

    c. $H_2N-CH_2-CH_2-CH_3$

    d. $CH_2-CH_2-CH_2-\underset{\underset{\displaystyle H}{|}}{C}=O$

39. On the basis of the functional groups listed in Table 20.5, identify the family of organic compounds to which each of the following belongs.

    a. $CH_3CH_2-O-CH_2CH_2CH_3$

    b. $CH_3CH_2CH_2CH_2-OH$

    c. $CH_3CH_2\underset{\underset{\displaystyle OH}{|}}{C}HCH_3$

    d. $CH_3CH_2CH_2CH_2COOH$

20.11 Alcohols

Questions

40. What functional group characterizes an alcohol? What ending is added to the name of the parent hydrocarbon to show that a molecule is an alcohol?

41. Distinguish among primary, secondary, and tertiary alcohols. Give a structural formula for an example of each type.

Problems

42. Give the systematic name for each of the following alcohols. Indicate whether the alcohol is primary, secondary, or tertiary.

    a. $CH_3CH_2CH_2CH_2CH_2-OH$

    b. $\underset{\underset{\displaystyle OH}{|}}{\overset{\overset{\displaystyle CH_3}{|}}{CH_3CCH_2CH_3}}$

    c. $CH_3CH_2\underset{\underset{\displaystyle OH}{|}}{C}HCH_2CH_3$

    d. $CH_3CH_2CH_2-OH$

43. Draw structural formulas for each of the following alcohols. Indicate whether the alcohol is primary, secondary, or tertiary.

    a. 1-pentanol

    b. 2-pentanol

    c. 3-pentanol

    d. 3-methyl-3-pentanol

20.12 Properties and Uses of Alcohols

Questions

44. Why is methanol sometimes called wood alcohol? Describe the modern synthesis of methanol. What are some uses of methanol?

45. Write the equation for the fermentation of glucose to form ethanol. Why can't ethanol solutions of greater than about 13% concentration be made directly by fermentation? How can the ethanol content be increased beyond this level in beverages?

46. Write the equation for the synthesis of ethanol from ethylene. What are some commercial uses of ethanol made by this process?

47. Give the names and structural formulas of two other commercially important alcohols. Cite the major use of each.

20.13 Aldehydes and Ketones

Questions

48. What functional group is *common* to both aldehydes and ketones?

49. What structural feature *distinguishes* aldehydes from ketones?

20.14 Naming Aldehydes and Ketones

Questions

50. Give the systematic name for each of the following:

    a. $CH_3-CH_2-CH_2-\underset{\underset{\displaystyle CH_2-CH_3}{|}}{C}=O$

    b. $CH_3-\underset{\underset{\displaystyle Cl}{|}}{C}H-\underset{\underset{\displaystyle Cl}{|}}{C}H-\underset{\underset{\displaystyle H}{|}}{C}=O$

    c. $CH_3-\underset{\underset{\displaystyle CH_3}{|}}{C}H-\overset{\overset{\displaystyle CH_3}{|}}{C}H-CH_2-\underset{\underset{\displaystyle H}{|}}{C}=O$

    d. $CH_3-\overset{\overset{\displaystyle CH_3}{|}}{C}H-\underset{\underset{\displaystyle H}{|}}{C}=O$

    e. $CH_3-CH_2-C=O$ (attached to benzene ring)

(c) 3-pentanol (secondary); (d) 1-propanol (primary)

43. (a) $CH_3-CH_2-CH_2-CH_2-CH_2-OH$ (primary)

(b)
$$CH_3-CH_2-CH_2-\underset{\underset{\displaystyle OH}{|}}{C}H-CH_3$$
(secondary)

(c)
$$CH_3-CH_2-\underset{\underset{\displaystyle OH}{|}}{C}H-CH_2-CH_3$$
(secondary)

(d)
$$CH_3-CH_2-\underset{\underset{\displaystyle OH}{|}}{\overset{\overset{\displaystyle CH_3}{|}}{C}}-CH_2-CH_3$$
(tertiary)

44. Methanol is sometimes called wood alcohol because it was formerly obtained by heating wood in the absence of air (also called destructive distillation of wood). Currently it is prepared by the catalyzed hydrogenation of carbon monoxide. Methanol is an important industrial chemical produced in large amounts every year. It is used as a starting material for the synthesis of acetic acid and of many other important substances. Methanol is also used as a motor fuel for high-performance engines.

45. $C_6H_{12}O_6 \rightarrow 2CH_3CH_2OH + 2CO_2$ (yeast is a catalyst). The yeast are killed if the concentration of alcohol is greater than 13%. To make more concentrated ethanol solutions, distillation is needed.

46. Although much ethanol is produced each year by means of the fermentation process, this compound is also produced synthetically by hydration of ethene (ethylene).

$CH_2{=}CH_2 + H_2O \rightarrow$
$\qquad\qquad CH_3-CH_2OH$

Ethanol is used in industry as a solvent and as a starting material for the synthesis of more complicated molecules. Mixtures of ethanol and gasoline are used as automobile motor fuels (gasohol).

47. Methanol (CH_3OH): starting material for synthesis of acetic acid and many plastics; isopropyl alcohol (2-propanol, $CH_3-CH(OH)-CH_3$): rubbing alcohol

48. Aldehydes and ketones both contain the carbonyl functional group.

(e) NO_3 (benzene ring with NO_3 groups)

37. (a) 1,2-dimethylbenzene (*o*-xylene is the common name); (b) 1,2,3,4,5,6-hexachlorobenzene; (c) anthracene; (d) 3,5-dichloro-1-methylbenzene (3,5-dichlorotoluene)

38. (a) alcohol (primary); (b) ketone; (c) amine; (d) aldehyde

39. (a) ether; (b) alcohol (primary); (c) alcohol (secondary); (d) organic (carboxylic) acid

40. Alcohols are characterized by the presence of the hydroxyl group, $-OH$. To name an alcohol, the final *-e* is dropped from the name of the parent hydrocarbon and the ending *-ol* is added. A locator may also be necessary to indicate the location of the hydroxyl group.

41. Primary alcohols have one hydrocarbon fragment (alkyl group) bonded to the carbon atom where the $-OH$ group is attached. Secondary alcohols have two alkyl groups attached, and tertiary alcohols contain three alkyl groups. Examples are

Ethanol (primary)	CH_3-CH_2-OH
2-Propanol (secondary)	$CH_3-\underset{\underset{\displaystyle OH}{|}}{C}H-CH_3$
2-Methyl-2-propanol (tertiary)	$CH_3-\underset{\underset{\displaystyle OH}{|}}{\overset{\overset{\displaystyle CH_3}{|}}{C}}-CH_3$

42. (a) 1-pentanol (primary); (b) 2-methyl-2-butanol (tertiary);

49. The location of the carbonyl group (C=O). Aldehydes contain the carbonyl group at the end of a hydrocarbon chain. Ketones contain the carbonyl group in the interior of a hydrocarbon chain.

50. (a) 3-hexanone (ethyl propyl ketone); (b) 2,3-dichlorobutanal (2,3-dichlorobutyraldehyde); (c) 3,4-dimethylpentanal; (d) 2-methylpropanal; (e) ethyl phenyl ketone

51. (a)

$$\varnothing-\overset{\overset{\displaystyle O}{\|}}{C}-CH_3 \quad (\varnothing = \text{phenyl group})$$

(b) $CH_3-CH_2-CH_2-\overset{\overset{\displaystyle O}{\|}}{C}-H$

(c) $CH_3-CH_2-\overset{\overset{\displaystyle O}{\|}}{C}-CH_3$

(d)

$CH_3-CH_2-CH_2-\overset{\overset{\displaystyle O}{\|}}{C}-CH_2-CH_2-CH_3$

(e)

$CH_3-CH_2-CH_2-\overset{\overset{\displaystyle O}{\|}}{C}-CH_2-CH_2-CH_3$

52. Carboxylic acids are typically weak acids.

$CH_3CH_2COOH + H_2O \rightleftharpoons$
$\quad CH_3CH_2COO^- + H_3O^+$

53. Acetylsalicylic acid is synthesized from salicylic acid (behaving as an alcohol through its —OH group) and acetic acid.

54. (a) 3-methylbutanoic acid; (b) benzoic acid; (c) 2-hydroxypropanoic acid; (d) 3,4-dimethylhexanoic acid

55. (a)

$CH_3-CH_2-\underset{\underset{\displaystyle CH_3}{|}}{CH}-CH_2-COOH$

(b) $H-\underset{\underset{\displaystyle O-CH_2-CH_3}{|}}{\overset{\overset{\displaystyle O}{\|}}{C}}$

(c)

$\varnothing-\underset{\underset{\displaystyle O-CH_3}{|}}{\overset{\overset{\displaystyle O}{\|}}{C}} \quad (\varnothing = \text{phenyl group})$

(d) $CH_3-CH_2-\underset{\underset{\displaystyle Br}{|}}{CH}-COOH$

(e)

$CH_3-CH_2-\underset{\underset{\displaystyle CH_3}{|}}{CH}-\underset{\underset{\displaystyle Cl}{|}}{CH}-\underset{\underset{\displaystyle CH_3}{|}}{CH}-COOH$

56. Polymers are large, usually chain-like, molecules that

---

51. Draw a structural formula for each of the following:
  a. phenyl methyl ketone
  b. butanal
  c. butanone
  d. dipropylketone
  e. 4-heptanone

20.15 Carboxylic Acids and Esters

Questions

52. Are carboxylic acids typically strong acids or weak acids? Write an equation showing the acid CH_3CH_2COOH ionizing in water.

53. Draw the structure of acetylsalicylic acid, and circle the portion of the molecule that shows that it is an ester. From what acid and alcohol is acetylsalicylic acid synthesized?

Problems

54. Give the systematic name for each of the following:

  a. $CH_3-\underset{\underset{\displaystyle CH_3}{|}}{CH}-CH_2-COOH$

  b.

  —COOH

  c. $CH_3-\underset{\underset{\displaystyle OH}{|}}{CH}-COOH$

  d.

  $CH_3-CH_2-CH-\underset{\underset{\displaystyle CH_3}{|}}{\overset{\overset{\displaystyle CH_3}{|}}{CH}}-CH_2-COOH$

55. Draw a structural formula for each of the following:
  a. 3-methylpentanoic acid
  b. ethyl methanoate
  c. methyl benzoate
  d. 2-bromobutanoic acid
  e. 3-chloro-2,4-dimethylhexanoic acid

20.16 Polymers

Questions

56. What, in general terms, is a polymer? What is a monomer?

57. What is a *polyester?* What structural feature characterizes polyesters? Give an example of a common polyester.

Problems

58. Draw the structures of acrylonitrile and butadiene. Also draw the structures of the basic repeating units when each of these substances polymerizes. Give several uses of each polymeric substance.

59. For the polymeric substances nylon and Dacron, sketch representations of the repeating unit in each.

Critical Thinking

60. Write the *general* formula for a normal alkane. How does a given alkane differ from the previous or the following member of the series?

61. Draw structural formulas for all isomeric alkanes having the general formula C_5H_{12}.

62. Give the systematic name of each of the following substituted alkanes.

  a. $CH_3-\underset{\underset{\displaystyle Cl}{|}}{CH}-CH_2-CH_3$

  b. $\underset{\underset{\displaystyle Br}{|}}{CH_2}-\underset{\underset{\displaystyle Br}{|}}{CH_2}$

  c. CHI_3

  d. $CH_3-\underset{\underset{\displaystyle Cl}{|}}{CH}-\underset{\underset{\displaystyle Cl}{|}}{CH}-\underset{\underset{\displaystyle Cl}{|}}{CH}-CH_3$

  e.

  $CH_3-\underset{\underset{\displaystyle Cl}{|}}{\overset{\overset{\displaystyle Cl}{|}}{C}}-CH_2-\underset{\underset{\displaystyle CH_3-CH-CH_3}{|}}{CH}-CH_2-CH_2-CH_3$

63. Write a structural formula for each of the following compounds.
  a. 2,3-dimethylheptane
  b. 2,2-dimethyl-3-chloro-1-octanol
  c. 2-chloro-1-hexene
  d. 1-chloro-2-hexene
  e. 2-methylphenol

64. Draw the structural formula(s) for, and give the name(s) of, the organic product(s) of each of the following reactions. If a mixture of several, similar products is expected, indicate the type of product expected.

  a. $CH_3-CH_3 + Cl_2 \xrightarrow{\text{Light}}$

  b. $CH_3-CH=CH-CH_3 + H_2 \xrightarrow{\text{Pt}}$

  c. $\underset{\displaystyle CH_3-CH_2}{\overset{\displaystyle CH_3-CH_2}{}}C=CH-CH_3 + Br_2 \longrightarrow$

---

are built from smaller molecules. The smaller molecules may combine and repeat in the chain of the polymer hundreds or thousands of times. The small molecules from which polymers are constructed are called monomers.

57. A polyester is a polymer in which the polymerization forms an ester group. The repeating unit is an ester; thus there are many esters, or "poly-esters." Dacron is an example.

58. Carpets, fabrics

Acrylonitrile

$H_2C=\overset{\overset{\displaystyle H}{|}}{\underset{\underset{\displaystyle CN}{|}}{C}}$

Polyacrylnitrile (PAN)

$-(CH_2-\overset{}{\underset{\underset{\displaystyle CN}{|}}{CH}})_{\overline{n}}$

Tire tread, coating resin

Butadiene

$H_2C=\overset{\overset{\displaystyle H}{|}}{C}-\overset{\overset{\displaystyle H}{|}}{C}=CH_2$

Polybutadiene

$-(CH_2CH=CHCH_2)_{\overline{n}}$

59. Nylon

Dacron

60. The general formula is C_nH_{2n+2}. Each successive alkane differs from the preceding or following alkane by CH_2 (a methylene unit).

65. The alcohol glycerol (glycerine), which is produced in the human body by the digestion of fats, has the following structure. Give the systematic name of glycerol.

$$CH_2-CH-CH_2$$
$$\;\;|\;\;\;\;\;\;|\;\;\;\;\;\;|$$
$$OH\;\;\;OH\;\;\;OH$$

66. The sugar glucose could conceivably be given the name 2,3,4,5,6-pentahydroxyhexanal (though this name is never used, because the actual sugar glucose is only one possible isomer having this name). Draw the structure implied by this name.

67. Draw a structure corresponding to each of the following names.
  a. 2-methylpentanal
  b. 3-hydroxybutanoic acid
  c. 2-aminopropanal
  d. 2,4-hexanedione
  e. 3-methylbenzaldehyde

68. On the basis of the functional groups listed in Table 20.5, identify the family of organic compounds to which each of the following belongs.

a. (benzene ring)$-CH_2-CH_2-C=O$ with OH

b. $CH_3-CH_2-CH_2-C=O$ attached to benzene ring

c. $CH_3-CH_2-C=O$ with $O-CH_2-CH_2-$(benzene ring)

d. (benzene ring with OH and CH_2-CH_3)

67. (a) $CH_3-CH_2-CH_2-CH-C=O$ with H and CH_3

(b) $CH_3-CH-CH_2-COOH$ with OH

(c) $CH_3-CH-C=O$ with H and NH_2

(d) $CH_3-C-CH_2-C-CH_2-CH_3$ with O, O

(e) $H-C=O$ attached to benzene ring with CH_3

68. (a) carboxylic acid; (b) ketone; (c) ester; (d) alcohol (phenol)

61. The carbon skeletons are

C—C—C—C—C

C—C—C—C with C below

C—C—C with C above and C below

62. (a) 2-chlorobutane; (b) 1,2-dibromoethane; (c) triiodomethane (common name: iodoform); (d) 2,3,4-trichloropentane; (e) 2,2-dichloro-4-isopropylheptane

63. (a) $CH_3-CH-CH-CH_2-CH_2-CH_2-CH_3$ with CH_3 CH_3

(b) $CH_3-CH_2-CH_2-CH_2-CH_2-CH-C-CH_2-OH$ with Cl CH_3 and CH_3

(c) $CH_3-CH_2-CH_2-CH_2-C=CH_2$ with Cl

(d) $CH_3-CH_2-CH_2-CH=CH-CH_2-Cl$

(e) (benzene ring with OH and CH_3)

64. (a) CH_3-CH_2Cl, chloroethane, CH_2Cl-CH_2Cl, 1,2-dichloroethane, and various other chlorosubstituted ethanes

(b) $CH_3-CH_2-CH_2-CH_3$, butane

(c) CH_3-CH_2, $CBr-CHBr-CH_3$, 2,2-dibromo-3-ethylpentane, CH_3-CH_2

65. 1,2,3-trihydroxypropane (1,2,3-propanetriol)

66. $CH_2-CH-CH-CH-CH-C=O$ with OH OH OH OH OH H

21 Biochemisty

	Section	Text Features & Components	Labs, Demonstrations & Activities
Teaching Segment 21A **1 block** **pp. 684–690**	21.1–21.2 ◖ Proteins Primary Structure of Proteins	🅛🅟 Lesson Plans (Sec 21.1–21.4)	🆃🅴 Mini Demo *p. 687*
	21.3 Secondary Structure of Proteins		
	21.4 Tertiary Structure of Proteins		🆃🅴 Mini Demo *p. 689*
Teaching Segment 21B **2 blocks** **pp. 690–697**	21.5–21.6 ● Functions of ◕ Proteins Enzymes	🆂🅴 Chemical Impact: Urine Farming *p. 692*	🆃🅴 Mini Demo *p. 691* 🆂🅴 Chemistry in the Laboratory: Enzymes in Food *p. 708* 🅛🅜 Experiment 90: Enzymes in Food Lab Manual Report Sheets Teacher's Lab Guide
	21.7 Carbohydrates	🆃🅴 Teaching Tips *p. 693* 🆂🅴 Top Ten Sugar–Consuming Countries *p. 693* 🆂🅴 Celebrity Chemical: Aspartame *p. 696*	🅛🅜 Experiment 91: Vitamin C in Juices Lab Manual Report Sheets Teacher's Lab Guidee
Teaching Segment 21C **1 block** **pp. 697–707**	21.8 Nucleic Acids	🅛🅟 Lesson Plans (Sec 21.8–21.9)	
	21.9 Lipids	🆂🅴 Chemical Impact: Faux Fats *p. 705*	🆂🅴 Chemistry in Action: Colorful Milk *p. 702*

Key

- 🆂🅴 Student Edition
- 🆃🅴 Teacher Edition
- 🆁🅿 Teacher Resource Package
- 🅛🅜 Lab Materials
- 🅛🅟 Lesson Plans
- 🅰🆁 Additional Resources
- Florida Specific

Technology and Media

 Transparencies
 Figure 21.5, 21.6, 21.19, 21.23

PowerPoint Slides

 Animation Soap

eEdition CD-ROM
 Easy Planner CD-ROM
 English Summaries CD
 Spanish Summaries CD

 Web Site classzone.com
 McDougal Littell Test Generator

Chapter Planning Guide

All Learners	Review & Assessment	Standards
TE Active Learning *p. 684* **TE** Teaching Tips *pp. 684–685* **AR** Less Proficient Students *p. 42*	**TE** Additional Examples *p. 687* **SE** Key Terms *p. 709* **SE** Questions and Problems *p. 710*	**TE** **NSES** UCP1, UCP3, UCP5, A1, A2, B2, C5 **SSS** SC.A.1.4.5, SC.H.3.4.5, SC.H.3.4.6
TE Teaching Tips *p. 688* **■** Transparency: Figure 21.5, 21.6 *p. 688* **AR** Less Proficient Students *p. 42*	**SE** Key Terms *p. 709* **SE** Questions and Problems *p. 710*	
RP Team Learning Worksheets (Sec 21.1–21.4) *p. 123* **AR** Less Proficient Students *p. 42*	**SE** Focus Questions (Sec 21.1–21.4) *p. 690* **SE** Key Terms *p. 709* **SE** Questions and Problems *p. 710*	
TE Active Learning *p. 690* **TE** Teaching Tips *p. 691* **AR** Less Proficient Students *p. 42*	**SE** What if . . . *p. 690* **SE** Key Terms *p. 709* **SE** Questions and Problems *p. 710*	**TE** **NSES** UCP1, UCP5, A1, A2, B2, B3, C5, E1, E2 **SSS** SC.H.1.4.1, SC.H.1.4.3, SC.H.1.4.4, SC.H.1.4.7, SC.A.1.4.2, SC.A.1.4.4, SC.B.1.4.1, SC.H.3.4.1
TE Teaching Tips *pp. 694, 696* **RP** Team Learning Worksheets (Sec 21.5–21.7) *p. 125* **AR** Less Proficient Students *pp. 42–43*	**SE** Focus Questions (Sec 21.5–21.7) *p. 697* **SE** Key Terms *p. 709* **SE** Questions and Problems *p. 711*	
SE Active Learning *p. 697* **■** Transparency: Figure 21.19 **TE** Teaching Tips *pp. 697, 699* **AR** Less Proficient Students *p. 43*	**SE** Key Terms *p. 709* **SE** Questions and Problems *p. 711*	**TE** **NSES** UCP1, UCP5, A1, A2, B2, C2, E1, E2, F6 **SSS** SC.H.1.4.1, SC.H.1.4.7, SC.A.1.4.2, SC.H.3.4.6
TE Teaching Tips *p. 701* **■** Transparency: Figure 21.23 **▤** Animation: Soap *p. 703* **RP** Team Learning Worksheets (Sec 21.8–21.9) *p.127* **AR** Less Proficient Students *p. 43*	**SE** Focus Questions (Sec 21.8–21.9) *p. 707* **SE** Key Terms *p. 709* **SE** Questions and Problems *p. 711*	

Chapter Materials

TE Reading Strategy
AR English/Spanish Summaries *pp. 35–37*
AR Challenge Projects/Problems *p. 37*
AR Less Proficient Students *p. 43*
◉ English Summary Audio
◉ Spanish Summary Audio
RP Chapter Review Worksheets (Basic, Review, Challenge)

SE Chapter Summary *p. 709*
SE Critical Thinking *p. 711*
RP Solutions Guide
RP Chapter Tests
RP Test Bank
▨ McDougal Littell Test Generator
AR Standardized Test Practice
● FCAT Test 10

Chapter 21: Using Prior Knowledge

Using prior knowledge is a reading strategy in which the students apply what they have already learned to help comprehend a new concept. This connection between prior knowledge and new material can be helpful in learning chemistry concepts, and in the integration of other subject areas with chemistry.

Point out that in this textbook, photographs of familiar items or scenes are used in the chapter openers and throughout the chapters. Tell the students that before reading a chapter, they should reflect on these visuals and the corresponding captions. This exercise will create awareness of the material, which will help the students to determine which previously learned concepts to review. For example, the photo in the chapter opener on page 682 shows a student dressed in gym clothes jumping in the air. Have the students brainstorm how this photo is related to the chapter title.

Identifying Course Concepts Previously Learned

As you introduce this chapter, point out that biochemistry is an extension of some of the concepts learned in chemistry and in biology. Encourage the students to skim the chapter and make a list of concepts they have previously learned in this course or in other courses. Guide the students to create and fill out a table, sorting the information they have learned by course. The students' tables should resemble the one shown below.

Course Concepts Previously Learned		
Chemistry	**Biology**	**Math**
elements	cells	permutations
polymers	DNA	
mass percent	RNA	
polar bonds	genes	
nonpolar bonds		

Encourage the students to review the concepts listed in their tables. Point out that biochemistry, chemistry, biology, and math are integrated. Explain that the skills learned previously in these courses will help the students understand the new material. Have the students read the chapter introduction. Discuss how concepts such as the cell and chemical elements are fundamental to learning about biochemistry.

Identifying Real-World Applications

Next, have the students skim the chapter and make a list of familiar, real-world examples and applications found in the text. The students' lists may include the following items.

> Energy, exercise, disease, insulin, protein, hair, muscle, cartilage, nutrients, wool, permanent hair wave, egg, X-ray, goats, yeast, carbohydrates, sugar, honey, fruits, artificial sweeteners, starch, fats, milk, beeswax, steroids, cholesterol

Tell the students to select three items from their lists and brainstorm reasons that these items are mentioned in the chapter. Point out that familiarity with these applications helps to explain a concept as practical and useful.

Point out that many of the chapter features in this textbook are designed to enhance the students' understanding of a concept. These features are important in reading assignments because they capture the students' interest with the use of real-world topics or applications.

Organize the students in small groups and have each group read the features in this chapter: Chemical Impact *Urine Farming*, page 692; Celebrity Chemical *Aspartame*, page 696; and Chemical Impact *Faux Fats*, page 705. Instruct each group to compare and contrast the effectiveness of the real-world material presented in the three features. Ask each group to write a response to the following questions.

- To which feature does your group relate best? Why?
- Which feature most interested the members of your group?
- Which feature helped your group better understand the corresponding section material? Why?
- Does your group think the features are an effective way to enhance the section material? Why or why not?
- What suggestions does your group have for another feature that may better explain one of the concepts in the chapter?

Encourage the students to add any real-world applications that occur to them to their notes as they read a section. This activity will engage the students in the reading assignment and help connect the text material with more familiar uses and applications of chemistry.

CHEMICAL IMPACT

Urine F

Nature is a very good chemist—organisms make hundreds of complex chemicals every second to survive. The rap-

CELEBRITY CHEMICAL

Aspartame (

CHEMICAL IMPACT

Faux

What's wrong with fat-free ice cream? Why doesn't it taste like the real thing? It doesn't have any fat, that's why. Fat plays a big role in making things taste good—smooth and flavorful. Fats also add sheen and color to foods and can make food tender, flaky, or creamy. They also help the body absorb fat-soluble vitamins and make us feel full.

Despite their good qualities, fats can be very bad for us. They have been implicated as factors causing cancer, heart disease, and other ailments. As a result, Americans have been told to reduce the fat content of their daily diets.

Overview

In this Chapter our goals are for the students to:

- Learn about proteins
- Understand the primary structure of proteins
- Understand the secondary structure of proteins
- Understand the tertiary structure of proteins
- Learn about the various functions served by proteins
- Understand how enzymes work
- Understand the fundamental properties of carbohydrates
- Understand the fundamental nucleic acid structure
- Learn the four classes of lipids

21 Biochemistry

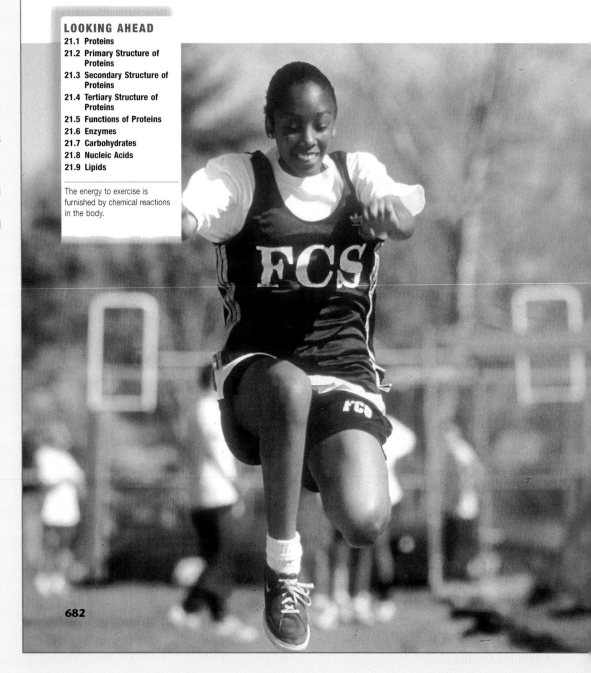

The energy to exercise is furnished by chemical reactions in the body.

682

Biochemistry, the study of the chemistry of living systems, is a vast and exciting field in which important discoveries about how life is maintained and how diseases occur are being made every day. In particular, there has been rapid growth in the understanding of how living cells manufacture and use the molecules necessary for life. This not only has been beneficial for detection and treatment of diseases but also has spawned a new field—**biotechnology,** which uses nature's "machinery" to synthesize desired substances. For example, insulin is a complex biomolecule that is used in the body to regulate the metabolism of sugars. People who have diabetes are deficient in natural insulin and must take insulin by injection or other means. In the past this insulin was obtained from animal tissues (particularly that of cows). However, our increased understanding of the biochemical processes of the cell has allowed us to "farm" insulin. We have learned to insert the "instructions" for making insulin into the cells of bacteria such as *E. coli* so that as the bacteria grow they produce insulin that can then be harvested for use by diabetics. Many other products, including natural pesticides, are also being produced by the techniques of biotechnology.

An understanding of biochemistry also allows our society to produce healthier processed foods. For example, the food industry is making great efforts to reduce the fat levels in food without destroying the good taste that fats bring to food. (See "Chemical Impact: Faux Fats," page 705.)

We cannot hope to cover all the important aspects of this field in this chapter; we will concentrate here on the major types of biomolecules that support living organisms. First, however, we will survey the elements found in living systems and briefly describe the constitution of a cell.

At present, 30 elements are definitely known to be essential to human life. These **essential elements** are shown in color in **Figure 21.1.** The most abundant elements are hydrogen, carbon, nitrogen, and oxygen; sodium, magnesium, potassium, calcium, phosphorus, sulfur, and chlorine are also

This sample of E. Coli bacteria has been genetically altered to produce human insulin. The insulin production sites are colored orange. The bacteria are cultured and pure human insulin is harvested from them.

Figure 21.1
The chemical elements essential for life. Those most abundant in living systems are shown as purple. Nineteen elements, called the trace elements, are shown as green.

Biochemistry **683**

present in relatively large amounts. Although present only in trace amounts, the first-row transition metals are essential for the action of many enzymes (biological catalysts). For example, zinc, one of the **trace elements,** is found in nearly 200 biologically important molecules. The functions of the essential elements are summarized in **Table 21.1.** In time, other elements will probably be found to be essential.

Life is organized around the functions of the **cell,** the smallest unit in living things that exhibits the properties normally associated with life, such as reproduction, metabolism, mutation, and sensitivity to external stimuli.

As the fundamental building blocks of all living systems, aggregates of cells form tissues, which in turn are assembled into the organs that make up complex living systems. Therefore, to understand how life is maintained and reproduced, we must learn how cells operate on the molecular level. This is the main thrust of biochemistry.

TABLE 21.1

Some Essential Elements and Their Major Functions

Element	Percent by Mass in the Human Body	Function
oxygen	65	in water and many organic compounds
carbon	18	in all organic compounds
hydrogen	10	in water and many inorganic and organic compounds
nitrogen	3	in both inorganic and organic compounds
calcium	1.5	in bone; essential to some enzymes and to muscle action
phosphorus	1.2	essential in cell membranes and to energy transfer in cells
potassium	0.2	cation in cell fluid
chlorine	0.2	anion inside and outside the cells
sulfur	0.2	in proteins
sodium	0.1	cation in cell fluid
magnesium	0.05	essential to some enzymes
iron	<0.05	in molecules that transport and store oxygen
zinc	<0.05	essential to many enzymes
cobalt	<0.05	found in vitamin B_{12}
iodine	<0.05	essential to thyroid hormones
fluorine	<0.01	in teeth and bones

21.1 Proteins

Objective: *To learn about proteins.*

In Chapter 20 we saw that many useful synthetic materials are polymers. A great many natural materials are also polymers: starch, hair, silk and cotton fibers, and the cellulose in woody plants, to name only a few.

In this section we introduce a class of natural polymers, the **proteins,** which make up about 15% of our bodies and have molar masses that range from approximately 6,000 to over 1,000,000 grams. Proteins have many functions in the human body. **Fibrous proteins** provide structural integrity and

Themes
Organization, Systems

Skills
Making comparisons, classifying, applying concepts

Student Preparation
Assign the students to read Sections 21.1 to 21.4 and to answer the Focus Questions at the end of Section 21.4 before coming to class.

Active Learning
After introducing the material in Sections 21.1 to 21.4 in class, place the students in groups and have them work together on Sections 21.1–21.4: Team Learning Worksheet. Answers and/or discussion of these questions are located in the *Teacher Resources.*

TEACHING TIP

Table 21.1 gives mass percents of elements and their functions. Reviewing it is an excellent way to emphasize the importance of chemistry in everyday life.

Striated muscle tissue.

strength for many types of tissue and are the main components of muscle, hair, and cartilage. Other proteins, usually called **globular proteins** because of their roughly spherical shape, are the "worker" molecules of the body. These proteins transport and store oxygen and nutrients, act as catalysts for the thousands of reactions that make life possible, fight invasion of the body by foreign objects, participate in the body's many regulatory systems, and transport electrons in the complex process of metabolizing nutrients.

21.2 Primary Structure of Proteins

Objective: *To understand the primary structure of proteins.*

The building blocks of all proteins are the α-**amino acids:**

$$\text{NH}_2-\overset{\overset{\displaystyle\text{H}}{|}}{\underset{\underset{\displaystyle\text{R}}{|}}{\text{C}}}-\text{C}\overset{\displaystyle\text{O}}{\underset{\displaystyle\text{OH}}{}}$$

α-Carbon

The R in this structure may represent H, CH_3, or more complex substituents. These molecules are called α-amino acids because the amino group (—NH_2) is always attached to the α-carbon, the one next to the carboxyl group (—COOH). The 20 amino acids most commonly found in proteins are shown in **Figure 21.2** on the following page.

Note from Figure 21.2 that the amino acids are grouped into polar and nonpolar classes on the basis of the composition of the R groups, also called the **side chains.** Nonpolar side chains contain mostly carbon and hydrogen atoms; polar side chains contain nitrogen and oxygen atoms. This difference is important because polar side chains are *hydrophilic* (water-loving), but nonpolar side chains are *hydrophobic* (water-fearing). This greatly affects the three-dimensional structure of the resulting proteins, because they exist in aqueous media in living things.

The protein polymer is built by reactions between amino acids. For example, two amino acids can react as follows, forming a C—N bond with the elimination of water.

At the pH in biological fluids, the amino acids shown in Figure 21.2 exist in a different form, with the proton of the —COOH group transferred to the —NH_2 group. For example, glycine would be in the form $^+H_3NCH_2COO^-$.

Peptide linkage

$$\text{(two amino acids)} \;\rightarrow\; \text{(peptide)} \;+\; H_2O$$

21.2 Primary Structure of Proteins **685**

TEACHING TIPS

- This section is an excellent place to review what causes a side group to be polar or nonpolar. Refer students back to the ideas they learned about bonding and work with them to determine why each side chain is classified as polar or nonpolar.

- The term "hydrophobic" is actually a misnomer. While the nonpolar side chains do not mix well with water, they do not repel the water. Instead, water molecules are simply more attracted to other water molecules than to the nonpolar side chains.

- When students first begin to make peptide linkages, they often link the carboxyl group on one amino acid to the R group of the next. Work through several examples of the linkages with students. It is helpful to mark the different parts of the amino acid (carboxyl, amine, R groups) with different colors so that students can more easily identify which groups should interact.

Figure 21.2
The 20 α-amino acids found in most proteins. The R group is shown in color.

The product shown at the bottom of page 685 is called a **dipeptide.** The term *peptide* comes from the structure

$$-\overset{\displaystyle \overset{O}{\|}}{C}-\overset{\displaystyle \overset{H}{|}}{N}-$$

which chemists call a **peptide linkage** or a peptide bond. The prefix *di-* indicates that two amino acids have been joined. Additional reactions lengthen the chain to produce a **polypeptide** and eventually a protein.

The 20 amino acids can be assembled in any order, which makes possible an enormous number of different proteins. This variety allows for the many types of proteins needed for the functions that organisms carry out.

The *order* or *sequence* of amino acids in the protein chain is called the **primary structure.** We indicate the primary structure by using three-letter codes for the amino acids (see Figure 21.2), where it is understood that the terminal carboxyl group is on the right and the terminal amino group is on the left. For example, one possible sequence for a tripeptide containing the amino acids lysine, alanine, and leucine is

which is represented in the shorthand notation (three-letter codes)as

lys-ala-leu

Example 21.1

Understanding Primary Structure

Write the sequences of all possible tripeptides composed of the amino acids tyrosine (tyr), histidine (his), and cysteine (cys).

Solution

There are six possible sequences:

tyr-his-cys	his-tyr-cys	cys-tyr-his
tyr-cys-his	his-cys-tyr	cys-his-tyr

A striking example of the importance of the primary structure of polypeptides can be seen in the differences between *oxytocin* and *vasopressin*. Oxytocin is a hormone that triggers contraction of the uterus and milk secretion. Vasopressin raises blood pressure and regulates kidney function. Both of these molecules are nine-unit polypeptides, and they differ by only two amino acids **(Figure 21.3)**; yet they have completely different functions in the human body.

cys-tyr-ile-gln-asn-cys-pro-leu-gly

(a)

cys-tyr-phe-gln-asn-cys-pro-arg-gly

(b)

Figure 21.3
The amino acid sequences in (a) oxytocin and (b) vasopressin. The differing amino acids are enclosed in boxes.

21.2 Primary Structure of Proteins **687**

MINI-DEMO

Use a set of children's pop beads to illustrate the primary structure of a protein. The differently shaped beads can represent different amino acids. The pop connections can represent peptide linkages. Have students translate your primary structure into the three-letter-coded structure by assigning a code sequence to each bead.

Additional Examples

Write the sequences of all possible tripeptides composed of the amino acids serine (ser), glutamic acid (glu), and arginine (arg).

ser-glu-arg	glu-arg-ser	arg-ser-glu
ser-arg-glu	glu-ser-arg	arg-glu-ser

TEACHING TIP

An excellent example of a secondary structure is the coiled cord from a telephone. Another possibility is to twist children's pop beads into a helix to represent the secondary structure while showing the primary structure by the order of the pop beads. A folded piece of paper can represent the pleated sheet secondary structure.

USING TECHNOLOGY

 Figure 21.5

 Figure 21.6

21.3 Secondary Structure of Proteins

Objective: *To understand the secondary structure of proteins.*

So far we have considered the primary structure of proteins—the order of amino acids in the chain **(Figure 21.4a).** A second level of structure in proteins is the arrangement in space of the chain of the long molecule. This is called the **secondary structure** of the protein **(Figure 21.4b).**

One common type of secondary structure resembles a spiral staircase. This spiral structure is called an α-helix **(Figure 21.5).** A spiral-like secondary structure gives the protein elasticity (springiness) and is found in the fibrous proteins in wool, hair, and tendons. Another type of secondary structure involves joining several different protein chains in an arrangement called a **pleated sheet,** as shown in **Figure 21.6.** Silk has this arrangement of proteins, making its fibers flexible but very strong and resistant to stretching. The pleated sheet is also found in muscle fibers.

As you might imagine, a molecule as large as a protein has a great deal of flexibility and can assume a variety of overall shapes. The function the protein is to serve influences the specific shape that it will have. For long, thin structures such as hair, wool and silk fibers, and tendons, an elongated shape is required. This may involve an α-helical secondary structure, as found in the protein α-keratin in hair and wool or in the collagen that occurs in tendons **(Figure 21.7a),** or it may involve a pleated-sheet secondary structure, as found in silk **(Figure 21.7b).** Many of the proteins in the body that have nonstructural functions (such as serving as enzymes) are globular. One is myoglobin **(Figure 21.8),** which absorbs an O_2 molecule and stores it for use by the cells as it is needed. Note that the secondary structure of myoglobin is basically α-helical. However, in the areas where the chain bends to give the protein its compact globular structure, the α-helix breaks down so that the protein can "turn the corner."

(a) Primary structure

(b) Secondary structure

Figure 21.4
(a) The primary structure of a protein describes the order of the amino acids in the chain. One example is shown. (b) The secondary structure of a protein describes the arrangement of the chain in space. A spiral (helical) arrangement of the protein chain is shown.

Figure 21.5
One type of secondary protein structure is like a spiral staircase and is called the α-helix. The spheres represent individual amino acids.

Figure 21.6
Two protein chains bound together in the pleated-sheet secondary structure. Each sphere represents an amino acid.

688   Chapter 21   Biochemistry

Figure 21.7
(a) Collagen, a protein found in tendons, consists of three protein chains (each with an α-helical structure) twisted together to form a super-helix. The result is a long, relatively narrow protein. (b) Many proteins are bound together in the pleated-sheet arrangement to form the elongated protein found in silk fibers.

(a)   (b)

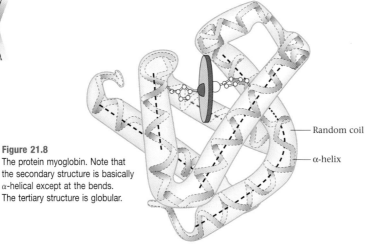

Figure 21.8
The protein myoglobin. Note that the secondary structure is basically α-helical except at the bends. The tertiary structure is globular.

— Random coil

— α-helix

21.4 Tertiary Structure of Proteins

Objective: *To understand the tertiary structure of proteins.*

The overall shape of the protein, long and narrow or globular, is called its **tertiary structure.** To make sure the difference between secondary and tertiary structure is clear, examine Figure 21.8 again. The secondary structure of the myoglobin protein is helical except in the regions where it bends back on itself to give the overall compact (globular) tertiary structure. If the bends did not occur, the tertiary structure would be like a long tube (tubular). In both tertiary arrangements (globular and tubular), the secondary structure of the protein is basically helical.

The amino acid *cysteine* (cys) plays a special role in stabilizing the tertiary structure of many proteins, because the —SH groups on two cysteines can react to form an S—S bond called a **disulfide linkage.**

Protein
chain

Chemicals used in permanent wave solutions create curls in hair.

Themes
Organization, Form and Function, Models

Skills
Classifying, making comparisons, developing models

MINI-DEMO

One way to illustrate the tertiary structure is to use a coiled phone cord or a Slinky. The coils represent the secondary structure of the protein, which can be bent, folded, or coiled to illustrate the tertiary structure.

Figure 21.9
The permanent waving of hair.

Natural cysteine
linkages in hair

Reduction

Chains shift

Hair set in curlers
alters tertiary structure

Oxidation

New cysteine linkages
in waved hair

The formation of a disulfide linkage can fasten together two parts of a protein chain to form and hold a bend in the chain, for example. A practical application of the chemistry of disulfide bonds is the permanent waving of hair **(Figure 21.9).** The S—S linkages in the protein of hair are broken by treatment with a reducing agent. Next the hair is set in curlers to change the tertiary protein structure to the desired shape. Then treatment with an oxidizing agent causes new S—S bonds to form, which make the hair protein retain the new structure.

Focus Questions **Sections 21.1–21.4**

1. What are the major types and functions of proteins?
2. Draw the general structure for an amino acid.
   a. Circle the side chain group.
   b. Draw a second amino acid next to the first and circle the water removed to form a peptide bond to link the two amino acids.
3. What are the differences among primary, secondary, and tertiary structure in proteins?

21.5 Functions of Proteins

Objective: *To learn about various functions served by proteins.*

The three-dimensional structure of a protein is crucial to its function. The process of breaking down this structure is called **denaturation (Figure 21.10).** For example, heat causes the denaturation of egg proteins when an egg is cooked. Any source of energy can cause denaturation of proteins and is thus potentially dangerous to living organisms. For example, ultraviolet radiation, X-ray radiation, or nuclear radioactivity can disrupt protein structure, which may lead to cancer or genetic damage. The metals lead and mercury, which have a very high affinity for sulfur, cause protein denaturation by disrupting disulfide bonds.

The tremendous variability in the several levels of protein structure allows proteins to be tailored specifically to serve a wide range of functions, some of which are given in **Table 21.2.**

Energy

Figure 21.10
A schematic representation of the thermal denaturation of a protein.

690   Chapter 21   Biochemistry

TEACHING TIP

Figure 21.9 shows how a permanent wave causes hair to curl. It provides an interesting way to introduce the denaturation of proteins and the disruption of protein function that can result. The formation of disulfide links demonstrates that R groups can play an active role in protein structure (other than in the primary structure).

 Answers to Focus Questions

1. The functions of proteins are summarized in Table 21.2.

2.

3. The primary structure is the order in which the amino acids are linked. The secondary structure involves the way the protein chain interacts with itself. The tertiary structure involves the overall shape of the protein, including how more remote regions on the protein interact.

 Section 21.5

Themes
Form and Function

Skills
Making comparisons, applying concepts

Student Preparation
Assign the students to read Sections 21.5 to 21.7 and to answer the Focus Questions at the end of Section 21.7 before coming to class.

Active Learning
After introducing the material in Sections 21.5 to 21.7 in class, place the students in groups and have them work together on Sections 21.5–21.7: Team Learning Worksheet. Answers and/or discussion of these questions are located in the *Teacher Resources.*

WHAT IF Comments

Hydrogen bonding in proteins largely determines the secondary structure of the proteins. These structures include the α-helix and the pleated sheet. Structures forming an α-helix include hair and tendons. Structures forming a pleated sheet are found in muscle fibers. Since these structures contribute to the performance of the proteins, your body could not function properly.

TABLE 21.2
Common Functions of Proteins

Function	Comment/Example
Structure	Proteins provide the strength of tendons, bones, and skin. Cartilage, hair, wool, fingernails, and claws are mainly protein. Viruses have an outer layer of protein.
Movement	Proteins are the major components of muscles and are directly responsible for the ability of muscles to contract. The swimming of sperm results from the contraction of protein filaments in their tails.
Catalysis	Nearly all chemical reactions in living organisms are catalyzed by enzymes, which are almost always proteins.
Transport	Oxygen is carried from the lungs to tissues by the protein hemoglobin in red blood cells.
Storage	The protein ferritin stores iron in the liver, spleen, and bone marrow.
Energy transformation	Cytochromes are proteins found in all cells. They extract energy from food molecules by transferring electrons in a series of oxidation–reduction reactions.
Protection	Antibodies are special proteins that are synthesized in response to foreign substances and cells, such as bacterial cells. They then bind to those substances or cells and provide us with immunity to various diseases. Interferon, a small protein made and released by cells when they are exposed to a virus, protects other cells against viral infection. Blood-clotting proteins protect against bleeding (hemorrhage).
Control	Many hormones are proteins produced in the body that have specific effects on the activity of certain organs.
Buffering	Because proteins contain both acidic and basic groups on their side chains, they can neutralize both acids and bases and thus provide buffering for blood and tissues.

21.6 Enzymes

Objective: *To understand how enzymes work.*

Enzymes are proteins that catalyze specific biological reactions. Without the several hundred enzymes now known, life would be impossible. Almost all of the critical biochemical reactions would occur far too slowly at the temperatures at which life exists. Enzymes are impressive for their tremendous efficiency (they are typically 1 to 10 million times as efficient as inorganic catalysts) and their incredible selectivity (an enzyme "ignores" the thousands of molecules in body fluids that are not involved in the reaction it catalyzes).

Although the mechanisms of enzyme activity are complex and not fully understood in most cases, a simple theory called the **lock-and-key model (Figure 21.11)** seems to fit many enzymes. This model postulates that the

Figure 21.11
Schematic diagram of the lock-and-key model of the functioning of an enzyme.

21.6   Enzymes   **691**

Integrating the
CHEMICAL
IMPACT

Urine Farming

This Chemical Impact provides an opportunity to discuss the implications of genetic engineering for society. The use of genetically modified products is currently the source of much controversy. Students could research this topic and debate the issue in class.

CHEMICAL IMPACT   Science, Technology, and Society

Urine Farming

A New Zealand goat, one of the animals used for urine farming.

Nature is a very good chemist—organisms make hundreds of complex chemicals every second to survive. The rapidly expanding science of biotechnology is learning more every day about how to use natural chemical pathways to make valuable molecules. For example, insulin for diabetics is now made almost exclusively by "farming" genetically altered *E. coli* or yeast.

Turning livestock into four-footed pharmaceutical factories has seemed an attractive option ever since we learned to carry out "genetic engineering." In fact, a great deal of effort has been expended on creating cows, sheep, and goats that are genetically modified to produce useful human proteins that are secreted into the animals' milk, from which they can then be harvested. None of these proteins has yet reached the market—tests are now under way to check their efficacy and safety—but a blood-clotting agent, antithrombin III, developed by Genzyme Transgenics Corporation of Framingham, Massachusetts, is close to commercial application. Creating a transgenic (genetically modified) animal is expensive (costing approximately $60,000), but

then standard breeding techniques can lead to an entire herd of animals programmed to produce commercially interesting molecules.

As a medium, milk has some disadvantages. It is produced only by mature females and contains a wide variety of proteins that complicate the purification process to obtain the desired product. Urine may be a better alternative. It contains fewer natural proteins and is produced at an early age by both male and female animals. Robert J. Wall and his colleagues at the U.S. Department of Agriculture in Beltsville, Maryland, have developed transgenic mice that produce human growth hormone in the walls of their bladders. For obvious reasons, mice are not ideal for large-scale production of chemicals, but Wall's experiments nevertheless show that the concept works. At present it is too early to know whether urine farming will prove feasible. Yields from the bladder are about 10,000 times lower than those from the mammary glands. In addition, collecting urine from farm animals could prove to be a very tricky business.

An enzyme often changes shape slightly as the substrate is bound. This "clamps" the substrate into place.

shapes of the reacting molecule (the **substrate**) and the enzyme are such that they fit together much as a key fits a specific lock. The substrate and enzyme attach to each other in such a way that the part of the substrate where the reaction is to occur occupies the **active site** of the enzyme. After the reaction occurs, the products are liberated and the enzyme is ready for a new substrate. We can represent enzyme catalysis by the following steps:

Step 1   The enzyme E and the substrate S come together.

$$E + S \rightleftharpoons E \cdot S$$

Step 2   The reaction occurs to give the product P, which is released from the enzyme.

$$E \cdot S \rightarrow E + P$$

After the product is released, the enzyme is free to engage another substrate.

Because this process occurs so rapidly, only a tiny amount of enzyme is required.

In some cases a substance other than the substrate can bind to the enzyme's active site. When this occurs, the enzyme is said to be *inhibited*. If the inhibition is permanent, the enzyme is said to be inactivated. Some of the most powerful toxins act by inhibiting, or inactivating, key enzymes.

Because enzymes are crucial to life and because we hope to learn how to mimic their efficiency in our industrial catalysts, the study of enzymes occupies a prominent place in chemical research.

21.7 Carbohydrates

Objective: *To understand the fundamental properties of carbohydrates.*

The **carbohydrates** are another class of biologically important molecules. Carbohydrates serve as food sources for most organisms and as structural materials for plants. Because many carbohydrates have the empirical formula CH_2O, it was originally believed that these substances were hydrates of carbon ($C \cdot H_2O$), which accounts for their name.

Like proteins, carbohydrates occur in almost bewildering varieties. Many of the most important carbohydrates are polymers—large molecules constructed by hooking together many smaller molecules. We have seen that proteins are polymers constructed from amino acids. The polymeric carbohydrates are constructed from molecules called **simple sugars** or, more precisely, **monosaccharides.** Monosaccharides are aldehydes or ketones that contain several hydroxyl (—OH) substituents. An example of a monosaccharide is fructose, with the structure

$$
\begin{array}{c}
CH_2OH \\
| \\
C{=}O \quad \leftarrow \text{Ketone} \\
| \\
HO-C-H \\
| \\
H-C-OH \\
| \\
H-C-OH \\
| \\
CH_2OH
\end{array}
$$

Fructose

Fructose is a sugar found in honey and fruits. Monosaccharides can have various numbers of carbon atoms, and we name them according to the number

Breads contain high levels of carbohydrates and fruits are a dietary source of fructose.

Section 21.7

Themes
Organization, Form and Function

Skills
Applying concepts, interpreting diagrams

Laboratory
Experiment 91:
Vitamin C in Juices, Microscale

TEACHING TIP

Use glucose and fructose to compare the structures of common monosaccharides. Both have six carbons, but glucose has an aldehyde functional group on carbon 1 and fructose has a ketone on carbon 2. Both have —OH groups on the remaining carbons.

21.7 Carbohydrates **693**

TABLE 21.3

The General Names of Monosaccharides

Number of Carbon Atoms	Prefix	General Name of Sugar
3	*tri-*	triose
4	*tetr-*	tetrose
5	*pent-*	pentose
6	*hex-*	hexose
7	*hept-*	heptose
8	*oct-*	octose
9	*non-*	nonose

of carbon atoms they contain by adding prefixes to the root *-ose*. The general names of monosaccharides are shown in **Table 21.3.** Notice that fructose is a ketone with six carbon atoms and five —OH substituents. Fructose is a member of the hexose family, where the prefix *hex-* means six.

The most important monosaccharides found in living organisms are pentoses and hexoses. The most common pentoses and hexoses are shown in **Table 21.4.**

Although we have so far represented the monosaccharides as straight-chain molecules, they usually form ring structures in aqueous solution. **Figure 21.12** shows how the ring forms for fructose. Note that a new bond is formed

Figure 21.12
The formation of a ring structure for fructose.

TEACHING TIPS

- It is helpful to illustrate how a sugar cyclizes by using a model. Build a model of glucose and then carefully close the ring, showing students what happens as you proceed.

- Point out that in glucose the aldehyde group reacts to form the ring, whereas in fructose the ketone group reacts to form the ring. This difference changes the number of atoms in the ring for the two sugars.

TABLE 21.4

Some Important Monosaccharides

Pentoses (five carbon atoms)

Hexoses (six carbon atoms)

(a) Glucose

(b) Fructose

(c) Sucrose

Figure 21.13
Sucrose (c) is a disaccharide formed from glucose (a) and fructose (b).

between the oxygen of a hydroxyl group and the carbon of the ketone group. In the cyclic form, fructose is a five-membered ring containing a C—O—C bond. Glucose, a hexose that is an aldehyde, forms a six-membered ring structure. The six-membered glucose ring is shown in **Figure 21.13a.** Note that the ring is nonplanar.

More complex carbohydrates are formed by the combining of monosaccharides. For example, two monosaccharides can combine to form a **disaccharide. Sucrose,** common table sugar, is a disaccharide formed from glucose and fructose by elimination of water to form a C—O—C bond between the rings that is called a **glycoside linkage (Figure 21.13c).** When sucrose is consumed in food, this reaction is reversed (the glycoside bond is broken). An enzyme in saliva catalyzes the breakdown of sucrose into its two monosaccharides.

Large polymers containing many monosaccharide units are called **polysaccharides** and can form when each ring forms two glycoside linkages, as shown in **Figure 21.14.** Three of the most important of these polymers are starch, cellulose, and glycogen. All of these substances are polymers of glucose; they differ in the way the glucose rings are linked together.

Figure 21.14
Starch is made by hooking together many glucose rings. Only a small part of the chain is shown here.

21.7 Carbohydrates **695**

CELEBRITY CHEMICAL

Aspartame ($C_{14}H_{18}N_2O_5$)

Have students bring in samples of items containing aspartame. Alternatively, have them find items containing aspartame in the grocery store and bring in a list of these products. Discuss the need to properly label products, as some people are sensitive to this chemical.

CELEBRITY CHEMICAL

Aspartame ($C_{14}H_{18}N_2O_5$)

A product containing aspartame.

Most humans love things that taste sweet—chocolate candy, cake, ice cream, and so on. The problem with sweet things is they have lots of calories and tend to make us gain weight. Wouldn't it be great to have sweets without the calories? Of course, this dream has now become reality through the magic of chemistry—artificial sweeteners, or molecules that taste sweet but do not add to the calorie count. Many molecules have a sweet taste—even sweeter than sugar. The earliest of these compounds were discovered in the late 1800s when tasting a new compound was accepted procedure. Most of the current artificial sweeteners were discovered by accident, however, when scientists were not observing proper lab hygiene.

Today the most widely used artificial sweetener is a compound called aspartame, which is formed by coupling together two amino acids naturally found in humans: aspartic acid and phenylalanine. Aspartame is 200 times sweeter than sugar and leaves no unpleasant after-taste. It is now found in most diet drinks and many other low-calorie products. One disadvantage of aspartame is that it decomposes at baking temperatures and thus cannot be used in products that are heated.

Like all artificial sweeteners, aspartame has had some critics. When this substance breaks down in the body it forms aspartic acid, phenylalanine, and methanol. The first two compounds are naturally present in the body and pose no hazard to most people. However, about one person in 15,000 suffers from a disease called phenylketonuria, which makes an individual sensitive to excess phenylalanine. People with this condition must avoid aspartame. Also, the fact that methanol is a product of the breakdown of aspartame makes some people nervous, because methanol is a toxic substance. Nevertheless, studies have shown that the small amount of methanol produced from aspartame poses no risk. In fact, a glass of natural fruit juice contains as much methanol as is produced from typical use of aspartame.

Although aspartame has been the subject of some criticism, all indications are that it is safe for virtually everyone. It continues to dominate the artificial sweetener market.

TEACHING TIP

Students often have difficulty seeing how starch and cellulose form from glucose. You will need to mark the molecules and number the carbons to show them each time an —OH from carbon 1 links with an —OH from carbon 4.

Starch (Figure 21.14) is the carbohydrate reservoir in plants. It is the form in which glucose is stored by the plant for later use as cellular fuel—both by the plants themselves and by organisms that eat plants.

Cellulose, the major structural component of woody plants and natural fibers such as cotton, is also a polymer of glucose. However, in cellulose the way in which the glucose rings are linked is different from the way they are linked in starch. This difference in linkage has very important consequences. The human digestive system contains enzymes that can catalyze breakage of the glycoside bonds between the glucose molecules in starch. These enzymes are *not* effective on the glycoside bonds of cellulose, however, presumably because the different structure causes a poor fit between the enzyme's active site and the carbohydrate. Interestingly, the enzymes necessary to cleave the glycoside linkages in cellulose are found in bacteria that exist in the digestive tracts of termites, cows, deer, and many other animals. Therefore, unlike humans, these animals can derive nutrition from the cellulose in wood, hay, and other similar substances.

Glycogen is the main carbohydrate reservoir in animals. For example, it is found in muscles, where it can be broken down into glucose units when energy is required for physical activity.

Focus Questions

Sections 21.5–21.7

1. What level of protein structure is changed by denaturation?
2. What role do enzymes play in biochemical reactions?
3. How is a protein different from a carbohydrate?
4. How are starch and cellulose similar? Why can't we digest cellulose?

21.8 Nucleic Acids

Objective: *To understand the fundamental nucleic acid structures.*

Life is possible only because each cell, when it divides, can transmit the vital information about what it is to the next generation of cells. It has been known for a long time that this process involves the chromosomes in the nucleus of the cell. Only since 1953, however, have scientists understood the molecular basis of this intriguing cellular "talent."

The substance that stores and transmits the genetic information is a polymer called **deoxyribonucleic acid (DNA)**, a huge molecule with a molar mass as high as several billion grams. Together with other similar nucleic acids called the **ribonucleic acids (RNA)**, DNA carries the information needed for the synthesis of the various proteins the cell requires to carry out its life functions. The RNA molecules, which are found in the cytoplasm outside the cell nucleus, are much smaller than DNA polymers, with molar mass values of only 20,000 to 40,000 grams.

Both DNA and RNA are polymers—they are constructed by the hooking together of many smaller units. The fundamental unit in these polymers is called a **nucleotide.** Each nucleotide in turn has three parts:

1. *A nitrogen-containing organic base*
2. *A five-carbon sugar*
3. *A phosphate group*

A nucleotide can be represented as follows:

Note that the prefix *de-* refers to the absence of the substance that follows. Thus deoxyribose means ribose with a missing oxygen (see Figure 21.15).

21.8 Nucleic Acids **697**

Figure 21.15
The structure of the pentoses (a) deoxyribose and (b) ribose. Deoxyribose is the sugar molecule present in DNA; ribose is found in RNA. The difference in these sugars is the substitution, in ribose, of an OH for one H in deoxyribose. This OH is shown in color.

In the DNA polymer, the five-cabon sugar is deoxyribose **(Figure 21.15a)**; in the RNA polymer, it is ribose **(Figure 21.15b).** This difference in the sugar molecules present in the polymers is responsible for the names DNA (deoxyribonucleic acid) and RNA (ribonucleic acid).

The organic base molecules in the nucleotides of DNA and RNA are shown in **Figure 21.16.** Notice that some of these bases are found only in DNA, some are found only in RNA, and some are found in both. The formation of a specific nucleotide containing the base adenine and the sugar ribose is shown in **Figure 21.17.** To form the DNA and RNA polymers, the nucleotides

Uracil (U)
RNA

Cytosine (C)
DNA
RNA

Thymine (T)
DNA

Adenine (A)
DNA
RNA

Guanine (G)
DNA
RNA

Figure 21.16
The organic bases found in DNA and RNA. Note that uracil is found only in RNA and that thymine is found only in DNA.

Figure 21.17
(a) Adenosine is formed by the reaction of adenine and ribose. (b) The reaction of phosphoric acid with adenosine to form the ester adenosine 5-phosphoric acid, a nucleotide. (At biological pH, the phosphoric acid would not be fully protonated as is shown here.)

Figure 21.18
A portion of a typical nucleic acid chain, half of the DNA double helix shown in Figure 21.19.

Repeating unit along DNA chain

A molecular model of part of the DNA structure.

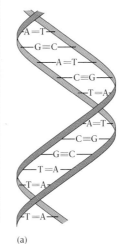

(a)

Figure 21.19
(a) The DNA double helix contains two sugar–phosphate backbones with the bases from the two strands hydrogen-bonded to each other. The (b) thymine–adenine and (c) cytosine–guanine pairs show complementarity. The hydrogen-bonding interactions are shown by dotted lines.

Thymine   Adenine

(b)

Cytosine   Guanine

(c)

are hooked together. DNA polymers can contain up to a *billion* nucleotide units. **Figure 21.18** shows a small portion of a DNA chain.

The key to DNA's functioning is its *double-helical structure with complementary bases on the two strands*. Complementary bases form hydrogen bonds to each other, as shown in **Figure 21.19.** Note that the structures of cytosine and guanine make them perfect partners (complementary) for hydrogen bonding and that they are *always* found as pairs on the two strands of DNA. Thymine and adenine form similar hydrogen-bonding pairs.

21.8   Nucleic Acids   **699**

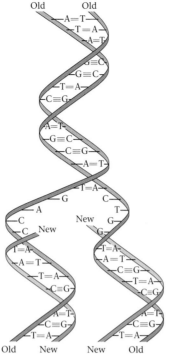

There is much evidence to suggest that the two strands of DNA unwind during cell division and that new complementary strands are constructed on the unraveled strands **(Figure 21.20).** Because the bases on the strands always pair in the same way—cytosine with guanine and thymine with adenine—each unraveled strand serves as a template for attaching each complementary base (along with the rest of its nucleotide). This process results in two new double-helix DNA structures that are identical to the original one. Each new double strand contains one strand from the original DNA double helix and one newly synthesized strand. This replication of DNA makes possible the transmission of genetic information when cells divide.

DNA and Protein Synthesis

Besides replication, the other major function of DNA is **protein synthesis.** The proteins consumed by an organism in its food are typically not the specific proteins that organism needs to maintain its existence. The nutrient proteins are broken down into their constituent amino acids, which are then used to construct those proteins that the organism needs. The information for constructing each protein needed by a particular organism is stored in that organism's DNA. A given segment of the DNA, called a **gene,** contains the code for a specific protein. This code for the primary structure of the protein (the sequence of amino acids) can be transmitted to the construction "machinery" of the cell.

DNA stores the genetic information, and RNA molecules are responsible for transmitting this information to cell components called ribosomes, where protein synthesis actually occurs. This process involves, first, the construction of a special RNA molecule called **messenger RNA (mRNA).** The mRNA is built in the cell nucleus, where a specific section of DNA (a gene) is used as the pattern. The mRNA then migrates from the nucleus into the cytoplasm of the cell, where, with the assistance of the ribosomes, the protein is synthesized.

Small RNA fragments, called **transfer RNA (tRNA)** molecules, attach themselves to specific amino acids and bring them to the growing protein chain as dictated by the pattern built into the mRNA. This process is summarized in **Figure 21.21.**

Figure 21.20
During cell division, the original DNA double helix unwinds and new complementary strands are constructed on each original strand. In this way, the two cells resulting from the division have exact copies of the DNA of the original cell.

Figure 21.21
The mRNA molecule, constructed from a specific gene on the DNA, is used as the pattern for construction of a given protein with the assistance of ribosomes. The tRNA molecules attach to specific amino acids and put them in place, as dictated by the patterns on the mRNA. This sequence (left to right) shows the protein chain growing.

700

21.9 Lipids

Objective: *To learn the four classes of lipids.*

The **lipids** are a group of substances defined in terms of their solubility characteristics. They are water-insoluble substances that can be extracted from cells by organic solvents such as benzene. The lipids found in the human body can be divided into four classes according to their molecular structure: fats, phospholipids, waxes, and steroids.

The most common **fats** are esters composed of the trihydroxy alcohol known as glycerol and long-chain carboxylic acids called **fatty acids (Table 21.5).** *Tristearin,* the most common animal fat, is typical of these substances.

Fats that are esters of glycerol are called **triglycerides** and have the general structure

where the three R groups may be the same or different and may be saturated or unsaturated. Vegetable fats tend to be unsaturated and usually occur as

TABLE 21.5

Some Common Fatty Acids and Their Major Sources

Name	Formula	Major Source
Saturated		
arachidic acid	$CH_3(CH_2)_{18}$—COOH	peanut oil
butyric acid	$CH_3(CH_2)_2$—COOH	butter
caproic acid	$CH_3(CH_2)_4$—COOH	butter
lauric acid	$CH_3(CH_2)_{10}$—COOH	coconut oil
stearic acid	$CH_3(CH_2)_{16}$—COOH	animal and vegetable fats
Unsaturated		
oleic acid	$CH_3(CH_2)_7CH{=}CH(CH_2)_7$—COOH	corn oil
linoleic acid	$CH_3(CH_2)_4CH{=}CH—CH_2—CH{=}CH(CH_2)_7$—COOH	linseed oil
linolenic acid	$CH_3CH_2CH{=}CH—CH_2CH{=}CH—CH_2—CH{=}CH—(CH_2)_7COOH$	linseed oil

701

Themes
Organization, Form and Function

Skills
Applying concepts, interpreting diagrams, making comparisons

TEACHING TIPS

- Now is a good time to discuss soaps and how they work. Figures 21.22 and 21.23 show how a micelle forms and then breaks down globules of fats. Making soap in the laboratory is a good way for students to learn more about this process as well.

- Formation of lipids involves the same reaction as does formation of an ester, discussed in Chapter 20. The glycerol is a multihydroxyalcohol.

- Fats containing more unsaturated fatty acids are liquids at room temperature.

CHEMISTRY

Unsaturated fats contain one or more C=C bonds.

CHEMISTRY

Like dissolves like.

oily liquids; most animal fats are saturated (contain only C—C single bonds) and occur as solids at room temperature.

Triglycerides can be broken down by treatment with aqueous sodium hydroxide. The products are glycerol and the fatty acid salts; the latter are known as soaps. This process is called **saponification.**

$$
\begin{array}{c}
CH_2-O-\overset{\displaystyle O}{\overset{\displaystyle \|}{C}}-R \\[4pt]
CH-O-\overset{\displaystyle O}{\overset{\displaystyle \|}{C}}-R' \quad + \quad 3NaOH \quad \rightarrow \\[4pt]
CH_2-O-\overset{\displaystyle O}{\overset{\displaystyle \|}{C}}-R''
\end{array}
\qquad
\begin{array}{c}
CH_2OH \; + \; RCOONa \\[4pt]
CHOH \; + \; R'COONa \\[4pt]
CH_2OH \; + \; R''COONa
\end{array}
$$

Triglyceride   Sodium   Glycerol   Soaps
                      hydroxide

Much of what we call greasy dirt is nonpolar. Grease, for example, consists mostly of long-chain hydrocarbons. However, water, the solvent most commonly available to us, is very polar and does not dissolve "greasy dirt." We need to add something to the water that is somehow compatible with both the polar water and the nonpolar grease. Fatty-acid anions are perfect for this role, because they have a long nonpolar tail and a polar head. For example, the stearate anion can be represented as

Nonpolar   Polar
tail   head

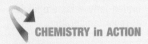

CHEMISTRY in ACTION

Colorful Milk

CHEMISTRY in ACTION
Colorful Milk

1. Half-fill a shallow colorless container with whole milk.
2. Add 1–2 drops of food coloring to the surface of the milk. Do not stir.
3. Add 1–2 drops of a different food coloring to the surface in a different area. Do not stir.
4. Without moving or shaking the container, observe the food coloring and record what you see.
5. Dip one end of a cotton swab in a liquid dishwashing detergent. Touch the center of the surface of the milk with this end of the swab. Be careful not to stir the milk.
6. Record your observations. If the motion stops, add another drop of the detergent (see step 5).
7. Compare what the food coloring did in the milk to what happens when you add food coloring to water (see "Chemistry in Action: Mysterious Mixing" on page 34.)
8. How did the detergent affect the food coloring in the milk? Explain.

702   Chapter 21   Biochemistry

Figure 21.22
A two-dimensional "slice" of the structure of a micelle of fatty-acid anions. Cations surround the negatively charged micelle.

Nonpolar tail   Polar head

○ Positive ion

 Water molecule

Such ions can be dispersed in water because they form **micelles (Figure 21.22).** These aggregates of fatty-acid anions have the water-incompatible tails in the interior; the anionic parts (the polar heads) point outward and interact with the polar water molecules. A soap solution does not contain *individual* fatty-acid anions dispersed in the water but rather groups of ions (micelles).

Soap dissolves grease by taking the grease molecules into the nonpolar interior of the micelle **(Figure 21.23),** so they can be carried away by the

Figure 21.23
Soap micelles absorb grease molecules into their interiors so that the molecules are suspended in the water and can be washed away.

703

USING TECHNOLOGY

▶ Figure 21.23

Animation and Video

Animation, Soap

Polar head   **Nonpolar tails**

Figure 21.24
Lecithin, a phospholipid, with its long nonpolar tails and polar substituted-phosphate head.

water. Soap thus acts to suspend the normally incompatible grease in the water. Because of this ability to assist water in suspending nonpolar materials, soap is also called a *wetting agent,* or **surfactant.**

A major disadvantage is that soap anions form precipitates in hard water (water that contains large concentrations of ions such as Ca^{2+} and Mg^{2+}). These precipitates occur because the Ca^{2+} and Mg^{2+} ions form insoluble solids with soap anions. These precipitates ("soap scum") dull clothes and drastically reduce soap's cleaning efficiency. To help alleviate this problem, a huge industry has developed to produce artificial soaps, called detergents. Detergents are similar to natural soaps in that they have a long nonpolar tail and an ionic head. However, detergent anions have the advantage of not forming insoluble solids with Ca^{2+} and Mg^{2+} ions.

Phospholipids are similar in structure to fats in that they are esters of glycerol. Unlike fats, however, they contain only two fatty acids. The third group bound to glycerol is a phosphate group, which gives phospholipids two distinct parts: the long nonpolar "tail" and the polar substituted-phosphate "head" **(Figure 21.24).**

Waxes are another class of lipids. Like fats and phospholipids, waxes are esters, but unlike these other lipids, they involve monohydroxy alcohols instead of glycerol. For example, *beeswax,* a substance secreted by the wax glands of bees, is mainly myricyl palmitate,

$$CH_3(CH_2)_{14}-\overset{\overset{\textstyle O}{\|}}{C}-O-(CH_2)_{29}-CH_3$$

formed from palmitic acid,

$$CH_3(CH_2)_{14}-C\overset{\displaystyle O}{\underset{\displaystyle OH}{\Big\langle}}$$

and carnaubyl alcohol

$$CH_3(CH_2)_{29}-OH$$

Waxes are solids that furnish waterproof coatings on leaves and fruit and on the skins and feathers of animals. Waxes are also important commercially.

704   Chapter 21   Biochemistry

Faux Fats

What's wrong with fat-free ice cream? Why doesn't it taste like the real thing? It doesn't have any fat, that's why. Fat plays a big role in making things taste good—smooth and flavorful. Fats also add sheen and color to foods and can make food tender, flaky, or creamy. They also help the body absorb fat-soluble vitamins and make us feel full.

Despite their good qualities, fats can be very bad for us. They have been implicated as factors causing cancer, heart disease, and other ailments. As a result, Americans have been told to reduce the fat content of their daily diets.

Can we design "faux fat"—a material that tastes and behaves like fat but doesn't hurt us? In fact, almost everyone in the food industry is trying to achieve this goal. Take a walk through a supermarket and you'll find that many products have a low-fat or fat-free alternative.

There are three types of fat substitutes: carbohydrate-based, protein-based, and fat-based. The carbohydrate-based fat substitutes appeared first on the market in the 1960s, and the protein-based substitutes followed in the late 1980s. Modified starches, gums, and proteins, chopped into tiny pieces ranging from 100 to 3000 nm, make up most of the fake fats on the market. For example, NutraSweet manufactures Simplesse, a whey-protein concentrate most often found in dairy and oil-based foods such as ice cream and salad dressing.

Although faux fats are widely used these days, they have yet to be perfected. One of the biggest problems with carbohydrate- and protein-based fat substitutes is that they decompose at high temperatures and therefore can't be used for frying foods. Another problem is that fat substitutes often alter the flavor of foods. Most aromatic chemicals, which greatly affect flavor, are soluble in fat, so the taste lasts much longer in foods made with real fat than in those that use substitutes. However, newly developed fake fats appear to counter some of these disadvantages.

Olestra is a "sucrose polyester" manufactured by Procter & Gamble. It is a fat-based substance, but while natural fats have three fatty acids attached to glycerol (see pages 701–703), olestra has six to eight fatty acids (all derived from vegetable oils) attached to a sucrose molecule (see Figure 21.13c). Because it will not fit the enzymes in the body that break down fats, sucrose polyester passes through the body undigested. Thus it is a non-nutritive fat —it produces no calories. In addition, because it is stable at high temperatures, olestra, marketed as Olean by Procter & Gamble, can be used for deep-frying. Although olestra was approved for use in snack foods by the Federal Drug Administration in 1996 and can be found in such products as Ruffles and Pringles potato chips, there remains controversy over the side effects. Because olestra isn't digested, consuming large quantities of these products may cause intestinal discomfort. Nevertheless, market reaction to these products has been quite positive. In the meantime the search for the perfect fat substitute continues.

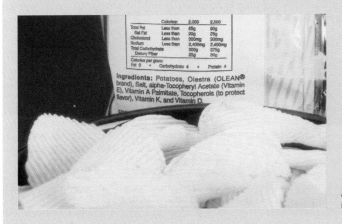

A product that contains no natural fats.

21.9 Lipids **705**

Beeswax in a honeycomb from Indonesia.

For example, whale oil is largely composed of the wax cetyl palmitate. It has been used in so many products, including cosmetics and candles, that the blue whale has been hunted almost to extinction.

Steroids are a class of lipids that have a characteristic carbon ring structure of the type

Steroids comprise four groups: cholesterol, adrenocorticoid hormones, sex hormones, and bile acids.

Cholesterol (Figure 21.25a) is found in virtually all organisms and is the starting material for the formation of the many other steroid-based molecules, such as vitamin D **(Figure 21.25b).** Although cholesterol is essential for human life, it has been implicated in the formation of plaque on the walls of arteries (a process called atherosclerosis, or hardening of the arteries), which can lead eventually to clogging. This effect seems especially important in the arteries that supply blood to the heart. Blockage of these arteries leads to heart damage that often results in death from a heart attack.

The **adrenocorticoid hormones,** such as cortisol **(Figure 21.25c),** are synthesized in the adrenal glands (glands that lie next to each kidney) and are involved in various regulatory functions.

Of the **sex hormones,** the most important male hormone is *testosterone* **(Figure 21.25d),** a hormone that controls the growth of the reproductive organs and hair and the development of the muscle structure and deep voice that are characteristic of males. There are two types of female sex hormones of particular significance: *progesterone* **(Figure 21.25e),** and a group of estrogens, one of which is *estradiol* **(Figure 21.25f).** Changes in the concentrations of these hormones cause the periodic changes in the ovaries and uterus that are responsible for the menstrual cycle. During pregnancy, a high level of progesterone is maintained, which prevents ovulation.

The **bile acids** are produced from cholesterol in the liver and stored in the gallbladder. The primary human bile acid is *cholic acid* **(Figure 21.25g),**

CH3
CH3
CH3
CH3
CH3

HO

(a) cholesterol

CH3
CH3
CH3
CH3
CH3
CH2

HO

(b) vitamin D₃

CH₂OH
C=O
OH   CH₃   OH
CH₃

O

(c) cortisol

OH
CH₃
CH₃

O

(d) testosterone

CH₃
C=O
CH₃
CH₃

O

(e) progesterone

OH
CH₃

HO

(f) estradiol

O
C—O—H
OH   CH₃
CH₃

HO   OH

(g) cholic acid

Figure 21.25
Several common steroids and steroid derivatives.

a substance that aids in the digestion of fats by emulsifying them in the intestine. Bile acids can also dissolve cholesterol ingested in food and are therefore important in controlling cholesterol in the body.

Focus Questions

Sections 21.8–21.9

1. What are the fundamental parts of a nucleotide?
2. In the double helix that forms DNA, what are the substances that form the steps in the ladder? How are they held together?
3. What are the major functions of DNA?
4. What are lipids? List the types of lipids and give a function of each.

Focus Questions   **707**

Answers to Focus Questions

1. The fundamental parts of a nucleotide are sugar, phosphate, and base.

2. The substances that form the steps are the base pairs. They are held together by hydrogen bonding.

3. The major functions of DNA are replication and protein synthesis.

4. Lipids are water-insoluble substances that can be extracted by nonpolar solvents. Four classes of lipids exist: fats, phospholipids, waxes, and steroids.

CHEMISTRY in the LABORATORY

Enzymes in Food

Objectives

1. To observe the effect of proteases on gelatin

2. To observe the effect of freezing and heating on the functioning of proteases

Skills

Observing, applying concepts, making comparisons, drawing conclusions

Materials

Goggles	Frozen pineapple
Apron	Fresh pineapple
Plastic cups	Canned
Toothpicks	pineapple
Microwave	Meat tenderizer
oven	Soft-contact
Dry gelatin	lens cleaner

Preparation Hints

You may wish to prepare the gelatin for the students. A four-serving package of gelatin will make enough to fill six 3-oz plastic cups (the cups will be three-fourths filled).

Prelab Discussion

Remind students that although they are working with food, they should not taste or eat anything in the lab.

Post-Lab Discussion

Have students present their results to the class. Conduct a class discussion on the effects of freezing, microwaving, and canning pineapple.

Disposal

Gather all materials from students and dispose of them properly.

Sample Data/Answers

Prelab Assignment

2. We use this sample as a control. It allows us to compare our results with the original sample.

Data/Observations

The gelatin surface is firm in cups 1, 3, and 5. The surface of the gelatin will be watery in cups 2, 4, 6, and 7.

Analysis and Conclusions

1. The fresh and frozen pineapple samples break down the structure of gelatin. Canned pineapple does not disrupt the gelatin structure.

2. The canned pineapple is more like the microwaved pineapple,

---

CHEMISTRY in the LABORATORY
Enzymes in Food

Problem

What is the effect of a type of enzyme called a protease on gelatin? How can we affect the functioning of proteases?

Introduction

Enzymes are proteins that act as catalysts for specific biological reactions. Without them, life would be impossible because important reactions in our bodies would occur far too slowly.

Enzymes called proteases break down certain proteins. As some fruits contain proteases, and gelatin is a network of protein molecules, we can use gelatin to experiment on the functioning of proteases.

Prelab Assignment

1. Read the entire lab experiment before you begin.

2. Why is there one sample of gelatin to which nothing was added?

Materials

Goggles
Apron
Plastic cups
Toothpicks
Microwave oven
Dry gelatin
Frozen pineapple
Fresh pineapple
Canned pineapple
Meat tenderizer
Soft contact lens cleaner

Procedure

Part I: Preparation of the Gelatin

1. Prepare the gelatin according to the directions on the package.

2. Divide the gelatin equally into seven plastic cups.

3. Allow the gelatin to set.

Part II: How Do Proteases Affect Gelatin?

1. Place a piece of fresh pineapple (about a 1-inch cube) in a microwave oven and cook it on the highest setting for one minute. Allow the pineapple to return to room temperature.

708

---

2. Test the effect of proteases on gelatin by placing the following on the surface of the gelatin in each cup:

Cup 1: nothing

Cup 2: a piece (1-inch cube) of fresh pineapple

Cup 3: a piece (1-inch cube) of canned pineapple

Cup 4: a piece (1-inch cube) of frozen pineapple

Cup 5: the piece of pineapple that was microwaved

Cup 6: a spoonful of meat tenderizer

Cup 7: a teaspoon of contact lens cleaner

3. Examine the cups every 5 minutes for 20 minutes. Be careful to return the pieces of pineapple to their original positions after looking under each piece.

4. Return the cups to the refrigerator.

5. Observe the cups the next day.

Cleaning Up

Clean up all materials and wash your hands thoroughly.

Data/Observations

List your observations for each cup.

Analysis and Conclusions

1. Why do many packages of gelatins state "do not use fresh or frozen pineapple"? Why do the packages not include the statement "do not used canned pineapple"?

2. Is canned pineapple more like fresh, frozen, or microwaved pineapple? What does this fact tell you about the canning process? Explain.

3. From your results, would you say meat tenderizers contain proteases?

4. From your results, would you say contact lens cleaners contain proteases?

5. Propose a theory of how meat tenderizers and contact lens cleaners work.

Something Extra

How do proteases affect the setting of gelatin? Carry out an experiment to answer this question.

---

which implies that the canning process involves heat. The heat denatures the protein.

3. Yes. The meat tenderizer breaks down the gelatin just like the fresh and frozen pineapple.

4. Yes. The contact lens cleaner breaks down the gelatin just like the fresh and frozen pineapple.

5. Meat contains proteins and the meat tenderizer breaks down these proteins. The residue on contact lenses must contain pro-

tein as well (which the contact lens cleaners break down).

Something Extra

Gelatin will not set if proteases are added to the gelatin before it has set. Students can test this idea by adding fresh or frozen pineapple to gelatin before it is set.

Chapter Review

Assign the students to work individually on the Chapter 21 Review Worksheet at the appropriate level (Basic, Standard, or Challenge). Answers are found in the *Teacher Resources.*

Assessment

Chapter 21 Test is found in the *Teacher Resources,* along with the answers for the test.

 Computerized Test Bank for Chapter 21

Answers to End of Chapter Problems

1. Oxygen is the element present in the human body in the largest percentage by mass (65%). Other elements present in the body and their uses are given in Table 21.1.

708

21 Chapter Review

Key Terms

biochemistry (p. 683)
biotechnology (p. 683)
essential elements (p. 683)
trace elements (p. 684)
cell (p. 684)
protein (21.1)
fibrous protein (21.1)
globular protein (21.1)
a-amino acid (21.2)
side chain (21.2)
dipeptide (21.2)
peptide linkage (21.2)
polypeptide (21.2)
primary structure (21.2)
secondary structure (21.3)
a-helix (21.3)
pleated sheet (21.3)
tertiary structure (21.4)
disulfide linkage (21.4)
denaturation (21.5)
enzyme (21.6)
lock-and-key model (21.6)
substrate (21.6)
active site (21.6)
carbohydrate (21.7)
monosaccharide (simple
    sugar) (21.7)
disaccharide (21.7)
sucrose (21.7)
glycoside linkage (21.7)

polysaccharide (21.7)
starch (21.7)
cellulose (21.7)
glycogen (21.7)
deoxyribonucleic acid
    (DNA) (21.8)
ribonucleic acid
    (RNA) (21.8)
nucleotide (21.8)
protein synthesis (21.8)
gene (21.8)
messenger RNA
    (mRNA) (21.8)
transfer RNA
    (tRNA) (21.8)
lipid (21.9)
fat (21.9)
fatty acid (21.9)
triglyceride (21.9)
saponification (21.9)
micelle (21.9)
surfactant (21.9)
phospholipid (21.9)
wax (21.9)
steroid (21.9)
cholesterol (21.9)
adrenocorticoid
    hormone (21.9)
sex hormone (21.9)
bile acid (21.9)

Summary

1. Thirty elements are currently known to be essential for life. The most abundant elements in the human body are hydrogen, carbon, nitrogen, and oxygen, but calcium, phosphorus, sodium, magnesium, potassium, sulfur, and chlorine are also present in large amounts. Other elements found only in trace amounts, such as zinc, are essential for the action of many enzymes.

2. Proteins are a class of natural polymers with molar masses ranging from 6000 to 1,000,000 grams. Fibrous proteins are employed in the human body for structural purposes in muscle, hair, and cartilage. Globular proteins are molecules that transport and store oxygen and nutrients, act as catalysts, help regulate the body's systems, fight foreign objects, and so on.

3. The building blocks of proteins are the α-amino acids, which are classified as polar or nonpolar, depending on whether the side chain (R group) attached to the α-carbon is hydrophilic or hydrophobic. A protein polymer is built by successive condensation reactions that produce peptide linkages:

4. The order or sequence of amino acids in the protein chain is called the protein's primary structure. Differences in primary structure are what enable proteins to be tailored for different and very specific functions.

5. The secondary structure is the arrangement of the protein chain in space. The two most common secondary structures are the α-helix and the pleated sheet.

6. The overall shape of the protein is called its tertiary structure. Energy sources and a variety of chemicals can cause the breakdown of tertiary protein structure, which is called denaturation.

7. Enzymes are proteins that act as catalysts in biological reactions.

8. Carbohydrates serve as food sources for most organisms and as structural materials for plants. Simple carbohydrates, called monosaccharides, are most commonly five-carbon and six-carbon polyhydroxy ketones and aldehydes.

9. Monosaccharides combine to form more complex carbohydrates. For example, sucrose is a disaccharide, and starch and cellulose are polymers of glucose (polysaccharides).

10. When a cell divides, the genetic information is transmitted via deoxyribonucleic acid (DNA), which has a double-helical structure. During cell division, the double helix unravels, and a new polymer forms along each strand of the original DNA, creating two double-helical DNA molecules. The DNA contains segments called genes, which store the primary structures of specific proteins. Various types of ribonucleic acid (RNA) molecules assist in protein synthesis.

11. Lipids are water-insoluble substances found in cells. They can be divided into four classes: fats, phospholipids, waxes, and steroids.

Chapter Review **709**

6. The structures of the amino acids are given in Figure 21.2. A side chain is nonpolar if it is mostly hydrocarbon in nature (like alanine). Polar side chains may contain the hydroxyl group (—OH), the sulfhydryl group (—SH), or a second amino (—NH$_3$) or carboxyl (—COOH) group.

7. Since most proteins exist in aqueous media (water) in living creatures, the presence of hydrophobic (water-fearing) and hydrophilic (water-loving) side chains on the amino acids in a protein will greatly influence how that protein's chain interacts with water. The three-dimensional structure of the protein is greatly influenced by what types of side chains are present in its constituent amino acids.

8. cys-ala-phe; cys-phe-ala; phe-ala-cys; phe-cys-ala; ala-cys-phe; ala-phe-cys

9. See *Solutions Guide* for labels.

(a) ile-ala-gly

(b) gln-ser

(c) ser-gln

(d) cys-asn-gly

10. phe-ala-gly

phe-gly-ala

ala-phe-gly

---

2. Proteins represent biopolymers of α-amino acids. Proteins make up about 15% of the human body by mass.

3. Molar masses of proteins range from a few thousand amu to more than 1 million amu. Such molar masses are consistent with proteins in that they are large polymeric molecules.

4. Fibrous proteins provide the structural material for many tissues in the body. They are the chief constituents of hair, cartilage, and

muscles. Fibrous proteins consist of lengthwise bundles of polypeptide chains (a fiber). Globular proteins consist of polypeptide chains folded into a spherical shape. They are found in the bloodstream, where they transport and store various substances, act as antibodies (fight infections), act as enzymes (catalysts), and participate in the body's various regulatory systems.

5. The general structural formula for the α-amino acids is

All α-amino acids contain the carboxyl group (—COOH) and the amino group (—NH$_2$) attached to the α-carbon atom as indicated. In this general formula, *R* represents the remainder of the amino acid molecule (side chain). It is this portion of the molecule that differentiates one amino acid from another.

ala-gly-phe

CH_3 H O H O CH_2

H_2N—C—C—N—C—C—N—C—COOH

N terminal H H H H H H C terminal

gly-phe-ala

H O CH_2 O CH_3

H_2N—C—C—N—C—C—N—C—COOH

N terminal H H H H H H C terminal

gly-ala-phe

H O CH_3 O CH_2

H_2N—C—C—N—C—C—N—C—COOH

N terminal H H H H H H C terminal

11. The secondary structure of a protein describes, in general, the arrangement in space of the protein's polypeptide chain. The most common secondary structures are the α-helix and the β pleated sheet.

12. Long, thin, resilient proteins (such as hair) typically contain elongated, elastic α-helical protein molecules. Other proteins (such as silk) that form sheets or plates typically contain protein molecules having the β pleated-sheet structure. Proteins without a structural function in the body (such as hemoglobin) typically have a globular structure.

13. A large number of similar polypeptide chains are arranged lengthwise next to each other to form a wide sheet of protein. The individual polypeptide chains contain the normal bond angles associated with the molecules involved and are not linear; when several chains are arranged next to each other to form a sheet, ripples ("pleats") appear in the overall sheet. Silk and muscle fibers have the pleated-sheet structure.

14. The polypeptide chain forms a coil or spiral. Such proteins are found in wool, hair, and tendons.

15. The tertiary structure represents the protein's specific overall shape in its natural environment. To distinguish between secondary and tertiary structures, consider a given protein with an α-helical secondary structure. In the body, this helix is folded and twisted by interactions with the protein's environment until it forms a tight sphere (tertiary structure).

Questions and Problems

All exercises with blue numbers have answers in the back of this book.

21.1 Proteins

Questions

1. What element is present in the human body in the largest percentage by mass? Name ten other elements essential to life and list their uses in the body.

2. What are proteins? What portion of the human body (by mass) consists of proteins?

3. Describe the range of molar masses shown by proteins in the body. Are such molar masses consistent with proteins being polymers?

4. What uses do *fibrous* and *globular* proteins have in the body? Describe the general shape of these types of proteins.

21.2 Primary Structure of Proteins

Questions

5. Sketch the general formula for an α-amino acid, indicating the α-amino carbon atom. Circle the portion of the structure that all α-amino acids have in common.

6. Write the formulas of two amino acids with polar side chains and of two amino acids with nonpolar side chains. Explain *why* the side chains you have chosen have their respective polarities.

7. Why is it important to distinguish between hydrophilic and hydrophobic side chains? What solvent forms the natural environment for proteins in the body?

8. Write the amino acid sequences possible for a tripeptide containing the amino acids *cys, ala,* and *phe,* with each amino acid being used only once in each tripeptide.

Problems

9. Given the formulas of the common amino acids in Figure 21.2, sketch the structures of the following simple peptides. Circle the peptide bonds in your structures. Label the terminal amino and carboxyl groups clearly.
   a. ile-ala-gly
   b. gln-ser
   c. ser-gln
   d. cys-asn-gly

10. Given the formulas of the common amino acids in Figure 21.2, sketch the structures of the six different tripeptides possible containing phenylalanine, alanine, and glycine (each taken only once). Circle the peptide bonds in your structures. Label the terminal amino and carboxyl groups clearly.

Chapter 21 Biochemistry

21.3 Secondary Structure of Proteins

Questions

11. In general terms, what does the secondary structure of a protein represent?

12. How is the secondary structure of a protein related to its function in the body? Give examples.

13. Describe the secondary protein structure known as the pleated sheet. Give two examples of materials containing proteins with this structure.

14. Describe the secondary protein structure known as the α-helix. What types of proteins have this secondary structure?

21.4 Tertiary Structure of Proteins

Questions

15. In general terms, what does the tertiary structure of a protein describe? Clearly distinguish between the secondary and tertiary structures.

16. Describe the function of the amino acid cysteine in influencing the tertiary structure of a protein.

21.5 Functions of Proteins

Questions

17. What is meant by *denaturation* of a protein? Give three examples of situations in which proteins are denatured.

18. Describe the structure of the protein *collagen*. What function does collagen have in the body?

19. What name is given to proteins that catalyze biochemical reactions in the cell?

20. What are antibodies? Give an example of an important antibody.

21. Give several examples of proteins that serve a protective function in the body.

22. How does a "permanent wave" change the structure of the protein of hair? What amino acid undergoes reaction during a permanent wave? Which level of structure for the hair protein is affected?

21.6 Enzymes

Questions

23. How does the efficiency of an enzyme compare to that of inorganic catalysts? Are enzymes more or less efficient?

24. What general name is given to the molecule acted on by an enzyme? What does it mean to say that an enzyme is *specific* for this molecule?

25. What name is given to the specific portion of the enzyme molecule where catalysis actually occurs?

26. Describe the *lock-and-key* model for enzymes. Why are the *shapes* of the enzyme and its substrate important in this model?

16. Cysteine contains the sulfhydryl (—SH) group in its side chain. It can therefore form disulfide linkages (—S—S—) with other cysteine molecules in the same polypeptide chain. This type of link produces a kink or a knot in the chain that leads to the tertiary structure (three-dimensional shape). For example, cysteine is responsible for the curling of hair.

17. Denaturation represents the breaking down of the protein's tertiary structure. Cooking a raw egg, adding heavy metal ions, and creating permanent hair waves are examples in which proteins are denatured.

18. Collagen has an α-helical secondary structure. Collagen functions as the raw material from which tendons are constructed.

19. enzymes

20. Antibodies are proteins made in the body in response to a foreign substance such as bacteria or viruses. Interferon is an important antibody because it offers general protection against viruses (many antibodies target specific invaders).

21. Antibodies are synthesized in the body in response to foreign substances such as bacteria. Interferon is a protein that helps to protect cells against viral infection. The process of blood clotting involves several proteins.

22. The cross-linkages between adjacent polypeptide chains of one

710

21.7 Carbohydrates

Questions

27. What functional groups are present in the simple sugars (monosaccharides)?

28. Sugars can be referred to as *polyhydroxy carbonyl* compounds. Explain this terminology.

29. In aqueous solution, the monosaccharides generally adopt a ring structure, rather than having "straight chains." Sketch representations for the ring forms of glucose and fructose.

30. Sketch the straight-chain structures of the following monosaccharides.
   a. glucose   c. ribulose
   b. ribose   d. galactose

21.8 Nucleic Acids

Questions

31. What molecule stores and transmits genetic information in the cell? How large is this molecule? Where in the cell is this molecule found?

32. Name the five nitrogen bases found in DNA and RNA. Which base is found commonly in RNA but not in DNA? Which base is found commonly in DNA but not in RNA?

33. Describe the double-helical structure of DNA. What type of bonding occurs *within* the chain of each strand of the double helix? What type of bonding exists *between* strands to link them together?

34. Describe the *complementary base pairing* between the two individual strands of DNA that forms the overall double-helical structure. How is complementary base pairing involved in the replication of the DNA molecule during cell division?

35. What name is applied to the specific section of the DNA molecule that contains the code for construction of a particular protein?

36. Explain the distinction between, and the functions of, messenger RNA and transfer RNA.

21.9 Lipids

Questions

37. Under what circumstances is a biomolecule classified as a *lipid*? Is the classification based on a particular characteristic structure or on some physical property?

38. Referring to Table 21.5, list several saturated and several unsaturated fatty acids. What is the general source of most unsaturated fatty acids?

39. What is *saponification*? Write a general equation for the saponification of a triglyceride. What are the ionic products of a saponification reaction more commonly called?

40. What is a *micelle*? How do the micelles formed by soap molecules suspend greasy dirt in a solution?

41. What steroid serves as the starting material in the body for the synthesis of other steroids? What dangers are involved in having too large a concentration of this substance in the body?

Critical Thinking

Matching

For exercises 42–63 choose one of the following terms to match the description given.

a. aldohexose   n. glycogen
b. saliva   o. glycoside linkage
c. antibody   p. hormone
d. cellulose   q. hydrophobic
e. CH_2O r. inhibition
f. cysteine   s. ketohexoses
g. denaturation   t. oxytocin
h. disaccharides   u. pleated sheet
i. disulfide   v. polypeptide
j. DNA   w. polysaccharides
k. enzymes   x. primary structure
l. fibrous   y. substrate
m. globular   z. sucrose

42. polymer consisting of many amino acids

43. linkage that forms between two cysteine species

44. peptide hormone that triggers milk secretion

45. proteins with roughly spherical shape

46. sequence of amino acids in a protein

47. silk protein secondary structure

48. water-repelling amino acid side chain

49. amino acid responsible for permanent wave in hair

50. biological catalysts

51. breakdown of a protein's tertiary and/or secondary structure

52. molecule acted on by an enzyme

53. occurs when an enzyme's active site is blocked by a foreign molecule

54. special protein synthesized in response to foreign substance

55. substance that has a specific effect on a particular target organ

56. animal polymer of glucose

57. —C—O—C— bond between rings in disaccharide sugars

58. empirical formula leading to the name carbo*hydrate*

59. where enzymes catalyzing the breakdown of glycoside link are found

60. six-carbon ketone sugars

61. structural component of plants, polymer of glucose

62. sugars consisting of two monomer units

63. six-carbon aldehyde sugars

---

droxyl groups (—OH).

29. See Figure 21.12.

30. (a)

(b)

(c)

(d)

31. DNA is responsible for coding and storing genetic information in the cell and for subsequently transmitting that information. It is found in the nucleus of each cell. The molar mass of DNA depends on the complexity of the species, but human DNA may have a molar mass as large as 2 billion g.

32. uracil (RNA only); cytosine (DNA, RNA); thymine (DNA only); adenine (DNA, RNA); guanine (DNA, RNA)

33. In a strand of DNA, the phosphate group and the sugar molecule of adjacent nucleotides become bonded to each other. The chain portion of the DNA molecule, therefore, consists of alternating phosphate groups and sugar molecules. The nitrogen bases are found sticking out from the side of this phosphate–sugar chain, being bonded to the sugar molecules.

(Please refer to page A14 in the back of this book to find answers to problems 34–63.)

---

protein are broken chemically and then re-formed chemically in a new location. The primary cross-linkage involved is a disulfide linkage between cysteine units in the polypeptide chain. The tertiary structure is mainly affected, although the secondary structure can also be affected if the waving lotion is left on too long (making the hair very "frizzy").

23. Enzymes are typically 1 to 10 million times more efficient than inorganic catalysts.

24. The molecule acted upon by an enzyme is referred to as the enzyme's substrate. If an enzyme is said to be specific for a particular substrate, it will catalyze the reactions of only that molecule.

25. active site

26. The lock-and-key model postulates that the structures of the enzyme and its substrate are complementary. In this way, the active site of the enzyme and the portion of the substrate to be acted upon can fit closely together. The structures of these portions of the molecules are unique to the particular enzyme–substrate pair. They fit together in the same way that a particular key is necessary to open a specific lock.

27. Simple sugars typically contain several hydroxyl groups as well as the carbonyl functional group.

28. Sugars contain an aldehyde or ketone functional group (carbonyl group, C=O) as well as several hy-

Appendices

Laboratory Safety Handbook

Appendix A

One of the first things a chemist learns is that working in a laboratory can be an exciting experience. But the laboratory can also be a dangerous place if safety rules are not followed. You must be responsible for your safety and the safety of others.

General Safety Rules

1. Read the directions for the experiment several times. Follow the directions exactly as they are written. If you have questions about any part of the procedure, ask your teacher for assistance.

2. Never perform any activities that are not authorized by your teacher. Do not work in the laboratory without teacher supervision.

3. Use the safety equipment provided for you. Safety goggles and a lab apron should be worn whenever you are working with chemicals or heating any substance.

4. Never eat or drink in the lab. Never inhale chemicals. Do not taste any chemicals.

5. Take care not to spill any material in the lab. If a spill occurs, immediately ask your teacher about the proper cleanup procedure. Do not pour chemicals or other substances into the sink or trash container.

6. Tie back long hair to keep it away from any chemicals, burners or other lab equipment.

7. Remove or tie back any articles of loose clothing or jewelry that can hang down and come in contact with chemicals or flames.

8. Know the locations and use of the safety showers and eyewashes.

First Aid in the Lab

Report any accidents or injury, no matter how minor, to your teacher.

Heating and Fire Safety

1. Maintain a clean work area and keep materials away from flames.

2. Never reach across an open flame.

3. Make sure you know how to use a Bunsen burner. Never leave a heat source unattended.

4. When heating a test tube, always point it away from you and others in case the substance bumps out of the tube.

5. Never heat a liquid in a sealed container. The increase in pressure could cause the container to break injuring you or others.

Injury	Response
Burns	Apply cold water. Call your teacher immediately.
Cuts and Abrasions	Stop any bleeding by applying direct pressure. Call your teacher immediately.
Foreign Matter in eye	Use eyewash to flush with plenty of water. Call your teacher immediately.
Fainting	Leave the person lying down. Loosen any tight clothing. Call your teacher immediately. Keep people away.
Poisoning	Note the suspected substance. Call your teacher immediately.
Spills on Skin	Flush with large amounts of water or use the safety shower. Call your teacher immediately.

6. Before picking up a container that has been heated hold the back of your hand close to the container. If you can feel heat on your hand the container is too hot to handle. Use a clamp, tongs or a hot pad. Remember hot glass looks just like cold glass.

7. If a fire should break out in the classroom or if your clothing catches fire smother it with a fire blanket or roll on the ground. NEVER RUN.

Working in the Laboratory Safely

1. Always use heat resistant (Pyrex) glassware for heating.

2. Use materials only from properly labeled containers. Read labels carefully before using chemicals.

3. Do not return chemicals to stock bottles. Discard extra chemicals as your teacher directs.

4. When diluting acids, *always add acid to water.*

5. Do not use the sink to discard matches, or any other solid material.

6. Use glycerine or a lubricant when inserting glass tubing or thermometers through rubber stoppers. Protect your hand with paper towel or a folded cloth.

7. Store backpacks, coats and other personal items away from the immediate lab bench area.

Cleaning Up the Laboratory

1. After working in the lab clean up your work area and return all equipment to its proper place.

2. Turn off all water and burners. Check that you have turned off the gas jet as well as the burner.

3. Dispose of chemicals and other materials as directed by your teacher.

4. Wash your hands thoroughly before leaving the lab.

Appendix B

Math Review

In solving chemistry problems you will use, over and over again, relatively few mathematical procedures. In this section we review the few algebraic manipulations that you will need.

Solving an Equation

In the course of solving a chemistry problem, we often construct an algebraic equation that includes the unknown quantity (the thing we want to calculate). An example is

$$(1.5)V = (0.23)(0.08206)(298)$$

We need to "solve this equation for V." That is, we need to isolate V on one side of the equals sign with all the numbers on the other side. How can we do this? The key idea in solving an algebraic equation is that *doing the same thing on both sides of the equals sign* does not change the equality. That is, it is always "legal" to do the same thing to both sides of the equation. Here we want to solve for V, so we must get the number 1.5 on the other side of the equals sign. We can do this by dividing *both sides* by 1.5.

$$\frac{(1.5)V}{1.5} = \frac{(0.23)(0.08206)(298)}{1.5}$$

Now the 1.5 in the denominator on the left cancels the 1.5 in the numerator:

$$\frac{(\cancel{1.5})V}{\cancel{1.5}} = \frac{(0.23)(0.08206)(298)}{1.5}$$

to give

$$V = \frac{(0.23)(0.08206)(298)}{1.5}$$

Using the procedures in "Using Your Calculator" for chain calculations, we can now obtain the value for V with a calculator.

$$V = 3.7$$

Sometimes it is necessary to solve an equation that consists of symbols. For example, consider the equation

$$\frac{P_1V_1}{T_1} = \frac{P_2V_2}{T_2}$$

Let's assume we want to solve for T_2. That is, we want to isolate T_2 on one side of the equation. There are several possible ways to proceed, keeping in mind that we always do the same thing on both sides of the equals sign. First we multiply both sides by T_2.

$$T_2 \times \frac{P_1V_1}{T_1} = \frac{P_2V_2}{\cancel{T_2}} \times \cancel{T_2}$$

This cancels T_2 on the right. Next we multiply both sides by T_1.

$$T_2 \times \frac{P_1V_1}{\cancel{T_1}} \times \cancel{T_1} = P_2V_2T_1$$

This cancels T_1 on the left. Now we divide both sides by P_1V_1.

$$T_2 \times \frac{\cancel{P_1V_1}}{\cancel{P_1V_1}} = \frac{P_2V_2T_1}{P_1V_1}$$

This yields the desired equation,

$$T_2 = \frac{P_2V_2T_1}{P_1V_1}$$

For practice, solve each of the following equations for the variable indicated.

a. $PV = k$; solve for P

b. $1.5x + 6 = 3$; solve for x

c. $PV = nRT$; solve for n

d. $\dfrac{P_1V_1}{T_1} = \dfrac{P_2V_2}{T_2}$; solve for V_2

e. $\dfrac{°F - 32}{°C} = \dfrac{9}{5}$; solve for $°C$

f. $\dfrac{°F - 32}{°C} = \dfrac{9}{5}$; solve for $°F$

Solutions

a. $\dfrac{P\cancel{V}}{\cancel{V}} = \dfrac{k}{V}$

$P = \dfrac{k}{V}$

b. $1.5x + 6 - 6 = 3 - 6$

$1.5x = -3$

$\dfrac{\cancel{1.5}x}{\cancel{1.5}} = \dfrac{-3}{1.5}$

$x = -\dfrac{3}{1.5} = -2$

c. $\dfrac{PV}{RT} = \dfrac{n\cancel{RT}}{\cancel{RT}}$

$\dfrac{PV}{RT} = n$

d. $\dfrac{P_1V_1}{T_1} \times T_2 = \dfrac{P_2V_2}{\cancel{T_2}} \times \cancel{T_2}$

$\dfrac{P_1V_1T_2}{T_1P_2} = \dfrac{\cancel{P_2}V_2}{\cancel{P_2}}$

$\dfrac{P_1V_1T_2}{T_1P_2} = V_2$

e. $\dfrac{°F - 32}{\cancel{°C}} \times \cancel{°C} = \dfrac{9}{5}°C$

$\dfrac{5}{9}(°F - 32) = \dfrac{\cancel{5}}{\cancel{9}} \times \dfrac{\cancel{9}}{\cancel{5}}°C$

$\dfrac{5}{9}(°F - 32) = °C$

f. $\dfrac{°F - 32}{\cancel{°C}} \times \cancel{°C} = \dfrac{9}{5}°C$

$°F - \cancel{32} + \cancel{32} = \dfrac{9}{5}°C + 32$

$°F = \dfrac{9}{5}°C + 32$

Appendix C

Scientific Notation

The numbers we must work with in scientific measurements are often very large or very small; thus it is convenient to express them using powers of 10. For example, the number 1,300,000 can be expressed as 1.3×10^6, which means multiply 1.3 by 10 six times, or

$$1.3 \times 10^6 = 1.3 \times \underbrace{10 \times 10 \times 10 \times 10 \times 10 \times 10}_{10^6 = 1\ million}$$

A number written in scientific notation always has the form:

> A number (between 1 and 10) times
> the appropriate power of 10

To represent a large number such as 20,500 in scientific notation, we must move the decimal point in such a way as to achieve a number between 1 and 10 and then multiply the result by a power of 10 to compensate for moving the decimal point. In this case, we must move the decimal point four places to the left.

$$2\underset{4\ 3\ 2\ 1}{0\,5\,0\,0}$$

to give a number between 1 and 10:

2.05

where we retain only the significant figures (the number 20,500 has three significant figures). To compensate for moving the decimal point four places to the left, we must multiply by 10^4. Thus

$$20{,}500 = 2.05 \times 10^4$$

As another example, the number 1985 can be expressed as 1.985×10^3. To end up with the number 1.985, which is between 1 and 10, we had to move the decimal point three places to the left. To compensate for that, we must multiply by 10^3. Some other examples are given in the accompanying left.

Number	Exponential Notation
5.6	5.6×10^0 or 5.6×1
39	3.9×10^1
943	9.43×10^2
1126	1.126×10^3

So far, we have considered numbers greater than 1. How do we represent a number such as 0.0034 in exponential notation? First, to achieve a number between 1 and 10, we start with 0.0034 and move the decimal point three places to the right.

$$0.\underset{1\ 2\ 3}{0\,0\,3\,4}$$

This yields 3.4. Then, to compensate for moving the decimal point to the right, we must multiply by a power of 10 with a negative exponent—in this case, 10^{-3}. Thus

$$0.0034 = 3.4 \times 10^{-3}$$

In a similar way, the number 0.00000014 can be written as 1.4×10^{-7}, because going from 0.00000014 to 1.4 requires that we move the decimal point seven places to the right.

Mathematical Operations with Exponents

We next consider how various mathematical operations are performed using exponents. First we cover the various rules for these operations; then we consider how to perform them on your calculator.

Multiplication and Division

When two numbers expressed in exponential notation are multiplied, the initial numbers are multiplied and the exponents of 10 are *added*.

$$(M \times 10^m)(N \times 10^n) = (MN) \times 10^{m+n}$$

For example (to two significant figures, as required),

$$(3.2 \times 10^4)(2.8 \times 10^3) = 9.0 \times 10^7$$

When the numbers are multiplied, if a result greater than 10 is obtained for the initial number, the decimal point is moved one place to the left and the exponent of 10 is increased by 1.

$$(5.8 \times 10^2)(4.3 \times 10^8) = 24.9 \times 10^{10}$$
$$= 2.49 \times 10^{11}$$
$$= 2.5 \times 10^{11} \qquad \text{(two significant figures)}$$

Division of two numbers expressed in exponential notation involves normal division of the initial numbers and *subtraction* of the exponent of the divisor from that of the dividend. For example,

$$\frac{4.8 \times 10^8}{\underset{\text{Divisor}}{2.1 \times 10^3}} = \frac{4.8}{2.1} \times 10^{(8-3)} = 2.3 \times 10^5$$

If the initial number resulting from the division is less than 1, the decimal point is moved one place to the right and the exponent of 10 is decreased by 1. For example,

$$\frac{6.4 \times 10^3}{8.3 \times 10^5} = \frac{6.4}{8.3} \times 10^{(3-5)} = 0.77 \times 10^{-2}$$
$$= 7.7 \times 10^{-3}$$

Addition and Subtraction

In order for us to add or subtract numbers expressed in exponential notation, *the exponents of the numbers must be the same.* For example, to add 1.31×10^5 and 4.2×10^4, we must rewrite one number so that the exponents of both are the same. The number 1.31×10^5 can be written 13.1×10^4: decreasing the exponent by 1 compensates for moving the decimal point one place to the right. Now we can add the numbers.

$$\begin{array}{r} 13.1 \times 10^4 \\ +\ \ 4.2 \times 10^4 \\ \hline 17.3 \times 10^4 \end{array}$$

In correct exponential notation, the result is expressed as 1.73×10^5.

To perform addition or subtraction with numbers expressed in exponential notation, we add or subtract only the initial numbers. The exponent of the result is the same as the exponents of the numbers being added or subtracted. To subtract 1.8×10^2 from 8.99×10^3, we first convert 1.8×10^2 to 0.18×10^3 so that both numbers have the same exponent. Then we subtract.

$$\begin{array}{r} 8.99 \times 10^3 \\ -\ 0.18 \times 10^3 \\ \hline 8.81 \times 10^3 \end{array}$$

Powers and Roots

When a number expressed in exponential notation is taken to some power, the initial number is taken to the appropriate power and the exponent of 10 is *multiplied* by that power.

$$(N \times 10^n)^m = N^m \times 10^{m \times n}$$

For example,

$$\begin{aligned} (7.5 \times 10^2)^2 &= (7.5)^2 \times 10^{2 \times 2} \\ &= 56. \times 10^4 \\ &= 5.6 \times 10^5 \end{aligned}$$

When a root is taken of a number expressed in exponential notation, the root of the initial number is taken and the exponent of 10 is divided by the number representing the root. For example, we take the square root of a number as follows:

$$\sqrt{N \times 10^n} = (N \times 10^n)^{1/2} = \sqrt{N} \times 10^{n/2}$$

For example,

$$\begin{aligned} (2.9 \times 10^6)^{1/2} &= \sqrt{2.9} \times 10^{6/2} \\ &= 1.7 \times 10^3 \end{aligned}$$

Using a Calculator to Perform Mathematical Operations on Exponents

In dealing with exponents, you must first learn to enter them into your calculator. First the number is keyed in and then the exponent. There is a special key that must be pressed just before the exponent is entered. This key is often labeled $\boxed{\text{EE}}$ or $\boxed{\text{exp}}$. For example, the number 1.56×10^6 is entered as follows:

Press	Display
1.56	1.56
EE or exp	1.56 00
6	1.56 06

To enter a number with a negative exponent, use the change-of-sign key $\boxed{+/-}$ after entering the exponent number. For example, the number 7.54×10^{-3} is entered as follows:

Press	Display
7.54	7.54
EE or exp	7.54 00
3	7.54 03
+/-	7.54 -03

Once a number with an exponent is entered into your calculator, the mathematical operations are performed exactly the same as with a "regular" number. For example, the numbers 1.0×10^3

and 1.0×10^2 are multiplied as follows:

Press	Display
1.0	1.0
EE or exp	1.0 00
3	1.0 03
$\times$	1 03
1.0	1.0
EE or exp	1.0 00
2	1.0 02
=	1 05

The answer is correctly represented as 1.0×10^5.

The numbers 1.50×10^5 and 1.1×10^4 are added as follows:

Press	Display
1.5	1.50
EE or exp	1.50 00
5	1.50 05
+	1.5 05
1.1	1.1
EE or exp	1.1 00
4	1.1 04
=	1.61 05

The answer is correctly represented as 1.61×10^5. Note that when exponential numbers are added, the calculator automatically takes into account any difference in exponents.

To take the power, root, or reciprocal of an exponential number, enter the number first, then press the appropriate key or keys. For example, the square root of 5.6×10^3 is obtained as follows:

Press	Display
5.6	5.6
EE or exp	5.6 00
3	5.6 03
$\sqrt{X}$	7.4833148 01

The answer is correctly represented as 7.5×10^1.

Practice by performing the following operations that involve exponential numbers. The answers follow the exercises.

a. $7.9 \times 10^2 \times 4.3 \times 10^4$ f. $\dfrac{1}{8.3 \times 10^2}$

b. $\dfrac{5.4 \times 10^3}{4.6 \times 10^5}$ g. $\log(1.0 \times 10^{-7})$

c. $1.7 \times 10^2 + 1.63 \times 10^3$ h. $-\log(1.3 \times 10^{-5})$

d. $4.3 \times 10^{-3} + 1 \times 10^{-4}$ i. $\sqrt{6.7 \times 10^9}$

e. $(8.6 \times 10^{-6})^2$

Solutions

a. 3.4×10^7 f. 1.2×10^{-3}

b. 1.2×10^{-2} g. -7.00

c. 1.80×10^3 h. 4.89

d. 4.4×10^{-3} i. 8.2×10^4

e. 7.4×10^{-11}

Appendix D

Graphing

In interpreting the results of a scientific experiment, it is often useful to make a graph. If possible, the function to be graphed should be in a form that gives a straight line. The equation for a straight line (a *linear equation*) can be represented in the general form

$$y = mx + b$$

where y is the *dependent variable*, x is the *independent variable*, m is the *slope*, and b is the *intercept* with the y axis.

To illustrate the characteristics of a linear equation, $y = 3x + 4$ is plotted in Figure A.1. For this equation $m = 3$ and $b = 4$. Note that the y intercept occurs when $x = 0$. In this case the y intercept is 4, as can be seen from the equation ($b = 4$).

The slope of a straight line is defined as the ratio of the rate of change in y to that in x:

$$m = \text{slope} = \frac{\Delta y}{\Delta x}$$

For the equation $y = 3x + 4$, y changes three times as fast as x (because x has a coefficient of 3). Thus the slope in this case is 3. This can be verified from the graph. For the triangle shown in Figure A.1,

$$\Delta y = 15 - 16 = 36 \qquad \text{and} \qquad \Delta x = 15 - 3 = 12$$

Thus

$$\text{Slope} = \frac{\Delta y}{\Delta x} = \frac{36}{12} = 3$$

This example illustrates a general method for obtaining the slope of a line from the graph of that line. Simply draw a triangle with one side parallel to the y axis and the other side parallel to the x axis, as shown in Figure A.1. Then determine the lengths of the sides to get Δy and Δx, respectively, and compute the ratio $\Delta y/\Delta x$.

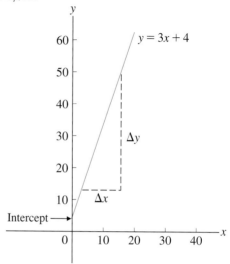

Figure A.1
Graph of the linear equation $y = 3x + 4$.

Appendix E

Naming Common Ions

Common Simple Cations and Anions			
Cation	**Name**	**Anion**	**Name***
H^+	hydrogen	H^-	hydride
Li^+	lithium	F^-	fluoride
Na^+	sodium	Cl^-	chloride
K^+	potassium	Br^-	bromide
Cs^+	cesium	I^-	iodide
Be^{2+}	beryllium	O^{2-}	oxide
Mg^{2+}	magnesium	S^{2-}	sulfide
Ca^{2+}	calcium		
Ba^{2+}	barium		
Al^{3+}	aluminum		
Ag^+	silver		

*The root is given in color.

Common Type II Cations		
Ion	**Systematic Name**	**Older Name**
Fe^{3+}	iron(III)	ferric
Fe^{2+}	iron(II)	ferrous
Cu^{2+}	copper(II)	cupric
Cu^+	copper(I)	cuprous
Co^{3+}	cobalt(III)	cobaltic
Co^{2+}	cobalt(II)	cobaltous
Sn^{4+}	tin(IV)	stannic
Sn^{2+}	tin(II)	stannous
Pb^{4+}	lead(IV)	plumbic
Pb^{2+}	lead(II)	plumbous
Hg^{2+}	mercury(II)	mercuric
Hg_2^{2+}*	mercury(I)	mercurous

*Mercury(I) ions always occur bound together in pairs to form Hg_2^{2+}.

Names of Common Polyatomic Ions

Ion	Name	Ion	Name
NH_4^+	ammonium	CO_3^{2-}	carbonate
NO_2^-	nitrite	HCO_3^-	hydrogen carbonate (bicarbonate is a widely used common name)
NO_3^-	nitrate	ClO^-	hypochlorite
SO_3^{2-}	sulfite	ClO_2^-	chlorite
SO_4^{2-}	sulfate	ClO_3^-	chlorate
HSO_4^-	hydrogen sulfate (bisulfate is a widely used common name)	ClO_4^-	perchlorate
OH^-	hydroxide	$C_2H_3O_2^-$	acetate
CN^-	cyanide	MnO_4^-	permanganate
PO_4^{3-}	phosphate	$Cr_2O_7^{2-}$	dichromate
HPO_4^{2-}	hydrogen phosphate	CrO_4^{2-}	chromate
$H_2PO_4^-$	dihydrogen phosphate	O_2^{2-}	peroxide

Appendix F

SI Units and Conversion Factors

These conversion factors are given with more significant figures than those typically used in the body of the text.

Length

SI Unit: Meter (m)

1 meter	= 1.0936 yards
1 centimeter	= 0.39370 inch
1 inch	= 2.54 centimeters (exactly)
1 kilometer	= 0.62137 mile
1 mile	= 5280. feet
	= 1.6093 kilometers

Volume

SI Unit: Cubic Meter (m³)

1 liter	= 10^{-3} m^3
	= 1 dm^3
	= 1.0567 quarts
1 gallon	= 4 quarts
	= 8 pints
	= 3.7854 liters
1 quart	= 32 fluid ounces
	= 0.94635 liter

Mass

SI Unit: Kilogram (kg)

1 kilogram	= 1000 grams
	= 2.2046 pounds
1 pound	= 453.59 grams
	= 0.45359 kilogram
	= 16 ounces
1 atomic mass unit	= 1.66057×10^{-27} kilograms

Pressure

SI Unit: Pascal (Pa)

1 atmosphere	= 101.325 kilopascals
	= 760.torr (mm Hg)
	= 14.70 pounds per square inch

Energy

SI Unit: Joule (J)

1 joule	= 0.23901 calorie
1 calorie	= 4.184 joules

Appendix G

Solubility Rules

General Rules for Solubility of Ionic Compounds (Salts) in Water at 25 °C

1. Most nitrate (NO_3^-) salts are soluble.
2. Most salts of Na^+, K^+, and NH_4^+ are soluble.
3. Most chloride salts are soluble. Notable exceptions are $AgCl$, $PbCl_2$, and Hg_2Cl_2.
4. Most sulfate salts are soluble. Notable exceptions are $BaSO_4$, $PbSO_4$, and $CaSO_4$.
5. Most hydroxide compounds are only slightly soluble.* The important exceptions are $NaOH$ and KOH. $Ba(OH)_2$ and $Ca(OH)_2$ are only moderately soluble.
6. Most sulfide (S^{2-}), carbonate (CO_3^{2-}), and phosphate (PO_4^{3-}) salts are only slightly soluble.*

*The terms *insoluble* and *slightly soluble* really mean the same thing: such a tiny amount dissolves that it is not possible to detect it with the naked eye.

Answers to End-of-Chapter Problems

Chapter 14 (continued)

42. The presence of a second metal's atoms in a metal's lattice changes the properties (usually making the alloy stronger because irregularities keep the crystal from being easily deformed). Steels with relatively high carbon content are exceptionally strong. Steels produced by alloying iron with nickel, chromium, and cobalt are more resistant to corrosion (rusting) than iron itself is.

43. m

44. j

45. g

46. f

47. i

48. d

49. e

50. a

51. c

52. l

53. Diethyl ether should have a higher vapor pressure because it does not exhibit hydrogen bonding, whereas 1-butanol does.

54. (a) KBr (ionic bonding); (b) NaCl (ionic bonding); (c) H_2O (hydrogen bonding)

55. Energy is required for a substance to evaporate (this energy is called the heat of vaporization). Applying rubbing alcohol to skin causes internal heat from the body to be absorbed as the heat of vaporization of the alcohol.

56. "Steel" is a general term applied to alloys consisting mostly of iron. Steel is much stronger and harder than iron, which is relatively soft, malleable, and ductile.

57. Dipole–dipole interactions are typically 1% as strong as a covalent bond.

58. London dispersion forces arise from instantaneous dipoles; they are weaker than dipole–dipole forces or covalent bonds.

59. (a) London dispersion forces; (b) hydrogen bonding and London dispersion forces; (c) London dispersion forces; (d) London dispersion forces

60. A volatile liquid is one that evaporates relatively easily. Such liquids generally have high vapor pressures because they have relatively weak intermolecular forces (London dispersion forces or weak dipole–dipole interactions).

61. In NH_3, strong hydrogen bonding can exist. Because CH_4 molecules are nonpolar, only the relatively weak London dispersion forces exist.

Chapter 19 (continued)

41. If the system used to cool a reactor core fails, the reactor may reach temperatures high enough to melt the core itself. It could become hot enough to melt through the bottom of the reactor and into the earth. A steam explosion is possible if the cooling system becomes blocked.

42. $^1_0n + ^{238}_{92}U \rightarrow ^{239}_{92}U$; $^{239}_{92}U \rightarrow ^{239}_{93}Np + ^{0}_{-1}e$; $^{239}_{93}Np \rightarrow ^{239}_{94}Pu + ^{0}_{-1}e$

43. Nuclear fusion is the process of combining two light nuclei into a larger nucleus, with an energy release larger even than that provided by fission processes.

44. The hydrogen nuclei are positively charged and therefore repel each other. Extremely high temperatures are needed to overcome this repulsion as they are shot into each other.

45. Fusion provides an enormous amount of energy per gram of fused material. If hydrogen can be fused, the earth possesses a large supply of the needed raw materials in the oceans. In addition, the product nuclei from the fusion of hydrogen (which are helium isotopes) are far less dangerous than those produced by fission processes.

46. Although the energy is small, it is enough to break chemical bonds, which may cause malfunctioning of cellular systems.

47. Somatic damage is damage directly to the organism itself. It causes nearly immediate sickness or death. Genetic damage is damage to the genetic machinery of the organism. It causes defects in future generations of offspring.

48. Alpha particles are stopped by the outermost layers of the skin; beta particles penetrate only about 1 cm into the body; gamma rays are deeply penetrating.

49. Alpha particles are much heavier than gamma rays, so they can ionize biological materials very effectively. Gamma rays can penetrate long distances but seldom cause ionization.

50. Nuclei of atoms that are chemically inert, or that are not ordinarily found in the body, tend to be excreted from the body quickly and do little damage. Nuclei of atoms that form a part of the body's structure or normal metabolic pro-cesses are likely to be incorporated into the body.

51. The exposure limits given in Table 19.5 as causing no detectable clinical effects are in the range of 0–25 rem. The total yearly exposures from natural and human-induced radioactive sources are estimated in Table 19.6 as less than 200 millirem (0.2 rem)—well within the acceptable limits.

52. alpha, beta, beta, alpha, alpha, alpha, alpha, alpha, beta, beta, alpha, beta, beta, alpha

53. (a) cobalt is a component of vitamin B_{12}; (b) bones consist partly of calcium phosphate; (c) red blood cells contain hemoglobin, an iron-protein compound; (d) mercury is absorbed by substances in the brain (part of the reason why mercury is so hazardous in the environment)

54. Nuclear waste has been generated for more than 40 years but no permanent disposal plan has been implemented yet. A major problem is that nuclear material has long half-lives, and we have not yet come up with equally long-lasting storage devices.

55. Al-27: 13 protons, 14 neutrons; Al-28: 13 protons, 15 neutrons; Al-29: 13 protons, 16 neutrons

56. ^{131}I is used in the diagnosis and treatment of thyroid cancer and other dysfunctions of the thyroid gland. The thyroid gland is the only organ in the human body that uses and stores iodine. ^{131}I that is administered concentrates there and can be used to create an image on a scanner or X-ray film. In higher doses it can selectively destroy cancer cells in the thyroid. ^{201}Tl concentrates in healthy muscle cells when administered and can be used to detect and assess damage to heart muscles after a heart attack; the damaged muscles show a lower uptake of ^{201}Tl than normal muscles do.

57. Breeder reactors convert nonfissionable U-238 into fissionable Pu-239. A combination of U-238 and U-235 is used. Excess neutrons from the U-235 fission are absorbed by U-238, converting it to Pu-239. The chemical and physical properties of Pu-239 make it very difficult and expensive to handle.

34. A comparison of the two strands of a DNA molecule shows that a given base in one strand is always paired with a particular base in the other strand. Because of the shapes and side atoms along the rings of the nitrogen bases, only certain parts can hydrogen-bond with one another in the double helix. Adenine is always paired with thymine; cytosine is always paired with guanine. When a DNA helix unwinds for replication during cell division, only the appropriate complementary bases are able to approach and bond to the nitrogen bases of each strand. For example, for a guanine–cytosine pair in the original DNA, when the two strands separate, only a new cytosine molecule can bond to the original guanine, and only a new guanine molecule can bond to the original cytosine.

35. gene

36. Messenger RNA molecules are synthesized to be complementary to a portion (gene) of the DNA molecule in the cell. They serve as the template or pattern upon which a protein will be constructed (a particular group of nitrogen bases on mRNA is able to accommodate and specify a particular amino acid in a particular location in the protein). Transfer RNA molecules are much smaller than mRNA, and their structure accommodates only a single, specific amino acid molecule. They "find" their specific amino acid in the cellular fluids and bring it to mRNA, where it is added to the protein molecule being synthesized.

37. Rather than having some common structural feature, substances are classified as lipids based on their solubility charactristics. Lipids are water-insoluble substances that can be extracted from cells by nonpolar organic solvents such as benzene or carbon tetrachloride.

38. Saturated: butyric acid, caproic acid, lauric acid, stear-ic acid; unsaturated: oleic acid, linoleic acid, linolenic acid. Most unsaturated fatty acids are derived from vegetable matter (plants).

39. Saponification is the production of a soap by treatment of a triglyceride with a strong base such as NaOH. triglyceride + 3NaOH → glycerol + 3Na$^+$soap$^-$

$$
\begin{array}{l}
CH_2-O-\overset{\overset{\displaystyle O}{\|}}{C}-R \\[6pt]
CH-O-\overset{\overset{\displaystyle O}{\|}}{C}-R' + 3NaOH \rightarrow \\[6pt]
CH_2-O-\overset{\overset{\displaystyle O}{\|}}{C}-R''
\end{array}
\qquad
\begin{array}{l}
CH_2-OH \quad RCOONa \\[6pt]
CH-OH + R'COONa \\[6pt]
CH_2-OH \quad R''COONa
\end{array}
$$

40. Soaps have a nonpolar nature and an ionic nature. In water, soap anions form aggregates called micelles, in which the hydrocarbon chains are oriented toward the interior of the aggregate and the ionic carboxyl groups are oriented toward the outside. The resulting micelle is able to interact with a grease molecule (pulling it into the hydrocarbon interior). See Figures 21.22 and 21.23.

41. Cholesterol is a naturally occurring steroid from which the body synthesizes other needed steroids. Because cholesterol is insoluble in water, having too large a concentration of this substance in the bloodstream may lead to buildup on the walls of blood vessels, causing their eventual blockage.

42. v   **43.** i

44. t   **45.** m

46. x   **47.** u

48. q   **49.** f

50. k   **51.** g

52. y   **53.** r

54. c   **55.** p

56. n   **57.** o

58. e   **59.** b

60. s   **61.** d

62. h   **63.** a

Glossary

Acid a substance that produces hydrogen ions in aqueous solution; a proton donor.

Acid–base indicator a substance that marks the end point of an acid–base titration by changing color.

Acid rain rainwater with an acidic pH, a result of air pollution by sulfur dioxide and nitrogen oxides.

Acidic oxide a covalent oxide that dissolves in water to give an acidic solution.

Actinide series a group of fourteen elements following actinium on the periodic table, in which the $5f$ orbitals are being filled.

Activation energy the threshold energy that must be overcome to produce a chemical reaction.

Air pollution contamination of the atmosphere, mainly by the gaseous products of transportation and the production of electricity.

Alcohol an organic compound in which the hydroxyl group is a substituent on a hydrocarbon.

Aldehyde an organic compound containing the carbonyl group bonded to at least one hydrogen atom.

Alkali metal a Group 1 metal.

Alkaline earth metal a Group 2 metal.

Alkane a saturated hydrocarbon with the general formula C_nH_{2n+2}.

Alkene an unsaturated hydrocarbon containing a carbon–carbon double bond. The general formula is C_nH_{2n}.

Alkyne an unsaturated hydrocarbon containing a carbon–carbon triple bond. The general formula is C_nH_{2n-2}.

Alloy a substance that contains a mixture of elements and has metallic properties.

Alloy steel a form of steel containing carbon plus metals such as chromium, cobalt, manganese, and molybdenum.

Alpha (α) particle a helium nucleus produced in radioactive decay.

Alpha-particle production a common mode of decay for radioactive nuclides in which the mass number changes.

Amine an organic base derived from ammonia in which one or more of the hydrogen atoms are replaced by organic groups.

α-Amino acid an organic acid in which an amino group, a hydrogen atom, and an R group are attached to the carbon atom next to the carboxyl group.

Ampere the unit of measurement for electric current; 1 ampere is equal to 1 coulomb of charge per second.

Amphoteric substance a substance that can behave either as an acid or as a base.

Anion a negative ion.

Anode in a galvanic cell, the electrode at which oxidation occurs.

Aqueous solution a solution in which water is the dissolving medium, or solvent.

Aromatic hydrocarbon one of a special class of cyclic unsaturated hydrocarbons, the simplest of which is benzene.

Arrhenius concept a concept postulating that acids produce hydrogen ions in aqueous solution, whereas bases produce hydroxide ions.

Atmosphere the mixture of gases that surrounds the earth's surface.

Atom the fundamental unit of which elements are composed.

Atomic mass (weight) the weighted average mass of the atoms in a naturally occurring element.

Atomic number the number of protons in the nucleus of an atom; each element has a unique atomic number.

Atomic radius half the distance between the atomic nuclei in a molecule consisting of identical atoms.

Atomic solid a solid that contains atoms at the lattice points.

Aufbau principle a principle stating that as protons are added one by one to the nucleus to build up the elements, electrons are similarly added to hydrogen-like orbitals.

Auto-ionization the transfer of a proton from one molecule to another of the same substance.

Avogadro's law equal volumes of gases at the same temperature and pressure contain the same number of particles (atoms or molecules).

Avogadro's number the number of atoms in exactly 12 grams of pure ^{12}C, equal to 6.022×10^{23}.

Ball-and-stick model a molecular model that distorts the sizes of atoms but shows bond relationships clearly.

Barometer a device for measuring atmospheric pressure.

Base a substance that produces hydroxide ions in aqueous solution; a proton acceptor.

Basic oxide an ionic oxide that dissolves in water to produce a basic solution.

Battery a group of galvanic cells connected in series.

Beta (β) particle an electron produced in radioactive decay.

Beta-particle production a decay process for radioactive nuclides in which the mass number remains constant and the atomic number increases by one. The net effect is to change a neutron to a proton.

Binary compound a two-element compound.

Binding energy (nuclear) the energy required to decompose a nucleus into its component nucleons.

Biochemistry the study of the chemistry of living systems.

Biomolecule a molecule that functions in maintaining and/or reproducing life.

Bond (chemical bond) the force that holds two atoms together in a compound.

Bond energy the energy required to break a given chemical bond.

Bond length the distance between the nuclei of the two atoms that are connected by a bond.

Bonding pair an electron pair found in the space between two atoms.

Boyle's law the volume of a given sample of gas at constant temperature varies inversely with the pressure.

Breeder reactor a nuclear reactor in which fissionable fuel is produced while the reactor runs.

Brønsted–Lowry model a model proposing that an acid is a proton donor and that a base is a proton acceptor.

Buffer capacity the ability of a buffered solution to absorb protons or hydroxide ions without a significant change in pH.

Buffered solution a solution that resists a change in its pH when either hydroxide ions or protons are added.

Buret a device for the accurate measurement of the delivery of a given volume of liquid.

Calorie a unit of measurement for energy; one calorie is the quantity of energy required to heat one gram of water by one Celsius degree.

Calorimetry the science of measuring heat flow.

Carbohydrate a polyhydroxyl ketone or polyhydroxyl aldehyde or a polymer composed of these.

Carbon steel an alloy of iron containing up to about 1.5% carbon.

Carboxyl group the—COOH group in an organic acid.

Carboxylic acid an organic compound containing the carboxyl group.

Catalyst a substance that speeds up a reaction without being consumed.

Cathode in a galvanic cell, the electrode at which reduction occurs.

Cathode rays the "rays" emanating from the negative electrode (cathode) in a partially evacuated tube; a stream of electrons.

Cathodic protection the connection of an active metal, such as magnesium, to steel to protect the steel from corrosion.

Cation a positive ion.

Cell potential (electromotive force) the driving force in a galvanic cell that pushes electrons from the reducing agent in one compartment to the oxidizing agent in the other.

Chain reaction (nuclear) a self-sustaining fission process caused by the production of neutrons that proceed to split other nuclei.

Charles's law the volume of a given sample of gas at constant pressure is directly proportional to the temperature in kelvins.

Chemical change the change of substances into other substances through a reorganization of the atoms; a chemical reaction.

Chemical equation a representation of a chemical reaction showing the relative numbers of reactant and product molecules.

Chemical equilibrium a dynamic reaction system in which the concentrations of all reactants and products remain constant as a function of time.

Chemical formula a representation of a molecule in which the symbols for the elements are used to indicate the types of atoms present and subscripts are used to show the relative numbers of atoms.

Chemical kinetics the area of chemistry that concerns reaction rates.

Chemical property the ability of a substance to change to a different substance.

Chemical stoichiometry the quantities of materials consumed and produced in a chemical reaction.

Colligative property a solution property that depends on the number of solute particles present.

Collision model a model based on the idea that molecules must collide to react; used to account for the observed characteristics of reaction rates.

Combustion reaction the vigorous and exothermic oxidation–reduction reaction that takes place between certain substances (particularly organic compounds) and oxygen.

Complete ionic equation an equation that shows as ions all substances that are strong electrolytes.

Compound a substance with constant composition that can be broken down into elements by chemical processes.

Condensation the process by which vapor molecules re-form a liquid.

Condensed states of matter liquids and solids.

Conjugate acid the species formed when a proton is added to a base.

Conjugate acid–base pair two species related to each other by the donating and accepting of a single proton.

Conjugate base what remains of an acid molecule after a proton is lost.

Continuous spectrum a spectrum that exhibits all the wavelengths of visible light.

Control rods in a nuclear reactor, rods composed of substances that absorb neutrons. These rods regulate the power level of the reactor.

Core electron an inner electron in an atom; one that is not in the outermost (valence) principal quantum level.

Corrosion the process by which metals are oxidized in the atmosphere.

Covalent bonding a type of bonding in which atoms share electrons.

Critical mass the mass of fissionable material required to produce a self-sustaining chain reaction.

Critical reaction (nuclear) a reaction in which exactly one neutron from each fission event causes another fission event, thus sustaining the chain reaction.

Crystalline solid a solid characterized by the regular arrangement of its components.

Dalton's law of partial pressures for a mixture of gases in a container, the total pressure exerted is the sum of the pressures that each gas would exert if it were alone.

Denaturation the breaking down of the three-dimensional structure of a protein, resulting in the loss of its function.

Density a property of matter representing the mass per unit volume.

Deoxyribonucleic acid (DNA) a huge nucleotide polymer having a double-helical structure with complementary bases on the two strands. Its major functions are protein synthesis and the storage and transport of genetic information.

Diatomic molecule a molecule composed of two atoms.

Dilution the process of adding solvent to lower the concentration of solute in a solution.

Dipole–dipole attraction the attractive force resulting when polar molecules line up such that the positive and negative ends are close to each other.

Dipole moment a property of a molecule whereby the charge distribution can be represented by a center of positive charge and a center of negative charge.

Disaccharide a sugar formed from two monosaccharides joined by a glycoside linkage.

Distillation a method for separating the components of a liquid mixture that depends on differences in the ease of vaporization of the components.

Double bond a bond in which two atoms share two pairs of electrons.

Dry cell battery a common battery used in calculators, watches, radios, and tape players.

Electrical conductivity the ability to conduct an electric current.

Electrochemistry the study of the interchange of chemical and electrical energy.

Electrolysis a process that involves forcing a current through a cell to cause a nonspontaneous chemical reaction to occur.

Electrolyte a material that dissolves in water to give a solution that conducts an electric current.

Electrolytic cell a cell that uses electrical energy to produce a chemical change that would not otherwise occur.

Electromagnetic radiation radiant energy that exhibits wave-like behavior and travels through space at the speed of light in a vacuum.

Electron a negatively charged particle that occupies the space around the nucleus of an atom.

Electronegativity the tendency of an atom in a molecule to attract shared electrons to itself.

Element a substance that cannot be decomposed into simpler substances by chemical or physical means. It consists of atoms all having the same atomic number.

Empirical formula the simplest whole-number ratio of atoms in a compound.

End point the point in a titration at which the indicator changes color.

Endothermic refers to a reaction in which energy (as heat) flows into the system.

Energy the capacity to do work or to cause the flow of heat.

Enthalpy at constant pressure, the change in enthalpy equals the energy flow as heat.

Enzyme a large molecule, usually a protein, that catalyzes biological reactions.

Equilibrium constant the value obtained when equilibrium concentrations of the chemical species are substituted into the equilibrium expression.

Equilibrium expression the expression (from the law of mass action) equal to the product of the product concentrations divided by the product of the reactant concentrations, each concentration having first been raised to a power represented by the coefficient in the balanced equation.

Equilibrium position a particular set of equilibrium concentrations.

Equivalence point (stoichiometric point) the point in a titration when enough titrant has been added to react exactly with the substance in solution that is being titrated.

Essential elements the elements known to be essential to human life.

Ester an organic compound produced by the reaction between a carboxylic acid and an alcohol.

Exothermic refers to a reaction in which energy (as heat) flows out of the system.

Exponential notation expresses a number in the form $N \times 10^{M}$; a convenient method for representing a very large or very small number and for easily indicating the number of significant figures.

Fat (glyceride) an ester composed of glycerol and fatty acids.

Fatty acid a long-chain carboxylic acid.

Filtration a method for separating the components of a mixture containing a solid and a liquid.

First law of thermodynamics a law stating that the energy of the universe is constant.

Fission the process of using a neutron to split a heavy nucleus into two nuclei with smaller mass numbers.

Fossil fuel a fuel that consists of carbon-based molecules derived from decomposition of once-living organisms; coal, petroleum, or natural gas.

Frequency the number of waves (cycles) per second that pass a given point in space.

Fuel cell a galvanic cell for which the reactants are continuously supplied.

Functional group an atom or group of atoms in hydrocarbon derivatives that contains elements in addition to carbon and hydrogen.

Fusion the process of combining two light nuclei to form a heavier, more stable nucleus.

Galvanic cell a device in which chemical energy from a spontaneous oxidation–reduction reaction is changed to electrical energy that can be used to do work.

Galvanizing a process in which steel is coated with zinc to prevent corrosion.

Gamma (γ) ray a high-energy photon produced in radioactive decay.

Gas one of the three states of matter; has neither fixed shape nor fixed volume.

Geiger–Müller counter (Geiger counter) an instrument that measures the rate of radioactive decay by registering the ions and electrons produced as a radioactive particle passes through a gas-filled chamber.

Gene a given segment of the DNA molecule that contains the code for a specific protein.

Greenhouse effect a warming effect exerted by certain molecules in the earth's atmosphere (particularly carbon dioxide and water).

Ground state the lowest possible energy state of an atom or molecule.

Group (of the periodic table) a vertical column of elements having the same valence electron configuration and similar chemical properties.

Haber process the manufacture of ammonia from nitrogen and hydrogen, carried out at high pressure and high temperature with the aid of a catalyst.

Half-life (of a radioactive sample) the time required for the number of nuclides in a radioactive sample to reach half the original number of nuclides.

Half-reactions the two parts of an oxidation–reduction reaction, one representing oxidation, the other reduction.

Halogen a Group 7 element.

Hard water water from natural sources that contains relatively large concentrations of calcium and magnesium ions.

Heat energy transferred between two objects because of a temperature difference between them.

Heating/cooling curve a plot of temperature versus time for a substance, where energy is added at a constant rate.

Heisenberg uncertainty principle a principle stating that there is a fundamental limitation to how precisely we can know both the position and the momentum of a particle at a given time.

Herbicide a pesticide applied to kill weeds.

Heterogeneous equilibrium an equilibrium involving reactants and/or products in more than one state.

Heterogeneous mixture a mixture that has different properties in different regions of the mixture.

Heterogeneous reaction reaction involving reactants in different phases.

Homogeneous equilibrium an equilibrium system in which all reactants and products are in the same state.

Homogeneous mixture a mixture that is the same throughout; a solution.

Homogeneous reaction reaction involving reactants in only one phase.

Hydration the interaction between solute particles and water molecules.

Hydrocarbon a compound of carbon and hydrogen.

Hydrocarbon derivative an organic molecule that contains one or more elements in addition to carbon and hydrogen.

Hydrogen bonding unusually strong dipole–dipole attractions that occur among molecules in which hydrogen is bonded to a highly electronegative atom.

Hydronium ion the H_3O^+ ion; a hydrated proton.

Hypothesis one or more assumptions put forth to explain observed phenomena.

Ideal gas a hypothetical gas that exactly obeys the ideal gas law. A real gas approaches ideal behavior at high temperature and/or low pressure.

Ideal gas law an equation relating the properties of an ideal gas, expressed as $PV = nRT$, where P = pressure, V = volume, n = moles of the gas, R = the universal gas constant, and T = temperature on the Kelvin scale. This equation expresses behavior closely approached by real gases at high temperature and/or low pressure.

Indicator a chemical that changes color and is used to mark the end point of a titration.

Intermolecular forces relatively weak interactions that occur between molecules.

Internal energy the sum of the kinetic and potential energies of all components of an object.

Intramolecular forces interactions that occur within a given molecule.

Ion an atom or a group of atoms that has a net positive or negative charge.

Ion-product constant (K_w) the equilibrium constant for the auto-ionization of water; $K_w = [H^+][OH^-]$. At 25 °C, K_w equals 1.0×10^{-14}.

Ionic bonding the attraction between oppositely charged ions.

Ionic compound a compound that results when a metal reacts with a nonmetal to form cations and anions.

Ionic solid a solid containing cations and anions that dissolves in water to give a solution containing the separated ions, which are mobile and thus free to conduct an electric current.

Ionization energy the quantity of energy required to remove an electron from a gaseous atom or ion.

Isomers species that have the same chemical formula but different properties.

Isotopes atoms of the same element (the same number of protons) that have different numbers of neutrons. They have identical atomic numbers but different mass numbers.

Joule a unit of measurement for energy; 1 calorie = 4.184 joules.

Ketone an organic compound containing the carbonyl group bonded to two carbon atoms.

Kinetic energy $\left(\frac{1}{2}mv^2\right)$ energy due to the motion of an object; dependent on the mass of the object and the square of its velocity.

Kinetic molecular theory a model that assumes that an ideal gas is composed of tiny particles (molecules) in constant motion.

Lanthanide series a group of fourteen elements following lanthanum on the periodic table, in which the $4f$ orbitals are being filled.

Lattice a three-dimensional system of points designating the positions of the centers of the components of a solid (atoms, ions, or molecules).

Law of chemical equilibrium a general description of the equilibrium condition; it defines the equilibrium expression.

Law of conservation of energy energy can be converted from one form to another but can be neither created nor destroyed.

Law of conservation of mass mass is neither created nor destroyed.

Law of constant composition a given compound always contains elements in exactly the same proportion by mass.

Law of mass action (also called the law of chemical equilibrium) a general description of the equilibrium condition; it defines the equilibrium expression.

Law of multiple proportions a law stating that when two elements form a series of compounds, the ratios of the masses of the second element that combine with one gram of the first element can always be reduced to small whole numbers.

Lead storage battery a battery (used in cars) in which the anode is lead, the cathode is lead coated with lead dioxide, and the electrolyte is a sulfuric acid solution.

Le Châtelier's principle if a change is imposed on a system at equilibrium, the position of the equilibrium will shift in a direction that tends to reduce the effect of that change.

Lewis structure a diagram of a molecule showing how the valence electrons are arranged among the atoms in the molecule.

Limiting reactant (limiting reagent) the reactant that is completely consumed when a reaction is run to completion.

Line spectrum a spectrum showing only certain discrete wavelengths.

Linear accelerator a type of particle accelerator in which a changing electrical field is used to accelerate a beam of charged particles along a linear path.

Lipids water-insoluble substances that can be extracted from cells by nonpolar organic solvents.

Liquid one of the three states of matter; has a fixed volume but takes the shape of its container.

London dispersion forces the relatively weak forces, which exist among noble gas atoms and nonpolar molecules, that involve an accidental dipole that induces a momentary dipole in a neighbor.

Lone pair an electron pair that is localized on a given atom; an electron pair not involved in bonding.

Main-group (representative) elements elements in the groups labeled 1,2,3,4,5,6,7, and 8 on the periodic table. The group number gives the sum of the valence s and p electrons.

Mass the quantity of matter in an object.

Mass number the total number of protons and neutrons in the atomic nucleus of an atom.

Mass percent the percent by mass of a component of a mixture or of a given element in a compound.

Matter the material of the universe.

Metal an element that gives up electrons relatively easily and is typically lustrous, malleable, and a good conductor of heat and electricity.

Metalloid an element that has both metallic and non-metallic properties.

Metallurgy the process of separating a metal from its ore and preparing it for use.

Millimeters of mercury (mm Hg) a unit of measurement for pressure, also called a torr; 760 mm Hg = 760 torr = 101,325 Pa = 1 standard atmosphere.

Mixture a material of variable composition that contains two or more substances.

Model (theory) a set of assumptions put forth to explain the observed behavior of matter. The models of chemistry usually involve assumptions about the behavior of individual atoms or molecules.

Moderator a substance used in a nuclear reactor to slow down the neutrons.

Molar heat of fusion the energy required to melt 1 mol of a solid.

Molar heat of vaporization the energy required to vaporize 1 mol of a liquid.

Molar mass the mass in grams of one mole of a compound.

Molar volume the volume of one mole of an ideal gas; equal to 22.42 liters at standard temperature and pressure.

Molarity moles of solute per volume of solution in liters.

Mole (mol) the number equal to the number of carbon atoms in exactly 12 grams of pure ^{12}C: Avogadro's number. One mole represents 6.022×10^{23} units.

Mole ratio (stoichiometry) the ratio of moles of one substance to moles of another substance in a balanced chemical equation.

Molecular equation an equation representing a reaction in solution and showing the reactants and products in undissociated form, whether they are strong or weak electrolytes.

Molecular formula the exact formula of a molecule, giving the types of atoms and the number of each type.

Molecular solid a solid composed of small molecules.

Molecular structure the three-dimensional arrangement of atoms in a molecule.

Molecular weight (molar mass) the mass in grams of one mole of a substance.

Molecule a bonded collection of two or more atoms of the same element or different elements.

Monoprotic acid an acid with one acidic proton.

Natural gas consists of mostly methane and is associated with petroleum deposits.

Natural law a statement that expresses generally observed behavior.

Net ionic equation an equation for a reaction in solution, representing strong electrolytes as ions and showing only those components that are directly involved in the chemical change.

Network solid an atomic solid containing strong directional covalent bonds.

Neutralization reaction an acid–base reaction.

Neutron a particle in the atomic nucleus with a mass approximately equal to that of the proton but with no charge.

Noble gas a Group 8 element.

Nonelectrolyte a substance that, when dissolved in water, gives a nonconducting solution.

Nonmetal an element that does not exhibit metallic characteristics. Chemically, a typical nonmetal accepts electrons from a metal.

Normal boiling point the temperature at which the vapor pressure of a liquid is exactly one atmosphere; the boiling temperature under one atmosphere of pressure.

Normal melting/freezing point the melting/freezing point of a solid at a total pressure of one atmosphere.

Normality the number of equivalents of a substance dissolved in a liter of solution.

Nuclear atom the modern concept of the atom as having a dense center of positive charge (the nucleus) and electrons moving around the outside.

Nuclear transformation the change of one element into another.

Nucleon a particle in an atomic nucleus, either a neutron or a proton.

Nucleus the small, dense center of positive charge in an atom.

Nuclide the general term applied to each unique atom; represented by $^{A}_{Z}X$, where X is the symbol for a particular element.

Octet rule the observation that atoms of nonmetals form the most stable molecules when they are surrounded by eight electrons (to fill their valence orbitals).

Orbital a representation of the space occupied by an eletron in an atom; the probability distribution for the electron.

Organic acid an acid with a carbon-atom backbone and a carboxyl group.

Organic chemistry the study of carbon-containing compounds (typically containing chains of carbon atoms) and their properties.

Oxidation an increase in oxidation state (a loss of electrons).

Oxidation–reduction (redox) reaction a reaction in which one or more electrons are transferred.

Oxidation states a concept that provides a way to keep track of electrons in oxidation–reduction reactions according to certain rules.

Oxidizing agent (electron acceptor) a reactant that accepts electrons from another reactant.

Oxyacid an acid in which the acidic proton is attached to an oxygen atom.

Ozone O_3, a form of elemental oxygen much less common than O_2 in the atmosphere near the earth.

Partial pressures the independent pressures exerted by different gases in a mixture.

Particle accelerator a device used to accelerate nuclear particles to very high speeds.

Pascal the SI unit of measurement for pressure; equal to one newton per square meter.

Percent yield the actual yield of a product as a percentage of the theoretical yield.

Periodic table a chart showing all the elements arranged in columns in such a way that all the elements in a given column exhibit similar chemical properties.

Petroleum a thick, dark liquid composed mostly of hydrocarbon compounds.

pH scale a log scale based on 10 and equal to $-\log[H^+]$; a convenient way to represent solution acidity.

Phenyl group the benzene molecule minus one hydrogen atom.

Photochemical smog air pollution produced by the action of light on oxygen, nitrogen oxides, and unburned fuel from auto exhaust to form ozone and other pollutants.

Photon a "particle" of electromagnetic radiation.

Physical charge a change in the form of a substance, but not in its chemical nature; chemical bonds are not broken in a physical change.

Physical property a characteristic of a substance that can change without the substance becoming a different substance.

Polar covalent bond a covalent bond in which the electrons are not shared equally because one atom attracts them more strongly than the other.

Polar molecule a molecule that has a permanent dipole moment.

Polyatomic ion an ion containing a number of atoms.

Polyelectronic atom an atom with more than one electron.

Polymer a large, usually chain-like molecule built from many small molecules (monomers).

Polymerization a process in which many small molecules (monomers) are joined together to form a large molecule.

Polyprotic acid an acid with more than one acidic proton. It dissociates in a stepwise manner, one proton at a time.

Positron production a mode of nuclear decay in which a particle is formed that has the same mass as an electron but opposite charge. The net effect is to change a proton to a neutron.

Potential energy energy due to position or composition.

Precipitation reaction a reaction in which an insoluble substance forms and separates from the solution as a solid.

Precision the degree of agreement among several measurements of the same quantity; the reproducibility of a measurement.

Primary structure (of a protein) the order (sequence) of amino acids in the protein chain.

Probability distribution (orbital) a representation indicating the probabilities of finding an electron at various points in space.

Product a substance resulting from a chemical reaction. It is shown to the right of the arrow in a chemical equation.

Protein a natural polymer formed by condensation reactions between amino acids.

Proton a positively charged particle in an atomic nucleus.

Pure substance a substance with constant composition.

Radioactive decay (radioactivity) the spontaneous decomposition of a nucleus to form a different nucleus.

Radiocarbon dating (carbon-14 dating) a method for dating ancient wood or cloth on the basis of the radioactive decay of the nuclide $^{14}_{6}C$.

Radiotracer a radioactive nuclide, introduced into an organism for diagnostic purposes, whose pathway can be traced by monitoring its radioactivity.

Random error an error that has an equal probability of being high or low.

Rate of decay the change per unit time in the number of radioactive nuclides in a sample.

Reactant a starting substance in a chemical reaction. It appears to the left of the arrow in a chemical equation.

Reactor core the part of a nuclear reactor where the fission reaction takes place.

Reducing agent (electron donor) a reactant that donates electrons to another substance, reducing the oxidation state of one of its atoms.

Reduction a decrease in oxidation state (a gain of electrons).

Rem a unit of radiation dosage that accounts for both the energy of the dose and its effectiveness in causing biological damage (from *r*oentgen *e*quivalent for *m*an).

Resonance a condition occurring when more than one valid Lewis structure can be written for a particular molecule. The actual electronic structure is represented not by any one of the Lewis structures but by the average of all of them.

Salt an ionic compound.

Salt bridge a U-tube containing an electrolyte that connects the two compartments of a galvanic cell, allowing ion flow without extensive mixing of the different solutions.

Saturated solution a solution that contains as much solute as can be dissolved in that solution.

Scientific method a process of studying natural phenomena that involves making observations, forming laws and theories, and testing theories by experimentation.

Scientific notation see *Exponential notation.*

Scintillation counter an instrument that measures radioactive decay by sensing the flashes of light that the radiation produces in a detector.

Secondary structure (of a protein) the three-dimensional structure of the protein chain (for example, α-helix, random coil, or pleated sheet).

SI units International System of units based on the metric system and on units derived from the metric system.

Sigma (σ) bond a covalent bond in which the electron pair is shared in an area centered on a line running between the atoms.

Significant figures the certain digits and the first uncertain digit of a measurement.

Silica the fundamental silicon–oxygen compound, which has the empirical formula SiO_2 and forms the basis of quartz and certain types of sand.

Silicates salts that contain metal cations and polyatomic silicon–oxygen anions that are usually polymeric.

Single bond a bond in which two atoms share one pair of electrons.

Solid one of the three states of matter; has a fixed shape and volume.

Solubility the amount of a substance that dissolves in a given volume of solvent or solution at a given temperature.

Solubility product the constant for the equilibrium expression representing the dissolving of an ionic solid in water.

Solute a substance dissolved in a solvent to form a solution.

Solution a homogeneous mixture.

Solvent the dissolving medium in a solution.

Somatic damage radioactive damage to an organism resulting in its sickness or death.

Specific heat another name for specific heat capacity.

Specific heat capacity the amount of energy required to raise the temperature of one gram of a substance by one Celsius degree.

Spectator ions ions present in solution that do not participate directly in a reaction.

Standard atmosphere a unit of measurement for pressure equal to 760 mm Hg or 101, 325 Pa.

Standard solution a solution the concentration of which is accurately known.

Standard temperature and pressure (STP) the condition 0 °C and 1 atmosphere of pressure.

State function a property that is independent of the pathway.

States of matter the three different forms in which matter can exist: solid, liquid, and gas.

Stoichiometric quantities quantities of reactants mixed in exactly the amounts that result in their all being used up at the same time.

Stoichiometry of a reaction the relative quantities of reactants and products involved in the reaction.

Strong acid an acid that completely dissociates (ionizes) to produce H^+ ion and the conjugate base.

Strong base a metal hydroxide compound that completely dissociates into its ions in water.

Strong electrolyte a material that, when dissolved in water, dissociates (ionizes) completely and gives a solution that conducts an electric current very efficiently.

Structural formula the representation of a molecule in which the relative positions of the atoms are shown and the bonds are indicated by lines.

Subcritical reaction (nuclear) a reaction in which fewer than one of the neutrons from each fission event causes another fission event and the process dies out.

Sublimation the process by which a substance goes directly from the solid state to the gaseous state without passing through the liquid state.

Substitution reaction (hydrocarbons) a reaction in which an atom, usually a halogen, replaces a hydrogen atom in a hydrocarbon.

Supercooling the process of cooling a liquid to a temperature below its freezing point without its changing to a solid.

Supercritical reaction (nuclear) a reaction in which more than one of the neutrons from each fission event causes another fission event. The process rapidly escalates to a violent explosion.

Superheating the process of heating a liquid to a temperature above its boiling point without its boiling.

Surroundings everything in the universe surrounding a thermodynamic system.

System (thermodynamic) that part of the universe on which attention is to be focused.

Systematic error an error that always occurs in the same direction.

Temperature measure of the random motions (average kinetic energy) of the components of a substance.

Tertiary structure (of a protein) the overall shape of a protein, long and narrow or globular, maintained by different types of intramolecular interactions.

Theoretical yield the maximum amount of a given product that can be formed when the limiting reactant is completely consumed.

Theory (model) a set of assumptions put forth to explain some aspect of the observed behavior of matter.

Thermodynamics a study of energy and its interactions.

Titration a technique in which one solution is used to analyze another.

Torr another name for millimeters of mercury (mm Hg).

Trace elements metals present only in trace amounts in the human body.

Transition metals several series of elements in which inner orbitals (d or f orbitals) are being filled.

Transuranium elements the elements beyond uranium that are made artificially by particle bombardment.

Triple bond a bond in which two atoms share three pairs of electrons.

Uncertainty (in measurement) the characteristic reflecting the fact that any measurement involves estimates and cannot be exactly reproduced.

Unit factor an equivalence statement between units that is used for converting from one set of units to another.

Universal gas constant the combined proportionality constant in the ideal gas law; 0.08206 L atm/K mol, or 8.314 J/K mol.

Unsaturated solution a solution in which more solute can be dissolved than is dissolved already.

Valence electrons the electrons in the outermost occupied principal quantum level of an atom.

Valence shell electron pair repulsion (VSEPR) model a model the main postulate of which is that the structure around a given atom in a molecule is determined principally by the tendency to minimize electron-pair repulsions.

Vapor pressure the pressure of the vapor over a liquid at equilibrium in a closed container.

Vaporization (evaporation) the change in state that occurs when a liquid evaporates to form a gas.

Viscosity the resistance of a liquid to flow.

Volt the unit of measurement for electric potential; it is defined as one joule of work per coulomb of charge transferred.

Wavelength the distance between two consecutive peaks or troughs in a wave.

Weak acid an acid that dissociates only to a slight extent in aqueous solution.

Weak base a base that reacts with water to produce hydroxide ions to only a slight extent in aqueous solution.

Weak electrolyte a material that, when dissolved in water, gives a solution that conducts only a small electric current.

Weight the force exerted on an object by gravity.

Work force acting over a distance.

Photo/Illustration Credits

Photographs by Sean Brady were arranged with the assistance of Professor Doug Sawyer.

Chapter 1

p. 2, Fred Hirschmann; p. 3, PhotoDisc; p. 4, Bart Eklund; p. 5, David Katzenstein/Corbis; p. 6, Sean Brady; p. 7, StockTrek/PhotoDisc; p. 8, Kaz Mori/The Image Bank; p. 10, Ken O'Donoghue; p. 13, Robert Harding Associates; p. 15, Michael Newman/PhotoEdit.

Chapter 2

p. 20, Fred Hirschmann; p. 21, Sean Brady; p. 22 (top), Sean Brady; p. 22 (center) IBM Almaden Research Center; p. 22 (bottom, left), Dr. Jeremy Burgess/Science Photo Library/Photo Researchers, Inc.; p. 22 (bottom, right), Chuck Place; p. 23, The Art Archive/Chicago Art Institute/Album/Joseph Martin; p. 25 (left), Don Farrall/PhotoDisc; p. 25 (right), Sean Brady; p. 27 (left), Lawrence Lawry/PhotoDisc); p. 27 (center), Lester V. Bergman/Corbis; p. 27 (right), Tom Pantages; p. 28, Fred Hirschmann; p. 29, Richard Megna/Fundamental Photographs; p. 30, Sean Brady; p. 31, Chip Clark; p. 33, Jim Pickerell/Tony Stone; p. 36, Ulrike Welsch/PhotoEdit; p. 37 (top), PhotoDisc; p. 37 (bottom), Richard Megna/Fundamental Photographs; p. 38, Richard Megna/Fundamental Photographs; p. 40, Fred Hirschmann.

Chapter 3

p. 46, Yann Arthus-Bertrand/Corbis; p. 47, The Granger Collection; p. 48, Ulf E. Wallin/The Image Bank; p. 50 (top), PhotoLink/Corbis; p. 50 (bottom), Archivo Iconografico, S.A./Corbis; p. 52, Reproduced by permission, Manchester Literary and Philosophical Society; p. 56, Bettmann/Corbis; p. 58, Cindy Charles/PhotoEdit; p. 62, Sean Brady; p. 66 (top), Bethnal Green Museum, London/Bridgeman Art Library, NY; p. 66 (bottom), API/Explorer/Photo Researchers, Inc.; p. 68, Dr. E.R. Degginger; p. 69 (both), Sean Brady; p. 70 (top), Sean Brady; p. 70 (bottom), Paul Silverman/Fundamental Photographs; p. 74, Dr. E.R. Degginger; p. 75, Dr. E.R. Degginger.

Chapter 4

p. 84, Randi Hirschmann; p. 85, Bob Daemmrich/The Image Bank; p. 87, Erich Lessing/Art Resource, NY; p. 90, Sean Brady; p. 96 (top photos), Sean Brady; p. 96 (bottom), Dr. Gopal Murti/Science Photo Library/Photo Researchers, Inc.; p. 103, Dan Suzio/Photo Researchers, Inc.

Chapter 5

p. 112, Phillip Hayson/Photo Researchers, Inc.; p. 113, Sean Brady; p. 114, Ray Simon/Photo Researchers, Inc.; p. 117, NASA, p. 120, Courtesy, Mettler-Toledo; p. 123, Ben Osborne/Stone; p. 124, Russel D. Curtis/Photo Researchers, Inc.; p. 138, Warner Brothers/Kobal Collection; p. 145, Dan McCoy/Rainbow; p. 146, Tom Pantages.

Chapter 6

p. 152, Adam Woolfitt/Corbis; p. 153 (top), Jeff Greenberg/Visuals Unlimited; p. 153 (bottom), Siede Preis/PhotoDisc; p. 159 (all), Ken O'Donoghue; p. 160, Ken O'Donoghue; p. 161, Sean Brady; p. 162, Sean Brady; p. 163, G.K. & Vikki Hart/The Image Bank; p. 168, Michael P. Gadomski/Photo Researchers, Inc.; p. 171, Sean Brady; p. 173, NASA; p. 174, The Art Archive/Victoria and Albert Museum London/Graham Brandon; p. 179, Grant Heilman/Grant Heilman Photography.

Chapter 7

p. 192, Charles Winters/Photo Researchers, Inc.; p. 193 (top), J.C. Allen/Stock, Boston; p. 193 (bottom, left), Stephen Derr/The Image Bank; p. 193 (bottom, right), Sean Brady; p. 194 (top, left), Sean Brady; p. 194 (center), Spencer Grant/PhotoEdit; p. 194 (right), Sean Brady; p. 195 (all), Richard Megna/Fundamental Photographs; p. 197 (all), Richard Megna/Fundamental Photographs; p. 199, Richard Megna/Fundamental Photographs; p. 202, Thomas Eisner and Daniel Aneshansley, Cornell University; p. 206, Richard Megna/Fundamental Photographs.

Chapter 8

p. 212, Richard Megna/Fundamental Photographs; p. 213, Dan McCoy/Rainbow; p. 214, Richard Megna/Fundamental Photographs; p. 220, Sean Brady; p. 225, Sean Brady; p. 227, Stephen P. Parker/Photo Researchers, Inc.; p. 228, Sean Brady; p. 230, Bruce Roberts/Photo Researchers, Inc.; p. 232, Richard Megna/Fundamental Photographs; p. 233, Sean Brady; p. 237, PhotoDisc; p. 238, (Figure 8.8) Reprinted with permission from *Chemical and Engineering News*, Vol. 66, Issue #38, September 19, 1998, pg. 9, Copyright © 1988 American Chemical Society, (Figure 8.9) Reprinted with permission from *Chemical and Engineering News*, Vol. 66, Issue #38, September 19, 1998, pg. 9, Copyright © 1988 American Chemical Society, (Figure 8.10) Courtesy, Morton Thiokol; p. 240, Michael Newman/PhotoEdit.

Chapter 9

p. 250, Paul S. Howell/Gamma Liaison; p. 251, Corbis Images/Picture Quest; p. 253, Bill Bachmann/PhotoEdit; p. 261 (both), Sean Brady; p. 264, NASA, p. 265, George Olson/The Photo File; p. 266, Larry Larimer/Artville/PictureQuest; p. 271, Grant Heilman/Grant Heilman Photography; p. 276, Ken O'Donoghue; p. 277, Sean Brady.

Chapter 10

p. 288, NASA, p. 289, Chad Ehler/Stock Connection/PictureQuest; p. 292, ElektraVision AG/PictureQuest; p. 295, Sean Brady; p. 297, Neil Lucas/BBC Wild; p. 301, AP Photo/Itsuo Inouye; p. 303, John Pinkston and Laura Stern/USGS, Menlo Park; p. 304, Argonne National Laboratory; p. 309, Alan Oddie/PhotoEdit; p. 311, Courtesy, National Biodiesel Fuel Board.

Chapter 11

p. 322, Robert Everts/Tony Stone; p. 323, AP Photo/Donna McWilliam; p. 326, Sean Brady; p. 327, Agricultural Research Service, USDA; p. 331, AIP Emilio Segre Visual Archives; p. 332, The Granger Collection; p. 333, AP Photo/Terry Renna; p. 342, Courtesy of Professor Andrey K. Geim/High Field Magnet Laboratory/University of Nijmegen; p. 346, Dan McCoy/Rainbow; p. 348, AP Photo/The Charleston Daily Mail, Chip Ellis; p. 351, PhotoLink/PhotoDisc/PictureQuest.

Chapter 12

p. 358, Digital Vision/Picture Quest; p. 359, Tino Hammid; p. 368, Courtesy, Fraunhofer Institute for Applied Materials Research; p. 372, The Bancroft Library, p. 377, Vince Streano/Corbis; p. 380 (both), Donald Clegg; p. 382 (all), Frank Cox.

Chapter 13

p. 398, Photo by Jurg Alean; p. 399, Photo by Jean-Francois Luy with the kind authorization of Breitling SA; p. 400 (both), Sean Brady; p. 402, Ken O'Donoghue; p. 406, Dave Jacobs/Tony Stone; p. 408, John A. Rizzo/PhotoDisc; p. 410, James L. Amos/Corbis; p. 420, Sean Brady; p. 423, Kurt Amsler/Vandystadt/AllsportUSA; p. 429, Based on Dr. Donald H. Stedman and Gary A. Bishiop, *Scientific News*, **157**, 166, March 11, 2000 p. 432, Courtesy, Ford Motor Corporation.

Chapter 14

p. 440, Fred Hirschmann; p. 441, Ryan McVay/Photodisc; p. 442, USDA Photo by Scott Bauer; p. 448, Flip Nicklin/Minden Pictures; p. 450, PhotoLink/PhotoDisc; p. 452, David Chasey/PhotoDisc; p. 454 (top left, center), Sean Brady; p. 454 (top, right), Mark A. Schneider/Visuals Unlimited; p. 454 (bottom), M. Freeman/PhotoLink/PhotoDisc; p. 457 (left), Ken O'Donoghue; p. 457 (right), Richard Megna/Fundamental Photographs; p. 458, Reshef Tenne/Department of Materials & Interfaces/Weizmann Institute/Israel; p. 459, T.J. Florian/Rainbow; p. 460 (all) Sean Brady.

Chapter 15

p. 466, Martin Rogers/Tony Stone; p. 467, Siede Preis/PhotoDisc; p. 470, AP Photo/Jon Reid; p. 471, Micheal Newman/PhotoEdit; p. 472, Charles D. Winters/Photo Researchers, Inc.; p. 473, D. Yeske/Visuals Unlimited; p. 479, Tom Pantages; p. 484, Tom Pantages; p. 486, Richard Megna/Fundamental Photographs; p. 487, Ken O'Donoghue; p. 490, Van Bucher/Photo Researchers, Inc.

Chapter 16

p. 502, S. Pearce/PhotoLink/PhotoDisc; p. 503 (top), PhotoLink/PhotoDisc; p. 503 (bottom), Sean Brady; p. 505, Sean Brady; p. 507, Sean Brady; p. 509, Sean Brady; p. 510, Agricultural Research Service/USDA; p. 517, Andrew Syred/Science Photo Library/Photo Researchers, Inc.; p. 518, David Woodfall/Tony Stone; p. 521 (left), Sean Brady; p. 521 (right), Richard Megna/Fundamental Photographs; p. 523, Copyright Los Angeles Times Syndicate. Photo from Chemical Heritage Foundation; p. 525 (top), Richard Megna/Fundamental Photographs; p. 525 (bottom), John Shaw/Tom Stack & Associates; p. 528, Hans Reinhard/Bruce Coleman, Inc.;

Chapter 17

p. 536, Rafael Macia/Photo Researchers, Inc.; p. 537 (top), Sean Brady; p. 537 (bottom), Ken O'Donoghue; p. 539, Delphi Automotive Systems; p. 540, AP Photo/NASA; p. 541, Amana; p. 542 (top), Tom Pantages: p. 542 (bottom), AP Photo/Cliff Schiappa; p. 543, C Squared Studios/PhotoDisc; p. 553 (both), Richard Megna/Fundamental Photographs; p. 555, Rod Planck/Photo Researchers, Inc.; p. 557, Paul Silverman/Fundamental Photographs; p. 558, Sean Brady; p. 562 (both), Sean Brady; p. 565, Science Photo Library/Photo Researchers, Inc.

Chapter 18

p. 574, Jeff J. Daly/Visuals Unlimited; p. 575, Sean Brady; p. 576, Sean Brady; p. 578, Gregg Otto/Visuals Unlimited; p. 587, Ken O'Donoghue; p. 590 (top), Richard Megna/Fundamental Photographs; p. 590, (bottom), Paul Chesley/Tony Stone; p. 593 (left), Spencer Grant/PhotoEdit; p. 593 (right), Corbis-Bettmann; p. 597, Courtesy, Ballard Power Systems; p. 598, Bruce Farnsworth/Place Stock Photography; p. 599, Runk/Schoenberger/Grant Heilman Photography; p. 600, The Granger Collection.

Chapter 19

p. 606, Argus Fotoarchiv/Peter Arnold, Inc.; p. 607, James L. Amos/Corbis; p. 609, Kopal/Mediamed Publiphoto/Photo Researchers, Inc.; p. 613, Culver Pictures; p. 616, Ken O'Donoghue; p. 617 (top), Mark A. Philbrick/BYU; p. 617 (bottom), Smithsonian Institution, Natural History Museum, Department of Mineral Sciences; p. 618 (both), SIU/Visuals Unlimited; p. 622, Roger Ressmeyer/Corbis; p. 624 (both), NASA; p. 626, (Figure 19.9)

Reprinted with permission from *Chemical and Engineering News,* Vol. 61, Issue #29, July 18, 1983, pp. 20-38. Copyright © 1983 American Chemical Society, (photo) AP Photo/Lennox McLendon.

Chapter 20

p. 632, Alan Becker/The Image Bank; p. 633, Tom Pantages; p. 635, Frank Cox; p. 637, Corbis Images/PictureQuest; p. 638, AFP/Corbis; p. 646, Tony Freeman/PhotoEdit; p. 649, Jeff Greenberg/PhotoEdit; p. 651, Ken O'Donoghue; p. 654, Inga Spence/Visuals Unlimited; p. 655, Sean Brady; p. 659, Agricultural Research/USDA. Photo by Scott Bauer; p. 663, Sean Brady; p. 668, Jeff Greenberg/PhotoEdit; p. 670 (top), John A. Rizzo/PhotoDisc; p. 670 (bottom), (Laguna Design/Science Photo Library/Photo Researchers, Inc.; p. 671, Ron Boardman/Frank Lane Picture Agency/Corbis; p. 673 (top), Dr. Harold Rose/Science Photo Library/Photo Researchers, Inc.; p. 673 (bottom), Sandia National Laboratories.

Chapter 21

p. 682, Michael Newman/PhotoEdit; p. 683, Volker Steger/Science Photo Library/Photo Researchers, Inc.; p. 685, Michael Abbey/Science Source/Photo Researchers, Inc.; p. 689, D. Yeske/Visuals Unlimited; p. 692, Courtesy, Genzyme Transgenics Corporation; p. 693 (left), USDA; p. 693 (right), Mitch Hrdlicka/PhotoDisc; p. 696, RDF/Visuals Unlimited; p. 699, M. Freeman/PhotoLink/PhotoDisc; p. 705, Sean Brady; p. 706, Will & Deni McIntyre/Photo Researchers, Inc.

Index

1A

1A								
1 **H** Hydrogen 1.008	**2A**							

Key

6 ——— Atomic number
C ——— Element symbol
Carbon ——— Element name
12.01 ——— Atomic mass

1	2
1 **H** Hydrogen 1.008	
3 **Li** Lithium 6.941	4 **Be** Beryllium 9.012
11 **Na** Sodium 22.99	12 **Mg** Magnesium 24.31

19 **K** Potassium 39.10	20 **Ca** Calcium 40.08	21 **Sc** Scandium 44.96	22 **Ti** Titanium 47.88	23 **V** Vanadium 50.94	24 **Cr** Chromium 52.00	25 **Mn** Manganese 54.94	26 **Fe** Iron 55.85	27 **Co** Cobalt 58.93
37 **Rb** Rubidium 85.47	38 **Sr** Strontium 87.62	39 **Y** Yttrium 88.91	40 **Zr** Zirconium 91.22	41 **Nb** Niobium 92.91	42 **Mo** Molybdenum 95.94	43 **Tc** Technetium (98)	44 **Ru** Ruthenium 101.1	45 **Rh** Rhodium 102.9
55 **Cs** Cesium 132.9	56 **Ba** Barium 137.3	57 **La** Lanthanum 138.9	72 **Hf** Hafnium 178.5	73 **Ta** Tantulum 180.9	74 **W** Tungsten 183.9	75 **Re** Rhenium 186.2	76 **Os** Osmium 190.2	77 **Ir** Iridium 192.2
87 **Fr** Francium (223)	88 **Ra** Radium 226.0	89 **Ac** Actinium (227)	104 **Rf** Rutherfordium (261)	105 **Db** Dubnium (262)	106 **Sg** Seaborgium (263)	107 **Bh** Bohrium (264)	108 **Hs** Hassium (265)	109 **Mt** Meitnerium (268)

58 **Ce** Cerium 140.1	59 **Pr** Praseodymium 140.9	60 **Nd** Neodymium 144.2	61 **Pm** Promethium (145)	62 **Sm** Samarium 150.4
90 **Th** Thorium 232.0	91 **Pa** Protactinium (231)	92 **U** Uranium 238.0	93 **Np** Neptunium (237)	94 **Pu** Plutonium (244)